BIBLE HISTORY
Old Testament

BIBLE HISTORY
Old Testament

ALFRED EDERSHEIM

WILLIAM B. EERDMANS PUBLISHING COMPANY
Grand Rapids, Michigan

The *Bible History, Old Testament,* by Alfred Edersheim was originally published in 1876-1887, in seven volumes. It went through several editions, some of which were bound in four volumes, and later in two volumes. The present edition is a reprint of that which appeared in 1890, complete and unabridged, containing all seven volumes, bound between two covers.

Reprinted, November 1992

One Volume Edition, Reprinted, December 1982
ISBN: 0-8028-8028-2
Printed in the United States of America

THE BIBLE HISTORY

VOLUME I

THE

WORLD BEFORE THE FLOOD,

AND THE

HISTORY OF THE PATRIARCHS

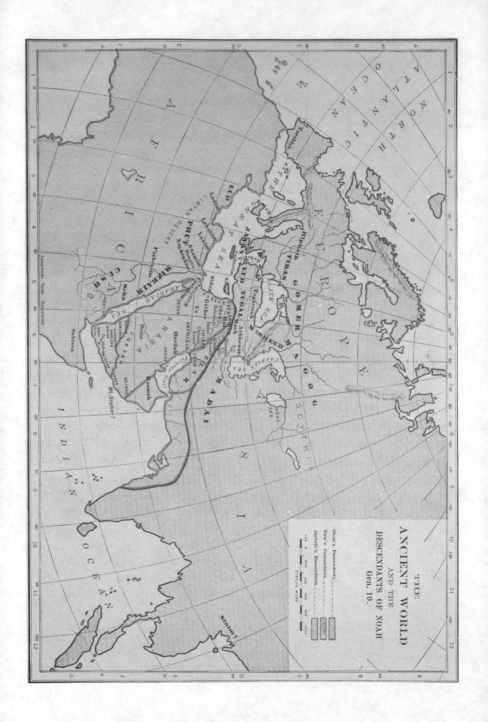

THE
ANCIENT WORLD
AND THE
DESCENDANTS OF NOAH
Gen. 10.

Shem's Descendants
Ham's Descendants
Japheth's Descendants

100 0 200 400 600 800 1000
STATUE MILES

PREFACE

—◦◦◦—

ONE of the most marked and hopeful signs of our time is the increasing attention given on all sides to the study of Holy Scripture. Those who believe and love the Bible, who have experienced its truth and power, can only rejoice at such an issue. They know that "the Word of God liveth and abideth for ever ;" that "not one tittle" of it "shall fail ;" and that it is "able to make wise unto salvation, through faith which is in Christ Jesus." Accordingly they have no reason to dread the results either of scientific investigation, or of searching inquiry into "those things which are most surely believed among us." For, the more the Bible is studied, the deeper will be our conviction that "the foundation of God standeth sure."

It is to help, so far as we can, the reader of Holy Scripture—not to supersede his own reading of it—that the series, of which this is the first volume, has been undertaken. In writing it I have primarily had in view *those who teach and those who learn,* whether *in the school or in the family.* But my scope has also been wider. I have wished to furnish what may be useful for *reading in the family,*—what indeed may, in some measure, serve the place of a popular exposition of the sacred history. More than this, I hope it may likewise prove *a book to put in the hands of young men,—* not only to show them what the Bible really teaches, but to defend them against the insidious attacks arising from misrepresentation and misunderstanding of the sacred text.

With this threefold object in view, I have endeavoured to write in a form so popular and easily intelligible as to be of use to the

Sunday-school teacher, the advanced scholar, and the Bible-class ; progressing gradually, in the course of this and the next volume, from the more simple to the more detailed. At the same time, I have taken up the Scripture narrative successively, chapter by chapter, always marking the portions of the Bible explained, that so, in family or in private reading, the sacred text may be compared with the explanations furnished. Finally, without mentioning objections on the part of opponents, I have endeavoured to meet those that have been raised, and that not by controversy, but rather by a more full and correct study of the sacred text itself in the Hebrew original. In so doing, I have freely availed myself not only of the results of the best criticism, German and English, but also of the aid of such kindred studies as those of Biblical geography and antiquities, the Egyptian and the Assyrian monuments, etc.

But when all has been done, the feeling grows only more strong that there is another and a higher understanding of the Bible, without which all else is vain. Not merely to know the meaning of the narratives of Scripture, but to realize their spiritual application ; to feel their eternal import ; to experience them in ourselves, so to speak,—this is the only profitable study of Scripture, to which all else can only serve as outward preparation. Where the result is "doctrine, reproof, correction, and instruction in righteousness," the Teacher must be He, by whose "inspiration all Scripture is given." "For what man knoweth the things of a man, save the spirit of man which is in him? even so the things of God knoweth no man, but the Spirit of God." But the end of all is Christ—not only "the end of the law for righteousness to every one that believeth," but also He in whom "all the promises of God are Yea and Amen."

A. E.

HENIACH, BOURNEMOUTH.

CONTENTS

History of the Patriarchs.

Contents.

DATES OF EVENTS

<small>RECORDED IN</small>

The Book of Genesis, according to HALES, USSHER, and KEIL.

Ussher.		Events.	Hales.		Keil.
Before Christ.	Year of the World.		Before Christ.	Year of the World.	Year after the immigration into Canaan.
4004	1	The Creation	5411	1	
3874	130	Birth of Seth	5181	230	
3769	235	Birth of Enos.........................	4976	435	
3679	325	Birth of Cainan	4786	625	
3609	395	Birth of Mahaleel	4616	795	
3074	930	Death of Adam......................	4481	930	
3544	460	Birth of Jared	4451	960	
3382	622	Birth of Enoch	4289	1122	
3317	687	Birth of Methuselah	4124	1287	
3130	874	Birth of Lamech	3937	1474	
3017	987	Translation of Enoch	3914	1487	
2948	1056	Birth of Noah	3755	1656	
2348–9	1656	Deluge	3155	2256	
2346	1658	Birth of Arphaxad	3153	2258	
2311	1693	Birth of Salah	3018	2393	
2281	1723	Birth of Heber	2888	2523	
1998	2006	Death of Noah	2805	2606	
2247	1757	Birth of Peleg	2754	2657	
2233	1771	Confusion of Tongues	2554	2857	
2217	1787	Birth of Reu	2624	2787	
2185	1819	Birth of Serug	2492	2919	
2155	1849	Birth of Nahor	2362	3049	
2126	1878	Birth of Terah	2283	3128	
1998	2006	Death of Noah	......	......	
1996	2008	Birth of Abram	2153	3258	
1921	2083	Abram arrives in Canaan	2078	3333	1
1910	2094	Birth of Ishmael	2067	3344	11
		Institution of Circumcision	......	.....	24
1896	2108	Birth of Isaac	2053	3358	25
		Death of Sarah	......	......	62
1856	2148	Marriage of Isaac	2013	3398	65
1836	2168	Birth of Esau and Jacob	1993	3418	85
		Death of Abraham	......	......	100
		Esau's Marriage	......	......	125
		Death of Ishmael	......	......	148
1760	2244	Jacob's flight to Padan Aram	1916	3495	162
		Jacob's Marriage	......	......	169

USSHER.		EVENTS.	HALES.		KEIL.
Before Christ.	Year of the World.		Before Christ.	Year of the World.	Year after the immigration into Canaan.
1745	2259	Birth of Joseph........................	1902	3509	176
1739	2265	Jacob's return to Canaan............	1896	3515	182
1732	2272	Jacob's arrival at Hebron	1889	3522	192
1728	2276	Joseph sold into Egypt..............	1885	3526	193
1716	2288	Death of Isaac	1873	3538	205
1715	2289	Joseph made Governor of Egypt...	1872	3539	206
1706	2298	Jacob goes to Egypt.................	1863	3548	215
1689	2315	Death of Jacob	1846	3565	232
1635	2369	Death of Joseph	1792	3619	286

The reader will find in ch. x. some explanations regarding the systems of Chronology by Ussher and Hales. Hales professes to follow the text of the Greek or LXX. Translation of the Old Testament, correcting it by the Jewish historian Josephus, whose dates, however, are often manifestly very inaccurate. Ussher professes to follow the Hebrew text. The modern Jewish chronology places the birth of Isaac, when Abraham was one hundred years old, in the year of the world 2048. With this latter very nearly agrees the chronology adopted by a celebrated modern German commentator, Professor Keil, who places it only two years earlier, viz. in 2046. We have given in the last column, according to the chronology of Keil, the succession of events *after the migration of Abram into Canaan.* Keil places the latter event in the year of the world 2021, and before Christ 2137. From this the reader will easily be able to calculate all the other dates according to the chronology of Keil, which on the whole seems to us the most reliable. He bases it on the following *data :* according to 1 Kings vi. 1, the Temple of Solomon was built 480 years after the Exodus, while the deportation of Israel into Babylon took place 406 years after the building of the Temple, that is, in all, 886 years after the Exodus. But as the commencement of the Exile must have fallen in the year 606 before Christ, we have the year 1492 before Christ (or 2666 after the Creation) as that of the Exodus. The year 606 before Christ is fixed as that of the commencement of the Babylonish exile, because it ended after 70 years, in the *first* year of the sole reign of Cyrus, which we know to have been the year 536 before Christ.

INTRODUCTION

THAT the "God of Abraham, Isaac, and Jacob" is also the "God and Father of our Lord and Saviour Jesus Christ," and that "they which are of faith, the same are the children of Abraham,"—these are among the most precious truths of revelation. They show us not only the faithfulness of our God, and the greatness of our privileges, but also the marvellous wisdom of the plan of salvation, and its consistency throughout. For the Bible should be viewed, not only in its single books, but in their connection, and in the unity of the whole. The Old Testament could not be broken off from the New, and each considered as independent of the other. Nor yet could any part of the Old Testament be disjoined from the rest. The full meaning and beauty of each appears only in the harmony and unity of the whole. Thus they all form links of one unbroken chain, reaching from the beginning to the time when the Lord Jesus Christ came, for whom all previous history had prepared, to whom all the types pointed, and in whom all the promises are "Yea and Amen." Then that which God had spoken to Abraham, more than two thousand years before, became a blessed reality, for "the Scripture, foreseeing that God would justify the heathen through faith, preached before the gospel unto Abraham, saying, In thee shall all nations be blessed. So then they which be of faith are blessed with faithful Abraham." That this one grand purpose should have been steadily kept in view, and carried forward through all the vicissitudes of history, changes of time, and stages of civilisation,—and that without requiring any alteration, only further unfolding and at last completion,—affords indeed the strongest confirmation to our faith. It is also a precious comfort to our hearts; for we see how God's purpose of mercy has been always the same ; and, walking the same pilgrim-way which "the fathers" had trod, and along which God had safely guided the Covenant, we rejoice to know that neither opposition of man nor yet unfaithfulness on the part of His professing people can make void the gracious counsel of God :—

> " He loved us from the first of time,
> He loves us to the last."

And this it is which we learn from the unity of Scripture.

But yet another and equally important truth may be gathered. There is not merely harmony but also close connection between the various parts of Scripture. Each book illustrates the other, taking up its teaching and carrying it forward. Thus the unity of Scripture is not like that of a stately building, however ingenious its plan or vast its proportions ; but rather, to use a Biblical illustration, like that of the light, which shineth more and more unto the perfect day. We mark throughout growth in its progress, as men were able to bear fuller communications, and prepared for their reception. The law, the types, the history, the prophecies, and the promises of the Old Testament all progressively unfold and develop the same truth, until it appears at last in its New Testament fulness. Though all testify of the same thing, not one of them could safely be left out, nor yet do we properly understand any one part unless we view it in its bearing and connection with the others. And so when at last we come to the close of Scripture, we see how the account of the creation and of the first calling of the children of God, which had been recorded in the book of Genesis, has found its full counterpart—its *fulfilment*—in the book of Revelation, which tells the glories of

the second creation, and the perfecting of the Church of God.
As one of the old Church teachers (St. Augustine) writes:

" Novum Testamentum in vetere latet,
Vetus in novo patet."[1]

That in a work composed of so many books, written under
such very different circumstances, by penmen so different, and
at periods so widely apart, there should be "some things hard
to be understood, which they that are unlearned and unstable
wrest," can surely not surprise us, more particularly when
we remember that it was God's purpose only to send the
brighter light as men were able to bear it. Besides, we must
expect that with our limited powers and knowledge we shall not
be able fully to understand the ways of God. But, on the other
hand, this may be safely said, that the more deep, calm, and
careful our study, the more ample the evidence it will bring to
light to confirm our faith against all attacks of the enemy.
Yet the ultimate object of our reading is not knowledge, but
experience of grace. For, properly understood, the Scripture
is all full of Christ, and all intended to point to Christ as our
only Saviour. It is not only the law, which is a schoolmaster
unto Christ, nor the types, which are shadows of Christ, nor
yet the prophecies, which are predictions of Christ; but the
whole Old Testament history is full of Christ. Even where
persons are not, *events* may be types. If any one failed to
see in Isaac or in Joseph a personal type of Christ, he could
not deny that the offering up of Isaac, or the selling of
Joseph, and his making provision for the sustenance of his
brethren, are typical of events in the history of our Lord. And
so indeed every event points to Christ, even as He is alike
the beginning, the centre, and the end of all history—"the
same yesterday, and to-day, and for ever." One thing follows
from this: only *that* reading or study of the Scriptures can be
sufficient or profitable through which we learn to know Christ

[1] " Only in the New Covenant does the Old unfold,
And hidden lies the New Testament in the Old."

—and that as "the Way, the Truth, and the Life" to *us*. And for this purpose we ought constantly to ask the aid and teaching of the Holy Spirit.

A few brief remarks, helpful to the study of patriarchal history, may here find a place.

In general, the Old Testament may be arranged into "The Law and the Prophets."[1] It was possibly with reference to this division that the Law consisted of the *five* books of Moses —ten being the symbolical number of completeness, and the Law with its commands being only half complete without "the Prophets" and the promises. But assuredly to the *fivefold* division of the Law answers the arrangement of the Psalms into five books, of which each closes with a benediction, as follows:—Book I. : Psa. i.–xli. ; Book II. : Psa. xlii.–lxxii. ; Book III. : Psa. lxxiii.–lxxxix. ; Book IV. : Psa. xc.–cvi. ; Book V. : Psa. cvii.–cl.,—the last Psalm standing as a grand final benediction.

The Law or the Five Books of Moses are commonly called the *Pentateuch*, a Greek term meaning the "fivefold," or "five-parted" Book. Each of these five books commonly bears a title given by the Greek translators of the Old Testament (the so-called LXX.), in accordance with the contents of each : *Genesis* (origin, creation), *Exodus* (going out from Egypt), *Leviticus*, *Numbers*, and *Deuteronomy* (Second Law, or the Law a second time). The Jews designate each book by the first or else the most prominent word with which it begins.

[1] Matt. xi. 13, xxii. 40; Acts xiii. 15, etc. The ordinary Jewish division is into the *Law* (five books of Moses); the *Prophets* (*earlier* : Joshua, Judges, 1 and 2 Sam., 1 and 2 Kings; and *later* : Isaiah, Jeremiah, Ezekiel, and the Twelve Minor Prophets) ; and "*The Writings*," or sacred writings, *hagiographa*,– which comprise The Psalms, Proverbs, and Job;—the "five rolls," read at special festivals in the Synagogue : the Song of Songs, Ruth, Lamentations, Ecclesiastes, and Esther;—Daniel, Ezra, Nehemiah, and 1 and 2 Chronicles (called in Heb. "Words, or Acts, of the Days," journals, or diaries). Comp. Luke xxiv. 44.

The book of *Genesis* consists of *two* great *parts*, each again divided into five sections. Every section is clearly marked by being introduced as "generations," or "originations"—in Hebrew *Toledoth*—as follows:

ART I.—THE HISTORY OF THE WORLD TO THE FINAL ARRANGE-MENT AND SETTLEMENT OF THE VARIOUS NATIONS.

General Introduction : Chap. I.-II. 3.
Section 1. Generations of the Heavens and the Earth, II. 4-IV.
   ,,   2. Book of the Generations of Adam, V.-VI. 8.
   .,   3. The Generations of Noah, VI. 9-IX.
   ,,   4. The Generations of the Sons of Noah, X.-XI. 9.
   ,,   5. The Generations of Shem, XI. 10-26.

PART II.—PATRIARCHAL HISTORY.

Section 1. The Generations of Terah (the father of Abraham), XI. 27-XXV. 11.
   ,,   2. The Generations of Ishmael, XXV. 12-18.
   ,,   3. The Generations of Isaac, XXV. 19-XXXV.
   ,,   4. The Generations of Esau, XXXVI.
   ,,   5. The Generations of Jacob, XXXVII.

These two parts make together *ten* sections— the number of completeness,—and each section varies in length with the importance of its contents, so far as they bear upon the history of the kingdom of God. For, both these parts, or rather the periods which they describe, have such bearing. In the first we are successively shown man's original position and relation-ship towards God; then his fall, and the consequent need of redemption; and next God's gracious provision of mercy. The acceptance or rejection of this provision implies the separation of all mankind into two classes—the Sethites and the Cainites. Again, the judgment of the flood upon the ungodly, and the preservation of His own people, are typical for all time ; while the genealogies and divisions of the various nations, and the separation of Shem, imply the selection of one nation, from whom salvation should spring for all mankind. *In this first part the interest of the history groups around events rather than persons.* It is otherwise in the second part, where the history of the Covenant and of the Covenant-people begins with the calling of Abraham, and is continued in Isaac, in Jacob, and in his descendants. *Here the interest centres in persons rather than events*, and we are successively shown God's rich promises as they unfold, and God's gracious dealings as they contribute to the training of the patriarchs. The book of Genesis, and with it the first period of the Covenant history, closes when the family had expanded into a nation. Finally, with reference to the special arrangement of the "generations" recorded throughout the book of Genesis, it will be noticed that, so to speak, the side branches are always cut off before the main branch is carried onwards. Thus the history of Cain and of his race precedes that of Seth and his race; the genealogy of Japheth and of Ham that of Shem; and the history of Ishmael and Esau that of Isaac and of Jacob. For the principle of election and selection, of separation and of grace, underlies from the first the whole history of the Covenant. It appears in the calling of Abraham, and is continued throughout the history of the patriarchs; and although the holy family enlarges into the nation, the promise narrows first to the house of David, and finally to one individual—the Son of David, the Lord Jesus Christ, the one Prophet, the one Priest, the one King, that in Him the kingdom of heaven might be opened to all believers, and from Him the blessings of salvation flow unto all men.

THE

WORLD BEFORE THE FLOOD

OR, THE

HISTORY OF THE ANTEDILUVIANS

~~~

CHAPTER I.

Creation—Man in the Garden of Eden—The Fall.
(GEN. I.—III.)

" HE that cometh unto God must believe that He is, and
that He is the rewarder of them that diligently seek
Him." Hence Holy Scripture, which contains the revealed
record of God's dealings and purposes with man, commences
with an account of the creation. "For the invisible things
of Him from the creation of the world are clearly seen, being
understood by the things that are made, even His eternal
power and Godhead."

Four great truths, which have their bearing on every part of
revelation, come to us from the earliest Scripture narrative,
like the four rivers which sprung in the garden of Eden. The
first of these truths is—*the creation of all things by the word of
God's power;* the second, *the descent of all men from our
common parents, Adam and Eve;* the third, *our connection with
Adam as the head of the human race, through which all mankind
were involved in his sin and fall;* and the fourth, that *One
descended from Adam, yet without his sin, should by suffering
free us from the consequences of the fall, and as the second Adam
become the Author of eternal salvation to all who trust in Him.*
To these four vital truths there might be added, as a fifth, the
institution of one day in seven to be a day of holy rest
unto God.

It is scarcely possible to imagine a greater contrast than

between the heathen accounts of the origin of all things and the scriptural narrative.   The former are so full of the grossly absurd that no one could regard them as other than fables ; while the latter is so simple, and yet so full of majesty, as almost to force us to "worship and bow down," and to " kneel before the Lord our Maker."   And as this was indeed the object in view, and not scientific instruction, far less the gratification of our curiosity, we must expect to find in the first chapter of Genesis simply the grand outlines of what took place, and not any details connected with creation.   On these points there is ample room for such information as science may be able to supply, when once it shall have carefully selected and sifted all that can be learned from the study of earth and of nature.   That time, however, has not yet arrived ; and we ought, therefore, to be on our guard against the rash and unwarranted statements which have sometimes been brought forward on these subjects.   Scripture places before us the successive creation of all things, so to speak, in an ascending scale, till at last we come to that of man, the chief of God's works, and whom his Maker destined to be lord of all.[1]   Some have imagined that the six days of creation represent so many periods, rather than literal days, chiefly on the ground of the supposed high antiquity of our globe, and the various great epochs or periods, each terminating in a grand revolution, through which our earth seems to have passed, before coming to its present state, when it became a fit habitation for man. There is, however, no need to resort to any such theory.   The first verse in the book of Genesis simply states the general fact, that " In the beginning "—whenever that may have been— " God created the heaven and the earth."   Then, in the second verse, we find earth described as it was at the close of the last great revolution, preceding the present state of things : " And the earth was without form and void ; and darkness was upon the face of the deep."   An almost indefinite space of time, and many changes, may therefore have intervened between the

[1] Psa. viii. 3–8.

creation of heaven and earth, as mentioned in ver. 1, and the chaotic state of our earth, as described in ver. 2. As for the exact date of the *first* creation, it may be safely affirmed that we have not yet the knowledge sufficient to arrive at any really trustworthy conclusion.

It is of far greater importance for us, however, to know that God "created all things by Jesus Christ;"[1] and further, that "all things were created by Him, and for Him,"[2] and that "of Him, and through Him, and to Him are all things."[3] This gives not only unity to all creation, but places it in living connection with our Lord Jesus Christ. At the same time we should also always bear in mind, that it is "through faith we understand that the worlds were framed by the word of God, so that things which are seen were not made of things which do appear."[4]

Everything as it proceeded from the hand of God was "very good,"[5] that is, perfect to answer the purpose for which it had been destined. "And on the seventh day God ended His work which He had made; and He rested on the seventh day from all His work which He had made. And God blessed the seventh day, and sanctified it : because that in it He had rested from all His work which God created and made." It is upon this original institution of the Sabbath as a day of holy rest that our observance of the Lord's day is finally based, the change in the precise day—from the seventh to the first of the week—having been occasioned by the resurrection of our Lord Jesus Christ, by which not only the first, but also the new creation was finally completed.[6]

[1] Eph. iii. 9. [2] Col. i. 16.
[3] Rom. xi. 36. See also 1 Cor. viii. 6; Heb. i. 2; John i. 3.
[4] Heb. xi. 3.
[5] It is noteworthy that in Gen. i. we always read, "And the evening and the morning were the first day," or second, or third day, etc. Hence the Jews calculate the day from evening to evening, that is, 1rom the first appearance of the stars in the evening to the first appearance of stars next evening, and not, as we do, from midnight to midnight.
[6] See Isa. lxv. 17.

Of all His works God only "created man in His own image : in the image of God created He him." This expression refers not merely to the intelligence with which God endowed, and the immortality with which He gifted man, but also to the perfect moral and spiritual nature which man at the first possessed. And all his surroundings were in accordance with his happy state. God "put him into the garden of Eden[1] to dress it and to keep it," and gave him a congenial companion in Eve, whom Adam recognized as bone of his bones, and flesh of his flesh. Thus as God had, by setting apart the Sabbath day, indicated *worship* as the proper relationship between man and his Creator, so He also laid in Paradise the foundation of civil society by the institution of *marriage* and of the family.[2]

It now only remained to test man's obedience to God, and to prepare him for yet higher and greater privileges than those which he already enjoyed. But evil was already in this world of ours, for Satan and his angels had rebelled against God. The scriptural account of man's trial is exceedingly brief and simple. We are told that "the tree of the knowledge of good and evil" had been placed "in the midst of the garden," and of the fruit of this tree God forbade Adam to eat, on pain of death. On the other hand, there was also "the tree of life" in the garden, probably as symbol and pledge of a higher life, which we should have inherited if our first parents had continued obedient to God. The issue of this trial came only too soon. The tempter, under the form of a serpent, approached Eve. He denied the threatenings of God, and deceived her

---

[1] Many different views have been broached as to the exact locality of *Eden,* which it would scarcely be suitable to discuss in this place. The two opinions deserving most attention are those which place it either near the northern highlands of Armenia, or else far south in the neighbourhood of the Persian Gulf. We know that two of the streams mentioned as issuing from Paradise were the *Tigris* and the *Euphrates,* and we can readily conceive that the changes subsequently produced by the flood may have rendered the other descriptions of the district inapplicable to its present aspect.   [2] Comp. Mark x. 6, 9.

as to the real consequences of eating the forbidden fruit. This, followed by the enticement of her own senses, led Eve first to eat, and then to induce her husband to do likewise. Their sin had its immediate consequence. They had aimed to be "as gods," and, instead of absolutely submitting themselves to the command of the Lord, acted independently of Him. And now their eyes were indeed opened, as the tempter had promised, "to know good and evil;" but only in their own guilty knowledge of sin, which immediately prompted the wish to hide themselves from the presence of God. Thus, their alienation and departure from God, the condemning voice of their conscience, and their sorrow and shame gave evidence that the Divine threatening had already been accomplished: "In the day that thou eatest thereof thou shalt surely die." The sentence of death which God now pronounced on our first parents extended both to their bodily and their spiritual nature—to their mortal and immortal part. In the day he sinned man died in body, soul, and spirit. And because Adam, as the head of his race, represented the whole ; and as through him we should all have entered upon a very high and happy state of being, if he had remained obedient, so now the consequences of his disobedience have extended to us all ; and as "by one man sin entered into the world, and death by sin," so " death passed upon all men, for that all have sinned." Nay, even "creation itself," which had been placed under his dominion, was made through his fall "subject to vanity," and came under the curse, as God said to Adam : " Cursed is the ground for thy sake ; in sorrow shalt thou eat of it all the days of thy life ; thorns also and thistles shall it bring forth to thee."

God, in His infinite mercy, did not leave man to perish in his sin. He was indeed driven forth from Paradise, for which he was no longer fit. But, before that, God had pronounced the curse upon his tempter, Satan, and had given man the precious promise that the seed of the woman should bruise the head of the serpent; that is, that our blessed Saviour, "born of a

woman," should redeem us from the power of sin and of
death, through His own obedience, death, and resurrection.
And even the labour of his hands, to which man was now
doomed, was in the circumstances a boon.   Therefore, when
our first parents left the garden of Eden, it was not without
hope, nor into outer darkness.   They carried with them the
promise of a Redeemer, the assurance of the final defeat of the
great enemy, as well as the Divine institution of a Sabbath on
which to worship, and of the marriage-bond by which to be
joined together into families.   Thus the foundations of the
Christian life in all its bearings were laid in Paradise.

There are still other points of practical interest to be
gathered up.   The descent of all mankind from our first
parents determines our spiritual relationship to Adam.   In
Adam all have sinned and fallen.   But, on the other hand,
it also determines our spiritual relationship to the Lord Jesus
Christ, as the second Adam, which rests on precisely the same
grounds.   For "as we have borne the image of the earthy,
we shall also bear the image of the heavenly," and "as in
Adam all die, even so in Christ shall all be made alive."
"For as by one man's disobedience many were made sinners,
so by the obedience of one shall many be made righteous."
The descent of all mankind from one common stock has in
times past been questioned by some, although Scripture expressly teaches that " He has made of one blood all nations,
for to dwell on the face of the earth."   It is remarkable that
this denial, which certainly never was shared by the most
competent men of science, has quite lately been, we may
say, almost universally abandoned, and the original unity of
the human race in their common descent is now a generally
accepted fact.

Here, moreover, we meet for the first time with that strange
resemblance to revealed religion which makes heathenism so
like and yet so unlike the religion of the Old Testament.   As
in the soul of man we see the ruins of what he had been
before the fall, so in the legends and traditions of the various

religions of antiquity we recognize the echoes of what men had originally heard from the mouth of God. Not only one race, but almost all nations, have in their traditions preserved some dim remembrance alike of an originally happy and holy state,—a so-called golden age—in which the intercourse between heaven and earth was unbroken, and of a subsequent sin and fall of mankind. And all nations also have cherished a faint belief in some future return of this happy state, that is, in some kind of coming redemption, just as in their inmost hearts all men have at least a faint longing for a Redeemer.

Meanwhile, this grand primeval promise, "The seed of the woman shall bruise the head of the serpent," would stand out as a beacon-light to all mankind on their way, burning brighter and brighter, first in the promise to Shem, next in that to Abraham, then in the prophecy of Jacob, and so on through the types of the Law to the promises of the Prophets, till in the fulness of time " the Sun of Righteousness " arose "with healing under His wings !"

CHAPTER II.

Cain and Abel—The Two Ways and the Two Races.

(GEN. IV.)

THE language in which Scripture tells the second great event in history is once more exceedingly simple. Two of the children of Adam and Eve are alone mentioned : *Cain* and *Abel.* Not that there were no others, but that the progress of Scripture history is connected with these two. For the Bible does not profess to give a detailed history of the world, nor even a complete biography of those persons whom it introduces. Its object is to set before us a *history of the kingdom of God*, and it only describes such persons and events as is necessary for that purpose. Of the two sons of Adam and Eve, *Cain* was the elder, and indeed, as we gather, the first-born of all their children. Throughout antiquity, and in the East to this day, proper names are regarded as significant of a deeper meaning. When Eve called her first-born son *Cain* ("gotten," or "acquired"), she said, "I have gotten a man from Jehovah." [1] Apparently she connected the birth of her son with the immediate fulfilment of the promise concerning the Seed, who was to bruise the head of the serpent. This expectation was, if we may be allowed the comparison, as natural on her part as that of the immediate return of our Lord by some of the early Christians. It also showed how deeply this hope had sunk into her heart, how lively was her faith in the fulfilment of the promise, and how ardent her longing for it. But if such had been her views, they must have been speedily disappointed. Perhaps for this very reason, or else because she had been more fully informed, or on other grounds with which we are not acquainted, the other son of Adam and Eve, mentioned in Scripture, was named *Abel*, that is "breath," or "fading away."

What in the history of these two youths is of scriptural importance, is summed up in the statement that "Abel was a keeper of sheep, but Cain was a tiller of the ground." We next meet them, each bringing an offering unto Jehovah; Cain "of the fruit of the ground," and Abel "of the firstlings of his flock, and of the fat thereof." Jehovah "had respect unto Abel and his offering," probably marking His acceptance by some outward and visible manifestation; "but unto Cain and his offering He had not respect." Instead of inquiring into the reason of his rejection, and trying to have it removed, Cain now gave way to feelings of anger and jealousy. In His mercy, God indeed brought before him his sin, warned him of its danger, and pointed out the way of escape. But Cain

[1] It may be well here to note that whenever the word *Lord* is printed in our English Bibles in capitals, its Hebrew equivalent is *Jehovah*—a term which marks the idea of the covenant God.

had chosen his course. Meeting his brother in the field, angry words led to murderous deed, and earth witnessed the first death, the more terrible that it was violent, and at a brother's hand. Once more the voice of Jehovah called Cain to account, and again he hardened himself, this time almost disowning the authority of God. But the mighty hand of the Judge was on the unrepenting murderer. Adam had, so to speak, broken the first great commandment, Cain the first and the second; Adam had committed sin, Cain both sin and crime. As a warning, and yet as a witness to all, Cain, driven from his previous chosen occupation as a tiller of the ground, was sent forth "a fugitive and a vagabond in the earth." So—if we may again resort to analogy—was Israel driven forth into all lands, when with wicked hands they had crucified and slain Him whose blood "speaketh better things than that of Abel." But even this punishment, though "greater" than Cain "can bear," leads him not to repentance, only to fear of its consequences. And "lest any finding him should kill him," Jehovah set a mark upon Cain, just as He made the Jews, amidst all their persecutions, an indestructible people. Only in their case the gracious Lord has a purpose of mercy; for they shall return again to the Lord their God—"all Israel shall be saved;" and their bringing in shall be as life from the dead. But as for Cain, he "went out from the presence of Jehovah, and dwelt in the land of Nod," that is, of "wandering" or "unrest." The last that we read of him is still in accordance with all his previous life: "he builded a city, and called the name of the city, after the name of his son, Enoch."

Now, there are some lessons quite on the surface of this narrative. Thus we mark the difference in the sacrifice of the two brothers—the one "of the fruit of the ground," the other an animal sacrifice. Again, the offering of Cain is described merely in general terms; while Abel's is said to be "of the *first-lings* of his flock"—*the first* being in acknowledgment that *all* was God's, "and of the *fat* thereof," that is, of the best. So also we note, how faithfully God warns, and how kindly He

points Cain to the way of escape from the power of sin. On
the other hand, the murderous deed of Cain affords a terrible
illustration of the words in which the Lord Jesus has taught us,
that angry bitter feelings against a brother are in reality murder,[1] showing us what is, so to speak, the full outcome of self-
willedness, of anger, envy, and jealousy. Yet another lesson
to be learned from this history is, that our sin will at the last
assuredly find us out, and yet that no punishment, however
terrible, can ever have the effect of changing the heart of a
man, or altering his state and the current of his life. To these
might be added the bitter truth, which godless men will perceive
all too late, that, as Cain was at the last driven forth from
the ground of which he had taken possession, so assuredly
all who seek their portion in this world will find their hopes
disappointed, even in those things for which they had sacrificed the "better part." In this respect the later teaching
of Scripture[2] seems to be contained in germ in the history
of Cain and Abel.

If from these obvious lessons we turn to the New Testament
for further light on this history, we find in the Epistle of Jude
(ver. 11) a general warning against going "in the way of Cain ;"
while St. John makes it an occasion of admonishing to
brotherly love : "Not as Cain, who was of that wicked one,
and slew his brother. And wherefore slew he him ? Because
his own works were evil, and his brother's righteous."[3] But
the fullest information is derived from the Epistle to the
Hebrews, where we read, on the one hand, that "without faith
it is impossible to please God," and, on the other, that "by
faith Abel offered unto God a more excellent sacrifice than
Cain, by which he obtained witness that he was righteous, God
testifying of his gifts : and by it he, being dead, yet speaketh."[4]
Scripture here takes us up, as it were, to the highest point in
the lives of the two brothers—their sacrifice—and tells us of
the presence of faith in the one, and of its absence in the
other. This showed itself alike in the manner and in the kind

[1] Matt. v. 22.   [2] Psa. xlix.   [3] 1 John iii. 12.   [4] Heb. xi. 4.

of their sacrifice. But the faith which prompted the sacrifice of Abel, and the want of faith which characterised that of Cain, must, of course, have existed and appeared long before. Hence St. John also says that Cain "was of that wicked one," meaning that he had all along yielded himself to the power of that tempter who had ruined our first parents. A little consideration will explain this, and, at the same time, bring the character and conduct of Cain into clearer light.

After the fall the position of man towards God was entirely changed. In the garden of Eden man's hope of being confirmed in his estate and of advancing upwards depended on his *perfect obedience.* But man disobeyed and fell. Henceforth his hope for the future could no longer be derived from perfect obedience, which, indeed, in his fallen state was impossible. So to speak, the way of "doing" had been set before him, and it had ended, through sin, in death. God in His infinite grace now opened to man another path. He set before him the hope of faith. The promise which God freely gave to man was that of a Deliverer, who would bruise the head of the serpent, and destroy his works. Now, it was possible either to embrace this promise by faith, and in that case to cling to it and set his heart thereon, or else to refuse this hope and turn away from it. Here, then, at the very opening of the history of the kingdom, we have the two different ways which, as the world and the kingdom of God, have ever since divided men. If we further ask ourselves what those would do who rejected the hope of faith, how they would show it in their outward conduct, we answer, that they would naturally choose the world as it then was; and, satisfied therewith, try to establish themselves in the earth, claim it as their own, enjoy its pleasures and lusts, and cultivate its arts. On the other hand, one who embraced the promises would consider himself a pilgrim and a stranger in this earth, and both in heart and outward conduct show that he believed in, and waited for, the fulfilment of the promise. We need scarcely say that the one describes the history of Cain and of his race; the other that of

Abel, and afterwards of Seth and of his descendants. For around these two—Cain and Seth—as their representatives, all the children of Adam would group themselves according to their spiritual tendencies.

Viewed in this light the indications of Scripture, however brief, are quite clear. When we read that "Cain was a tiller of the ground," and "Abel was a keeper of sheep," we can understand that the choice of their occupations depended not on accidental circumstances, but quite accorded with their views and character. Abel chose the pilgrim-life, Cain that of settled possession and enjoyment of earth. The nearer their history lay to the terrible event which had led to the loss of Paradise, and to the first giving of the promise, the more significant would this their choice of life appear. Quite in accordance with this, we afterwards find Cain, not only building a city, but calling it after the name of his own son, to indicate settled proprietorship and enjoyment of the world as it was. The same tendency rapidly unfolded in his descendants, till in Lamech, the fifth from Cain, it had already assumed such large proportions that Scripture deems it no longer necessary to mark its growth. Accordingly the separate record of the Cainites ceases with Lamech and his children, and there is no further specific mention made of them in Scripture.

Before following more in detail the course of these two races—for, in a spiritual sense, they were quite distinct—we mark at the very threshold of Scripture history the introduction of sacrifices. From the time of Abel onwards, they are uniformly, and with increasing clearness, set before us as the appointed way of approaching and holding fellowship with God, till, at the close of Scripture history, we have the sacrifice of our blessed Lord and Saviour Jesus Christ, to which all sacrifices had pointed. And not only so, but as the dim remembrance of a better state from which man had fallen, and of a hope of deliverance, had been preserved among all heathen nations, so also had that of the necessity of sacrifices. Even the bloody rites of savages, nay, the cruel sacrifices of best-beloved children, what were they but a cry of despair in the felt need of reconciliation to God through sacrifice—the giving up of what was most dear in room and stead of the offerer? These are the terribly broken pillars of what once had been a temple ; the terribly distorted traditions of truths once Divinely revealed. Blessed be God for the light of His Gospel, which has taught us " the way, the truth, and the life," even Him who is "the Lamb of God, which taketh away the sin of the world."

CHAPTER III.

Seth and his Descendants—The Race of Cain.

(GEN. IV.)

THE place of Abel could not remain unfilled, if God's purpose of mercy were to be carried out. Accordingly He gave to Adam and Eve another son, whom his mother significantly called "Seth," that is, "appointed," or rather "compensation ;" "for God," said she, "hath appointed me ('compensated me with') another seed instead of Abel, whom Cain slew." Before, however, detailing the history of Seth and his descendants, Scripture traces that of Cain to the fifth and sixth generations. Cain, as we know, had gone into the land of "Nod"—"wandering," "flight," "unrest,"—and there built a city, which has been aptly described as the laying of the first foundations of that kingdom in which "the spirit of the beast" prevails.[1] We must remember that probably centuries had elapsed since the creation, and that men had already multiplied on the earth. Beyond this settle-

---

[1] A modern commentator holds that the words of Gen. iv. 17, only imply that Cain " was building," not that he had finished the building of his city.

ment of Cain, nothing seems to have occurred which Scripture has deemed necessary to record, except that the names of
the "Cainites" are still singularly like those of the "Sethites."
Thus we follow the line of Cain's descendants to *Lamech*, the
fifth from Cain, when all at once the character and tendencies
of that whole race appear fully developed. It comes upon us,
almost by surprise, that within so few generations, and in the
lifetime of the first man, almost every commandment and institution of God should already be openly set aside, and violence,
lust, and ungodliness prevail upon the earth. The first direct
breach of God's arrangement of which we here read, is the
introduction of polygamy. "Lamech took unto him two
wives." Assuredly, "from the beginning it was not so."
But this is not all. Scripture preserves to us in the address
of Lamech to his two wives the earliest piece of poetry. It
has been designated "Lamech's Sword-song," and breathes
a spirit of boastful defiance, of trust in his own strength,
of violence, and of murder.[1] Of God there is no further
acknowledgment than in a reference to the avenging of Cain,
from which Lamech augurs his own safety. Nor is it without
special purpose that the names of Lamech's wives and of his
daughter are mentioned in Scripture. For their names point
to "the lust of the eye, and the lust of the flesh," just as the
occupations of Lamech's sons point to "the pride of life."
The names of his wives were "Adah," that is, "beauty," or
"adornment;" and "Zillah," that is, "the shaded," perhaps
from her tresses, or else "sounding," perhaps from her song;
while "Naamah," as Lamech's daughter was called, means

---

[1] A modern critic has rendered Lamech's Sword-song thus :

" Adah and Zillah, hear my voice : ye wives of Lamech, hearken unto
    my speech ;
Yea, I slay men for my wound, and young men for my hurt.
For *if* Cain is avenged sevenfold, Lamech seventy and sevenfold"—

referring to the invention of Tubal-Cain, and meaning that if God avenged
Cain, he would with his sword avenge himself seventy and sevenfold for
every wound and every hurt.

"pleasant, graceful, lovely." And here we come upon another and most important feature in the history of the "Cainites." The pursuits and inventions of the sons of Lamech point to the culture of the arts, and to a settled and permanent state of society. His eldest son by Adah, "Jabal, was the father of such as dwell in tents, and of such as have cattle," that is, he made even the pastoral life a regular business. His second son, "Jubal, was the father of all such as handle the harp (or cithern), and the flute (or sackbut)," in other words, the inventor alike of stringed and of wind instruments; while Tubal-Cain,[1] Lamech's son by Zillah, was "an instructor of every artificer in brass and iron." Taken in connection with Lamech's sword-song, which immediately follows the scriptural account of his sons' pursuits, we are warranted in designating the culture and civilisation introduced by the family of Lamech as essentially godless. And that, not only because it was that of ungodly men, but because it was pursued independent of God, and in opposition to the great purposes which He had with man. Moreover, it is very remarkable that we perceive in the Cainite race those very things which afterwards formed the characteristics of heathenism, as we find it among the most advanced nations of antiquity, such as Greece and Rome. Over their family-life might be written, as it were, the names Adah, Zillah, Naamah; over their civil life the "sword-song of Lamech," which indeed strikes the key-note of ancient heathen society; and over their culture and pursuits, the abstract of the biographies which Scripture furnishes us of the descendants of Cain. And as their lives have been buried in the flood, so has a great flood also swept away heathenism—its life, culture, and civilisation from the earth, and only left on the mountain-top that ark into which God had shut up them who believed His warnings and His promises.

The contrast becomes most marked as we turn from this record of the Cainites to that of Seth and of his descendants.

[1] Perhaps "Tubal, the smith."

Even the name which Seth gave to his son—*Enos*, or "frail"[1]—stands out as a testimony against the assumption of the Cainites. But especially does this vital difference between the two races appear in the words which follow upon the notice of Enos' birth : " Then began men to call upon the name of Jehovah." Of course, it cannot be supposed that before that time prayer and the praise of God had been wholly unknown in the earth. Even the sacrifices of Cain and of Abel prove the contrary. It must therefore mean, that the vital difference which had all along existed between the two races, became now also outwardly manifest by a distinct and open profession, and by the praise of God on the part of the Sethites. We have thus reached the first great period in the history of the kingdom of God—that of an outward and visible separation between the two parties, when those who are " of faith" "come out from among" the world, and from the kingdom of this world. We remember how many, many centuries afterwards, when *He* had come, whose blood speaketh better things than that of Abel, His followers were similarly driven to separate themselves from Israel after the flesh, and how in Antioch they were first called Christians. As that marked the commencement of the history of the New Testament Church, so this introduction of an open profession of Jehovah on the part of the Sethites, the beginning of the history of the kingdom of God under the Old Testament.

And yet this separation and coming out from the world, this " beginning to call upon the name of Jehovah," is what to this day each one of us must do for himself, if he would take up the cross, follow Christ, and enter into the kingdom of God.

[1] The word is used for " man," from his frailty, in such passages as Psa. viii. 4 ; xc. 3 ; ciii. 15, etc.

CHAPTER IV.

Genealogy of the Believing Race, through Seth.

(GEN. V.)

ONE purpose of Scripture has now been fulfilled. The tendencies for evil of the Cainite race have been traced to their full unfolding, and "the kingdom of this world" has appeared in its real character. On the other hand, the race of Seth have gathered around an open profession of their faith in the promises, and of their purpose to serve God, and they have on this ground separated themselves from the Cainites. The two ways are clearly marked out, and the character of those who walk in them determined. There is, therefore, no further need to follow the history of the Cainites, and Scripture turns from them to give us an account of "the elders" who "by faith" "obtained a good report."

At first sight it seems as if the narrative here opened with only a "book," or account, "of the generations of Adam," containing here and there a brief notice interspersed; but in truth it is otherwise. At the outset we mark, as a significant contrast, that whereas we read of Adam that "in the like-ness of God made He him," it is now added that "he begat a son in his own likeness, after his image." Adam was created pure and sinless in the likeness of God; Seth inherited the fallen nature of his father. Next, we observe how all the genealogies, from Adam downwards, have this in common, that they give first the age of the father at the birth of his eldest son,[1] then the number of years which each of them lived after that event, and finally their total age at the time

---

[1] With the exception of Seth, who, of course, was not the eldest son of Adam.

of death.   Altogether, *ten* "elders" are named from the crea
tion to the time of the flood, and thus grouped : [1]

Names.	Age at Birth of Son.	Number of Years after that event.	Total Age.	Year of Birth from Creation.	Year of Death from Creation.
Adam	130	800	930	1	930
Seth	105	807	912	130	1042
Enos	90	815	905	235	1140
Cainan	70	840	910	325	1235
Mahaleel	65	830	895	395	1290
Jared	162	800	962	460	1422
Enoch	65	300	365	622	987
Methuselah	187	782	969	687	1656
Lamech	182	595	777	874	1651
Noah	500	450	950	1056	2006
Thence to the Flood ...	100				
Sum total	1656				

On examining them more closely, what strikes us in these
genealogical records of the Patriarchs is, that the details
they furnish are wanting in the history of the Cainites,
where simply the *birth* of *seven* generations are mentioned,
viz. : Adam, Cain, Enoch, Irad, Mehajael, Methusael, Lamech,
and his sons.   The reason of this difference is, that whereas
the Cainites had really no future, the Sethites, who "called
upon the name of Jehovah," were destined to carry out the
purpose of God in grace unto the end.   Next, in two cases
the same names occur in the two races—Enoch and Lamech.
But in both, Scripture furnishes characteristic distinctions
between them.   In opposition to the Enoch after whom
Cain called his city, we have the Sethite Enoch, "who
walked with God, and was not; for God took him;" and
in contradistinction to the Cainite Lamech, with his boastful

[1] Such are the numbers according to the Hebrew text.   There are
differences between this and the Greek translation of the so-called LXX
(the Septuagint), and also the Samaritan text.   For further particulars we
refer to ch. x., where also the difference between the chronologies of
Ussher and Hales is explained.

ode to his sword, we have the other Lamech, who called his son Noah, "saying, This same shall comfort us concerning our work and toil of our hands, because of the ground which Jehovah hath cursed." Thus the similarity of their names only brings out the more clearly the contrast of their character. Finally, as the wickedness of the one race comes out most fully in Lamech, who stands *seventh* in the genealogy of the Cainites, so does the godliness of the other in Enoch, who equally stands *seventh* in that of the Sethites.

Passing from this comparison of the two genealogies to the table of the Sethites, we are reminded of the saying, that these primeval genealogies are " monuments alike of the faithfulness of God in the fulfilment of His promise, and of the faith and patience of the fathers." Every generation lived its appointed time ; they transmitted the promise to their sons ; and then, having finished their course, they all " died in faith, not having received the promises, but having seen them afar off, and were persuaded of them, and embraced them, and confessed that they were strangers and pilgrims on the earth." That is absolutely all we know of the majority of them. But the emphatic and seemingly needless repetition in each case of the words, " And he died," with which every genealogy closes, tells us that " death reigned from Adam unto Moses,"[1] with all the lessons which it conveyed of its origin in sin, and of its conquest by the second Adam. Only one exception occurs to this general rule—in the case of Enoch ; when, instead of the usual brief notice how many years he "lived" after the birth of his son, we read that " he walked with God after he begat Methuselah three hundred years ;" and instead of the simple closing statement that " he died," we are not only a second time told that " Enoch walked with God," but also that " he was not ; for God took him." Thus both his life and his translation are connected with his " walk with God." This expression is unique in Scripture, and except in reference to Noah[2] only occurs again in connection with the

---

[1] Rom. v. 14.   [2] Gen. vi. 9.

priest's intercourse with God in the holy place.[1]   Thus it indicates a peculiarly intimate, close, and personal converse with Jehovah.   Alike the life, the work, and the removal of Enoch are thus explained in the Epistle to the Hebrews : " By faith Enoch was translated that he should not see death; and was not found, because God had translated him : for before his translation he had this testimony, that he pleased God."[2]   His translation was like that of Elijah,[3] and like what that of the saints shall be at the second coming of our blessed Lord.[4]   In this connection it is very remarkable that Enoch "prophesied" of the very thing which was manifested in his own case, "saying, Behold, the Lord cometh with ten thousands of His saints, to execute judgment upon all, and to convince all that are ungodly among them of all their ungodly deeds which they have ungodly committed, and of all their hard speeches which ungodly sinners have spoken against Him."[5]

When Enoch was "translated" only Adam had as yet died : Seth, Enos, Cainan, Mahalaleel, and Jared were still alive.   On the other hand, not only Methuselah, the son of Enoch, but also his grandson Lamech, who at the time was one hundred and thirteen years old, must have witnessed his removal. Noah was not yet born.   But how deep on the godly men of that period was the impression produced by the prophecy of Enoch, and by what we may call its anticipatory and typical fulfilment in his translation, appears from the circumstance that Lamech gave to his son, who was born sixty-nine years after the translation of Enoch, the name of Noah—"rest" or "comfort"—"saying, This same shall comfort us concerning our work and toil of our hands, because of the ground which

---

[1] Mal. ii. 6.   [2] Heb. xi. 5.   [3] 2 Kings ii. 10.   [4] 1 Cor. xv. 51, 52. [5] Jude 14, 15.   This quite accords with what was generally known about Enoch.   One of the Old Testament apocryphal works, written before the time of Christ (Ecclesiasticus xliv. 16), has it that " Enoch was translated, being an example of repentance to all generations ;" while another book (B. of En. i. 9) expressly states, that he prophesied the coming of the Lord for judgment upon the ungodly.

Jehovah hath cursed." Evidently Lamech felt the burden of toil upon an earth which God had cursed, and looked forward to a gracious deliverance from the misery and corruption existing in consequence of it, by the fulfilment of the Divine promise concerning the Deliverer. In longing hope of this he called his son *Noah*. A change, indeed, *did* come; but it was by the destruction of that sinful generation, and by the commencement of a new period in the covenant-history. We mark that, in the case of Noah, Scripture no longer mentions, as before, only one son; but it gives us the names of the *three* sons of Noah, to show that henceforth the one line was to divide into three, which were to become the founders of human history.

It is most instructive, also, to notice that *Enoch*, who seems to have walked nearest to God, only lived on earth altogether three hundred and sixty-five years—less than half the time of those who preceded and who succeeded him. An extraordinary length of life may be a blessing, as affording space for repentance and grace; but in reference to those most dear to God, it may be shortened as a relief from the work and toil which sin has brought upon this world. Indeed, the sequel will show that the extraordinary duration of life, though necessary at the first, yet by no means proved a source of good to a wicked and corrupt generation.

CHAPTER V.

The Universal Corruption of Man—Preparation for the Flood.

(GEN. VI.)

IT is a remarkable circumstance that all nations should have preserved in their traditions notices of the extraordinary length to which human life was at the first protracted. We can understand that knowledge of such a fact would be most readily handed down. But we should remember, that before the "flood" the conditions of vigour, constitution, climate, soil, and nourishment were quite different from those on which the present duration of life depends. A comparison between the two is therefore impossible, for the best of all reasons, that we have not sufficient knowledge of the primitive state of matters. But this we can clearly see, that such long continuance of life was absolutely necessary, if the earth was to be rapidly peopled, knowledge to advance, and, above all, the worship of God and faith in that promise about a Deliverer which He had revealed, to be continued. As it was, each generation could hand down to remote posterity what it had learned during the centuries of its continuance. Thus Adam was alive to tell the story of Paradise and the fall, and to repeat the word of promise, which he had heard from the very mouth of the Lord, when Lamech was born ; and though none of the earlier "fathers" could have lived to see the commencement of building the ark, which took place in the year 1536 from the creation, yet Lamech died only five years before "the flood," and his father Methuselah—the longest-lived man—in the very year of the deluge. If we try to realise how much information even in our own days, when intercourse, civilisation, and the means of knowledge have so far advanced, can be gained from personal intercourse with the chief actors in great events, we shall understand the importance of man's longevity in the early ages of our race.

But, on the other hand, it was possible to pervert this long duration of life to equally evil purposes. The rare occurrence, during so many centuries, of death with its terrors would tend still more to blunt the conscience ; the long association of evil men would foster the progress of corruption and evil ; and the apparently indefinite delay of either judgment or deliverance would strengthen the bold unbelief of scoffers. That such was the case appears from the substance of Lamech's prophecy ; from the description of the state of the

earth in the time of Noah, and the unbelief of his cotem-
poraries; and from the comparison by our Lord[1] between
"the days of Noe" and those of "the coming of the Son
of man," when, according to St. Peter,[2] there shall be "scoffers,
walking after their own lusts, and saying, Where is the promise
of His coming? for since the fathers fell asleep, all things
continue as they were from the beginning of creation."

The corruption of mankind reached its highest point when
even the difference between the Sethites and the Cainites
became obliterated by intermarriages between the two parties,
and that from sensual motives. We read that "the sons of
God saw the daughters of men that they were fair; and they
took them wives of all which they chose."[3] At that time
the earth must have been in a great measure peopled,[4] and
its state is thus described, "And God saw that the wickedness
of man was great in the earth, and that every imagination of
the thoughts of his heart was only evil continually." This
means more than the total corruption of our nature, as we
should now describe it, and refers to the universal prevalence
of open, daring sin, and rebellion against God, brought about
when the separation between the Sethites and the Cainites
ceased. With the exception of Noah there was none in
that generation "to call upon the name of Jehovah." "In
those days there were 'giants' (in Hebrew: *Nephilim*) in the
earth . . . . the same were the mighty men (or heroes) which
were of old, the men of renown." Properly speaking, these
Nephilim were "men of violence," or tyrants, as Luther renders
it, the root of the word meaning, "to fall upon."[5] In short, it

---

[1] Matt. xxiv. 37–39 ; Luke xvii. 26.   [2] 2 Peter iii. 3, 4.

[3] Other theories concerning the "sons of God" have been broached, but
cannot be maintained on careful and accurate investigation. Any reader
curious on the subject may see it discussed in my edition of Kurtz's *History
of the Old Covenant*," vol. i., p. 96, etc.

[4] The most exaggerated estimates of the number of the human race at
that time have been made, showing the fallacy of such calculations.

[5] The word *Nephilim* occurs once again in Num. xiii. 33, in the report
of the men of gigantic stature, whom the spies saw in Canaan. But though

was a period of violence, of might against right, of rapine, lust, and universal unbelief of the promise. With the virtual extinction of the Sethite faith and worship no further hope remained, and that generation required to be wholly swept away in judgment.

And yet, though not only the justice of God, but even His faithfulness to His gracious promise demanded this, the tender loving-kindness of Jehovah appears in such expressions as these : "It repented Jehovah that He had made man on the earth, and it grieved Him"—literally, "it pained into His heart." The one term, of course, explains the other. When we read that God repented, it is only our human way of speaking, for, as Calvin says, "nothing happens by accident, or that has not been foreseen." It brings before our minds "the sorrow of Divine love over the sins of man," in the words of Calvin, "that when the terrible sins of man offend God, it is not otherwise than as if His heart had been wounded by extreme sorrow." The consequence was, that God declared He would destroy "from the face of the earth both man and beast,"—the latter, owing to the peculiar connection in which creation was placed with man, as being its lord, which involved it in the ruin and punishment that befel man. But long before that sentence was actually executed, God had declared, "My Spirit shall not always strive with man,"—or rather, "dwell with man," "bear rule," or "preside," among them,—"for that he also is flesh," or, as some have rendered it, "since in his erring," or aberration, he has become wholly "carnal, sensual, devilish;" "yet his days shall be an hundred and twenty years;" that is, a further space of a hundred and twenty years would in mercy be granted them, before the final judgments should burst. It was during these hundred and twenty years that "the long-suffering of God waited," "while the ark was

the *Nephilim* in those days may have been men of gigantic proportions, it does not follow that *Nephilim* means "giants." Lastly, there is nothing in the text which shows that they were exclusively the offspring of the sons of God.

a preparing, wherein few, that is, eight souls, were saved by water."

For, to the universal corruption of that generation, there was *one* exception—*Noah.* It needs no more than simply to put together the notices of Noah, in the order in which Scripture places them: "But Noah found grace in the eyes of Jehovah;" and again: "Noah was a just man, and perfect"—as the Hebrew word implies, spiritually upright, genuine, inwardly entire and complete, one whose heart had a single aim—"in his generations," or among his contemporaries; and lastly, "Noah walked with God,"—this expression being the same as in the case of Enoch. The mention of his finding grace in the eyes of Jehovah precedes that of his "justice," which describes his moral bearing towards God; while this justice was again the outcome of inward spiritual rectitude, or of what under the fuller light of the New Testament we would designate a heart renewed by the Holy Spirit. The whole was summed up and completed in an Enoch-like walk with God. The statement that Noah found grace is like the forth-bursting of the sun in a sky lowering for the storm. Three times the sacred text repeats it, that the earth was corrupt, adding that it was full of violence, just as if the watchful eye of the Lord, who "looked upon the earth," had been searching and trying the children of men, and was lingering in pity over it, before judgment was allowed to descend.

Nor was this all. Even so, "the long-suffering of God waited" for one hundred and twenty years, "while the ark was a preparing;" and during this time, especially, Noah must have acted as "a preacher of righteousness." The building of the ark commenced when Noah was four hundred and eighty years old; that is, before any of his three sons, Shem, Ham, and Japheth, had been born,—in fact, just twenty years before the birth of Shem. Thus the great faith of Noah appeared not only in building an ark in the midst of a scoffing and unbelieving generation, and that against all human probability of its ever being needed, and one hun-

dred and twenty years before it was actually required, but
in providing room for "his sons" and his "sons' wives,"
while as yet he himself was childless! Indeed, the more we
try to realise the circumstances, the more grand appears the
unshaken confidence of the patriarch. The words in which
God announced His purpose were these: "The end of all
flesh is come before Me,"—that is, as some have explained
it, the extreme limit of human depravity;—"for the earth
is filled with violence through them,"—that is, violence proceeding from them ("from before their faces"),—"and, behold,
I will destroy them with the earth." Noah and his family
were alone to be preserved, and that by means of an "ark,"—
an expression which only occurs once more in reference to the
ark of bulrushes in which Moses was saved.[1] Noah was to
construct his ark of "gopher," most likely cypress wood, and
to "pitch it within and without with pitch." The ark was to
be three hundred cubits long, fifty broad, and thirty high; that
is, reckoning the cubit at one foot and a half, four hundred
and fifty feet long, seventy-five broad, and forty-five high.[2] As
the wording of the Hebrew text implies, there was all around
the top, one cubit below the roof, an opening for light and
for air (rendered in our version "window"), in which, it has
been suggested, some translucent substance like our glass may
have been inserted. Here there seems also to have been a
regular "window," which is afterwards specially referred to
(ch. viii. 6). The door was to be in the side of the ark, which
was arranged in three stories of rooms (literally "cells"), or
the accommodation of all the animals in the ark, and the

[1] Ex. ii. 3–5.

[2] Some have calculated the cubit at twenty-one inches, which would giv-
a length of five hundred and twenty-five feet, a width of eighty-seven and a
half, and a height of fifty-two and a half. St. Augustine calculates that
the proportions of the ark were the same as those of a perfect human
figure, "the length of which from the sole to the crown is six times the
width across the chest, and ten times the depth of the recumbent figure,
measured in a right line from the ground." Smith's *Dictionary of the
Bible*, vol. ii. p. 566, *note.*

storage of food. For "of every living thing" Noah was to bring with him into the ark,—seven pairs, in the case of "clean beasts," and one pair of those that were not clean. Then, when the appointed time for it came, God would "bring a flood of waters upon the earth, to destroy all flesh, wherein is the breath of life, from under heaven." But with Noah God would "establish" His "covenant," that is, carry out through him His purpose in the covenant of grace, which was to issue in the birth of the Redeemer. Accordingly, Noah, his wife—for here there is no trace of polygamy,—his sons, and his sons' wives were to go into the ark, and there to be kept alive during the general destruction of all around.

Thus far the directions of Scripture. Much needless ingenuity has been wasted on a calculation of the exact space in the ark, of its internal arrangements, and of the accommodation it contained for the different species of animals then existing. Such computations are essentially unreliable, as we can neither calculate the exact room in the ark, nor yet the exact number of *species* which required to be accommodated within its shelter. Scripture, which sets before us the history of God's kingdom, never gratifies such idle and foolish inquiries. But of this we may be quite sure, that the ark which God provided was literally and in every sense quite sufficient for the purposes for which it was intended, and that these purposes were fully secured. It may perhaps help us to realise this marvellous structure if we compare it to the biggest ship known—the *Great Eastern*, whose dimensions are six hundred and eighty feet in length, eighty-three in breadth, and fifty-eight in depth; or else if we describe it as nearly half the size of St. Paul's Cathedral in London. It should be borne in mind that the ark was designed not for navigation, but chiefly for storage. It had neither masts, rudder, nor sails, and was probably flat at the bottom, resembling a huge floating chest. To show how suitable its proportions were for storage, we may mention that a Dutchman, Peter Jansen, built in 1604 a ship on precisely the same proportions (not, of course, the same figures), which was found to hold one-third more lading than any other vessel of the same tonnage.

All other questions connected with the building of the ark may safely be dismissed as not deserving serious discussion. But the one great fact would stand out during that period : Noah preaching righteousness, warning of the judgment to come, and still exhibiting his faith in his practice by continuing to provide an ark of refuge. To sum up Noah's life of faith, Noah's preaching of faith, and Noah's work of faith in the words of Scripture : " By faith Noah, being warned of God of things not seen as yet, moved with fear, prepared an ark to the saving of his house ; by the which he condemned the world, and became heir of the righteousness which is by faith." [1]

CHAPTER VI.

The Flood.

(GEN. VII.—VIII. 15.)

THERE is a grandeur and majestic simplicity about the scriptural account of " The Flood " which equally challenges and defies comparison. Twice only throughout the Old Testament is the event again referred to—each time in the grave, brief language befitting its solemnity. In Ps. xxix. 10 we read : " Jehovah sitteth upon the flood ; yea, Jehovah sitteth King for ever,"—a sort of Old Testament version of " Jesus Christ, the same yesterday, and to-day, and for ever." Then, if we may carry out the figure, there is an evangelical application of this Old Testament history in Isa. liv. 9, 10 : " For this is as the waters of Noah unto Me : for as I have sworn that the waters of Noah should no more go over the earth ; so have I sworn that I would not be wroth

---

[1] Heb. xi. 7.

with thee, nor rebuke thee. For the mountains shall depart, and the hills be removed; but My kindness shall not depart from thee, neither shall the covenant of My peace be removed, saith Jehovah that hath mercy on thee."

The first point in the narrative of " The Flood " which claims our attention is an emphatic mention, twice repeated, of Noah's absolute obedience, " according unto all that Jehovah commanded him." [1] Next, we mark a " solemn pause of seven days " before the flood actually commenced, when " all the fountains of the great deep were broken up, and the windows of heaven were opened ;" in other words, the floodgates alike of earth and heaven thrown wide open. The event happened " in the sixth hundredth year of Noah's life, in the second month, the seventeenth day of the month ;" that is, if we calculate the season according to the beginning of the Hebrew civil year, about the middle or end of our month of November. Then Noah and his wife, his three sons—Shem, Ham, and Japheth—and their wives, and all the animals, having come into the ark, " Jehovah shut him in," and for forty days and forty nights "the rain was upon the earth," while, at the same time, the fountains of the great deep were broken up. The flood continued for one hundred and fifty days, [2] when it began to subside. The terrible catastrophe is thus described : "And the flood was forty days upon the earth ; and the waters increased, and bare up the ark, and it was lift up above the earth. And the waters prevailed, and were increased greatly upon the earth ; and the ark went upon the face of the waters. And the waters prevailed exceedingly upon the earth ; and all the high hills, that were under the whole heaven, were covered. Fifteen cubits upward did the waters prevail ; and the mountains were covered. And all flesh died that moved upon the earth, both of fowl, and of cattle, and of

[1] Gen. vi. 22 ; vii. 5.

[2] Gen. viii. 3, 4, compared with vii. 11, seems to imply that the forty days of rain must be included in these one hundred and fifty days, and not added to them.

beast, and of every creeping thing that creepeth upon the earth,
and every man : all in whose nostrils was the breath of life, of
all that was in the dry land, died. And every living substance
was destroyed which was upon the face of the ground, both
man, and cattle, and the creeping things, and the fowl of the
heaven; and they were destroyed from the earth : and
Noah only remained alive, and they that were with him in
the ark."

The remarks of a recent writer on this subject are every way
so appropriate that we here reproduce them : " The narrative
is vivid and forcible, though entirely wanting in that sort of
description which in a modern historian or poet would have occupied the largest space. We see nothing of the death-struggle ; we
hear not the cry of despair ; we are not called upon to witness
the frantic agony of husband and wife, and parent and child,
as they fled in terror before the rising waters.   Nor is a word
said of the sadness of the one righteous man who, safe himself,
looked upon the destruction which he could not avert.   But
an impression is left upon the mind with peculiar vividness
from the very simplicity of the narrative, and it is that of utter
desolation.   This is heightened by the repetition and contrast
of two ideas.   On the one hand, we are reminded no less than
six times in the narrative[1] who the tenants of the ark were, the
favoured and rescued few ; and, on the other hand, the total
and absolute blotting out of everything else is not less
emphatically dwelt upon."[2]

We will not take from the solemnity of the impressive stillness, amid which Scripture shows us the lonely ark floating on
the desolate waters that have buried earth and all that belonged
to it,[3] by attempting to describe the scenes that must have

[1] Gen. vi., vii., viii.

[2] Gen. vi. 13, 17 ; vii. 4, 21–23. Mr. Perowne, in Smith's *Dictionary
of the Bible*, art. "Noah."

[3] Mr. Perowne quotes from Lyell's *Principles of Geology*, as an illustrative instance of the effects of an inundation, of course, on quite a
different scale, "what occurred in the Runn of Cutch, on the eastern area

ensued. Only the impression is left on our minds that the words "Jehovah shut him in," may be intended to show that Noah, even if he would, could not have given help to his perishing contemporaries. At the end of the one hundred and fifty days it is said, in the peculiarly touching language of Scripture, "God remembered Noah, and every living thing, and all the cattle that was with him in the ark." A drying wind was made to pass over the earth, the flood " was restrained," "and the waters returned from the earth continually." On the seventeenth day of the seventh month, that is, exactly five months after Noah had entered it, the ark was found to be resting " upon the mountains of Ararat,"—not necessarily upon either the highest peak, which measures seventeen thousand two hundred and fifty feet, nor yet, perhaps, upon the second highest, which rises to about twelve thousand feet, but upon that mountain range. Still the waters decreased ; and seventy-three days later, or on the first day of the tenth month, the mountain-tops all around became visible. Forty days more, and Noah "sent forth a raven," which, finding shelter on the mountain-tops, and food from the floating carcases, did not return into the ark. At the end of seven days more "he sent forth a dove from him to see if the waters were abated from off the face of the ground," that is, from the low ground in the valleys. " But the dove found no rest for the sole of her foot, and she returned unto him into the ark." Yet another week, and he sent her forth a second time, when she returned again in the evening, bearing in her mouth an olive-leaf. It is a remarkable fact, as bearing indirect testimony to this narrative, that the olive has been ascertained to bear leaves under water. A third time Noah put forth the messenger of peace, at the end of another week, and she "returned not again unto him any more." "No picture in natural history," says the writer already quoted, "was ever drawn with more exquisite

of the Indus, in 1819, when the sea flowed in, and in a few hours converted a tract of land, two thousand square miles in area, into an inland sea or lagoon."

beauty and fidelity than this. It is admirable alike for its poetry and its truth." On the first day of the first month, in the sixth hundredth and first year, " the waters were dried up from off the earth ; and Noah removed the covering of the ark, and looked, and, behold, the face of the ground was dry. And in the second month, on the twenty-seventh day of the month, was the earth dried,"—just one year and ten days after Noah had entered the ark.

Thus far the scriptural narrative. It has so often been explained that the object of the Bible is to give us the history of the kingdom of God, not to treat of curious or even scientific questions, that we can dismiss a matter too often discussed of late in an entirely unbecoming spirit, in these words of a recent writer :[1] " It is a question among theologians and men of science whether the flood was absolutely universal, or whether it was universal only in the sense of extending over all the part of the world then inhabited. We do not here enter into this controversy ; but we may notice the remarkable fact that the district lying to the east of Ararat, where the ark rested, bears traces of having at one time been under water. It is a peculiarly depressed region, lying lower than the districts around, and thus affording peculiar facilities for such a submersion."

But there is another matter connected with the flood so marked and striking as to claim our special attention. It is that the remembrance of the flood has been preserved in the traditions of so many nations, so widely separated and so independent of each other, that it is impossible to doubt that they have all been derived from one and the same original source. As might be expected, they contain many legendary details, and they generally fix the locality of the flood in their own lands ; but these very particulars mark them as corruptions of the real history recorded in the Bible, and carried by the different nations into the various countries where they settled. Mr. Perowne has grouped these traditions into those of *Western Asia*, including the Chaldean, the Phenician, that of the so-

[1] Dr. Blaikie, *Bible History*, p. 29.

called "Sibylline Oracles," the Phrygian, the Syrian, and the Armenian stories; then those of *Eastern Asia*, including the Persian, Indian, and Chinese; and, thirdly, those of the *American nations*—the Cherokee, and the various tribes of Mexican Indians, with which—strange though it may seem— he groups those of the Fiji Islands. To these he adds, as a fourth cycle, the similar traditions of the *Greek nations*. But the most interesting of all these traditions is the *Chaldean* or *Babylonian*, which deserves more than merely passing notice.

Though it needs not such indirect confirmations to convince us of the truth of the narratives in the Bible, it is very remarkable how all historical investigations, when really completed and rightly applied, confirm the exactness of what is recorded in the Holy Scriptures. But their chief value to us must always be this, that they tell us of that Ark which alone rides on the waters of the deluge, and preserves for ever safe them who are "shut in" there by the hand of Jehovah.

CHALDEAN NARRATIVE OF THE DELUGE.—In general we may say that we have two Chaldean accounts of the flood. The one comes to us through Greek sources, from Berosus, a Chaldean priest in the third century before Christ, who translated into Greek the records of Babylon. This, as the less clear, we need not here notice more particularly. But a great interest attaches to the far earlier cuneiform inscriptions, first discovered and deciphered in 1872 by Mr. G. Smith, of the British Museum, and since further investigated by the same scholar.[1] These inscriptions cover twelve tablets, of which as yet only part has been made available. They may broadly be described as embodying the Babylonian account of the flood, which, as the event took place in that locality, has a special value. The narrative is supposed to date from two thousand to two thousand five hundred years before Christ. The history of the flood is related by a hero, preserved through it, to a monarch whom Mr. Smith calls *Izdubar*, but whom he supposes to have been the Nimrod of Scripture. There are, as one might have expected, frequent differences between the Babylonian and the Biblical account of the flood. On the other hand, there are striking points of agreement between them, which all the more confirm the scriptural account, as showing that the event had become a

---

[1] See *Assyrian Discoveries*, by George Smith. London, 1875.

distinct part of the history of the district in which it had taken place. There are frequent references to Erech, the city mentioned in Gen. x. 10; allusions to a race of giants, who are described in fabulous terms ; a mention of Lamech, the father of Noah, though under a different name, and of the patriarch himself as a sage, reverent and devout, who, when the Deity resolved to destroy by a flood the world for its sin, built the ark. Sometimes the language comes so close to that of the Bible that one almost seems to read disjointed or distorted quotations from Scripture. We mention, as instances, the scorn which the building of the ark is said to have called forth on the part of contemporaries ; the pitching of the ark without and within with pitch ; the shutting of the door behind the saved ones , the opening of the window, when the waters had abated ; the going and returning of the dove since "a resting-place it did not find," the sending of the raven, which, feeding on corpses in the water, " did not return ;" and, finally, the building of an altar by Noah. We sum up the results of this discovery in the words of Mr. Smith :

"Not to pursue this parallel further, it will be perceived that when the Chaldean account is compared with the Biblical narrative, in their main features the two stories fairly agree ; as to the wickedness of the antediluvian world, the Divine anger and command to build the ark, its stocking with birds and beasts, the coming of the deluge, the rain and storm, the ark resting on a mountain, trial being made by birds sent out to see if the waters had subsided, and the building of an altar after the flood. All these main facts occur in the same order in both narratives, but when we come to examine the details of these stages in the two accounts, there appear numerous points of difference ; as to the number of people who were saved, the duration of the deluge, the place where the ark rested, the order of sending out the birds, and other similar matters."[1]

We conclude with another quotation from the same work, which will show how much of the primitive knowledge of Divine things, though mixed with terrible corruptions, was preserved among men at this early period :

"It appears that at that remote age the Babylonians had a tradition of a flood which was a Divine punishment for the wickedness of the world ; and of a holy man, who built an ark, and escaped the destruction ; who was afterwards translated and dwelt with the gods. They believed in hell, a place of torment under the earth, and heaven, a place of glory in the sky ; and their description of the two has, in several points, a striking likeness to those in the Bible. They believed in a spirit or soul distinct from the body, which was not destroyed on the death of the mortal frame ; and they represent this ghost as rising from the earth at the bidding of one of the gods, and winging its way to heaven."

---

[1] *Assyrian Discoveries*, p. 218.

HISTORY OF THE PATRIARCHS

CHAPTER VII.

After the Flood—Noah's Sacrifice—Noah's Sin—Noah's Descendants.

(GEN. VIII. 15—IX. 28.)

RIGHTLY considered, the destruction of "all flesh" by the deluge was necessary for its real preservation. Death was needful for its new life. The old world was buried in the flood, that a new order of things might rise from its grave. For, manifestly, after the mixing up of the Sethite with the Cainite race, an entirely new commencement required to be made if the purpose of God in grace was to be carried to its goal. Hence, also, God once more pronounced upon Noah the blessing of fruitfulness which he had spoken to Adam, and gave him dominion over creation, yet, as we shall see, with such modifications as the judgment that had just passed, and the new state of things which had commenced, implied.

It deserves our notice that, even after the earth was quite dry, Noah awaited the express command of God before leaving the ark. His first act after that was to build "an altar unto Jehovah," and there to offer "burnt-offerings" "of every clean beast, and of every fowl." Nor was it merely in gratitude and homage to God, but also in spiritual worship that he thus commenced his life anew, and consecrated earth unto Jehovah. In bringing an animal sacrifice Noah followed the example of Abel; in calling upon the name of Jehovah he once again and solemnly adopted the profession of the Sethites. But there was this difference between his and any preceding sacrifice, that now for the first time we read of building an altar. While

Paradise was still on earth, men probably turned towards it as the place whence Jehovah held intercourse with man. But when its site was swept away in the flood, God, as it were, took up His throne in heaven, and from thence revealed Himself unto men and held intercourse with them.[1] And the truth, that our hearts and prayers must rise upwards to Him who is in heaven, was symbolised by the altar on which the sacrifice was laid. Scripture significantly adds, that "Jehovah smelled a sweet savour," or rather "a savour of rest," "of satisfaction;" in other words, He accepted the sacrifice. "And Jehovah said in His heart," that is, He resolved, "I will not again curse the ground for man's sake, for (or because) the imagination of man's heart is evil from his youth." Both Luther and Calvin have remarked on the circumstance that men's universal sin fulness, which formerly had been the cause of the judgment of the flood, should now be put forward as the reason for not again cursing the ground. But in fact this only marks another difference between the state of man before and after the flood. If we may so say, God now admitted the fact of universal sin-fulness as existing, and made it an element of His future government. He looked upon man as a miserable and wretched sinner, with whom in His compassion and long-suffering He would bear, delaying His second and final judgment till after He should have accomplished all that He had promised to do for the salvation of men. Putting aside Israel, as God's special people, the period between Noah and Christ may be described, in the words of St. Paul, as "the times of this ignorance" which "God winked at,"[2] or as those when "through the forbearance of God" sins were passed over.[3]

Having thus explained the fundamental terms on which the Lord would deal with the nations of the earth during the period between the flood and the coming of the Saviour, that is, during the Jewish dispensation, we proceed to notice, in the words which God addressed to Noah, some other points of difference

[1] See also Gen. xi. 5, 7.   [2] Acts xvii. 30.
[3] Rom. iii. 25, see marginal rendering.

between the former and the new state of things. First of all, the gracious announcement that, while the earth remained, seed-time and harvest, cold and heat, summer and winter, day and night were not to cease, implies not only His purpose to spare our earth, but also that man might henceforth reckon upon a regular succession of seasons, and that he was to make this earth for the present his home, to till it, and to possess it. Hence it was quite another matter when Noah became an "husbandman," from what it had been when Cain chose to be "a tiller of the ground." Next, as already stated, God renewed the blessing of fruitfulness in much the same terms in which He had spoken it originally to Adam, and once more conferred dominion over the lower creation. But in this new grant there was this essential difference—that man's dominion would now be one of force, and not, as formerly, of willing subjection. If God had at the first brought "every beast" and "every fowl" before Adam, as it were, to do homage to him, and to receive from him their names, it was now said to Noah and to his descendants, "The fear of you and the dread of you shall be upon every beast of the earth ; . . . into your hand are they delivered."

Perhaps we ought also to notice in this connection that, whatever may have been the common practice before, now for the first time the use of animal food was expressly permitted, with the exception of the blood, and that probably for the reason afterwards mentioned in the case of sacrifices, that the blood was the seat of life.[1] Another and most important change is marked by the solemn prohibition of murder, with this addition, that " whoso sheddeth man's blood, by man shall his blood be shed." Such crimes were no longer to be avenged directly by God Himself, but He delegated His authority to man.[2] As Luther rightly says, " In these words the civil magistracy is instituted, and the Divine right of bearing the sword." For when it is added, as a reason why murder should be punished with death, that God made man in His own image, it seems to convey that vengeance might not be taken by any

---

[1] Lev. xvii. 11, 14.   [2] Rom. xiii. 1, 2.

one at his own will, but that this belonged to those who on earth represented the authority of God, or were His delegates ; whence also they are called in Psa. lxxxii. 6, 'gods," or rather "*Elohim.*"[1] And, as Luther rightly argues, "If God concedes to man the power over life and death, assuredly this carries with it authority over that which is less than life, such as goods, family, wife, children, servants, and land." Thus the words spoken by the Lord to Noah contain the warrant and authority of those who are appointed rulers and judges over us. In later times the Jews have been wont to speak of what they called the seven Noachic commandments, which, according to them, were binding upon all Gentile proselytes. These were a prohibition (1) of idolatry, (2) of blasphemy, (3) of murder, (4) of incest, (5) of robbery and theft, (6) of eating blood and strangled animals, and (7) an injunction of obedience to magistrates.[2]

In confirmation of what God had spoken, He "established" His "covenant" with Noah and his sons, and in "token" thereof "set," or "appointed," His "bow in the cloud." It may have been so, that the rainbow was then seen for the first time, although this does not necessarily follow from the words of Scripture. They only tell us that henceforth the rainbow was to be a "token" or visible symbol to man of God's promise no more to destroy all flesh by a flood, and also that He Himself would "look upon it" as such, so that He might "remember the everlasting covenant between God and every living creature." The symbol of the rainbow was therefore to be both a sign and a seal of God's promise. And we can readily understand how impressive, whenever a storm burst upon the earth, this symbol would have appeared to those who had witnessed the flood. In the poetical language of a German writer, " The rainbow, caused by the influence of

---

[1] Two terms are chiefly used in the Hebrew for God : the one, *Elohim*, which refers to His power as Ruler and Lord ; the other, *Jehovah*, to His character as the covenant-God.

[2] Comp. also Acts xv. 20.

the sun upon the dark clouds, would show to man, that what was from heaven would penetrate that which rose from earth; and as it spanned the gulf between heaven and earth, it would seem to proclaim peace between God and man; while even the circumstance that it bounded the horizon would symbolize, how the covenant of mercy extended to earth's utmost bounds."

From this scene of intercourse between Noah and God we have to pass to an event in his history, alas, of a very different character. When Noah—with his three sons, Shem, Ham, and Japheth—left the ark to become an husbandman, he planted a vineyard, as Jewish legend has it, from a slip of the vine that had strayed out of Paradise. But it may boldly be asserted that, except the forbidden fruit itself, none has brought more sin, ruin, and desolation upon our earth. Whether Noah was unacquainted with the intoxicating property of the vine, or neglected proper moderation, the sad spectacle is presented of the aged patriarch, so lately rescued from the flood, not only falling a victim to drunkenness, but exposing himself in that state to the impious and vile conduct of his son Ham. As Luther says, " Ham would not have mocked his father, when overcome with wine, if he had not long before cast from his soul that reverence which, according to God's command, children should cherish towards their parents." It is a relief to find the other sons of Noah, so far from sharing their brother's sin, reverently defending their father from the unnatural vileness of Ham. As we might have expected, the conduct of the brothers received meet reward,—the curse descended on Ham, while a blessing, suited to each, was given to Shem and Japheth. But, in the words of the patriarch, the curse lights specially upon Canaan, the son of Ham, not to the exclusion of his other sons, but probably because as Noah had suffered from his son, so Ham was to experience his punishment in his son; and Canaan may have been specially singled out, either because he fully entered into the spirit of his father, or more probably because of the later connection between Israel and the Canaanites, in whom they would see alike the spirit and the curse of Ham fully realised. In connection with this we mark, that, twice before, [1] when Ham is mentioned, it is added that he was "the father of Canaan."

Shem, Ham, and Japheth, who were to repeople the earth, seem to have impressed their own characteristics on their descendants. Their very names are symbolical and prophetic. *Shem* means splendour or glory, *Ham* burning heat, and *Japheth* enlargement. Bearing this in mind, we listen to the words of the patriarch :

> " Cursed be Canaan,
> A servant of servants shall he be to his brethren ;"

and we know that this has been the fate of the children of Ham, or the races of Africa ; while, strangely, the name of *Canaan* has been interpreted as meaning "he who is subject. " Again,

> " Blessed be Jehovah, the God of Shem,
> And Canaan shall be their slave :"

a prophecy most signally fulfilled when Israel took possession of the land of Canaan ; and, lastly,

> " God (Elohim) shall enlarge Japheth (enlargement) ;
> And he shall dwell in the tents of Shem,
> And Canaan shall be their slave."

This latter prophecy consists of three parts. It promises from God, as the God of power, that enlargement to Japheth which is the characteristic of his descendants, the European nations. And it adds that Japheth (not, as some have read it, God) shall dwell in the tents of Shem, that is, as St. Augustine has said, "in the churches which the apostles, the sons of the prophets, reared ;" thus referring to the blessing which was to flow to all nations through the Hebrew race. [2] Lastly, Canaan

---

[1] Gen. ix. 18, 22.

[2] As a German writer expresses it : " What are we all but descendants of Japheth, who dwell in the tents of Shem ; and what is the language of the New Testament, but that of Javan spoken in the dwellings of Shem ?"

was to be the servant of Japheth, as seen in the subjection to Greece and Rome, of Tyre and Carthage, the ancient centres of wealth and merchandise, and of Egypt, the empire of might and of the oldest civilisation.

But the words spoken to Shem, the ancestor of the Hebrew race, deserve special notice. The blessing here begins quite differently from that of Japheth. It opens with a thanksgiving to God, for, as Luther says, " Noah sees it to be such that he cannot express it in words, therefore he turns to thanksgiving." Then, the blessing of Shem is not outward, but spiritual ; for Jehovah is to be the God of Shem. To speak in an anticipatory figure, Shem's portion, in the widest sense, is that to be hereafter assigned to Levi, amongst the Jews ; and Japheth is to dwell in his tents,—in other words, Israel is to be the tribe of Levi to all nations. More than that, whereas Elohim is to give enlargement to Japheth, Jehovah the covenant-God is to be the God of Shem. Thus the primitive promise to Adam is now both further defined and enlarged. The promised Deliverer is to come through Shem, as the ancestor of the chosen race, in the midst of whom Jehovah is to dwell ; and through Shem, Japheth is to share in the coming spiritual blessing. Here, then, is clearly defined the separation of the Jews and the Gentiles, and the mission of each : the one from Jehovah, the other from Elohim ; the one in the Church, the other in the world.

CHAPTER VIII.

Genealogy of Nations—Babel—Confusion of Tongues.

(GEN. X.—XI. 10.)

IT was the Divine will, that after the flood the whole earth should be repeopled by the descendants of Noah. For this purpose they must, of course, have separated and spread, so as to form the different nations and tribes among whom the world should be apportioned. Any attempted unity on their part would not only be contrary to the Divine purpose, but also, considering the universal sinfulness of man, prove dangerous to themselves, and even be untrue, since their inward separation had already appeared in the different characters and tendencies of Ham and his brothers. But before recording the judgment by which the Divine purpose was enforced, Scripture gives us the genealogy of the different nations, and this with a threefold object—to show how the earth was all peopled from the descendants of Noah; to define the relation of Israel towards each nationality; and, best of all, to register, as it were, their birth in the book of God, thereby indicating, that, however "in time past He suffered all nations to walk in their own ways,"[1] they also were included in the purposes of mercy, and intended finally to "dwell in the tents of Shem."

In accordance with the general plan on which Holy Scripture is written, we read after the prophecy of Noah, which fixed the future of his sons, no more of that patriarch than that he "lived after the flood three hundred and fifty years," and that he died at the age of nine hundred and fifty years. Regarding the division of earth among his three sons, it may be said generally, that Asia was given to Shem, Africa to Ham, and Europe to Japheth. In the same general manner a modern scholar has traced all existing languages to three original sources, themselves, no doubt, derived from a primeval spring, which may have been lost in the "confusion of tongues," though its existence is attested by constant and striking points of connection between the three great families of languages. The more we think of the allotment of Europe, Asia, and Africa among the three sons of Noah, the more clearly do we see the fulfilment of prophecy regarding them. As we run our eye down the catalogue of nations in Gen. x., we have little difficulty in recognising them; and beginning with the youngest, *Japheth*, we find of those known to the

[1] Acts xiv. 16.

general reader, the Cymry of Wales and Brittany (*Gomer*), the Scythians (*Magog*), the Medes (*Madai*), the Greeks (*Ionians, Javan*), and the Thracians (*Tiras*). Among their descendants, the Germans, Celts, and Armenians have been traced to the three sons of Gomer. It is not necessary to follow this table farther, though all will remember Tarshish, or Spain, and the Kittim, or "inhabitants of the isles."

Passing next to *Shem* (ver. 21), we notice that he is called "the father of all the children of Eber," because in Eber the main line divided into that of Peleg, from whom the race of Abraham sprang, and the descendants of Joktan (ver. 25). The descendants of Shem are exclusively Asiatic nations, among whom we only notice Asshur or Assyria, and Uz, as the land which gave birth to Job.

We have reserved *Ham* for the last place, because of the connection of his story with the dispersion of all nations. His sons were Cush or Ethiopia, Mizraim or Egypt, Phut or Lybia, and Canaan, which, of course, we know. It will be noticed, that the seats of all these nations were in Africa, except that of Canaan, whose intrusion into the land of Palestine was put an end to by Israel. But yet another of Ham's descendants had settled in Asia. Nimrod, the founder of the Babylonian empire, the conqueror of Assyria, and the builder of Nineveh (ver. 11), was the son of Cush. Altogether this "mighty one in the earth," who founded the first world-empire, reminds us of Cain and of his descendant Lamech. Leaving out of view the possible meaning of his name, which some have explained as being "we will rebel," boastful violence and rebellion certainly constitute the characteristics of his history. Most strangely have the Assyrian tablets of the royal successors of Nimrod been made to furnish an explanation of his description as "a mighty hunter"—for this is the title given in them to the great conquering warrior-monarchs, as "hunting the people." Thus we gather the full meaning of the expression, "he began to be a mighty one in the earth." From Babylon, which was "the beginning of his kingdom,"

Nimrod "went out into Assyria" (ver. 11, marginal rendering),
"and builded Nineveh"—the remarkable circumstance here
being that each time four cities are mentioned in connection with Nimrod : first, the four cities of his Babylonian empire,
of which Babel was the capital, and then the four cities
of his conquered Assyrian empire, of which Nineveh was the
capital.   Now all this tallies in the most striking manner with
what we read in ancient history, and with those Assyrian
monuments which within our own lifetime have by the labours
of Layard and Loftus been exhumed from their burial of many
centuries, to give witness for the Bible.   For, first, we now know
that the great Asiatic empire of Babylon was of *Cushite*
origin.   Nay, even the name Nimrod occurs in the list of
Egyptian kings.   Secondly, we are made aware that Babel was
the original seat of the empire ; and, strangest of all, that the
earliest Babylonian kings bore a title which is supposed to
mean "four races," in reference to "the quadruple groups of
capitals"[1] of Babylonia and Assyria.   Lastly, we know that,
as stated in the Bible, "the Babylonian empire extended
its sway northwards" to Assyria, where Nineveh was founded,
which in turn succeeded to the empire once held by Babel.
In all these respects, therefore, the latest historical investigations have most strikingly confirmed the narrative of Scripture.

Of the magnificence of Babel, the capital of the empire of
Nimrod, "the mighty hunter," it is difficult to convey an
adequate conception, without entering into details foreign to
our purpose.   But some idea of it may be formed from its
extent, which according to the *lowest* computation, covered no
less than one hundred square miles, or about five times the size
of London; while the highest computation would make it cover
two hundred square miles, or ten times the extent of London ![2]
Such was the world-city, the first "beginning" of which at least

[1] See Mr. Bevan's article in Smith's *Dictionary of the Bible*, vol. ii.,
pp. 544, etc.

[2] Mr. Smith, however, regards these accounts as exaggerated.

Nimrod had founded. No wonder that the worldly pride of that age should have wished to make such a place the world-capital of a world-empire, whose tower "may reach unto heaven!" The events connected with the discomfiture of their plan took place in the days of Peleg, the grandson of Shem.[1] As Peleg was born one hundred years after the flood, and lived two hundred and thirty-nine years, there must have been already a considerable population upon the earth.

If evidence were required that the flood had indeed destroyed sinners but not sin, it would be found in the bearing and language of men in the days of Nimrod and Peleg. After leaving the ark, they had "journeyed eastward" (ch. xi. 2) till they reached the extensive well-watered plain of Shinar, where they settled. Being still all "of one language and of one speech," they resolved to build themselves there "a city, and a tower whose top may reach unto heaven," for the twofold purpose of making themselves "a name," and lest they "be scattered abroad upon the face of the whole earth." Such words read singularly like those which a Nimrod would employ, and they breathe the spirit of "Babylon" in all ages. Assuredly their meaning is: "Let us rebel!"—for not only would the Divine purpose of peopling the earth have thus been frustrated, but such a world-empire would in the nature of it have been a defiance to God and to the kingdom of God, even as its motive was pride and ambition. A German critic has seen in the words "let us make us a *name*"—in Hebrew, *sheen*—a kind of counterfeit of the *Shem* in whom the promises of God centred, or, if one might so express it, the setting up of an anti-Christ of worldly power. Something of this kind seems certainly indicated in what God says of the attempt (ver. 6): "And this they begin to do: and now nothing will be restrained from them which they have imagined to do." These words seem to imply that the building of Babel was only intended as the commencement of a further course of rebellion. The gathering of all material forces into one common centre would have led

[1] Gen. x. 25.

to universal despotism and to universal idolatry,—in short, to
the full development of what as anti-Christ is reserved for the
judgment of the last days.   We read, that "Jehovah came
down to see the city and the tower," that is, using our human
modes of expression, to take judicial cognisance of man's
undertaking.   In allusion to the boastful language in which
the builders of Babel and of its tower had in their self-confidence stated their purpose: "Go to, let us make brick," etc.
(ver. 3), Jehovah expressed *His* purpose of defeating their folly,
using the same words: "Go to, let us go down, and there
confound their language."   And by this simple means, without
any outward visible interference, did the Lord arrest the
grandest attempt of man's rebellion, and by confounding
their language, "scattered them abroad from thence upon
the face of all the earth."   "Therefore is the name of it
called Babel, or confusion."   What a commentary does this
history afford to the majestic declarations of the second
Psalm !

Of the tower of Babel no certainly ascertained remains have
as yet been discovered.   It has commonly been identified with
the ruins called *Birs Nimrud*, about six miles to the south-
west of the site of 'ancient Babylon.   Birs Nimrud is "a
pyramidical mound, crowned apparently by the ruins of a
tower, rising to the height of one hundred and fifty-five and a
half feet above the level of the plain, and in circumference
somewhat more than two thousand feet."[1]   Its distance from
Babylon, however, seems opposed to the idea that these are
the ruins of the tower spoken of in Scripture.   But even so,
Birs Nimrud can only be a few centuries younger than the
tower of Babel; and its construction enables us to judge what
the appearance of the original tower must have been.   Birs
Nimrud faced north-east, and formed a sort of "oblique
pyramid, built in seven receding stages.   The platform on
which these stages rested was of crude brick ; the stages themselves of burnt brick, painted in different colours in honour of

[1] Professor Rawlinson, in Smith's *Dictionary of the Bible*, vol. i.

gods or planets—each stage as it was placed on the other receding, so as to be considerably nearer the back of the building, or the south-west." The first stage, painted *black* in honour of Saturn, was a square of two hundred and seventy-two feet, and twenty-six feet high; the second stage, *orange* coloured, in honour of Jupiter, was a square of two hundred and thirty feet, and twenty-six high; the third stage, *bright red*, in honour of Mars, was a square of one hundred and eighty-eight feet, and also twenty-six high; the fourth stage, *golden*, for the Sun, was one hundred and forty-six feet square, and fifteen high; the fifth stage, *pale yellow*, for Venus, was one hundred and four feet square, and fifteen high; the sixth stage, *dark blue*, for Mercury, was sixty-two feet square, and fifteen high; and the seventh stage, *silver*, for the Moon, was twenty feet square, and fifteen high. The whole was surmounted by a chapel, which must have nearly covered the whole top. The whole height, as already stated, was one hundred and fifty-three feet; or about one-third that of the great pyramid of Egypt, which measures four hundred and eighty feet. It is also interesting to notice, how exactly what we know of early Babylonian architecture tallies with what we read in Scripture : " Let us make brick, and burn them thoroughly. And they had brick for stone, and slime (or rather, bitumen) had they for mortar." The small burnt bricks, laid in bitumen, are still there ; not only in the tower, but in the still existing ruins of the ancient palace of Babel, which was coeval with the building of the city itself.

Holy Scripture does not inform us whether " the tower " was allowed to stand after the dispersion of its builders ; nor yet does it furnish any details as to the manner in which " Jehovah did there confound the language of all the earth." All this would have been beyond its purpose. But there, at the very outset, when the first attempt was made to found, in man's strength, a vast kingdom of this world, which God brought to naught by confounding the language of its builders, and by scattering them over the face of the earth, we see a typical judgment, of which the counterpart in blessing was granted on the day of Pentecost; when, by the outpouring of the Holy Spirit, another universal kingdom was to be founded, the first token of which was that gift of tongues, which pointed forward to a reunion of the nations, when the promise would be fulfilled that they should all be gathered into the tents of Shem !

----•◦•----

CHAPTER IX.

The Nations and their Religion—Job.

A MODERN German writer has well said: " The birth of heathenism may be dated from the moment when the presumptuous statement was uttered, ' Go to, let us build a city and a tower whose top may reach unto heaven, and let us make us a name.' "   Even Josephus, the ancient Jewish historian, regards Nimrod as the father of heathenism, the characteristic of which is to find strength and happiness in sin, and not in God.   Its essential principle is to reject all that is not seen, and to cling to that which is temporal.   Thus we also may be heathens in heart, even though we are not such in mind, and do not worship stocks or stone.   Indeed, it is very remarkable, that neither nation nor tribe has ever been discovered which did not acknowledge and worship some superior Being ; and yet from the most savage barbarians to the most refined philosopher, they have all been destitute of the knowledge of the one living and true God.   The only exception in the world has been that of Israel, to whom God specially revealed Himself; and even Israel required constant teaching, guidance, and discipline from on high to keep them from falling back into idolatry.   Idolatry is

the religion of sight in opposition to that of faith. Instead
of the unseen Creator, man regarded that which was visible—
the sun, the moon, the stars—as the cause and the ruler of all ;
or he assigned to everything its deity, and thus had gods many
and lords many; or else he converted his heroes, real or
imaginary, into gods. The worship of the heavens, the worship of nature, or the worship of man—such is heathenism and
idolatry. And yet all the while man felt the insufficiency
of his worship, for behind these gods he placed a dark, im-
moveable, unsearchable *Fate*, which ruled supreme, and con-
trolled alike gods and men. It was indeed a terrible exchange
to make—to leave our heavenly Father and His love for such
delusions and disappointments. The worst of it was, that man
gradually became conformed to his religion. He first imputed
his own vices to his gods, and next imitated the vices of his
gods. Assuredly, the heathen nations were the younger son
in the parable,[1] who had left his father's house with the portion
of goods that belonged to him—heathen science, art, literature,
and power—to find himself at the last driven to eat the husks
on which the swine do feed, and yet not able to satisfy the
cravings of his hunger ! Blessed be God for that revelation of
Himself in Christ Jesus, which has brought the prodigal back
to the Father's home and heart !

But even so, God did not leave Himself without a witness.
The inward searching of man after a God, the accusing voice
of his conscience, the attempt to offer sacrifices, and the
remnants of ancient traditions of the truth among men—all
seemed to point upward. And then, as all were not Israel
who were of Israel, so God also had at all times His own, even
among the Gentile nations. Job, Melchizedek, Rahab, Ruth,
Naaman, may be mentioned as instances of this. It will be
readily understood that the number of those "born out of
season," as it were, from among the Gentiles, must have been
largest the higher we ascend the stream of time, and the nearer
we approach the period when early traditions were still pre-

[1] Luke xv. 12.

served in their purity in the earth. The fullest example of this is set before us in the book of Job, which also gives a most interesting picture of those early times.

Two things may be regarded as quite settled about the book of Job. Its scene and actors are laid in patriarchal times, and outside the family or immediate ancestry of Abraham. It is a story of Gentile life in the time of the earliest patriarchs. And yet anything more noble, grand, devout, or spiritual than what the book of Job contains is not found, "no, not in Israel." This is not the place to give either the history of Job, or to point out the depth of thought, the vividness of imagery, and the beauty and grandeur of language with which it is written. It must suffice to take the most rapid survey of the religious and social life which it sets before us. Without here referring to the sayings of Elihu, Job had evidently perfect knowledge of the true God; and he was a humble, earnest worshipper of Jehovah. Without any acquaintance with "Moses and the prophets," he knew that of which Moses and the prophets spoke. Reverent, believing acknowledgment of God, sub-mission, and spiritual repentance formed part of his experience, which had the approval of God Himself. Then Job offered sacrifices; he speaks about the great tempter; he looks for the resurrection of the body; and he expects the coming of Messiah.

We have traced the barest outlines of the religion of Job. The friends who come to him, if they share not his piety, at least do not treat his views as something quite strange and previously unheard. This, then, is a blessed picture of at least a certain class in that age. How far culture and civilisation must have advanced in those times we gather from various allusions in the book of Job. Job himself is a man of great wealth and high rank. In the language of a recent writer :[1] "The chieftain lives in considerable splendour and dignity. . . . Job visits the city frequently, and is there received with

---

[1] Canon Cook, in Smith's *Dictionary of the Bible*, vol. i., p. 1097.

high respect as a prince, judge, and distinguished warrior.[1] There are allusions to courts of justice, written indictments, and regular forms of procedure.[2] Men had begun to observe and reason upon the phenomena of nature, and astronomical observations were connected with curious speculations upon primeval traditions. We read of mining operations, great buildings, ruined sepulchres. . . . Great revolutions had occurred within the time of the writer; nations, once independent, had been overthrown, and whole races reduced to a state of misery and degradation."

Nor ought we to overlook the glimpses of social life given us in this history. While, indeed, there was violence, robbery, and murder in the land, there is happily also another side to the picture. "When I went out to the gate through the city, when I prepared my seat in the street, the young men saw me, and hid themselves; and the aged arose and stood up." Along with such becoming tribute of respect paid to worth, we find that the relationship between the pious rich and the poor is thus described : "When the ear heard me, then it blessed me; and when the eye saw me, it gave witness to me : because I delivered the poor that cried, and the fatherless, and him that had none to help him. The blessing of him that was ready to perish came upon me, and I caused the widow's heart to sing for joy." Assuredly there is nothing in all this which we could wish to see altered even in New Testament times ! But the more terrible in contrast must have been the idolatry and the corruption of the vast majority of mankind ; an idolatry which they had probably inherited from before the flood, and which soon attained gigantic proportions, and a corruption which went on ever increasing during the "times of this ignorance."

[1] Job xxix. 7, 9.   [2] Job xiii. 26; xxxi. 28.

CHAPTER X.

The Chronology of the Early History of the Bible—Commencement of the History of God's Dealings with Abraham and his Seed.

B EFORE further proceeding with our history some brief explanation may be desirable of the chronological table given in this volume, and in general of the early chronology of the Bible. It will be noticed, first, that the years are counted from " B. C.," that is, from " before Christ;" the numbers, of course, becoming smaller the farther we come down from the creation of the world, and the nearer we approach the birth of our Saviour. Thus, if the year of creation be computed at 4004 before Christ, the deluge, which happened 1656 years later, would fall in the year 2348 B. C. Further, it will be observed that we have given two chronological tables of the same events, which differ by many hundreds of years—the one "according to Hales," the other "according to Ussher," which latter is that of "the dates in the margin of English Bibles," and, we may add, corresponds with the Hebrew text of the Old Testament. The explanation of the difference between them is that our calculations of Biblical dates may be derived from one of three sources. We have, in fact, the five books of Moses in three different forms before us. First, we have the original Hebrew text of the Old Testament; next, there exists a translation of it in Greek, completed long before the time of our Lord, which was commonly used by the Jews at the time of Christ, for which reason also it is generally quoted in the New Testament. This version is known as that of the " LXX," or " Seventy," from the supposed number of translators. Finally, we have the Samaritan Pentateuch, or that in use among the Samaritans. Now, as the genealogies differ in these three in regard to the ages of the patriarchs, the question arises which of them should be adopted ? Each in turn has had its defenders, but the most learned critics are now almost unanimous in concluding, as indeed we might have expected, that the Hebrew text contains the true chronology. Of the other two, the Samaritan is so untrustworthy that for practical purposes we may leave it entirely out of view. The Septuagint chronology differs from that of the Hebrew text in prolonging the ages of the patriarchs, partially before the deluge, but chiefly between the deluge and the calling of Abraham,—the result being that the flood is thrown five hundred and eighty - six years later than in the Hebrew text; and the birth of Abraham yet other eight hundred and seventy-eight years—the total difference amounting to no less than one thousand two hundred and forty-five years ! It is not difficult to guess the reason why the Greek translators had thus altered the original numbers. It was evidently their wish to throw the birth of Abraham as late as possible after the flood. Of these two chronologies, that of the Hebrew text may, for convenience sake, be designated as the short, and that of the "LXX" as the long chronology ; and, in a general way, it may be said that (with certain modifications which it would take too long to explain) Hales has adopted the long, or Greek, and Ussher the short, or Hebrew chronology.

This may suffice on a matter which has engaged only too much discussion.[1] It is far more important to think of the kingdom of God, the history of which is given us in the Holy Scriptures ; for now we are at the beginning of its real appearance. If God had at the first dealt with mankind generally, then with one part of the race, and lastly with one division of nations, He now chose and raised up for Himself a peculiar people, through whom His purposes of mercy towards all men were to be carried out. This people was to be trained from its cradle until it had fulfilled its mission, which was when He came who was the Desire of all nations. Three points here claim our special attention :—

[1] The modern Jews count the year of the Creation from 3761 B.C., so that, in order to calculate the Jewish era, we have to add to our Christian era the number 3761.

1. The *election* and *selection* of what became the people of God. Step by step we see in the history of the patriarchs this electing and separating process on the part of God.   Both are marked by this twofold characteristic : that all is accomplished, not in the ordinary and natural manner, but, as it were, super-naturally ; and that all is of grace.   Thus Abram was called alone out of his father's house—he was elected and selected. The birth of Isaac, the heir of the promises, was, in a sense, supernatural ; while, on the other hand, Ishmael, the elder son of Abram, was rejected.   The same election and selection appears in the history of Esau and Jacob, and indeed through-out the whole patriarchal history. For at the outset the chosen race was to learn what is the grand lesson of all Scripture—that everything comes to us from God, and is of grace,—that it is not man's doing, but God's working; not in the ordinary manner, but by His special interposition.   Nor should we fail to mark another peculiarity in God's dealings.   To use a New Testament illustration, it was the grain of mustard-seed which was destined to grow into the tree in whose branches all the birds of the air were to find lodgment.   In Abram the stem was cut down to a single root.   This root first sprang up into the patriarchal *family*, then expanded into the *tribes* of Israel, and finally blossomed and bore fruit in the chosen *people*.   But even this was only a means to an end.   Israel had possessed, so to speak, the three crowns separately.   It had the priesthood in Aaron, the royal dignity in David and his line, and the prophetic office.   But in the "last days" the triple crown of priest, king, and prophet has been united upon Him Whose it really is, even Jesus, a "Prophet like unto Moses," the eternal Priest "after the order of Melchizedek," and the real and ever reigning "Son of David."   And in Him all the promises of God, which had been given with increasing clearness from Adam onwards to Shem, then to Abraham, to Jacob, in the law, in the types of the Old Testament, and, finally, in its prophecies, have become "Yea and amen," till at the last all nations shall dwell in the tents of Shem.

2. We mark a *difference* in the mode of Divine revelation in the patriarchal as compared with the previous period. Formerly, God had spoken to man, either on earth or from heaven, while now He actually appeared to them, and that specially as the Angel of Jehovah, or the Angel of the Covenant. The first time Jehovah "appeared" unto Abram was when he entered the land of Canaan, in obedience to that Divine call which singled him out to become the ancestor of the people of God.[1] After that a fresh appearance of Jehovah, and of the Angel of the Covenant, in whom He manifested Himself, marked each stage of the Covenant history. And this appearance was not only granted to Abraham and to Hagar, to Jacob, to Moses, to Balaam, to Gideon, to Manoah and to his wife, and to David, but even towards the close of Jewish history this same Angel of Jehovah is still found pleading for rebellious, apostate Israel in these words : "O Jehovah of Hosts, how long wilt Thou not have mercy on Jerusalem?"[2] The more carefully we follow His steps, the more fully shall we be convinced that He was not an ordinary Angel, but that Jehovah was pleased to reveal Himself in this manner under the Old Testament. We shall have frequent occasion to return to this very solemn subject. Meantime it may be interesting to know that of old the Jews also regarded Him as the *Shechinah*, or visible presence of God,—the same as appeared in the pillar of the cloud and of fire, and afterwards in the temple, in the most holy place ; while the ancient Church almost unanimously adored in Him the Son of God, the Second Person of the blessed Trinity. We cannot conceive any subject more profitable, or likely to be fraught with greater blessing, than reverently to follow the footsteps of the Angel of Jehovah through the Old Testament.

3. The one grand characteristic of the patriarchs was their *faith*. The lives of the patriarchs prefigure the whole history of Israel and their Divine selection. In the words of a recent German writer, amidst all varying events, the one constant

---

[1] Gen. xii. 7.   [2] Zech. i. 12.

trait in patriarchal history was "faith which lays hold on
the word of promise, and on the strength of this word
gives up that which is seen and present for that which is
unseen and future." Thus "Abraham was the man of joyous,
working faith; Isaac of patient, bearing faith; Jacob of contending and prevailing faith." But all lived and " died in
faith, not having received the promises, but having seen them
afar off, and were persuaded of them, and embraced them, and
confessed that they were strangers and pilgrims in the earth."
And it is still so. Without ignoring the great privilege of those
who are descended from Abraham, yet, in the true sense, only
"they which are of faith, the same are the children of
Abraham;" "and if ye be Christ's, then are ye Abraham's
seed, and heirs according to the promise." To adapt the
words of a German poet:

> " What marks each one within the fold
>   Is faith that does not see;
> And yet, as if it did behold,
>   Trusts, unseen Lord, to Thee !"

———

CHAPTER XI.

The Calling of Abram—His Arrival in Canaan, and Temporary Removal to Egypt.

(GEN. XI. 27—XIII. 4.)

WITH Abram an entirely new period may be said to begin.
He was to be the ancestor of a new race in whom the
Divine promises were to be preserved, and through whom they
would finally be realised. It seemed, therefore, necessary that,
when Abram was called, he should forsake his old home, his
family, his country, and his people. Not to speak of the
dangers which otherwise would have beset his vocation, a
new beginning required that he should be cut off from all
that was "behind." Had he remained in Ur of the Chaldees,

he would at best only have been a new link in the old chain. Besides, the special dealings of God, and Abram's faith and patience, as manifested in his obedience to the Divine command, were intended to qualify him for being the head of the new order of things, "the father of all who believe." Lastly, it was intended that the history of Abram, as that of his seed after him, should prepare the way for the great truths of the Gospel, and exhibit as in a figure the history of all who through faith and patience inherit the promises.

Hitherto, God had only interposed, as in the flood, and at the confounding of tongues, to arrest the attempts of man against His purposes of mercy. But when God called Abram, He personally and actively interfered, and this time in mercy, not in judgment. The whole history of Abram may be arranged into four stages, each commencing with a personal revelation of Jehovah. The *first,* when the patriarch was called to his work and mission;[1] the *second,* when he received the promise of an heir, and the covenant was made with him;[2] the *third,* when that covenant was established in the change of his name from Abram to Abraham, and in circumcision as the sign and seal of the covenant;[3] the *fourth,* when his faith was tried, proved, and perfected in the offering up of Isaac.[4] These are, so to speak, the high points in Abram's history, which the patriarch successively climbed, and to which all the other events of his life may be regarded as the ascent.

Descending the genealogy of Shem, Abram stands tenth among "the fathers" after the flood. He was a son—apparently the third and youngest—of Terah, the others being Haran and Nahor. The family, or perhaps more correctly the tribe or clan of Terah, resided in Chaldæa, which is the southern part of Babylonia. "Ur of the Chaldees," as recently again discovered,[5] was one of the oldest, if not the most ancient,

---

[1] Gen. xii.—xiv.   [2] Gen. xv., xvi.
[3] Gen. xvii.—xxi.   [4] Gen. xxii.—xxv. 11.
[5] See the article *Ur,* in Smith's *Bible Dictionary.* The view previously

among the cities of Chaldæa. It lies about six miles away from the river Euphrates, and, curious to relate, is at present somewhere near one hundred and twenty-five miles from the Persian Gulf, though it is supposed, that at one time it was actually washed by its waters, the difference being accounted for by the rapid deposit of what becomes soil, or of *alluvium*, as it is called. Thus Abram must in his youth have stood by the seashore, and seen the sand innumerable, to which his posterity in after ages was likened. Another figure, under which his posterity is described, must have been equally familiar to his mind. It is well known that the brilliancy of a starlit sky in the East, and especially where Abram dwelt, far exceeds anything which we witness in our latitudes. Possibly this may have first led in those regions to the worship of the heavenly bodies. And Abram must have béen the more attracted to their contemplation, as the city in which he dwelt was "wholly given" to that idolatry; for the real site of Ur has been ascertained from the circumstance that the bricks still found there bear the very name of *Hur* on them. Now this word points to *Hurki*, the ancient moon-god, and Ur of the Chaldees was the great "Moon-city," the very centre of the Chaldean moon-worship! The most remarkable ruins of that city are those of the old moon-temple of Ur, which from the name on the bricks are computed to date from the year 2000 before Christ. Thus bricks that are thirty-eight centuries old have now been brought forward to bear witness to the old city of Abraham, and to the tremendous change that must have passed over him when, in faith upon the Divine word, he obeyed its command.

Jewish tradition has one or two varying accounts to show how Abram was converted from the surrounding idolatry, and what persecutions he had to suffer in consequence Scripture does not indulge our fancy with such matters; but, true to its uniform purpose, only relates what belongs

---

adopted, which finds *Ur* in quite a different district, is evidently erroneous.

to the history of the kingdom of God. We learn, however, from Josh. xxiv. 2, 14, 15, that the family of Terah had "in old time, on the other side of the flood," or of Euphrates, "served other gods;" and we can readily understand what influence their surroundings must, in the circumstances, have exercised upon them. It was out of this city of Ur that God called Abram. Previously to this, *Haran*, Abram's eldest brother, had died. We read, that "Terah took Abram, his son, and Lot the son of Haran his son's son, and Sarai his daughter-in-law, his son Abram's wife, and they went forth with them from Ur of the Chaldees, *to go into the land of Canaan;* and they came unto Haran, and dwelt there." The words which we have italicised leave no room for doubt, that the first call of God had come to Abram long before the death of Terah, and when the clan were still at Ur.[1] From the circumstance that Haran is afterwards called "the city of Nahor,"[2] we gather that Nahor, Abraham's brother, and his family had also settled there, though perhaps at a later period, and without relinquishing their idolatry. It is a remarkable confirmation of the scriptural account, that, though this district belongs to Mesopotamia, and not to Chaldæa, its inhabitants are known to have for a long time retained the peculiar Chaldæan language and worship. Haran has preserved its original name, and at the time of the Romans was one of the great battle-fields on which that power sustained a defeat from the Parthians.

The journey from Ur, in the far south, had been long, wearisome, and dangerous; and the fruitful plains around Haran must have held out special inducements for a pastoral tribe to settle. But when the Divine command came, Abram was "not disobedient unto the heavenly vision." Perhaps the arrival and settlement of Nahor and his family, bringing with them their idolatrous associations, may have formed an additional incentive for departing. And so far, God had in His providence made it easier for Abram to leave, since his

---

[1] Comp. Acts vii. 2.   [2] Gen. xxiv. 10; comp. xxvii. 43.

father Terah had died in Haran, at the age of two hundred
and five years. The *second* call of Jehovah to Abram, as given
in Gen. xii. 1–3, consisted of a *fourfold command*, and a *fourfold promise.* The command was quite definite in its terms :
"Get thee out of thy country, and from thy kindred, and
from thy father's house, unto a land that I will shew thee ;"
leaving it, however, as yet undecided which was to be the
place of his final settlement. This uncertainty must have
been an additional and, in the circumstances, a very
serious difficulty in the way of Abram's obedience. But the
word of promise reassured him. It should be distinctly
marked, that on this, as on every other occasion in Abram's
life, his *faith* determined his *obedience.* Accordingly, we read,
"By faith Abraham, when he was called to go out into a place
which he should after receive for an inheritance, obeyed ; and
he went out, not knowing whither he went."[1] The promise
upon which he trusted assured to him these four things : "I
will make of thee a great nation ;" "I will bless thee," with
this addition (in ver. 3), "and thou shalt be a blessing, and
I will bless them that bless thee, and curse him that curseth
thee ;" "I will make thy name great ;" and, lastly, "In thee
shall all families of the earth be blessed."

When we examine these promises more closely, we at once
perceive how they must have formed yet another trial of
Abram's faith ; since he was not only going, a stranger into
a strange land, but was at the time wholly childless. The
promise that he was to "be a blessing," implied that blessing
would, so to speak, be identified with him ; so that happiness
or evil would flow from the relationship in which men would
place themselves towards Abram. On the other hand, from
the peculiar terms "them that bless thee," in the plural, and
"him that curseth thee," in the singular, we gather that the
Divine purpose of mercy embraced *many,* "of all nations,
kindreds, and tongues." Lastly, the great promise, "In thee
shall all families of the earth be blessed," went far beyond

---

[1] Heb. xi. 8.

the personal assurance, " I will make thy name great." It resumed and made more definite the previous promises of final deliverance, by fixing upon Abram as the spring whence the blessing was to flow. Viewed in this light, all mankind appear as only so many families, but of one and the same father; and which were to be again united in a common blessing *in* and *through* Abram. Repeated again and again in the history of Abram, this promise contained already at the outset the whole fulness of the Divine purpose of mercy in the salvation of men. Thus was the prediction to be fulfilled : " God shall enlarge Japheth, and he shall dwell in the tents of Shem," as is shown by St. Peter in Acts iii. 25, and by St. Paul in Gal. iii. 8, 14.

Abram was seventy-five years old " when he departed out of Haran," accompanied by Lot and his family. Putting aside the various traditions which describe his prolonged stay at Damascus, and his supposed rule there, we learn from Scripture that Abram entered the land of promise, as many years afterwards his grandson Jacob returned to it, leaving on his right the majestic Lebanon, and on his left the pastures of Gileac and the mountain-forests of Bashan. Straight on he passed over hills and through valleys, till he reached the delicious plain of Moreh, or rather the spreading terebinth-tree of Moreh, in the valley of Sichem. Travellers have spoken in the most enthusiastic terms of this vale. " All at once," writes Professor Robinson, " the ground sinks down to a valley running towards the west, with a soil of rich, black vegetable mould. Here a scene of luxuriant and almost unparalleled verdure burst upon our view. The whole valley was filled with gardens of vegetables, and orchards of all kinds of fruits, watered by several fountains, which burst forth in various parts, and flow westward in refreshing streams. It came upon us suddenly, like a scene of fairy enchantment. We saw nothing to compare with it in all Palestine." Another traveller [1] says : " Here there are no wild thickets; yet there is always verdure, always

[1] Van de Velde.

shade,—not of the oak, the terebinth, or the garoub-tree, but of
the olive-grove, so soft in colour, so picturesque in form, that
for its sake we can willingly dispense with all other wood."
Such was the first resting-place of Abram in the land of promise, in the plain, or rather in the wood of Moreh, which probably derived its name from the Canaanitish proprietor of the
district. For, as shown by the remark of the sacred writer,
"and the Canaanite was then in the land," the country was not
tenantless, but occupied by a hostile race ; and if Abram was
to enter on its possession, it must once more be by faith in the
promises.

Here it was that Jehovah actually "appeared" unto Abram,
under some visible form or other ; and now for the first time
in sight of the Canaanite was the promise conveyed, "unto thy
seed will I give this land." It is added that Abram "there
builded an altar unto Jehovah who appeared unto him." Thus,
the soil on which Jehovah had been seen, and which He had
just promised to Abram, was consecrated unto the Lord ; and
Abram's faith, publicly professed in the strange land, grasped
Jehovah's promise, solemnly given.

From Shechem, Abram removed, probably for the sake of
pasturage, southwards to a mountain on the east of Bethel,
pitching his tent between Bethel and Ai. This district is, in
the words of Robinson, "still one of the finest tracts for
pasturage in the whole land." In the glowing language of
Dean Stanley : " We here stand on the highest of a succession
of eminences, . . . its topmost summit resting, as it were, on
the rocky slopes below, and distinguished from them by the
olive-grove, which clusters over its broad surface above. From
this height, thus offering a natural base for the patriarchal altar,
and a fitting shade for the patriarchal tent, Abram and Lot
must be conceived as taking the wide survey of the country . .
such as can be enjoyed from no other point in the neighbourhood." What met their astonished gaze from this point will be
described in the following chapter. Meantime, we note that
here, also, Abram "builded an altar unto Jehovah ;" and,

though He does not seem to have visibly appeared unto him, yet the patriarch called upon the name of Jehovah. After a residence, probably of some time, Abram continued his journey, "going on still toward the south,"—a pilgrim and a stranger " in the land of promise ; " his possession of it only marked by the altars which he left on his track.

A fresh trial now awaited the faith of Abram. Strong as it always proved in what concerned the kingdom of God, it failed again and again in matters personal to himself. A famine was desolating the land, and, as is still the case with the Bedouin tribes under similar circumstances, Abram and his family "went down into Egypt," which has at all times been the granary of other nations. It does not become us to speculate whether this removal was lawful, without previous special directions from God ; but we know that it exposed him to the greatest danger. As we must not underrate the difficulties of the patriarchs, so neither must we overrate their faith and their strength. Abram "was a man of like passions with us," and of like weaknesses. When God spoke to him he believed, and when he believed then he obeyed. But God had said nothing as yet to him, directly, about Sarai ; and, in the absence of any special direction, he seems to have taken the matter into his own hands, after the manner of those times and countries. From Gen. xx. 13 we learn that when he first set out from his father's house, an agreement had been made between the two, that Sarai was to pass as his sister, because, as he said, " the fear of God " was not among the nations with whom they would be brought in contact ; and they might slay Abram for his wife's sake.[1] The deceit—for such it really was—seemed scarcely such in their eyes, since Sarai was so closely related to her husband that she might almost be called his sister. In

[1] There is in the British Museum an ancient Egyptian "papyrus," which, although of somewhat later date than that of Abram, proves that his fears, on entering Egypt, were at least not groundless. It relates how a Pharaoh, on the advice of his councillors, sent armies to take away a man's wife by force, and then to murder her husband.

short, as we all too ofttimes do, it was deception, commencing
with self-deception ; and though what he said might be true in
the letter, it was false in the spirit of it. But we must not
imagine that Abram was so heartless as to endanger his wife
for the sake of his own safety. On the contrary, it seemed the
readiest means of guarding her honour also ; since, if she
were looked upon as the sister of a mighty chief, her hand
would be sought, and certain formalities have to be gone
through, which would give Abram time to escape with his
wife. This is not said in apology, but in explanation of the
matter.

Ancient Egyptian monuments here again remarkably confirm the scriptural narrative. They prove that the immigra-
tion of distinguished foreigners, with their families and de-
pendents, was by no means uncommon. One of them, dating
from the time of Abram, represents the arrival of such a
" clan," and their presentation and kindly reception by Pharaoh.
Their name, appearance, and dress show them to be a pastoral tribe of Semitic origin.[1] Another ancient tablet records
how such foreigner attained the highest dignities in the land.
So far, then, Abram would meet with a ready welcome. But
his device was in vain, and Sarai " was taken into the house
of Pharaoh." As the future brother-in-law of the king, Abram
now rapidly acquired possessions and wealth. These presents Abram could, of course, not refuse, though they increased his guilt, as well as his remorse and sense of shame.
But he had committed himself too deeply to retrace nis
steps ; and the want of faith, which had at the first given
rise to his fears, may have gone on increasing. Abram had
given up for a time the promised land, and he was now in
danger of losing also the yet greater promise. But Jehovah
did not, like Abram, deny her who was to be the mother of

---

[1] Another curious coincidence is, that the name of this "chief" is *Abshah*,
"father of land," which reminds us of *Abraham*, the "father of a multitude."
The whole bearing of the Egyptian monuments on the narratives of the
Bible will be fully discussed in the next volume.

the promised seed. He visited " Pharaoh and his house with great plagues," which by-and-by led to their ascertaining the true state of the case—possibly from Sarai herself. Upon this the king summoned Abram, and addressed him in words of reproach, which Abram must have the more keenly felt that they came from an idolater. Their justice the patriarch acknowledged by his silence. Yet the interposition of God on behalf of Abram induced Pharaoh to send him away with all his possessions intact ; and, as the wording of the Hebrew text implies, honourably accompanied to the boundary of the land.

It is a true remark, made by a German writer, that while the occurrence of a famine in Canaan was intended to teach Abram that even in the promised land nourishment depended on the blessing of the Lord,—in a manner teaching him beforehand this petition, " Give us this day our daily bread,"—his experience in Egypt would also show him that in conflict with the world fleshly wisdom availed nothing, and that help came only from Him who " suffered no man to do them wrong : yea, He reproved kings for their sakes; saying, Touch not Mine anointed, and do My prophets no harm," [1] thus, as it were, conveying to Abram's mind these two other petitions : " Lead us not into temptation, but deliver us from evil." And so Abram once more returned to Bethel, "unto the place where his tent had been at the beginning ; unto the place of the altar which he had made at the first : and there Abram called on the name of Jehovah." In one respect this incident is typical of what afterwards befel the children of Israel. Like him, they went into Egypt on account of a famine ; and, like him, they left it under the influence of " fear of them which fell" upon the Egyptians—yet laden with the riches of Egypt.

[1] Psalm cv. 14, 15.

CHAPTER XII.

The Separation of Abram and Lot—Abram at Hebron—Sodom plundered—Lot rescued—The Meeting with Melchizedek.

(GEN. XIII., XIV.)

HITHERTO Abram had been accompanied by Lot in all his wanderings. But a separation must take place between them also. For Abram and his seed were to be kept quite distinct from all other races, so that the eye of faith might in future ages be fixed upon the father of the faithful, as on him from whom the promised Messiah was to spring. Like so many of God's most marked interpositions, this also was brought about by what seemed a series of natural circumstances, and probably Abram himself was ignorant of the Divine purpose in what at the time must have been no small trial to him. The increase of their wealth, and especially of their herds and flocks in Egypt, led to disputes between the herdmen of Abram and of Lot, which were the more painful that, as the Bible notes, "the Canaanite and the Perizzite dwelled then in the land," and must have been witnesses to this "strife" between "brethren." To avoid all occasion of it, Abram now proposed a voluntary separation, allowing Lot, though he was the younger and the inferior, the choice of district—and this not merely from *generosity*, but in *faith*, leaving it to the Lord to determine the bounds of his habitation.

As the two stood on that highest ridge between Bethel and Ai, the prospect before them was indeed unrivalled. Looking back northwards, the eye would rest on the mountains which divide Samaria from Judæa; westwards and southwards, it would range over the later possession of Benjamin and Judah, till in the far distance it descried the slope on which Hebron lay. But the fairest vision was eastward : in the extreme distance, the dark mountains of Moab; at their foot, the Jordan, winding through a valley of untold fertility; and in the immediate foreground, the range of hills above Jericho. As the patriarchs gazed upon it, the whole cleft of the Jordan valley was rich with the most luxuriant tropical vegetation, the sweetest spot of all being around the Lake of Sodom, at that time probably a sweetwater lake, the "circuit" of the plain resembling in appearance, but far exceeding in fertility and beauty, the district around the Sea of Galilee. In this "round" of Jordan, and by the waters of Sodom, rich cities had sprung up, which, alas! were also the seat of the most terrible corruption. As Lot saw this "round" or district, fair like Paradise, green with perennial verdure, like the part of Egypt watered by the Nile, his heart went out after it, unmindful of, or not caring to inquire into, the character of its inhabitants. The scene might well have won the heart of any one whose affections were set on things beneath. Lot's heart was so set; and he now vindicated by his choice the propriety of his being separated from Abram. Assuredly their aims went asunder, as the ways which they took. Yet, even thus, God watched over Lot, and left him not to reap the bitter fruit of his own choice.

Nor was Abram left in that hour without consolation. As most he needed it when alone, and with apparently nothing but the comparatively barren hills of Judæa before him, Jehovah once more renewed to him, and enlarged the promise of the land, far as his eye could range, bestowing it upon Abram and his "seed for ever." For the terms of this promise were not made void by the seventy years which Judah spent in the captivity of Babylon, nor yet are they annulled by the eighteen centuries of Israel's present unbelief and dispersion. The promise of the land is to Abram's "seed for ever." The land and the people God has joined together; and though now the one lies desolate, like a dead body, and the other wanders unresting, as it were a disembodied spirit, God will again bring them to each other in the days when His promise shall be finally established.

So Abram must have understood the word of Jehovah. And when, so to speak, he now took possession by faith of the promised land, he was directed to walk through it. In the course of these wanderings he reached Hebron, one of the most ancient cities of the world, where in the wood of one, Mamre, he pitched his tent under a spreading terebinth, and built an altar unto Jehovah. This place seems through the rest of his life to have continued one of the centres of his movements.

Meanwhile Lot had taken up his abode in a district which, like the rest of Canaan at the time of Joshua's conquest, was subdivided among a number of small kings, each probably ruling over a city and the immediately surrounding neighbourhood. For twelve years had this whole district been tributary to *Chedorlaomer.* In the thirteenth year they rebelled; and, in the fourteenth, the hordes of Chedorlaomer and of his three confederates swept over the intervening district, carrying desolation with them, till they encountered the five allied monarchs of the "round of Jordan," in the vale of Siddim, the district around what afterwards became the Dead Sea. Once more victory attended the invaders—two of the Canaanitish kings were killed, the rest fled in wild confusion ; Sodom and Gomorrah were plundered, and their inhabitants—Lot among them—carried away captives by the retreating host. This was the first time—at least in Scripture history—that the world-kingdom, as founded by Nimrod, was brought into contact with the people of God, and that on the soil of Palestine. For Chedorlaomer and his confederates occupied the very land and place where afterwards the Babylonian and Assyrian empires were.[1] It became necessary, therefore, that Abram should interfere. God had given him the land, and here was its hereditary enemy; and God now called and fitted him, though but a stranger and a pilgrim on its soil, to become

---

[1] Gen. x. 10. There is frequent reference to the kingdom of *Elam* on the Assyrian monuments, confirmatory of Scripture, and Mr. Smith inserts the names of Chedorlaomer and of his three confederates in his "list of Babylonian monarchs" (see *Assyrian Discoveries,* pp. 441, 442).

its deliverer; while alike the mode and the circumstances of this deliverance were to point forward to those realities of which it was the type.

One who had escaped from the rout brought Abram tidings of the disaster. He immediately armed his own trained servants, three hundred and eighteen in number; and being joined by Aner, Eshcol, and Mamre, the chieftains to whom the district around Hebron belonged, followed in pursuit of Chedorlaomer and his allies. Probably, as is common in such warfare, victory had made them careless. They may have feasted, or their bands, laden with captives and spoil, may have been straggling, and without order. Certainly they were ignorant of any coming danger, when Abram, having divided his force, fell upon them, in the dead of night, from several sides at the same time, inflicted a great slaughter, and pursued them to close by Damascus. All the spoil and all the captives, among them Lot also, were rescued and brought back. As the returning host of Abram entered the valley of Shaveh, close under the walls of what afterwards became Jerusalem, they were met by two persons bearing very different characters, and coming from opposite directions. From the banks of Jordan the new king of Sodom, whose predecessor had fallen in battle against Chedorlaomer, came up to thank Abram, and to offer him the spoils he had won; while from the heights of *Salem*—the ancient Jerusalem—the priest-king *Melchizedek* descended to bless Abram, and to refresh him with "bread and wine." This memorable meeting seems to have given the valley its name, "the king's dale;" and here, in later times, Absalom erected for himself a monumental pillar.[1] But now a far different scene ensued, and one so significant in its typical meaning as to have left its impress alike on the prophecies of the Old and in the fulfilment of the New Testament. Melchizedek appears like a meteor in the sky—suddenly, unexpectedly, mysteriously,—and then as suddenly disappears. Amid the abundance of genealogical details of that period

[1] 2 Sam. xviii. 18.

we know absolutely nothing of his descent; in the roll of kings and their achievements, his name and reign, his birth and death remain unmentioned. Considering the position which he occupies towards Abram, that silence must have been intentional, and its intention typical; that is, designed to point forward to corresponding realities in Christ. Still more clearly than its silence does the information which Scripture furnishes about Melchizedek show the deep significance of his personality. His name is " King of Righteousness," his government that of the " Prince of Peace ;" he is a priest," neither in the sense in which Abram was, nor yet "after the order of Aaron," his priesthood being distinct and unique ; he blesses Abram, and his blessing sounds like a ratification of the bestowal of the land upon the patriarch ; while Abram gives "him tithes of all." There is in this latter tribute an acknowledgment of Melchizedek both as king and priest—as priest in giving him " tithes," and as king in giving him these tithes of all the spoil, as if he had royal claim upon it ; while Abram himself refuses to touch any of it, and his allies are only allowed to "take their portion."

This is not the place to discuss the typical meaning of this story ; yet the event and the person are too important to pass them unnoticed. Twice again we meet Melchizedek in Scripture : once in the prophecy of Psa. cx. 4 : " Thou art a priest for ever after the order of Melchizedek ;" the other time in the application of it all to our blessed Saviour, in Heb. vii. 3. That Melchizedek was not Christ Himself is evident from the statement that he was "made like unto the Son of God" (or "likened unto" Him, Heb. vii. 3); while it equally appears from these words, and from the whole tenor of Scripture, that he was a type of Christ. In fact, we stand here at the threshold of two dispensations. The covenant with Noah had, so to speak, run its course, or rather was merging into that with Abram. As at the commencement of the New Testament, John gave testimony to Jesus, and yet Jesus was baptised by John ; so here Melchizedek gave testimony to Abram, and yet received tithes from Abram. If we add, that in our view Melchizedek was probably the last representative of the race of *Shem* in the land of Canaan, which was now in the hands of the Canaanites, who were children of *Ham*, as well as that he was the last representative of the *faith* of Shem, in the midst of idolatry—being a "priest of the most high God,"—the relation between them will become more clear. It was the old transferred to the new, and enlarged in it; it was the rule and the promise of Shem, solemnly handed over to Abram by the last representative of Shem in the land, who thus gave up his authority in the name of "the most high God, possessor of heaven and earth," "which hath delivered" Abram's enemies into his hands. It has been well observed, that "Abram's greatness consisted in his hopes, that of Melchizedek in his present possession." Melchizedek was both a priest and a king,—Abram only a prophet; Melchizedek was recognised as the rightful possessor of the country, which as yet was only promised to Abram. True, the future will be infinitely greater than the present,—but then it was as yet *future*. Melchizedek owned its reality by blessing Abram, and transferring his title, as it were, to him; while Abram recognised the present, by giving tithes to Melchizedek, and bending to receive his blessing. Thus Melchizedek, the last representative of the Shenitic order, is the type of Christ, as the last representative of the Abrahamic order. What lay in germ in Melchizedek was to be gradually unfolded—the priesthood in Aaron, the royalty in David—till both were most gloriously united in Christ. Melchizedek was, however, only a shadow and a type ; Christ is the reality and the antitype. It is for this reason that Scripture has shut to us the sources of historical investigation about his descent and duration of life, that by its silence it might point to the heavenly descent of Jesus. For the same reason also Abram, who so soon afterwards vindicated his dignity and position in the language of superiority with which he declined the king of Sodom's offer of the spoils, bent lowly before Melchizedek, that in his blessing

he might receive the spiritual inheritance which he now be-
queathed him.   Nor will the attentive reader fail to remark
the language in which Melchizedek spake of God as "the most
high," and the "possessor of heaven and earth "—terms which
Abram adopted, but to which he added the new name of
" *Jehovah*," as that of "the most high God, the possessor of
heaven and earth "—a name which indicated that covenant of
grace of which Abram was to be the representative and the
medium.   It is quite in accordance with this whole transaction
that Abram put aside the offer of the king of Sodom : "Give
me the persons, and take the goods to thyself."   Assuredly,
it had not been as an ally of the king of Sodom, but to vindicate
his position, and that of all connected with him, that the Lord
had summoned Abram to the war, and given him the victory.
And so these figures part, never to meet again : the king of
Sodom to hasten to the judgment, already lingering around
him ; the king of Salem to wait for the better possession promised, which indeed was already commencing.

CHAPTER XIII.

The twofold Promise of "a Seed" to Abraham—Eshmael
—Jehovah visits Abraham — The Destruction of
Sodom—Abraham's Sojourn at Gerar—His Covenant
with Abimelech.

(Gen. xv.—xx., xxi. 22—34.)

HIGH times of success and prosperity are only too often
followed by seasons of depression.   Abram had indeed
conquered the kings of Assyria, but his very victory might
expose him to their vengeance, or draw down the jealousy of
those around him.   He was but a stranger in a strange land,
with no other possession than a promise,—and not even an

heir to whom to transmit it. In these circumstances it was that " Jehovah came unto Abram in a vision," saying, " I am thy shield, and thy exceeding great reward"—that is, Myself am thy defence from all foes, and the source and spring whence thy faith shall be fully satisfied with joy. It was but natural, and, as one may say, childlike, that Abram should in reply have opened up before God all his wants and his sorrow, as he pointed, not in the language of doubt, but rather of question, to his own childless state, which seemed to leave Eliezer, his servant, his only heir. But Jehovah assured him that it was to be otherwise than it seemed ; nay, that his seed should be numberless as the stars in the sky. "And he believed in Jehovah : and He counted it to him for righteousness." The remark stands solitary in the narrative, as if to call attention to a great fact; and its terms indicate, on the part of Abram, not merely faith in the word, but trustfulness in the person of Jehovah as his Covenant-God. Most touching and sublime is the childlikeness of that simple believing without seeing, and its absolute confidence. Ever since, through thousands of years, it has stood out as the great example of faith to the church of God. And from this faith in the living God sprang all the obedience of Abram. Like the rod of Aaron, his life budded and blossomed and bore fruit "within the secret place of the Most High."

To confirm this faith Jehovah now gave to Abram a sign and a seal, which yet were such once more only to his faith. He entered into a covenant with him. For this purpose the Lord directed Abram to bring an heifer, a she-goat, and a ram, each of three years old, also a turtle-dove and a young pigeon. These sacrifices—for they were all representatives of the kinds afterwards used as sacrifices—were to be divided, and the pieces laid one against the other, as the custom was in making a covenant, the covenanting parties always passing between them, as it were to show that now there was no longer to be division, but that what had been divided was to be considered as one between them. But here, at the first, no covenanting

party appeared at all to pass between the divided sacrifices.
All day long, as it seemed to Abram, he sat watching lonely,
only driving from the carcases the birds of prey which came
down upon them. So it seemed to the eye of sense! Presently
even gathered around, and a deep sleep and a horror of great
darkness fell upon Abram. The age of each sacrificed animal,
the long, lonely day, the birds of prey swooping around, and
the horror that had come with the night, all betokened what
Jehovah now foretold : how for three generations the seed of
Abram should be afflicted in Egypt; but in the fourth, when
the measure of the iniquity of the present inhabitants of
Canaan would be full, they were to return, and enter on the
promised possession of the land. As for Abram himself, he
was to go "to his fathers in peace." Then it was that the
covenant was made; not, as usually, by both parties passing
between the divided sacrifice, but by Jehovah alone doing so,
since the covenant was that of *grace*, in which one party alone
—God—undertook all the obligations, while the other received
all the benefits.

For the first time did Abram see passing between those
pieces the smoking furnace and the burning lamp—the Divine
brightness enwrapt in a cloud, just as Moses saw it in the bush,
and the children of Israel on their wilderness march, and as it
afterwards dwelt in the sanctuary above the mercy-seat, and
between the cherubim. This was the first vision vouchsafed
to Abram, the first stage of the covenant into which God
entered with him, and the first appearance of the glory of the
Lord. At the same time, what may be called the personal
promise to Abram was also enlarged, and the boundaries of
the land clearly defined as stretching from the Nile in the west,
to the Euphrates in the east, an extent, it may be here
observed, which the Holy Land has never yet attained, not
even in the most flourishing days of the Hebrew monarchy.

Precious as the promise of God to Abram had been, it had
still left one point undetermined—who the *mother* of the promised seed was to be. Instead of waiting for the direction of

God in this respect also, Sarai seems in her impatience to have anticipated the Lord; and, as we always do when taking things into our own hands, in a manner contrary to the mind of God, as well as to her own sorrow and disappointment. Ten years had elapsed since Abram had entered Canaan, when Sarai, despairing of giving birth to the heir of the promise, followed the common custom of those days and countries, and sought a son by an alliance between her husband and Hagar, her own Egyptian maid. The consequences of her folly were dispeace in her home, then reproaches, and the flight of Hagar. What else might have followed it is difficult to tell, had not the Lord in mercy interposed. None less than the Angel of the Covenant Himself appeared to the fugitive slave, as she rested by a fountain in the wilderness that led down into her native Egypt. He bade her return to her mistress, promised to the son whom she was to bear that liberty and independence of bearing which has ever since characterised his descendants, and gave him the name of *Ishmael*—the Lord heareth,—as it were thus binding him alike by his descent, and by the Providence that had watched over him, to the God of Abram. Hagar also learned there for the first time to know Him as the God who seeth, the living God, whence the fountain by which she had sat henceforth bore the name of " The Well of the Living, who beholdeth me." So deep are the impressions which a view of the Lord maketh, and so closely should we always connect with them the events of our lives.

Hagar had returned to Abram's house, and given birth to Ishmael. And now ensued a period which we must regard as of most sore trial to Abram's faith. Full thirteen years elapsed without apparently any revelation on the part of God. During this time Ishmael had grown up, and Abram may almost insensibly have accustomed himself to look upon him as the heir, even though in all probability he knew that he had not been destined for it. Abram was now ninety-nine years old, and Sarai stricken in years. For every human hope and prospect must be swept away, and the heir be, in the fullest sense, the child of the promise, that so faith might receive directly from God that for which it had waited. It was in these circumstances that Jehovah at last once more appeared in visible form to Abram,—this time to establish and fulfil the covenant which He had formerly made.[1] Hence also now the admonition : "Walk before Me, and be thou perfect," which follows but can never precede the covenant. In token of this established covenant, God enjoined upon Abram and his descendants the rite of circumcision as a *sign* and a *seal;* at the same time changing the name of *Abram*, "father of elevation" (noble chief?), into *Abraham*, "the father of a multitude," and that of *Sarai*, "the princely," into *Sarah*, or "the princess,"[2] to denote that through these two the promise was to be fulfilled, and that from them the chosen race was to spring. These tidings came upon Abraham with such joyous surprise that, as in humble worship, he "fell upon his face," he "laughed," as he considered within himself the circumstances of the case,—as Calvin remarks, not from doubt or disbelief, but in gladness and wonder. To perpetuate the remembrance of the wonder, the promised seed was to bear the name of Isaac, or "laughter." Thus, as afterwards, at the outset of the calling of the Gentiles, the name of Saul was changed into Paul— probably after the first-fruits of his ministry,—so here, at the outset of Israel's calling, we have three new names, indicative of the power of God, which lay at the root of all, and of the simple faith which received the promise. The heir of the promises was indeed to be the child of Sarah ; but over Ishmael also would the Lord watch, and "multiply him exceedingly," and "make him a great nation." Ever since those days has the sign of circumcision remained to bear testimony to the covenant with Abraham. On the eighth day, as the first full

[1] The expression "I will make My covenant" (Gen. xvii. 2) is quite different from that rendered by the same words in Gen. xv. 18. In the latter case it is "to *make*"—literally, to "*cut* a covenant ;" while the terms in Gen. xvii. 2 are, "I will *give* My covenant," *i.e.*, establish, fulfil it.

[2] Others have derived the name *Sarah* from a root, meaning "to be fruitful."

period of seven has elapsed, a new period is, as it were, to begin; and each Jewish child so circumcised is a living witness to the transaction between God and Abraham more than three thousand years ago. But, better far, it pointed forward to the fulfilment of the covenant-promise in Christ Jesus, in whom there is now no other circumcision needed than that of the heart.

While Abraham's faith was thus exercised and blessed, the "evil men and seducers," among whom Lot had chosen his dwelling, had been waxing worse and worse, and rapidly filling up the measure of their iniquity. That judgment which had long hung over them like a dark cloud was now to burst in a terrible tempest. Abram was sitting "in the tent door in the heat of the day," when Jehovah once more appeared in visible form to him. This time it was, as it seemed, three wayfarers, whom the patriarch hastened to welcome to the rest and refreshment of his abode. But the heavenly Guests were the Lord Himself[1] and two angels, who were to be the ministers of His avenging justice. There can be no doubt that Abraham recognised the character of his heavenly Visitors, though, with the delicacy and modesty so peculiarly his, he received and entertained them according to the manner in which they presented themselves to him. The object of their visit was twofold—the one bearing reference to Sarah, the other to Abraham. If Sarah was to become the mother of the promised seed, she also must learn to believe.[2] Probably she had not received quite in faith the account which Abraham had given of his last vision of Jehovah. At any rate, the first inquiry of the three was after Sarah. The message of the birth of a son was now addressed directly to her; and as her non-belief appeared in her laughter, it was first reproved and then removed. The first object of their visit accomplished, the Three pursue their way towards Sodom, accompanied by Abraham. Now it was that Jehovah Himself[3] opened to the patriarch the other purpose of their coming. It was to tell him the impending doom of the cities of the plain,

---

[1] See Gen. xviii. 13.   [2] Heb. xi. 11.   [3] Gen. xviii. 17.

and that for two reasons : because Abraham was the heir to the promises, and because he would " command his children and his household after him, and they shall keep the way of Jehovah, to do justice and judgment." From the latter words we gather that the doom of Sodom was communicated to Abraham that it might serve as a warning to the children of Israel.   It was not to be regarded as an isolated judgment ; but the scene of desolation, which was for ever to occupy the site of the cities of the plain, would also for ever exhibit to Israel the consequences of sin, and be to them a type of future judgment.   It is in this light that the Scriptures both of the Old and the New Testament present to us the destruction of Sodom and Gomorrah.   On the other hand, as God had in the covenant made gift of the land to Abraham and to his seed, it seemed fitting that he should know of the terrible desolation which was so soon to spread over part of it ; and that in his character as the *medium* of blessing to all, he should be allowed to intercede for their preservation, as formerly he had been called to fight for their deliverance.   It was therefore neither on account of the intimate converse between God and Abraham, nor yet because Lot, the nephew of Abraham, was involved in the catastrophe, but strictly in accordance with God's covenant-promise, that God made a communication of the coming judgment to Abraham, and that he was allowed to plead in the case.

Mercy, indeed, *was* extended to Lot ; but he did not escape the consequences of his selfish and sinful choice of a portion in this world.   A second time was he to be taught that it is not in the abundance of the things which a man hath that wealth or happiness consists.   Jehovah so far listened to the pleading of Abraham, whose believing urgency reminds us of the holy "importunity,"[1] characteristic of all true prayer, that He promised to spare the cities of the plain if even ten righteous men were found in them.   But the result of the trial by the two angels who went to Sodom was even more terrible

---

[1] Luke xi. 8.

than could have been anticipated. The last brief night of horror in Sodom was soon past; and, as the morning glow lay on the hills of Moab, the angels almost constrained Lot and his family to leave the doomed city. Lingering regret for it led Lot's wife to look behind her, when judgment overtook her also, and she was changed into a pillar of salt. Tradition has since pointed out a mountain of salt, at the southern extremity of the Dead Sea, as the spot where the occurrence had taken place. It need scarcely be said that, like most traditions, which only import a disturbing element into our thinking, this also is not founded on fact. The judgment which descended on the doomed cities is described in the sacred text as a "rain of brimstone and fire from Jehovah out of heaven," by which the whole district was overthrown. This account in all its literality has been again confirmed by the late investigations of Canon Tristram, made on the spot. The whole neighbourhood of the Dead Sea abounds with sulphur and bitumen, furnishing the materials for the terrible conflagration which ensued when the lightning from heaven struck it, probably accompanied by an earthquake, which would throw up fresh masses of combustible matter. Far and wide the smoke of the burning country was seen to ascend; and as Abraham watched it on the height beyond Hebron, where the evening before he had spoken the last pleading words to Jehovah, it seemed like a vast furnace, from which the cloud of smoke rose to heaven.

The basin of the Dead Sea has been specially examined by an American expedition under Lieutenant Lynch. The results of their soundings have brought to light the remarkable fact that it really consists of two lakes, the one, thirteen, the other one thousand three hundred feet deep,—the former being regarded as the site of the doomed cities, and the latter as probably a sweetwater lake, whose waters had washed their shores. In that case, the suggestion is that the catastrophe was brought about by volcanic agency. But whatever changes in the appearance of the country the judgment from heaven may have produced, the most trustworthy authorities have given up the view that the cities of the plain have been submerged by volcanic agency, and are satisfied that the account which Scripture gives of this catastrophe ought to be taken in its utmost literality.

It is equally sad and instructive to notice how little effect mere judgments, however terrible, are capable of producing even upon those most nearly affected by them.   Lot and his daughters had been allowed to retire to Zoar, a little town not far from Sodom.   But the same weakness of faith which had made them at the first reluctant to leave their own doomed city, now induced them to forsake Zoar, though safety had been promised them there. Far worse than that, they fell into the most grievous and abominable sin, the issue of which was the birth of the ancestors of Israel's hereditary enemies—Moab and Ammon.[1] But even this is not all. Whether from a dislike to a neighbourhood so lately visited by such judgments, or in quest of better pasturage for his flocks, Abraham left the district of Mamre, and travelled in a south-easterly direction, where he settled in the territory of Abimelech, king of Gerar, in the land of the Philistines.   Abimelech seems to have been a royal title, like that of Pharaoh.[2]   But in this instance, as we gather from Scripture, the possessor of this title was far different from the king of Egypt.   In fact, he appears to have been not merely true and upright in character, but to have feared the Lord.   Accordingly, when Abraham was once more guilty of the same dissimulation as formerly in Egypt, passing off his wife for his sister from fear for his own life, God directly communicated to Abimelech in a dream the real state of matters.   Upon this, Abimelech hastened to amend the wrong he had, unwittingly, so nearly committed.   In comparison to the Gentile king, Abraham occupies indeed an unfavourable position.   He is unable to vindicate his conduct on other grounds than what amounts to a want of faith.   But, as God had informed Abimelech, Abraham, despite his weakness, was "a prophet;" and in that capacity, as already

[1] Deut. xxiii. 3, 4.   [2] Comp. Gen. xxvi. 1, 8.

quoted," He suffered no man to do them wrong; yea, He reproved kings for their sakes, saying, Touch not Mine anointed, and do My prophets no harm." The alliance with Abraham which Abimelech had sought by marriage, was shortly afterwards concluded by a formal covenant between the two, accompanied by a sacrifice of the sacred number of seven ewe lambs.[1] To show that this was intended not as a private but as a public alliance, Abimelech came accompanied by his chief captain, or phichol,[2] at the same time expressly stating it as the motive in the public step which he took, that God was with Abraham in all that he did. In similar manner, the sympathy on these points between Abimelech and his people had formerly been shown, when the king had communicated to "all his servants" what God had told him about Abraham, "and the men were sore afraid." In these circumstances we do not wonder that Abraham should have made the land of the Philistines the place of lengthened residence, pitching his tent close by Beersheba, "the well of the oath," with Abimelech, or rather "the well of the seven" ewe lambs,—and there he once more "called on the name of Jehovah, the everlasting God."

CHAPTER XIV.

Birth of Isaac—Ishmael sent away—Trial of Abraham's Faith in the Command to sacrifice Isaac—Death of Sarah—Death of Abraham.

(GEN. XXI.—XXV. 18.)

A T last the time had come when the great promise to Abraham should receive its fulfilment. The patriarch was in his hundredth and Sarah in her ninetieth year when Isaac was born to them. Manifestly, it had been the Divine

[1] Gen. xxi. 22.   [2] Comp. Gen. xxvi. 26.

purpose to protract as long as possible the period before that event; partly to exercise and mature Abraham's faith, and partly that it should appear the more clearly that the gift of the heir to the promises was, in a manner, supernatural. As we have seen, the very name of their child was intended to perpetuate this fact; and now Sarah also, in the joyousness of her heart, said, "God hath made me to laugh, so that all that hear will laugh with me,"—literally, "Laughter has God prepared for me; every one that heareth it will (joyously) laugh with me." Thus, as Abraham's laughter had been that of faith in its surprise, so the laughter of Sarah was now in contrast to that of her former weakness of trust, one of faith in its gratitude. But there might be yet a third kind of laughter, —neither of faith, nor even of unbelief, but of disbelief: the laughter of mockery, and it also would receive its due recompense. According to God's direction,[1] Abraham had circumcised Isaac on the eighth day. When the period for weaning him arrived, the patriarch made, after the manner of those times, a great feast. We can scarcely say what the age of the child was,—whether one year, or, as Josephus implies, three years old. In either case, Ishmael must have been a lad, springing into manhood—at least fifteen, and possibly seventeen years of age. "And Sarah saw the son of Hagar, the Egyptian, which she had born unto Abraham, mocking,"— literally, "that he was a mocker." As a German writer observes: "Isaac, the object of holy laughter, serves as the target of his unholy wit and profane banter. He does not laugh; he makes merry. 'What! this small, helpless Isaac, the father of nations!' Unbelief, envy, and pride in his own carnal pre-eminence,—such were the reasons of his conduct. Because he does not understand, 'Is anything too hard for Jehovah?' therefore he finds it laughable to connect such great issues with so small a beginning." It was evidently in this light that the apostle viewed it, when describing the conduct of Ishmael in these words: "As then he that was born after the flesh persecuted him that was born after the Spirit."[1] On this ground, and not from jealousy, Sarah demanded that the bondwoman and her son should be " cast out." But Abraham, who seems to have misunderstood her motives, was reluctant to comply, from feelings of paternal affection quite natural in the case, till God expressly directed him to the same effect. The expulsion of Ishmael was necessary, not only from his unfitness, and in order to keep the heir of the promise unmixed with others, but also for the sake of Abraham himself, whose faith must be trained to renounce, in obedience to the Divine call, everything,—even his natural paternal affection. And in His tender mercy God once more made the trial easier, by bestowing the special promise that Ishmael should become "a nation." Therefore, although Hagar and her son were literally cast forth, with only the barest necessaries for the journey—water and bread,—this was intended chiefly in trial of Abraham's faith, and their poverty was only temporary. For, soon afterwards we read in Scripture, that, before his death, Abraham had enriched his sons (by Hagar and Keturah) with " gifts ;"[2] and at his burying Ishmael appears, as an acknowledged son, by the side of Isaac, to perform the last rites of love to their father.[3]

Thus " cast out," Hagar and her son wandered in the wilderness of Beersheba, probably on their way to Egypt. Here they suffered from what has always been the great danger to travellers in the desert—want of water. The lad's strength failed before that of his mother. At length her courage and endurance also gave way to utter exhaustion and despondency. Hitherto she had supported the steps of her son ; now she let him droop "under one of the shrubs," while she went "a good way off," not to witness his dying agony, yet still remaining within reach of him. To use the pictorial language of Scripture, "She lift up her voice and wept." Not *her* cry, however, but that of Abraham's son went up into the ears of the Lord ; and once more was Hagar directed to a well of water, but this time

[1] Gal. iv. 29.   [2] Gen. xxv. 6.   [3] Gen. xxv. 9.

by an "angel of God," not, as before, by the "Angel of Jehovah."
And now also, to strengthen her for the future, the same
assurance concerning Ishmael was given to Hagar which had
previously been made to Abraham.   This promise of God has
been abundantly fulfilled.   The lad dwelt in that wide district
between Palestine and Mount Horeb, called "the wilderness of
Paran," which to this day is the undisputed dominion of his
descendants, the Bedouin Arabs.

Bitter as the trial had been to "cast out" Ishmael, his son,
it was only a preparation for a far more severe test of Abraham's
faith and obedience.   For this—the last, the highest, but also
the steepest ascent in Abraham's life of faith—all God's previous leadings and dealings had been gradually preparing and
qualifying him.   But even so, it seems to stand out in Scripture
alone and unapproached, like some grand mountain-peak,
which only one climber has ever been called to attain.   No,
not one ; for yet another and far higher mountain peak, so
lofty that its summit reacheth into heaven itself, has been
trodden by the "Seed of Abraham," Who has done all, and far
more than Abraham did, and Who has made that a blessed
reality to us which in the sacrifice of the patriarch was only a
symbol.   And, no doubt, it was when on Mount Moriah—the
mount of God's true " provision"—Abraham was about to offer
up his son, that, in the language of our blessed Lord,[1] he saw
the day of Christ, "and was glad."

The test, trial, or "temptation" through which Abraham's
faith had now to pass, that it might be wholly purified as " gold
in the fire," came in the form of a command from God to
bring Isaac as a burnt-offering.   Nothing was spared the
patriarch of the bitterness of his sorrow.   It was said with
painful particularity : "Take now thy son, thine only son,
whom thou lovest ;" and not a single promise of deliverance
was added to cheer him on his lonely way.   The same inde-
finiteness which had added such difficulty to Abraham's first
call to leave his father's house marked this last trial of the

[1] John viii. 56.

obedience of his faith. He was only told to get him "into the land of Moriah," where God would further tell him upon which of the mountains around he was to bring his strange " burnt-offering." Luther has pointed out, in his own terse language, how to human reason it must have seemed as if either God's promise would fail, or else this command be of the devil, and not of God. From this perplexity there was only one issue—to bring " every thought into captivity to the obedience of Christ." And Abraham " staggered not" at the word of God ; doubted it not ; but was " strong in faith," " accounting"—yet not knowing it—" that God was able to raise up Isaac even from the dead ; from whence he also received him in a figure." For we must not detract from the trial by importing into the circumstances our knowledge of the issue. Abraham had absolutely no assurance and no knowledge beyond that of his present duty. All he had to lay hold upon was the previous promise, and the character and faithfulness of the covenant God, who now bade him offer this sacrifice. Sharp as the contest must have been, it was brief. It lasted just one night ; and next morning, without having taken "counsel with flesh and blood," Abraham, with his son Isaac and two servants, were on their way to " the land of Moriah." We have absolutely no *data* to determine the exact age of Isaac at the time ; but the computation of Josephus, that he was twenty-five years old, makes him more advanced than the language of the Scripture narrative seems to convey to our minds. Two days they had travelled from Beersheba, when on the third the " mountains round about Jerusalem" came in sight. From a gap between the hills, which forms the highest point on the ordinary road, which has always led up from the south, just that one mountain would be visible on which afterwards the temple stood. This was " the land of Moriah," and that the hill on which the sacrifice of Isaac was to be offered ! Leaving the two servants behind, with the assurance that after they had worshipped they would " come again"—for faith was sure of victory, and anticipated it,—father and son pursued their solitary road, Isaac carrying the wood, and Abraham the sacrificial knife and fire. "And they went both of them together. And Isaac spake unto Abraham his father, and said, My father : and he said, Here am I, my son. And he said, Behold the fire and the wood : but where is the lamb for a burnt-offering ? And Abraham said, My son, God will provide himself a lamb for a burnt-offering : so they went both of them together." Nothing further is said between the two till they reach the destined spot. Here Abraham builds the altar, places on it the wood, binds Isaac, and lays him upon the altar. Already he has lifted the sacrificial knife, when the Angel of Jehovah, the Angel of the Covenant, arrests his hand. Abraham's faith has now been fully proved, and it has been perfected. "A ram caught in the thicket" will serve for "a burnt-offering in the stead of his son;" but to Abraham all the previous promises are not only repeated and enlarged, but "confirmed by an oath," "that by two immutable things, in which it was impossible for God to lie," he "might have a strong consolation." "For when God made promise to Abraham, because He could swear by no greater, He sware by Himself."[1] This "oath" stands out alone and solitary in the history of the patriarchs; it is afterwards constantly referred to,[2] and, as Luther observes, it became really the spring whence all flowed that was promised "by oath" unto David, in Psa. lxxxix. 35 ; cx. 4 ; cxxxii. 11. No wonder Abraham called the place "*Jehovah Jireh*," "Jehovah seeth," or "Jehovah provideth," which means that He seeth *for us*, for, as even the term implieth, His providence, or providing, is just His seeing for us, *what, where*, and *when* we do not see for ourselves. As we remember that on this mountain-top the temple of the Lord afterwards stood, and that from it rose the smoke of accepted sacrifices, we can understand all the better what the inspired writer adds by way of explanation : "As it is said to this day, In the mount where Jehovah is seen,"—where

[1] Heb. vi. 13.

[2] Gen. xxiv. 7 ; xxvi. 3 ; l. 24 ; Ex. xiii. 5, 11 ; xxxiii. 1, etc.

He seeth and is seen,—whence also the name of *Moriah* is derived.

But before passing from this event, it is necessary to view it in its bearings *upon Abraham, upon Isaac,* and even *upon the Canaanites,* as well as in its higher *typical or symbolical application.* It is very remarkable that a German writer who has most strenuously opposed the truth of this scriptural narrative, has been compelled to some extent to admit the deeper bearing of this history on the faith of Abraham. He writes : " Hitherto even Isaac, that precious gift so long promised, had been only a natural blessing to Abraham. A son like any other, although the offspring of Sarah, he had been born and educated in his house. Since his birth Abraham had not been called to bear for him the pangs of a soul struggling in faith, and yet every blessing becomes only spiritual and truly lasting, if we appropriate it in the contest of faith." At God's bidding Abraham had necessarily given up country, kindred, and home, and then his paternal affection towards Ishmael. It yet remained to give up even Isaac after the flesh, so as to receive him again spiritually ; to give up not merely "his only son, the goal of his longing, the hope of his life, the joy of his old age"—all that was dearest to him ; but the heir of all the promises, and that in simple, absolute faith upon God, and in perfect confidence, that God could raise him even from the dead. Thus was the promise purged, so to speak, from all of the flesh that clung to it ; and thus Abraham's faith was perfected, and his love purified. Upon Isaac, also, the event had a most important bearing. For when he resisted not his father, and allowed himself to be bound and laid on the altar, he entered into the spirit of Abraham, he took upon himself his faith, and thus showed himself truly the heir to the promises. Nor can we forget how this surrender of the first-born was the first of that dedication of all the first-born unto God, which afterwards the law demanded, and which meant that in the first-born we should consecrate all and everything unto the Lord. Perhaps the lesson which the Canaanites might learn from the event will seem to some quite secondary, as compared with these great truths.   Yet we must bear in mind, that all around cruel human sacrifices were offered on every hill, when God gave His sanction to a far different offering, by for ever substituting animal sacrifices for that surrender of the best beloved which human despair had prompted for an atonement for sin.   And yet God Himself gave up His beloved, His own only begotten Son for us,—and of this the sacrifice of Isaac was intended to be a glorious type; and as Abraham received this typical sacrifice again from the dead "in a figure," so we in reality, when God raised up His own Son, Jesus Christ, from the dead, and has made us sit together with Him in heavenly places.

After the offering up of Isaac, Abraham lived many years; yet scarcely any event worth record in Scripture occurred during their course.   The first thing we afterwards read is the death of Sarah, at the age of one hundred and twenty-seven.   She is the only woman whose age is recorded in Scripture, the distinction being probably due to her position towards believers, as stated in 1 Pet. iii. 6. Isaac was at the time thirty-seven years old, and Abraham once more resident in Hebron.   The account of Abraham's purchase of a burying-place from " the children of Heth" is exceedingly pictorial.   It also strikingly exhibits alike Abraham's position in the land as a stranger and a pilgrim, and yet his faith in his future possession thereof.   The treaty for the field and cave of *Machpelah* (either " the double" cave, or else " the separated place," or " the undulating spot"), which Abraham wished to purchase for "a burying-place," was carried on in public assembly, "at the gate of the city," as the common Eastern fashion is.   The patriarch expressly acknowledged himself " a stranger and a sojourner" among " the children of Heth;" and the sacred text emphatically repeats again and again how "Abraham stood up, and bowed himself to the people of the land."   On the other hand, they carry on their negotiations in the true Eastern fashion, first offering any of their own sepulchres, since Abraham was confessedly among them " a prince of God" (rendered in our version "a mighty prince"), then refusing any payment for Machpelah, but finishing up by asking its fullest value, in this true oriental manner : "My lord, hearken unto me : the land is worth four hundred shekels of silver (about fifty guineas[1]); what is that betwixt me and thee?" In contrast, Abraham truly stands out prince-like in his courtesy and in his dealings. And so the field and cave were secured to him—a "burying-place," Abraham's only "possession" in a land that was to be his for ever! But even in this purchase of a permanent family burying-place, Abraham showed his faith in the promise ; just as, many centuries later, the prophet Jeremiah showed his confidence in the promised return of Judah from Babylon, by purchasing a field in Anathoth.[2] In this cave of Machpelah lie treasured the remains of Abraham and Sarah, of Isaac and Rebekah, of Leah also, and the embalmed bodies of Jacob and perhaps Joseph.[3] No other spot in the Holy Land holds so much precious dust as this; and it is, among all the so-called "holy places," the only one which to this day can be pointed out with perfect certainty. Since the Moslem rule, it has not been accessible to either Christian or Jew. The site over the cave itself is covered by a Mahomedan sanctuary, which stands enclosed within a quadrangular building, two hundred feet long, one hundred and fifteen wide, and fifty or sixty high, the walls of which are divided by pilasters, about five feet apart, and two and a half feet wide. This building, with its immense stones, one of which is no less than thirty-eight feet long, must date from the time of David or of Solomon. The mosque within it was probably anciently a church ; and in the cave below its floor are the patriarchal sepulchres.

Three years after the death of Sarah, Abraham resolved to fill the gap in his own family and in the heart of Isaac, by seeking a wife for his son. To this we shall refer in connection with the life of Isaac. Nothing else remains to be told of the thirty-eight years which followed the death of Sarah.

[1] A very considerable price for those times   [2] Jer. xxxii. 7, 8.
[3] See "*Those Holy Fields ;*" *Palestine illustrated by Pen and Pencil*, p. 39.

We read, indeed, that Abraham "took a wife," Keturah, and that she bore him six sons, but we are not sure of the time when this occurred. At any rate, the history of these sons is in no wise mixed up with that of the promised seed. They became the ancestors of Arab tribes, which are sometimes alluded to in Holy Writ. And so, through the impressive silence of so many years as make up more than a generation, Scripture brings us to the death of Abraham, at the " good old age" of one hundred and seventy-five, just seventy-five years after the birth of Isaac. To quote the significant language of the Bible, he " was gathered to his people," an expression far different from dying or being buried, and which implies reunion with those who had gone before, and a firm and assured belief in the life to come. And as his sons Isaac and Ishmael, both aged men, stand by his sepulchre in the cave of Machpelah, we seem to hear the voice of God speaking it unto all times : " These all died in faith, not having received the promises, but having seen them afar off, and were persuaded of them, and embraced them, and confessed that they were strangers and pilgrims on the earth."[1]

CHAPTER XV.

The Marriage of Isaac—Birth of Esau and Jacob— Esau sells his Birthright—Isaac at Gerar—Esau's Marriage.

(GEN. XXIV. ; XXV. 19—XXVI.)

THE sacred narrative now turns to the history of Isaac, the heir to the promises, still marking in its course the same dealings on the part of God which had characterised the life of Abraham. Viewed in connection with the Divine promises, the marriage of Isaac would necessarily appear a subject of the deepest importance to Abraham. Two things were quite firmly settled in the mind of the patriarch : Isaac must on no

[1] Heb. **xi. 13.**

account take a wife from among the Canaanites around,—he must not enter into alliance with those who were to be dispossessed of the land ; and Jehovah, who had so often proved a faithful God, and in obedience to whose will he now refused what might have seemed highly advantageous connections, would Himself provide a suitable partner for Isaac. These two convictions determined Abraham's conduct, as they also guided that of "his eldest servant," whom Abraham commissioned to execute his wishes, and who, in general, seems to have been deeply imbued with the spirit of his master.

Some time before[1] Abraham had been informed that his brother Nahor, whom he left behind in Haran, had been blessed with numerous descendants. To him the patriarch now despatched "his servant, the elder of his house, who ruled over all that was his"—generally supposed to have been Eliezer of Damascus,[2] though at that time he must, like his master, have been far advanced in years. But before departing, he made him swear by *Jehovah*—since this matter concerned the very essence of the covenant—to avoid every alliance with the Canaanites, and to apply to his "kindred." And when the servant put before him the possibility, that the execution of this wish might render it necessary for Isaac to return to the land whence Abraham had come, the patriarch emphatically negatived the suggestion, as equally contrary to the Divine will, while his faith anticipated no difficulty, but calmly trusted the result in God's hands. In all this Abraham had no fresh revelation from heaven ; nor needed he any. He only applied to present circumstances what he had formerly received as the will of God, just as in all circumstances of life we need no fresh communication from above—only to understand and to apply the will of God as revealed to us in His holy word.

The result proved how true had been Abraham's expectations. Arrived at Haran, Abraham's servant made it a matter of prayer that God would "prosper his way," for even when in the way of God's appointment, we must seek and ask His

---

[1] Gen. xxii. 20. [2] Gen. xv. 2.

special blessing.   There, as he stood outside the city by the well
to which, according to the custom of the East, the maidens
would resort at even to draw water for their households, it
naturally occurred to him to connect in his prayer a mark of
that religious courtesy, hospitality, and kindness to which he
had been accustomed in his master's house, with the kindred
of Abraham, and hence with the object of his journey.   His
prayer was scarcely finished when the answer came.   "Before
he had done speaking"[1] *Rebekah*, the daughter of Bethuel, the
son of Nahor, Abraham's brother, came to the well by which
the stranger stood with his camels.   Her appearance was
exceedingly prepossessing ("the damsel was very fair to look
upon"), and her bearing modest and becoming.   According to
the sign on which he had fixed in his own mind, he asked her
for water to drink; and according to the same sign, she exceeded
his request by drawing for his camels also.   But even so
Abraham's servant did not yield to his first impressions; only
at the literality of the answer to his prayer, "the man wondering at her, held his peace, to know whether Jehovah had made
his way prosperous or not."   Before asking further who her
kindred were, and seeking their hospitality, he rewarded her
kindness by splendid presents.   But when the answers of
Rebekah showed him that Jehovah had actually led him
straight "to the house of his master's brethren," the man, fairly
overcome by his feelings, "bowed down his head, and worshipped Jehovah."

The description of what now ensued is not only exceedingly
graphic, but true to the life.   It is said that Rebekah "ran and
told her mother's house," that is, evidently to the female portion of the household.   Next, Laban, Rebekah's brother,
seeing the jewels and hearing her tale, hastens to invite the
stranger with true Eastern profusion of welcome.   But the
terms in which Laban, partially at least an idolater, addressed
Abraham's servant : "Thou blessed of Jehovah," remind us
how easily the language of Abraham—in other words, religious

[1] Comp. Dan. ix. 20, 21.

language, is picked up by those who have really no claim to use it. The servant of Abraham, on the other hand, is quite like his master in his dignified bearing and earnestness of purpose. Before accepting hospitality at the hands of Bethuel and Laban, he will have an answer to the commission on which he has been sent, nor can persuasions or entreaty prevail on him to prolong his stay, even over the following day. With the full consent of Rebekah, the caravan returns to Canaan. Once more it is evening when the end of the journey is reached. It so happens that Isaac has " gone out to meditate in the field" —an expression which implies religious communion with God, probably in connection with this very marriage—when he meets the returning caravan. Rebekah receives her future husband with the becoming modesty of an Eastern bride, and the heart-happiness of the son of promise is secured to him in union with her whom the Lord Himself had "provided" as his wife. Isaac was at the time of his marriage forty years old.

In the quiet retirement of his old age Abraham not only witnessed the married happiness of his son, but even lived fifteen years beyond the birth of Esau and Jacob. As for Isaac, he had settled far from the busy haunts of the Canaanites, at the well *Lahai-Roi*, a retreat suited to his quiet, retiring disposition. For twenty years the union of Isaac and Rebekah had remained unblessed with children, to indicate that here also the heir to the promises must be a gift from God granted to expectant faith. At last Jehovah listened to Isaac's "entreaty," "for his wife," or rather, literally, "over against his wife," for, as Luther strikingly remarks : " When I pray for any one, I place him right in view of my heart, and neither see nor think of anything else, but look at him alone with my soul ;" and this is true of all intercessory prayer. Rebekah was now to become the mother of twin sons. But even before their birth a sign occurred which distressed her, and induced her " to inquire of Jehovah" its meaning, though we know not in what precise manner she did this. The answer of God indicated this at least quite clearly, that of her children " the elder shall serve the younger;" that is, that, contrary to all usual expectation, the firstborn should *not* possess the birthright which the Divine promise had conveyed to the family of Abraham.   The substitution of the younger for the elder son was indeed in accordance with God's previous dealings, but it seemed strange where the two were sons of the same parents.   It is not only reasonable, but quite necessary for the understanding of the subsequent history, to believe that Rebekah communicated the result of her inquiry to her husband, and that afterwards both Esau and Jacob were also made acquainted with the fact.   This alone fully accounts for the conduct of Jacob and of his mother in seeking to appropriate the birthright, contrary to what would otherwise have been the natural arrangement.   When the two children were born, the red and hairy appearance of the elder procured for him the name of *Esau*, or "hairy;" while the younger was called *Jacob*, or he " who takes hold by the heel," because "his hand took hold by Esau's heel"—a name which afterwards was adapted to mean "a supplanter,"[1] since he who takes hold by the heel " trips up " the other.

The appearance of the children did not belie their character when they grew up.   The wild disposition of Esau, which found occupation in the roaming life of a hunter, reminds us of Ishmael ; while Jacob, gentle and domestic, sought his pleasures at home.   As is so often the case, Isaac and Rebekah made favourites of the sons who had the opposite of their own disposition.   The quiet, retiring Isaac preferred his bold, daring, strong, roaming elder son ; while Rebekah, who was naturally energetic, felt chiefly drawn to her gentle son Jacob.   Yet at bottom Esau also was weak and easily depressed, as appeared in his tears and impotent reproaches when he found himself really deprived of the blessing ; while Jacob, too, like his mother, impetuous, was ever ready to take matters into his own hands.   We repeat it, that all parties must at the time have been aware that, even before the birth of the children, the word of God had designated *Jacob* as heir of the promises.

[1] Gen. xxvii. 36.

But Isaac's preference for Esau made him reluctant to fall in with the Divine arrangement; while the impetuosity of Rebekah and of Jacob prompted them to bring about in their own way the fulfilment of God's promise, instead of believingly waiting to see when and how the Lord would do it. Thus it came that Jacob, watching his opportunities, soon found occasion to take advantage of his brother. One day Esau returned from the chase "faint" with hunger. The sight of a mess of lentils, which to this day is a favourite dish in Syria and Egypt, induced him, unaccustomed and unable as he was to control the desires of the moment, to barter away his birthright for this "red" pottage. The circumstances become the more readily intelligible when we remember, besides the unbridled disposition of Esau, that, as Lightfoot has pointed out, it was a time of commencing famine in the land. For, immediately afterwards,[1] we read that "there was a famine in the land," greater even than that at the time of Abraham, and which compelled Isaac for a season to leave Canaan. From this event, so characteristic and decisive in his history, Esau, after the custom of the East, obtained the name of *Edom*, or "red," from the colour of "the mess of pottage" for which he had sold his birthright.

In regard to the conduct of the two brothers in this matter, we must note, that Scripture in no way excuses nor apologises for that of Jacob. According to its wont, it simply states the facts, and makes neither comment nor remark upon them. *That* it leaves to "the logic of facts;" and the terrible trials which were so soon to drive Jacob from his home, and which kept him so long a bondsman in a strange land, are themselves a sufficient Divine commentary upon the transaction. Moreover, it is very remarkable that Jacob never in his after-life appealed to his purchase of the birthright. But so far as Esau is concerned only one opinion can be entertained of his conduct. We are too apt to imagine that because Jacob wronged or took advantage of Esau, therefore Esau was right. The opposite of

[1] Gen. xxvi. 1.

this is the case. When we ask ourselves what Jacob intended to purchase, or Esau to sell in the "birthright," we answer that in later times it conveyed a double share of the paternal possessions.[1] In patriarchal days it included "lordship" over the rest of the family, and especially succession to that spiritual blessing which through Abraham was to flow out into the world,[2] together with possession of the land of Canaan and covenant-communion with Jehovah.[3] What of these things was spiritual, we may readily believe, Esau discredited and despised, and what was temporal, but yet future, as his after conduct shows, he imagined he might still obtain either by his father's favour or by violence. But that for the momentary gratification of the lowest sensual appetites he should have been ready to barter away such unspeakably precious and holy privileges, proved him, in the language of the Epistle to the Hebrews,[4] to have been "a profane person," and therefore quite unfitted to become the heir of the promises. For profanity consists in this : for the sensual gratification or amusement of the moment to give up that which is spiritual and unseen ; to be careless of that which is holy, so as to snatch the present enjoyment,—in short, practically not to deem anything holy at all, if it stands in the way of present pleasure. Scripture puts it down as the bitter self-condemnation which Esau, by his conduct, pronounced upon himself : "and he did eat and drink, and rose up, and went his way ; thus Esau despised his birthright."

Before farther following the history of Isaac's trials and joys, it seems desirable to make here a few general remarks, for the purpose of explaining the conduct alike of Isaac and of Jacob, and its bearing on the history of the covenant. It has been common to describe Abraham as the man of *faith*, Isaac as the model of *patient bearing*, and Jacob as the man of *active working* ; and in the two latter cases to connect the spiritual fruits, which were the outcome of their faith, with their natural cha-

[1] Deut. xxi. 17.   [2] Gen. xxvii. 27 29.
[3] Gen. xxviii. 4.   [4] Heb. xii. 16

racters also. All this is quite correct; but, in our opinion, it is necessary to take a broader view of the whole matter. Let it be borne in mind, that God had both made and established His covenant with Abraham. The history of Isaac and Jacob, on the other hand, rather represents *the hindrances to the covenant.* These are just the same as we daily meet in our own walk of faith. They arise from opposite causes, according as in our weakness we either lag behind, or in our haste go before God. Isaac lagged behind, Jacob tried to go before God; and their history exhibits the dangers and difficulties arising from each of these causes, just as, on the other hand, God's dealings with them show how mercifully, how wisely, and yet how holily He knew to remove these hindrances out of the way, and to uproot these sins from their hearts and lives. Accordingly, we shall consider the history of Isaac and Jacob as that of the hindrances of the covenant and of their removal.

Viewed in this light we understand all the better, not only Jacob's attempt to purchase the "birthright"—as if Esau had had the power of selling it !—but what followed that transaction? It seems that a grievous famine induced Isaac to leave his settlement, and it naturally occurred to him in so doing to follow in the wake of his father Abraham, and to go into Egypt. But when he had reached Gerar, the residence of Abimelech, king of the Philistines, where Abraham had previously sojourned, "Jehovah appeared unto him," and specially directed him to remain there, at the same time renewing to him the promises He had made to Abraham. Both in this direction and in the renewal of blessing we recognise the kindness of the Lord, Who would not expose Isaac to the greater trials of Egypt, and would strengthen and encourage his faith. Apparently, he had on reaching Gerar not said that Rebekah was his wife ; and when he was, at last, "asked" about it, the want of courage which had prompted the equivocation, ripened into actual falsehood. Imitating in this the example of Abraham, he passed off his wife as his sister. But here also the kindness of the Lord interposed to spare him a trial greater than he might have been able to bear. His deceit was detected before his wife had been taken by any one ; and an order given by Abimelech—whether the same who ruled at the time of Abraham, or his successor—secured her future safety. The famine seems now to have become so intense, that Isaac began to till land for himself. And God blessed him with an unusually large return—still further to encourage his faith amidst its trials. Commonly, even in very fruitful parts of Palestine, the yield is from twenty-five to fifty times that which had been sown ; and in one small district, even eighty times that of wheat, and one hundred times that of barley. But Isaac at once "received an hundredfold "—to show him that even in a year of famine God could make the most ample provision for His servant. The increasing wealth of Isaac excited the envy of the Philistines. Disputes arose, and they stopped up the wells which Abraham had digged. At last, even Abimelech, friendly as he was, advised him to leave the place. Isaac removed to the valley of Gerar. But there also similar contentions arose ; and Isaac once more returned to Abraham's old settlement at Beersheba. Here Jehovah again appeared unto him, to con- firm, on his re-entering the land, the promises previously made. Beersheba had also its name given it a second time. For Abimelech, accompanied by his chief captain and his privy councillor, came to Isaac to renew the covenant which had for- merly been there made between the Philistines and Abraham. Isaac was now at peace with all around. Better still, "he builded an altar" in Beersheba, "and called upon the name of Jehovah." But in the high day of his prosperity fresh trials awaited him. His eldest son Esau, now forty years old, took two Canaanitish wives, "which were a grief of mind unto Isaac and to Rebekah." Assuredly, if Isaac had not "lagged far behind," he would in this have recognised the final and full unfitness of Esau to have "the birthright." But the same ten- dency which had hitherto kept him at best undecided, led, ere it was finally broken, to a further and a far deeper sorrow than any he had yet experienced.

CHAPTER XVI.

Isaac's Blessing obtained by Jacob deceitfully—Esau's Sorrow—Evil Consequences of their error to all the members of their family—Jacob is sent to Laban—Isaac renews and fully gives him the Blessing of Abraham.

(GEN. XXVII.—XXVIII. 9.)

IF there is any point on which we should anxiously be on our guard, it is that of "tempting God." We do so tempt the Lord when, listening to our own inclinations, we put once more to the question that which He has already clearly settled. Where God *has* decided, never let us doubt, nor lag behind. But if anything might be described as clearly settled by God, it was, surely, the calling of Jacob and the rejection of Esau. It had been expressly foretold in prophecy even before the children were born ; and Esau had also afterwards proved himself wholly unfit to be the heir of the promise, first by his light-minded profanity, and next by his alliance with the Canaanites, than which nothing could have more directly run counter to the will of God, and to the purposes of the covenant. Despite these clear indications, Isaac *did* lag behind, reluctant to follow the direction of God. In truth, he had thrown his natural affections as a makeweight into the scale. As we shall presently show, Isaac hesitated, indeed, to allot unto Esau the *spiritual* part of the blessing; but what he regarded as the natural rights of the first-born appeared to him inalienable, and these he meant now formally to recognise by bestowing upon him the blessing.

A German writer aptly observes : " This is one of the most remarkable complications of life, showing in the clearest manner that a higher hand guides the threads of history, so that neither

sin nor error can ultimately entangle them.   Each one weaves
the threads which are committed to him according to his own
views and desires; but at last, when the texture is complete,
we behold in it the pattern which the Master had long devised,
and towards which each labourer had only contributed one or
another feature."   At the time of which we write Isaac was one
hundred and thirty-seven years old[1]—an age at which his half-
brother Ishmael had died, fourteen years before; and though
Isaac was destined to live yet forty-three years longer,[2] the
decay of his sight, and other infirmities, brought the thought
of death very near to him.   Under these circumstances he resolved formally to bestow the privileges naturally belonging to
the first-born upon Esau.   With this, however, he coupled, as
a sort of preliminary condition, that Esau should bring and
prepare for him some venison.   Possibly he regarded the finding of the game as a sort of providential sign, and the preparation of it as a token of affection.   There would be nothing
strange in this, for those who believe in God, and yet for some
reason refuse implicitly to follow His directions, are always on
the outlook for some "sign" to justify them in setting aside
the clear intimations of His will.   But Rebekah had overheard
the conversation between her husband and her son.   Probably she had long been apprehensive of some such event, and
on the outlook for it.   And now the danger seemed most pressing.   Another *hour*, and the blessing might for ever be lost
to Jacob.   Humanly speaking, safety lay in quick resolution
and decided action.   It mattered not what were the means
employed, if only the end were attained.   Had not God dis-

[1] The age of Isaac is thus ascertained: When Joseph stood before
Pharaoh (Gen. xli. 46), he was thirty years old, and hence thirty-nine when
Jacob came into Egypt.   But at that time Jacob was one hundred and
thirty years of age (Gen. xlvii. 9).   Hence Jacob must have been ninety-
one years old when Joseph was born; and as this happened in the fourteenth year of Jacob's stay with Laban, Jacob's flight from his home must
have taken place in the seventy-seventh year of his own, and the one hundred and thirty-seventh of his father Isaac's life.
[2] Gen. xxxv. 28.

tinctly pointed out Jacob as heir to the promises? Had not Esau proved himself utterly unfit for it, and that even before he married those Canaanitish women? She could only be fulfilling the will of God when she kept her husband from so great a wrong, and secured to her son what God had intended him to possess. Thus Rebekah probably argued in her own mind. To be sure, if she had had the faith of Abraham, who was ready on Mount Moriah to offer up his own son, believing that, if it were to be so, God was able to raise him from the dead, she would not have acted, not even felt, nor feared, as she did. But then her motives were very mixed, even though she kept the promise steadily in view, and her faith was weak and imperfect, even though she imagined herself to be carrying out the will of God. Such hours come to most of us, when it almost seems as if necessity obliged and holy wisdom prompted us to accomplish, in our own strength, that which, nevertheless, we should leave in God's hand. If once we enter on such a course, it will probably not be long before we cast to the winds any scruples about the means to be employed, so that we secure the object desired, and which possibly may seem to us in accordance with the will of God. Here also *faith* is the only true remedy: faith, which leaves God to carry out His own purposes, content to trust Him absolutely, and to follow Him whithersoever *He* leadeth. And God's way is never through the thicket of human cunning and devices. "He that believeth shall not make haste;" nor need he, for God will do it all for him.

In pursuance of her purpose, Rebekah proposed to Jacob to take advantage of his father's dim sight, and to personate Esau. He was to put on his brother's dress, which bore the smell of the aromatic herbs and bushes among which he was wont to hunt, and to cover his smooth skin with a kind of fur; while Rebekah would prepare a dish which his father would not be able to distinguish from the venison which Esau was to make ready for him. It is remarkable, that although Jacob at first objected, his scruples were caused rather by fear of detection

than from a sense of the wrong proposed. But Rebekah
quieted his misgivings,—possibly trusting, that since she was
doing, as she thought, the will of God, she could not but succeed. In point of fact, Jacob found his part more difficult
than he could have expected. Deceit, equivocation, and
lying, repeated again and again, were required to allay the
growing suspicions of the old man. At last Jacob succeeded—
with what shame and remorse we can readily imagine—in
diverting his father's doubts ; and Isaac bestowed upon him
"the blessing," and with it the birthright. But it deserves
special notice, that while this blessing assigned to him both
the land of Canaan and lordship over his brethren, there is in
it but the faintest allusion to *the* great promise to Abraham.
The only words which can be supposed to refer to it are
these : "Cursed be every one that curseth thee, and blessed
be he that blesseth thee."[1] But this is manifestly very different from the blessing of Abraham, "In thee and in thy seed
shall all the nations of the earth be blessed."[2] It is clear that
Isaac imagined he had blessed Esau, and that he did not dare
confer upon him the spiritual privileges attached to the birthright. So, after all, Jacob and Rebekah did *not* attain that
which they had sought !

Jacob had scarcely left the presence of his father, when
Esau entered with the venison he had prepared. If Isaac,
Rebekah, and Jacob had been each wrong in their share in the
transaction, Esau deserves at least equal blame. Not to speak
of his previous knowledge of the will of God on this point,
he disguised from his brother Jacob that he was about to
obtain from his father's favour that which he had actually
sold to Jacob ! Surely, there was here quite as great dishonesty, cunning, and untruthfulness as on the part of Jacob.
When Isaac now discovered the deceit which had been practised upon him, he "trembled very exceedingly," but he refused
to recall the blessing he had pronounced : "I have blessed
him—yea, and he shall be blessed." Now, for the first time,

---

[1] Gen. xxvii. 29.   [2] Gen. xxii. 18.

the mist which in this matter had so long hung about Isaac's spiritual vision, seems dispelled. He sees the finger of God, who had averted the danger which his own weakness had caused. Thus, while all parties in the transaction had been in error and sin, God brought about His own purpose, and Isaac recognised this fact. Now, for the first time also, Esau obtained a glimpse of what he had *really* lost. We read, that " afterwards, when he would have inherited the blessing, he was rejected : for he found no place of repentance, though he sought it diligently with tears."[1] At his earnest entreaty for some kind of blessing, Isaac pronounced what in reality was a prophecy of the future of Edom. Translating it *literally*, it reads :

> " Behold, thy dwelling shall be without fatness of the earth,
> And without the dew of heaven from above."

This describes the general aspect of the sterile mountains of Edom ; after which the patriarch continues, by sketching the future history of the Edomites :

> " But by thy sword shalt thou live, and shalt serve thy brother ;
> Yet it shall come to pass that, as thou shakest it, thou shalt break
> his yoke from off thy neck."

The last sentence, it has been well remarked, refers to the varying success of the future struggles between Israel and Edom, and introduces into the blessing of Jacob an element of judgment. And when we compare the words of Isaac with the history of Israel and Edom, down to the time when Herod, the Idumean, possessed himself of the throne of David, we see how correctly the whole has been summed up in the Epistle to the Hebrews (xi. 20) : " By faith Isaac blessed Jacob and Esau concerning things to come."

For, that Isaac was now acting in *faith*, and that he discerned how, without knowing it, he had blessed, not according to his own inclination, but according to the will and purpose of God, appears from the subsequent history. It seems that Esau, full

[1] Heb. xii. 17.

of hatred and envy, resolved to rid himself of his rival by mur-
dering his brother, only deferring the execution of his purpose
till after the death of his father, which he also believed to be
near at hand. Somehow Rebekah, ever watchful, obtained
tidings of this; and knowing her elder son's quick temper,
which, however violent, did not long harbour anger, she resolved to send Jacob away to her brother Laban, for "a few
days," as she fondly imagined, after which she would "send
and fetch" him "from thence." But kindness towards her
husband prompted her to keep from him Esau's murderous
plan, and to plead as a reason for Jacob's temporary departure
that which, no doubt, was also a strong motive in her own
mind, that Jacob should marry one of her kindred. For,
as she said, "If Jacob take a wife of the daughters of Heth,
such as these of the daughters of the land, what good shall
my life be to me?" Petulant as was her language, her reasoning was just, and Isaac knew it from painful experience of
Esau's wives. And now Isaac expressly sent Jacob to Laban,
to seek him a wife; and in so doing, this time consciously and
wittingly, renewed the blessing which formerly had been fraudu-
lently obtained from him. Now also the patriarch speaks
clearly and unmistakably, not only reiterating the very terms of
the covenant-blessing in all their fulness, but especially adding
these words : "God Almighty . . . . give thee the blessing of
Abraham, to thee, and to thy seed with thee." Thus Isaac's
dimness of spiritual sight had at last wholly passed away. But
the darkness around Esau seems to only have grown deeper
and deeper. Upon learning what charge Isaac had given his
son, and apparently for the first time awakening to the fact that
"the daughters of Canaan pleased not Isaac [1] his father," he
took "Mahalath, the daughter of Ishmael" as a third wife—as
if he had mended matters by forming an alliance with him
whom Abraham had, by God's command, "cast out!" Thus

[1] There is no mention here that Esau dreaded *God's* displeasure, or even
thought of it. We may remember our earthly, and yet, alas, forget our
heavenly Father.

the spiritual incapacity and unfitness of Esau appeared at every step, even where he tried to act kindly and dutifully.

To conclude, by altering and adapting the language of a German writer : After this event Isaac lived other forty-three years. But he no more appears in this history. Its thread is now taken up by Jacob, on whom the promise has devolved. Scripture only records that Isaac was gathered to his fathers when one hundred and eighty years old, and full of days, and that he was buried in the cave of Machpelah by Esau and Jacob, whom he had the joy of seeing by his death-bed as reconciled brothers. When Jacob left, his father dwelt at Beersheba. The desire to be nearer to his father's burying-place may have been the ground of his later settlement in Mamre, where he died.[1] Rebekah, who at parting had so confidently promised to let Jacob know whenever Esau's anger was appeased, may have died even before her favourite son returned to Canaan. At any rate the promised message was never delivered, nor is her name mentioned on Jacob's return.

CHAPTER XVII.

Jacob's Vision at Bethel—His Arrival at the House of Laban—Jacob's double Marriage and Servitude— His Flight from Haran—Pursuit of Laban, and Reconciliation with Jacob.

(GEN. XXVIII. 10—XXXI.)

IT had been a long and weary journey that first day when Jacob left his home at Beersheba.[2] More than forty miles had he travelled over the mountains which afterwards

---

[1] Gen. xxxv. 27–29.

[2] We infer from the sacred text that Jacob made his first night's quarters at Bethel.

were those of Judah, and through what was to become the
land of Benjamin. The sun had set, and its last glow faded
out from the grey hills of Ephraim, when he reached "an
uneven valley, covered, as with gravestones, by large sheets of
bare rock,—some few here and there standing up like the
cromlechs of Druidical monuments."[1] Here, close by a wild
ridge, the broad summit of which was covered by an olive
grove, was the place where Abraham had first rested for some
time on entering the land, and whence he and Lot had, before
their separation, taken a survey of the country. There, just
before him, lay the Canaanitish *Luz;* and beyond it, many
days' journey, stretched his weary course to Haran.[2] It was a
lonely, weird place, this valley of stones, in which to make
his first night's quarters. But perhaps it agreed all the better
with Jacob's mood, which had made him go on and on, from
early morning, forgetful of time and way, till he could no
longer pursue his journey. Yet, accidental as it seemed—for
we read that "he lighted upon a certain place,"—the selection
of the spot was assuredly designed of God. Presently Jacob
prepared for rest. Piling some of the stones, with which the
valley was strewed, he made them a pillow, and laid him down
to sleep. Then it was, in his dream, that it seemed as if these
stones of the valley were being builded together by an unseen
hand, step upon step, "a ladder"—or, probably more correctly,
"a stair." Now, as he watched it, it rose and rose, till it reached
the deep blue star-spangled sky, which seemed to cleave for its
reception. All along that wondrous track moved angel-forms,
"ascending and descending upon it;" and angel-light was shed
upon its course, till quite up on the top stood the glorious
Jehovah Himself, Who spake to the lonely sleeper below : "I
am Jehovah, the God of Abraham thy father, and the God of
Isaac." Silent in their ministry, the angels still passed up and
down the heaven-built stairs, from where Jacob lay to where Jehovah spake. The vision and the words which the Lord spoke

[1] Stanley, *Sinai and Palestine,* p. 217.
[2] The journey from Beersheba to Haran is quite four hundred miles.

explain each other, the one being the *symbol* of the other.   On
that first night, when an outcast from his home, and a fugitive,
heavy thoughts, doubts, and fears would crowd around Jacob;
when, in every sense, his head was pillowed on stones in the
rocky valley of Luz, Jehovah expressly renewed to him, in the
fullest manner, the promise and the blessing first given to
Abraham, and added to it this comfort, whatever might be
before him : " I am with thee, and will keep thee in all places
whither thou goest, and will bring thee again into this land ;
for I will not leave thee until I have done that which I have
spoken to thee of."   And what Jacob heard, that he also saw
in symbolic vision.   The *promise* was the real God-built stair,
which reached from the lonely place on which the poor wanderer lay quite up to heaven, right into the very presence of
Jehovah ; and on which, all silent and unknown by the world,
lay the shining track of angel-ministry.   And so still to each
one who is truly of Israel is the promise of that mysterious
"ladder" which connects earth with heaven.   Below lies poor,
helpless, forsaken man ; above, stands Jehovah Himself, and
upon the ladder of promise which joins earth to heaven, the
angels of God, in their silent, never-ceasing ministry, descend,
bringing help, and ascend, as to fetch new deliverance.   Nay,
this "ladder" is Christ,[1] for by this "ladder" God Himself has
come down to us in the Person of His dear Son, Who is, so to
speak, the Promise become Reality, as it is written : " Hereafter ye shall see heaven open, and the angels of God ascending
and descending upon the Son of Man."[2]

"And Jacob awaked out of his sleep, and he said, Surely
Jehovah is in this place, and I knew it not."   Quite another fear
now came upon him from that of loneliness or of doubt.   It
was awe at the conscious presence of the ever-watchful, ever-
mindful covenant-God which made him feel, as many a wanderer
since at such discovery : " How dreadful is this place !   This
is none other but the house of God, and this is the gate of
heaven."   And early next morning Jacob converted his stony

---

[1] So both Luther and Calvin understood it.   [2] John i. 51.

pillow into a memorial pillar, and consecrated it unto God.
Henceforth this rocky valley would be to him no more the
Canaanitish Luz, but *Beth-el*, "the house of God;" just as John
the Baptist declared that God could of such stones raise up
children to Abraham. At the same time Jacob vowed a vow,
that when God had fulfilled His promise, and brought him back
again " in peace," he would, on his part also, make the place a
Beth-el, by dedicating it to God, and offering unto the Lord a
tenth of all that He should give him, which also he did.[1]

No further incident worth recording occurred till Jacob
reached the end of his journey in " the land of the people of
the East." Here he found himself at a " well," where, contrary
to the usual custom, three flocks were already in waiting, long
before the usual evening time for watering them. Professor
Robinson has made this personal observation, helpful to our
understanding of the circumstances: "Over most of the cisterns
is laid a broad and thick flat stone, with a round hole cut in
the middle, forming the mouth of the cistern. This hole we
found in many cases covered with a heavy stone, which it
would require two or three men to roll away." We know not
whether these flocks were kept waiting till sufficient men had
come to roll away the stone, or whether it was the custom to
delay till all the flocks had arrived. At any rate, when Jacob
had ascertained that the flocks were from Haran, and that the
shepherds knew Laban, the brother of Rebekah, and when he
saw the fair Rachel, his own cousin, coming with her flock, he
rolled away the stone himself, watered his uncle's sheep, and in
the warmth of his feelings at finding himself not only at the goal
of his journey, but apparently God-directed to her whose very
appearance could win his affections, he embraced his cousin.
Even in this little trait the attentive observer of Jacob's natural
character will not fail to recognise "the haste" with which he
always anticipated God's leadings. When Laban, Rachel's
father, came to hear of all the circumstances, he received Jacob
as his relative. A month's trial more than confirmed in the

[1] Gen. xxxv. 6, 7.

mind of that selfish, covetous man the favourable impression of Jacob's possible use to him as a shepherd, which his first energetic interference at the "well" must have produced. With that apparent frankness and show of liberality under which cunning, selfish people so often disguise their dishonest purposes, Laban urged upon Jacob to name his own "wages." Jacob had learned to love Rachel, Laban's younger daughter. Without consulting the mind of God in the matter, he now proposed to serve Laban seven years for her hand. This was just the period during which, among the Hebrews, a Jewish slave had to serve ; in short, he proposed becoming a bondsman for Rachel. With the same well-feigned candour as before, Laban agreed : "It is better that I give her to thee, than that I should give her to another man (to a stranger)." The bargain thus to sell his daughter was not one founded on the customs of the time, and Laban's daughters themselves felt the degradation which they could not resist, as appears from their after statement, when agreeing to flee from their father's home : "Are we not counted of him strangers ? for he has sold us."[1]

The period of Jacob's servitude seemed to him rapidly to pass, and at the end of the seven years he claimed his bride. But now Jacob was to experience how his sin had found him out. As he had deceived his father, so Laban now deceived him. Taking advantage of the Eastern custom that a bride was always brought to her husband veiled, he substituted for Rachel her elder sister Leah. But, as formerly, God had, all unknown to them, overruled the error and sin of Isaac and of Jacob, so He did now also in the case of Laban and Jacob. For Leah was, so far as we can judge, the one whom God had intended for Jacob, though, for the sake of her beauty, he had preferred Rachel. From Leah sprang *Judah*, in whose line the promise to Abraham was to be fulfilled. Leah, as we shall see in the sequel, feared and served Jehovah ; while Rachel was attached to the superstitions of her father's house ; and even the natural character of the elder sister fitted her better for her new calling

[1] Gen. xxxi. 14, 15.

than that of the somewhat petulant, peevish, and self-willed, though beautiful younger daughter of Laban. As for the author of this deception, Laban, he shielded himself behind the pretence of a national custom, not to give away a younger before a first-born sister. But he readily proposed to give to Jacob Rachel also, in return for other seven years of service. Jacob consented, and the second union was celebrated immediately upon the close of Leah's marriage festivities, which in the East generally last for a week. It were an entire mistake to infer from the silence of Scripture that this double marriage of Jacob received Divine approbation. As always, Scripture states facts, but makes no comment. *That* sufficiently appears from the lifelong sorrow, disgrace, and trials which, in the retributive providence of God, followed as the consequence of this double union.

The sinful weakness of Jacob appeared also in his married life, in an unkind and unjust preference for Rachel, and God's reproving dealings in that He blessed the "hated" wife with children, while he withheld from Rachel a boon so much desired in a family where all that was precious stood connected with an heir to the promises. At the same time, this might also serve to teach again the lesson, given first to Abraham and then to Isaac, how especially in the patriarchal family this blessing was to be a direct gift from the Lord.[1] Leah bore in rapid succession four sons, whom she significantly named *Reuben* (" behold ! a son"), saying, " Surely *Jehovah* hath looked upon my affliction ;" *Simeon* ("hearing"), "Because *Jehovah* hath heard that I was hated ;" *Levi* (" cleaving," or " joined "), in the hope "Now this time will my husband cleave to me ;" and *Judah* ("praised," viz., be Jehovah), since she said : "Now will I praise *Jehovah*." It deserves special notice, that in the birth of at least three of these sons, Leah not only recognised God, but specially acknowledged Him as *Jehovah*, the covenant-God.

We do not suppose that Rachel, who had no children of her own, waited all this time without seeking to remove what she

[1] See also Psa. cxxvii. 3.

enviously and jealously regarded as her sister's advantage. Indeed, the sacred text nowhere indicates that the children of Jacob were born in the exact succession of time in which their names are recorded. On the contrary, we have every reason to suppose that such was not the case. It quite agrees with the petulant, querulous language of Rachel, that she waited not so long, but that so soon as she really found herself at this disadvantage compared with her sister, she persuaded her husband to make her a mother through *Bilhah*, her own maid, as Sarah had done in the case of Hagar. Thus the sins of the parents too often reappear in the conduct of their successors. Instead of waiting upon God, or giving himself to prayer, Jacob complied with the desire of his Rachel, and her maid successively bore two sons, whom Rachel named "*Dan*," or "judging," as if God had judged her wrong, and "*Naphtali*," or "my wrestling," saying: "With great wrestling have I wrestled with my sister, and I have prevailed." In both instances we mark her gratified jealousy of her sister; and that, although she owned God, it was not as *Jehovah*, but as *Elohim*, the God of nature, not the covenant God of the promise.

Once again the evil example of a sister, and its supposed success, proved infectious. When Leah perceived that she no longer became as before, a mother, and probably without waiting till both Rachel's adopted sons had been born, she imitated the example of her sister, and gave to Jacob her own maid *Zilpah* as wife. Her declension in faith further appears also in the names which she chose for the sons of *Zilpah*. At the birth of the eldest, she exclaimed, "Good fortune cometh,"[1] and hence called him "*Gad*," or "good fortune;" the same idea being expressed in the name of the second, *Asher*, or "happy." Neither did Leah in all this remember God, but only thought of the success of her own device. But the number of children now granted to the two sisters neither removed their mutual jealousies, nor restored peace to the house of Jacob. Most

[1] This is the correct translation; or else, after another reading: "With good luck!"

painful scenes occurred ; and when at length *Leah* again gave
birth to two sons, she recognised, indeed, God in their names,
but now, like her sister, only *Elohim*, not *Jehovah;* while she
seemed to see in the first of them a reward for giving Zilpah to
her husband, whence the child's name was called *Issachar*
(" he gives," or "he brings reward "); while she regarded her
last-born son, *Zebulun*, or "dwelling," as a pledge that since
she had borne him six sons, her husband would now dwell
with her !

It has already been stated that we must not regard the order
in which the birth of Jacob's children is mentioned as indicating their actual succession.[1] They are rather so enumerated,
partly to show the varying motives of the two sisters, and
partly to group together the sons of different mothers. That
the scriptural narrative is not intended to represent the actual
succession of the children appears also from the circumstance,
that the birth of an only daughter, *Dinah* ("judgment") is
mentioned immediately after that of Zebulun. The wording
of the Hebrew text here implies that Dinah was born at a later
period ("afterwards"), and, indeed, she alone is mentioned on
account of her connection with Jacob's later history, though we
have reason to believe that Jacob had other daughters,[2] whose
names and history are not mentioned.

And now at last better thoughts seem to have come to Rachel.
When we read that in giving her a son of her own, " God
hearkened to her," we are warranted in inferring that believing
prayer had taken in her heart the former place of envy and
jealousy of her sister. The son whom she now bore, in the
fourteenth year of Jacob's servitude to Laban, was called *Joseph*,
a name which has a double meaning : " the remover," because,
as she said, "God hath taken away my reproach," and " adding," since she regarded her child as a pledge that God—this

[1] In Jacob's last blessing (Gen. xlix.) we find quite a different succession
of his sons ; this time also with a view to the purposes of the narrative,
rather than to chronological order.
[2] See Gen. xxxvii. 35, and xlvi. 7.

time "Jehovah"—"shall add to me another son." The object
of Jacob's prolonged stay with his father-in-law was now accomplished. Fourteen years' servitude to Laban left him as poor as
when first he had come to him. The wants of his increasing
family, and the better understanding now established in his
family, must have pointed out to him the desirableness of returning to his own country. But when he intimated this wish
to his father-in-law, Laban was unwilling to part with one by
whom he had so largely profited. With a characteristic confusion of heathen ideas with a dim knowledge of the being of
Jehovah, Laban said to Jacob (we here translate literally):
"If I have found grace in thy sight (*i.e.* tarry), for I have
divined [1] (ascertained by magic), and Jehovah hath blessed
me for thy sake." The same attempt to place Jehovah as the
God of Abraham by the side of the god of Nahor—not denying, indeed, the existence of Jehovah, but that He was the
only true and living God—occurs again later when Laban made
a covenant with Jacob.[2] It also frequently recurs in the later
history of Israel. Both strange nations and Israel itself, when
in a state of apostasy, did not deny that Jehovah was God, but
they tried to place Him on a level with other and false deities.
Now, Scripture teaches us that to place any other pretended
God along with the living and true One argues as great ignorance, and is as great a sin, as to deny Him entirely.

In his own peculiar fashion Laban, with pretended candour
and liberality, now invited Jacob to name his wages for the
future. But this time the deceiver was to be deceived. Basing
his proposal on the fact that in the East the goats are mostly
black and the sheep white, Jacob made what seemed the very
modest request, that all that were spotted and speckled in the

---

[1] It is a very remarkable circumstance that the Hebrew word for *divining*
is the same as that for *serpent*. In heathen rites also the worship of the
serpent was connected with magic; and in all this we recognise how all
false religion and sorcery is truly to be traced up to the "old serpent,"
which is Satan.

[2] Gen. xxxi. 53.

flock were to be his share. Laban gladly assented, taking care to make the selection himself, and to hand over Jacob's portion to his own sons, while Jacob was to tend the flocks of Laban. Finally, he placed three days' journey betwixt the flocks of Jacob and his own. But even so, Jacob knew how, by an artifice well understood in the East, to circumvent his father-in-law, and to secure that, though ordinarily "the ringstraked, speckled, and spotted" had been an exception, now they were the most numerous and the strongest of the flocks. And the advantage still remained on the side of Jacob, when Laban again and again reversed the conditions of the agreement.[1] This clearly proved that Jacob's artifice could not have been the sole nor the real reason of his success. In point of fact, immediately after the first agreement with Laban, the angel of God had spoken to Jacob in a dream, assuring him that, even without any such artifices, God would right him in his cause with Laban.[2] Once more, then, Jacob acted, as when in his father's house. He "made haste;" he would not wait for the Lord to fulfil his promise; he would use his own means—employ his cunning and devices—to accomplish the purpose of God, instead of committing his cause unto Him. And as formerly he had had the excuse of his father's weakness and his brother's violence, so now it might seem as if he were purely on his defence, and as if his deceit were necessary for his protection —the more so as he resorted to his device only in spring, not in autumn,[3] so that the second produce of the year belonged chiefly to his father-in-law.

The consequences proved very similar to those which followed his deceit in his father's house. The rapidly growing wealth of Jacob during the six years of this bargain so raised the enmity and envy of Laban and of his sons, that Jacob must have felt it necessary for his own safety to remove, even if he had not received Divine direction to that effect. But this put

---

[1] Gen. xxxi. 7.   [2] Gen. xxxi. 12, 13.
[3] Thus we understand Gen. xxx. 41, 42. The spring-produce is supposed to be stronger than that of autumn.

an end to all hesitancy; and having communicated his purpose to his wives, and secured their cordial consent, he left secretly, while Laban was away at the sheep-shearing, which would detain him some time.   Three days elapsed before Laban was informed of Jacob's flight.   He immediately pursued after him, " with his brethren," his anger being further excited by the theft of his household gods, or " *teraphim*," which Rachel, unknown, of course, to Jacob, had taken with her.   On the seventh day Laban and his relatives overtook Jacob and his caravan in Mount Gilead.   The consequences might have been terrible, if God had not interposed to warn Laban in a dream, not to injure nor to hurt Jacob.   Being further foiled in his search after the missing *teraphim*, through the cunning of his own daughter, Laban, despite his hypocritical professions of how affectionate their leave-taking might have been if Jacob had not "stolen away," stood convicted of selfishness and unkindness.   In fact, if the conduct of Jacob, even in his going away, had been far from straightforward, that of Laban was of the most unprincipled kind.   However, peace was restored between them, and a covenant made, in virtue of which neither party was to cross for hostile purposes the memorial pillar which they erected, and to which Laban gave a Chaldee and Jacob a Hebrew name, meaning "the heap of witness."

Hypocritically as in the mouth of Laban the additional name of *Mizpah* sounds, which he gave to this pillar, it is a very significant designation to mark great events in our lives, especially our alliances and our undertakings.   For *Mizpah* means " watchtower," and the words which accompanied the giving of this name were :

"Jehovah watch between me and thee, when we are absent one from another."

CHAPTER XVIII.

Jacob at Mahanaim—The Night of Wrestling—Recon-
ciliation between Jacob and Esau—Jacob settles at
Shechem—Jacob proceeds to Bethel to pay his Vow—
Death of Rachel—Jacob settles at Hebron.

(GEN. XXXII.—XXXVI.)

WE are now nearing what may be described as the high
point in the spiritual history of Jacob. Quite different
as the previous history of Abraham had been from that of
Jacob, yet, in some sense, what Mount Moriah was to Abraham, that the fords of Jabbok became to his grandson : a place
of trial and of decision,—only that while the one went to it,
the other only left it, with a new name, and all that this
implied.

One dreaded meeting was past, and its apprehended dangers averted. Jacob had in his fear "stolen away" from
Laban. He had been pursued as by an enemy, but God had
brought peace out of it all. Standing by his "Mizpah," he
had seen Laban and his confederates disappearing behind the
range of Gilead, their spears and lances glistening in the sunlight, as they wound through the pine and oak forests which
cover the mountain side. One enemy was now behind him ;
but another and far more formidable had yet to be encountered. In dealing with Laban, Jacob could justly plead his
long service and the heartless selfishness of his employer. But
what could he say to Esau in excuse or palliation of the past ?
How would he meet him ? and did his brother still cherish the
purpose of revenge from which he had fled twenty years ago ?
To these questions there was absolutely no answer, except
the one which faith alone could understand : that if he now
returned to his own country, and faced the danger there

awaiting him, it was by the express direction of the Lord Himself. If so, Jacob must be safe. Nor was he long in receiving such general assurance of this as might strengthen his faith. Leaving the mountains of Gilead, Jacob had entered the land of promise, in what afterwards became the possession of *Gad*. A glorious prospect here opened before him. Such beauty, fruitfulness, freshness of verdure, and richness of pasturage ; dark mountain forests above, and rich plains below, as poor Palestine, denuded of its trees, and with them of its moisture— a land of ruins—has not known these many, many centuries! And there, as he entered the land, "the angels of God met him." Twenty years before they had, on leaving it, met him at Bethel, and, so to speak, accompanied him on his journey. And now in similar pledge they welcomed him on his return Only then, they had been angels ascending and descending on their ministry, while now they were " angel hosts" to defend him in the impending contest, whence also Jacob called the name of that place *Mahanaim*, " two hosts," or " two camps." And if at Bethel he had seen them in a " dream," they now appeared to him when waking, as if to convey yet stronger assurance.

Such comfort was, indeed, needed by Jacob. From Mahanaim he had sent to his brother Esau a message intended to conciliate him. But the messengers returned without any reply, other than that Esau was himself coming to meet his brother, and that at the head of a band of four hundred men. This certainly was sufficiently alarming, irrespective of the circumstance that since Esau was (as we shall presently show) just then engaged in a warlike expedition against Seir, the four hundred men with whom he advanced, had probably gathered around his standard for plunder and bloodshed, just like those wild Bedouin tribes which to this day carry terror wherever they appear. Even to receive no reply at all would, in itself, be a great trial to one like Jacob. Hitherto he had by his devices succeeded in removing every obstacle, and evading every danger. But now he was absolutely helpless, in face of an enemy from whom he could neither retreat nor escape. It is said in the sacred text: "Then Jacob was greatly afraid and distressed." The measures to which he resorted prove this. He divided his caravan into two bands, in the hope that if Esau attacked the one, the other might escape during the fray. The result thus aimed at was very doubtful, and, at the best, sad enough. Jacob must have deeply felt this, and he betook himself to prayer. Mingling confession of his utter unworthiness with entreaty for deliverance from the danger before him, he successively pleaded before God His express command to return to Canaan, His past mercies, and His gracious promises, at the same time addressing God as Jehovah, the covenant-God of Abraham and of Isaac. Not one of these pleas could fail. That cry of despair was the preparation for what was to follow: Jacob was now learning to obtain, otherwise than by his own efforts, that which Jehovah had promised to give.

We know, with almost perfect certainty, the exact spot where the most important transaction in the life of Jacob took place. It was at the ford of *Jabbok*, the confluence of the two streams which flow from the East into Jordan, between the Sea of Galilee and the Dead Sea, and almost midway between these two points. Indeed, there is only one ford of Jabbok "practicable," "and even here," as a recent traveller records, "the strong current reached the horse's girths."[1] The beauty and richness of the whole district is most striking—park-like scenery alternating with sweet glades, covered with rich crops; "trees and shrubs grouped in graceful variety;" then peeps into the great Jordan valley, with its almost tropical vegetation, and of the hills of Palestine beyond. Looking down upon the ford, the brook Jabbok is almost invisible from the thicket of oleander which covers its banks; while on the steeper sides, up either way, forests of oak and of evergreen oak merge into the darker pine. It was night in this solitude. Overhead shone the innumerable stars—once the pledge of the promise to Abraham. The impressive silence was only broken by the

[1] See the description in Canon Tristram's *Land of Israel*, pp. 470 563.

rushing of Jabbok, and the lowing of the flocks and herds, as they passed over the brook, or the preparations for transporting the women, children, and servants. Quite a large number of the cattle and sheep Jacob now sent forward in separate droves, that each, as it successively came to Esau as a gift from his brother, might tend to appease his feelings of anger, or satisfy the cupidity of his followers. At last they were all gone, each herdsman bearing a message of peace. The women also and children were safely camped on the south side of Jabbok. Only Jacob himself remained on the northern bank. It was a time for solitude—" and Jacob was left alone," quite alone, as when first he left his father's house. There on the oleander banks of Jabbok occurred what has ever since been of the deepest significance to the church of God. "There wrestled with him a man till the breaking of day." That "Man" was the Angel of Jehovah in Whom was His Presence. "And when He saw that He prevailed not against him, He touched the hollow of his thigh; and the hollow of Jacob's thigh was out of joint, as he wrestled with Him." The contest by wrestling must now have become impossible. But a far other contest ensued. "And He said, Let Me go, for the day breaketh. And he (Jacob) said, I will not let Thee go, except Thou bless me." Jacob had now recognised the character of his opponent and of the contest, and he sought quite another victory, and by quite other means than before. He no longer expected to prevail in his own strength. He asked to be *blessed* by Him with whom he had hitherto only wrestled, that so he might prevail. That blessing was given. But first the Lord brought before him what had been his old name as expressive of his old history—*Jacob*, " the cunning, self-helpful supplanter;" then He bestowed on him a new name, characteristic of his new experience and better contest by prayer : *Israel*, "a prince with God." In that new character would he have " power with God and men," and "prevail" against all enemies. But the mysterious name of the Angel he must not yet know; for "the mystery of godliness" was not to be fully revealed till all the purposes for which Jacob was to become Israel had been fulfilled. And now "He blessed him there." "And Jacob called the name of the place *Peniel* (the face of God): for I have seen God face to face, and my soul has recovered.[1] And as he passed over Penuel the sun rose upon him, and he halted upon his thigh. Therefore the children of Israel eat not of the sinew which shrank, which is upon the hollow of the thigh, unto this day." And "to this day," literally, is this custom observed among "the children of Israel."

Now what was the meaning of this solemn transaction? Assuredly, it was *symbolical*—but of what? It was a real transaction, but symbolical of Jacob's past, present, and future. The "man" who wrestled with Jacob "until the breaking of day" was Jehovah. Jacob had, indeed, been the believing heir to the promises, but all his life long he had wrestled with God—sought to attain success in his own strength and by his own devices. Seeming to contend with man, he had really contended with God. And God had also contended with him. At last farther contest was impossible : Jacob had become disabled, for God had touched the hollow of his thigh. In the presence of Esau Jacob was helpless. But before he could encounter his most dreaded earthly enemy, he must encounter God, with Whom he had all along, though unwittingly, contended by his struggles and devices. The contest with Esau was nothing; the contest with Jehovah everything. The Lord could not be on Jacob's side, till he had been disabled, and learned to use other weapons than those of his own wrestling. Then it was that Jacob recognised with whom he had hitherto wrestled. Now he resorted to other weapons, even to prayer; and he sought and found another victory, even in the blessing of Jehovah and by His strength. Then also, truly at "the breaking of day," he obtained a new name, and with it new power, in which he prevailed with God and man. Jacob, indeed, "halted upon his thigh;" but he was now Israel, a

---

[1] So the words are rendered by one of the ablest German critics.

prince with God. And still to all ages this contest and this victory, in despair of our own efforts, and in the persevering prayer, "I will not let Thee go except Thou bless me," have been and are a most precious symbol to the children of God. May we not also add, that as the prophet Hosea pointed to it as symbolical of Israel's history,[1] so it shall be fully realised when "they shall look upon Me Whom they have pierced, and they shall mourn?"[2]

As Jacob passed over Jabbok in the early morn, the glittering of spears and lances in the sunlight, among the dark pine forests, betokened the approach of Esau with his four hundred men. But Jacob had nothing more to fear: the only real contest was over. It was necessary, when Jacob returned to take possession of the land and of the promises, that all that was past in his history should be *past*—and it was so! Never, after that night, did Jacob again contend with carnal weapons; and though the old name of Jacob reappears again and again by the side of his new designation, it was to remind both him and us that Jacob, though halting, is not dead, and that there is in us always the twofold nature, alike of Jacob and of Israel. What now followed we cannot tell better than in the words of a recent German writer: "Jacob, who in his contest with the Angel of Jehovah had prevailed by prayer and entreaty, now also prevails by humility and modesty against Esau, who comes to meet him with four hundred men." As already hinted, Esau had probably been just engaged in that warlike expedition to Mount Seir, which resulted in his conquest of the land, where he afterwards settled.[3] This accounts for his appearance at the head of an armed band. Possibly, he may, at the same time, have wished to have the revenge of giving anxiety to his brother, and of showing him the contrast between their respective positions; or he may to the last have been undecided how to act towards his brother. At any rate, under the overruling guidance of God, and "overcome by the humility of Jacob, and by the kindliness of his own heart,

---

[1] Hos. xii. 4.   [2] Zech. xii. 10.   [3] Gen. xxxvi. 6, 7.

Esau fell upon the neck of his brother, embraced and kissed him.   With reluctance he accepted the rich presents of Jacob, and he offered to accompany him to the end of his journey with his armed men—a proposition which Jacob declined in a friendly spirit.   Thus the two brothers, long separated in affection, were reconciled to each other.   Their good understanding remained undisturbed till the day of their death."

There was nothing in Jacob's language to his brother which, when translated from Eastern to our Western modes of conduct and expression, is inconsistent with proper self-respect. If he declined the offer of an armed guard, it was because he felt he needed not an earthly host to protect him.   Besides, it was manifestly impossible for cattle and tender children to keep up with a Bedouin warrior band.   While Esau, therefore, returned to Mount Seir, there to await a visit from his brother, Jacob turned in a north-westerly direction to *Succoth*, a place still east of Jordan, and afterwards in the possession of the tribe of Gad.   Here he probably made a lengthened stay, for we read that "he built him an house, and made booths for his cattle," whence also the name of *Succoth*, or "booths."   At last Jacob once more crossed the Jordan, "and came in peace[1] to the city of Shechem, which is in the land of Canaan."   The words seem designedly chosen to indicate that God had amply fulfilled what Jacob had asked at Bethel : to "come again in peace."[2] But great changes had taken place in the country.   When Abram entered the land, and made this his first resting-place, there was no city there, and it was only "the place of Shechem."[3] But now the district was all cultivated and possessed, and a city had been built, probably by "Hamor the Hivite," the father of Shechem, who called it after his son.[4]   From "the children of Hamor" Jacob bought the field on which he "spread his tent."   This was "the portion" which Jacob afterwards gave to his son Joseph,[5] and here the "bones of Joseph, which the children of Israel brought out of Egypt," were,

---

[1] So the words should be translated.   [2] Gen. xxviii. 21.
[3] Gen. xii. 6.   [4] Comp. Gen. iv. 17.   [5] Gen. xlviii. 22.

at least at one time, buried.[1] Far more interesting than this, we know that by the well which Jacob there dug, sat, many centuries afterwards, "David's greater Son," to tell the poor sinning woman of Samaria concerning the "well of water springing up unto everlasting life"—the first non-Jewess blessed to taste the water of which "whosoever drinketh" "shall never thirst."[2] Here Jacob erected an altar, and called it *El-elohe-Israel*, "God, the God of Israel."

But his stay at Shechem was to prove a fresh source of trial to Jacob. Dinah, his daughter, at that time (as we gather) about fifteen years of age, in the language of the sacred text, "went out to see the daughters of the land," or, as Josephus, the Jewish historian, tells us, to take part in a feast of the Shechemites. A more terrible warning than that afforded by the results of her thoughtless and blameworthy participation in irreligious and even heathen festivities could scarcely be given. It led to the ruin of Dinah herself, then to a proposal of an alliance between the Hivites and Israel, to which Israel could not, of course, have agreed ; and finally to vile deceit on the part of Simeon and Levi, for the purpose of exacting bloody revenge, by which the whole male population of Shechem were literally exterminated. How deeply the soul of Jacob recoiled from this piece of Eastern cruelty, appears from the fact, that even on his deathbed, many years afterwards, he reverted to it in these words :—

"Simeon and Levi are brethren ;
Their swords are weapons of iniquity.
O my soul, come not thou into their council ;
Unto their assembly, mine honour, be not thou united ! "[3]

But one, though undesigned, consequence of the crime proved a further blessing to Jacob. It was quite clear that he and his family must remove from the scene of Simeon's and Levi's teachery and cruelty. Then it was that God directed Jacob to return to Beth-el, and fulfil the promise which he had there made on fleeing from the face of Esau his brother. About

---

[1] Josh. xxiv. 32.   [2] John iv. 14.   [3] Gen. xlix. 5, 6.

ten years must have elapsed since the return of Jacob from Mesopotamia, and yet he had not paid his vows unto the Lord ! From what follows, we infer that, in all probability, the reason of this delay had been that the family of Jacob had not been purged from idolatry, and that hitherto Jacob had been too weak to remove from his household what must have rendered his appearance at Beth-el morally impossible. But now we read, that " he said unto his household, and to all that were with him, Put away the strange gods that are among you, and be clean, and change your garments" (this as a symbol of purification) : " and let us arise, and go up to Bethel." And all the *teraphim* and idolatrous "charms" were buried deep down below a terebinth-tree "which was by Shechem." A touching incident is recorded immediately on their arrival at Beth-el. "Deborah, Rebekah's nurse, died, and she was buried beneath Beth-el, under an oak, and the name of it was called Allon-bachuth (the oak of weeping)." Thus Deborah's long and faithful service in the household of Isaac, and the family-mourning over the old, tried family friend, are deemed worthy of perpetual memorial in the Book of God ! But from the circumstance that Deborah died in the house of Jacob, we infer not only that her mistress Rebekah was dead, but that there must have been some intercourse between Isaac and Jacob since his return to Canaan. Most probably Jacob had visited his aged parent, though Scripture does not mention it, because it in no way affects the history of the covenant. At Bethel God again appeared to Jacob ; and while He once more bestowed on him the name of Israel and the covenant-promises previously given, Jacob also paid his vow unto the Lord, and on his part likewise renewed the designation of the place as Beth-el.

From Bethel they continued their journey towards *Mamre*, the place of Isaac's residence. On the way, some distance from *Ephrath*, "the fruitful," which in later times was called *Bethlehem*, "the house of bread,"[1] Rachel died in giving birth to Jacob's twelfth son. His mother wished to call her

[1] Micah v. 2.

child *Ben-oni,* "the son of my sorrow;" but his father named him *Benjamin,* which has been variously interpreted as meaning "son of the right hand," "son of days, *i.e.* of old age," and "son of happiness," because he completed the number of twelve sons. From Jer. xxxi. 15, we gather that Rachel actually died in *Ramah.* "Jacob set a pillar upon her grave." As the oak, or rather the terebinth, of Deborah was still known at the time of the Judges, when Deborah's greater namesake dwelt under its shadow, "between Ramah and Bethel in Mount Ephraim,"[1] so the pillar which marked Rachel's grave was a landmark at the time of Samuel.[2] Another crime yet stained the family of Jacob at *Migdal Eder,* "the watchtower of the flock," in consequence of which Reuben was deprived of the privileges of the firstborn.[3] At last Jacob came to his journey's end, "unto Isaac his father, unto Mamre, unto the city of Arbah, which is Hebron, where Abraham and Isaac sojourned." Here Scripture pauses to record, by way of anticipation, the death of Isaac, at the age of one hundred and eighty years, although that event took place twelve years after Jacob's arrival at Hebron; and, indeed, Isaac had lived to share his son's sorrow, when Joseph was sold into Egypt, having only died ten years before Jacob and his sons settled in Egypt.[4] But the course of sacred history has turned from Isaac, and, in fact, Jacob himself is now but a secondary actor in its events. The main interest henceforth centres in *Joseph,* the elder son of Rachel, with whose life the progress of sacred history is identified.

---

[1] Judg. iv. 5.   [2] 1 Sam. x. 2, 3.   [3] Gen. xlix. 4.

[4] As Jacob was seventy-seven years old when he went into Mesopotamia, he must have been one hundred and eight on his return to Hebron; while Isaac was at the time only one hundred and sixty-eight years old, since Jacob was born in the sixtieth year of his father's age, as appears from Gen. xxv. 26. It is, however, fair to add that Dr. Harold Browne proposes another chronology of Jacob's life (after Kennicott and Horsley), which would make him twenty years younger, or fifty-seven years of age, at the time of his flight to Padan-Aram. (See *Bible Commentary,* vol. i. pp. 177, 178.)

CHAPTER XIX.

Joseph's Early Life—He is Sold by his Brethren into Slavery—Joseph in the House of Potiphar—Joseph in Prison.

(GEN. XXXVII.—XXXIX.)

FOR the proper understanding of what follows it is necessary to bear in mind that what may be called the *personal* history of the patriarchs ceases with Jacob; or rather that it now merges into that of the *children* of Israel—of the family, and of the tribes. The purpose of God with the patriarchs as *individuals* had been fulfilled, when Jacob had become father of the twelve, who were in turn to be the ancestors of the chosen people. Hence the personal manifestations of God to individuals now also ceased. To this there is only a solitary exception, when the Lord appeared unto Jacob as he went into Egypt, to give him the needful assurance that by His will Israel removed from Canaan, and that in His own good time He would bring them back to the land of promise. By way of anticipation, it may be here stated that this temporary removal was in every respect necessary. It formed the fulfilment of God's prediction to Abram at the first making of the covenant; [1] and it was needful in order to separate the sons of Jacob from the people of the land. How readily constant contact with the Canaanites would have involved even the best of them in horrible vices appears from the history of Judah, when, after the selling of Joseph, he had left his father's house, and, joining himself to the people of the country, both he and his rapidly became conformed to the abominations around. [2] It was necessary also as a preparation for the later history of Israel, when the Lord God would bring them out from their

[1] Gen. xv. 12–17.　　　　[2] Gen. xxxviii.

house of bondage by His outstretched arm, and with signs and wonders. As this grand event was to form the foundation and beginning of the history of Israel as a nation, so the servitude and the low estate which preceded it were typical, and that not only of the whole history of Israel, but of the Church itself, and of every individual believer also, whom God delivers from spiritual bondage by His mighty grace. Lastly, all the events connected with the removal into Egypt were needful for the training of the sons of Israel, and chiefly for that of Joseph, if he were to be fitted for the position which God intended him to occupy. Nor can we fail to recognise, that, although Joseph is not personally mentioned in the New Testament as a type of Christ, his *history* was eminently typical of that of our blessed Saviour, alike in his betrayal, his elevation to highest dignity, and his preserving the life of his people, and in their ultimate recognition of him and repentance of their sin. Yet, though "known to God" were all these "His works from the beginning," all parties were allowed, in the free exercise of their own choice, to follow their course, ignorant that all the while they were only contributing their share towards the fulfilment of God's purposes. And in this lies the mystery of Divine Providence, that it always worketh wonders, yet without seeming to work at all—whence also it so often escapes the observation of men. Silently, and unobserved by those who live and act, it pursues its course, till in the end all things are seen "to work together" for the glory of God, and "for good to them that love God, that are the called according to His purpose."

The scriptural history of Joseph opens when he is seventeen years of age. Abundant glimpses into the life of the patriarchal family are afforded us. Joseph is seen engaged in pastoral occupations, as well as his brethren. But he is chiefly with the sons of Bilhah and Zilpah, the maids of Leah and Rachel. Manifestly also there is ill feeling and jealousy on the part of the sons of Leah towards the child of Rachel. This must have been fostered by the difference in their natural disposition, as well as by the preference which Jacob showed for the son of his beloved wife. The bearing of the sons of Jacob was rough, wild, and lawless, without any concern for their father's wishes or aims. On the other hand, Joseph seems to have united some of the best characteristics of his ancestors. Like Abraham, he was strong, decided, and prudent; like Isaac, patient and gentle; like Jacob, warmhearted and affectionate. Best of all, his conduct signally differed from that of his brethren. On the other hand, however, it is not difficult to perceive how even the promising qualities of his natural disposition might become sources of moral danger. Of this the history of Joseph's ancestors had afforded only too painful evidence. How much greater would be the peril to a youth exposed to such twofold temptation as rooted dislike on the part of brothers whom he could not respect, and marked favouritism on that of his father! The holy reticence of Scripture—which ever tells so little of man and so much of God—affords us only hints, but these are sufficiently significant. We read that "Joseph brought unto his father" the "evil report" of his brethren. That is one aspect of his domestic relations. Side by side with it is the other: "Now Israel loved Joseph more than all his children." Even if "the coat of many colours," which he gave to "the son of his old age," had been merely a costly or gaudy dress, it would have been an invidious mark of favouritism, such as too often raises bitter feelings in families. For, as time is made up of moments, so life mostly of small actions whose greatness lies in their combination. But in truth it was *not* a "coat of many colours," but a tunic reaching down to the arms and feet, such as princes and persons of distinction wore,[1] and it betokened to Joseph's brothers only too clearly, that their father intended to transfer to Joseph the right of the first-born.

---

[1] Mr. R. S. Poole (in the article on *Joseph*, in Smith's *Dictionary of the Bible*) writes : "The richer classes among the ancient Egyptians wore long dresses of white linen. The people of Palestine and Syria, represented on the Egyptian monuments as enemies or tributaries, wore similar dresses, partly coloured, generally with a stripe round the skirts and the borders of the sleeves."

We know that the three oldest sons of Leah had unfitted themselves for it—Simeon and Levi by their cruelty at Shechem, and Reuben by his crime at the "watch-tower of the flock." What more natural than to bestow the privilege on the first-born of her whom Jacob had intended to make his only wife? At any rate, the result was that "his brethren hated him," till, in the expressive language of the sacred text, "they could not get themselves to address him unto peace,"[1] that is, as we understand it, to address to him the usual Eastern salutation : "Peace be unto thee !"

It needed only an occasion to bring this state of feeling to an outbreak, and that came only too soon. It seems quite natural that, placed in the circumstances we have described, Joseph should have dreamt two dreams implying his future supremacy. We say this, even while we recognise in them a distinct Divine direction. Yet Scripture does not say, either, that these dreams were sent him as a direct communication from God, or that he was directed to tell them to his family. The imagery of the first of these dreams was taken from the *rustic*, that of the second from the *pastoral* life of the family. In the first dream Joseph and his brothers were in the harvest-field—which seems to imply that Jacob, like his father Isaac, had tilled the ground—and Joseph's sheaf stood upright, while those of his brothers made obeisance. In the second dream they were all out tending the flock, when the sun and moon and the eleven stars made obeisance to Joseph. The first of these dreams was related only unto his brethren, the second both to his father and to his brothers. There must have been something peculiarly offensive in the manner in which he told his dreams, for we read not only that "they hated him yet the more for his dreams," but also "*for his words.*" Even Jacob saw reason to reprove him, although it is significantly added that he observed the saying. As we now know it, they *were* prophetic dreams ; but, at the time, there were no means of judging whether they were so or not, especially as Joseph had

[1] This is the literal translation.

so "worded" them, that they might seem to be merely the effect of vanity in a youth whom favouritism had unduly elated. The future could alone show this ; but, meantime, may we not say that it was needful for the sake of Joseph himself that he should be removed from his present circumstances to where that which was holy and divine in him would grow, and all of self be uprooted? But such results are only obtained by one kind of training—*that of affliction.*

The sons of Jacob were pasturing their flocks around She-chem, when the patriarch sent Joseph to inquire of their welfare. All unconscious of danger the lad hastened to execute the commission. Joseph found not his brethren at Shechem itself, but a stranger directed him to "*Dothan,*" the two wells, whither they had gone. "Dothan was beautifully situated, about twelve miles from Samaria. Northwards spread richest pasture-lands ; a few swelling hills separated it from the great plain of Esdrae-lon. From its position it must have been the key to the passes of Esdraelon, and so, as guarding the entrance from the north, not only of Ephraim, but of Palestine itself. On the crest of one of those hills the extensive ruins of Dothan are still pointed out, and at its southern foot still wells up a fine spring of living water. Is this one of the two wells from which Dothan derived its name? From these hills Gideon afterwards descended upon the host of Midian. It was here that Joseph overtook his brethren, and was cast into the dry well. And it was from that height that the sons of Jacob must have seen the Arab caravan slowly winding from Jordan on its way to Egypt, when they sold their brother, in the vain hope of binding the word and arresting the hand of God." [1]

But we are anticipating. No sooner did his brothers descry Joseph in the distance, than the murderous plan of getting rid of him, where no stranger should witness their deed, occurred to their minds. This would be the readiest means of disposing alike of "the dreamer" and of his "dreams." Reuben alone

[1] Our quotation here is from the present writer's book on *Elisha the Prophet, a Type of Christ* (ch. xix. "An Unseen Host," p. 225).

shrunk from it, not so much from love to his brother as from consideration for his father. On pretence that it would be better not actually to shed their brother's blood, he proposed to cast him into one of those cisterns, and leave him there to perish, hoping, however, himself secretly to rescue and to restore him to his father. The others readily acceded to the plan. A Greek writer has left us a graphic account of such wells and cisterns. He describes them as regularly built and plastered, narrow at the mouth, but widening as they descend, till at the bottom they attain a width sometimes of one hundred feet. We know that when dry, or covered with only mud at the bottom, they served as hiding-places, and even as temporary prisons.[1] Into such an empty well Joseph was now cast, while his brothers, as if they had finished some work, sat down to their meal. We had almost written, that it so happened—but truly it was in the providence of God, that just then an Arab caravan was slowly coming in sight. They were pursuing what we might call the world-old route from the spice district of Gilead into Egypt—across Jordan, below the Sea of Galilee, over the plain of Jezreel, and thence along the sea-shore. Once more the intended kindness of another of his brothers well-nigh proved fatal to Joseph. Reuben had diverted their purpose of bloodshed by proposing to cast Joseph into "the pit," in the hope of being able afterwards to rescue him. Judah now wished to save his life by selling him as a slave to the passing Arab caravan. But neither of them had the courage nor the uprightness frankly to resist the treachery and the crime. Again the other brothers hearkened to what seemed a merciful suggestion. The bargain was quickly struck. Joseph was sold to "the Ishmaelites" for twenty shekels—the price, in later times, of a male slave from five to twenty years old,[2] the medium price of a slave being thirty shekels of silver, or about four pounds, reckoning the shekel of the sanctuary, which was twice the common shekel,[3] at two shillings and eight-pence. Reuben was not present when the sale was made. On

---

[1] Jer. xxxviii. 6 ; Is. xxiv. 22. [2] Lev. xxvii. 5. [3] Ex. xxi. 32.

his return he "rent his clothes" in impotent mourning. But the others dipped Joseph's princely raiment in the blood of a kid, to give their father the impression that Joseph had been " devoured by a wild beast." The device succeeded. Jacob mourned him bitterly and "for many days," refusing all the comfort which his sons and daughters hypocritically offered. But even his bitterest lamentation expressed the hope and faith that he would meet his loved son in another world—for, he said : " I will go down into the grave (or into *Sheol*) unto my son, mourning."

Except by an incidental reference to it in the later con-fession of his brothers,[1] we are not told either of the tears or the entreaties with which Joseph vainly sought to move his brethren, nor of his journey into Egypt. We know that when following in the caravan of his new masters, he must have seen at a distance the heights of his own Hebron, where, all unsuspecting, his father awaited the return of his favourite. To that home he was never again to return. We meet him next in the slave-market. Here, as it might seem in the natural course of events, " Potiphar, an officer of Pharaoh, captain of the guard, an Egyptian, bought him of the hands of the Ishmaelites." The name *Potiphar* frequently occurs on the monuments of Egypt (written either Pet-Pa-Ra, or Pet-P-Ra), and means : " Dedicated to *Ra*," or the sun. According to some writers, " at the time that Joseph was sold into Egypt, the country was not united under the rule of a single native line, but governed by several dynasties, of which the fifteenth dynasty of Shepherd-kings was the predominant one, the rest being tributary to it."[2]   At any rate, he would be carried

---

[1] Gen. xlii. 21,

[2] R. S. Poole, as above.   We have here stated the ordinarily received view.   But Canon Cook has urged strong and, as it seems to us, con-vincing reasons for supposing that the sale of Joseph took place at the close of the twelfth dynasty, or under the original Pharaohs, before the foreign domination of the Shepherd-kings had commenced.   The question will be fully discussed in the next volume.   Meantime, the curious reader must be referred to the essay on Egyptian history at the close of vol. i. of *The Speaker's Commentary.*

into that part of Egypt which was always most connected with Palestine. Potiphar's office at the court of Pharaoh was that of "chief of the executioners," most probably (as it is rendered in our Authorised Version) captain of the king's body-guard. In the house of Potiphar it went with Joseph as formerly in his own home. For it is not in the power of circumstances, prosperous or adverse, to alter our characters. He that is faithful in little shall also be faithful in much ; and from him who knoweth not how to employ what is committed to his charge, shall be taken even that he hath. Joseph was faithful, honest, upright, and conscientious, because in his earthly, he served a heavenly Master, Whose presence he always realised. Accordingly " Jehovah was with him," and " Jehovah made all that he did to prosper in his hand." His master was not long in observing this. From an ordinary domestic slave he promoted him to be " overseer over his house, and all that he had he put into his hand." The confidence was not misplaced. Jehovah's blessing henceforth rested upon Potiphar's substance, and he "left all that he had in Joseph's hand ; and he knew not aught that he had, save the bread which he did eat." The sculptures and paintings of the ancient Egyptian tombs bring vividly before us the daily life and duties of Joseph. " The property of great men is shown to have been managed by scribes, who exercised a most methodical and minute supervision over all the operations of agriculture, gardening, the keeping of live stock, and fishing. Every product was carefully registered, to check the dishonesty of the labourers, who in Egypt have always been famous in this respect. Probably in no country was farming ever more systematic. Joseph's previous knowledge of tending flocks, and perhaps of husbandry, and his truthful character, exactly fitted him for the post of overseer. How long he filled it we are not told."[1]

It is a common mistake to suppose that earnest religion and uprightness must necessarily be attended by success, even

---

[1] R. S. Poole, as above.

in this world. It is, indeed, true that God will not withhold any good thing from those whose Sun and Shield He is; but then success may not always be a good thing for them. Besides, God often tries the faith and patience of His people—and that is the meaning of many trials. Still oftener are they needed for discipline and training, or that they may learn to glorify God in their sufferings. In the case of Joseph it was both a temptation and a trial by which he was prepared, outwardly and inwardly, for the position he was to occupy. The beauty which Joseph had inherited from his mother exposed him to wicked suggestions on the part of his master's wife, which will surprise those least who are best acquainted with the state of ancient Egyptian society. Joseph stood quite alone in a heathen land and house. He was surrounded only by what would blunt his moral sense, and render the temptation all the more powerful. He had also, as compared with us, a very imperfect knowledge of the law of God in its height and depth. Moreover, what he had seen of his older brothers would not have elevated his views. Still, he firmly resisted evil, alike from a sense of integrity towards his master, and, above all, from dread " of this great wickedness and sin against God." Yet it seemed only to fare the worse with him for his principles. As so often, the violent passion of the woman turned into equally violent hatred, and she maliciously concocted a false charge against him.[1] We have reason to believe that Potiphar could not in every respect have credited the story of his wife. For the punishment awarded in Egypt to the crime of which she accused him, was far more severe than that which Joseph received. Potiphar consigned him to the king's prison, of which, in his capacity as chief of the body-guard, he was the superintendent. How bitterly it fared

---

1 Quite a similar Egyptian story exists, entitled "The Two Brothers," which has lately been translated. It resembles so closely the biblical account that we are disposed to regard it as at least founded upon the trial of Joseph. Differing in this from Mr. Poole, we hold that the weight of evidence is in favour of the supposition.

there with him at the first, we learn from these words of Psalm cv. 17, 18 :—

> "He sent before them a man:
> Sold for a slave was Joseph,
> They afflicted with fetters his feet,
> The iron entered into his soul."[1]

The contrast could scarcely be greater than between his former prophetic dreams and his present condition. But even so Joseph remained stedfast. And, as if to set before us the other contrast between sight and faith, the sacred text expressly states it : "But"—a word on which our faith should often lay emphasis—"Jehovah was with Joseph, and showed him mercy, and gave him favour in the sight of the keeper of the prison." By-and-by, as his integrity more and more appeared, the charge of the prisoners was committed unto him; and as "what he did Jehovah made to prosper," the whole management of the prison ultimately passed into Joseph's hands. Thus, here also Jehovah proved Himself a faithful covenant-God. A silver streak was lining the dark cloud. But still must "patience have her perfect work."

CHAPTER XX.

Joseph in Prison—The Dream of Pharaoh's Two Officers—The Dream of Pharaoh—Joseph's Exaltation—His Government of Egypt.

(GEN. XL., XLI. ; XLVII. 13—26.)

ELEVEN years had passed since Joseph was sold into Egypt, and yet the Divine promise, conveyed in his dreams, seemed farther than ever from fulfilment. The greater part of this weary time had probably been spent in prison, without other prospect than that of such indulgence as his services to "the keeper of the prison" might insure, when an event

[1] This is the literal translation.

occurred which, for a brief season, promised a change in Joseph's condition. Some kind of " offence "—real or ima-ginary—had, as is so often the case in the East, led to the sudden disgrace and imprisonment of two of Pharaoh's chief officers. The charge of " the chief of the butlers "—or chief of the cupbearers—and of " the chief of the bakers " naturally devolved upon " the captain of the guard,"—a successor, as we imagine, of *Potiphar*, since he appointed Joseph to the respon-sible post of their personal attendant. They had not been long in prison when, by the direct leading of Divine Providence, both dreamed in the same night a dream, calculated deeply to impress them. By the same direct guidance of Providence, Joseph was led to notice in the morning their anxiety, and to inquire into its cause. We regard it as directly from God, that he could give them at once and unhesitatingly the true meaning of their dreams.

We are specially struck in this respect with the manner in which Joseph himself viewed it. When he found them in distress for want of such " interpreter " as they might have consulted if free, he pointed them straight to God : " Do not interpretations belong to God?" thus encouraging them to tell, and at the same time preparing himself for reading their dreams, by casting all in faith upon God. In short, whether or not he were eventually enabled to understand their dreams, he would at least not appear like the Egyptian magicians— he would not claim power or wisdom ; he would own God, and look up to Him.

We say it the more confidently, that Joseph's interpretation came to him directly from God, that it seems so easy and so rational. For, it is in the supernatural direction of things natural that we ought most to recognise the direct interposition of the Lord. The dreams were quite natural, and the interpre-tation was quite natural—yet both were directly of God. What more natural than for the chief butler and the chief baker, three nights before Pharaoh's birthday, on which, as they knew, he always " made a feast unto all his servants," to dream that

they were each again at his post? And what more natural
than that on such an occasion Pharaoh should consider,
whether for good or for evil, the case of his absent imprisoned
officers? Or, lastly, what more natural than that the chief
butler's consciousness of innocence should suggest in his dream
that he once more waited upon his royal master; while the
guilty conscience of the chief baker saw only birds of prey
eating out of the basket from which he had hitherto supplied
his master's table?

Here, then, it may be said, we have all the elements of
Joseph's interpretation to hand, just as we shall see they
were equally obvious in the dreams which afterwards troubled
Pharaoh. Yet as then none of the magicians and wise men of
Egypt could read what, when once stated, seems so plainly
written, so here all seems involved in perplexity till God
gives light.

As already stated, the two dreams were substantially the
same. In each case the number *three*, whether of clusters in
the vine from which the chief butler pressed the rich juice into
Pharaoh's cup, or of baskets in which the chief baker carried
the king's bakemeat, pointed to the three days intervening
before Pharaoh's birthday. In each case also their dreams
transported them back to their original position before any
charge had been brought against them, the difference lying in
this : that, in the one dream, Pharaoh accepted the functions
of his officer; while, in the other, birds which hover about
carcases ate out of the basket. It is also quite natural that, if
the chief butler had a good conscience towards his master, he
should have been quite ready at the first to tell his dream;
while the chief baker, conscious of guilt, only related his when
encouraged by the apparently favourable interpretation of his
colleague's. Perhaps we ought also to notice, in evidence of
the truthfulness of the narrative, how thoroughly Egyptian in
all minute details is the imagery of these dreams. From the
monuments the growth and use of the vine in Egypt, which had
been denied by former opponents of the Bible, have been

abundantly proved. From the same source we also learn that bakery and confectionery were carried to great perfection in Egypt, so that we can understand such an office as a royal chief baker. Even the bearing of the baskets furnishes a characteristic trait; as in Egypt men carried loads on their heads, and women on their shoulders.[1]

The event proved the correctness of Joseph's interpretation. On Pharaoh's birthday-feast, three days after their dreams, the chief butler was restored to his office, but the chief baker was executed. When interpreting his dream, Joseph had requested that, on the chief butler's restoration, he, who had himself suffered from a wrongful charge, should think on him, who, at first " stolen away out of the land of the Hebrews," had so long been unjustly kept in apparently hopeless confinement. This wording of Joseph's petition seems to indicate that, at most, he only hoped to obtain liberty; and that probably he intended to return to his father's house. So ignorant was he as yet of God's further designs with him ! But what was a poor Hebrew slave in prison to a proud Egyptian court official ? It is only like human nature that, in the day of his prosperity, " the chief butler did not remember Joseph, but forgat him !"

Two other years now passed in prison — probably more dreary and, humanly speaking, more hopeless than those which had preceded. At length deliverance came, suddenly and unexpectedly. This time it was Pharaoh who dreamed successively two dreams. In the first, seven fat kine were feeding among the rich "marsh-grass"[2] on the banks " of the Nile." But presently up came from " the river" seven lean kine, which devoured the well-favoured, without, however, fattening by them. The second dream showed one stalk of corn with seven ears, " full and good," when up sprang beside it another stalk, also with seven ears, but " blasted with the east wind ;" "and the thin ears devoured the seven good ears." So vivid

---

[1] This would not have been true of other countries. Thus, in Italy and Spain, women carry their loads on their heads.

[2] So the literal rendering.

had been the dream that it seemed to Pharaoh like reality—
"and Pharaoh awoke, and, behold, it was a dream." Only
a dream! and yet the impression of its reality still haunted
him, so that he sent for "the magicians of Egypt, and all the
wise men thereof" to interpret his dreams. But these sages
were unable to suggest any explanation satisfactory to the mind
of Pharaoh; for we can scarcely believe that they did not
attempt some interpretation. In this perplexity, his memory
quickened by Oriental terror at his master's disappointment, the
chief of the cup-bearers suddenly remembered his own and the
chief baker's dreams just two years before, and Joseph's
interpretation of them. The event becomes all the more
striking and also natural if we may take the date literally as
"at the end of two full years," or on the third anniversary
of that birthday of Pharaoh.

Before proceeding, we notice some of the particulars which
give the narrative its vivid colouring, and at the same time
wonderfully illustrate its historical truthfulness. And, first of
all, we again mark the distinctly Egyptian character of all.
The "river" is "the Nile," the sacred stream of Egypt, on
which its fertility depended—and Pharaoh stands on its banks.
Then the term which we have rendered "marsh-grass," or "reed-
grass,"[1] is certainly an Egyptian word for which there is no.
Hebrew equivalent, because that to which it applied was peculiar to the banks of the Nile. Next, the whole complexion of
the dreams is Egyptian, as we shall presently show. Moreover,
it is remarkable how closely recent independent inquiries have
confirmed the scriptural expressions about "the magicians"
and "the wise men" of Egypt. It has been always known
that there was a special priestly caste in Egypt, to whom not
only the religion but the science of the country was entrusted.
But of late we have learned a great deal more than this. We
know not only that magic formed part and parcel of the religion
of Egypt, but we have actually restored to us their ancient
magical *Ritual* itself! We know their incantations and their

[1] "Meadow" in our Authorised Version, Gen. xli. 2

amulets, with a special reference to the dead; their belief in lucky and unlucky days and events, and even in the so-called "evil eye." But what is most to our present purpose, we know that the care of the magical books was entrusted to *two* classes of learned men, whose titles exactly correspond to what, for want of better designation, is rendered as "magicians," or perhaps "scribes," and "wise men!" It was before this assemblage, then, of the wisest and most learned, the most experienced in "magic," and the most venerable in the priesthood, that Pharaoh vainly related his dreams. Most wise truly in this world, yet most foolish; most learned, yet most ignorant! What a contrast between the hoary lore of Egypt and the poor Hebrew slave fetched from prison : they professedly claiming, besides their real knowledge, supernatural powers; he avowedly, and at the outset, disclaiming all power on his part, and appealing to God ! A grander scene than this Scripture itself does not sketch; and what an illustration of what was true then, true in the days of our Lord, true in those of St. Paul, and to the end of this dispensation : "Where is the wise? where is the scribe? where is the disputer of this world? Hath not God made foolish the wisdom of this world?"

And yet when we hear the interpretation through the lips of Joseph, how simple, nay, how obvious does it appear, quite commanding Pharaoh's implicit conviction. Clearly, the two dreams are *one*—the first bearing on the pastoral, the other on the agricultural life of Egypt. The dreams are about the flocks and the crops. In both cases there is first sevenfold fatness, and then sevenfold leanness, such as to swallow up the previous fatness, and yet to leave no trace of it. The second dream *illustrates* the first; and yet the first bears already its own interpretation. For the kine were in Egypt reverenced as symbol of *Isis*, the goddess of earth as the nourisher; and in the hieroglyphics the cow is taken to mean earth, agriculture, and nourishment. And then these kine were feeding by the banks of that Nile, on whose inundations it solely depended whether the year was to be one of fruitfulness or of famine. Equally

Egyptian is the description of the stalk with many ears, which is just one of the kinds of wheat still grown in Egypt. But, we repeat it, obvious as all this now seems to us, the wise men of Egypt stood speechless before their monarch ! And what a testimony, we again say, for God, when Joseph is " brought hastily out of the dungeon !" To the challenge of Pharaoh : " I have heard of thee, to wit : Thou hearest a dream to interpret it "—that is, thou only requirest to hear, in order to interpret a dream,—he answers, simply, emphatically, but believingly : " Ah, not I " (" not to me," " it does not belong to me"), " God will answer the peace of Pharaoh ;"[1] *i.e.,* what is for the peace of the king. Nor can we omit to notice one more illustration of the accuracy of the whole narrative, when we read that, in preparation for his appearance before Pharaoh, Joseph " shaved himself." This we know from the monuments was peculiarly Egyptian under such circumstances ; whereas among the Hebrews, for example, shaving was regarded as a mark of disgrace.

The interpretation, so modestly yet so decidedly given by Joseph, that the dreams pointed to seven years of unprecedented fruitfulness followed by an equal number of famine, so grievous that the previous plenty should not be known, approved itself immediately to the mind of Pharaoh and "of all his servants." With this interpretation Joseph had coupled most sagacious advice, for the source of which, in so trying a moment, we must look far higher than the ingenuity of man.[2] He counselled the king to exact in the years of plenty a tax of one-fifth of the produce of the land, and to have it stored under royal supervision against the seven years of famine. Viewed as an impost, this was certainly not heavy, considering that they were years of unexampled plenty ; viewed as a fiscal measure, it was most beneficial as compared with what we may suppose to have been previously a mere arbitrary system of taxation, which in reality was tyrannical exaction;

[1] We again translate the Hebrew text literally.
[2] See Matt. x. 18, 19.

while at the same time it would preserve the people from absolute destruction.   Lastly, regarded in the light of a higher arrangement, it is very remarkable that this proportion of giving, on the part of Pharaoh's subjects, afterwards became the basis of that demanded from Israel by Jehovah, their heavenly King.[1]   We can scarcely wonder that Pharaoh should have at once appointed such a councillor to super- intend the arrangements he had proposed.   In point of fact he naturalised him, made him his grand vizier, and publicly proclaimed him "ruler over all the land."   Once more every trait in the description is purely Egyptian.   Pha- raoh gives him his signet, which " was of so much importance with the ancient Egyptian kings, that their names were always enclosed in an oval which represented an elongated signet."[2] He arrays him " in vestures of *byssus*,"[3] the noble and also the priestly dress ; he puts the chain, or "the collar of gold"[4] "about his neck," which was always the mode of investiture of high Egyptian officials; he makes him ride "in the second chariot which he had," and he has it proclaimed before him : "*Avrech*," that is, "fall down," "bend the knee," or "do obei- sance."[5]   To complete all, on his naturalisation Joseph's name is changed to *Zaphnath-paaneah*, which most probably means "the supporter of life," or else "the food of the living," although others have rendered it "the saviour of the world," and the Rabbis, but without sufficient reason, "the revealer of secrets."   Finally, in order to give him a position among the highest nobles of the land, Pharaoh " gave him to wife *Asenath*" (probably "she who is of *Neith*," the Egyptian god-

[1] This will be fully shown in a future volume, when the religious and charitable contributions of Israel are explained.

[2] Mr. R. S. Poole, as above.

[3] The *byssus* was the Egyptian "white, shining" linen, or rather a peculiar stuff of purely Egyptian growth.

[4] Literally, "a collar, that of gold," not merely indefinitely, "a collar of gold."

[5] Canon Cook renders it, " Rejoice, then," and supposes the people or the attendants to have shouted this.   *The Speaker's Comment.*, vol. i., p. 482.

dess of wisdom[1]), "the daughter of Poti-pherah ("dedicated to the sun"), priest of On," that is, the chief priest of the ancient ecclesiastical, literary, and probably also political capital of the land,[2] "the City of the Sun." This is the more noteworthy, as the chief of the priesthood was generally chosen from among the nearest relatives of Pharaoh. Yet in all this story there is really nothing extraordinary. As Egypt depends for its produce entirely on the waters of the Nile, the country has at all times been exposed to terrible famines ; and one which lasted for exactly seven years is recorded in A.D. 1064—1071, the horrors of which show us the wisdom of Joseph's precautionary measures. Again, so far as the sudden elevation of Joseph is concerned, Eastern history contains many such instances, and indeed, a Greek historian tells us of an Egyptian king who made the son of a mason his own son-in-law, because he judged him the cleverest man in the land. What is remarkable is the marvellous Divine appointment in all this, and the equally marvellous Divine choice of means to bring it about.

Joseph was exactly thirty years old on his elevation, the same age, we note, on which our blessed Lord entered on His ministry as "the Saviour of the world," "the Supporter of life," and "the Revealer of secrets." The history of Joseph's administration may be traced in a few sentences. During the seven years of plenty, "he gathered corn as the sand of the sea, very much, until he left numbering," a notice which remarkably agrees with "the representations of the monuments, which show that the contents of the granaries were accurately noted by scribes when they were filled." Then, during the years of famine, he first sold corn to the people for money.

[1] We must here differ from Mr. Poole, who regards *Asenath* as a Hebrew, not an Egyptian name, meaning "storehouse," and as parallel to the Hebrew name of *Bithiah* (1 Chron. iv. 18), a "daughter," or "servant of Jehovah," which an Egyptian woman adopted on her marriage to Mered, or rather on her conversion unto the Lord. But in the case of *Asenath* the text seems to imply that the name was Egyptian.

[2] Mr. Poole, as above. This, as the ordinary chronological supposition ; but see the note on the subject in the previous chapter.

When all their money was exhausted, they proposed of their own accord to part with their cattle to Pharaoh, and lastly with their land. In the latter case exception was made in favour of the priestly caste, who derived their support directly from Pharaoh. Thus Pharaoh became absolute possessor of all the money, all the cattle, and all the land of Egypt, and that at the people's own request. This advantage would be the greater, if there had been any tendency to dissatisfaction against the reigning house as an alien race. Nor did Joseph abuse the power thus acquired. On the contrary, by a spontaneous act of royal generosity he restored the land to the people on condition of their henceforth paying one-fifth of the produce in lieu of all other taxation. Besides the considerations already stated in favour of such a measure, it must be borne in mind that in Egypt, where all produce depends on the waters of the Nile, a system of canals and irrigation, necessarily kept up at the expense of the State, would be a public necessity.[1] But the statement of Scripture, which excepts from this measure of public taxation "the land of the priests only, which became not Pharaoh's," remarkably tallies with the account of secular historians.

Two things here stand out in the history of Joseph. The same gracious Hand of the Lord, which, during his humiliation, had kept him from sin, disbelief, and despair, now preserved him in his exaltation from pride, and from lapsing into heathenism, to which his close connection with the chief priest of Egypt might easily have led him. More than that, he considered himself "a stranger and a pilgrim" in Egypt. His heart was in his father's home, with his father's God, and on his father's promises. Of both these facts there is abundant evidence. His Egyptian wife bore him two sons "before the years of famine came." He gave to both of them *Hebrew*, not

---

[1] In point of fact, we know that a monarch of the twelfth dynasty, Amenemha III., first established a complete system of canalisation, and made the immense artificial lake of Moeris to receive and again distribute the superfluous waters of the Nile.

Egyptian names. By the first, *Manasseh*, or " he that maketh forget," he wished to own the goodness of God, who had made him forget his past sorrow and toil. By the second, *Ephraim*, or "double fruitfulness," he distinctly recognized that, although Egypt was the land in which God had caused him " to be fruitful," it was still, and must ever be, not the land of his joy but that of his "affliction !" If it be asked why, in his prosperity, Joseph had not informed his father of his life and success, we answer, that in such a history safety lay in quiet waiting upon God. If Joseph had learned the great lesson of his life, it was this, that all in the past had been of God. Nor would He now interfere with further guidance on His part. The Lord would show the way, and lead to the end.[1] But as for him, he believed, and therefore made no haste. Thus would God be glorified, and thus also would Joseph be kept in perfect peace, because he trusted in Him.

CHAPTER XXI.

𝕿𝖍𝖊 𝕾𝖔𝖓𝖘 𝖔𝖋 𝕵𝖆𝖈𝖔𝖇 𝖆𝖗𝖗𝖎𝖛𝖊 𝖎𝖓 𝕰𝖌𝖞𝖕𝖙 𝖙𝖔 𝕭𝖚𝖞 𝕮𝖔𝖗𝖓— 𝕵𝖔𝖘𝖊𝖕𝖍 𝕽𝖊𝖈𝖔𝖌𝖓𝖎𝖟𝖊𝖘 𝖍𝖎𝖘 𝕭𝖗𝖔𝖙𝖍𝖊𝖗𝖘—𝕴𝖒𝖕𝖗𝖎𝖘𝖔𝖓𝖒𝖊𝖓𝖙 𝖔𝖋 𝕾𝖎𝖒𝖊𝖔𝖓—𝕿𝖍𝖊 𝕾𝖔𝖓𝖘 𝖔𝖋 𝕵𝖆𝖈𝖔𝖇 𝖈𝖔𝖒𝖊 𝖆 𝖘𝖊𝖈𝖔𝖓𝖉 𝖙𝖎𝖒𝖊, 𝖇𝖗𝖎𝖓𝖌𝖎𝖓𝖌 𝕭𝖊𝖓𝖏𝖆𝖒𝖎𝖓 𝖜𝖎𝖙𝖍 𝖙𝖍𝖊𝖒—𝕵𝖔𝖘𝖊𝖕𝖍 𝖙𝖗𝖎𝖊𝖘 𝖍𝖎𝖘 𝕭𝖗𝖊- 𝖙𝖍𝖗𝖊𝖓—𝕳𝖊 𝖒𝖆𝖐𝖊𝖘 𝖍𝖎𝖒𝖘𝖊𝖑𝖋 𝖐𝖓𝖔𝖜𝖓 𝖙𝖔 𝖙𝖍𝖊𝖒—𝕵𝖆𝖈𝖔𝖇 𝖆𝖓𝖉 𝖍𝖎𝖘 𝕱𝖆𝖒𝖎𝖑𝖞 𝖕𝖗𝖊𝖕𝖆𝖗𝖊 𝖙𝖔 𝖉𝖊𝖘𝖈𝖊𝖓𝖉 𝖎𝖓𝖙𝖔 𝕰𝖌𝖞𝖕𝖙.

(GEN. XLII.—XLV.)

WE are now approaching a decisive period in the history of the house of Israel. Yet once again everything seems to happen quite naturally, while in reality everything is supernatural. The same causes which led to a diminution of rain in the Abyssinian mountains, and with it of the waters of the

---

[1] There is no evidence, that at that time Joseph knew that God purposed to reunite him again to his family, far less that they were to come to him into Egypt.

Nile, brought drought and famine to Palestine.   It is quite in character that, in such straits, the wild, lawless sons of Jacob should have stood helplessly despondent, while the energies of their father were correspondingly roused.   "Why do ye look one upon another? . . . I have heard that there is corn in Egypt: get you down thither, and buy for us from thence." The ten sons of Jacob now departed on this errand.   But Benjamin, who had taken the place of Joseph in his father's heart, was not sent with them, perhaps from real fear of "mischief" by the way, possibly because his father did not quite trust the honest intentions of his sons.

The next scene presents to us the Hebrew strangers among a motley crowd of natives and foreigners, who had come for corn ; while Joseph, in all the state of the highest Egyptian official, superintends the sale.   In true Eastern fashion the sons of Jacob make lowest obeisance before " the governor over the land."   Of course they could not have recognised in him, who looked, dressed, and spoke as an Egyptian noble, the lad who, more than twenty years before, had, in "the anguish of his soul," "besought" them not to sell him into slavery.   The same transformation had not taken place in them, and Joseph at once knew the well-remembered features of his brethren.   But what a change in their relative positions ! As he saw them bending lowly before him, his former dreams came vividly back to him.   Surely, one even much less devout than Joseph would, in that moment, have felt that a Divine Hand had guided the past for a Divine purpose.   Personal resentment or pique could not have entered into his mind at such a time.   If, therefore, as some have thought, severity towards his brethren partially determined his conduct, this must have been quite a subordinate motive.   At any rate, it is impossible to suppose that he cherished any longer feelings of anger, when shortly afterwards, on their expression of deep penitence, " he turned himself about from them and wept." But we prefer regarding Joseph's conduct as consistent throughout.   The appearance of his brothers before him seemed to imply that God had not meant to separate him from his family, nor yet that he should return to them, but that they should come to him, and that he had been sent before to keep them alive.   But for such a re-union of the family it was manifestly needful, that their hearts and minds should have undergone an entire change from that unscrupulous envy which had prompted them to sell him into slavery.   This must be ascertained before he made himself known to them.   Moreover, its reality must be tested by the severest trial to which their altered feelings could be subjected.

Thus viewing it, we can understand the whole conduct of Joseph.   Of course, his first object would be to separate the sons of Jacob from the crowd of other purchasers, so as to deal specially with them, without, however, awakening their suspicions ; his next to ascertain the state of matters at home.   Then he would make them taste undeserved sorrow by the exercise of an arbitrary power, against which they would be helpless— even as Joseph had been in their hands.   Thus they might see their past sin in their present sorrow.   All these objects were attained by one and the same means.   Joseph charged them with being spies, who, on pretence of buying corn, had come to find out the defenceless portions of the land.   The accusation was not unreasonable in the then state of Egypt, nor uncommon in Eastern countries.   It was not only that this afforded a pretext for dealing separately with them, but their answer to the charge would inform Joseph about the circumstances of his family.   For, naturally, they would not only protest their innocence, but show the inherent improbability of such an imputation.   Here no argument could be more telling than that they were "all one man's sons," since no one would risk the lives of *all* his children in so dangerous a business.   But this was not enough for Joseph.   By reiterating the charge, he led them to enter into further details, from which he learned that both his father and Benjamin were alive.   Still their reference to himself as one "who is not," seemed to imply persistence in their former deceit, and must have strengthened his doubts as to their state of mind. But now experience of violence would show them not only their past guilt, but that, however God might seem to delay, He was the avenger of all wrong. More than that, if Benjamin were placed relatively to them in the same circumstances of favouritism as Joseph had been ; and if, instead of envying and hating him, they were prepared, even when exposed through him to shame and danger, not only to stand by him, but to suffer in his stead, then they had repented in the truest sense, and their state of mind was the opposite of what it had been twenty years ago.[1] Proceeding on this plan, Joseph first imprisoned all the ten, proposing to release one of their number to fetch Benjamin, in order to test, as he said, the truthfulness of their statements. This excessive harshness was probably intended to strike terror into their hearts ; and, at the end of three days, he so far relented as to retain only one of their number as an hostage ; at the same time encouraging them both by the statement that, in so doing, his motive was " fear of God," and by the assurance that, once satisfied of their innocence, he cherished no evil design against them. The reference to "fear of God" on the part of an Egyptian, and this apparent shrinking from needless rigour, must have cut them to the heart, as it brought out in contrast their own implacable conduct towards Joseph. Simeon was chosen to remain behind as hostage, because he was the next oldest to Reuben, who was not detained, since he had endeavoured to save the life of Joseph. This also must have contributed to remind them of their former wrong ; and, for the first time, they avow to one another their bitter guilt in the past, and how God was now visiting it. So poignant were their feelings that, in the presence of Joseph, they spoke of it, in their own Hebrew, ignorant that Joseph, who had conversed with them through an interpreter, understood their words. Joseph was obliged hastily to withdraw, so as not to betray himself ; but he wavered not in his purpose. Simeon was

---

[1] This is substantially the view taken by Luther, and presented in his usual quaint and forcible language.

bound before their eyes, and the rest were dismissed; but each with ample provender for the journey, besides the corn they had bought, and with the purchase-money secretly restored to them.

The terror with which the unexpected turn of events had inspired them was deepened when, at their first night's quarters, one of them discovered the money in his sack. But, as before, the impression was wholesome. They traced in this also the avenging hand of God: "What is this that God hath done unto us?"

The narrative which, on their return, they had to tell their father was sufficiently sad. But the discovery they now made, that the money which they had paid had been secretly put back into each man's sack, seemed to imply some deep design of mischief, and filled Jacob and his sons with fresh fears. If the condition of their again appearing before the ruler of Egypt was, that they must bring Benjamin with them, then he, who had already lost two sons, would refuse to expose to such a risk his darling, the last remaining pledge of his Rachel. Reuben, indeed, volunteered the strange guarantee of his own two sons: "Slay my two sons, if I bring him not to thee." But this language was little calculated to reassure the heart of Jacob. For a time it seemed as if Jacob's former sorrow was to be increased by the loss of Simeon, and as if Joseph and his family were never again to meet.

If we ask ourselves why Joseph should have risked this, or added to his father's sorrow, we answer, to the first question, that, since Joseph now knew the circumstances of his family, and had Simeon beside him, he could at any time, on need for it appearing, have communicated with his father. As to the second difficulty, we must all feel that this grief and care could not be spared to his father if his brothers were to be tried, proved, and prepared for their mission. And did it not seem as if Joseph had rightly understood the will of God in this matter, since the heart of his brethren had been at once touched to own their past sin and the Hand of God? Could he not then still further commit himself to God in well-doing, and trust Him? Nay, could he not also trust Jacob's faith to bear up under this trial? At most it would be short, and how blessed to all the fruits expected from it! Once more the event próved the correctness of his views. As the stock of provisions, which the sons of Jacob had brought, became nearly exhausted, a fresh application to the royal granaries of Egypt was absolutely necessary. This time it was Judah who offered *himself* in surety for Benjamin. His language was so calm, affectionate, and yet firm, as to inspire Jacob with what confidence can be derived from the earnest, good purpose of a true man. But he had higher consolation—that of prayer and faith : " God Almighty give you mercy before the man, that he may send away your other brother, and Benjamin." Yet, even if God had otherwise appointed,—if He saw fit to take from him his children, his faith would rise to this also : " And I, if I am bereaved, I am bereaved !"—good is the will of the Lord, and he would bow before it.

It is touching, as it were, to watch the trembling hands of the old man as he makes feeble attempts to ward off the wrath of the dreaded Egyptian. It was a famine-year, and, naturally, there would be scarcity of the luxuries which were usually exported from the East to Egypt. Let them, then, take a present of such dainties to the Egyptian—" a little balm, and a little honey, spices, and myrrh, nuts, and almonds." As for the money which had been put back into their sacks, it might have been an oversight. Let them take it again with them, along with the price of what corn they were now to purchase. And so let them go forth in the name of the God of Israel— Benjamin, and all the rest. He would remain behind alone, as at the fords of Jabbok,—no, not alone; but in faith and patience awaiting the issue. Presently the ten brothers, with more anxious hearts than Joseph ever had on his way to Egypt. or in the slave-market, are once more in the dreaded presence of the Egyptian. Joseph saw the new-comers, and with them what he judged to be his youngest brother, whom he had left in his home a child only a year old. Manifestly, it was neither the time nor the place to trust himself to converse with them. So he gave his steward orders to take them to his house, and that they should dine with him at noon. Joseph had spoken in Egyptian, which seems to have been unknown to the sons of Jacob. When they saw themselves brought to the house of Joseph, it immediately occurred to them that they were to be charged with theft of the former purchase-money. But the steward with kindly words allayed the fears which made them hesitate before entering " at the door of the house."

The sight of Simeon, who was at once restored to them, must have increased their confidence. Presently preparations were made for the banquet. It was a deeply trying scene for Joseph which ensued when he met his brethren on his return home. Little could they imagine what thoughts passed through his mind, as in true Oriental fashion they laid out the humble presents his father had sent, and lowly " bowed themselves to him to the earth." His language ill concealed his feelings. Again and again he inquired for his father, and as they replied : " Thy servant our father is in good health; he is yet alive," they again " bowed down their heads, and made obeisance." But when he fastened his eyes on Benjamin, his own mother's son, and had faltered it out, so unlike an Egyptian : " God be gracious unto thee, my son," he was obliged hastily to withdraw, " for his bowels did yearn upon his brother." Twenty-two years had passed since he had been parted from his brother, and Benjamin now stood before him—a youth little older than he when his bitter bondage in prison had commenced. Would they who had once sacrificed him on account of jealousy, be ready again to abandon his brother for the sake of selfishness?

At the banquet a fresh surprise awaited the sons of Jacob. Of course, after the Egyptian fashion, Joseph ate by himself, and the Egyptians by themselves : he as a member of the highest caste, and they from religious scruples. We know from secular history that the Egyptians abstained from certain kinds of meat, and would not eat with the knives and forks, nor from the cooking utensils which had been used by those of any other nation.   But it must have seemed unaccountable, that at the banquet their places were arranged exactly according to their ages.   How could the Egyptian have known them, and what mysterious circumstances surrounded them in his presence?   Yet another thing must have struck them.   In their father's house the youngest of their number, the son of Rachel, had been uniformly preferred before them all.   And now it was the same in the Egyptian palace !   If the Egyptian ruler " sent messes unto them from before him," "Benjamin's mess was five times so much as any of theirs."   Why this mark of unusual distinction, as it was regarded in ancient times ?[1]

However, the banquet itself passed pleasantly, and early next morning the eleven, gladsome and thankful, were on their way back to Canaan.   But the steward of Joseph's house had received special instructions.   As before. each "bundle of money" had been restored in every man's sack.   But, besides, he had also placed in that of Benjamin, Joseph's own cup, or rather his large silver bowl.   The brothers had not travelled far when the steward hastily overtook them.   Fixing upon the eleven the stain of base ingratitude, he charged them with stealing the "bowl" out of which "his lord drank, and whereby, indeed, he divined."   Of course this statement of the steward by no means proves that Joseph actually *did* divine by means of this " cup."   On the contrary, such could *not* have been the case, since it was of course impossible to divine, out of a cup that had been stolen from him, that it was stolen (ver. 15) !   But, no doubt, there was in Joseph's house, as in that of all the great sages of Egypt, the silver bowl, commonly employed for divination, in which unknown events were supposed to appear in reflection from the water, sometimes after

[1] Among the Spartans a double, among the Cretans a fourfold portion was set before princes and rulers.   In Egypt the proportion seems to have been five times.

gems or gold (with or without magical inscriptions and incantations) had been cast into the cup, to increase the sheen of the broken rays of light. Similar practices still prevail in Egypt.

The charge of treachery and of theft so took the brothers by surprise, that, in their conscious innocence, they offered to surrender the life of the guilty and the liberty of all the others, if the cup were found with any of them. But the steward had been otherwise instructed. He was to isolate Benjamin from the rest. With feigned generosity he now refused their proposal, and declared his purpose only to retain the guilty as bondsman. The search was made, and the cup found in the sack of Benjamin. Now the first great trial of their feelings ensued. They were all free to go home to their own wives and children ; Benjamin alone was to be a bondsman : the cup had been found in *his* sack ! Granting that, despite appearances, they knew him to be innocent, why should they stand by him ? At home he had been set before them as the favourite; nay, for fear of endangering him, their father had well nigh allowed them all, their wives and their children, to perish from hunger. In Egypt, also, he, the youngest, the son of another mother, had been markedly preferred before them. They had formerly got rid of one favourite, why hesitate now, when Providence itself seemed to rid them of another? What need, nay, what business had they to identify themselves with him? Was it not enough that he had been put before them everywhere; must they now destroy their whole family, and suffer their little ones to perish for the sake of one who, to say the best, seemed fated to involve them in misery and ruin? So they might have reasoned. But so they did not reason, nor, indeed, did they reason at all; for in all matters of duty reasoning is ever dangerous, and only absolute, immediate obedience to what is right, is safe. "They rent their clothes, and laded every man his ass, and returned to the city."

The first trial was past; the second and final one was to commence. In the presence of Joseph, "they fell before him on the ground" in mute grief. Judah is now the spokesman, and right well does his advocacy prefigure the pleading of his great Descendant. Not a word does he utter in extenuation or in plea. This one thought only is uppermost in his heart : "God hath found out the iniquity of thy servants." Not guilty indeed on *this* charge, but guilty before God, who hath avenged their iniquity ! How, then, can they leave Benjamin in his undeserved bondage, when not he, but they have really been the cause of this sorrow ? But Joseph, as formerly his steward, rejects the proposal as unjust, and offers their liberty to all except Benjamin. This gives to Judah an opening for pleading, in language so tender, graphic, and earnest, that few have been able to resist its pathos. He recounts the simple story, how the great Egyptian lord had at the first inquired whether they had father or brother, and how they had told him of their father at home, and of the child of his old age who was with him, the last remaining pledge of his wedded love, to whom the heart of the old man clave. Then the vizier had asked the youth to be brought, and they had pleaded that his going would cost the life of his father. But the famine had compelled them to ask of their father even this sacrifice. And the old man had reminded them of what they knew only too well : how his wife, the only one whom even now he really considered such, had borne him two sons ; one of those had gone out from him, just as it was now proposed Benjamin should go, and he had not seen him since, and he had said : "Surely he is torn in pieces." And now, if they took this one also from him, and mischief befell him, his grey hairs would go down with sorrow to the grave. What the old man apprehended had come to pass, no matter how. But could he, Judah, witness the grief and the death of his old father ? Was he not specially to blame, since upon his guarantee he had consented to part with him ? Nay, he had been his surety ; and he now asked neither pardon nor favour, only this he entreated, to be allowed to remain as bondsman instead of the lad, and to let him go back with his brethren. He besought slavery as a boon, for how could he "see the evil" that should "come on his father?"

Truly has Luther said : "What would I not give to be able to pray before the Lord as Judah here interceded for Benjamin, for it is a perfect model of prayer, nay, of the strong feeling which must underlie all prayer." And, blessed be God, One has so interceded for us, Who has given Himself as our surety, and become a bondsman for us.[1] His advocacy has been heard; His substitution accepted; and His intercession for us is ever continued, and ever prevails. The Lord Jesus Christ is "the Lion of the tribe of Juda, the Root of David," and "hath prevailed to open the book, and to loose the seven seals thereof."

The last trial was now past. Indeed, it had been impossible to continue it longer, for Joseph "could not refrain himself." All strangers were hastily removed, and Joseph, with all tenderness of affection and delicacy of feeling, made himself known to them as the brother whom they had sold into Egypt, but whom in reality God had sent before for the purpose not only of saving their lives, but of preserving their posterity, that so His counsel of mercy with the world might be accomplished. Then let them not be grieved, for God had overruled it all. Three times must he speak it, and prove his forgiveness by the most loving marks, before they could credit his words or derive comfort from them. But one object Joseph had now in view : to bring his father and all his family to be near him, that he might nourish them; for as yet only two out of the seven years of famine had passed. And in this purpose he was singularly helped by Divine Providence. Tidings of what had taken place reached Pharaoh, and the generous conduct of his vizier pleased the king. Of his own accord he also proposed what Joseph had intended; accompanying his invitation with a royal promise of ample provision, and sending "wagons" for the transport of the women and children. On his part, Joseph added rich presents for his father. When the eleven returned, first alone, to their father, and told him all, "the heart of Jacob fainted, for he believed them not." Pre-

[1] Psalm xl. 6, 7 ; Phil. ii. 6–8.

sently, as he saw the Egyptian "wagons" arriving, a great reaction took place. "The spirit of Jacob their father revived." The past, with its sorrows and its sin, seemed blotted out from his memory. Once more it was not, as before, Jacob who spoke, but "Israel" (the prince with God and man) who said, "It is enough, Joseph my son is yet alive : I will go and see him before I die."

CHAPTER XXII.

Departure of Jacob and his Family into Egypt—Jacob's Enterview with Pharaoh—His last Illness and command to be buried in Canaan—Adoption of Ephraim and Manasseh among the Sons of Israel.

(GEN. XLVI.—XLVIII.)

A DIFFICULT path lay before the patriarch Jacob. As yet he had had no direct intimation from God that he should remove with his family to Egypt. But, on the other hand, God's dealings with Joseph, the invitation of Pharaoh, and the famine in Canaan served to point it out as the period of which God had spoken to Abram,[1] when his seed should leave Canaan, and become strangers and enslaved in a land that was not theirs. He knew that two things must take place before the return of Israel to, and their final possession of the promised land. "The iniquity of the Amorites" must be "full," and the *family* of Israel must have grown into a *nation*. The former was still future, and as for the latter it is easy to see that any further stay in Canaan would have been hindering and not helpful to it. For at the time Canaan was divided among numerous independent tribes, with one or

[1] Gen. xv. 13.

more of whom the sons of Jacob, as they increased in numbers, must either have coalesced or entered into warfare Still more dangerous to their religion would have been their continuance among and intercourse with the Canaanites. It was quite otherwise in Egypt. Thither they went professedly as sojourners, and for a temporary purpose. The circumstance that they were shepherds, and as such "an abomination to the Egyptians," kept them separate, alike politically, religiously, and socially, from the rest of the people, and, indeed, caused them to be placed in a district by themselves. Yet "the land of Goshen" was the best for the increase of their substance in flocks and herds. These may be designated as the outward reasons for their removal into Egypt at that time; the higher and spiritual bearings of the event have already been stated.

The assurance which Jacob needed for his comfort was granted him, as he reached Beersheba, the southern boundary of the promised land. There the patriarch offered "sacrifices unto the God of his father Isaac," and there the faithful Lord spake to him "in the visions of the night." His words gave Jacob this fourfold assurance, that God *was* the covenant-God, and that Jacob need not fear to go down into Egypt; that God would *there* make of him a great nation, in other words, that the transformation from the family to the nation should take place in Egypt; that God would go down with him; and, lastly, that He would surely bring him up again. And each of these four assurances was introduced by an emphatic *I*, to indicate the personal and direct source of all these blessings. Thus strengthened, Israel pursued his journey in confidence of spirit.

As so often in Scripture, a very important lesson is conveyed to us in this connection, though in a manner to escape superficial observation. It has been repeatedly remarked, that the Bible does not furnish the history of individuals as such, but gives that of the kingdom of God. This appears most clearly in the list, which is introduced at this stage, of "the names of the children of Israel which came into Egypt." Manifestly, it is

not to be taken as literally the catalogue of those who com-
panied with Jacob on his journey to Egypt. For one thing,
some of them, such as Joseph himself, and his sons Ephraim
and Manasseh, and their children, if at the time they had any,
were already in Egypt. Then, some of the grandsons and
great-grandsons of Jacob, mentioned in this catalogue, must
have been born after the sons of Jacob came into Egypt;
while, on the other hand, there must have been others who are
not mentioned, since it is impossible to imagine that all the
families of those whose further descendants are not named
became extinct. But if the principle is kept in view, that only
what concerns the kingdom of God is recorded, then all
becomes plain. We now regard this *not as a biographical list,
but as a genealogical table*, drawn up with a special object in
view. That object is, to enumerate first the ancestors of the
tribes of Israel, and then such of their descendants as founded
the separate and distinct "*families*" in each tribe. Accordingly
this genealogical table contains, besides the names of such
descendants of Jacob as literally went with him into Egypt,
also those of such as became "heads of houses." This appears
quite clearly from a comparison with Numb. xxvi., where the
"families" of Israel are specially enumerated. Among their
founders not one single name appears that had not been previously given in the earlier table. Certain names, however,
have dropped out in the second table, viz., that of a son of
Simeon, and of one of Asher, and those of three sons of Benjamin—no doubt, either because they became extinct, or else
because they were removed from their places through some
judgment. Nor does it seem strange to find the names of the
future heads of families beforehand enumerated in this catalogue. Do we not similarly read, that in Abraham yet unborn
generations of Levi had given tithes to Melchizedek? Indeed,
Scripture constantly expresses itself on this wise. Thus we
read that God said to Abraham, to Isaac, and to Jacob: "I
will give thee the land," when, as yet, they were but strangers
and pilgrims in it; and, many centuries before the event took

place: "In *thee* shall all nations of the earth be blessed;" while to Jacob himself God spake : "I will bring *thee* up again," from Egypt. For with God nothing is, in the real sense, future. "He seeth the end from the beginning." But when the sacred text sums up the genealogical table with the statement tnat "all the souls" were "threescore and ten," we think ot the significance of the number, seven times ten, seven being the sacred covenant number, and ten that of perfectness.[1]

On his journey Jacob sent Judah in advance, to inform Joseph of his arrival. He hastened to receive his father in the border-land of Goshen. Their meeting, after so long a parting, was most affectionate and touching. The Hebrew expression, rendered in our Authorised Version : "Joseph . . . presented himself unto him," implies extraordinary splendour of appear ance. But when in the presence of his Hebrew father, the great Egyptian lord was once more only the lad Joseph. He "fell on his neck, and wept on his neck a good while." It now became the duty of Joseph to inform Pharaoh of the actual arrival of his family in Egypt, so as to obtain at the same time a fresh welcome, and a temporary concession of the land of Goshen for their settlement. For this purpose Joseph went first alone to the king, and next introduced five of his brothers. Both he and they laid stress on the fact that by occupation the family were shepherds. This would secure their stay in Goshen, as the district was most suitable for pasturage, and at the same time most remote and most isolated from the great bulk of the people. For the Egyptian monuments show that shepherds were considered as the lowest class or caste, probably because their nomadic habits were

---

[1] The Greek version of the LXX gives the number at seventy-five, and from it, as best known among the Jews at the time, St. Stephen quotes (Acts vii. 14). This number results, of course, from a slightly different arrangement of the table. That in the Hebrew text names of *Leah :* Six sons, twenty-five grandsons, and two great-grandsons, besides Dinah ; of *Zilpah :* Two sons, eleven grandsons, two great-grandsons, and one daughter ; of *Rachel :* Two sons, and twelve grandsons ; and of *Bilhah :* Two sons and five grandsons. The two "daughters" are inserted for special reasons.

so opposed to the settled civilisation of the country. Another point which the sons of Jacob were specially to bring out before Pharaoh was this, that they had come only "to *sojourn*," not to settle in the land, so that, as they had arrived at the first upon the express invitation of the king, they might be at liberty freely to depart when the time for it came. It is of importance to notice this in connection with the wrong afterwards done in the forcible detention of their descendants. It happened as Joseph had expected. Pharaoh assigned to them a dwelling-place "in the best of the land," that is, in the portion most suitable, in fact, in almost the only district suitable for pasturage—in the borderland between Canaan and Egypt, the land of Goshen, or of Rameses, as it is sometimes called from the city of that name. A careful and able scholar [1] has thus expressed himself on the subject : "The land of Goshen lay between the eastern part of the ancient Delta, and the western border of Palestine; it was scarcely a part of Egypt Proper, was inhabited by other foreigners besides the Israelites, and was in its geographical names rather Semitic than Egyptian; it was a pasture-land, especially suited to a shepherd people, and sufficient for the Israelites, who there prospered, and were separate from the main body of the Egyptians." [2]

Before settling him in Goshen, Joseph presented his father to Pharaoh, who received him with the courtesy of an Eastern monarch, and the respect which the sight of age, far exceeding the ordinary term of life in Egypt, would ensure. In acknowledgment of Pharaoh's kindness, "Jacob blessed" him ; and in answer to the question about his age, compared "the days of the years" of *his* own "pilgrimage" with those of his fathers.

[1] Mr. Grove, in Smith's *Dictionary of the Bible*, vol. i., p. 711.

[2] It is well known that one of the Egyptian monuments exhibits so striking an illustration of this entrance of the children of Israel into Egypt, that some have regarded it, though on insufficient grounds, as an actual representation of the event. The strangers are evidently of Semitic race, and came with their wives and children.

Abraham had lived one hundred and seventy-five, Isaac one hundred and eighty years; while Jacob was at the age of only one hundred and thirty, apprehending the approach of death. Compared to theirs, his days had not only been "few" but "evil," full of trial, sorrow, and care, ever since his flight from his father's house. Yet, however differing in outward events, the essential character of their lives was the same. His and theirs were equally a "pilgrimage." For, "these all died in faith, not having received the promises, but having seen them afar off, and were persuaded of them, and embraced them, and confessed that they were strangers and pilgrims on the earth. For they that say such things declare plainly that they seek a country, ... a better country, that is, an-heavenly : wherefore God is not ashamed to be called their God : for He hath prepared for them a city."[1] And in such wise also must each of our lives, whatever its outward history, be to us only a "pilgrimage."

But seventeen more years were granted to Israel in his quiet retirement of Goshen. Feeling that now the time of his departure had really come, he sent for Joseph. It was not to express weak regrets, nor even primarily to take such loving farewell as, under such circumstances, might be proper and fitting. Israel, as he is here again characteristically named,[2] was preparing for another great act of faith. On his dying bed, he still held fast by the promises of God concerning the possession of Canaan, and all that was connected with it ; and he exacted an oath from his son to bury him with his fathers, in the cave of Machpelah. Having obtained this solemn promise, it is said,[3] "he bowed himself in worship over the head of the bed."

[1] Heb. xi. 13, 14, 16.

[2] It is most instructive to notice in this history the frequent change of the names of *Jacob* and *Israel*.

[3] We translate literally. The Greek translators, or LXX, from whom the quotation is made in Heb. xi. 21, have, by the slightest change in the Hebrew word, rendered it, "worshipped, *leaning* upon the top of his staff." The meaning is substantially the same.

One thing still remained to be done. As yet the sons of Joseph had not been formally adopted into the family of Israel. But the two oldest of them, Manasseh and Ephraim, were to become heads of separate tribes; for Joseph was to have this right of the firstborn—*two* portions in Israel. Therefore, when, shortly after his interview with his father, Joseph was informed that the last fatal sickness had come upon him, he hastened to bring his two sons that they might be installed as co-heirs with the other sons of Jacob. In this Joseph signally showed his faith. Instead of seeking for his sons the honours which the court of Egypt offered them, he distinctly renounced all, to share the lot of the despised shepherd race. For the first time we here find the blessing accompanied with the laying on of hands.[1] But Jacob's eyes were dim, and when Joseph had brought his two sons close to his father, placing Manasseh, as the eldest, to his father's right hand, and Ephraim, as the younger, to his left, he ascribed it to failure of sight when Israel crossed his hands, laying the right on Ephraim and the left on Manasseh. But Jacob had been "guiding his hands wittingly." In fact, he had done it prophetically. The event proved the truth of this prophecy. At the time of Moses, indeed, Manasseh still counted twenty thousand men more than Ephraim.[2] But this comparative relationship was reversed in the days of the Judges; and ever afterwards Ephraim continued, next to Judah, the most powerful tribe in Israel. What, however, chiefly impresses us is, to see how intensely all the feelings, remembrances, and views of the dying man are intertwined with his religion. No longer does he cherish any hard thoughts about his "evil" days in the past. His memory of former days is now only of the gentleness and the goodness of God, Who had led him all through his pilgrimage. His feelings come out most fully in the words of blessing which he spake:

---

[1] The laying on of hands formed also an essential part in offering sacrifices. The offerer laid his hands on the victim, and confessed his sins,—thus transferring them, and constituting the sacrifice his substitute.

[2] Numb. xxvi. 34, 37.

"The God,[1] before Whose face walked my fathers, Abraham and Isaac; the God Who pastured[2] me from my existence on unto this day; THE ANGEL Who redeemed me from all evil, bless the lads; and let my name, and the name of my fathers, Abraham and Isaac, be named upon them, and let them increase to a multitude in the midst of the land." In this threefold reference to God as the covenant-God, the Shepherd and the Angel-Redeemer, we have a distinct anticipation of the truth concerning the blessed Trinity.

The blessing having been spoken, "Jacob gave to his son Joseph," as a special gift, "that parcel of ground" by Sychar,[3] the ancient Shechem, which he had originally bought of "the children of Heth;"[4] but which, as he prophesied, he —that is, his descendants—would have to take again[5] with sword and bow out of the hand of the Amorite. In this possession of Joseph, many centuries later, rested the Redeemer-Shepherd, when, even in His weariness, He called and pastured His flock.[6] But as for Jacob, the last assurance which he gave to his son was emphatically to repeat this confession of his faith: "Behold, I die: but God shall be with you, and bring you again unto the land of your fathers." For men pass away, but the word and purpose of the Lord abide for ever!

---

[1] The Hebrew puts it *with* the article—not merely God, but *the* God.

[2] Or "shepherded," like Psa. xxiii. 1; xxviii. 9. See also its fulness in John x. 11.

[3] John iv. 5.   [4] Gen. xxxiii. 19.

[5] The tense in verse 22 is the *prophetic past*, in which the future is seen as already achieved.

[6] John iv.

CHAPTER XXIII.

The Last Blessing of Jacob—Death of Jacob—Death of Joseph.

(GEN. XLIX. I.)

THE last scene had now come, and Jacob gathered around his dying couch his twelve sons. The words which he spake to them were of mingled *blessing* and *prediction*. Before him, in prophetic vision, unrolled, as it were, pictures of the tribes of which his sons were to be the ancestors; and what he saw he sketched in grand outlines. It is utterly impossible to regard these prophetic pictures as exact representations of any one definite period or even event in the history of Israel. They are sketches of the tribes in their grand characteristics, rather than predictions, either of special events, or of the history of Israel as a whole. And to them applies especially the description which one has given of prophetic visions generally, that "*they are pictures drawn without perspective,*"—that is, such that you cannot discern the distance from you of the various objects.

Two other general remarks may be helpful to the reader. It will be observed that, generally, in the "blessing" spoken, the *name* of the ancestor seems to unfold the future character and history of the tribe. Secondly, as against all cavillers, it may be said deliberately, that these words of blessing must have been spoken by Jacob himself. When we attempt to imagine them as spoken at any other period in the history of Israel, we find ourselves surrounded by insuperable difficulties. For these words can only apply to the tribes as Jacob viewed them. They could not have been written at any other period, since in that case every later writer would have said something quite inapplicable to one or other of the tribes, so that he could not have used this precise language concerning them all. With these brief prefatory remarks we address ourselves to the words of " blessing :"[1]

> REUBEN, my firstborn thou,
> My might and the firstling of my strength,
> Pre-eminence of dignity and pre-eminence of power—

Such *should* have been the position of Reuben, as the firstborn, had it not been for the "upboiling" of his passions and his consequent sin. Hence Jacob continues :

> Upboiling like water,
> Thou shalt not have the pre-eminence,
> Because thou wentest up thy father's bed,
> Then defiledst thou it—
> He went up my couch !

The sons next in age to Reuben were Simeon and Levi. Their wanton cruelty at Shechem, from which Jacob recoiled with horror even on his death-bed, had made them "brethren," or companions in evil. As they had united for evil, so God would *scatter* them in Israel, so that they should not form independent and compact tribes. In point of fact, we know that even at the second numbering of Israel,[2] Simeon had sunk to be the smallest tribe. In the last blessing of Moses,[3] no mention at all is made of Simeon. Nor does this tribe seem to have obtained any well-defined portion in the land, but only to have held certain cities within the possession of Judah.[4] Lastly, we know that such of the families of Simeon as largely increased and became powerful, afterwards left the Holy Land, and settled outside its boundaries.[5] The tribe of Levi also received not any possession in Israel; only that their scattering was changed from a curse into a blessing by their election to the priesthood. This scattering of two tribes was the significant answer which God in His righteous providence made to their ancestors' attempt at vindicating the honour of their race by carnal means and weapons.

---

[1] We always translate literally.   [2] Numb. xxvi. 14.   [3] Deut. xxxiii.
[4] Josh. xix. 1-9.   [5] 1 Chron. iv. 38-43.

SIMEON and LEVI are brethren;
Instruments of violence are their swords;
Into their council come not thou, oh my soul,
Unto their assembly be not thou united, mine honour;
For in their anger they slew men,
And in their self-will they hamstrung oxen.
Cursed be their anger, for it was fierce,
And their wrath, for it was cruel.
I will divide them in Jacob,
And scatter them in Israel.

The three older brothers being thus dispossessed, and Joseph receiving the twofold territorial portion, the other privileges of the birthright are solemnly transferred to *Judah.* He is to be the leader, "the lion." As the lion is king of the forest, so was Judah to have royal sway, through David onwards to the Son of David, the *Shiloh,* unto Whom, as "the Lion of the tribe of Judah," all nations should render homage and obedience. Similarly, fulness of earthly riches was to distinguish the lot of Judah, these earthly blessings being themselves emblems of the spiritual riches dispensed in the portion of Judah. The whole description here is full of Messianic allusions, which were afterwards taken up in the prophecy of Balaam;[1] then applied to David;[2] and from him carried forward in prophecy, through Psa. lxxii., Isa. ix., xi., to Ezek. xxi. 27, and Zech. ix. 9, till they were finally realised in Jesus Christ, "sprung out of Juda,"[3] "our peace, who hath made both one,"[4] and who "must reign till He hath put all enemies under His feet,"[5] "the Lion of the tribe of Juda, the Root of David," Who "hath prevailed."[6]

In the blessing upon Judah we note, for the first time, how the prophetic significance of the *name* unfolds and appears :

JUDAH thou ! Thy brethren shall praise thee !
Thy hand in the neck of thine enemies,
Thy father's sons shall bow down before thee.

---

[1] Numb. xxiii. 24 ; xxiv. 9, 17   [2] Psalm lxxxix. 20-37.
[3] Heb. vii. 14.   [4] Eph. ii. 14.
[5] 1 Cor. xv. 25.   [6] Rev. v. 5.

> A lion's whelp[1] is Judah;
> From the prey, my son, thou art gone up:
> He stoopeth down, he coucheth like a lion,[1]
> And like a lioness[1]—who shall rouse him?
> *The sceptre shall not depart from Judah,*
> *Nor the ruler's staff from between his feet,*
> *Until* SHILOH [2] *come,*
> *And to* HIM *willing obedience of the nations!*
> He bindeth unto the vine his foal,
> And unto the choice vine his ass's colt;
> He washeth his garments in wine,
> And in the blood of grapes his raiment;
> Sparkling his eyes from wine,
> And white his teeth from milk.

As local illustrations of this richness of the portion of Judah, the reader will remember that the best wine in Palestine grew near Hebron and Engedi,[3] and that some of the best pasture-land was south of Hebron, about Tekoa and Carmel.[4]

The next blessing also connects itself with the *name* of *Zebulun*, or "dwelling," although it requires to be borne in mind, in further illustration of the fact that it was not intended as a literal prediction, that the possessions of the tribe of Zebulun, so far as we can judge from Josh. xix. 10–16, never *actually* touched the Mediterranean nor the Sea of Galilee, nor yet literally bordered on Zidon:

> ZEBULUN—by the coast of seas shall he dwell,
> And that, by the coast of ships,
> And his side towards Zidon.

The name of *Issachar*, "reward," or "hire," is also emblematical of the character of the tribe, as, in its rich portion of

---

[1] A young lion for agility and grace; a full-grown lion for strength and majesty; a lioness whose fierceness defends her offspring.

[2] This is not the place for critical discussion; but we state it as our deliberate conviction, that the term *Shiloh* can only refer to a personal designation of the Messiah, whatever the derivative meaning of the word may be.

[3] Numb. xiii. 23, etc.; Sol. Song i. 14.

[4] 1 Sam. xxv. 2; 2 Chron. xxvi. 10; Amos i. 1.

Lower Galilee, it preferred labour with quietude, to power and
domination :

> ISSACHAR is a bony ass,
> Crouching between the folds.
> He saw rest, that *it was* a boon,
> And the land, that *it was* pleasant,
> And he bent his shoulder to bear,
> And became a tributary servant.

The allusion in the case of *Dan*, or "judgment," is again to
the name.   Although Dan was only the son of a bondmaid, he
should not be behind his brethren, but "give judgment" to his
people, that is, to Israel—the reference being possibly to such
men as Samson, though also generally to the character of the
tribe.   There is another mysterious and most important allusion here, to which we shall immediately advert :

> DAN shall give judgment to his people,
> As one of the tribes of Israel.
> Dan shall be a serpent by the way,
> An adder in the path,
> Which biteth the heels of the horse
> So that backwards falleth his rider.

We shall not presume to offer an authoritative explanation
of this comparison of Dan to a serpent, and to that kind of
adder which, being of the colour of the sand, remains unobserved till it has given its deadly bite.   We only put it as
a suggestion, whether this may not contain an allusion
to apostasy or to the Antichrist,[1] at the same time noting
that the name of Dan is omitted from the list of the tribes in
Rev. vii. 5–8.

It is also significant that, immediately after the mention of
these contests in connection with Dan, Jacob bursts forth in a
prayer, intended, as says Calvin, not only to express his own
personal faith and hope, but his confidence for his descendants.
Quite the oldest Jewish commentary, or rather paraphrase,[2]

---

[1] Many of the Fathers have regarded this "serpent" as referring to
Antichrist.

[2] The Jerusalem Targum in its most correct recension.

puts it this way : " My soul waiteth not for the deliverance of Gideon, the son of Joash, for it was only temporal ; nor for that of Samson, for it was but transient ; but for the redemption by the Messiah, the Son of David, which in Thy word Thou hast promised to send to Thy people, the children of Israel ; for this, Thy salvation, my soul waiteth."

For Thy salvation wait I, oh Jehovah !

In reference to *Gad*, we have a threefold allusion to a kindred word, signifying oppression. To the prediction itself we cannot attach any definite historical fulfilment :

GAD—a press presseth upon him,
But he presseth on their heel.

In the case of *Asher*, the reference is evidently to the most fertile possession of that tribe, extending from Mount Carmel to the land of Tyre, the district richest in corn and oil :[1]

Out of ASHER fatness : his bread—
And he yieldeth royal dainties.

The allusion as to *Naphtali* is to the graceful agility and fleetness of the people, and also to their mental ability and quickness :

NAPHTALI is a hind let loose—
He uttereth words of beauty.

At last Jacob comes to the name of his loved son Joseph. Then it seems as if his whole heart were indeed overflowing. First, he sketches his fruitfulness, like that of a fruit-tree " planted by rivers of water,"[2] whose boughs run over the wall ;[3] then he describes his strength, as derived from God Himself ; and, lastly, he pours forth richest blessings, richer far than any his ancestors had bestowed :

Son of a fruit-tree (a fruitful bough) is JOSEPH,
Son of a fruit-tree by a well,
Whose daughters (branches) spread over the wall.

---

[1] I Kings v. II.   [2] Psalm i. 3.   [3] Comp. Psalm lxxx. 8-11.

> The archers harass him,
> They shoot at him, and hate him ;
> But his bow abideth in firmness,
> And the arms of his hands remain supple
> From the Hands of the Strong One of Jacob,
> From thence, from the Shepherd, from the Rock of Israel,
> From the God of thy father—may He help thee !
> And from the Almighty—may He bless thee !
> Blessings of heaven from above !
> Blessings of the deep that lieth beneath !
> Blessings of the breasts and of the womb !
> The blessings of thy father exceed
> The blessings of my ancestors
> Unto the bound of the everlasting hills—[1]
> May they come on the head of Joseph,
> And on the crown of the head of him who is separated[2] among
>   his brethren !

The allusions to *Benjamin* will be understood by a reference to *Ehud*,[3] to Judges v. 14; xx. 16; 1 Chron. viii. 40; xii. 2; 2 Chron. xiv. 8; xvii. 17, and to the history of Saul and of Jonathan :

> BENJAMIN—a wolf who ravins :
> In the morning he devoureth prey,
> And at even he divideth spoil !

And now, having spoken these his last blessings, Jacob once more charged his sons to bury him in the cave of Machpelah. Then he gathered up his feet into the bed, laid him peace fully down, and without sigh or struggle yielded up the ghost, and was " gathered unto his people."

Such was the end of Jacob—the most pilgrim-like of the pilgrim fathers. His last wishes were obeyed to the letter. The first natural outburst of grief on the part of Joseph past, he " commanded his servants, the physicians, to embalm his father"—either to do the work themselves or to superintend it.

[1] That is, as far as the mountains overtop the plains, so the blessings which Joseph now receives exceed those which any of Jacob's ancestors had bestowed.

[2] That is, in dignity. The term in the Hebrew is *Nasir*.

[3] Judges iii. 15.

Forty days the process lasted,[1] and seventy days, as was their wont, the Egyptians mourned. At the end of that period Joseph, as in duty bound, applied to Pharaoh, though not personally, since he could not appear before the king in the garb of mourning, craving permission for himself and his retinue to go up and bury his father in the land of Canaan. The funeral procession included, besides Joseph and "all his house," "his brethren, and his father's house," also "all the servants of Pharaoh, the elders of his house, and all the elders of the land of Egypt,"—that is, the principal state and court officials, under a guard of both "chariots and horsemen." So influential and "very great a company" would naturally avoid, for fear of any collisions, the territory of the Philistines, through which the direct road from Egypt lay. They took the circuitous route through the desert and around the Dead Sea—significantly, the same which Israel afterwards followed on their return from Egypt—and halted on the Eastern bank of Jordan, at *Goren-ha-Atad*, "the buckthorn threshing-floor," or perhaps "the threshing-floor of *Atad*." The account of the funeral, as that of the embalming, and indeed every other allusion, is

---

[1] Everything here is truly Egyptian : the number of physicians in Joseph's service, since in Egypt every physician treated only one special kind of disease; the mourning, which always lasted seventy days ; and the process of embalming, which took from forty to seventy days. There were two modes of embalming, besides that for the poor—the most elaborate costing about two hundred and fifty pounds, and a simpler one about eighty-one pounds. The brain was first taken out through the nostrils; then an incision made in the left side, and all the intestines extracted, except the kidneys and the heart. The body was next filled with various spices—except frankincense,—sewed up, and steeped in *natrum*, which is found in the natrum lakes of Egypt, and consists of carbonate, sulphate, and muriate of soda. We here purposely omit a great number of particulars, such as the use of palm-wine in washing the internal parts, the occasional staining of the nails, the elaborate wrapping of the body in *byssus*, and other varying details. It is remarkable how well all parts of the body, and even the features, were preserved by this process. The body was laid either in an oblong case, or more frequently in one that had the shape of the mummy itself. Our description applies chiefly to the costliest mode of embalming.

strictly in accordance with what we learn from Egyptian monuments and history. The custom of funeral processions existed in every province of Egypt, and representations of such are seen in the oldest tombs. As a German scholar remarks: "When we look at the representations upon the monuments, we can almost imagine that we actually see the funeral train of Jacob." At *Goren-ha-Atad* other mourning rites were performed during seven days. The attention of the inhabitants of the district was naturally attracted to this "grievous mourning to the Egyptians," and the locality henceforth bore the name of *Abel Mizraim*, literally "meadow of the Egyptians," but, by slightly altering the pronunciation : "mourning of the Egyptians." Here the Egyptians remained behind, and none but the sons and the household of Jacob stood around his grave at Machpelah.

On their return to Egypt an unworthy suspicion seems to have crossed the minds of Joseph's brethren. What if, now that their father was dead, Joseph were to avenge the wrong he had sustained at their hands? But they little knew his heart, or appreciated his motives. The bare idea of their cherishing such thoughts moved Joseph to tears. Even if bitter feelings had been in his heart, was he "in the place of God " to interfere with His guidance of things? Had it not clearly appeared that, whatever evil *they* might have thought to do him, "God meant it unto good?" With such declarations, and the assurance that he would lovingly care for them and their little ones, he appeased their fears.

Other fifty-four years did Joseph live in Egypt. He had the joy of seeing his father's blessing commence to be fulfilled. Ephraim's children of the third generation, and Manasseh's grandchildren " were brought up upon his knees." At the good old age of one hundred and ten years, as he felt death approaching, he gathered "his brethren" about him. Joseph was full of honours in Egypt; he had founded a family, than which none was more highly placed. Yet his last act was to disown Egypt, and to choose the lot of Israel—poverty, contempt, and pilgrimage : to renounce the present, in order to cleave unto the future. It was a noble act of faith, true like that of his fathers ! His last words were these : " I die : and God will surely visit you, and bring you out of this land unto the land which He sware to Abraham, to Isaac, and to Jacob." And his last deed was to take a solemn oath of the children of Israel, to carry up his bones with them into the land of promise. In obedience to his wishes they embalmed his body, and laid it in one of those Egyptian coffins, generally made of sycamore wood, which resembled the shape of the human body. And there, through ages of suffering and bondage, stood the figure-like coffin of Joseph, ready to be lifted and carried thence when the sure hour of deliverance had come. Thus Joseph, being dead, yet spake to Israel, telling them that they were only temporary sojourners in Egypt, that their eyes must be turned away from Egypt unto the land of promise, and that in patience of faith they must wait for that hour when God would certainly and graciously fulfil His own promise.

When at the close of this first period of the Covenant-history we look around, we feel as if now indeed " the horror of great darkness " were fast falling upon Israel, which Abraham had experienced as he was shown the future of his descendants.[1] Already personal intercourse between heaven and earth had ceased. From the time that Jacob had paid his vow in Bethel,[2] no personal manifestation of God, such as had often gladdened his fathers and him, was any more vouchsafed, except on his entrance into Egypt,[3] and then for a special purpose. Nor do we read of any such during the whole eventful and trying life of Joseph. And now long centuries of utter silence were to follow. During all that weary period, with the misery of their bondage and the temptation of idolatry around constantly increasing, there was neither voice from heaven nor visible manifestation to warn or to cheer the children of Israel in Egypt. One mode of guidance was for a time withdrawn. Israel had now only the past to sustain and direct them.

[1] Gen. xv. 12.   [2] Gen. xxxv. 15.   [3] Gen. xlvi. 2–4.

But that past, in its history and with its promises, was sufficient. Besides, the torch of prophecy, which the hands of dying Jacob had held, cast its light into the otherwise dark future. Nay, the fact that Joseph's life, which formed the great turning-point in Israel history, had been allowed to pass without visible Divine manifestations to him and to them was in itself significant. For even as his unburied body seemed to preach and to prophesy, so his whole life would appear like a yet unopened or only partially opened book,—a grand unread prophecy, which the future would unfold. And not merely the immediate future, as it concerned Israel; but the more distant future as it concerns the whole Church of God. For, although not the person of Joseph,[1] yet the leading events of his life are typical of the great facts connected with the life and the work of Him who was betrayed and sold by His brethren, but whom "God exalted with His right hand to be a Prince and a Saviour."

[1] It deserves notice that the *person of Joseph* is not mentioned in the Old or the New Testament as a type of Christ. This, of course, does not apply to the facts of his life in their bearing on the future, as these were unquestionably typical.

THE BIBLE HISTORY

VOLUME II

THE EXODUS

AND

THE WANDERINGS IN THE WILDERNESS

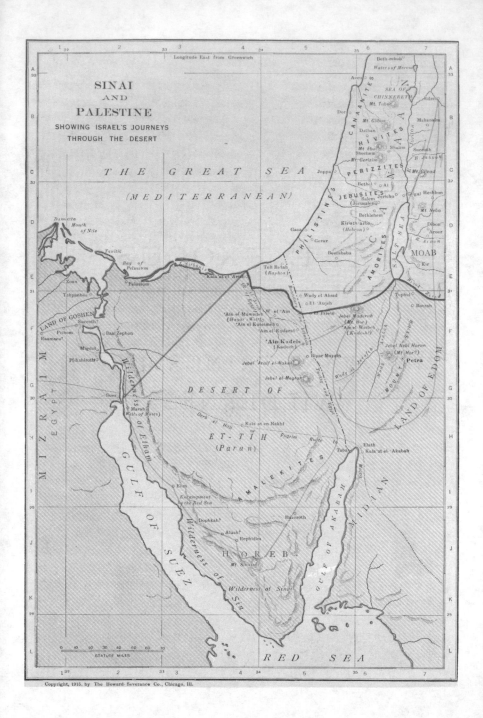

SINAI
AND
PALESTINE

SHOWING ISRAEL'S JOURNEYS
THROUGH THE DESERT

THE GREAT SEA

(MEDITERRANEAN)

PREFACE

THE period covered by the central books of the Pentateuch is, in many respects, the most important in Old Testament history, not only so far as regards Israel, but the Church at all times. Opening with centuries of silence and seeming Divine forgetfulness during the bondage of Egypt, the pride and power of Pharaoh are suddenly broken by a series of miracles, culminating in the deliverance of Israel and the destruction of Egypt's host. In that Paschal night and under the blood-sprinkling, Israel as a nation is born of God, and the redeemed people are then led forth to be consecrated at the Mount by ordinances, laws, and judgments. Finally, we are shown the manner in which Jehovah deals with His people, both in judgment and in mercy, till at the last He safely brings them to the promised inheritance. In all this we see not only the history of the ancient people of God, but also a grand type of the redemption and the sanctification of the Church. There is yet another aspect of it, since this narrative exhibits the foundation of the Church in the Covenant of God, and also the principles of Jehovah's government. for all time. For, however great the difference in the development, the essence and character of the covenant of grace are ever the same. The Old and New Testaments are essentially one—not two covenants but one, gradually unfolding into full perfectness, "Jesus Christ Himself being the chief corner stone" of the foundation which is alike that of the apostles and prophets.[1]

There is yet a further consideration besides the intrinsic

[1] Eph. ii. 20.

importance of this history. It has, especially of late, been so boldly misrepresented, and so frequently misunderstood, or else it is so often cursorily read—neither to understanding nor yet to profit—that it seemed desirable to submit it anew to special investigation, following the sacred narrative consecutively from Chapter to Chapter, and almost from Section to Section. In so doing, I have endeavoured to make careful study of the original text, with the help of the best critical appliances. So far as I am conscious, I have not passed by any real difficulty, nor yet left unheeded any question that had a reasonable claim to be answered. If this implied a more detailed treatment, I hope it may also, with God's blessing, render the volume more permanently useful. Further, it has been my aim, by the aid of kindred studies, to shed additional light upon the narrative, so as to render it vivid and pictorial, enabling readers to realise for themselves the circumstances under which an event took place. Thus I have in the first two chapters sought to read the history of Israel in Egypt by the light of its monuments, and also to portray the political, social, and religious state of the people prior to the Exodus. Similarly, when following the wanderings of Israel up to the eastern bank of the Jordan, I have availed myself of the best recent geographical investigations, that so the reader might, as it were, *see* before him the route followed by Israel, the scenery, and all other accessories.

It need scarcely be said, that in studying this narrative *the open Bible should always be at hand.* But I may remind myself and others, that the only real understanding of any portion of Holy Scripture is that conveyed to the heart by the Spirit of God. And, indeed, throughout, my great object has been, not to supersede the constant and prayerful use of the Bible itself, but rather to lead to those Scriptures, which alone "are able to make wise unto salvation through faith which is in Christ Jesus."

A. E.

HENIACH, BOURNEMOUTH
February, 1876.

CONTENTS.

The Exodus.

CHAPTER VI.

CHAPTER VII.

The Wanderings in the Wilderness.

CHAPTER VIII.

CHAPTER IX.

CHAPTER X.

CHAPTER XI.

CHAPTER XII.

CHAPTER XIII.

CHAPTER XIV.

CHAPTER XV.

CHAPTER XVI.

CHAPTER XVII.

CHAPTER XVIII.

CHAPTER XIX.

CHAPTER XX.

CHAPTER XXI.

THE EXODUS

CHAPTER I.

Egypt and its History during the Stay of the Children of Israel, as Illustrated by the Bible and Ancient Monuments.

(Exodus I. 1–7.)

THE devout student of history cannot fail to recognise it as a wonderful arrangement of Providence, that the beginning and the close of Divine revelation to mankind were both connected with the highest intellectual culture of the world. When the apostles went forth into the Roman world, they could avail themselves of the Greek language, then universally spoken, of Grecian culture and modes of thinking. And what Greece was to the world at the time of Christ, that and much more had Egypt been when the children of Israel became a God-chosen nation. Not that in either case the truth of God needed help from the wisdom of this world. On the contrary, in one sense, it stood opposed to it. And yet while history pursued seemingly its independent course, and philosophy, science, and the arts advanced apparently without any reference to Revelation, all were in the end made subservient to the furtherance of the kingdom of God. And so it always is. God marvellously uses natural means for supernatural ends, and maketh all things work together to His glory as well as for the good of His people.

It was, indeed, as we now see it, most important that the
children of Israel should have been brought into Egypt, and
settled there for centuries before becoming an independent
nation.   The early history of the sons of Jacob must have
shown the need alike of their removal from contact with the
people of Canaan, and of their being fused in the furnace of
affliction, to prepare them for inheriting the land promised unto
their fathers.   This, however, might have taken place in any
other country than Egypt.   Not so their training for a nation.
For that, Egypt offered the best, or rather, at the time, the only
suitable opportunities.   True, the stay there involved also
peculiar dangers, as their after history proved.   But these would
have been equally encountered under any other circumstances,
while the benefits they derived through intercourse with the
Egyptians were peculiar and unique.   There is yet another
aspect of the matter.   When standing before King Agrippa,
St. Paul could confidently appeal to the publicity of the history
of Christ, as enacted not in some obscure corner of a barbarous
land, but in full view of the Roman world : " For this thing
was not done in a corner."[1]   And so Israel's bondage also and
God's marvellous deliverance took place on no less conspicuous
a scene than that of the ancient world-empire of Egypt.

Indeed, so close was the connection between Israel and
Egypt, that it is impossible properly to understand the history
of the former without knowing something of the latter.   We
shall therefore devote this preliminary chapter to a brief
description of Egypt.   In general, however historians may differ
as to the periods when particular events had taken place, the
land itself is full of reminiscences of Israel's story.   These have
been brought to light by recent researches, which almost year
by year add to our stock of knowledge.   And here it is specially
remarkable, that every fresh historical discovery tends to shed
light upon, and to confirm the Biblical narratives.   Yet some
of the principal arguments against the Bible were at one time
derived from the supposed history of Egypt !   Thus while

[1] Acts xxvi. 26.

men continually raise fresh objections against Holy Scripture, those formerly so confidently relied upon have been removed by further researches, made quite independently of the Bible, just as an enlarged knowledge will sweep away those urged in our days. Already the Assyrian monuments, the stone which records the story of Moab,[1] the temples, the graves, and the ancient papyri of Egypt have been made successively to tell each its own tale, and each marvellously bears out the truth of the Scripture narrative. Let us see what we can learn from such sources of the ancient state of Egypt, so far as it may serve to illustrate the history of Israel.

The connection between Israel and Egypt may be said to have begun with the visit of Abram to that country. On his arrival there he must have found the people already in a high state of civilisation. The history of the patriarch gains fresh light from monuments and old papyri. Thus a papyrus (now in the British Museum), known as *The Two Brothers*, and which is probably the oldest work of fiction in existence, proves that Abram had occasion for fear on account of Sarai. It tells of a Pharaoh, who sent two armies to take a fair woman from her husband and then to murder him. Another papyrus (at present in Berlin) records how the wife and children of a foreigner were taken from him by a Pharaoh. Curiously enough, this papyrus dates from nearly the time when the patriarch was in Egypt. From this period also we have a picture in one of the tombs, representing the arrival of a nomad chief, like Abram, with his family and dependants, who seek the protection of the prince. The new-comer is received as a person of distinction. To make the coincidence the more striking—though this chief is not thought to have been Abram—he is evidently of Semitic descent, wears a "coat of many colours," is designated *Hyk*, or prince, the equivalent of the modern *Sheich*, or chief of a tribe, and even bears the name of *Ab-shah*, "father of sand," a term resembling that of *Ab-raham*, the "father of a multitude."[2] Another

[1] 2 Kings iii.

[2] We have here to refer to the masterly essay on "The Bearings of

Egyptian story—that of *Sancha*, "the son of the sycomoie,"
—reminds us so far of that of Joseph, that its hero is a foreign
nomad, who rises to the highest rank at Pharaoh's court and
becomes his chief counsellor. These are instances how
Egyptian history illustrates and confirms that of the Bible.

Of the forced employment of the children of Israel in
building and repairing certain cities, we have, as will presently
be shown, sufficient confirmation in an Egyptian inscription
lately discovered. We have also a pictorial representation of
Semitic captives, probably Israelites, making bricks in the manner
described in the Bible; and yet another, dating from a later
reign, in which Israelites—either captives of war, or, as has been
recently suggested, mercenaries who had stayed behind after
the Exodus—are employed for Pharaoh in drawing stones, or
cutting them in the quarries, and in completing or enlarging the
fortified city of Rameses, which their fathers had formerly
built. The builders delineated in the second of these representations are expressly called *Aperu*, the close correspondence
of the name with the designation *Hebrew*, even in its English
form, being apparent. Though these two sets of representations
date, in all probability, from a period later than the Exodus,
they remarkably illustrate what we read of the state and the
occupations of the children of Israel during the period of their
oppression. Nor does this exhaust the bearing of the Egyptian
monuments on the early history of Israel. In fact, we can
trace the two histories almost contemporaneously, and see how
remarkably the one sheds light upon the other.

In general, our knowledge of Egyptian history is derived
from the *monuments*, of which we have already spoken, from
certain references in *Greek historians*, which are not of much
value, and especially from the historical work of *Manetho*,
an Egyptian priest who wrote about the year 250 B.C. At

Egyptian History upon the Pentateuch," appended to vol. i. of what is
commonly known as *The Speaker's Commentary*. For an engraving of this
remarkable fresco, see *The Land of the Pharaohs: Egypt and Sinai,
Illustrated by Pen and Pencil*, p. 102 (Religious Tract Society).

that time the monuments of Egypt were still almost intact. Manetho had access to them all; he was thoroughly conversant with the ancient literature of his country, and he wrote under the direction and patronage of the then monarch of the land. Unfortunately, however, his work has been lost, and the fragments of it preserved exist only in the distorted form which Josephus has given them for his own purposes, and in a chronicle, written by a learned Christian convert of the third century (*Julius Africanus*). But this latter also has been lost, and we know it only from a similar work written a century later (by *Eusebius*, bishop of Cæsarea), in which the researches of Africanus are embodied.[1] Such are the difficulties before the student! On the other hand, both Africanus and Eusebius gathered their materials in Egypt itself, and were competent for their task; Africanus, at least, had the work of Manetho before him; and, lastly, by universal consent, the monuments of Egypt remarkably confirm what were the undoubted statements of Manetho. Like most heathen chronologies, Manetho's catalogue of kings begins with gods, after which he enumerates thirty dynasties, bringing the history down to the year 343 B.C. Now some of these dynasties were evidently not successive, but contemporary, that is, they present various lines of kings who at one and the same time ruled over different portions of Egypt. This especially applies to the so-called 7th, 8th, 9th, 10th, and 11th dynasties. It is wholly impossible to conjecture what period of time these may have occupied. After that we have more solid ground. We know that under the 12th dynasty the whole of Egypt was united under one sway. As we gather from the monuments, the country was in a very high state of prosperity and civilisation. At the beginning of this dynasty we suppose the visit of Abram to have taken place. The reign of this 12th dynasty lasted more than two centuries,[2] and either at its close or at the

---

[1] Even this exists only in its Armenian translation, not in the original.

[2] We must again refer those who wish fuller information to the essay already mentioned, the conclusions of which we have virtually adopted.

beginning of the 13th dynasty we place the accession and rule of Joseph. From the fourth king of the 13th to the accession of the 18th dynasty Egyptian history is almost a blank. That period was occupied by the rule of the so-called *Hyksos*, or Shepherd kings, a foreign and barbarous race of invaders, hated and opposed by the people, and hostile to their ancient civilisation and religion. Although Josephus represents Manetho as assigning a very long period to the reign of "the Shepherds," he gives only six names. These and these only are corroborated by Egyptian monuments, and we are warranted in inferring that these alone had really ruled over Egypt. The period occupied by their reign might thus amount to between two and three centuries, which agrees with the Scripture chronology.

"The Shepherds" were evidently an eastern race, and probably of Phenician origin. Thus the names of the two first kings in their list are decidedly Semitic (*Salatis*, "mighty," "ruler," and *Beon*, or *Benon*, "the son of the eye," or, the "beloved one"); and there is evidence that the race brought with it the worship of Baal and the practice of human sacrifices—both of Phenician origin. It is important to keep this in mind, as we shall see that there had been almost continual warfare between the Phenicians along the west coast of Palestine and the Hittites, and the native Egyptian kings, who, while they ruled, held them in subjection. This constant animosity also explains why, not without good reason, "every shepherd was an abomination" unto the real native Egyptians.[1] It also explains why the Shepherd kings left the Israelitish shepherds unmolested in the land of Goshen, where they found them. Thus a comparison of Scripture chronology with the history of Egypt, and the evidently peaceful, prosperous state of the country, united under the rule of one king, as described in the Bible, lead us to the conclusion that Joseph's stay there must have taken place at the close of the 12th, or, at latest, at the commencement of the 13th dynasty. He could not have come during the rule of the Hyksos, for then Egypt was in a distracted, divided, and

---

[1] Gen. xlvi. 34.

chaotic state; and it could not have been later, for after the
Shepherd kings had been expelled and native rulers restored,
no "new king," no new dynasty, "arose up over Egypt." On
the other hand, the latter description exactly applies to a king
who, on his restoration, expelled the Hyksos.

And here the monuments of Egypt again afford remarkable
confirmation of the history of Joseph. For one thing, the
names of three of the Pharaohs of the 13th dynasty bear a
striking resemblance to that given by the Pharaoh of the Bible
to Joseph (Zaphnath-paaneah). Then we know that the Pharaohs
of the 12th dynasty stood in a very special relationship to the
priest city of On,[1] and that its high-priest was most probably
always a near relative of Pharaoh. Thus the monuments of
that period enable us to understand the history of Joseph's
marriage. But they also throw light on a question of far
greater importance—how so devout and pious a servant of the
Lord as Joseph could have entered into such close relationship
with the priesthood of Egypt. Here our knowledge of the
most ancient religion of Egypt enables us to furnish a complete
answer. Undoubtedly, all mankind had at first some knowledge of the one true God, and a pure religion inherited from
Paradise. This primeval religion seems to have been longest
preserved in Egypt. Every age indeed witnessed fresh corruptions, till at last that of Egypt became the most abject
superstition. But the earliest Egyptian religious records, as
preserved in that remarkable work, *The Ritual for the Dead*,
disclose a different state of things. There can be no doubt
that, divested of all later glosses, they embodied belief in
"the unity, eternity, and self-existence of the unknown Deity,"
in the immortality of the soul, and in future rewards and punishments, and that they inculcated the highest duties of morality.
The more closely we study these ancient records of Egypt,
the more deeply are we impressed with the high and pure
character of its primeval religion and legislation. And when
the children of Israel went into the wilderness, they took, in

[1] Gen. xli. 45.

this respect also, with them from Egypt many lessons which had not to be learned anew, though this one grand fundamental truth had to be acquired, that the Deity unknown to the Egyptians was *Jehovah*, the living and the true God. We can therefore understand how such close connection between Joseph and the Egyptian priesthood was both possible and likely.

But this is not all. Only under a powerful native ruler could the redivision of the land and the rearrangement of taxation, which Joseph proposed, have taken place. Moreover, we know that under the rule of the last great king of this native dynasty (the 13th) a completely new system of Nile-irrigation *was* introduced, such as we may well believe would have been devised to avoid another period of famine, and, strangest of all, a place by the artificial lake made at that time bears the name *Pi-aneh*, "the house of life," which is singularly like that given by Pharaoh to Joseph. If we now pass over the brief 14th dynasty and the Hyksos period, when we may readily believe Israel remained undisturbed in Goshen, we come to the restoration of a new native dynasty (the so-called 18th). After the "Shepherds" had been expelled, the Israelitish population, remaining behind in the borderland of Goshen, would naturally seem dangerously large to the "new king," the more so as the Israelites were kindred in descent and occupation to the "Shepherds,"[1] and had been befriended by them. Under these circumstances a wise monarch might seek to weaken such a population by forced labour. For this purpose he employed them in building fortress-cities, such as Pithom and Raamses.[2] *Raamses* bears the name of the district in which it is situated, but *Pithom* means "the fortress of foreigners," thus indicating its origin. Moreover, we learn from the monuments that this "new king" (Aahmes I.) employed in building his fortresses what are called the *Fenchu*— a word meaning "bearers of the shepherd's staff," and which therefore would exactly describe the Israelites.

[1] Ex. i. 9, 10.　　　　　[2] Ex. i. 11.

The period between the " new king " of the Bible (Aahmes I.) and Thothmes II. (the second in succession to him), when we suppose the Exodus to have taken place, quite agrees with the reckoning of Scripture. Now this Thothmes II. began his reign very brilliantly. But after a while there is a perfect blank in the monumental records about him. But we read of a general revolt after his death among the nations whom his father had conquered. Of course, one could not expect to find on Egyptian monuments an account of the disasters which the nation sustained at the Exodus, nor how Pharaoh and his host had perished in the Red Sea. But we do find in his reign the conditions which we should have expected under such circumstances, viz., a brief, prosperous reign, then a sudden collapse; the king dead; no son to succeed him; the throne occupied by the widow of the Pharaoh, and for twenty years no attempt to recover the supremacy of Egypt over the revolted nations in Canaan and east of the Jordan. Lastly, the character of his queen, as it appears on the monuments, is that of a proud and bitterly superstitious woman, just such as we would have expected to encourage Pharaoh in "hardening his heart" against Jehovah. But the chain of coincidences does not break even here. From the Egyptian documents we learn that in the preceding reign—that is, just before the children of Israel entered the desert of Sinai—the Egyptians ceased to occupy the mines which they had till then worked in that peninsula. Further, we learn that, during the latter part of Israel's stay in the wilderness, the Egyptian king, Thothmes III., carried on and completed his wars in Canaan, and that just immediately before the entry of Israel into Palestine the great confederacy of Canaanitish kings against him was quite broken up. This explains the state in which Joshua found the country, so different from that compact power which forty years before had inspired the spies with such terror; and also helps us to understand how, at the time of Joshua, each petty king just held his own city and district, and how easily the fear of a nation, by which even the dreaded

Pharaoh and his host had perished, would fall upon the inhabitants of the land (compare also Balaam's words in Numb.
xxiii. 22 ; xxiv. 8).   We may not here follow this connection
between the two histories any farther.   But all through the
troubled period of the early Judges down to Barak and
Deborah, Egyptian history, as deciphered from the monuments,
affords constant illustration and confirmation of the state of
Canaan and the history of Israel, as described in the Bible.
Thus did Providence work for the carrying out of God's
purposes, and so remarkably does He in our days raise up
witnesses for His Word, where their testimony might least have
been expected.

We remember that Abram was at the first driven by famine
into Egypt.   The same cause also led the brothers of Joseph
to seek there corn for their sustenance.   For, from the earliest
times, Egypt was the great granary of the old world.   The
extraordinary fertility of the country depends, as is well
known, on the annual overflow of the Nile, caused in its turn
by rains in the highlands of Abyssinia and Central Africa.   So
far as the waters of the Nile cover the soil, the land is like a
fruitful garden ; beyond it all is desolate wilderness.   Even in
that "land of wonders," as Egypt has been termed, the Nile is
one of the grand outstanding peculiarities.   Another, as we
have seen, consists in its monuments.   These two landmarks
may conveniently serve to group together what our space will
still allow us to say of the country and its people.

The name of the country, Egypt (in Greek *Ai-gyptos*),
exactly corresponds to the Egyptian designation *Kah-Ptah*,
"the land of Ptah"—one of their gods—and from it the name
of *Copts* seems also derived.   In the Hebrew Scriptures its
name is *Mizraim*, that is, "the two *Mazors*," which again
corresponds with another Egyptian name for the country,
Chem (the same as "the land of Ham"[1]), both *Mazor* and
Chem meaning in their respective languages the red mud or
dark soil of which the cultivated part of the country consisted.

[1] Ps. cv. 23, 27.

It was called "the two Mazors," probably because of its ancient division into Upper and Lower Egypt. The king of Upper Egypt was designated by a title whose initial sign was a bent reed, which illustrates such passages as 2 Kings xviii. 21 ; Isaiah xxxvi. 6 ; Ezekiel xxix. 6 ; while the rulers of Lower Egypt bore the title of " bee," which may be referred to in Isaiah vii. 18.[1] The country occupies less than 10,000 square geographical miles, of which about 5,600 are at present, and about 8,000 were anciently, fit for cultivation. Scripture history has chiefly to do with Lower Egypt, which is the northern part of the country, while the most magnificent of the monuments are in Upper, or Southern, Egypt.

As already stated, the fertility of the land depends on the overflowing of the Nile, which commences to rise about the middle of June, and reaches its greatest height about the end of September, when it again begins to decrease. As measured at Cairo, if the Nile does not rise twenty-four feet, the harvest will not be very good; anything under eighteen threatens famine. About the middle of August the red, turbid waters of the rising river are distributed by canals over the country, and carry fruitfulness with them. On receding, the Nile leaves behind it a thick red soil, which its waters had carried from Central Africa, and over this rich deposit the seed is sown. Rain there is none, nor is there need for it to fertilise the land. The Nile also furnishes the most pleasant and even nourishing water for drinking, and some physicians have ascribed to it healing virtues. It is scarcely necessary to add that the river teems with fish. Luxuriously rich and green, amidst surrounding desolation, the banks of the Nile and of its numerous canals are like a well-watered garden under a tropical sky. Where climate and soil are the best conceivable, the fertility must be unparalleled. The ancient Egyptians seem to have also bestowed great attention on their fruit and flower gardens, which, like ours, were attached to their villas. On the monuments we see gardeners presenting handsome bouquets;

See also the article " Egypt " in Dr. Smith's *Dictionary of the Bible.*

gardens traversed by alleys, and adorned with pavilions and colonnades; orchards stocked with palms, figs, pomegranates, citrons, oranges, plums, mulberries, apricots, etc. ; while in the vineyards, as in Italy, the vines were trained to meet across wooden rods, and hang down in rich festoons. Such was the land on which, in the desolate dreariness and famine of the wilderness, Israel was tempted to look back with sinful longing !

When Abram entered Egypt, his attention, like that of the modern traveller, must have been riveted by the Great Pyramids. Of these about sixty have been counted, but the largest are those near the ancient Memphis, which lay about ten miles above Cairo. Memphis—in Scripture Noph[1]—was the capital of Lower, as Thebes that of Upper, Egypt—the latter being the Pathros of Scripture.[2] It is scarcely possible to convey an adequate idea of the pyramids. Imagine a structure covering at the base an area of some 65,000 feet, and slanting upwards for 600 feet;[3] or, to give a better idea than these figures convey, "more than half as long on every side as Westminster Abbey, eighty feet higher than the top of St. Paul's, covering thirteen acres of ground, and computed to have contained nearly seven million tons of solid masonry !"[4] We cannot here enter on the various purposes intended by these wonderful structures, some of which, at any rate, were scientific. Not far from the great pyramids was the ancient On, connected with the history of Joseph, and where Moses probably got his early training. But all hereabout is full of deepest interest—sepulchres, monuments, historical records, and sites of ancient cities. We are in a land of dreams, and all the surroundings bear dreamy outlines ; gigantic in their proportions, and rendered even more gigantic by the manner in which they are disposed. Probably the most magnificent of these monuments in Upper Egypt—the Pathros of Scripture

[1] Is. xix. 13 ; Jer. ii. 16 ; xlvi. 14, 19 ; Ezek. xxx. 13, 16.
[2] Is. xi. 11 ; Jer. xliv. 1, 15.   [3] The perpendicular height is 479 feet.
[4] Canon Trevor, *Ancient Egypt*, p. 40.

—are those of its capital, Thebes, the No, or No Amon of the Bible.[1] It were impossible in brief space to describe its temple. The sanctuary itself was small, but opposite to it a court opened upon a hall into which the great cathedral of Paris might be placed, without touching the walls on either side! One hundred and forty columns support this hall, the central pillars being sixty-six feet high, and so wide that it would take six men with extended arms to embrace one of them. The mind gets almost bewildered by such proportions. All around, the walls bear representations, inscriptions, and records—among others, those of Shishak, who captured Jerusalem during the reign of Rehoboam. But the temple itself is almost insignificant when compared with the approach to it, which was through a double row of sixty or seventy ram-headed sphinxes, placed about eleven feet apart from each other. Another avenue led to a temple which enclosed a lake for funeral rites; and yet a third avenue of sphinxes extended a distance of 6000 feet to a palace. These notices are selected to give some faint idea of the magnificence of Egypt.

It would be difficult to form too high an estimate of the old-world culture and civilisation, here laid open before us. The laws of Egypt seem to have been moderate and wise; its manners simple and domestic; its people contented, prosperous, and cultured. Woman occupied a very high place, and polygamy was almost the exception. Science, literature, and the arts were cultivated; commerce and navigation carried on, while a brave army and an efficient fleet maintained the power of the Pharaohs. Altogether the country seems old in its civilisation, when alike the earliest sages of Greece and the lawgivers of Israel learned of its wisdom. But how different the use which Israel was to make of it from that to which the philosophers put their lore! What was true, good, and serviceable was to enter as an element into the life of Israel. But this life was formed and moulded quite .differently from that of Egypt. Israel as a nation was born of God; redeemed

[1] Jer. xlvi. 25 ; Ezek. xxx. 14–16 ; Nah. iii. 8.

by God; brought forth by God victorious on the other side the flood; taught of God; trained by God; and separated for the service of God. And this God was to be known to them as Jehovah, the living and the true God. The ideas they had gained, the knowledge they had acquired, the life they had learned, even the truths they had heard in Egypt, might be taken with them, but, as it were, to be baptised in the Red Sea, and consecrated at the foot of Sinai. Quite behind them in the far distance lay the Egypt they had quitted, with its dreamy, gigantic outlines. As the sand carried from the desert would cover the land, so did the dust of superstition gradually bury the old truths. We are ready to admit that Israel profited by what they had seen and learned. But all the more striking is the final contrast between Egyptian superstition, which ultimately degraded itself to make gods of almost everything in nature, and the glorious, spiritual worship of the Israel of God. That contrast meets us side by side with the resemblance to what was in Egypt, and becomes all the more evident by the juxtaposition. Never is the religion of Israel more strikingly the opposite to that of Egypt than where we discover resemblances between the two; and never are their laws and institutions more really dissimilar than when we trace an analogy between them. Israel may have adopted and adapted much from Egypt, but it *learned* only from the Lord God, who, in every sense of the expression, *brought out* His people with a mighty hand, and an outstretched arm!

NOTE ON THE BOOK OF EXODUS.

For a clearer understanding, a general outline of the Book of Exodus may here be given. Like Genesis (see *Hist. of the Patriarchs*, Introd. p. xv.), it consists of two great Parts, the first describing the *redemption* of Israel, and the ·second the *consecration* of Israel as the *people of God*. The first Part (ch. i.–xv. 21) appropriately ends with "the Song of Moses;" while, similarly, the second Part closes with the erection and consecration of the Tabernacle, in which Jehovah was to dwell in the midst of His people, and to hold fellowship with them.

Again, each of these two Parts may be arranged into *seven* Sections (*seven* being the covenant number), as follows :

Part I. : 1. Preparatory : Israel increases, and is oppressed in Egypt (i.) ; birth and preservation of a deliverer (ii.) ;

2. The calling and training of Moses (iii. iv.) ;

3. His mission to Pharaoh (v.–vii. 7) ;

4. The signs and wonders (vii. 8–xi.) ;

5. Israel is set apart by the Passover, and led forth (xii.–xiii. 16) ;

6. Passage of the Red Sea and destruction of Pharaoh (xiii. 17–xiv.) ;

7. Song ot triumph on the other side (xv. 1–21).

The seven sections of Part II. are as follows :

1. March of the children of Israel to the Mount of God (xv. 22–xvii. 7) ;

2. Twofold attitude of the Gentile nations towards Israel : the enmity of Amalek, and the friendship of Jethro (xvii. 8–xviii.) ;

3. The covenant at Sinai (xix.–xxiv. 11) ;

4. Divine directions about making the Tabernacle (xxiv. 12–xxxi.) ;

5. Apostasy of Israel, and their restoration to be the people of God (xxxii.–xxxiv.) ;

6. Actual construction of the Tabernacle and of its vessels (xxxv.–xxxix.);

7. The setting up and consecration of the Tabernacle (xl.), the latter corresponding, as closing section of Part II., to the Song of Moses (xv.), with which the first part had ended (see Keil, *Bibel Com.*, vol. i., pp. 302–311).

The reader will note these parts and sections in his Bible, and mark what grandeur and unity there is in the plan of the Book of Exodus, and how fully it realises the idea of telling the story ot the kingdom of God.

CHAPTER II.

The Children of Israel in Egypt—Their Residences, Occupations, Social Arrangements, Constitution, and Religion—"A new King who knew not Joseph."

(EXODUS I. to end.)

THREE centuries and a half intervened between the close of the Book of Genesis and the events with which that of Exodus opens. But during that long period the history of the children of Israel is almost an entire blank. The names of their families have come down to us, but without any chronicle of their history; their final condition at the time of the Exodus is marked, but without any notice of their social or national development. Except for a few brief allusions scattered through the Old Testament, we should know absolutely nothing of their state, their life, or their religion, during all that interval. This silence of three and a half centuries is almost awful in its grandeur, like the loneliness of Sinai, the mount of God.

Two things had been foretold as marking this period, and these two alone appear as outstanding facts in the Biblical narrative. On the boundary of the Holy Land the Lord had encouraged Israel :· "Fear not to go down into Egypt; for I will there make of thee a great nation."[1] And the Book of Exodus opens with the record that this promise had been fulfilled, for "the children of Israel were fruitful, and increased abundantly, and multiplied, and waxed exceeding mighty ; and the land was filled with them."[2] Yet another prediction, made centuries before to Abram, was to be fulfilled. His seed was to be "a stranger in a land not theirs," to be enslaved and afflicted.[3] And as the appointed centuries were drawing to a close, there "arose up a new king over Egypt," who "evil entreated our fathers."[4] Thus, in the darkest period of their

[1] Gen. xlvi. 3.   [2] Ex. i. 7.   [3] Gen. xv. 13-16.   [4] Acts vii. 19.

bondage, Israel might have understood that, as surely as these two predictions had been literally fulfilled, so would the twofold promise also prove true : " I will bring thee up again," and that " with great substance." And here we see a close analogy to the present condition of the Jews. In both cases the promised future stands in marked contrast to the actual state of things. But, like Israel of old, we also have the "more sure word of prophecy," as a "light that shineth in a dark place until the day dawn."

The closing years of the three and a half centuries since their entrance into Egypt found Israel peaceful, prosperous, and probably, in many respects, assimilated to the Egyptians around. " The fathers " had fallen asleep, but their children still held undisturbed possession of the district originally granted them. The land of Goshen, in which they were located, is to this day considered the richest province of Egypt, and could, even now, easily support a million more inhabitants than it numbers.[1] Goshen extended between the most eastern of the ancient seven mouths of the Nile and Palestine. The border-land was probably occupied by the more nomadic branches of the family of Israel, to whose flocks its wide tracts would afford excellent pasturage ; while the rich banks along the Nile and its canals were the chosen residence of those who pursued agriculture. Most likely such would also soon swarm across to the western banks of the Nile, where we find traces of them in various cities of the land.[2] There they would acquire a knowledge of the arts and industries of the Egyptians. It seems quite natural that, in a country which held out such inducements for it, the majority of the Israelites should have forsaken their original pursuits of shepherds, and become agriculturists. To this day a similar change has been noticed in the nomads who settle in Egypt. Nor was their new life entirely foreign to their history. Their ancestor, Isaac, had, during his stay among the Philistines, sowed and reaped.[3] Besides, at their

---

[1] Robinson's *Bibl. Res.* (2nd ed.) vol. i., p. 54.
[2] **Ex.** xii. [3] Gen. xxvi. 12.

settlement in Egypt, the grant of land—and that the best in
the country—had been made to them "for a possession," a term
implying fixed and hereditary proprietorship.[1]   Their later
reminiscences of Egypt accord with this view.   In the wilderness
they looked back with sinful longing to the time when they had
cast their nets into the Nile, and drawn them in weighted with
fish ; and when their gardens and fields by the waterside had
yielded rich crops—" the cucumbers, and the melons, and the
leeks, and the onions, and the garlick."[2]   And afterwards, when
Moses described to them the land which they were to inherit,
he contrasted its cultivation with their past experience of
Egypt, "where thou sowedst thy seed, and wateredst it with
thy foot, as a garden of herbs."[3]   As further evidence of this
change from pastoral to agricultural pursuits, it has also been
remarked that, whereas the patriarchs had possessed camels,
no allusion is made to them in the narrative of their descendants.   No doubt this change of occupation served a higher
purpose.   For settlement and agriculture imply civilisation, such
as was needed to prepare Israel for becoming a nation.

In point of fact, we have evidence that they had acquired most
of the arts and industries of ancient Egypt.   The preparation
of the various materials for the Tabernacle, as well as its construction, imply this.   Again, we have such direct statements,
as, for example, that some of the families of Judah were "carpenters"[4] (1 Chron. iv. 14), "weavers of fine Egyptian linen"
(ver. 21), and "potters" (ver. 23).   These must, of course, be
regarded as only instances of the various trades learned in
Egypt.   Nor was the separation between Israel and the
Egyptians such as to amount to isolation.   Goshen would, of
course, be chiefly, but not exclusively, inhabited by Israelites.
These would mingle even in the agricultural districts, but,
naturally, much more in the towns, with their Egyptian neighbours.   Accordingly, it needed the Paschal provision of the

[1] Gen. xlvii. 11, 27.   [2] Numb. xi. 5.   [3] Deut. xi. 10.
[4] The reference is probably to "guilds," such as in Egypt. The word
rendered in our Authorised Version "craftsmen," means "carpenters."

blood to distinguish the houses of the Israelites from those of the Egyptians ;[1] while Exodus iii. 22 seems to imply that they were not only neighbours, but perhaps, occasionally, residents in the same houses. This also accounts for the "mixed multitude" that accompanied Israel at the Exodus, and, later on, in the wilderness, for the presence in the congregation of offspring from marriages between Jewish women and Egyptian husbands.[2]

While the greater part of Israel had thus acquired the settled habits of a nation, the inhabitants of the border-district between Goshen and Canaan continued their nomadic life. This explains how the tribes of Reuben, Gad, and Manasseh possessed so much larger flocks than their brethren, as afterwards to claim the wide pasture-lands to the east of Jordan.[3] We have, also, among the records of "ancient stories,"[4] a notice of some of the descendants of Judah exercising lordship in Moab, and we read of a predatory incursion into Gath on the part of some of the descendants of Ephraim, which terminated fatally.[5] It is but fair to assume that these are only instances, mentioned, the one on account of its signal success, the other on that of its failure, and that both imply nomadic habits and incursions into Canaan on the part of those who inhabited the border-land.

But whether nomadic or settled, Israel preserved its ancient *constitution* and *religion*, though here also we notice modifications and adaptations, arising from their long settlement in Egypt. The original division of Israel was into *twelve tribes*, after the twelve sons of Jacob, an arrangement which continued, although the sons of Joseph became two tribes (Ephraim and Manasseh), since the priestly tribe of Levi had no independent political standing. These twelve tribes were again subdivided into *families* (or rather clans), mostly founded by the grandsons of Jacob, of which we find a record in Numb. xxvi., and which amounted in all to sixty. From Joshua vii. 14 we learn that

---

[1] Ex. xii. 13.
[2] Lev. xxiv. 10.
[3] Numb. xxxii. 1–4.
[4] I Chron. iv. 22.
[5] The passage I Chron. vii. 21 is involved and difficult. But the best critics have understood it as explained in the text.

those "families" had at that time, if not earlier, branched into
"households," and these again into what is described by the
expression "man by man" (in the Hebrew, *Gevarim*). The
latter term, however, is really equivalent to our "family," as
appears from a comparison of Josh. vii. 14 with vers. 17, 18.
Thus we have in the oldest times *tribes* and *clans*, and in those
of Joshua, if not earlier, the clans again branching into *households* (kin) and *families*. The "heads" of those clans and
families were their chiefs; those of the *tribes*, "the princes."[1]
These twelve princes were "the rulers of the congregation."[2]
By the side of these rulers, who formed a *hereditary aristocracy*,
we find two classes of *elective officials*,[3] as "representatives" of
"the congregation."[4] These are designated in Deut. xxix. 10,
as the "elders" and the "officers," or, rather, "scribes." Thus
the rule of the people was jointly committed to the "princes,"
the "elders," and the "officers."[5] The institution of "elders"
and of "scribes" had already existed among the children of
Israel in Egypt before the time of Moses. For Moses "gathered
the elders of Israel together," to announce to them his Divine
commission,[6] and through them he afterwards communicated
to the people the ordinance of the Passover.[7] The mention of
"scribes" as "officers" occurs even earlier than that of elders,
and to them, as the lettered class, the Egyptian taskmasters
seem to have entrusted the superintendence of the appointed
labours of the people.[8] From the monuments of Egypt we
know what an important part "the scribes" played in that

---

[1] Numb. i. 4, 16, 44; ii. 3, etc.; vii. 10.

[2] Ex. xxxiv. 31; Numb. vii. 2; xxx. 1; xxxi. 13; xxxii. 2; xxxiv. 18.

[3] Comp. Deut i. 9–14.   [4] Numb. xxvii. 2.

[5] See also Deut. xxxi. 28. In the wilderness a meeting of these three
classes of rulers seems to have been called by blowing the *two* silver
trumpets, while blasts from one summoned only a council of the princes
(Numb. x. 3, 4). It deserves special notice that this mixed rule of hereditary
and elective officials continued the constitutional government of the people,
not only during the period of the Judges, but under the Kings. We find
its analogy also in the rule of the Synagogue.

[6] Ex. iii. 16; iv. 29.   [7] Ex. xii. 21.   [8] Ex. v. 6, 14, 15, 19.

country, and how constantly their mention recurs. Possibly, the order of scribes may have been thus introduced among Israel. As the lettered class, the scribes would naturally be the intermediaries between their brethren and the Egyptians. We may, therefore, regard them also as the representatives of learning, alike Israelitish and Egyptian. That the art of writing was known to the Israelites at the time of Moses is now generally admitted. Indeed, Egyptian learning had penetrated into Canaan itself, and Joshua found its inhabitants mostly in a very advanced state of civilisation, one of the towns bearing even the name of *Kirjath-sepher*, the city of books, or *Kirjath-sannah*, which might almost be rendered " university town."[1]

In reference to the *religion* of Israel, it is important to bear in mind that, during the three and a half centuries since the death of Jacob, all direct communication from Heaven, whether by prophecy or in vision, had so far as we know, wholly ceased. Even the birth of Moses was not Divinely intimated. In these circumstances the children of Israel were cast upon that knowledge which they had acquired from "the fathers," and which, undoubtedly, was preserved among them. It need scarcely be explained, although it shows the wisdom of God's providential arrangements, that the simple patriarchal forms of worship would suit the circumstances in Egypt much better than those which the religion of Israel afterwards received. *Three great observances* here stand out prominently. Around them the faith and the worship alike of the ancient patriarchs, and afterwards of Israel, may be said to have clustered. They are : *circumcision, sacrifices*, and the *Sabbath*. We have direct testimony that the rite of circumcision was observed by Israel in Egypt.[2] As to *sacrifices*, even the proposal to celebrate a great sacrificial feast in the wilderness,[3] implies that sacrificial worship had maintained its hold upon the people. Lastly, the direction to gather on the Friday two days' provision of manna,[4] and the introduction of the Sabbath command by the word

[1] Josh. xv. 15, 49. [2] Ex. iv. 24-26 ; Josh. v. 5.
[3] Ex. viii. 25-28. [4] Ex. xvi. 22.

"Remember,"[1] convey the impression of previous *Sabbath observance* on the part of Israel. Indeed, the manner in which many things, as, for example, the practice of vows, are spoken of in the law, seems to point back to previous religious rites among Israel.

Thus far for those outward observances, which indicate how, even during those centuries of silence and loneliness in Egypt, Israel still cherished the fundamental truths of their ancestral religion. But there is yet another matter, bearing reference not to their articles of belief or their observances, but to the religious life of the family and of individuals in Israel. This appears in the *names* given by parents to their children during the long and hard bondage of Egypt. It is well known what significance attaches in the Old Testament to *names*. Every spiritually important event gave its new and characteristic name to a person or locality. Sometimes—as in the case of Abram, Sarai, and Jacob—it was God Himself Who gave such new name ; at others, it was the expression of hearts that recognised the special and decisive interposition of God, or else breathed out their hopes and experiences, as in the case of Moses' sons. But any one who considers such frequently recurring names among "the princes" of Israel, as *Eliasaph* (my God that gathers), *Elizur* (my God a rock), and others of kindred import, will gather how deep the hope of Israel had struck its roots in the hearts and convictions of the people. This point will be further referred to in the sequel. Meantime, we only call attention to the names of the chiefs of the three families of the Levites : *Eliasaph* (my God that gathers), *Elizaphan* (my God that watcheth all around), and *Zuriel* (my rock is God)—the Divine Name (*El*) being the same by which God had revealed Himself to the fathers.

Besides their own inherited rites, the children of Israel may have learned many things from the Egyptians, or been strengthened in them. And here, by the side of resemblance, we also observe marked contrast between them. We have already seen

[1] Ex. xx. 8.

that, originally, the religion of the Egyptians had contained much of truth, which, however, was gradually perverted to super stition. The Egyptians and Israel might hold the same truths, but with the difference of understanding and application between dim tradition and clear Divine revelation. Thus, both Israel and the Egyptians believed in the great doctrines of the immortality of the soul, and of future rewards and punishments. But, in connection with this, Israel was taught another lesson, far more difficult to our faith, and which the ancient Egyptians had never learned, that God is the God of the *present* as well as of the future, and that even here on earth He *reigneth*, dispensing good and evil. And perhaps it was owing to this that the temporal consequences of sin were so much insisted upon in the Mosaic law. There was no special need to refer to the consequences in another life. The Egyptians, as well as Israel, acknowledged the latter, but the Egyptians knew not the former. Yet this new truth would teach Israel constantly to realise Jehovah as the living and the true God. On the other hand, the resemblances between certain institutions of Israel and of Egypt clearly prove that the Law was not given at a later period, but to those who came out from Egypt, and immediately upon their leaving it. At the same time, much evil was also acquired by intercourse with the Egyptians. In certain provisions of the Pentateuch we discover allusions, not only to the moral corruptions witnessed, and perhaps learned, in Egypt, but also to the idolatrous practices common there. Possibly, it was not the gorgeous ritual of Egypt which made such deep impression, but the services constantly there witnessed may have gradually accustomed the mind to the worship of nature. As instances of this tendency among Israel, we remember the worship of the golden calf,[1] the warning against sacrificing unto the "he-goat,"[2] and the express admonition, even of Joshua (xxiv. 14), to "put away the strange gods" which their "fathers served on the other side of the flood." To the same

[1] Ex. xxxii.
[2] Lev. xvii. 7. Erroneously rendered in our Authorised Version "devils."

effect is the retrospect in Ezek. xx. 5–8, in Amos v. 26, and in
the address of Stephen before the Jewish council.[1]   Yet it is
remarkable that, although the forms of idolatry here referred to
were all practised in Egypt, there is good reason for believing
that they were not, so to speak, strictly Egyptian in their origin,
but rather foreign rites imported, probably from the Phenicians.[2]

Such then was the political, social, and religious state of
Israel, when their long peace was suddenly interrupted by
tidings that Aahmes I. was successfully making war against the
foreign dynasty of the Hyksos.   Advancing victoriously, he at
last took Avaris, the great stronghold and capital of the
Shepherd kings, and expelled them and their adherents from
the country.   He then continued his progress to the borders of
Canaan, taking many cities by storm.   The memorials of the
disastrous rule of the Shepherds were speedily removed; the
worship which they had introduced was abolished, and the old
Egyptian forms were restored.   A reign of great prosperity now
ensued.

Although there is difference of opinion on the subject, yet
every likelihood (as shown in the previous chapter) seems to
attach to the belief that the accession of this new dynasty was
the period when the "king arose who knew not Joseph."[3]   For
reasons already explained, one of the first and most important
measures of his internal administration would necessarily be to
weaken the power of the foreign settlers, who were in such vast
majority in the border province of Goshen.   He dreaded lest,
in case of foreign war, they might join the enemy, "and get

[1] Acts vii. 43.

[2] This is very ably argued by Mr. R. J. Poole in Smith's *Dict. of the
Bible*, vol. iii. "Remphan."

[3] The Hebrew word "arose" is almost always used to describe a new
commencement (as in Deut. xxxiv. 10); the word "new" occurs in
connection with an entire change (as in Deut. xxxii. 17; Judges v. 8),
while the expression, "knew not" (Deut. xxviii. 36) is applied not so much
to absolute want of knowledge, as to the absence of *friendly* acquaintance-
ship.   If this king began a new dynasty, he must have been either the
first of the Hyksos or else of those who expelled them.   As the former
assumption is almost impossible, we are shut up to the latter.

them up out of the land." The latter apprehension also shows that the king must have known the circumstances under which they had at first settled in the land. Again, from the monuments of Egypt, it appears to have been at all times the policy of the Pharaohs to bring an immense number of captives into Egypt, and to retain them there in servitude for forced labours. A somewhat similar policy was now pursued towards Israel. Although allowed to retain their flocks and fields, they were set to hard labour for the king. Egyptian "taskmasters" were appointed over them, who "made the children of Israel serve with rigour," and did "afflict them with their burdens." A remarkable illustration of this is seen in one of the Egyptian monuments. Labourers, who are evidently foreigners, and supposed to represent Israelites, are engaged in the various stages of brickmaking, under the superintendence of four Egyptians, two of whom are apparently superior officers, while the other two are overseers armed with heavy lashes, who cry out, " Work without fainting !" The work in which the Israelites were employed consisted of brickmaking, artificial irrigation of the land, including, probably, also the digging or restoring of canals, and the building, or restoring and enlarging of the two " magazine-cities "[1] of Pithom and Raamses, whose localities have been traced in Goshen, and which served as depôts both for commerce and for the army. According to Greek historians it was the boast of the Egyptians that, in their great works, they only employed captives and slaves, never their own people. But Aahmes I. had special need of Israelitish labour, since we learn from an inscription, dating from his twenty-second year, that he was largely engaged in restoring the temples and buildings destroyed by the " Shepherds."

But this first measure of the Pharaohs against Israel produced the opposite result from what had been expected. So far from diminishing, their previous vast growth went on in increased ratio, so that the Egyptians " were sorely afraid[2] (alarmed) because of

---

[1] This, and not "treasure-cities," is the literal rendering.

[2] The expression is the same as in Numb. xxii. 3, and implies " to be struck with awe."

the children of Israel."[1] Accordingly Pharaoh resorted to a second measure, by which all male children, as they were born, were to be destroyed, probably unknown to their parents. But the two Hebrew women, who, as we suppose, were at the head of "the guild" of midwives, do not seem to have communicated the king's order to their subordinates. At any rate, the command was not executed. Scripture has preserved the names of these courageous women, and told us that their motive was "fear of God" (in the Hebrew with the article, "the God," as denoting the living and true God). And as they were the means of "making" or upbuilding the houses of Israel, so God "made them houses." It is true that, when challenged by the king. they failed to speak out their true motive ; but, as St. Augustine remarks, "God forgave the evil on account of the good, and rewarded their piety, though not their deceit."

How little indeed any merely human device could have averted the ruin of Israel, appears from the third measure which Pharaoh now adopted. Putting aside every restraint, and forgetting, in his determination, even his interests, the king issued a general order to cast every Jewish male child, as it was born, into the Nile. Whether this command, perhaps given in anger, was not enforced for any length of time, or the Egyptians were unwilling permanently to lend themselves to such cruelty, or the Israelites found means of preserving their children from this danger, certain it is, that, while many must have suffered, and all needed to use the greatest precautions, this last ruthless attempt to exterminate Israel also proved vain.

Thus the two prophecies *had* been fulfilled. Even under the most adverse circumstances Israel had so increased as to fill the Egyptians with alarm ; and the "affliction" of Israel had reached its highest point. And now the promised deliverance was also to appear. As in so many instances, it came in what men would call the most unlikely manner.

[1] Ex. i. 12.

CHAPTER III.

The Birth, and the Training of Moses, both in Egypt and in Midian, as Preparatory to his Calling.

(EXODUS II.)

To the attentive reader of Scripture it will not seem strange—only remarkable—that the very measure which Pharaoh had taken for the destruction of Israel eventually led to their deliverance. Had it not been for the command to cast the Hebrew children into the river, Moses would not have been rescued by Pharaoh's daughter, nor trained in all the wisdom of Egypt to fit him for his calling. Yet all throughout, this marvellous story pursues a *natural* course; that is, natural in its progress, but supernatural in its purposes and results.

A member of the tribe of Levi, and descendant of Kohath,[1] *Amram* by name, had married *Jochebed*, who belonged to the same tribe. Their union had already been blessed with two children, Miriam and Aaron,[2] when the murderous edict of Pharaoh was issued. The birth of their next child brought them the more sorrow and care, that the " exceeding fairness " of the child not only won their hearts, but seemed to point him out as destined of God for some special purpose.[3] In this struggle of affection and hope against the fear of man, they obtained the victory, as victory is always obtained, " by faith." There was no special revelation made to them, nor was there need for it. It was a simple question of faith, weighing the

[1] Ex. vi. 20 ; Numb. xxvi. 59.
[2] The narrative implies that they were born before the murderous edict. Aaron was three years older than Moses (Ex. vii. 7), while Miriam was grown up when Moses was exposed (Ex. ii. 4).
[3] The expression in Acts vii. 20 is " fair before God."

command of Pharaoh against the command of God and their own hopes. They resolved to trust the living God of their fathers, and to brave all seeming danger. It was in this sense that " by faith Moses, when he was born, was hid three months of his parents, because they saw he was a proper child ; and they were not afraid of the king's commandment." Longer concealment at home being impossible, the same confidence of faith now led the mother to lay the child in an ark made, as at that time the light Nile-boats used to be, of " bulrushes," or papyrus—a strong three-cornered rush, that grew to a height of about ten or fifteen feet.[1] The "ark"—a term used in Scripture only here and in connection with the deliverance of Noah by an " ark "—was made tight within by " slime "— either Nile-mud or asphalt—and impenetrable to water by a coating of " pitch." Thus protected, the " ark," with its precious burden, was deposited among " the flags " in the brink, or lip of the river, just where Pharaoh's daughter was wont to bathe, though the sacred text does not expressly inform us whether or not this spot was purposely chosen.

The allusion in Ps. lxxviii. 12, to the " marvellous things " done " in the field of Zoan," may perhaps guide us to the very scene of this deliverance. Zoan, as we know, was the ancient *Avaris*, the capital of the Shepherd kings, which the new dynasty had taken from them. The probability that it would continue the residence of the Pharaohs, the more so as it lay on the eastern boundary of Goshen, is confirmed by the circumstance that in those days, of all the ancient Egyptian residences, Avaris or Zoan alone lay on an arm of the Nile which was not infested by crocodiles, and where the princess therefore could bathe. There is a curious illustration on one of the Egyptian monuments of the scene described in the rescue of

---

[1] Everything here is strictly Egyptian ; even some of the terms used in the Hebrew are derived from the Egyptian. The papyrus no longer grows below Nubia, but the Egyptian monuments exhibit many such " arks " and boats made of the plant, and similarly prepared. The " flags " were a smaller species of papyrus.

Moses. A noble lady is represented bathing in the river with four of her maidens attending upon her, just like the daughter of Pharaoh in the story of Moses. But to return—the discovery of the ark, and the weeping of the babe, as the stranger lifted him, are all true to nature. The princess is touched by the appeal of the child to her woman's feelings. She compassionates him none the less that he is one of the doomed race. To have thrown the weeping child into the river would have been inhuman. Pharaoh's daughter acted as every woman would have done in the circumstances.[1] To save *one* Hebrew child could be no very great crime in the king's daughter. Moreover, curiously enough, we learn from the monuments, that just at that very time the royal princesses exercised special influence—in fact, that two of them were co-regents. So when, just at the opportune moment, Miriam, who all along had watched at a little distance, came forward and proposed to call some Hebrew woman to nurse the weeping child—this strange gift, bestowed as it were by the Nile-god himself on the princess,[2]—she readily consented. The nurse called was, of course, the child's own mother, who received her babe now as a precious charge, entrusted to her care by the daughter of him who would have compassed his destruction. So marvellous are the ways of God.

One of the old church-writers has noted that "the daughter of Pharaoh is the community of the Gentiles," thereby meaning to illustrate this great truth, which we trace throughout history, that somehow the salvation of Israel was always connected with the instrumentality of the Gentiles. It was so in the history of Joseph, and even before that; and it will continue so till at the last, through their mercy, Israel shall obtain mercy.

[1] In what is commonly known as *The Speaker's Commentary*, an illustration of this is given from the so-called *Ritual for the Dead*, the most ancient existing religious record of Egypt. It seems that one of the things which the disembodied spirit had to answer before the Lord of truth was this: "I have not afflicted any man ; I have not made any man weep ; I have not withheld milk from the mouth of sucklings."

[2] The Egyptians worshipped the Nile as a god.

But meanwhile a precious opportunity was afforded to those believing Hebrew parents to mould the mind of the adopted son of the princess of Egypt. The three first years of life, the common eastern time for nursing, are often, even in our northern climes, where development is so much slower, a period decisive for after life. It requires no stretch of imagination to conceive what the child Moses would learn at his mother's knee, and hear among his persecuted people. When a child so preserved and so trained found himself destined to step from his Hebrew home to the court of Pharaoh—his mind full or the promises made to the fathers, and his heart heavy with the sorrows of his brethren,—it seems almost natural that thoughts of future deliverance of his people through him should gradually rise in his soul. Many of our deepest purposes have their root in earliest childhood, and the lessons then learnt, and the thoughts then conceived, have been steadily carried out to the end of our lives.

Yet, as in all deepest life-purpose, there was no rashness about carrying it into execution. When Jochebed brought the child back to the princess, the latter gave her adopted son the Egyptian name "Moses," which, curiously enough, appears also in several of the old Egyptian papyri, among others, as that of one of the royal princes. The word means " brought forth," or " drawn out," " because," as she said in giving the name, " I drew him out of the water."[1] But for the present Moses would probably not reside in the royal palace at Avaris. St. Stephen tells us[2] that he " was instructed in all the wisdom of the Egyptians." In no country was such value attached to education, nor was it begun so early as in Egypt. No sooner was a child weaned than it was sent to school, and instructed by regularly appointed scribes. As writing was not by letters, but by hieroglyphics, which might be either pictorial representations, or symbols (a sceptre for a king,

---

[1] Others have derived it from two old Egyptian words which literally mean, " water," " saved."

[2] Acts vii. 22.

etc.), or a kind of phonetic signs, and as there seem to have been hieroglyphics for single letters, for syllables, and for words, that art alone must, from its complication, have taken almost a lifetime to master it perfectly. But beyond this, education was carried to a very great length, and, in the case of those destined for the higher professions, embraced not only the various sciences, as mathematics, astronomy, chemistry, medicine, etc., but theology, philosophy, and a knowledge of the laws. There can be no doubt that, as the adopted son of the princess, Moses would receive the highest training. Scripture tells us that, in consequence, he was " mighty in his words and deeds," and we may take the statement in its simplicity, without entering upon the many Jewish and Egyptian legends which extol his wisdom, and his military and other achievements.

Thus the first forty years of Moses' life passed. Undoubtedly, had he been so minded, a career higher even than that of Joseph might have been open to him. But, before entering it, he had to decide that one great preliminary question, with whom he would cast in his lot—with Egypt or with Israel, with the world or the promises. As so often happens, the providence of God here helped him to a clear, as the grace of God to a right, decision. In the actual circumstances of Hebrew persecution it was impossible at the same time " to be called the son of Pharaoh's daughter " and to have part, as one of them, " with the people of God." The one meant " the pleasures of sin " and " the treasures of Egypt "—enjoyment and honours, the other implied " affliction " and " the reproach of Christ "— or suffering and that obloquy which has always attached to Christ and to His people, and at that time especially, to those who clung to the covenant of which Christ was the substance.

But " faith," which is " the substance of things hoped for, the evidence of things not seen," enabled Moses not only to "refuse" what Egypt held out, but to " choose rather the affliction," and, more than that, to " esteem the reproach of Christ greater riches than the treasures of Egypt," because " he had respect unto the recompence of the reward."[1]   In this spirit " he went out unto his brethren, and looked on their burdens." [2]   But his faith, though deep and genuine, was as yet far from pure and spiritual. The ancient Egyptians were noted for the severity of their discipline, and their monuments represent the " taskmasters " armed with heavy scourges, made of tough bending wood, which they unmercifully used.   The sight of such sufferings, inflicted by menials upon his brethren, would naturally rouse the utmost resentment of the son of the Princess Royal.   This, together with the long-cherished resolve to espouse the cause of his brethren, and the nascent thought of becoming their deliverer, led him to slay an Egyptian, whom he saw thus maltreating " an Hebrew, one of his brethren."   Still it was not an access of sudden frenzy, for " he looked this way and that way," to see " that there was no man " to observe his deed ; rather was it an attempt to carry out spiritual ends by carnal means, such as in the history of Moses' ancestors had so often led to sin and suffering.   He would become a deliverer before he was called to it of God ; and he would accomplish it by other means than those which God would appoint.   One of the fathers has rightly compared this deed to that of Peter in cutting off the ear of the high-priest's servant ; at the same time also calling attention to the fact, that the heart both of Moses and Peter resembled a field richly covered with weeds, but which by their very luxuriance gave promise of much good fruit, when the field should have been broken up and sown with good seed.

In the gracious dispensation of God, that time had now come. Before being transplanted, so to speak, Moses had to be cut down.   He had to strike root downwards, before he could spring upwards.   As St. Stephen puts it, " his brethren understood not how that God, by his hand, would give them deliverance "—what his appearance and conduct among them really meant ; and when next he attempted to interfere in a quarrel between two Hebrews, the wrong-doer in harsh terms disowned his authority,

[1] Heb. xi. 24-26.   [2] Ex. ii. 11.

and reproached him with his crime. It was now evident that the matter was generally known. Presently it reached the ears of Pharaoh. From what we know of Egyptian society, such an offence could not have remained unpunished, even in the son of a princess, and on the supposition that she who had originally saved Moses was still alive, after the lapse of forty years, and that the then reigning Pharaoh was her father. But, besides, Moses had not only killed an official in the discharge of his duty, he had virtually taken the part of the Hebrews, and encouraged them to rebellion. That Moses commanded such position of influence that Pharaoh could not at once order his execution, but " sought to slay him," only aggravated the matter, and made Moses the more dangerous. Open resistance to Pharaoh was of course impossible. The sole hope of safety now seemed to lie in renouncing all further connection with his people. That or flight were the only alternatives. On the other hand, flight might further provoke the wrath of the king, and it was more than doubtful whether any of the neighbouring countries could, under such circumstances, afford him safe shelter. It was therefore, indeed, once more an act of " faith " when Moses " forsook Egypt, not fearing the wrath of the king, for he endured " (or remained stedfast, viz., to his choice and people), " as seeing the Invisible One," that is, as one who, instead of considering the king of Egypt, looked by faith to the King invisible.[1]

Like Jacob of old, and Joseph under similar circumstances, Moses must now go into a strange land. All that Egypt could teach him, he *had* acquired. What he still needed could only be learned in loneliness, humiliation, and suffering. Two things would become manifest in the course of his history. That which, in his own view, was to have freed his people from their misery, had only brought misery to himself. On the other hand, that which seemed to remove him from his special calling, would prepare the way for its final attainment. And so it often happens to us in the most important events of our lives, that

[1] 1 Tim. i. 17.

thus we may learn the lessons of faith and implicit self-surrender, and that God alone may have the glory.

Disowned by his people, and pursued by the king, the gracious Providence of God prepared a shelter and home for the fugitive. Along the eastern shore of the Red Sea the Midianites, descended from Abraham through Keturah,[1] had their settlements, whence, as nomads, they wandered, on one side to the southern point of the peninsula of Sinai, and on the other, northward, as far as the territory of Moab. Among the Midianites it happened to Moses, as of old to Jacob on his flight. At the "well" he was able to protect the daughters of Reuel, "the priest of Midian," against the violence of the shepherds, who drove away their flocks.[2] Invited in consequence to the house of Reuel, he continued there, and eventually married Zipporah, the daughter of the priest. This, and the birth of his two sons, to which we shall presently refer, is absolutely all that Moses himself records of his forty years' stay in Midian.

But we are in circumstances to infer some other and important details. The father-in-law of Moses seems to have worshipped the God of Abraham, as even his name implies : *Reuel*, the "friend of El ;" the latter the designation which the patriarchs gave to God, as *El Shaddai*, "God Almighty."[3] This is further borne out by his after-conduct.[4] Reuel is also called *Jethro* and *Jether*,[5] which means "excellency," and was probably his official title as chief priest of the tribe, the same as the *Imam* of the modern Arabs, the term having a kindred meaning.[6]

[1] Gen. xxv. 2–4.

[2] Both in Ex. ii. 16, and iii. 1, the Hebrew expression for "flocks" implies that they consisted of sheep and goats, not of cattle, and thus affords another indirect testimony to the truth of the narrative, as only such flocks would be ordinarily pastured in that district.

[3] Ex. vi. 3.　　　　[4] Ex. xviii.　　　　[5] Ex. iii. 1 ; iv. 18.

[6] We must distinguish *Reuel* Jethro from *Hobab*, who seems to have been the son of Reuel, and brother-in-law of Moses, and to have accompanied Israel on their journey (see Judges iv. 11). There is a little difficulty here, as the word rendered in our Authorised Version "father-in-law," really means every relative by marriage.

But the life of Moses in the house of Reuel must have been one of humiliation and loneliness. From her after-conduct [1] we infer that Zipporah was a woman of violent, imperious temper, who had but little sympathy with the religious convictions of her husband. When she first met him as "an Egyptian," his bravery may have won her heart. But further knowledge of the deepest aims of his life might lead her to regard him as a gloomy fanatic, who busied his mind with visionary schemes. So little indeed does she seem to have had in common with her husband that, at the most trying and noble period of his life, when on his mission to Pharaoh, he had actually to send her away.[2] Nor could there have been much confidence between Moses and his father-in-law. His very subordinate position in the family of Jethro (iii. 1); the fact of his reticence in regard to the exact vision vouchsafed him of God (iv. 18); and the humble manner in which Moses was sent back into Egypt (ver. 20), all give a saddening view of the mutual relations. What, however, all this time were the deepest feelings and experiences of his heart, found expression in the names which he gave to his two sons. The elder he named *Gershom* (expulsion, banishment),[3] "for he said, I have been a stranger in a strange land;"[4] the second he called *Eliezer*, "my God is help" (xviii. 4). Banished to a strange land, far from his brethren and the land of promise, Moses longs for his real home. Yet this feeling issues not in despondency, far less in disbelief or distrust. On the contrary, "the peaceable fruits of righteousness," springing from the "chastening" of the Lord, appear in the name of his second son; "for the God of my fathers," said he, "is mine help, and delivered me from the sword of Pharaoh." The self-confidence and carnal zeal manifest in his early attempt to deliver his brethren in Egypt have been quenched in the land of his banishment, and in the school of

[1] Ex. iv. 25. [2] Ex. xviii. 2, 3.

[3] Mr. Cook regards it as a compound of a Hebrew and an Egyptian word meaning "a stranger" in "a foreign land."

[4] Ex. ii. 22.

sorrow. And the result of all he has suffered and learned has been absolute trustfulness in the God of his fathers, the God of the promises, Who would surely fulfil His word.

———◦◦◦———

CHAPTER IV.

The Call of Moses—The Vision of the Burning Bush—The Commission to Pharaoh and to Israel—and the three "Signs," and their Meaning.

(EXODUS II. 23 ; IV. 17.)

WHEN God is about to do any of His great works, He first silently prepares all for it. Not only the good seed to be scattered, but the breaking up of the soil for its reception is His. Instrumentalities, unrecognised at the time, are silently at work ; and, together with the good gift to be bestowed on His own, He grants them the felt need and the earnest seeking of it. Thus prayers and answers are, as it were, the scales of grace in equipoise.

It was not otherwise when God would work the great deliverance of His people from Egypt. Once more it seemed as if the clouds overhead were just then darkest and heaviest. One king had died and another succeeded ;[1] but the change of government brought not to Israel that relief which they had probably expected. Their bondage seemed now part of the settled policy of the Pharaohs. Not one ray of hope lit up their sufferings other than what might have been derived from faith. But centuries had passed without any communication or revelation from the God of their fathers ! It must therefore be considered a revival of religion when, under such circumstances, the people, instead of either despairing or plotting rebellion against Pharaoh, turned in earnest prayer unto the

[1] Ex. ii. 23. We must ask the reader to read this chapter with the open Bible beside him.

Lord, or, as the sacred text puts it, significantly adding the definite article before God,[1] "cried" "unto the God," that is, not as unto one out of many, but unto *the* only true and living God.   This spirit of prayer, now for the first time appearing among them, was the first pledge and harbinger, indeed, the commencement of their deliverance.[2]   For though only "a cry," so to speak, spiritually inarticulate, no intervening period of time divided their prayer from its answer.   " Anc God heard their groaning, and God remembered His covenant with Abraham, with Isaac, and with Jacob.   And God looked upon the children of Israel, and God had respect unto them " —literally, He "knew them," that is, recognised them as the chosen seed of Abraham, and, recognising, manifested His love towards them.

The southern end of the peninsula of Sinai, to which the sacred narrative now takes us, consists of a confused mass of peaks (the highest above 9,000 feet), some of dark green porphyry, but mostly red granite of different hues, which is broken by strips of sand or gravel, intersected by wadies or glens, which are the beds of winter torrents, and dotted here and there with green spots, chiefly due to perennial fountains.   The great central group among these mountains is that of Horeb, and one special height in it Sinai, the " mount of God."   Strangely enough, it is just here amidst this awful desolateness that the most fertile places in " the wilderness " are also found.   Even in our days part of this plateau is quite green.   Hither the Bedouin drive their flocks when summer has parched all the lower districts.   Fruit-trees grow in rich luxuriance in its valleys, and " the neighbourhood is the best watered in the whole peninsula, running streams being found in no less than four of the adjacent valleys."[3]   It was thither that Moses, probably in the early summer,[4] drove Reuel's flock for pasturage and water.   Behind him, to the east, lay the desert;

---

[1] Ex. ii. 23.   [2] Ex. iii. 7 ; Deut. xxvi. 7.
[3] Palmer's *Desert of the Exodus*, vol. i. p. 117.
[4] This will be shown when describing the ten plagues.

before him rose in awful grandeur the mountain of God. The stillness of this place is unbroken; its desolateness only relieved by the variety of colouring in the dark green or the red mountain peaks, some of which "shine in the sunlight like burnished copper." The atmosphere is such that the most distant outlines stand out clearly defined, and the faintest sound falls distinctly on the ear. All at once truly a "strange sight" presented itself. On a solitary crag, or in some sequestered valley, one of those spiked, gnarled, thorny acacia trees, which form so conspicuous a feature in the wádies of "the desert," of which indeed they are "the only timber tree of any size,"[1] stood enwrapped in fire, and yet "the bush was not consumed." At view of this, Moses turned aside "to see this great sight." And yet greater wonder than this awaited him. A vision which for centuries had not been seen now appeared; a voice which had been silent these many ages again spoke. "The Angel of Jehovah" (ver. 2), who is immediately afterwards Himself called "Jehovah" and "God" (vers. 4, 5), spake to him "out of the midst of the bush." His first words warned Moses to put his shoes from off his feet, as standing on holy ground; the next revealed Him as the same Angel of the Covenant, who had appeared unto the fathers as "the God of Abraham, the God of Isaac, and the God of Jacob." The reason of the first injunction was not merely reverence, but it was prompted by the character of Him who spoke. For in the East shoes are worn chiefly as protection from defilement and dust, and hence put off when entering a sanctuary, in order, as it were, not to bring within the pure place defilement from without. But the place where Jehovah manifests Himself— whatever it be—*is* "holy ground;" and he who would have communication with Him must put aside the defilement that clings to him. In announcing Himself as the God of the fathers, Jehovah now declared the continuity of His former purpose of mercy, His remembrance of Israel, and His speedy

---

[1] See the illustration and description in Canon Tristram's *Natural History of the Bible*, pp. 391, 392.

fulfilment of the promises given of old.   During these centuries
of silence He had still been the same, ever mindful of His
covenant, and now, just as it might seem that His purpose had
wholly failed, the set time had come, when He would publicly
manifest Himself as the God of Abraham, Isaac, and Jacob.[1]
The same truth was symbolically expressed by the vision of
the burning bush.   Israel, in its present low and despised
state, was like the thorn-bush in the wilderness (comp. Judges
ix. 15), burning in the fiery "furnace of Egypt,"[2] but "not
given over unto death," because Jehovah, the Angel of the
Covenant, was "in the midst of the bush"—a God who
chastened, but did "not consume."   And this vision was intended not only for Moses, but for all times.   It symbolises the
relationship between God and Israel at all times, and similarly
that between Him and His Church.   For the circumstances in
which the Church is placed, and the purpose of God towards it,
continue always the same.   But this God, in the midst of the
flames of the bush, *is* also a consuming fire, alike in case of
forgetfulness of the covenant on the part of His people,[3] and
as "a fire" that "burneth up His enemies round about."[4]
This manifestation of God under the symbol of fire, which on
comparison will be seen to recur through all Scripture, shall
find its fullest accomplishment when the Lord Jesus shall come
to judge—"His eyes as a flame of fire, and on His head many
crowns."[5]   But as for Moses, he "hid his face; for he was
afraid to look upon God."

The vision vouchsafed, and the words which accompanied it,
prepare us for the further communication which the Lord was
pleased to make to His servant.   He had heard the cry of His
people; He knew their sorrows, and He had come to deliver

---

[1] Even the expression, "I am the God of thy father," in the singular
number, implies the identity of His dealings throughout.   All the fathers
were but as one father before Him.   So closely should we study the
wording of Scripture.

[2] Deut. iv. 20.   [3] Deut. iv. 24.   [4] Ps. xcvii. 3.

[5] Rev. xix. 12.

and bring them into the Land of Promise, "a good land," it
is added, "and a large," a land "flowing with milk and
honey"—large and fruitful enough to have been at the time
the territory of not fewer than six Canaanitish races (ver. 8).
Finally, the Lord directed Moses to go to Pharaoh in order to
bring His people out of Egypt.

Greater contrast could scarcely be conceived than between
the Moses of forty years ago and him who now pleaded to be
relieved from this work. If formerly his self-confidence had
been such as to take the whole matter into his own hands, his
self-diffidence now went the length of utmost reluctance to act,
even as only the Lord's messenger and minister. His first and
deepest feelings speak themselves in the question, "Who am I,
that I should go unto Pharaoh, and that I should bring forth
the children of Israel out of Egypt?" (ver. 11). But the
remembrance of former inward and outward failure was no
longer applicable, for God Himself would now be with him.
In token of this he was told, "When thou hast brought forth
the people out of Egypt, ye shall serve God upon this mountain." Evidently this "token" appealed to his *faith*, as indeed
every "sign" does, whence their misunderstanding by those
"who are not of the household of faith" (comp. Matt. xii.
38, 39; Luke xvi. 31). Similarly, long afterwards, a distantly
future event—the birth of the Virgin's Son—was to be a sign
to the house of Ahaz of the preservation of the royal line of
David.[1] Was it then that underneath all else God saw in the
heart of Moses a want of realising faith, and that He would
now call it forth?

This first difficulty, on the part of Moses, had been set aside.
His next was: What should he say in reply to this inquiry of
Israel about God: "What is His Name?" (ver. 13). This
means, What was he to tell them in answer to their doubts and
fears about God's purposes towards them? For, in Scripture,
the *name* is regarded as the manifestation of character or of
deepest purpose, whence also a *new name* was generally given

[1] Isa. vii. 10-14.

after some decisive event, which for ever after stamped its character upon a person or place.

In answer to this question, the Lord explained to Moses, and bade him tell Israel, the import of the Name *Jehovah*, by which He had at the first manifested Himself, when entering into covenant with Abraham.[1] It was, "I am that I am"—words betokening His unchangeable nature and faithfulness. The "I am" had sent Moses, and, as if to remove all doubt, he was to add: "the God of your fathers, of Abraham, Isaac, and Jacob." "This," the Lord declares, "is my Name for ever, and this is my memorial to all generations;" in other words, as such He would always prove Himself, and as such He willeth to be known and remembered, not only by Israel, but "to all generations." Here, then, at the very outset, when the covenant with Abraham was transferred to his seed, the promise also, which included all nations in its blessing, was repeated.

In further preparation for his mission, God directed Moses on his arrival in Egypt to "gather" the elders of Israel together, and, taking up the very words of Joseph's prophecy when he died,[2] to announce that the promised time had come, and that God had "surely visited" His people. Israel, he was told, would hearken to his voice; not so Pharaoh, although the original demand upon him was to be only to dismiss the people for a distance of three days' journey into the wilderness. Yet Pharaoh would not yield, "not even by a strong hand" (ver. 19)—that is, even when the strong hand of God would be upon him. But, at the last, the wonder-working power of Jehovah would break the stubborn will of Pharaoh; and when Israel left Egypt it would not be as fugitives, but, as it were, like conquerors laden with the spoil of their enemies.

Thus the prediction clearly intimated that only after a long and severe contest Pharaoh would yield. But would the faith of Israel endure under such a trial? This is probably the meaning of Moses' next question, seemingly strange as put at

[1] Gen. xv. 7. [2] Gen. i. 24.

this stage : " But, behold, they will not believe me, nor hearken unto my voice : for they will say, Jehovah hath not appeared unto thee."[1] To such doubts, whether on the part of Israel, of Pharaoh, or of the Egyptians, a threefold symbolical reply was now furnished, and that not only to silence those who might so object, but also for the encouragement of Moses himself. This reply involved the bestowal of power upon Moses to work miracles. We note that here, *for the first time* in Old Testament history, this power was bestowed upon man, and that the occasion was the first great conflict between the world and the Church. These miracles were intended to be like "a voice" from heaven, bearing direct testimony to the truth of Moses' commission. So we read in Exodus iv. 8 of Israel "hearkening unto" and "believing" "the voice" of the signs, and in Psalm cv. 27 (marginal reading) that Moses and Aaron "shewed the words of His signs among them." But while this was the general purpose of *the three signs* now displayed— first to Moses himself—each had also its special reference : the first to Pharaoh, the second to Israel, and the third to the might of Egypt.

In the *first sign* Moses was bidden to look at the rod in his hand. It was but an ordinary shepherd's staff. At God's command he was to cast it on the ground, when presently it was changed into a serpent, from which Moses fled in terror. Again God commands, and as Moses seized the serpent by the tail, it once more "became a rod in his hand." The meaning of this was plain. Hitherto Moses had wielded the shepherd's crook. At God's command he was to cast it away ; his calling was to be changed, and he would have to meet "the serpent"—not only the old enemy, but the might of Pharaoh, of which the serpent was the public and well-known Egyptian emblem.[2] "The serpent was the symbol of royal and divine

---

[1] Ex. iv. 1.

[2] Scripture frequently uses the serpent as a symbol of the power hostile to the kingdom of God, and applies the figure not only to Egypt (as in Ps. lxxiv. 13 ; Is. li. 9), but also to Babylon (Is. xxvii. 1).

power on the diadem of every Pharaoh "[1]—the emblem of the land, of its religion, and government. At God's command, Moses next seized this serpent, when it became once more in his hand the staff with which he led his flock—only that now the flock was Israel, and the shepherd's staff the wonder-working " rod of God."[2]   In short, the humble shepherd, who would have fled from Pharaoh, should, through Divine strength, overcome all the might of Egypt.

The *second sign* shown to Moses bore direct reference to Israel. The hand which Moses was directed to put in his bosom became covered with leprosy ; but the same hand, when a second time he thrust it in, was restored whole. This miraculous power of inflicting and removing a plague, uni-versally admitted to come from God, showed that Moses could inflict and remove the severest judgments of God. But it spoke yet other "words" to the people. Israel, of whom the Lord had said unto Moses, " Carry them in thy bosom,"[3] was the leprous hand. But as surely and as readily as it was restored when thrust again into Moses' bosom, so would God bring them forth from the misery and desolateness of their state in Egypt, and restore them to their own land.

The *third sign* given to Moses, in which the water from the Nile when poured upon the ground was to become blood, would not only carry conviction to Israel, but bore special reference to the land of Egypt. The Nile, on which its whole fruitfulness depended, and which the Egyptians worshipped as divine, was to be changed into blood. Egypt and its gods were to be brought low before the absolute power which God would manifest.

These " signs," which could not be gainsayed, were surely sufficient. And yet Moses hesitated. Was he indeed the proper agent for such a work? He possessed not the elo-quence whose fire kindles a nation's enthusiasm and whose force sweeps before it all obstacles. And when this objection

---

[1] *Speaker's Commentary*, vol. i. p. 265.
[2] Ex. iv. 20   [3] Numb. xi. 12.

also was answered by pointing him to the need of direct dependence on Him who could unloose the tongue and open eyes and ears, the secret reluctance of Moses broke forth in the direct request to employ some one else on such a mission. Then it was that "the anger of the Lord was kindled against Moses." Yet in His tender mercy He pitied and helped the weakness of His servant's faith. For this twofold purpose God announced that even then Aaron was on his way to join him, and that he would undertake the part of the work for which Moses felt himself unfit. Aaron would be alike the companion and, so to speak, "the prophet" of Moses.[1] As the prophet delivers the word which he receives, so would Aaron declare the Divine message committed to Moses. "AND MOSES WENT."[2]

Two points yet require brief explanation at this stage of our narrative. For, *first*, it would appear that the request which Moses was in the first place charged to address to Pharaoh was only for leave "to go three days' journey into the wilderness," whereas it was intended that Israel should for ever leave the land of Egypt. *Secondly*, a Divine promise was given that Israel should "not go empty," but that God would give the people favour in the sight of the Egyptians, and that every woman should " borrow of her neighbour," so that they would "spoil the Egyptians."

At the outset, we observe the more than dutiful manner in which Israel was directed to act towards Pharaoh. Absolutely speaking, Pharaoh had no right to detain the people in Egypt. Their fathers had *avowedly* come not to settle, but temporarily " to sojourn,"[3] and on that understanding they had been received. And now they were not only wrongfully oppressed, but unrighteously detained. But still they were not to steal away secretly, nor yet to attempt to raise the standard of rebellion. Nor was the Divine power with which Moses was armed to be at the first employed either in avenging their past wrongs or in securing their liberty. On the contrary, they

---

[1] Ex. vii. 1.   [2] Ex. iv. 18.   [3] Gen. xlvii. 4.

were to apply to Pharaoh for permission to undertake even so harmless an expedition as a three days' pilgrimage into the wilderness to sacrifice unto God—a request all the more reasonable, that Israel's sacrifices would, from a religious point of view, have been "an abomination" to the Egyptians,[1] and might have led to disturbances. The same almost excess of regard for Pharaoh prompted that at the first only so moderate a demand should be made upon him. It was infinite condescension to Pharaoh's weakness, on the part of God, not to insist from the first upon the immediate and entire dismissal of Israel. Less *could not* have been asked than was demanded of Pharaoh, nor could obedience have been made more easy. Only the most tyrannical determination to crush the rights and convictions of the people, and the most daring defiance of Jehovah, could have prompted him to refuse such a request, and that in face of all the signs and wonders by which the mission of Moses was accredited. Thus at the first his submission was to be tried where it was easiest to render it, and where disobedience would be " without excuse."

There might have been some plea for such a man as Pharaoh to refuse at once and wholly to let those go who had so long been his bondsmen ; there could be absolutely none for resisting a demand so moderate and supported by such authority. Assuredly such a man was ripe for the judgment of hardening ; just as, on the other hand, if he had at the first yielded obedience to the Divine will, he would surely have been prepared to receive a further revelation of His will, and grace to submit to it. And so God in His mercy always deals with man. " He that is faithful in that which is least, is faithful also in much : and he that is unjust in the least, is unjust also in much." The demands of God are intended to try what is in us. It was so in the case of Adam's obedience, of Abraham's sacrifice, and now of Pharaoh ; only that in the latter case, as in the promise to spare Sodom if even ten righteous men were found among its wicked inhabitants, the Divine forbearance

---

[1] Ex. viii. 62.

went to the utmost verge of condescension. The same principle of government also appears in the New Testament, and explains how the Lord often first told of " earthly things," that unbelief in regard to them might convince men of their unfitness to hear of " heavenly things." Thus the young ruler [1] who believed himself desirous of inheriting eternal life, and the scribe who professed readiness to follow Christ,[2] had each only a test of " earthly things " proposed, and yet each failed in it. The lesson is one which may find its application in our own case—for only " then shall we know if we follow on to know the Lord."

The second difficulty about the supposed direction to Israel to " borrow jewels of silver, and jewels of gold, and raiment," and so to " spoil the Egyptians,"[3] rests upon a simple misunderstanding of the text. Common sense even would indicate that, under the circumstances in which the children of Israel, at the last, left the land, no Egyptian could have contemplated a temporary loan of jewels, soon to be repaid. But, in truth, the word rendered in our Authorised Version by " borrowing," does not mean a loan, and is not used in that sense in a single passage in which it occurs throughout the Old Testament. It *always* and only means " to ask " or " to request." This " request," or " demand "—as, considering the justice of the case, we should call it—was readily granted by the Egyptians. The terror of Israel had fallen on them, and instead of leaving Egypt as fugitives, they marched out like a triumphant host, carrying with them " the spoil " of their Divinely conquered enemies.

It is of more importance to notice another point. *Moses was the first to bear a Divine commission to others. He was also the first to work miracles.* Miracles present to us the union of the Divine and the human. All miracles pointed forward to the greatest of all miracles, " the mystery of godliness, into which angels desire to look;" *the* union of the Divine with the human, in its fullest appearance in the Person

[1] Matt. xix. 16.   [2] Matt. viii. 19.   [3] Ex. iii. 22.

of the God-Man. Thus in these two aspects of his office, as well as in his mission to redeem Israel from bondage and to sanctify them unto the Lord, Moses was an eminent type of Christ. "Wherefore" let us "consider the Apostle and High Priest of our profession, Christ Jesus; who was faithful to Him that appointed Him, as also Moses *was faithful* in all his house. . . . as a servant, for a testimony of those things which were to be spoken after; but Christ as a Son over His own house; whose house are we, if we hold fast the confidence and the rejoicing of the hope firm unto the end."[1]

CHAPTER V.

Moses Returns into Egypt—The Dismissal of Zipporah — Moses meets Aaron — Their Reception by the Children of Israel — Remarks on the Hardening of Pharaoh's Heart.

(EXODUS IV. 17–31.)

SCRIPTURE-HISTORY is full of seemingly strange contrasts. Unintelligible to the superficial observer, the believing heart rejoices to trace in them, side by side, the difference between what appears to the eye of man and what really is before God; and then between the power of God, and the humbleness of the means and circumstances through which He chooses to manifest it. The object of the one is to draw out our faith, and to encourage it in circumstances which least promise success; that of the other, to give all the glory to God, and ever to direct our eye from earth to heaven. So it was, when, in the days of His flesh, neither Israel nor the Gentiles recognised the royal dignity of Christ in Him who entered Jerusalem, "meek, and riding upon an ass and the colt of an ass." And so it also appeared, when, in the simple

[1] Heb. iii. 1, 2, 5, 6.

language of Scripture, " Moses took his wife and his sons, and
set them upon an ass, and he returned to the land of Egypt :
and Moses took the rod of God in his hand."[1] What a
contrast! He who bears in his hand the rod of God is
dismissed in this mean manner—his wife and sons, and all
their goods láden on one ass, and himself humbly walking by
their side ! Who would have recognised in this humble guise
him who carried that by which he would smite down the pride
of Pharaoh and the might of Egypt?

On his return from " the mount of God," Moses had simply
announced to his father-in-law his purpose of revisiting Egypt.
Probably Jethro had not sufficient enlightenment for Moses to
communicate to him the Divine vision. Besides, the relations
between them at the time (as we gather even from the manner
in which Jethro allowed him to depart) seem not to have been
such as to invite special confidence ; possibly, it might have only
raised hindrances on the part of Jethro or of Zipporah. But it
was an indication that God furthered his way, when alike his
father-in-law and his wife so readily agreed to an expedition
which, in the circumstances, might have been fraught with
great danger. And this was not all. *After he had resolved to
go, but before he actually set out,* God encouraged him by the
information that all the men were dead who had sought his
life. Again, while on his journey, He gave him threefold
strengthening for the work before him. First, He pointed him
to the Divine rod in his hand, with which he was to attest by
miracles his mission to Pharaoh.[2] Secondly, lest he should be
discouraged by the failure of these signs to secure Pharaoh's
submission, God not only foretold the hardening of the king's
heart, but by saying, "I will harden his heart" (ver. 21),
proved that that event also was under His own immediate
control and direction. Lastly, in the message which he was to
bear to Pharaoh a double assurance was conveyed (vers. 22, 23).
Jehovah demanded freedom for the people, because " Israel is
my son, even my firstborn," and He threatened, in case of

[1] Ex. iv. 20.   [2] Ex. iv. 21.

Pharaoh's refusal, "to slay" his "son," even the king's "firstborn." So terrible a threat was to prove the earnestness of the Divine demand and purpose. On the other hand, the title given to Israel implied that God would not leave " His firstborn" in the bondage of Egypt. In the contest with Pharaoh Jehovah would surely prevail. That precious relationship between God and His people, which was fully established in the covenant at Mount Sinai,[1] might be said to have commenced with the call of Abraham. Israel was " the son of God" by election, by grace, and by adoption.[2] As such, the Lord would never withdraw His love from him,[3] but pity him even as a father his children;[4] and, although He would chastise the people for their sins, yet would He not withdraw His mercy from them. Such a relationship is nowhere else in the Old Testament indicated as subsisting between God and any other nation. But it is exceedingly significant that Israel is only called "the firstborn." For this conveys that Israel was not to be alone in the family of God, but that, in accordance with the promise to Abraham, other sons should be born into the Father's house. Thus even the highest promise spoken to Israel included in it the assurance of future blessing to the Gentiles.

And yet he who was to declare Israel the heir to this precious legacy was himself at the time living in neglect of the sign of that very covenant! His own second son[5] had not been circumcised according to the Divine commandment[6]— whether from neglect, owing to faith discouraged, or, more probably, as we gather from the subsequent conduct of Zipporah, on account of his wife's opposition, which in his depressed circumstances he could not overcome. But judgment must begin at the house of God; and no one is fit to be employed as an instrument for God who in any way lives in neglect of His

[1] Ex. xix. 5.   [2] Deut. xxxii. 18 ; Is. lxiv. 8 ; Jer. iii. 4 ; Mal. i. 6 ; ii. 10.
[3] Hos. xi. 1 ; Jer. xxxi. 9–20.   [4] Ps. ciii. 13.
[5] From Ex. iv. 25, we gather that only one son required to be circumcised. This would, of course, be the younger of the two.
[6] Gen. xvii. 14.

commandments. God met even His chosen servant Moses as an enemy. His life was in imminent danger, and Zipporah had to submit, however reluctantly, to the ordinance of God. But her mood and manner showed that as yet she was not prepared to be Moses' helpmate in the work before him. He seems to have understood this, and to have sent her and the children back to his father-in-law. Only at a later period, when he had "heard of all that God had done for Moses and for Israel His people," did Jethro himself bring them again to Moses.[1]

Thus purged from the leaven of sin, Moses continued his journey. Once more God had anticipated His servant's difficulties; we might almost say, the fulfilment of His own promises. Already He had directed Aaron "to go into the wilderness to meet Moses." At the mount of God the two brothers met, and Aaron willingly joined the Divine mission of Moses. Arrived in Egypt, they soon "gathered together all the elders of the children of Israel." At hearing of the gracious tidings which Aaron announced, and at sight of "the signs" with which he attested them, it is said: "they bowed their heads and worshipped." Then God had not forsaken His people whom He foreknew! So then, not Moses' unbelieving fears (iv. 1), but God's gracious promise (iii. 18), had in this respect also been amply realised. Neither their long stay in Egypt nor their bondage had extinguished their faith in the God of their fathers, or their hope of deliverance. However grievously they might afterwards err and sin, the tidings that "Jehovah had visited" His people came not upon them as strange or incredible. More than that, their faith was mingled with humiliation and worship.

Before we pass to an account of the wonders by which Moses was so soon to prove before Pharaoh the reality of his mission, it may be convenient here briefly to consider a very solemn element in the history of these transactions—we mean, the hardening of Pharaoh's heart. Not that we can ever hope fully to understand what touches the counsels of God, the

[1] Ex. xviii, 1–7.

administration of His government, the mysterious connection between the creature and the Creator, and the solemn judgments by which He vindicates His power over the rebellious. But a reverent consideration of some points, taken directly from the text itself, may help us at least, like Israel of old, to "bow our heads and worship." We have already noticed, that before Moses had returned into Egypt,[1] God had declared of Pharaoh, "I will harden his heart," placing this phase in the foreground, that Moses might be assured of God's overruling will in the matter. For a similar purpose, only much more fully expressed, God now again announced to Moses, *before the commencement of the ten plagues,*[2] "I will harden Pharaoh's heart, and multiply My signs and My wonders in the land of Egypt." These are the two first statements about the hardening of Pharaoh's heart. In both cases the agency is ascribed to God; but in both cases the event is yet future, and the announcement is only made in order to explain to Moses what his faith almost needed to know.

Twice ten times in the course of this history does the expression *hardening* occur in connection with Pharaoh. Although in our English version only the word "harden" is used, in the Hebrew original three different terms are employed, of which one (as in Ex. vii. 3) literally means *to make hard* or *insensible,* the other (as in x. 1) *to make heavy,* that is, unimpressionable, and the third (as in xiv. 4), *to make firm* or *stiff,* so as to be immovable. Now it is remarkable, that of the twenty passages which speak of Pharaoh's hardening, exactly ten ascribe it to Pharaoh himself, and ten to God,[3] and that in

---

[1] Ex. iv. 21.   [2] Ex. vii. 3.

[3] Perhaps we ought to mark that *ten* is the number of completeness. The ten passages in which the hardening is traced to Pharaoh himself are: Ex. vii. 13 (" the heart of Pharaoh was firm " or " stiff"); ver. 14 ("was heavy"); ver. 22 ("firm"); viii. 15 ("made heavy"); ver. 19 (was "firm"); ver. 32; ix. 7, 34 ("heavy"); ver. 35 ("firm"); xiii. 15 (" Pharaoh made hard," viz., his heart). The ten passages in which it is traced to the agency of God are: Ex. iv. 21; vii. 3; ix. 12; x. 1; x. 20; x. 27; xi. 10; xiv. 4; xiv. 8; xiv. 17.

both cases precisely the same three terms are used. Thus the making "hard," "heavy," and "firm" of the heart is exactly as often and in precisely the same terms traced to the agency of Pharaoh himself as to that of God. As a German writer aptly remarks: "The effect of the one is the hardening of man to his own destruction; that of the other, the hardening of man to the glory of God." Proceeding further, we find that, with the exception of the two passages[1] in which the Divine agency in hardening is beforehand announced to Moses for his instruction, the hardening process is during the course of the actual history, in the first place, traced only to Pharaoh himself. Thus, before the ten plagues, and when Aaron first proved his Divine mission by converting the rod into a serpent,[2] "the heart of Pharaoh was hardened," that is, by himself (vers. 13, 14).[3] Similarly, after each of the first five plagues (vii. 22; viii. 15; viii. 19; viii. 32; ix. 7) the hardening is also expressly attributed to Pharaoh himself. Only when still resisting after the sixth plague do we read for the first time, that "the Lord made firm the heart of Pharaoh" (ix. 12). But even so, space for repentance must have been left, for after the seventh plague we read again (ix. 34) that "Pharaoh made heavy his heart;" and it is only after the eighth plague that the agency is exclusively ascribed to God.

Moreover, we have to consider the *progress* of this hardening on the part of Pharaoh, by which at last his sin became ripe for judgment. It was not only that he resisted the demand of Moses, even in view of the miraculous signs by which his mission was attested; but that, step by step, the hand of God became more clearly manifest, till at last he was, by his own confession, "inexcusable." If the first sign of converting the rod into a serpent could in a certain manner be counterfeited by the Egyptian magicians, yet Aaron's rod swallowed up theirs (vii. 12). But after the third plague, the magicians

---

[1] Ex. iv. 21 and vii. 3.   [2] Ex. vii. 10.

[3] The rendering in our Authorised Version conveys a wrong impression, as if *God* had hardened Pharaoh's heart.

themselves confessed their inability to carry on the contest, declaring: "This is the finger of God" (viii. 19). If any doubt had still been left upon his mind, it must have been removed by the evidence presented after the fifth plague (ix. 7), when "Pharaoh sent, and, behold, there was not one of the cattle of the Israelites dead." Some of the Egyptians. at least, had profited by this lesson, and on the announcement of the seventh plague housed their cattle from the predicted hail and fire (ix. 20, 21). Lastly, after that seventh plague, Pharaoh himself acknowledged his sin and wrong (ix. 27), and promised to let Israel go (ver. 28). Yet after all, on its removal, he once more hardened his heart (ver. 35)! Can we wonder that such high-handed and inexcusable rebellion should have been ripe for the judgment which appeared in the Divine hardening of his heart? Assuredly in such a contest between the pride and daring of the creature and the might of the Lord God, the truth of this Divine declaration had to be publicly manifested: "Even for this purpose have I raised thee up, that I might show My power in thee, and that My name might be declared throughout all the earth."[1]

For the long-suffering and patience of God will not always wait. It is indeed most true, that "God hath no pleasure in the death of the wicked, but rather that he be converted and live;"[2] and that He "will have all men come to the knowledge of the truth and be saved."[3] But "he that being often reproved hardeneth his neck, shall suddenly be destroyed, and that without remedy."[4] The same manifestation of God which to the believing is "a savour of life unto life," is to those who resist it "a savour of death unto death." As one has written, "the sunlight shining upon our earth produces opposite results according to the nature of the soil." In Scripture language:[5] "the earth which drinketh in the rain that cometh

[1] Rom. ix. 17. [2] Ezek. xxxiii. 11.
[3] 1 Tim. ii. 4, comp. 2 Pet. iii. 9. [4] Prov. xxix. 1.
[5] Heb. vi. 7, 8.

oft upon it, and bringeth forth herbs meet for them by whom it is dressed, receiveth blessing from God: but that which beareth thorns and briars is rejected, and is nigh unto cursing; whose end is to be burned." Or, as a German writer puts it: "It is the curse of sin that it makes the hard heart ever harder against the gracious drawing of the Divine love, patience, and long-suffering." Thus they who harden themselves fall at last under the Divine judgment of hardening, with all the terrible consequences which it involves.

Hitherto we have only traced this as it appears in the course of Pharaoh's history. There are, however, deeper bearings of the question, connected with the Divine dealings, the sovereignty, and the power of God. For such inquiries this is obviously not the place. Suffice it to draw some practical lessons. First and foremost, we learn the insufficiency of even the most astounding miracles to subdue the rebellious will, to change the heart, or to subject a man unto God. Our blessed Lord Himself has said of a somewhat analogous case, that men would not believe even though one rose from the dead.[1] And His statement has been only too amply verified in the history of the world since His own resurrection. Religion is matter of the heart, and no intellectual conviction, without the agency of the Holy Spirit, affects the inmost springs of our lives Secondly, a more terrible exhibition of the daring of human pride, the confidence of worldly power, and the deceitfulness of sin than that presented by the history of this Pharaoh can scarcely be conceived. And yet the lesson seems to have been overlooked by too many! Not only sacred history but possibly our own experience may furnish instances of similar tendencies; and in the depths of his own soul each believer must have felt his danger in this respect, for "the heart is deceitful above all things, and desperately wicked." Lastly, resistance to God must assuredly end in fearful judgment. Each conviction suppressed, each admonition stifled, each loving offer rejected, tends towards increasing spiritual in-

[1] Luke xvi. 31.

sensibility, and that in which it ends. It is wisdom and safety to watch for the blessed influences of God's Spirit, and to throw open our hearts to the sunlight of His grace.

———•◇•———

CHAPTER VI.[1]

𝔐oses and 𝔄aron deliver their 𝔐essage to 𝔓haraoh— 𝔍ncreased 𝔒ppression of 𝔍srael—𝔇iscouragement of 𝔐oses—𝔄aron shows a 𝔖ign—𝔊eneral view and 𝔄nalysis of each of the 𝔗en "𝔖trokes," or 𝔓lagues.

(EXODUS V.–XII. 30.)

THE predicted trial was soon to come. Provoked through the daring of man, who would measure his strength against that of the living God, it was to establish two facts for all ages and to all mankind. In sight of Egypt (Ex. vii. 5) and of Israel (x. 2) it was to evidence that God was Jehovah, the only true and the living God, far above all power of men and of gods.[2] This was one aspect of the judgments which were to burst upon Egypt.[3] The other was, that He was the faithful Covenant-God, who remembered His promises, and would bring out His people " with a stretched-out arm and with great judgments," to take them to Himself for a people, and to be to them a God (vi. 1–8). These are the eternal truths which underlie the history of Israel's deliverance from Egypt. How Israel had understood and taught them to their children, appears from many passages of Scripture, especially from Ps. lxxviii. and cv. Nor is their application less suited to our wants. It exhibits alike the Law and the Gospel—the severity and the goodness of God—and may be summed up in that grand proclamation unto all the world : " Jehovah reigneth."[4]

[1] The understanding of this chapter especially will be greatly enhanced by comparing it throughout with the Bible-text. The object has been not only to tell the history, but, so far as might be within our limits, to explain the statements of Scripture.

[2] Ex. ix. 14.   [3] Rom. ix. 17.   [4] Ps. xcix. 1.

The sacred narrative here consists of two parts : the one pre-paratory, so far as all parties in this history are concerned—Pharaoh, Israel, and Moses ; the other describing the successive " signs " in which Jehovah manifested Himself and His power, and by which He achieved both the deliverance of Israel and His judgments upon Pharaoh and Egypt. And here we shall notice successive progress : *externally* in the character of the *plagues* sent by God, and *internally* in their effect upon Pharaoh and his people.

Twice, before the plagues laid low the pride of Egypt, Moses and Aaron had to appear before Pharaoh : once with a simple message (v. 1–5), the second time both with a message and a sign to attest their mission (vi. 10–13 ; vii. 8–13). In this also we mark the Divine condescension and goodness. If at the first interview the king could say : " Who is Jehovah, that I should obey His voice to let Israel go ? I know not Jehovah, neither will I let Israel go " (v. 2), it became impossible to urge this plea, when, at the king's challenge, " Shew a miracle for you " (vii. 9), Aaron's rod was changed into a serpent. This proved beyond doubt that Jehovah was God, and that He had commissioned His servants, since they wielded His power. The only question still possible was, whether the gods whom Pharaoh served were equal to the Lord. For this purpose the king summoned his magicians, who imitated, in a certain way, the miracle of Aaron. But even so, the inferiority of their power was proved when " Aaron's rod swallowed up their rods." This assuredly— even taking their own profession of miracle-working—should have been sufficient to indicate to Pharaoh that " Jehovah, He is God "—had his hardness of heart admitted of such conviction. But as between Moses' and Aaron's first and second interview with Pharaoh important events occurred, it may be well briefly to record them again in their order.

After the first interview, in which Moses and Aaron had simply delivered the Divine command, Pharaoh, who had pleaded ignorance of Jehovah (that is, of His Deity and claims), professed to regard the demand of Moses as a mere pretence to procure a series of holidays for the people. They were "vain words" (v. 9) "to let the people from their works" (ver. 4). As "the people of the land"—that is, the Israelites, the labouring class—were "many," to "make them rest from their burdens" (ver. 5) would inflict great damage upon the king. To prevent their having either time or inclination to listen to such suggestions, the king ordered that, while the old amount of work should continue to be exacted, the straw needful for making the sun-dried bricks (such as we find on the monu- ments of Egypt) should no longer be supplied. The time requisite for gathering "stubble instead of straw" prevented, of course, their fulfilling their "daily tasks." The punishment then fell upon the Israelitish "officers," or rather "scribes," whom the Egyptian "taskmasters" had set over the work and held responsible for it. An appeal to Pharaoh only explained the cause of his increased severity, and the "officers" of a people which but lately had acknowledged that God had visited them, not seeing that visitation, but rather seemingly the opposite, ventured in their unbelief to appeal to Jehovah against Moses and Aaron! So rapidly do the results of a faith which cometh only by the hearing of the ear give way before discouragements.

As for Moses, the hour of his severest trial had now come. With the words of Israel's complaint he went straight to the Lord, yet, as St. Augustine remarks, not in the language of contumacy or of anger, but of inquiry and prayer. To his question : "Lord, wherefore hast Thou so evil entreated this people?" (v. 22)—as so often to our inquiries into God's "Wherefore"—no reply of any kind was made. "What I do thou knowest not now, but thou shalt know hereafter." To us, indeed, the "need be" of making the yoke of Egypt as galling as possible seems now evident, as we remember how the heart of the people clung to the flesh-pots of Egypt, even after they had tasted the heavenly manna ;[1] and the yet higher "need be

[1] Numb. xi.

for it," since the lower Israel's condition and the more tyrannical Pharaoh's oppression, the more glorious the triumph of Jehovah, and the more complete the manifestation of His enemy's impotence. But in Moses it only raised once more, at this season of depression, the question of his fitness for the work which he had undertaken. For when Satan cannot otherwise oppose, he calls forth in us unbelieving doubts as to our aptitude or call for a work. The direction which Moses now received from God applies, in principle, to all similar cases. It conveyed a fresh assurance that God would certainly accomplish His purpose ; it gave a fuller revelation of His character as Jehovah, with the special promises which this implied (vi. 2–8); and it renewed the commission to Moses to undertake the work, accompanied by encouragements and assurances suitable in the circumstances.

One point here claims special attention, not only on account of the difficulties which it presents to the general reader, but also because its lessons are so precious. When, on the occasion just referred to, God said to Moses (Ex. vi. 2, 3) : " I am Jehovah : and I appeared unto Abraham, unto Isaac, and unto Jacob in *El Shaddai* (God Almighty), but *as to* My name *Jehovah* was I not known to them,"[1] it cannot, of course, mean, that the patriarchs were ignorant of the special designation *Jehovah*, since it frequently occurs in their history.[2] To understand this passage aright, we must bear in mind the meaning of the expression " name " as applied to God, and that of the term " Jehovah." By the " name of God " we are of course to understand not a mere appellation of God, but that by which He makes Himself known to man. Now Scripture teaches us that we only *know* God in so far as He *manifests*, or reveals Himself. Hence the peculiar *name* of God indicates the peculiar manner in which He had manifested Himself, or, in other

[1] Such is the literal rendering, which in part may remove some of the difficulties.

[2] This view is, however, entertained by some—notably by Josephus, who holds that the name Jehovah was first revealed to Moses.

words, the character or His dealings at the time. Now the character of God's dealings—and therefore His name—was in patriarchal times unquestionably *El Shaddai* (Gen. xvii. 1; xxxv. 11; xlviii. 3). But His manifestation as Jehovah—the dealings by which, in the sight of all men, He made Himself known as such—belonged not to that, but to a later period. For the term "Jehovah" literally means, "He who is," which agrees with the explanation given by God Himself: "He who is that He is."[1] As here used, the word "*to be*" refers not to the essential nature of God, but to His relationship towards man. In that relationship God manifested Himself, and He was known as Jehovah—as "He who is that He is," in other words, as unchangeable—when, after centuries of silence, and after the condition of Israel in Egypt had become almost hopeless, He showed that He had not forgotten His promise given to the fathers, that He had all along been preparing its fulfilment; and that neither the resistance of Pharaoh nor the might of Egypt could stay His hand. Viewed in this light, the distinction between the original El Shaddai manifestation to the patriarchs and the Jehovah knowledge vouchsafed to the children of Israel becomes both clear and emphatic.

But to return. The first interview of Moses with Pharaoh had served to determine the relationship of all parties in reference to the Divine command. It had brought out the enmity of Pharaoh, ripening for judgment; the unbelief of Israel, needing much discipline; and even the weakness of Moses. There, at the outset of his work, even as the Lord Jesus at the commencement of His ministry, he was tempted of the adversary, and overcame by the word of God. Yet how great in this also, is the difference between the type and the Antitype!

Still, though hardly fought, the contest was gained, and Moses and Aaron confronted a second time the king of Egypt. On this occasion Aaron, when challenged by Pharaoh, proved his right to speak in the name of God. He cast down his rod, and it became a serpent, and although "the magicians of

[1] Ex. iii. 14.

Egypt" "did in like manner with their enchantments," the superiority of Aaron appeared when his "rod swallowed up their rods." Without here entering into the general question of *magic* before the coming of our Lord, or of the power which the devil and his agents may have wielded on earth before our Saviour subdued his might, and led captivity captive, there was really nothing in what the Egyptian magicians did that Eastern jugglers do not profess to this day. To make a serpent stiff and to look like a rod, and then again suddenly to restore it to life, are among the commonest tricks witnessed by travellers. St. Paul mentions the names of Jannes and Jambres as those who "withstood Moses,"[1] and his statement is not only confirmed by Jewish tradition, but even referred to by the Roman writer Pliny. Both their names are Egyptian, and one of them occurs in an ancient Egyptian document. In this connection it is also important to notice, that the Hebrew term for "the serpent," into which Aaron's rod was changed, is not that commonly used, but bears a more specific meaning. It is not the same term as that for the serpent (*nachash*) by which Moses was to accredit his mission before his own people,[2] but it indicated the kind of serpent (*tannin*) specially used by Egyptian conjurers, and bore pointed reference to the serpent as the great symbol of Egypt.[3] Hence also the expression "dragon," which is the proper rendering of the word, is frequently in Scripture used to denote Egypt.[4] Accordingly Pharaoh should have understood that, when Aaron's rod swallowed up the others, it pointed to the vanquishment of Egypt, and the executing of judgment "against all the gods of Egypt."[5] Wilfully to shut his eyes to this, and to regard Aaron and Moses as magicians whom his own equalled in

[1] 2 Tim. iii. 8.　　　　　[2] Ex. iv. 3, 4.

[3] "It occurs in the Egyptian ritual, c. 163, nearly in the same form, 'Tanem,' as a synonym of the monster serpent which represents the principle of antagonism to light and life."—*Speaker's Commentary*, vol. i, p. 276, *note* 10.

[4] Ps. lxxiv. 13 ; Is. xxvii. 1 ; li. 9 ; Ezek. xxix. 3 ; xxxii. 2.

[5] Ex. xii. 12.

power, was to harden his heart, and to call down those terrible plagues which ushered in the final judgment upon Pharaoh and his people.

Before describing in detail the plagues of Egypt, a few general remarks will be helpful to our understanding of the subject.

1. The plagues were *miraculous*—yet not so much in themselves as in the time, the manner, and the measure in which they came upon Egypt. None of them was wholly unknown in Egypt, but had visited the land at some time or other, and in some measure. As so often, the Lord here employed ordinary natural events. The supernaturalness of the plagues consisted in their severity, their successive occurrence, their coming and going at the word of Moses, their partial extent, and the unusual seasons and manner in which they appeared.

2. We mark in them a regular arrangement and steady progress. Properly speaking, there were only nine plagues (3 × 3), the tenth "stroke"[1] being in reality the commencement of judgment by Jehovah Himself, when *He* went out "into the midst of Egypt" to slay its firstborn. Of these nine, the first three were in connection with that river and soil which formed the boast of Egypt, and the object of its worship. They extended over the *whole country*, and at the third the magicians confessed: "This is the finger of God." By them the land was laid low in its pride and in its religion. The other six came exclusively upon the Egyptians, as the Lord had said: "I will put a division between My people and thy people," "to the end that thou mayest know that I am Jehovah in the midst of the land."[2] If the first three plagues had shown the impotence of Egypt, the others proved that Jehovah reigned even in the midst of Egypt. Finally, the three last "strokes" were not only far more terrible than any

[1] This is the literal meaning of the word rendered "plague," Ex. xi. 1. Philo, however, and most interpreters, speak of ten plagues, and regard that number as symbolical of completeness.

[2] Ex. viii. 22, 23. So literally, and not "earth."

of the others, but intended to make Pharaoh know "that there is none like Me in all the earth."[1] To show that Jehovah, He is God; that He was such in the midst of Egypt; and finally, that there was none like Him in the midst of all the earth—or, that Jehovah was the living and the true God—such was the threefold object of these "strokes."

3. In reference to the duration of these strokes, the interval between them, and the length of time occupied by all, we know that the first plague lasted seven days,[2] and that the killing of the firstborn and the Passover occurred in the night of the fourteenth *Abib* (or *Nisan*), corresponding to about the beginning of April. In reference to the seventh plague (that of the hail), we have this statement to guide us as to its time:[3] "the flax and the barley was smitten: for the barley was in the ear, and the flax was bolled (or in blossom). But the wheat and the rice (or rather the spelt) were not smitten: for they were not grown." This would fix the time as about the end of January or the beginning of February, giving an interval of at least eight weeks between the seventh and the tenth stroke, or, if we might take this as an average, of more than two weeks between each plague. Computed at this rate, the first "stroke" would have fallen in September or October, that is, after the cessation of the annual overflow of tne Nile. But this seems unlikely, not only because the red colouring ordinarily appears in the river at the *commencement* of its increase, but because the expressions (vii. 19, 21) seem to imply that the river was then at its rise (and not on the decrease), and especially because just before this the Israelites are represented as gathering "stubble" for their bricks, which must have been immediately after the harvest, or about the end of April. Hence it seems more likely (as most interpreters suppose) that the first "stroke" fell upon Egypt about the middle of June, in which case from the first "plague" an interval of about ten months would have elapsed prior to the slaying of the firstborn. All this time did the Lord deal with Egypt, and Pharaoh was on his trial!

[1] Ex. ix. 14.   [2] Ex. vii. 25.   [3] Ex. ix. 31, 32.

There is, as we have already indicated, a terrible irony about "the plagues" of Egypt, since in the things in which Egypt exalted itself it was laid low. We seem to hear it throughout: "He that sitteth in the heavens shall laugh : the Lord shall have them in derision."[1] This will appear more clearly as we briefly consider each of the "strokes."

The first "stroke," or "plague." Early in the morning, during the rise of the Nile, Pharaoh went down to the river to offer unto its waters the customary Divine worship. Probably, he was accompanied by his wise men and magicians. Here he was confronted by Moses with the message of God. On his refusal to listen, Moses smote, as he had threatened, the waters with the rod of God, and the Nile, in all its branches, canals, cisterns, and reservoirs,[2] becomes red, like blood. Such a change of colour in the Nile was by no means uncommon, or Pharaoh would scarcely have quite hardened his heart against the miracle. In ordinary times this appearance of the river arises partly from the red earth, which the swollen waters carry with them, and partly from the presence of small cryptogamic plants and animalcules (infusoria). The supernaturalness of the event lay in its suddenness, in its appearance at the command of Moses, and in the now altered qualities of the water. "The fish that was in the river died"—thus depriving the people of one of the main staples of their food ; "and the river stank, and the Egyptians could not drink of the water of the river," thus cutting off the main supply of their drink. Somehow the magicians, however, contrived to imitate this miracle, probably on some of the water that had been drawn before "the rod" had smitten the river. And so for seven days, throughout the whole land of Egypt, the blood-like, un-drinkable water in every household "vessel of wood" or of earthenware, and in the large stone troughs which stood for general use in the corners of streets and on village-roads, bore testimony for Jehovah. And the Egyptians had to dig round

[1] Ps. ii. 4.
[2] This is the correct rendering of the expressions in Ex. vii. 19.

about the river, that their drinking-water might be filtered for use. But "Pharaoh turned and went into his house, neither did he set his heart to this also."

The second "stroke" or "plague"—that of the frogs—was also in connection with the river Nile. At the same time it must be remembered that the frog was also connected with the most ancient forms of idolatry in Egypt, so that what was the object of their worship once more became their curse. Here also a natural occurrence, not uncommon in Egypt, rendered Pharaoh's unbelief not impossible. After the annual inundation of the Nile the mud not uncommonly produces thousands of frogs—called by the Arabs to this day by the name corresponding to the term used in the Bible. These frogs "are small, do not leap much, are much like toads, and fill the whole country with their croaking. They are rapidly consumed by the ibis, which thus preserves the land from the stench described in Ex. viii. 14."[1] The supernaturalness of the visitation lay in their extraordinary number and troublesomeness (viii. 3), and in their appearance at the bidding of Moses. The magicians here also succeeded in imitating Moses upon a small scale. But apparently they were wholly unable to remove the plague, and Pharaoh had to ask the intercession of Moses, at the same time promising to let the people go. To give the king yet further proof that "the stroke" was not natural but of God, Moses left Pharaoh the option of himself fixing what time he pleased for their removal: "Glory over me : when shall I entreat for thee ?" (viii. 9)—that is, let *me* not fix a time, but let me yield to *thee* the glory of fixing the exact time for the cessation of the plague. "But when Pharaoh saw that there was respite (literally, enlargement, breathingspace), he made heavy his heart."

The third stroke, as always the third in each of the three series of plagues, *came unannounced* to Pharaoh, and consisted, not exactly of what we call "lice," but rather of a kind of small insects, scarcely visible, but which penetrate

---

[1] *Speaker's Commentary*, vol. i. p. 279, *note.*

everywhere and cause the most intense inconvenience. Sir S. Baker describes this visitation of vermin, which is not uncommon after the rice-harvest, in almost the words of Scripture : " It is as though the very dust were turned into lice." The " plague" came when Aaron, as directed by God, had smitten the dust of the earth with his rod. As twice before the river, so now the fertile soil, which the Egyptians also worshipped, became their curse. In vain the magicians tried to imitate this miracle. Their power was foiled. But, to neutralise the impression, they " said unto Pharaoh, This is the finger of Elohim" (viii. 19)—the result of the power of a God. *He* has done this. Therefore, being in no way due to Moses and Aaron, it cannot confirm their demand. *We* are vanquished, yet not by Moses and Aaron, but by a Divine power equally superior to them and to us. Therefore " Pharaoh's heart was hardened" (" made firm " and insensible).

And now in the second series of plagues commenced the distinction between the Egyptians and Israel,[1] the latter being exempted from " the strokes," to show that it was not " the finger of Elohim merely," but that He was "Jehovah in the midst of the land" of Egypt (viii. 22). For the same reason, Moses and Aaron were not used as instruments in the fourth and fifth plagues. They were simply *announced* to Pharaoh by the messengers of Jehovah, but inflicted by God Himself, to show that they came directly from His hand.

The fourth stroke consisted of swarms of so-called dog-flies, which not only infested the houses, but " corrupted the land" by depositing everywhere their eggs. This " plague"[2] is to this day most troublesome, painful, and even dangerous, as these animals fasten upon every uncovered surface, especially the eyelids and corners of the eyes, and their bites cause

---

[1] The word does not properly mean "division" (as in our Authorised Version, viii. 23), but, in the first place, *deliverance, salvation*, and also separation, distinction, and selection. Thus the Hebrew term, as the reality, connects the two ideas of salvation and separation.

[2] Comp. Ps. lxxviii. 45.

severe inflammation. It was announced to Pharaoh, as he went to the river early in the morning (viii. 20), as has been suggested, probably "with a procession, in order to open the solemn festival which was held one hundred and twenty days after the first rise" of the Nile (*i.e.* about the end of October or early in November). Although it wrung from Pharaoh consent for the people to go, yet on its removal, "he hardened his heart at this time also"—perhaps because in this and the next plague he did not see the instrumentality of Moses, and therefore fell back upon the theory of the magicians about "the finger of Elohim."

The *fifth stroke* was a very grievous murrain (not uncommon in Egypt), which has been supposed to have been of the same kind as the "cattle-plague" in our own country, only far more extensive. But although Pharaoh ascertained, by special inquiry, that Israel had been exempted from this plague, his heart was hardened.

The *sixth stroke* was again made to descend by the instrumentality of Moses and Aaron. As the third in the second series, it came without any warning to the king. Moses and Aaron were directed to take "ashes of the furnace"—probably in reference to the great buildings and pyramids in which Egypt took such pride—and to "sprinkle it up towards heaven; and it became a boil breaking forth with blains upon man and upon beast" (ix. 10). Such "burning tumours breaking into pustulous ulcers," but exclusively confined to man, are not uncommon in the valley of the Nile.[1] Even the magicians seem now to have yielded (ver. 11), but the judgment of hardening had already come upon Pharaoh.

The *sixth plague* had struck not only the pride and the possessions of the Egyptians, but their persons. But the three which now followed in rapid succession, stroke upon stroke, were far more terrible than any that had preceded, and indeed represented "all" God's "plagues" (ver. 14). They were ushered

---

[1] A modern writer has supposed them to have been the black-looking, foul ulcers symbolized by the black, rusty ashes of the furnaces.

in by a most solemn warning, unheeded by him who was nigh
unto destruction (vers. 15–18). The reason why God did
not at once destroy Pharaoh and his people is thus stated
by the Lord Himself:[1] "For now if I had stretched forth
My hand and smitten thee and thy people with the pestilence, then hadst thou been cut off from the earth. But
now in very deed for this cause have I let thee stand (made
thee stand, raised thee up),[2] for to show in thee My power
(perhaps, to let thee see or experience it—this is the first
reason; the second)—and that My Name may be declared
throughout all the earth." That this actually was the result we
gather from Exodus xv. 14. Nay, the tidings spread not only
among the Arabs, but long afterwards among the Greeks and
Romans, and finally, through the Gospel, among all nations
of the earth.

Only one day for thought and repentance was granted to
Pharaoh (ix. 18) before the *seventh stroke* descended. It consisted of such hail as had never been seen in Egypt, mingled
with thunder and fiery lightning. The cattle in Egypt are
left out to graze from January to April, and such of the
Egyptians as gave heed to the warning of Moses withdrew
their cattle, and servants into shelter, and so escaped the
consequences; the rest suffered loss of men and beasts. That
some "among the servants of Pharaoh" "feared the word of
Jehovah" (ix. 20) affords evidence of the spiritual effect of
these "strokes." Indeed Pharaoh himself now owned: "I
have sinned this time" (ver. 27). But this very limitation, and
the hardening of his heart when the calamity ceased, show
that his was only the fear of consequences, and, as Moses had
said, "that ye will not yet fear Jehovah Elohim" (ver. 30).

A very decided advance is to be marked in connection with
the *eighth stroke*. For Moses and Aaron, on the ground of
Pharaoh's former confession of sin, brought this message
from God to him: "How long wilt thou refuse to humble

[1] Ex. ix. 15, 16. We give the correct rendering of the passage.
[2] Rom. ix. 17.

thyself before Me?"[1]   Similarly, "Pharaoh's servants," warned
by previous judgments, now expostulated with the king (x. 7),
and he himself seemed willing to let the male Israelites go for
a short season, provided they left their families and flocks
behind.   On the other hand, the hardening of Pharaoh's heart
had also so far advanced, that, on Moses' refusal to submit to
conditions, the king burst into such daring taunts as (vers.
10, 11):[2] "So be it! Jehovah be with you as I will let go
you and your little ones.   Look! for evil is before your faces"
(*i.e.* your intentions are evil; or, perhaps, it may be rendered:
See to it! for beware, danger is before you).   "Not so! Go
then, ye men, for that ye are seeking" (the language evidently
ironical).   And they were driven out from Pharaoh's presence.

And thus it came, that when "Moses stretched forth his rod
over the land of Egypt, Jehovah brought an east wind upon
the land all that day, and all that night; and when it was
morning the east wind brought[3] the locusts."   Once more they
were natural means which the Lord used.   For the plague of
locusts was common in Egypt; yet even the heathen used to
regard this as a special visitation of God.   In Scripture it
serves as the emblem of the last judgments coming upon our
earth.[4]   This "plague," so much dreaded at all times, came
now slowly, from far-off Arabia,[5] upon the doomed land, more
grievous than such visitation had ever been known, and to the
utter destruction of every green thing still left in Egypt—
Goshen alone being again excepted.   Pharaoh felt it, and for
the first time not only confessed his sin, but asked forgiveness, and entreated that "this death" might be taken away
(x. 16, 17).   Not for want of knowledge, then, did Pharaoh
harden himself after that.   Yet now also it was not repentance,
but desire for removal of "this death," that had influenced

[1] Ex. x. 3.   [2] We give the literal translations.
[3] Or "carried."   The storm literally carries the swarm of locusts.
[4] Rev. ix. 3–10.
[5] Generally, it is not the east but the south wind that brings the locusts,
from Ethiopia or Lybia.   It was purposely from a long distance that they
were sent, to show that Jehovah reigned everywhere.

Pharaoh. No sooner had his request been granted, than his rebellion returned.

Once more unannounced came the *ninth stroke*, more terrible than any that had preceded. A thick darkness covered the whole land, except Goshen. There was this peculiar phenomenon about it, that, not only were the people unable to see each other, but "neither rose any from his place for three days." It was literally, as Scripture has it, a "darkness which might be felt"—the darkness of a great sand-storm, such as the *Chamsin* or south-west wind sometimes brings in early spring, only far more severe, intense, and long. Let us try to realise the scene. Suddenly and without warning would the *Chamsin* rise. The air, charged with electricity, draws up the fine dust and the coarser particles of sand till the light of the sun is hid, the heavens are covered as with a thick veil, and darkness deepens into such night that even artificial light is of no avail. And the floating dust and sand enter every apartment, pervade every pore, find their way even through closed windows and doors. Men and beasts make for any kind of shelter, seek refuge in cellars and out-of-the-way places from the terrible plague. And so, in utter darkness and suffering, three weary nights and long days pass, no one venturing to stir from his hiding. Once more, Pharaoh now summoned Moses. This time he would let all the people go, if only they would leave their flocks behind as pledge of their return. And when Moses refused the condition, the king "said unto him, Get thee from me, take heed to thyself; see my face no more; for in that day thou seest my face thou shalt die" (x. 28). It was a challenge which sounded not strange in Moses' ears, for before this interview God had informed him what would happen,[1] and directed that Israel

[1] The three first verses of Ex. xi. must have been spoken to Moses *before* his last interview with Pharaoh. Verse 1 should be rendered: "And Jehovah had said unto Moses," etc. They are inserted after x. 29, because they account for and explain the confident reply with which Moses met the challenge of Pharaoh. Evidently, xi. 4, and what follows, form part of that reply of Moses to Pharaoh which begins in x. 29.

should prepare to leave. And Moses now took up the king's challenge, and foretold how after those terrible three days' darkness "at midnight," Jehovah Himself would "go out into the midst of Egypt," and smite every firstborn of man and beast. Then would rise through the night a great lament al' over the land, from the chamber of the palace, where Pharaoh's only son[1] lay a-dying, to that of the hut where the lowliest maidservant watched the ebbing tide of her child's life.

But in Goshen all these three days was light and festive joy. For while thick darkness lay upon Egypt, the children of Israel, as directed by God, had already on the tenth of the month—four days before the great night of woe—selected their Paschal lambs, and were in waiting for their deliverance. And alike the darkness and the light were of Jehovah—the one symbolical of His judgments, the other of His favour.

—— ·•◦•· ——

CHAPTER VII.

The Passover and its Ordinances—The Children of Israel leave Egypt—Their First Resting-place—The Pillar of Cloud and of Fire—Pursuit of Pharaoh—Passage through the Red Sea—Destruction of Pharaoh and his Host—The Song "on the other side."

(EXODUS XII.–XV. 21.)

EVERY ordinance had been given to Israel about the Paschal feast,[2] and observed by them. On the tenth day of the month *Abib* (the month of ears, so called, because in it the ears of wheat first appear), or, as it was afterwards

---

[1] If, as we have argued in this volume, the monarch under whom the Exodus took place was Thothmes II., it is remarkable that he left no son, but was succeeded by his widow ; so that in that night Pharaoh's only son was slain with the firstborn of Egypt.

[2] Later Jewish ordinances distinguish between the so-called "Egyptian Passover"- that is, as it was enjoined for the first night of its celebration—

called, *Nisan*,[1] the "Passover" sacrifice was chosen by each household.

This was *four* days before the "Passover" actually took place—most probably in remembrance of the prediction to Abraham,[2] that "in the fourth generation" the children of Israel should come again to the land of Canaan. The sacrifice might be a lamb or a kid of goats,[3] but it must be "without blemish, a male of the first year." Each lamb or kid should be just sufficient for the sacrificial meal of a company, so that if a family were too small, it should join with another.[4] The sacrifice was offered "between the evenings" by each head of the company, the blood caught in a basin, and some of it "struck" "on the two side-posts and the upper door-post of the houses" by means of "a branch of hyssop." The latter is not the hyssop with which we are familiar, but most probably the *caper*, which grows abundantly in Egypt, in the desert of Sinai, and in Palestine. In ancient times this plant was regarded as possessing cleansing properties. The direction, to sprinkle the entrance, meant that the blood was to be applied to the house itself, that is, to make atonement for it, and in a sense to convert it into an altar. Seeing this blood, Jehovah, when He passed through to smite the Egyptians, would "pass over the door," so that it would "not be granted[5] the destroyer to come in" unto their dwellings.[6] Thus the term "Passover," or *Pascha*, literally expresses the meaning and object of the ordinance.

---

and the "Permanent Passover," as it was to be observed by Israel after their possession of the Land of Promise. The sacrificial lamb was to be offered "between the evenings" (Ex. xii. 6, marginal rendering), that is, according to Jewish tradition, from the time the sun begins to decline to that of its full setting, say, between 3 and 6 o'clock P.M.

[1] Esther iii. 7 ; Neh. ii. 1.   [2] Gen. xv. 16.

[3] The Hebrew word means either of the two. See Ex. xii. 5 ; Deut. xvi. 2.

[4] Later Jewish ordinances fixed the number of a company at a *minimum* of ten, and a *maximum* of twenty, persons.

[5] Such is the literal rendering.   Ex. xii. 23.

While all around the destroyer laid waste every Egyptian household, each company within the blood-sprinkled houses of Israel was engaged in the sacrificial meal. This consisted of the Paschal lamb, and "unleavened bread with," or rather "upon, bitter herbs," as if in that solemn hour of judgment and deliverance they were to have set before them as their proper meal the symbol of all the bitterness of Egypt, and upon it the sacrificial lamb and unleavened bread to sweeten and to make of it a festive supper. For everything here was full of deepest meaning. The sacrificial lamb, whose sprinkled blood protected Israel, pointed to Him whose precious blood is the only safety of God's people; the hyssop (as in the cleansing of the leper, and of those polluted by death, and in Psalm li. 7) was the symbol of purification; and the unleavened bread that "of sincerity and truth," in the removal of the "old leaven" which, as the symbol of corruption, pointed to "the leaven of malice and wickedness."[1] More than that, the spiritual teaching extended even to details. The lamb was to be "roast," neither eaten "raw," or rather not properly cooked (as in the haste of leaving), nor yet "sodden with water"—the latter because nothing of it was to pass into the water, nor the water to mingle with it, the lamb and the lamb alone being the food of the sacrificial company. For a similar reason it was to be roasted and served up whole— complete, without break or division, not a bone of it being broken,[2] just as not even a bone was broken of Him who died for us on the cross.[3] And this undividedness of the Lamb pointed not only to the entire surrender of the Lord Jesus, but also to our undivided union and communion in and with Him.[4] So also none of this lamb was to be kept for another meal, but that which had not been used must be burnt. Lastly, those who gathered around this meal were not only all Israelites, but must all profess their faith in the coming deliverance; since they were to sit down to it with loins girded, with shoes on

[1] I Cor. v. 7, 8.   [2] Ex. xii. 46.
[3] John xix. 33, 36.   [4] I Cor. x. 17,

their feet and a staff in their hand, as it were, awaiting the signal of their redemption, and in readiness for departing from Egypt.

A nobler spectacle of a people's faith can scarcely be conceived than when, on receiving these ordinances, "the people bowed the head and worshipped" (xii. 27).[1] Any attempt at description either of Israel's attitude or of the scenes witnessed when the Lord, passing through the land "about midnight," smote each firstborn from the only son of Pharaoh to the child of the maidservant and the captive, and even the firstborn of beasts, would only weaken the impression of the majestic silence of Scripture. Such things cannot be described—at least otherwise than by comparison with what is yet to follow. Suffice then, that it was a fit emblem of another "midnight," when the cry shall be heard: "Behold, the Bridegroom cometh."[2] In that midnight hour did Jehovah execute "judgment against all the gods of Egypt,"[3] showing, as Calvin rightly remarks, how vain and false had been the worship of those who were now so powerless to help. That was also the night of Israel's birth as a nation: of their creation and adoption as the people of God.[4] Hence the very order of the year was now changed. The month of the Passover (*Abib*) became henceforth the first of the year.[5] The Paschal supper was made a perpetual institution, with such new rules as to its future observance as would suit the people when settled in the land;[6]

[1] Not only in faith but in thanksgiving.

[2] Matt. xxv. 6.   [3] Ex. xii. 12.   [4] Isa. xliii. 15.

[5] The later Jews had a twofold computation of the year— the *ecclesiastical year*, which began with the month *Abib*, or Nisan, and by which all the festivals were arranged ; and the *civil year*, which began in autumn, in the seventh month of the sacred year. In Egypt the year properly began with the summer equinox, when the Nile commenced to rise.

[6] The arrangement of Ex. xii. should be noted : vers. 1–14 contain the Divine directions to Moses for the observance of the first Passover ; vers 15–20 give instructions for the *future* celebration of the feast, enjoined later (ver. 17), but inserted here in their connection with the history; in vers. 21–27 Moses communicates the will of God to the people ; while ver. 28 records the obedience of Israel.

and its observance was to be followed by a "feast of unleavened bread," lasting for seven days, when all leaven should
be purged out of their households.[1] Finally, the fact that
God had so set Israel apart in the Paschal night and redeemed
them to Himself, was perpetuated in the injunction to
"sanctify" unto the Lord "all the firstborn both of man and
of beast."[2]

When at last this "stroke" descended upon Egypt, Pharaoh
hastily called for Moses and Aaron. In that night of terror he
dismissed the people unconditionally, only asking that, instead
of the curse, a "blessing" might be left behind (xii. 32).
"And the Egyptians were urgent upon the people that they
might send them out of the land in haste, for they said, We be
all dead men." Ere the morning had broken, the children of
Israel were on their march from Rameses, around which most of
them had probably been congregated. Their "army" consisted
in round numbers[3] of "600,000 on foot—men, beside children"
(xii. 37), or, as we may compute it, with women and
children, about two millions. This represents a by no means
incredible increase during the four hundred and thirty years
that had elapsed since their settlement in Egypt,[4] even irrespective of the fact that, as Abraham had had three hundred
and eighteen "trained servants born in his own house,"[5]
and therefore afterwards circumcised (Gen. xvii. 13), whom

---

[1] The *Exodus* brought Israel into a new life. Hence, all that was of the
old, and sustained it, must be put away (1 Cor. v. 8). To have eaten of
leaven would have been to deny, as it were, this great fact. The feast of
unleavened bread, which followed the Passover-night, lasted seven days,
both as commemorative of the creation of Israel, and because the number
seven is that of the covenant.

[2] Ex. xiii. 1–7.

[3] "About 600,000 on foot" (comp. Numb. i. 46; iii. 39). "On foot,'
an expression used of an army; for Israel went out, not as fugitives, but as
an army in triumph.

[4] Calculations have again and again been made to show the reasonable-
ness of these numbers; and the question may indeed be considered as
settled. Nor must we forget that a special blessing attached to Israel, in
fulfilment of the promise, Gen. xlvi. 3.   [5] Gen. xiv. 14.

he could arm against the invaders of Sodom, so the sons of Jacob must have brought many with them who were afterwards incorporated in the nation. With these two millions of Israelites also went up a mixed multitude of varied descent, drawn in the wake of God's people by the signs and wonders so lately witnessed—just as a mixed crowd still follows after every great spiritual movement, a source of hindrance rather than of help to it,[1] ever continuing strangers, and at most only fit to act as "hewers of wood and drawers of water."[2] But a precious legacy of faith did Israel bear, when they took with them out of Egypt the bones of Joseph,[3] which all those centuries had waited for the fulfilment of God's promise. As Calvin aptly writes : "In all those times of adversity the people could never have forgotten the promised redemption. For if, in their communings, the oath which Joseph had made their fathers swear had not been remembered, Moses could in no wise have been aware of it."

Such a sight had never been witnessed in the land of Egypt as when the nation, so delivered, halted for their first night-quarters at *Succoth,* or "booths." The locality of this and the following station, *Etham,* cannot be exactly ascertained ; nor is this the place to discuss such questions. Succoth may have been fixed upon as the general rendezvous of the people, while at Etham they had reached "the edge of the wilderness," which divides Egypt from Palestine. The straight road would have brought them shortly into the land of the Philistines, face to face with a warlike race, against which even Egypt could often scarcely stand. Of course they would have contested the advance of Israel. To such test God in His mercy would not expose a people so unprepared for it, as was Israel at that time. Accordingly, they were directed to "turn" southward, and march to "*Pi-hahiroth,* between *Migdol* and the sea," where they were to encamp.

Two events, as we understand it, marked Etham, the second stage of their journey. It was apparently here, at the edge of

[1] Numb. xi. 4.   [2] Deut. xxix. 11.   [3] Ex. xiii. 19.

the wilderness,[1] that Jehovah first "went before" His people "by day in a pillar of cloud, to lead them the way; and by night in a pillar of fire, to give them light, to go by day and night," that is, to enable them at all times to march onward. In Exodus xiii. 17, 18, we read that "God (Elohim) led the people," but now *Jehovah,* as it were, took command (ver. 21),[2] and, by a sensible sign of His Presence, ensured their safety. This pillar was at the same time one "of fire and of the cloud" (xiv. 24), "of light" and "of cloud and darkness" (ver. 20). Ordinarily, by day only the cloud was visible, but by night the fire, which the cloud had enwrapped, shone out.[3] In this cloud Jehovah was visibly present in the "Angel" of the covenant;[4] there the glory of Jehovah appeared (xvi. 10; xl. 34; Numb. xvi. 42); thence He spoke to Moses and to Israel; and this was the *Shechinah,* or visible Presence, which afterwards rested upon the Most Holy Place. And this pledge and symbol of His visible Presence appears once more in the description of the last days—only then "upon every dwelling-place of Mount Zion."[5]

Secondly, it was probably from Etham, as they turned south-wards, that tidings were carried to Pharaoh, which made him hope that Israel had, by this sudden backward movement, "entangled" themselves as in a net, and would fall a ready prey to his trained army.[6] Perhaps now also, for the first time, he realised that the people had "fled" (ver. 5)—not merely gone for a few days to offer sacrifice, as they might have done, close by Etham, but left entirely and for ever. The sacred text does not necessarily imply that from Etham to Pi-hahiroth there was only one day's march. Indeed, opinions as to the exact locality of each of the stages to the Red Sea[7] are still

---

[1] Ex. xiii. 21.

[2] The expression is the more noteworthy, as, both on a monument and in one of the ancient Egyptian documents, the general is compared to "a flame in the darkness," "streaming in advance of his soldiers."

[3] Numb. ix. 15, 16.   [4] Ex. xiv. 19.   [5] Isa. iv. 5.

[6] Ex. xiv. 2–4.

[7] In the Hebrew it is called "the sea of reeds," but in the Greek transla-

divided, though the general route is sufficiently ascertained. While Israel thus pursued their journey, Pharaoh quickly gathered his army, the principal strength of which lay in its " six hundred chosen chariots." Each of these was drawn by two fiery, trained horses, and contained two warriors, one bearing the shield and driving, the other fully armed. A most formidable array it would have been under any circumstances; much more so to an untrained multitude, encumbered with women and children, and dispirited by centuries of slavery to those very Egyptians, the flower of whose army they now saw before them.

It must have been as the rays of the setting sun were glinting upon the war chariots, that the Israelites first descried the approach of Pharaoh's army. It followed in their track, and came approaching them from the north. There was no escape in that direction. Eastward was the sea; to the west and south rose mountains. Flight was impossible; defence seemed madness. Once more the faith of Israel signally failed, and they broke into murmuring against Moses. But the Lord was faithful. What now took place was not only to be the final act of sovereign deliverance by God's arm alone, nor yet merely to serve ever afterwards as a memorial by which Israel's faith might be upheld, but also to teach, by the judgments upon Egypt, that Jehovah was a righteous and holy Judge.

There are times when even prayer seems unbelief, and only to go forward in calm assurance is duty. "Wherefore criest thou unto Me? Speak unto the children of Israel that they go forward." Yet this forward movement was to be made only after Moses had stretched the rod of God over the sea, and the Angel of the Lord gone behind the host, casting the light of the pillar upon Israel's path, while, with the darkness of the cloud, he kept Egypt apart from them. Then blew the " strong east

tion of the LXX, and in the New Testament, "the Red Sea." The name is differently derived either from the *red coral* in its waters, or from *Edom*, which means " red "—as it were, the sea of the red men, or Edomites.

wind all that night," as never it had swept across those waters before.[1] They divided, and formed on each side a wall, between which Israel passed dry-shod. When the host of Egypt reached the seashore, night had probably fallen, and the Israelites were far advanced on the dry bed of the sea. Their position would be seen by the fire from the cloud which threw its light upon the advancing multitude. To follow where they had dared to go, seemed dictated by military honour, and victory within easy reach. Yet, read in the light of what was to follow, it sounds like Divine irony that "the Egyptians pursued and went in after them in the midst of the sea." And so the long night passed. The grey morning light was breaking on the other side of the waters, when a fiercer sun than that about to rise on the horizon cast its glare upon

---

[1] Rev. xv. 2, 3. The following extract from Palmer's *Desert of the Exodus* (vol. i. p. 37) may be interesting : " A strong wind blowing from the east, at the moment of the setting in of the ebb-tide, might so drive back the waters that towards the sea they would be some feet higher than on the shore side. Such a phenomenon is frequently observed in lakes and inland seas; and if there were, as there would very probably be, at the head of the gulf, any inequality in the bed of the sea, or any chain of sand-banks dividing the upper part of the gulf into two basins, that portion might be blown dry, and a path very soon left with water on either side. As the parting of the sea was caused by an east wind, the sudden veering of this wind to the opposite quarter at the moment of the return tide would bring the waters back with unusual rapidity. This seems to have been actually the case, for we find that the waters returned, not with a sudden rush, overwhelming the Egyptians at once, but gradually, and at first, as we might expect, saturating the sand, so that 'it took off their chariot-wheels that they drave them heavily.' In the hurricane and darkness of the night this would naturally cause such a panic and confusion as to seriously retard them in their passage ; but, in the meantime, the waters were too surely advancing upon them, and when morning broke 'Israel saw the Egyptians dead upon the sea-shore.' The verse last quoted seems to show conclusively that the wind did veer round to the west, for otherwise, with the east wind still blowing, the corpses of Pharaoh and his host would have been driven away from the Israelites, and thrown upon the opposite shore." Parallel instances are referred to by Dean Stanley (*Sinai and Palestine*, p. 34), notably that of the bed of the river Rhone being blown dry by a strong north-west wind.

the Egyptians. "Jehovah looked unto" them "through the pillar of fire and of the cloud, and troubled the host of the Egyptians." It was the fire of His Divine Presence, bursting suddenly through the pillar of the cloud, which threw them into confusion and panic. The wheels of their chariots became clogged, the sand beneath them seemed to soften under the fiery glow, and they drave heavily. With that light from the fiery cloud, the conviction flashed upon them that it was Jehovah who fought for Israel and against them. They essayed immediate flight. But already Moses had, at God's command, once more stretched his hand over the sea. In that morning watch, the wind veered round; the waters returned, and Pharaoh, with the flower of his host, sank, buried beneath the waves. Thus, in the language of Scripture, "Jehovah shook off¹ the Egyptians in the midst of the sea."²

Incidental confirmations of this grand event are not wanting. Throughout the Old Testament, it is constantly appealed to, and forms, so to speak, the foundation on which God rests His claim upon His people. Local tradition also has preserved its memory. Nor has anything yet been urged to shake our faith in the narrative. Although the exact spot of the passage through the Red Sea is matter of discussion, yet all are agreed that it must have taken place near Suez, and that the conditions are such as to make it quite possible for the host of Israel to have safely crossed during that night. Moreover, it is a curious fact, illustrating the history of Pharaoh's overthrow, that, according to Egyptian documents, seventeen years elapsed after the death of Thothmes II. (whom we regard as the Pharaoh of this narrative) before any Egyptian expedition was undertaken into the Peninsula of Sinai, and twenty-two years before any attempt was made to recover the power over Syria which Egypt seems to have lost. And thus, also, it was that Israel could safely pursue their march through the wilderness, which had hitherto been subject to the Egyptians.

But Moses and the children of Israel sang on the other side

¹ So literally, as in the margin.   ² Ex. xiv. 27.

of the sea a song of thanksgiving and triumph, which, repeated every Sabbath in the Temple,[1] when the drink-offering of the festive sacrifice was poured out, reminded Israel that to all time the kingdom was surrounded by the hostile powers of this world; that there must always be a contest between them; and that Jehovah would always Himself interpose to destroy His enemies and to deliver His people. Thus that great event is really not solitary, nor yet its hymn without an echo. For all times it has been a prophecy, a comfort, and a song of anticipated sure victory to the Church. And so at the last, they who stand on the "sea of glass mingled with fire," who have "gotten the victory," and have "the harps of God," "sing the song of Moses, the servant of God, and the song of the Lamb."

---

[1] Tradition informs us that the "Song of Moses" was sung in sections (one for each Sabbath) in the Temple, at the close of the Sabbath-morning service. The Song of Moses consists of three stanzas (Ex. xv. 2–5, 6–10, and 11–18), of which the first two show the power of Jehovah in the destruction of His enemies, while the third gives thanks for the result, in the calling of Israel to be the kingdom of God, and their possession of the promised inheritance.

THE

WANDERINGS IN THE WILDERNESS

CHAPTER VIII.

𝔗he 𝔚ilderness of 𝔖hur—𝔗he 𝔖inaitic 𝔓eninsula—𝔌ts
𝔖cenery and 𝔙egetation—𝔌ts 𝔠apabilities of 𝔖upport-
ing a 𝔓opulation—𝔗he 𝔚ells of 𝔐oses—𝔗hree 𝔇ays'
𝔐arch to 𝔐arah—𝔈lim—𝔅oad to the 𝔚ilderness of
𝔖in—𝔌srael's 𝔐urmuring—𝔗he 𝔐ira.ulous 𝔓rovision
of the 𝔔u.ils—𝔗he 𝔐anna.

(EXODUS XV. 22 ; XVI.)

WITH the song of triumph on the other side the sea, the
first part of the Book of Exodus ends. Israel has now
become a nation. God has made it such by a twofold deliverance. He has, so to speak, "created" it for Himself. It only
remains that this new-born people of God shall be consecrated
to Him at the mount. And the second part of Exodus describes
their wilderness-journey to Sinai, and their consecration there
unto God. In this also it may serve to us as the pattern of
heavenly things on our passage through the wilderness to the
mount.

As Israel looked in the morning light across the now quiet
sea, into which Jehovah had so lately shaken the pursuers of
His people, their past danger must have seemed to them greater
than ever. Along that defile, the only practicable road, their
enemies had followed them. Assuredly the sea was the only
pathway of safety to them, and in that sea they had been bap-
tized unto Moses, and unto Moses' God. And now, as they
turned towards the wilderness, there seemed to stand before
them, and to extend all along their line of vision, east and north,

a low range of bare limestone hills, that bounded the prospect, rising like a wall. Accordingly they called this the wilderness of *Shur*, or of " the wall."[1] This then was the wilderness,
fresh, free, and undisputed ! But this also was that " great and
terrible wilderness," so full of terror, danger, and difficulty,[2]
through which they must now pass. Under the shadow of that
mass of rocky peaks, along the dry torrent-beds which intersect
them, through the unbroken stillness of that scenery, of which
grandeur and desolateness are the characteristics, led their way.
A befitting road to such a sanctuary as Sinai ! But what contrast
in all around to the Egypt they had left behind only a few hours !

When we think of the desert through which Israel journeyed,
we must not picture to ourselves a large, flat, sandy tract, wholly
incapable of cultivation. In fact it is in almost every particular
quite the contrary. That tract of land which bears the name of
the Peninsula of Sinai, extends between the Gulf of Suez on the
west, and that of Akaba (or the Persian Gulf) on the east. Its
configuration is heart-shaped, the broader part lying towards
Palestine, the narrower, or apex, stretching southwards into the
sea. It really consists of three distinct portions. The northern,
called the Wilderness of *Tih*, or, " of the Wandering," is pebbly,
high table-land, the prevailing colour being that of the grey
limestone. Next comes a broad belt of sandstone and yellow
sand, the only one in the desert of the Exodus. To the south
of it, in the apex of the peninsula, lies the true Sinaitic range.
This portion bears the name of the *Tor*, and consists in the
north chiefly of red sandstone, and in the centre of red granite
and green porphyry. The prevailing character of the scenery
is that of an irregular mass of mountains, thrown together in
wild confusion. The highest peak rises to about 9000 feet.
Between these wind what seem, and really are, torrent-beds,
filled, perhaps, for a very short time in winter, but generally
quite dry. These are called *Wâdies*, and they form the highway through the wilderness. Here and there, where either a
living spring rises, or the torrent has left its marks, or where

---

[1] Ex. xv. 22.   [2] Deut. viii. 15 ; xxxii. 10.

the hand of man is at work, cultivated patches, fair and fruitful, are found; palm-trees spring up, even gardens and fields, and rich pasture ground. But, generally, the rocky mountain-sides are bare of all vegetation, and their bright colouring gives the scenery its peculiar character. The prevailing tints are red and green; but this is varied by what seems a purple, rose, or crimson-coloured stream poured down the mountain side, while, occasionally, the green of the porphyry deepens into black. Over all this, unbroken silence prevails, so that the voice is heard in the pure air at extraordinary distances. Besides the cultivated or fruitful spots already mentioned, and tiny rock-flowers, and aromatic herbs, the vegetation of the wilderness consists chiefly of the caper-plant, the hyssop of the Bible, which springs from the clefts of the rocks and hangs down in gay festoons; the " thorn," a species of acacia ; another species of the same tree, the *Shittim*-wood of Scripture, of which the framework of the Tabernacle was made; the white broom, or juniper of Scripture ; and the tamarisk, which, at certain seasons of the year, produces the natural manna. This leads us to say, that it were a mistake to suppose that the wilderness offered no means of support to those who inhabited it. Even now it sustains a not inconsiderable population, and there is abundant evidence that, before neglect and ravages had brought it to its present state, it could, and did, support a very much larger number of people. There were always Egyptian colonies engaged in working its large copper, iron, and turquoise mines, and these settlers would have looked well to its springs and cultivated spots. Nor could the Israelites, any more than the modern Bedouin, have had difficulty in supporting, in the desert, their numerous herds and flocks. These would again supply them with milk and cheese, and occasionally with meat. We know from Scripture that, at a later period, the Israelites were ready to buy food and water from the Edomites,[1] and they may have done so from passing caravans as well. Similarly, we gather from such passages as Lev. viii. 2, 26, 31 ; ix. 4 ; x. 12 ;

---

[1] Deut. ii. 6

xxiv. 5; Numb. vii. 13, and others, that they must have had a
supply of flour, either purchased, or of their own sowing and
reaping, during their prolonged stay in certain localities, just as
the modern Bedouin still cultivate what soil is fit for it.

Such was the wilderness on which Israel now entered.
During the forty years that Moses had tended the flocks of
Jethro, its wádies and peaks, its pastures and rocks must have
become well known to him. Nor could the Israelites themselves have been quite ignorant of its character, considering the
constant connection between Egypt and the desert. We are
therefore the more disposed to attach credit to those explorers
who have tried to ascertain what may have been the most
likely route taken by the children of Israel. This has of late
years been made the subject of investigation by scholars
thoroughly qualified for the task. Indeed, a special professional
survey has been made of the Desert of Sinai.[1] The result is,
that most of the stations on the journey of Israel have been
ascertained, while, in reference to the rest, great probability
attaches to the opinion of the explorers.

The first camping-place was, no doubt, the modern *Ayûn
Mûsa* (Wells of Moses), about half an hour from the sea-shore.
Even now the care of the foreign consuls has made this a most
pleasant green and fresh summer retreat. One of the latest
travellers has counted nineteen wells there, and the clumps of
palm-trees afford a delightful shade. There is evidence that,
at the time of Moses, the district was even more carefully cultivated than now, and its water-supply better attended to. Nor
is there any doubt as to the next stage in Israel's wilderness-
journey. The accounts of travellers quite agree with the
narrative of the Bible. Three days' journey over pebbly ground
through desert wádies, and at last among bare white and black

---

[1] A regular Ordnance Survey has been made, under the direction of
Sir Henry James, R.E., by Capts. Wilson and Palmer, R.E., four non-
commissioned officers of the Royal Engineers, the Rev. F. W. Holland, and
Messrs. Wyatt and Palmer. The result has been published in a splendid
folio volume, with maps and photographic illustratiors, and an excellent
introduction by Canon Williams.

limestone hills, with nothing to relieve the eye except, in the distance, the " shur," or wall of rocky mountain which gives its name to the desert, would bring the weary, dispirited multitude to the modern *Hawwárah,* the " Marah " of the Bible. Worse than fatigue and depression now oppressed them, for they began to suffer from want of water. For three days they had not come upon any spring, and their own supplies must have been well-nigh exhausted. When arrived at Hawwárah they found indeed a pool, but, as the whole soil is impregnated with nitre, the water was bitter (Marah) and unfit for use. Luther aptly remarks that, when our provision ceases, our faith is wont to come to an end. It was so here. The circumstances seemed indeed hopeless. The spring of Hawwárah is still considered the worst on the whole road to Sinai, and no means have ever been suggested to make its waters drinkable. But God stilled the murmuring of the people, and met their wants by a miraculous interposition. Moses was shown a tree which he was to cast into the water, and it became sweet. Whether or not it was the thorny shrub which grows so profusely at Hawwárah, is of little importance. The help came directly from heaven, and the lesson was twofold. " There He made for them a statute and an ordinance, and there He proved them."[1] The " statute," or principle, and " the ordinance," or right, was this, that in all seasons of need and seeming impossibility the Lord would send deliverance straight from above, and that Israel might expect this during their wilderness-journey. This " statute " is, for all times, the *principle* of God's guidance, and this " ordinance " the *right* or privilege of our heavenly citizenship. But He also ever " proves " us by this, that the enjoyment of our right and privilege is made to depend upon a constant exercise of faith.

From Hawwárah, or Marah, a short march would bring Israel to a sweet and fertile spot, now known as *Wády Gharandel,* the *Elim* of Scripture, " where were twelve wells of water, and threescore and ten palm-trees ; and they encamped there by the

---

[1] Ex. xv 25.

waters." This spot was suitable for a more lengthened encampment. In point of fact, we find that quite a month passed before their next stage in the wilderness of *Sin*.[1] Even now this valley, watered by a perennial stream, has rich pasturage for cattle, and many shrubs and trees. Here, and in the neighbourhood, the flocks and herds would find good sustenance, and the people rest. Leaving Elim, the character of the scenery changes. Instead of dreary level plains of sand, as hitherto, we are now entering among the mountains, and the bright green of the caper-plant forms a striking contrast to the red sandstone of the rocks. Hitherto the route of Israel had been directly southward, and in pursuing it, they had successively skirted the Tih, and near Elim a belt of sand. But now the host was to enter on the Sinaitic range itself. From Numb. xxxiii. 10, we know that from Elim their journey first brought them again to the shore of the "Sea of Weeds." The road which they would follow would be from Wády Gharandel through the Wády Taiyebeh, in a south westerly direction. Here the sandstone again gives place to chalk hills and rocks. Where the road descends to the sea (at Rás Abu Zenimeh) it would touch, probably, the most dreary, flat, and desolate place in the whole wilderness. This spot was the next camping-ground of the children of Israel after Elim. From the shore of the Red Sea the next halting-place brought them into the Wilderness of *Sin* itself.[2] That name applies to the whole extensive sandy plain, which runs along the shore of the Red Sea, from the camping-place of Israel to the southern end of the Sinaitic Peninsula.[3] On leaving the Wilderness of Sin,[4] we

---

[1] Ex. xvi. 1.　　　　　[2] Numb. xxxiii. 11.

[3] From the Wády Gharandel *two* roads lead to Sinai—the so-called upper and the lower. Each of these has been ably and learnedly represented as that followed by the Children of Israel. After considerable research and consideration, we have arrived at the conclusion that the balance of evidence is decidedly in favour of the lower road, which, accordingly, has been described in the text. This conclusion has also been unanimously adopted by the Scientific Ordnance Survey Expedition, which investigated the question on the spot. It is of importance for the localization of Rephidim.　　　　　[4] Numb. xxxiii. 12–14.

read of two stations, *Dophkah* and *Alush*, before the Israelites reached *Rephidim*. The Wilderness of Sin, the modern *El Markhá*, is a dreary, desolate tract, which obtains its name from a long ridge of white chalk hills. In this inhospitable desert, the provisions which Israel had brought from Egypt, and which had now lasted a month, began to fail. Behind them, just above the range of chalk cliffs, they would see, in the distance, the purple streaks of those granite mountains which form the proper Sinaitic group. To the west lay the sea, and across it, in the dim mist, they could just descry the rich and fertile Egypt, which they had for ever left behind. Once more their unbelief broke forth. True, it was only against Moses that their murmurs rose. But in reality their rebellion was against God. To show this, and thereby "to prove them, whether they would walk in the law of God or no,"[1] that is, follow Him implicitly, depending upon, and taking such provision as He sent, and under the conditions that He dispensed it, God would now miraculously supply their wants. Bread and meat would be given them, both directly sent from God, yet both so given that, while unbelief was inexcusable, it should still be possible. To show the more clearly that these dealings were from the Lord, they were bidden "come near before Jehovah," and "behold the glory of Jehovah," as it "appeared in the cloud."[2] That Presence ought to have prevented their murmuring, or rather changed it into prayer and praise. And so it always is, that, before God supplies our wants, He shows us that His presence had been near, and He reveals His glory. That Presence is in itself sufficient; for no good thing shall be wanting to them that trust in Him.

As evening gathered around the camp, the air became darkened. An extraordinary flight of quails, such as at that season of the year passes northward from the warmer regions of the interior, was over the camp. It is a not uncommon occurrence that, when wearied, these birds droop and settle down for rest, so as to be easily clubbed with sticks, and even caught by

[1] Ex. xvi. 4.　　　　　[2] Ex. xvi. 9, 10.

the hand. The miracu'ousness chiefly consisted in the extraordinary number, the seasonable arrival, and the peculiar circumstances under which these quails came. But greater wonder
yet awaited them on the morrow. While passing through the
Wády Gharandel they might have observed that the tamarisk,
when pricked by a small insect, exuded drops of white, sweet,
honey-like substance, which melted in the sun. This was the
natural *manna* (a name perhaps derived from the Egyptian),
which, in certain districts, is found from the middle of May to
about the end of July. But "can *God* furnish a table in the
wilderness?" Can He command the clouds from above, and
open the doors of heaven? Can He rain down manna upon
them to eat? That would indeed be to give them of the corn
of heaven! Truly, this were angels' food, the provision, direct
from God, "the bread of heaven!"[1] The Lord did this, and far
more. As in the evening, He had "caused an east wind to
blow in the heavens; and by His power He brought in the
south wind; He rained flesh also upon them as dust, and
feathered fowls like as the sand of the sea ;" so, in the morning,
as the dew that had lain rose in white vapour, and was
carried towards the blue sky, there lay on the face of the ground
" a small round thing, as small as the hoar frost." " It was like
coriander seed, white ; and the taste of it was like wafers made
with honey."[2] The children of Israel said, Manna! What is
that? It *was* manna, and yet it was not manna; not the
manna which the wilderness produced, and yet in some respects
like it; it was the manna from heaven, the bread which God
gave them to eat. Thus it recalls our present condition. We
are in the wilderness, yet not of the wilderness; our provision is like the wilderness food, yet not the wilderness manna ;
but, above all, it is sent us directly from God.

Such assuredly must have been the lessons which Israel was,
and which we to this day are, called to learn. The very resemblance in some points of the natural to the heaven-sent manna
would suggest a truth. But the difference between them was

[1] P . Ixxviii. 19–27 ; cv 40.   [2] Ex. xvi. 21.

even greater and more patent than their likeness. On this point let there be no mistake. Israel could never have confounded the heaven-sent with the natural manna. The latter is seen in but a few districts of the desert, and only at certain seasons—at most during three months; it is produced by the prick of an insect from the tamarisks; it is not the least like coriander-seed; nor yet capable of being baked or seethed (xvi. 23); and the largest produce for a whole year throughout the Peninsula amounts to about 700 lbs., and would therefore not have sufficed to feed the host of Israel even for one day, far less at all seasons and during all the years of their wanderings! And so, in measure, it is still with the provision of the believer. Even the "daily bread" by which our bodies are sustained, and for which we are taught to pray, is, as it were, manna sent us directly from heaven. Yet our provision looks to superficial observers as in so many respects like the ordinary manna, that they are apt to mistake it, and that even we ourselves in our unbelief too often forget the daily dispensation of our bread from heaven.

There is yet another point in which the miraculous provision of the manna, continued to Israel during all the forty years of their wilderness-journey, resembles what God's provision to us is intended to be. The manna was so dispensed that " he that gathered much had nothing over, and he that gathered little had no lack; they gathered every man according to his eating."[1] For this marks the true purpose of God's giving to us, which-ever interpretation of the verse just quoted we adopt: whether we regard it as describing the final result of each man's work, that, however much or little he had gathered, it was found, when measured, just sufficient for his want; or understand it to mean that all threw into a common store what they had gathered, and that each took from it what he needed.

By two other provisions did God sanctify His daily gift. First, the manna came not on the Sabbath. The labour of the previous day provided sufficient to supply the wants of God's day of holy rest. But on ordinary days the labour of gathering

[1] Ex. xvi. 18.

the bread which God sent could not be dispensed with. What was kept from one day to the other only "bred worms and stank" (xvi. 20). Not so on the Lord's day. This also was to be to them "a statute" and an "ordinance" of faith, that is, a principle of God's giving and a rule of their receiving. Secondly, "an omer full of manna" was to be "laid up before Jehovah" in a "golden pot." Together with "Aaron's rod that budded, and the tables of the covenant," it was afterwards placed in the Holiest of all, within the ark of the covenant, over-shadowed by "the cherubim of glory."[1]

Thus, alike in the "rain of bread from heaven," in the ordinance of its ingathering, and in the Sabbath law of its sanctified use, did God prove Israel—even as He now proves us: whether we will "walk in His law or no."[2]

———◦◦———

CHAPTER IX.

Rephidim—The Defeat of Amalek, and its meaning—
The Visit of Jethro and its symbolical import.

(EXODUS XVII. XVIII.)

A SWEETER spot or grander scenery can scarcely be imagined than *Wády Feiran.* Here we are at last among those Sinaitic mountains which rise in such fantastic shapes and exhibit every variety of colouring. Following the windings of Wády Feiran we come upon a wide fertile plain, seemingly all shut in by mountains. This is *Rephidim,* the battle-field where Israel, fighting under the banner of Jehovah, defeated Amalek. The place is too full of interest to be cursorily passed by.

Just before reaching the plain of Rephidim, the children of Israel would, on their way from the Wilderness of Sin, pass a large, bare, outstanding rock. This, according to an Arab tradition, to which considerable probability attaches, is the rock which Moses smote, and whence the living water gushed. Now

———

[1] Heb. ix. 4.   [2] Ex. xvi. 4.

we know that, when Israel reached that spot, they must have been suffering from thirst, since, all the way from the Red Sea, these three days, they would not have passed a single spring, while their march in early May through that wilderness must have been peculiarly hot and weary. Again, it is quite certain that they must have passed by that rock, and under its shadow they would in all likelihood halt. For at that moment the valley of Rephidim before them with its living springs was held by Amalek, who, as the modern Bedouin would do in similar circumstances, had gathered around their wells and palms, waiting to attack the enemy as he came up thirsty, weary, and wayworn. Here then probably was the scene of the miracle of the smitten rock. Beyond it lay the battle-field of Rephidim.

Before following the Biblical narrative, let us try to realise the scene. Advancing from the rock just described upon that broad plain, we seem to be in a sort of dreamy paradise, shut in by strange walls of mountains. As the traveller now sees Rephidim, many a winter's storm has carried desolation into it. For this is the region of sudden and terrific storms, when the waters pour in torrents down the granite mountains, and rush with wild roar into the wádies and valleys, carrying with them every living thing and all vegetation, uprooting palms, centuries old, and piling rocks and stones upon each other in desolate grandeur. At present the stillness of the camp at night is often broken by the dismal howl of wolves, which in winter prowl about in search of food, while in the morning the mark of the leopard's foot shows how near danger had been. But in the days of the Exodus Rephidim and its neighbourhood were comparatively inhabited districts. Nothing, however, can have permanently changed the character of the scenery. Quite at the north of the valley are groves of palms, tamarisks and other trees, offering delicious shade. Here the voice of the bulbul is heard, and, sweeter still to the ear of the traveller, the murmur of living water. This beautiful tract, one of the most fertile in the peninsula, extends for miles along the valley. To the north, some 700 feet above the valley, rises a mountain (Jebel Táhúneh), which, not without much probability, is regarded as that on which Moses stood when lifting up to heaven his hand that held the rod, while in the valley itself Israel fought against Amalek.   As a sort of background to it we have a huge basin of red rock, gneiss and porphyry, above which a tall mountain-peak towers in the far distance.   Turning the other way and looking south, across the battle-field of Rephidim, the majestic Mount Serbal, one of the highest in the Peninsula (6690 feet), bounds the horizon.   On either side of it two valleys run down to Rephidim.   Between them is a tumbled and chaotic mass of mountains of all colours and shapes.   Lastly, far away to the south-east from where Moses stood, he must have descried, through an opening among the hills, the blue range of Sinai.

But before us lies the highland valley of Rephidim itself, nearly 1500 feet above the level of the sea.   Here in close proximity, but in striking contrast to sweet groves and a running river, are all around fantastic rocks of gorgeous diversity of colour, white boulders, walls of most lovely pink porphyry, from the clefts of which herbs and flowers spring and wind, and grey and red rocks, over which it literally seems as if a roseate stream had been poured.   In this spot was the fate of those who opposed the kingdom of God once and, viewing the event prophetically, for ever decided.

Wonderful things had Israel already experienced.   The enemies of Jehovah had been overthrown in the Red Sea ; the bitter waters of Marah been healed ; and the wants of God's people supplied in the wilderness.   But a greater miracle than any of these—at least one more palpable—was now to be witnessed, for the purpose of showing Israel that no situation could be so desperate but Jehovah would prove "a very present help in trouble."   That this was intended to be for all time its meaning to Israel, appears from the name *Massah* and *Meribah*, temptation and chiding, given to the place, and from the after references to the event in Deut. vi. 16 ; Psalms lxxviii. 15 ; cv. 41, and especially in Psalm cxiv. 8.   The admonition (Psalm xcv. 8) "Harden not your heart, as in Meribah, as in the day of

Massah in the wilderness, when your fathers tempted Me, proved Me, and saw My work," refers, however, primarily, to a later event, recorded in Numb. xx. 2, and only secondarily to the occurrence at Rephidim. At the same time it is true, that when the children of Israel chode with Moses on account of the want of water in Rephidim, it was virtually a tempting of Jehovah. Judgment did not, however, at that time follow. Once more would God prove Himself, and prove the people. Moses was directed to take with him of the elders of Israel, and in their view to smite the rock in *Horeb* (that is, "dry," "parched"). God would stand there before him—to help and to vindicate His servant. And from the riven side of the parched rock living waters flowed—an emblem this of the "spiritual rock which followed them;" an emblem also to us —for " that Rock was Christ."[1]

It was probably while the advanced part of the host were witnessing the miracle of the Smitten Rock that Amalek fell upon the worn stragglers, " and smote the hindmost, . . . even all that were feeble," . . . when Israel was "faint and weary."[2] It was a wicked deed, for Israel had in no way provoked the onset, and the Amalekites were, as descendants of Esau, closely related to them. But there is yet deeper meaning attaching both to this contest and to its issue. For, first, we mark the record of God's solemn determination " utterly to put out the remembrance of Amalek from under heaven,"[3] and His proclamation of "war of Jehovah with Amalek from generation to generation" (xvii. 16). Secondly, we have in connection with this the prophetic utterance of Balaam to this effect:[4] " Amalek the firstfruits of the heathen" (the beginning of the Gentile power and hostility), " but his latter end even to destruction;" while, lastly, we notice the brief but deeply significant terms in which Scripture accounts for the cowardly attack of Amalek:[5] " he feared not God." The contest of Amalek therefore must have been intended, not so much against Israel simply as a

---

[1] I Cor. x. 4.   [2] Deut. xxv. 18.   [3] Ex. xvii. 14.
[4] Numb. xxiv. 20.   [5] Deut. xxv. 18.

nation, as against Israel in their character as the people of God. It was the first attack of the kingdoms of this world upon the kingdom of God, and as such it is typical of all that have followed. Strange as it may sound, in such a contest God will not fight for Israel as at the Red Sea. Israel itself must also fight, though success will be granted only so long as their fight is carried on under the banner of God. That banner was the rod which Moses had received, and with which he was to perform miracles. This rod represented the wonder-working Presence of Jehovah with His people as their Shepherd, their Ruler and their Leader. Yet in the fight which Israel waged, it was not enough simply to stretch forth the rod as over the Red Sea. The hand that holds the rod must also be lifted up to heaven— the faith that holds the symbol of God's wonder-working presence must rise up to heaven and draw down in prayer the pledged blessing, to give success to Israel's efforts, and ensure victory to their arms. Thus we understand this history. Moses chose a band to fight against Amalek, placing it under the command of *Hoshea*, a prince of the tribe of Ephraim,[1] whose name, perhaps, from that very event, was changed to *Joshua* (Jehovah is help). In the mean time Moses himself took his position on the top of a hill, with the rod of God in his hand. So long as this rod was held up Israel prevailed, but when Moses' hands drooped from weariness, Amalek prevailed. Then Aaron and Hur—the latter a descendant of Judah, and the grandfather of Bezaleel,[2] who seems to have held among the laity a position akin to that of Aaron[3]—stayed the hands of Moses until the going down of the sun, and the defeat of Amalek was complete.

This holding up of Moses' hands has been generally regarded as symbolical of prayer. But if that were all, it would be difficult to understand why it was absolutely needful to success that

[1] Numb. xiii. 8, 16 ; Deut. xxxii. 44.

[2] 1 Chron. ii. 18, 19. According to Jewish tradition Hur was the husband of Miriam, Moses' sister. His father Caleb must not be confounded with Caleb, the son of Jephunneh.

[3] Ex. xxiv. 14.

his hands should be always upheld, so that when they drooped, merely from bodily weariness, Amalek should have immediately prevailed. Moreover, it leaves unexplained the holding up of the *rod* towards heaven. In view of this difficulty it has been suggested by a recent commentator, that the object of holding up the hands was not prayer, but the uplifting of the God-given, wonder-working rod, as the banner of God, to which, while it waved above them, and only so long, Israel owed their victory. With this agrees the name of the memorial-altar, which Moses reared to perpetuate the event—*Jehovah-nissi*, "the Lord my banner." But neither does this explanation quite meet the statements of Scripture. Rather would we combine both the views mentioned. The rod which Moses held up was the banner of God—the symbol and the pledge of His presence and working; and he held it up, not over Israel, nor yet over their enemies, but towards heaven in prayer, to bring down that promised help in their actual contest.[1] And so it ever is: Amalek opposes the advance of Israel; Israel must fight, but the victory is God's; Israel holds the rod of almighty power in the hand of faith; but that rod must ever be uplifted toward heaven in present application for the blessing secured by covenant-promise.

If the attack of Amalek represented the hostility of the world to the kingdom of God, the visit of Jethro, which followed Israel's victory, equally symbolised the opposite tendency. For Jethro came not only as Moses' father-in-law to bring back his wife and children—although even this would have expressed his faith in Jehovah and the covenant-people,—but he "rejoiced for all the goodness which Jehovah had done to Israel." More than that, he professed: "Now I know that Jehovah is greater than all gods; for He has shown Himself great in the thing wherein they (the Egyptians) had dealt proudly against them

---

[1] This view seems implied in Ex. xvii. 15, and explains the otherwise obscure words of ver. 16, which we literally render: "And Moses built an altar, and called the name of it Jehovah-nissi; and he said, For the hand upon the throne of Jehovah! War with Amalek from generation to generation!"

(the Israelites)" (Ex. xviii. 11). As this acknowledgment of God led Jethro to praise Him, so his praise found expression in burnt-offerings and sacrifices, after which Jethro sat down with Moses and Aaron, and the elders of Israel, to the sacrificial meal of fellowship with God and with each other. Thus Jethro may be regarded as a kind of firstfruits unto God from among the Gentiles, and his homage as an anticipating fulfilment of the promise ;[1] "And many people shall go and say, Come ye, and let us go up to the mountain of Jehovah, to the house of the God of Jacob; and He will teach us of His ways, and we will walk in His paths."

A very marked advantage was immediately derived from the presence of Jethro. Just as after the conversion of the Gentiles to Christianity, the accumulated learning and research of heathenism were to be employed in the service of the Gospel, so here the experience of Jethro served in the outward arrangements of the people of God. Hitherto every case in dispute between the people had been brought to Moses himself for decision. The consequence was, that Moses was not only in danger of "wearing away," from the heaviness of the work, but the people also (xviii. 18), since the delay which necessarily ensued was most tedious, and might easily have induced them to take justice into their own hands. Now the advice which Jethro offered was to teach the people "ordinances and laws," and to "shew them the way wherein they must walk, and the work they must do." Whatever questions arose to which the ordinances, laws, and directions, so taught them, would find a ready application, were to be considered "small matters," which might be left for decision to subordinate judges, whom Moses should "provide out of all the people—able men, such as fear God, men of truth, hating covetousness" (ver. 21). Whatever came not within range of a mere application of these known laws were "great matters," which Moses should reserve for his own decision, or rather, "bring the causes unto God." And this wise advice was given so modestly and with such ex-

[1] Isa. ii. 3.

press acknowledgment that it only applied "if God command" him so, that Moses heard in it the gracious direction of God Himself. Nor would it be possible to imagine a more beautiful instance of the help which religion may derive from knowledge and experience, nor yet a more religious submission of this world's wisdom to the service and the will of God, than in the advice which Jethro gave, and the manner in which he expressed it. From Deut. i. 12–18 we learn that Moses carried out the plan in the same spirit in which it was proposed. The election of the judges was made by the people themselves, and their appointment was guided, as well as their work directed, by the fear and the love of the Lord.

CHAPTER X.

Israel at the foot of Mount Sinai—The Preparations for the Covenant—The "Ten Words," and their meaning.

(Ex. xix.-xx. 17.)

IT was the third month after leaving Egypt when the children of Israel reached that innermost mountain-group from which the Peninsula of Sinai derives its name. Roughly speaking, the whole district occupies about twice the area of Yorkshire.[1] Running through it, like roads, pass very many wádies, all seemingly leading up to the grand central sanctuary, where God was about to give His law to His people. This mountain district bears in Scripture two distinct names—*Horeb* and *Sinai*—the former applying probably to the whole group, the latter to one special mountain in it. The meaning of the name Horeb is probably "mountain of the dried-up ground," that of Sinai "mountain of the thorn." At present the whole Sinaitic group is known by the designation of *Jebel Músa*. It

[1] According to the Ordnance Survey the triangle of the Sinaitic Peninsula covers an area of 11,600 square miles.

forms " a huge mountain-block, about two miles in length and
one mile in breadth, with a narrow valley on either side, . . .
and a spacious plain at the north-eastern end."[1] That plain,
at present known as *Er Ráhah*, is computed to be capable of
accommodating a host of two millions. Right before it rises
Jebel Músa, from which protrudes a lower bluff, visible from
all parts of the plain. This is the modern *Rás Sufsáfeh*
(Willow-head), and was in all probability the Sinai upon which
the Lord came down, and whence He spake " the ten words."
In that case the plain of Er Ráhah must have been that on
which Israel stood, and the mound in front, on the ascent to
Rás Sufsáfeh, the spot where Moses " separated from the elders
who had accompanied him so far on his ascent."

On leaving Rephidím the main body of the Israelites would
pass through what is known as Wády es Sheikh, a broad open
valley, containing tamarisk trees, and " cut right through the
granitic wall."   As a turn in the road is reached, " the journey
lies entirely through granite rocks, the sharp, rugged outlines of
which, as well as the increasing height and sombre grey colouring of the mountains, impart much more solemn grandeur to
the scenery."   A late eloquent traveller[2] thus describes the
approach to Sinai : " At each successive advance these cliffs
disengaged themselves from the intervening and surrounding
hills, and at last they stood out—I should rather say, the
columnar mass, which they form, stood out—alone against the
sky. On each side the infinite complications of twisted and
jagged mountains fell away from it. On each side the sky
compassed it round, as though it were alone in the wilderness.
And to this great mass we approached through a wide valley,
a long-continued plain, which, enclosed as it was between two
precipitous mountain ranges of black and yellow granite, and
having always at its end this prodigious mountain-block, I
could compare to nothing else than the immense avenue

---

[1] *Desert of the Exodus*, vol. i. p. 111. The quotations, when not otherwise
marked, are all from the same work.

[2] Dean Stanley, in his *Sinai and Palestine*, p. 72.

through which the approach was made to the great Egyptian temples."

As we try to realise the scene presented at the giving of the Law, we can well understand how " all the people that was in the camp trembled."[1] The vast plain of Er Ráhah, and all the neighbouring valleys and glens, were dotted with the tents of Israel. No more suitable camping-ground could have been found than this, the best-watered neighbourhood in the whole peninsula, where " running streams are found in no less than four of the adjacent valleys." The plain itself is nearly 5000 feet above the level of the sea. Right in front, cut off by intervening valleys from all around, rises the Horeb group (its highest point 7363 feet), and from it projects into the valley, like some gigantic altar or pulpit, the lower bluff of Rás Sufsáfeh (6830 feet)—" the nether part of the mount "—that Sinai from which the voice of the living God was heard. In front is the mound on which Moses parted from the elders. So abruptly does Sufsáfeh rise, " that you may literally stand under it and touch its base ;" and so thoroughly is the mountain range separated from all around, that there could be no difficulty whatever in " setting bounds unto the people round about," to prevent their going up into the mount, or even touching the border of it.[2] Behind Sufsáfeh, on some peak or cleft, Moses was forty days with the Lord, and descending into the adjacent valley, he would—as the members of the Ordnance Survey record they had frequently experienced—hear the sound from the camp without being able to see what passed in it.

But now as the people gazed on it, " Mount Sinai was altogether on smoke."[3] That vast isolated mountain-block— two miles in length and one in breadth—seemed all on fire ! As " the smoke of a furnace " it rose to heaven, " and the whole mount quaked greatly," and " there were thunders and lightnings," and " the voice of the trumpet exceeding loud." But, more awful than any physical signs, " Jehovah came down upon Mount Sinai," " and Jehovah called Moses to the top of the

[1] Ex. xix. 16.   [2] Ex. xix. 12.   [3] Ex. xix. 18.

mount," and God Himself "spake all these words " of the commandments. For three days had the people been preparing by continued sanctification, and now they stood in readiness at the foot of, although shut off from, the mountain. But even so, " when the people saw it, they removed, and stood afar off. And they said unto Moses, Speak thou with us, and we will hear : but let not God speak with us, lest we die."[1]

This outward sanctification of Israel had been preceded by inward and spiritual preparation. As always, the demand and the command of God had been preceded by His promise. For He ever gives what He asks. It is, as St. Augustine beautifully expresses it, "Give what Thou commandest, and command what Thou wilt." Arrived at the foot of Mount Sinai, Moses had gone up to a lower peak, as if to ask the commands of his Lord, and Jehovah had spoken to him from the top of the mountain. He was directed, before the people prepared to receive the Law, to remind them of their gracious deliverance from Egypt, of the judgments of God's hand, and of the mercy and kindness which they had received. For as " on eagle's wings" had Jehovah borne them, God's dealings being compared to the eagle, who spreads his strong pinions under the young birds when they take their first flight, lest, weary or faint, they be dashed on the rocks (comp. Deut. xxxii. 11). Yet all this mercy—Moses was to tell Israel—was but the pledge of far richer grace. For now would the Lord enter into covenant with them. And if Israel obeyed His voice, and kept the covenant, then, in His own words, "Ye shall be to Me a precious possession[2] from among all nations—for Mine is all the earth. And ye shall be unto Me a kingdom of priests and a holy nation."[3]

The promise thus conveyed was both special and universal ; and it described alike the character of God's people and their

---

[1] Ex. xx. 18, 19.

[2] The word is the same as for " choice treasure" (1 Chron. xxix. 3 ; Eccles. ii. 8). We have translated the whole verse literally.

[3] Ex. xix 5, 6.

destination. All the earth was God's, not only by right of creation and possession, but as destined yet to own Him its Lord. Herein lay a promise of universal blessing to all man-kind And with this the mission of Israel was closely bound up. But while all the earth was the Lord's, Israel was to be His "precious possession from among all nations," His choice treasure—for this the Hebrew expression implies—or, as St. Paul[1] and St. Peter[2] explain it, "a peculiar people." The manner in which this dignity would appear, is explained by the terms in which Israel is described as "a kingdom of priests and a holy nation." The expression "kingdom of priests" means a kingdom whose citizens are priests, and as such possess royal dignity and power, or, in the language of St. Peter, "a royal priesthood." So far as Israel was concerned, the outward and visible theocracy, which God established among them, was only the *means* by which this end was to be obtained, just as their observing the covenant was the *condition* of it. But the promise itself reached far beyond the Old Covenant, and will only be fulfilled in its completeness when "the Israel of God"—whom already the Lord Jesus, "the First-begotten of the dead and the Prince of the kings of the earth," "hath made kings and priests unto God and His Father"[3]—shall share with Him His glory and sit with Him on His throne. Thus the final object of the royal priesthood of Israel were those nations, from among whom God had chosen His people for a precious possession. Towards them Israel was to act as priests. For, just as the priest is the intermediary between God and man, so Israel was to be the intermediary of the knowledge and salvation of God to all nations. And this their priesthood was to be the foundation of their royalty.

A still more solemn description of Israel, and of us who are called "the Israel of God," is that of "holy nation." As Calvin rightly observes: "This designation was not due to the piety or holiness of the people, but because God distinguished them by peculiar privileges from all others. But this sanctification

Tit. ii. 14.   [2] 1 Pet. ii. 9.   [3] Rev. i. 5, 6; v. 10.

implies another, viz., that they who are so distinguished by God's grace should cultivate holiness, so that in turn they sanctify God." The Hebrew term for " holy " is generally supposed to mean " separated, set apart." But this is only its secondary signification, derived from the purpose of that which is holy. Its primary meaning is to be *splendid, beautiful, pure,* and *uncontaminated.* God is holy—as the Absolutely Pure, Resplendent, and Glorious One. Hence this is symbolised by the light. God dwelleth in light that is unapproachable;[1] He is " the Father of light, with Whom is no variableness, neither shadow of turning "—light which never can grow dimmer, nor give place to darkness.[2] Christ is the light that shineth in the darkness of our world, " the true light which lighteth every man."[3] And Israel was to be a holy people as dwelling in the light, through its covenant-relationship to God. It was not the selection of Israel from all other nations that made them holy, but the relationship to God into which it brought the people. The call of Israel, their election and selection, were only the *means.* Holiness itself was to be attained through the *covenant*, which provided forgiveness and sanctification, and in which, by the discipline of His law and the guidance of His Holy Arm, Israel was to be led onward and upward. Thus, if God showed the excellence of His name or His glory in creation,[4] the way of His holiness was among Israel.[5]

This detailed consideration of what Moses was charged to say, will help us to understand both the preparations for the covenant, and the solemn manner in which it was inaugurated. When Moses intimated to the people the gracious purpose of God, they declared their readiness to obey what God had spoken. But as the Lord could only enter into covenant with the people through the mediation of Moses, on account of their weakness and sinfulness, He spoke in a thick cloud with His servant before them all, so that they might see and hear, and for ever afterwards believe. As previously indicated, the out-

[1] I Tim. vi. 16. [2] James. i. 17. [3] John i. 5, 9. [4] Ps. viii.
[5] Ps. lxxvii. 13 ; comp. also Ps. civ. with Ps. ciii.

ward preparations of the people were twofold. First, they underwent certain purifications, symbolical of inward cleansing. Secondly, bounds were set round Sinai, so that none might break through nor touch the mountain,[1] Then, on the third day,[2] Moses led forth the men, and placed them "at the nether part of the mount," "that burned with fire." There God proclaimed His holy and eternal law amidst portentous signs, which indicated that He was great and terrible in His holiness, and a jealous God, though the fire of His wrath and zeal was enwrapt in a dense cloud.

The revelation of God's will, which Israel heard from Mount Sinai, is contained in the ten commandments, or, as they are called in the Hebrew original, "the ten words."[3] These were prefaced by this declaration of what Jehovah was and what He had done : " I am Jehovah thy God, which have brought thee out of the land of Egypt, out of the house of bondage."[4] This (as Calvin says) "to prepare the souls of the people for obedience." The " ten words" were afterwards written on two tables of stone, which were to be kept within the ark of the covenant, "the mercy-seat" being significantly placed over them.[5] It is not easy to say how they were arranged on these two tables, but not improbably the first four "words" with "the Preface" (in ver. 1) may have occupied the first, and the other six commandments the second Table of the Law.[6] But we only

[1] When we read in Ex. xix. 24, "let not the priests and the people break through," we are to understand by the former expression not the Aaronic priesthood, which had not yet been instituted, but those who hitherto discharged priestly functions—probably the heads of houses.

[2] According to Jewish tradition this was the day of Pentecost, fifty days after the Passover.

[3] The Decalogue, comp. Ex. xxxiv. 28 ; Deut. iv. 13.

[4] Ex. xx. 2.   [5] Ex. xxv. 16; xl. 20.

[6] Most likely not the whole of each commandment, but in every case only the actual direction (such as "Thou shalt not steal") was graven on the tables. This would give in the Hebrew, for the first four commandments, along with the " Preface," seventy-three words, and for the other six commandments thirty-one words. It is well known that the Roman Catholics

know for certain, that "the tables were written on both their sides : on the one side and on the other were they written And the tables were the work of God, and the writing was the writing of God, graven upon the tables."[1]

Considering more closely these "ten words" "of the covenant," we notice, first, their number : *ten*, as that of completeness. Next, we see that the fifth commandment (to honour our parents) forms a transition from the first to the second table— the first table detailing our duties towards God ; the second those towards man. But our duty to our parents is higher than that towards men generally; indeed, in a certain sense is Divine, just as the relationship to an earthly father symbolises that to our Father in heaven. Hence the command is to *honour*, whereas our duty to men only requires us to *love* them. Again, almost all the commands are put in a *negative* form (" thou shalt not "), implying that transgression, not obedience, is natural to us. But "the commandment is exceeding broad," and requires a corresponding right state of mind. Accordingly we find that the law of the ten commandments is summed up in this : " Thou shalt love the Lord thy God with all thy heart, and with all thy soul, and with all thy strength ; and thy neighbour as thyself." Lastly, the first five "words" have always some reason or motive attached to them. Not so those of the second

---

and the Lutheran Church combine the two first commandments into one, and divide the tenth into two. But for this there is not the shadow of ground or authority, either in the Hebrew text or even in Jewish tradition.

[1] Ex. xxxii. 15, 16. When we read that the law was "received by the ministration of angels " (Acts vii. 53 ; Gal. iii. 19 ; Heb. ii. 2), we are not to understand by it that God Himself did not speak all these words, but either to refer it to those "ten thousands" of angels who were His attendants when He spake on Sinai (Deut. xxxiii. 2 ; Ps. lxviii. 17) ; or, more probably, to the difference between the Old and the New Testament dispensations. In the former, the Second Person of the Blessed Trinity appeared only in the Angel of the Covenant ; in the latter, He became incarnate in the Person of Jesus Christ, the God-Man.

table, which are mostly put quite generally, to show that such commands as, not to kill, not to commit adultery, not to steal, not to bear false witness, are intended to apply to all possible cases, and not only to friends or fellow-citizens.

Passing from general considerations to particulars, we find that the "*first word*" not only forbids all idolatry in thought, word, and deed, but enjoins to love, fear, serve, and cleave to the Lord.[1] The *second word* shows the *manner* in which the Lord will be served—more particularly, not under any image or by any outward representation. As Calvin remarks, it condemns "all fictitious worship which men have invented according to their own minds," and not according to the word of God. The *third word* forbids the profaning of the name of Jehovah, in which He has manifested His glory, by using it either for untruth or in vain words, that is, either in false or idle swearing, in cursing, in magic, or such like. The *fourth word*, which implies a previous knowledge of the Sabbath on the part of Israel, enjoins personal, domestic, and public rest from all manner of labour on God's holy day, which is to be spent in His service and for His glory. The *fifth word* directs honour to parents as (in the language of Luther) "the vicars of God," and hence implies similar reverence towards all God's representatives, especially magistrates and rulers. The *Second Table* progresses from outward deed (in the sixth, seventh, and eighth "words") to speech (ninth commandment), and finally to thought and desire. The *sixth, seventh, and eighth words* apply equally to what may injure *our own* life, chastity, or property, and those of others. The *ninth word* should be literally translated: "Thou shalt not answer against thy neighbour as a false witness" (or "as a witness of falsehood"). Comparing this with the statement in Deut. v. 20, where the expression is "a witness of vanity," we gather that not only all untrue, but all unfounded statements against our neighbour are included in this commandment. Lastly, the *tenth word* sounds the inmost depths of our hearts, and forbids all

[1] Deut. vi. 5, 13; x. 12, 20.

wrong and inordinate desires in reference to anything that is
our neighbour's.[1]

Such law was never given by man ; never dreamed of in his
highest conceptions.   Had man only been able to observe it,
assuredly not only life hereafter but happiness and joy here
would have come with it. As it was, it brought only knowledge
of sin.   Yet, for ever blessed be God : " The law was given by
Moses, but grace and truth came by Jesus Christ."[2]

———◇———

CHAPTER XI.

Civil and Social Ordinances of Israel as the People of God—Their Religious Ordinances in their National Aspect—The "Covenant made by Sacrifice," and the Sacrificial Meal of Acceptance.

(Ex. xx. 18–xxiv. 12.)

THE impression produced upon the people by the phenomena accompanying God's revelation of His law was so
deep, that they entreated that any further Divine communication
might be made through the mediatorship of Moses. As Peter,
when the Divine power of the Lord Jesus suddenly burst upon
him,[3] felt that he, a sinful man, could not stand in the presence
of his Lord, so were the children of Israel afraid of death, if
they continued before God. But such feelings of fear have
nothing spiritual in themselves.   While Moses acceded to their
request, he was careful to explain that the object of all they
had witnessed had not been the excitement of fear (Ex. xx. 20),
but such searching of heart as might issue, not in slavish
apprehension of outward consequences, but in that true fear of
God, which would lead to the avoidance of sin.

---

[1] In Deut. v. 21 two different expressions are used—the "desire" being
awakened from without by that which is seen to be beautiful ; while the
" coveting" springs from within--from the evil inclinations or supposed
requirements of him who covets.   [2] John i. 17.   [3] Luke v. 8.

And now Moses stood once more alone in the " thick darkness, where God was." The ordinances then given him must
be regarded as the final preparation for that covenant which
was so soon to be ratified.[1] For, as the people of God, Israel
must not be like the other nations. Alike in substance and in
form, the conditions of their national life, the fundamental principles of their state, and the so-called civil rights and ordinances
which were to form the groundwork of society, must be Divine.
To use a figure : Israel was God's own possession. Before
hallowing and formally setting it apart, God marked it out, and
drew the boundary-lines around His property. Such was the
object and the meaning of the ordinances,[2] which preceded the
formal conclusion of the covenant, recorded in Exodus xxiv.
Accordingly the principles and " judgments" (xxi. 1), or rather
the "rights" and juridical arrangements, on which national
life and civil society in Israel were based, were not only
infinitely superior to anything known or thought of at the
time, but such as to embody the solid and abiding principles
of national life for all times. And in truth they underlie all
modern legislation, so that the Mosaic ordinances are, and will
remain, the grand model on which civil society is constructed.[3]

Without entering into details, we note the general arrangement of these ordinances. They were preceded by a general
indication of *the manner in which Israel was to worship God.*[4]
As God had spoken to Israel " from heaven," so they were not
to make any earthly representation of what was heavenly. On
the other hand, as God would " come unto " them—from heaven
to earth, and there hold intercourse with them, the altar which
was to *rise* from earth towards heaven was to be simply " an
altar of earth " (ver. 24), or if of stones, of such as were in the
condition in which they had been found in the earth. Moreover, as the altar indicated that place on earth where God

[1] Ex. xxiv.   [2] Ex. xx. 22–xxiii.
[3] Fully to understand the sublime principles of the Mosaic, or rather
the Divine Law, they must be examined in detail. This, of course, is
impossible in this place.   [4] Ex. xx. 22–26.

would appear for the purpose of blessing Israel, it was only to be reared where *God* recorded His name, that is, where *He* appointed it. In other words, their worship was to be regulated by His manifestation in grace, and not by their own choice or preferences. For grace lies at the foundation of all praise and prayer. The sacrifices and worship of Israel were not to procure grace; grace had been the originating cause of their worship. And so it ever is. "We love Him, because He first loved us," and the gift of His dear Son to us sinners is free and unconditional on the part of the Father, and makes our return unto Him possible. And because this grace is free, it becomes man all the more to serve God with holy reverence, which should show itself even in outward demeanour (ver. 26).

"The judgments" next communicated to Moses determined, first, *the civil and social position of all in Israel relatively to each other* (Ex. xxi. 1–xxiii. 12), and then *their religious position relatively to the Lord* (xxiii. 13–19)."

The Divine legislation *begins*, as assuredly none other ever did, not at the topmost but at the lowest rung of society. It declares in the first place *the personal rights of such individuals as are in a state of dependence—male* (xxi. 2–6) and *female slaves* (vers. 7–11). This is done not only with a sacred regard for the rights of the person, but with a delicacy, kindness, and strictness beyond any code ever framed on this subject. If slavery was still tolerated, as a thing existent, its real principle, that of making men chattels and property, was struck at the root, and the institution became, by its safeguards and provisions, quite other from what it has been among any nation, whether ancient or modern.

Then follow "judgments" guarding *life* (vers. 12–14), with crimes against which, the maltreatment and the cursing of parents (vers. 15, 17), and man-stealing (ver. 16), are put on a level. It is the *sanctity of life*, in itself, in its origin, and in its free possession, which is here in question, and the punishment awarded to such crimes is neither intended as warning nor as correction, but strictly as punishment, that is, as retribution.

From the *protection of life* the law passes to that *of the body* against all injuries, whether *by man* (vers. 18–27) or *by beast* (vers. 28–32). The principle here is, so far as possible, *compensation*, coupled with punishment in grave offences.

Next, the safety of *property* is secured. But before entering upon it, the Divine law, Divine also in this, protects also the life of a beast.[1] Property is dealt with under various aspects. First, we have the *theft of cattle*—the most important to guard against among an agricultural people—a different kind of protection being wisely allowed to owners by day and by night (xxii. 1–4). Then, *damage to fields or their produce* is considered (vers. 5, 6). After that, *loss or damage of what had been entrusted* for safe keeping (vers. 7–15), and along with it *loss of honour* (vers. 16, 17) are dealt with.

The statutes which follow (vers. 18–30) are quite different in character from those which had preceded. This appears even from the omission of the " *if*," by which all the previous ordinances had been introduced. In truth, they do not contemplate, as the others, any possible case, but they state and ordain what must never be allowed to take place. They are beyond the province of ordinary civil legislation, and concern Israel as being specially *the people of God*. As such they express what Jehovah expects from His own people, bound to Him by covenant. And this, perhaps, is the most wonderful part of the legislation, regulating and ordering what no civil rule has ever sought to influence. As before, the series of statutes begins by interdicting what is contrary to the God-consecrated character of the nation. Thus, at the outset all *magic* is exterminated (ver. 18), and with it *all unnatural crimes* (ver. 19), and *idolatrous practices* (ver. 20). In short, as before in worship, so now in life, heathenism, its powers, its vileness, and its corruptions are swept aside. On the other hand, in opposition to all national exclusiveness, the stranger (though not the strange god) is to be kindly welcomed (ver. 21) ; widows and the fatherless are not

---

[1] Ex. xxi. 33–36.

to be " humiliated "[1] (vers. 22–24) ; those in temporary need not
to be vexed by usury (vers. 25–27) ; God as the supreme Lawgiver
is not to be reviled, nor yet are those appointed to rule under
Him to be cursed (ver. 28) ; the tribute due to the Lord as
King is to be cheerfully given (vers. 29, 30) ; and the holy dignity
of His people not to be profaned even in their daily habits (ver.
31). Again, nothing that is untrue, unloving, or unjust is to be
said, done, or attempted (xxiii. 1–3), and that not merely in
public dealings, but personal dislike is not to influence conduct.
On the contrary, all loving help is to be given even to an enemy
in time of need (vers. 4, 5) ; the poor and persecuted are not to
be unjustly dealt with ; no bribe is to be taken, " for the gift
maketh open eyes blind, and perverteth the causes of the righteous,"[2] and the same rule is to apply to the stranger as to Israel
(vers. 6–9). Finally in this connection, the seventh year's and
the seventh day's rest are referred to, not so much in their
religious character as in their bearing upon the poor and the
workers (vers. 10–12).

Passing from the statutes fixing the civil and social position
of all in Israel to *their religious position relatively to Jehovah,*[3]
we have first of all an injunction of the three great annual feasts.
Although strictly religious festivals, they are here viewed,
primarily, not in their symbolical and typical meaning (which is
universal and eternal), but *in their national bearing:* the Paschal
feast as that of Israel's deliverance from Egypt, the feast of
weeks as that " of harvest, the firs fruit of thy labours," and
the feast of tabernacles as that of final " ingathering" (vers.
14–17). Of the three ordinances which now follow (vers. 18–19),
the first refers to the Paschal sacrifice (comp. Exodus xii. 15,
20 ; xiii. 7 ; xxxiv. 25), and the second to the feast of firstfruits
or of weeks. From this it would follow, that the prohibition
to " seethe a kid in its mother's milk " (ver. 19) must, at least
primarily, have borne some reference to the festivities of the

---

[1] This, not "afflicted," as in the Authorised Version, is the right translation, the command extending beyond oppression to all unkind treatment.
[2] So verse 8 literally.   [3] Ex. xxiii. 13–19.

week of tabernacles ; perhaps, as the learned Rabbinical commentator Abarbanel suggests, because some such practices were connected with heathen, idolatrous rites at the time of the ingathering of fruits.[1]

The "judgments" which the Lord enjoins upon His people are appropriately followed by *promises* (xxiii. 20–33), in which, as their King and Lord, He undertakes their guidance and protection, and their possession of the land He had assigned to them. First and foremost, assurance is given them of the personal presence of Jehovah in that ANGEL, in Whom is the Name of the Lord (ver. 20). This was no common angel, however exalted, but a manifestation of Jehovah Himself, prefigurative of, and preparatory to His manifestation in the flesh in the Person of our Lord and Saviour Jesus Christ. For all that is here said of Him is attributed to the Lord Himself in Exodus xiii. 21 ; while in Exodus xxxiii. 14, 15, He is expressly designated as "the Face" of Jehovah ("My Face"—in the Authorised Version "My presence"). Accordingly, all obedience is to be shown to His guidance, and every contact with idolatry and idolaters avoided. In that case the Lord would fulfil every good and gracious promise to His people, and cause them to possess the land in all its extent.

Such were the terms of the covenant which Jehovah made with Israel in *their national capacity.* When the people had ratified them by acceptance,[2] Moses wrote all down in what was called "the book of the covenant" (xxiv. 7). And now the covenant itself was to be inaugurated by sacrifice, the sprinkling

[1] From our ignorance of the circumstances, this is perhaps one of the most difficult prohibitions to understand. The learned reader will find every opinion on the subject discussed in *Bocharti Hierozoicon,* vol. i. pp. 634, 635. It is well known that the modern Jews understand it as implying that nothing made of milk is to be cooked or eaten along with any kind of meat, even knives and dishes being changed, and most punctilious precautions taken against any possible intermixture of the two. Most commentators find the reason of the prohibition in the cruelty of seething a kid in its mother's milk. But the meaning must lie deeper.

[2] Ex. xxiv. 3.

of blood, and the sacrificial meal. This transaction was the most important in the whole history of Israel. By this one sacrifice, never renewed, Israel was formally set apart as the people of God ; and it lay at the foundation of all the sacrificial worship which followed. Only *after* it did God institute the Tabernacle, the priesthood, and all its services. Thus this one sacrifice prefigured the one sacrifice of our Lord Jesus Christ for His Church, which is the ground of our access to God and the foundation of all our worship and service. Most significantly, an altar was now built at the foot of Mount Sinai, and surrounded by twelve pillars " according to the twelve tribes of Israel." Ministering youths—for as yet there was no priesthood—offered the burnt, and sacrificed the peace offerings unto Jehovah. Half of the blood of the sacrifices was put into basins, with the other half the altar was sprinkled, thus making reconciliation with God. Then the terms of the covenant were once more read in the hearing of all, and the other half of the blood, by which reconciliation *had* been made, sprinkled on the people with these words : " Behold the blood of the covenant which Jehovah hath made with you upon all these words (or terms)."[1]

As a nation Israel was now reconciled and set apart unto God—both having been accomplished by the " blood of sprinkling." Thereby they became prepared for that fellowship with Him which was symbolised in the sacrificial meal that followed.[2] There God, in pledge of His favour, fed His people upon the sacrifices which He had accepted. The sacrificial meal meant the fellowship of acceptance ; its joy was that of the consciousness of this blessed fact. And now Moses and Aaron, and his two sons (the future priests), along with seventy of the elders

[1] Further details are furnished in Heb. ix. 19–22, where also transactions differing in point of time are grouped together, as all forming part of this dedication of the first Covenant by blood. That this is the meaning of the passage appears from Heb. ix. 22. The sprinkling of the book and the people, as afterwards of the Tabernacle and its vessels, was made in the manner described in ver. 19.

[2] Ex. xxiv. 9–11

of Israel, went up into the mount, "and did eat and drink" at that sacrificial meal, in the seen presence of the God of Israel—not indeed under any outward form,[1] but with heaven's own brightness underneath the Shechinah. Thus "to see God, and to eat and drink," was a foretaste and a pledge of the perfect blessedness in beholding Him hereafter. It was also a symbol and a type of what shall be realised when, as the Alleluia of the "great multitude" proclaims the reign of the "Lord God omnipotent," the gladsome, joyous bride of the Lamb now made ready for the marriage, and adorned with bridal garments, hears the welcome sound summoning her to "the marriage supper of the Lamb."[2]

CHAPTER XII.

The Pattern seen on the Mountain—The Tabernacle, the Priesthood, and the Services in their arrangement and typical meaning—The Sin of the Golden Calf—The Divine Judgment—The Plea of Moses—God's gracious forgiveness—The Vision of the Glory of the Lord vouchsafed to Moses.

(Ex. xxiv. 12.-xxxiii.)

NEVER assuredly have we stronger proof of the Divine origin of what we call grace, and of the weakness and unprofitableness of human nature, than in the reaction which so often follows seasons of religious privilege. Readers of the New Testament will recall many instances of this in the Gospel-history, and will remember how our Lord, ever and again, at such times took His disciples aside into some desert place for quietness and prayer. But perhaps the saddest instance of how near the great enemy lingers to our seasons of spiritual enjoyment, and how great our danger of giddiness, when standing on such heights, is furnished by the history of Israel, immediately after the solemn covenant had been ratified.

[1] Deut. iv. 12, 15. [2] Rev. xix. 6-9.

Now that God had set apart His reconciled people unto Himself, it was necessary to have some definite place where He would meet with, and dwell among them, as also to appoint the means by which they should approach Him, and the manner in which He would manifest Himself to them. To reveal all this, as well as to give those "tables of stone," on which the commandments were graven, God now called Moses once more "up into the mount." Accompanied by "Joshua, his minister," he obeyed the Divine behest, leaving the rule of the people to Aaron and Hur. For six days he had to wait, while "the glory of Jehovah abode upon the mount." On the seventh, Moses was summoned within the bright cloud, which, to the children of Israel beneath, seemed "like a devouring fire"—Joshua probably remaining near, but not actually with him. "Forty days and forty nights" "Moses was in the mount," without either eating bread or drinking water.[1] The new revelation which he now received concerned the *Tabernacle* which was to be erected, the *priesthood* which was to serve in it, and the *services* which were to be celebrated. Nay, it extended to every detail of furniture, dress, and observance. And for what was needful for this service, the *free-will offerings* of Israel were to be invited.[2]

We have it upon the highest authority, that, not only in its grand outlines, but in all minutest details, everything was to be made "after the pattern" which God showed to Moses on the mount.[3] And so we also read in Acts vii. 44, and Hebrews viii. 5 ; ix. 23, teaching us, that Moses was shown by God an actual pattern or model of all that he was to make in and for the sanctuary. This can convey only one meaning. It taught far more than the general truth, that only that approach to God is lawful or acceptable which He has indicated. For, God showed Moses every detail to indicate that every detail had its special meaning, and hence could not be altered in any, even the minutest, particular, without destroying that meaning, and losing that significance which alone made it of importance.

[1] Deut. ix. 9.   [2] Ex. xxv. 1-8.   [3] Ex. xxv. 9.

Nothing here was intended as a mere ornament or ceremony, all was *symbol* and *type*. As symbol, it indicated a present truth; as type, it pointed forward (a prophecy by deed) to future spiritual realities, while, at the same time, it already conveyed to the worshipper the firstfruits, and the earnest of their final accomplishment in "the fulness of time." We repeat, everything here had a spiritual meaning—the material of which the ark, the dresses of the priesthood, and all else was made; colours, measurements, numbers, vessels, dresses, services, and the priesthood itself—and all proclaimed the same spiritual truth, and pointed forward to the same spiritual reality, viz., God in Christ in the midst of His Church. The Tabernacle was "the tent of meeting" (*Ohel Moëd*) where God held intercourse with His people, and whence He dispensed blessing unto them. The priesthood, culminating in the high-priest, was the God-appointed mediatorial agency through which God was approached and by which He bestowed His gifts; the sacrifices were the means of such approach to God, and either intended to restore fellowship with God when it had been dimmed or interrupted, or else to express and manifest that fellowship. But alike the priesthood, the sacrifices, and the altar pointed to the Person and the work of the Lord Jesus Christ. So far as the Tabernacle itself was concerned, the court with the altar of burnt-offering was the place by which Israel *approached* God; the Holy Place that in which they held communion with God; and the Most Holy Place that in which the Lord Himself visibly dwelt among them in the Shechinah, as the covenant-God, His Presence resting on the mercy-seat which covered the Ark.

It is most instructive to mark the *order* in which the various ordinances about the Tabernacle and its furniture were given to Moses. First, we have the directions about the *Ark*, as the most holy thing in the Most Holy Place;[1] then, similarly, those about the *table of shewbread* and the *golden candlestick* (xxv. 23–40), not only as belonging to the furniture of the Holy

[1] Ex. xxv. 10–22.

Place, but because spiritually the truths which they symbolized
—life and light in the Lord—were the outcome of God's
Presence between the cherubim. After that, the dwelling
itself is described, and the position in it of Ark, table, and
candlestick.[1] Then only comes the *altar of burnt-offering*, with
the court that was to surround the sanctuary (xxvii. 1–19).
We now enter, as it were, upon a different section, *that of
ministry*. Here directions are first given about *the burning of
the lamps* on the seven-branched candlestick (xxvii. 20, 21);
after which we have the institution of, and all connected with,
the priesthood.[2] The last, because the highest, point in the
ministry is that about the *altar of incense* and its service
(xxx. 1–10). This symbolized *prayer*, and hence could only
come in after the institution of the mediatorial priesthood.
Thus far it will be noticed, that the arrangement is always *from
within outwards*—from the Most Holy Place to the court of
the worshippers, symbolizing once more that all proceeds from
Him Who is the God of grace, Who, as already quoted in the
language of St. Augustine, "gives what He commands,"[3] and
that the highest of all service, to which everything else is
subservient, or rather to which it stands related as the means
towards the end, is that of fellowship in prayer—the worshipful
beholding of God.

These directions are followed by some others strictly connected with the character of Israel as the people of God.
Israel is His firstborn among the nations,[4] and, as such, must
be redeemed, like the firstborn son of a family,[5] to indicate,
on the one hand, that the people are really His own property, and that the life entrusted to them belongeth to Him;
and, on the other hand, to express that, in the firstborn, all the

---

[1] Ex. xxvi.   [2] Ex. xxviii.; xxix.

[3] "Da quod jubes, et jube quod vis"—Give what Thou commandest,
and command what Thou wilt; a principle, we cannot too often repeat,
applicable throughout the economy of grace, where all originates with
God.   [4] Ex. iv. 22, 23.

[5] Ex. xxii. 29; xxxiv. 20; Numb. iii. 12, 13, 16.

family is hallowed to God.[1] This was the import of the
"*atonement money.*"[2] But even so, each approach to Him
needed special *washing*—hence the *laver* (xxx. 17–21). Again,
within Israel, the priests were to be the sacred representatives
of the people. As such, they, and all connected with their
service, must be *anointed* with a peculiar oil, symbolical of the
Holy Spirit, all counterfeit of which was to be visited with such
punishment as reminds us of that following upon the sin
against the Holy Ghost (vers. 22–33). Lastly, the *material*
for the highest symbolical service, that of *incensing*, is described
(vers. 34–38). The whole section closes by designating the
persons whom the Lord had raised up for doing all the work
connected with the preparation of His Sanctuary.[3]

The institutions thus made were, in reality, the outcome
and the consequences of the covenant which the Lord had
made with Israel. As "*a sign*" of this covenant between
Jehovah and the children of Israel,[4] God now ordered anew
the *observance of the Sabbath* (xxxi. 12–17)—its twofold provision of rest and of sanctification (ver. 15) being expressive of
the civil and the religious aspects of that covenant, and of
their marvellous combination. Thus furnished with all needful
directions, Moses finally received, at the Hand of the Lord,
the "two tables of testimony," "written with the finger of
God" (ver. 18).

While these sacred transactions were taking place on the
mount, a far different scene was enacted below in the camp of
Israel. Without attempting the foolish and wrongful task of
palliating the sin of making the Golden Calf,[5] it is right that
the matter should be placed in its true light. The prolonged
absence of Moses had awakened peculiar fears in the people.
They had seen him pass more than a month ago into the
luminous cloud that covered the mount. "And the sight of
the glory of Jehovah was like a devouring fire on the top of
the mount in the eyes of the children of Israel."[6] What more

---

[1] Rom. xi. 16.   [2] Ex. xxx. 11–16.   [3] Ex. xxxi. 1–11.
[4] Ex. xxxi. 17.   [5] Ex. xxxii. 1–6.   [6] Ex. xxiv. 17.

natural than for those who waited, week after week, in unexplained solitude, within sight of this fire, to imagine that
Moses had been devoured by it? Their leader was gone, and
the visible symbol of Jehovah was high up on the mountain
top, like "a devouring fire." They must have another leader;
that would be Aaron. But they must also have another symbol
of the Divine Presence. One only occurred to their carnal
minds, besides that which had hitherto preceded them. It was
the Egyptian Apis, who, under the form of a calf, represented
the powers of nature. To his worship they had always been
accustomed; indeed, its principal seat was the immediate
neighbourhood of the district in Egypt where, for centuries,
they and their fathers had been settled. Probably, this also
was the form under which many of them had, in former days,
tried, in a perverted manner, to serve their ancestral God,
combining the traditions of the patriarchs with the corruptions
around them (compare Joshua xxiv. 14; Ezekiel xx. 8; xxiii.
3, 8). It is quite evident that Israel did not mean to forsake
Jehovah, but only to serve Him under the symbol of Apis.
This appears from the statement of the people themselves on
seeing the Golden Calf:[1] "This is thy God,"[2] and from the
proclamation of Aaron (xxxii. 5): "To-morrow is a feast to
Jehovah." Their great sin consisted in not realizing the Presence of an unseen God, while the fears of their unbelief led
them back to their former idolatrous practices, unmindful that
this involved a breach of the second of those commandments so
lately proclaimed in their hearing, and of the whole covenant
which had so solemnly been ratified. Some expositors have
sought to extenuate the guilt of Aaron by supposing that, in
asking for their golden ornaments to make "the calf," he had
hoped to enlist their vanity and covetousness, and so to turn
them from their sinful purpose. The text, however, affords no
warrant for this hypothesis. It is true that Aaron was, at the

---

[1] Ex. xxxii. 4.

[2] Both here and in ver. 1 the rendering should be in the *singular*
("God"), and not in the *plural* ("Gods"), as in the Authorised Version.

time, not yet in the priesthood, and also that his proclamation
of "a feast to Jehovah" may have been intended to bring it
out distinctly, that the name of Jehovah was still, as before,
acknowledged by Israel. But his culpable weakness—to say
the least of it—only adds to his share in the people's sin.
Indeed, this appears from Aaron's later confession to Moses,[1]
than which nothing more humiliating is recorded, even throughout this sad story. Perhaps, however, it was well that, before
his appointment to the priesthood, Aaron, and all after him,
should have had this evidence of natural unfitness and unworthiness, that so it might appear more clearly that the character of all was typical, and in no way connected with the
worthiness of Aaron or of his house.

While Israel indulged in the camp in the usual licentious
dances and orgies which accompanied such heathen festivals
yet another trial awaited Moses. It had been God Himself
Who informed Moses of the "quick" apostasy of His people
(xxxii. 7, 8), accompanying the announcement by these words:
"Now therefore let Me alone, that My wrath may wax hot
against them, and that I may consume them : and I will make of
thee a great nation" (ver. 10). One of the fathers has already
noticed, that the Divine words, "Now therefore let Me alone,"
seemed to imply a call to Moses to exercise his office as
intercessor for his people. Moreover, it has also been remarked, that the offer to make of Moses a nation even greater
than Israel,[2] was, in a sense, a real temptation, or rather a
trial of Moses' singleness of purpose and faithfulness to his
mission. We know how entirely Moses stood this trial, and
how earnestly, perseveringly, and successfully he pleaded for
Israel with the Lord (vers. 11–14). But one point has not
been sufficiently noticed by commentators. When, in announcing the apostasy of Israel, God spake of them not as His own
but as Moses' people—"thy people, whom thou broughtest out
of the land of Egypt" (ver. 7)—He at the same time furnished
Moses with the right plea in his intercession, and also indi-

---

[1] Ex. xxxii. 21–24.   [2] Deut. ix. 14.

cated the need of that severe punishment which was afterwards
executed, lest Moses might, by weak indulgence, be involved
in complicity with Israel's sin. The latter point is easily understood. As for the other, we see how Moses, in his intercession,
pleaded the argument with which God had furnished him.
Most earnestly did he insist that Israel was *God's* people, since
their deliverance from Egypt had been wholly God-wrought.
Three special arguments did he use with God, and *these three
may to all time serve as models* in our pleading for forgiveness
and restoration after weaknesses and falls. These arguments
were: *first*, that Israel was God's property, and that His past
dealings had proved this (ver. 11); *secondly*, that God's own
glory was involved in the deliverance of Israel in the face of
the enemy (ver. 12); and, *thirdly*, that God's gracious promises
were pledged for their salvation (ver. 13). And such pleas God
never refuses to accept (ver. 14).

But, although informed of the state of matters in the camp
of Israel, Moses could have been scarcely prepared for the
sight which presented itself, when, on suddenly turning an
eminence,[1] the riotous multitude, in its licentious merriment,
appeared full in view. The contrast was too great, and as
" Moses' wrath waxed hot, he cast the tables out of his hands,
and brake them beneath the mount" (ver. 19). It is not
necessary to suppose that what follows in the sacred text is
related in the strict order of time. Suffice it, that, after a short
but stern reproof to Aaron, Moses took his station "in the gate
of the camp," summoning to him those who were " on the side
of Jehovah." All the sons of Levi obeyed, and were directed
to go through the camp and "slay every man his brother, and
every man his companion, and every man his neighbour"
(ver. 27). On that terrible day no less than 3,000 men fell

[1] "Often in descending this" (the so-called "Hill of the Golden Calf,"
close by the spot whence the Law was given), "while the precipitous sides
of the ravine hid the tents from my gaze, have I heard the sound of voices
from below, and thought how Joshua had said unto Moses as *he* came down
from the mount, 'There is a noise of war in the camp.'"—Mr. Palmer in
The Desert of the Exodus, vol. i. p. 115.

under the sword of Levi. As for the Golden Calf, its wooden framework was burnt in the fire and its gold covering ground to powder, and strewed upon the brook which descended from Sinai.[1] Of this Israel had to drink, in symbol that each one must receive and bear the fruits of his sin, just as, later on, the woman suspected of adultery was ordered to drink the water into which the writing of the curses upon her sin had been washed.[2]

There is one point here which requires more particular inquiry than it has yet received. As commonly understood, the slaughter of these 3,000 stands out as an unexplained fact. Why just *these* 3,000? Did they fall simply because they happened to stand by nearest, on the principle, as has been suggested, of decimating an offending host; and why did no one come to their aid? Such indiscriminate punishment seems scarcely in accordance with the Divine dealings. But the text, as it appears to us, furnishes hints for the right explanation. When Moses stood in the camp of Israel and made proclamation for those who were on Jehovah's side, we read that "he saw that the people were naked" (ver. 25), or unreined, *licentious* (comp. ver. 6; 1 Cor. x. 7, 8). In short, there stood before him a number of men, fresh from their orgies, in a state of licentious attire, whom even his appearance and words had not yet sobered into quietness, shame, and repentance. These, as we understand it, still thronged the open roadway of the camp, which so lately had resounded with their voices; these were met by the avenging Levites, as, sword in hand, they passed from gate to gate, like the destroying angel through Egypt on the Paschal night; and these were the 3,000 which fell on that day, while the vast multitude had retired to the quietness of their tents in tardy repentance and fear, in view of him whose presence among them betokened the nearness of that holy and jealous God, Whose terrible judgments they had so much cause to dread.

[1] Deut. ix. 21. The learned reader will find every possible suggestion in *Bocharti Hieroz.*, vol. i. pp. 349, etc. [2] Numb. v. 24.

Thus ended the day of Moses' return among his people. On the morrow he gathered them to speak, not in anger but in sorrow, of their great sin.   Then returning from them to the Lord, he entreated forgiveness for his brethren, with an intensity and self-denial of love (vers. 31, 32), unequalled by that of any man except St. Paul.[1] Thus far he prevailed, that the people were not to be destroyed, nor the covenant to cease; but God would not personally go in the midst of a people so incapable of bearing His holy Presence ; He would send a created angel to be henceforth their leader.   And still would this sin weight the scale in the day of visitation, which the further rebellion of this people would only too surely bring.   The first words of the final sentence, that their carcases were to fall in the wilderness,[2] were, so to speak, already uttered in this warning of the Lord on the morrow of the slaughter of the 3,000 : " Nevertheless in the day when I visit I will visit their sin upon them."   " Thus," in the language of Scripture (ver. 35), " Jehovah smote the people, because they made the calf, which Aaron made."[3]

That the Lord would not go personally with Israel because of their stiffneckedness, was, indeed, felt to be " evil tidings."[4] The account of the people's repentance and of God's gracious forgiveness[5] forms one of the most precious portions of this history.   The first manifestation of their godly sorrow was the putting away of their " ornaments," not only temporarily but permanently.   Thus we read : " The children of Israel stripped themselves of their ornaments from the mount Horeb onward " (xxxiii. 6).[6] Israel was, so to speak, in permanent mourning, ever after its great national sin.   Next, as the Lord would not per-

---

[1] Rom. ix. 3.   "It is not easy," writes Bengel, "to estimate the love of a Moses or a Paul.   Our small measure of capacity can scarcely take it in, just as an infant cannot realise the courage of a hero."

[2] Numb. xiv. 29.

[3] The text does *not* necessarily imply (as the Authorised Version would naturally suggest) that any further special "plagues" were at *that* time sent upon the people.   [4] Ex. xxxiii. 4.

[5] Ex. xxxiii.   [6] So literally.

sonally be in the midst of Israel, Moses removed the tent—probably his own—outside the camp, that there he might receive the Divine communications, when "the cloudy pillar descended," "and Jehovah talked with Moses." Moses called this "the tent of meeting" (rendered in the Authorised Version "the tabernacle of the congregation :" ver. 7). It is scarcely necessary to say, that this was not "the Tabernacle" (as the Authorised Version might lead one to infer), since the latter was not yet constructed. To this "tent of meeting" all who were of the true Israel, and who regarded Jehovah not merely as their national God, but owned Him personally and felt the need of Him, were wont to go out. This must not be looked upon as either a protest or an act of separation on their part, but as evidence of true repentance and of their desire to meet with God, who no longer was in the camp of Israel. Moreover, all the people, when they saw the cloudy pillar descend to Moses, "rose up and worshipped." Altogether, this was perhaps the period of greatest heart-softening during Israel's wanderings in the wilderness.

And God graciously had respect to it. He had already assured Moses that he stood in special relationship to Him ("I know thee by name"), and that his prayer for Israel had been heard ("thou hast also found grace in My sight"). But as yet the former sentence stood, to the effect that an angel, not Jehovah Himself, was to be Israel's future guide. Under these circumstances Moses now entreated Jehovah to show him His way, that is, His present purpose in regard to Israel, adding, that if God would bring them into the Land of Promise, He would "consider that this is Thy people," and hence He their God and King. This plea also prevailed, and the Lord once more promised that His own presence would go with them, and that He Himself would give them the rest of Canaan (ver. 14; comp. Deut. iii. 20; Heb. iv. 8). And Moses gave thanks by further prayer, even more earnest than before, for the blessing now again vouchsafed (vers. 15, 16).

But one thing had become painfully evident to Moses by

what had happened.   However faithful in his Master's house,[1] he was but a servant; and a servant knoweth not the will of his master.   The threat of destruction if Jehovah remained among Israel, and the alternative of sending with them an angel, must have cast a gloom over his future mediatorship. It was, indeed, only that of a servant, however highly favoured, not of a son.[2]   Oh, that he could quite understand the Being and character of the God of Israel—see, not His likeness, but His glory![3]   Then would all become clear, and, with fuller light, joyous assurance fill his heart.   That such was the real meaning of Moses' prayer, "Show me Thy glory" (ver. 18), appears from the mode in which the Lord answered it.   "And He said, I will make all My goodness pass before thee, and I will proclaim the Name of Jehovah before thee."   Then was Moses taught, that the deepest mystery of Divine grace lay not in God's *national*, but in His *individual* dealings, in sovereign mercy: "And I will be gracious to whom I will be gracious, and will show mercy on whom I will show mercy" (ver. 19). Yet no man could see the *face*—the full outshining of Jehovah. Neither flesh nor spirit, so long as it dwelt in the flesh, could bear such glory.   While that glory passed by, God would hold Moses in a clift of the rock, perhaps in the same in which a similar vision was afterwards granted to Elijah,[4] and there He would support, or "cover" him with His hand.   Only "the back parts"—the after-glory, the luminous reflection of what Jehovah really was—could Moses bear to see.   But what Moses witnessed, hid in the clift of the rock, and Elijah, the representative of the prophets, saw more clearly, hiding his face in his mantle, while he worshipped, appears fully revealed to us in the Face of Jesus Christ, in Whom "the whole fulness of the Godhead dwelleth bodily."

[1] Heb. iii. 5.   [2] Heb. iii. 5, 6.
[3] Ex. xxxiii. 18.   [4] 1 Kings xix. 9.

CHAPTER XIII.

Moses a Second Time on the Mount—On his return his Face shineth—The rearing of the Tabernacle—Its Consecration by the seen Presence of Jehovah.

(Ex. xxxiv.–xl.)

THE covenant relationship between God and Israel having been happily restored, Moses was directed to bring into the mount other two tables—this time of his own preparing—instead of those which he had broken, that God might once more write down the "ten words."[1] Again he passed forty days and forty nights on Sinai without either eating or drinking (xxxiv. 28). The communications which he received were preceded by that glorious vision of Jehovah's brightness, which had been promised to him. What he *saw* is nowhere told us ; only what he *heard*, when Jehovah " proclaimed" before him what Luther aptly designates as " the sermon about the name of God." It unfolded His inmost being, as that of love unspeakable—the cumulation of terms being intended to present that love in all its aspects. And, in the words of a recent German writer : " Such as Jehovah here proclaimed, He also manifested it among Israel at all times, from Mount Sinai till He brought them into the land of Canaan ; and thence till He cast them out among the heathen. Nay, even now in their banishment, He is 'keeping mercy for thousands, who turn to the Redeemer that has come out of Zion.'"

When Moses thus fully understood the character of Jehovah, he could once more plead for Israel, now converting into a plea for forgiveness even the reason which had seemed to make the presence of Jehovah among Israel dangerous—that they were a

[1] Ex. xxxiv. 1–4.

stiff-necked people (ver. 9).   In the same manner had the Lord, in speaking to Noah, made the sin of man, which had erst provoked judgment, the ground for future forbearance.[1]   And the Lord now graciously confirmed once more His covenant with Israel.   In so doing He reminded them of its two conditions, the one negative, the other positive, but both strictly connected, and both applying to the time when Moses should be no more, and Israel had entered on possession of the Promised Land.   These two conditions were always to be observed, if the covenant was to be maintained.   The one was avoidance of all contact with the Canaanites and their idolatry (vers. 11–16) ; the other, observance of the service of Jehovah in the manner prescribed by Him (vers. 17–26).

Another confirmation of the Divine message which Moses bore from the mount, appeared on his return among Israel. All unknown to himself, the reflection of the Divine glory had been left upon him, and " the skin of his face shone[2] (shot out rays) because of His (God's) talking with him."[3]   As Aaron and the children of Israel were afraid of this reflection of the Divine glory, Moses had to use a covering for his face while speaking to them, which he only removed when conversing with the Lord.   It is to this that the apostle refers[4] when he contrasts the Old Testament glory on the face of Moses, which " was to be done away "—at any rate at the death of Moses— and which was connected with what, after all, was " the ministration of death," with " the ministration of the Spirit " and its exceeding and enduring glory.   Moreover, the vail with which Moses had to cover his face was symbolical of the vail covering the Old Testament, which is only " done away in Christ " (2 Cor. iii. 13, 14).

Everything was now ready for the construction of the Taber-

---

[1] Gen. vi. 5, 6, comp. with Gen. viii. 21.

[2] The Hebrew word is derived from *a horn*, and some versions actually translate : " he wist not that his face was *horned*."   From this the representation of Moses with horns on his forehead has had its origin.

[3] So literally.   [4] 2 Cor. iii. 7.

nacle and of all requisite for its services. We can understand how, especially in view of the work before them, the Sabbath rest should now be once more enjoined.[1] Then a proclamation was made for voluntary contributions of all that was needful, to which the people responded with such " willing offerings" (xxxv. 29), that soon not only " sufficient" but " too much" " for all the work" was gathered.[2] The amount of gold and silver actually used is expressly mentioned in Exodus xxxviii. 24–26. The sum total of the *gold* amounts in present value to at least 131,595*l.*, and that of tl e silver to about 75,444*l.*, or both together to 207,039*l.* And it must be borne in mind, that this sum does not indicate the whole amount offered by Israel —only that actually employed. In regard to the silver, either less of it was offered or none at all may have been required, since the 75,444*l.* in silver represent the exact amount of the "ransom money"[3] which every Israelite had to pay on their being first numbered (xxxviii. 26). Nor was it only gold, silver, and other material which the people brought. All "wise-hearted" men and women " whose heart the Lord stirred up "—that is, all who understood such work, and whose zeal was kindled by love for God's sanctuary—busied themselves, according to their ability, under the direction of Bezaleel, the grandson of Hur, and Aholiab, of the tribe of Dan. But what chiefly impresses us in the sacred narrative is the evidence of spiritual devotion, which appeared alike in the gifts and in the labour of the people. "And Moses did look upon all the work, and, behold, they had done it as Jehovah had commanded, even so had they done it : and Moses blessed them."[4]

Under such willing hands, the whole work was completed within an almost incredibly short period. On comparing Exodus xix. 1, which fixes the arrival of Israel at Mount Sinai as in the third month (of the first year), with Exodus xl. 2, which informs us that the Tabernacle was ready for setting up "on the first day of the first month" (of the second year), we find

---

[1] Ex. xxxv. 2, 3.   [2] Ex. xxxvi. 5–7.   [3] Ex. xxx. 12.
[4] Ex. xxxix. 43.

that an interval of nine months had elapsed.　From this, however, must be deducted twice forty days, during which Moses was on the mount, as well as the days when Israel prepared for the covenant, and those when it was ratified and the law given, and also the interval between Moses' first and second stay on the mountain.　Thus the whole of the elaborate work connected with the Tabernacle and its services must have been done *within six months.*　And now that "the Tabernacle was reared up," Moses first placed within the Most Holy Place the Ark holding "the testimony," and covered it with the mercy-seat; next, he ranged in the Holy Place, to the north, the table of shewbread, setting "the bread in order upon it before the Lord;" then, to the south, "the candlestick," lighting its lamps before the Lord; and finally "the golden altar" "before the vail" of the Most Holy Place, "and he burnt sweet incense thereon."　All this being done, and the curtain at the entrance to the Tabernacle hung up,[1] the altar of burnt-offering was placed "by the door of the Tabernacle," and "the laver" between it and that altar, although probably not in a straight line, but somewhat to the side of the altar of burnt-offering. And on the altar smoked the burnt and the meat-offering, and the laver was filled with water, in which Moses, and Aaron, and his sons washed their hands and their feet.

All was now quite in readiness—means, ordinances, and appointed channels of blessing, and all was in waiting.　One thing only was needed; but upon that the meaning and the efficacy of everything else depended.　But God was faithful to His promise.　As in believing expectancy Israel looked up, "the cloud covered the tent of the congregation, and the glory of Jehovah filled the Tabernacle."　Outside, visible to all, rested "upon the tent" that Cloud and Pillar, in which Jehovah had hitherto guided them, and would continue so to do. For, as the cloud by day and the appearance of fire by night tarried over the Tabernacle, the children of Israel "abode in their tents," "and journeyed not."　But "when it was taken

[1] Ex. xl. 28.

up," then Israel's camp was speedily broken up, and, journeying, they followed their Divine Leader (comp. Numbers ix. 15–23). A *constant*, *visible*, and *guiding* Presence of Jehovah this among His professing people, resting above the outer tent that covered the Tabernacle. But within that Tabernacle itself there was yet another and unapproachable Presence. For "the glory of Jehovah filled the Tabernacle. And Moses was not able to enter into the tent of the congregation, because the cloud abode thereon, and the glory of Jehovah filled the Tabernacle."[1] Presently it withdrew within the Most Holy Place, into which none could enter but the high-priest once a year, and that on the day and for the purpose of atonement, and where it rested between thc cherubim of glory, above the mercy-seat, that covered the ark with the testimony. For "the way into the holiest of all was not yet made manifest." " But Christ being come an high-priest of good things to come, by a greater and more perfect tabernacle, not made with hands, that is to say, not of this building; neither by the blood of goats and calves, but by His own blood He entered in once into the holy place, having obtained eternal redemption for us."[2]

CHAPTER XIV.

Analysis of the Book of Leviticus—The Sin of Nadab and Abihu—Judgment upon the Blasphemer.

(LEVITICUS.)

THE Book of Exodus was intended to tell how the Lord God redeemed and set apart for Himself " a peculiar people." Accordingly, it appropriately closes with the erection of the Tabernacle and the hallowing of it by the visible Presence of Jehovah in the Holy Place. It yet remained to show the other aspect of the covenant. For the provisions and the

[1] Ex. xl. 34, 35.   [2] Heb. ix. 8, 11, 12.

means of grace must be accepted and used by those for whom
they are designed, and the "setting apart" of the people by
Jehovah implied, as its converse, consecration on the part of
Israel. And this forms the subject matter of the Book of
Leviticus,[1] which a recent German writer has aptly described as
"the code regulating the spiritual life of Israel, viewed as the
people of God." To sum up its general contents—it tells
us in its first Part (i.–xvi.) how Israel was to *approach* God,
together with what, symbolically speaking, was inconsistent with
such approaches; and in its second Part (xvii.–xxvii.) how,
having been brought near to God, the people were to maintain,
to enjoy, and to exhibit the state of grace of which they had
become partakers. Of course, all is here symbolical, and we
must regard the directions and ordinances as conveying in an
outward form so many spiritual truths. Perhaps we might go
so far as to say, that Part I. of Leviticus exhibits, in a symbolical form, the doctrine of *justification*, and Part II. that of
sanctification; or, more accurately : the manner of *access to God*,
and the *holiness* which is the result of that access.

It has already been pointed out, that the Book of Leviticus
consists of two Parts ; the one ending with chapter xvi. ; the
other, properly speaking, with chapter xxv. ; chapter xxvi. being
a general conclusion, indicating the blessings of faithful adherence to the covenant, while chapter xxvii., which treats of
vowing unto the Lord, forms a most appropriate *appendix*.
At the close of the book itself,[2] and of the chapter which, for
want of a better name, we have termed its *appendix* (xxvii.
34), we find expressions indicating the purpose of the whole,
and that the book of Leviticus forms in itself a special and
independent part of the Pentateuch. We repeat it : the Book

---

[1] The Book of *Leviticus*, or about the Levitical ordinances, derives its
designation from the corresponding Greek term in the LXX translation, and
its Latin name in the Vulgate. It corresponds to the Rabbinical designation
of "Law of the Priests," and "Book of the Law of Offerings." Among
the Jews it is commonly known as *Vajikra*, from the first word in the
Hebrew text : " *Vajikra*," "He called."

[2] Lev. xxvi. 46.

of Leviticus is intended for Israel as the people of God; it is the statute-book of Israel's spiritual life; and, on both these grounds, it is neither simply legal, in the sense of ordinary law, nor yet merely ceremonial, but *throughout symbolical and typical.* Accordingly, its deeper truths apply to all times and to all men.

Part I. (i.–xvi.), which tells Israel *how to approach God so as to have communion with Him,* appropriately opens with a description of the *various kinds of sacrifices.*[1] It next treats of the *priesthood.*[2] The thoroughly symbolical character of all, and hence the necessity of closest adherence to the directions given, are next illustrated by the judgment which befell those who offered incense upon "strange fire."[3] From the priesthood the sacred text passes to *the worshippers.*[4] These must be *clean —personally* (xi. 1–47), in their *family-life,*[5] and as a *congregation.*[6] Above and beyond all is the *great cleansing* of the *Day of Atonement,*[7] with which the *first part* of the book, concerning access to God, closes.

The *Second Part* of the Book of Leviticus, which describes, in symbolical manner, the *holiness* that becometh the people of God, treats, first, of *personal holiness,*[8] then of *holiness in the family,*[9] of *holiness in social relations,*[10] and of *holiness in the priesthood.*[11] Thence the sacred text proceeds to *holy seasons.*[12] As the duty of close adherence to the Divine directions in connection with the priesthood had been illustrated by the judgment upon Nadab and Abihu,[13] so now the solemn duty, incumbent on all Israel, to treat the Name of Jehovah as holy, is exhibited in the punishment of one who had blasphemed it.[14] Finally, Leviticus xxv. describes the *holiness of the land.* Thus Part II. treats more especially of *consecration.* As Part I., describing access to God, had culminated in the ordinance of the Day of Atonement, so Part II. in that of the Jubilee Year. Lastly, Leviticus xxvi. dwells on the blessing attaching to

[1] Lev. i.–vii.
[2] Lev. viii.–x.
[3] Lev. x. 1–6.
[4] Lev. xi.–xv.
[5] Lev. xii.
[6] Lev. xiii.–xv.
[7] Lev. xvi.
[8] Lev. xvii.
[9] Lev. xviii.
[10] Lev. xix. xx.
[11] Lev. xxi. xxii.
[12] Lev. xxiii. xxiv.
[13] Lev. x. 1–6.
[14] Lev. xxiv. 10 to end.

faithful observance of the covenant; while Leviticus xxvii., reaching, as it were, beyond ordinary demands and consecrations, speaks of the free-will offerings of the heart, as represented by vows.

It now only remains to describe the two illustrative instances already referred to—the one connected with the priesthood, the other with the people. Aaron and his sons had just been solemnly consecrated to their holy office, and the offering, which they had brought, consumed in view of the whole people by fire from before Jehovah, to betoken His acceptance thereof.[1] All the more did any transgression of the Lord's ordinance, especially if committed by His priests, call for signal and public punishment. But *Nadab* and *Abihu*, the two eldest sons of Aaron, attempted to offer " strange fire before Jehovah, which He commanded them not."[2] Some writers have inferred from the prohibition of wine or of any strong drink to the priests during the time of their ministry, which immediately follows upon the record of this event (x. 8–11), that these two had been under some such influence at the time of their daring attempt. The point is of small importance, comparatively speaking. It is not easy to say what the expression "strange fire" exactly implies. Clearly, the two were going to offer incense on the golden altar (ver. 1), and as clearly this service was about to be done at a time *not* prescribed by the Lord. For a comparison of vers. 12 and 16 shows that it took place between the sacrifice offered by Aaron[3] and the festive meal following that sacrifice; whereas incense was only to be burnt at the morning and evening sacrifices. Besides, it may be, that they also took " strange fire" in the sense of taking the burning coals otherwise than from the altar of burnt-offering. In the ceremonial for the Day of Atonement the latter is expressly prescribed,[4] and it is a fair inference that the same direction applied to every time of incensing. At any rate, we know that such was the invariable rule in the Temple at the time of Christ.

[1] Lev. ix.   [2] Lev. x. 1.   [3] Lev. ix.   [4] Lev. xvi. 12.

But Nadab and Abihu were not allowed to accomplish their purpose. The same fire, which a little ago had consumed the accepted sacrifice,[1] now struck them, "and they died before Jehovah," that is, in front of His dwelling-place—most probably in the court (comp. Leviticus i. 5), just as they were about to enter the Holy Place. Thus, on the very day of their consecration to the priesthood, did the oldest sons of Aaron perish, because they had not sanctified the Lord in their hearts, but had offered Him a worship of their own devising, instead of that holy incense consumed by fire from off the altar, which symbolised prayer, offered up on the ground of accepted sacrifice. And this twofold lesson did the Lord Himself teach in explanation of this judgment (x. 3). So far as the priesthood was concerned—"I will sanctify Myself in those who stand near to Me,[2] and" (so far as all the people were concerned) "before all the people I will glorify Myself." In other words, if those who had been consecrated to Him would not sanctify Him in heart and life, He would sanctify Himself in them by judgments (comp. also Ezekiel xxxviii. 16), and thus glorify His Name before all, as the Holy One, Who cannot with impunity be provoked to anger.

So deeply was Aaron solemnized, that, in the language of Scripture, he "held his peace." Not a word of complaint escaped his lips; nor yet was a token of mourning on his part, or on that of his sons, allowed to cast the shadow of personal feelings, or of latent regret, upon this signal vindication of Divine holiness (x. 6). Only their "brethren, the whole house of Israel" were permitted to "bewail this burning (of His anger) which Jehovah hath kindled."

The history of the judgment upon the blasphemer[3] was inserted in the portion of Leviticus where it stands, either because it happened at the time when the laws there recorded were given, or else because it forms a suitable introduction to, and illustration of, the duty of owning Jehovah, which finds its fullest outward expression in the rest of the Sabbatical and in the

---

[1] Lev. ix. 24.   [2] So literally.   [3] Lev. xxiv. 10–14.

arrangements of the Jubilee Year, enjoined in Leviticus xxv.
It also affords another instance of the dangers accruing to
Israel from the presence among them of that "mixed multitude"
which had followed them from Egypt.[1]   There seems no reason
to doubt the Jewish view, that the latter occupied a separate
place in the camp; the children of Israel being ranged according to their tribes, "every man by his own standard, with the
ensign of their father's house."[2]   But as the blasphemer was
only the son of a Danite *mother*—Shelomith, the daughter of
Dibri—his father having been an Egyptian,[3] he would not
have been entitled to pitch his tent among the tribe of Dan.
Hebrew tradition further states, that this had been the cause of
the quarrel, when the blasphemer " went out among the children
of Israel ; and this son of the Israelitish woman and a man of
Israel strove together in the camp."   Finally, it adds, that the
claim to dwell among the Danites having been decided by
Moses against him, the man "blasphemed the Name[4] (*of
Jehovah*), and cursed."   Whatever truth, if any, there be in this
tradition, the crime itself was most serious.   If even cursing
one's parents was visited with death, what punishment could
be too severe upon one who had "reviled" Jehovah, and
"cursed!"   But just because the case was so solemn, Moses
did not rashly adjudicate in it (comp. the corresponding delay

---

[1] Ex. xii. 38.   [2] Numb. ii. 2.

[3] A very ancient Jewish tradition has it, that the father of this blasphemer
was the Egyptian whom Moses slew on account of his maltreatment of an
Hebrew (Ex. ii. 11, 12).   Legendary details are added about the previous
offences of that Egyptian, which need not be here repeated.   Their evident
object is, on the one hand, to render the passionate anger of Moses excus-
able, and, on the other, to account for the fact that an Egyptian was the
father of a child of which a Hebrewess was the mother.

[4] The Rabbis and the LXX version render the expression "blasphemed"
by "uttered distinctly," and Jewish traditionalism has based upon this
rendering the prohibition ever to pronounce the name *Jehovah*—an ordinance
so well observed that even the exact pronunciation of the word is not certainly known.   Most probably it should be pronounced *Jahveh*.   In our
English Version, as in the LXX and Vulgate, it is rendered by "the LORD,"
the latter word being printed in capitals.

in Numbers xv. 34) "They put him in ward to determine about them (*i.e.* about blasphemers), according to the mouth (or command) of Jehovah."[1] Then by Divine direction the blasphemer was taken without the camp; those who had heard his blasphemy laid "their hands upon his head," as it were to put away the blasphemy from themselves, and lay it on the head of the guilty (comp. Deut. xxi. 6) ; and the whole congregation shared in the judgment by stoning him.

But the general law which decreed the punishment of death upon blasphemy[2] was to apply to native Israelites as well as to the stranger, as indeed all crimes that carried retributive punishment—specially those against the life or the person—were to be equally visited, whether the offender were a Jew or a foreigner. This is the object of the repetition of these laws in that connection.[3] For Jehovah was not a national deity, like the gods of the heathen ; nor were Israel's privileges those of exceptional favour in case of offences ; but Jehovah was the Holy One of Israel, and holiness became His house for ever.

CHAPTER XV.

Analysis of the Book of Numbers—The Numbering of Israel, and that of the Levites—Arrangement of the Camp, and its Symbolical Import—The March.

(NUMB. I.–IV. ; X. I–II.)

THE Book of Numbers[4] reads almost like a chronicle of the principal events during the thirty-eight years which elapsed between Israel's stay in the wilderness of Sinai, and

---

[1] So literally.   [2] Lev. xxiv. 16.   [3] Lev. xxiv. 17–22.
[4] This designation of the Fourth Book of Moses, from the numbering of the people, is derived from its title in the LXX and in the Vulgate translation. The Jews commonly call it either *Vajedabber*, from the first word in the text, "And He (the Lord) spake ;" or else *Bammidbar*, "in the wilderness."

their arrival on the borders of Canaan. What took place during the journey to Mount Sinai had been intended to prepare the people for the solemn events there enacted. Similarly, the thirty-eight years' wanderings which followed were designed to fit Israel for entering on possession of the Land of Promise. The outward history of the people during that period exhibited, on the one hand, the constant care and mercy of Jehovah, and on the other, His holiness and His judgments; while the laws and ordinances given them were needful for the organisation of the commonwealth of Israel in its future relations. A brief analysis of the whole book will show the connection of all.

In general, the Book of Numbers seems to consist of *three parts*—the *first*,[1] detailing *the preparations for the march* from Sinai; the *second*,[2] *the history of the journeyings* of Israel through the wilderness; and the *third*,[3] *the various occurrences on the east of the Jordan.* If we examine each of these parts separately, we find that Part I. *consists of four sections*, detailing —1. The numbers and the outward arrangement of each of the tribes,[4] and the appointment of the Levites to their service (iii., iv.); 2. Laws concerning the higher and spiritual order of the people, culminating in the priestly blessing (v., vi.); 3. The three last occurrences before leaving Mount Sinai (vii., viii., ix. 1–14); 4. The signals for the march in the wilderness (ix. 15–x. 10).

Part II. tells the history of *the wanderings* of Israel, in *their three stages*—1. From Sinai to Paran, near Kadesh, detailing all that happened there (x. 10–xiv.); 2. From the announcement of the death of the generation which had come out from Egypt to the re-assembling of the people at Kadesh in the fortieth year after the Exodus (xv.–xix.); 3. The march from Kadesh to Mount Hor, with the events during its course (xx., xxi.). Lastly, Part III. *consists of five sections* detailing—1. The attempts of Moab and Midian against Israel

[1] Numb. i.–x. 10.   [2] Numb. x. 11.–xxi.
[3] Numb. xxii.–xxvi.   [4] Numb. i., ii.

(xxii.–xxv.); 2. A fresh census and the ordinances connected with it (xxv.–xxvii.); 3. Certain sacred laws given in view of settling in Palestine (xxviii.–xxx.); 4. The victory over Midian, the division of the territory gained, along with a review of the past (xxxi.–xxxiii. 49); 5. Some prospective directions on taking possession of the Land of Promise (xxxiii. 50–xxxvi.).[1]

Before leaving the encampment at Mount Sinai, God directed Moses and Aaron to take a *census* of all who constituted the host of Israel—in the language of Scripture: "All that are able to go forth to war," "their armies,"[2] that is, "every male from twenty years old and upwards." In this they were to be assisted by one delegate from each tribe, "every one head of the house of his fathers" (i. 4); or, as they are designated in ver. 16, "the called (representatives) of the congregation, princes of their paternal tribes, heads of thousands in Israel."[3] The latter expression indicates that the census was taken on the plan proposed by Jethro,[4] by which Israel was arranged into thousands, hundreds, fifties, and tens. This also accounts for the *even numbers* assigned to each tribe as the final result of the numbering. Manifestly, the census was made on the basis of the poll taken, nine months before, for the purpose of the "atonement money."[5] This poll had yielded a total of 603,550,[6] which is precisely the same number as that in Numbers i. 46. Probably, therefore, the census was substantially only a re-arrangement and registration of the people according to their tribes, in thousands, hundreds, fifties, and tens, made with the co-operation of the hereditary rulers of the tribes. The above number of men capable of bearing arms would, if we may apply modern statistical results, imply a total population of upwards of *two millions*. Thirty-eight years later,

---

[1] We have substantially followed the arrangement of Keil, which agrees with that of the best modern commentators. In our remarks as to the numbering of the tribes, we have also availed ourselves of the same help.

[2] Numb. i. 3.   [3] This is the real meaning of the passage.

[4] Ex. xviii. 21, 25.   [5] Ex. xxx. 11–16.   [6] Ex. xxxviii. 26.

just before entering upon possession of the land, a *second census* was taken,[1] which yielded a total number of 601,730 capable of bearing arms (xxvi. 51), thus showing a *decrease* of 1820 during the years of wandering in the wilderness. Arranging these two census according to the tribes, and placing them side by side, we gather some interesting information:

First Census (Ex. xxx. ; Numb. i.).		Second Census (Numb. xxvi.).
REUBEN . 46,500 (Prince *Elizur,* "My God the Rock.") . . .		43,730
Simeon . 59,300 („ *Shelumiel,* "God my Salvation.") .		22,200
Gad . . 45,650 („ *E iasaph,* "My God that gathers.")		40,500
JUDAH[2] . 74,600 („ *Nahshon,* " The Diviner.") . .		76,500
Issachar . 54,400 („ *Nethaneel,* "God the Giver.")		64,300
Zebulon . 57,400 („ *Eliab,* "My God the Father.")		60,500
EPHRAIM 40,500 („ *Elishama,* "My God the Hearer.") .		32,500
Manasseh 32,200 („ *Gamaliel,* " My God the Rewarder.") .		52,700
Benjamin 35,400 („ *Abidan,* "My Father is Judge.") .		45,600
DAN . . 62,700 („ *Ahiezer,* " My Brother is Help.") .		64,400
Asher . . 41,500 („ *Pagiel,* either "My fate is God," or "My prayer-God.")		53,400
Naphtali . 53,400 („ *Ahira,* "My Brother is Friend.") .		45,400
603,550		601,730

A comparison of the foregoing figures will show, that, while some of the tribes remarkably *increased*, others equally remarkably *decreased*, during the thirty-eight years' wanderings. Thus, for example, Issachar *increased* nineteen *per cent.*, Benjamin and Asher twenty-nine *per cent.*, and Manasseh about sixty-three *per cent.*;[3] while Reuben *decreased* six *per cent.*, Gad twelve *per cent.*, Naphtali fifteen *per cent.*, and Simeon almost sixty-three *per cent.* Some interpreters have connected the large decrease in the latter tribe with the judgment following upon the service of Baal Peor; the fact that Zimri, a prince of the tribe of Simeon, had been such a notable offender[4] leading to the

[1] Numb. xxvi.

[2] The names printed in capitals are those of the standard-bearers (see further on). It will be seen that of the twelve princes he of Judah bears a peculiar name. The name *Nahshon* is derived from a *serpent.* Without indulging in fanciful speculations, we may be allowed to suggest that this *may* bear prophetic reference to the Great Prophet who was to bruise the head of the *serpent.* With this also agrees the name of his father *Amminadab,* "my people is noble."

[3] The variations in population are very remarkable.

[4] Numb. xxv. 6–14.

inference that the tribe itself had been largely implicated in the sin.

It has already been noted, that the Levites were taken for the ministi y of the sanctuary in place of the firstborn of Israel.[1] The number of the latter amounted to 22,273.[2] But this statement is not intended to imply that, among all the Jewish males, amounting to upwards of a million[3] of all ages—from the grandfather to the infant lately born—there were only 22,273 "firstborns." The latter figure evidently indicates only the number of the firstborn since the departure from Egypt. With reference to those born previously to the Exodus we are expressly told :[4] "all the firstborn are Mine ; on the day that I smote all the firstborn of Egypt I hallowed unto Me all the firstborn in Israel." Hence the fresh hallowing of the firstborn of Israel, and their subsequent numbering with a view to the substitution of the Levites for them, must have dated from *after the Paschal night.* Thus the 22,273 firstborn sons, for whom the Levites were substituted, represent those born *after* the departure from Egypt. If this number seems proportionally large, it should be remembered that the oppressive measures of Pharaoh would tend to diminish the number of marriages during the latter part of Israel's stay in Egypt, while the prospect of near freedom would, in a corresponding manner, immensely increase them.[5] Besides, it is a well-known fact that even now the proportion of boys to girls is very much greater among

---

[1] Numb. iii. 11, 12.   [2] Numb. iii. 43.

[3] The total number of the people being computed at about two millions, about one million of males would be the ordinary proportion.

[4] Numb. iii. 13 ; viii. 17.

[5] It is indeed unsafe to draw from *present* statistical *data* definite inferences as to the state of Israel at that time. But nothing is so remarkable as the influence of outward circumstances upon the annual number of marriages. Thus in Austria there were, in 1851, 361,249 marriages among a population of 36½ millions ; while in 1854, among a population of upwards of 37 millions, only 279,202 occurred. In England the population increased between 1866 and 1869 by about a million, while in the latter year there were nearly 11,000 marriages less than in the former.

Jews than among Gentiles.[1] Viewed in this light, the account of Scripture on this subject presents no difficulties to the careful reader.[2]

As already explained, the Levites were not numbered with the other tribes, but separately,[3] and appointed ministers to Aaron the priest "for the service of the Tabernacle," in room of the firstborn of Israel (iii. 5–13). Not being regarded as part of the *host*, they were counted "from a month old and upward," the number of their males amounting to 22,000, which at the second census (after the thirty-eight years' wanderings) had increased to 23,000.[4] This has been computed to imply about 13,000 men, from twenty years and upwards—a number less than half that of the smallest of the other tribes (Benjamin, 35,400). With this computation agrees the statement[5] that the number of Levites "from thirty years old and upwards, even unto fifty years old, every one that came to do the service of the ministry," amounted in all to 8,580.[6] The same proportion between Levi and the rest of the people seems to have continued in after times, as we gather from the results of the census taken by King David,[7] when Levi had only increased

[1] The proportion of boys to girls born in England varies most curiously from year to year, and in different counties. The lowest during the last ten years has been in Huntingdonshire in the year 1868, when it descended to 94·3 boys to 100 girls. But the mean proportion during the last ten years shows from 102 to 106 boys (the latter number in Cornwall) to 100 girls. In the year 1832 the proportion in Geneva was 157 boys born to 100 girls. Among the Jews in some places the *mean* proportion has, on an average of 16 years, been as high as 145 boys to 100 girls. The reader who is curious on this and similar subjects is referred to my article, " On certain Physical Peculiarities of the Jewish Race," in the *Sunday Magazine* for 1869, pp. 315, etc.

[2] The views of the Jews on the redemption of the firstborn at the time of Christ differed from those of the Bible. See my *Temple, its Ministry and Services at the time of Christ*, p. 302.

[3] Numb. iii. 15.   [4] Numb. iii. 39 ; xxvi. 62.   [5] Numb. iv. 48.

[6] We cannot here enter into further numerical details. But this we can and do assert, that all supposed difficulties on this subject vanish before a careful study of the sacred text.

[7] 1 Chron. xxiii. 3.

from 23,000 to 38,000, while the rest of the tribes had more than doubled. The Levites were arranged into families after their ancestors, *Gershon, Kohath,* and *Merari,* the three sons of Levi.[1] The *Gershonites* (again subdivided into two families, and amounting to 7,500), under their leader Eliasaph—"My God that gathers"[2]—had charge of "the Tabernacle," or rather of "the dwelling-place;" of "the tent;" of "the covering thereof;" and of "the hanging (or curtain) for the door of the tent of meeting;" as also of "the hangings of the court" (in which the Tabernacle stood) ; of the curtain for its door ; and of all the cordage necessary for these "hangings." We have been particular in translating this passage, because it proves that the common view, which places the curtains "of fine twined linen, and blue, and purple, and scarlet,"[3] *outside* the boards that constituted the framework of the Tabernacle, is entirely erroneous. Evidently *these hangings,* and not the boards, constituted "the Tabernacle," or rather "the dwelling"[4]—"the tent," outside the framework, consisting of the eleven curtains of goats' hair,[5] and "the covering" of the whole being twofold—one "of rams' skins dyed red," and another "of badgers' skins."[6]

Whilst the Gershonites had charge of "the dwelling," "the tent," and the hangings of the outer court, the care of the "boards of the dwelling," with all that belonged thereto, and of "the pillars of the court round about"—in short, of all the outer solid framework of the Tabernacle and of the court—devolved upon the Merarites, under their chief, Zuriel ("My Rock is God"). Finally, the most important charge—that of the contents and vessels of the sanctuary—was committed to the Kohathites, under their chief Elizaphan ("My God watcheth round about").

Viewed as a whole, the camp of Israel thus formed a threefold

[1] Numb. iii. 14-43.

[2] The significance of the names of "the princes," as indicative of the spiritual hopes of Israel while in Egypt, has already been pointed out in a former chapter.   [3] Ex. xxvi. 1.

[4] So it should be rendered both in Numb. iii. 25 and in Ex. xxvi. 1, 5.

[5] Ex. xxvi. 7.   [6] Ex. xxvi. 14.

square—a symbolical design, further developed in the Temple
of Solomon, still more fully in that of Ezekiel, and finally shown
in all its completeness in "the city that lieth foursquare."[1] The
innermost square—as yet elongated and therefore not perfect
in its *width* (or comprehension), nor yet having the perfect
form of a cube, except so far as the Most Holy Place itself
was concerned (which was a cube)—was occupied by "the
dwelling," covered by "the tent," and surrounded by its "court."
Around this inner was another square, occupied by the
ministers of the Tabernacle—in the *East*, or at the entrance
to the court, by Moses, Aaron, and his sons; in the *South* by
the Kohathites, who had the most important Levitical charge;
in the *West* by the Gershonites; and in the *North* by the
Merarites. Finally, there was a third and outermost square,
which formed the camp of Israel. The *eastern* or most important place here was occupied by *Judah*, bearing the standard
of the division. With Judah were Issachar and Zebulon (the
sons of Leah), the three tribes together a host of 186,400
men. The *southern* place was held by *Reuben*, with the
standard of that division, camped probably nearest to Zebulon,
or at the south-eastern corner. With Reuben were Simeon
and Gad (the sons of Leah and of Zilpah, Leah's maid),
forming altogether a host of 151,450 men. The *western* post
was occupied by *Ephraim*, with the standard of his division,
being probably camped nearest to Gad, or at the south-western
corner. With Ephraim were Manasseh and Benjamin (in
short, the three descendants of Rachel), forming altogether
a host of 108,100 men. Lastly, the *northern* side was occupied by *Dan*, with his standard, camping probably nearest to
Benjamin, or at the north-western corner. With Dan were
Asher and Naphtali (the sons of Bilhah and Zilpah), forming
altogether a host of 157,600 men. This was also the order

---

[1] Rev. xx 9; xxi. 16. We cannot here enter further into this subject.
But the symbolism of the threefold square, and the symbolical meaning of
the prophetic visions in Ezekiel and the Book of Revelation will readily
present themselves to the thoughtful student of Scripture.

of march, Judah with his division leading, after which came
Reuben, with his division, then the sanctuary with the Levites
in the order of their camping, the rear consisting of the
divisions of Ephraim and of Dan. The sacred text does not
specially describe the *banners* carried by the four leading
tribes. According to Jewish tradition they bore as emblems
"the likeness of the four living creatures," seen by Ezekiel
in his vision of the *Chariot*,[1] the *colour* of the standard being
the same as that of the precious stones on the high-priest's
breastplate, on which the names of the standard-bearing tribes
were graven.[2] In that case *Judah* would have had on its
standard a *lion* on a *blood-red ground* (the sardian stone or
sard), *Reuben* the head of a man on a ground of *dark red*
colour (the ruby or carbuncle), *Ephraim* the head of a bullock
on a ground of hyacinth (the ligury, according to some, Ligurian
amber), and *Dan* an eagle on a ground of bright yellow, like
gold (the ancient chrysolith, perhaps our topaz). This, supposing the names to have been graven in the order in which the
tribes camped. But Josephus and some of the Rabbis range
the names on the breastplate in the same order as on the
ephod of the high-priest,[3] that is, "according to their birth."
In that case Reuben would have been on the sardian stone or
sard, *Judah* on the ruby or carbuncle, *Dan* on a sapphire, or
perhaps lapis-lazuli (blue), and *Ephraim* on an onyx, or else a
beryl,[4] the colour of the banners, of course, in each case corresponding. Altogether the camp is supposed to have occupied
about three square miles.

The direction either for marching or for resting was, as
explained in a former chapter, given by the Cloud in which
the Divine Presence was. But for actual signal to move, two
silver trumpets were to be used by the sons of Aaron. A

[1] Ezek. i. 10.　　[2] Ex. xxviii. 15-21.　　[3] Ex. xxviii. 10.
[4] It will be perceived that interpreters differ as to the exact equivalent of
the precious stones mentioned in the sacred text. As to the arrangement
of the stones on the high-priest's breastplate, we prefer the view that the
order in the camp indicated that of the names on the breastplate.

prolonged alarm indicated the commencement of the march.
At the first alarm the eastern, at the second the southern part
of the camp was to move forward, then came the Tabernacle
and its custodians, the western, and finally the northern part of
the camp, Naphtali closing the rear. On the other hand,
when an assembly of the people was summoned, the signal was
only *one blast* of the trumpets in short, sharp tones. In
general, and for all times, the blast of these silver trumpets,
whether in war, on festive, or on joyous occasions, had this
spiritual meaning: "ye shall be remembered before Jehovah
your God."[1] In other words, Israel was a host, and as such
summoned by blast of trumpet. But Israel was a host of
which Jehovah was Leader and King, and the trumpets that
summoned this host were silver trumpets of the sanctuary,
blown by the priests of Jehovah. Hence these their blasts
brought Israel as the Lord's host in remembrance before their
God and King.

CHAPTER XVI.

The Offerings of the "Princes"—The setting apart of the
Levites—And the Second Observance of the Passover.

(NUMB. VII.-IX.)

THREE other occurrences are recorded, before the camp of
Israel broke up from Mount Sinai, although they may
not have taken place in the exact order in which, for special
reasons, they are told in the sacred text. These events were:
the offering of certain gifts on the part of "*the princes*" of
Israel:[2] the *actual setting apart of the Levites* to the service for
which they had been already previously designated;[3] and a
second observance of the Passover.[4]

[1] Numb. x. 1-10.   [2] Numb. vii.
[3] Numb. viii.   [4] Numb. ix. 1-14.

The offerings of the princes of Israel commenced immediately after the consecration of the tabernacle.[1] But their record is inserted in Numbers vii., partly in order not to interrupt the consecutive series of Levitical ordinances, which naturally followed upon the narrative of the consecration of the tabernacle,[2] and partly because one of the offerings of the princes bore special reference to the wilderness-journey, which was then about to be immediately resumed. Probably these offerings may have been brought on some of the days on which part of the Levitical ordinances was also proclaimed. We know that the presentation of gifts by the princes occupied, altogether, the mornings of twelve, or rather of thirteen days.[3] On the first day[4] they brought in common "six covered waggons and twelve oxen," for the transport of the Tabernacle during the journeyings of the children of Israel. Four of these waggons with eight oxen were given to the *Merarites,* who had charge of the heavy framework and of the pillars ; the other two waggons and four oxen to the *Gershonites,* who had the custody of the hangings and curtains. As for the vessels of the sanctuary, they were to be carried by the *Kohathites* on their shoulders. Then, during the following twelve days "the princes" offered successively each the same gift, that so "there might be equality," anticipating in this also the New Testament principle.[5] Each offering consisted of a "silver charger," weighing about four and a half pounds, a "silver bowl," weighing about two and a quarter pounds, both of them full of fine flour mingled with oil for a meat-offering, and a "golden spoon," about a third of a pound in weight, "full of incense." These gifts were accompanied by burnt, sin, and peace-offerings, which no doubt were sacrificed each day, as the vessels were presented in the sanctuary. And as they

[1] Lev. viii. 10–ix. 1 ; comp. Numb. vii. 1.

[2] Lev. xi. to the end of the book.

[3] With the help of a Paragraph Bible it would be easy to arrange the Levitical ordinances (Lev. xi.–end) in twelve or thirteen sections for as many days. [4] Numb. vii. 1–9.

[5] 2 Cor. viii. 14.

brought their precious offerings, with humble confession of sin over their sacrifices, with thanksgiving and with prayer, the Lord graciously signified His acceptance by speaking unto Moses "from off the mercy-seat," "from between the cherubim."[1]

The second event was *the formal setting apart of the Levites,*[2] which was preceded by a significant direction to Aaron in reference to the lighting of the seven-branched candlestick in the sanctuary. To make the meaning of this symbol more clear, it was added : "the seven lamps shall give light over against the candlestick"—that is, each of the seven lamps (the number being also significant) shall be so placed as to throw its light into the darkness *over against it.* Each separately— and yet each as part of the one candlestick in the Holy Place, and burning the same sacred oil, was to shed light into the darkness over against the candlestick. For the light on the candlestick was symbolical of the mission of Israel as the people of God, and the Levites were really only the repre- sentatives of all Israel, having been substituted instead of their firstborn.[3] On this account, also, the Levites were not specially "hallowed," as the priests had been,[4] but only "cleansed" for their ministry, and after that presented to the Lord. The first part of this symbolical service consisted in sprinkling on them "water of sin" (rendered in our Authorised Version "water of purifying"), alike to confess the defilement of sin and to point to its removal. After that they were to shave off all their hair and to wash their clothes. The Levites were now "unsinned" (viii. 21),[5] so far as their persons were concerned. Then followed

---

[1] Numb. vii. 89.   [2] Numb. viii. 5, etc.   [3] Numb. iii. 11-13.

[4] We read in Ex. xxix. 1, in reference to Aaron and his sons, " Hallow them to minister unto Me in the priest's office "—literally, " consecrate them to priest unto Me " (we use the word " priest " as a verb). In the case of the Levites there was neither consecration nor priesting, but cleansing unto ministry or service. Of course, the Aaronic priesthood pointed to and nas ceased in Christ, our one great High-Priest.

[5] This is the literal rendering of the Hebrew term, which is the same as that used by David in Ps. li. 9.

their dedication to the work. For this purpose the Levites were led "before the Tabernacle" (viii. 9), that is, probably into the outer court, bringing with them two young bullocks—the one for a burnt, the other for a sin-offering, and each with its meat-offering. The people, through their representatives—the princes—now laid their hands upon them, as it were to constitute them their substitutes and representatives. Then Aaron took them "before Jehovah" (ver. 10), that is, into the Holy Place, and "waved them for a wave-offering of the children of Israel"[1]—probably by leading them to the altar and back again—after which, the Levites would lay their hands upon the sacrifices which were now offered by Aaron, who so "made an atonement for them" (ver. 21). The significance of all these symbols will be sufficiently apparent. "And after that, the Levites went in to do service in the Tabernacle of the congregation" (ver. 22).

The third event recorded was a second celebration of the Passover on the anniversary of Israel's deliverance from Egypt —"in his appointed season, according to all the rites of it, and according to all the ceremonies thereof."[2] We specially mark how the Lord now again directed all—the injunction to "keep the Passover" being expressly repeated here, perhaps to obviate the possibility of such a misunderstanding as that the Passover was not to be observed from year to year. Again, when certain men, "defiled by a dead body," complained that they had thereby been excluded from the feast, Moses would not decide the matter himself, but brought their case before God. The direction given was, that, under such or similar circumstances, the Passover should be observed exactly a month later, it being at the same time added, to guard against any wilful, not necessary, neglect, that whoever omitted the ordinance without such reason should "be cut off from among His people."[3] For, as the significance of symbolical rites

---

[1] Rendered in our Authorised Version, "Aaron shall offer the Levites for an offering." [2] Numb. ix. 3.

[3] Numb. ix. 13.

depended upon their entirety, so that if any part of them, however small, had been omitted, the whole would have been nullified, so, on the other hand, Israel's compliance with the prescribed rites required to be complete in every detail to secure the benefits promised to the obedience of faith. But not to receive these benefits was to leave an Israelite outside the covenant, or exposed to the Divine judgment. More than that, being caused by unbelief or disobedience, it involved the punishment due to open rebellion against God and His Word.

CHAPTER XVII.

Departure from Sinai—March into the Wilderness of Paran—At Taberah and Ribroth-hattaabah.

(NUMB. X. 29–XI.)

A T length, on the twentieth day of the second month,[1] the signal for departure from Sinai was given. The cloud which had rested upon the Tabernacle moved; the silver trumpets of the priests summoned "the camps" of Israel to their march, and as the Ark itself set forward, Moses, in joyous confidence of faith, spake those words of mingled prayer and praise which, as they marked the progress of Israel towards the Land of Promise, have ever been the signal in every forward movement of the Church :[2]

> Arise, O Jehovah, let Thine enemies be scattered :
> Let them also that hate Thee flee before Thee.

The general destination of Israel was, in the first place, "the wilderness of Paran," a name known long before.[3] This tract

---

[1] That is, the month after the Passover ; probably about the middle of May.

[2] Ps. lxviii. 1.   "In order to arm the Church with confidence, and to strengthen it with alacrity against the violent attacks of enemies."—*Calvin.*

[3] Gen. xiv. 6; xxi. 21.

may be described as occupying the whole northern part of the Sinaitic peninsula, between the so-called Arabah[1] on the east, and the wilderness of Shur in the west,[2] which separates Philistia from Egypt. Here Israel was, so to speak, hedged in by the descendants of Esau—on the one side by the Edomites, whose country lay east of the Arabah, and on the other by the Amalekites, while right before them were the Amorites. The whole district still bears the name Bádiet et Tíh, "the desert of the wanderings." Its southern portion seems, as it were, driven in wedgeways into the Sinaitic peninsula proper, from which it is separated by a belt of sand. Ascending from the so-called Tor, which had been the scene of the first year of Israel's pilgrimage and of the Sinaitic legislation, the Tíh might be entered by one of several passes through the mountains which form its southern boundary. The Et Tíh itself "is a limestone plateau of irregular surface."[3] It may generally be described as " open plains of sand and gravel . . . broken by a few valleys," and is at present "nearly waterless, with the exception of a few springs, situated in the larger wádies," which, however, yield rather an admixture of sand and water than water.. " The ground is for the most part hard and unyielding, and is covered in many places with a carpet of small flints, which are so worn and polished . . . as to resemble pieces of black glass." In spring, however, there is a scanty herbage even here, while in the larger wádies there is always sufficient for camels, and even " a few patches of ground available for cultivation." Such was " that great and terrible wilderness, wherein were fiery serpents, and scorpions,[4] and drought, where there was no water,"[5] through which Jehovah their God safely led Israel !

[1] The deep valley which runs from the Dead Sea to the Gulf of Akabah.

[2] Gen. xvi. 7 ; Ex. xv. 22.

[3] When not otherwise stated, the quotations within inverted commas are from Palmer's *Desert of the Exodus*.

[4] " In the course of the day we caught and bottled a large specimen of the cerastes, or horned snake, a very poisonous species, which abounds in the desert."—*Desert of the Exodus*, p. 310.

[5] Deut. viii. 15.

A still earlier retrospect on the part of Moses brings the events about to be described most vividly before us. Addressing Israel, he reminds them :[1] "when we departed from Horeb, we went through all that great and terrible wilderness, which ye saw by the way of the mountain of the Amorites, as Jehovah our God commanded us ; and we came to Kadesh-barnea." This "mountain of the Amorites" is the most interesting spot in the whole Et Tíh, or "wilderness of the wanderings." Arrived there, it seemed as if Israel were just about to take possession of the Promised Land. Thence the spies went forth to view the land. But here also the sentence was spoken which doomed all that unbelieving, faint-hearted generation to fall in the wilderness, and thither Israel had to return at the end of their forty years' wanderings to start, as it were, anew on their journey of possession. "The mountain of the Amorites" is a mountain plateau in the north-east of the Et Tíh, about seventy miles long, and from forty to fifty broad, which extends northward to near Beersheba. It contains many spots known to us from patriarchal history, and also celebrated afterwards. According to the description of travellers, we are here, literally, in a land of ruins, many of them dating far back, perhaps from the time of the Exodus, if not earlier. Even the old name of the Amorites is still everywhere preserved as 'Amir and 'Amori. It leaves a peculiar impression on the mind to find not only the old Scripture names of towns continued these thousands of years, but actually to hear the wells which Abraham and Isaac had dug still called by their ancient names ! About half way towards Beersheba the whole character of the scenery changes. Instead of the wilderness we have now broad valleys, with many and increasing evidences of former habitation all around. Indeed, we are now in the *Negeb*, or "south country" (erroneously rendered "the south" in our Authorised Version), which extends from about Kadesh to Beersheba. If "certain primeval stone remains" found throughout the Sinaitic peninsula have been regarded by the latest travellers as marking the

[1] Deut. i. 19.

journeyings, or rather the more prolonged settlements of Israel in " the wilderness," there is one class of them which deserves special attention. These are the so-called " Hazeroth," or " fenced enclosures," consisting of " a low wall of stones in which thick bundles of thorny acacia are inserted, the tangled branches and long needle-like spikes forming a perfectly impenetrable hedge around the encampment" of tents and cattle which they sheltered. These " Hazeroth," so frequently referred to in Scripture, abound in this district.

Such then was the goal and such the line of march before Israel, when, on that day in early summer, the Ark and the host of the Lord moved forward from the foot of Sinai. At the reiterated request of Moses, Hobab, the brother-in-law of Moses, had consented to accompany Israel, and to act as their guide in the wilderness, in the faith of afterwards sharing " what goodness Jehovah" would do unto IIis people.[1] This we learn from such passages as Judges i. 16; 1 Samuel xv. 6; xxvii. 10; xxx. 29. Although the pillar of cloud was the real guide of Israel in all their journeying, yet the local knowledge of Hobab would manifestly prove of the greatest use in indicating springs and places of pasturage. And so it always is. The moving of the cloud or its resting must be our sole guide ; but under its direction the best means which human skill or knowledge can suggest should be earnestly sought and thankfully used.

For three days Israel now journeyed without finding " a resting-place." By that time they must have fairly entered upon the " great and terrible wilderness." The scorching heat of a May sun reflected by such a soil, the fatigues of such a march, with probably scarcity of water and want of pasturage for their flocks—all combined to depress those whose hearts were not strong in faith and filled with longing for the better country. Behind and around was the great wilderness, and, so far as could be seen, no " resting-place" before them ! In truth, before inheriting the promises, Israel had now to pass through a trial of faith analogous to that which Abraham had

[1] Numb. x. 32.

undergone. Only as in his case each victory had been marked
by increasing encouragements, in theirs each failure was
attended by louder warnings, till at last the judgment came
which deprived that unbelieving generation of their share in
the enjoyment of the promise. Three days' journey under
such difficulties,[1] and " the people were as they who complain
of evil in the ears of Jehovah."[2]   But as this really reflected
upon His guidance, it displeased the Lord, and a fire, sent by
Jehovah, " consumed in the ends of the camp."   At the intercession of Moses "the fire was quenched."   But the lesson
which might have been learned, and the warning conveyed in
the judgment which had begun in the uttermost parts of the
camp, remained unnoticed.   Even the name *Taberah* (burning),
with which Moses had intended to perpetuate the memory of
this event, was unheeded.   Possibly, the quenching of the fire
may have deadened their spiritual sensibility, as formerly the
removal of the plagues had hardened the heart of Pharaoh and
of his people.   And so Taberah soon became *Kibroth-hattaavah*,[3]
and the fire of wrath that had burned in the uttermost parts
raged fiercely within the camp itself.

The sin of Israel at Kibroth-hattaavah was due to lust, and
manifested itself in contempt for God's provision and in a desire
after that of Egypt.   The " mixed multitude " which had come
up with Israel were the first to lust.   From them it spread to
Israel.   The past misery of Egypt—even its cruel bondage
—seemed for the moment quite forgotten, and only the lowest
thoughts of the abundant provision which it had supplied for
their carnal wants were present to their minds.   This impatient
question of disappointed lustfulness, " Who shall give us flesh to
eat?" repeated even to weeping, can only be accounted for by

[1] The distance of "three days' journey" (Numb. x. 33) prevents our
accepting Professor Palmer's theory, who identifies Taberah with the
present Erweis el Ebeirig.—*Desert of the Exodus*, pp. 257, 312.

[2] Numb. xi. 1.

[3] The locality of the two is evidently the same, as appears even from the
omission of Taberah from the list of encampments in Numb. xxxiii. 16.

such a state of feeling. But if it existed, it was natural that God's gracious provision of manna should also be despised. As if to mark their sin in this the more clearly, Scripture here repeats its description of the manna, and of its miraculous provision.[1] When Moses found "the weeping" not confined to any particular class, but general among the people (xi. 10), and that "the anger of Jehovah was kindled greatly," his heart sank within him. Yet, as has been well observed, he carried his complaint to the Lord in prayer, and therefore his was not the language of unbelief, only that of utter depression. Rightly understood, these words of his, "Have I conceived all this people? have I begotten them?" implied that not *he* but *God* was their father and their provider,[2] and that therefore he must cast their care upon the Lord. But even so the trial of Moses had in this instance become a temptation, although God gave him "with the temptation a way of escape."

Two things would the Lord do in answer to the appeal of Moses. First, He would, in His tender mercy, support and encourage His servant, and then manifest His power and holiness. With this twofold purpose in view, Moses was directed to place seventy of the elders of Israel—probably in a semi-circle—around the entrance to the Tabernacle. These "elders" were henceforth to help Moses in bearing the burden of the people. He had wished help, and he was now to receive it, although he would soon experience that the help of man was vain, and God alone the true helper. And then, to show in sight of all men that He had appointed such help, *yet only as a help to Moses*, God "came down in a cloud," spake unto Moses, and then put of his spirit upon these "elders." In manifestation of this new gift "they prophesied," by which, however, we are to understand not the prediction of future events, but probably that "speaking in the spirit" which in the New Testament also is designated as "prophesying."[3] Further, lest in the mind of the people this should be connected with any miraculous power inherent in Moses, the same spirit descended, and with the same

---

[1] Numb. xi. 7–9.   [2] Ex. iv. 22 ; Isa. lxiii. 16.   [3] 1 Cor. xii. ; xiv.

effect, upon two (Eldad and Medad) who had been "written," that is, designated for the office, but who for some reason had been prevented from appearing at the door of the Tabernacle. The lesson, it was evident, was required, for even Joshua had misunderstood the matter. When he found that Eldad and Medad prophesied "in the camp," he deemed the authority of his master compromised, and wished to "forbid them," since these men had not received the gift through Moses. We are here reminded of the similar conduct of John, who would have forbidden one "casting out devils" in the name of Christ, because he followed not with the other disciples, and of the Lord's rebuke of such mistaken zeal[1]—a mistake too often repeated, and a rebuke too much forgotten in the Christian Church at all times. Far different were the feelings of Moses. As a faithful servant, he emphatically disclaimed all honour for himself, and only expressed the fervent wish that the same spiritual gifts might be shared by all the Lord's people.

One thing was still required. God would manifest His power in providing for the wants of the people, and His holiness in taking vengeance on their lust. The lesson was specially needed, for even Moses had, when first told, questioned the full promise of providing for the whole people flesh sufficient to last for a month.[2] And now the Lord again showed how easily He can bring about supernatural results by what we call natural means. As explained in a former chapter, in spring the quails migrate in immense numbers from the interior of Africa northwards. An east wind, blowing from the Arabian Gulf, now drove them, in vast quantities, just over the camp of Israel. Here they fell down exhausted by the flight, and lay, to the distance of a day's journey "on this side and on that," in some places two cubits high. It is the same lesson which we have so often learned in this history. The "wind" which brought the quails "went forth from the Lord," and the number brought was far beyond what is ordinarily witnessed, although such a flight and drooping of birds are by no means uncommon.

---

[1] Mark ix. 38 ; Luke ix. 49.   [2] Numb. xi. 18-23.

And so God can, by means unthought of, send sudden deliverance—unexpectedly, even to one like Moses. But as for Israel, they had now their wishes more than gratified. The supply of flesh thus provided sufficed not only for the present, but was such that the greater part of it was preserved for after use (xi. 32). Thus had God shown the folly of those who murmured against His provision or questioned His ability. It still remained to punish the presumption and sin of their conduct. " While the flesh was yet between their teeth, ere it was chewed, the wrath of Jehovah was kindled against the people, and Jehovah smote the people with a very great plague. And he called the name of that place Kibroth-hattaavah (the graves of lust) : because there they buried the people that lusted." But how deeply the impression of this judgment sunk into the hearts of the godly in Israel appears from such passages as Psalm lxxviii. 26–31, while its permanent lesson to all times is summed up in these words : " He gave them their request ; but sent leanness into their soul."[1]

CHAPTER XVIII.

Murmuring of Miriam and Aaron—The Spies sent to Canaan — Their " Evil Report" — Rebellion of the People, and Judgment pronounced upon them — The Defeat of Israel " unto Hormah."

(NUMB. XII.-XIV.)

HITHERTO the spirit of rebellion on the part of the people had been directed against Jehovah Himself. If Moses had lately complained of continual trials in connection with those to whom he stood in no way closely related,[2] he was now to experience the full bitterness of this : " A man's foes shall be they of his own household."[3] From Kibroth-hattaavah

[1] Ps. cvi. 15. [2] Numb. xi. 12. [3] Matt. x. 36.

Israel had journeyed to Hazeroth, a station the more difficult to identify from the commonness of such "fenced enclosures" in that neighbourhood.[1] Here Miriam and—apparently at her instigation[2]—Aaron also "spake against Moses," as it is added, "because of the Ethiopian woman whom he had married," referring most likely to a second marriage which Moses had contracted after the death of Zipporah. For the first time we here encounter that pride of Israel after the flesh and contempt for all other nations, which has appeared throughout their after history, and in proportion as they have misunderstood the spiritual meaning of their calling. Thus, as Calvin remarks, Miriam and Aaron now actually boasted in that prophetic gift, which should have only wrought in them a sense of deep humility.[3] But Moses was *not* like any ordinary prophet, although in his extreme meekness he would not vindicate his own position (xii. 3). He "was faithful," or approved, "to Him that appointed him,"[4] not merely in any one special matter, but "in all the house" of Jehovah, that is, in *all* pertaining to the kingdom of God. And the Lord now vindicated His servant both by public declaration, and by punishing Miriam with leprosy. At the entreaty of Aaron, who owned his sister's and his own guilt, and at the intercession of Moses, this punishment was indeed removed. But the isolation of Miriam from the camp of Israel would teach all, how one who had boasted in privileges greater than those of others might be deprived even of the ordinary fellowship of Israel's camp.

The seven days of Miriam's separation were past, and Israel again resumed the march towards the Land of Promise. They had almost reached its boundary, when the event happened

---

[1] For the reason mentioned in a previous chapter we are unable to accept Professor Palmer's identification of Hazeroth with 'Ain Hadherah, however interesting the notices. See *Desert of the Exodus*, vol. i., pp. 256, 259, 261, and vol. ii., pp. 289, 313, etc.

[2] We gather this from the name of Miriam being first mentioned, and from the fact that Numb. xii. 1 reads in the original : "And she spake, Miriam and Aaron, against Moses."

[3] Numb. xii. 2.   [4] Heb. iii. 2, 5.

which not only formed the turning-point in the history of that generation, but which, more than any other, was typical of the future of Israel. For as that generation in their unbelief refused to enter the Land of Promise when its possession lay open before them, and as they rebelled against God and cast off the authority of Moses, so did their children reject the fulfilment of the promises in Christ Jesus, disown Him whom God had exalted a Prince and a Saviour, and cry out: " Away with Him ! away with Him !" And as the carcases of those who had rebelled fell in the wilderness, so has similar spiritual judgment followed upon the terrible cry : " His blood be upon us and upon our children !" But, blessed be God, as mercy was ultimately in store for the descendants of that rebellious generation, so also, in God's own time, will Israel turn again unto the Lord and enjoy the promises made unto the fathers.

The scene of this ever-memorable event was " the wilderness of Paran," or, to define the locality more exactly, *Kadesh-barnea.*[1] The spot has first been identified by Dr. Rowlands and Canon Williams,[2] and since so fully described by Professor Palmer, that we can follow the progress of events, step by step. Kadesh is the modern *'Ain Gadis*, or spring of Kadesh, and lies in that north-eastern plateau of the wilderness of Paran, which formed the stronghold of the Amorites.[3] A little north of it begins the Negeb or " south country " of Palestine,[4] which, as already explained, reaches to about Beersheba, and where the Promised Land really begins. The district is suited for pasturage, and contains abundant traces of former habitation, and, in the north, also evidence of the former cultivation of vines. Here, and

---

[1] Numb. xiii. 26 ; Deut. i. 19.

[2] The merit of the discovery unquestionably belongs to Dr. Rowlands and Canon Williams. See Williams, *Holy City*, vol. i., p. 464.

[3] Kadesh was formerly called *En Mishpat*, " Well of Judgment," Gen. xiv. 7. The recurrence of the *En* in the earlier name identifies it more closely with the *'Ain* Gadis of Canon Williams, Mr. Wilton, and Professor Palmer.

[4] The rendering "south," in our Authorised Version, is apt to confuse the general reader.

not, as is usually supposed, in the neighbourhood of Hebron, we must look for that valley of *Eshcol*,[1] whence the spies afterwards on their return brought the clusters of grapes, as specimens of the productiveness of the country.   Kadesh itself is the plain at the foot of the cliff whence the 'Ain Gadis springs. To the east is a ridge of mountains, to the west stretches a wide plain, where the Canaanites had gathered to await the advance of Israel.   Hence, if the spies were to "get up this Negeb" ("south country"), they had "to go up by the mountain,"[2] in order to avoid the host of Canaan.   In so doing they made a detour, passing south of 'Ain Gadis, through what is called in Scripture the wilderness of Zin (xiii. 21), from which they ascended into the mountains.   Thus much seems necessary to understand the localisation of the narrative.

But to return.   From Deut. i. 22, we gather that the proposal of sending spies "to search out the land" had originally come from the people.   By permission of the Lord, Moses had agreed to it,[3] adding, however, a warning to "be of good courage" (Numb. xiii. 20), lest this should be associated with fear of the people of the land.   Twelve persons, seemingly the most suitable for the work,—spiritually and otherwise—were chosen from "the rulers" of the tribes.[4]   Of these we only know *Caleb* and *Joshua*, the "minister of Moses," whose name Moses had formerly changed from *Hoshea*, which means "*help*," to Joshua, or "Jehovah is help."   Detailed and accurate directions having been given them, the spies left the camp of Israel "at the time of the first-ripe grapes," that is, about the end of July.   Thus far they were successful.   Eluding the Canaanites, they entered Palestine, and searched the land to its northernmost boundary, "unto Rehob, as men come to Hamath," that is, as far as the plain of Coele-Syria.   On their way back, coming from the north, they would of course not be suspected.   Accordingly they now

---

[1] *Eshcol* means in Hebrew a bunch of grapes.

[2] Numb. xiii. 17, 22.   [3] Numb. xiii. 1.

[4] Not from the "princes," as appears by a comparison of names.   Comp Numb. xiii. 4-15 with i. 5, etc. ; vii. 12, etc.

descended by Hebron, and explored the route which led into the Negeb by the western edge of the mountains. "In one of these extensive valleys—perhaps in Wády Hanein, where miles of grape-mounds even now meet the eye—they cut the gigantic cluster of grapes, and gathered the pomegranates and figs, to show how goodly was the land which the Lord had promised for their inheritance."[1] After forty days' absence the spies returned to camp. The report and the evidence of the fruitfulness of the land which they brought, fully confirmed the original promise of God to Israel.[2] But they added:[3] "Only that the people is strong which occupieth the land, and the cities fortified, very great, and also descendants of the Anak have we seen there,"[4] whom, in their fear, they seem to have identified (ver. 33) with the *Nephilim* of the antediluvian world.[5]

This account produced immediate terror, which Caleb sought in vain to allay. His opposition only elicited stronger language on the part of the other "spies," culminating in their assertion, that, even if Israel were to possess the land, it was one " that eateth up its inhabitants," that is, a country surrounded and peopled by fierce races in a state of constant warfare for its possession. Thus the most trustworthy and the bravest from among their tribes, with only the exception of Caleb and of Joshua (whose testimony might be set aside on the ground of his intimate relationship to Moses), now declared their inability either to conquer or to hold the land, for the sake of which they had left the comforts of Egypt and endured the hardships and dangers of "the great and terrible wilderness!" A night of complete demoralisation followed—the result being open revolt against Moses and Aaron, direct rebellion against Jehovah, and a proposal to elect a fresh leader and return to Egypt! In vain

[1] Palmer's *Desert of the Exodus*, vol. ii., p. 512.

[2] Ex. iii. 8. [3] Numb. xiii. 28.

[4] So literally. "The Anak" were probably a race or tribe, perhaps remnants of the original inhabitants of Palestine before the Canaanites took possession of it. The meaning of *Anak* is probably ' long-necked."

[5] Gen. vi. 4. Rendered in the Authorised Version "giants," in Numb. xiii. 33.

Moses and Aaron "fell on their faces" before God in sight of all the congregation ; in vain Joshua and Caleb "rent their clothes" in token of mourning, and besought the people to remember that the Presence of Jehovah with them implied certain success.   The excited people only "spake" of stoning them, when of a sudden "the glory of Jehovah visibly appeared in the tent of meeting to all the children of Israel."[1]   Almost had the Lord destroyed the whole people on the spot, when Moses again interposed—a type of the great Leader and Mediator of His people.   With pleadings more urgent than ever before, he wrestled with God—his language in its intensity consisting of short, abrupt sentences, piled, as it were, petition on petition, but all founded on the glory of God, on His past dealings, and especially on the greatness of His mercy, repeating in reference to this the very words in which the Lord had formerly condescended to reveal His inmost Being, when proclaiming His "Name" before Moses.[2]   Such plea could not remain unheeded ; it was typical of the great plea and the great Pleader.   But as, when long afterwards Israel called down upon themselves and their children the blood of Jesus, long and sore judgments were to befall the stiffnecked and rebellious, even although ultimately all Israel should be saved, so was it at Kadesh.   According to the number of days that the spies had searched the land, were to be the years of their wanderings in the wilderness, and of all that generation which had come out from Egypt, at the age of twenty and upwards, not one was to enter the Land of Promise,[3] but their carcases were to fall in that wilderness, with the exception of Caleb and Joshua.[4]   But

---

[1] Numb. xiv. 10.   [2] Ex. xxxiii. 17, 19.

[3] It may be instructive to know that Numb. xiv. 21 should be rendered : "but as truly as I live, and all the earth shall be filled with the glory of Jehovah."

[4] As the tribe of Levi was not numbered with the rest (Numb. i.), they did not apparently fall within the designation of those who were to die in the wilderness (Numb. xiv. 29).   Comp. Josh. xiv. 1, etc.   The Rabbis enumerate literally ten temptations on the part of Israel (Numb. xiv. 22) ; it need scarcely be said, very fancifully.

as for the other ten searchers of the land, quick destruction overtook them, and they "died by the plague before Jehovah."

This commencement of Divine judgment, coupled as it was with abundant evidence of its reality—especially in the immediate destruction of the ten spies, while Caleb and Joshua were preserved alive—produced an effect so strange and unlooked for, that we could scarcely understand it, but for kindred experience in all ages of the Church. It was now quite plain to Israel what they might, and certainly would have obtained, had they only gone forward. Yesterday that Land of Promise— in all its beauty and with all its riches—so close at hand as to be almost within sight of those mountain ranges, was literally theirs. To-day it was lost to them. Not one of their number was even to see it. More than that, their carcases were to fall in that wilderness! All this simply because they would not go forward yesterday! Let them do so to-day. If they had then done wrong, let them do the opposite to-day, and they would do right. Moreover, it was to Israel that God had pledged His word, and as Israel He would have brought them into the land. They were Israel still: let them now go forward and claim Israel's portion. But it was not so; and never is so in kindred circumstances. The wrong of our rebellion and unbelief is not turned into right by attempting the exact opposite. It is still the same spirit, which prompted the one, that influences the other. The obedience which is not of simple faith is of self-confidence, and only another kind of unbelief and self-righteousness. It is not the doing of this or that, nor the circumstance of outwardly belonging to Israel, which secures victory over the enemy, safety, or possession of the land. It is that "Jehovah is among us."[1] And the victory is ever that of faith. Not a dead promise to the descendants of Jacob after the flesh, but the presence of the living God among His believing Israel secured to them the benefits of the covenant. And Israel's determination to go up on the morrow, and so to retrieve the past, argued as great spiritual ignorance and unfit-

[1] Numb. xiv. 42.

ness, and involved as much rebellion and sin, as their former faint-heartedness and rebellion at the report of the spies.

In vain Moses urged these considerations on the people. The people " presumed[1] to go up to the head of the mountain," although Moses and the Ark of the Covenant of Jehovah remained behind in the camp. From Kadesh it is only about twenty miles to *Hormah*, to which place their enemies afterwards "smote and discomfited them." As we know from the descriptions of travellers, increasing fertility, cultivation, and civilisation must have met the host as it advanced into the Negeb. The Israelites were in fact nearing what they must have felt home-ground—sacred to them by association with Abraham and Isaac. For a little to the north of Hormah are the wells of Rehoboth, Sitnah, and Beersheba, which Abraham and Isaac had dug, the memory of which is to this day preserved in the modern names of Ruheibeh, Shutneh, and Bir Sebâ. Abraham himself had "journeyed toward the Negeb, and dwelled between Kadesh and Shur,"[2] and Isaac had followed closely in his footsteps.[3] And of the next occupants of the land, the Amorites, we find almost constantly recurring mementoes, and nowhere more distinctly than in the immediate neighbourhood of Hormah. From Judges i. 17, we know that that city, or probably rather the fort commanding it, had originally borne the name of Zephath, which simply means "watch-tower." The name Hormah, or "banning," was probably given it on a later occasion, when, after the attack of the king of Arad, Israel had "vowed the vow" utterly to destroy the cities of the Canaanites (Numb. xxi. 1-3). But, as Dr. Rowlands and Canon Williams have shown, the name Zephath has been preserved in the ruins of Sebaita, while Professor Palmer has discovered, close by, the ancient "watch-tower," which was a strong fort on the top of a hill commanding Sebaita. It is intensely interesting, amid the ruins of later fortifications,

---

[1] "Raised themselves up to go." This rendering seems the best. Others have translated, "they despised, so as," etc., or, "they persistently contended."

[2] Gen. xx. 1.   [3] Gen. xxvi. 17 to end.

to come upon these primeval remains, which mark not only the ancient site of Zephath, but may represent the very fort behind which the Amorites and Canaanites defended themselves against Israel, and whence they issued to this war. As if to make it impossible to mistake this "mountain of the Amorites," the valley north of Sebaita bears to this day the name Dheigat el 'Amerin, or Ravine of the Amorites, and the chain of mountains to the south-west of the fort that of Rás Amir, "head" or top " of the Amorites."[1]

Israel had presumed to go up into this mountain-top without the presence of Jehovah, without the Ark of the Covenant, and without Moses. Yesterday they had been taught the lesson that their seeming weakness would be real strength, if Jehovah were among them. To-day they had in bitter experience to find out this other and equally painful truth—that their seeming strength was real weakness. Smitten and discomfited by their enemies, they fled " even unto Hormah."

CHAPTER XIX.

The Thirty-eight Years in the Wilderness—The Sabbath-breaker—The Gainsaying of Korah and of his Associates—Murmuring of the People; the Plague, and how it was stayed—Aaron's Rod budding, blossoming, and bearing Fruit.

(NUMB. XV.; XXXIII. 19–37; DEUT. I. 46–II. 15; NUMB. XVI., XVII.)

MORE than thirty-seven years of " wanderings" were now to be passed in " the wilderness of Paran," till a new generation had risen to enter on possession of the Land of Promise. Of that long period scarcely more than one single record is left us in Scripture. As a German writer observes : The host of Israel, being doomed to judgment, ceased to be

[1] *Desert of the Exodus,* vol. ii. p. 380.

the subject of sacred history, while the rising generation, in whom the life and hope of Israel now centred, had, as yet, no history of its own.   And so we mark all this period rather by the death of the old than by the life of the new, and the wanderings of Israel by the graves which they left behind, as their carcases fell in the wilderness.

Still, we may profitably gather together the various notices scattered in Scripture. First, then, we learn that Israel " abode in Kadesh many days,"[1] and that thence their direction was " towards the Red Sea."[2] Their farthest halting-place from Kadesh seems to have been *Ezion-gaber*, which, as we know, lay on the so-called Elanitic Gulf of the Red Sea.   Thence they returned, at the end of the forty years' wanderings, once more to " the wilderness of Zin, which is Kadesh."[3]   The " stations" on their wanderings from Kadesh to Ezion-gaber are marked in Numbers xxxiii. 18–35.   There are just seventeen of them, after leaving *Rithmah*—a name derived from *retem*, a broom-bush, and which may therefore signify the valley of the broom-bushes.   If we rightly understand it, this was the original place of the encampment of Israel near Kadesh.   In point of fact, there is a plain close to 'Ain Gadis or Kadesh which to this day bears the name of Abu Retemet.   As for Kadesh itself—or the Holy Place, the place of " sanctifying "— which originally bore the name En Mishpat, "well of judgment,"[4] we imagine that it derived its peculiar name from the events that there took place, the additional designation of Barnea—Kadesh Barnea—either marking a former name of the place, or more probably meaning " the land of moving to and fro."[5] We presume that the encampment in " the broom-valley" was in all probability determined by the existence and promise of vegetation there, which, no doubt, was due to the presence

[1] Deut. i. 46.   [2] Deut. ii. 1.
[3] Numb. xxxiii. 36.   [4] Gen. xiv. 7.
[5] Or " wandering," or "being shaken."   Bishop Harold Browne suggests the query whether there may be any allusion to this in Ps. xxix. 8: "The Lord shaketh the wilderness of Kadesh."

of watercourses. Indeed, an examination of the names of the seventeen stations occupied by Israel during their wanderings shows, that all the encampments were similarly selected in the neighbourhood of water and vegetation. Thus we have *Rimmon-parez*, "the pomegranate breach"—perhaps the place where Korah's rebellion brought such terrible punishment; *Libnah*, "whiteness," probably from the white poplar trees growing there; *Rissah*, "dew;" *Mount Shapher*, "the mount of beauty," or "of goodliness;" *Mithcah*, "sweetness," in reference to the water; *Hashmonah*, "fatness," "fruitfulness," where to this day there is a pool full of sweet living water, with abundant vegetation around; *Bene-jaakan*, or, as in Deut. x. 6,[1] *Beeroth Bene-jaakan*, "the wells of the children of Jaakan," probably the wells which the Jaakanites had dug on their expulsion by the Edomites from their original homes;[2] *Jotbathah*, "goodness;" and *Ebronah*, probably "fords." The other names are either derived from peculiarities of scenery, or else from special events, as *Kehelathah*, "assembling;" *Makheloth*, "assemblies;" *Haradah*, "place of terror," etc.[3]

[1] In Deut. x. 6, 7, *four* of these stations are again mentioned, but in the inverse order from Numb. xxxiii. Evidently in Numb. xxxiii. we have the camps from Kadesh to Ezion-gaber during the thirty-seven years of wandering; while in Deut. x. 6, 7 the reference is to the march from Kadesh to Mount Hor in the fortieth year (after the *second* stay at Kadesh) on the journey of Israel to take possession of the land. But the apparently strange insertion of verses 6 and 7 in Deut. x., interrupting a quite different narrative, requires explanation. In vers. 1–5 Moses reminds the people how, in answer to his prayer, God had restored His covenant. Verses 6 and 7 are then inserted to show that not only the covenant, but also the mediatorial office of the high-priesthood had been similarly granted anew. God had not only continued it to Aaron, but, on his death at Mosera, Eleazar had been invested with the office, and under his ministry the tribes had continued their onward march. Instead of explaining all this in detail, Moses simply reminds the children of Israel (vers. 6, 7) of the historical facts of the case, which would speak for themselves.

[2] Gen. xxxvi. 27 ; 1 Chron. i. 42.

[3] Many of these stations have been identified—at least, with a great degree of probability. But an account of the various suggestions of modern explorers would lead too much into details.

The first impression which we derive, alike from the fewness of these stations, and from their situation, is, that the encampments were successively occupied for lengthened periods. More than that, we infer from the peculiar wording of some expressions in the original, that, during these thirty-eight years, the people were scattered up and down, the Tabernacle with the Levites forming, as it were, a kind of central camp and rallying-place. It is also quite certain that, at that period, the district in which the wanderings of Israel lay was capable of supporting such a nomadic population with their flocks and herds. Indeed, the presence of water, if turned to account, would always transform any part of that wilderness into a fruitful garden. In this respect the knowledge of irrigation, which the Israelites had acquired in Egypt, must have been of special use. Lastly, the people were not quite isolated. Not only were they near what we might call the direct highway between the East and Egypt, but they were in contact with other tribes, such as the Bene-jaakan. Deut. ii. 26–29 seems to imply that at times it was possible to purchase provisions and water, while Deut. ii. 7 shows that Israel had not only "lacked nothing" during "these forty years," but that they had greatly increased in substance and wealth. Such passages as Deut. viii. 14, etc.; xxix. 5; and Neh. ix. 21 prove in what remarkable manner God had cared for all the wants of His people during that period; and there can be no doubt that in the prophetic imagery of the future, especially by Isaiah, there is frequent retrospect to God's gracious dealings with Israel in the wilderness.[1]

Brief as is the record of these thirty-eight years, it contains a notice of two events—both in rebellion against the Lord. The first gives an account of a man who had openly violated the

---

[1] See *Speaker's Commentary*, vol. ii. p. 720, *note*. The clearest indication of this is found in Isa. xliii. 16-21. But I think it a mistake to trace in Ps. lxxiv. 14, an allusion to a supply of fish from the Elanitic Gulf of the Red Sea, although it is true that several of the encampments of Israel were on, or quite close to, its shores.

Divine law by gathering "sticks upon the Sabbath day."[1] Although the punishment of death had been awarded to such a "presumptuous sin,"[2] the offender was, in the first place, "put in ward," partly to own the Lord by specially asking His direction, since only the punishment itself but not its mode had been previously indicated, and partly perhaps to impress all Israel with the solemnity of the matter. Due observance of the Lord's day was, indeed, from every point of view, a question of deepest importance to Israel, and the offender was, by Divine direction, "brought without the camp, and stoned with stones, and he died." We are not told at what particular period of the wanderings of Israel this event had occurred. It is apparently inserted as an instance and illustration, immediately after the warning against "presumptuous sins" (literally, "sins with a hand uplifted," viz., against Jehovah). These sins in open contempt of God's word involved the punishment of being "cut off" from the people of the Lord.

Nor have we any precise date by which to fix the other and far more serious instance of rebellion on the part of Korah and of his associates,[3] in which afterwards the people, as a whole, were implicated.[4] There is, however, reason to suppose that it occurred at an early period of "the wanderings"—perhaps, as already suggested, at Rimmon-parez. The leaders of this rebellion were Korah, a Levite—a descendant of Izhar, the brother of Amram,[5] and therefore a near relative of Aaron—and three Reubenites, Dathan, Abiram, and On. But as the latter is not further mentioned, we may suppose that he early withdrew from the conspiracy. These men gained over to their side no fewer than two hundred and fifty princes from among the other tribes,[6] all of them members of the national representative

[1] Numb. xv. 32–36.
[2] Ex. xxxi. 14, etc. ; xxxv. 2.
[3] Numb. xvi.
[4] Numb. xvi. 41–50.
[5] Ex. vi. 18.
[6] The statement that Zelophehad, a Manassite, had not been "in the company of Korah" (Numb. xxvii. 3), implies that his fellow-conspirators belonged to the various tribes.

council,[1] and "men of renown," or, as we should express it, well-known leading men. Thus the movement assumed very large proportions, and evidenced wide-spread disaffection and dissatisfaction. The motives of this conspiracy seem plain enough. They were simply jealousy and disappointed ambition, though the rebels assumed the language of a higher spirituality. As descended from a brother of Aaron, Korah disliked, and perhaps coveted, what seemed to him the supremacy of Aaron, for which he could see no valid reason. He had also a special grievance of his own. True, he was one of that family of the Kohathites to whom the chief Levitical charge in the sanctuary had been committed; but then the Kohathites numbered four families,[2] and the leadership of the whole was entrusted not to any of the older branches, but to the youngest, the Uzzielites (Numb. iii. 30). Was there not manifest wrong and injustice in this, probably affecting Korah personally? It speaks well for the Levites as a whole, that, notwithstanding all this, Korah was unable to inveigle any of them in his conspiracy. But close to the tents of the Kohathites and of Korah was the encampment of the tribe of Reuben, who held command of the division on the south side of the camp. Possibly—and indeed the narrative of their punishment seems to imply this—the tent of Korah and those of the Reubenite princes, Dathan, Abiram, and On, were contiguous. And Reuben also *had* a grievance; for was not Reuben Jacob's firstborn, who should therefore have held the leadership among the tribes? It was not difficult to kindle the flame of jealousy in an Eastern breast. What claim or right had Moses, or rather the tribe of Levi whom he represented, to supremacy in Israel? Assuredly this was a grievous wrong and an intolerable usurpation, primarily as it affected Reuben, and secondarily all the other tribes. This explains the ready

---

[1] The Authorised Version (Numb. xvi. 2) translates "famous," but the literal rendering is "called to the meeting," evidently members of the national representative council. See Numb. i. 16.

[2] Numb. iii. 27.

participation of so many of the princes in the conspiracy, the expostulation of Moses with Korah (xvi. 8–11), and his indignant appeal to God against the implied charges of the Reubenites (ver. 15). Indeed, the conspirators expressly stated these views as follows (ver. 3) : " Sufficient for you !"—that is, You, Moses and Aaron, have long enough held the priesthood and the government; " for the whole congregation, all are holy, and in the midst of them Jehovah. And why exalt ye yourselves over the convocation[1] of Jehovah ?" It will be observed that the pretence which they put forward to cover their selfish, ambitious motives was that of a higher spirituality, which recognised none other than the spiritual priesthood of all Israel. But, as we shall presently show, their claim to it was not founded on the typical mediatorship of the high-priest, but on their standing as Israel after the flesh.

The whole of this history is so sad, the judgment which followed it so terrible—finding no other parallel than that which in the New Testament Church overtook Ananias and Sapphira—and the rebellion itself is so frequently referred to in Scripture, that it requires more special consideration. The rebellion of Korah, as it is generally called, from its prime mover, was, of course, an act of direct opposition to the appointment of God. But this was not all. The principle expressed in their gainsaying (ver. 3) ran directly counter to the whole design of the old covenant, and would, if carried out, have entirely subverted its typical character. It was, indeed, quite true that all Israel were holy and priests, yet not in virtue of their birth or national standing, but through the typical priesthood of Aaron, who " brought them nigh " and

---

[1] We have rendered the term literally by " convocation." Two different terms are used in this chapter. One of these—*edah*—means, literally, *congregation*, and may be said to designate Israel as the outward and visible Church. The other term is *kahal*, literally " the called," or convocation, and refers to the spiritual character of Israel as called of God. Thus the distinction of an outward and visible and a spiritual Church had its equivalent in the Old Testament. In this chapter the term *kahal* occurs only in ver. 3, and again in ver. 33.

was their intermediary with God. Again, this priesthood of
Aaron, as indeed all similar selections – such as those of the
place where, and the seasons when God would be worshipped,
of the composition of the incense, or of the sacrifices—although
there may have been secondary and subordinate reasons for
them, depended in the first place and mainly upon God's appointment. "Him whom the Lord hath chosen will He cause to come
near unto Him" (xvi. 5); "whom the Lord doth choose, he
shall be holy" (ver. 7). Every other service, fire, or place
than that which *God* had chosen, would, however well and
earnestly intended, be "strange" service, "strange" fire, and a
"strange" place. This was essential for the *typical* bearing of
all these arrangements. It was God's appointment, and not the
natural fitness of a person or thing which here came into consideration. If otherwise, they would have been natural *sequences*,
not *types*—constituting a rational rather than a Divine service.
It was of the nature of a type that God should appoint the
earthly emblem with which He would connect the spiritual
reality. The moment Israel deviated in any detail, however
small, they not only rebelled against God's appointment, but
destroyed the meaning of the whole by substituting the human
and natural for the Divine. The types were, so to speak,
mirrors of God's own fitting, which exhibited, as already
present, future spiritual realities with all their blessings. In
Christ all such types have ceased, because the reality to which
they pointed has come.

This digression seemed necessary, alike for the proper understanding of the history of Korah and for that of the typical
arrangements of the Old Testament. But to return. On the
morning following the outbreak of the rebellion, Korah and
his two hundred and fifty associates presented themselves, as
Moses had proposed, at the door of the Tabernacle. Here
"they took every man his censer, and put fire in them, and
laid incense thereon." Indeed, Korah had gained such influence,
that he was now able to gather there "all the congregation"
as against Moses and Aaron. Almost had the wrath of God,

Whose glory visibly appeared before all, consumed "this congregation" in a moment, when the intercession of Moses and
Aaron once more prevailed. In these words : "O God, the
God of the spirits of all flesh, shall one man sin, and wilt Thou
be wroth with all the congregation?" (as Calvin remarks)
Moses made his appeal "to the general grace of creation,"
praying that, "as God was the Creator and Maker of the
world, He would not destroy man whom He had created, but
rather have pity on the work of His hands." And so there is
a plea for mercy, and an unspeakable privilege even in the fact
of being the creatures of such a God !

Leaving the rebels with their censers at the door of the
Tabernacle—perhaps panic-struck—Moses next repaired to the
tents of Dathan and Abiram, accompanied by the elders, and
followed by the congregation.[1] On the previous day the two
Reubenites had refused to meet Moses, and sent him a
taunting reply, suggesting that he only intended to blind the
people.[2] And now when Dathan and Abiram, with their
wives and children, came out and stood at the door of their
tents, as it were, to challenge what Moses could do, the people
were first solemnly warned away from them. Then a judgment, new and unheard of, was announced, and immediately
executed. The earth opened her mouth and swallowed up
these rebels and their families, with all that appertained to
them, that is, with such as had taken part in their crime. As
for Korah, the same fate seems to have overtaken him. But
it is an emphatic testimony alike to the truth of God's declaration, that He punisheth not men for the sins of their
fathers,[3] and to the piety of the Levites, that the sons of
Korah did not share in the rebellion of their father, and

---

[1] From Numb. xvi., and the reference in Numb. xxvi. 10, 11, I am led
to infer that Korah followed also in the train, perhaps to see what would
come of it, leaving the two hundred and fifty princes at the door of the
Tabernacle. If Korah's tent was contiguous to those of Dathan and
Abiram, we can form a clearer conception of the whole scene.

[2] Literally rendering xvi. 14 : " Wilt thou put out the eyes of these men?"

[3] Jer. xxxi. 30 ; Ezek. xviii. 19, 20.

consequently died not with him.[1]   More than this, not only were Samuel and afterwards Heman descendants of Korah,[2] but among them were some of those "sweet singers of Israel," whose hymns, Divinely inspired, were intended for the Church at all times.   And all the Psalms "of the sons of Korah"[3] have this common characteristic, which sounds like an echo of the lesson learned from the solemn judgment upon their house, that their burden is praise of the King Who is enthroned at Jerusalem, and longing after the services of God's sanctuary.[4] But as for "the two hundred and fifty men that offered incense," "there came out a fire from the Lord and consumed" them, as, on a former occasion, it had destroyed Nadab and Abihu.[5] Their censers, which had been "hallowed," by being presented before the Lord,[6] were converted into plates for covering the altar of burnt offering, that so they might be a continual "memorial unto the children of Israel" of the event and its teaching.

This signal judgment of God upon the rebels had indeed struck the people who witnessed it with sudden awe, but it led not to that repentance[7] which results from a change of heart. The impression passed away, and "on the morrow" nothing remained but the thought that so many princes of tribes, who had sought to vindicate tribal independence, had been cut off for the sake of Moses !   It was in their cause, the people would argue, that these men had died ; and the mourning in the tents of the princes, the desolateness which marked what had but yesterday been the habitations of Korah, Dathan, and Abiram, would only give poignancy to the feeling that with this event a yoke of bondage had been for ever riveted upon the nation. For they recognised not the purpose and meaning of God ; this

---

[1] Numb. xxvi. 11.   [2] 1 Sam. i. 1 ; 1 Chron. vi. 33-38.

[3] Wrongly translated in the Authorised Version, "for the sons of Korah."

[4] The following are the eleven Psalms designated as those of the sons of Korah : Ps. xlii., xliv.–xlix., lxxxiv., lxxxv., lxxxvii., and lxxxviii. The following are further references to the history of the sons of Korah : 1 Chron. ix. 19 ; xii. 6 ; xxvi. 1-19 ; 2 Chron. xx. 19 ; Neh. xi. 19.

[5] Lev. x. 2.   [6] Numb. xvi. 37.   [7] Ps. iv. 4.

would have implied spiritual discernment; only that, if judgment had proceeded from Jehovah, it had come, if not at the instigation of, yet in order to vindicate Moses and Aaron. In their ingratitude they even forgot that, but for the intercession of these two, the whole congregation would have perished in the gainsaying of Korah. So truly did that generation prove the justice of the Divine sentence that none of their number should enter into the land of Canaan, and so entirely unfit did their conduct (as of old that of Esau) show them for inheriting the promises!

But as for Moses and Aaron, when the congregation was once more gathered against them with this cruel and unjust charge on their lips, "Ye have killed the people of Jehovah," they almost instinctively "faced towards the tent of meeting,"[1] as the place whence their help came and to which their appeal was now made. Nor did they look in vain. Denser and more closely than before did the cloud cover the tabernacle, and from out of it burst visibly the luminous glory of Jehovah. And as Moses and Aaron entered the court of the tabernacle, "Jehovah spake unto Moses, saying, Get you up from among this congregation, and I will consume them as in a moment. And they fell upon their faces." But what was Moses to plead? He knew that "already" was "wrath gone forth from Jehovah," and "the plague" had "begun." What could he now say? In the rebellion at Mount Horeb,[2] again at Kadesh,[3] and but the day before at the gainsaying of Korah, he had exhausted every argument. No similar plea, nor indeed any plea, remained. Then it was, in the hour of deepest need, when every argument that even faith could suggest had been taken away, and Israel was, so to speak, *lost*, that the all-sufficiency of the Divine provision in its vicarious and mediatorial character appeared. Although as yet only *typical*, it proved all sufficient. The incense kindled on the coals taken from the altar of burnt-offering, where the sacrifices had been brought,

---

[1] This is the literal rendering.

[2] Ex. xxxii. 31.   [3] Numb. xiv. 13, etc.

typified the accepted mediatorial intercession of our great High-priest. And now, when there was absolutely no plea upon earth, this typical pleading of His perfect righteousness and intercession prevailed. Never before or after was the Gospel so preached under the Old Testament[1] as when Aaron, at Moses' direction, took the censer, and, having filled it from the altar, "ran into the midst of the congregation," "and put on incense, and made an atonement for the people" (xvi. 47). And as he stood with that censer "between the dead and the living," "the plague," which had already swept away not less than 14,700 men, "was stayed." Thus if Korah's assumption of the priestly functions had caused, the exercise of the typical priesthood now removed, the plague.

But the truth which God now taught the people was not to be exhibited only in judgment. After the storm and the earthquake came the "still, small voice," and the typical import of the Aaronic priesthood was presented under a beautiful symbol. By direction of God, "a rod" for each of the twelve tribes, bearing the respective names of their princes,[2] was laid up in the Most Holy Place, before the Ark of the Covenant. And on the morrow, when Moses entered the sanctuary, "behold the rod of Aaron for the house of Levi had budded, and brought forth buds, and bloomed blossoms, and yielded almonds." The symbolical teaching of this was plain. Each of these "rods" was a ruler's staff, the emblem of a tribe and its government. This was the natural position of

---

[1] The only similar instance was the lifting up of the brazen serpent, which typically represented another part of the work of our Redeemer. Even the prophecies of Isaiah were not clearer than these two sermons by outward deed, as we may call them—the one declaring the typical meaning of the Aaronic priesthood, and the efficacy of that to which it pointed ; the other, the character and the completeness of God's provision for the removal of guilt.

[2] According to the more common view, twelve rods were presented, Ephraim and Manasseh being counted only one tribe, that of Joseph. According to others, there were twelve rods, exclusively of that of Levi, which bore the name of Aaron.

all these princes of Israel.   But theirs as well as Aaron's were rods *cut off from the parent-stem*, and therefore incapable of putting forth verdure, bearing blossom, or yielding fruit in the sanctuary of God.   By nature, then, there was absolutely no difference between Aaron and the other princes; all were equally incapable of the new life of fruitfulness.   What distinguished Aaron's rod was the selection of God and the miraculous gift bestowed upon it.   And then, typically in the old, but really in the new dispensation, that rod burst at the same time into branches, into blossom, and even into fruit—all these three combined, and all appearing at the same time. And so these princes "took every man his rod;" but Aaron's rod was again brought before the Ark of the Covenant, and kept there "for a token." [1]   Nor was even the choice of the almond, which blossoms first of trees, without its deep meaning.   For the almond, which bursts earliest into flower and fruit, is called in Hebrew "*the waker*" (*shaked*, comp. Jer. i. 11, 12). Thus, as the "early waker," the Aaronic priesthood, with its buds, blossoms, and fruit, was typical of the better priesthood, when the Sun of Righteousness would rise "with healing in His wings." [2]

[1] Apparently, both the pot of manna and Aaron's rod were lost when the ark returned from the Philistine cities (see 1 Kings viii. 9).   This loss also was deeply significant—as it were, God's unspoken comment on the state of Israel.

[2] The significance of the Levitical sections, as they follow upon Numb. xvii., will be apparent to the attentive reader.   But this is not the place to enter further on the subject.

CHAPTER XX.

The Second Gathering of Israel in Kadesh—The Sin of Moses and Aaron—Embassy to Edom—Death of Aaron—Retreat of Israel from the borders of Edom—Attack by the Canaanitish King of Arad.

(NUMB. XX.; XXI. 1-3.)

I T was indeed most fitting that, at the end of the thirty-seven years' wanderings, Israel should once more gather at Kadesh. There they had been scattered, when the evil report which the spies had brought led to their unbelief and re-bellion; and thence had the old generation carried, as it were, its sentence of death back into the wilderness, till during these long and weary years its full terms had been exhausted. And now a new generation was once more at Kadesh. From the very spot where the old was broken off was the fresh start to be made. God is faithful to His purpose; *He* never breaks off. If the old was interrupted, it had been by man's unbelief and rebellion, not by failure on the part of God; and when He resumed His work, it was exactly where it had been so broken off. And man also must return to where he has departed from God, and to where sentence has been pronounced against him, before he enters on his new journey to the Land of Promise. But what solemn thoughts might not have been expected in this new generation, as they once more stood ready to resume their journeying on the spot where that of their fathers had been arrested. As *He* had sanctified His Name in Kadesh by judgment, would *they* now sanctify it by their faith and willing obedience?

Besides Joshua and Caleb, to whom entrance into the land

had been specially promised, only three of the old generation still remained. These were Miriam, Moses, and Aaron. And now, just at the commencement of this fresh start, as if the more solemnly to remind them of the past, Miriam, who had led the hymn of thanksgiving and triumph on their first entering the desert,[1] was taken away. Only Moses and Aaron were now left—weary, wayworn pilgrims, to begin a new journey with new pilgrims, who had to learn afresh the dealings of Jehovah. And this may help us to understand what happened at the very outset of their pilgrimage. Israel was in *Kadesh*, or rather in the desert of Zin, the name Kadesh applying probably to the whole district as well as to a special locality. So large a number of people gathered in one place would naturally soon suffer from want of water. Let it also be remembered, that that generation knew of the wonders of the Lord chiefly by the hearing of the ear, but of His judgments by what they had seen of death sweeping away all who had come out of Egypt. In the hardness of their hearts it now seemed to them as if the prospect before them were hopeless, and they destined to suffer the same fate as their fathers. Something of this unbelieving despair appears in their cry: "Would God that we had died when our brethren died before Jehovah"[2]— that is, by Divine judgment, during these years of wandering. The remembrance of the past with its disappointments seems to find expression in their complaints (xx. 5). It is as if they contrasted the stay of their nation in Egypt, and the hopes awakened on leaving it, with the disappointment of seeing the good land almost within their grasp, and then being turned back to die in the wilderness! And so the people broke forth in rebellion against Moses and against Aaron.

Feelings similar to theirs seem to have taken hold even on Moses and Aaron—only in a different direction. The people despaired of success, and rebelled against Moses and Aaron. With them as leaders they would never get possession of the Land of Promise. On the other hand, Moses and Aaron also

[1] Ex. xv. 31. [2] Numb. xx. 3.

despaired of success, and rebelled, as it were, against the people. Such an unbelieving people, rebelling at the very outset, would never be allowed to enter the land. The people felt as if the prospect before them were hopeless, and so did Moses and Aaron, although on opposite grounds. As we have said, the people rebelled against Moses and Aaron, and Moses and Aaron against the people. But at bottom, the ground of despair and of rebellion, both on the part of the people and of Moses, was precisely the same. In both cases it was really unbelief of God. The people had looked upon Moses and not upon God as their leader into the land, and they had despaired. Moses looked at the people as they were in themselves, instead of thinking of God Who now sent them forward, secure in His promise, which He would assuredly fulfil. This soon appeared in the conduct and language of Moses. By Divine direction he was to stand in sight of the people at "the rock before their eyes" with "the rod from before Jehovah"—no doubt the same with which the miracles had been wrought in Egypt, and under whose stroke water had once before sprung from the rock at Rephidim.[1]

It is generally thought that the sin of Moses, in which Aaron shared, consisted in his *striking* the rock—and doing so twice—instead of merely *speaking* to it, "and it shall give forth its water;" and also, in the hasty and improper language which he used on the occasion: "Hear now, ye rebels, must we fetch you water out of this rock?"[2] But it seems difficult to accept this view. On the one hand, we can scarcely imagine that unbelief should have led Moses to strike, rather than to speak to the rock, as if the former would have

[1] Ex. xvii. 6.

[2] The great Rabbinical interpreter Rashi accounts for the twice striking by supposing that Moses went to the wrong rock, when, at the first stroke, only a few drops came, but at the second abundance of water. He finds the sin of Moses in his striking instead of speaking, since the people would, in the latter case, have argued—If the rock which neither speaks, hears, nor needs nourishment, obeys the voice of God, how much more are we bound so to do. The Jerusalem Targum has it, that at the first stroke blood came from the rock.

been more efficacious than the latter. On the othe1 hand, it seems strange that Moses should have been directed to "take the rod," if he were not to have used it, the more so as this had been the Divinely sanctioned mode of proceeding at Rephidim.[1] Lastly, how, in that case, could Aaron have been implicated in the sin of Moses? Of course, the striking the rock *twice* was, as we read in Psalm cvi. 32, 33, evidence that they had "angered" Moses, and that "his spirit was provoked." This also showed itself in his language, which Scripture thus characterises: "he spake unadvisedly with his lips"—or, as the word literally means, "he babbled."[2] Be it observed, that Moses *is not anywhere in Scripture blamed* for striking instead of speaking to the rock, while it is expressly stated that the people "angered him also at the waters of strife, so that it went ill with Moses for their sakes."

The other aspect of the sin of Moses was afterwards expressly stated by the Lord Himself, when He pronounced on Moses and Aaron the sentence that they should not "bring this congregation into the land," which He had given them, on this ground: "Because ye believed Me not, to sanctify Me in the eyes of the children of Israel" (xx. 12). Thus in their rebellion against Moses and Aaron, the people had not believed that Jehovah would bring them into the land which He had given them; while, in their anger at the people, Moses and Aaron had not believed God, to sanctify Him in His power and grace in the eyes of the children of Israel. Israel failed as the people of God; Moses as their mediator. Hitherto Moses had, under every provocation, been faithful as a steward over his charge, and pleaded with God and prevailed, because he believed. Now for the first time Moses failed, as we all fail, through unbelief, looking at the sin of the people, and thence inferring the impossibility of their inheriting the promises, instead of looking at the grace and power of God which

[1] Ex. xvii. 6.
[2] The word, whether written *bata* or *bada*, means to talk foolishly, or rashly, *to babble*, also to boast.

made all things possible, and at the certainty of the promise. Unlike Abraham in similar circumstances, " he staggered at the promises." And having through unbelief failed as mediator of the people, his office was to cease, and the conduct of Israel into the land to devolve upon another.

It is only in this sense that we can accept the common statement, that the sin of Moses was *official* rather than *personal.* For these two —office or work, and person—cannot be separated either as regards responsibility or duty. Rather would we think of Moses and Aaron as aged pilgrims, worn with the long way through the wilderness, and footsore with its roughnesses and stones, whose strength momentarily failed when the weary journey was once more resumed, and who in their weariness stumbled at the rock of offence. Yet few events possess deeper pathos than this " babbling " at the waters of Meribah. Its true parallel is found not in the Old but in the New Testament. It is true that, in similar circumstances, Elijah also despaired of Israel, and was directed to " the mount of God," there to learn the same lesson as Moses—before, like him, he was unclothed of his office. But the full counterpart to the temptation of Moses is presented in the history of John the Baptist, when doubting, not the Person but the mode of working of the Messiah, and despairing, from what he saw and heard, of the fulfilment of the promise at that time and among that generation, he sent his disciples on that memorable embassy, just before he also was unclothed of his office. This is not the place to follow the subject further. Suffice it to point out, on the one hand, Moses, Elijah, John the Baptist, and, on the other, Joshua, Elisha, and our blessed Lord, as the types and antitypes presented to us in Scripture.

Before leaving Kadesh, Moses sent messengers to the king of Edom, and also, as we learn from Judges xi. 17, to the king of Moab,[1] whose dominions lay on the north of Edom, asking

---

[1] The reply of the king of Moab is not mentioned in Scripture, because, upon the refusal of Edom, even his permission would have been of no use, as the road to Moab lay through Edom.

permission for Israel to pass through their countries. A glance
at the map will show that this would have been the most direct
route, if Palestine was to be entered from the other side Jordan
at Jericho. Certainly it was the easiest route, as it avoided
contact with those who held the Negeb, or south country,
who thirty-seven years before had met Israel in hostile conflict and signally defeated them.[1] But in vain Moses urged
upon Edom the claims of national kinship, Israel's past sufferings in Egypt, and their marvellous deliverance and guidance
by The Angel of Jehovah. In vain also did he limit his
request to permission to use the ordinary caravan road—"the
king's highway"—without straying either to the right or the
left, adding the promise of payment for the use of the wells.[2]
The children of Esau not only absolutely refused, but hastily
gathered an army of observation on their borders. Meantime,
while the messengers of Moses had gone on their embassy, the
camp of Israel had moved forward to what may be described
as "the uttermost of the border" of Edom. A day's journey
eastward from Kadesh, through the wide and broad Wády
Murreh, suddenly rises a remarkable mountain, quite isolated
and prominent, which Canon Williams describes as "singularly
formed," and the late Professor Robinson likens to "a lofty
citadel." Its present name Moderah preserves the ancient
Biblical Moserah, which, from a comparison of Numb. xx. 22–29
with Deut. x. 6, we know to have been only another desig
nation for Mount Hor. In fact, "Mount Hor" or *Hor-ha-Hor*
("mountain, the mountain") just means "the remarkable mountain." This was the natural route for Israel to take, if they
hoped to pass through Edom by the king's highway—the
present Wády Ghuweir,—which would have led them by way
of Moab, easily and straight, to the other side of Jordan. It
was natural for them here to halt and await the reply of the
king of Edom. For while Moderah lies at the very boundary,
but still outside Edom, it is also at the entrance to the various
wádies or roads, which thence open east, south, and south-west,

[1] Numb. xiv. 44, 45.   [2] Numb. xx. 14–17.

so that the children of Israel might thence take any route which circumstances would indicate. Moreover, from the height of Moderah they would be able to observe any hostile movement that might be directed against them, whether from the east by Edom, or from the north and west by the Amalekites and Canaanites. From what has been said, it will be gathered that we regard this as the Mount Hor where Aaron died.[1]

Thus speedily, within a day's journey of the place of his sin, was the Divine sentence upon Aaron executed. There is a solemn grandeur about this narrative, befitting the occasion and in accordance with the locality. In the sight of all the con-

[1] The traditional site for Mount Hor is Jebel Harûn, close by Petra, the capital of Edom. To state is already to refute a supposition which implies that Israel had asked leave to pass through Edom, and then, without awaiting the reply, marched into the heart of Edom, and camped for thirty days close by its capital ! Moreover, it is difficult to understand what could have been the object of going so far south, if Israel hoped—as at the time they did—to strike through the nearest practicable wády, the road that led northward through Edom and Moab to the ford of Jordan. In that case Jebel Harûn would have been far out of their way. Finally, it is impossible to arrange the chronological succession of events as given in the Bible, except on the supposition that Moderah was Mount Hor. For, if the camp of Israel had been near Petra, there could have been no reason for the king of Arad to dread their forcing their way through his territory (Numb. xxi. 1), even as it seems most unlikely that he should have marched so far south-east as Petra to attack Israel. Accordingly, interpreters who regard Jebel Harûn as Mount Hor are obliged to suppose that the attack of the king of Arad had taken place earlier, say, at the period indicated in Numb. xx. 22. But in that case it is difficult to imagine how the king could have heard that Israel was " coming by the way of the spies," seeing they were taking exactly the opposite direction, and had just requested permission to pass through Edom. Against these weighty reasons we have only the authority of tradition in favour of Harûn. On the other hand, all becomes plain, and easily understood, if we regard Moderah as Mount Hor ; and the whole narrative in its chronological succession in Scripture is just what we should have expected. The reader who wishes further information is referred to the admirable work of the late Rev. E. Wilton on *The Negeb, or South Country of Scripture* (pp. 126-134), and to the excellent map attached to it.

gregation these three, Moses, Aaron, and Eleazar, went up the mount. In his full priestly dress walked Aaron to his burial. He knew it, and so did all in that camp, who now, for the last time, reverently and silently looked upon the venerable figure of him who, these forty years, had ministered unto them in holy things.[1] There was no farewell. In that typical priesthood all depended on the unbroken continuance of the office, not of the person. And hence on that mountain-top Aaron was first unclothed of his priestly robes, and Eleazar, his son, formally invested with them. Thus the priesthood had not for a moment ceased when Aaron died. Then, not as a priest but simply as one of God's Israel, was he "gathered unto his people." But over that which passed between the three on the mount has the hand of God drawn the veil of silence. And so the new priest, Eleazar, came down from the solemn scene on Mount Hor to minister amidst a hushed and awe-stricken congregation. "And when all the congregation saw that Aaron was dead, they mourned for Aaron thirty days, even all the house of Israel."

Serious tidings were now in store for Israel. The messengers returned from Edom bringing absolute refusal to the request of passage through that country. Not only so, but the large army of Edom was assembling on the frontier, close to the camping-ground of Israel. If, according to the Divine command, Edom was not to be attacked, then Israel must rapidly *retreat.* The ordinary route from Mount Hor "to compass the land of Edom," so as to advance northwards, by the east of Edom, would have led Israel straight down by the Wády El-Jeib, and so through the northern part of the Arabah. But this route touched the western boundary of Edom, just where, as we gather from the Scriptural narrative, the army of Edom was *echeloned.* To avoid them, it became therefore necessary, in the first place, to retrace their steps again through

---

[1] According to Numb. xxxiii. 37, etc., Aaron died on the first day of the fifth month of the fortieth year after the Exodus, and at the age of one hundred and twenty-three years.

part of the Wády Murreh, in order thence to strike in a south-
easterly direction through what are now known as "the mountains of the 'Azâzimeh," the ancient dukedom of Teman, or
Mount Paran. By this detour Israel would strike the Arabah
far south of where the army of Edom awaited them, passing
through the modern Wádies Ghudhâghidh and 'Adbeh. In
point of fact, we learn from Deut. x. 7 that Gudgodah and
Jotbath were the two stations reached next after the retreat
from Mount Hor. But just at the point where the host of
Israel would turn southwards from Wády Murreh, they were
also in almost a straight line for the territory of the king of
Arad. Of course, he would be informed that Israel had been
refused a passage through Edom, and, finding them on the
flank of his territory, would naturally imagine that they intended to invade it. "And the Canaanitish king of Arad,
which dwelt in the Negeb"[1] (or south country), "heard tell that
Israel came by the way of the spies" (or, more probably, "the
way of the merchants," the caravan road);[2] "then he fought
against Israel, and took of them prisoners"—having probably
fallen on their rearguard. The event is mentioned for this
twofold reason: to show the unprovoked enmity of Canaan
against Israel, and the faithfulness of God. For Israel at that
time "vowed a vow" utterly to destroy the cities of the
Canaanites. And God hearkened and heard. Many years
afterwards He gave the prayed-for victory,[3] when the name of
Hormah or ban—utter destruction—given in prophetic anticipation of God's faithfulness, became a reality.[4]

[1] So literally. Arad is the modern Tell Arad, about twenty miles south
of Hebron. So tenaciously do names cling to localities in the East.

[2] So Mr. Wilton rightly renders it, and not "the way of the spies,"
i.e., of the twelve men who had, thirty-eight years before, gone up to spy the
land. Others translate, "the beaten track."

[3] Judges i. 17.

[4] Some commentators imagine that even at the first a great victory had
been gained by the Israelites over the Canaanites. But the supposition is
incompatible alike with the narrative and with other portions of Scripture.

CHAPTER XXI.

Journey of the Children of Israel in "compassing the land of Edom—The "Fiery Serpents" and the "Brazen Serpent"—Israel enters the land of the Amorites—Victories over Sihon and over Og, the kings of the Amorites and of Bashan—Israel camps in "the lowlands of Moab," close by the Jordan.

(NUMB. XXI. 3-35 ; XXXIII. 35-49; DEUT. II.–III. 11.)

THE opposition of Edom and the unprovoked attack of the Canaanite king of Arad must have convinced Israel that the most serious difficulties of their march had now commenced. It was quite natural that, during the thirty-eight years when they were scattered up and down in the Sinaitic peninsula, their powerful neighbours should have left them unmolested, as the wandering Bedawin are at this day.[1] But when Israel again gathered together and moved forward as a host, then the tidings of the marvellous things which God had done for them, communicated with all the circumstantiality common in the east, would excite mingled terror and a determination to resist them. The latter probably first; the former as resistance was seen to be vain, and the God of Israel realised as stronger than all other national deities. Eastern idolaters would naturally thus reason; and the knowledge of this will help our understanding of the Scriptural narrative.

The general direction of Israel's march, in order to "compass" the land of Edom, was first to the head of the Elanitic Gulf of the Red Sea, or the Gulf of 'Akabah. Thence they would, a

---

[1] This is well brought out in Palmer's *Desert of the Exodus*, Part ii., pp. 517, etc.

few hours north of Ezion-gaber (the giant's backbone), enter the mountains, and then pass northwards, marching to Moab " by the road which runs between Edom and the limestone plateau of the great eastern desert "[1] (comp. Deut. ii. 8). Probably they were prepared to contend for every fresh advance which they made northwards. But the first part of their journey was otherwise trying. That deep depression of the Arabah through which they marched—intensely hot, bare of vegetation, desolate, rough, and visited by terrible sandstorms—was pre-eminently " that great and terrible wilderness," of which Moses afterwards reminded the people.[2] What with the weariness of the way, the want of water, and of all food other than the manna, " the soul of the people was much discouraged," " and the people spake against God and against Moses." The judgment of " fiery serpents" which the Lord, " in punishment, sent among the people," and of which so many died bore a marked resemblance to all His former dealings. Once more He did not create a new thing for the execution of His purpose, but only disposed sovereignly of what already existed. Travellers give remarkable confirmation and illustrations of the number and poisonous character of the serpents in that district.[3] Thus one writes of the neighbourhood of the gulf: " The sand on the shore showed traces of snakes on every hand. They had crawled there in various directions. Some of the marks appeared to have been made by animals which could not have been less than two inches in diameter. My guide told me that snakes were very common in these regions." Another traveller on exactly the route of the children of Israel states : " In the afternoon a large and very mottled snake was brought to us, marked with *fiery* spots and spiral lines, which evidently belonged, from the formation of its teeth, to one of the most poisonous species. . . . . The Bedouins say that these snakes, of which they have great dread, are very

---

[1] *Desert of the Exodus,* vol. ii. p. 523.   [2] Deut. i. 19.
[3] For many and very apt Scripture illustrations we would here refer to Mr. Wilton's *Negeb,* p. 47, etc.

numerous in this locality."[1] From the fact that the brazen serpent is also called "*fiery*" (a *Saraph*), we infer that the expression describes rather the appearance of these "fire-snakes" than the effect of their bite.

Two things are most marked in this history—the speedy repentance of Israel, couched in unwonted language of humility,[2] and the marvellous teaching of the symbol, through which those who had been mortally bitten were granted restoration to life and health. Moses was directed to make a fiery serpent of brass, and to set it upon a pole, and whosoever looked upon it was immediately healed. From the teaching of our Lord[3] we know that this was a direct type of the lifting up of the Son of Man, "that whosoever believeth in Him should not perish, but have eternal life." The *simplicity* of the remedy— only to look up in faith, its *immediateness* and its *completeness* as well as the fact that this was the *only* but also the *all-sufficient* remedy for the deadly wound of the serpent—all find their counterpart in the Gospel. But for the proper understanding both of the type and of the words of our Lord, we must inquire in what manner Israel would view and understand the lifting up of the brazen serpent and the healing that flowed from it. Undoubtedly, Israel would at once connect this death through the fiery serpents with the introduction of death into Paradise through the serpent.[4] And now a brazen serpent was lifted up, made in the *likeness* of the fiery serpent, yet *without its poisonous bite*. And this was for the healing of Israel. Clearly then, the deadly poison of the fiery serpent was removed in the uplifted brazen serpent! All this would carry back the mind to the promise given when first the poisonous sting of the serpent was felt, that the Seed of the Woman should bruise the head of the serpent, and that in so doing His own heel should be bruised. In this sense even the apocryphal Book of Wisdom (xvi. 6)

---

[1] Kurtz' *History of the Old Covenant*, vol. iii. pp. 343, 344, English translation.

[2] Numb. xxi. 7.   [3] John iii. 14, 15.

[4] Both the Jerusalem and the Jonathan Targum contain an allusion to this.

designates the brazen serpent "a symbol of salvation." And
so we are clearly taught that "God sending His own Son in
the likeness of sinful flesh, and for sin, *condemned sin in the
flesh;*"[1] that "He hath made Him to be sin for us, who knew
no sin ;"[2] and that "His own self bare our sins in His own
body on the tree."[3] The precious meaning of the type is thus
deduced by Luther from the three grand peculiarities of this
"symbol of salvation :" "First, the serpent which Moses made
at the command of God had to be of brass or copper, that is,
red, and like those fiery serpents, which were red, and burning
in their bite—yet without poison. Secondly, the brazen serpent
had to be set up on a pole for a sign" (comp. Col. ii. 14, etc.).
"Thirdly, those who would be healed of the fiery serpents' bite
must look up to the brazen serpent, lifted up on the pole"
(perceive, and believe), "else they could not recover nor live."
Similarly a modern German critic thus annotates John iii. 14:
"Christ is the antitype of this serpent, inasmuch as He took
upon Himself and vicariously bore sin, the most noxious of all
noxious powers."

It is of the deepest interest to follow the march of the children
of Israel, when every day's journey brought them nearer to the
Land of Promise as their goal. To them it was not, as to us,
a land of ruins and of memories, but of beauty and of hope.
To a people who had all their lives seen and known nothing
but "the wilderness," the richness, fertility, and varied beauty
of Palestine, as it then was, must have possessed charms such
as we can scarcely imagine. Then every step in advance was,
so to speak, under the direct leading of God, and, in a sense, a
miracle, while every such leading and miracle was itself a pledge
of others yet to follow. The researches of modern travellers[4]

---

[1] Rom. viii. 3.   [2] 2 Cor. v. 21.   [3] 1 Pet. ii. 24.

[4] We cannot, of course, here enter on a description of these localities
as illustrative of the Bible, however interesting the subject. For further
information we direct the reader, besides the works of Professor Robinson,
Canon Williams, Mr. Wilton, and Professor Palmer, to Canon Tristram's
Land of Moab, as specially illustrative of this part of our history.

enable us almost to company with Israel on this their march. As already stated, the wonderful tenacity with which old names keep their hold in the far East helps us to discover the exact spots of Biblical scenes ; while, on the other hand, descriptions of the localities throw most vivid light on the Scriptural narratives, and afford evidence of their trustworthiness.

The reader ought to remember that the route which lay before Israel was in part the same as that still traversed by the great caravans from Damascus to Mecca. The territories which they successively passed or entered were occupied as follows. First, Israel skirted along the *eastern* boundary of Edom, leaving it on their left. The *western* boundary of Edom, through which Israel had sought a passage when starting from Kadesh,[1] would from its mountainous character and few passes have been easily defended against the Israelites. But it was otherwise with the *eastern* line of frontier, which lay open to Israel, had they not been Divinely directed not to fight against Edom.[2] This, however, explains the friendly attitude which the Edomites found it prudent to adopt along their eastern frontier,[3] although their army had shortly before been prepared to fight on the western. At *Ije Abarim,*[4] "the ruins," or "the hills of the passages," or "of the sides"—perhaps "the lateral hills"—the Israelites were approaching the wilderness which lay to the east of Moab. The brook or Wády Zared[5] here forms the boundary between Edom and Moab. But as Israel had been also commanded not to fight against Moab,[6] they left their territory equally untouched, and, continuing straight northwards, passed through the wilderness of Moab, till they reached the river Arnon, the modern Wády Mojib, which formed the boundary between the Moabites and the Amorites. The territory of the Amorites stretched from the Arnon to the Jabbok. It had originally belonged to the

---

[1] Numb. xx. 18. [2] Deut. ii. 4–6. [3] Deut. ii. 29.
[4] There is reason to suppose that *Abarim,* or "passages," was a generic name for the mountains which bordered the territory of Moab.
[5] Numb. xxi. 12. [6] Deut. ii. 9.

Moabites ;[1] but they had been driven southwards by the
Amorites.   No command of God prevented Israel from warring
against the Amorites, and when Sihon, their king, refused to
give them a free passage through his territory, they were Divinely
directed to that attack which issued in the destruction of Sihon,
and the possession of his land by Israel.

At the brook Zared—on the southern boundary of Moab—
the Israelites had already been in a line with the Dead Sea,
leaving it, of course, far on their left.   The river Arnon also,
which formed the boundary between Moab and the Amorites,
flows into the Dead Sea almost opposite to Hazazon-tamar, or
En-gedi.   This tract, which now bears the name of el-Belkah,
is known to the reader of the Old Testament as the *land of
Gilead*, while in New Testament times it formed the province
of *Perea*.   Lastly, the district north of the Jabbok and east of
the Jordan was the ancient *Bashan*, or the modern Hauran.
The fact that the country north of the Arnon had, before its
possession by the Amorites, been so long held by Moab explains
the name "Fields of Moab" (rendered in the Authorised Version
" country of Moab," Numbers xxi. 20) as applied to the upland
hills of Gilead, just as the western side of Jordan similarly bore
the name of " the plains of Moab," or rather " the lowlands of
Moab."[2]   The children of Israel were still camped on the *south*
side of the Arnon when they sent the embassy to Sihon,
demanding a passage through his territory.   Canon Tristram
has given a most vivid description of the rift through which the
Arnon flows.   Its width is calculated at about three miles from
crest to crest, and its depth at 2150 feet from the top of the
southern, and at 1950 from that of the northern bank.   Of
course, the army of Israel could not have passed the river
here, but higher up, to the east, " in the wilderness."[3]   They
probably waited till the messengers returned from Sihon.   How
high their courage and confidence in God had risen, when
tidings arrived that Sihon with all his army was coming to
meet them, appears even from those extracts of poetic pieces

[1] Numb. xxi. 26.   [2] Numb. xxii 1   [3] Numb. xxi 13.

which form so marked a peculiarity of the Book of Numbers, and which read like stanzas of war-songs by the camp-fires.[1] From the banks of the Arnon the route of Israel was no doubt northward till they reached *Bamoth* or *Bamoth Baal*, "the heights of Baal,"[2] one of the stations afterwards taken up by Balak and Balaam.[3] "And from Bamoth (they marched) to the valley, which is in the fields of Moab (on the plateau of Moab), on the height of Pisgah, and looks over to the face of the wilderness,"[4] that is, over the tract of land which extends to the north-eastern shore of the Dead Sea.[5]

From this plateau on the mountains of the Abarim, of which Pisgah and Nebo were peaks, Israel had its first view of the Land of Promise, and especially of that mysterious Sea of Salt whose glittering surface and deathlike surroundings would recall such solemn memories and warnings. At last then the goal was in view! The decisive battle between Sihon and Israel was fought almost within sight of the Dead Sea. The victory at Jahaz, in which Sihon was smitten "with the edge of the sword"—that is, without quarter or sparing,—gave Israel possession of the whole country, including Heshbon and "all the daughters thereof"—or daughter-towns,—from the Arnon to the upper Jabbok (the modern Nahr Amman). The latter river formed the boundary between the Amorites and the Ammonites. Beyond this the Amorites had not penetrated, because "the border of the children of Ammon was strong."[6] And Israel also forbore to penetrate farther, not on the same ground as the Amorites, but because of an express command of God.[7] Leaving untouched therefore the country of Ammon, the Israelites next moved northward, defeated Og, king of

---

[1] Not less than three of these "songs" are quoted in Numb. xxi. We cannot here refer further to these deeply interesting compositions. Similarly, it is impossible to enter into fuller geographical details, or to compare the list of stations in Numb. xxi. with that in chap. xxxiii. and in Deut. ii. But the most perfect harmony prevails between them.

[2] Numb. xxi. 19.

[3] Numb. xxii. 41.

[4] So literally.

[5] Numb. xxi. 20.

[6] Numb. xxi. 24.

[7] Deut. ii. 19.

Bashan, and took possession of his territory also, and of the mountains of Gilead.[1]   The whole country east of the Jordan was now Israel's, and the passage of that river could not be disputed.

Before actually entering upon their long-promised inheritance, some great lessons had, indeed, yet to be learned.   An event would take place which would for ever mark the relation between the, kingdom of God and that of this world.   The mission of Moses, the servant of the Lord, must also come to an end, and the needful arrangements be made for possessing and holding the land of Palestine.   But all these belong, strictly speaking, to another period of Israel's history.   When the camp was pitched in *Shittim,* "on this side Jordan by Jericho," waiting for the signal to cross the boundary-line, *the wanderings of the children of Israel* were really at an end.

[1] These territories and their ancient sites have of late been visited and described by such travellers as Canon Tristram, Professor Palmer, and others.

THE BIBLE HISTORY

VOLUME III

ISRAEL IN CANAAN

UNDER

JOSHUA AND THE JUDGES

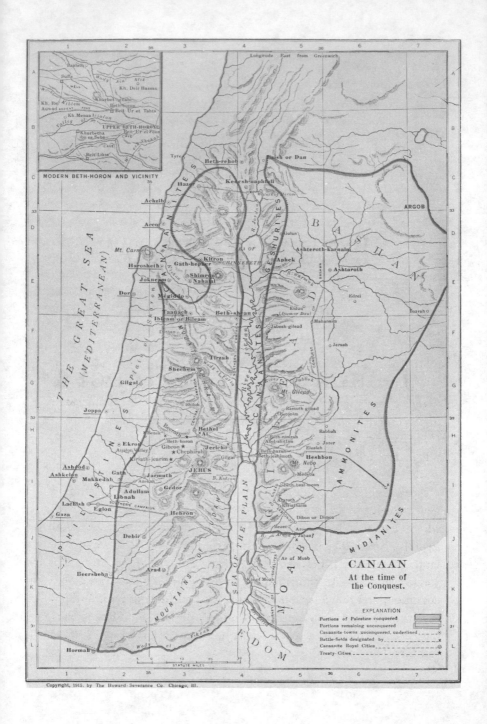

CANAAN
At the time of
the Conquest.

EXPLANATION

Portions of Palestine conquered
Portions remaining unconquered
Canaanite-towns unconquered, underlined . . . . . . ⊚
Battle-fields designated by . . . . ×
Canaanite Royal Cities . . . . ⊚
Treaty-Cities . . . . ★

MODERN BETH-HORON AND VICINITY

UPPER BETH-HORON

PREFACE

———◦◦◦———

THE history of Israel as a nation may be said to commence with their entrance into their own land. All previous to this—from the Paschal night on which Israel was born as a people to the overthrow of Sihon and of Og, the last who would have barred Israel's way to their home—had been only preparatory. During the forty years' wanderings the people had, so to speak, been welded together by the strong hand of Jehovah. But now, when the Lion of Judah couched by the banks of Jordan, Israel was face to face with its grand mission, and the grand task of its national life commenced : to dispossess heathenism, and to plant in its stead the kingdom of God (Ps. lxxx. 8–11), which was destined to strike root and to grow, till, in the fulness of time, it would extend to all nations of the world.[1]

Accordingly, when the camp of Israel was pitched at Shittim, a new period commenced. Its history records, first, certain events which had to take place immediately before entering the Land of Promise ; next, the conquest, and then the apportionment of the land among the tribes of Israel ; and, lastly, in the time of the Judges, side by side, the unfolding of Israel's religious and national condition, and the assertion of those fundamental principles which underlay its very existence as a God-called people. These principles are :—The special relationship of Israel as the people of God towards Jehovah, and Jehovah's special dealings towards them as

[1] Comp. such a Missionary Psalm as the 87th ; also such passages as Ps. lxxxvi. 9 ; Is. xliv. 5.

their King.[1] The history of the wilderness period had, indeed, been shaped by this two-fold relationship, but its consequences appeared more clearly under Joshua, and most fully in the time of the Judges. When not only Moses, but Joshua, and even the elders who had been his contemporaries had passed away, the people, now settled in the land, were left free to develop those tendencies which had all along existed.   Then ensued that alternation of national apostacy and judgment, and of penitent return to God and deliverance, which constitutes, so to speak, the framework on which the Book of Judges is constructed. This part of Israel's history attained alike its highest and its lowest point in Samson, with whom the period of the Judges appropriately closes. For, the administration of Samuel forms only the transition to, and preparation for the establishment of royalty in Israel. But the spiritual import of the whole history of that period is summed up in these words of Holy Scripture (Ps. xliv. 2–4) : " Thou didst drive out the heathen with Thy hand, and plantedst them : Thou didst afflict the people, and cast them out. For they got not the land in possession by their own sword, neither did their own arm save them, but Thy right hand, and Thine arm, and the light of Thy countenance, because Thou hadst a favour unto them. Thou art my King, O God : command deliverances for Jacob."

The Books of Joshua and of the Judges form the two first portions of what in the Hebrew Canon are designated as the " Former Prophets."[2] This, not because their narratives are largely connected with the rise and activity of the prophets, nor yet because their authors were prophets, but rather because the character and contents of these books are prophetic. They give the history of Israel from the prophet's point of view—not a succinct and successive chronicle of the nation, but a history of the Kingdom of God in Israel. This also explains its peculiarities of form and style. For, neither are the Judges, for example, mentioned in the order

---

[1] Some modern negative critics have even broached the theory—of course, wholly unfounded—that originally the Book of Joshua had formed with the five books of Moses ℈ *Hexateuch*.

[2] The others are the Books of Samuel and of the Kings.

of their succession, nor must it be supposed that they ruled over all the tribes of Israel. Similarly, there are evidently large blanks left in the history of the times, and while some events or reigns of considerable duration are only cursorily mentioned, very detailed and circumstantial narratives are given of persons and occurrences, which only occupied the scene for a comparatively short period. But as, from the frequent references to authorities, and from their evident knowledge of details, the writers of these books must have had at command ample material for a full history, we conclude that the selection, Divinely guided, was made in accordance with the "Spirit of Prophecy," to mark the progress of the Kingdom of God in connection with Israel.

From what has been said it will be readily understood, that the history traced in this volume offers peculiar difficulties—from its briefness, its abruptness, its rapid transitions, the unusual character of its incidents, and its sudden and marked Divine interpositions. These difficulties are not so much exegetical or critical—although such are certainly not wanting—but rather concern the substance of the narratives themselves, and touch the very essence of Holy Scripture. For myself, I am free to confess that I entered on my present undertaking, I shall not say with apprehension, but with great personal diffidence. I knew, indeed, that what appears a difficulty might find its full and satisfactory solution, even though I were not able to indicate it, and that a narrative might have its Divine meaning and spiritual purpose, even though I should fail to point it out. Yet I imagine that most readers of the Books of Joshua and Judges will in some measure understand and sympathise with my feelings. All the more is it now alike duty and privilege, at the close of these investigations, to express it joyously and thankfully, that the more fully these narratives are studied, the more luminous will they become ; the more will their Divine meaning appear ; and the more will they carry to the mind conviction of their truthfulness, and to the heart lessons of their spiritual import. Perhaps I may be allowed in illustration of these statements to point to my study of the characters of Balaam and Joshua, and of the histories of Gideon, of Jephthah, and especially of Samson.

From this circumstance, and faithful to the plan, which I proposed to myself in this series, of gradually leading a reader onwards, the sacred narrative has received in this volume more full treatment —the discussion of such textual questions as fell within its scope, being, however, chiefly thrown into the *foot-notes*. Many questions; indeed, on which I could have earnestly wished to enter, lay quite outside the purport of the present series, and had therefore reluctantly to be left aside. These concern chiefly the *antiquity* and the *authenticity* of these books of Holy Scripture. I venture to think, that a great deal yet remains to be said on these points—the chief defect of former treatises lying, in my opinion, in this, that they rather busy themselves with refuting the arguments of opponents, than bring forward what I would call the *positive* evidence. That such positive evidence abundantly exists, a somewhat careful study has increasingly convinced me. I am not ashamed to own my belief that, notwithstanding confident assertions of writers on the opposite side, we may trustfully and contentedly walk in "the old paths;" and the present volume is intended as a reverent contribution, however inadequate, towards the better understanding of what, I verily believe, "holy men of old spake as they were moved by the Spirit," and that, "for doctrine, for reproof, for correction, for instruction in righteousness."

ALFRED EDERSHEIM.

LODERS VICARAGE, BRIDPORT.
February 23, 1877.

CONTENTS

—◆—

CHAPTER I.

CHAPTER II.

CHAPTER III.

CHAPTER IV.

CHAPTER V.

CHAPTER VI.

CHAPTER VII.

CHAPTER VIII.

CHAPTER IX.

CHAPTER X.

CHAPTER XI.

CHAPTER XII.

CHAPTER XIII.

CHAPTER XIV.

CHRONOLOGICAL TABLE,

ACCORDING TO PROFESSOR KEIL, FROM THE EXODUS TO THE BUILDING OF THE TEMPLE BY SOLOMON.

(Comp. Judges xi. 26 and 1 Kings vi. 1.)

PRINCIPAL EVENTS.	Years of their duration.	Date before Christ.
The Exodus	..	.. 1492
Giving of the Law on Mount Sinai	..	{ from 1492 to 1491
Death of Moses and Aaron	{ in the 40th year	.. 1453
Conquest of Canaan by Joshua	7	1452 ,, 1445
Division of Canaan to the invasion of Chushan Rishathaim	10	1445 ,, 1435
Death of Joshua	..	about 1442
Wars of Israel against the Canaanites	..	from 1442
Expedition against Benjamin (Judges xx.) . . .	..	about 1436
Oppression by Chushan Rishathaim.	8	1435 to 1427
Othniel, and rest of Israel	40	1427 ,, 1387
Oppression by the Moabites	18	1387 ,, 1369
Ehud, and rest of Israel	80	1369 ,, 1289
Victory of Shamgar over the Philistines. . . .	..	.. ..
Oppression by Jabin	20	1289 ,, 1269
Deborah and Barak, and rest of Israel	40	1269 ,, 1229
Oppression by the Midianites	7	1229 ,, 1222
Gideon, and rest	40	1222 ,, 1182
Abimelech	3	1182 ,, 1179
Tola	23	1179 ,, 1156
Jair	22	1156 ,, 1134
Eli for forty years	..	1154 ,, 1114
Then : *In the East.* *In the West.*		
Oppression by the Ammon- {By the Philistines . ites, 18 years : 1134–1116 {Loss of the Ark . .	40	1134 ,, 1094
	..	about 1114
Jephthah, 6 years : 1116– {Samson's deeds . .	..	1116 to 1096
1110 . . . . . {Samuel as a prophet.	..	from 1114
Ibzan, 7 years : 1110–1103 Samuel judge . .	19	1094 to 1075
Elon, 10 years : 1103–1093 Saul king. . .	20	1075 ,, 1055
Abdon, 8 years : 1093–1085 David at Hebron .	7	1055 ,, 1048
David at Jerusalem .	33	1048 ,, 1015
Solomon to the build- } ing of Temple . }	3	1015 ,, 1012
Total . .	480 years.	

ISRAEL IN CANAAN

JOSHUA AND THE JUDGES

CHAPTER I.

Israel about to take Possession of the Land of Promise — Decisive Contest showing the real Character of Heathenism—Character and History of Balaam.

(NUMB. XXII.)

THE wilderness-life and the early contests of Israel were over. Israel stood on the threshold of the promised possession, separated from it only by the waters of Jordan. But, before crossing that boundary-line, it was absolutely necessary that the people should, once and for all, gain full knowledge of the real character of heathenism in its relation to the kingdom of God. Israel must learn that the heathen nations were not only hostile *political* powers, opposing their progress, but that heathenism itself was in its nature antagonistic to the kingdom of God. The two were incompatible, and therefore no alliance could ever be formed with heathenism, no intercourse cultivated, nor even its presence tolerated. This was the lesson which, on the eve of entering Palestine, Israel was to learn by painful experience in connection with the history of Balaam. Its importance at that particular period will readily be understood. Again and again was the same lesson taught throughout the history of Israel, as each alliance or even contact with the kingdoms of this world

brought fresh sorrow and trouble.   Nor is its application to
the Church of God, so far as concerns the danger of com-
mixture with, and conformity to the world, less obvious.   And
so the history of Balak and of Balaam has, besides its direct
lessons, a deep meaning for all times.

With the decisive victories over Sihon and over Og, all who
could have barred access to the Land of Promise had been
either left behind, or else scattered and defeated.   And now
the camp of Israel had moved forward, in the language of
Scripture, to " the other side Jordan from Jericho."[1]   Their
tents were pitched in rich meadow-land, watered by many
streams, which rush down from the neighbouring mountains—
the *Arboth*, or lowlands of *Moab*, as the country on this and that
side the river was still called, after its more ancient inhabitants.[2]
As the vast camp lay scattered over a width of several miles,
from *Abel Shittim*, " the meadow of the acacias," in the north,
to *Beth Jeshimoth*, " the house of desolations," on the edge of
the desert, close to the Dead Sea, in the south,[3] it might have
seemed as if the lion of Judah were couching ready for his
spring on the prey.   But was he the lion of Judah, and were
the promises of God to him indeed " yea and amen ?"   A
fiercer assault, and one in which heathenism would wield other
arms than those which had so lately been broken in their hands,
would soon decide that question.

We can perceive many reasons why Moab, though apparently
not immediately threatened, should, at that special moment,
have come forward as the champion and representative of
heathenism.[4]   True, Israel had left their land untouched, restrained by express Divine command from invading it.[5]   But
their close neighbourhood was dangerous.   Besides, had not all
that land north of the Arnon, which Israel had just wrested from

[1] Or, " across the Jordan of Jericho," *i.e.*, that part of the Jordan which
watered Jericho.

[2] The name *Arboth* still survives in the *Arabah*, which stretches from a
little farther south to the Elanitic Gulf of the Red Sea.

[2] Numb. xxxiii. 49.   [4] Numb. xxii. 1-3.   [5] Deut. ii. 9.

the Amorites, been till lately Moabitish—the very name of Moab still lingering on mountain-plateau and lowland plains ; and might not Moab again have what once it held ? But there was far more involved than either fear or cupidity suggested. The existence alike of heathen nations and of heathenism itself depended on the issue. There can be no doubt that the prophetic anticipation of the song of Moses [1] had already in great part been fulfilled. " The nations" *had* "heard" of God's marvellous doings for Israel, and were afraid ; " the mighty men of Moab, trembling " *had* taken " hold upon them." Among the wandering tribes of the east, tidings, especially of this kind, travel fast. Jethro had heard them long before,[2] and the testimony of Rahab[3] shows how fear and dread had fallen upon the inhabitants of the land. Force of arms had been tried against them. The Amorites, who had been able to wrest from Moab all the land north of the Arnon, had boldly marched against Israel under the leadership of Sihon their king, and been not only defeated but almost exterminated. A similar fate had befallen the brave king of Bashan and his people. There could be no question that so far Jehovah, the God of Israel, had proved true to His word, and stronger than the gods of the nations who had been subdued. Farther progress, then, in the same direction might prove fatal alike to their national existence, their national deities, and their national religion.

In trying to realise the views and feelings of heathenism under such circumstances, we must beware of transporting into them our modern ideas. In our days the question is as to the acknowledgment or else the denial of Jehovah God. In those days it turned upon the acknowledgment or the opposite of Jehovah as the *only* true and living God, as this is expressed in the first commandment. Heathenism would never have thought of denying the existence or power of Jehovah as the national God of the Hebrews (see, for example, 1 Kings xx. 23 ; 2 Kings xviii. 25, 33–35). What it controverted was, that Jehovah was the *only* God—all others being merely idols,

[1] Ex. xv. 14–16.   [2] Ex. xviii. 1.   [3] Josh. ii. 9.

the work of men's hands. Prepared as they were to acknowledge Jehovah as the national Deity of the Hebrews, the question
before them would be, whether *He* or their gods were the
more powerful. It was a point of the deepest interest to them,
since, if anything were known of Jehovah, it would be this,
that He was "a jealous God," and that the rites by which He
was worshipped were so different from theirs, as to involve
an entire change, not only of religion, but of popular habits and
manners. From what has been stated, it will be understood
why, in attempting to break the power of Israel, whose God
had hitherto—whether from accident, fate, or inherent power—
proved Himself superior to those of the nations, the king of
Moab had, in the first place, recourse to "divination," and why
he was so specially anxious to secure the services of Balaam.

Balaam, or rather Bileam, the son of Beor,[1] belonged apparently to a family of magicians who resided at Pethor, possibly,
as has been suggested, a city of professional soothsayers or
students of that craft, but certainly situated in "Aram" or
Mesopotamia, and on the banks of the Euphrates.[2] His name,
which means "devourer," or "swallower up," and that of his
father, which means "burner up," or "destroyer"—whether given
them at birth, or, as is so common in the East, from their
supposed characteristics—indicate alike the claims which they
put forth and the estimate in which they were popularly held.[3]
If, as has been conjectured,[4] Balak, the king of Moab, was of
Midianitish origin (his father having been a Midianitish usurper),
it becomes all the more intelligible that in his peculiar circumstances he would apply for advice and help to the Midianites;

[1] By a peculiar Aramaic interchange of letters, St. Peter writes the name
Bosor : 2 Pet. ii. 15.

[2] Numb. xxii. 5 ; xxiii. 7 ; Deut. xxiii. 4.

[3] It is of curious interest, that precisely the same names occur in the
royal Edomitish family : Gen. xxxvi. 32.

[4] By Bishop Harold Browne, from the analogy of his father's name to
that of later Midianite chiefs—the name *Zippor,* "bird," reminding us of
Oreb, "crow," and *Zeeb,* "wolf." The later Targumim also regard Balak
as of Midianitish origin.

that he would ally himself with them; and that through them
he would come to know of, and along with them send for,
Balaam.[1]   At any rate, those Midianite wanderers of the desert
which stretched between Mesopotamia and the dominions of
Moab would, like modern Bedawîn under similar circumstances,
not only know of the existence of a celebrated magician like
Balaam, but probably greatly exaggerate his power.   Moreover, being themselves unable to attack Israel, they would
nevertheless gladly make common cause with Moab, and that,
although for the present their territory was not directly
threatened, any more than that of the Moabites.   This explains
the alliance of Moab and Midian and their common embassy
to Balaam.

The object in view was twofold.   As already explained, the
success of Israel as against the nations, or rather that of
Israel's God against their deities, might, in their opinion, arise
from one of two causes.   Either their own national deities—
Chemosh and Baal—had not been sufficiently propitiated—
sufficient influence or power had not been brought to bear
upon them; or else Jehovah was *really* stronger than they.
In either case Balaam would bring invaluable, and, if he only
chose to exert it, *sure* help.   For, according to heathen views,
a magician had absolute and irresistible power with the gods;
power was inherent in him or in the incantations which he
used.   And herein lay one of the fundamental differences
between heathenism and the Old Testament, between magic
and miracles.   In the former it was all of man, in the latter it
was shown to be all of God.   No prophet of the Lord ever
had or claimed power, like the magicians; but in every case
the gracious influence was specially, and for that time, transmitted directly from God.   Only the God-Man had power in
Himself, so that His every contact brought health and life.
And in the Christian dispensation also, however much of the
supernatural there may be experienced and witnessed, nothing
is magical; there is no mere exercise of power or of authority;

[1] Numb. xxii. 4, 7, etc.

but all is conveyed to us through the free promises of God, and in the dispensation of His grace.

But to return. Supposing that Jehovah were really superior to Chemosh and Baal, the king of Moab and his associates would none the less desire the aid of Balaam. For it was a further principle of heathenism, that national deities might be induced to transfer their blessing and protection from one nation to another. Thus the ancient Romans were wont, when laying siege to a foreign city, solemnly to invite its special gods to come out to them and join their side,[1] promising them in return not only equal but higher honours than they had hitherto enjoyed. And if something of this kind were now needful—if influence was to be exerted on the God of the Israelites, who was so capable of it as Balaam, both from his profession as a dealer with the gods, and from his special qualifications? And this leads up to the principal personage in this history, to his character, and to the question of his religion.[2]

What has been said of the knowledge which the king of Moab must have possessed of Jehovah's dealings in reference to Israel[3] applies, of course, with much greater force to Balaam himself. As a professional magician, belonging to a family of magicians, and residing at one of their chief seats, it was alike

[1] See the proof passages in Kurtz' *History of the Old Covenant*, vol. iii. p. 399 ; and the very interesting discussion on the subject by Döllinger, in his splendid work, *Heidenthum u. Judenthum*.

[2] As this is not the place for theological or critical discussion, I will only remark, that I cannot accept either of the opposing views of Balaam's character—that he was a true prophet of Jehovah, or that he was simply " a prophet of the devil," " who was *compelled* by God, against his will, to bless." But as little do I profess myself able to receive, or even properly to under-stand, the view of recent critics (Hengsterberg, Kurtz, Keil, Bishop Harold Browne, etc.), that Balaam "was in a transition state from one to the other," that " he knew and confessed Jehovah, sought and found him ;" but that, " on the other hand, he was not sufficiently advanced in the know-ledge and service of Jehovah to throw overboard every kind of heathen augury." I have, therefore, subjected the whole question to fresh investiga-tion, the results of which are given in the text.

[3] Ex. xv. 14–16.

his duty and his interest to acquaint himself with such matters. Moreover, we ought not to forget that, in the place of his residence, traditions of Abraham would linger with that Eastern local tenacity which we have already had so frequent occasion to notice. Indeed, we have positive evidence that Balaam's inquiries had gone back far beyond the recent dealings of Jehovah to His original covenant-relationship towards His people. A comparison of the promise of God to Abraham in Gen. xiii. 16 with the mode of expression used by Balaam in Numb. xxiii. 10; still more—the correspondence between Gen. xlix. 9 and Numb. xxiii. 24, xxiv. 9 in his description of Judah; but most of all, the virtual repetition of the prophecy Gen. xlix. 10 in Numb. xxiv. 17, prove beyond doubt that Balaam had made himself fully acquainted with the promises of Jehovah to Israel. That a professional soothsayer like Balaam should have been quite ready, upon a review of their whole history, to acknowledge Jehovah as the national God of Israel, and to enter—if the expression may be allowed—into professional relationship with such a powerful Deity, seems only natural in the circumstances. This explains *his* conduct in speaking to and of Jehovah, and apparently owning Him. *But in all this Balaam did not advance a step beyond the mere heathen point of view*, any more than Simon Magus when, " beholding the miracles and signs which were done," " he was baptised ;"[1] nor did his conduct bring him nearer to the true service of Jehovah than were those seven sons of Sceva to that of Christ, when they endeavoured to cast out evil spirits in the name of the Lord Jesus.[2] In fact, Scripture designates him uniformly by the word *Kosem*, which is the distinctive term for heathen soothsayers in opposition to prophets of the Lord. And with this his whole conduct agrees. Had he possessed even the most elementary knowledge of Jehovah as *the only true and living God*, or the most rudimentary understanding of His covenant-purposes, he could not, *considering his acquaintance with previous prophecy*, have for a moment entertained the idea of allying himself with

---

[1] Acts viii. 13.   [2] Acts xix. 13, 14.

Balak against Israel. On the other hand, if, according to his view of the matter, he could have succeeded in making the God of Israel, so to speak, one of his patron-deities, and if, upon his own terms, he could have become one of His prophets; still more, if he could have gained such influence with Him as to turn Him from His purpose regarding Israel, then would he have reached the goal of his ambition, and become by far the most powerful magician in the world. Thus, in our opinion, from the time when we first meet him, standing where the two roads part, to the bitter end of his treachery, when, receiving the reward of Judas, he was swept away in the destruction of Midian, his conduct was throughout consistently *heathen*, and his progress rapid in the downward course.

Where the two roads part! In every great crisis of history, and, we feel persuaded, in the great crisis of every individual life, there is such a meeting and parting of the two ways—to life or to destruction. It was so in the case of Pharaoh, when Moses first brought him the summons of the Lord to let His people go free, proving his authority by indubitable signs. And Balaam stood at the meeting and parting of the two ways that night when the ambassadors of Balak and the elders of Midian were for the first time under his roof. *That embassy was the crisis in his history.* He had advanced to the knowledge that Jehovah, the God of Israel, was God. The question now came: Would he recognise Him as the only true and living God, with Whom no such relationship could exist as those which heathenism supposed; towards Whom every relationship must be moral and spiritual, not magical—one of heart and of life service, not of influence and power? To use New Testament language, in his general acknowledgment of Jehovah, Balaam had advanced to the position described in the words: " he that is not against us is for us."[1] But this is only, as it were, the meeting and parting of the two roads. The next question which comes is far deeper, and decisive, so far as each individual is concerned. It

[1] Luke ix. 50.

refers to our relationship to the Person of Christ. And in regard to this we read : " He that is not with Me is against Me."[1]

As always in such circumstances, God's great mercy and infinite patience and condescension were not wanting to help Balaam in the crisis of his life. There could, at least, be no doubt on two points. Balak's avowed wish had been, by the help of Balaam, to " smite" Israel and "drive them out of the land ;"[2] and his expressed conviction, " he whom thou blessest is blessed, and he whom thou cursest is cursed." Now, not to speak of the implied magical power thus attributed to him, Balaam must have known that Balak's intention ran directly counter to Jehovah's purpose, while the words, in which the power of blessing and cursing was ascribed to Balaam, were not only a transference to man of what belonged to God alone, *but must have been known to Balaam* as the very words in which Jehovah had originally bestowed the blessing on Abraham : " I will bless them that bless thee, and curse him that curseth thee."[3] That Balaam so knew these words appears from his own quotation of them in Numb. xxiv. 9. The proposal of Balak therefore ran directly counter to the fundamental purpose of God, as Balaam knew it—and yet he could hesitate even for a single moment ! But this is not all. In His infinite long-suffering, not willing that any should perish, God even now condescended to Balaam. He had proposed to the ambassadors of Balak that they should "lodge" with him that night, and that on the morrow he would make his reply, as Jehovah would speak unto him. And Jehovah did condescend to meet Balaam in his own way, and that night fully communicated to him His will. The garbled and misrepresenting account of it, which Balaam in the morning gave to his guests, finally marked his choice and decided his fate.

But why did Jehovah God appear to, or deal with such an one as Balaam ? Questions like these ought, with our limited knowledge of God's purposes, not always to be entertained. In the present instance, however, we can suggest at least some

---

[1] Matt. xii. 30.   [2] Numb. xxii. 6.   [3] Gen. xii. 3.

answer. Of God's purpose, so far as Balaam's personal condition was concerned, we have already spoken. But a wider issue was here to be tried. Balak had sent for Balaam in order through his magic to destroy Israel, or rather to arrest and turn aside the wonder-working power of Jehovah. It was, therefore, really a contest between heathenism and Israel as the people of God, which would exhibit and decide the real relationship between Israel and the heathen world, or in other words, between the Church of God and the kingdoms of this world. And as formerly God had raised up Pharaoh to be the instrument of bringing down the gods of Egypt, so would He now decide this contest through the very man whom Balak had chosen as its champion—using him as a willing instrument, if he yielded, or as an unwilling, if he rebelled, but in any case as an *efficient* instrument for carrying out His own purposes. It is in this manner that we regard God's meeting Balaam, and His speaking both to him and through him.

Three brief but emphatic utterances had God in that first night made to Balaam : " Thou shalt not go with them ; thou shalt not curse the people : for they are blessed."[1] Of these Balaam, in his reply to the ambassadors next morning, had deliberately suppressed the last two (xxii. 13). Yet they were the most important, as showing the utter hopelessness of the undertaking, and the utter powerlessness of any man to control or influence the purpose of God. He thus withheld knowledge of the utmost importance for understanding alike the character of the true God and that of His true servants, who simply obey, but do not seek to control, His will. But even in what he did repeat of God's message there was grievous misrepresentation. For this statement, " Jehovah refuses to give me leave to go with you " (xxii. 13), implied an ungrounded arbitrariness on the part of God ; confirmed Balak in his heathen views ; and perhaps encouraged him to hope for better results under more favourable circumstances. As for Balaam himself, we may be allowed to infer, that he misunderstood God's appearance to, and conversa-

[1] Numb. xxii. 12.

tion with him, as implying a sort of league with, or acknowledgment of him, while all the time he had irrevocably departed from
God, and entered the way of sin and of judgment. Accordingly,
we find Balaam thenceforth speaking of Jehovah as " my God,"
and confidently assuming the character of His servant. At the
same time, he secured for himself the presents of Balak, while,
in his reply, he took care not to lose the favour of the king,
but rather to make him all the more anxious to gain his aid,
since he *was* owned of Jehovah, Who had only refused a leave
which on another occasion He might grant.

It was under these circumstances that a second embassy from
Balak and Midian, more honourable than the first, and with
almost unlimited promises, came again to ask Balaam " to curse
this people " (ver. 17). The king had well judged. With no
spiritual, only a heathen acknowledgment of Jehovah, covetousness and ambition were the main actuating motives of Balaam.
In the pithy language of the New Testament,[1] he "loved the
wages of unrighteousness." But already his course was sealed.
Refusing to yield himself a willing, he would now be made the
unwilling instrument of exalting Jehovah. And thus God gave
him leave to do that on which he had set his heart, with this
important reservation, however : " But yet the word which I
shall say unto thee, that shalt thou do." Balaam, whose blinded
self-satisfaction had already appeared in his profession to the
ambassadors, that he could " not go beyond the word of
Jehovah his God," understood not the terrible judgment upon
himself implied in this " let him alone," which gave up the false
prophet to his own lusts. He had no doubt been so far honest,
although he was grossly and wilfully ignorant of all that concerned Jehovah, when he proposed to consult God a second
time, whether he might curse Israel. And now it seemed as
if God had indeed inclined to him. Balaam was as near reaching the ideal of a magician, and having " power," as was Simon
Magus when he offered the apostles money to bestow on him
the power of imparting the Holy Ghost.

[1] 2 Pet. ii. 15.

It was no doubt on account of this spirit of deluded self-satisfaction, in which next morning he accompanied the ambassadors of Balak, that "God's anger was kindled because he went,"[1] and that "the angel of Jehovah stood in the way for an adversary against him"—significantly, the angel of the covenant with a drawn sword, threatening destruction. The main object of what happened to him on the journey was, if possible, to arouse Balaam to a sense of his utter ignorance of, and alienation from Jehovah. And so even "the dumb ass, speaking with man's voice, forbad the madness of the prophet."[2] We know, indeed, that animals are often more sensitive to the presence or nearness of danger than man—as it were, perceive what escapes our senses. But in this case the humiliating lesson was, that while the self-satisfied prophet had absolutely seen nothing, his ass had perceived the presence of the angel, and, by going out of the way, or falling down, saved the life of his master ; and that, even so, Balaam still continued blinded, perverse, and misunderstanding, till God opened the mouth of the dumb animal, so that with man's voice it might forbid the madness of the prophet. To show Balaam himself as he really was, and the consequences of his conduct ; and to do so in the strongest, that is, in this case, in the most humiliating manner, such was the object of the apparition of the angel, and of the human language in which Balaam heard the ass reproving him.[3]

But even this produced no real effect—only an offer on the part of Balaam to get him back again, if it displeased the angel of Jehovah (xxii. 34). The proposal was as blundering, and argued as deep ignorance, as his former readiness to go with the ambassadors. For the question was not simply one of

---

[1] Literally, "because he was going." Keil rightly points out that the use of the participle here implies, that God's anger was kindled by the spirit and disposition in which he was going, rather than by the fact of his going.

[2] 2 Pet. ii. 16.

[3] This is not the place to enter into critical discussions. The great matter is to understand the meaning and object of this narrative, in whatever manner the "man's voice" may have issued from the "dumb ass," or the human language have reached the consciousness of Balaam.

going or not going, but of glorifying God, and acknowledging the supremacy of His covenant-purpose. Balaam might have gone and returned without doing this; but Jehovah would now do it Himself through Balaam. And already the elders of Moab and Midian had hurried on along with Balaam's own servants, to announce the arrival of the prophet. Presently from the lonely, terrible interview with the angel was he to pass into the presence of the representative of that heathenism against which the drawn sword in the angel's hand was really stretched out.

CHAPTER II.

The "Prophecies" of Balaam—The End of Balaam—Parallel between Balaam and Judas.

(NUMB. XXII. 36–XXV.; XXXI. 1–20.)

THE meeting between the king of Moab and the soothsayer took place at Ir Moab, the "city" or capital of Moab, close by its northern boundary.[1] It commenced with gentle reproaches on the part of the monarch, which, Eastern-like, covered large promises, to which the soothsayer replied by repeating his old profession of being only able to speak the word that God would put in his mouth. There is no need of assuming hypocrisy on his part; both monarch and soothsayer acted quite in character and quite consistently. From Ir Moab they proceeded to Kirjath Huzoth, "the city of streets," the later Kiriathaim.[2] Here, or in the immediate neighbourhood, the first sacrifices were offered, Balaam as well as "the princes" taking part in the sacrificial meal. Next morning

---

[1] Canon Tristram identifies this with the old *Ar,* or *Rabbath Moab* (*Land of Moab*, p. 110). But this latter seems too far south for the requirements of the text.

[2] Josh. xiii. 19; Ezek. xxv. 9, etc. See the description of the place, and of the prospect from it, in Tristram, *u.s.*, pp. 270, 276.

Balak took the soothsayer to the lofty heights of Mount Attarus, to *Bamoth Baal*, "the heights of Baal," so-called because that plateau was dedicated to the service of Baal. The spot, which also bears the names of Baal-meon, Beth Baal-meon, and Beth-meon, commands a magnificent view. Although "too far recessed to show the depression of the Dead Sea," the view northwards stretches as far as Jerusalem, Gerizim, Tabor, Hermon, and Mount Gilead.[1] But, although the eye could sweep so far over the Land of Promise, he would, from the conformation of the mountains, only see "the utmost part of the people,"[2] that is, the outskirts of the camp of Israel.

In accordance with the sacred significance which, as Balaam knew, attached to the number *seven* in the worship of Jehovah, seven altars were now built on the heights of Baal, and seven bullocks and seven rams offered upon them—a bullock and a ram on each altar. Leaving Balak and the princes of Moab by the altars, Balaam went forth in the regular heathen manner, in the hope of meeting Jehovah,[3] which is explained by Numb. xxiv. 1 as meaning "to seek auguries," such as heathen soothsayers saw in certain natural appearances or portents. And there, on the top of "a bare height,"[4] God did meet Balaam, not in auguries, but by putting "a word in Balaam's mouth." As the man shared not in it otherwise than by being the outward instrument of its communication, this "word" was to him only "a parable," and is designated as such in Scripture. Never before so clearly as in presence of the powers of heathenism, assembled to contend against Israel, did Jehovah show forth His almighty power, alike in making use of an instrument almost passive in His hand, and in disclosing His eternal purpose.[5]

[1] Tristram, p. 304.   [2] Numb. xxii. 41.
[3] Numb. xxiii. 3.   [4] So literally ; Numb. xxiii. 3.
[5] The prophecies of Balaam certainly go far beyond the range of the prophetic vision of that time. Could it be, because Balaam was so entirely passive, as it were transmitting, without absorbing, any of the rays of light, nor yet mingling them with the colouring in his own mind?

FIRST " PARABLE " OF BALAAM.[1]

From Aram brought me Balak,
The king of Moab from the mountains of the east—
Come, curse me Jacob,
And come, threaten [2] Israel !
How shall I curse whom God doth not curse,
And how shall I threaten whom Jehovah threatens not ?
For, from the top of the rocks I see him,
And from the hills I behold him :
Lo, a people dwelling [3] alone,
And not reckoning itself among the nations (the Gentiles) !
Who can count the dust of Jacob,
And the number of the fourth part [4] of Israel ?
Let me die the death of the righteous, [5]
And let my latter end be like his !

Two things will be noted, without entering into special criticism. First, as to the form of this parable : each thought is
embodied in two sentences, with rapid, almost abrupt, transitions from one thought to the other. Secondly, the outward
and inward separation of Israel (the former as symbol of the
latter) is singled out as the grand characteristic of God's
people—a primary truth this of the Old Testament, and, in its
spiritual application, of the New Testament also. But even in
its literality it has proved true in the history of Israel of old,
and still applies to them, showing us that Israel's history is
not yet finished ; that God has not forgotten His people ; and
that a purpose of mercy yet awaits them, in accordance with
His former dealings. Such a people Balaam could not curse.
On the contrary, he could only wish that his death should
be like theirs whom God's ordinances and institutions kept

---

[1] Of course, we translate literally.
[2] Literally : pronounce wrath.
[3] We have put it so as to include both the present and the future tense.
[4] Bishop H. Browne prefers the rendering "progeny." But "the fourth
part " seems to refer to the square arrangement of the camp of Israel, each
side of the square being occupied by three tribes.
[5] In the *plural* number, referring to Israel.

separate outwardly, and made righteous inwardly, referring in this, of course, to Israel not as individuals, but in their totality as the people of God. In the language of a German critic,[1] "The pious Israelite could look back with calm satisfaction, in the hour of his death, upon a life rich in proofs of the blessing, forgiving, protecting, delivering, saving mercy of God. With the same calm satisfaction would he look upon his children, and children's children, in whom he lived again, and in whom also he would still take part in the high calling of his nation, and in the ultimate fulfilment of the glorious promise which it had received from God. . . . And for himself, the man who died in the consciousness of possessing the mercy and love of God, knew also that he would carry them with him as an inalienable possession, a light in the darkness of Sheol. He knew that he would be 'gathered to his fathers'—a thought which must have been a very plenteous source of consolation, of hope, and of joy."

THE SECOND "PARABLE" OF BALAAM.

It was but natural that Balak should have been equally surprised and incensed at the words of the soothsayer. The only solution he could suggest was, that a fuller view of the camp of Israel might change the disposition of the magician. "Come, I pray thee, with me unto another place, from whence thou mayest see them (viz., in their totality); only the end (utmost part) of them seest thou, but the whole of them thou seest not—and from thence curse me them."[2] The station now selected was on "the field of the watchers," on the top of Pisgah, affording not only a full view of the camp, but of the Land of Promise itself. Here Moses, not long afterwards, took his farewell prospect of the goodly heritage which the Lord had assigned to His people.[3] The same formalities as before

---

[1] Kurtz, *History of the Old Covenant*, vol. iii. p. 432, Engl. Trans.

[2] Numb. xxiii. 13. So literally; the critical discussion see in Keil, *Bible Commentary*, vol. ii. p. 313.

[3] A description of the view from Pisgah is given in a subsequent chapter.

having been gone through, in regard to altars and sacrifices, Balaam once more returned to Balak with the following message :

> Rise up, Balak, and hear,
> Hearken to me, son of Zippor !
> Not man is God that He should lie,
> Nor a son of man that He should repent !
> Hath He said, and shall He not do it,
> Hath He spoken, and shall He not fulfil it ?
> Behold, to bless, I have received—
> And He hath blessed, and I cannot turn it back !
> He beholdeth not iniquity in Jacob,
> And He looketh not upon distress in Israel :
> Jehovah his God is with him,
> And the king's jubilee in the midst of him.[1]
> God bringeth them out of Egypt—
> As the unwearied strength of the buffalo is his.[2]
> For, no augury in Jacob, no soothsaying [3] in Israel,
> According to the time it is said to Jacob and to Israel what God doeth.[4]
> Behold, the people, like a lioness it riseth,
> And like a lion it raiseth itself up—
> He shall not lie down, till he has eaten the prey,[5]
> And drink the blood of the slain.

The meaning of this second "parable" needs no special explanation. Only it will be noticed, that the progress of thought is successively marked by *four lines*—the last two always expressing the ground, or showing the foundation of the two first. The centre couplet is the most important. It marks for ever, that the Covenant-Presence of God in Israel, or, as we should now express it, that the grace of God, is the ultimate cause of the forgiveness of sins, and that the happy realisation of Jehovah

[1] That is, the shout of jubilee on account of the abiding presence of Jehovah as their King is in the midst of the camp of Israel. This is symbolised by the blast of the trumpets, which is designated by the same word as that rendered "jubilee."

[2] Viz., Israel's.

[3] The same word by which Balaam himself is uniformly designated as "the soothsayer."

[4] In due time God reveals by His word to Israel His purpose.

[5] Literally, "the torn," what he had torn in pieces.

as the King is the ground of joy. Whenever and wherever that Presence is wanting only unforgiven sin is beheld; wherever that shout is not heard only misery is felt.

THE THIRD "PARABLE" OF BALAAM.

In his despair Balak now proposed to try the issue from yet a third locality. This time a ridge somewhat farther north was selected—"the top of Peor that looketh toward Jeshimon." A third time seven altars were built and sevenfold sacrifices offered. But there was a marked difference in the present instance. Balaam went no more "as at other times to seek for auguries."[1] Nor did Jehovah now, as formerly (xxiii. 5, 16), "put a word in his mouth." But "the Spirit of God came upon him" (xxiv. 2), in the same manner as afterwards upon Saul[2]—he was in the ecstatic state, powerless and almost unconscious, or, as Balaam himself describes it, with his *outward* eyes shut (ver. 3), and "falling," as if struck down, while seeing "the vision of the Almighty," and "having his (inner) eyes opened" (ver. 4).

> Saith Balaam, the son of Beor,
> And saith the man with closed eye,[3]
> Saith he, hearing the words of God,
> Beholding the vision of the Almighty : he beholdeth—falling down—
> and with open eyes !
> How good are thy tabernacles, Jacob,
> Thy dwellings, O Israel—
> Like (watered) valleys they stretch, like gardens by a river,
> Like aloes Jehovah planted, like cedars by the waters.[4]
> Flow waters from his twin buckets—and his seed by many waters,
> Higher than Agag[5] shall be his king—and his kingdom be exalted.

---

[1] Numb. xxiv. 1.   [2] 1 Sam. xix. 23.

[3] The Targum Onkelos, however, renders, "the man who saw clearly."

[4] Targum Onkelos : "as rivers flowing onward ; as the watered garden by Euphrates—as aromatic shrubs planted by the Lord ; as cedars by the waters."

[5] *Agag*—literally, "the fiery"—was not the name of one special king (1 Sam. xv. 8), but the general designation of the kings of Amalek, as Abimelech that of the kings of Philistia, and Pharaoh of Egypt.

God brings him from Egypt—his the unwearied strength of the buffalo—
He shall eat the nations (Gentiles) his enemies—and their bones shall he
   gnaw—and his arrows shall he split.[1]
He coucheth, lieth down like a lion and like a lioness—who shall rouse
   him ?
Blessed he that blesseth thee, and cursed he that curseth thee !

We can scarcely wonder that the bitter disappointment of
Balak should now have broken forth in angry reproaches.
But Balaam had not yet finished his task. Before leaving the
king he must deliver another part of the message, which he
had already received from Jehovah,[2] but not yet spoken.
"Come, I will advise thee what this people shall do to thy
people in the latter days " (xxiv. 14).

PROPHETIC MESSAGE THROUGH BALAAM IN FOUR
"PARABLES."

*First "parable," descriptive first of the " latter days," and
then referring to Moab,* as the representative of heathenism :

Saith Balaam, the son of Beor, and saith the man with closed eye,
Saith he, hearing the words of God, and knowing the knowledge of the
   Most High,
Beholding the vision of the Almighty : he beholdeth—falling down—
   and with open eyes :
I behold Him, but not now—I descry Him, but not nigh !
Cometh[3] a Star from Jacob, and rises a Sceptre from Israel,
And dasheth the two sides of Moab, and overthroweth the sons of
   tumult.[4]

---

[1] The rendering of this clause is exceedingly difficult and doubtful. I
have taken the verb in its original meaning, *divide, split,* as in Judges v. 26,
"When she had split and stricken through his temples."

[2] This we gather from the addition of the words, "knowing the knowledge of the Most High" (xxiv. 16) besides, "beholding the vision of the
Almighty" (ver. 4).

[3] Literally, makes its way.

[4] Among all nations "the star" has been associated with the future
glory of great kings. The application of it to the Messiah is not only
constant in Scripture, but was universally acknowledged by the ancient

And Edom shall be a possession, and a possession shall be Seir[1]—his
    enemies[2]—
And Israel is doing mighty things![3]
And shall come from Jacob (a ruler)
And shall destroy what remaineth out of the cities.

Second "parable" against Amalek—as the representative of
heathenism in its *first* contest against Israel:

And he beheld Amalek, and he took up his parable, and said:
First of the Gentiles Amalek—and his latter end even unto destruction.

Third "parable" in favour of the Kenites as the friends and
allies of Israel:

And he beheld the Kenites, and he took up his parable, and said:
Durable thy dwelling-place, and placed on the rock thy nest.
For shall Kajin be for destruction,
Until Asshur shall lead thee away?

Fourth "parable" concerning the Assyrian empire, and the
kingdoms of this world, or prophecy of "the end," appropriately beginning with a "*woe:*"

And he took up his parable, and said:[4]
Woe! who shall live when God putteth this?[5]
And ships from the side of Chittim—and afflict Asshur, and afflict
    Eber—
And he also unto destruction!

This latter may, indeed, be characterised as the most wonderful of prophecies. More than a thousand years before the
event, not only the rising of the great world-empire of the West

---

Jews. Both the Targum Onkelos and that of Jonathan apply it in this
manner. "The two sides of Moab," *i.e.*, from end to end of the land.
"The sons of tumult," *i.e.*, the rebellious nations.

[1] Edom is the people; Seir the country.
[2] "His enemies," viz., those of Israel; the language is very abrupt.
[3] Onkelos: "prosper in riches."
[4] Of course, the Assyrian empire was as yet in the far future, and could
not therefore be "beheld" like Moab, Amalek, and the Kenites.
[5] Who shall be able to abide when God doeth all this?

is here predicted, with its conquest of Asshur and Eber (*i.e*, of the descendants of Eber),[1] but far beyond this the final destruction of that world-empire is foretold! In fact, we have here a series of prophecies, commencing with the appearance of the Messiah and closing with the destruction of Anti-Christ. To this there is no parallel in Scripture, except in the visions of Daniel. No ingenuity of hostile criticism can take from, or explain away the import of this marvellous prediction.

And now the two parted—the king to go to his people, the soothsayer, as we gather from the sequel, to the tents of Midian. But we meet Balaam only too soon again. One who had entered on such a course could not stop short of the terrible end. He had sought to turn away Jehovah from His people, and failed. He would now endeavour to turn the people from Jehovah. If he succeeded in this, the consequences to Israel would be such as Balak had desired to obtain. By his advice[2] the children of Israel were seduced into idolatry and all the vile abominations connected with it.[3] In the judgment which ensued, not fewer than 24,000 Israelites perished, till the zeal of Phinehas stayed the plague, when in his representative capacity he showed that Israel, as a nation, abhorred idolatry and the sins connected with it, as the greatest crime against Jehovah. But on "the evil men and seducers" speedy judgment came. By God's command the children of Israel were avenged of the Midianites. In the universal slaughter of Midian, Balaam also perished.

The figure of Balaam stands out alone in the history of the Old Testament. The only counterpart to it is that of Judas, the traitor. Balaam represented the opposition of heathenism; Judas that of Judaism. Both went some length in following the truth; Balaam honestly acknowledged the God of Israel, and followed His directions: Judas owned the Messianic appearance in Jesus, and joined His disciples. But in the

[1] Gen. x. 21.   [2] Numb. xxxi. 16; Rev. ii. 14.
[3] The service of Baal-Peor represents the vilest form of idolatry. See Fürst, Dict. *sub voce.*

crisis of their inner history, when that came which, in one form or another, must be to every one the decisive question —each failed. Both had stood at the meeting and parting of the two ways, and both chose that course which rapidly ended in their destruction. Balaam had expected the service of Jehovah to be quite other from what he found it; and, trying to make it such as he imagined and wished, he not only failed, but stumbled, fell, and was broken. Judas, also, if we may be allowed the suggestion, had expected the Messiah to be quite other than he found Him; disappointment, perhaps failure in the attempt to induce Him to alter His course, and an increasingly widening gulf of distance between them, drove him, step by step, to ruin. Even the besetting sins of Balaam and of Judas—covetousness and ambition—are the same. And as, when Balaam failed in turning Jehovah from Israel, he sought —only too successfully—to turn Israel from the Lord; so when Judas could not turn the Christ from His purpose towards His people, he also succeeded in turning Israel, as a nation, from their King. In both instances, also, for a moment a light more bright than before was cast upon the scene. In the case of Balaam we have the remarkable prophetic utterances, reaching far beyond the ordinary range of prophetic vision; at the betrayal of Judas, we hear the prophetic saying of the High-priest going far beyond the knowledge of the time, that Jesus should die, not only for His own people, but for a ruined world. And, lastly, in their terrible end, they each present to us most solemn warning of the danger of missing the right answer to the great question—that of absolute and implicit submission of mind, heart, and life to the revealed Covenant-Will of God.

CHAPTER III.

The Second Census of Israel—The "daughters of Zelophehad"—Appointment of Moses' Successor—Sacrificial Ordinances—The war against Midian—Allocation of Territory East of the Jordan—Levitical and Cities of Refuge.

(NUMB. XXVI.–XXXVI.)

BEFORE describing the closing scene of Moses' life, we may here conveniently group together brief notices of the events intervening between the judgment of "the plague" on account of Israel's sin (Numb. xxv.) and the last discourses of Moses recorded in the Book of Deuteronomy.

1. A *second census* of Israel was taken by Divine direction (Numb. xxvi.). The arrangements for it were in all probability the same as those at the *first census*, thirty-eight years before (Numb. i.).[1] The "plague" had swept away any who might yet have remained of the old doomed generation, which had come out of Egypt. At any rate, none such were now left (Numb. xxvi. 64). This may have been the reason for taking a new *census*. But its main object was in view of the approaching apportionment of the land which Israel was so soon to possess. Accordingly, the census was not taken as before (Numb. i.), according to the number of individuals in each tribe, but according to "families." This corresponded in the main[2] with the names of the grandsons and great-grandsons of Jacob, enumerated in Gen. xlvi. In reference to the future

[1] The results of that census, as compared with the first, have been stated in a previous volume.

[2] The reason of any divergences has been explained in the first volume of this series (*History of the Patriarchs*, p. 174).

division of the land, it was arranged that the *extent* of the
" inheritance " allotted to each tribe should correspond to its
numbers (Numb. xxvi. 52–54). But the exact locality assigned
to each was to be determined "by lot " (vers. 55, 56), so that
each tribe might feel that it had received its " possession"
directly from the Lord Himself.

The proposed division of the land brought up a special
question of considerable importance to Israel. It appears that
one Zelophehad, of the tribe of Manasseh, and of the family of
Gilead, had died—not in any special judgment, but along with
the generation that perished in the wilderness. Having left no
sons, his daughters were anxious to obtain a " possession," lest
their father's name should be " done away from among his
family " (Numb. xxvii.). By Divine direction, which Moses
had sought, their request was granted,[1] and it became " a statute
of judgment " in Israel—a juridical statute—that daughters, or—
in their default—the nearest kinsman, should enter upon the inheritance of those who died without leaving sons. In all such
cases, of course the children of those who obtained the possession would have to be incorporated, not with the tribe to
which they originally belonged, but with that in which their " inheritance " lay. Thus the " name " of a man would not " be
done away from among his family." Nor was this " statute "
recorded merely on account of its national bearing, but for
higher reasons. For this desire to preserve a name in a
family in Israel sprang not merely from feelings natural in
such circumstances, but was connected with the hope of the
coming Messiah. Till *He* appeared, each family would fain
have preserved its identity. Several instances of such changes
from one tribe to another, through maternal inheritance, are
recorded in Scripture (comp. 1 Chron. ii. 34, 35 ; Numb.
xxxii. 41, and Deut. iii. 14, 15, and 1 Chron. ii. 21–23 ; and

[1] To prevent the possibility of the possession of Zelophehad passing, in
the year of Jubilee, away from the tribe to which Zelophehad had belonged,
it was determined (Numb. xxxvi.) that his daughters should not marry out
of their father's tribe ; and this was afterwards made a general law.

notably, even in the case of priests, Ezra ii. 61, 62, and Nehem. vii. 63 and 64).

2. God intimated once more to Moses his impending death, before actual entrance into the Land of Promise (Numb. xxvii. 12–14). In so doing, mention of the sin which had caused this judgment was repeated, to show God's holiness and justice, even in the case of His most approved servants. On the other hand, this second reminder also manifested the faithfulness of the Lord, Who would have His servant, as it were, set his house in order, that he might meet death, not at unawares, but with full consciousness of what was before him. It is touching to see how meekly Moses received the sentence. Faithful to the end in his stewardship over God's house, his chief concern was, that God would appoint a suitable successor, so " that the congregation of the Lord be not as sheep which have no shepherd " (vers. 15–17). To this office Joshua, who had the needful spiritual qualifications, was now set apart by the laying on of Moses' hands, in presence of Eleazar the priest and of the congregation. Yet only part of Moses' " honour "— so much as was needful to ensure the obedience of Israel— was put upon Joshua, while his public movements were to be directed by " the judgment of the Urim " and Thummim. Thus did God not only vindicate the honour of His servant Moses, but also show that the office which Moses had filled was, in its nature, unique, being typical of that committed in all its fulness to the Great Head of the Church.

3. Now that the people were about to take possession of the land, the sacrificial ordinances were once more enjoined, and with full details. The daily morning and evening sacrifice had already been previously instituted in connection with the altar of burnt-offering (Ex. xxix. 38–42). To this daily consecration of Israel were now added the special sacrifices of the Sabbath—symbolical of a deeper and more special dedication, on God's own day. The Sabbatic and the other festive sacrifices were always brought in addition to the daily offering Again, the commencement of every month was marked by a

special sacrifice, with the addition of a sin-offering, while the blast of the priests' trumpets was intended, as it were, to bring Israel's prayers and services in remembrance before the Lord. If the beginning of each month was thus significantly consecrated, the feast of unleavened bread (from the 15th to the 21st of Abib), which made that month the beginning of the year, was marked by the repetition *on each of its seven days* of the sacrifices which were prescribed for every "new moon." The Paschal feast (on the 14th of Abib) had no general congregational sacrifice, but only that of the lamb for the Paschal supper in each household. Lastly, the sacrifices for *the feast of weeks* were the same as those for the feast of un-leavened bread, *with the addition* of the two "wave loaves" and their accompanying sacrifices prescribed in Lev. xxiii. 17–21.[1] This concluded the first festive cycle in the year.

The second cycle of feasts took place in the seventh or sacred month—seven being the sacred number, and that of the covenant. It began with new moon's day when, besides the daily, and the ordinary new moon's offerings, special festive sacrifices were brought (Numb. xxix. 1–6). Then on the 10th of that month was the "Day of Atonement," while on the 15th commenced the feast of tabernacles, which lasted seven days, and was followed by an octave. All these feasts had their appropriate sacrifices.[2] The laws as to sacrifices appropriately close with directions about "vows" (Numb. xxx.). In all the ordinances connected with the sacred seasons, the attentive reader will mark the symbolical significance attaching to the number *seven*—alike in the feasts themselves, in their number,

---

[1] That the sacrifices prescribed in Lev. xxiii. 17–21 were not the same as those in Numb. xxviii. 26–31, is not only established by the unanimous testimony of Jewish tradition, but appears from a comparison of the dif-ferences between the sacrifices ordained in these two passages. Thus the feast of weeks or "of first-fruits" had threefold sacrifices—the ordinary daily, the ordinary festive, and the special festive sacrifice.

[2] For details as to the manner in which these feasts were observed at the time of Christ, I have to refer the reader to my book on *The Temple: its Ministry, and Services at the Time of Christ.*

their sacrifices, and in that of the days appointed for holy convocation. Indeed, the whole arrangement of time was ordered on the same principle, ascending from the Sabbath of days, to the Sabbath of weeks, of months, of years, and finally to the Sabbath of Sabbatic years, which was the year of Jubilee. And thus all time pointed forward and upward to the "Sabbatism," or sacred rest, that remaineth for "the people of God" (Heb. iv. 9).

4. All that has hitherto been described occurred *before* the expedition against Midian, by which Israel was "avenged" for the great sin into which they had by treachery been seduced. That expedition which was accompanied by Phinehas, whose zeal had formerly stayed the plague (Numb. xxv. 7, 8), was not only completely successful, but executed all the Divine directions given. The Midianites seem to have been taken by surprise, and made no resistance. The five kings of Midian, or rather the five chieftains of their various tribes (comp. Numb. xxv. 15), all of whom seem to have been tributaries of Sihon (comp. Josh. xiii. 21), were killed, as well as the great bulk of the population, and "their cities," and "tent-villages" (erroneously rendered in the Authorised Version "goodly castles") "burnt with fire." Besides a large number of prisoners, immense booty was taken. To show their gratitude for the marvellous preservation of the people, who had probably surprised their enemies in one of their wild licentious orgies, the princes offered as an "oblation" to the sanctuary all the golden ornaments taken from the Midianites. The value of these amounted, according to the present standard of money, to considerably upwards of 25,000*l.*

The destruction of the power of Midian, who might have harassed them from the east, secured to Israel the quiet possession of the district east of Jordan, which their arms had already conquered. All along, from the river Arnon in the south, which divided Israel from Moab, to the river Jabbok and far beyond it, the land of Gilead[1] and of Bashan,

---

[1] Numb. xxxii. 1 speaks of "the Land of Jazer and of Gilead." "Jazer."

their borders were safe from hostile attacks. The accounts of travellers are unanimous in describing that district as specially suited for pastoral purposes. We read of magnificent park-like scenery, of wide upland pastures, and rich forests, which everywhere gladden the eye. No wonder that those of the tribes which had all along preserved their nomadic habits, and whose flocks and herds constituted their main possessions and their wealth, should wish to settle in those plains and mountains. To them they were in very truth the land of promise. suited to their special wants, and offering the very riches which they desired. The other side Jordan had little attraction for them ; and its possession would have been the opposite of advantageous to a strictly pastoral people. Accordingly, "the children of Gad," and "the children of Reuben" requested of Moses : "Let this land be given unto thy servants for a possession, and bring us not over Jordan" (Numb. xxxii. 5).

If this proposal did not actually imply that those tribes intended henceforth quietly to settle down, leaving their brethren to fight alone for the conquest of Palestine proper, it was at least open to such interpretation. Moses seems to have understood it in that sense. But, if such had been their purpose, they would not only have separated themselves from the Lord's work and leading, but, by discouraging their brethren, have re-enacted, only on a much larger scale, the sin of those unbelieving spies who, thirty-eight years before, had brought such heavy judgment upon Israel. And the words of Moses prevailed. Whether from the first their real intentions had been right, or the warning of Moses had influenced them for good, they now solemnly undertook to accompany their brethren across Jordan, and to stand by them till they also had entered on their possession. Until then they would only restore

---

or "Jaazer" (Numb. xxi. 32) was a town on the way between Heshbon in the south and Bashan in the north. It gave its name to the district, and was probably specially mentioned by the Reubenites as perhaps the township east of Jordan nearest to the camp of Israel. It is supposed to be the modern Seir—almost in a line with Jericho, east of the Jordan.

the " folds "[1] for their sheep, and rebuild the destroyed cities,[2] to afford safe dwelling-places for their wives and children, and, of course, for such of their number as were either left behind for defence, or incapable of going forth to war. On this express promise, their request was granted, and the ancient kingdoms of Sihon and of Og were provisionally assigned to Reuben, Gad, and half the tribe of Manasseh, which latter had made special conquests in Gilead (Numb. xxxii. 39). But the actual division of the district among these tribes was left over for the period when the whole country should be allocated among the children of Israel (Josh. xiii.).

5. The arrangements preparatory to possession of the land appropriately concluded with two series of ordinances.[3] The *first* of these (Numb. xxxiii. 50–xxxiv.) directed the extermination of the Canaanites and of all traces of their idolatry, re-enjoining, at the same time, the partition of the now purified land, by lot, among the tribes of Israel (Numb. xxxiii. 50–56). Next, the boundary lines of Palestine were indicated, and the persons named who were to superintend the partition of the country (Numb. xxxiv.). This duty was intrusted to Eleazar the high-priest, and to Joshua, along with ten representative " priests, one from each of the ten tribes, Reuben and Gad having already received their portion on the other side Jordan.

The *second* series of ordinances now enacted (Numb. xxxv., xxxvi.) was, if not of greater importance, yet of even deeper symbolical meaning. According to the curse that had been pronounced upon Levi, that tribe was destined to be "divided in Jacob" (Gen. xlix. 7). But, in the goodness of God, this was now converted into a blessing alike to Levi and to all

[1] These are not "Hazzeroth," but rubble walls for sheep, made of loose stones.

[2] These cities were rebuilt before the apportionment of the country among these two and a half tribes. This appears from the fact that, for example, *Dibon* and *Aroer* were built by "the children of Gad" (Numb. xxxii. 34, 35), but afterwards allocated to Reuben (Josh. xiii. 16, 17)

[3] Each of these two series is marked by a special preface—the first, Numb. xxxiii. 50; the second, Numb. xxxv. 1.

Israel. The Levites, the special property and election of the
Lord, were to be scattered among all the other tribes, to recall
by their presence everywhere the great truths which they symbolised, and to keep alive among the people the knowledge
and service of the Lord. On the other hand, they were not to
be quite isolated, but gathered together into cities, so that by
fellowship and intercourse they might support and strengthen
one another. For this purpose forty-eight cities were now
assigned to the Levites—of course not exclusive of any other
inhabitants, but "to dwell in," that is, they were to have as
many houses in them as were required for their accommodation.
Along with these houses certain "suburbs," also, or "commons"
for their herds and flocks, were to be assigned them—covering
in extent on each side a distance of 1000 cubits (1500 feet)
round about their cities (Numb. xxxv. 4). Besides, around
this inner, another outer circle of 2000 cubits was to be drawn
in every direction. These were to be the fields and vineyards
of the Levites[1] (ver. 5). The number of these cities in each
tribe varied according to the size of its territory. Thus Judah
and Simeon had to furnish nine cities, Naphtali only three, and
each of the other tribes four (Josh. xxi.). Lastly, the thirteen
Levitical cities in the territories of Judah, Simeon, and Benjamin were specially assigned to the priests, the descendants
of the house of Aaron, while six of the Levitical cities—three
east and three west of the Jordan—were set apart as "cities of
refuge," for the unintentional manslayer. It is interesting to
notice, that even the number of the Levitical cities was
significant. They amounted in all to forty-eight, which is a
multiple of four, the symbolical number of the kingdom of God
in the world, and of twelve, the number of the tribes of Israel.

In regard to the "cities of refuge," for the protection of the
unintending manslayer, it must not be imagined that the simple
plea of unintentional homicide afforded safety. The law, indeed,

[1] Very varied interpretations of these two difficult verses have been
proposed. That adopted in the text is in accordance with Jewish tradition,
and the most simple, while it meets all the requirements of the text.

provided that the country both east and west of the Jordan should be divided in three parts—each with its " city of refuge," the roads to which were always to be kept in good repair. But, according to the sacred text (Numb. xxxv. 25, comp. Josh. xx. 4), a homicide would, on arriving at the gates of a city of refuge, first have to plead his cause before the elders of that city, when, if it approved itself to their minds, they would afford him provisional protection. If, however, afterwards, the " avenger of blood " claimed his extradition, the accused person would be sent back under proper protection to his own city, where the whole case would be thoroughly investigated. If the homicide was then proved to have been unintentional, the accused would be restored to the " city of refuge," and enjoy its protection, till the death of the high priest set him free to return to his own city.[1] As for the duty of " avenging blood," its principle is deeply rooted in the Old Testament, and traced up to the relation in which God stands to our world. For, the blood of man, who is God's image, when shed upon earth, which is God's property, " crieth " unto God (Gen. iv. 10)—claims payment like an unredeemed debt. Hence the expression " avenger of blood," which should be literally rendered " redeemer of blood." On the other hand, the symbolical meaning of the cities of refuge will readily be understood. There—in the place of God's merciful provision—the manslayer was to find a refuge, sheltered, as it were, under the wings of the grace of God, till the complete remission of the punishment at the death of the high priest—the latter symbolically pointing forward to the death of Him Whom God has anointed our great High Priest, and Who " by His one oblation of Himself once offered," hath made " a full, perfect, and sufficient sacrifice, oblation, and satisfaction " for the sins of the world.

[1] Perek II. of the Mishnic tractate *Maccoth* treats on this subject, and expounds at length the application of this law.

CHAPTER IV.

Death and Burial of Moses.

(DEUT. III. 23–29; NUMB. XXVII. 15–23; DEUT. XXXIV.)

ALL was now ready, and Israel about to cross the Jordan and take possession of the Promised Land! It was only natural—one of those traits in the history of the great heroes of the Bible, so peculiarly precious, as showing in their weakness their kinship to our feelings—that Moses should have longed to share in what was before Israel. Looking back the long vista of these one hundred and twenty years—first of life and trial in Egypt, then of loneliness and patient faith while feeding the flocks of Jethro, and, lastly, of labour and weariness in the wilderness, it would indeed have been strange, had he not wished now to have part in the conquest and rest of the goodly land. He had believed in it; he had preached it; he had prayed for it; he had laboured, borne, fought for it. And now within reach and view of it *must* he lay himself down to die?

Scripture records,[1] with touching simplicity, what passed between Moses and his Heavenly Father.[2] "And I entreated grace from the Lord at that time, saying: Lord Jehovah, Thou hast begun to show Thy servant Thy greatness and Thy strong hand. For what God is there in heaven or in the earth which doeth like Thy doings and like Thy might? Oh, that I might now go over and see the good land which is on the other side Jordan, this goodly mountain and the Lebanon! And Jehovah was wroth with me on account of you, and hearkened not unto me. And God said to me: Let it now

---

[1] Deut. iii. 23–26.   [2] We translate literally.

suffice thee[1]--continue not to speak to Me any more on this matter." The deep feelings of Moses had scarcely bodied themselves in the language of prayer. Rather had it been the pouring forth of his inmost desires before his Father in heaven—a precious privilege which His children possess at all times. But even so Moses had in this also, though but " as a steward " and "afar off," to follow Him whose great type he was, and to learn the peaceful rest of this experience, after a contest of thought and wish : " Nevertheless, not my will, but Thine be done." And it was the good will of God that Moses should lay himself down to rest without entering the land. Although it came in punishment of Israel's and of Moses' sin at the waters of Meribah, yet it was also better that it should be so—better for Moses himself. For on the top of Pisgah God prepared something better for Moses than even entrance into the land of earthly promise.

And now calmly, as a father setteth his house in order, did Moses prepare for his departure. During his life all his thoughts had been for Israel ; and he was faithful even unto the death. His last care also had been for the people whom he had loved, and for the work to which he had been devoted— that Jehovah would provide for His congregation " a shepherd " "who may lead them out and bring them in."[2] Little else was left to be done. In a series of discourses, Moses repeated, and more fully re-stated, to Israel the laws and ordinances of God their King. His last record was " a song " of the mercy and truth of God ;[3] his last words a blessing upon Israel.[4] Then, amid the respectful silence of a mourning people, he set out alone upon his last pilgrim-journey. All the way up to the highest top of Pisgah the eyes of the people must have followed him. They could watch him as he stood there in the sunset, taking his full view of the land—there to see for himself how true and faithful Jehovah had been. Still could they descry

---

Literally : Enough (sufficient) for thee. [2] Numb. xxvii. 16, .7.
[3] Deut. xxxii. [4] Deut. xxxiii.

his figure, as, in the shadows of even, it moved towards a valley apart. After that no mortal eye ever beheld him, till, with Elijah, he stood on the mount of transfiguration. Then indeed was the longing wish of Moses, uttered many, many centuries before, fulfilled far beyond his thinking or hoping at the time. He *did* stand on "the goodly mountain" within the Land of Promise, worshipping, and giving testimony to Him in "Whom all the promises are yea and amen." It was a worthy crowning this of such a life. Not the faithful steward of Abraham, Eliezer of Damascus, when he brought to his master's son the God-given bride, could with such joy see the end of his faithful stewardship when the heir entered on his possession, as this "steward over God's house," when on that mountain he did homage to "the Son in His own house."

But to Israel down in the valley had Moses never so preached of the truth and faithfulness of Jehovah, and of His goodness and support to His people, as from the top of Pisgah. There was a strange symbolical aptness even in the ascent of the mount, 4,500 feet up, which is "rapid" but "not rugged."[1] Standing on the highest crest, the prospect would, indeed, seem almost unbounded. *Eastwards*, stretching into Arabia, rolls a boundless plain—one waving ocean of corn and grass. As the eye turns *southwards*, it ranges over the land of Moab, till it rests on the sharp outlines of Mounts Hor and Seir, and the rosy granite peaks of Arabia. To the *west* the land descends, terrace by terrace, to the Dead Sea, the western outline of which can be traced in its full extent. Deep below lies that sea, "like a long strip of molten metal, with the sun mirrored on its surface, waving and undulating in its further edge, unseen in its eastern limits, as though poured from some deep cavern beneath." Beyond it would appear the ridge of Hebron, and

---

[1] Our description here, and of the view from the top is from Canon Tristram's *Land of Israel*, pp. 539–543, of course, in a shortened form. We must content ourselves with this general acknowledgment without always the formality of inverted commas.

then as the eye travelled northwards, successively the sites
of Bethlehem and of Jerusalem. The holy city itself would be
within range of view—Mount Moriah, the Mount of Olives ; on
the one side of it the gap in the hills leading to Jericho, while
on the other side, the rounded heights of Benjamin would be
clearly visible. Turning *northwards*, the eye follows the winding course of Jordan from Jericho, the city of palm-trees, up
the stream. Looking across it, it rests on the rounded top of
Mount Gerizim, beyond which the plain of Esdraelon opens,
and the shoulder of Carmel appears. That blue haze in the
distance is the line of " the utmost sea." Still farther northwards rise the outlines of Tabor, Gilboa, the top of snow-clad
Hermon, and the highest range of Lebanon. In front are the
dark forests of Ajalon, Mount Gilead, then the land of Bashan
and Bozrah. "And Jehovah shewed Moses all the land of
Gilead, unto Dan, and all Naphtali, and the land of Ephraim,
and Manasseh, and all the land of Judah, unto the utmost sea,
and the Negeb, and the plain of the valley of Jericho, the city
of palm-trees, unto Zoar."[1]

Such was the prospect which, from that mountain-top, spread
before Moses. And when he had satiated his eyes upon it,
he descended into that valley apart to lay him down to rest.
Into the mysterious silence of that death and burial at the
hands of Jehovah we dare not penetrate. Jewish tradition,
rendering the expression (Deut. xxxiv. 5) literally, has it that
" Moses the servant of Jehovah died there . . . at the mouth
of Jehovah," or, as they put it, by the kiss of the Lord. But
from the brief saying of Scripture[2] may we not infer that
although Moses also received in death the wages of sin, yet his
body passed not through corruption, however much " the
devil," contending as for his lawful prey, "disputed" for its
possession, but was raised up to be with Elijah the first to
welcome the Lord in His glory? For " men bury a body that
it may pass into corruption. If Jehovah, therefore, would not
suffer the body of Moses to be buried by men, it is but natural

[1] Deut. xxxiv. 1–3.   [2] Jude 9.

to seek for the *reason* in the fact that He did not intend to leave him to corruption." [1]

But "*there arose not a prophet since in Israel like unto Moses, whom Jehovah knew face to face, in all the signs and the wonders, which Jehovah sent him to do in the land of Egypt to Pharaoh, and to all his servants, and to all his land, and in all that mighty hand, and in all the great terror which Moses showed in the sight of all Israel.*"[2]

"AND MOSES VERILY WAS FAITHFUL IN ALL HIS HOUSE, AS A SERVANT, FOR A TESTIMONY OF THOSE THINGS WHICH WERE TO BE SPOKEN AFTER; BUT CHRIST AS A SON OVER HIS OWN HOUSE; WHOSE HOUSE ARE WE, IF WE HOLD FAST THE CONFIDENCE AND THE REJOICING OF THE HOPE FIRM UNTO THE END."[3]

CHAPTER V.

The Charge to Joshua—Despatch of the two Spies to Jericho—Rahab.

(JOSH. I. II.)

A WIDE, rich plain at the foot of the mountains of Moab, carpeted with wild flowers springing in luxuriant beauty, watered by many rivulets and rills, here and there covered by acacia trees, where birds of brightest plumage carol, and beyond, to the south, by the banks of streams, where scented oleanders rise to a height of twenty-five feet, their flower-laden boughs bending like those of the willow—such is Abel-Shittim, "the meadow of acacias." Beyond it are the fords of Jordan, and the western heights; in the distance southwards, the hills of Judæa, on which the purple light rests. Climate and vegetation are tropical, on the eastern even more than on the western

---

[1] Kurtz, *History of the Old Covenant*, vol. iii. p. 495 (English translation).
[2] Deut. xxxiv. 10-12.　　　　　[3] Heb. iii. 5, 6.

banks of the Jordan.   Many memories hallow the place
Somewhere here must Elijah have smitten the waters of Jordan,
that they parted, ere the fiery chariot wrapt him from the
companionship of Elisha.   In this district also was the scene
of John's baptism, where the Saviour humbled Himself to
fulfil all righteousness.   And on this " meadow of acacias "
did an early summer shed its softness when, about the month
of March, forty years after the Exodus, the camp of Israel kept
thirty days' solemn mourning for Moses (Deut. xxxiv. 8).
Behind them rose that mountain-top, from which "that saint
of God" had seen his last of Israel and of the goodly land,
which they were so soon to possess ; before them lay the Land
of Promise which they were presently to enter.

Such a leader as Moses had been would Israel never more
see ; nor yet one with whom God had so spoken, " mouth to
mouth," as a man with his friend.   A feeling of loneliness and
awe must have crept over the people and over their new leader,
Joshua, like that which Elisha felt, when, alone, he turned
him back with the mantle of Elijah that came to him from
heaven, to test whether now also the waters would divide at
the bidding of the Lord God of Elijah.   And the faithful
Covenant-God was with Joshua, as he waited, not unbelievingly,
but expectantly, in that mourning camp of Abel-Shittim, for
a fresh message from God.   Though he had been previously
designated by God, and set apart to the leadership, it was well
he should so wait, not only for his own sake, but also " that
the people might afterwards not hesitate gladly to follow his
leadership, who had not moved a foot without the leading of
God."[1]   And in due time the longed-for direction came: not
in doubtful language, but renewing alike the commission of
Joshua and the promises to Israel.   Far as the eye could
reach, to the heights of Anti-Lebanon in the extreme distance, to the shores of the Great Sea, to the Euphrates in
the East—all was theirs, and not a foeman should withstand
them, for God would "not fail nor forsake" their leader.

[1] Calvin.

Only two things were requisite : that, in his loving obedience, the word and commands of God should be precious to Joshua ; and that in strong faith he should be " very courageous." This latter command was twice repeated, as it were to indicate alike the inward courage of faith and the outward courage of deed.

That this call had found a response in the hearts not only of Joshua, but also of the people, appears from the answer of Reuben, Gad, and the half tribe of Manasseh, when reminded of their obligation to share in the impending warfare of their brethren.   While professing their readiness to acknowledge in all things the authority of Joshua, they also expressly made the latter conditional on the continued direction of Jehovah, and re-echoed the Divine admonition to be " strong and of a good courage."   So much does success in all we undertake depend on the assurance of faith !   " For he that wavereth is like a wave of the sea driven with the wind and tossed.   For let not that man think that he shall receive anything of the Lord" (James i. 6, 7).

Thus directed and encouraged, Joshua gave orders that the people should provide themselves with the necessary victuals to begin, if occasion should offer, their forward march on the third day.   In point of fact, however, it was at least five days before that movement could be made.   For Joshua had deemed it prudent to adopt proper preparatory measures, although, or rather just because he was assured of Divine help, and trusted in it.   Accordingly he had sent, unknown to the people,[1] two spies " to view the land and Jericho."[2] The reason of this secrecy lay probably both in the nature of their errand, and in the sad remembrance of the discouragement which evil report by the spies had formerly wrought among the people (Numb. xiv. 1).   As the two spies

---

[1] In Josh. ii. 1, the accentuation connects the words "secretly" and "saying," which are separated by commas in our Authorised Version, showing that the commission was intrusted to them secretly.

[2] The meaning really is "especially Jericho," which fortress was the key to the western bank of Jordan.

stealthily crept up the eight miles of country from the western bank of the Jordan to " the city of palm trees," they must have been struck with the extraordinary " beauty and luxuriance of the district. Even now there is a bright green oasis of several miles square which marks the more rich and populous groves of Jericho."[1] Its vegetation is most rich and rare; almost every tree is tenanted by the bulbul or Palestinian nightingale, with the " hopping thrush," " the gorgeous Indian blue kingfisher, the Egyptian turtle-dove, and other singing birds of Indian or Abyssinian affinity." " On the plain above are the desert larks and chats, while half an hour's walk takes us to the Mount of Temptation, the home of the griffon, where beautifully plumed partridges, rock-swallows, rock-doves, and other birds abound. But, beyond all others, Jericho is the home of the lovely sun-bird, ... resplendent with all the colours of the humming-bird"—its back brilliant green, its throat blue, and its breast purple, " with a tuft of rich red, orange, and yellow feathers at each shoulder." The little stream—which Elisha healed from its after curse—swarms with fish, while climate and prospect are equally delicious in that early summer-like spring, when the spies visited it. And what the wealth and beauty of this plain must have been when it was crowded with feathery palms, and scented balsam gardens, we learn from the descriptions of Josephus (*Ant.* xv. 4, 2). This paradise of Canaan was guarded by the fortress of Jericho— one of the strongest in the whole land.[2] Behind its walls and battlements immense wealth was stored, partly natural and partly the result of civilisation and luxury. This appears even from the character and value of the spoil which one individual—Achan—could secrete from it (Josh. vii. 21).

As the spies neared the city, the setting sun was casting his rays in richest variegated colouring on the limestone mountains which surrounded the ancient Jericho like an amphitheatre,

[1] Tristram, *Land of Israel*, pp. 203 and following.

[2] This impression is irresistibly conveyed to the mind by a comparison of the Scriptural account of Jericho with that of the other cities in Canaan.

rising closest, and to the height of from 1200 to 1500 feet, in the north, where they bear the name of *Quarantania*, marking the traditional site of the forty days of our Lord's temptation; and thence stretching with widening sweep towards the south. Friend or ally there was none in that city, whose hospitality the two Israelites might have sought. To have resorted to a khan or inn would have been to court the publicity which most of all they wished to avoid. Under these circumstances, the choice of the house of Rahab, the harlot, was certainly the wisest for their purpose. But even so, in the excited state of the public mind, when, as we know (Josh. ii. 11), the terror of Israel had fallen upon all, the arrival of two suspicious-looking strangers could not remain a secret. So soon as the gates were shut, and escape seemed impossible, the king sent to make captives of what he rightly judged to be Israelitish spies. But Rahab had anticipated him. Arriving at the same conclusion as the king, and expecting what would happen, she had " hid them "—perhaps hastily —"with the stalks of flax which she had laid in order upon the roof," after the common Eastern fashion of drying flax on the flat roofs of houses. By the adroit admission of the fact that two men, previously unknown to her, had indeed come, to which she added the false statement that they had with equal abruptness left just before the closing of the gates, she succeeded in misleading the messengers of the king. The story of Rahab sounded likely enough; she had seemingly been frank, nor was there any apparent motive for untruthfulness on her part, but quite the opposite, as the same danger threatened all the inhabitants of Jericho. As Rahab had suggested, the messengers " pursued quickly " in the supposed wake of the Jewish emissaries, which would have been "the way to Jordan, unto the fords," by which they must return to the camp of Israel, and the gates were again shut, to make escape from Jericho impossible, if, after all, they had not quitted the city.

Thus far the device of Rahab had succeeded. So soon as night settled upon the city, she repaired to the roof, and acquainted the spies, who were ignorant of any danger, with what had taken place. At the same time she explained the motives of her conduct. They must indeed have listened with wonder, not unmingled with adoring gratitude, as she told them how they, in Canaan, had heard what Jehovah had done for Israel at the Red Sea, and that, by His help, the two powerful kings of the Amorites had been " utterly destroyed." The very language, in which Rahab described the terror that had fallen upon her countrymen, was the same as that uttered prophetically forty years before, when Moses and the children of Israel sang the new song on the other side of the Red Sea, Ex. xv. 14–16 (comp. Ex. xxiii. 27 ; Deut. ii. 25 ; xi. 25). But the effect of this knowledge of Jehovah's great doings differed according to the state of mind of those who heard of them. In the Canaanites it called forth the energy of despair in resisting Israel, or rather Israel's God. But in Rahab's heart it awakened far other feelings. She knew that Jehovah had given to Israel the land—and far better than even this, that " Jehovah your God, He is God in heaven above and in earth beneath." Knowing God's purpose, she would shelter the spies, and so further their errand ; knowing that He alone was God, she and all near and dear to her must not take part in the daring resistance of her countrymen, but seek safety by separating themselves from them and joining the people of God. And so she implored mercy for herself and her kindred in the day when Jehovah would surely give Israel the victory. Such a request could not be refused, evidenced as its genuineness had been by her " works." The two spies solemnly acceded to it, but on condition that she would prove true to the end, helping on their work by still keeping their mission secret, and evidencing her faith by gathering on the day of trial all her kindred within her house. That house should be distinguished from all other dwellings in Jericho by exhibiting the same " scarlet cord," with which she let down the spies over the city wall upon which her house was built. All throughout, this story is full of deepest symbolical meaning. And in truth, one, prepared so to act, was in heart "an Israelite indeed," and her household already belonged to the "household of faith."

We are now in circumstances to appreciate the faith by which the harlot Rahab perished not with them that were disobedient,[1] when she had "received the spies with peace," a faith which, as St. James argues, evidenced itself "by works" (James ii. 25). In so doing, it is not necessary either to represent her in her former life as other than she really was,[2] or even to extenuate her sin in returning a false answer to the king of Jericho. Nor, on the other hand, do we wish to exaggerate the spiritual condition to which she had attained. Remembering who, and what, and among whom she had been all her life-time, her emphatic confession, that Jehovah, the God of Israel, "He is God in heaven above, and in earth beneath;" her unwavering faith in the truth of His promises, which moved her to self-denying action at such danger and sacrifice, and supported her in it; her separation from her countrymen; her conduct towards the spies at the risk of her life—all show her to have had that faith which "is the substance of things hoped for, the evidence of things unseen;" not a "dead faith," "without works," but one which "wrought with her works, and by works was made perfect." And He Who "giveth more grace" to them who wisely use what they have, marvellously owned and blessed this "firstfruits" from among the Gentiles. Her history, which, in all its circumstances, bears a remarkable analogy to that of the woman of Samaria (John iv.), is recorded for the instruction of the Church. And, as in the case of the Hebrew midwives who had preserved Israel (Ex. i. 21), God also "made her a house." She became the wife of Salmon, a prince of the tribe of Judah, and from her sprang in direct line both David (Ruth iv. 21) and David's Lord (Matt. i. 4).[3]

[1] Heb. xi. 31, marginal rendering.
[2] So Josephus and the Rabbis, who represent her as simply an innkeeper.
[3] The learned reader who is curious to know the Rabbinical fables about

But as for the two Israelitish spies, they hid themselves, according to Rahab's advice, for three days among the limestone caves and grottoes which abound in Mount Quarantania, while their pursuers vainly searched for them in the opposite direction of the fords of Jordan. When the fruitless pursuit had ceased, they made their way back to Joshua, expressing to him their conviction, as the result of their mission : " Truly Jehovah hath delivered into our hands all the land ; for even all the inhabitants of the country do faint because of us."

———◆———

CHAPTER VI.

Miraculous Parting of the Jordan, and the Passage of the Children of Israel—Gilgal and its meaning—The first Passover on the soil of Palestine.

(Josh. iii.-v. 12.)

THE morrow after the return of the spies, the camp at Shittim was broken up, and the host of Israel moved forward. It consisted of all those tribes who were to have their possessions west of the Jordan, along with forty thousand chosen warriors from Reuben, Gad, and the half tribe of Manasseh.[1] A short march brought them to the brink of Jordan. Strictly speaking, the Jordan has a threefold bank ; the largest at the water's edge, which, in spring, is frequently inundated, owing to the melting of snow on Hermon ; a middle bank, which is covered with rich vegetation, and an upper

---

Rahab, will find them in Lightfoot, *Hor. Hebr. et Talmud. ;* and in Wetstein, *Nov. Test.*, in the notes on Matt. i. 5 ; also in Meuschen, *Nov. Test. ex Talm. illustr.*, p. 40.

[1] As, according to Numb. xxvi. 7, 18, 34, the total number of the men of war in the tribes Reuben and Gad, and those of half Manasseh amounted to 110,580, it follows that 70,580 must have been left behind for the protection of the territory east of the Jordan.

bank, which overhangs the river. The people now halted for three days, first to await the Divine direction as to the passage of the river, and then to prepare for receiving in a proper spirit the manifestation of Divine power about to be manifested in the miraculous parting of Jordan. For, as one has remarked, the expression used by Joshua, "the living God is among you" (Josh. iii. 10), does not merely imply the presence of God among Israel, but, as the event proved, the operations by which He shows Himself both *living* and *true*.

All that was to be done by Israel was Divinely indicated to Joshua, and all was done exactly as it had been[1] directed. First, proclamation was made throughout Israel to " sanctify " themselves, and that not only outwardly by symbolic rites, but also inwardly by turning unto the Lord, in expectant faith of "the wonders " about to be enacted. These were intimated to them beforehand (Josh. iii. 5, 13). Thus passed three days. It was "the tenth day of the first month" (Josh. iv. 19), the anniversary of the day on which forty years before Israel had set apart their Paschal lambs (Ex. xii. 3), that the miraculous passage of the Jordan was accomplished, and Israel stood on the very soil of the promised land. Before the evening of that anniversary had closed in, the memorial stones were set up in Gilgal. All between those two anniversaries seemed only as a grand historical parenthesis. But the kingdom of God has no blanks or interruptions in its history; there is a grand unity in its course, for Jehovah reigneth. With feelings stirred by such remembrances, and the expectancy of the great miracle to come, did Israel now move forward. First went the Ark, borne by the priests, and, at a reverent distance of 2000 cubits, followed the host. For, it was the Ark of the Covenant which was to make a way for Israel through the waters of Jordan, and they were to keep it in sight, so as to mark the miraculous road, as it

---

[1] We mark in this narrative *three sections*, each commencing with a Divine command (Josh. iii. 7, 8; iv. 2, 3; and iv. 15, 16), followed by Joshua's communication thereof to the people, and an account of its execution. This to connect each stage with the Lord Himself.

was gradually opened to them. It is to this that the Divine words refer (Josh. iii. 4) : " that ye may know," or rather come to know, recognise, understand, "the way by which ye must go : for ye have not passed this way heretofore." With the exception of Caleb and Joshua, none, at least of the laity,[1] had been grown up at the time, and seen it, when the Lord parted the waters of the Red Sea at the Exodus. Then it had been the uplifted wonder-working rod of Moses by which the waters were parted But now it was the Ark at whose advance they were stayed. And the difference of the means was quite in accordance with that of the circumstances. For now the Ark of the Covenant was the ordinary symbol of the Divine Presence among Israel; and God commonly employs the ordinary means of grace for the accomplishment of His marvellous purposes of mercy.

It was early spring, in that tropical district the time of early harvest (Josh iii. 15), and the Jordan had overflown its lowest banks. As at a distance of about half a mile the Israelites looked down, they saw that, when the feet of those who bore the Ark touched the waters, they were arrested."[2] Far up " beyond where they stood, at the city of Adam that is beside Zarethan,"[3] did the Divine Hand draw up the waters of Jordan, while the waters below that point were speedily drained into the Dead Sea. In the middle of the river-bed the priests with the Ark [4] halted till the whole people had passed over dryshod. Then twelve men, who had previously been detailed for the

---

[1] See *The Exodus and the Wanderings in the Wilderness*, p. 168.

[2] In Josh. iii. 11 and 13 it is significantly designated, "the Ark of Jehovah, the Lord of all the earth," as Calvin remarks, to show the subjection of all to God, and to increase the trust of Israel.

[3] This, and not, as in our Authorised Version, "very far from the city of Adam," is the correct rendering. The sites of these two cities have not been identified. From the nature of the banks, the inundation caused by this miracle would not lead to serious consequences.

[4] The attentive reader will notice that, throughout the Scripture narrative, the main stress is laid on the presence of the Ark, the priests being only introduced as the bearers of it.

purpose,[1] took up twelve large stones from where the priests
had stood in the river-bed, to erect them a solemn memorial to
all times of that wondrous event. Only after that did the
priests come up from Jordan. And when "the soles of the
priests' feet were lifted up unto the dry land" (literally, were
detached, viz., from the clogging mud, "upon the dry"),
"the waters of Jordan returned unto their place, and flowed
over all his banks, as before." It must have been towards
evening when the rest of the march was accomplished—a
distance of about five miles—and Israel's camp was pitched at
what afterwards became *Gilgal*, "in the east border of Jericho,"
about two miles from the latter city.[2]

The object and meaning of this "notable miracle" are
clearly indicated in the sacred text. We know that it was
as absolutely necessary in the circumstances as formerly the
cleaving of the Red Sea had been. For, at that season of the
year, and with the means at their disposal, it would have been
absolutely impossible for a large host with women and children to cross the Jordan. But, besides, it was fitting that a
miracle similar to that of the Exodus from Egypt should mark
the entrance into the Land of Promise ; fitting also, that the
commencement of Joshua's ministry should be thus Divinely
attested like that of Moses (Josh. iii. 7). Finally, it would be
to Israel a glorious pledge of future victory in the might of
their God (ver. 10), while to their enemies it was a sure
token of the judgment about to overtake them (Josh. v. 1).

Two things yet remained to be done, before Israel could
enter upon the war with Canaan. Although the people of
God, Israel had been under judgment for nearly forty years,
and those born in the wilderness bore not the covenant mark
of circumcision. To renew that rite in their case was the

---

[1] The rendering of Josh. iv. 1–3 in our Authorised Version does not give
that impression, but alike Rabbinical and the best Christian authorities
regard these verses as a parenthesis, and translate, in ver. 1, "ar d the Lord
had spoken to Joshua."

[2] Tristram, *Land of Israel*, p. 219.

first necessity, so as to restore Israel to its full position as the covenant-people of God.[1] After that, a privilege awaited Israel which for thirty-eight years they had not enjoyed. Probably the Passover at the foot of Sinai (Numb. ix. 1) had been the last, as that feast would not have been observed by the people in their uncircumcision. But at Gilgal their reproach was " rolled away," and the people of God renewed the festive remembrance of their deliverance from Egypt. Truly, that first Passover on the soil of Palestine had a twofold meaning. Even the circumstances recalled its first celebration. As the night of the first Passover was one of terror and judgment to Egypt, so now, within view of the festive camp of Gilgal, " Jericho was straitly shut up because of the children of Israel : none went out, and none came in" (Josh. vi. 1). And now also the Divine wilderness-provision of the "manna which had clung to them with the tenacity of all God's mercies," ceased on " the morrow after they had eaten of the old corn of the land : neither had the children of Israel manna any more ; but they did eat of the fruits of the land of Canaan that year." And so also have miraculous gifts ceased in the Church, because their continuance has become unnecessary. Similarly will our manna-provision for daily life-need cease, when we at the last enter upon the land of promise, and for ever enjoy its fruits !

---

[1] Of course, the survivors of those who, having come out from Egypt, were at the time of the sentence in Kadesh under twenty years old (Numb. xiv. 29)—in short, all in Gilgal who were thirty-eight years and upwards—*had been* circumcised. Reckoning the total of males at Gilgal at about one million, the proportion of the circumcised to the uncircumcised would have been about 280,000 to 720,000. The former would suffice to prepare the Paschal lambs, and, if needful, to defend the camp at Gilgal, although the terror consequent upon the dividing of Jordan would probably have protected Israel from all hostile attacks. See Keil, *Bibl. Comm.*, vol. ii. pp. 38, 39.

CHAPTER VII.

The "Prince of the Host of Jehovah" appears to Joshua
—The miraculous fall of Jericho before the Ark of
Jehovah.

(JOSH. V. 13; VI. 27).

AT first sight it may seem strange, that, when such fear
had fallen upon the people of the land, any attempt
should have been made to defend Jericho. But a fuller
consideration will help us not only to understand this, but
also by-and-by to see special reasons, why this one fortress
should have been miraculously given to Israel. Not to
mention motives of honour, which would at least have some
influence with the men of Jericho, it was one of the main
principles of heathenism, that each of their "gods many" was
limited in his activity to one special object. But what the
Canaanites had heard of Jehovah showed Him to be the God
of nature, who clave the Red Sea and arrested the waters of
Jordan, and that He was so far also the God of battles, as to
give Israel the victory over the Amorite kings. But was His
strength also the same as against their gods in reducing strong
fortresses? Of that at any rate they had no experience.
Trivial as such a question may sound in our ears, we have
evidence that it was seriously entertained by heathendom. To
mention only one instance, we know that a similar suggestion
was made at a much later period, not by obscure men, but by
the servants and trusted advisers of Ben-hadad, and that it was
acted upon by that monarch in the belief that "Jehovah is God
of the hills, but he is not God of the valleys" (1 Kings xx. 28).
At any rate, it was worth the trial, and Jericho, as already

stated, was the strongest fortress in Canaan, and the key to the whole country.

This latter consideration could not but have weighed on the mind of Joshua, as from the camp of Gilgal he "viewed the city." As yet no special direction had been given him how to attack Jericho, and, assuredly, the people whom he commanded were untrained for such work. While such thoughts were busy within him, of a sudden, "as he lifted up his eyes and looked, there stood over against him," not the beleaguered city, but "a man with his sword drawn in his hand." Challenged by Joshua : "Art thou for us, or for our adversaries ?" the strange warrior replied : "No ! But I am the Captain (or Prince) of the host of Jehovah, now I am come."[1] Here His speech was interrupted—for Joshua fell on his face before Him, and reverently inquired His commands. The reply : "Loose thy shoe from off thy foot, for the place whereon thou standest is holy,"[2] must have convinced Joshua that this Prince of the host of Jehovah was none other than the Angel of the Covenant, Who had spoken to Moses out of the burning bush (Ex. iii. 4), and Who was co-equal with Jehovah. Indeed, shortly afterwards, we find Him expressly spoken of as Jehovah (Josh. vi. 2). So then the mission of Joshua was substantially the continuation and completion of that of Moses. As at the commencement of the latter, the Angel of the Covenant had appeared and spoken out of the burning bush, so He now also appeared to Joshua, while the symbolical act of "loosing the shoe off his foot," in reverent acknowledgment of the Holy One of Israel, recalled the vision of Moses, and at the same time connected it with that of his successor. Having assured Joshua of complete victory, the Angel of Jehovah gave him detailed directions how Israel was to compass Jericho, under the leadership of the Ark of the Lord, and how, when the wall of the city had fallen, the people were to act. Implicit obedience

---

[1] This is the correct rendering of Josh. v. 14; that in our Authorised Version does not fully express the pictorial import of the original.

[2] For an explanation of the meaning of this symbol, see *The Exodus, etc.*

of what in its nature was symbolical, was absolutely requisite, and Joshua communicated the command of the Lord both to priests and people.

And now a marvellous sight would be witnessed from the walls of Jericho. Day by day, a solemn procession left the camp of Israel. First came lightly armed men,[1] then followed seven priests blowing continually, not the customary silver trumpets, but large horns, the loud sound of which penetrated to the far distance, such as had been heard at Sinai (Ex. xix. 16, 19; xx. 18). The same kind of horns were to be used on the first day of the seventh month (Lev. xxiii. 24), and to announce the year of Jubilee (Lev. xxv. 9). Thus heralded, came the Ark of Jehovah, borne by the priests, and after it "the rereward" of Israel. So they did for six days, each day once encompassing the walls of Jericho, but in solemn silence, save for the short sharp tones, or the long-drawn blasts of the priests' horns. The impression made by this long, solemn procession, which appeared and disappeared, and did its work, in solemn silence, only broken by the loud shrill notes of the horns, must have been peculiar. At length came the seventh day. Its work began earlier than on the others—"about the dawning of the day." In the same order as before, they encompassed the city, only now seven times. "And it came to pass at the seventh time, when the priests blew with the trumpets, Joshua said unto the people, Shout; for Jehovah hath given you the city." "And it came to pass, when the people heard the sound of the trumpet, and the people shouted with a great shout, that the wall fell down flat, so that the people went up into the city, every man straight before him, and they took the city." As for Jericho itself, Joshua had by Divine command declared it "*cherem*," or "devoted" to Jehovah

---

[1] Josh. vi. 9 implies that the host of Israel was divided into two parts: "the armed men" preceding, and "the rereward following the Ark." As the Hebrew "for armed men" is the same term as that in Josh. iv. 13 ("prepared for war"), it has been suggested by Rabbinical interpreters that "the armed men" consisted of Reuben, Gad, and the half tribe of Manasseh.

(Josh. vi. 17). In such cases, according to Lev. xxvii. 28, 29, no redemption was possible, but, as indicated in Deut. xiii. 16, alike the inhabitants and all the spoil of the city was to be destroyed, " only the silver, and the gold, and the vessels of brass and of iron" being reserved and " put into the treasury of the house of Jehovah" (Josh. vi. 24 ; comp. Numb. xxxi. 22, 23, 50–54). This was not the ordinary sentence against *all* the cities of Canaan. In all other cases the inhabitants alone were " smitten with the edge of the sword" (Josh. viii. 26 ; x. 28 ; comp. Deut. ii. 34 ; iii. 6 ; viii. 2 ; xx. 16), while the cattle and the spoil were preserved. But in the case of Jericho, for reasons to be afterwards stated, the whole city, with *all* that it contained, was *cherem.* Only Rahab, "and her father's household, and all that she had," were saved from the general wreck.

It lies on the surface of the Scriptural narrative that " a notable miracle," unparalleled in history, had in this case been "wrought" by Jehovah for Israel. As a German writer puts it : It would have been impossible to show it more clearly, that Jehovah had *given* the city to Israel. First, the river was made to recede, to allow them entrance into the land ; and now the walls of the city were made to fall, to give them admission to its first and strongest city. Now such proofs of the presence and help of Jehovah, so soon after Moses' death, must have convinced the most carnal among Israel, that the same God who had cleft the Red Sea before their fathers was still on their side. And in this light must the event also have been viewed by the people of Canaan. But, besides, a deeper symbolical meaning attached to all that had happened. The first and strongest fortress in the land Jehovah God bestowed upon His people, so to speak, as a free gift, without their having to make any effort, or to run any risk in taking it. A precious pledge this of the ease with which all His gracious promises were to be fulfilled. Similarly, the manner in which Israel obtained possession of Jericho was deeply significant. Evidently, the walls of Jericho fell, not before Israel, but before the Ark of Jehovah, or rather, as it is expressly said in Josh. vi. 8, before Jehovah Himself, whose presence among His people was connected with the Ark of the Covenant. And the blast of those jubilee-horns all around the doomed city made proclamation of Jehovah, and was, so to speak, the summons of His kingdom, proclaiming that the labour and sorrow of His people were at an end, and they about to enter upon their inheritance. This was the symbolical and typical import of the blasts of the jubilee-horns, whenever they were blown. Hence also alike in the visions of the prophets and in the New Testament the final advent of the kingdom of God is heralded by the trumpet-sound of His angelic messengers (comp. 1 Cor. xv. 52 ; 1 Thess. iv. 16 ; Rev. xx. and xxi.). But, on the other hand, the advent of the kingdom of God always implies destruction to His enemies. Accordingly, the walls of Jericho must fall, and all the city be destroyed. Nor will the reader of this history fail here also to notice the significance of the number *seven*—seven horns, seven priests, seven days of compassing the walls, repeated seven times on the seventh day ! The *suddenness* of the ruin of Jericho, which typified the kingdom of this world in its opposition to that of God, has also its counterpart at the end of the present dispensation. For "the day of the Lord cometh as a thief in the night ; and when they shall say, Peace and safety, then sudden destruction cometh upon them, as travail upon a woman with child ; and they shall not escape."

Lastly, it was fitting that Jericho should have been *entirely* devoted unto the Lord ; not only that Israel might gain no immediate spoil by what the Lord had done, but also because the city, as the firstfruits of the conquest of the land, belonged unto Jehovah, just as all the first, both in His people and in all that was theirs, was His—in token that the whole was really God's property, Who gave everything to His people, and at Whose hands they held their possessions. But, to indicate the state of heart and mind with which Israel compassed the city, following the Ark in solemn silence, we recall this emphatic testimony of Scripture (Heb. xi. 30): "By faith the walls of Jericho fell down, after they were compassed about seven days." In this instance also, as just before the Lord cleft the Red Sea, and again afterwards, when in answer to Jehoshaphat's prayer God destroyed the heathen combination against His people, the Divine call to them was, "Stand ye still" (in expectant faith) "and see the salvation of Jehovah" (Ex. xiv. 13, 2 Chron. xx. 17). And so it ever is to His believing people in similar circumstances.

CHAPTER VIII.

Unsuccessful Attack upon Ai—Achan's Sin, and Judgment—Ai attacked a second time and taken.

(JOSH. VII.–VIII. 29.)

THE conquest of Jericho without fight on the part of Israel had given them full pledge of future success. But, on the other hand, also, might it become a source of greatest danger, if the gracious promises of God were regarded as national rights, and the presence of Jehovah as secured, irrespective of the bearing of Israel towards Him. It was therefore of the utmost importance, that from the first it should appear that victory over the enemy was Israel's only so long as the people were faithful to the covenant of their God.

In their progress towards the interior of the land, the fortress next to be taken was *Ai*. Broken up as the country seems to have been into small territories, each under an independent chieftain or "king," who reigned in his fortified city and held sway over the district around,[1] a series of sieges rather than of pitched battles was to be expected. *Ai*, situated on a

---

[1] In Josh. xii. 7–24, no less than thirty-one such "kings" are enumerated, as vanquished by Joshua. And it must be remembered that their territories did not by any means cover the whole of Palestine west of the Jordan.

conical hill about ten miles to the west of Jericho, was a com
paratively smaller city, numbering only 12,000 inhabitants
(Josh. viii. 25). Yet its position was exceedingly important.
Southwards it opened the road to Jerusalem, which is only a
few hours distant ; northwards it commanded access to the heart
of the country, so that, as we find in the sequel, a victorious
army could march thence unopposed into the fertile district of
Samaria. Moreover, the fate of Ai virtually decided also that
of Bethel. The latter city, ruled by another independent
"king," [1] lay to the west of Ai, being separated from it by a high
intervening hill. This hill, about midway between Bethel and
Ai, possessed special interest. It was the site of Abram's altar,
when he first entered the land (Gen. xii. 8). Here also had
the patriarch stood with Lot, overlooking in the near distance
the rich luxuriance of the Jordan valley, when Lot made his
fatal choice of residence (Gen. xiii. 4, 10). Standing on this
hill, a valley is seen to stretch westward to Bethel, while
eastward, around Ai, "the wadys which at first break down
steeply . . . descend gradually for about three quarters of a
mile, before taking their final plunge to the Jordan valley.
The gently sloping ground is well studded with olive trees."[2]
This rapid sketch of the locality will help us to realise the
events about to be recorded.

The advance now to be made by Israel was so important,
that Joshua deemed it a proper precaution to send "men to
view Ai." Their report satisfied him that only an army-corps
of about 3000 men was requisite to take that city. But the

---

[1] Josh. xii. 16. From the position of the king of Bethel in the list of
vanquished " kings," we are led to infer that Bethel was taken somewhat
later than Ai. But, from Josh. viii. 17, we learn that there was a league
between the two cities. Their armies must have either moved in accord,
or have been at the disposal of the king of Ai. In either case the men of
Bethel may have made their way back to their own city when Israel
turned against Ai.

[2] We are here indebted to a very interesting paper by Canon Williams,
read before the Church Congress at Dublin in 1868, and to Capt. Wilson's
Notes upon it.

expedition proved far from successful. The men of Ai issued from the city, and routed Israel, killing thirty-six men, pursuing the fugitives as far as "Shebarim" ("mines," or perhaps "quarries" where stones are broken), and smiting them "in the going down," that is, to about a mile's distance, where the wadys, descending from Ai, take "their final plunge" eastwards. Viewed in any light, the event was terribly ominous. It had been Israel's first fight west of the Jordan— and their first defeat. The immediate danger likely to accrue was a combination of all their enemies round about, and the utter destruction of a host which had become dispirited. But there was even a more serious aspect than this. Had God's pledged promises now failed? or, if this could not even for a moment be entertained, had the Lord given up His gracious purpose, His covenant with Israel, and the manifestation of His "Name" among all nations, connected therewith?[1] Feelings like these found expression in Joshua's appeal to God, when, with rent clothes and ashes upon their heads, he and the elders of Israel lay the livelong day, in humiliation and prayer, before the Lord, while in the camp "the hearts of the people" had "melted and became as water." We require to keep in view this contrast between the impotent terror of the people and the praying attitude of their leaders, to realise the circumstances of the case; the perplexity, the anxiety, and the difficulties of Joshua, before we judge of the language which he used. It fell indeed far short of the calm confidence of a Moses; yet, in its inquiry into the reason of God's dealings, which were acknowledged, faith, so to speak, wrestled with doubt (Josh. vii. 7), while rising fear was confronted by trust in God's promises (ver. 9). Best of all, the inward contest found expression in prayer. It was therefore, after all, a contest of faith, and faith is "the victory over the world."

Strange, that amidst this universal agitation, one should have remained unmoved, who, all the time, knew that he was the cause of Israel's disaster and of the mourning around. Yet his

[1] See the remarks on Ex. vi. 3 in *The Exodus*, etc.

conscience must have told him that, so long as it remained, the curse of his sin would follow his brethren, and smite them with impotence. It is this hardness of impenitence—itself the consequence of sin—which, when properly considered, vindicates, or rather demonstrates, the rightness of the Divine sentence afterwards executed upon Achan.[1] His sin was of no ordinary character. It had not only been a violation of God's express command, but daring sacrilege and profanation. And this under circumstances of the most aggravated character. Besides, Joshua had, just before the fall of Jericho, warned the people of the danger to themselves and to all Israel of taking "of the accursed thing" (Josh. vi. 18). So emphatic had been the ban pronounced upon the doomed city, that it was extended to all time, and even over the whole family of any who should presume to restore Jericho as a fortress (vi. 26).[2] And, in face of all this, Achan had allowed himself to be tempted! He had yielded to the lowest passion. One of those Babylonish garments, curiously woven with figures and pictures (such as classical writers describe), a massive golden ornament, in the shape of a tongue, and a sum of silver, amounting to about 25*l.* in a city the walls of which had just miraculously fallen before the Lord, had induced him to commit this daring sin! More than that, when it had come

---

[1] The Divine sentence needs no justification. Achan's was a sin which involved its peculiar punishment. But, as in the case of Esau, his history showed the fitness of the Divine sentence which debarred him of the "inheritance" of the promise, so was it also in the case of Achan. In studying the history of *events* we are too apt to overlook that of *persons* and *characters*.

[2] It is a common mistake to suppose that Jericho was never to be rebuilt. This evidently could not have been the meaning of Joshua, as among other cities he assigned Jericho to the tribe of Benjamin (Josh. xviii. 21). Similarly, we read of "the city of palm-trees" in Judges iii. 13, and by its own name in 2 Sam. x. 5. The ban of Joshua referred not to the rebuilding of Jericho, but to *its restoration as a fortified city*. This also appears from the terms used by Joshua ("set up the gates of it," Josh. vi. 26), and again reiterated when the threatened judgment afterwards came upon the family of Hiel (1 Kings xvi. 34).

true, as Joshua predicted (vi. 18), that such theft would "make the camp of Israel a curse, and trouble it," Achan had still persisted in his sin.

It will be remembered that, forty years before, at the brink of the Red Sea, "the Lord said unto Moses: Wherefore criest thou unto Me? speak unto the children of Israel, that they go forward!" (Ex. xiv. 15). As then, so now, when Joshua and the elders of Israel lay on their faces before the Lord, not prayer, but action was required. In the one case it was not exercise of faith to pray where *obedience* was called for ; nor yet, in the other, had prayer any meaning, nor could it expect an answer, while sin remained unremoved. And so it ever is. The cause of Israel's disaster lay, not in want of faithfulness on the part of the Lord, but on that of Israel. Their sin must now be searched out, and "the accursed" be "destroyed from among them." For, although the sin of Achan was that of an individual, it involved all Israel in its guilt. The sinner was of Israel, and his sin was in Israel's camp. It is needless here to discuss the question, how one guilty of sin should involve in its consequences those connected with him, whether by family or social ties. It is simply a *fact*, admitting no discussion, and is equally witnessed when God's law in nature, and when His moral law is set at defiance. The deepest reason of it lies, indeed, in this, that the God of nature and of grace is also the founder of society; for, the family and society are not of man's devising, but of God's institution, and form part of His general plan. Accordingly, God deals with us not merely as individuals, but also as families and as nations. To question the rightness of this would be to question alike the administration, the fundamental principles, and the plan of God's universe. But there is reason for devout thankfulness, that we can, and do recognise the presence of God in both nature and in history. The highest instance of the application of this law, is that which has rendered our salvation possible. For just as we had sinned and destroyed ourselves through our connection with the first Adam, so are we saved

through the second Adam—the Lord from heaven, Who has
become our Substitute, that in Him we might receive the
adoption of children.

The tidings, that the sin of one of their number had involved
Israel in judgment, must have rapidly spread through the
camp of Israel.   But even this knowledge and the summons to
sanctify themselves, that on the morrow the transgressor might
be designated by the Lord, did not move Achan to repentance
and confession.   And now all Israel were gathered before the
Lord.   First approached the princes of the twelve tribes.
Each name of a tribe had been written separately,[1] when " the
lot " that " came up," or was drawn, bore the name of Judah.
Thus singled out, the heads of the various clans of Judah
next presented themselves, when the lot designated that of
Zarhi.   And still the solemn trial went on, with increasing
solemnity, as the circle narrowed, when successively the
families of Zabdi, and finally, among them, the household of
Achan was singled out by the hand of God.   All this time
had Achan kept silence.   And now he stood alone before
God and Israel, that guilty one who had "troubled" all.
Would he at the last confess, and " give glory to Jehovah " by
owning Him as the God who seeth and knoweth all sin, however deeply hidden?   It was in the language of sorrow, not
of anger, that Joshua adjured him.   It wrung from Achan a
full admission of his crime.   How miserable the whole thing
must have sounded in his own ears, when he had put the facts
of his sin into naked words ; how paltry the price at which he
had sold himself, when it was brought into the broad sunlight
and "laid out before the Lord," in the sight of Joshua and of
all Israel.   One thing more only remained to be done.   They

---

[1] We infer that the guilty tribe, kindred, family, and individual household (being the four divisions according to which all Israel was arranged)
was designated by the *lot*, from the fact that the expression rendered
"*taken*" in Josh. vii. is exactly the same as that word in I Sam. x. 20, and
xiv. 41, 42.   Again, the expressions "the lot came up " (Josh. xviii. 11)
or " came forth " (xix. 1), seems to indicate that the lot was drawn—probably out of an urn—in the manner described in the text.

led forth the wretched man, with all his household, and all that belonged to them, and all Israel stoned him.[1] And then they burned the dead body,[2] and buried all beneath a heap of stones, alike as a memorial and a warning. But the valley they called that of "Achor," or *trouble*—while the echoes of that story sounded through Israel's history to latest times, in woe and in weal, for judgment and for hope (Is. lxv. 10; Hos. ii. 15).

The sin of Israel having been removed, God once more assured Joshua of His presence to give success to the undertaking against Ai. In pledge thereof He was even pleased to indicate the exact means which were to be used in reducing the city. A corps of 30,000 men was accordingly detailed, of whom 5000 were placed in ambush on the west side of Ai,[3] where, under shelter of the wood, their presence was concealed from Ai, and, by the intervening hill, from Bethel. While the main body of the Israelites under Joshua were to draw away the defenders of Ai by feigned flight, this corps was at a given signal to take the city, and after having set it on fire, to turn against the retreating men. Such was the plan of attack,

[1] Most commentators read Josh. vii. 24, 25, as implying that the sons and daughters of Achan were stoned with him, supposing that his family could not have been ignorant of their father's sin. Of the latter there is, however, no indication in the text. It will also be noticed that in ver. 25 the *singular* number is used : "All Israel stoned him ;" "and they raised over him a great heap of stones." In that case, the plural number which follows ("and burned them," etc.) would refer only to the oxen, asses, and sheep, and to all that Achan possessed.

[2] This was an aggravation of the ordinary punishment of death, Lev. xx. 14. We may here also explain that the expression "wrought folly in Israel" (Josh. vii. 15), refers to that which is opposed to the character and dignity of God's people, as in Gen. xxxiv. 7.

[3] Interpreters have found considerable difficulties in Josh. viii. 3, as compared with vers. 10–12, and accordingly suggested, that as the two letters ה and ל—the one indicating the number five, the other thirty—are very like each other, there may have been a mistake in copying ver. 3, where it should read 5000 instead of 30,000. But there really is no need for resorting to this theory, and I believe that the narrative, fairly read, conveys the meaning expressed by me in the text.

and it was closely adhered to. "The ambush" lay on the west of Ai, while the main body of the host pitched north of the city, a valley intervening between them and Ai. Next, Joshua moved into the middle of that valley. Early the following morning the king of Ai discovered this advance of the Israel-itish camp, and moved with his army to the "appointed place,"[1] right in front of "the plain," which, as we know from the description of travellers, was covered by olive trees. The battlefield was well chosen, since Ai occupied the vantage-ground on the slope, while an advance by Israel would be checked and broken by the olive plantation which they would have to traverse. Joshua and all Israel now feigned a retreat, and fled in an easterly direction towards the wilderness. Upon this, all the people that were in Ai, in their eager haste to make the victory decisive, "allowed themselves to be called away"[2] to pursue after Israel, till they were drawn a considerable distance from the city. The olive plantation now afforded those who had lain in ambush shelter for their advance. The precon-certed signal was given. Joshua, who probably occupied a height apart, watching the fight, lifted his spear. As the out-posts of the ambush saw it, and reported that the signal for their advance had been given, a rush would be made up the steep sides of the hill towards the city. But the signal would also be perceived and understood by the main army of Israel, and they now anxiously watched the result of movements which they could not follow. They had not long to wait. Above the dark green olive trees, above the rising slopes, above the white walls, curled slowly in the clear morning air the smoke of the burning city. Something in the attitude and movements of Israel must have betrayed it, for "the men of Ai looked behind them," only to see that all was lost, and no means of escape left them. And now the host of Israel "turned again," while those who had

[1] Not "time," as in our Authorised Version, which would give no meaning.

[2] This is the real meaning of the form of the Hebrew verb, and makes the narrative most pictorial.

set Ai on fire advanced in an opposite direction. Between these two forces the men of Ai were literally crushed. Not one of them escaped from that bloody plain and slope. The slaughter extended to the district around. Finally, the king of Ai was put to death, and his dead body " hanged upon a tree till eventide." [1] But of what had been Ai " they made a *Tel* (or heap) for ever." Never was Scripture saying more literally fulfilled than this. For a long time did modern explorers in vain seek for the site of Ai, where they knew it must have stood. " The inhabitants of the neighbouring villages," writes Canon Williams, to whom the merit of the identification really belongs, " declared repeatedly and emphatically that this was *Tel*, and nothing else. I was satisfied that it should be so when, on subsequent reference to the original text of Josh. viii. 28, I found it written, that ' Joshua burnt Ai, and made it a *Tel* for ever, even a desolation unto this day !' There are many *Tels* in modern Palestine, that land of *Tels*, each *Tel* with some other name attached to it to mark the former site. But the site of Ai has no other name ' unto this day.' It is simply *et-Tel—the heap* ' par excellence.' "

---

[1] It does not appear that "hanging" was one of the modes of execution under the Mosaic Law. From Deut. xxi. 22, we learn that in certain cases the criminal was put to death, and *after that* his dead body hung on a tree till eventide. This is fully confirmed by Josh. x. 26. The Rabbinical Law (Sanh. vii. 3 ; xi. 1) recognises strangulation, but not hanging, as a mode of execution in the lightest cases to which the punishment of death attached. Full details are given as to the manner in which the punishment was to be administered.

CHAPTER IX.

Solemn Dedication of the Land and of Israel on Mounts Ebal and Gerizim—The Deceit of the Gibeonites.

(JOSH. VIII. 30, IX.)

BY the miraculous fall of Jericho God had, so to speak, given to His people the key to the whole land; with the conquest of Ai they had themselves entered, in His strength, upon possession of it. The first and most obvious duty now was, to declare, by a grand national act, in what character Israel meant to hold what it had received of God. For, as previously explained, it could never have been the Divine object in all that had been, or would be done, merely to substitute one nation for another in the possession of Palestine; but rather to destroy the heathen, and to place in their room His own redeemed and sanctified people, so that on the ruins of the hostile kingdom of this world, His own might be established. To mark the significance of the act by which Israel was to declare this, it had before been prescribed by Moses as a first duty (Deut. xxvii. 2), and detailed directions given for it (Deut. xxvii.). The act itself was to consist of *three parts*. The law—that is, the commands, "statutes," and "rights," contained in the Pentateuch—was to be written on "great stones," previously covered with "plaster," in the manner in which inscriptions were made on the monuments of Egypt.[1] Then sacrifices were to be offered on an altar of "whole stones." The memorial stones were to be set up, and

---

[1] In the drier climate of Palestine such inscriptions would of course last much longer than in our own country. Still, they could not have been so durable as if *graven* on these stones. May it not be, that this "profession" was intended for that, rather than for all future generations? For, though

the sacrifices offered on Mount Ebal. But the third was to be the most solemn part of the service. The priests[1] with the Ark were to occupy the intermediate valley, and six of the tribes (Simeon, Levi, Judah, Issachar, Joseph, and Benjamin)—those which had sprung from the lawful wives of Israel—were to stand on Mount Gerizim, while the other six (of whom five had sprung from Leah's and Rachel's maids, Reuben being added to them on account of his great sin, Gen. xlix. 4) were placed on Mount Ebal. Then, as the priests in the valley beneath read the words of blessing, the tribes on Mount Gerizim were to respond by an *Amen;* and as they read the words of the curses, those on Mount Ebal were similarly to give their solemn assent —thus expressly taking upon themselves each obligation, with its blessing in the observance, and its curse in the breach thereof. An historical parallel here immediately recurs to our minds. As, on his first entrance into Canaan, Abraham had formally owned Jehovah by rearing an altar unto Him (Gen. xii. 7), and as Jacob had, on his return, paid the vow which he had recorded at Bethel (Gen. xxxv. 7), so Israel now consecrated its possession of the land by receiving it as from the Lord, by recording His name, and by taking upon itself all the obligations of the covenant.

A glance at the map will enable us to realise the scene. From Ai and Bethel the direct route northwards leads by Shiloh to Shechem (Judges xxi. 19). The journey would occupy altogether about eleven hours. Of course, Israel could not have realised at the time that they were just then travelling along what would become the great highway from Galilee to Jerusalem, so memorable in after-history. Leaving the sanctuary of Shiloh a little aside, they would climb a rocky ridge. Before them a noble prospect spread. This was the

---

it was indeed binding upon all succeeding generations—as the record of the transaction in Scripture shows—yet each generation must take up for itself the profession to be the Lord's.

[1] That this devolved not upon the Levites generally, but specially upon the priests, appears from Josh. viii. 33.

future rich portion of Ephraim : valleys covered with corn, hills terraced to their tops, the slopes covered with vines and olive-yards. Onwards the host moved, till it reached a valley, bounded south and north by mountains, which run from west to east. This was the exact spot on which Abram had built his first altar (Gen. xii. 7) ; here, also, had Jacob's first settlement been (Gen. xxxiii. 19). Not a foe molested Israel on their march right up the middle of the land, partly, as previously explained, from the division of the land under so many petty chieftains, but chiefly because God had a favour unto them and to the work to which they had set their hands. Travellers speak in rapturous terms of the beauty of the valley of Shechem, even in the present desolateness of the country. It is a pass which intersects the mountain-chain, that runs through Palestine from south to north. To the south it is bounded by the range of Gerizim, to the north by that of Ebal. From where the priests with the Ark took up their position on the gentle rise of the valley, both Gerizim and Ebal appear hollowed out, forming, as it were, an amphitheatre,[1] while "the limestone strata, running up in a succession of ledges to the top of the hills, have all the appearance of benches." Here, occupying every available inch of ground, were crowded the tribes of Israel : men, women, and children, "as well the strangers, and he that was born among them." As they stood close together, the humblest in Israel by the side of the "officers," "elders," and "judges," all eagerly watching what passed in the valley, or solemnly responding to blessing or curse, a scene was enacted, the like of which had not before been witnessed upon earth, and which could never fade from the memory.[2]

[1] This peculiarity was noticed by Canon Williams, and also specially referred to by Capt. Wilson, R.E., from whom the quotation within inverted commas is made.

[2] *All* travellers are agreed on two points : 1. That there could be no difficulty whatever in distinctly hearing both from Ebal and Gerizim anything that was spoken in the valley. 2. That these two mountains afforded sufficient standing-ground for all Israel. We note these two points in answer to possible objections. Happily in the present instance we have

It is noteworthy that, on Mount Ebal, whence came the
responses to the curses, the great stones were set up on which
" the law" was written, and that there also the sacrifices were
offered. This is in itself characteristic. Perhaps even the
circumstance is not without significance, that they who stood
on Mount Ebal must have had their view *bounded* by the
mountains of Benjamin. Not so they who occupied Gerizim,
the mount whence came the responses to the blessings. For
the view which greeted those who at early morn crowded
the top of the Mount of Blessings, was only second to that
vouchsafed to Moses from the summit of Pisgah. If less in
extent than the latter, it was more distinct and detailed.[1] All
Central Palestine lay spread like a map before the wondering gaze of Israel. Tabor, Gilboa, the hills of Galilee rose in
succession; in the far-distance snow-capped Hermon bounded
the horizon, with sweet valleys and rich fields intervening.
Turning to the right, they would descry the Lake of Galilee, and
follow the cleft of the Jordan valley, marking beyond it Bashan,
Ajalon, Gilead, and even Moab; to their left, the Mediterranean
from Carmel to Gaza was full in view, the blue outline far
away dimly suggesting thoughts of the "isles of the Gentiles,"
and the blessings in store for them. Far as the eye could
reach—and beyond it, to the uttermost bounds of the earth—
would the scene which they witnessed in that valley below be
repeated; the echo of the blessings to which they responded
on that mount would resound, till, having wakened every
valley, it would finally be sent back in songs of praise and
thanksgiving from a redeemed earth. And so did Israel on
that spring morning consecrate Palestine unto the LORD,
taking sea and lake, mountain and valley—the most hallowed
spots in their history—as witnesses of their covenant.

From this solemn transaction the Israelites moved, as we

express and independent testimony to put such cavils out of court. According to Dr. Thomson (*The Land and the Book*, i. p. 203), the valley is about
sixty rods wide.

[1] Comp. Canon Tristram's *Land of Israel*, p. 153.

gather from Josh. ix. 6, to Gilgal, where they seem to have formed a permanent camp. The mention of this place in Deut. xi. 30, where it is described as " beside the oaks of Moreh,"[1] that is, near the spot of Abram's first altar (Gen. xii. 7), implies a locality well-known at the time, and, as we might almost conjecture from its after history, a sort of traditional sanctuary. This alone would suffice to distinguish this Gilgal from the first encampment of Israel east of Jericho, which only obtained its name from the event which there occurred. Besides, it is impossible to suppose that Joshua marched back from Shechem to the banks of Jordan (ix. 6; x. 6, 7, 9, 15, 43), and, again, that he did so a second time, after the battles in Galilee, to make apportionment of the land among the people by the banks of Jordan (xiv. 6). Further, the localisation of Gilgal near the banks of Jordan would be entirely incompatible with what we know of the after-history of that place. Gilgal was one of the three cities where Samuel judged the people (1 Sam. vii. 16); here, also, he offered sacrifices, when the Ark was no longer in the tabernacle at Shiloh (1 Sam. x. 8; xiii. 7-9; xv. 21); and there, as in a central sanctuary, did all Israel gather to renew their allegiance to Saul (1 Sam. xi. 14). Later on, Gilgal was the great scene of Elisha's ministry (2 Kings ii. 1), and still later it became a centre of idolatrous worship (Hos. iv. 15; ix. 15; xii. 11; Amos iv. 4; v. 5). All these considerations lead to the conclusion, that the Gilgal which formed the site of Joshua's encampment is the modern *Jiljilieh*, a few miles from Shiloh, and about the same distance from Bethel—nearly equi-distant from Shechem and from Jerusalem.[2]

In this camp at Gilgal a strange deputation soon arrived. Professedly, and apparently, the travellers had come a long distance. For their garments were worn, their sandals clouted, their provisions dry and mouldy,[3] and the skins in which their

---

[1] This is the correct rendering.
[2] Comp. Robinson's *Biblical Researches*, vol. ii. p. 243.
[3] Literally, "dotted over."

wine had been were rent and "bound up" (like purses), as in the East wine-bottles of goat's skin are temporarily repaired on a long journey. According to their own account, they lived far beyond the boundaries of Palestine, where their fellow-townsmen had heard what the Lord had done in Egypt, and again to Sihon and to Og, wisely omitting from the catalogue the miraculous passage of Jordan and the fall of Jericho, as of too recent date for their theory. Attracted by the name of Jehovah, Israel's God, who had done such wonders, they had been sent to make "a league" with Israel. It must have been felt that the story did not sound probable—at least, to any who had learned to realise the essential enmity of heathenism against the kingdom of God, and who understood that so great a change as the report of these men implied could not be brought about by "the hearing of the ear." Besides, what they proposed was not to make submission to, but a league with, Israel; by which not merely life, but their land and liberty, would be secured to them.[1] But against any *league* with the inhabitants of Canaan, Israel had been specially warned (Ex. xxiii. 32; xxxiv. 12; Numb. xxxiii. 55; Deut. vii. 2). What if, after all, they were neighbours? The suspicion seems to have crossed the minds of Joshua and of the elders, and even to have been expressed by them, only to be set aside by the protestations of the pretended ambassadors. It was certainly a mark of religious superficiality and self-confidence on the part of the elders of Israel to have consented on such grounds to "a league." The sacred text significantly puts it : "And the men (the elders of Israel) took of their victuals (according to the common Eastern fashion of eating bread and salt with a guest who is received as a friend), but they asked not counsel at the mouth of Jehovah."

Their mistake soon became apparent. Three days later, and Israel found that the pretended foreigners were in reality neighbours! Meanwhile, the kings or chieftains who ruled in Western Palestine had been concerting against Israel a

[1] In Josh. ix. 15, we read indeed : "Joshua . . . made a league with them, to let them live."

combined movement of their forces from " the hills," or high-lands of Central Palestine, from " the valleys," or the *Shephelah* (low country), between the mountain-chain and the sea, and " from the coasts of the great sea over against Lebanon," that is, from Joppa northwards by the sea-shore. The existence of the small confederate republic of Gibeon with its three associate cities in the midst of small monarchies throws a curious light upon the state of Palestine at the time ; and the jealousy which would naturally exist between them helps to explain alike the policy of the Gibeonites, and the revenge which the Canaanitish kings were shortly afterwards preparing to take. The history of the republic of Gibeon is interesting. " Gibeon was a great city, as one of the royal cities . . . . greater than Ai, and all the men thereof were mighty" (Josh. x. 2). Its inhabitants were " Hivites" (xi. 19). Afterwards Gibeon fell to the lot of Ben-jamin, and became a priest-city (xviii. 25 ; xxi. 17). When Nob was destroyed by Saul, the tabernacle was transported to Gibeon, where it remained till the temple was built by Solomon (1 Chron. xvi. 39 ; xxi. 29 ; 1 Kings iii. 4 ; 2 Chron. i. 3).[1] It lay about two hours to the north-west of Jerusalem, and is represented by the modern village of *el-Jib.* Its three associate towns were *Chephirah*, about three hours' west from Gibeon, the modern *Kefir ; Beeroth*, about ten miles north of Jerusalem, the modern *el-Bireh*—both cities afterwards within the possession of Benjamin ; and *Kirjath-Jearim*, " the city of groves," probably

---

[1] The following historical notice in the *Mishnah* is so interesting, that we give its translation : "When they went to Gilgal, high places were allowed (for ordinary worship) ; the most holy offerings were eaten ' within,' between the veils ; the less holy ones in every place. When they went to Shiloh, the high places were forbidden. There were not there beams (for the house of God), but a building of stones below (a kind of foundation) and the curtains (tabernacle) above, and that was (in Scripture-language) ' rest.' Then the most holy offerings were eaten ' within,' between the veils, and the less holy and the second tithe anywhere within sight (of Shiloh). When they went to Nob and to Gibeon, high places were allowed. Then the most holy offerings were eaten ' within,' between the veils, and the less holy ones in all the cities of Israel" (Sevachim xiv. 5, 6, 7).

so called from its olive, fig, and other plantations, as its modern representative, *Kuriet-el-Enab*, is from its vineyards. The latter city, which was afterwards allotted to Judah, is about three hours from Jerusalem; and there the Ark remained from the time of its return from the Philistines to that of David (1 Sam. vii. 2 ; 2 Sam. vi. 2 ; 1 Chron. xiii. 5, 6).

When the people learned the deceit practised upon them, they "murmured against the princes;" but the latter refused to break their solemn oath, so far as it insured the lives and safety of the Gibeonites. If they had sworn rashly and presumptuously "by Jehovah, God of Israel," it would have only added another and a far more grievous sin to have broken their oath ; not to speak of the effect upon the heathen around. The principle applying to this, as to similar rash undertakings, is, that a solemn obligation, however incurred, must be considered binding, *unless its observance involve fresh sin.*[1] But in this instance it manifestly did *not* involve fresh sin. For the main reason of the destruction of the Canaanites was their essential hostility to the kingdom of God. The danger to Israel, accruing from this, could be avoided in a solitary instance. With a view to this, the Gibeonites were indeed spared, but attached as " bond-men " to the sanctuary, where they and their descendants performed all menial services [2] (Josh. ix. 23). Nor, as the event proved, did they ever betray their trust, or lead Israel into idolatry.[3] Still, as a German writer observes, the rashness of Israel's princes, and the conduct of the Gibeonites, conveys to the church at all times solemn warning against the devices and the deceit of the world, which, when outward advantage offers, seeks a friendly alliance with, or even reception into, the visible kingdom of God.

[1] As for example in the case of monastic vows.

[2] From the concluding words of Josh. ix. 27, it has been rightly inferred that the Book of Joshua must date from a period previous to the building of the temple by Solomon.

[3] From 2 Sam. xxi. 1, we gather that, in his carnal zeal, Saul had broken the oath of the princes—with what result appears from the narrative.

CHAPTER X.

The Battle of Gibeon—Conquest of the South of Canaan —The Battle of Merom—Conquest of the North of Canaan—State of the land at the close of the seven years' war

(JOSH. X.-XII.)

THE surrender of Gibeon would fill the kings of Southern Canaan with dismay. It was, so to speak, treason within their own camp; it gave Israel a strong position in the heart of the country and within easy reach of Jerusalem; while the possession of the passes leading from Gibeon would throw the whole south of Canaan open to their incursion. In the circumstances it was natural that the chieftains of the south would combine, in the first place, for the retaking of Gibeon. The confederacy, which was under the leadership of *Adoni-Zedek*,[1] king of Jerusalem,[2] embraced *Hoham*,[3] king of Hebron (about seven hours' south of Jerusalem); *Piram*,[4] king of Jarmuth, the present *Jarmuk*, about three hours' to the south-west of Jerusalem; *Japhia*,[5] king of Lachish, and *Debir*,[6] king of Eglon, both cities close to each other, and not far from Gaza, to the south-west of Hebron. The march of the combined kings was evidently rapid, and the danger pressing, for it seems to have found the Gibeonites wholly unprepared,

[1] The reader will notice the significant change from Melchi-Zedek, "My King righteousness," to Adoni-Zedek, "My Lord righteousness," marking the change of dynasties. See *History of the Patriarchs*, p. 86.

[2] Jerusalem, either the *habitation of peace*, or the *possession of peace*— perhaps originally the *habitation of Shalem*.

[3] *Hoham*: "the Jehovah of the multitude."

[4] *Piram*: "coursing about," wild and free.

[5] *Japhia*: exalted.   [6] *Debir*: scribe.

and their entreaty to Joshua for immediate succour was of the most urgent kind. That very night Joshua marched to their relief with "all the people of war, that is, the mighty men of valour."[1] The relieving army came upon the enemy as "suddenly" as they had appeared in sight of Gibeon. It was probably very early in the morning when Joshua and his warriors surprised the allied camp. Gibeon lay in the east, surrounded, as in a semicircle, north, west, and south, by its three confederate cities. The five kings had pushed forward within that semicircle, and camped in the "open ground at the foot of the heights of Gibeon." Animated by the assurance which God had expressly given Joshua: "Fear them not: for I have delivered them into thine hand; there shall not a man of them stand before thee," the host of Israel fell upon them with an irresistible rush. The Canaanites made but a short stand before their unexpected assailants; then fled in wild confusion towards the pass of Upper Beth-horon, "the house of caves." They gained the height before their pursuers, and were hurrying down the pass of the Nether Beth-horon, when a fearful hail-storm, such as not unfrequently sweeps over the hills of Palestine, burst upon them. It was in reality "the Lord" who, once more miraculously employing natural agency, "cast down great stones from heaven upon them;" "and they were more which died from the hailstones than they whom the children of Israel slew with the sword."[2] It was but noon; far behind Israel in the heaven stood the sun over Gibeon, and before them over Ajalon in the west hung the crescent moon. The tempest was extinguishing day and light, and the work was but half done. In the pass to Nether Beth-horon Israel might be readily divided; at any rate, the enemy might escape before their crushing defeat had assured safety to Gibeon, and given the south of Palestine to Israel. Now, or never, was the time

[1] We have so rendered the Hebrew particle "and" which is here used explanatively.
[2] A German writer has noticed that a similar hailstorm determined the battle of Solferino against the Austrians in 1859.

to pursue the advantage. Oh, that the sun would once more burst forth in his brightness ; oh, that the all too short day were protracted " until the people had avenged themselves upon their enemies !" Then it was that Joshua burst into that im-passioned prayer of faith, which is quoted in the sacred text from the " Book of Jasher,"—or " Book of the Pious,"—apparently, as we infer from 2 Sam. i. 18, a collection of poetical pieces, connected with the sublimest scenes in the history of the heroes of the kingdom of God. In this instance the quotation begins, as we take it, Josh. x. 12, and ends with ver. 15. This is proved by the insertion in ver. 15 of a notice, which in the historical narrative occurs only in ver. 43. For it is evident that Joshua did *not* return to Gilgal immediately after the battle of Gibeon (ver. 21), but pursued the war, as described in the rest of ch. x., till the whole south of Palestine was reduced. Thus verses 12–15 are a quotation from " the Book of the Pious," inserted within the Book of Joshua, the narrative of which is resumed in ver. 16. The quotation reads as follows :

"Then spake Joshua to Jehovah,
In the day Jehovah gave the Amorite before the sons of Israel,
And he spake in the sight of Israel
Sun, on Gibeon rest still,[1]
And moon, on the valley of Ajalon !
And still rested the sun,
And the moon stood,
Till the people were avenged on their foes.

(Is not this written in the ' Book of the Pious ?')

And the sun stood in mid-heaven,
And hasted not to go—like (as on) a complete day.[2]

---

[1] The word probably means "to become dumb." Accordingly, a recent Italian writer has regarded it as a poetical expression for "ceasing to shine," and treated the event as an eclipse of the sun. But the context shows that this view is untenable, and that "to become dumb" means here to rest silent or stand still.

[2] That is, like any ordinary complete day. We attach considerable im-portance to our rendering as here proposed.

And there was not like that day, before or after,
That Jehovah hearkened to the voice of man—
For Jehovah warred for Israel !

And Joshua returned, and all Israel with him to the camp, to Gilgal."[1]

And God hearkened to the voice of Joshua. Once more the sun burst forth, and the daylight was miraculously protracted till Israel was avenged of its enemies. Onwards rolled the tide of fugitives, hotly pursued by Israel, through the pass of Nether Beth-horon to Azekah, and thence to Makkedah.[2] Here tidings were brought to Joshua, that the five kings had hid themselves in one of the caves with which that district abounds. But Joshua would not be diverted from his object. He ordered large stones to be rolled to the mouth of the cave, and its entrance to be guarded by armed men, while the rest of the army followed the enemy and smote their " rearguard." Only broken remnants of the fugitives found shelter in the " fenced cities." Joshua himself had camped before the city of Makkedah. Thither the pursuing corps returned, and thence the war was afterwards carried on (x. 21, 29). On the morning after the victory, the five confederate kings were brought from their hiding-place. In a manner not uncommon in ancient times,[3] Joshua made his

[1] It is impossible here to enter on a detailed criticism. Substantially our view is that of all the best critics, except that some regard the five lines after the parenthesis as the remarks of him who inserted in the Book of Joshua the quotation from the Book of Jasher. But the poetical terms used in these five last lines render this view, to say the least of it, *most* improbable. Poetical expressions, similar to those used in the text, will recur to the reader, specially Judges v. 20 : " the stars fought out of their courses (not " *in* their courses," as in Authorised Version) against Sisera." See also Ps. xviii. 10 ; xxix. 6 ; cxiv. 4–6 ; Isa. xxxiv. 3 ; lv. 12 ; lxiv. 1 ; Amos ix. 13 ; Mic. i. 4. The passage Hab. iii. 11 does not refer to the event in the text, as its correct rendering is : " The sun and moon enter into their habitation," that is, go into shadow. Our view does not, of course, militate against a miraculous intervention on the part of God.

[2] The locality of these two places has not been ascertained.

[3] It seems even to have been practised by the Byzantine emperors long after the Christian era. See the reference given, *Bynaeus* in Kid's *Commentary*, p. 81.

captains put their feet upon the necks of the prostrate kings, who had so lately gone forth boastfully in all the pride and pomp of war. But the lesson which Israel was to learn from their victory was not one of self-confidence in their supposed superiority, but of acknowledgment of God and confidence in Him : " Fear not, nor be dismayed, be strong and of good courage : for thus shall Jehovah do to all your enemies against whom ye fight."

The death of these five kings proved only the beginning of a campaign which may have lasted weeks, or even months, for we find that successors of these five kings afterwards shared their fate. In the end, the whole south of Canaan was in the hands of Israel, though some of the cities taken appear to have been afterwards again wrested from them, and occupied by the Canaanites.[1] The extent of the conquest is indicated (x. 41) by a line drawn south and north, westwards—"from Kadesh-barnea even unto Gaza"—and eastwards, "from the district of Goshen[2] unto Gibeon."

The campaign thus finished in the south had soon to be renewed in the north of Canaan. The means, the help, and the result were the same as before. Only, as the danger was much greater, from the multitude of Israel's opponents—" even as the sand that is upon the sea-shore,"—and from their formidable mode of warfare ("horses and chariots very many"), hitherto unknown to Israel, the Lord once more gave express assurance of victory : " I will deliver them up all slain before Israel." At the same time He enjoined " to hough (or hamstring) their horses, and burn their chariots with fire," lest Israel should be tempted to place in future their trust in such weapons. The allied forces of the northern enemy were under

---

[1] Such as Gezer (x. 33), Hebron, and Debir (xiv. 12 ; xv. 13-17; comp. Judges i. 10-15). Masius rightly observes, that in this expedition Joshua had rather rapidly swept over the south of Palestine than permanently and wholly occupied the country.

[2] Of course not the province of that name in Egypt, but a district in the south of Judah, probably deriving its name from the town of that name (xv. 51).

the leadership of Jabin,[1] king of Hazor,[2] which " beforetimes was the head of all those kingdoms." They consisted not only of the three neighbouring " kings " (or chieftains) of Madon, Shimron, and Achshaph,[3] but of all the kings " in the north and (on the mountain " (of Naphtali, Josh. xx. 7), of those in the Arabah, south of the Lake of Gennesaret, of those " in the plains," or valleys that stretched to the Mediterranean, and in " the heights of Dor," at the foot of Mount Carmel—in short, of all the Canaanite tribes from the Mediterranean in the south-west up to Mizpeh[4] "the view") under Mount Hermon in the far north-east.

With the rapidity and suddenness which characterised all his movements, Joshua fell upon the allied camp by the Lake Merom (the modern *el-Huleh*), and utterly routed the ill-welded mass of the enemy. The fugitive Canaanites seem to have divided into three parts, one taking the road north-west to "Zidon the Great," another that west and south-west to the "smelting-pits by the waters" (Misrephoth-Maim), and the third that to the east leading to the valley of Mizpeh. In each direction they were hotly pursued by the Israelites. One by one all their cities were taken. Those in the valleys were burnt, but those on the heights, with the exception of Hazor, left standing, as requiring only small garrisons for their occupation. Altogether the war in the south and north must have occupied at least seven years,[5] at the end of which the whole country was

---

[1] *Jabin* seems to have been the title of the kings of Hazor (Judges iv. 2).

[2] Hazor in the mountains, north of Lake Merom, was afterwards rebuilt, and again became the seat of royalty (Judges iv. 2 ; 1 Sam. xii. 9). Thence Sisera issued against Israel.

[3] The locality of these three places has not been ascertained ; but they seem to have been in the neighbourhood of Hazor.

[4] There were several places throughout the land bearing the name of "Mizpeh" or "view." This Mizpeh was probably the modern village *Mutulleh*, which also means "prospect," situated on a hill two hundred feet high, north of Lake Merom, whence there is a splendid view.

[5] This we gather from Josh. xiv. 10. From it we learn that forty-five years had elapsed since the spies returned to Kadesh. But as thirty-eight of these were spent in the wanderings in the wilderness, it follows that the wars for the occupation of Canaan must have lasted seven years.

in the possession of Israel, from the "smooth mountain (Mount Halak) that goeth up to Seir,"—that is, the white chalk mountains in the chain of the Azazimeh, in the Negeb—as far north as " Baal-gad," the town dedicated to " Baal " as god of "fortune," the Cæsarea Philippi of the Gospels (xi. 16–18). More than that, Joshua also drove the Anakim, who had inspired the spies with such dread, from their original seats in the mountains,[1] and in and around Hebron, Debir, and Anab into the Philistine cities of Gaza, Gath, and Ashdod. From ch. xv. 14 we infer that they shortly afterwards returned, but were conquered by that veteran hero, Caleb.

To sum up all, we find that the wars under Joshua put Israel into possession of Canaan and broke the power of its inhabitants, but that the latter were not exterminated, nor yet all their cities taken by Israel (xiii. 1–6 ; xvii. 14, etc. ; xviii. 3 ; xxiii. 5, 12). Indeed, such a result could scarcely have been desirable, either in reference to the country or to Israel, while, from Ex. xxiii. 28–30 and Deut vii. 22, we know that from the beginning it had not been the Divine purpose. But there was also a higher object in this. It would teach that a conquest, begun in the power of God and in believing dependence on Him, must be completed and consolidated in the same spirit. Only thus could Israel prosper as a nation. Canaan had been given to Israel by God, and given to their faith. But much was left to be done which only the same faith could achieve.

---

[1] In Josh. xi. 21 a distinction is made between "the mountains of Judah " and "the mountains of Israel." This, strange as it may sound, affords one of the undesigned evidences of the early composition of the Book of Joshua. "When Judah entered on his possession," observes a German critic, " all the other tribes were still in Gilgal (xiv. 6 ; xv. 1). Afterwards, when Ephraim and Manasseh entered on theirs, all Israel, except Judah, were camped in Shiloh (xvi. 1 ; xviii. 1), these two possessions being separated by the still unallotted territory which later was given to Benjamin (xviii. 11). What more natural than that 'the mountain' given to the ' children of Judah' should have been called ' the mountain of Judah,' and that where all the rest of Israel camped, ' the mountain of Israel,' and also ' the mountain of Ephraim' (xix. 50; xx. 7), because it was afterwards given to that tribe ?"

Any conformity to the heathen around, or tolerance of heathenism, any decay of the spirit in which they had entered the land, would result not only in weakness, but in the triumph of the enemy. And so it was intended of the Lord. The lesson of all this is obvious and important. To us also has our Joshua given entrance into Canaan, and victory over our enemies—the world, the flesh, and the devil. We have *present* possession of the land. But we do not yet hold all its cities, nor are our enemies exterminated. It needs on our part constant faith ; there must be no compromise with the enemy, no tolerance of his spirit, no cessation of our warfare. Only that which at first gave us the land can complete and consolidate our possession of it.

CHAPTER XI.

Distribution of the land—Unconquered districts—Tribes east of the Jordan—"The lot"—Tribes west of the Jordan—The inheritance of Caleb—Dissatisfaction of the sons of Joseph—The Tabernacle at Shiloh—Final division of the land.

(JOSH. XIII.–XXI.)

THE continuance of unsubdued races and districts soon became a source of danger, although in a direction different from what might have been anticipated. Sufficient had been gained by a series of brilliant victories to render the general tenure of the land safe to Israel. The Canaanites and other races were driven to their fastnesses, where for the time they remained on the defensive. On the other hand, a nation like Israel, accustomed to the nomadic habits of the wilderness, would scarcely feel the need of a fixed tenure of land, and readily grow weary of a desultory warfare in which each tribe had separately to make good its boundaries. Thus it came that Joshua had grown old, probably ninety or a hundred years, while the work intrusted to him was far from completed. In the far south and along the sea-shore the whole district from the brook of Egypt[1] to Ekron was still held, in the south-west and south-east, by the Geshurites and the Avites, while the territory farther north from Ekron to Gaza was occupied by the five lords of the Philistines (Josh. xiii. 2, 3). According to the Divine direction, all these, though not descended from Canaan (Gen. x. 14), were to be "counted to the Canaanites," that is, treated as such. Travelling still farther northwards along the sea-shore, the whole "land of the Canaanites" or of the Phœnicians far up to the celebrated "cave"[2] near Sidon, and beyond it to Aphek[3] and even "to the borders of the Amorites"[4] was still unconquered. Thence eastward across Lebanon as far as Baal-gad and "the entering into Hamath,"[5] and again back from Mount Lebanon, across country, to the "smelting-pits on the waters," was subject to the Sidonians or Phœnicians.[6] Yet all this belonged by Divine gift to Israel. That it was still unoccupied by them, and that Joshua was now old, constituted the ground for the Divine command to make immediate distribution of the land among the tribes. It was as if, looking to His promise, God would have bidden Israel consider the whole land as theirs, and simply

[1] Literally : "from Shichor, in the face of Egypt," or rather "from the black (river) to the east of Egypt." This was the brook *Rhinocorura*, the modern *el-Arish*.

[2] Left untranslated (*Mearah*) in the Authorised Version. The cave, which is east of Sidon, still serves as a hiding-place to the Druses.

[3] The modern *Afkah*, on a terrace of Mount Lebanon, by the principal source of the river Adonis, in a lovely situation.

[4] The explanation of this is doubtful. Possibly it means : as far east as the territory of Og, king of Bashan, which formerly belonged to the Amorites.

[5] *Hamath*, a district in Syria, with a capital of the same name on the Orontes.

[6] The particle "*and,*" put in *italics* in our Authorised Version, is not in the text of Josh. xiii. 6. The clause, "all the Sidonians" is explanatory, not additional.

go forward, in faith of that promise and in obedience to His command.[1]

It will be remembered that only nine and a half tribes remained to be provided for, since " unto the tribe of Levi He gave none inheritance," other than what came from the sanctuary, while Reuben, Gad, and half Manasseh had had their portions assigned by Moses east of the Jordan.[2] That territory was bounded by Moab along the *south-eastern* shores of the Dead Sea, while the *eastern* border of Reuben and Gad was held by Ammon. Both these nations were by Divine command not to be molested by Israel (Deut. ii. 9, 19). The southernmost and smallest portion of the district east of the Jordan belonged to Reuben. His territory extended from the river Arnon, in the south, to where Jordan flowed into the Dead Sea, and embraced the original kingdom of Sihon. Northward of it, the Ammonites had once held possession, but had been driven out by Sihon. That new portion of Sihon's kingdom was given not to Reuben but to Gad. The territory of that tribe ran along the Jordan as far as the Lake of Gennesaret—the upper portion (from Mahanaim) narrowing almost into a point. North of this was the possession of the half tribe of Manasseh, which embraced the whole of Bashan. It occupied by far the largest extent of area. But from its position it also lay most open to constant nomadic incursions, and possessed comparatively few settled cities.

The division of the land among the nine and a half tribes[3] was, in strict accordance with Divine direction (Numb. xxvi. 52–56; xxxiii. 54; xxxiv. 2–29), made by Eleazar, Joshua, and one representative from each of the ten tribes. It was

---

[1] With the register of the defeated kings (Josh. xii.) the first part of the Book of Joshua ends, and Part II. begins with ch. xiii.

[2] Although geographical details may seem dry to some, they are most important for the proper understanding of the Bible narrative. They may also be made alike interesting and spiritually useful, if the history of these places is traced in the various passages of Scripture where they are mentioned.

[3] The children of Joseph were counted two tribes.

decided by the "lot," which probably, however, only determined the *situation* of each inheritance, whether north or south, inland or by the sea-shore, not its *extent* and precise boundaries. These would depend upon the size of each tribe. In point of fact, the original arrangements had in some cases to be afterwards modified, not as to tribal localisation, which was unalterably fixed by the Divine lot, but as to extent of territory. Thus Judah had to give up part of its possession to Simeon (Josh. xix. 9), while Dan, whose portion proved too small, obtained certain cities both from Judah and from Ephraim.[1] As regards the lot, we may probably accept the Rabbinical tradition, that two urns were set out, one containing the names of the ten (or rather nine and a half) tribes, the other the designation of the various districts into which the country had been arranged, and that from each a lot was successively drawn, to designate first the tribe, and then the locality of its inheritance.

This is not the place, however interesting the task, to

---

[1] In connection with this we may note the curious and undesigned evidence, that we have in the text the real and original allotment of the land by Joshua himself. As so often, it is derived from an objection suggested. For there are strange divergencies in the sacred text. In describing the lots of *Judah* and of *Benjamin, the boundaries are accurately marked,* and a *complete list of cities* is given ; in those of *Ephraim* and *half Manasseh* there is *no register of cities ;* in those of *Simeon* and *Dan* only lists of cities : in those of the other tribes evidently an incomplete tracing of boundaries and lists of cities. Now when we consider the history, we conclude that this is just what we would have expected in a contemporary document. Josh. xv. xvi. assigns a definite portion to Judah ; ch. xvii. to Ephraim and half Manasseh, about which, however, they complain as being partly occupied by Canaanites whom they dared not attack (ver. 16). Hence in their case there is no register of cities. On the other hand, the lot of Benjamin, being between Judah and Joseph (xviii. 11), was completely occupied, and the register is complete. The territories of Simeon and Dan have no boundary mark, only a register of cities, because they really formed part of the territories of Judah and Ephraim. Lastly, the defectiveness in the description of the other tribal lots arises from so much of the country being still in the hands of the Canaanites. It is evident that such a register could not have dated from a later period, when the tribes were in full possession, but must be the original register of Joshua.

describe the exact boundaries and cities of each tribe. We can only attempt the most general outline, which the reader must fill up for himself. Beginning in the far south, at Kadesh in the wilderness, and along the borders of Edom, we are within the territory of Simeon; north of it, bounded on the west by the land of the Philistines, and on the east by the Dead Sea, is the possession of Judah; beyond it, to the east, that of Benjamin, and to the west, that of Dan; north of Dan we reach Ephraim, and then Manasseh, the possession of Issachar running along the east of these two territories, and ending at the southern extremity of the Lake of Gennesaret; by the shore of that lake and far beyond it is the territory of Naphtali, first a narrow slip, then widening, and finally merging into a point. Asher occupied the seaboard, north of Manasseh; while, lastly, Zebulon is as it were wedged in between Issachar, Manasseh, Asher, and Naphtali.

It only remains briefly to notice the incidents recorded in connection with the territorial division of the land.

1. It seems that before the first lot was drawn in the camp at Gilgal, Caleb, the son of Jephunneh, came forward with a special claim. It will be remembered, that of the twelve princes sent from Kadesh only he and Joshua had brought "a good report of the land," in the spiritual sense of the expression, as encouraging the people to go forward. And when the Divine sentence doomed that rebellious generation to death in the wilderness, Caleb and Joshua alone were excepted. Strictly speaking, no more than this might have been implied in the promise by Moses, now claimed by Caleb: "Surely the land whereon thy feet have trodden shall be thine inheritance" (Josh. xiv. 9), since to have survived was to obtain the inheritance.[1] But there seems to have been more than merely a promise of survival, although it alone is mentioned in Numb. xiv. 24, 30. For we infer from the words and the attitude of

---

[1] Even these words (xiv. 12): "Now therefore give me this mountain, whereof Jehovah spake in that day;" do not necessarily imply that that 'mountain" was actually assigned to Caleb on "that day."

Caleb, and from the similar privileges afterwards accorded to Joshua (xix. 49, 50), that Moses had, by direction of the Lord, given these two a right of special and personal choice. This on account of their exceptional faithfulness, and as the sole survivors of the generation to whom the land had been given. It was as if the surviving proprietors might choose their portion,[1] before those who, so to speak, were only next of kin had theirs allotted to them. Of this Caleb now reminds Joshua, and in words of such vigorous faith, as make us love still better the tried old warrior of Jehovah. Appearing at the head of "the house of fathers," in Judah, of which he was the head,[2] he first refers to the past, then owns God's faithfulness in having preserved him to the age of eighty-five, with strength and courage undiminished for the holy war. From xiv. 9 we infer that, when the twelve spies distributed themselves singly over the land, for the purposes of their mission, Caleb specially "searched" that "mountain," which was the favourite haunt of the dreaded Anakim. If this be so, we discover a special meaning and special faith on the part of Caleb, when he, rather than Joshua, attempted to "still the people before Moses, and said, Let us go up at once" (Numb. xiii. 30). In that case there was also special suitableness in the Divine bestowal made then and there : "Surely the land whereon thy feet have trodden shall be thine inheritance" (Josh. xiv. 9, 12). But even if otherwise, the courage and faith of the old warrior shine only the more brightly,

[1] It is difficult to arrive at a certain conclusion, whether at Kadesh districts were actually assigned to Caleb and to Joshua, or to Caleb alone, or whether the choice of districts was accorded to both, or to one of them. The reader will infer our conclusion from the text.

[2] "Caleb, the son of Jephunneh the Kenazite," that is, a son of Kenaz, who was a descendant of Hezron, the son of Pharez, a grandson of Judah (1 Chron. ii. 5, 18). The name "Kenaz" seems to have been rather marked in the family, as it recurs again later, 1 Chron. iv. 15. Caleb was the chieftain or head of one of "the houses of fathers" in Judah, and to the presence of this his "house"—not of the whole tribe—refer the words (Josh. xiv. 6) : "Then the children of Judah came unto Joshua."

as, recalling the terror formerly inspired by the Anakim and the strength of their cities, he claims that very portion for his own. Yet his courage bears no trace of self-sufficiency,[1] only of believing dependence upon the Lord. "If so be Jehovah will be with me, and I shall drive them out" (ver. 12).

The claim thus made was immediately acknowledged, Joshua adding his blessing on Caleb's proposed undertaking. But it was some time later that the expedition was actually made,[2] when Caleb offered the hand of his daughter, Achsah, as the prize of taking the great stronghold of Debir, the ancient Kirjath-sepher, or "book-city,"—probably the fortified depository of the sacred books of the Anakim. The prize was won by a near kinsman, Othniel,[3] who, after the death of Joshua, was the first "judge" of Israel (Judges iii. 9). The history of the campaign, with its accompanying incidents, is inserted in Josh. xv. 13–19, because, both geographically and historically, it fits into that part of the description of the inheritance of Judah.[4]

2. The first signs of future weakness and disagreement appeared so early as when the lot designated the possession of the children of Joseph (Ephraim and half the tribe of Manasseh).

---

[1] In this sense the words must be understood (Josh. xiv. 7) : "I brought word again, as it was in mine heart," that is, according to my conscientious conviction. Similarly the expression (ver. 8) : "but I wholly followed the Lord," means, that his allegiance to the Lord was not shaken either by the evil report of the other spies, or by the murmuring and threatening of the people.

[2] It seems to have taken place after the death of Joshua, and is recorded in Judges i. 11, etc.

[3] It is not easy to decide whether Othniel was the son of Kenaz, who was a younger brother of Caleb, or whether he was himself Caleb's younger brother (Judges iii. 9). The punctuation of the Masorethists is in favour of the latter view, nor was the marriage of an uncle with his niece contrary to the Mosaic law.

[4] Two other critical remarks may here find a place. 1. Our present Hebrew text seems incomplete between Josh. xv. 59 and 60. Here the LXX. insert, no doubt from a more perfect MS., a list of other eleven cities, among them Bethlehem. 2. The closing notice of ver. 63 helps us to fix the date of the Book of Joshua.

Theirs was the richest and most fertile in the land, including
the plain of Sharon, capable of producing almost boundless
store, and of becoming the granary of the whole land. On that
ground then no complaint could be made. Nor could any
reasonable objection be taken to the size of their lot,[1] provided they were prepared to go forward in faith and occupy it
as against the Canaanites, who still held the principal towns
in the valley, all the way from Bethshean by the Jordan to
the plain of Jezreel and farther. But the children of Joseph
were apparently afraid of such encounter because of the iron
chariots of their enemies. Equally unwilling were they to
clear the wooded heights of Ephraim, which connect the range
north of Samaria with Mount Carmel, and where the Perizzites
and the Rephaim had their haunts. Rather did they clamour
for an additional "portion" (xvii. 14). Their demands were,
of course, refused; Joshua turning the boastful pride in which
they had been made into an argument for action on their
part against the common enemy (ver. 18).[2] But this murmuring
of the children of Joseph, and the spirit from which it proceeded, gave sad indications of dangers in the near future.
National disintegration, tribal jealousies, coupled with boastfulness and unwillingness to execute the work given them of
God, were only too surely foreboded in the conduct of the
children of Joseph.

3. If such troubles were to be averted, it was high time to
seek a revival of religion. With that object in view, "the
whole congregation of the children of Israel" were now

[1] Ephraim numbered 32,500 and half Manasseh 26,350 men capable of
bearing arms (Numb. xxvi. 34, 37), or, both together, 58,850, while Judah
numbered 76,500, and even Dan and Issachar respectively 64,400 and
64,300.

[2] The Authorised Version renders the last clause of ver. 18: "though
they have iron chariots, and though they be strong." The true rendering is
not "though," but "for." Most commentators regard this as an irony,
implying that it needed such strong tribes as the sons of Joseph! But I
regard it as rather a covert appeal to their faith—"just because it is so, ye
shall drive them out."

gathered at *Shiloh*, and the tabernacle set up there (xviii. 1). The choice of Shiloh was, no doubt, Divinely directed (Deut. xii. 11). It was specially suitable for the purpose, not only from its central situation—about eight hours' north of Jerusalem, and five south of Shechem—but from its name, which recalled *rest*[1] and the promised rest-giver (Gen. xlix. 10). Then Joshua solemnly admonished the assembled people as to their "slackness" in taking possession of the land which Jehovah had given them. To terminate further jealousies, he asked the people to choose three representatives from each of the seven tribes whose inheritance had not yet been allotted. These were to "go through the land and describe it," that is, to make a general estimate and valuation, rather than an accurate survey, "with reference to their inheritance,"[2] that is, in view of their inheriting the land. After their return to Shiloh these twenty-one delegates were to divide the land into seven portions, when the lot would assign to each tribe the place of its inheritance.

4. The arrangement thus made was fully carried out.[3] After its completion Joshua, who, like Caleb, had received a special promise, was allowed to choose his own city within his tribal inheritance of Ephraim.[4] Finally, the cities of refuge, six in number; the Levitical cities, thirty-five in number; and the thirteen cities of the priests,[5] the sons of Aaron, were formally set aside.

[1] *Shiloh* means rest.   [2] So literally.

[3] According to Josephus, it took seven months; according to the Rabbis, seven years. It need scarcely be said, that both suppositions are equally void of foundation. Josephus also imagines, that there was only one deputy from each tribe—or seven in all—to whom he adds three men expert in surveying (*Ant.* v. 1, 20, 21).

[4] Considering that Joshua was himself a descendant of Joseph, his reply to the complaints of his tribe show the more clearly his uprightness and fitness for his calling.

[5] Of the six cities of refuge three were west of the Jordan : *Kadesh* (Naphtali—north), *Shechem* (Ephraim—centre), and *Hebron* (Judah—south); three east of the Jordan : *Bezer* (Reuben—south), *Ramoth* (Gad—centre), and *Golan* (Manasseh—north). The number of cities assigned to the Levites

Thus, *so far as the Lord was concerned, He* " gave unto Israel all the land which He sware to give unto their fathers ; and they possessed it, and dwelt therein.   And Jehovah gave them rest round about, according to all that He sware unto their fathers : and there stood not a man of all their enemies before them ; Jehovah delivered all their enemies into their hand.   There failed not ought of any good thing Jehovah had spoken unto the house of Israel ; all came to pass " (Josh xxi. 43–45).

CHAPTER XII.

Return of the two and a half Tribes to their Homes—
Building of an Altar by them—Embassy to them—
Joshua's Farewell Addresses — Death of Joshua —
Review of his Life and Work.

(JOSH. XXII.–XXIV.)

YET another trial awaited Joshua, ere he put off the armour and laid him down to rest.   Happily, it was one which he rather dreaded than actually experienced.   The work given him to do was ended, and each of the tribes had entered on its God-given inheritance.   And now the time had come for those faithful men who so truly had discharged their undertaking to

---

(thirty-five) cannot be regarded as too large.   The second census gave the number of male Levites at 23,000.   This, with a proportionate number of females, has been calculated to give a population of about 1300 for each of the thirty-five towns.   Besides, it should be remembered, that *the Levites were not the sole inhabitants of such towns.*   This should also be taken into account in regard to the assignment of thirteen cities to the descendants of Aaron, although their number has been computed at the time at two hundred families.   Probably this is exaggerated, even admitting that as Aaron's two sons had 24 descendants (1 Chron. xxiv.), the next generation might have numbered 144 males, and the next again (at the time of Joshua) between 800 and 900 descendants.   But, irrespective of this, the law had to provide not for that period, but for all time to come.

recross Jordan, and " get unto to the land of their possession."
These many years had the men of Reuben, Gad, and Manasseh
fought and waited by the side of their brethren.   And now that
God had given them rest, Joshua dismissed the tried warriors
with a blessing, only bidding them fight in their own homes
that other warfare, in which victory meant loving the Lord,
walking in His ways, keeping His commandments, and cleaving
unto and serving Him.

It must have been with a heavy heart that Joshua saw them
depart from Shiloh.[1] It was not merely that to himself it
would seem like the beginning of the end, but that misgivings
and fears could not but crowd upon his mind.   They parted
from Shiloh to comparatively far distances, to be separated from
their brethren by Jordan, and scattered amid the wide tracts, in
which their nomadic pastoral life would bring them into frequent and dangerous contact with heathen neighbours.   They
were now united to their brethren ; they had fought by their
side; would this union continue ?   The very riches with which
they departed to their distant homes (xxii. 8) might become a
source of danger.   They had parted with Jehovah's blessing
and monition from the central sanctuary at Shiloh.   Would it
remain such to them, and they preserve the purity of their faith
at a distance from the tabernacle and its services?   Joshua
remembered only too well the past history of Israel; he knew
that even now idolatry, although publicly non-existent, had still
its roots and fibres in many a household as a sort of traditional
superstition (xxiv. 23).   Under such circumstances it was
that strange tidings reached Israel and Joshua.   Just before
crossing Jordan the two and a half tribes had built an altar
that could be seen far and wide, and then departed without
leaving any explanation of their conduct.   At first sight this
would have seemed in direct contravention of one of the

---

[1] From Josh. xxii. 9 we learn that they " departed out of Shiloh," hence
after the land had been finally apportioned among the tribes. Of course,
this does not imply that the *same* warriors had continued all through the
wars without changing.

first principles of Israel's worship. Place, time, and manner of it were all God-ordained and full of meaning, and any departure therefrom, even in the slightest particular, destroyed the meaning, and with it the value of all. More especially would this appear an infringement of the express commands against another altar and other worship (Lev. xvii. 8, 9; Deut. xii. 5–7), to which the terrible punishment of extermination attached (Deut. xiii. 12–18). And yet there was something so strange in rearing this altar on the *western* side of the Jordan,[1] and not on the eastern, and in their own possession, that their conduct, however blameworthy, might possibly bear another explanation than that of the great crime of apostasy.

It was an anxious time when the whole congregation gathered, by their representatives, at Shiloh, not to worship, but to consider the question of going to war with their own brethren and companions in arms, and on such grounds. Happily, before taking decided action, a deputation was sent to expostulate with the two and a half tribes. It consisted of ten princes, representatives, each of a tribe, and all " heads of houses of their fathers," though, of course, not the actual chiefs of their tribes. At their head was Phinehas, the presumptive successor to the high priesthood, to whose zeal, which had once stayed the plague of Peor, the direction might safely be left. We are not told how they gathered the representatives of the offending tribes, but the language in which, as recorded, the latter were addressed, is quite characteristic of Phinehas.

The conduct of the two and a half tribes had been self-willed and regardless of one of the first duties—that of not giving offence to the brethren, nor allowing their liberty to become a stumbling-block to others. For a doubtful good they had committed an undoubted offence, the more unwarranted,

---

[1] This we gather from xxii. 10: " And when they came to the circle (circuits) of Jordan, that is in the land of Canaan " (in contrast to " the land of Gilead "), ver. 9. Again in ver. 11: " built an altar in face (or, in front) of the land of Canaan (that is, at its extreme boundary, looking towards it), in the circuits of Jordan, by the side of (or, ' over against') the children of Israel."

that they had neither asked advice nor offered explanation. Phinehas could scarcely help assuming that they had "committed unfaithfulness towards the God of Israel."[1] He now urged upon them the remembrance, yet fresh in their minds, of the consequences of the sin of Peor, and which had, alas! still left its bitter roots among the people.[2] If, on account ot their uncleanness, they felt as if they needed nearer proximity to the altar, he invited them back to the western side of the Jordan, where the other tribes would make room for them. But if they persisted in their sin, he reminded them how the sin of the one individual, Achan, had brought wrath on all the congregation. If so, then the rest of Israel must take action, so as to clear themselves from complicity in their "rebellion."

In reply, the accused tribes protested, in language of the most earnest expostulation, that their conduct had been wholly misunderstood.[3] So far from wishing to separate from the tabernacle and worship of Jehovah, this great altar had been reared as a witness to all ages that they formed an integral part of Israel, lest in the future they might be debarred from the service of Jehovah. That, and that alone, had been their meaning, however ill expressed. The explanation thus offered was cause of deep thankfulness to the deputies and to all Israel. Thus, in the good providence of God, this cloud also passed away.

A twofold work had been intrusted to Joshua : to *conquer the land* (Josh. i. 8), and to *divide it by inheritance* among the

[1] So literally, and not, as in Authorised Version (xxii. 16) : "What trespass is this that ye have committed?" This sin is very significantly viewed here as an "unfaithfulness" towards the God of Israel.

[2] So in Josh. xxii. 17. Such a judgment as the death of 24,000 (Numb. xxv. 9) must have left many painful gaps in Israel. But this was not the saddest consequence. For, evidently, the worship of Baal-Peor had struck root among the people, even although for the present it was outwardly suppressed.

[3] There is a fervency of utterance in their protestation, which appears even in the accumulation of the names of God The particle rendered "if" is here used as the formula for an oath.

people[1] (i. 6). Both had been done, and in the spirit of
strength, of courage, and of believing obedience enjoined at
the outset (i. 7). Unlike his great predecessor and master,
Moses, he had been allowed to finish his task, and even to rest
after its completion.[2] And now he had reached one hundred
and ten years, the age at which his ancestor Joseph had died
(Gen. l. 26). Like a father who thinks of and seeks to
provide for the future of his children after his death;[3] like
Moses when he gathered up all his life, his mission, and his
teaching in his last discourses ; as the Apostle Peter, when he
endeavoured that Christians might " be able after his Exodus[4]
to have these things always in remembrance," so did Joshua
care for the people of his charge. On two successive occasions
he gathered all Israel, through their representative " elders," [5]
to address to them last words. They are in spirit and even
in tenor singularly like those of Moses, as indeed he had no
new truth to communicate.

The first assembly must have taken place either in his own
city of Timnath-serah,[6] or else at Shiloh. The address there
given had precisely the same object as that afterwards delivered
by him, and indeed may be described as preparatory to the
latter. Probably the difference between the two lies in this,
that the first discourse treated of the future of Israel rather in
its political aspect, while the second, as befitted the circum-

---

[1] So also the Book of Joshua is divided into two parts: the first (ch. i.–xii.),
descriptive of the *conquest*, the second of the *division* of the land.

[2] Joshua seems to have lived about fifteen years after the final division
of the land.

[3] This idea is suggested by Calvin.

[4] The word used by the apostle (2 Pet. i. 15) is " *Exodus*," the same as
employed in the conversation on the Mount of Transfiguration (Luke ix. 31),
to which St. Peter in his epistle makes pointed reference (2 Pet. i. 16–18).

[5] All Israel were summoned through their *elders*, which is a generic name
including the three divisions : " heads" of tribes, clans, and houses of
fathers, " judges," and " officers."

[6] Literally " the possession of the sun "—properly *Timnath serach*, also
called *Timnath-Cheres* (Judges ii. 9) by a transposition of letters, not uncommon in the Hebrew.

stances, chiefly dwelt on the past mercies of Jehovah, and urged upon the people decision in their spiritual choice. Both discourses are marked by absence of all self-exaltation or reference to his own achievements. It is the language of one who, after long and trying experience, could sum up all he knew and felt in these words : " As for me and my house, we will serve Jehovah."

The first discourse of Joshua consisted of two parts (xxiii. 2–13, and 14–16), each beginning with an allusion to his approaching end, as the motive of his admonitions. Having first reminded Israel of all God's benefits and of His promises, in case of their faithfulness, he beseecheth them : " Take heed very much to your souls to love Jehovah your God " (ver. 11), the danger of an opposite course being described with an accumulation of imagery that shows how deeply Joshua felt the impending danger. Proceeding in the same direction, the second part of Joshua's address dwells upon the absolute certainty with which judgment would follow, as surely as formerly blessing had come.

The second address of Joshua, delivered to the same audience as the first, was even more solemn. For, this time, the assembly took place at Shechem, where, on first entering the land, Israel had made solemn covenant by responding from Mounts Ebal and Gerizim to the blessings and the curses enunciated in the law. And the present gathering also was to end in renewal of that covenant. Moreover, it was in Shechem that Abraham had, on entering Canaan, received the first Divine promise, and here he had built an altar unto Jehovah (Gen. xii. 6, 7). Here also had Jacob settled after his return from Mesopotamia, and purged his household from lingering idolatry, by burying their Teraphim under an oak (Gen. xxxiii. 20 ; xxxv. 2, 4). It was truly a " sanctuary of Jehovah " (Josh. xxiv. 26), and they who came to it " gathered before God "[1] (ver. 1). In language the most tender and impressive, reminding us of Stephen's last speech before the

---

[1] In the Hebrew with the article "the God," to indicate that it was the only true and living *Elohim*.

Sanhedrim (Acts vii.), Joshua recalled to them the mercies of
God (Josh. xxiv. 2–13), specially in those five great events : the
calling of Abraham, the deliverance from Egypt, the defeat of
the Amorites and of the purpose of Balaam,[1] the miraculous
crossing of Jordan and taking of Jericho, and finally, the
Divine victory[2] given them over all the nations of Canaan.
On these grounds he now earnestly entreated them to make
decisive choice of Jehovah as their God.[3] And they replied
by solemnly protesting their determination to cleave unto the
Lord, in language which not only re-echoed that of the preface
to the ten commandments (Ex. xx. 2 ; Deut. v. 6), but also
showed that they fully responded to Joshua's appeals. To
bring the matter to a clear issue, Joshua next represented to them
that they could not serve Jehovah (xxiv. 19)—that is, in their
then state of heart and mind—"in their own strength, without
the aid of grace ; without real and serious conversion from all
idols ; and without true repentance and faith."[4] To attempt
this were only to bring down judgment instead of the former
blessing. And when the people still persevered in their profession, Joshua, having made it a condition that they were to put
away the strange gods from among them and "direct" their
hearts "unto Jehovah, God of Israel,"[5] made again solemn

---

[1] In xxiv. 9 : "Then Balak . . . . arose and warred against Israel ;" not
with outward weapons, but through Balaam.

[2] The expressive figure is here used : "And I sent the hornet before
you," to designate that which carries terror among the inhabitants of a
place. Comp. Ex. xxiii. 28 ; Deut. vii. 20.

[3] The call to "choose this day " whom they would serve (ver. 15), does
not place the duty of their allegiance to Jehovah in any doubt, but is rather
the strongest and most emphatic mode of enforcing the admonition of
ver. 14, especially followed, as it is, by the declaration : "but as for me
and my house, we will serve Jehovah."

[4] So in substance J. H. Michaelis in his notes on the passage.

[5] Keil argues that the expression (ver. 23), "put away the strange gods
which are among you," means "in your hearts." But this interpretation
is critically untenable, while such passages as Amos v. 26 and Acts vii. 43
prove the existence of idolatrous rites among the people, even though they
may have been discarded in public.

covenant with them. Its terms were recorded in a document which was placed within the book of the Law,[1] and in memory thereof a great stone was set up under the memorable tree at Shechem which had been the silent witness of so many solemn transactions in the history of Israel.

With this event the history of Joshua closes.[2] Looking back upon it, we gather the lessons of his life and work, and of their bearing upon the future of Israel. Born a slave in Egypt, he must have been about forty years old at the time of the Exodus. Attached to the person of Moses, he led Israel in the first decisive battle against Amalek (Ex. xvii. 9, 13), while Moses, in the prayer of faith, held up to heaven the God-given "rod." It was no doubt on that occasion that his name was changed from *Oshea*, "help," to *Jehoshua*, "Jehovah is help" (Numb. xiii. 16). And this name is the key to his life and work. Alike in bringing the people into Canaan, in his wars, and in the distribution of the land among the tribes—from the miraculous crossing of Jordan and taking of Jericho to his last address—he was the embodiment of his new name : " Jehovah is help !" To this outward calling his character also corresponded. It is marked by singleness of purpose, directness, and decision. There is not indeed about him that elevation of faith, or comprehensiveness of spiritual view which we observed in Moses. Witness Joshua's despondency after the first failure at Ai. Even his plans and conceptions lack breadth and depth. Witness his treaty with the Gibeonites, and the commencing disorganisation among the tribes at Shiloh. His strength always lies in his singleness of purpose. He sets an object before him, and unswervingly follows it. So in his campaigns : he marches rapidly, falls suddenly upon the enemy, and follows up the victory with unflagging energy. But there

[1] He took, as we would say, "Minutes" of this transaction, which were placed inside the roll of the law of Moses.

[2] The deaths of Joshua and Eleazar were, of course, chronicled at a later period. According to the Talmud (Baba Bathra, 15 a), the former was written down by Eleazar, and the latter by Phinehas.

he stops—till another object is again set before him, which
he similarly pursues. The same singleness, directness, and
decision, rather than breadth and elevation, seem also to
characterise his personal religion.

There is another remarkable circumstance about Joshua.
The conquest and division of the land seem to have been his
sole work. He does not appear to have even ruled as a judge
over Israel. But so far also as the conquest and division of
the land were concerned, his work was not complete, nor,
indeed, *intended* to be complete. And this is characteristic of
the whole Old Testament dispensation, that no period in its
history sees its work completed, but only begun and pointing
forward to another yet future,[1] till at last all becomes complete
in the "fulness of time" in Christ Jesus. Thus viewed, a fresh
light is cast upon the name and history of Joshua. Assuredly
Joshua did not give "*rest*" even to his own generation, far less
to Israel as a nation. *It was rest begun, but not completed*—a
rest which even in its temporal aspect left so much unrest ;
and as such it pointed to Christ. What the one Joshua could
only begin, not really achieve, even in its outward typical
aspect, pointed to, and called for the other Joshua, the Lord
Jesus Christ,[2] in Whom and by Whom all is reality, and all
is perfect, and all is rest for ever. And so also it was only
after many years that *Oshea* became Joshua, while the name
Joshua was given to our Lord by the angel before His birth
(Matt. i. 21). The first *became*, the second *was* Joshua. And
so the name and the work of Joshua pointed forward to the
fulness in Christ, alike by what it was and by what it was not,
and this in entire accordance with the whole character and
object of the Old Testament.

[1] See some interesting remarks in Herzog's *Real Encycl.*, vol. vii. p. 41.
If any reader, able to follow out such questions, should feel interested in
"the higher criticism" of the Book of Joshua, we would direct him to the
masterly essay by L. König, in *Alttest. Studien*, part i.

[2] Jesus is the Greek equivalent for Joshua.

CHAPTER XIII.

Summary of the Book of Judges—Judah's and Simeon's Campaign—Spiritual and national Decay of Israel—"from Gilgal to Bochim."

(Judges i.-iii. 4.)

IF evidence were required that each period of Old Testament history points for its completion to one still future, it would be found in the Book of Judges. The history of the three and a half centuries which it records brings not anything new to light, either in the life or history of Israel; it only continues what is already found in the Book of Joshua, carrying it forward to the Books of Samuel, and thence through Kings, till it points in the dim distance to *the King* of Israel, the Lord Jesus Christ, Who gives perfect rest in the perfect kingdom. In the Book of Joshua we see two grand outstanding facts, one explaining the outer, the other the inner history of Israel. As for the latter, we learn that ever since the sin of Peor, if not before, idolatry had its hold upon the people. Not that the service of the Lord was discarded, but that it was combined with the heathen rites of the nations around. But as true religion was really the principle of Israel's national life and unity, "unfaithfulness" towards Jehovah was also closely connected with tribal disintegration, which, as we have seen, threatened even in the time of Joshua. Then, as for the outer history of Israel, we learn that the completion of their possession of Canaan was made dependent on their faithfulness to Jehovah. Just as the Christian can only continue to stand by the same faith in which, in his conversion to God, he first had access to Him (Rom. v. 2), so Israel could only retain the land and complete its conquest by the same faith in which they had at first entered it. For faith is never a thing of the past. And for this reason God allowed a remnant of those nations to continue in the land "to prove Israel by them"[1] (Judges iii. 1), so that, as Joshua had forewarned them (Josh. xxiii. 10–16, comp. Judges ii. 3), "faithfulness" on their part would lead to sure and easy victory, while the opposite would end in terrible national disaster. Side by side with these two facts, there is yet a third, and that the most important: the unchanging faithfulness of the Lord, His unfailing pity and lovingkindness, according to which, when Israel was brought low and again turned to Him, He "raised them up judges, . . . and delivered them out of the hand of their enemies all the days of the judge" (Judges ii. 18).

The exhibition of these three facts forms the subject-matter of Israel's history under the Judges, as clearly indicated in Judges ii. 21, iii. 4. Accordingly, we must not expect in the Book of Judges a complete or successive history of Israel during these three and half centuries, but rather the exhibition and development of those three grand facts. For Holy Scripture furnishes *not* —like ordinary biography or history—a chronicle of the lives of individuals, or even of the successive history of a period, save in so far as these are connected with the progress of the kingdom of God. Sacred history is primarily that of the kingdom of God, and only secondarily that of individuals or periods. More particularly is this the reason why we have no record at all of five of the Judges[2]—not even that Jehovah had raised them up. For this cause also some events are specially selected in the sacred narrative, which, to the superficial reader, may seem trivial; sometimes even difficult or objectionable. But a more careful study will show that the real object of these narratives is, to bring into full view one or other of the great principles of

[1] This is not in any way inconsistent with Ex. xxiii. 29, etc., Deut. vii. 22. For, as Keil rightly remarks, there is a vast difference between exterminating the whole of the ancient inhabitants of the land, say, in one year, and suspending even their gradual extermination.

[2] *Tola* (x. 1), *Jair* (x. 3), *Ibzan, Elon,* and *Abdon* (xii. 8–15).

the Old Testament dispensation. For the same reason also we must not look for strict chronological arrangement in the narratives. In point of fact, the Judges ruled only over one or several of the tribes, to whom they brought special deliverance. Accordingly, the history of some of the Judges overlaps each other, their reign having been contemporaneous in different parts of the land. Thus while in the far east across Jordan the sway of the children of Ammon lasted for eighteen years, till Jephthah brought deliverance (Judges x. 6–xii. 7), the Philistines at the same time oppressed Israel in the far south-west. This circumstance renders the chronology of the Book of Judges more complicated.

The Book of Judges divides itself into three parts : *a general introduction* (i.–iii. 6), *a sketch of the period of the Judges* (iii. 7–xvi. 31), arranged in six groups of events (iii. 7–11 ; iii. 12–31 ; iv., v. ; vi.–x. 5 ; x. 6–xii. 15 ; xiii.–xvi.), *and a double Appendix* (xvii.–xxi.). The two series of events, recorded in the latter, evidently took place at the *commencement* of the period of the Judges. This appears from a comparison of Judges xviii. 1 with i. 34, and again of Judges xx. 28 with Josh. xxii. 13 and xxiv. 33. The first of the two narratives is mainly intended to describe the *religious*, the second the *moral* decadence among the tribes of Israel. In these respects they throw light upon the whole period. We see how soon, after the death of Joshua and of his contemporaries, Israel declined—*spiritually*, in combining with the heathen around, and mingling their idolatrous rites with the service of Jehovah ; and *nationally*, the war with the Canaanites being neglected, and the tribes heeding on every great occasion only their private interests and jealousies, irrespective of the common weal (v. 15–17, 23 ; viii. 1–9), until "the men of Ephraim" actually levy war against Jephthah (xii. 1–6), and Israel sinks so low as to deliver its *Samson* into the hands of the Philistines (xv. 9–13) !

Side by side with this decay of Israel we notice a similar decline in the *spiritual* character of the Judges from an *Othniel* and a *Deborah* down to *Samson*. The mission of these Judges was, as we have seen, chiefly local and always temporary, God raising up a special deliverer in a time of special need. It is quite evident that such special instruments were not necessarily always under the influence of spiritual motives. God has at all periods of history used what instruments He pleased for the deliverance of His people—a Darius, a Cyrus, a Gamaliel, and in more modern times often what appeared the most unlikely, to effect His own purposes. Yet in the history of the Judges it seems always the best and most religious whom the locality or period affords who is chosen, so that the character of the Judges affords also an index of the state of a district or period. And in each of them we mark the presence of real faith (Heb. xi.), acting as the lever-power in their achievements, although their faith is too often mingled with the corruptions of the period. *The Judges were Israel's representative men*—representatives of its faith and its hope, but also of its sin and decay. Whatever they achieved was " by faith." Even in the case of Samson, all his great deeds were achieved in the faith of God's gift to him as a Nazarite, and when "the Spirit of the Lord came upon him." Hence the Judges deserved to be enrolled in the catalogue of Old Testament "worthies." Besides, we must not forget the necessary influence upon them of the spirit of their age. For we mark in the Bible a progressive development, as the light grew brighter and brighter unto the perfect day. In truth, if this were not the case, one of two inferences would follow. Either we would be tempted to regard its narratives as partial, or else be driven to the conclusion that these men could not have been of the period in which they are placed, since they had nothing in common with it, and hence could neither have been leaders of public opinion, nor even been understood by it.

From these brief preliminary observations we turn to notice, that there were altogether twelve, or rather, including Deborah (Judges iv. 4), thirteen Judges over Israel. Of only eight of these are any special deeds recorded. The term Judge must not, however, be regarded as primarily referring to the ordinary judicial functions, which were discharged by the elders and

officers of every tribe and city. Rather do we regard it as equivalent to *leader* or *ruler*. The period of the Judges closes with
Samson. Eli was mainly high priest, and only in a secondary
sense "Judge," while Samuel formed the transition from the
Judges to royalty. With Samson the period of the Judges
reached at the same time its highest and its lowest point. It
is as a *Nazarite*, devoted to God before his birth, that he is
"Judge," and achieves his great feats—and it is as a Nazarite
that he falls and fails through selfishness and sin. In both
respects he is the representative of Israel—God-devoted, a
Nazarite people, and as such able to do all things, yet falling
and failing through spiritual adultery. And thus the period of
the Judges ends as every other period. It contains the germ
of, and points to something better ; but it is imperfect, incomplete, and fails, though even in its failure it points forward.
Judges must be succeeded by kings, and kings by *the* King—
the true Nazarite, the Lord Jesus Christ.

The period between the death of Joshua and the first
"Judge" is summarised in Judges i.–iii. 6. It appears, that
under the influence of Joshua's last address, deepened no
doubt by his death, which followed soon afterwards, the "holy
war" was resumed. In this instance it was purely aggressive
on the part of Israel, whereas formerly, as a matter of fact, the
attack always came from the Canaanites (except in the case of
Jericho and of Ai). But the measure of the sin of the nations
who occupied Palestine was now full (Gen. xv. 13–16), and the
storm of judgment was to sweep them away. For this purpose
Israel, to whom God in His mercy had given the land, was
to be employed—but only in so far as the people realised
its calling to dedicate the land unto the Lord. On the ruins
of what not only symbolised, but at the time really was the
kingdom of Satan,[1] the theocracy was to be upbuilt. Instead

---

[1] It is difficult to resist the impression that Canaan was not only the
focus of ancient heathenism in its *worst* abominations, but the centre
whence it spread. Very much in the mythology, and almost all the vileness
of Greek and Roman heathenism is undoubtedly of Canaanitish origin.

of that focus whence the vilest heathenism overspread the world, the kingdom of God was to be established, with its opposite mission of sending the light of truth to the remotest parts of the earth. Nor can it be difficult to understand how, in such circumstances, at such a time, and at that period of religious life, any compromise was impossible—and every war must be one of extermination.

Before entering on this new "war," the children of Israel asked Jehovah, no doubt through the *Urim* and *Thummim*, which tribe was to take the lead. In reply, Judah was designated, in accordance with ancient prophecy (Gen. xlix. 8). Judah, in turn, invited the co-operation of Simeon, whose territory had been parcelled out of its own. In fact, theirs were common enemies. The two tribes encountered and defeated the Canaanites and Perizzites in *Bezek*, a name probably attaching to a district rather than a place, and, as the word seems to imply, near the shore of the Dead Sea.[1] In the same locality *Adoni-bezek*[2] appears to have made a fresh stand, but with the same disastrous result. On that occasion a remarkable, though most cruel retaliation overtook him. As chieftain of that district he must have been equally renowned for his bravery and cruelty. After a custom not uncommon in antiquity,[3] the many chieftains whom he had subdued were kept, like dogs "for lengthened sport,"[4] under the banqueting table of the proud conqueror in a mutilated condition, their thumbs and great toes cut off, in token that they could never

---

Indeed, we may designate the latter as the only real *missionary* heathenism at the time in the world. Consider the significance of planting in its stead the kingdom of God, with its untold missionary influences and its grand purpose to the world! We must also bear in mind, that the spread of Canaanitish idolatry would be greatly promoted by the chain of colonies which extended from Asia Minor into Europe.

[1] Cassel derives the name from the slimy nature of the soil.

[2] According to Cassel : "My god is splendour," perhaps a sun worshipper.

[3] Cassel enumerates many such.

[4] " *In longum sui ludibrium,*" Curtius de Rebus : Alex. v. 5, 6.

again handle sword and bow, nor march to war. It need scarcely be said. that the Mosaic law never contemplated such horrors. Nevertheless the allied tribes now inflicted mutilation upon Adoni-bezek. The victors carried him to Jerusalem, where he died. On that occasion the city itself, so far as it lay within the territory of Judah, was taken and burnt. But the boundary line between Judah and Benjamin ran through Jerusalem, the Upper City and the strong castle, which were held by the Jebusites, being within the lot of Benjamin. In the war under Joshua, the Jebusites had foiled Judah (Josh. xv. 63). Now also they retired to their stronghold, whence the Benjamites did not even attempt to dislodge them (Judges i. 21). From Jerusalem the tribes continued their victorious march successively to "the mountain," or highlands of Judah, then to the *Negeb*, or south country, and finally to the *Shephelah*, or lowlands, along the sea-shore. Full success attended the expedition, the tribes pursuing their victories as far south as the utmost borders of the ancient kingdom of Arad, where, as their fathers had vowed (Numb. xxi. 2), they executed the ban upon *Zephath* or *Hormah*. The descendants of Hobab (Judges iv. 11) the Kenite,[1] the brother-in-law of Moses, who had followed Israel to Canaan (Numb. x. 29), and had since pitched their tents near Jericho, now settled in this border land, as best suited to their nomadic habits and previous associations (Judges i. 8–11, 16). The campaign ended[2] with the incursion into the *Shephelah*, where Judah wrested from the Philistines three out of their five great cities. This conquest, however, was not permanent (xiv. 19; xvi. 1), nor were the inhabitants of the valley driven out, "because they had chariots of iron."[3]

But the zeal of Israel did not long continue. In fact, all

---

[1] This notice is here inserted, probably, because the event happened between the taking of Debir (i. 11) and that of Zephath (i. 17).

[2] Only Gaza, Ashkelon, and Ekron seem to have been taken, but neither Gath nor Ashdod.

[3] These were armed with scythes on their wheels.

that follows after the campaign of Judah and Simeon is a
record of failure and neglect, with the single exception of the
taking of Bethel by the house of Joseph.   Thus the tribes were
everywhere surrounded by a fringe of heathenism.   In many
parts, Israelites and heathens dwelt together, the varying proportions among them being indicated by such expressions as
that the "Canaanites dwelt among" the Israelites, or else the
reverse.   Sometimes the Canaanites became tributary.   On the
other hand, the Amorites succeeded in almost wholly [1] driving
the tribe of Dan out of their possessions, which induced a
considerable proportion of the Danites to seek fresh homes in
the far north (Judges xviii.).

Israel was settling down in this state, when their false rest
was suddenly broken by the appearance among them of "the
Angel of Jehovah." [2]   No Divine manifestation had been vouchsafed them since the Captain of Jehovah's host had stood before
Joshua in the camp at Gilgal (Josh. v. 13-15).   And now, at
the commencement of a new period, and that one of spiritual
decay, He "came" from Gilgal to Bochim, not to announce
the miraculous fall of a Jericho before the ark of Jehovah, but
the continuance of the heathen power near them in judgment
upon their unfaithfulness and disobedience.   "From Gilgal to
Bochim !"   There is much in what these names suggest—and
that even although Gilgal may have been the permanent
camp,[3] where leading representatives of the nation were always
assembled, to whom "the Angel of Jehovah" in the first place
addressed Himself, and *Bochim*, or "weepers," the designation
given afterwards to the meeting-place by the ancient sanctuary
(either Shechem or more probably Shiloh), where the elders of
the people gathered to hear the Divine message.   And truly
what had passed between the entrance into Canaan and that

[1] They drove them out of the valley (i. 35) which constituted the
principal part of the possession of Dan (Josh. xix. 40).   The Amorites even
" dared to dwell " in Har-Heres, in Aijalon, and in Shaalbim (Judges i. 35),
although they were afterwards made tributary by the house of Joseph.

[2] Cassel erroneously regards this as a human messenger from God.

[3] For the situation of this Gilgal, comp. a previous chapter.

period might be thus summed up: " From Gilgal to Bochim !"
The immediate impression of the words of the Angel of Jehovah
was great. Not only did the place become *Bochim*, but a sacrifice
was offered unto Jehovah, for wherever His presence was manifested, there might sacrifice be brought (comp. Deut. xii. 5 ;
Judges vi. 20, 26, 28 ; xiii. 16 ; 2 Sam. xxiv. 25).

But, alas ! the impression was of but short continuance.
Mingling with the heathen around, "they forsook Jehovah,
and served Baal and Ashtaroth."[1] Such a people could only
learn in the school of sorrow. National unfaithfulness was
followed by national judgments. Yet even so, Jehovah, in
His mercy, ever turned to them when they cried, and raised
up "deliverers." In the truest sense these generations "had
not known all the wars of Canaan" (Judges iii. 1). For the
knowledge of them is thus explained in the Book of Psalms
(Ps. xliv. 2, 3): "Thou didst drive out the heathen with
Thy hand, and plantedst them ; Thou didst afflict the nations,
and cast them out. For they got not the land in possession
by their own sword, neither did their own arm save them :
but Thy right hand, and Thine arm, and the light of Thy
countenance, because Thou hadst a favour unto them." This
lesson was now to be learned in bitter experience by the
presence and power of the heathen around : "to prove Israel
by them, to know whether they would hearken unto the
commandments of Jehovah, which He commanded their fathers
by the hand of Moses" (Judges iii. 4).

[1] *Ashtaroth* is the "star-goddess" of the night, *Astarte*, whose symbol,
properly speaking, was the *Asherah*. It is impossible to detail the vileness of her service. Mention ot it occurs so early as in Gen. xiv. 5, where
we read of *Ashteroth Karnaim*, the "star-goddess of the horns," *i.e.*, the
quarter of the moon.

CHAPTER XIV.

Othniel—Ehud—Shamgar.

(JUDGES III. 5-31.)

THE first scene presented in the history of the Judges is that of Israel's intermarriage with the heathen around, and their doing "evil in the sight of Jehovah," forgetting Him, and serving "Baalim and the groves."[1] And the first "judgment" on their apostacy is, that they are "sold" by the Lord into the hand of "Chushan-rishathaim, king of Mesopotamia," or rather of "Aram-naharaim," "the highland by the two streams" (Euphrates and Tigris). Curiously enough, there is an ancient Persian tradition, according to which the monarchs of Iran, who held dominion "by the streams," waged war against Egypt, Syria, and Asia Minor. Of their heroes, who are described as *Cushan*, or from the land of *Chusistan* (= Scythians, Parthians?), the most notable is *Kustan* or *Rastam*, a name evidently akin to Rishathaim.[2] And so ancient heathen records once more throw unexpected light upon the historical narratives of the Old Testament.

The oppression had lasted full eight years when Israel "cried[3] unto Jehovah." The deliverer raised up for them was *Othniel*, the younger brother of Caleb, whose bravery had formerly gained him the hand of his wife (i. 12-15). But his success now was not due to personal prowess. "The Spirit of

---

[1] "Baalim and the Astartes" (Ashtaroth or Asheroth). So literally.

[2] See Cassel's *Comm.* p. 33. Jewish tradition and most commentators translate the name: "twofold sin," in supposed allusion to a twofold wrong against Israel. But this is, to say the least, a very strained explanation.

[3] The same word as that used of Israel in Ex. ii. 23.

Jehovah was [1] upon him, and he judged Israel, and went out to war." For the first time in the Book of Judges we meet here the statement, that "the Spirit of Jehovah" "was upon," or "clothed," or else "came upon" a person. We naturally connect the expression with what we read of "the manifold gifts of the Spirit" as these are detailed in Is. xi. 2, which were distributed to each as God pleased, and according to the necessity of the time (I Cor. xii. 11). But, in thinking of these influences, we ought to bear two things in mind. *First:* although, in each case, the influence came straight from above—from the Spirit of God— for the accomplishment of a special purpose, it was *not* necessarily, as under the New Testament dispensation, a sanctifying influence. *Secondly:* this influence must not be regarded as the same with the *abiding* presence of the Holy Spirit in the heart. This also belongs to the New Testament dispensation. In short, these gifts of the Holy Spirit were *miraculous*, rather than *gracious*—like the gifts in the early Church, rather than as "the promise of the Father." In the case of Othniel, however, we note that the Spirit of God "*was* upon" him, and that, under His influence, "he judged" Israel, even "before he went out to war." And so, while ancient Jewish tradition in all other instances paraphrases the expression, "the Spirit of the Lord," by "the spirit of strength," in the case of *Othniel*— "the lion of God"[2]—it renders it : "the spirit of prophecy." A war so undertaken must have been successful, and "the land had rest forty years."[3]

[1] The expression here and in xi. 29 is, "was upon" him ; in vi. 34, it is "clothed him ;" in xiv. 6, 19 ; xv. 14, "came upon" or "lighted upon." The attentive reader will note the important difference of meaning in each of these terms. In the first case there is permanence—at least to carry out a special purpose ; in the second, the idea is of surrounding, protecting, or enduing ; and, in the third, of suddenness, implying a power, wholly from without, descending unexpectedly at the right moment, and then withdrawn. All have, however, this in common, that the influence comes straight from the Spirit of God.

[2] This, or else "my lion is God," is the rendering of the name.

[3] The text does not make it clear whether Othniel died at the end of these forty years ; only that he died after the land had obtained rest.

The next judgment to rebellious Israel came likewise from the east. Quite on the eastern boundary of Reuben and of Gad lay the land of Moab. One of the chieftains of its tribes, Eglon,[1] now allied himself with the old enemies of Israel, Ammon and Amalek, the former occupying the territory south of Reuben, the latter the districts in the far south-west, below Philistia. Eglon swept over the possessions of the trans-Jordanic tribes, crossed the river, and made Jericho, which was probably re-built as a town, though not as a fortress, his capital. Having thus cut the land, as it were, into two, and occupied its centre and garden, Eglon reduced Israel for eighteen years to servi-tude. At the end of that period the people once more " cried unto the Lord," and " the Lord raised them up a deliverer," although Holy Scripture does *not* say that in his mode of deliverance he acted under the influence of the Spirit of the Lord. In the peculiar circumstances of the case this silence is most significant.

The "deliverer" was "Ehud (probably, the praised one), the son of Gera, a Benjamite, a man left-handed," or, as the original has it, " shut up "[2] or "weak" "as to his right hand." The conspiracy against Eglon was well planned. Ehud placed himself at the head of a deputation charged to bring Eglon "a present," or, more probably, the regular tribute, as we gather from the similar use of the word in 2 Sam. viii. 2, 6 ;

[1] We infer that Eglon was not the king of all Moab, because in that case he would not have exchanged its capital Rabbath Moab for Jericho, and also from the fact that, after the death of Eglon and the destruction of his garrison, the war does not seem to have been carried on by either party.

[2] Not paralysed—the term occurs in Ps. lxix. 15. Cassel has some very curious remarks on this subject. *Benjamin* means " son of the right hand ;" yet it seems a peculiarity of Benjamin to have had left-handed warriors (see Judges xx. 16). Similarly we read of certain African races, that they mostly fought with the left hand (Stobæus, *Ecl. phys.* i. 52). The Roman hero, who, like Ehud, delivered his country of its foreign oppressor, was *Scævola*—left-handed. The left was in ancient times the place of honour, because it was the weaker and less protected side (Xenoph. Cyrop. viii. 4). Similarly, the sea (in Hebrew, *yam*) was always regarded as the *right* side of a country—that of liberty, as it were.

2 Kings xvii. 3, 4. But Ehud carried under his raiment a two-edged dagger, a cubit long ; according to the LXX translation, about three-quarters of a foot. The tribute was delivered, no doubt with many protestations of humility and allegiance [1] on the part of Ehud, and the deputation graciously dismissed. It was needful for his plan, and probably in accordance with his wish to involve no one else in the risk, that the rest should be done by Ehud alone. Having seen his fellow-countrymen safely beyond " the quarries that were by Gilgal," or, rather, as the term implies, beyond " the terminal columns " (always objects of idolatrous worship), that divided the territory of Eglon from that of Israel, he returned to the king, whose confidence his former appearance had no doubt secured. The narrative here is exceedingly graphic. The king is no longer in the palace where the deputation had been received, but in his " upper chamber of cooling," [2] a delicious summer-retreat built out upon the end of the flat roof. Ehud professes to have "a secret errand," which had brought him back when his companions were gone. All the more that he does not ask for the withdrawal of the king's attendants does Eglon bid him be " Silent !" in their presence, which, of course, is the signal for their retirement. Alone with the king, Ehud saith, in a manner not uncommon in the East : " I have a message from God unto thee," on which Eglon, in token of reverence, rises from his seat.[3] This is the favourable moment, and, in an instant, Ehud has plunged his dagger up to the hilt into the lower part of his body, with such force that the blade came out behind.[4] Not pausing for a moment, Ehud retires, closes and locks the doors upon the murdered king, and escapes beyond the boundary. Meanwhile the king's attendants, finding the room locked, have waited, till,

[1] The term used here is the same as ordinarily employed for the offering of gifts and sacrifices to the Deity.

[2] So literally.

[3] It was common in antiquity to rise when receiving a direct message from the king. This is the origin of the liturgical practice of rising when the Gospel is read.

[4] The text means only this, and not as in the Authorised Version.

at last, they deem it necessary to break open the doors. The
horror and confusion consequent upon the discovery of the
murder have given Ehud still further time. And now the preconcerted signal is heard. The shrill blast of the trumpet in
Seirath (perhaps the "hairy" or "wooded") wakes the echoes of
Mount Ephraim. All around from their hiding troop the men
of Israel. The first object is to haste back towards Jericho
and take the fords of Jordan, so as to allow neither help to
come, nor fugitives to escape ; the next to destroy the garrison
of Moab. In both, Israel are successful, and, " at that time "—
of course, not on that precise day—10,000 of Moab are slain,
all of them, as we should say, fine men and brave soldiers.
" And the land had rest fourscore years."

Ancient history, both Greek and Roman, records similar
stories,[1] and, where the murderer has been a patriot, elevates
him to the highest pinnacle of heroism. Nay, even Christian
history records like instances, as in the murder of Henry III.
and Henry IV. of France, the former, even in its details, so like
the deed of Ehud. But strikingly different from the toleration,
and even commendation, of such deeds by the Papacy[2] is the
judgment of the Old Testament. Its silence is here severest
condemnation. It needed not cunning and murder to effect
deliverance. Not one word of palliation or excuse is said for
this deed. It was *not* under the influence of "the Spirit of
Jehovah" that such deliverance was wrought, nor is it said of
Ehud, as of Othniel, that he "judged Israel." Even Jewish
tradition[3] compares Ehud to the " ravening wolf," which had
been the early emblem of his tribe, Benjamin (Gen. xlix. 27).

It must have been during this period of eighty years' rest,[4]
that another danger at least threatened Benjamin. This time
it came from an opposite direction—from the west, where the

[1] Thucyd. vi. 56; Polyb. v. 81 ; Plut. Cæsar, 86; Curtius, vii. 2, 27 ;
comp. Cassel, *u.s.*
[2] Ranke, *Französ. Gesch.* i. p. 171 ; 473.
[3] Ber. Rabba, c. 89.
[4] This view is also taken by Jewish interpreters, though not by Josephus.

Philistines held possession. " After" Ehud (iii. 31), that is, after his example, a notable exploit was performed by *Shamgar* (" the name of a stranger " ?). Under the impulse of sudden sacred enthusiasm, he seized, as the first weapon to hand, an ox-goad, commonly used to urge on the oxen in ploughing. The weapon is formidable enough, being generally about eight feet long, and six inches round at the handle, which is furnished with an iron horn to loosen the earth off the plough, while the other end is armed with a long iron spike. With this weapon he slew no fewer than 600 Philistines, whom, probably, panic seized on his appearance.[1] The exploit seems to have been solitary, and we read neither of further war, nor yet of Shamgar's rule, only that for the time the danger of a Philistine incursion was averted.

CHAPTER XV.

𝕿𝖍𝖊 𝕺𝖕𝖕𝖗𝖊𝖘𝖘𝖎𝖔𝖓 of 𝕵𝖆𝖇𝖎𝖓 𝖆𝖓𝖉 𝕾𝖎𝖘𝖊𝖗𝖆—𝕯𝖊𝖇𝖔𝖗𝖆𝖍 𝖆𝖓𝖉 𝕭𝖆𝖗𝖆𝖐 —𝕿𝖍𝖊 𝕭𝖆𝖙𝖙𝖑𝖊 of 𝕿𝖆𝖆𝖓𝖆𝖈𝖍—𝕿𝖍𝖊 𝕾𝖔𝖓𝖌 of 𝕯𝖊𝖇𝖔𝖗𝖆𝖍.

(JUDGES IV., V.)

DARKER and darker are the clouds which gather around Israel, and stranger and more unexpected is the deliverance wrought for them. It had begun with *Othniel*, truly a " lion of God." But after the " lion of God " came one left-handed, then a woman, then the son of an idolater, and then an outlaw of low birth, as if it were ever to descend lower and lower, till the last stage is reached in the Nazarite, Samson, who, as Nazarite, is the typical representative of Israel's calling and strength, and, as Samson, of Israel's weakness and spiritual adultery. Yet each period and each deliverance has its characteristic features and high points.

The narrative opens as if to resume the thread of Israel's

[1] Greek legend has a similar story of Lycurgos chasing Dionysos and the Bacchantes with an ox-goad (*Il.* vi. 135).

continuous history, only temporarily broken by Ehud's life:
" And the children of Israel continued[1] to do evil in the eyes
of Jehovah—and Ehud was dead." This furnished a long
wished-for opportunity. It had been about a century before
when a Jabin ("the prudent" or " understanding,"—no doubt
the monarch's title, like Pharaoh or Abimelech) had marshalled
the chieftains of Northern Palestine against Joshua, and been
signally defeated (Josh. xi. 1–10). Since then his capital had
been restored and his power grown, till now it seemed the
fitting moment to recover his ancient empire. As we understand the narrative, the hosts of Jabin had swept down from
Hazor in the far north, and occupied the possessions of
Naphtali, Zebulun, and Issachar. While Jabin himself continued
in his capital, his general, *Sisera* ("mediation," "lieutenant"?)
held the southern boundary of the annexed provinces, making
his head-quarters at *Harosheth ha Gojim*—"the smithy of the
nations"—perhaps so called from being the arsenal where his
iron war-chariots, armed with scythes, were made. The site of
this place is probably somewhere in the neighbourhood of
Bethshean, which afterwards formed the southernmost point of
Galilee. Evidently it must have been south of Mount Tabor,
to which Barak afterwards marched from Kedron, in the north
of Naphtali. For, irrespective of the utterly helpless state of
the country, as described in Judges v. 6, Sisera would not have
allowed Barak to turn his flank or to march on his rear.[2] The
occupation of the north of Palestine by Sisera had lasted twenty
years. Relief must have seemed well-nigh hopeless. On the
one hand, the population was wholly disarmed (Judges v. 8);
on the other, Sisera had no less than nine hundred war-chariots
—means of attack which Israel most dreaded. But as often
before, so now, suffering led Israel to cry unto the Lord—and
help was soon at hand.

[1] So literally, and very significantly for the history of Israel.
[2] For this reason I cannot adopt the localisation proposed by Dr.
Thomson (*Land and Book*, ch. xxix.), north of the hills that bound the
Plain of Jezreel, although the suggestion is supported by Mr. Grove.

One of the most painful circumstances in the history of the Judges is the utter silence which all this time seems to envelop Shiloh and its sanctuary. No help comes from the priesthood till quite the close of this period. Far away in Mount Ephraim God raised up a woman, on whom He had poured the spirit of prophecy. It is the first time in this history that we read of the prophetic gift. The sacred text conveys, that she exercised it in strict accordance with the Divine law, for it is significantly added in connection with it, that "she judged Israel at that time." *Deborah*, "the bee,"[1] is described as a "burning woman."[2] The meeting-place for all in Israel who sought judgment at her hands was between Ramah and Bethel, under a palm-tree,[3] which afterwards bore her name. Thence she sent for Barak ("lightning,") the son of Abinoam ("my father"—God—"is favour"), from the far north, from Kadesh in Naphtali. His ready obedience proved his preparedness. But when Deborah laid on him the Divine command "gradually to draw"[4] an army of 10,000 men to Mount Tabor, Barak shrank from it, unless Deborah would accompany him. This evidently proved distrust in the result of the undertaking, which in turn showed that he looked for success to the presence of man, rather than entirely to the power of God. Accordingly, he must learn the folly of attaching value to man; and Deborah predicted, that not Israel's leader, but a woman, wholly unconnected with the battle, would have the real triumph.

[1] Although there may be differences as to the mode of its derivation, there is none as to the real import of the name.

[2] The Authorised Version translates "the wife of Lapidoth." The latter word means "torches," and the meaning, as brought out by Cassel, seems to be "a woman of a torch-like spirit;" the Hebrew for wife and woman being the same. Jewish tradition has it, that she was the wife of *Barak*, "lightning," Barak and Lapidoth being, of course, closely connected terms.

[3] The palm-tree was the symbol of Canaan; and the name *Phœnician* is derived from its Greek equivalent.

[4] This is the meaning of the word, as appears from Ex. xii. 21.

Accompanied by Deborah, Barak now returned to Kadesh, whither he summoned the chiefs[1] of Naphtali and Zebulon. All plans being concerted, the combatants converged in small companies, from all roads and directions, "on foot,"[2] towards the trysting-place. About six or eight miles east of Nazareth rises abruptly a beautifully-shaped conical mountain, about 1000 feet high. This is Mount Tabor ("the height"), its sloping sides covered with trees, and affording from its summit one of the most extensive and beautiful prospects in Palestine. Here the army under Barak and Deborah gathered. Tidings soon reached the head-quarters of Sisera. His chariots could of course only fight to advantage in the valleys, and he naturally marched north-west to the plain of Jezreel or Esdraelon. This has ever been, and will prove in the final contest (Rev. xvi. 16), the great battle-field of Israel. It was now the first of many times that its fertile soil was to be watered with the blood of men.

Sisera had chosen his position with consummate skill. Marching in almost straight line upon the plain of Megiddo, his army was now posted at its entrance, resting upon the ancient Canaanitish town of Taanach (Judges v. 19, comp. Josh. xii. 21). Behind, and at his left flank, were the mountains of Manasseh, before him opened the basin of the valley, merging into the plain of Esdraelon, watered by the Kishon. Into this plain must Barak's army descend "on foot," badly armed, without experienced officers, without cavalry or chariots—and here his own 900 war-chariots would operate to best advantage. It was not even like one of those battles in which mountaineers hold their own fastnesses, or swoop down on their enemies in narrow defiles. On the contrary, all seemed to tell against Israel—all but this, that God had previously promised to draw

---

[1] This we infer, as it could not have served any purpose to have gathered the tribes themselves so far north, while it would certainly have attracted the attention of the enemy.

[2] So, and not as the Authorised Version renders it: "he went up with 10,000 men at his feet."

Sisera and his army to the river Kishon, and to deliver them into Barak's hand. Then once more did the Lord appear as "a man of war," and fight on the side of His people. It is said : "And Jehovah discomfited," or rather, "threw into confusion, Sisera and all his chariots, and all his host." The expression is the same as when Jehovah fought against Egypt (Ex. xiv. 25), and again when before Gibeon Joshua bade sun and moon stand still (Josh. x. 10). It indicates the direct interference of the Lord through terrible natural phenomena ; (comp. also its use in 2 Sam. xxii. 15 ; Ps. xviii. 14 ; cxliv. 6). As we gather from Judges v. 20–22, a fearful storm swept down from heaven in face of the advancing army.[1] The battle must have drawn towards Endor, where its fate was finally decided (Ps. lxxxiii. 9, 10). Presently the war-chariots were thrown into confusion, and instead of being a help became a source of danger. The affrighted horses carried destruction into the ranks of the host. Soon all were involved in a common panic. A scene of wild confusion ensued. It was impossible to retreat, and only in one direction could flight be attempted. And now the waters of Kishon had swollen into a wild torrent which swept away the fugitives ![2]

To escape capture, Sisera leaped from his chariot, and fled on foot northwards towards Hazor. Already he had passed beyond Kadesh, and almost reached safety. There the boundary of Naphtali was marked by what was known as " the oakwood at the twin tents of wandering" (Elon be-Zaanannim[3]). Here Heber the Kenite had pitched his tent, having separated from his brethren, who had settled in the extreme south at Arad (Judges i. 16). Living quite on the boundary of Jabin's dominion, and not being really Israelites, the clan of Heber had been left unmolested, and " there was peace between Jabin, king of Hazor, and the house of Heber the Kenite."

---

[1] So also Josephus (*Ant.* v. 5, 6).

[2] The battle must be read in connection with the song of Deborah (Judges v.), which furnishes its details.

[3] Comp. Josh. xix. 33.

Only outward, not real peace ! There is something wild and
weird about the appearance of these Kenites on the stage of
Jewish history. Originally an Arab tribe,[1] they retain to the
last the fierceness of their race. Though among Israel, they
never seem to amalgamate with Israel, and yet they are more
keenly Israelitish than any of the chosen race. In short,
these stranger-converts are the most intense in their allegiance
to the nation which they have joined, while at the same time
they never lose the characteristics of their own race. We
mark all this, for example, in the appearance of Jehonadab,
the son of Rechab (2 Kings x. 15), and again much later
during the troubles that befell Judah in the time of Jeremiah
(Jer. xxxv.). Jael, "the chamois," the wife of Heber, was
among the Kenites what Deborah, the "torch-woman," was
in Israel, only with all the characteristics of her race developed to the utmost. At her tent-door she meets the fugitive
Sisera. She disarms his suspicions; she invites him to rest and
security; she even sacrifices the sacred rights of hospitality
to her dark purpose. There is something terrible and yet
grand about that fierce woman, to whom every other consideration is as nothing, so that she may avenge Israel and
destroy its great enemy. All seems lawful to her in such an
undertaking; every means sanctified by the end in view. She
has laid the worn warrior to rest; she has given him for
refreshment of the best her tent affords. And now, as he lies
in heavy sleep, she stealthily withdraws one of the long iron
spikes to which the tent-cords are fastened, and with a heavy
hammer once, again, and yet a third time, strikes it into his
temples. It is not long before Barak—a "lightning" in pursuit
as in battle—has reached the spot. Jael lifts aside the tent-
curtain and shows him the gory corpse. In silence Barak turns
from the terrible spectacle. But the power of Jabin and his
dominion are henceforth for ever destroyed.

There is, as it seems to us, not a word in Scripture to express

---

[1] They were Midianites, descendants of Abraham by Keturah—undoubtedly a Bedouin tribe.

its approbation of so horrible a deed of deceit and violence—no, not even in the praise which Deborah in her song bestows upon Jael. It was not like Deborah's war, nor like Barak's battle, but strictly Kenite. Her allegiance to the cause of the people of God, her courage, her zeal, were Israelitish; their fanatical, wild, unscrupulous manifestation belonged to the race from which she had sprung, to the traditions amidst which she had been nurtured, and to the fiery blood which coursed in her veins—they were not of God nor of His word, but of her time and race. Heathen history tells of similar deeds, and records them with highest praise;[1] Scripture with solemn silence. Yet even so Jehovah reigneth, and the fierce Arab was the sword in His hand !

1. "Then sang Deborah and Barak on that day, saying :

2. For the loose flowing of the long hair,[2]
   For the free dedication of the people,
   Praise ye Jehovah !

3. Hear O kings, hearken O rulers,[3]
   I—to Jehovah will I sing,
   Will psalmody[4] to Jehovah, the God of Israel !

4. Jehovah, when Thou didst come forth from Seir,
   When Thou marchedst from out the fields of Edom,
   The earth trembled, also the heavens dropped,
   Even the clouds dropped water.[5]

---

[1] For example in the case of Aretaphila in Cyrene (Plutarch, *The Virtues of Women*, 19).

[2] The language is extremely difficult, and the most different interpretations have been proposed. We have adopted the ingenious view of Cassel, which represents Israel, as it were, taking the Nazarite vow for God and against His enemies.

[3] Comp. Ps. ii. 2—these, of course, are kings and princes of the heathen.

[4] Always used of sacred song with instrumental accompaniment.

[5] Deborah begins with the record of God's great doings of old in the wilderness, the later parallel being in Ps. lxviii. 7, 8. Comp. here especially Ex. xix. and Deut. xxxiii. 2, and for the expressions, Ps. xlvii. 5 ; cxiv. 7 ; Isa. lxiii. 12 ; lxiv. 2 ; Jer. x. 10 ; Joel iii. 16.

5. The mountains quaked before Jehovah—
   This Sinai before Jehovah, the God of Israel.[1]

---

6 In the days of Shamgar, the son of Anath,
   In the days of Jael,[2] the highways ceased,[3]
   And they who went on paths, went by roundabout ways.

7. Deserted was the open country[4] in Israel—deserted—
   Till I arose, Deborah,
   I arose a mother in Israel!

8. Chose they new gods—
   Then war at the gates—
   If shield was seen or spear
   Among forty thousand in Israel![5]

---

9. My heart towards the rulers of Israel,
   Those who freely vowed (dedicated) themselves among the people.
   Praise ye Jehovah!

10. Ye that ride on white[6] she-asses,
    Ye that sit on coverings,[7]
    Ye that walk by the way—consider![8]

11. From the noise (sound, voice) of the archers between the draw-wells[9]—

---

[1] Here the *first* stanza of the *first* division of this song ends. There are in all three sections, each of three stanzas. The reader will have no difficulty in marking the progress of thought.

[2] Cassel, as I think fancifully, regards "Jael," not as referring to the wife of Heber, but as a poetic name for Shamgar or Ehud.

[3] Or were deserted.

[4] That is, the country with open villages and towns, in opposition to walled cities.

[5] That is, "shield and spear were *not* seen." So low had the fortunes of Israel fallen before their enemies.

[6] The expression is not without difficulty; Cassel would render it by pack-saddled.

[7] The reference here is evidently to abiding in tents, whether the word be rendered mats, carpets, garments, or coverings.

[8] Viz., the contrast between the insecurity of former times and the present happy condition. Cassel happily points out that, as in Ps. i. 1, the reference is to the three classes : those who sit, who stand, and who go.

[9] The language is very difficult. To us it seems to indicate the contrast between the noise of battle and the peaceful scene of the maidens, who can now go without fear outside the gates to draw water.

There they rehearse the righteous deeds[1] of Jehovah,
The mighty deeds of His open country[2] in Israel—
Then went down to the city gates the people of Jehovah !

PART II.

12. Awake, awake, Deborah,
Awake, awake—utter the song ;
Arise, Barak, and lead captive thy captives, son of Abinoam !

13. Then went down a remnant of the mighty, of the people,
Jehovah went down for me among the heroes !

14. From out of Ephraim—his root in Amalek ;[3]
After thee : Benjamin among thy nations[4]—
From Machir[5] come down they who bear rule,
From Zebulon who draw out with the staff of the writer.[6]

---

15. But the princes of Issachar *were* with Deborah—
And Issachar the foundation[7] of Barak,
Pouring on foot into the valley !
By the brooks of Reuben great resolves of heart—[8]

16. Why abodest thou among the folds
To hear the flutes of the flocks ?
By the brooks of Reuben great ponderings of heart !

17. Gilead dwells on the other side Jordan ![9]
And Dan, why pass upon ships ?

---

[1] The righteous deeds are here the *mighty* deeds, and so we have rendered it in the next line.

[2] Seems to mean : His mighty deeds in reference to, or as seen in the villages and unwalled towns of Israel.

[3] There seems an allusion here to the *ancient* glory of the tribes : Ephraim, from which sprang Joshua, the conqueror of Amalek.

[4] " Nations," here equivalent to heathens, and the reference is to Ehud.

[5] Machir is Manasseh, Gen. 1. 23.

[6] These two tribes then distinguished for peaceful avocations. Such was the *former* glory of Israel. In the next stanza Deborah proceeds to sketch the *present* state of the tribes.

[7] In his territory the battle was fought—the rendering " foundation " is after the Jewish commentaries.

[8] Here begins the censure of the tribes who should have taken part

[9] Such is its plea.

Asher sitteth by the sea-shore,
And by its bays resteth !

18. Zebulon a people that jeoparded its life unto death,
And Naphtali on the heights of the field !

19. Came kings—warred—
Then warred the kings of Canaan,
In Taanach, by the waters of Megiddo—
Spoil of silver took they none !

20. From heaven warred,
The stars out of their paths warred against Sisera !

21. The river Kishon swept them away,
River of encounters,[1] river Kishon !
March forth my soul in strength !

22. Then clattered the hoofs of the horse
From the racing and chasing[2] of his mighty.

23. Curse ye Meroz,[3] saith the Angel of Jehovah,
Curse ye—cursed its inhabitants,
For they came not to the help of Jehovah,
The help of Jehovah against the mighty !

PART III.

24. Blessed among women, Jael,
The wife of Heber, the Kenite,
Among women in the tent[4] blessed !

25. Water asked he—milk she gave,
In the cup of the noble[5] brought she thickened milk[6]—

---

[1] The common rendering is "ancient river ;" Cassel translates "river of help." I prefer "battle," the root being : to meet or to encounter, *obviam ire*. *Kishon*, "the winding one." Ancient Jewish tradition has it that this battle was fought on the Passover, which is not unlikely, as the Kishon is swollen during the rainy season, but quite dry in summer.

[2] In their flight. In the original the word is simply repeated.

[3] Probably a place near Endor, whose inhabitants joined not in the pursuit of Sisera.

[4] Such women as live in tents—pastoral and nomadic, as all the Kenites were.

[5] The cup used on state occasions, as it were.

[6] Cream, or thickened milk (it is a mistake of interpreters to suppose that it was thickened to make him intoxicated) ; or else camel's milk.

26. Her hand to the tent-nail sendeth forth,
    And her right hand to the ponderous hammer of workmen—
    Hammers[1] she Sisera, shivers[1] his head,
    Cleaves[1] and pierces his temple !

27. Between her feet he winds—he falls—he lies—
    Between her feet he winds—he falls—
    Where he winds there he falls desolated![2]

---

28. High up through the window spies—anxiously she calls,
    The mother of Sisera—cut through the lattice :
    ' Why tarrieth his chariot to come,
    Why linger the steps of his war-chariots ?'

29. The wise of her princesses answer—
    Nay, she herself answers her words to herself :

30. ' Are they not finding—dividing spoil—
    A maiden—twain maidens to the head of the warriors—
    Spoil of dyed garments to Sisera,
    Spoil of dyed garments—many-coloured kerchief—
    A dyed garment, twain many-coloured kerchiefs for the necks
    of the prey !'[3]

---

31. So perish all Thine enemies, Jehovah—
    And let those who love Him be like the going forth of the sun
    in his strength !

And the land had rest forty years."

[1] We almost seem to hear the three strokes of the hammer by which her bloody work is done.

[2] The description of the effects corresponding to the three strokes of the hammer.

[3] With each captive maiden the warrior would also receive one dyed garment and twain many-coloured kerchiefs. In the arduous task of translating this, one of the most difficult passages of Scripture, Cassel's *Commentary* has been of greatest use, although its suggestions are too often fanciful.

CHAPTER XVI.

Midianitish Oppression—The Calling of Gideon—Judgment begins at the House of God—The Holy War—The Night-battle of Moreh.

(JUDGES VI.–VII. 22.)

WITH the calling of Gideon commences the *second* period in the history of the Judges. It lasted altogether less than a century. During its course events were rapidly hastening towards the final crisis. Each narrative is given with full details, so as to exhibit the peculiarity of God's dealings in every instance, the growing apostacy of Israel, and the inherent unfitness even of its best representatives to work real deliverance.

The narrative opens, as those before, with a record of the renewed idolatry of Israel. Judgment came in this instance through the Midianites, with whom the Amalekites and other "children of the east" seem to have combined. It was two hundred years since Israel had avenged itself on Midian (Numb. xxxi. 3–11). And now once more, from the far east, these wild nomads swept, like the modern Bedawîn, across Jordan, settled in the plain of Jezreel, and swooped down as far as Gaza in the distant south-west. Theirs was not a permanent occupation of the land, but a continued desolation. No sooner did the golden harvest stand in the field, or was stored into garners, than they unexpectedly arrived. Like the plague of locusts, they left nothing behind. What they could not carry away as spoil, they destroyed. Such was the feeling of insecurity to life and property, that the people made them "mountain-dens, and caves, and strongholds," where to seek safety for themselves and their possessions. Seven years had this terrible scourge impoverished the land, when the people once more bethought themselves of Jehovah, the God of their fathers, and cried unto Him. This time, however, before granting deliverance, the Lord sent a prophet to bring Israel to a knowledge of their guilt as the source of their misery. The call to repentance was speedily followed by help.

1. *The calling of Gideon.*—Far away on the south-western border of Manasseh, close by the boundary of Ephraim, was the little township of *Ophrah,*[1] belonging to the family of *Abiezer*[2] (Josh. xvii. 2; 1 Chron. vii. 18), apparently one of the smallest clans in Manasseh (Judges vi. 15). Its head or chief was *Joash*—"Jehovah strength," or "firmness." As such he was lord of Ophrah. In such names the ancient spiritual faith of Israel seems still to linger amidst the decay around. And now, under the great oak by Ophrah, suddenly appeared a heavenly stranger. It was the Angel of Jehovah, the Angel of the Covenant, Who in similar garb had visited Abraham at Mamre (Gen. xviii.). Only there He had come, in view of the judgment about to burst, to confirm Abraham's faith—to enter into fellowship with him, while here the object was to call forth faith, and to prove that the Lord was ready to receive the vows and prayers of His people, if they but turned to Him in the appointed way. This may also explain, why in the one case the heavenly visitor joined in the meal,[3] while in the other fire from heaven consumed the offering (comp. Judges xiii. 16; 1 Kings xviii. 38; 2 Chron. vii. 1).

Close by the oak was the winepress of Joash, and there his son *Gideon*[4] was beating out the wheat with a stick.[5] Alike the place and the manner of threshing were quite unusual, and

---

[1] *Ophrah* means township. This Ophrah is to be distinguished from that in Benjamin.   [2] "My father *is* help."

[3] The *Targum* puts it: "they seemed to eat," and Cassel argues that, as theirs was not real humanity, neither was their eating. This, of course, is quite different from the eating on the part of our Lord, which was real— since His humanity and His body were real and true.

[4] "One who cuts down," a warrior.

[5] The term in the original conveys this.

only accounted for by the felt need for secrecy, and the constant apprehension that at an unexpected moment some wild band of Midianites might swoop down upon him. If, as we gather from the Angel's salutation, Gideon was a strong hero, and if, as we infer from his reply, remembrances and thoughts of the former deeds of Jehovah for Israel had burned deep into his heart, we can understand how the humiliating circumstances under which he was working in his father's God-given posses- sion, in one of the remotest corners of the land, must have filled his soul with sadness and longing. It is when "the strong warrior" is at the lowest, that the Messenger of the Covenant suddenly appears before him.   Not only the brightness of His face and form, but the tone in which He spake, and still more His words, at once struck the deepest chords in Gideon's heart. "Jehovah with thee, mighty hero !" Then the speaker was one of the few who looked unto Jehovah as the help-giver ; and he expressed alike belief and trust ! And was there not in that appellation "mighty warrior" a sound like the echo of national expectations—like a call to arms? One thing at least the Angel immediately gained. It was—what the Angel of His Presence *always* first gains—*the confidence of Gideon's heart.* To the unknown stranger he pours forth his inmost doubts, sorrows, and fears. It is not that he is ignorant of Jehovah's past dealings, nor that he questions His present power, but that he believes that, if Jehovah had not withdrawn from Israel, their present calamities could not have rested upon them. The conclusion was right and true, so far as it went ; for Israel's prosperity or sufferings depended on the presence or the absence of Jehovah. Thus Gideon's was in truth *a confession of Israel's sin,* and of *Jehovah's justice.* It was *the beginning of repentance.* But Gideon had yet to learn another truth—that Jehovah would turn from His anger, if Israel only turned to Him ; and yet another lesson *for himself :* to *put personal trust in the promise of God,* based as it was on His covenant of love, and that whether the outward means to be employed seemed adequate or not.

But Gideon was prepared to learn all this; and, as always, *gradually* did the Lord teach His servant, both by word, and by the sight with which He confirmed it. The reply of the Angel could leave no doubt on the mind of Gideon that a heavenly messenger was before him, Who promised that through him Israel should be saved, and that simply because *He* sent him. It is not necessary to suppose that Gideon understood that this messenger from heaven was the Angel of the Covenant. On the contrary, the revelation was very gradual. Nor do the questions of Gideon seem strange—for such they are rather than doubts. Looking around at his tribe, at his clan, and at his own position in it, help through him seemed most unlikely, and, if we realise all the circumstances, was so. Only one conclusive answer could be returned to all this: "I shall be with thee." The sole doubt now left was: Who was this great I AM?—and this Gideon proposed to solve by "asking for a sign," yet not a sign to his unbelief, but one connected with worship and with sacrifice. Jehovah granted it. As when Moses sought to know God, He revealed not His being but His character and His ways (Ex. xxxiii. 18; xxxiv. 6), so now He revealed to Gideon not only Who had spoken to him, but also that His "Name" was "Jehovah, Jehovah God, merciful and gracious, longsuffering, and abundant in goodness and truth, keeping mercy for thousands, forgiving iniquity, and transgression, and sin."

It would be almost fatal to the proper spiritual understanding of this, as of other Biblical narratives, if we were to transport into it our present knowledge, ideas, and views. Remembering the circumstances of the nation, of Gideon, and of Israel; remembering also the stage of spiritual knowledge attainable at that period, and the difficulty of feeling really sure *Who* the speaker was, we can understand Gideon's request (vi. 1–17): "Work for me a sign that THOU (art He) Who art speaking with me."[1] It is difficult to imagine what special sign Gideon was expecting. Probably he had formed no

[1] So literally.

definite idea. Suffice it, he would bring a sacrificial gift; the rest he would leave to Him. And he brought of the best. It was a kid of the goats, while for the "cakes," to be offered with it, he took a whole ephah of flour, that is, far more than was ordinarily used. But he does all the ministry himself; for no one must know of it. To dispense with assistance, he puts the meat and the cakes in the "bread-basket,"[1] "and the broth in a pot." Directed by the Angel, he spreads his offering on a rock. Then the Angel touches it with the end of His staff; fire leaps out of the rock and consumes the sacrifices; and the Angel has vanished out of his sight. There was in this both a complete answer to all Gideon's questions, and also deep symbolic teaching. But a fresh fear now fills Gideon's heart. Can one like him, who has seen God, live? To this also Jehovah gives an answer, and that for all times: "Peace to thee—fear not—thou shalt not die!" And in perpetual remembrance thereof—not for future worship— Gideon built an altar there,[2] and attached to it the name, "Jehovah-Peace!"

2. One part was finished, but another had to begin. Jehovah had called—would Gideon be ready to obey? For *judgment must now begin at the house of God.* No one is fit for His work in the world till he has begun it in himself and in his own house, and put away all sin and rebellion, however hard the task. It was night when the command of Jehovah came. This time there was neither hesitation nor secrecy about Gideon's procedure. He obeyed God's directions literally and imme- diately. Taking ten of his servants, he first threw down the altar of Baal, and cut down the *Asherah*—the vile symbol of the vile service of Astarte—that was upon it.[3] One altar was de- stroyed, but another had to be raised. For, the altar of Jehovah

---

[1] This is the uniform meaning of the word.

[2] The added notice as to its continuance at the time of the writer throws light upon the date of the authorship of the book.

[3] The two were very generally connected, and formed the grossest con- trast to the pure service of Jehovah.

could not be reared till that of Baal had been cast down.
It was now built, and that not in some secret hiding-place, but
on "the top of this defence"—either on the top of the hill
on which the fort stood, or perhaps above the place where
the people were wont to seek shelter from the Midianites.
Upon this altar Gideon offered his father's "second bullock
of seven years old"—the age being symbolical of the time of
Midian's oppression—at the same time using the wood of the
Asherah in the burnt-sacrifice. Such a reformation could not,
and was not intended to be hidden. The Baal's altar and its
Asherah were indeed Joash's, but only as chief of the clan.
And when on the following morning the Abiezrites clamoured
for the death of the supposed blasphemer, Joash, whose courage
and faith seem to have been re-awakened by the bold deed of
his son, convinced his clan of the folly of their idolatry by
an unanswerable argument, drawn from their own conduct.
"What !" he exclaimed, in seeming condemnation, "will ye
strive for Baal ? Or will ye save him? He that will strive for
him let him die until the morrow !¹ If he be a god, let him
strive for himself, because he has thrown down his altar. And
they called him on that day Jerubbaal² ('let Baal strive'), that
is to say, Let the Baal strive with him, because he has thrown
down his altar."

3. *The Holy War.*—Gideon had now purified himself and
his house, and become ready for the work of the Lord. And
yet another important result had been secured. The test to
which Baal had been put had proved his impotence. Idolatry
had received a heavy blow throughout the land. In Ophrah
at least the worship of Jehovah was now alone professed.

---

¹ That is, if any should seek to vindicate Baal to-day let him die ; wait
till to-morrow to give him time !

² In 2 Sam. xi. 21 he is called Jerubbesheth—*besheth*, "shame," being
an opprobrious name instead of Baal. May this throw any light on the
names of Ishbosheth and Mephibosheth? In 1 Chron. viii. 33, ix. 39, at
least Ishbosheth is called Ish-baal, while in 1 Chron. viii. 34 we have
Meribbaal ("strife of," or else "against Baal") instead of Mephibosheth
("glory" or "utterance" of Baal).

Moreover, the whole clan Abiezer, and, beyond it, all who had heard of Gideon's deed, perpetuated even in his name, were prepared to look to him as their leader. The occasion for it soon came. Once more the Midianitish Bedawîn had swarmed across Jordan; once more their tents covered the plain of Jezreel. Now or never—now, before their destructive raids once more began, or else never under Gideon—must Israel arise! Yet not of his own purpose did he move. In the deeply expressive language of Scripture: " The Spirit of Jehovah clothed Gideon," [1] like a garment round about, or rather like an armour. Only after that he blew the trumpet of alarm. First, his own clan Abiezer " was called after him." Next, swift messengers bore the tidings all through Manasseh, and that tribe gathered. Other messengers hastened along the coast (to avoid the Midianites) through Asher northwards to Zebulun and Naphtali, and they as well as Asher, which formerly had not fought with Barak, obeyed the summons.

All was ready—yet one thing more did Gideon seek. It was not from unbelief, nor yet in weakness of faith, that Gideon asked a sign from the Lord, or rather a token, a pledge of His presence. Those hours in the history of God's heroes, when, on the eve of a grand deed of the sublimest faith, the spirit wrestles with the flesh, are holy seasons, to which the superficial criticism of a glib profession, that has never borne the strain of utmost trial, cannot be applied without gross presumption. When in such hours the soul in its agony is seen to cast its burden upon the Lord, we feel that we stand on holy ground. It is like a stately ship in a terrific gale, every beam and timber strained to the utmost, but righting itself at last, and safely reaching port.[2] Or rather it is like a close following of Jesus into the Garden of Gethsemane— with its agony, its prayer, and its victory. In substance, though not in its circumstances, it was the same struggle as

[1] So, Judges vi. 34, literally.

[2] The thought is beautifully carried out in one of the Hymns of St. Joseph of the Studium (translated by Dr. Neale in his *Hymns of the Eastern Church*).

that which was waged in the night when Jacob prayed : " I will not let Thee go except Thou bless me ; " the same as when, many centuries afterwards, the Baptist sent his disciples to ask Jesus : " Art Thou He, or do we wait for another ? "

The " sign " was of Gideon's own choosing, but graciously accorded him by God. It was twofold. On the first night the fleece of wool spread on the ground was to be full of dew, but the ground all around dry. This, however, might still admit of doubt, since a fleece would naturally attract the dew. Accordingly, the next night the sign was reversed, and the fleece alone remained dry, while the ground all around was wet with dew. The symbolical meaning of the sign is plain. Israel was like that fleece of wool, spread on the wide extent of the nations. But, whereas all the ground around was dry, Israel was filled with the dew, as symbol of the Divine blessing.[1] And the second sign meant, that it was equally of God, when, during Israel's apostacy, the ground all around was wet, and the fleece of Jehovah's flock alone left dry.

4. *The battle: " For Jehovah and for Gideon !"*—The faith which had made such trial of God was to be put to the severest trial. Israel's camp was pitched on the height ; probably on a crest of Mount Gilboa, which seems to have borne the name of Gilead. At its foot rose " the spring Harod "— probably the same which now bears the name *Jalood*. Beyond it was the hill *Moreh* (from the verb " to indicate," " to direct "), and north of it, in the valley,[2] lay the camp of Midian, 135,000 strong (Judges viii. 10), whereas the number of Israel amounted to only 22,000. But even so they were too many—at least for Jehovah " to give the Midianites into their hand, lest Israel vaunt themselves against Me, saying, Mine own hand hath saved me." In accordance with a previous Divine direction (Deut. xx. 8), proclamation was made for all who were

---

[1] Gen. xxvii. 28 ; Deut. xxxiii. 13 ; Prov. xix. 12 ; Isa. xxvi. 19 ; Hos. xiv. 5 ; Mic. v. 7.

[2] " And they camped upon the spring Harod, and the camp of Midian was to him from the north, from the height of Moreh in the valley " (Judges vii. 1).

afraid, to " turn and wind about [1] from Mount Gilead."[2]   Still, Gideon must have been surprised, when, in consequence, he found himself left with only 10,000 men.   But even these were too many.   To " purify them " (as by refining—for such is the meaning of the word), Gideon was now to bring them down to the spring Harod, where those who were to go to battle would be separated from the rest.[3]   All who lapped the water with the tongue out of their hands (out of the hollow hand), as a dog lappeth water, were to go with Gideon, the rest to return, each to his own place.   Only three hundred were now left, and with these God declared He would save, and deliver the Midianites into Gideon's hand.   If we ask about the rationale of this means of distinction, we conclude, of course, that it indicated the bravest and most ardent warriors,[4] who would not stoop to kneel, but hastily quenched their thirst out of the hollow of their hands, in order to hasten to battle.   But Jewish tradition assigns another and deeper meaning to it.   It declares that the practice of kneeling was characteristic of the service of Baal, and hence that kneeling down to drink when exhausted betrayed the habit of idolaters.   Thus the three hundred would represent those in the host of Israel—" all the knees which have not bowed unto Baal " (1 Kings xix. 18).[5]   They who had been selected now " took victuals from the people [6] in their hands, and the trumpets "—the rest were sent away.

[1] So literally ; possibly referring to circuitous routes.

[2] Gilead was probably another name for Gilboa.   Cassel suggests that it may stand for *Manasseh.*

[3] First the Divine promise, and *then* the Divine command to our faith (Judges vii. 7).   So it is always.

[4] Josephus (*Ant.* v. 6, 3) holds, that the three hundred were the most fainthearted.   But it is surely unreasonable to suppose that, when all who feared had been dismissed, the most fainthearted should in the end have been chosen.

[5] Cassel attempts to find a special meaning in the comparison : " as a dog licketh," as referring to a kind of dog (of which the ancients and the Talmud speak), which was wont, when the crocodile was asleep, to throw itself into its gullet and to kill it.

[6] This seems to be the real meaning of Judges vii. 8, whether or not it be deemed needful to emendate the text.

That night the small company of Israel occupied an advanced position on the brow of the steep mountain, that overhangs the valley of Jezreel.[1] Effectually concealed, probably by the shelter of wood or vineyards, the vast straggling camp of Midian spread right beneath them. That night came the Divine command to Gideon to go down to the camp, for God had given it into his hand. And yet, alike in condescension to Gideon's weakness, and to show how thoroughly the Lord had prepared the victory, He first allowed him to ascertain for himsel the state of matters in the camp of Midian. Quietly Gideon and his page *Phurah* (" the branch ") crept from rock to rock, over where the last patrol of the advance-guard[2] kept watch around the camp-fire. Here they overheard the tale of a strange dream. Alike the dream and its interpretation are peculiarly Eastern and in character. Both would make the deepest impression on those sons of the desert, and, communicated to the next patrol, as the first watch was relieved by the second, must have prepared for that panic which, commencing with the advance-guard, was so soon to spread through the whole camp of Midian. The dream was simply this : " Behold, a loaf of barley-bread rolled itself into the camp of Midian, and it came to the tent (the principal one, that of the general), and struck it, and it fell, and it turned from above[3] —and it was fallen !" To which his neighbour (comrade) replied : " This is nothing else but the sword of Gideon, the son of Joash, a man of Israel ; given hath the God[4] into his hand Midian and all his camp." So wondrous seemed the dream and its interpretation, that, when Gideon and his armour-bearer heard it, they bent in silent worship, assuredly knowing that God had given them the victory. In truth, with the tale of this dream the miracle of the victory had already begun.

[1] So we understand the expression : " And the camp of Midian was beneath him in the valley."

[2] Judges vii. 11 : " The end of the advance-guard ;" the latter seems to be the meaning of *Chamushim*. See Josh. i. 14.

[3] So that the upper part was downwards.

[4] " The Elohim," emphatically, with the article.

There is such pictorialness and such truthfulness of detail about all this narrative, that we almost seem to see the events enacted before us. That camp of Bedouins, like locusts in number—with their wives, children, and camels, like the sand by the seashore; then the watchfire by which alone they keep guard; the talk over the camp-fire; the dream so peculiarly Bedouin, and its rapid interpretation, no less characteristically Eastern—and yet the while all ordered and arranged of God— while that small band of three hundred Israelites lies concealed on the neighbouring height, and Gideon and his "young man," are close by, behind the great shadows which the watch-fire casts, hidden perhaps in the long grass! Then the dream itself! It was all quite natural, and yet most unnatural. The Midian- ites—especially the advanced-guard, that lay nearest to Israel, could not be ignorant that Gideon and his host occupied yonder height. Fame would spread, probably exaggerate, the "mighty valour" of Gideon, and the valour of his followers— while the diminished numbers of Gideon would, of course, not be known, as they had retired by circuitous routes. Moreover, the Midianites must also have been aware that this was to Israel a religious war; nor can they have been ignorant of the might of Jehovah. The fears which all this inspired appear in the interpretation of the dream. But the dream itself was the result of the same feelings. Barley-bread was deemed the poorest food; yet a loaf of this despised provision of slaves rolls itself into Midian's camp, strikes the tent of the leader, turns it upside down, and it falls! Here is a dream-picture of Israel and its victory—all quite natural, yet marvellously dreamed and told just at that peculiar time. And still, often do dreams, excited by natural causes, link themselves, in God's appointment, to thoughts that come supernaturally. We have throughout this history marked how often what seemed to happen quite naturally, was used by God miraculously, and how the supernatural linked itself to what, more or less, had its counterpart in the ordinary course of nature. It had been so in the history of Moses and of Israel; it was so when Joshua defeated the allied kings before Gibeon, and when Barak en countered the invincible chariots of Sisera. In each case it was the Lord, Who gave miraculous victory through terrific tempest. So also it had been in an hour, when thoughts of Israel's past and present must have burned deepest into the heart of Gideon, that the Angel stood before him, even as it was by means most natural that God separated from the rest the three hundred who had not bent the knee to Baal, and who alone were to go to the holy war. Thoughts like these do not detract from, they only make the supernatural the more marvellous. Yet they seem also to bring it nearer to us, till we feel ourselves likewise within its circle, and can realise that even our "daily bread" comes to us straight from heaven !

Gideon and Phurah have returned to the waiting host. In whispered words he has told what they had witnessed. And now the three hundred are divided into three companies. It is not the naked sword they grasp, for in that night not Israel, but Jehovah is to fight. In one hand each man holds a trumpet, in the other, concealed in a pitcher, a burning torch. Each is to do exactly as the leader. Silently they creep round to three different parts of Midian's camp. The guard has just been re lieved, and the new watchers have settled quietly by the watch fire. Suddenly a single trumpet is heard, then three hundred— here, there, everywhere the sound of war is raised. The night is peopled with terrors. Now with loud crash three hundred pitchers are broken ; three hundred torches flash through the darkness ; three hundred voices shout : "The sword for Jehovah and for Gideon !" Then is the enemy all around the camp ! No one can say in what numbers. Again and again rings the trumpet-sound ; wave the torches. The camp is roused. Men, women, children, camels rush terror-stricken through the dark night. No one knows but that the enemy is in the very midst of them, and that the neighbour whom he meets is an Israelite, for all around still sounds the war-trumpet, flash the torches, and rises the war-cry. Each man's sword is turned against his neighbour. Multitudes are killed or trampled down, and their cries and groans increase the terror of that wild night. A hopeless panic ensues, and ere morning-light, the site of the camp and the road of the fugitives towards Jordan are strewed with the slain.[1]

CHAPTER XVII.

Farther Course of Gideon—The Ephod at Ophrah— Death of Gideon—Conspiracy of Abimelech—The Parable of Jotham—Rule and End of Abimelech.

(JUDGES VII. 23–IX.)

THE tide of battle had rolled towards the Jordan. The fugitives seem to have divided into two main bodies. The quickest, under the leadership of Zebah and Zalmunna, succeeded in crossing the Jordan, and hastened towards the wilderness, while the main body of the army, encumbered with women and cattle, fled in a south-easterly direction, trying to gain the more southern fords of the Jordan within the possession of Issachar, and almost in a straight line with that of Ephraim. The two kings were the object of Gideon's own pursuit, in which he was joined by those of Naphtali, Asher, and Manasseh, who had shortly before been dismissed from the battle. To overtake the other body of fugitives, Gideon summoned the Ephraimites, directing them to occupy "the waters," or tributaries of Jordan, unto Beth-barah (the house of springs) and the Jordan. The success of Ephraim was complete. A great battle seems to have been fought (Is. x. 26), in which the leaders of the Midianites, Oreb and Zeeb ("the raven" and "the wolf") were taken and slain. The Ephraimites continued the pursuit of the fugitives to the other side of the Jordan,

---

[1] It is interesting to notice, that both classical and modern history record similar night-surprises, with ensuing panic and slaughter, though, of course, not of the miraculous character of this narrative.

bringing with them to Gideon the gory heads of Oreb and Zeeb. Strange and sad, that their first meeting with Gideon after this victory should have been one of reproaches and strife, on account of their not having been first summoned to the war— strife, springing from that tribal jealousy which influenced for such evil the whole history of Ephraim. Nor was the reply of Gideon much more satisfactory than their noisy self-assertion (viii. 1–3). To us at least it savours more of the diplomacy of an Oriental, than the straightforward bearing of the warrior of God.

While Ephraim occupied " the waters " and the fords of the Jordan, Gideon himself had crossed the river at the spot where Jacob of old had entered Canaan on his return from Padan-Aram. "Faint yet pursuing," the band reached *Succoth;* but its "princes" refused even the most useful provisions to Gideon's men. The people of the neighbouring Penuel acted in the same heartless manner—no doubt from utter lack of interest in the cause of God, from cowardice, and, above all, from scorn for the small band of 300, with which Gideon had gone in pursuit of the flower of Midian's army. They had calculated the result by the outward means employed, but were destined soon to feel the consequences of their folly. Making a detour eastwards, through the wilderness, Gideon advanced on the rear of Midian, and fell unexpectedly upon the camp at Karkor, which was held by 15,000 men under the command of Zebah and Zalmunna ("sacrifice" and " protection refused "). The surprise ended in defeat and flight, the two Midianite leaders being made prisoners and taken across Jordan. On his way,[1] Gideon "taught the men of Succoth," by punishing their rulers[2]— seventy-seven in number, probably consisting of either seven,

[1] In Judges viii. 13 the rendering should be, "from the ascent of Heres," probably a mountain-road by which he came—instead of " before the sun was up."

[2] The notice in viii. 14 (literally rendered), that the lad "wrote down for him " the names of the princes, is interesting as showing the state of education at the time even in so remote a district.

or else five " princes," and of seventy or else seventy-two elders—while in the case of Penuel, which seems to have offered armed resistance to the destruction of its citadel, " the men of the city " were actually slain.

The fate of Gideon's princely captives did not long remain doubtful. It seems that he would have spared their lives, if they had not personally taken part in the slaughter of his brothers, which may have occurred at the commencement of the last campaign, and while the Midianites held Jezreel— possibly under circumstances of treachery and cruelty, prompted perhaps by tidings that Gideon had raised the standard of resistance. It may have been to investigate the facts on the spot, that Gideon had brought back [1] the two princes, or he may have only heard of it on his return. At any rate, the two Midianites not only confessed, but boasted of their achievement. By the law of retaliation they were now made to suffer death, although the hesitation of Gideon's son spared them the humiliation of falling by the hand of a young lad.

The deliverance of Israel was now complete. It had been wrought most unexpectedly, and by apparently quite inadequate means. In the circumstances, it was natural that, in measure as the people failed to recognise the direct agency of Jehovah, they should exalt Gideon as the great national hero. Accordingly, they now offered him the hereditary rule over, at least, the northern tribes. Gideon had spiritual discernment and strength sufficient to resist this temptation. He knew that he had only been called to a temporary work, and that the " rule " which they wished could not be made hereditary. Each " judge " must be specially called, and qualified by the influence of the Holy Spirit. Besides, the latter was not, as since the ascension of our Blessed Saviour, a permanent indwelling of the Holy Spirit as a Person, but consisted in certain effects produced by His agency. The proposal of Israel could therefore only arise from carnal misunderstanding, and must be refused.

[1] We gather that this took place either in Jezreel or at Ophrah from the circumstance that Gideon's son had joined him : viii. 20.

But Gideon himself was not proof against another temptation and mistake. God had called him not only to temporal, but to spiritual deliverance of Israel. He had thrown down the altar of Baal; he had built up that of Jehovah, and offered on it accepted sacrifice. Shiloh was deserted, and the high priest seemed set aside. Ophrah had been made what Shiloh should have been, and Gideon had taken the place of the high priest. All this had been by express Divine command— and without any reference to the services of the tabernacle. Moreover, Gideon's office had never been recalled. Should it not now be made permanent, at least, in his own person? The keeping of Israel's faith had been committed to his strong hand; should he deliver it up to the feeble grasp of a nominal priesthood which had proved itself incapable of such a trust? It was to this temptation that Gideon succumbed. when he asked of the people the various golden ornaments, taken as spoil from the enemy.[1] The gold so obtained amounted to seventeen thousand shekels—or nearly the weight of fifty pounds. With this Gideon made an ephod, no doubt with the addition of the high-priestly breastplate and its precious gems, and of the Urim and Thummim. Here, then, was the commencement of a spurious worship. Presently, Israel went to Ophrah, " a whoring after it," while to Gideon himself and to his house this " thing became a snare."[2]

In truth, the same spiritual misunderstanding which culmi- nated in Gideon's arrogating to himself high-priestly functions, had appeared almost immediately after that night-victory of Jehovah over Midian. Even his reply to the jealous wrangling of Ephraim does not sound like the straightforward language of one who had dismissed the thousands of Israel to go to

[1] It is well known that the Midianites delighted in that kind of orna- -ments. We recognise in this, even to the present day, the habits of the Bedawîn. If we bear in mind that the host of Midian consisted of 150,000 men, the weight of gold will by no means appear excessive.

[2] The Rabbis find here tribal jealousies against Ephraim, within whose territory were Shiloh and the tabernacle.

battle with only three hundred. Again, there is what at least looks like petty revenge about his dealings with Succoth and Penuel; while it is difficult to understand upon what principle, other than that of personal retaliation, he had made the lives of Zebah and Zalmunna wholly dependent upon their conduct towards his own family. And the brief remarks or Scripture about the family-life of Gideon, after he had made the ephod, only tend to confirm our impressions. But, meantime, for "forty years in the days of Gideon," "the country was in quietness," and, however imperfect in its character, the service of Jehovah seems to have been, at least outwardly, the only one professed. Matters changed immediately upon his death. Presently the worship of Baalim becomes again common, and especially that of the "Covenant-Baal" (Baal-berith). There is a sad lesson here. If Gideon had made a spurious ephod, his people now chose a false "covenant-god." And, having first forsaken the Covenant-Jehovah, they next turned in ingratitude from their earthly deliverer, "neither showed they kindness to the house of Jerubbaal." Thus sin ever brings its own punishment.

Not far from Ophrah, but in the territory of Ephraim, was the ancient *Shechem*, connected with so much that was most solemn in the history of Israel. We know the long-standing tribal jealousy of Ephraim and their desire for leadership. Moreover, as we learn from Judges ix. 28, Shechem seems to have retained among its inhabitants the lineal representatives of Hamor, the original "prince" and founder of Shechem in the days of Jacob (Gen. xxxiii. 19; xxxiv. 2; comp. Josh. xxiv. 32). These would represent, so as speak, the ancient feudal heathen aristocracy of the place, and, of course, the original worshippers of Baal. As perhaps the most ancient city in that part of the country, and as the seat of the descendants of Hamor, Shechem seems to have become the centre of Baal worship. Accordingly we find there the temple of the "Covenant-Baal" (Judges ix. 4). Possibly the latter may have been intended to express and perpetuate the union of the original heathen with the more modern Israelitish, or "Shechem" part of the population. Here then were sufficient elements of mischief ready: tribal jealousy; envy of the great and ancient Shechem towards little Ophrah; hatred of the rule of the house of Gideon; but, above all, the opposition of heathenism. It is very characteristic of this last, as the chief motive at work, that throughout all the intrigues against the house of Gideon, he is never designated by his own name, but always as *Jerubbaal*—he that contended against Baal. Contending against Baal had been the origin of Gideon's power; and to the heathen mind it seemed still embodied in that Jehovah-Ephod in the possession of Gideon's sons at Ophrah. The present rising would in turn be the contending of Baal against the house of Gideon, and his triumph its destruction. It only needed a leader. Considering the authority which the family of Gideon must still have possessed, none better could have been found than one of its own members.

Gideon had left no fewer than seventy sons. If we may judge from their connivance at the worship of Baal around, from the want of any recognised outstanding individuality among them, and especially from their utter inability to make a stand even for life against an equal number of enemies, they must have sadly degenerated; probably were an enervated, luxurious, utterly feeble race. There was one exception, however, to this; one outside their circle, and yet of it—Abimelech, not a legitimate son of Gideon's, but one by "a maid-servant," a native of Shechem. Although we know not the possible peculiarities of the case, it is, in general, quite consistent with social relations in the East, that Abimelech's slave-mother should have had influential connections in Shechem, who, although of an inferior grade,[1] could enter into dealings with "the citizens" of the place. Abimelech seems to have

---

[1] This appears from the whole account of their transactions, in which the others are always designated as "lords" of Shechem, in our Authorised Version, "men of Shechem," or rather, probably, the citizens—what we would call the "house-owners" of Shechem.

possessed all the courage, vigour, and energy of his father; only coupled, alas! with restless ambition, reckless unscrupulousness, and daring impiety. His real name we do not know;[1] for *Abimelech*, father-king, or else king-father, seems to have been a by-name, probably suggested by his natural qualifications and his ambition. The plot was well contrived by Abimelech. At his instigation his mother's relatives entered into negotiations with the "citizens" or "householders" of Shechem. The main considerations brought to bear upon them seem to have been: hatred of the house of Gideon, and the fact that Abimelech was a fellow-townsman. This was sufficient. The compact was worthily ratified with Baal's money. Out of the treasury of his temple they gave Abimelech seventy shekels. This wretched sum, somewhere at the rate of half-a-crown a person, sufficed to hire a band of seventy reckless rabble for the murder of Gideon's sons. Such was the value which Israel put upon them! Apparently unresisting, they were all slaughtered upon one stone, like a sacrifice—all but one, Jotham ("Jehovah [is] perfect"), who succeeded in hiding himself, and thus escaped.

This is the first scene. The next brings us once more to "the memorial by the vale"[2] which Joshua had set up, when, at the close of his last address, the people had renewed their covenant with Jehovah (Josh. xxiv. 26, 27). It was in this sacred spot that "the citizens of Shechem and the whole house of Millo"[3] were now gathered to make Abimelech king! Close by, behind it, to the south, rose Gerizim, the Mount of Blessings. On one of its escarpments, which tower 800 feet above the valley, Jotham, the last survivor of Gideon's house, watched the scene. And now his voice rose above the shouts

---

[1] This is rightly inferred by Keil from the meaning of the verb, insufficiently rendered in our Authorised Version: "whose name he called Abimelech" (viii. 31).

[2] Wrongly rendered in our version "by the plain of the pillar," ix. 6.

[3] That is, the inhabitants of Millo. Millo was no doubt the castle or citadel close to Shechem.

of the people. In that clear atmosphere every word made its
way to the listeners below. It was a strange parable he told,
peculiarly of the East, that land of parables, and in language so
clear and forcible, that it stands almost unique. It is about
the Republic of Trees, who are about to elect a king. In turn
the olive, the fig tree, and the vine, the three great representatives of fruit-bearing trees in Palestine,[1] are asked. But each
refuses; for each has its own usefulness, and inquires with
wonder: "Am I then to lose" my fatness, or my sweetness, or
my wine, "and to go to flutter above the trees?"[2] The expressions are very pictorial, as indicating, on the one hand, that
such a reign could only be one of unrest and insecurity, a
"wavering" or "fluttering" above the trees, and that, in order
to attain this position of elevation above the other trees, a tree
would require to be uprooted from its own soil, and so lose
what of fatness, sweetness, or refreshment God had intended it
to yield. Then, these noble trees having declined the offer,
and apparently all the others also,[3] the whole of the trees next
turn to the thornbush, which yields no fruit, can give no shadow,
and only wounds those who take hold of it, which, in fact, is only
fit for burning. The thornbush itself seems scarcely to believe
that such a proposal could seriously be made to it. "If in
truth" (that is, "truly and sincerely") "ye anoint me king
over you, come, put your trust in my shadow;[4] but if not (that
is, if you fear so to do, or else find your hopes disappointed),
let fire come out of the thornbush and devour the cedars of
Lebanon."[5] The application of the parable was so evident,

---

[1] The Rabbis understand the three trees as referring to Othniel, Deborah,
and Gideon.

[2] So literally.

[3] This we gather from the fact that "the trees" successively solicit the
olive, the fig, and the vine, while afterwards "*all* the trees" are said to
turn to the thorn, as if all of them had been successively asked, and had
declined.

[4] Seek shelter under my shadow.

[5] That is, the noblest and the best. The thorn is easily set on fire—
indeed, fit for nothing else.

that it scarcely needed the pungent sentences in which Jotham in conclusion set before the people their conduct in its real character.

Jotham had not spoken as a prophet, but his language was prophetic. Three years, not of kingdom, but of rule,[1] and the judgment of God, which had been slumbering, began to descend. Scripture marks distinctly both the Divine agency in the altered feeling of Shechem towards Abimelech, and its import as boding judgment. The course of events is vividly sketched. First, the citizens post "liers in wait" in all the mountain passes, in the vain hope of seizing Abimelech. The consequence is universal brigandage. This device having failed, they next invite, or at least encourage the arrival among them of a freebooting adventurer with his band. It is the season of vintage, and, strange and terrible as it may sound, a service, specially ordered by Jehovah, is observed, but only to be prostituted to Baal. According to Lev. xix. 24, the produce of the fourth year's fruit planting was to be brought as "praise-offerings" (*Hillulim*) to Jehovah. And now these men of Shechem "made praise offerings"[2] (Hillulim), but went with them into the house of Baal-berith. At the sacrificial feast which followed, wine soon loosened the tongues. It is an appeal to Baal as against the house of Jerubbaal; a revolt of old Shechem against modern Shechem; in favour of the old patrician descendants of Hamor against Abimelech and his lieutenant Zebul.[3] This insulting challenge, addressed in true Oriental fashion to the absent, is conveyed by secret messengers

---

[1] The expression in ix. 22 is *not* that Abimelech reigned as a king, but that he lorded it.

[2] Our Authorised Version translates wrongly ix. 27 : "And they went out into the fields, ... and made merry." This last clause should be rendered, " and made *Hillulim*—praise offerings."

[3] The language is very pictorial in its contrast of young Shechem with old Shechem, or rather Hamor ; and in laying emphasis upon the name Jerubbaal. The challenge to Abimelech is, of course, not to be regarded as delivered to himself, but, as so common in the East, addressed to an imaginary Abimelech.

to Abimelech.[1] That night he and his band move forward. Divided into four companies, they occupy all the heights around Shechem. Ignorant how near was danger, Gaal stands next morning in the gate with his band, in the same spirit of boastfulness as at the festival of the previous night. He is still, as it were, challenging imaginary foes. Zebul is also there. As Abimelech's men are seen moving down towards the valley, Zebul first tries to lull Gaal's suspicions. And now they are appearing in all directions—from the mountains, "from the heights of the land," and one company "from the way of the terebinth of the magicians."[2] Zebul now challenges Gaal to make good his boasting. A fight ensues in view of the citizens of Shechem, in which Gaal and his band are discomfited, and he and his adherents are finally expelled from the town. If the Shechemites had thought thus to purchase immunity, they were speedily undeceived. Abimelech was hovering in the neighbourhood, and, when the unsuspecting people were busy in their fields, he surprised and slaughtered them, at the same time occupying the city, which was razed to the ground and sowed with salt. Upon this the citizens of the tower, or of Millo, sought refuge in the sacred precincts of "the hall of the god Berith." But in vain. Abimelech set it on fire, and 1000 persons perished in the flames. Even this did not satisfy his revenge. He next turned his forces against the neighbouring town of Thebez. Reduced to the utmost straits, its inhabitants fled to the strong tower within the city. Thither Abimelech pursued them. Almost had the people of Thebez shared the fate of the citizens of Millo, when Abimelech's course was strangely arrested. From the top of the tower a woman cast down upon him an "upper millstone."[3] As the Rabbis put it, he, that had slaughtered his brothers upon a stone, was killed

[1] The message of Zebul (ix. 31) was : "they raise the city against thee," viz., in rebellion—not, as in our Authorised Version, "they fortify the city against thee."

[2] In the Authorised Version (ver. 37) "the plain of the Meonenim."

[3] In the Authorised Version (ver. 53) "a piece of a millstone."

by a stone.   Abimelech died as he had lived.   Feeling himself
mortally wounded, ambitious warrior to the last, he had himself
run through by the sword of his armour-bearer, to avoid the
disgrace of perishing by the hand of a woman.   But his epitaph,
and that of the men of Shechem who had perished by his
hand, had been long before written in the curse of Jotham.

CHAPTER XVIII.

Successors of Abimelech—Chronology of the Period—
Israel's renewed Apostacy, and their Humiliation before
Jehovah—Oppression by the Ammonites—Jephthah—
His History and Vow—The Successors of Jephthah.

(JUDGES X.–XII.)

THE sudden and tragic end of Abimelech seems to have
awakened repentance among the people.   It is thus
that we explain the mention of his name (x. 1) in connection
with three judges, who successively ruled over the northern
tribes.   The first of these was *Tola* (" scarlet-worm "),[1] the son
of *Puah* (probably " red dye ") and grandson of Dodo, a man
of Issachar.   His reign lasted twenty-three years, and was
followed by that of *Jair* (" Enlightener "); who judged twenty-
two years.   The family notice of the latter indicates great
influence, each of his thirty sons appearing as a " chief "
(riding on " ass-colts "), and their property extending over
thirty out of the sixty cities (1 Kings iv. 13 ; 1 Chron. ii. 23)
which formed the ancient Havoth-Jair, or circuits of Jair[2]
(Numb. xxxii. 41 ; Deut. iii. 14).

---

[1] Some have translated this by the son of " his uncle," viz., the uncle of
Abimelech.   But this seems unlikely, as Gideon was of Manasseh, and Tola
of Issachar.   The names of *Tola* and *Puah*, or Phuvah (Gen. xlvi. 13 ;
Numb. xxvi. 23), as well as that of *Jair*, were *tribal* names.

[2] Certain critics have imagined a discrepancy between the earlier notice

Chronology of the period.   153

These forty-five years of comparative rest conclude the second period in the history of the Judges. The third, which commences with fresh apostacy on the part of Israel, includes the contemporaneous rule of *Jephthah* and his successors—Ibzan, Elon, and Abdon (xii. 8–15)—in the north and east, and of *Samson* in the south and west. While in the north and east Jephthah encountered the Ammonites, Samson warred against the Philistines in the south-west. The oppression of Ammon over the eastern and northern tribes lasted eighteen years (x. 8, 9); the rule of Jephthah six years (xii. 7); that of his three successors twenty-five years—covering in all a period of forty-nine years. On the other hand, the oppression of the Philistines lasted in all forty years (xiii. 1), during twenty years of which (xv. 20) Samson "began to deliver Israel" (xiii. 5), the deliverance being completed only twenty years later under Samuel, when the battle of Ebenezer was gained (1 Sam. vii.). Thus Abdon, Jephthah's last successor in the north, must have died nine years after the battle of Ebenezer. These dates are of great importance, not only on their own account, but because they show us the two parallel streams of Israel's history in the north and the south. Again, the coincidence of events in the south with those in the north casts fresh light upon both. Thus, as Eli's high-priestly administration, which in a general sense is designated as "judging Israel," lasted forty years (1 Sam. iv. 18), and his death took place about twenty years and seven months before the victory of Samuel over the Philistines (1 Sam. vi. 1; vii. 2), it is evident that the first twenty years of Eli's administration were contemporary with that of Jair in the east, while the last twenty were marked by the Philistine oppression, which continued forty years. In that case Samson must

---

in Numb. xxxii. 41, etc., and that in the text. But the text does *not* say that the Havoth-Jair obtained its name in the period of the Judges—rather the opposite, as will appear from the following rendering of Judges x. 4: "and they had thirty cities (of) those which are called the circuit of Jair *even* unto this day."

have been born, and have grown up during the high priesthood of Eli, and most of his exploits, as judging Israel for
twenty years, taken place under Samuel, who gained the battle
of Ebenezer, and so put an end to Philistine oppression, a
short time after the death of Samson. In connection with
this we may note, that Samuel's period of judging is only
mentioned *after* the battle of Ebenezer (1 Sam. vii. 15).

There is another and very important fact to be considered.
The terrible fate which overtook the house of Gideon, culminating in the death of Abimelech, seems for ever to have put
an end to the spurious ephod-worship of Jehovah, or to that
in any other place than that He had chosen, or through any
other than the Levitical priesthood. *Accordingly, the sanctuary
of Shiloh and its ministers now come again, and permanently,
into prominent notice.* This not only in the case of Eli and
Samuel, but long before that. This appears from the sacred
text. For when, previous to the calling of Jephthah, the children of Israel repented, we are told that they " cried unto
the Lord," and that the Lord spake unto them, to which they
in turn made suitable reply (Judges x. 10, 11, 15). But the
peculiar expressions used leave no doubt on our mind, that
the gathering of Israel before the Lord had taken place in
His sanctuary at Shiloh, and the answer of Jehovah been made
by means of the Urim and Thummim (comp. Judges i. 1).

For clearness' sake, it may be well to explain, that
Judges x. 6–18 forms a general introduction, alike to the history
of Jephthah and his successors, and to that of Samson. In
ver. 6 *seven* national deities are mentioned whom Israel had
served, besides the Baalim and Ashtaroth of Canaan. This in
opposition to the *sevenfold* deliverance (vers. 11, 12) which
Israel had experienced at the hands of Jehovah.[1] Then

---

[1] Israel's unfaithfulness is represented as keeping measure, so to speak,
with God's mercy and deliverance. The significance of the number seven
should not be overlooked. Instead of "the Maonites" in ver. 12 the LXX.
read " Midianites," which seems the more correct reading. Otherwise it
must refer to the tribe mentioned 2 Chron. xxvi. 7 ; comp. 1 Chron. iv. 41.

follows, in ver. 7, a general reference to the twofold contemporaneous oppression by the Ammonites in the east and
north, and by the Philistines in the south and west. In ver. 8
the account of the Ammonites' oppression[1] commences with
the statement, that "they ground down and bruised the
children of Israel that year," and in a similar manner for
eighteen years. In fact, the Ammonites, in their successful
raids across the Jordan, occupied districts of the territory of
Judah, Benjamin, and Ephraim, which bordered either on
the Dead Sea or on the fords of Jordan.[2] Next, we have in
verses 10–15 an account of Israel's humiliation and entreaty
at Shiloh, and of the Lord's answer by the Urim and
Thummim. Finally, ver. 16 informs us, how the genuineness
of their repentance appeared not in professions and promises,
but in the putting away of all " strange gods," and that when
there was no immediate prospect of Divine help. After this,
to reproduce the wonderful imagery of Scripture : " His soul
became short on account of the misery of Israel." That misery
had lasted too long ; He could not, as it were, be any longer
angry with them, nor bear to see their suffering. For, as a
German writer beautifully observes : " The love of God is not
like the hard and fast logical sequences of man ; it is ever
free. . . . The parable of the prodigal affords a glimpse of the
marvellous 'inconsistency' of the Father, who receives the
wanderer when he suffered the consequences of his sin. . . .
Put away the strange gods, and the withered rod will burst
anew into life and verdure." And such is ever God's love—full
and free. For, in the words of the author just quoted : " Sin
and forgiveness are the pivots of all history, specially of that
of Israel, including in that term the spiritual Israel."

Now, indeed, was deliverance at hand. For the first time
these eighteen years that Ammon had camped in Gilead, the
children of Israel also camped against them in Mizpeh, or, as it is

[1] That of the Philistines commences xiii. 1.
[2] I do not suppose that the Ammonites traversed the land, but that they
made raids across the fords of Jordan, and laid waste the contigucus districts.

otherwise called (Josh. xiii. 26 ; xx. 8), in Ramath-Mizpeh or Ramoth-Gilead (the modern *Salt*), a city east of the Jordan, in an almost direct line from Shiloh. The camp of Israel could not have been better chosen. Defended on three sides by high hills, Mizpeh lay "on two sides of a narrow ravine, half way up, crowned by a (now) ruined citadel,"[1] which probably at all times defended the city. "Ramoth-Gilead must always have been the key of Gilead, at the head of the only easy road from the Jordan, opening immediately on to the rich plateau of the interior, and with this isolated cone rising close above it, fortified from very early times, by art as well as by nature." All was thus prepared, and now the people of Gilead, through their "princes," resolved to offer the supreme command to any one who had already begun to fight against the children of Ammon—that is, who on his own account had waged warfare, and proved successful against them. This notice is of great importance for the early history of Jephthah.

Few finer or nobler characters are sketched even in Holy Scripture than *Jephthah*, or rather Jiphthach ("the breaker through"). He is introduced to us as "a mighty man of valour"—the same terms in which the angel had first addressed Gideon (vi. 12). But this "hero of might" must first learn to conquer his own spirit. His history is almost a parallel to that of Abimelech—only in the way of *contrast*. For, whereas Abimelech had of his own accord left his father's house to plan treason, Jephthah was wrongfully driven out by his brothers from his father's inheritance. Abimelech had appealed to the citizens of Shechem to help him in his abominable ambition; Jephthah to the "elders of Gilead" for redress in his wrong, but apparently in vain (xi. 7). Abimelech had committed unprovoked and cruel murder with his hired band; Jephthah withdrew to the land of *Tob*, which, from 2 Sam. x. 6, 8, we know to have been on the northern boundary of Peræa between Syria and the land of Ammon. There he gathered

---

[1] The description is taken from Canon Tristram's *Land of Israel*, pp. 557, 560.

around him a number of freebooters, as David afterwards in
similar circumstances (1 Sam. xxii. 2) ; not, like Abimelech,
to destroy his father's house, but, like David, to war against the
common foe. This we infer from Judges x. 18, which shows
that, before the war between Gilead and Ammon, Jephthah had
acquired fame as contending against Ammon. This life of
adventure would suit the brave Gileadite and his followers;
for he was a wild mountaineer, only imbued with the true spirit
of Israel. And now, when war had actually broken out, " the
elders of Gilead " were not in doubt whom to choose as their
chief. They had seen and repented their sin against Jehovah,
and now they saw and confessed their wrong towards Jephthah,
and appealed to his generosity. In ordinary circumstances
he would not have consented ; but he came back to them, as
the elders of Gilead had put it, because they were in distress.
Nor did he come in his own strength. The agreement made
with the elders of Israel was solemnly ratified before Jehovah.

He that has a righteous cause will not shrink from having
it thoroughly sifted. It was not because Jephthah feared the
battle, but because he wished to avoid bloodshed, that he twice
sent an embassy of remonstrance to the king of Ammon. The
claims of the latter upon the land between the Arnon and the
Jabbok were certainly of the most shadowy kind. That country
had, at the time of the Israelitish conquest, belonged to Sihon,
king of the Amorites. True, the Amorites were not its original
owners, having wrested the land from Moab (Numb. xxi. 26).
Balak might therefore have raised a claim ; but, although he
hired Balaam to protect what still remained of his kingdom
against a possible attack by Israel, which he dreaded, he never
attempted to recover what Israel had taken from the Amorites,
although it had originally been his. Moreover, even in dealing
with the Amorites, as before with Edom and Moab, whose
territory Israel had actually avoided by a long circuit, the
utmost forbearance had been shown. If the Amorites had
been dispossessed, theirs had been the unprovoked attack, when
Israel had in the first place only asked a passage through

their country.   Lastly, if 300 years'[1] undisputed possession of the land did not give a prescriptive right, it would be difficult to imagine by what title land could be held.   Nor did Jephthah shrink from putting the matter on its ultimate and best ground.   Addressing the Ammonites, as from their religious point of view they could understand it, he said : " And now Jehovah God of Israel hath dispossessed the Amorites from before His people, and shouldest thou possess it ?   Is it not so, that which Chemosh[2] thy god giveth thee to possess, that wilt thou possess; and all that which Jehovah our God shall dispossess before us, that shall we possess ?"   We do not wonder that of a war commenced in such a spirit we should be told : " And the Spirit of the Lord came upon Jephthah."   Presently Jephthah passed all through the land east of the Jordan, and its people obeyed his summons.

We are now approaching what to many will appear the most difficult part in the history of Jephthah—perhaps among the most difficult narratives in the Bible.   It appears that, before actually going to war, Jephthah solemnly registered this vow : " If thou indeed givest the children of Ammon into mine hand—and it shall be, the outcoming (one), that shall come out from the door of my house to meet me on my returning in peace from the children of Ammon, shall be to Jehovah, and I will offer that a burnt offering."   We know that the vow *was* paid.   The defeat of the Ammonites was thorough and crushing. But on Jephthah's return to his house the first to welcome him was his only daughter—his only child—who at the head of the maidens came to greet the victor.   There is a terrible irony about those " timbrels and dances," with which Jephthah's daughter went, as it were, to celebrate her own funeral obsequies, while the fond father's heart was well-nigh breaking.   But the

---

[1] Of course these are round numbers, and not to be regarded as strictly arithmetical.

[2] *Chemosh*—the destroyer or desolater—the Moabite god of war.   He is represented on coins with a sword in his right hand, a spear and lance in his left ; the figure being flanked by burning torches.

noble maiden was the first to urge his observance of the vow unto Jehovah. Only two months did she ask to bewail her maidenhood with her companions upon the mountains. But ever after was it a custom for the maidens in Israel to go out every year for four days, "to praise[1] the daughter of Jephthah."

Such is the story; but what is its meaning? What did Jephthah really intend by the language of his vow; and did he feel himself bound by it in the literal sense to offer up his daughter as a burnt sacrifice? Assuredly, we shall make no attempt either to explain away the facts of the case, or to disguise the importance of the questions at issue. At the outset we are here met by these two facts: that up to that period Jephthah had both acted and spoken as a true worshipper of Jehovah, and that his name stands emblazoned in that roll of the heroes of the faith which is handed down to us in the Epistle to the Hebrews (xi. 32). But it is well-nigh impossible to believe that a true worshipper of Jehovah could have either vowed or actually offered a human sacrifice—not to speak of the sacrifice being that of his own and only child. Such sacrifices were the most abhorrent and opposed to the whole spirit and letter of the Law of God (Lev. xviii. 21 ; xx. 2–5 ; Deut. xii. 31 ; xviii. 10), nor do we find any mention of them till the reigns of the wicked Ahaz and Manasseh. Not even Jezebel had ventured to introduce them; and we know what thrill of horror ran through the onlookers, when the *heathen* king of Moab offered his son an expiatory sacrifice on the walls of his capital (2 Kings iii. 26, etc.). But the difficulty becomes well-

---

[1] This is the correct rendering, and not "lament," as in our Authorised Version. There was a curious custom in Israel in the days of our Lord. Twice in the year, " on the 15th of Ab, when the collection of wood for the sanctuary was completed, and on the Day of Atonement, the maidens of Jerusalem went in white garments, specially lent them for the purpose, so that rich and poor might be on an equality, into the vineyards close to the city, where they danced and sung" (see my *Temple: its Services and Ministry at the time of Jesus Christ*, p. 286). Could this strange practice have been a remnant of the maidens' praise of the daughter of Jephthah ?

nigh insuperable, when we find the name of Jephthah recorded in the New Testament among the heroes of the faith.
Surely, no one guilty of such a crime could have found a
place there! Still, these are considerations which, though
most important, are outside the narrative itself, and in any
truthful investigation the latter should, in the first place, be
studied by itself.

In so doing we must dismiss, as irrelevant and untruth-
ful, such pleas as the roughness of those times, the imperfect-
ness of religious development, or that of religious ignorance
on the part of the outlaw Jephthah, who had spent most of
his life far from Israel. The Scripture sketch of Jephthah
leaves, indeed, on the mind the impression of a genuine,
wild, and daring Gilead mountaineer—a sort of warrior-Elijah.
But, on the other hand, he acts and speaks throughout as
a true worshipper of Jehovah. And his vow, which in the
Old Testament always expresses the highest religious feeling
(Gen. xxviii. 20; 1 Sam. i. 11; Ps. cxvi. 14; Is. xix. 21), is so
sacred *because* it is made to Jehovah. Again, in his embassy
to the king of Ammon, Jephthah displays the most intimate
acquaintance with the Pentateuch, his language being repeatedly almost a literal quotation from Numb. xx. He who knew
so well the details of Scripture history could not have been
ignorant of its fundamental principles. Having thus cleared
the way, we observe:

1. That the language of Jephthah's vow implied, from the
first, at least the possibility of some human being coming
out from the door of his house, to meet him on his return.
The original conveys this, and the evident probabilities of the
case were strongly in favour of such an eventuality. Indeed,
Jephthah's language seems to have been designedly chosen in
such general terms as to cover all cases. But it is impossible
to suppose that Jephthah would have deliberately *made a vow*
in which he contemplated human sacrifice; still more so, that
Jehovah would have connected victory and deliverance with
such a horrible crime.

2. In another particular, also, the language of Jephthah's vow is remarkable. It is, that "the outcoming (whether man or beast) shall be to Jehovah, and I will offer that a burnt-offering." The great Jewish commentators of the Middle Ages have, in opposition to the Talmud, pointed out that these two last clauses are *not* identical. It is never said of an *animal* burnt-offering, that it "shall be to Jehovah"—1or the simple reason that, as a burnt-offering, *it is* such. But where human beings are offered to Jehovah, there the expression is used, as in the case of the first-born among Israel and of Levi (Numb. iii. 12, 13). But in these cases it has never been suggested that there was actual human sacrifice.

3. It was a principle of the Mosaic law, that burnt sacrifices were to be exclusively *males* (Lev. i. 3).

4. If the loving daughter had devoted herself to *death*, it is next to incredible that she should have wished to spend the two months of life conceded to her, not with her broken-hearted father, but in the mountains with her companions.

5. She bewails not her "maiden age," but her "maidenhood" —not that she dies so young, but that she is to die unmarried. The Hebrew expression for the former would have been quite different from that used in Scripture, which only signifies the latter.[1] But for an only child to die unmarried, and so to leave a light and name extinguished in Israel, was indeed a bitter and heavy judgment, viewed in the light of pre-Messianic times. Compare in this respect especially such passages as Lev. xx. 20 and Psalm lxxviii. 63. The trial appears all the more withering when we realise, how it must have come upon Jephthah and his only child in the hour of their highest glory, when all earthly prosperity seemed at their command. The greatest and happiest man in Israel becomes in a moment the poorest and the most stricken. Surely, in this vow and sacrifice was the lesson of vows and sacrifices taught to victorious Israel in a manner the most solemn.

[1] The Hebrew expression is *bethulim.* If it meant maiden age it would probably, as Keil remarks, have been *neurim* (comp. Lev. xxi. 13).

6. It is very significant that in xi. 39 it is only said, that Jephthah " did with her according to his vow "—not that he actually offered her in sacrifice, while in the latter case the added clause, " and she knew no man," would be utterly needless and unmeaning. *Lastly*, we may ask, Who would have been the priest by whom, and where the altar on which, such a sacrifice could have been offered unto Jehovah ?

On all these grounds—its utter contrariety to the whole Old Testament, the known piety of Jephthah, the blessing following upon his vow, his mention in the Epistle to the Hebrews, but especially the language of the narrative itself—we feel bound to reject the idea of any human sacrifice. In what special manner, besides remaining unmarried,[1] the vow of her dedication to God was carried out, we do not feel bound to suggest. Here the principle, long ago expressed by Clericus, holds true : " We are not to imagine that, in so small a volume as the Old Testament, *all* the customs of the Hebrews are recorded, or the full history of all that had taken place among them. Hence there are necessarily allusions to many things which cannot be fully followed out, because there is no mention of them elsewhere."

Yet another trial awaited Jephthah. The tribal jealousy of Ephraim, which treated the Gileadites (more especially the half tribe of Manasseh) as mere runaways from Ephraim, who had no right to independent tribal action, scarcely to independent existence—least of all to having one of their number a " Judge," now burst into a fierce war. Defeated in battle, the Ephraimites tried to escape to the eastern bank of the Jordan ; but Gilead had occupied the fords. Their peculiar pronunciation[2] betrayed Ephraim, and a horrible massacre ensued.

---

[1] In general, the Mishnah condemns in unmeasured terms female asceticism (Sotah iii. 4). But in the Talmud (Sotah 22a) one instance at least is recorded with special praise, in which a virgin wholly devoted herself to prayer. See Cassel in *Herzog's Encyclop.* vi. p. 475, note.

[2] *Shibboleth* means stream, which the Ephraimites pronounced Sibboleth.

Six years of rest—"then died Jephthah the Gileadite, and was buried in one of the cities of Gilead." We know not the locality, nor yet the precise place where he had lived, nor the city in which his body was laid. No father's home had welcomed him; no child was left to cheer his old age. He lived alone, and he died alone. Truly, as has been remarked, his sorrow and his victory are a type of Him Who said : "Not my will, but Thine be done."

It almost seems as if Jephthah's three successors in the judgeship of the eastern and northern tribes were chiefly mentioned to mark the contrast in their history. Of Ibzan of Bethlehem,[1] of Elon the Zebulonite, and of Abdon the Pirathonite, we know alike the dwelling and the burying-place. They lived honoured, and died blessed—surrounded, as the text emphatically tells us, by a large and prosperous number of descendants. But their names are not found in the catalogue of worthies whom the Holy Ghost has selected for our special example and encouragement.

CHAPTER XIX.

Meaning of the History of Samson—His Annunciation and early History—The Spirit of Jehovah "impels him"—His Deeds of Faith.

(JUDGES XIII.-XV.)

THERE is yet another name recorded in the Epistle to the Hebrews among the Old Testament "worthies," whose title to that position must to many have seemed at least doubtful. Can Samson claim a place among the spiritual

---

[1] The Bethlehem here spoken of is, of course, not that in Judah, but that in Zebulon (Josh. xix. 15). The situation of *Ajalon*, the modern *Salem*, quite in the north of Zebulon, and of *Pirathon* in Ephraim, the modern *Ferata*, six miles west of Nablus, has been ascertained.

heroes, who "through faith subdued kingdoms, wrought righteousness, obtained promises?" The question cannot be dismissed
with a summary answer, for if, as we believe, the Holy Spirit
pronounced such judgment on his activity as a judge, then
careful and truthful study of his history must bear it out. But
then also must that history have been commonly misread and
misunderstood. Let it be remembered, that it is of Samson's
activity as a Judge, and under the impulse of the Spirit of God,
we are writing, and *not* of every act of his life. In fact, we shall
presently distinguish two periods in his history; the first, when
he acted under the influence of that Spirit; the second, when,
yielding to his passions, he fell successively into sin, unfaithfulness to his calling, and betrayal of it, followed by the
desertion of Jehovah and by His judgment. And, assuredly, the
language of the Epistle to the Hebrews could not apply to the
period of Samson's God-desertion and of his punishment, but
only to that of his first activity or of his later repentance.

It was in the days of Eli the high priest. Strange and
tangled times these, when once again principles rather than
men were to come to the front, if Israel was to be revived
and saved. The period of the Judges had run its course to
the end. The result had been general disorganisation, an
almost complete disintegration of the tribes, and decay of the
sanctuary. But now, just at the close of the old, the new was
beginning; or rather, old principles were once more asserted.
In Eli the Divine purpose concerning the priesthood, in Samson
that concerning the destiny and mission of Israel, were to
reappear. In both cases, alike in their strength and in their
weakness—in the faithfulness and in the unfaithfulness of its
representatives. The whole meaning of Samson's history is,
that he was a Nazarite. His strength lay in being a Nazarite; his
weakness in yielding to his carnal lusts, and thereby becoming
unfaithful to his calling. In both respects he was not only a
type of Israel, but, so to speak, a mirror in which Israel could
see itself and its history. Israel, the Nazarite people—no
achievement, however marvellous, that it could not and did

not accomplish! Israel, unfaithful to its vows and yielding to spiritual adultery—no depth of degradation so low, that it would not descend to it! The history of Israel was the history of Samson; his victories were like theirs, till, like him, yielding to the seductions of a Delilah, Israel betrayed and lost its Nazarite strength. And so also with Samson's and with Israel's final repentance and recovery of strength. Viewed in this light, we can not only understand this history, but even its seeming difficulties become so many points of fresh meaning. We can see why his life should have been chronicled with a circumstantiality seemingly out of proportion to the deliverance he wrought; and why there was so little and so transient result of his deeds. When the Spirit of God comes upon him, he does supernatural deeds; not in his own strength, but as a Nazarite, in the strength of God, by Whom and for Whom he had been set apart before his birth. All this showed the meaning and power of the Nazarite; what deliverance God could work for His people even by a single Nazarite, so that, in the language of prophecy, one man could chase a thousand! Thus also we understand the peculiar and almost spasmodic character of Samson's deeds, as also the reason why he always appears on the scene, not at the head of the tribes, but alone to battle.

If the secret of Samson's strength lay in the faithful observance of his Nazarite vow, his weakness sprung from his natural character. The parallel, so far as Israel is concerned, cannot fail to be seen. And as Samson's sin finally assumed the form of adulterous love for Delilah, so that of his people was spiritual unfaithfulness. Thus, if the period of the Judges reached its highest point in Samson the Nazarite, it also sunk to its lowest in Samson the man of carnal lusts, who yielded his secret to a Delilah. As one has put it : " The strength of the Spirit of God bestowed on the Judges for the deliverance of their people was overcome by the power of the flesh lusting against the Spirit." Yet may we, with all reverence, point from Samson, the Nazarite for life,[1] to the great antitype in Jesus

[1] The ordinary Nazarite vow was only for a period. But the later Rabbis

Christ, the "Nazarite among His brethren,"[1] in Whom was fulfilled that "which was spoken by the prophets, He shall be called a Nazarite"[2] (Matt. ii. 23). And it is at any rate remarkable that ancient Jewish tradition, in referring to the blessing spoken to Dan (Gen. xlix. 17, 18), applies this addition : "I have waited for Thy salvation, Jehovah," through Samson the Danite, to the Messiah.[3]

1. *Samson's birth.* According to the chronological arrangement already indicated, we infer that Samson was born under the pontificate of Eli, and *after* the commencement of the Philistine oppression, which lasted forty years. If so, then his activity must have begun one or two years before the disastrous battle in which the ark fell into the hands of the Philistines, and in consequence of which Eli died (1 Sam. iv. 18).

While in the east and north the Ammonites oppressed Israel, the same sin had brought on the west and south of Palestine the judgment of Philistine domination. Then it was, that once more the Angel of Jehovah came, to teach the people, through Samson, that deliverance could only come by recalling and realising their Nazarite character as a priestly kingdom unto Jehovah ; and that the Lord's Nazarite, so long as he remained such, would prove all-powerful through the strength of his God. The circumstances connected with the annunciation of Samson were supernatural. In the "secluded mountain village" of Zorah,[4] the modern *Surah*, about six hours west of Jerusalem, within the possession of Dan, lived *Manoah* ("resting") and his wife. Theirs, as we judge from the whole history, was the humble, earnest piety which, despite much apostasy, still lingered in Israel. It is to be observed that, like Sarah in the

---

distinguish between the ordinary Nazarite and the "Samson" or life-Nazarite. See my *Temple: its Ministry and Services at the time of Christ*, p. 328.

[1] Gen. xlix. 26.
[2] We have purposely adopted this rendering.
[3] Comp. Cassel, p. 122.
[4] Thomson, *The Land and the Book*, vol. ii. p. 361.

Old, and the mother of the Baptist in the New Testament, Manoah's wife was barren. For the child about to be born was not only to be God-devoted but God-given—and that in another sense even from his contemporary, Samuel, who had been God-asked of his mother. But in this case the Angel of the Covenant Himself came to announce the birth of a child, who should be "a Nazarite unto God from the womb," and who *as such* should "begin to deliver Israel out of the hand of the Philistines."[1] Accordingly, He laid on the mother, and still more fully on the unborn child, the Nazarite obligations as these are detailed in Numb. vi. 1–8, with the exception of that against defilement by contact with the dead, which evidently would have been incompatible with his future history.

The appearance of the Angel and His unnamedness had carried to the woman thoughts of the Divine, though she regarded the apparition as merely that of a man of God. Manoah had not been present; but in answer to his prayer a second apparition was vouchsafed. It added nothing to their previous knowledge, except the revelation of the real character of Him Who had spoken to them. For, when Manoah proposed to entertain his guest, he learned that He would not eat of his food, and that His name was "Wonderful." The latter, of course, in the sense of designating His character and working, for, as in the parallel passage, Is. ix. 6, such names refer not to the being and nature of the Messiah, but to His activity and manifestation—not to what He *is*, but to what He *does*. As suggested by the Angel, Manoah now brought a burnt-offering unto Jehovah—for, wherever He manifested Himself, there sacrifice and service might be offered. And when the Angel "did wondrously;" when fire leaped from the altar, and the Angel ascended in the flame that consumed the burnt-offering, then Manoah and his wife, recognising His nature, fell worshipping on the ground. No further revelation was granted

---

[1] The conjunction of the two in the text (Judges xiii. 5) indicates that they were to be regarded as cause and effect

them; but when Manoah, in the spirit of the Old Testament, feared lest their vision of God might render it impossible for them to live on earth, his wife, more fully enlightened, strove to allay such doubts by the inference, that what God had begun in grace He would not end in judgment. An inference this, applying to all analogous cases in the spiritual history of God's people. And so months of patient, obedient waiting ensued, when at last the promised child was born, and obtained the name of Samson, or rather (in the Hebrew) *Shimshon.*[1] His calling soon appeared, for as the child grew up under the special blessing of the Lord, " the Spirit of Jehovah began to impel him in the camp of Dan, between Zorah and Eshtaol."[2]

2. About an hour south-west from Zorah, down[3] the rocky mountain-gorges, lay *Timnath,* within the tribal possession of Dan, but at the time held by the Philistines. This was the scene of Samson's first exploits. The " occasion " was his desire to wed a Philistine maiden. Against such union,. as presumably contrary to the Divine will (Ex. xxxiv. 16; Deut. vii. 3), his parents remonstrated, not knowing " that it was of Jehovah, for he was seeking an occasion from (or on account of) the Philistines." Strictly speaking, the text only implies that this " seeking occasion on account of the Philistines" was directly from the Lord ; his proposed marriage would be so only indirectly, as *affording* the desired occasion. Here then we again come upon man's individuality—his personal choice, as the motive power of which the Lord makes use for higher purposes. We leave aside the question, whether or not Samson had, *at the outset,* realised a higher Divine purpose in it all, and mark two points of vital importance in

[1] The name has been variously interpreted. By the Rabbis it is rendered "sunlike," in allusion to Ps. lxxxiv. 11. Others render it "mighty," " daring," or "he who lays waste."

[2] The exact locality cannot be ascertained. The Spirit of Jehovah began to *push,* to *drive,* or *impel* him.

[3] Hence the expression " Samson went down to Timnath." See Thomson.

this history. *First*, whenever Samson consciously subordinated his will and wishes to national and Divine purposes, he acted as a Nazarite, and "by faith;" whenever national and Divine purposes were made subservient to his own lusts, he failed and sinned. Thus we perceive throughout, side by side, *two elements* at work: the Divine and the human; Jehovah and Samson; the supernatural and the natural—intertwining, acting together, influencing each other, as we have so often noticed them throughout the course of Scripture history. *Secondly*, the influences of the Spirit of God upon Samson come upon him as *impulses* from without—sudden, mighty, and irresistible by himself and by others.

The misunderstanding and ignorance of Samson's motives on the part of his parents cannot fail to recall a similar opposition in the life of our Blessed Lord, even as, reverently speaking, this whole history foreshadows, though "afar off," that of our great Nazarite. But to return. Yielding at last to Samson, his parents, as the custom was, go with him to the betrothal at Timnath. All here and in the account of the marriage is strictly Eastern, and strictly Jewish. Nay, such is the tenacity of Eastern customs, that it might almost serve as descriptive of what would still take place in similar circumstances. But, under another aspect, we are here also on the track of direct Divine agency, all unknown probably to Samson himself. To this day "vineyards are very often far out from the villages, climbing up rough wádies and wild cliffs." [1] In one of these, precisely in the district where he would be likely to meet wild beasts, Samson encountered a young lion. "And the Spirit of Jehovah came mightily upon him," or "lighted upon him," the expression being notably the same as in 1 Sam. x. 10; xi. 6; xvi. 13; xviii. 10. Samson rent him, as he would have torn a kid. [2] This circumstance became "the occasion against the

[1] Thomson.
[2] Besides the parallel cases in Scripture (1 Sam. xvii. 34; 2 Sam. xxiii. 20), such writers as Winer and Cassel have collated many similar instances from well-accredited history.

Philistines." For, when soon afterwards Samson and his parents returned once more for the actual marriage, he found a swarm of bees in the dried skeleton of the lion. The honey,[1] which he took for himself and gave to his parents, became the occasion of a riddle which he propounded, after a custom usual in the East, to the "thirty companions" who acted as "friends of the bridegroom." The riddle proved too hard for them. Unwilling to bear the loss incurred by their failure—each "a tunic" and a "change-garment,"[2] these men threatened Samson's wife and her family with destruction. The woman's curiosity had from the first prompted her to seek the answer from her husband. But now her importunity, quickened by fear, prevailed. Of course, she immediately told the secret to her countrymen, and Samson found himself deceived and betrayed by his wife. But this was the "occasion" sought for. Once more "the Spirit of Jehovah lighted upon Samson." There was not peace between Israel and the Philistines, only an armed truce. And so Samson slew thirty men of them in Ashkelon, and with their spoil paid those who had answered his riddle. In his anger at her treachery he now forsook for a time his bride, when her father, as it were in contempt, immediately gave her to the first of the "bridegroom's friends."

This circumstance gave "occasion" for yet another deed. Samson returns again to his wife. Finding her the wife of another, he treats this as Philistine treachery against Israel, and declares to his father-in-law and to others around:[3] "This time I am blameless before the Philistines when I do evil unto them." The threatened "evil" consists in tying together, two and two, three hundred jackals, tail to tail, with a burning torch between them, and so sending the maddened animals

---

[1] Cassel notes the affinity between the Hebrew *devash*, honey, and the Saxon *wahs* or wax ; and again between the Hebrew *doneg*, wax, and the Saxon *honec* or honey.

[2] These " change-garments " were costly raiment, frequently changed.

[3] Cassel thinks that the words were addressed by Samson to his Jewish countrymen ; but this seems contrary to the whole context.

into the standing corn of the Philistines, which was just being harvested, into their vineyards, and among their olives. The destruction must have been terrible, and the infuriated Philistines took vengeance not upon Samson, but upon his wife and her family, by burning "her and her father with fire." This was cowardly as well as wicked, upon which Samson "said unto them, If (since) ye have done this, truly when I have been avenged upon you, and after that I will cease." The result was another great slaughter. But Samson, knowing the cowardice of his countrymen, felt himself now no longer safe among them, and retired to "the rock-cleft (rock-cave) *Etam*" (" the lair of wild beasts ").

Samson's distrust had not been without sufficient ground. Afraid to meet Samson in direct conflict, the Philistines invaded the territory of Judah and spread in *Lehi*. Upon this, his own countrymen, as of old, not understanding "how that God by his hand would deliver them," actually came down to the number of 3000, to deliver Samson into the hand of the Philistines. Another parallel this, "afar off," to the history of Him whom His people delivered into the hands of the Gentiles! Samson offered no resistance, on condition that his own people should not attack him. Bound with two new cords, he was already within view of the hostile camp at Lehi; already he heard the jubilant shout of the Philistines, when once more "the Spirit of Jehovah came mightily upon him." Like flax at touch of fire, "flowed his bonds from off his hands."[1] This sudden turn of affairs, and manifestation of Samson's power, caused an immediate panic among the Philistines. Following up this effect, Samson seized the weapon readiest to hand, the jawbone of an ass, and with it slew company after company, "heap upon heap," till, probably in various en- counters, no less than 1000 of the enemy strewed the ground. Only one more thing was requisite. All "this great deliverance" had evidently been given by Jehovah. But had Samson owned Him in it; had he fought and conquered "by faith," and as a

[1] So literally translated.

true Nazarite? Once more it is through the operation of natural causes, supernaturally overruled and directed, that Samson is now seen to have been the warrior of Jehovah, and Jehovah the God of the warrior. Exhausted by the long contest with the Philistines and the heat of the day, Samson sinks faint, and is ready to perish from thirst. Then God cleaves first, as it were, the rock of Samson's heart, so that the living waters of faith and prayer gush forth, before He cleaves the rock at Lehi. Such plea as his could not remain unheeded. Like that of Moses (Ex. xxxii. 31), or like the reasoning of Manoah's wife, it connected itself with the very covenant purposes of Jehovah and with His dealings in grace. After such battle and victory Samson could not have been allowed to perish from thirst ; just as after our Lord's victory, He could not fail to see of the travail of His soul and be satisfied ; and as it holds true of the Christian in his spiritual thirst, after the great conquest achieved for him : "He that spared not His own Son, but delivered Him up for us all, how shall He not with Him also freely give us all things ? " (Rom. viii. 32.) Then, in answer to Samson's prayer, " God clave the hollow place which is in Lehi,"[1] probably a cleft in the rock, as erst He had done at Horeb (Ex. xvii. 6) and at Kadesh (Numb. xx. 8, 11). But the well which sprang thence, and of which, in his extremity, Samson had drunk, ever afterwards bore the significant name *En-hakkore*, the well of him that had called—nor had called in vain !

[1] This is *unquestionably* the meaning of the text, and not, as in the Authorised Version, "a hollow place that was in the jaw." The mistake has arisen from the circumstance that *Lehi* means a jaw-bone, the locality having obtained the name from Samson's victory with the jaw-bone (*Ramath-lehi*, "the hill or height of the jaw-bone," Judges xv. 17). The name *Lehi* is used *proleptically* in ver. 9, 14, that is, by anticipation.

CHAPTER XX.

The Sin and Fall of Samson—Jehovah departs from him —Samson's Repentance, Faith, and Death.

(JUDGES XVI.)

THE closing verse of Judges xv. marks also the close of this period of Samson's life. Henceforth it is a record of the terrible consequences, first of using God's gift, intrusted for the highest and holiest purposes, for self-indulgence, and then of betraying and losing it. And this betrayal and loss are ever the consequence of taking for self what is meant for God, just as in the parable of the prodigal son the demand for the portion of goods which belonged to him is followed by the loss of all, by want and misery.

And here, in this its second stage, the history of Samson closely follows that of Israel. As Israel claimed for self, and would have used for self the gifts and calling of God ; as it would have boasted in its Nazarite-strength and trusted in it, irrespective of its real meaning and the object of its bestowal, so now Samson. He goes down to Gaza, one of the fortified strongholds of the Philistines, *not* impelled by the Spirit of Jehovah, but for self-indulgence,[1] confident and boastful in what he regards as his own strength. Nor does that strength yet fail him, at least outwardly. For God is faithful to His promise, and so long as Samson has not cast away His help, it shall not fail him. But already he is on the road to it, and the night at Gaza must speedily be followed by the story of Delilah. Meanwhile, the men of Gaza and Samson must learn

---

[1] Cassel tries to prove that the place to which Samson went in Gaza was merely a hostelry—and so the ancient commentaries understood it But the language of the text does not bear out such interpretation.

another lesson—so far as they are capable of it. All night the guards are posted by the gates to wait for the dawn, when, as they expect, with the opening of the gates, Samson will leave the city, and they take him prisoner. During the night, however, they may take their sleep; for are not the gates strong and securely fastened? But, at midnight, Samson leaves the city, carrying with him its gates, and putting them down on " the top of a hill which faces towards Hebron,"¹ that is, at a distance of about half an hour to the south-east of Gaza.

Samson had once more escaped the Philistines; but the hour of his fall was at hand. To regard the God-intrusted strength as his own, and to abuse it for selfish purposes, was the first step towards betraying and renouncing that in which it really lay. Samson had ceased to be a Nazarite in heart before he ceased to be one outwardly. The story of Delilah ² is too well known to require detailed repetition. Her very name—" the weak " or " longing one "—breathes sensuality, and her home is in the valley of Sorek, or of the choice red grape. The Philistine princes have learned it at last, that force cannot prevail against Samson, until by his own act of unfaithfulness he has deprived himself of his strength. It is the same story as that of Israel and its sin with Baal-Peor. The same device is adopted which Balaam had suggested for the ruin of Israel, and, alas! with the same success. The five princes of the Philistines promise each to give Delilah 1000 and 100 shekels, or 5500 in all, about £700, as the reward of her treachery. Three times has Samson eluded her persistency to find out his secret. Each time she has had watchers in an adjoining apartment ready to fall upon him, if he had really lost his strength. But the third time he had, in his trifling with sacred things, come dangerously near his fall, as in her hearing he

¹ So the text literally, and not, as in the Authorised Version, "the top of an hill that is before Hebron," for which, besides, the distance would have been far too great.

² The Rabbis have it, that if her name had not been Delilah, she would have obtained it, because she softened and weakened Samson's strength.

connected his strength with his hair. And yet, despite all warnings, like Israel of old, he persisted in his sin.

At last it has come. He has opened all his heart to Delilah, and she knows it. But Scripture puts the true explanation of the matter before us, in its usual emphatic manner, yet with such manifest avoidance of seeking for effect, that only the careful, devout reader will trace it. The facts are as follows: When Samson betrays his secret to Delilah, he says (xvi. 17): "If I be shaven, then my strength will go from me," whereas, when the event actually takes place, Scripture explains it: "He wot not that Jehovah was departed from him." In this contrast between his fond conceit about *his own* strength and the fact that it was due to *the presence of Jehovah*, lies the gist of the whole matter. As one writes: "The superhuman strength of Samson lay not in his uncut hair, but in this, that Jehovah was with him. But Jehovah was with him only so long as he kept his Nazarite vow." Or, in the words of an old German commentary: "The whole misery of Samson arose from this, that he appropriated to himself what God had done through him. God allows his strength to be destroyed, that in bitter experience he might learn, how without God's presence he was nothing at all. And so our falls always teach us best." But, as ever, sin proves the hardest taskmaster. Every indignity is heaped on fallen Samson. His eyes are put out; he is loaded with fetters of brass, and set to the lowest prison work of slaves. And here, also, the history of Samson finds its parallel in that of blinded Israel, with the judgment of bondage, degradation, and suffering, consequent upon their great national sin of casting aside their Nazarite vow.

But, blessed be God, neither the history nor its parallel stops here. For "the gifts and callings of God are without repentance." The sacred text expressly has it: "And the hair of his head began to grow, as it was shorn"—that is, *so soon* as it had been shorn. Then began a period of godly sorrow and repentance, evidenced both by the return of God to him, and by his last deed of faith, in which for his people he sacrificed his life ; herein also following the great Antitype, though " afar off." We imagine,[1] that "the lad" who led him to the pillars on which the house of Dagon rested was a Hebrew, cognisant of Samson's hopes and prayers, and who, immediately after having placed him in the fatal position, left the temple, and then carried the tidings to Samson's " brethren " (xvi. 31).

It is a high day in Gaza. From all their cities have the princes of the Philistines come up ; from all the country around have the people gathered. The temple of the god *Dagon*—the fish-god, protector of the sea—is festively adorned and thronged. Below, the lords of the Philistines and all the chief men of the people are feasting at the sacrificial meal ; above, along the roof, the gallery all around is crowded by three thousand men and women who look down on the spectacle beneath. It is a feast of thanksgiving to Dagon, of triumph to Philistia, of triumph against Jehovah and His people, and over captive Samson. The image of Dagon—the body of a fish with the head and hands of a man— which less than twenty years before had fallen and been broken before the ark of Jehovah (1 Sam. v. 4), stands once more proudly defying the God of Israel. And now the mirth and revelry have reached their highest point : Samson is brought in, and placed in the middle of the temple, between the central pillars which uphold the immense roof and the building itself. A few words whispered to his faithful Hebrew servant, and Samson's arms encircle the massive pillars. And then an unuttered agonising cry of repentance, of faith from the Nazarite, once more such, who will not only subordinate self to the nation and to his calling, but surrender life itself ! Blind Samson is groping for a new light—and the brightness of another morning is already gilding his horizon. With all his might he bows himself. The pillars reel and give way. With one terrible crash fall roof and gallery, temple and image of Dagon ; and in the ruins perish with Samson the lords of the Philistines and the flower of the people.

It has been told in Zorah. Gaza and Philistia are hushed

[1] The suggestion was first made by Cassel.

in awe and mourning. Samson's brethren and his father's house
come down. From the ruins they search out the mangled
body of the Nazarite. No one cares to interfere with them.
Unmolested they bear away the remains, and lay them to rest
in the burying-place of Manoah his father.

And so ends the period of the judges. Samson could have
had no successor—he closed an epoch. But already at Shiloh
a different reformation was preparing; and with different
weapons will repentant Israel, under Samuel, fight against the
Philistines, and conquer!

CHAPTER XXI.

Social and Religious Life in Bethlehem in the Days of the Judges—The Story of Ruth—King David's Ancestors.

(THE BOOK OF RUTH.)

YET another story of a very different kind from that of
Samson remains to be told. It comes upon us with
such sweet contrast, almost like a summer's morning after a night
of wild tempest. And yet without this story our knowledge
of that period would be incomplete.

It was "in the days when the judges judged"[1]—near the close
of that eventful period. West of the Jordan, Jair and Eli held
sway in Israel, while east of the river the advancing tide of
Ammon had not yet been rolled back by Jephthah, the Gileadite.
Whether the incursions of the Ammonites had carried want
and wretchedness so far south into Judah as Bethlehem
(Judges x. 9), or whether it was only due to strictly natural

---

[1] Critics differ widely as to the exact time when the events recorded in
the Book of Ruth took place. Keil makes Boaz a contemporary of Gideon;
but we have seen no reason to depart from the account of Josephus, who
lays this history in the days of Eli.

causes, there was a "famine in the land," and this became, in
the wonder-working Providence of God, one of the great links
in the history of the kingdom of God.[1]

Bearing in mind the general characteristics of the period,
and such terrible instances of religious apostacy and moral
degeneracy as those recorded in the two Appendices to the Book
of Judges (Judges xvii.–xxi.), we turn with a feeling of intense
relief to the picture of Jewish life presented to us in the Book
of Ruth.[2] Sheltered from scenes of strife and semi-heathenism,
the little village of Bethlehem had retained among its inhabitants
the purity of their ancestral faith and the simplicity of primitive
manners. Here, embosomed amidst the hills of Judah, where
afterwards David pastured his father's flocks, and where shepherds heard angels hail the birth of "David's greater Son,"
we seem to feel once again the healthful breath of Israel's spirit,
and we see what moral life it was capable of fostering alike in
the individual and in the family. If Boaz was, so to speak,
the patriarch of a village, in which the old Biblical customs
were continued, the humblest homes of Bethlehem must have
preserved true Israelitish piety in its most attractive forms.
For, unless the Moabitess Ruth had learned to know and love
the land and the faith of Israel in the Bethlehemite household
of Elimelech, transported as it was for a time into the land of
Moab, she would not have followed so persistently her mother-
in-law, away from her own home, to share her poverty, to work,
if need be, even to beg, for her. And from such ancestry,
nurtured under such circumstances, did the shepherd king of
Israel spring, the ancestor and the type of the Lord and Saviour

[1] The Book of Ruth occupies an intermediate position between that of
the Judges and those of Samuel—it is a supplement to the former and an
introduction to the latter. So much "romance" has been thrown about
the simple narrative of this book, as almost to lose sight of its real purport.

[2] The Book of Ruth numbers just eighty-five verses. In the Hebrew
Bible it is placed among the *Hagiographa*, for dogmatic reasons on which
it is needless to enter. In Hebrew MSS. it is among the five *Megilloth*
"rolls" (Song, Ruth, Lamentations, Ecclesiastes, and Esther). Among
the Jews it is very significantly read on the feast of weeks.

of men. These four things, then, seem the object of the Book of Ruth: to present a supplement by way of contrast to the Book of Judges; to show the true spirit of Israel; to exhibit once more the mysterious connection between Israel and the Gentiles, whereby the latter, at the most critical periods of Israel's history, seem most unexpectedly called in to take a leading part; and to trace the genealogy of David. Specially perhaps the latter two. For, as one has beautifully remarked:[1] If, as regards its contents, the Book of Ruth stands on the threshold of the history of David, yet, as regards its spirit, it stands, like the Psalms, at the threshold of the Gospel. Not merely on account of the genealogy of Christ, which leads up to David and Boaz, but on account of the spirit which the teaching of David breathes, do we love to remember that Israel's great king sprang from the union of Boaz and Ruth, which is symbolical of that between Israel and the Gentile world.

Everything about this story is of deepest interest—the famine in Bethlehem, "the house of bread," evidently caused, as after-wards its removal, by the visitation of God (Ruth i. 6); the hints about the family of Elimelech; even their names: Elim-elech, "my God is king;" his wife, Naomi, "the pleasant," and their sons Mahlon (or rather Machlon) and Chilion (rendered by some "the weak," "the faint;" by others "the jubilant," "the crowned").[2] The family is described as "Ephrathites of Beth-lehem-judah." The expression is apparently intended to convey, that the family had not been later immigrants, but original Jewish settlers—or, as the Jewish commentators have it, patrician burghers of the ancient Ephrath, or "fruitfulness" (Gen. xxxv. 19; xlviii. 7; comp. 1 Sam. xvii. 12; Micah v. 2). At one time the family seems to have been neither poor nor of inconsiderable standing (Ruth i. 19–21; ii.; iii.). But now, owing to "the

[1] Professor Cassel in his *Introduction to the Book of Ruth.*
[2] The rendering of the names by Josephus is evidently fanciful. The widely differing translations, which we have given in the text, show the divergence of critics, who derive the name from so very different roots.

famine," Ephrath was no onger "fruitfulness," nor yet Bethlehem "the house of bread;" and Elimelech, unable, on account ot the troubles in the west, to go for relief either into Philistia or into Egypt, migrated beyond Jordan, and the reach of Israel's then enemies, to "sojourn" in Moab.

There is no need to attempt excuses for this separation from his brethren and their fate on the part of Elimelech, nor for his seeking rest among those hereditary enemies of Israel, outside Palestine, on whom a special curse seems laid (Deut. xxiii. 6). We have only to mark the progress of this story to read in it the judgment of God on this step. Of what befel the family in Moab, we know next to nothing. But this we are emphatically told, that Elimelech died a stranger in the strange land. Presently Machlon and Chilion married Moabite wives— Machlon, Ruth (Ruth iv. 10); Chilion, Orpah.[1] So other ten years passed. Then the two young men died, each childless, and Naomi was left desolate indeed. Thus, as one has re-marked: "The father had feared not to be able to live at home. But scarcely had he arrived in the strange land when he died. Next, the sons sought to found a house in Moab; but their house became their grave. Probably, they had wished not to return to Judah, at least till the famine had ceased— and when it had ceased, they were no more. The father had gone away to have more, and to provide for his family—and his widow was now left without either children or possession!" Similarly, we do not feel it needful to attempt vindicating the marriage of these two Hebrew youths with Moabite wives. For there really was no express command against such unions. The instances in Scripture (Judges iii. 6; 1 Kings xi. 1; Neh. xiii. 23), which are sometimes quoted as proof to the contrary, are not in point, since they refer to the marriage of Hebrews *in the land of Israel*, not to that of those resident outside its boundaries (comp. Deut. vii. 3), and in the case of such marriages this is evidently an important element.

[1] Professor Cassel renders Ruth "the rose;" and Orpah "the hind." The *Midrash* makes Ruth a daughter of king Eglon.

And now tidings reached Moab, that " Jehovah had visited his people to give them bread." Naomi heard in it a call to return to her own land and home. According to eastern fashion, her daughters-in-law accompanied her on the way. When Naomi deemed that duty of proper respect sufficiently discharged, she stopped to dismiss them—as she delicately put it—to their " mother's " houses, with tenderly spoken prayer, that after all their sorrow the God of Israel would give them rest in a new relationship, as they had dealt lovingly both with the dead and with her. Closely examined, her words are found to convey, although with most exquisite delicacy, that, if her daughters-in-law went with her, they must expect to remain for ever homeless and strangers. She could offer them no prospect of wedded happiness in her own family, and she wished to convey to them, that no Israelite in his own land would ever wed a daughter of Moab. It was a noble act of self-denial on the part of the aged Hebrew widow by this plain speaking to strip herself of all remaining comfort, and to face the dark future, utterly childless, alone, and helpless. And when one of them, Orpah, turned back, though with bitter sorrow at the parting, Naomi had a yet more trying task before her. Ruth had, indeed, fully understood her mother-in-law's meaning ; but there was another sacrifice which she must be prepared to make, if she followed Naomi. She must not only be parted from her people, and give up for ever all worldly prospects, but she must also be prepared to turn her back upon her ancestral religion. But Ruth had long made her choice, and the words in which she intimated it have deservedly become almost proverbial in the church. There is such ardour and earnestness about them, such resolution and calmness, as to lift them far above the sphere of mere natural affection or sense of duty. They intimate the deliberate choice of a heart which belongs in the first place to Jehovah, the God of Israel (i. 17), and which has learned to count all things but loss for the excellency of this knowledge. Although the story of Ruth has been invested with romance from its sequel, there is nothing romantic about her present resolve. Only the sternest prose of poverty is before her. Not to speak of the exceedingly depressing influence of her language (i. 13, 20, 21), Naomi had been careful to take from her any hope of a future, such as she had enjoyed in the past. In truth, the choice of Ruth is wholly unaccountable, except on the ground that she felt herself in heart and by conviction one of a Hebrew household—an Israelitish woman in soul and life, and that although she should in a sense be disowned by those with whom she had resolved to cast in her lot.

There was stir in the quiet little village of Bethlehem—especially among the women[1]—when Naomi unexpectedly returned after her long absence, and that in so altered circumstances. The lamentations of the widow herself made her even repudiate the old name of *Naomi* for *Mara* ("bitter"), for that "Jehovah" had "testified against," and "Shaddai"[2] afflicted her. Whether or not Naomi and her acquaintances really understood the true meaning of this "testifying" on the part of Jehovah, certain it is, that the temporary excitement of her arrival soon passed away, and the widow and her Moabite companion were left to struggle on alone in their poverty. Apparently no other near relatives of Elimelech were left, for Boaz himself is designated in the original as "an acquaintance to her husband,"[3] though the term indicates also relationship. And thus through the dreary winter matters only grew worse and worse, till at last early spring brought the barley-harvest.

It was one of those arrangements of the law, which, by its exquisite kindness and delicacy—in such striking contrast to the

[1] The Hebrew text significantly marks "they said," "call me not" (Ruth i. 20) with the *feminine* gender.

[2] Professor Cassel quotes parallel passages from Genesis to show that *Shaddai* means specially the God Who gives fruitfulness and increase.

[3] Not, as in the Authorised Version, "a kinsman of her husband's." The Rabbis make him a nephew of Elimelech, with as little reason as they represent Naomi and Ruth arriving just as they buried the first wife of Boaz ! The derivation of the word *Boaz* is matter of dispute. We still prefer that which would render the name : "in him strength."

heathen customs of the time—shows its Divine origin, that what was dropped, or left, or forgotten in the harvest, was not to be claimed by the owner, but remained, as a matter of right, for the poor, the widows, and *emphatically* also for the " stranger." As if to confute the later thoughts of Jewish narrowness, " the stranger " alone is mentioned in *all* the three passages where this command occurs (Lev. xix. 9, 10 ; xxiii. 22 ; Deut. xxiv. 19–22).[1] Thus would the desolate share in Israel's blessings— and that as of Divine right rather than of human charity, while those who could no longer work for others might, as it were, work for themselves. Yet it must have been a bitter request, when Ruth, as if entreating a favour, asked Naomi's leave to go and glean in the fields, in the hope that she might " find favour " in the sight of master and reapers, so as not to be harshly spoken to, or roughly dealt with. And this was all —all that Ruth had apparently experienced of the " blessed- ness of following the Lord," for Whose sake she had left home and friends ! But there is a sublimeness in the words of Scripture which immediately follow—a carelessness of effect, and yet a startling surprise characteristic of God's dealings. As Ruth went on her bitter errand, not knowing whither, Scripture puts it :—" her hap happened the portion of field belonging to Boaz "—the same Divine " hap " by which sleep fled from Ahasuerus on that decisive night ; the same " hap " by which so often, what to the careless onlooker seems a chance " occurrence," is sent to us from God directly.

The whole scene is most vividly sketched. Ruth has come to the field of Boaz ; she has addressed herself to " the servant that was set over the reapers," and obtained his leave to " glean " after the reapers, and to " gather in the sheaves."[2] From early morn she has followed them, and, as the overseer afterwards

---

[1] May we ask those who doubt the early authorship of Deuteronomy, how they account for this circumstance ?

[2] Professor Cassel has pointed out the distinction between the expression "in the sheaves " (ii. 7) and " between the sheaves " (ver. 15), the former being *after* the reapers, the latter *among* them.

informs Boaz (ii. 7), " her sitting in the house," whether for rest or talk, had been " but little."[1]   And now the sun is high up in the heavens, when Boaz comes among his labourers.   In true Israelitish manner he salutes them: "Jehovah with you !" to which they respond, " Jehovah bless thee !"   He could not but have known "all the poor" (in the conventional sense) in Bethlehem, and Ruth must have led a very retired life, never seeking company or compassion, since Boaz requires to be informed who the Moabite damsel was.   But though a stranger to her personally, the story of Ruth was well known to Boaz. Seen in the light of her then conduct and bearing, its spiritual meaning and her motives would at once become luminous to Boaz.   For such a man to know, was to do what God willed.   Ruth was an Israelite indeed, brave, true, and noble. She must not go to any other field than his ; she must not be treated like ordinary gleaners, but remain *there*, where he had spoken to her, "by the maidens," so that, as the reapers went forwards, and the maidens after them to bind the sheaves, she might be the first to glean ; she must share the privileges of his household ; and he must take care that she should be unmolested.

It is easier, even for the children of God, to bear adversity than prosperity, especially if it come after long delay and unexpectedly.   But Ruth was " simple" in heart ; or, as the New Testament expresses it, her " eye was single," and God preserved her.   And now, in the altered circumstances, she still acts quite in character with her past.   She complains not of her poverty ; she explains not how unused she had been to such circumstances ; but she takes humbly, and with surprised gratitude, that to which she had no claim, and which as a " stranger" she had not dared to expect.   Did she, all the while, long for a gleam of heaven's light—for an Israelitish welcome, to tell her that all this came from the God of Israel, and for His sake ?   It was granted her, and that more fully

---

[1] So correctly, and not as in the Authorised Version, which misses the meaning.

than she could have hoped. Boaz knew what she had done for man, and what she had given up for God. Hers, as he now assured her, would be recompense for the one, and a *full* reward of the other, and that from Jehovah, the God of Israel, under Whose wings she had come to trust. And now for the first time, and when it is past, the secret of her long-hidden sorrow bursts from Ruth, as she tells it to Boaz : " Thou hast consoled me, and spoken to the heart of thine handmaid."

What follows seems almost the natural course of events—natural, that Boaz should accord to her the privileges of a kins-woman ; natural also, that she should receive them almost unconscious of any distinction bestowed on her—keep and bring home part even of her meal to her mother-in-law (ii. 18), and still work on in the field till late in the evening (ver. 17). But Naomi saw and wondered at what Ruth's simplicity and modesty could have never perceived. Astonished at such a return of a day's gleaning, she had asked for details, and then, without even waiting to hear her daughter's reply, had invoked God's blessing on the yet unknown dispenser of this kindness. And so Ruth the Moabitess has begun to teach the language of thanksgiving to her formerly desponding Hebrew mother ! But when she has told her story, as before to Boaz, so now to Naomi its spiritual meaning becomes luminous. In her weakness, Naomi had murmured; in her unbelief, she had complained ; she had deemed herself forsaken of God and afflicted. All the while, however she and hers might have erred and strayed, God had never left off His kindness either to the living or to the dead ![1] And it is only after she has thus given thanks, that she explains to the astonished Ruth : " The man is near unto us—he *is one* of our redeemers" (comp. Lev. xxv. 25 ; Deut. xxv. 5). Still even so, no further definite thoughts seem to have shaped themselves in the mind of either of the women. And so Ruth continued in quiet work

---

[1] It has been rightly observed, that this acknowledgment implied belief in the immortality of the soul—that the dead had not perished, but only gone from hence.

in the fields of Boaz all the barley-harvest and unto the end of the wheat-harvest, a period of certainly not less than two months.

But further thought and observation brought a new resolve to Naomi. The two months which had passed had given abundant evidence of the utter absence of all self-consciousness on the part of Ruth, of her delicacy and modesty in circumstances of no small difficulty. If these rare qualities must have been observed by Naomi, they could not have remained unnoticed by Boaz, as he daily watched her bearing. Nor yet could Ruth have been insensible to the worth, the piety, and the kindness of him who had been the first in Israel to speak comfort to her heart. That, in such circumstances, Naomi, recognising a true Israelitess in her daughter-in-law, should have sought " rest " for her—and that rest in the house of Boaz, was alike to follow the clear indications of Providence, and what might be called the natural course of events. Thus, then, all the actors in what was to follow were prepared to take their parts. The manner in which it was brought about must not be judged by our western notions, although we are prepared to defend its purity and delicacy in every particular. Nor could Naomi have well done otherwise than counsel as she did. For the law which fixed on the next-of-kin the duty of redeeming a piece of land (Lev. xxv. 25), did *not* connect with it the obligation of marrying the childless widow of the owner, which (strictly speaking) only devolved upon a brother-in-law (Deut. xxv. 5) ; although such seems to have been the law of custom in Bethlehem, and this, as we believe, in strict accordance with the *spirit* and object, if not with the *letter* of the Divine commandment. Thus Naomi had no *legal* claim upon Boaz—not to speak of the fact, of which she must have been aware, that there was a nearer kinsman than he of Elimelech in Bethlehem. Lastly, in accordance with the law, it was not Naomi but Ruth who must lay claim to such marriage (Deut. xxv. 7, 8).

Yet we should miss the whole spirit of the narrative, if, while admitting the influence of other matters, we were not to recognise that the law of redemption and of marriage with a childless widow, for the purpose of "not putting out a name in Israel," had been the guiding principle in the conduct of all these three—Naomi, Ruth, and Boaz. And, indeed, of the value and importance of this law there cannot be fuller proof than that furnished by this story itself—bearing in mind that from this next-of-kin-union descended David, and, "according to the flesh," the Lord Jesus Christ, the Son of David.

Keeping all this in view, we proceed to gather up the threads of our story. By the advice of her mother-in-law, Ruth puts off alike her widow's and her working dress. Festively arrayed as a bride—though, assuredly, not to be admired by Boaz, since the transaction was to take place at *night*—she goes to the threshing-floor, where, as the wind sprang up at even, Boaz was to winnow his barley. Unobserved, she watcheth where he lies down, and, softly lifting the coverlet, lays herself at his feet. At midnight, accidentally touching the form at his feet, Boaz wakes with a start—and " bent down, and, behold a woman lying at his feet!" In reply to his inquiry, the few words she speaks—exquisitely beautiful in their womanly and Scriptural simplicity—explain her conduct and her motive. Two things here require to be kept in mind: Boaz himself sees nothing strange or unbecoming in what Ruth has done ; on the contrary, he praises her conduct as surpassing all her previous claims to his respect. Again, the language of Boaz implies that Ruth, although daring what she had felt to be right, had done it with the fear which, in the circumstances, womanly modesty would prompt. We almost seem to hear the low whispered tones, and the tremor of her voice, as we catch the gentle, encouraging words of Boaz' reply : " My daughter," and as he stills the throbbing of her heart with his kindly-spoken, fatherly : " Fear not !" No thought but of purity and goodness,[1] and of Israel's law intruded on

[1] Professor Cassel reminds us of a legal determination in the *Mishnah* (*Yebam.* ii. 8), which the learned reader may compare. The reference,

the midnight converse of those who were honoured to become the ancestors of our Lord.

And now he, on his part, has explained to Ruth, how there is yet a nearer kinsman, whose claims must first be set aside, if the law is to be strictly observed. And, assuredly, if observance of the law of redemption, with all that it implied in Israel, had not been the chief actuating motive of Boaz and Ruth, there would have been no need first to refer the matter to the nearer kinsman, since there could be no possible hindrance to the union of those whose hearts evidently belonged to each other.

The conduct of each party having been clearly determined, they lie down again in silence. What remained of the short summer's night soon passed. Before the dawn had so far brightened that one person could have recognised another, she left the threshing-floor, bearing to her mother the gift of her kinsman, as if in pledge that her thoughts had been understood by him, and that her hope concerning the dead and the living would be realised.[1]

The story now hastens to a rapid close. Early in the morning Boaz goes up to the gate, the usual place for administering law, or doing business. He sits down as one party to a case; calls the unnamed nearer kinsman, as he passes by, to occupy the place of the other party, and ten of the elders as witnesses or umpires—the number *ten* being not only symbolical of completeness, but from immemorial custom, and afterwards by law, that which constituted a legal assembly. To understand what passed between Boaz and the unnamed kinsman, we must offer certain explanations of the

---

though apt, however, rather breaks in as prose upon the sublime beauty of the scene. It needed not such determinations to guard the purity of the threshing-floor of Boaz.

[1] We mention, without pronouncing any opinion upon it, that some— alike Jews and Christians—have seen a symbolism in the number *six* of the measures of barley which Ruth brought with her, as if days of work and toil were done, and "rest" about to be granted.

state of the case and of the law applying to it, different from any hitherto proposed. For the difficulty lies in the sale of the property by Naomi—nor is it diminished by supposing that she had not actually disposed of, but was only offering it for sale. In general we may here say, that the law (Numb. xxvii. 8, 11) does *not* deal with any case precisely similar to that under consideration. It only contemplates one of two things, the death of a childless man, when his next-of-kin (speaking broadly) *is bound* to marry his widow (Deut. xxv. 5) ; or else a forced sale of property through poverty, when the next-of-kin of the original proprietor may redeem the land (Lev. xxv. 25). It is evident, that the former must be regarded as a *duty*, the latter as a *privilege* attaching to kinship, the object of both being precisely the same, the preservation of the family (rather than of the individual) in its original state. But although the law does not mention them, the same principle would, of course, apply to all analogous cases. Thus it might, for example, be, that a man would marry the widow, but be unable to redeem the property. On the other hand, he never could claim to redeem property without marrying the widow, to whom as the representative of her dead husband the property attached. In any case the property of the deceased husband was vested in a childless widow. In fact, so long as the childless widow lived, no one could have any claim on the property, since she was potentially the heir of her deceased husband. All authorities admit, that in such a case she had the use of the property, and a passage in the Mishnah (*Yebam.* iv. 3) declares it lawful for her to sell possessions, though it does seem very doubtful whether the expression covers the sale of her deceased husband's *land*. Such, however, would have been in strict accordance with the principle and the spirit of the law. In the case before us then, the property still belonged to Naomi, though in reversion to Ruth as potentially representing Elimelech and Machlon, while the claim to be married to the next-of-kin could, of course, in the circumstances, only devolve upon Ruth. Thus the property still held by Naomi went, in equity and in law, with the hand of Ruth, nor had any one claim upon the one without also taking the other. No kinsman had performed the kinsman's *duty* to Ruth, and therefore no kinsman could claim the *privilege* of redemption connected with the land. With the hand of Ruth the land had, so to speak, been repudiated. But as the kinsman had virtually refused to do his part, and Naomi was unable to maintain her property, she disposed of it, and that quite in the spirit of the law. There was no wrong done to any one. The only ground for passing the land to a kinsman would have been, that he would preserve the name of the dead. But this he had virtually refused to do. On the other hand, it was still open to him to redeem the land, if, at the same time, he would consent to wed Ruth. It would have been the grossest injustice to have allowed the privilege of redeeming a property to the kinsman who refused to act as kinsman. Instead of preserving a name in Israel, it would in reality have extinguished it for ever.

This was precisely the point in discussion between Boaz and the unnamed kinsman. Boaz brought, first, before him the *privilege* of the kinsman: redemption of the land. This he accepted. But when Boaz next reminded him, that this privilege carried with it a certain *duty* towards Ruth, and that, if the latter were refused, the former also was forfeited, he ceded his rights to Boaz.[1] The bargain was ratified according to ancient custom in Israel by a symbolical act, of which we find a modification in Deut. xxv. 9. Among all ancient nations the " shoe" was a symbol either of departure (Ex. xii. 11), or of taking possession (comp. Psalm lx. 8).[2] In this instance

---

[1] The reason which he assigns (Ruth iv. 6), admits of different interpretations. Upon the whole I still prefer the old view, that his son by Ruth would have been the sole heir—the more so, that in this particular case (as we find in the sequel, iv. 15) Ruth's son would be obliged to be "the nourisher " of Naomi's "old age."

[2] A popular illustration of the former is the custom of throwing a shoe after a bride on her departure from her father's home. This also explains the custom of kissing the Pope's slipper, as claiming possession of, and dominion in the Church.

the kinsman handed his shoe to Boaz—that is, ceded his possession to him. Alike the assembled elders, and those who had gathered around to witness the transaction, cordially hailed its conclusion by wishes which proved, that "all the city knew that Ruth was a virtuous woman," and were prepared to receive the Moabitess as a mother in Israel, even as Thamar had proved in the ancestry of Boaz.

It had all been done in God and with God, and the blessing invoked was not withheld. A son gladdened the hearts of the family of Bethlehem. Naomi had now a "redeemer," not only to support and nourish her, nor merely to "redeem" the family property, but to preserve the name of the family in Israel. And that "redeemer"—a child, and yet not a child of Boaz; a redeemer-son, and yet not a son of Naomi —was the father of Jesse. And so the story which began in poverty, famine, and exile leads up to the throne of David. Undoubtedly this was the main object for which it was recorded: to give us the history of David's family; and with his genealogy, traced not in every link but in symbolical outline,[1] the Book of Ruth appropriately closes. It is the only instance in which a book is devoted to the domestic history of a woman, and that woman a stranger in Israel. But that woman was the Mary of the Old Testament.

[1] This is not the place to enter into the question of the Old Testament genealogies, but it is evident that five names cannot cover the period of 430 years in Egypt, nor yet other five that from the Exodus to David. On the other hand, it deserves notice that the names mentioned amount exactly to ten—the number of perfection, and that these are again arranged into twice five, each division covering very nearly the same length of period.

THE BIBLE HISTORY

VOLUME IV

ISRAEL

UNDER

SAMUEL, SAUL, AND DAVID,

TO THE BIRTH OF SOLOMON.

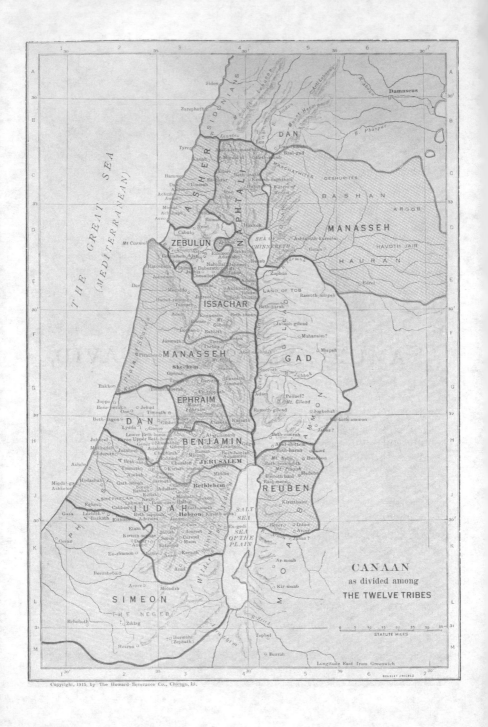

CANAAN
as divided among
THE TWELVE TRIBES

PREFACE

HE history of Israel, viewed as the Theocracy, or Kingdom of
God, consists of three periods : *First*, that *under the guidance
of Prophets* (from Moses to Samuel) ; *secondly*, that *under the rule
of Kings* (from Saul to the Babylonish Captivity) ; and, *thirdly*,
that *under the reign of High-priests* (from Ezra to the birth of
Jesus Christ). Thus the Theocracy had passed through its full
typical development in all its stages, when He came, to Whom
they all pointed : Jesus Christ, the Prophet, King, and High-priest
of the Kingdom of God. The period described in the present
volume closes one of these stages, and commences another. The
connecting link between them was Samuel — who alone fully
realised the mission of the Judges, and who was also Divinely
appointed to inaugurate the new institution of royalty in Israel.
That royalty next appeared in its twofold possibility—or, as we
might express it, in its negative and positive aspects. Saul
embodied the royal ideal of the people, while David represented
the Scriptural ideal of royalty in its conscious subjection to the
will of the Heavenly King. Saul was, so to speak, the king after
Israel's, David after God's own heart. But with the actual introduction of monarchy the first period had come to an end, and a
new era begun, which was intended to continue till the third and
last preliminary stage was reached, which prepared the way for the
Advent of Him, Who was the fulfilment of the typical meaning
of all.

From what has been said it will be inferred that the period
about to be described must have witnessed the birth of new
ideas, and the manifestation of new spiritual facts ; otherwise

spiritual advancement would not have kept pace with outward progress. But it is in the rhythm of these two that the real meaning of Scripture history lies, marking, as it does, the *pari passu* inner and outer development of the kingdom of God. On the other hand, the appearance of new ideas and spiritual facts would necessarily bring out in sharper contrast the old that was passing away, and even lead to occasional antagonism. Of course, these new ideas and facts would not at first be fully understood or realised. They rather pointed towards a goal which was to be reached in the course of history. For nothing could be more fatal to the proper understanding of Holy Scripture, or of the purposes of God in His dealings with His ancient people, than to transport into olden times the full spiritual privileges, the knowledge of Divine truth, or even that of right and duty, which we now enjoy. It is not to do honour, but dishonour, to the Spirit of God to overlook the educational process of gradual development, which is not only a necessity of our nature, but explains our history. A miracle of might could, indeed, have placed the age of Samuel on the same spiritual level with that of the New Testament, at least so far as regards the communication of the same measure of truth. But such an exhibition of power would have eliminated the *moral element* in the *educational* progress of Israel, with the discipline of wisdom, mercy, and truth which it implied, and, indeed, have rendered the whole Old Testament history needless.

What has been stated will lead the student to expect certain special difficulties in this part of the history. These concern, in our opinion, the substance more than the form or letter of the text, and raise doctrinal and philosophical rather than critical and exegetical questions. The calling and later rejection of Saul ; his qualification for the work by the influence of the Spirit of God, and afterwards the sending of a spirit of evil from the Lord ; in general, the agency of the Spirit of God in Old Testament times, as distinguished from the abiding Presence of the Comforter under the Christian dispensation, and, in connection with it, the origin and the character of the Schools of the Prophets and of prophetic inspiration—these will readily occur to the reader as instances of what we mean. As examples of another class of difficulties, he will recall such questions as those connected with the ban upon Amalek, the consultation of the witch of Endor, and in general with the lower moral standpoint evidently occupied by those of that time, even by David himself. Such questions could not be passed over. They are inseparably connected with the Scriptural narratives, and they touch the very foundations of our faith. In accordance with the plan of progressive advance which I set before myself in the successive volumes of this *Bible History*, I have endeavoured to discuss them as fully as the character of this work allowed. Whether or not I may always succeed in securing the conviction of my readers, I can at least say, that, while I have never written what was not in accordance with my own conscientious conviction, nor sought to invent an explanation merely in order to get rid of a difficulty, my own reverent belief in the authority of the Word of God has not in any one case been the least shaken. It sounds almost presumptuous to write down such a confession. Yet it seems called for in days when the enumeration of difficulties, easily raised, owing to the distance of these events, the great difference of circumstances, and the necessary scantiness of our materials of knowledge—whether critical, historical, or theological,—so often takes the place of sober inquiry ; and high-sounding phrases which, logically tested, yield no real meaning, are substituted for solid reasoning.

As in the course of this volume I have strictly kept by the Biblical narratives to be illustrated, I may perhaps be allowed here to add a bare statement of three facts impressed on me by the study of early Old Testament history. *First,* I would mark the difference between the subjective and objective aspects of its theology. However low, comparatively speaking, may have been the stage occupied by Israel in their conceptions of, and dealings with God, yet the manifestations of the Divine Being are always so sublime that we could not conceive them higher at any later period. As we read their account we are still as much overawed and solemnised as they who had witnessed them. In illustration, we refer to the Divine manifestations to Elijah and Elisha. In fact, their sublimeness increases in proportion as the human element, and consequently the Divine accommodation to it, recedes. *Secondly,* even as regards man's bearing towards the Lord, the Old Testament never presents what seems the fundamental character of all ancient heathen religions. The object of Israel's worship and services was never to *deprecate,* but to *pray.* There was no malignant deity or fate to be averted, but a Father Who claimed love and a King Who required allegiance. *Lastly,* there is never an exhibition of mere power on the part of the Deity, but always a moral purpose

conveyed by it, which in turn is intended to serve as germ of further
spiritual development to the people. We are too prone to miss this
moral purpose, because it is often conveyed in a form adapted to
the standpoint of the men of that time, and hence differs from that
suited to our own.

Of course, there are also many and serious critical and exegetical
questions connected with such portions of the Bible as the two
Books of Samuel and the first Book of Chronicles. To these I have
endeavoured to address myself to the best of my power, so far as
within the scope of a volume like this. Whether or not I may have
succeeded in this difficult task, I am at least entitled to address a
caution to the reader. Let him not take for granted that bold assertions of a negative character, made with the greatest confidence,
even by men of undoubted learning and ability, are necessarily
true. On the contrary, I venture to say, that their trustworthiness
is generally in inverse ratio to the confidence with which they are
made. This is not the place to furnish proof of this,—and yet it
seems unfair to make a charge without illustrating it at least by
one instance. It is chosen almost at random from one of the latest
works of the kind, written expressly for English readers, by one of
the ablest Continental scholars, and the present leader of that
special school of critics.[1] The learned writer labours to prove that
the promise in Gen. iii. 15 "must lose the name of ' Proto-Evan-
gelium,' which it owes to a positively incorrect view " of the passage. Accordingly he translates it : " I will put enmity between thee
(the serpent) and the woman, and between thy seed and her seed :
this (seed) shall lie in wait for thy head, and thou shalt lie in wait
for his heel "—or, as he explains it : " man aims his attack at the
head of the serpent, while it tries to strike man in the heel." It
may possibly occur to ordinary readers that it scarcely needed what
professes to be a record of Divine revelation to acquaint us with
such a fact. Very different are the views which the oldest Jewish
tradition expresses on this matter. But this is not the point to
which I am desirous of directing attention. Dr. Kuenen supports
his interpretation by two arguments. *First,* he maintains that the
verb commonly rendered "bruise," means "to lie in wait for,"
"according to the Septuagint and the Targum of Onkelos,"—and
that accordingly it cannot bear a Messianic reference. *Secondly,*

---

[1] *Prophets and Prophecy in Israel.* By Dr. A. Kuenen. London, 1877.

he, of course, implies that it is used in this sense by Onkelos in the passage in question. Now, the answer to all this is very simple, but quite conclusive. *First,* the Hebrew verb referred to is always used in the Targumim for " bruise," or " rub off," as will be seen by a reference to Levy's well-known *Dictionary of the Targumim,* Vol. II., pp. 462*b*, 463*a*.[1] *Secondly,* neither the word nor the rendering in question occurs in the Targum Onkelos, nor anything at all like it[2] (as implied in the language of Kuenen); while, *thirdly,* it *is* used, not indeed in the Targum Onkelos, but in the so-called Targum (Pseudo-) Jonathan and in the Jerusalem Targum (which in the whole of this history closely follow Jewish traditionalism), but in the sense of " bruise," with evident mystic reference—and what is more, *with express mention of its application to Messiah the King!*

I will not be so rash as to say, *Ex uno disce omnes,* but this instance may at least point the moral to our caution. In conclusion, I can only repeat the apostolic assurance, as in this sense also expressive of the feelings with which I close the present part of my investigations : " NEVERTHELESS THE FIRM FOUNDATION OF GOD STANDETH !"

ALFRED EDERSHEIM

LODERS VICARAGE, BRIDPORT.

[1] Comp. also the full discussion in Roediger's *Gesenii Thes.*, Vol. III., p. 1380 *b*—the *positive* part of which it has not suited Dr. Kuenen to notice.
[2] Onkelos paraphrases : "He will remember what thou hast done to him at the beginning, and thou shalt keep in mind against him to the end."

Contents of the First Book of Chronicles (*to beginning of Chap.* XX.), *and List of the Parallel Narratives in the two Books of Samuel.*

------ ✦ ------

CONTENTS.

ISRAEL:

UNDER SAMUEL, SAUL, AND DAVID.

CHAPTER I.

Purport and Lessons of the Books of Samuel—Eli—Hannah's Prayer and Vow—The Birth of Samuel—Dedication of the Child—Hannah's Song.

(I SAM. I.—II. II.)

ONCE more, after long and ominous silence, the interest of the sacred story turns towards the Tabernacle which God had pitched among men, and the Priesthood which He had instituted. The period of the Judges had run its full course, and wrought no deliverance in Israel. In this direction, evidently, help or hope was not to be looked for. More than that, in the case of Samson, it had appeared how even the most direct aid on the part of God might be frustrated by the self-indulgence of man. A new beginning had again to be made; but, as we have hitherto noticed in all analogous cases in sacred history, not wholly new, but one long foreshadowed and prepared.

Two great institutions were now to be prominently brought forward and established, both marking a distinct advance in the history of Israel, and showing forth more fully than before its typical character. These two institutions were: *the Prophetic Order* and *the Monarchy*. Both are connected with the history of Samuel. And this explains alike why the books which record this part of sacred history bear the name of *Samuel*, and why they close not with the death of David. as might have been expected in a biography or in a history of his reign, but with the final establishment of his kingdom (2 Sam. xx.).   At the close of 2 Sam. four chapters (xxi.–xxiv.) are added as a sort of appendix, in which various events are ranged, not chronologically, but in accordance with the general plan and scope of the work, which is : to present Israel as the kingdom of God, and as under the guidance of the spirit of prophecy.   This also explains two other peculiarities.   In a work compiled with such an object constantly in view, we do not expect, nor do we find in it, a *strictly chronological arrangement* of events.   Again, we notice large gaps in the history of Samuel, Saul, and David, long periods and important facts being omitted, with which the author *must* have been acquainted,—and to which, indeed, in some instances, he afterwards expressly refers,—while other periods and events are detailed at great length.   All these peculiarities are not accidental, but designed, and in accordance with the general plan of the work.   For, we must bear in mind, that as in the case of other parts of Holy Scripture, so in the Books of Samuel, we must not look for biographies, as of Samuel, Saul, and David, nor yet expect merely an account of their administration, but *a history of the kingdom of God* during a new period in its development, and in a fresh stage of its onward movement towards the end.   That end was the establishment of the kingdom of God in Him to Whom alike the Aaronic priesthood, the prophetic order, and Israel's royalty were intended to point.   These three institutions were prominently brought forward in the new period which opens in the books of Samuel. First, we have in the history of Eli a revival of the interest attaching to the priesthood.   Next, we see in Samuel the real commencement of the Old Testament prophetic order.   Not that the idea of it was new, or the people unprepared for it. We can trace it so early as in Gen. xx. 7 (comp. Psa. cv. 15) ; and we find not only Moses (Deut. xxxiv. 10), but even Miriam (Ex. xv. 20 ; Numb. xii. 2) designated by the title of prophet ; while the character and functions of the office (if " office " and not "mission" be the correct term) are clearly defined in Deut. xiii. 1–5 ; xviii. 9–22.[1] And although Joshua was not himself a prophet, yet the gift of prophecy had not ceased in his time. In proof we point not only to Deborah (Judg. iv. 4), but also to other instances (Judg. vi. 8). But on the other hand, the *order* of prophets as such evidently began with Samuel. The same remarks apply to the institution of royalty in Israel. It had been contemplated and prepared for from the first. Passing from the promise to Abraham (Gen. xvii. 6, 16), with its prophetic limitation to Judah (Gen. xlix. 10), we find the term kingdom applied to Israel, as marking its typical destiny (Ex. xix. 6), centering of course in *the* King (Num. xxiv. 17, 19). And as the character of the prophetic order, so that of this royalty also was clearly defined in Deut. xvii., while from Judg. viii. 23 we learn, that the remembrance and expectation of this destiny were kept alive in Israel. It was, however, during the period which we are about to describe, that royalty was first actually introduced in Israel. It appeared, if we may so express it, in Saul in its *negative*, and in David in its *positive* aspect ; and to the latter all the promises and types applied which were connected with its establishment. Nor is it without the deepest significance in this respect that in the books of Samuel the designation "Jehovah of Hosts," occurs for the first time, and that Hannah, who was the first to use this title in her prayer (1 Sam. i. 11), prophesied of that King (ii. 10) in Whom all Israel's hopes were fulfilled, and Whose kingdom is the subject of grateful praise alike by the Virgin-mother, and by the father of the Baptist (Luke ii.).[2]

But to turn to the history itself. Once more the Sanctuary had been restored to its former and God-destined position, and Eli the high-priest judged in Israel.[3] Once more God

---

[1] This is well brought out in Ewald, *Gesch. d. V. Isr.*, vol. ii. (3rd ed.) p. 596.

[2] Comp. Auberlen, as quoted by Keil, *Bibl. Comm.*, vol. ii. s. 2, p. 17.

[3] Ewald suggests that Eli had attained the dignity of judge owing to some outward deliverance, like that of the other judges. But the Scriptural narrative of Eli, which is very brief, gives us no indication of any such event.

had visibly interposed to own the institution of Nazarites, which, more than any other, symbolised Israel's spiritual calling of voluntary self-surrender to God. Alone, and unaided by man, the Nazarite Samson had made war for God against the Philistines. In the miraculous strength supplied from on high, he had prevailed against them. But neither priest nor Nazarite of that time had realised the spirituality of their calling. Both had been raised up to show what potentiality for good there was in God's institutions ; and both were removed to prove that even God's institutions were powerless, except by a continuous and living connection with Him on Whose presence and blessing depended their efficacy. But already God was preparing other instrumentalities—a prophet, who should receive and speak His Word, and another Nazarite, voluntarily devoted to God by his mother, and who would prevail not in the strength of his own arm, but by the power of prayer, and by the influence of the message which he brought from God. That prophet, that Nazarite was Samuel. His birth, like that of Samson, was Divinely announced ; but, in accordance with the difference between the two histories this time by prophecy, not as before, by angelic message. Samuel was God-granted, Samson God-sent ; Samuel was God-dedicated, Samson was God-demanded. Both were Nazarites ; but the one spiritually, the other outwardly ; both prevailed : but the one spiritually, the other outwardly. The work of Samson ended in self-indulgence, failure, and death ; that of Samuel opened up into the royalty of David, Israel's great type-king.

Up in Mount Ephraim, due west from Shiloh,[1] lay *Ramah,* "the height," or by its full name, *Ramathaim Zophim,* "the twin heights of the Zophites." [2]   From Josh. xxi. 20, we know

---

[1] Notwithstanding high authority, I cannot look for *Ramah,* as most modern writers do, anywhere within the ancient territory of Benjamin. The expression, "Mount Ephraim," might indeed be taken in a wider sense ; but then there is the addition "an Ephrathite," that is, an Ephraimite.   Keil's suggestion that Elkanah was originally an Ephraimite, but had migrated into Benjamin, is wholly unsupported.

[2] Some of the Rabbis fancifully render it, "the watchers," or prophets.

that, amongst others, certain districts within the tribal possession of Ephraim were assigned to the Levitical families which descended from Kohath. One of these—that of Zophai or Zuph (1 Chron. vi. 25, 35)—had given its name to the whole district, as "the land of Zuph" (1 Sam. ix. 5). From this family sprang *Elkanah*, "the God-acquired," or "purchased," a name which characteristically occurs in the Old Testament only in Levitical families.[1] It was not in accordance with what "was from the first," that Elkanah had two wives,[2] *Hannah* ("favour," "grace") and *Peninnah* ("pearl," or "coral"). Perhaps the circumstance that Hannah was not blessed with children may have led to this double marriage. "Yearly"—as has been inferred from the use of the same peculiar expression in Ex. xiii. 10— "at the Feast of the Passover,"[3] the one above all others to which families as such were wont to "go up" (Luke ii. 41), Elkanah came to Shiloh with his household for the twofold purpose of "worshipping" and of "sacrificing" peace-offerings according to the law (Ex. xxiii. 15; xxxiv. 20; Deut. xvi. 16). Although, Eli being old, the chief direction of the services devolved upon his unworthy sons, Hophni and Phinehas, yet these were joyous occasions (Deut. xii. 12; xvi. 11; xxvii. 7), when the whole household would share in the feast upon the thank-offering. At that time Elkanah was wont to give to Peninnah and to her children their "portions;" but to Hannah he gave "a portion for two persons,"[4] as if to indicate that he loved her just as if she had borne him a son. Whether from jealousy or from malevolence, Peninnah made those joyous seasons times of pain and bitter emotion to Hannah, by grieving

[1] With one exception—2 Chron. xxviii. 7—Levites seem in civic respects to have been reckoned with the tribes in whose territories they were located, as Judg. xvii. 7. This would be a further undesigned fulfilment of Gen. xlix. 7.

[2] The Mosaic Law tolerated and regulated, but nowhere approved it, and in practice polygamy was chiefly confined to the wealthy.

[3] If the inference be admitted, Judg. xi. 40; xxi. 19, must also refer to the Feast of the Passover. On the observance of this feast during the period of the Judges, comp. Hengstenberg, *Beitr.* iii. 79, etc.

[4] This in all probability is the correct rendering.

and trying to make her dissatisfied and rebellious against God. And so it happened each year : Hannah's sorrow, as time passed, seeming ever more hopeless. In vain Elkanah tried to comfort her by assurance of his own affection. The burden of her reproach, still unrolled from her, seemed almost too heavy to bear.

It was surely in the noble despair of faith—as if in her own way anticipating the New Testament question: "Lord, to whom shall we go?"—that Hannah rose from the untasted sacrificial feast, with the resolve to cast upon the Lord the burden she could not bear. It was early evening in spring time, and the aged high-priest Eli (a descendant not of Eleazar, but of Ithamar, to whom the high-priesthood seems to have been transferred from the elder branch of the Aaronic family, comp. Josephus' *Antiquities*, v. 11. 5)[1] sat at the entrance probably to the holy place, when a lonely woman came and knelt towards the sanctuary. Concealed by the folds of the curtain, she may not have noticed him, though he watched every movement of the strange visitor. Not a sound issued from her lips, and still they moved faster and faster as, unburdening the long secret, she poured out her hear[2] in silent prayer. And now the gentle rain of tears fell, and then in spirit she believingly rose to the vow that the child she sought from the Lord should not be cherished for the selfish gratification of even a mother's sacred love. He would, of course, be a Levite, and as such bound from his twenty-fifth or thirtieth year to service when his turn for it came. But her child should wholly belong to God. From

[1] That Eli was a descendant of Ithamar, not of Eleazar, appears from I Chron. xxiv. 1, Abimelech being the great-great-grandson of Eli. Ewald suggests that Eli was the first high-priest of that branch of the family of Aaron, and that he was invested with the office of high-priest in consequence of his position as judge. Other writers have offered different explanations of the transference of the priesthood to the line of Ithamar (comp. Keil, *Bibl. Comm.* ii. 2, pp. 30, 31). But the Scriptural narrative affords no *data* on the subject. It gives not the personal history of Eli, nor even that of the house of Aaron, but of the kingdom of God.

[2] Ver. 13, literally rendered : "She was speaking to her heart."

earliest childhood, and permanently, should he be attached to
the house of the Lord. Not only so—he should be a Nazarite,
and that not of the ordinary class, but one whose vow should
last for life (Num. vi. 2 ; comp. Judg. xiii. 5).

It leaves on us the twofold sad impression that such prayerful converse with God must have been rare in Shiloh, and
that the sacrificial feasts were not unfrequently profaned by
excesses, when such a man as Eli could suspect, and roughly
interrupt Hannah's prayer on the supposition of her drunkenness. But Eli was a man of God ; and the modest, earnest
words which Hannah spake soon changed his reproof into a
blessing. And now Hannah comes back to those she had left
at the sacrificial feast. The brief absence had transformed her,
for she returns with a heart light of sorrow and joyous in
faith. Her countenance [1] and bearing are changed. She eats
of the erst untasted food, and is gladsome. She has already
that for which to thank God, for she is strong in faith. Another
morning of early worship, and the family return to their quiet
home. But God is not unmindful of her. Ere another Pass
over has summoned the worshippers to Shiloh, Hannah has the
child of her prayers, whom significantly she has named *Samuel*,
the God-answered (literally : heard of God—*Exauditus a Deo*).
This time Hannah accompanied not her husband, though he
paid a vow which he seems to have made [2] if a son were
granted ; no, nor next time. But the third year, when the
child was fully weaned,[3] she presented herself once more
before Eli. It must have sounded to the old priest almost
like a voice from heaven when the gladsome mother pointed
to her child as the embodiment of answered prayer : " For this
boy have I prayed ; and Jehovah gave me my asking which
I asked of Him. And now I (*on my part*) make him the asked

[1] Ver. 18, literally : " And her face was the same face no more to her."
[2] This we infer from the addition, "and his vow," in ver. 21.
[3] The period of suckling was supposed to last three years (2 Macc. vii.
27). A Hebrew child at that age would be fit for some ministry, even
though the care of him might partially devolve on one of the women who
served at the door of the tabernacle.

one unto Jehovah all the days that he lives : he is 'the asked one' unto Jehovah !"[1] And as she so vowed and paid her vow, one of the three bullocks which they had brought was offered a burnt-offering, symbolic of the dedication of her child.[2]

Once more Hannah "prayed;" this time not in the language of sorrow, but in that of thanksgiving and prophetic anticipation. For was not Samuel, so to speak, the John the Baptist of the Old Testament? and was it not fitting that on his formal dedication unto God, she should speak words reaching far beyond her own time, and even furnishing what could enter into the Virgin-mother's song?

"And Hannah prayed and said :

1 " My heart rejoiceth in Jehovah—
   Uplifted my horn in Jehovah,
   Wide opened my mouth upon my foes
   For I rejoice in Thy salvation ![3]
2 None holy as Jehovah—for none *is* beside Thee,
   Nor *is* there rock as our God !
3 Multiply not speech lofty, lofty—
   (Nor) insolence come out of your mouth,
   For God of all knowledge [4] is Jehovah,
   And with Him deeds are weighed.[5]
4 Bow-heroes are broken,[6]
   And the stumbling girded with strength.

[1] This literal rendering will sufficiently bring out the beautiful meaning of her words. It is difficult to understand how our Authorised Version came to translate "lent."

[2] They had brought with them *three* bullocks—two for the usual burnt and thank-offerings, and the third as a burnt sacrifice at the formal dedication of Samuel. The meat-offering for each would have been at least $\frac{3}{10}$ of an ephah of flour (Num. xv. 8).

[3] Possibly it would be more accurate here to translate, "deliverance."

[4] In the original, "knowledge" is in the plural; I have rendered this by "all knowledge."

[5] Many interpreters understand this not of man's but of *God's* deeds, as meaning that God's doings were fixed and determined. But this seems very constrained. I would almost feel inclined to discard the Masoretic correction of our Hebrew text, and retaining the *Chethîb* to translate interrogatively, "And are not deeds weighed?"

[6] The verb which agrees with *heroes* is used both in a literal and a metaphorical sense—in the latter for confounded, afraid.

5 "The full hire themselves out for bread
And the hungry cease—
Even till the barren bears seven,
And the many-childed languisheth away!

6 Jehovah killeth and maketh alive,[1]
He bringeth down to Sheol, and bringeth up.

7 Jehovah maketh poor and maketh rich,
He layeth low and lifteth up.

8 He lifteth from the dust the weak,
And from the dunghill raiseth the poor,
To make them sit down with nobles.[2]
And seats of honour will He assign them—
For Jehovah's are the pillars of the earth,
And He hath set on them the habitable world.

9 The feet of His saints will He keep,[3]
And the wicked in darkness shall be put to silence,
For not by strength shall man prevail![4]

10 Jehovah—broken they that strive with Him,
Above him (over such) in the heavens shall He thunder;
Jehovah shall judge the ends of the earth,
And give strength to His King,
And lift on high the horn of His Anointed!"

And so the child and his parents parted—where parting is ever best: leaving him "ministering unto the Lord." But yearly, as they came up to the twice-loved service in Shiloh, they saw again the child, still serving in the courts of the Lord's house, "girded with a linen ephod." And the gift they brought him each year from home was that with which Hannah's love best liked to connect her absent child—"a little Meïl,"[5] or priestly robe in which to do his service. She had made him "the God-asked," and present or absent he was ever such in her loving thoughts. But, as Eli had prayed, instead of the "asked one," who was "asked" for Jehovah, three sons and two daughters gladdened Hannah's heart. "But the boy Samuel grew up with Jehovah" (1 Sam. ii. 21).

[1] Cp. Deut. xxxii. 39; Psa. xxx. 3; lxxi. 20; lxxxvi. 13.
[2] Cp. Psa. cxiii. 7, 8.   [3] Psa. lvi. 13; cxvi. 8; cxxi. 3, and others.
[4] Psa. xxxiii. 16, 17.
[5] The *Meïl* was properly the high-priestly robe (Ex. xxviii. 31). Of course, Samuel's was of different material, and without border.

CHAPTER II.

The Sin of Eli's Sons—Eli's Weakness—A Prophet's Message—Samuel's First Vision—His Call to the Prophetic Office.

(1 Sam. II. 12—III. 21.)

QUITE another scene now opens before us, and one which, as it shows the corruptness of the priestly family, also argues a very low religious state among the people.[1] The high-priest Eli was "very old,"[2] and the administration of the sanctuary was left in the hands of his two sons, Hophni and Phinehas. The energy, amounting almost to severity, which, even in his old age, Eli could display, as in his undeserved reproof of Hannah, was certainly not exercised towards his sons. They were "sons of Belial," and "knew not Jehovah" in His character and claims.[3] Their conduct was scandalous even in a decrepid age, and the unblushing frankness of their vices led "the people of the Lord to transgress," by "bringing into contempt"[4] the sacrificial services of the sanctuary. The main element of hope and the prospect of a possible revival lay in the close adherence of the people to these services. But the sons of Eli seemed determined to prove that these ordinances were mainly designed for the advantage of the priesthood, and therefore not holy, of Divine significance, and unalterably fixed. Contrary to the Divine insti-

---

[1] See the pertinent remarks of Ewald, *u.s.*, p. 10.

[2] The mention of this in Scripture is not intended to represent Eli as a man whose faculties were gone, but to account for the absolute rule of his sons, and for that indulgence which men in their old age are apt to show towards their children.

[3] *Belial* means literally *lowness*, that is, vileness.

[4] So literally.

tution, "the priest's right," as he claimed it,[1] was to take, if necessary by force, parts of the sacrifices before these had really been offered unto the Lord (Lev. iii. 3–5 ; comp. vii. 30–34).

Nor was this all. The open immorality of the high-priest's sons was as notorious as their profanity.[2] The only step which the aged high-priest took to put an end to such scandals was mild expostulation, the truisms of which had only so far value as they expressed it, that in offences between man and man, Elohim would, through the magistracy, restore the proper balance, but who was to do that when the sin was against Jehovah? Such remonstrances could, of course, produce no effect upon men so seared in conscience as to be already under sentence of judicial hardening (ver. 25).

But other and more terrible judgments were at hand. They were solemnly announced to Eli by a prophet (comp. Judg. xiii. 6), since by his culpable weakness he shared the guilt of his sons. As so often in His dealings with His own people, the Lord condescended to reason, not only to exhibit the rightness of His ways, but to lay down principles for all time for the guidance of His church. Had He not dealt in special grace with the house of Aaron? He had honoured it at the first by special revelation; He had singled it out for the privilege of ministering unto Him at the altar; for the still higher function of presenting in the incense the prayers of His people; and for that highest office of "wearing the ephod" in the solemn mediatorial services of the Day of Atonement. Moreover, He had made ample provision for all their wants. All this had been granted in perpetuity to the house of Aaron (Ex. xxix. 9). It had been specially confirmed to Phinehas on account of his zeal for the honour of

---

[1] Notwithstanding high authority, I cannot accept the view which would connect the *first* clause of 1 Sam. ii. 13 (of course, without the words in *italics*) with the last clause of ver. 12.

[2] Ver. 22. "The women that assembled at the door of the tabernacle" were, no doubt, officially engaged in some service, although we know not wherein it consisted. Comp. Ex. xxxviii. 8.

God (Num. xxv. 13). But even the latter circumstance, as well as the nature of the case, indicated that the whole rested on a moral relationship, as, indeed, the general principle holds true : "Them that honour Me I will honour, and they that despise Me shall be lightly esteemed." In accordance with this, Eli and his house would become subjects of special judgment: none of his descendants, so long as they held office, should attain old age (1 Sam. ii. 31); in punishment of their own insolence of office they would experience constant humiliation (ver. 32);[1] another and more faithful line of priests should fill the highest office (ver. 35);[2] and the deposed family would have to seek at their hands the humblest places for the sake of the barest necessaries of life (ver. 36). Thus justice would overtake a family which, in their pride of office, had dared to treat the priesthood as if it were absolutely their own, and to degrade it for selfish purposes. As for the chief offenders, Hophni and Phinehas, swift destruction would overtake them in one day; and their death would be the sign of the commencement of those judgments, which were to culminate in the time of Solomon (1 Kings ii. 27; comp. Josephus' *Antiq.* v. 11, 5; viii. 1, 3).

But, uncorrupted by such influences around, "the child Samuel grew, and was in favour both with Jehovah and with men,"—in this respect also the type of the "faithful Priest," the great Prophet, the perfect Nazarite (Luke ii. 52). It was

[1] The Authorised Version renders, evidently incorrectly : "Thou shalt see an enemy in My habitation, in all the wealth which God shall give Israel." But the suggestions of modern critics are not more satisfactory. I would venture to propose the following rendering of these difficult expressions : "And thou shalt see adversity to the tabernacle in all that benefits Israel ;" *i.e.*, constant humiliation of the priesthood during the prosperity of Israel, a prediction amply fulfilled in the history of the priesthood under Samuel, Saul, and latterly under David, until the deposition of the line of Ithamar.

[2] I venture to think that this promise should be applied impersonally rather than personally. Thus it includes, indeed, Samuel and afterwards Zadok, but goes beyond them, and applies to the priesthood generally, and points for its final fulfilment to the Lord Jesus Christ.

in many respects as in the days of the Son of man. " The
word of Jehovah" by prophetic revelation "was precious," it
was rare, and prophetic "vision was not spread."[1] Meanwhile
Samuel had grown into a youth, and was, as Levite, "ministering unto Jehovah before Eli." But as yet, beyond humble
faithful walk before God, heart-fellowship with Him, and outward ministrations in His sanctuary, Samuel had not other
knowledge of Jehovah, in the sense of personal revelation or
reception of His message (iii. 7). The sanctuary in Shiloh
had become permanent, and we are warranted in inferring
that "the dwelling," which formerly was adapted to Israel's
wanderings, had lost somewhat of its temporary character.
The "curtains" which in the wilderness had formed its
enclosure, had no doubt been exchanged for buildings for
the use of the priesthood in their ministry and for the many
requirements of their services. Instead of the "veil" at the
entrance to the outer court there would be doors, closed at
even and opened to the worshippers in the morning. The
charge of these doors seems to have devolved upon Samuel,
who as "minister" and guardian lay by night within the
sacred enclosure, in the court of the people—or, at least, close
to it, as did the priests on duty in later times. The aged high-
priest himself seems to have lain close by, probably in one of
the rooms or halls opening out upon the sanctuary.

It was still night, though the dawn was near.[2] The holy oil
in the seven-branched candlestick in the holy place was burning low, but its light had not yet gone out, when a voice calling
Samuel by his name wakened him from sleep. As Eli's eyes
had begun to "wax dim," so that he would require the aid of
the young Levite on ministry, it was natural to infer that it
was the voice of the aged high-priest that had called him.[3]

---

[1] So 1 Sam. iii. 1, literally rendered.

[2] The expression, "ere the lamp of God went out in the temple of the
Lord," seems intended to mark the time, as indicated by us in the text.

[3] This seems to be the reason why the fact is mentioned, that Eli's eyes
had begun to wax dim.

But it was not so, and Samuel again laid him down to rest. A second time the same voice called him, and a second time he repaired in vain to Eli for his commands. But when yet a third time the call was repeated, the high-priest understood that it was not some vivid dream which had startled the youth from his sleep, but that a voice from heaven commanded his attention. There is such simplicity and child-like faith, such utter absence of all intrusive curiosity, and such entire self-forgetfulness on the part of Eli, and on that of Samuel such complete want of all self-consciousness, as to render the surroundings worthy of the scene about to be enacted. Samuel no longer seeks sleep; but when next the call is heard, he answers, as directed by his fatherly teacher : "Speak,[1] for Thy servant heareth." Then it was that not, as before, merely a voice, but a vision was granted him,[2] when Jehovah repeated in express terms, this time not in warning prediction, but as the announcement of an almost immediate event, the terrible judgment impending upon Eli and his sons.

With the burden of this communication upon him, Samuel lay still till the grey morning light; nor, whatever thoughts might crowd upon him, did the aged high-priest seek to intrude into what might pass between that Levite youth and the Lord, before Whom he had stood for so many years in the highest function of the priestly office, and into Whose immediate Presence in the innermost sanctuary he had so often entered. Suffice it, the vision and the word of Jehovah had passed from himself—passed not to his sons and successors in the priesthood, but to one scarce grown to manhood, and whose whole history, associated as it was with that very

[1] It is remarkable, as indicative of Samuel's reverential fear, that his reply differs from that taught him by Eli in the omission of the word "Jehovah."

[2] This is implied in the words, "Jehovah came and stood" (1 Sam. iii. 10). The "voice" had come from out of the most holy place, where the Lord dwelt between the Cherubim; the "vision" or appearance, in whatever form it may have been, was close before Samuel. In the one case Samuel had been asleep, in the other he was fully awake

tabernacle, stood out so vividly before him. This itself was judgment. But what further judgment had the voice of the Lord announced to His youthful servant?

And now it was morning, and Samuel's duty was to open the gates of the sanctuary. What was he to do with the burden which had been laid upon him? In his reverence for his teacher and guide, and in his modesty, he could not bring himself unbidden to speak of that vision; he trembled to repeat to him whom most it concerned the words which he had heard. But the sound of the opening gates conveyed to Eli, that whatever might have been the commission to the young prophet, it had been given, and there could be no further hesitation in asking its import. Feeling that he and his family had been its subject, and that, however heavy the burden, it behoved him to know it, he successively asked, entreated, and even conjured Samuel to tell it in all its details. So challenged, Samuel dared not keep back anything. And the aged priest, however weak and unfaithful, yet in heart a servant of the Lord, received it with humiliation and resignation, though apparently without that resolve of change which alone could have constituted true repentance (1 Sam. iii. 17, 18).

By the faithful discharge of a commission so painful, and involving such self-denial and courage, Samuel had stood the first test of his fitness for the prophetic office. Henceforth "the word of the Lord" was permanently with him. Not merely by isolated commissions, but in the discharge of a regular office, Samuel acted as prophet in Israel. A new period in the history of the kingdom of God had commenced; and all Israel, from Dan to Beer-sheba, knew that there was now a new link between them and their Heavenly King, a living centre of guidance and fellowship, and a bond of union for all who were truly the Israel of God.

CHAPTER III.

Expedition against the Philistines—The Two Battles of Eben-ezer—Death of Eli's Sons, and Taking of the Ark—Death of Eli—Judgment on the Philistine Cities—The Return of the Ark.

(1 SAM. IV.—VII. 1.)

TIME had passed; but in Shiloh it was as before. Eli, who had reached the patriarchal age of ninety-seven, was now totally blind,[1] and his sons still held rule in the sanctuary. As for Samuel, his prophetic "word was to all Israel."[2] Some effect must have been produced by a ministry so generally acknowledged. True, it did not succeed in leading the people to repentance, nor in teaching them the spiritual character of the relationship between God and themselves, nor yet that of His ordinances in Israel. But whereas the conduct of Eli's sons had brought the sanctuary and its services into public contempt (1 Sam. ii. 17), Samuel's ministry restored and strengthened belief in the reality of God's presence in His temple, and in His help and power. In short, it would tend to keep alive and increase *historical*, although not *spiritual* belief in Israel. Such feelings, when uncombined with repentance, would lead to a revival of religiousness rather than of religion; to confidence in the possession of what, dissociated from their higher bearing,

---

[1] Literally, "his eyes stood" (1 Sam. iv. 15). Through a mistake, probably in reading the numeral letters (ע for צ), the Arabic and Syrian versions represent Eli as seventy-eight instead of ninety-eight years old.

[2] We regard the first clause of 1 Sam. iv. 1 as entirely unconnected with the account of Israel's expedition against the Philistines. Keil, following other interpreters, connects the two clauses, and assumes, as it appears to me, erroneously, that the war was undertaken in obedience to Samuel's word. But in that case he would have been the direct cause of Israel's disaster and defeat.

were merely externals; to a confusion of symbols with reality; and to such a reliance on their calling and privileges, as would have converted the wonder-working Presence of Jehovah in the midst of His believing people into a magic power attaching to certain symbols, the religion of Israel into mere externalism, essentially heathen in its character, and the calling of God's people into a warrant for carnal pride of nationality. In truth, however different in manifestation, the sin of Israel was essentially the same as that of Eli's sons. Accordingly it had to be shown in reference to both, that neither high office nor yet the possession of high privileges entitles to the promises attached to them, irrespective of a deeper relationship between God and His servants.

It may have been this renewed, though entirely carnal confidence in the Presence of God in His sanctuary, as evidenced by the prophetic office of Samuel, or else merely a fresh outbreak of that chronic state of warfare between Israel and the Philistines which existed since the days of Samson and even before, that led to the expedition which terminated in the defeat at Eben-ezer. At any rate, the sacred text implies that the Philistines held possession of part of the soil of Palestine; nor do we read of any recent incursion on their part which had given them this hold. It was, therefore, as against positions which the enemy had occupied for some time that "Israel went out to battle" in that open "field," which from the monument erected after the later deliverance under Samuel (1 Sam. vii. 12), obtained the name of *Eben-ezer*, or stone of help The scene of action lay, as we know, in the territory of Benjamin, a short way beyond *Mizpeh*, "the look out," about two hours to the north-west of Jerusalem.[1] The Philistines had pitched a short way off at *Aphek*, "firmness," probably a fortified position. The battle ended in the entire defeat of Israel, with a loss of four thousand men, not fugitives, but in the "battle-

---

[1] For reasons too numerous here to detail, I still hold by the old identification of *Mizpeh*, notwithstanding the high authority of Dean Stanley, and Drs. Grove and H. Bonar.

array"[1] itself. They must have been at least equal in numbers to
the Philistines, and under favourable circumstances, since at
the council of war after their defeat, " the elders of Israel "
unhesitatingly ascribed the disaster not to secondary causes,
but to the direct agency of Jehovah. It was quite in accordance
with the prevailing religious state that, instead of inquiring into
the causes of God's controversy with them, they sought safety
in having among them " the ark of the covenant of the Lord,"
irrespective of the Lord Himself and of the terms of His covenant. As if to mark, in its own peculiarly significant manner,
the incongruity of the whole proceeding, Scripture simply puts
together these two things in their sharp contrast : that it was
" the ark of the covenant of Jehovah of Hosts, which dwelleth
between the cherubim," and that " Hophni and Phinehas were
there with the ark of the covenant of God " (1 Sam. iv. 4).

Such an event as the removal of the ark from the sanctuary,
and its presence in the camp, had never happened since the
settlement of Israel in Canaan.   Its arrival, betokening to their
minds the certain renewal of miraculous deliverances such as
their fathers had experienced, excited unbounded enthusiasm
in Israel, and caused equal depression among the Philistines.
But soon another mood prevailed.[2] Whether we regard ver.
9 as the language of the leaders of the Philistines, addressed
to their desponding followers, or as the desperate resolve of
men who felt that all was at stake, this time they waited not to
be attacked by the Israelites. In the battle which ensued, and
the flight of Israel which followed, no less than thirty thousand
dead strewed the ground. In the number of the slain were
Hophni and Phinehas, and among the booty the very ark of
God was taken ! Thus fearfully did judgment commence in
the house of Eli ; thus terribly did God teach the lesson that
even the most sacred symbol connected with His immediate

---

[1] So literally in 1 Sam. iv. 2 : "They slew in the battle-array in the field
about four thousand men."

[2] In vers. 7 and 8 the Philistines speak of God in the plural number,
regarding Him from their polytheistic point of view.

Presence was in itself but wood and gold, and so far from being capable of doing wonders, might even be taken and carried away.

Tidings of this crushing defeat were not long in reaching Shiloh. Just outside the gate of the sanctuary, by the way which a messenger from the battle-field must come, sat the aged high-priest. His eyes were "stiffened" by age, but his hearing was keen as he waited with anxious heart for the expected news. The judgment foretold, the presence of his two sons with the army in the field, the removal of the ark, without any Divine authority, at the bidding of a superstitious people, must have filled him with sad misgivings. Had he been right in being a consenting party to all this? Had he been a faithful father, a faithful priest, a faithful guardian of the sanctuary? And now a confused noise as of a tumult reached him. Up the slopes which led to Shiloh, "with clothes rent and earth upon his head," in token of deepest meaning, ran a Benjamite, a fugitive from the army. Past the high-priest he sped, without stopping to speak to him whose office had become empty, and whose family was destroyed. Now he has reached the market-place; and up and down those steep, narrow streets fly the tidings. They gather around him; they weep, they cry out in the wildness of their grief, and "the noise of the crying" is heard where the old man sits alone still waiting for tidings. The messenger is brought to him. Stroke upon stroke falls upon him the fourfold disaster: "Israel is fled!" "a great slaughter among the people!" "thy two sons are dead!" "the ark of God is taken!" It is this last most terrible blow, rather than anything else, which lays low the aged priest. As he hears of the ark of God, he falls backward unconscious, and is killed in the fall by "the side of the gate" of the sanctuary. Thus ends a judgeship of forty years![1]

Yet another scene of terror. Within her house lies the wife

---

[1] The LXX. give it as twenty years, probably misreading the numeral letter מ for י

of Phinehas, with the sorrows and the hopes of motherhood upon her. And now these tidings have come into that darkened chamber also. They gather around her as the shadows of death. In vain the women that are about try to comfort her with the announcement that a son has been born to her. She answers not, neither regards it. She cannot forget her one great sorrow even in this joy that a man is born into the world. She has but one word, even for her new-born child: " *I-chabod,*" " no glory." To her he is Ichabod —for the glory is departed from Israel. And with that word on her lips she dies. The deepest pang which had wrought her death was, as in the case of her father-in-law, that the ark, the glory of Israel, was no more.[1] Two have died that day in Shiloh of grief for the ark of God—the aged high-priest and the young mother; two, whose death showed at least their own fidelity to their God and their heart-love for His cause and presence.

But although such heavy judgment had come upon Israel, it was not intended that Philistia should triumph. More than that, in the hour of their victory the heathen must learn that their gods were not only wholly powerless before Jehovah, but merely idols, the work of men's hands. The Philistines had, in the first place, brought the ark to Ashdod, and placed it in the temple of Dagon as a votive offering, in acknowledgment of the victory which they ascribed to the agency of their national god. Had not the ark of God been brought into the camp of Israel, and had not the God of Israel been defeated and led captive in His ark through the superior power of Dagon? But they were soon to feel that it was not so; and when on the morn of its arrival at Ashdod, the priests opened the temple doors, they found the statue of their god thrown upon its face in front of the ark. It might have been some accident; and

---

[1] As I understand the narrative, her only words, as quoted in the text, were Ichabod, as the name of the child, and the explanation which she gave of it in ver. 22. All the rest is added by the narrator of the sad tragedy.

the statue, with its head and bust of a bearded man, and body in the form of a fish,[1] was replaced in the *cella* at the entrance of the temple. But next morning the head and hands, which were in human form, were found cut off and lying on the threshold, as if each entrant should in contempt tread upon these caricatures of ideal humanity; and nothing but the Dagon itself,[2] the fish-body, was left, which once more lay prostrate before the ark.

But this was not all. If the gods of Philistia were only vanity, the power and strength in which the people may have boasted, were likewise to appear as unavailing before the Lord. He "laid waste" the people of Ashdod—as we infer from 1 Sam. vi. 4, 11, 18—by that terrible plague of southern countries, field-mice, which sometimes in a single night destroy a harvest, and are known to have driven whole tribes from their dwelling-places.[3] While thus the towns and villages around Ashdod were desolated, the inhabitants of that city itself and of its neighbourhood, suffered from another plague, possibly occasioned by the want caused by famine, in the form of an epidemic—probably a malignant skin disease,[4] highly infectious and fatal in its character. As we gather from the context, Philistia consisted at that time of a federation of five "cities," or cantons, under the oligarchical rule of "lords," or princes, with this provision, that no great public measure (such as the removal of the ark, which had been placed at Ashdod by common decree) might be taken without the consent of all. Accordingly, on an appeal of the people of Ashdod, the lords of the Philistines ordered the removal of the ark to Gath, probably judging, that the calamities complained of were due rather to natural causes than to its presence. But in

---

[1] See the description and representation in Layard's *Nineveh and Babylon*, pp. 343, 350. Dagon was the male god of fertility.

[2] *Dagon* means the "fish-form," from *dag*, a fish.

[3] Comp. the quotations in Bochart, *Hieroz.* i., pp. 1017–1019.

[4] Judging from the derivation of the word, and from its employment (in Deut. xxviii. 27) in connection with other skin diseases, we regard it as a kind of pestilential boils of a very malignant character.

Gath the same consequences also followed ; and when on its further transportation to Ekron the public sufferings were even greater and more sudden than before,[1] the cry became universal to return the ark to the land of Israel.

The experience of these seven months during which the ark had been in their land, not only convinced the lords of the Philistines of the necessity of yielding to the popular demand, but also made them careful as to the manner of handling the ark when returning it to its place.   Accordingly they resolved to consult their priests and soothsayers on this question : " What shall we do in reference to the ark of Jehovah—instruct us with what we shall send it to its place?"   The reply was to this effect, that if the ark were returned it should be accompanied by a " trespass-offering " (in expiation of their wrong (Lev. vi. 5 ; Num. v. 7),[2]—consisting, according to common heathen custom,[3] of votive offerings in gold, representing that wherein or whereby they had suffered.   Never perhaps did superstition more truly appear in its real character than in the advice which these priests pressed upon their people.   Evidently they were fully acquainted with the judgments which the God of Israel had executed upon the Egyptians when hardening their hearts, and with solemn earnestness they urge the return of the ark and a trespass-offering.   And yet they are not quite sure whether, after all, it was not mere chance that had happened to them ; and they propose a curious device by which to decide that question (1 Sam. vi. 7–9).

The advice of the priests was literally followed.   The ark,

[1] From the text it appears that the Ekronites, immediately on the arrival of the ark, entreated its removal ; but that before the necessary steps could be taken, they were visited with plagues similar to those in Ashdod and Gath, but more intense and widespread even than before. Thus the strokes fell quicker and heavier as the Philistines resisted the hand of God.

[2] The last clause of 1 Sam. vi. 3 should be rendered : " If ye shall then be healed, it will be known to you, why His hand is not removed from you," viz., not until you had returned the ark and brought a trespass-offering.

[3] This custom, it is well known, has since passed into the Roman Catholic Church.

with its trespass-offerings,[1] was placed on a new cart, which had never served profane purposes. To this were attached two milch cows, on whom never yoke of other service had been laid, and from whom their calves had just been taken. No force was to be used to keep them from returning to their calves; no guidance to be given what road to take. And, behold, it happened as the priests had suggested it would, if it were God Who had smitten them. "Though lowing as they went" for their calves, the kine took the straight road to the nearest Israelitish border-city, *Beth-shemesh* ("the house of the Sun"), followed by the wondering lords of the Philistines. The boundary was reached, and the Philistines waited to see what would happen.

About fourteen miles west of Jerusalem, on the northern boundary of the possession of Judah, about two miles from the great Philistine plain, and seven from Ekron, lay the ancient "sun city," Beth-shemesh. It was one of those allotted by Joshua to the priests (Josh. xxi. 16), though, of course, not exclusively inhabited by them. To reach it from Ekron, the great plain has first to be traversed. Then the hills are crossed which bound the great plain of Philistia. Ascending these, and standing on the top of a steep ridge, a valley stretches beneath, or rather "the junction of two fine plains."[2] This is "the valley of Beth-shemesh," where on that summer afternoon they were reaping the wheat-harvest (1 Sam. vi. 13); and beyond it, on "the plateau of a low swell or mound," was the ancient Beth-shemesh itself.

A fit place this to which to bring the ark from Philistia, right in view of Zorah, the birth-place of Samson. Here, over

[1] In 1 Sam. vi. 4, we read of "five" golden mice as part of the trespass-offering, the priests computing the number according to that of the five Philistine capitals. But from ver. 18 we infer that, in point of fact, their number was *not* limited to five, but that these votive offerings were brought not only for the five cities, but also for all "fenced cities" and "country villages," the plague of the mice having apparently been much wider in its ravages than that of the pestilential boils.

[2] Comp. Robinson's *Bibl. Researches*, ii. pp. 223-225; iii. p. 153.

these ridges, he had often made those incursions which had
carried terror and destruction to the enemies of Israel. The
sound of the approaching escort—for, no doubt, the Philistine
"lords" were accompanied by their retainers, and by a multi
tude eager to see the result—attracted the attention of the
reapers below. As, literally, "they lifted up their eyes" to
the hill whence it slowly wound down, the momentary fear
at seeing the Philistine escort gave place first to astonishment and then to unbounded joy, as they recognised their
own ark heading the strange procession. Now it had reached
the boundary—probably marked by a "great stone" in the
field of Joshua.[1] The Philistines had remained reverently
within their own territory, and the unguided kine stood still
by the first landmark in Israel. The precious burden they
brought was soon surrounded by Beth-shemites. Levites were
called to lift it with consecrated hands, and to offer first the
kine that had been devoted by the Philistines to the service of
the Lord, and then other "burnt-offerings and sacrifices"
which the men of Beth-shemesh had brought. But even so,
on its first return to the land, another lesson must be taught
to Israel in connection with the ark of God. It *was* the
symbol to which the Presence of Jehovah in the midst of
His people attached. Alike superstition and profanity would
entail judgment at His Hand. What the peculiar desecration
or sin of the Beth-shemites may have been, either on that day of
almost unbounded excitement, or afterwards, we cannot tell.[2]

---

[1] In vers. 14, 15 we read of a "great stone," while in ver. 18 it is called
"the great Avel." Interpreters regard this as a clerical error of the
copyist—אבל for אבן, AVeL for EVeN. But may it not be that this "great
stone" obtained the name *Avel*, "mourning," as marking the boundary-
line towards Philistia?

[2] The Authorised Version translates in ver. 19, "they had looked into
the ark," following in this the Rabbis. But this view is scarcely tenable.
Nor is the rendering of other interpreters satisfactory : "They looked (in
the sense of curious gazing) at the ark," although this assuredly comes within
the range of the warning, Num. iv. 20. But the whole text here seems
corrupted. Thus in the statement that "He smote threescore and ten men,"
the addition "of the people, 50,000," has—judging it both on linguistic and

Suffice it that it was something which the people themselves felt to be incompatible with the "holiness" of Jehovah God (ver. 20), and that it was punished by the death of not less than seventy persons.[1] In consequence the ark was, at the request of the Beth-shemites, once more removed, up the heights at the head of the valley to the "city of forest-trees," *Kirjath-jearim*, where it was given in charge to *Abinadab*, no doubt a Levite; whose son *Eleazar* was set apart to the office of guardian, not priest, of the ark.[2] Here this sacred symbol remained, while the tabernacle itself was moved from Shiloh to Nob, and from Nob to Gibeon, till David brought it, after the conquest of Jerusalem, into his royal city (2 Sam. vi. 2, 3, 12). Thus for all this period the sanctuary was empty of that which was its greatest treasure, and the symbol of God's Personal Presence removed from the place in which He was worshipped.

---

rational grounds—unquestionably crept into the text by the mistake of a copyist. But Thenius points out other linguistic anomalies, which lead to the inference that there may be here some farther corruption of the text. Accordingly, he adopts the reading from which the LXX. translated : "And the sons of Jechonias rejoiced not among the men of Beth-shemesh, that they saw the ark of the Lord."

[1] See previous note.

[2] It is difficult to say why the ark was not carried to Shiloh. Ewald thinks that the Philistines had taken Shiloh, and destroyed its sanctuary ; Keil, that the people were unwilling to restore the ark to a place which had been profaned by the sons of Eli ; Erdmann, that it was temporarily placed at Kirjath-jearim for safety, till the will of God were known. The latter seems the most satisfactory explanation, especially as Kirjath-jearim was the first large town between Beth-shemesh and Shiloh, and the priesthood of Shiloh had proved themselves untrustworthy guardians of the ark.

CHAPTER IV.

Samuel as Prophet—The Gathering at Mizpeh—Battle of Eben-ezer; Its Consequences—Samuel's Administration—The Demand for a King.

(1 SAM. VII., VIII.)

PERHAPS the most majestic form presented, even among the heroes of Old Testament history, is that of Samuel, who is specially introduced to us as a man of prayer (Psa. xcix. 6). Levite, Nazarite, prophet, judge—each phase of his outward calling seems to have left its influence on his mind and heart. At Shiloh, the contrast between the life of self-denial of the young Nazarite and the unbridled self-indulgence of Eli's sons must have prepared the people for the general acknowledgment of his prophetic office. And Nazarite—God-devoted, stern, unbending, true to his calling, whithersoever it might direct him,—such was ever the life and the character of Samuel![1]

It needed such a man in this period of reformation and transition, when all the old had signally failed, not through inherent weakness, but through the sin of the people, and when the forms of the new were to be outlined in their Divine perfectness.[2] The past, the present, and the future of the people seemed to meet in his history; and over it the figure

[1] Second, probably, only to Moses, if such comparisons are lawful. But even so, Samuel seems at times more majestic even than Moses—more grand, unbending, and unapproachable. Ewald compares Samuel with Luther.

[2] In the New Testament dispensation the outward calling is the result of, or at least intimately connected with, the inner state. The reverse was the case under the Old Testament, where the outward calling seems to mould the men. Even the prophetic office is not quite an exception to this rule.

of the life-Nazarite cast its shadow, and through it the first voice from the prophetic order was heard in Israel.

The sanctuary, destitute of the ark, and tended by a decrepid priesthood, over which the doom had been pronounced, had apparently fallen into utter disregard. The ark, carried captive into Philistia, but having proved a conqueror there, had indeed been restored to Israel, but was rather a witness of the past than the symbol of present help. The only living hope of Israel centred in the person of Samuel. Although, since the death of Eli, no longer attached to the sanctuary, which indeed his mission to a certain extent set aside, his spiritual activity had not been interrupted. Known and owned as prophet, he closely watched, and at the proper time decisively directed the religious movement in Israel. That decisive hour had now come.

Twenty years had passed since the return of the ark—a period, as we gather from the subsequent history, outwardly of political subjection to the Philistine, and spiritually of religious depression, caused by the desolateness of their sanctuary, and the manifest absence of the Lord from among His people. It was no doubt due to the influence of Samuel that these feelings led them towards the Lord. In the language of Scripture, they "lamented after Jehovah."[1] But this was only preparatory. It was Samuel's work to direct to a happy issue the change which had already begun. His earnest message to all Israel now was: "If with all your hearts you are returning to Jehovah,"—implying in the expression that repentance was primarily of the heart, and by the form of the Hebrew verb, that that return had indeed commenced and was going on—"put away the strange gods (*Baalim*, ver. 4), and the Ashtaroth, and make firm your hearts towards Jehovah" —in opposition to the former vacillation and indecision—

---

[1] As Schmid puts it : " One who follows another, and lamentingly entreats till he obtains,"—as did the Syrophenician woman. Thenius imagines that there is a *hiatus* between vers. 2 and 3 ; while Ewald regards vers. 3, 4 as a later addition. Impartial students, however, will fail to perceive either, but will be content to leave these two assertions to refute one another.

"and serve Him alone."¹ To Israel so returning with their *whole heart*, and repenting alike by the removal of their sin, and by exercising lively faith, Jehovah would, as of old, prove a Saviour—in the present instance, from the Philistines.

The words of Samuel produced the marks of at least full outward repentance. The next step was to call the people to one of those solemn national gatherings, in which, as on former occasions (Josh. xxiii. 2, etc. ; xxiv. 1, etc.), they would confess national sins and renew national obligations towards Jehovah. On its mountain height,² *Mizpeh*, the "look out" of Benjamin, was among those ancient sanctuaries in the land, where, as in *Shechem* (Josh. xxiv. 26), in *Gilgal* (Josh. v. 2–12, 15), and in *Bethel* (Judg. xx. 18, 23, 26 ; xxi. 2), the people were wont to assemble for solemn deliberation (Judg. xi. 11 ; xx. 1). But never before, since the days of Moses, had Israel so humbled itself before the Lord in confession of sin.³ It was thus that Samuel would prepare for his grand act of intercession on their behalf, and it was under such circumstances that he publicly exercised, or more probably that he began his office of "judge" (1 Sam. viii. 6), in its real meaning, by setting right what was wrong within Israel, and by becoming the means of their deliverance from the enemy.

The assembly had met in Mizpeh, not with any thought of war, far less in preparation for it. In fact, when Israel in Mizpeh heard of the hostile approach of the Philistines, "they were afraid" (ver. 7). But as rebellion had caused their desertion, so would return bring them help from the Lord. As

¹ So 1 Sam. vii. 3, rendered literally.
² The ancient Mizpeh, as we have identified it, lay about 2848 feet above the level of the sea. It seems to us impossible, from the localisation of this assembly and of the battle which followed, to identify Mizpeh with the hill Scopus, close to Jerusalem.
³ The ceremony of drawing and pouring out water, which accompanied Israel's fast and confession, has been regarded by most interpreters as a symbol of their sorrow and contrition. But may it not have been a ceremonial act, indicative not only of penitence, but of the purification and separation of the service of Jehovah from all foreign elements around? Comp. here also the similar act of Elijah (1 Kings xviii. 33–35).

so generally in this history, all would happen naturally in the ordinary succession of cause and effect; and yet all would be really and directly of God in the ordering and arrangement of events. Israel must not go to war, nor must victory be due to their own prowess. It must be all of God, and the Philistines must rush on their own fate. Yet it was quite natural that when the Philistines heard of this grand national gathering at Mizpeh, after twenty years of unattempted resistance to their rule, they should wish to anticipate their movements; and that, whether they regarded the assembly as a revival of distinctively national religion or as preparatory for war. Similarly, it was natural that they would go on this expedition not without serious misgivings as to the power of the God of Israel, which they had experienced during the stay of the ark in their land; and that in this state of mind they would be prepared to regard any terrible phenomenon in nature as His interposition, and be affected accordingly.

All this actually took place, but its real causes lay deeper than appeared on the surface. While Israel trembled at the approach of the Philistines, Samuel prayed,[1] and "Jehovah answered him." The great thunder-storm on that day, which filled the Philistines with panic, was really the Lord's thundering. It was a wild mass of fugitives against which Israel went out from Mizpeh, and whom they pursued and smote until under the broad meadows of Beth-car, "the house of the lamb." And it was to mark not only the victory, but

---

[1] In the text we read : "And Samuel took a *sucking* lamb, and offered it for a burnt-offering *wholly* unto Jehovah : and Samuel cried unto Jehovah for Israel" (1 Sam. vii. 9). The two words which we have italicised require brief comment. The "sucking lamb" would, according to Lev. xxii. 27, be, of course, seven days old. It was chosen so young as symbol of the new spiritual life among Israel. The expression, "a burnt-offering wholly unto Jehovah," is regarded by Keil as implying that the sacrifice was not, as ordinarily, cut up, but laid undivided on the altar. But this view is, on many grounds, untenable; and the expression, which is also otherwise used (Lev. vi. 22; Deut. xxxiii. 10; Psa. li. 19) is probably intended to point to the symbolical meaning of the burnt-offering, as wholly consumed (Lev. i. 9).

its cause and meaning, that Samuel placed the memorial-stone on the scene of this rout, between "the look out" and *Shen,* "the tooth," probably a rocky crag on the heights down which the Philistines were hurled in their flight. That stone he named "Eben-ezer, saying, Hitherto hath Jehovah helped us."

Helped—but only "hitherto!" For all Jehovah's help is only "hitherto"—from day to day, and from place to place — not unconditionally, nor wholly, nor once for all, irrespective of our bearing. But even so, the outward consequences of this Philistine defeat were most important. Although their military possession of certain posts, and their tenure of these districts still continued (comp. 1 Sam. x. 5; xiii. 4, 11–21; xiv. 21), yet the advancing tide of their incursions was stemmed, and no further expeditions were attempted such as that which had been so signally defeated.[1] More than that. In the immediate vicinity of the field of battle, all the cities which the Philistines had formerly taken from Israel, "with the coasts thereof,"—that is, with their surroundings—were restored to Israel, along the whole line extending north and south from Ekron to Gath.[2] Moreover, "the Amorites," or Canaanitish tribes in that neighbourhood, had withdrawn from their alliance with the Philistines : "And there was peace between Israel and the Amorites."

Similarly, order was introduced into the internal administration of the land, at least so far as the central and the southern portions of it were concerned. Samuel had his permanent residence in Ramah, where he was always accessible to the people. But, besides, "he went from year to year in circuit"

---

[1] It is thus that we understand 1 Sam. vii. 13. Indeed, the expression : "the hand of Jehovah was against (or rather, upon) the Philistines all the days of Samuel," implies that the hostilities between the two parties continued, although no further incursions were attempted, and the Philistines stood on the defensive rather than took the offensive.

[2] Of course, *outside* these two cities. The expression, "with the coasts thereof, " refers to the towns restored to Israel, and not to Ekron or Gath.

—to Bethel, thence to Gilgal,[1] returning by Mizpeh to his own home. In each of these centres, sacred, as we have seen, perhaps from time immemorial, he "judged Israel,"—not in the sense of settling disputes between individuals, but in that of the spiritual and national administration of affairs, as the centre and organ of the religious and political life of the people.

We have no means of judging how long this happy state of things lasted. As usually, Holy Scripture furnishes not details even of the life and administration of a Samuel. It traces the history of the kingdom of God. As we have no account of events during the twenty years which preceded the battle of Eben-ezer (1 Sam. vii. 2), so we are left in ignorance of those which followed it. From the gathering at Mizpeh, with its consequences, we are at once transported to Samuel's old age.[2] He is still "the judge;" the same stern, unbending, earnest, God-devoted man as when in the full vigour of manhood. But he has felt the need of help in matters of detail; and his two sons are now made "judges," with residence in Beer-sheba,[3] the ancient "well of the seven," or " of the oath," on the southern boundary of the land. Their office seems to have been chiefly, if not exclusively, that of civil administration, for which in the border district, and so near a nomadic or semi-nomadic population, there must have been ample need. Unfortunately, they were quite unlike their father. Although not guilty of the wicked practices of Eli's sons, yet among a pastoral and nomadic population there would be alike frequent opportunity for, and abundant temptation to, bribery; nor would any other charge against a judge so quickly spread, or be so keenly

[1] Of course, not the Gilgal in the Jordan-valley, but that formerly referred to in Josh. xii. 23.

[2] According to Jewish tradition, Samuel, like Solomon, died at the age of fifty-two. He is said to have become prematurely old.

[3] Josephus adds "Bethel" (*Ant.*, vi. 3, 2), implying that one of the two sons "judged" at Bethel, the other at Beersheba. But this suggestion— for it amounts to no more than that—is wholly unsupported.

resented as this.[1] Soon the murmurs became a complaint ; and that loud enough to bring about a meeting of that most ancient and powerful institution in Israel, "the eldership," or local and tribal oligarchy. Probably it was not merely discontent with this partial administration of justice that led to the proposal of changing the form of government from a pure theocracy to hereditary monarchy. Other causes had long been at work. We know that a similar proposal had been made to Gideon (Judg. viii. 22), if not to Jephthah (Judg. xi. 6). Although in both instances these overtures had been declined, the feeling which prompted it could only have gained strength. An hereditary monarchy seemed the only means of combining the tribes into one nation, putting an end to their mutual jealousies, and subordinating tribal to national interests. All nations around had their kings ; and whether for war or in peace, the want of a strong hand wielding a central power for the common good must have been increasingly felt.

Moreover, the ancient God-given constitution of Israel had distinctly contemplated and provided for a monarchy, when once the people had attained a settled state in the land. It must be admitted that, if ever, circumstances now pointed to this as the proper period for the change. The institution of "judges," however successful at times and in individuals, had failed as a whole. It had neither given external security nor good government to the people. Manifestly, it was at an end. Samuel must soon die ; and what after him ? Would it not be better to make the change under his direction, instead of leaving the people in charge of two men who could not even keep their hands from taking bribes ? Many years had elapsed since the battle of Mizpeh, and yet the Philistines were not driven out of the land. In fact, the present administration held out no prospect of any such result. This then, if ever,

---

[1] The rendering of the Authorised Version, they "perverted judgment," is stronger than the original, which means, "they inclined," or "bent," judgment.

was the proper time to carry out the long-desired and much-needed reform.

It cannot be denied that there was much force in all these considerations; and yet we find that not only Samuel resented it, but that God also declared it a virtual rejection of Himself. The subject is so important as to require careful consideration.

First, as to the facts of the case. The "elders of Israel" having formally applied to Samuel: "Make us now a king to judge us, like all the nations," on the ground of his own advanced age and the unfitness of his sons, "the thing was evil in the eyes of Samuel as they spake *it*,[1] Give us a king to judge us." But instead of making an immediate reply, Samuel referred the matter to the Lord in prayer. The view which Samuel had taken was fully confirmed by the Lord, Who declared it a rejection of Himself, similar to that of their fathers when they forsook Him and served other gods. Still He directed His prophet to grant their request, with this twofold proviso: to "bear strong testimony against them"[2] in reference to their sin in this matter, and to "declare to them the right of the king,"—not, of course, as God had fixed it, but as exercised in those heathen monarchies, the like of which they now wished to inaugurate in Israel. Samuel having fully complied with the Divine direction, and the people still persisting in their request, the prophet had now only to await the indication from on high as to the person to be appointed king—till which time the deputies of Israel were dismissed to their homes.

Keeping in view that there was nothing *absolutely* wrong in Israel's desire for a monarchy (Deut. xvii. 14, etc.; comp. even Gen. xvii. 6, 16; xxxv. 11), nor yet, so far as we can judge, *relatively*, as concerned the time when this demand was made, the explanation of the difficulty must lie in the motives

[1] The word "it" seems necessary to give the sense of the Hebrew correctly.

[2] This is the nearest approximation to a full rendering of the Hebrew expression.

and the manner rather than in the fact of the "elders," request.   In truth, it is precisely this—the "*wherefore*" and the
"*how*," not the thing itself,—not *that* they spake it, but "*as*
they spake it," which was "evil in the eyes of Samuel."[1] Israel
asked "a king" to "judge" them, such as those of all the
nations.   We know what the term "judge" meant in Israel.
It meant implicit reliance for deliverance from their enemies
on an individual, specially God-appointed—that is, really
on the unseen God.   It was this to which the people had
objected in the time of Gideon, and which they would no
longer bear in the days of Samuel.   Their deliverance was
unseen, they wanted it seen; it was only certain to *faith*, but
quite uncertain to them in their state of mind; it was in
heaven, they wanted it upon earth; it was of God, they
wanted it visibly embodied in a man.   In this aspect of the
matter, we quite understand why God characterised it as a
rejection of Himself, and that in reference to it He directed
Samuel to "bear strong testimony against them."

But sin is ever also folly.   In asking for a monarchy like
those around them, the people were courting a despotism
whose intolerable yoke it would not be possible for them to
shake off in the future (1 Sam. viii. 18).   Accordingly, in
this respect Samuel was to set before them "the right of
the king" (vers. 9, 11),[2] that is, the royal rights, as claimed
by heathen monarchs.   But whether from disbelief of the
warning, or the thought that, if oppressed, they would be
able to right themselves, or, as seems to us, from deliberate
choice in view of the whole case, the "elders" persisted in
their demand.   And, truth to say, in the then political circumstances of the land, with the bond of national unity al-

---

[1] It is noteworthy that Samuel introduces no personal element, nor
complains of their charges against his sons. If I have not remarked in
the text on the absence of all prayer before making such an application, as
contrasted with the conduct of Samuel, it is not that I am insensible to it,
but that I wish to present the matter in its objective rather than its subjective aspect.

[2] Not the manner of the king.

most dissolved, and in the total failure of that living realisation of the constant Presence of the Divine "Judge,"
which, if it had existed, would have made His "reign" seem
the most to be desired, but, when wanting, made the present
state of things appear the most incongruous and undesirable,
their choice seems to us only natural. In so doing, however,
they became openly unfaithful to their calling, and renounced
the principle which underlay their national history. Yet even
so, it was but another phase in the development of this history, another stage in the progress towards that end which had
been viewed and willed from the first.[1]

CHAPTER V.

*The Calling of Saul—Occasion of his Interview with Samuel—Samuel
Communes with Saul—Saul is Anointed King—The Three "Signs"—
Their Deeper Significance.*

(1 Sam ix.—x. 16.)

THE Divine direction for which prophet and people were
to wait was not long withheld. It came, as so often,
through a concurrence of natural circumstances, and in the
manner least expected. Its object, if we may venture to
judge, was to embody in the person of the new king the

---

[1] This account of the origin of monarchy in Israel seems to us to have
also another important bearing. It is impossible to regard it as either
unauthentic or of much later origin. For the manifest tendency of the
Jewish mind in later periods increasingly was to surround existing institutions with a halo of glory in their origin. This would especially be the
case in reference to the origin of monarchy, associated as it was in later
times with the house of David. Of anti-monarchical tendencies we discover
no real trace. An account so disparaging to royalty would never have
been *invented*, least of all in later times. The thoughtful reader will find
in what we have just marked a principle which has a wide application in
the criticism of Old Testament history.

ideal which Israel had had in view in making their demand for a monarchy. He should possess all the natural attractions and martial qualities which the people could desiderate in their king; he should reflect their religious standpoint at its best; but he should also represent their national failings and the inmost defect of their religious life : that of combining zeal for the religion of Jehovah, and outward conformity to it, with utter w..nt of real heart submission to the Lord, and of true devotedness to Him.

Thus viewed, we can understand alike the choice of Saul at the first, his failure afterwards, and his final rejection. The people obtained precisely what they wanted ; and because he who was their king so corresponded to their ideal, and so reflected the national state, he failed. If, therefore, it is with a feeling of sadness that we follow this story, we must remember that its tragic element does not begin and end with Saul ; and that the meaning of his life and career must be gathered from a deeper consideration of the history of his people. In truth, the history of Saul is a summary and a reflection of that of Israel. A monarchy such as his must first succeed, and finally fail when, under the test of trials, its inmost tendencies would be brought to light. Such a reign was also necessary, in order to bring out what was the real meaning of the people's demand, and to prepare Israel for the king of God's election and selection in the person of David.

Of all the tribes in Israel perhaps the most martial, although the smallest, was that of Benjamin. The " family " of Abiel [1] was, indeed, not famous for wealth or influence. But it must have occupied a prominent place in Benjamin for the manly qualities and the military capacity of its members,.since within a narrow circle it numbered such men as Saul, Jonathan,

---

[1] It is only such a view of the character of Saul which, I venture to think, satisfactorily accounts for his choice in the first instance, and then for his fall and final rejection. But thus read, there is a strict unity about his whole history, and his outward religiousness and the deeper defects of this religion appear consistent with each other.

and Abner.[1] The whole of this history gives such sketches of primitive life in Israel as to prove that it was derived from early and authentic sources. Kish, the father of Saul, and Ner, the father of Abner, were brothers, the sons of Abiel.[2] The former is described in the text as "a hero of might," by which, as in the case of Boaz, who is similarly designated (Ruth ii. 1), were meant in those times men stalwart, strong, and true, worthy representatives and, if need were, defenders of their national rights and of their national religion. Such, no doubt, was also the father of Abner. And yet there was exquisite simplicity about the family-life of these great, strong men. Kish had lost his she-asses—a loss of some consequence in times of such poverty that a man would consider "the fourth part of a shekel," or a *sus*—about $6\frac{1}{2}d$. of our money—as quite an adequate gift to offer a "seer" in return for consulting him (1 Sam. ix. 8). To find, if possible, the straying animals, Saul, the only son of Kish,[3] as we infer from the text, was sent in company with a servant. Saul, "the asked-for,' was not only "choice[4] and goodly," like all his race, but apparently as handsome as any man in the land, and taller than any by head and shoulders. In any country and age this would tell in favour of a popular leader, but especially in ancient times,[5] and more particularly in Israel at that period

---

[1] 1 Sam. ix. 1; comp. xiv. 51. The notice, therefore, in 1 Chron. viii. 33, ix. 39, must probably be a clerical error, though Keil suggests that, as in other places, the reference is to a "grandfather," or even more remote ancestor.

[2] Comp. 1 Sam. xiv. 51.

[3] Critics infer from the name *Shaul*—"the asked for"—that he was the *firstborn*. But I rather conclude from the use of the term in such passages as Gen. xlvi. 10, 1 Sam. i. 17, 27, that Kish had long been childless, and that Saul was the child of prayer; while from the absence of the mention of any other children, I would infer that he was the only son of Kish.

[4] Most critics render the term by "young." But I prefer the rendering "choice"—not, however, in the sense of the *Vulgate: electus*, chosen. From xiii. 1–3 we know that Jonathan was at the time capable of taking a command, so that Saul his father must have been at least forty years old.

[5] For quotations from the Classics, see the Commentaries.

From his home at Gibeah[1] Saul and his servant passed in a north-westerly direction over a spur of Mount Ephraim. Thence they turned in their search north-eastward to "the land of *Shalishah*," probably so called from the circumstance that three *Wadys* met there,[2] and then eastwards to the land of *Shaalim*—probably "the hollow," the modern *Salem*. Having traversed another district, which is called "the land of *Yemini*,"—either "the right hand," or else "of Benjamin," though apparently not within the territory of Benjamin—they found themselves in the district of *Zuph*, where Samuel's home at Ramah was.[3]

For three days had the two continued their unsuccessful search, when it occurred to Saul that their long absence might cause his father more anxiety than the straying of the she-asses. But before returning home, Saul's servant suggested that since they were just in view of the city where "the seer" lived, they might first consult him as to "the way" they "should go" in order to find the she-asses.[4] Having ascer-

---

[1] Our Authorised Version renders 1 Sam. x. 5, "the hill of God," and again, ver. 10, "the hill." In both cases it is Gibeah; and, as we infer from the familiarity of the people with Saul (ver. 11), either the place where Saul lived or quite close by it.

[2] The modern Wady Kurawa (see Keil, p. 66).

[3] "The land *Yemini*" could not have been intended to designate the tribal territory of Benjamin. It is never so employed, and the analogy of the expressions "land Shalishah," "land Shaalim," "land Zuph," forbids us to regard it as other than *a district*. Again, it is said, "he passed through the land of Benjamin." From where, and whither? Certainly not into Ephraim, for he came thence; and as certainly not into Judah. But the whole question of the localisation of the *Ramah* of Samuel and of the journey of Saul is amongst the most difficult in Biblical geography. There is another important consideration in regard to this subject to which we shall refer in a subsequent Note.

[4] There can be no reasonable doubt that this "city" was Ramah, the ordinary residence of Samuel. The question and answer in vers. 10 and 11 imply this; so does the circumstance that Samuel had a house there. Lastly, how could Saul's servant have known that the "seer" was in that city, if it had not been his ordinary residence? These two points, then, seem established: Saul's residence was at Gibeah, and he first met Samuel in Ramah. But if so, it seems impossible, in view of 1 Sam. x. 2,

tained that the seer was not only in the city, but that the people had had "a sacrifice" on the "height" outside, where, as we know (1 Sam. vii. 17), Samuel had built an altar, the two hastened on, in the hope of finding him in the city itself, before he went up " to bless," or speak the prayer of thanksgiving, with which the sacrificial meal would begin. For, amidst the guests gathered there, the two strangers could have little expectation of finding access to the president of the feast. They had just entered the city itself, and were "in the gate," or wide place inside the city-entrance, where the elders used to sit and popular assemblies gathered, when they met Samuel coming from an opposite direction on his way to the "*Bamah*," or sacrificial "height." To Saul's inquiry for "the seer's house," Samuel replied by making himself known.[1] He had expected him—for the day before the Lord had expressly intimated it to him.   Indeed, Samuel had prepared for it by ordering the choicest piece of that which was to be eaten of the sacrifice to be set aside for his guest—so sure was he of his arrival.   And now when he saw before him in the gate the stateliest and finest-looking man in all Israel, the same voice which had led him to expect, indicated that this was the future leader of God's people.

---

to identify the Ramah of Samuel with the Ramah of Benjamin, or to regard it as the modern *Neby Samuel*, four miles north-west of Jerusalem.

[1] We may here give a curious extract from *Siphre*, all the more readily that this commentary on Numbers and Deuteronomy, which is older than the Mishnah, is so little quoted even by those who make Rabbinical literature their study.   In *Siphre* 69a, by way of enforcing the duty of modesty, the expression of Samuel, "I am the seer" (1 Sam. ix. 19), is thus commented on : "The Holy One, blessed be He, said to him, Art thou the seer? by thy life, I shall shew thee that thou art not a seer.   And how did He shew it to him ?   At the time when it was said : Fill thy horn with oil, and go, I will send thee to Jesse, the Bethlehemite," etc.   Upon which 1 Sam. xvi. 6 is quoted, when the Holy One reminded Samuel that he had said : "I am a seer," while nevertheless he was entirely mistaken on the subject of the choice of Eliab !

The bearing of Samuel towards Saul was precisely such as the circumstances required. Moreover, it was consistent throughout, and dignified. An entirely new office, involving the greatest difficulties and responsibilities, was most unexpectedly to be almost thrust upon Saul ; an office, besides, the reality of which would not only be soon tested by such enemies as the Philistines, but to which he had neither family nor personal claims, and which would be sure to excite tribal jealousies and personal envies. To prepare Saul, it was necessary to call forth in him expectations, it might be vague, of great things ; to inspire him with absolute confidence in Samuel as the medium through whom God spake ; and finally, by converse on the deepest concerns of Israel, to bring out what lay inmost in his heart, and to direct it to its proper goal. Accordingly, Samuel invited Saul first to the feast and then to his house, at the outset intimating that he would tell him all that was in his heart (ver. 19). This assuredly could not have reference to the finding of the she-asses, since he immediately informed Saul about them, as evidence that he was " a seer," whose words must, therefore, be received as a message coming from God. Mysterious as was the allusion to what was in Saul's heart, the remark which accompanied his intimation of the finding of the she-asses sounded even more strange. As if treating such a loss as a very small matter, he added (ver. 20) : " And whose is all that is desirable in Israel ? Is it not thine and thy father's house ?"[1] The remark was so strange both in itself and as coming from "the seer," that Saul, feeling its seeming incongruity, could only answer by pointing to the fact that Benjamin was the smallest tribe, and his own family among the least influential in it. Saul was undoubtedly aware that Israel had demanded and were about to receive from Samuel a king. His reply leaves the impression on us, that, although probably he did not exactly formulate it in his own mind, yet Samuel's words had called up in him thoughts of the

[1] This is the correct rendering.

kingdom. Else why the reference to the size of his tribe and the influence of his family? And this was exactly what Samuel had wished : gradually to prepare him for what was coming.

Apparently the " seer " made no answer to what Saul had said. But at the sacrificial feast he pursued the same course towards his guest. To the Ephraimites there assembled he was, of course, unknown. But even they must have been surprised at finding that, while the mass of the people feasted outside, among the thirty principal guests who were bidden into "the parlour," not only was the chief place given to this stranger, but that the principal portion of the sacrifice had, as a mark of special honour, been reserved for him.

The feast was past, and Saul followed his host to his house. There on the flat roof,[1] so often the scene of private converse in the East, Samuel long "communed" with Saul, no doubt of "all that was in his heart ;" not, indeed, of the office about to be conferred on him, but of the thoughts which had been called up in Saul that day : of Israel's need, of Israel's sin, of Israel's help, and of Israel's God. After such " communing," neither of them could have found much sleep that night. It was grey dawn when they rose ; and as the morning broke, Samuel called up to Saul on the roof that it was time to depart. He himself convoyed him through the town ; then, sending forward the servant, he stopped to deliver the message of God. Taking a vial of oil,[2] he "anointed" Saul, thus placing the institution of royalty on the same footing as that of the sanctuary and the priesthood (Ex. xxx. 23, etc., Lev. viii. 10, etc), as appointed and consecrated by God and for God, and intended to be the medium for receiving and transmitting

---

[1] The LXX. translators in this, as in several other passages in this section, either had a Hebrew text somewhat varying from ours or else altered it in their translation. Notwithstanding the views of some critics (notably Thenius), we have seen no reason to depart from the *textus receptus*.

[2] The Hebrew word indicates a narrow-necked vessel from which the oil would come by drops.

blessing to His people. And with this, a kiss, in token of homage (Psa. ii. 12), and the perhaps not quite unexpected message : " Is it not that Jehovah hath anointed thee to be prince over His inheritance ?" Saul was appointed the first king in Israel.

In order to assure Saul of the Divine agency in all this, Samuel gave him three signs. Each was stranger than the other, and all were significant of what would mark the path of Israel's king. After leaving Samuel, coming from Ephraim, he would cross the northern boundary of Benjamin by the grave of Rachel.[1] There he would meet two men who would inform him of the finding of the she-asses and of his father's anxiety on his account. This, as confirming Samuel's words, would be a pledge that it was likewise by God's appointment he had been anointed king. Thus the first sign would convey that *his royalty was of God.* Then as he passed southwards, and reached " the terebinth Tabor,"[2] three men would meet him, coming from an opposite direction, and " going up to God, to Bethel," bearing sacrificial gifts. These would salute him, and, unasked, give him a portion of their sacrificial offerings—two loaves, probably one for himself, another for his servant. If, as seems likely, these three men belonged to " the sons of the prophets," the act was even more significant. It meant homage on the part of the godly in Israel, yet such as did not supersede nor swallow up the higher homage due to God—only two loaves out of all the sacrificial gifts being presented to Saul. To Saul this, then, would indicate *royalty in subordination to God.* The last was the strangest, but, rightly understood, also the most significant sign of all. Arrived at *Gibeah Elohim*, his own city, or else the hill close by, where the Philistines kept a garrison,[3] he would, on entering the city, meet " a band of prophets " coming down

---

[1] The traditional site of Rachel's grave near Bethlehem must be given up as wholly incompatible with this passage. The reasons have been fully explained in my *Sketches of Jewish Social Life,* p. 60.

[2] The locality cannot be identified. The suggestion of Thenius and Ewald, who regard *Tabor* as equivalent for *Deborah,* is scarcely tenable.

[3] Thenius and Böttcher render it, "a pillar ; " Ewald, "a tax-collector." But the rendering in the text seems the correct one (comp. xiii. 3, 4).

from the *Bamah,* or sacrificial height, in festive procession, preceded by the sound of the *nevel,* lute or guitar, the *thof,* or tambourine (Ex. xv. 20), the flute, and the *chinnor* [1] or hand-harp, themselves the while "prophesying." Then 'the Spirit of Jehovah" would "seize upon him," and he would "be turned into another man." The obvious import of this " sign," in combination with the others, would be : royalty not only *from* God and *under* God, but *with* God. And all the more significant would it appear, that Gibeah, the home of Saul, where all knew him and could mark the change, was now held by a garrison of Philistines ; and that Israel's deliverance should there commence [2] by the Spirit of Jehovah mightily laying hold on Israel's new king, and making of him another man. When all these "signs happen to thee," added the prophet, " do to thyself what thy hand findeth " (as circumstances indicate, comp. Judg. ix. 33) ; concluding therefrom : " for God is with thee."

The event proved as Samuel had foretold. Holy Scripture passes, indeed, lightly over the two first signs, as of comparatively less importance, but records the third with the more full detail. It tells how, immediately on leaving Samuel, " God turned to Saul another heart " (ver 9) ; how, when he met the band of prophets at Gibeah (ver. 10, not "the hill," as in our Authorised Version), " the Spirit of Elohim " " seized " upon him, and he " prophesied among them ;" so that those who had so intimately known him before exclaimed in astonishment : " What is this that has come unto the son of Kish ? Is Saul also among the prophets ?" Upon which " one from thence," more spiritually enlightened than the rest, answered : " And who is their father ?" implying that, in the case of the other prophets also, the gift of prophecy was not of

---

[1] The difference between the *nevel* and the *chinnor* is explained in my volume on *The Temple,* etc., p. 55. The *chinnor* differed from our harp in that it was carried in the hand (comp. 2 Sam. vi. 5).

[2] In the original the clause—" which there a garrison of the Philistines" —reads like an emphatic parenthesis, altogether meaningless except for the purpose indicated in the text.

hereditary descent.[1] Thus the proverb arose : "Is Saul also
among the prophets?" to indicate, according to circumstances,
either a sudden and almost incredible change in the outward
religious bearing of a man, or the possibility of its occurrence.

But there are deeper questions here which must, at least
briefly, be answered.   Apparently, there were already at that
time prophetic associations, called "schools of the prophets."
Whether these owed their origin to Samuel or not, the movement received at least a mighty impulse from him, and henceforth became a permanent institution in Israel.   But this
"prophesying" must not be considered as in all cases prediction.   In the present instance it certainly was not such,
but, as that of the "elders" in the time of Moses (Num. xi.
25), an ecstatic state of a religious character, in which men
unreservedly poured forth their feelings.   The characteristics
of this ecstatic state were entire separation from the circumstances around, and complete subjection to an extraordinary
influence from without, when thoughts, feelings, words, and
deeds were no longer under personal control, but became,
so to speak, passive instruments.   Viewing it in this light,
we can understand the use made of music, not only by true
prophets, but even among the heathen.   For the effect of
music is to detach from surrounding circumstances, to call
forth strong feelings, and to make us yield ourselves implicitly
to their influence.   In the case of the prophets at Gibeah and
in that of Saul, this ecstatic state was under the influence of
the "Spirit of Elohim."[2]   By this, as in the case of the
judges,[3] we are, however, not to understand the abiding and
sanctifying Presence of the Holy Ghost dwelling in the heart
as His temple.   The Holy Ghost was peculiarly "the gift of
the Father" and "of the Son," and only granted to the Church

---

[1] This is the view of Bunsen, and especially of Oehler, and seems to
afford the only correct interpretation of the saying.

[2] Samuel speaks of "the Spirit of Jehovah," while in the actual narrative we read of the "Spirit of Elohim."   Can the change of term have
been intentional?

[3] See Vol. III. of this History, p. 115.

in connection with, and after the Resurrection of our Blessed Lord. Under the Old Testament, only the manifold influences of the Spirit were experienced, not His indwelling as the Paraclete. This appears not only from the history of those so influenced, and from the character of that influence, but even from the language in which it is described. Thus we read that the Spirit of Elohim "seized upon" Saul, suddenly and mightily laid hold on him,—the same expression being used in Judg. xiv. 6, 19 ; xv. 14 ; 1 Sam. xvi. 13 ; xviii. 10.

But although they were only "influences" of the Spirit of Elohim, it need scarcely be said that such could not have been experienced without deep moral and religious effect. The inner springs of the life, thoughts, feelings, and purposes must necessarily have been mightily affected. It was so in the case of Saul, and the contrast was so great that his fellow-townsmen made a proverb of it. In the language of Holy Scripture. his "heart," that is, in Old Testament language, the spring of his feeling, purposing, and willing, was "turned into another" from what it had been, and he was "turned into another man," with quite other thoughts, aims, and desires than before. The difference between this and what in the New Testament is designated as "the new man," is too obvious to require detailed explanation. But we may notice these two as important points :• as in the one case it was only an overpowering influence of the Spirit of Elohim, not the abiding Presence of the Paraclete, so the moral effects produced through that influence were not primary, but secondary, and, so to speak, reflex, while those of the Holy Ghost in the hearts of God's people are direct, primary, and permanent.[1]

The application of these principles to "the spiritual gifts" in the early Church will readily occur to us. But perhaps it is more important to remember that we are always—and now more than ever—prone to confound the influences of

---

[1] If I may express it by a play upon two Latin words : In the one case it is *affectus* ab *effectu ;* in the other, if there is *effectus*, it is *effectus* ab *affectu.*

the Spirit of God with His abiding Presence in us, and to mistake the undoubted moral and religious effects, which for a time may result from the former, for the entire inward change, when "all old things have passed away," and "all things have become new," and are "of Christ." Yet the one is only the reflex influence of the spirit of man, powerfully influenced by the Spirit of Elohim ; the other the direct work of the Holy Ghost on the heart.

One of the effects of the new spiritual influence which had come upon Saul was, that when his uncle, Ner, met him upon the *Bamah*, or high place (ver. 14), probably joining him in his worship there to find out the real meaning of a change which he must have seen more clearly than any other, and which it would readily occur to him to connect with the visit to Samuel, he forbore to gratify a curiosity, probably not unmixed with worldly ambition and calculations.

But yet another charge had Samuel given to Saul before parting (ver. 8), and that not only a charge, but a life-direction, a warning, and a test of what was in him. That he understood it, is evident from 1 Sam. xiii. 7, 8. But would he submit to it, or rather to God? That would be to him the place and time when the two ways met and parted—and his choice of either one or the other would be decisive, both so far as his life and his kingdom were concerned.

CHAPTER VI.

Saul Chosen King at Mizpeh—His Comparative Privacy—Incursion of Nahash—Relief of Jabesh-gilead—Popular Assembly at Gilgal—Address of Samuel.

(1 Sam. x. 17—xii. 25.)

IN answer to the people's demand, Saul had been selected as their king. The motives and views which underlay their application for a king were manifest. They had been clearly set before the representatives of Israel by Samuel; and they had not gainsaid the correctness of his statement. They wanted not only a king, but royalty like that of the nations around, and for the purpose of outward deliverance; thus forgetting God's dealings in the past, disclaiming simple trust in Him, and disbelieving the sufficiency of His leadership. In fact, what they really wanted was a king who would reflect and embody their idea of royalty, not the ideal which God had set before them. And no better representative of Israel could have been found than Saul, alike in appearance and in military qualification; nor yet a truer reflex of the people than that which his character and religious bearing offered. He was the typical Israelite of his period, and this neither as regarded the evil-disposed or "sons of Belial," nor yet, of course, the minority of the truly enlightened, but the great body of the well-disposed people. If David was the king "after God's own heart," Saul was the king after the people's own heart. What they had asked, they obtained; and what they obtained, must fail; and what failed would prepare for what God had intended.

But as yet the choice of Saul had been a secret between the messenger of the Lord and the new king. As in every other case, so in this,[1] God would give the person called to most difficult work every opportunity of knowing His will, and every encouragement to do it. For this purpose Samuel had first called up great thoughts in Saul; then "communed" with him long and earnestly; then given him undoubted evidence that the message he bore was God's; and, finally, embodied in one significant direction alike a warning of his danger and guidance for his safety. All this had passed secretly between the two, that, undisturbed by influences from without, Saul might consider his calling and future course, and this in circumstances most favourable to a happy issue, while the transaction was still, as it were, between God and himself, and before he could be led astray by the intoxicating effect of success or by popular flattery.

And now this brief period of preparation was past, and what had been done in secret must be confirmed in public.[2] Accordingly Samuel summoned the people—no doubt by their representatives—to a solemn assembly "before Jehovah" in Mizpeh. Here the first great victory over the Philistines had been obtained by prayer (vii. 5), and here there was an "altar unto Jehovah" (ver. 9). As so often before, the lot was solemnly cast to indicate the will of God. But before so doing, Samuel once more presented to the people what the leadership of the Lord had been in the past, and what their choice of another leadership implied. This not with the view of annulling the proposed establishment of royalty, but with that of leading the people to repentance of their sin in connection with it. But the people remained unmoved. And now the lot was drawn.[3]

---

[1] Thus, for example, in the case of Balaam, and even of Pharaoh.

[2] Thenius and other writers regard this account of the election of Saul as incompatible with that of the previous interview between him and Samuel. They accordingly speak of two different accounts here incorporated into one narrative. But the thoughtful reader will agree with Ewald that closer consideration will convince us that Saul's appointment would have been incomplete without the public selection at Mizpeh.

[3] We note that the lot was, in this instance, not cast but drawn, evidently out of an urn. This is implied in the expression "taken," or rather "taken out," vers. 20, 21 (comp. Lev. xvi. 8; Numb. xxxiii. 54:

It fell on Saul, the son of Kish. But although he had come to Mizpeh, he could not be found in the assembly. It was a supreme moment in the history of Israel when God had indicated to His people, gathered before Him, their king by name. In circumstances so urgent, inquiry by the *Urim* and *Thummim* seemed appropriate. The answer indicated that Saul had concealed himself among the baggage on the outskirts of the encampment. Even this seems characteristic of Saul. It could have been neither from humility nor modesty [1] —both of which would, to say the least, have been here misplaced. It is indeed true that this was a moment in which the heart of the bravest might fail,[2] and that thoughts of what was before him might well fill him with anxiety.[3] Saul must have known what would be expected of him as king. Would he succeed in it? He knew the tribal and personal jealousies which his election would call forth. Would he be strong enough to stand against them? Such questions were natural. The only true answer would have been a *spiritual* one. Unable to give it, Saul withdrew from the assembly. Did he wonder whether after all it would come to pass or what would happen, and wait till a decision was forced upon him? The people, at any rate, saw nothing in his conduct that seemed to them strange ; and so we may take it that it was just up to the level of their own conceptions, though to us it appears very different from what a hero of God would have done.[4]

And so the newly-found king was brought back to the

Josh. vii. 14). The election was evidently first of tribes, then of clans, (here that of Matri), then of families, and lastly of individuals in the family selected. As the name of *Matri* does not otherwise occur, Ewald suggests that it is a copyist's error for *Bichri,* 2 Sam. xx. 1.

[1] So Keil.

[2] This is the suggestion of Nägelsbach.

[3] This is Ewald's view.

[4] The reluctance of Moses and of Jeremiah in similar circumstances afford no parallel, although that of the former, at least, was the result of weakness in faith. But their hesitation was before God, not before men.

assembly. And when Samuel pointed to him as he stood there, "from his shoulders upward" overtopping every one around, the people burst into a shout : "Let the king live !" For thus far Saul seemed the very embodiment of their ideal of a king. The transaction was closed by Samuel explaining to .the people, this time not "the right of the king" (1 Sam. viii. 9, 11), as claimed among other heathen nations whom they wished to imitate, but "the right of the kingdom"[1] (x. 25), as it should exist in Israel in accordance with the principles laid down in Deut. xvii. 14–20. This was put in writing, and the document solemnly deposited in the tabernacle.

For the moment, however, the establishment of the new monarchy seemed to bring no change. Saul returned to his home in Gibeah, attended indeed on his journey, by way of honour, by "a band whom Elohim had touched in their hearts," and who no doubt "brought him presents" as their king. But he also returned to his former humble avocations. On the other hand, "the sons of Belial" not only withheld such marks of homage, but openly derided the new king as wanting in tribal influence and military means for his office. When we bear in mind that these represented a party, possibly belonging to the great tribes of Judah and Ephraim, so strong as openly to express their opposition (1 Sam. xi. 12), and sufficiently numerous not to be resisted by those who thought otherwise, the movement must have been formidable enough to dictate as a prudential measure the retirement of Saul till the time when events would vindicate his election. And so complete was that privacy, that even the Philistine garrison in Gibeah remained in ignorance of the fact of Saul's new office, and of what it implied ; and that in the east, across the Jordan, the Ammonite king who waged war with Israel was

---

[1] Our Authorised Version translates, both here and 1 Sam. viii. 9, 11, "the manner ;" but the word can only mean "right," in the sense of right belonging to, or claimed by, any one. Thenius speaks of this as the establishment of a *constitutional* monarchy. But if "constitution" there was, it was God-given, not man-made.

apparently wholly unaware of any combined national movement on the part of the people, or of any new centre of union and resistance against a common enemy.

This expedition on the part of Nahash, king of the Ammonites, to which we have just referred, is otherwise also of interest, as showing that the desire of Israel after a king must have sprung from other and deeper motives than merely the age of Samuel, or even the conduct of his sons. From 1 Sam. xii. 12 it appears that the invasion by Nahash commenced before Israel's demand for a king, and was, indeed, the cause of it; thus proving that, as Samuel charged them, distrust of their heavenly Leader was the real motive of their movement. The expedition of Nahash had no doubt been undertaken to renew the claims which his predecessor had made, and to avenge the defeat which Jephthah had inflicted upon him (Judg. xi. 13, 33). But Nahash had penetrated much farther into Israelitish territory than his predecessor. His hordes had swarmed up the lovely rich valley of the Jabesh, laying bare its barley-fields and olive plantations, and wasting its villages; and they were now besieging the capital of Gilead—Jabesh-gilead—which occupied a commanding position on the top of an isolated hill overhanging the southern crest of the valley. In their despair, the people of Jabesh offered to surrender, but Nahash, in his insolence, insisted that he would thrust out their right eyes, avowedly to "lay it as a shame upon all Israel." Terrible as these conditions were, the "elders" of Jabesh saw no means of resisting, and only begged seven days' respite, to see whether any were left in Israel able and willing to save them. In the foolhardiness of his swagger, Nahash consented, well assured that if Israel were, as he fully believed, incapable of a combined movement for the relief of Jabesh, the whole land would henceforth be at his mercy, and between Philistia in the west and Ammon in the east, Israel—their land and their God —would lie helpless before the heathen powers.

It is, to say the least, a curious coincidence that Jabesh was the only town in Israel which had not taken part in the exter-

minating warfare against the tribe of Benjamin (Judg. xxi. 9).
But it was not on that ground, but because tidings had no
doubt reached them of the new royal office in Israel,[1] that
their messengers went straight to Gibeah. It was evening when
Saul returned home "behind the oxen," with which he had
been working,[2] to find Gibeah strangely moved. The tidings
which the men of Jabesh had brought had filled the place
with impotent lamentation, not roused the people to action.
So low had Israel sunk ! But now, as he heard it, once more
"the Spirit of Elohim seized upon Saul." He hewed in pieces
the "yoke of oxen" with which he had just returned, and sent
—probably by the messengers from Jabesh—these pieces
throughout the land, bidding those know who had no higher
thoughts than self, that thus it would be done to their oxen
who followed not after Saul and Samuel in the general war
against Ammon.

This, if ever, was the time when the Divine appointment of
Saul must be vindicated ; and to indicate this he conjoined with
himself Samuel, the venerated prophet of God, so long the
judge of Israel. It is said that "the terror of Jehovah" fell
upon the people.[3] From all parts of the land armed men
trooped to the trysting-place at Bezek, within the territory
of Issachar, near to Bethshan, and almost in a straight line to
Jabesh.   Three hundred thousand from Israel, and thirty

[1] Most critics seem to imagine that they had first gone all round Israel,
and only ultimately arrived at Gibeah, where they addressed themselves
to the people, and not to Saul.   But this account is in no way borne out by
the text, nor would it leave sufficient time for the measures taken by Saul
(ver. 7).   The statement of the elders of Jabesh (ver. 3) was evidently
intended to mislead Nahash.

[2] This is evidently the meaning, and not that conveyed in our Authorised
Version.

[3] Curiously enough, Keil seems to have overlooked that the Hebrew
word here used is that for "terror," or "awe," not fear.   The sacred
text ascribes the origin of this terror to the agency of Jehovah—not in the
sense of a miracle, but because it always traces up effects to Him as
their first cause.

thousand from Judah [1] (for that territory was in part held by the Philistines), had obeyed the summons of Saul. It was not an army, but a ban—a *landsturm*—an armed rising of the people. From the brow of the hill on which Bethshan lay, in the plain of Jezreel, you might look across Jordan and see Jabesh-gilead on its eminence. A very few hours would bring relief to the beleaguered city, and so they bade them know and expect. A feigned promise of subjection on the morrow made Nahash and his army even more confident than before. And what, indeed, had they to fear when all Israel lay so helplessly prostrate?

It was night when Saul and the armed multitude which followed him broke up from Bezek. Little did he know how well the brave men of Jabesh would requite the service; how, when on that disastrous day on Mount Gilboa he and his sons would fall in battle, and the victorious Philistines fasten their dead bodies to the walls of Bethshan, these brave men of Jabesh would march all night and rescue the fallen heroes from exposure (1 Sam. xxxi. 8–13). Strange that Saul's first march should have been by night from Bethshan to Jabesh, the same route by which at the last they carried his dead body at night.

But no such thoughts disturbed the host as they crossed the fords of the Jordan, and swarmed up the other bank. A few hours more, and they had reached the valley of the Jabesh. Following the example of Gideon (Judg. vii. 16), Saul divided the people "into three companies." From the rear and from either flank they fell upon the unsuspecting Ammonites when most secure—"in the morning watch," between three and six o'clock. A general panic ensued; and before the rout was ended not two of the enemy were left together. The revulsion of popular feeling toward Saul was complete. They would even have killed those who had formerly derided the new

---

[1] It almost appears as if we here met the first traces of a separation of the people into Israel and Judah. Similarly xvii. 52 ; xviii. 16 ; 2 Sam. ii. 9 ; iii. 10 ; v. 1–5 ; xix. 41, etc. ; xx. 2, 4.

monarchy. But Saul refused such counsel. Rather did Samuel make different use of the new state of feeling. On his proposal the people followed him and Saul to Gilgal, to which place so many sacred memories clung. Here they offered thank and peace-offerings, and greatly rejoiced as they renewed "the kingdom," and, in the sense of real and universal acknowledgment, "made Saul king before Jehovah."[1]

Although all his lifetime Samuel never ceased to judge Israel, yet his official work in that capacity had now come to an end. Accordingly he gave a solemn and public account of his administration, calling alike the Lord and His anointed to witness of what passed between him and the people. Leaving his sons to bear the responsibility[2] of their own doings, he challenged any charge against himself. But, as a faithful servant of the Lord, and ruler in Israel, he went further. Fain would he bring them to repentance for their great sin in the manner wherein they had demanded a king.[3] One by one he recalled to them the "righteous doings" of Jehovah in the fulfilment of His covenant-promises in the past.[4] In contrast to this never-failing help, he pointed to their unbelief, when, unmindful of what God had done and distrustful of what He would do, they had, on the approach of serious danger, virtually said concerning His leadership, "Nay, but a king shall reign over us." And God had granted their desire. But upon their and their king's bearing towards the Lord, not upon the fact that they had now a king, would the future of Israel depend. And this truth, so difficult for them to learn, God

---

[1] Some writers have imagined that Saul was anointed a second time. But for this there is no warrant in the text.

[2] It is thus that I understand I Sam. xii. 2 : "And, behold, my sons, they are with you."

[3] That Samuel did not blame Israel for wishing a king, but for the views and motives which underlay their application, appears (as Hengstenberg has shown) from the circumstance that when the people are repentant (ver. 19), he does not labour to make them recall what had been done, but only to turn unto the Lord (vers. 20–25).

[4] In the list of the judges mentioned by Samuel we find the name of *Bedan* (ver. 11). In all probability this is a copyist's mistake for *Barak*.

would now, as it were, *prove* before them in a symbol. Did they think it unlikely, nay, well-nigh impossible, to fail in their present circumstances? God would bring the unlikely and seemingly incredible to pass in a manner patent to all. Was it not the time of wheat-harvest,[1] when in the east not a cloud darkens the clear sky? God would send thunder and rain to convince them, by making the unlikely real, of the folly and sin of their thoughts in demanding a king.[2] So manifest a proof of the truth of what Samuel had said, and of the nearness of God and of His personal interposition, struck terror into the hearts of the people, and led to at least outward repentance. In reply to their confession and entreaty for his continued intercession, Samuel assured them that he would not fail in his duty of prayer for them, nor yet God, either in His faithfulness to His covenant and promises, or in His justice and holiness if they did wickedly.

And so the assembly parted—Israel to their tents, Saul to the work of the kingdom which lay to his hands, and Samuel to the far more trying and difficult duty of faithfully representing and executing the will of God as His appointed messenger in the land.

[1] That is—the months of May and June.

[2] We have ventured to suggest this explanation of the miraculous occurrence, because it meets all the requirements of the case, and because, even during the preparatory dispensation of the Old Testament, miracles were not mere exhibitions of *power* without moral purpose or meaning. At the same time, we fully and frankly accept the fact that in Biblical times, and till after the outpouring of the Holy Ghost, personal interposition on the part of God—miracle and prophetic inspiration—was the rule, not the exception, in God's dealings with His people.

CHAPTER VII.

Saul Marches against the Philistines—Position of the two Camps—Jona-
than's Feat of Arms—Saul Retreats to Gilgal—Terror among the
People—Saul's Disobedience to the Divine Command, and Rejection of
his Kingdom.

(1 SAM. XIII.)

A T Gilgal Saul had been accepted by the whole people as
their king,[1] and it now behoved him to show himself such
by immediately taking in hand as his great work the liberation
of the land from Israel's hereditary enemy the Philistines.
For this purpose he selected from the armed multitude at
Gilgal three thousand men, of whom two thousand under his
own command were posted in Michmash and in Mount Bethel,
while the other thousand advanced under Jonathan to Gibeah
of Benjamin (or Gibeah of Saul). Close to this, a little

---

[1] Accordingly the commencement of Saul's reign was dated from Gilgal.
Hence 1 Sam. xiii. 1 had opened, as the history of all other kings (comp.
2 Sam. ii. 10; v. 4; 1 Kings xiv. 21; xxii. 42; 2 Kings viii. 26; etc.),
with the statistical data of his age at the commencement, and the duration
of his reign. But unfortunately the numeral letters have wholly fallen
out of the first, and partially out of the second clause of ver. 1, which,
as they stand in our present Hebrew text, may be thus represented:
"Saul was . . . years old when he was made king, and he reigned two
. . . years over Israel." All other attempts at explanation of this verse—
notably that of our Authorised Version—are incompatible with the Hebrew
and with history. According to Jewish tradition (Jos., *Antiq.*, vi. 14, 9),
Saul reigned for forty years. This is also the time mentioned by St. Paul
(Acts xiii. 21). There is no sufficient reason for the view of certain critics
that the "original narrative" is here resumed from x. 16. In fact, if such
were the case, we would require some explanation of the phrase: "Saul
chose him three thousand men of Israel" (xiii. 2). Whence and where did
he choose them, if not from the assembly at Gilgal? Certainly, more
unlikely circumstances for this could not be found than those in which Saul
is left in x. 16, when, so far from selecting three thousand men, he ventures
not to confide the secret of his elevation even to his uncle !

to the north, at Geba, the Philistines had pushed forward an advanced post, perhaps from Gibeah, to a position more favourable than the latter.   Unable, with the forces at his disposal, to make a regular attack, it seems to have been Saul's purpose to form the nucleus of an army, and meanwhile to blockade and watch the Philistines in Geba.   So far as we can judge, it does not appear to have lain within his plan to attack that garrison, or else the enterprise would have been undertaken by himself, nor would it have caused the surprise afterwards excited by Jonathan's success.

As it is of considerable importance for the understanding of this history to have a clear idea of the scene where these events took place, we add the most necessary details.   Geba, the post of the Philistines, lay on a low conical eminence, on the western end of a ridge which shelves eastwards towards the Jordan.   Passing from Geba northwards and westwards we come to a steep descent, leading into what now is called the Wady-es-Suweinit.   This, no doubt, represents the ancient "passage of Michmash" (1 Sam. xiii. 23).   On the opposite steep brow, right over against Geba, lies Michmash, at a distance of barely three miles in a north-westerly direction.   This Wady-es-Suweinit is also otherwise interesting.   Running up in a north-westerly direction towards Bethel, the ridge on either side the wady juts out into two very steep rock-covered eminences—one south-west, towards Geba, the other north-west, towards Michmash.   Side wadys, trending from north to south behind these two eminences, render them quite abrupt and isolated.   These two peaks, or "teeth," were respectively called *Bozez*, "the shining," and *Seneh*, either "the tooth-like," "the pointed," or perhaps "the thorn," afterwards the scene of Jonathan's daring feat of arms (1 Sam. xiv. 1–13).   Bethel itself lies on the ridge, which runs in a north-westerly direction from Michmash.   From this brief sketch it will be seen that, small as Saul's army was, the Philistine garrison in Geba was, to use a military term, completely *enfiladed* by it, since Saul with his two thousand men occupied Michmash and Mount Bethel to

the north-east, north, and north-west, threatening their communications through the Wady-es-Suweinit with Philistia, while
Jonathan with his thousand men lay at Gibeah to the south
of Geba.

But the brave spirit of Jonathan could ill brook enforced
idleness in face of the enemy. Apparently without consultation with his father, he attacked and "smote" the Philistine
garrison in Geba. The blow was equally unexpected by Philistine and Israelite. In view of the preparations made by the
enemy, Saul now retired to Gilgal—probably not that in which
the late assembly had been held, but the other Gilgal near
Jericho.[1] Hither "the people were called together after Saul."
But the impression left on us is, that from the first the people
were depressed rather than elated, frightened rather than
encouraged by Jonathan's feat of arms. And no wonder,
considering not only the moral unpreparedness of the people,
but their unfitness to cope with the Philistines, alike so far as
arms and military training were concerned. The hundreds of
thousands who had followed Saul to Jabesh were little better
than an undisciplined mob that had seized any kind of weapons.
Such a multitude would be rather a hindrance than a help
in a war against disciplined infantry, horsemen, and war-
chariots. In fact, only three thousand of them were fit to
form the nucleus of an army, and even they, or what at
last remained of them to encounter the Philistines, were so
badly equipped that they could be truthfully described as
without either "sword or spear" (xiii. 22).[2]

[1] I have put this hypothetically, for I feel by no means sure that it was
not the other Gilgal. The argument of Keil, that in that case Saul would
have had to attack the Philistines at Michmash before reaching Gibeah
(ver. 15), is not convincing, since there was a road to the latter place to the
west of Michmash. On the other hand, however, the Gilgal near Jericho
was no doubt a more safe place of retreat where to collect an army, and
the wadys open directly upon it from Geba and Gibeah ; while, lastly, the
remark, that " Hebrews went over Jordan to the land of Gad and Gilead"
(ver. 7), seems to point to a camp in the immediate neighbourhood of that river.

[2] Of course, the expression must be taken in a general sense, and not
absolutely, and refers to the total want of regular armament.

The army with which the Philistines now invaded the land was the largest and best appointed[1] which they had yet brought into the field. Avoiding the former mistake of allowing their opponents to take them in flank by camping in Michmash, the Philistines now occupied that post themselves, their line extending thither from Beth-aven.[2] From their position at Gilgal the Israelites could see that mighty host, and under the influence of terror rapidly melted away. Some passed across the Jordan, the most part hid themselves in the caves and pits and rocks with which the whole district around the position of the Philistines abounds. The situation was indeed becoming critical in the extreme. Day by day the number of deserters increased, and even those who yet remained "behind him," "were terrified."[3] And still Saul waited from day to day for that without which he had been told he must not move out of Gilgal, and which now was so unaccountably and, as it would seem to a commander, so fatally delayed !

It will be remembered that on parting from Saul, immediately after his anointing, Samuel had spoken these somewhat mysterious words (1 Sam. x. 7, 8) : "And it shall be when these signs shall come unto thee, do for thyself as thine hand shall find, for Elohim is with thee. And when thou goest down before me to Gilgal,—and behold I am going down to thee,[4]—to offer burnt-offerings and to sacrifice sacrifices of peace-

[1] Our Hebrew text has " thirty thousand chariots."—a number not only disproportionate to the horsemen but unheard of in history. The copyist's mistake evidently arose in this manner. Writing, " And the Philistines gathered themselves together to fight with Israel," the copyist by mistake repeated the letter *l*, which in Hebrew is the numeral sign for 30, and so wrote what reads " *thirty* thousand chariots," instead of " one thousand chariots," as had been intended.

[2] This Beth-aven is mentioned in Josh. vii. 2, and must not be confounded with Bethel, east of which it evidently lay, between Bethel and Michmash. At the same time the word rendered "*eastward* from Beth-aven" (ver. 5) does not *necessarily* mean "eastwards," but might also be rendered "in front of," or "over against."

[3] So ver. 7 literally.

[4] I have so punctuated in accordance with most critics, to indicate that the offering of sacrifices refers to *Saul's* purpose in going to Gilgal,

offerings, seven days shalt thou tarry till I come to thee, and shew thee what thou shalt do." The first part of Samuel's injunction—to do as his hand should find—Saul had followed when making war against Nahash. It is the second part which sounds so mysterious. It will be remembered that, immediately after the defeat of Nahash, Saul and the people had, on the suggestion of Samuel, gone to Gilgal, there to "renew the kingdom." Manifestly that visit to Gilgal could not have been meant, since, so far from having to wait seven days for the arrival of Samuel, the prophet had accompanied Saul thither. It can, therefore, only have been intended to apply to this retreat of Saul upon Gilgal in preparation for his first great campaign against the Philistines.[1] And what to us sounds so mysterious in the language of Samuel may not have been so at the time to Saul. During that communing on the roof of Samuel's house, or afterwards, the two may have spoken of a great war against the Philistines, and of the necessity of gathering all Israel in preparation for it to Gilgal, not only for obvious military reasons, but as the place where the ʳeproach of Israel had first been rolled away (Josh. v. 9), and whence appro-

---

and that the sentence about Samuel's coming down is intercalated. But on this point I do not feel sure. It would make no difference, however, so far as regards the meaning of Samuel, whose injunction was intended to warn Saul not to interfere with the functions of the priestly office. I have, of course, translated the passage literally. The rendering of our Authorised Version, "and thou shalt go down," is impossible. We have our choice between the imperative and the conditional mood, and the balance of argument is strongly in favour of the latter.

[1] Of course, two other theories are possible. The one, a suggestion that the verse 1 Sam. x. 8 may be displaced in our Hebrew text, and should stand somewhere else, is a wild and vague hypothesis. The other suggestion, that all between x. 17 and xiii. 2 is intercalated from another narrative will not bear investigation. If the reader tries to piece ch. x. 16 to xiii. 3, he will at once perceive that there would be a felt gap in the narrative. Besides, how are we to account for the selection of three thousand men, and the going to war against the Philistines on the part of a man who is made the target of wit in his own place, and who dares not tell even his own uncle of his secret elevation to the royal office?

priately the re-conquest of the land should commence by
sacrifices and seeking the direction of the Lord.

But even if at the time when first uttered by Samuel it had
seemed mysterious to Saul, there could be no doubt that
the injunction applied to the circumstances in which the king
and his followers now found themselves. What should he do?
Day by day passed without tidings of Samuel, and still his
followers decreased, and the hearts of those who remained
waxed more feeble. Yet Saul *did* wait the full seven days
which Samuel had appointed. But when the seventh day was
drawing to a close[1] he forbore no longer; and although, as he
said, most reluctantly, he had the sacrifices offered, no doubt
by the regular priesthood (comp. 2 Sam. xxiv. 25 ; 1 Kings iii. 4 ;
viii. 63). No sooner had the sacrifices been offered, than on a
sudden Samuel himself appeared—as we understand it, before
the full term which he had set for his arrival had actually been
passed. Whether simply to brave it, or, as seems to us more
likely, from real ignorance of the import of what he had done,
Saul went to meet and salute Samuel. But the prophet came
as God's messenger. He denounced the *folly* of Saul, and his
sin in disobeying the express command of the Lord, and intimated that, had he stood the test, his kingdom, or royal line,
would have been established, whereas now his throne would
pass to a worthier successor. Not, therefore, his personal rejection, nor even that of his title to the throne, but only that of
his "kingdom," or line, as unfit to be "captains" over
"Jehovah's people"—such was the sentence which Samuel had
to announce on that day.

The "folly" of Saul's conduct must, indeed, have been
evident to all. He had not waited long enough, and yet too
long, so far as his following was concerned, which, after the
sacrifice, amounted to only about six hundred men (1 Sam.
xiii. 15). On the other hand, the only motive which, even
politically speaking, could have brought numbers to his ranks

---

[1] The context seems to imply that Saul offered his sacrifice and Samuel
came before the actual termination of the seven days.

or fired them with courage, was a religious belief in the help of Jehovah, of which Saul's breach of the Divine command and the defection of Samuel would threaten to deprive Israel. But still there are questions involved in the Divine punishment of Saul which require most earnest attention, not only for the vindication, but even for the proper understanding of this history.

To the first question which arises, why Samuel thus unduly delayed his journey to Gilgal, apparently without necessary reason, we can, in fairness, only return the answer, that his delay seems to have been *intentional,* quite as much as that of our blessed Lord, after He had heard of the sickness of Lazarus, and when He knew of his death (John xi. 6, 14, 15). But if intentional, its object can only have been to test the character of Saul's kingdom. Upon this, of course, the permanency of that kingdom would depend. We have already seen that Saul represented the kind of monarchy which Israel wished to have established. Saul's going down to Gilgal to offer sacrifices, and yet not offering them properly; his unwillingness to enter on the campaign without having entreated the face of Jehovah, and yet offending Him by disobedience; his waiting so long, and not long enough; his trust in the help of Jehovah, and yet his distrust when his followers left him ; his evident belief in the absolute efficacy of sacrifices as an outward ordinance irrespective of the inward sacrifice of heart and will—are all exactly representative of the religious state of Israel. But although Israel had sought, and in Saul obtained a monarchy "after *their own* heart," yet, as Samuel had intimated in Gilgal (xii. 14, 20–22, 24), the Lord, in His infinite mercy, was willing to forgive and to turn all for good, if Israel would only "fear the Lord and serve Him in truth." Upon this conversion, so to speak, of Israel's royalty into the kingdom of God the whole question turned. For, either Israel must cease to be the people of the Lord, or else the principle on which its monarchy was founded must become spiritual and Divine; and consequently any government that contravened this must be swept away to give place to another. If it be asked, what this Divine principle of monarchy was to be, we have no hesitation in answering, that it was intended to constitute a kingdom in which *the will of the earthly should be in avowed subjection to that of the heavenly King.* This was right in itself; it was expressive of the covenant-relationship by which Jehovah became the God of Israel, and Israel the people of Jehovah; and it embodied the typical idea of the kingdom of God, to be fully realised in the *King* of the Jews, Who came not to do His own will, but that of His Father in heaven, even to the bitter agony of the cup in Gethsemane. and the sufferings of Golgotha. *Saul was the king after Israel's own heart* (1 Sam. xii. 13); *David the king after God's own heart,* not because of his greater piety or goodness, but because, despite his failings and his sins, he fully embodied the Divine idea of Israel's kingdom; and for this reason also he and his kingdom were the type of our Lord Jesus Christ and of His kingdom.

In what has been said the second great difficulty, which almost instinctively rises in our minds on reading this history, has in part been anticipated. It will easily be understood that this great question had, if ever, to be tested and decided at the very commencement of Saul's reign, and before he engaged in any great operations, the success or failure of which might divert the mind. If to be tried at all, it must be on its own merits, and irrespective of results. Still, it must be admitted, that the first feeling with most of us is that, considering the difficulties of Saul's position, the punishment awarded to him seems excessive. Yet it only seems, but is not such. Putting aside the idea of his personal rejection and dethronement, neither of which was implied in the words of Samuel, the sentence upon Saul only embodied this principle, that no monarchy could be enduring in Israel which did not own the supreme authority of God. As Adam's obedience was tested in a seemingly small matter, and his failure involved that of his race, so also in the case of Saul. His partial obedience and his anxiety to offer the sacrifices as, in his mind, in themselves efficacious, only rendered it the more necessary to bring to the foreground the great question of absolute, unquestioning, and believing submission to the will of the Heavenly King. Saul's kingdom had shown itself not to be God's kingdom, and its continuance was henceforth impossible. However different their circumstances, *Saul was as unfit for the inheritance of the kingdom*, with the promises which this implied and the typical meaning it bore, *as Esau had been* for the inheritance of the first-born, with all that it conveyed in the present, in the near, and in the distant future.

CHAPTER VIII.

Camps of Israel and of the Philistines—Jonathan and his Armour-bearer —Panic among the Philistines, and Flight—Saul's Rash Vow—The "Lot" cast at Ajalon—Cessation of the War.

(I SAM. XIII. 15—XIV. 46.)

WHEN, after Samuel's departure, Saul with his six hundred men marched out of Gilgal, he found the Philistines occupying the range at Michmash which he had formerly held. With such weak following as he could command, it was wise on his part to take up a position in the "uttermost part of Gibeah" (xiv. 2), that is, as we gather from the context, to the north of the town itself, and on the outskirts of Geba[1] and its district (xiii. 16). Geba is only about an hour and a quarter north of Gibeah. We may therefore suppose Saul's camp to have been about two miles to the north of the latter city, and to have extended towards Geba. His head-quarters were under a pomegranate tree at a place called Migron—probably a "land-slip;" and there, besides his principal men, he had the then

[1] Our Authorised Version erroneously corrects, "*Gibeah,*" apparently following the LXX.

occupant of the high-priesthood, Ahiah,[1] the son of Ahitub, an elder brother of I-chabod, "wearing an ephod," or discharging the priestly functions. From Geba itself Michmash, which lay on the opposite ridge, was only divided by the intervening Wady-es-Suweinit. How long the Israelites had lain in thal position we are not informed. But we are told that "the spoilers," or rather "the destroyers," "went out of the camp of the Philistines in three bands" (xiii. 17),—one "facing" in a north-easterly direction by Ophrah towards the district of Shual, the "fox-country," the other "facing" westwards towards Beth-horon, and the third south-eastwards, "the way to the district that overlooketh the valley of Zeboim" ("raveners," [2] viz., wild beasts) "toward the wilderness" (of Judah). Thus the only direction left untouched was south and south-west, where Saul and Jonathan held the strong position of Gibeah-Geba. If the intention had been to draw them thence into the open, it failed. But immense damage must have been inflicted upon the country, while a systematic raid was made upon all smithies, so as to render it impossible not only to prepare weapons, but so much as to have the means of sharpening the necessary tools of husbandry.

In these circumstances it is once more the noble figure of Jonathan which comes to the foreground. Whatever fitness he might have shown for "the kingdom," had he been called to it, a more unselfish, warm-hearted, genuine, or noble character is not presented to us in Scripture than that of Jonathan. Weary of the long and apparently hopeless inactivity, trustful in Jehovah, and fired by the thought that with Him there was "no hindrance to save, by much or by little," he planned single-handed an

[1] This Ahiah, or rather *Achijah* ("brother," "friend of Jehovah"), is supposed to be the same as *Achimelech* ("brother," "friend of the King," viz., Jehovah), 1 Sam. xxii. 9, etc. Ewald (*Gesch.*, ii., 585, Note 3) regards the two names as interchangeable, like Elimelech and Elijahu. Keil suggests that Achimelech may have been a brother of Achijah.

[2] The Chaldee paraphrast has "serpents"—this valley being supposed to have been their lurking-place. But I have taken the more general meaning of the term.

expedition against the Philistine outpost at Michmash.   As he put it, it was emphatically a deed of faith, in which he would not take counsel either with his father or with any of the people, only with God, of Whom he would seek a sign of approbation before actually entering on the undertaking.   The sole com- panion whom he took was, as in the case of Gideon (Judg. vii. 9, 10), his armour-bearer, who seems to have been not only entirely devoted to his master, but like-minded.   In the Wady-es-Suweinit, which, as we have seen, forms "the passage" between the ridge of Geba, where Jonathan was, and that of Michmash, now occupied by the Philistines, were the two conical heights, or "teeth of rock," called Bozez and Seneh. One of these, as we gather from the text, faced Jonathan and his armour-bearer toward the north over against Michmash.   This we suppose to have been *Bozez,* "the shining one," probably so called from its rocky sides and top.   It is figuratively described in the text as cast [1] like metal.   Here, on the top of a sharp, very narrow ledge of rock, was the Philistine outpost. The "tooth of rock" opposite, on which Jonathan and his armour-bearer " discovered " themselves to their enemies, was *Seneh,* "the thornlike," or "pointed," or else "the tooth." [2] All around there was thick wood, or rather forest (xiv. 25), which stretched all the way towards Bethel (2 Kings ii. 23, 24). Standing on the extreme point of Seneh, the Philistines would probably only see Jonathan, with, at most, his armour-bearer ; but they would be ignorant what forces might lurk under cover of the trees.   And this was to be the sign by which Jonathan and his companion were to discern whether or not God favoured their enterprise.   If, when they " discovered" themselves to the Philis- tines, these would challenge them to stay and await their coming over to fight, then Jonathan and his companion would forbear,

---

[1] 1 Sam. xiv. 5, literally, "the one tooth poured "—"or a pillar"— "towards the north before" (or "over against") "Michmash."
[2] Dean Stanley supposes the name to be derived from a thorn-bush on the top of the eminence. But it may simply mean the "thorn-like," or moie probably, "the pointed."

while, if the challenge were the other way, they would infer
that Jehovah had delivered them into their hand.   The one, of
course, would argue courage on the part of the Philistines, the
other the want of it.   What followed is graphically sketched in
the sacred text.   From the point of "the thorn," or "tooth of the
rock," Jonathan "discovered" himself to the Philistines.   This
open appearance of the Hebrews was as startling as unexpected,
nor could the Philistines have imagined that two men alone
would challenge a post.   Manifestly the Philistine post had no
inclination to fight an unknown enemy; and so with genuine
Eastern boastfulness they heaped abuse on them, uttering the
challenge to come up.   This had been the preconcerted signal;
and, choosing the steepest ascent, where their approach would
least be looked for, Jonathan and his armour-bearer crept up
the ledge of the rock on their hands and feet.   Up on the top
it was so narrow that only one could stand abreast.   This we
infer not only from the language of the text, but from the
description of what ensued.   As Jonathan reached the top, he
threw down his foremost opponent, and the armour-bearer,
coming up behind, killed him.   There was not room for two to
attack or defend in line.   And so twenty men fell, as the text
expresses it, within "half a furrow of a yoke of field,"[1]—that is,
as we understand it, within the length commonly ploughed by
a yoke of oxen, and the width of about half a furrow, or more
probably half the width that would be occupied in ploughing a
furrow.   All this time it would be impossible, from the nature of
the *terrain*, to know how many assailants were supporting Jonathan and his armour-bearer.   This difficulty would be still more
felt in the camp and by those at a little farther distance, since it
would be manifestly impossible for them to examine the steep
sides of Bozez, or the neighbouring woods.   The terror, probably
communicated by fugitives, who would naturally magnify the

[1] Both Keil and Erdmann refer for a similar feat to Sallust, *Bell. Jugurth.*
c. 89, 90.   The quotation is so far erroneous that the story is told in c. 93,
94; but the feat of the Ligurian, however magnificent, was scarcely equal to
that of Jonathan.   Still, the one story is certainly parallel to the other.

danger, perhaps into a general assault, soon became a panic, or, as the text expresses it, a "terror of Elohim." Presently the host became an armed rabble, melting away before their imaginary enemy, and each man's sword in the confusion turned against his neighbour.   At the same time the Hebrew auxiliaries, whom cowardice or force had brought into the camp of the Philistines, turned against them, and the noise and confusion became indescribable.

From the topmost height of Gibeah the outlook, which Saul had there posted, descried the growing confusion in the Philistine camp.   Only one cause could suggest itself for this. When Saul mustered his small army, he found that only Jonathan and his armour-bearer were missing.   But the king sufficiently knew the spirit of his son not to regard as impossible any undertaking on his part, however seemingly desperate. What was he to do?   One thing alone suggested itself to him.   He would take counsel of the Lord by the well-known means of the Urim and Thummim.[1]   But while preparations were making for it, the necessity of its employment had evidently ceased.   It was not a sudden commotion, but an increasing panic among the Philistines that was observed. Presently Saul and his men, as they came to battle, found that the enemy himself had been doing their work.   And now it became a rout.   The Hebrews from the Philistine camp had joined the pursuers, and, as the well-known notes of the trumpet wakened the echoes of Mount Ephraim, the men who were in hiding crept out of their concealment. and followed in the chase. And so the tide of battle rolled as far as Beth-aven.

[1] Our present *textus receptus* has, in 1 Sam. xiv. 18, two copyist's errors. The one is emendated in our Authorised Version, which reads, "*with* the children of Israel," instead of, as in the *textus receptus*, "*and* the children of Israel," which would give no meaning.   The second error is emendated in the LXX., who seem to have had the correct text, according to which the word "Ephod" should be substituted for "ark."   The letters of these two words in the Hebrew are somewhat like each other, whence the error or the copyist.   The ark was at Kirjath Jearim, nor was it "brought hither" to ascertain the will of God.

But, though the battle was chiefly pursuit of the fleeing foe, already "the men of Israel were distressed," or rather "pressed," by weariness and faintness. For quite early in the day, and in the absence of Jonathan, Saul had yielded to one of his characteristic impulses. When he ascertained the real state of matters as regarded the Philistines, he put the people under a vow—to which, either by an "Amen," or else by their silence they gave assent—not to taste food until the evening, till he had avenged himself of his enemies. It need scarcely be said, that in this Saul acted without Divine direction. More than that, it is difficult to discern in it any religious motive, unless it were, that the enemies on whom Saul wished personally to be avenged were also the hereditary foes of Israel. And yet in the mind of Saul there was no doubt something religious about this rash vow. At any rate the form in which his impetuous Eastern resolve was cast, was such, and that of a kind which would peculiarly commend itself to an Israelite like Saul. Foolish and wrong as such a vow had been, still, as Israel had at least by their silence given consent, it lay as a heavy obligation upon the people. However faint, none dared break the fast during that long and weary day, when they followed the enemy as far as the western passes of Ajalon that led down into the Philistine plains. But Jonathan had not known it, till one told him of his father's vow after he had paused in the forest to dip his staff into honey that had dropped from the combs of wild bees. For such an offence Jonathan was certainly not morally responsible. Considering how small an amount of nourishment had helped him in his weariness, he could only deplore the rashness of his father, whose vow had, through the faintness which it entailed on the people, defeated the very object he had sought.

At last the weary day closed in Ajalon, and with it ended the obligation upon the people. The pursuit was stopped; and the people, ravenous for food, slew the animals "on the ground," felling them down, and eating the meat without being careful to remove the blood. It is true that, when Saul heard of it, he reproved the people for the sin which this involved, and took immediate steps to provide a proper slaughtering-place. Still this breach of an express Divine command (Lev. xix. 26) must in fairness be laid to the charge of Saul's rash vow. Nor could the building of a memorial-altar on the spot be regarded as altering the character of what had taken place that day.

Night was closing around Ajalon. The place, the circumstances, nay, his very vow, could not but recall to Saul the story of Joshua, and of his pursuit of the enemies of Israel (Josh. x. 12, 13). His proposal to follow up the Philistines was willingly taken up by the people, who had meanwhile refreshed themselves and were eager for the fray. Only the priests would first ask counsel of God. But no answer came, though sought by Urim and Thummim. Some burden must lie upon Israel, and Saul with his usual rashness would bring it to the test with whom lay the guilt, at the same time swearing by Jehovah that it should be avenged by death, even though it rested on Jonathan, the victor of that day, who had "wrought this great salvation in Israel," nay, who "had wrought with God" that day. But the people, who well knew what Jonathan had done, listened in dull silence. It must have been a weird scene as they gathered around the camp fire, and the torches cast their fitful glare on those whose fate the lot was to decide. First it was to be between all the people on the one side, and Saul and Jonathan on the other. A brief, solemn invocation, and the lot fell upon Saul and his son. A second time it was cast, and now it pointed to Jonathan. Questioned by his father, he told what he had done in ignorance. Still Saul persisted that his vow must be fulfilled. But now the people interposed. He whom God had owned, and who had saved Israel, must not die. But the pursuit of the Philistines was given up, and the campaign abruptly closed. And so ended in sorrow and disappointment what had been begun in self-willed disobedience to God and distrustfulness of Him.

CHAPTER IX

The War against Amalek—Saul's Disobedience, and its Motives—Samuel commissioned to announce Saul's Rejection—Agag Hewn in Pieces.

(I SAM. XIV. 47-52; XV.)

THE successful war against the Philistines had secured Saul in possession of the throne.[1] Henceforth his reign was marked by wars against the various enemies of Israel, in all of which he proved victorious.[2] These expeditions are only indicated, not described, in the sacred text, as not forming constituent elements in the history of the kingdom of God, however they may have contributed to the prosperity of the Jewish state. The war against Amalek alone is separately told (ch. xv.), alike from its character and from its bearing on the kingdom which God would establish in Israel. Along with these outward successes the sacred text also indicates the seeming prosperity of Saul, as regarded his family-life.[3] It almost appears as if it had been intended to place before us, side by side in sharp contrast, these two facts : Saul's prosperity

[1] We take this to be the meaning of the expression : "So Saul took the kingdom" (xiv. 47).

[2] The sacred text has it (vers. 47, 48) : "and whithersoever he turned himself, he vexed them"—the latter word being used of sentences pronounced by a judge,—"and he wrought might," that is, he displayed power.

[3] Only those three sons are mentioned whose story is identified with that of Saul himself, and who fell with him in the fatal battle of Gilboa (xxxi. 2). "*Ishui*" is evidently the same as *Abinadab*. We will not venture on any conjecture of the reason of the interchange of these two names (comp. I Chron. viii. 33 ; ix. 39). In the genealogies in Chronicles, a fourth son, *Esh-baal*, is mentioned, who was evidently the same as *Ishbosheth*. Merab and Michal are introduced with a view to their after-story. Ewald says : "With ch. xiv. Saul ceases to be the true king, in the prophetic meaning of that term. Hence the history of his reign is here closed with the usual general remarks."

both at home and abroad, and his sudden fall and rejection, to show forth that grand truth which all history is evolving: Jehovah reigneth!

Israel's oldest and hereditary enemies were the Amalekites. Descended from Esau (Gen. xxxvi., 12, 16; 1 Chron. i. 36; comp. Josephus' *Antiq.* ii., 1, 2), they occupied the territory to the south and south-west of Palestine. They had been the first wantonly to attack Israel in the wilderness[1] (Ex. xvii. 8, etc.), and "war against Amalek from generation to generation," had been the Divine sentence upon them. Besides that first attack we know that they had combined with the Canaanites (Num. xiv. 43–45), the Moabites (Judg. iii. 12, 13), and the Midianites (Judg. vii. 12) against Israel. What other more direct warfare they may have carried on, is not expressly mentioned in Scripture, because, as frequently observed, it is not a record of the national history of Israel. But from 1 Sam. xv. 33 we infer that, at the time of which we write, they were not only in open hostility against Israel, but behaved with extreme and wanton cruelty. Against this unrelenting hereditary foe of the kingdom of God the ban had long been pronounced (Deut. xxv. 17–19). The time had now arrived for its execution, and Samuel summoned Saul in the most solemn manner to this work. It was in itself a difficult expedition. To be carried out in its full sweep as a "ban," it would, in Saul's then state of mind, have required peculiar self-abnegation and devotion. Looking back upon it from another stage of moral development and religious dispensation, and in circumstances so different that such questions and duties can never arise,[2] and that they seem immeasurably far behind, as the dark valley to the traveller

---

[1] See Vol. II. of this History, pp. 101–103.

[2] This accommodation of the law to each stage of man's moral state, together with the continuous moral advancement which the law as a schoolmaster was intended to bring about, and which in turn was met by progressive revelation, renders it impossible to judge of a Divine command by trying to put it as to our own times, and as applicable to us. If we put forward the finger-hand on the dial of time, and the clock still strikes the old hour, we must not infer that the clock is out of order, but rather that

who has climbed the sunlit height, or as perhaps events and phases in our own early history, many things connected with the "ban" may appear mysterious to us. But the history before us is so far helpful as showing that, besides its direct meaning as a judgment, it had also another and a moral aspect, implying, as in the case of Saul, self-abnegation and real devotedness to God.

Thus viewed, the command to execute the "ban" upon Amalek was the second and final test of Saul's fitness for being king over God's people. The character of this kingdom had been clearly explained by Samuel at Gilgal in his address to king and people (1 Sam. xii. 14, 20, 21, 24). There is evidently an internal connection between the first (1 Sam. xiii. 8–14) and this second and final trial of Saul. The former had brought to light his want of faith, and even of simple obedience, and it had been a *test of his moral qualification for the kingdom;* this second was *the test of his moral qualification for being king.* As the first trial, so to speak, developed into the second, so Saul's *want* of moral qualification had ripened into absolute *dis*qualification— and as the former trial determined the fate of his line, so this second decided his own as king. After the first trial his line was rejected; after the second his own standing as theocratic king ceased. As God-appointed king he was henceforth rejected; Jehovah withdrew the sanction which He had formerly given to his reign by the aid of His power and the Presence of His Spirit. Henceforth "the Spirit of Jehovah departed from Saul "(1 Sam. xvi. 14), and he was left, in the judgment of God, to the influence of that evil spirit to whom his natural disposi-

---

we have unskilfully meddled with it. The principle for which we have here contended is clearly laid down in the teaching of our blessed Lord about divorce (Matt. xix. 8), and also implied in what St. Paul saith about the law (Gal. iii. 24). The whole of this subject is most admirably and exhaustively treated by Canon Mozley in his *Ruling Ideas in Early Ages, and their Relation to Old Testament Faith.* See especially Lecture VIII., on "The Law of Retaliation," and Lecture X., "The End the Test of a Progressive Revelation."

tion and the circumstances of his position laid him specially open (comp. Matt. xii. 43–45).

In view of the great moral trial which this expedition against Amalek would involve, Samuel had been careful to make it clear that the call to it came by Divine authority, reminding the king that he had been similarly sent to anoint him (1 Sam. xv. 1). From the circumstance that Saul seems to have marched against Amalek, not with a chosen host, but to have summoned the people as a whole [1] to execute the "ban," we infer that he had understood the character of his commission. Moving from *Telaim* ("the place of lambs" [2]), probably in the eastern part of the south country, he came to "the city of Amalek," which is not named, where he "laid an ambush in the valley." Before proceeding farther, he found means to communicate with that branch of the tribe of the Kenites who, from ancient times, had been on terms of friendship with Israel [3] (Num. x. 29; Judg. i. 16). In consequence they removed from among the Amalekites. Then a general slaughter began, which is described as "from Havilah," in the south-east, on the boundaries of Arabia, to the wilderness of Shur "over against," or eastward of Egypt. Every Amalekite who fell into their hands was destroyed,[4] with the notable exception, however, of Agag,[5] their king. And as they spared him, so also "the best of the sheep, and of the oxen, and of those of the second sort,[6] and the (wilderness-) fed lambs,

[1] So we understand the figures (1 Sam. xv. 4), which otherwise would be disproportionately large.

[2] Perhaps the same as *Telem* (Josh. xv. 24). Rashi has it, that Saul numbered the people by making each pick out a lamb, since it was unlawful to number the people directly.

[3] Another branch of that tribe was hostile to Israel: comp. Numb. xxiv. 21, etc.

[4] Of course, not literally *all* the Amalekites, but all who fell into their hands: comp. xxvii. 8; xxx. 1; 2 Sam. viii. 12; 1 Chron. iv. 43.

[5] Not a personal but an appellative name, like Pharaoh. Agag means "the fiery."

[6] The word must be rendered either so, or else, according to some of the Rabbis, "animals of the second birth" (*animalia secundo partu edita*), which are supposed to be better than the first-born.

and all that was good." The motives for the latter are, of course, easily understood ; not so that for sparing Agag. Did they wish to have in his person a sort of material guarantee for the future conduct of Amalek,—or did it flatter the national as well as the royal vanity to carry with them such a captive as Agag,—or did they really wish a sort of alliance and fraternity with what remained of Amalek ? All these motives may have operated. But of the character of the act as one of rebellion and disobedience there could be no doubt, in view of the direct Divine command (xv. 3).

If in the case of Saul's first failure it was difficult to with-hold sympathy, however clearly his sin and unfitness for the theocratic kingdom appeared, it is not easy even to frame an excuse for his utterly causeless disregard of so solemn a command as that of "the ban." All Jewish history, from Achan downwards, rose in testimony against him ; nay, re-membering his proposal to kill even Jonathan, when he had unwittingly infringed his father's rash vow, Saul stood con-victed out of his own mouth ! Nor was there any tangible motive for his conduct, nor anything noble or generous either about it, or about his after-bearing towards Samuel. Rather, quite the contrary. What now follows in the sacred narrative is tragic, grand, and even awful. The first scene is laid at night in Samuel's house at Ramah. It is God Who speaketh to the aged seer. " It repenteth Me that I have made Saul king, for he has returned from after Me, and My Word he has not executed " (literally, set up). " And it kindled in Samuel" (intense feeling, wrath), " and he cried unto Jehovah the whole night." [1] It is one of the most solemn, even awful thoughts— that of the Divine repentance, which we should approach with

---

[1] The distinction generally made, that the expression in ver. 11 is used *anthropopathically* (ἀνθρωποπαθῶς),—after the feelings of man—while that in ver. 29 is θεοπρεπῶς (*theoprepos*, according to the dignity and character of God), seems but partially correct. Better is the remark of Theodoret : Divine repentance is a change of His dispensation (re-arrangement of His household)—μεταμέλεια θεοῦ ἡ τῆς οἰκονομίας μεταβολή.

worshipful reverence.   God's repentance is not like ours, for
"the Strength of Israel will not lie, nor repent ; for He is not
a man that He should repent."   Man's repentance implies a
change of mind, God's a change of circumstances and relations.
He has not changed, but is ever the same ; it is man who has
changed in his position relatively to God.   The Saul whom
God had made king was not the same Saul whom God repented
to have thus exalted ; the essential conditions of their relationship were changed.   God's repentance is the unmovedness of
Himself, while others move and change.   The Divine finger
ever points to the same spot; but man has moved from it
to the opposite pole.   But as in all repentance there is sorrow,
so, reverently be it said, in that of God.   It is God's sorrow
of love, as, Himself unchanged and unchanging, He looks at the
sinner who has turned from Him.   But, although not wholly
unexpected, the announcement of this change on the part of
Saul, and of his consequent rejection, swept like a terrible
tempest over Samuel, shaking him in his innermost being.
The greatness of the sin, the terribleness of the judgment, its
publicity in the sight of all Israel, who knew of his Divine
call, and in whose presence Samuel, acting as Divine messenger,
had appointed him,—all these thoughts "kindled within him"
feelings which it would be difficult to analyse, but which led
to a "cry" all that long night, if perchance the Lord would
open a way of deliverance or of pardon.

With the morning light came calm resolve and the terrible
duty of going in search of Saul on this errand of God.   Nor
did the stern Nazarite now shrink from aught which this might
imply, however bitterly he might have to suffer in consequence.
Saul had returned to Gilgal, as if in his infatuation he had
intended to present himself in that place of so many sacred
memories before the God Whose express command he had
just daringly set aside.   By the way he had tarried at Carmel,[1]

---

[1] The modern Kurmul, three hours south of Hebron, the place of Nabal's
possessions (xxv. 2, 5, 7, 40).

where he "had set him·up a monument"[1] of his triumph over Agag. And now as Samuel met him, he anticipated his questions by claiming to have executed Jehovah's behest. But the very bleating of the sheep and lowing of the oxen betrayed his failure, and the excuse which he offered was so glaringly untrue,[2] that Samuel interrupted him[3] to put the matter plainly and straightforwardly in its real bearing: "Was it not when thou wast small in thine own eyes thou becamest head of the tribes of Israel?"—implying this as its counterpart: Now that thou art great in thine own eyes, thou art rejected, for it was God Who appointed thee, and against Him thou hast rebelled. Once more Saul sought to cloak his conduct by pretence of greater religiousness, when Samuel, in language which shows how deeply the spiritual meaning of ritual worship was understood even in early Old Testament times,[4] laid open the mingled folly and presumption of the king, and announced the judgment which the Lord had that night pronounced in his hearing. And now the painful interest of the scene still deepens. If there had been folly, hypocrisy, and meanness in Saul's excuses, there was almost incredible weakness also about his attempt to cast the blame upon the people. Evidently Saul's main anxiety was not about his sin, but about its consequences, or rather about the effect which might be produced upon the people if Samuel

---

[1] Ver. 12, erroneously rendered in our Authorised Version : "he set him up a place." The word literally means "a hand," and is again used for "monument" in 2 Sam. xviii. 18. Phœnician monuments have been found with *hands* on them.

[2] Besides its obvious falsehood, Saul must, of course, have known that all that was "banned" by that very fact belonged unto God (Lev. xxvii. 29), and could not, therefore, be again offered unto Him (Deut. xiii. 16).

[3] "Stay" (ver. 16), that is, "Stop! cease!"

[4] It is scarcely necessary to indicate, that the words of Samuel (vers. 22, 23) do *not* imply that sacrifices were not of primary importance. This would have run counter not only to his own practice, but to the whole Old Testament economy. But sacrifices, irrespective of a corresponding state of mind, and in actual rebelliousness against God,—religiousness without religion,—were not only a mere *opus operatum*, but a gross caricature, essentially heathen, not Jewish. Comp. Psa. l. 8–14; li. 17, 19; Isa. i. 11; Jer. vi. 20; Hos. vi. 6; Micah vi. 6–8.

were openly to disown him.   He entreated him to gc with him, and when Samuel refused, and turned to leave, he laid such hold on the corner of his mantle that he rent it.   Not terrified by the violence of the king, Samuel only bade him consider this as a sign of how Jehovah had that day rent the kingdom from him.

At last the painful scene ended.   Saul gave up the pretence of wishing Samuel's presence from religious motives, and pleaded for it on the ground of honouring him before the elders of his people.   And to this Samuel yielded.   Throughout it had not been a personal question, nor had Samuel received directions about Saul's successor, nor would he, under any circumstances, have fomented discord or rebellion among the people. Besides, he had other and even more terrible work to do ere that day of trial closed.   And now the brief service was past, and Samuel prepared for what personally must have been the hardest duty ever laid upon him.   By his direction Agag was brought to him.   The unhappy man, believing that the bitterness of death, its danger and pang were past, and that probably he was now to be introduced to the prophet as before he had been brought to the king, came "with gladness." [1]   So far as Agag himself was concerned, these words of Samuel must have recalled his guilt and spoken its doom : "As thy sword has made women childless, so be thy mother childless above (ordinary) women." [2]   But for Israel and its king, who had transgressed the "ban" by sparing Agag, there was yet another lesson, whatever it might cost Samuel.   Rebellious, disobedient king and people on the one side, and on the other Samuel the prophet and Nazarite alone for God—such, we take it, was the meaning of Samuel having to hew Agag in pieces before Jehovah in Gilgal.

From that day forward Samuel came no more to see Saul. God's ambassador was no longer accredited to him ; for he

---

[1] This, and not "delicately," as in our Authorised Version, is the meaning of the Hebrew word (comp. Prov. xxix. 21).

[2] More than ordinary women, or rather most of women, since her son was king of his people.

was no longer king of Israel in the true sense of the term. The Spirit of Jehovah departed from him. Henceforth there was nothing about him royal even in the eyes of men—except his death. But still Samuel mourned for him and over him; mourned as for one cut off in the midst of life, dead while living, a king rejected of God. And still "Jehovah repented that He had made Saul king over Israel."

CHAPTER X.

Samuel Mourns for Saul—He is directed to the house of Jesse—Anointing of David—Preparation of David for the Royal Office—The "Evil Spirit from the Lord" upon Saul—David is sent to Court—War with the Philistines—Combat between David and Goliath—Friendship of David and Jonathan.

(1 SAM. XVI.—XVIII. 4.)

IF the tragic events just recorded, and the share which Samuel had in them, had left on the mind a lingering feeling as of harshness or imperiousness on the part of the old prophet, the narrative which follows must remove all such erroneous impressions. So far from feeling calm or satisfied under the new state of things which it had been his duty to bring about, Samuel seems almost wholly absorbed by sorrow for Saul personally, and for what had happened; not unmixed, we may suppose, with concern for the possible consequences of his rejection.[1] It needed the voice of God

[1] Calvin remarks: "We see here the prophet affected as other men. As Samuel beholds the vessel which God's own hand had made, more than broken and minished, he is deeply moved. In this he showed pious and holy affection. But he was not wholly free from sin in the matter —not that the feeling itself was wrong, but that it exceeded the proper measure, and that he too much indulged in personal grief."

to recall the mind of the prophet to the wider interests of the theocracy, and to calm him into complete submission by showing how the difficulties which he anticipated had been provided for.   A new king had already been fixed upon, and the duty was laid on Samuel to designate him for that office.   Accordingly Samuel was now sent to anoint one of the sons of Jesse to be Saul's successor.   From the first, and increasingly, Samuel's public career had been difficult and trying.   But never before had his faith been so severely tested as by this commission.   He who had never feared the face of man, and who so lately had boldly confronted Saul at Gilgal, now spake as if afraid for his life, in case Saul, who no doubt was already under the influence of the " evil spirit," or rather the spirit of evil, should hear of what might seem an attempt to dethrone him.   But, as always in such circumstances, the fears, which weakness suggested, proved groundless.   As in the case of Saul, so in that of David, it was not intended that the anointing should be followed by immediate outward consequences.   Hence there was no need for publicity ; on the contrary, privacy served important purposes.   The chief present object seems to have been a solemn call to David to prepare himself, as having been set apart for some great work.   Besides, in view of the meaning of this symbol, and of its results in Saul and David (1 Sam. xvi. 13), the anointing may be regarded as an ordinance in connection with the gift of the Spirit of God, Who alone qualified for the work.   In view of all this, God directed Samuel to combine the anointing of Jesse's son with a sacrificial service at Bethlehem, the home of Jesse.   Only the latter, or public service, required to be made generally known. Many reasons will suggest themselves why the other part of Samuel's commission should have remained secret, probably not fully understood by Jesse, or even by David himself.[1]

[1] There is not a trace of attempted prevarication in the narrative. Calvin and others have given too much attention to a cavil which is best refuted by an attentive study of the history.

The narrative also affords some interesting glimpses into the history of the time. Thus we infer that Samuel had been in the habit of visiting various places in the land for the purpose of sacrifice and instruction. The former was quite lawful, so long as the ark was not in its central sanctuary.[1] On the other hand, it needs no comment to show the importance of such periodical visits of the prophet at a time when religious knowledge was necessarily so scanty, and the means of grace so scarce. It helps us to understand how religion was kept alive in the land. Again, the narrative implies that the family of Jesse must have occupied a leading place in Bethlehem, and been known as devoted to the service of the Lord. Nor do we wonder at this, remembering that they were the immediate descendants of Boaz and Ruth.

As we follow Samuel to Bethlehem, we seem to mark the same primitive simplicity and life of piety as of old. When the " elders " hear of Samuel's coming, they go to meet him, yet with fear lest the unexpected visit betoken some unknown sin resting on their quiet village. This apprehension is removed by Samuel's explanation, and they are invited to attend the " sacrifice." But the sacrificial meal which usually followed was to be confined to Jesse and his family, in whose house, as we infer, Samuel was a welcome guest. It would appear that Samuel himself was not acquainted with all that was to happen, the Lord reserving it for the proper moment to point out to His servant who was to be Israel's future king. And this, as we judge, partly because the aged prophet had himself a lesson to learn in the matter, or rather to unlearn what of the ideas of his time and people unconsciously clung to him.

All this appears from the narrative. One by one the sons of Jesse were introduced to Samuel. The manly beauty of Eliab, the eldest, and his rank in the family, suggested to the prophet that he might be " Jehovah's anointed." But

---

[1] See our quotation on this subject from the *Mishnah* in Vol. III. of this History, p. 78.

Samuel was to learn that Jehovah's judgment was "not as what man seeth" (looketh to), "for man looketh to the eyes but Jehovah looketh to the heart."[1] And so the others followed in turn, with a like result. Evidently, Samuel must have expressed it to Jesse that on that day one of his family was to be chosen by Jehovah, but for what purpose seems not to have been known to them. Nor did Jesse himself, nor even David, apparently understand what was implied in the rite of anointing. No words of solemn designation were uttered by the prophet, such as Samuel had spoken when he anointed Saul (1 Sam. x. 1). Besides, as Saul was the first king anointed, and as none had been present when it took place, we may reasonably suppose that alike the ceremony and its meaning were unknown to the people. Both Jesse and David may have regarded it as somehow connected with admission to the schools of the prophets, or more probably as connected with some work for God in the future, which at the proper time would be pointed out to them.[2] And thus was David in this respect also a type of our Lord, Whose human consciousness of His calling and work appears to have been, in a sense, progressive ; being gradually manifested in the course of His history.

But to return. The seven sons of Jesse had successively passed before Samuel, yet he was not among them whom the prophet had been sent to anoint. But for all that his mission had not failed : he had only learned to own the sovereignty of God, the failure of his own judgment, and the fact that he was simply a passive instrument to carry out, not his own views, but the will of the Lord. For, the youngest of the family still remained. So unlikely did it seem to his

[1] So 1 Sam. xvi. 7, rendered literally.

[2] A full knowledge of his being anointed to the kingdom is incompatible alike with his after position in his father's house, and the bearing of his brothers towards him. In general, we infer that each of the brothers only passed before Samuel, or was introduced to him, and then left his presence when no further direction in regard to him was given to the prophet.

father that he could be called to any great work, that he had been left in the field to tend the sheep. But when, at the bidding of Samuel, he came, his very bearing and appearance seemed to speak in his favour. In the language of the text, " he was reddish,[1] and fair of eyes, and goodly to look at." And now the command to anoint him was given, and immediately and unquestioningly obeyed by Samuel.[2]

The sacrifice past, and the sacrificial meal over, Samuel returned to Ramah, and David to his humble avocation in his father's household. And here also we love to mark the print of our Lord's footsteps, and to see in the history of David the same humble submission to a lowly calling, and faithful discharge of menial toil, and the same subjectness to his parents, as we adoringly trace in the life of Him Who humbled Himself to become David's son. But there was henceforth one difference in the life of the son of Jesse. From the day of his anointing forward, " the Spirit of Jehovah seized upon David," as formerly upon Saul, to qualify him by might and by power for the work of " God's anointed." But from Saul, who was no longer the king of God's appointment, had the Spirit of Jehovah departed, not only as the source of " might and of power," but even as " the Spirit of a sound mind." At his anointing, the Spirit then given him had made him " another man" (1 Sam. x. 6, 10). But Saul had resisted and rebelled, nor had he ever turned from his pride and disobedience in repentance to the Lord. And now the Spirit of God not only departed from him, but in judgment God sent an " evil spirit," or rather " a spirit of evil," to " terrify "[3] Saul. Not that God ever sends a spirit who is evil. The angels whom God sends are all good, though their commission may be in judgment to bring evil upon

[1] So ver. 12, literally. The expression, "reddish," or perhaps rather "auburn," refers to the colour of the hair, which is rare in Palestine.

[2] The Authorised Version renders ver. 13 : "And Samuel anointed him in the midst of his brethren." But the word may mean either "in the midst " or "among," in the sense of "from among." The latter is evidently the meaning in this instance.

[3] So literally, as in the margin of our Authorised Version.

us.[1] As one has rightly remarked, "God sends good angels to punish evil men, while to chastise good men, evil angels claim the power." The "evil spirit" sent from God was the messenger of that evil which in the Divine judgment was to come upon Saul, visions of which now affrighted the king, filled him with melancholy, and brought him to the verge of madness—but not to repentance. It is thus also that we can understand how the music of David's harp soothed the spirit of Saul, while those hymns which it accompanied—perhaps some of his earliest Psalms—brought words of heaven, thoughts of mercy, strains of another world, to the troubled soul of the king.

Had he but listened to them, and yielded himself not temporarily but really to their influence! But he was now the old Saul, only sensibly destitute of the Divine help, presence, and Spirit, and with all the evil in him terribly intensified by the circumstances. He had all the feelings of a man cast down from his high estate through his own sin, disappointed in his hopes and ambition, and apprehensive that at any moment the sentence of rejection, pronounced against him, might be executed, and that "better" one appear to whom his kingdom was to be given. And now an angel of evil from the Lord affrighted him with thoughts and visions of what would come to pass. For man can never withdraw himself from higher influences. As one of the fathers has it, "When the Spirit of the Lord departs, an evil spirit takes His place. And this should teach us to pray with David: 'Take not Thy Holy Spirit from me.'"

Yet, in the wonder-working providence of God, this very circumstance led David onwards towards his destination. The quiet retirement of the shepherd's life was evidently of deepest importance to him immediately after his anointing. We can understand what dangers—inward and outward—would have

[1] Comp. Delitzsch, *Comm. ü. d. Psalter*, vol. I., p. 601 ; Hofmann, *Schriftbeweis*, vol. i., pp. 188, 189. If the expression, "evil spirit," had been intended to convey that it was a spirit in itself evil, Saul's servants would have scarcely spoken of him as in 1 Sam. xvi. 15.

beset a sudden introduction to publicity or rush into fame. On the other hand, humble avocations, retirement, thought, and lonely fellowship with God would best develop his inner life in constant dependence upon God, and even call out those energies and that self-reliance which, in conjunction with the higher spiritual qualifications, were so necessary in his after-calling.   Nor was it time lost even so far as his outward influence was concerned.   It was then that the Spirit-helped youth acquired in the neighbouring country, and far as Eastern story would carry it, the reputation of " a mighty, valiant man, and a man of war," when, all unaided and un-armed, he would slay " both the lion and the bear " that had attacked the flock which he tended.   But, above all, it is to this period of inward and spiritual preparation in soli-tary communion with God that we trace the first of those Psalms which have for ever made " the sweet singer," in a sense, the " shepherd " of all spiritual Israel.   And here also we love to connect the plains and the shepherds of Bethlehem, who heard angels hymning the birth of our dear Lord, with His great ancestor and type, and to think how in those very plains the shepherd-king may have watched his flock in the quiet of the starlit night, and poured forth in accents of praise what is the faith and hope of the Church in all times.   No doubt this talent of David also, though probably only viewed as a worldly gift, became known in the neighbourhood.   And so, when the courtiers [1] of Saul suggested music as the well-known remedy in antiquity for mental disturbances, such as those from which the king suffered through the " evil spirit," one of the servant-men in attendance, probably a native of the district around Bethlehem, could from personal knowledge recommend David as " cunning in playing, . . . knowing of speech,[2] . . . and Jehovah is with him."

[1] Our Authorised Version renders the word used in 1 Sam. xvi. 15, 16, 17, and that in ver. 18 alike by "servants."   But the original marks that the former were the courtiers and officials around Saul, while in ver. 18 it is "one of the lads "—belonging to the class of man-servants

[2] So ver. 18, literally.

The words, seemingly casually spoken, were acted upon, and David was sent for to court. He came, bringing such gifts as the primitive habits of those times suggested to Jesse as fitting for a loyal subject to offer to his monarch. And as he stood before Saul in all the freshness of youth, with conscience clear, and in the Spirit-holpen vigour of a new life —so like the ideal of what Saul might have become, like him even in stature—the king's past and better self seems to have come back to him, "the king loved David greatly," and took him into his service.[1] And God's blessing rested on it : for, when the king heard, as it were, the sound of the rushing wings of the spirit of evil, and almost felt the darkness as he spread them over him, then, as David's hands swept the harp of praise, and it poured forth its melody of faith and hope, it seemed as if heaven's light fell on those wings, and the evil spirit departed from Saul. And thus we learn once more the precious lesson, how

> " God moves in a mysterious way
>   His wonders to perform."

What, if the result alone had been announced, would have seemed impossible, and hence miraculous in its accomplishment, was brought about by a chain of events, each linked to the other by natural causation. It is this naturalness, in many cases, of the supernatural which most shows that " Jehovah reigneth." What He has promised in His grace that He bringeth about in His providence. Next to inward humility and strength in dependence on the Lord, erhaps the most important lessons which David could learn for his future guidance would be those which at the court of Saul, and yet not of the court, he would derive from daily observation of all that passed in the government, standing in so near and confidential relationship to the king as to know all—the good and the evil, the danger and

---

[1] The text has it, that David was made "armour-bearer" to Saul. Probably the rank was little more than nominal. We know that in military monarchies, such as in Russia, every civil official has also a nominal military rank.

the difficulty—and yet being so wholly independent as to remain unbiassed in his estimate of persons and judgment of things.

So time passed. But in the intervals of calmness, when Saul needed not the ministry of David, the young Bethlehemite was wont to return to his father's home and to his humble avocations,—to find in quiet retirement that rest and strength which he needed (1 Sam. xvii. 15). And now once more had the dark cloud of war gathered over the land. It was again Israel's hereditary enemy the Philistines, who, probably encouraged by their knowledge of Saul's state, had advanced as far into Judah as the neighbourhood of Bethlehem. About ten miles to the south-west of that city lay Shochoh (or Sochoh), the modern Shuweikeh. Here a broad wady, or valley, marking a water-course, runs north for about an hour's distance. This is the modern Wady-es-Sumt, the valley of the acacias, the ancient valley of Elah, or of the terebinth. At the modern village of Sakarieh, the ancient Shaarim, the wady divides, turning westwards towards Gath, and northwards by the Wady Surar towards Ekron. Shochoh and Ephes-Dammim, the modern Damum, about three miles north-east of Shochoh, between which two points the Philistine camp was pitched, lay on the *southern* slope of the wady, while the host of Israel was camped on the *northern* slope, the two being separated by the deep part of the wady. But no longer did the former God-inspired courage fire Israel. The Spirit of God had departed from their leader, and his followers seemed to share in the depression which this consciousness brought. In such a warfare, especially among Easterns, all depended on decision and boldness. But unbelief makes cowards; and Saul and his army were content with a merely defensive position, without venturing to attack their enemies. Day by day the two armies gathered on the opposite slopes, only to witness what was for Israel more than humiliation, even an open defiance of their ability to resist the power of Philistia—by implication, a defiance of the covenant-people as such, and of Jehovah, the covenant-God, and a challenge to a fight between might in the flesh and power in the Spirit.   And truly Israel, under the leadership of a Saul, was ill prepared for such a contest. But herein also lay the significance of the Philistine challenge, and of the manner in which it was taken up by David, as well as of his victory.   It is not too much to assert that this event was a turning-point in the history of the theocracy, and marked David as the true king of Israel, ready to take up the Philistine challenge of God and of His people, to kindle in Israel a new spirit, and, in the might of the living God, to bring the contest to victory.

Forty days successively, as the opposing armies had stood marshalled in battle-array, Goliath of Gath—a descendant of those giants that had been left at the time of Joshua (Josh. xi. 21, 22)—had stepped out of the ranks of the Philistines to challenge a champion of Israel to single combat, which should decide the fate of the campaign, and the subjection of either Israel or the Philistines.   Such challenges were common enough in antiquity.   But it indicated a terrible state of things when it could be thrown down and not taken up,—a fearful "reproach" when an "uncircumcised Philistine" could so "defy the armies of the living God" (1 Sam. xvii. 8–10, 26, 36).   And yet as Goliath left the ranks of his camp, and "came down" (ver. 8) into the valley that separated the two hosts, and, as it were, shook his hand in scorn of high heaven and of Israel, not a man dared answer; till at last the Philistine, rendered more and more bold, began to cross the wady, and "came up" the slopes towards where Israel stood (ver. 25), when at sight of him they "fled," and "were sore afraid."

For, where the realising sense of God's presence was wanting, the contest would only seem one of strength against strength.   In that case, the appearance and bearing of the Philistine must have been sufficiently terrifying to Orientals. Measuring about nine feet nine inches,[1] he was covered

---

[1] This measurement is of course approximative, as we are not quite sure of the exact equivalent of Hebrew measures and weights.   Pliny mentions an Arab giant who measured exactly the same as Goliath, and a man and a

front and back by a coat of mail of brass, consisting of scales overlapping each other, such as we know were used in ancient times,[1] but weighing not less than about one hundred and fifty-scvcn pounds.[2] That armour, no doubt, descended to his legs, which were cased in "greaves of brass," while a helmet of the same material defended his head. As weapons of offence he carried, besides the sword with which he was girded (ver. 51 ; xxi. 9), an enormous javelin[3] of brass, which, after the manner of the ancient soldiers, was slung on his back, and a spear, the metal head of which weighed about seventeen or eighteen pounds.

Such was the sight which David beheld, when sent by his father to the army to inquire after the welfare of his three elder brothers,[4] who had followed Saul into the war, and at the same time, in true Oriental fashion, to carry certain provisions to them, and to bring a present from the dairy produce[5] to their commanding officer. The description of what follows is so vivid that we can almost see the scene. All is truly Oriental in its cast, and truly Scriptural in its spirit.

David, who had never been permanently in Saul's service,

---

woman in the time of Augustus who were even an inch taller (*Hist. Nat.*, vii. 16).   Josephus speaks of a Jew who was even taller (*Ant.*, xviii. 4, 5) ; and Keil refers to a giant of nearly the same proportions who visited Berlin in 1859.   The LXX., however, characteristically change the measurement from six to four cubits.

[1] A corselet of this kind, belonging to Rameses III., is in the British Museum.

[2] A mediæval corselet preserved in Dresden weighs more than a third of that of Goliath, which seems proportionate to his size.

[3] This is the meaning of the word, and not "target," as in our Authorised Version.

[4] The expression, ver. 18, "take a pledge of them," need not, as by most commentators, be taken literally, but may be a figurative expression for bringing back an assurance of their welfare.

[5] "Ten cheeses," or rather, "cuts of curdled milk ;" possibly resembling our so-called cream-cheese.

had, on the outbreak of the war, returned to his home.[1]
When he now arrived at the "trench" which ran round
the camp, to trace and defend it, the army of Israel was
being put in battle-array against that of the Philistines on
the opposite hill.   In true Oriental fashion, they were raising
a shout of defiance while not venturing on an attack.   David
left his baggage with the keeper of the baggage, and ran
forward to the foremost ranks, where, as he knew, the position of Judah, and therefore of his brothers, must be (Num.
ii. 3 ; x. 14).   While conversing with them, the scene previously described was re enacted.   As Goliath approached
nearer and nearer, the order of battle was dissolved before
him.   It is quite characteristic that these fear-stricken Israelites should have tried to excite one another by dwelling
on the insult offered to Israel, and the rewards which Saul had
promised to the victorious champion of his people.   Quite

[1] There is considerable difficulty about the text as it now stands.
That the narrative is strictly historical cannot be doubted.   But, on the
other hand, vers. 12–14, and still more vers. 55–58, read as if the writer
had inserted this part of his narrative from some other source, perhaps from a
special chronicle of the event.   The LXX. solve the difficulty by simply
leaving out vers. 12–31, and again vers. 55–58 ; that is, they boldly
treat that part as an interpolation ; and it must be confessed that the narrative reads easier without it.   And yet, on the other hand, if these verses
are interpolated, the work has been clumsily done ; and it is not easy to see
how any interpolator would not have at once seen the difficulties which he
created, especially by the addition of vers. 55–58.   Besides, the account,
vers. 12–31, not only fits in very well with the rest of the narrative—bating
some of the expressions in vers. 12–14—but also bears the evident impress of truthfulness.   The drastic method in which the LXX. dealt with the
text, so early as about two centuries before Christ, at least proves that, even
at that time, there were strong doubts about the genuineness of the text.
All this leads to the suggestion, that somehow the text may have become
corrupted, and that later copyists may have tried emendations and additions,
by way of removing difficulties, which, as might be expected in such a
case, would only tend to increase them.   On the whole, therefore, we
are inclined to the opinion that, while the narrative itself is strictly authentic, the text, as we possess it, is seriously corrupted in some of the
expressions, especially in the concluding verses of the chapter.   At the
same time it should be added, that its correctness has been defended by
very able critics.

characteristic also, from what we know of him, was the bearing of David. We need not attempt to eliminate from the narrative the personal element, as we may call it, in the conduct of David. God appeals to outward motives, even in what is highest—such as the loss or gain of our souls,— and the tale of what was " to be done " to him who wrought such deliverance in Israel might well fire a spirit less ardent than that of David to realise Israel's great need. But what was so distinctive in David—who probably knew Saul too well confidently to expect the literal fulfilment of his promises—was the spiritual response to the challenge of the Philistine which sprung unbidden to his lips (ver. 26), and which, when the hour for personal action came, was felt to be a deep reality to which his faith could confidently appeal (vers. 36, 37). Truly we seem to breathe another atmosphere than that hitherto in the camp of Israel ; nor could his public career be more appropriately begun,- who was to pasture Israel according to the integrity of his heart, and to lead them "by the skilfulness of his hands " (Psa. lxxviii. 70–72).

And here we have another instance of the prefigurative character of the history of David. As "the brothers " and near kinsfolk of our blessed Lord misunderstood His motives, and could not enter into the spirit of His work, so Eliab, when he imputed to David a dissatisfied ambition that could not rest contented with humble avocations, and when he characterised his God-inspired courage and confidence as carnal, and a delight in war and bloodshed for its own sake (ver. 28). But it was too late to arrest David by such objections. Putting them aside, as making a man an offender for a word, but without retaliating by convicting Eliab of his own uncharitableness, worldliness, and unbelief, David turned away to repeat his inquiries. Tidings of the young champion, who had displayed quite another banner against the Philistine than that of Saul, were soon brought to the king. In the interview which followed, the king bade the shepherd think of his youth and inexperience in a contest with such a warrior as Goliath. Yet he seems to speak like one who was half convinced by the bearing and language of this strange champion, and easily allowed himself to be persuaded ; not so much, we take it, by the account of his prowess and success in the past as by the tone of spiritual assurance and confidence in the God of·Israel with which he spake.

Once more thoughts of the past must have crowded in upon Saul. There was that in the language of this youth which recalled the strength of Israel, which seemed like the dawn of another morning, like a voice from another world. But if he went to the combat, let it be at least in what seemed to Saul the most fitting and promising manner—arrayed in the king's own armour,—as if the whole meaning of David's conduct—nay, of the combat itself and of the victory—had not lain in the very opposite direction : in the confessed inadequacy of all merely human means for every such contest, and in the fact that the victory over Goliath must appear as the Lord's deliverance, achieved through the faith of a personal, realising, conscious dependence on Him.   And so Saul's armour must be put aside as that which had " not been proved " in such a contest, of which the champion of the Lord had never made trial in such encounters—and of which he never could make trial.   A deep-reaching lesson this to the Church and to believers individually, and one which bears manifold application, not only spiritually, but even intellectually.   The first demand upon us is to be spiritual ; the next to be genuine and true, without seeking to clothe ourselves in the armour of another.

A few rapid sketches, and the narrative closes. Goliath had evidently retired within the ranks of the Philistines, satisfied that, as before, his challenge had remained unanswered.   And now tidings that a champion of Israel was ready for the fray once more called him forth.   As he advanced, David waited not till he had crossed the wady and ascended the slope where Israel's camp lay, but hastened forward, and picked him five stones from the dry river-bed in the valley.   And now the Philistine had time to take, as he thought, the full measure of his opponent. Only a fair-looking, stout, unarmed shepherd-youth, coming against him with his shepherd's gear, as if he were a dog! Was this, then, the champion of Israel? In true Eastern fashion, he advanced, boasting of his speedy and easy victory; in true heathen spirit the while cursing and blaspheming the God in Whose Name David was about to fight. But David also must speak. To the carnal confidence in his own strength which Goliath expressed, David opposed the Name—that is, the manifestation—of *Jehovah Zevaoth*, the God of heaven's hosts, the God also of the armies of Israel. That God, Whom Goliath had blasphemed and defied, would presently take up the challenge. He would fight, and deliver the giant into the hand of one even so unequal to such contest as an unarmed shepherd. Thus would "all the earth"—all Gentile nations—see that there was a God in Israel; thus also would "all this assembly" (the *kahal*, the called)—all Israel—learn that too long forgotten lesson which must underlie all their history, that "not by sword or spear, saith Jehovah: for Jehovah's is the war, and He gives you into our hands."

Words ceased. Slowly the Philistine giant advanced to what seemed easy victory. He had not even drawn the sword, nor apparently let down the visor of his helmet,—for was not his opponent unarmed? and a well-directed thrust of his spear would lay him bleeding at his feet. Swiftly the shepherd ran to the encounter. A well-aimed stone from his sling—and the gigantic form of the Philistine, encased in its unwieldy armour, mortally stricken, fell heavily to the ground, and lay helpless in sight of his dismayed countrymen, while the unarmed David, drawing the sword from the sheath of his fallen opponent, cut off his head, and returned to the king with the gory trophy. All this probably within less time than it has taken to write it down. And now a sudden dismay seized on the Philistines. Their champion and pride so suddenly swept down, they fled in wild disorder. It was true, then, that there was a God in Israel! It was true that the war was Jehovah's, and that He had given them into Israel's hand! Israel and Judah

raised a shout, and pursued the Philistines up that ravine, through
that wady, to Shaarim, and beyond it to the gates of Gath, and
up that other wady to Ekron.   But while the people returned
to take the spoil of the Philistine tents, David had given a
modest account of himself to the jealous king and his chief
general; had won the generous heart of Jonathan; and had
gone to lay up the armour of the Philistine as his part of the
spoil in his home.   But the head of the Philistine he nailed
on the gates of Jerusalem, right over in sight of the fort which
the heathen Jebusites still held in the heart of the land.

<center>~~~~~</center>

CHAPTER XI.

*Saul's Jealousy, and Attempts upon David's Life—David marries Michal—
Ripening of Saul's Purpose of Murder—David's Flight to Samuel—
Saul among the Prophets—David finally leaves the Court of Saul.*

(1 SAM. XVIII. 4—XX.)

THE friendship between Jonathan and David, which dated
from the victory over Goliath, and the modest, genuine
bearing of the young conqueror, is the òne point of light in a
history which grows darker and darker as it proceeds.   We
can imagine how a spirit so generous as that of Jonathan
would be drawn towards that unaffected, brave youth, so
free from all self-consciousness or self-seeking, who would
seem the very embodiment of Israelitish valour and piety.
And we can equally perceive how gratitude and admiration
of such real nobleness would kindle in the heart of David
an affection almost womanly in its tenderness.   Ancient
history records not a few instances of such love between
heroes, ratified like this by a "covenant," and betokened by
such gifts as when Jonathan put on David his "mantle," his

"armour-coat,"[1] and even his arms,—but none more pure and elevated, or penetrated, as in this instance, by the highest and best feelings of true piety.

There can be no doubt that this friendship was among the means which helped David to preserve that loyalty to Saul which was the grand characteristic of his conduct in the very trying period which now ensued. How these trials called out his faith, and consequently his patience; how they drew him closer to God, ripened his inner life, and so prepared him for his ultimate calling, will best appear from a comparison of the Psalms which date from this time. The events, as recorded in the sacred text, are not given in strict chronological order, but rather in that of their internal connection. As we understand it, after David's victory over Goliath, he was taken into the permanent employ of Saul. This and his general success[2] in all undertakings, as well as his prudence and modesty, which, at least during the first period, disarmed even the jealousy of Saul's courtiers, are indicated in general terms in 1 Sam. xviii. 5. But matters could not long progress peacefully. On the return of the army from the pursuit of the Philistines, the conquerors had, after the custom of the times, been met in every city through which they passed by choruses of women, who, with mimic dances, sung antiphonally[3] the praise of the heroes, ascribing the victory over thousands to Saul, and over ten thousands to David. It was quite characteristic of the people, and it implied not even conscious preference for David, least of all danger to Saul's throne. But it sufficed

[1] The same term is used in 1 Sam. xvii. 38, 39; Judg. iii. 16; 2 Sam. xx. 8. But I cannot see how (as in *The Speaker's Commentary*, vol. ii., p. 325) it can be supposed to comprise "the sword, bow, and girdle." These three are expressly connected with it by a threefold repetition of the expression, "even to."

[2] The expression in our Authorised Version, "behaved himself wisely," includes both skilfulness and success.

[3] In ver. 6 we have it, that they went to meet Saul "with hand-drums, with joy (that is, with pæans of joy), and with triangles." The picture is vivid, and true to the custom of the times.

to kindle in Saul deep and revengeful envy. Following upon what the spirit of evil from the Lord had set before him as his own fate, sealed as it was by his solemn rejection from the kingdom and the conscious departure of the Spirit of God, the popular praise seemed to point out David as his rival. And every fresh success of David, betokening the manifest help of God, and every failure of his own attempts to rid himself of this rival, would only deepen and embitter this feeling, and lead him onwards, from step to step, until the murderous passion became all engrossing, and made the king not only forgetful of Jehovah, and of what evidently was His purpose, but also wholly regardless of the means which he used. Thus Saul's dark passions were ultimately concentrated in the one thought of murder. Yet in reality it was against Jehovah that he contended rather than against David. So true is it that all sin is ultimately against the Lord; so bitter is the root of self; and so terrible the power of evil in its constantly growing strength, till it casts out all fear of God or care for man. So true also is it that "he that hateth his brother is a murderer," in heart and principle. On the other hand, these constant unprovoked attempts upon the life of David, regardlessly of the means employed, till at last the whole forces of the kingdom were used for no other purpose than to hunt down an innocent fugitive, whose only crime was that God was with him, and that he had successfully fought the cause of Israel, must have had a very detrimental effect upon the people. They must have convinced all that he who now occupied the throne was unfit for the post, while at the same time they could not but demoralise the people in regard to their real enemies, thus bringing about the very results which Saul so much dreaded.

It deserves special notice, that Saul's attempts against the life of David are in the sacred text never attributed to the influence of the spirit of evil from the Lord, although they were no doubt made when that spirit was upon him. For God never tempts man to sin; but he sinneth when he is drawn away by his own passion, and enticed by it. If proof were needed that the spirit whom God sent was not evil in himself, it would be found in this, that while formerly David's music could soothe the king, that power was lost when Saul had given way to sin. On the first occasion of this kind, Saul, in a maniacal [1] fit, twice poised [2] against David the javelin, which, as the symbol of royalty, he had by him (like the modern sceptre); and twice " David turned (bent) aside from before him." [3] The failure of his purpose only strengthened the king's conviction that, while God had forsaken him, He was with David. The result, however, was not repentance, but a feeling of fear, under which he removed David from his own presence, either to free himself of the temptation to murder, or in the hope, which he scarcely yet confessed to himself, that, promoted to the command over a thousand men, David might fall in an engagement with the Philistines. How this also failed, or rather led to results the opposite of those which Saul had wished, is briefly marked in the text.

With truest insight into the working of such a mind, the narrative traces the further progress of this history. Perhaps to test whether he really cherished ambitious designs, but with the conscious wish to rid himself of his dreaded rival, Saul now proposed to carry out his original promise to the conqueror of Goliath, by giving David his eldest daughter Merab to wife, at the same time professing only anxiety that his future son-in-law should fight " the battles of Jehovah." The reply given might have convinced him, that David had no

---

[1] Our Authorised Version renders ver. 10, "and he prophesied in the midst of the house;" and the word undoubtedly means this. But in the present instance it refers not to " prophecy," but to the ecstatic state which often accompanied it, even in false prophets : comp. 1 Kings xxii. 22; Acts xvi. 16; xix. 15. Saul was in a state of maniacal ecstasy.

[2] Apparently Saul did not actually throw the javelin, as in xix. 10.

[3] So literally. Our Authorised Version gives the impression that David had left the presence of Saul.

exaggerated views of his position in life.[1]   It is idle to ask
why Saul upon this so rapidly transferred Merab to one[2]
who is not otherwise known in history.   The affection of
Michal, Saul's younger daughter, for David, promised to
afford Saul the means of still further proving David's views,
and of bringing him to certain destruction.   The plan was
cleverly devised.   Taught by experience, David took no
further notice of the king's personal suggestion of such an
alliance.[3]   At this the courtiers were instructed secretly to
try the effect of holding out a prospect so dazzling as that
of being the king's son-in-law.   But the bait was too clumsily
put,—or rather it failed to take, from the thorough integrity
of David.   Next came not the suggestion merely, but a
definite proposal through the courtiers, to give the king as
dowry within a certain specified time a pledge that not less
than a hundred heathen had fallen in "the Lord's battles."
If the former merely general admonition to fight had not led
to David's destruction, a more definite demand like this might
necessitate personal contests, in which, as Saul imagined, every
chance would be against David's escape.   But once more the
king was foiled.   David, who readily entered on a proposal so
much in harmony with his life-work, executed within less than
the appointed time double the king's requirements, and Michal
became his wife.

And still the story becomes darker and darker.   We have
marked the progress of murderous thought in the king's mind,
from the sudden attack of frenzy to the scarcely self-confessed
wish for the death of his victim, to designed exposure of his life,

---

[1] The expression in ver. 18, "my life," probably means my *status* in life.
The rendering proposed by some, "my people," is linguistically unsupported, and implies a needless repetition.

[2] The suggestion of Keil, that it was due to want of affection on her part,
is as arbitrary as that (in *The Speaker's Commentary*) of a large dowry on
the part of Adriel.

[3] Ver. 21 had probably best be rendered : "Thou shalt this day be my
son-in-law in a second (another) manner ;" or else, become such "a
second time."

and lastly to a deliberate plan for his destruction. But now all restraints were broken through. Do what he might, David prospered, and all that Saul had attempted had only turned out to the advantage of the son of Jesse. Already he was the king's son-in-law ; Michal had given her whole heart to him ; constant success had attended those expeditions against the heathen which were to have been his ruin ; nay, as might be expected in the circumstances, he had reached the pinnacle of popularity. One dark resolve now settled in the heart of the king, and cast it shadow over every other considera-tion. David must be murdered. Saul could no longer dis-guise his purpose from himself, nor keep it from others. He spoke of it openly—even to Jonathan, and to all around him. So alarming had it become, that Jonathan felt it necessary to warn David, who, in his conscious integrity, seemed still unsuspicious of real danger. Yet Jonathan himself would fain have believed that his father's mood was only the outcome of that dreadful disease of which he was the victim. Accordingly, almost within hearing of David, who had secreted himself near by, he appealed to his father, and that in language so telling and frank, that the king himself was for the moment won. So it had been only frenzy—the outburst of the moment, but not the king's real heart-purpose—and David returned to court !

The hope was vain. The next success against the Philis-tines rekindled all the evil passions of the king. Once more, as he yielded to sin, the spirit of evil was sent in judg-ment—this time from Jehovah. As Saul heard the rushing of his dark pinions around him, it was not sudden frenzy which seized him, but he attempted deliberate murder. What a con-trast : David with the harp in his hand, and Saul with his spear ; David sweeping the chords to waken Divine melody in the king's soul, and the king sending the javelin with all his might, so that, as it missed its aim, it stuck in the wall close by where David had but lately sat. Meanwhile David escaped to his own house, apparently unwilling even now to believe in the king's deliberate purpose of murder. It was Saul's **own** daughter who had to urge upon her husband the terrible fact of her father's planned crime and the need of immediate flight, and with womanly love and wit to render it possible. How great the danger had been; how its meshes had been laid all around and well nigh snared him—but chiefly what had been David's own feelings, and what his hope in that hour of supreme danger : all this, and much more for the teaching of the Church of all ages, we gather from what he himself tells us in the fifty-ninth Psalm.[1]

The peril was past; and while the cowardly menials of Saul —though nominally of Israel, yet in heart and purpose, as in their final requital, "heathens" (Psa. lix. 6, 8)—prowled about the city and its walls on their terrible watch of murder, "growling" like dogs that dare not bark to betray their presence, and waiting till the dawn would bring their victim, lured to safety, within reach of their teeth, Michal compassed the escape of her husband through a window—probably on the city-wall. In so doing she betrayed, however, alike the spirit of her home and that of her times. The daughter of Saul, like Rachel of old (Gen. xxxi. 19), seems to have had *Teraphim*—the old Aramæan or Chaldean household gods, which were probably associated with fertility. For, despite the explicit Divine prohibition and the zeal of Samuel against all idolatry, this most ancient form of Jewish superstition appears to have continued in Israelitish households (comp. Judg. xvii. 5; xviii. 14; 1 Sam. xv. 23; Hos. iii. 4; Zech. x. 2). The *Teraphim* must have borne the form of a man; and Michal now placed this image in David's bed, arranging about the head "the plait of camel's hair,"[2] and covering the whole

---

[1] Our space prevents not only an analysis but even a literal translation of this Psalm. The reader should compare it with this history. Those who are able to avail themselves of it, will find much help in Professor Delitzsch's *Commentary on the Psalms* (German Ed., vol. i., pp. 441-448); translated in Clark's *Foreign Theological Library*.

[2] The Hebrew expression is somewhat difficult, and may imply that Michal used it to cover David's face, or that she put it about the Teraphim to appear like hair. I have translated the words literally.

"with the upper garment" (as coverlet), to represent David lying sick. The device succeeded in gaining time for the fugitive, and was only discovered when Saul sent his messengers a second time, with the peremptory order to bring David in the bed. Challenged by her father for her deceit, she excused her conduct by another falsehood, alleging that she had been obliged by David to do so on peril of her life.

Although we are in no wise concerned to defend Michal, and in general utterly repudiate, as derogatory to Holy Scripture, all attempts to explain away the apparent wrong-doing of Biblical personages, this instance requires a few words of plain statement. First, it is most important to observe, that Holy Scripture, with a truthfulness which is one of its best evidences, simply relates events, whoever were the actors, and whatever their moral character. We are somehow prone to imagine that Holy Scripture approves all that it records, at least in the case of its worthies—unless, indeed, the opposite be expressly stated. Nothing could be more fallacious than such an inference Much is told in the Bible, even in connection with Old Testament saints, on which no comment is made, save that of the retribution which, in the course of God's providence, surely follows all wrong-doing. And here we challenge any instance of sin which is not followed by failure, sorrow, and punishment. It had been so in the case of Abraham, of Isaac, and of Jacob; and it was so in that of David, whose every attempt to screen himself by untruthfulness ended in failure and sorrow. Holy Scripture never conceals wrong-doing—least of all seeks to palliate it. In this respect there is the most significant contrast between the Bible and its earliest (even pre-Christian) comments. Those only who are acquainted with this literature know with what marvellous ingenuity Rabbinical commentaries uniformly try, not only to palliate wrong on the part of Biblical heroes, but by some turn or alteration in the expression, or suggestion of motives, to present it as actually right.

But we must go a step further. He who fails to recognise

the gradual development of God's teaching, and regards the earlier periods in the history of God's kingdom as on exactly the same level as the New Testament, not only most seriously mistakes fundamental facts and principles, but misses the entire meaning of the preparatory dispensation. The Old Testament never places truth, right, or duty on any lower basis than the New. But while it does not lower, it does not unfold in all their fulness the principles which it lays down. Rather does it adapt the application of truths, the exposition of rights, and the unfolding of duties, to the varying capacities of each age and stage. And this from the necessity of the case, in highest wisdom, in greatest mercy, and in the interest of the truth itself. The principle : " When I was a child, I spake as a child, I understood as a child, I thought as a child," applies to the relation between the Old and the New Testament stand-point, as well as to all spiritual and even intellectual progress. The child is ignorant of all the bearings of what he learns; the beginner of the full meaning and application of the axioms and propositions which he is taught. Had it been otherwise in spiritual knowledge, its acquisition would have been simply impossible.

Here also we have to distinguish between what God *sanctioned* and that with which *He bore* on account of the hardness of the heart of those who had not yet been spiritually trained in that "time of ignorance," which "God overlooked." To come to the particular question in hand. Nothing could be more clear in the Old Testament than the Divine insistance on truthfulness. He Himself condescends to be His people's example in this. The command not to lie one to another (Lev. xix. 11) is enforced by the consideration, "I am Jehovah," and springs as a necessary sequence from the principle : "Be ye holy: for I Jehovah your God am holy." It is scarcely requisite to add, that in no other part of Holy Scripture is this more fully or frequently enforced than in the Book of Psalms. And yet, when occasion arose, David himself seems not to have scrupled to seek safety through falsehood, though with what little success appears in his history. It appears as if to his mind untruth had seemed only that which was false in the intention or in its object, not that which was simply untrue in itself, however good the intention might be, or however desirable the object thereby sought.[1] And in this connection it deserves notice, how among the few express moral precepts which the New Testament gives—for it deals in principles rather than in details ; it gives life, not law,—this about lying recurs with emphatic distinctness and frequency.[2]

As might almost have been anticipated, David's destination in his flight was Ramah. To tell Samuel, who had anointed him, all that had happened ; to ask his guidance, and seek refreshment in his company, would obviously suggest itself first to his mind. For greater safety, the two withdrew from the city, to " Naioth," " the dwellings," which seems to have been a block of dwellings within a compound, occupied by an order of prophets, of which Samuel was the " president," [3] and, we may add, the founder. Not that " prophetism " (if the term may be used) commenced with Samuel. In the sense of being the bearers of God's message, the patriarchs are called "prophets" (Gen. xx. 7 ; Psa. cv. 15). But in its strict sense the term first applied to Moses (Num. xi. 25 ; Deut. xxxiv. 10 ; Hos. xii. 13). Miriam was a prophetess (Ex. xv. 20 ; comp. Num. xii. 2). In the days of the Judges there were prophets (Judg. iv. 4 ; vi. 8). At the time of Eli, prophetic warning came through a " man of God " (1 Sam. ii. 27) ; and although " the word of God " (or prophecy) " was rare " in those days (1 Sam. iii. 1), yet it came

[1] The Germans speak of "lies of necessity" (*Nothlüge*), which to me seems a contradiction of terms, since no one duty (or moral necessity) can ever contravene another.

[2] I am bound to add that even Talmudical writings insist on the need of absolute truthfulness, though in terms far other than the New Testament.

[3] In the Authorised Version, 1 Sam. xix. 20, "Samuel standing *as appointed over them ;*" in the original, "Standing as president over them."

not upon the people as a strange and unknown manifestation (comp. also 1 Sam. ix. 9). Here, however, we must make distinction between the *prophetic gift* and the *prophetic office*. The latter, so far as appears, began with Samuel. A further stage is marked in the days of Elijah and Elisha. Then they were no longer designated "prophets," as at the time of Samuel, but "sons of the prophets," or "disciples" (1 Kings xx. 35; 2 Kings iv. 38; vi. 1). Lastly, whereas we read of only one prophetic community, Naioth, in the time of Samuel, and that close to his residence at Ramah, there were several such in the days of Elisha, in different parts of the country—as at Gilgal, Bethel, and Jericho. Whether there was a continuous succession in this from Samuel to Elijah can scarcely be determined, though the probability seems in its favour (comp. 1 Kings xviii. 13).

It is of more importance to understand the difference between "prophets" and "sons of the prophets," the circumstances under which these orders or unions originated, and the peculiar meaning attached to this prophetic calling. The first point seems sufficiently clear. The "sons of the prophets" were those who of set purpose devoted themselves to this work, and were, on the one hand, disciples of prophets, and on the other, the messengers or ministers to carry out their behests. Dedication and separation to the work (symbolised even by a common abode, and by a distinctive appearance and dress), religious instruction, and, above all, implicit obedience, are the historical features of those "sons of the prophets." Quite other was the "union," "company," or rather "congregation[1] of prophets" (1 Sam. xix. 20) near Ramah. There is no evidence of their having all permanently dedicated themselves to the office; the contrary seems rather implied. No doubt from among them sprung those who were afterwards "seers," such as Gad, Nathan, and Iddo; but the majority seem to have joined the union under a

---

[1] The *Lahakah*, which evidently is only an inversion of the letters of the word *Kahalah*, which generally designates "the congregation."

temporary constraining influence of the mighty Spirit of God.
And although, as we gather from many passages of Holy
Scripture (as 1 Sam. xxii. 5 ; 1 Chron. xxix. 29, and other
passages in the Books of Kings), they were occupied with the
composition and the study of sacred history, and no doubt
with that of the law also, as well as with the cultivation of
hymnology, it would be a great mistake to regard them as a
class of students of theology, or to represent them as a monastic
order.

In point of fact, the time of Samuel, and that of Elijah and
Elisha, were great turning-points, periods of crisis, in the history of the kingdom of God. In the first, the tabernacle, the
priesthood, and the God-appointed services had fallen into
decay, and, for a time, may be said to have been almost in
abeyance. Then it was that God provided other means of
grace, by raising up faithful, devoted men, who gathered into
a living sanctuary, filled not by the Shechinah, but by the
mighty Spirit of God. Under the direction of a Samuel, and
the influence of a "spiritual gift,"—like those of apostolic days
—their presence and activity served most important purposes.
And, as in apostolic days, the spiritual influence under which
they were seems at times to have communicated itself even to
those who were merely brought into contact with them. This,
no doubt, to prove its *reality* and *power*, since even those who
were strangers to its spiritual purpose, and unaffected by it,
could not resist its might, and thus involuntarily bore witness to it. And something analogous to this we also witness
now in the irresistible influence which a spiritual movement
sometimes exercises even on those who are and remain strangers
to its real meaning.[1]

[1] As there is unity in all God's working, we mark a similar law prevailing in the physical and intellectual world. The general influence of
physical forces and causes—even atmospheric—is sufficiently known, nor
can it be necessary, in these days, to attempt proving that of "the spirit of
the times," which intellectually and even morally affects us all more or less,
whether consciously or unconsciously, willingly or unwillingly.

Thus far as regards "the congregation of prophets ın the days of Samuel. In the time of Elijah, Israel—as distinct from Judah—was entirely cut off from the sanctuary, and under a rule which threatened wholly to extinguish the service of God, and to replace it by the vile and demoralising rites of Baal. Already the country swarmed with its priests, when God raised up Elijah to be the breaker-up of the way, and Elisha to be the restorer of ancient paths.   The very circumstances of the time, and the state of the people, pointed out the necessity of the revival of the ancient "order," but now as "sons of the prophets" rather than as prophets.

Nor did this change of designation imply a retrogression. What on superficial inquiry seems such, is, on more careful consideration, often found to mark real progress.   In earliest patriarchal, and even in Mosaic times, the communications between Jehovah and His people were chiefly by *Theophanies,* or Personal apparitions of God ; in the case of the prophets, by *inspiration ;* in the New Testament Church, by the *indwelling of the Holy Ghost.*   It were a grievous mistake to regard this progress in the spiritual history of the kingdom of God as a retrogression.   The opposite is rather the case.   And somewhat similarly we may mark, in some respects, an advance in the succession of "sons of the prophets" to the order of "prophetics," or "prophesiers," as we may perhaps designate them by way of distinction.   " But all these things worketh one and the self-same Spirit, dividing to every man " (and to every period in the Church's history) " severally as He will," and adapting the agencies which He uses to the varying necessities and spiritual stages of His people.

What has been stated will help to explain how the three embassies which Saul sent to seize David in the Naioth were in turn themselves seized by the spiritual influence, and how even Saul, when attempting personally to carry out what his messengers had found impossible, came yet more fully and manifestly than they under its all-subduing power.[1]   It proved

[1] The difference between the influence on Saul and on his messengers

incontestably that there was a Divine power engaged on behalf of David, against which the king of Israel would vainly contend, which he could not resist, and which would easily lay alike his messengers and himself prostrate and helpless at its feet. If, after this, Saul continued in his murderous designs against David, the contest would manifestly be not between two men, but between the king of Israel and the Lord of Hosts, Who had wrought signs and miracles on Saul and his servants, and that in full view of the whole people. It is this latter consideration which gives such meaning to the circumstances narrated in the sacred text, that the common report, how the spiritual influence had subdued and constrained Saul, when on his murderous errand against David, led to the renewal of the popular saying : " Is Saul also among the prophets ?" For all Israel must know it, and speak of it, and wonder as it learns its significance.

Thus at the end, as at the beginning of his course, Saul is under the mighty influence of the Spirit of God—now to warn, and, if possible, to reclaim, as formerly to qualify him for his work. And some result of this kind seems to have been produced. For, although David fled from Naioth on the arrival of Saul, we find him soon again near the royal residence (xx. 1), where, indeed, he was evidently expected by the king to take part in the festive meal with which the beginning of every month seems to have been celebrated (vers. 5, 25, 27). The notice is historically interesting in connection with Num. x. 10; xxviii. 11–15,[1] as also that other one (1 Sam. xx. 6, 29), according to which it appears to have been the practice in those days

---

may be thus marked. It seized him *before* he arrived at Naioth (ver. 23); and it was more powerful and of longer duration (ver. 24). The statement that "he stripped off his clothes," and "lay down naked," refers, of course, only to his upper garments. In the excitement of the ecstacy he would put these away (comp. 2 Sam. vi. 14, 16, 20).

[1] The statement that the festive meal took place on two successive days must, of course, not be understood as implying that the religious festival lasted two days.

of religious unsettledness for families to have had a yearly
"sacrifice" in their own place, especially where, as in Bethlehem, there was an altar (comp. xvi. 2, etc.).

But, whatever had passed, David felt sure in his own mind
that evil was appointed against him, and that there was but a
step between him and death.   Yet on that moral certainty alone
he did not feel warranted to act.   Accordingly he applied to
Jonathan, whom he could so fully trust, expressly placing his
life, in word as in deed, in his hands, if he were really guilty of
what the king imputed to him (ver. 8).   With characteristic
generosity, Jonathan, however, still refused to believe in any
settled purpose of murder on the part of his father, attributing
all that had passed to the outbursts of temporary madness.
His father had never made a secret of his intentions and movements.   Why, then, should he now be silent, if David's
suspicions were well founded?   The suggestion that Jonathan
should excuse David's absence from the feast by his attendance
on the yearly family-sacrifice at Bethlehem, for which he had
asked and obtained Jonathan's leave, was well calculated to
bring out the feelings and purposes of the king.   If determined to evil against David, he would in his anger at the
escape of his victim, and his own son's participation in it, give
vent to his feelings in language that could not be mistaken,
the more so, if, as might be expected, Jonathan pleaded with
characteristic warmth on behalf of his absent friend.   But who
could be trusted to bring tidings to David as he lay in hiding,
"or" tell him "what" Saul would "answer" Jonathan
"roughly"—or, in other words, communicate the details of the
conversation?

To discuss the matter, unendangered by prying eyes and ears,
the two friends betook themselves "to the field."   The account
of what passed between them—one of the few narratives of
this kind given in Scripture—is most pathetic.   It was not
merely the outflowing of personal affection between the two,
or perhaps it would not have been recorded at all.   Rather
is it reported in order to show that, though Jonathan had never

spoken of it, he was fully aware of David's future destiny ; more than that, he had sad presentiment of the fate of his own house. And yet, in full view of it all, he believingly submitted to the will of God, and still lovingly clave to his friend ! There is a tone of deep faith toward God, and of full trust in David, in what Jonathan said. Far more fully and clearly than his father does he see into the future, alike as regards David and the house of Saul. But there is not a tinge of misunderstanding of David, not a shadow of suspicion, not a trace of jealousy, not a word of murmur or complaint. More touching words, surely, were never uttered than this charge which Jonathan laid on David as *his* part of their covenant, in view of what was to come upon them both : "And not only if I am still alive—not only shalt thou do with me the mercy of Jehovah" (show towards me Divine mercy) "that I die not; but thou shalt not cut off thy mercy from my house—not even" (at the time) "when Jehovah cutteth off the enemies of David, every one from the face of the earth " (xx. 14, 15). [1]

The signal preconcerted between the friends was, that on the third day David should lie in hiding at the same spot where he had concealed himself "in the day of business "— probably that day when Jonathan had formerly pleaded with his father for his friend (xix. 2–7)—beside the stone Ezel, perhaps "the stone of demarcation," marking a boundary. Jonathan was to shoot three arrows. If he told the lad in attendance that they lay nearer than he had run to fetch them, David might deem himself safe, and come out of hiding. If, on the contrary, he directed him to go farther, then David should conclude that

---

[1] The original is very difficult in its structure. We have rendered it as literally as the sense would allow. Of the other proposed translations only these two deserve special notice. "And (wilt thou) not if I am still alive, wilt thou not show the kindness of the Lord towards me, that I die not ?" Or else, "And mayest thou, if I am still alive—mayest thou show towards me the kindness of the Lord—and (if) not, if I die, not withdraw thy mercy from my house for ever." But the first rendering implies, besides other difficulties, a change from a question in ver. 14 to an assertion in ver. 15, while the second necessitates a change in the Hebrew words.

his only safety lay in flight. The result proved that David's fears had been too well grounded. Saul had evidently watched for the opportunity which the New Moon's festival would offer to destroy his hated rival. On the first day he noticed David's absence, but, attributing it to some Levitical defilement, made no remark, lest his tone might betray him. But on the following day he inquired its reason in language which too clearly betokened his feelings. It was then that Jonathan repeated the false explanation which David had suggested. Whether or not the king saw through the hollowness of the device, it certainly proved utterly unavailing. Casting aside all restraint, the king turned on his son, and in language the most insulting to an Oriental, bluntly told him that his infatuation for David would cause his own and his family's ruin. To the command to send for him for the avowed purpose of his murder, Jonathan with characteristic frankness and generosity replied by pleading his cause, on which the fury of the king rose to such a pitch, that he poised his javelin against his own son, as formerly against David.

Jonathan had left the feast in moral indignation at the scene which had taken place before the whole court. But deeper far was his grief for the wrong done to his friend. That day of feasting became one of fasting to Jonathan. Next morning he went to give the preconcerted signal of danger. But he could not so part from his friend. Sending back the lad to the city with his bow, quiver, and arrows, the two friends once more met, but for a moment. There was not time for lengthened speech; the danger was urgent. They were not unmanly tears which the two wept, "till David wept loudly."[1] The parting must be brief—only just sufficient for Jonathan to remind his friend of their covenant of friendship in God, to Whose care he now commended him. Then Jonathan retraced his lonely way to the city, while David hastened on his flight southward to Nob. Only once again, and that in sadly altered circumstances, did these two noblest men in Israel meet.

[1] So literally, and not as in the Authorised Version.

CHAPTER XII.

David at Nob—Observed by Doeg—Flight to Gath—David feigns Madness —The Cave of Adullam—Shelter in Moab—Return to the land of Israel—Jonathan's Last Visit—Persecutions by Saul.

(1 SAM. XXI.—XXIII.)

A MIDST the many doubts which must have beset the mind of David, one outstanding fact, however painful, was at least clear. He must henceforth consider himself an outlaw, whom not even the friendship of a Jonathan could protect. As such he must seek some shelter—best outside the land of Israel, and with the enemies of Saul. But the way was far, and the journey beset by danger. On all accounts—for refreshment of the body, for help, above all, for inward strengthening and guidance—he would first seek the place whither he had so often resorted (1 Sam. xxii. 15) before starting on some perilous undertaking.

The Tabernacle of the Lord was at that time in Nob, probably the place that at present bears a name which some have rendered "the village of Esau" (or Edom)—reminding us of its fatal celebrity in connection with Doeg the Edomite. The village is on the road from the north to Jerusalem —between Anathoth and the Holy City, and only about one hour north-west from the latter. Here Ahimelech (or Ahiah, 1 Sam. xiv. 3), the great-grandson of Eli, ministered as high-priest—a man probably advanced in years, with whom his son Abiathar (afterwards appointed high-priest by David, 1 Sam. xxx. 7) was, either for that day or else permanently,[1] conjoined in the sacred

---

[1] It is thus that we explain the notice in Mark ii. 26. This would also account for Abiathar's flight on the first tidings of his father's death (1 Sam. xxii. 20), whereas the other priests would deem themselves safe, and so fall into the hands of their murderer.

service. Nob was only about an hour to the south-east of
Gibeah of Saul. Yet it was not immediately on parting with
Jonathan that David appeared in the holy place. We can readily
understand that flight along that road could not have been
risked by day—nor, indeed, anywhere throughout the boundaries
of the district where Saul's residence was. We therefore conclude that David lay in hiding all that night. It was the morning of a Sabbath when he suddenly presented himself, alone,
unarmed, weary, and faint with hunger before the high-priest.
Never had he thus appeared before Ahimelech; and the high-
priest, who must, no doubt, have been aware of dissensions in
the past between the king and his son-in-law, was afraid of what
this might bode. But David had a specious answer to meet
every question and disarm all suspicion. If he had come
unarmed, and was faint from hunger, the king's business had
been so pressing, and required such secrecy, that he had avoided
taking provisions, and had not even had time to arm himself.
For the same reasons he had appointed his followers to meet
him at a trysting-place, rather than gone forth at the head of
them.

In truth, David's wants had become most pressing.[1] He
needed food to support him till he could reach a place of safety.
For he dared not show himself by day, nor ask any man for
help. And he needed some weapon with which, in case of
absolute necessity, to defend his life. We know that it was
the Sabbath, because the shewbread of the previous week, which
was removed on that day, had to be eaten during its course.
It affords sad evidence of the decay into which the sanctuary
and the priesthood had fallen, that Ahimelech and Abiathar
could offer David no other provisions for his journey than
this shewbread ; which, according to the letter of the law, only
the priests might eat, and that within the sanctuary (Lev.

[1] The whole history tends to show that David was alone, alike in Nob
and afterwards in Gath, though from Mark ii. 25, 26, we infer that a few
faithful friends may have kept about him to watch over his safety till he
reached the border of Philistia.

xxiv. 9). But there was the higher law of charity (Lev. xix. 18), which was rightly regarded as overruling every merely levitical ordinance, however solemn (comp. Matt. xii. 5 ; Mark ii. 25). If it was as David pretended, and the royal commission was so important and so urgent, it could not be right to refuse the necessary means of sustenance to those who were engaged on it, provided that they had not contracted any such levitical defilement as would have barred them from access to the Divine Presence (Lev. xv. 18). For, viewed in its higher bearing, what were the priests but the representatives of Israel, who were all to be a kingdom of priests? This idea seems indeed implied in the remark of David (xxi. 5) : "And though the manner" (the use to which it is put) "be not sacred, yet still it will be made" (become) "sacred by the instrument,"—either referring to himself as the Divine instrument about to be employed,[1] or to the "wallet" in which the bread was to be carried, as it were, on God's errand. By a similar pretence, David also obtained from the high-priest the sword of Goliath, which seems to have been kept in the sanctuary wrapt in a cloth, behind the ephod, as a memorial of God's victory over the might of the heathen. Most important of all, David, as we infer from xxii. 10, 15, appears to have "enquired of the Lord," through the high-priest—whatever the exact terms of that inquiry may have been. In this also there was nothing strange, since David had done so on previous occasions, probably before entering on dangerous expeditions (xxii. 15).

But already David's secret was betrayed. It so happened in the Providence of God, that on this special Sabbath, one of Saul's principal officials, the "chief over the herdsmen," was in Nob, "detained before Jehovah." The expression implies that Doeg was obliged to remain in the sanctuary in consequence of some religious ceremony—whether connected with his admission as a proselyte, for he was by birth an Edomite, or with

---

[1] The passage in the Hebrew is very difficult. The word which we have rendered "instrument" is applied to *human* instrumentality in Gen. xlix. 5 ; Isa. xiii. 5 ; xxxii. 7 ; Jer. l. 25 ; comp. also Acts ix. 15.

a vow, or with some legal purification.   Such a witness could not be excluded, even if David had chosen to betray his secret to the priest.   Once committed to the fatal wrong of his false-hood, David had to go on to the bitter end, all the while feeling morally certain that Doeg was his enemy, and would bring report of all to Saul (xxii. 22).   His feelings as con-nected with this are, as we believe, expressed in Ps. vii.[1]

At first sight it may seem strange that on his further flight from Nob, David should have sought shelter in Gath, the city of Goliath, whom he had killed in single combat.   On the other hand, not only may this have been the place most readily accessible to him, but David may have imagined that in Gath, especially, the defection of such a champion from the hosts of Saul would be hailed as a notable triumph, and that accordingly he would find a welcome in seeking its pro-tection.   The result, however, proved otherwise.   The courtiers of Achish, the king,—or, to give him his Philistine title, the Abimelech (my father king) of Gath (comp. Gen. xx. 2 ; xxvi. 8) —urged on him the high position which David held in popular estimation in Israel, and his past exploits, as presumably in-

---

[1] The Psalm evidently refers to the time of Saul's persecutions.   On this point critics are almost unanimous.   Most of them, however, take the word *" Cush "* as the name of a *person* (though it nowhere else occurs), and date his otherwise *unknown "report"* in the period between 1 Sam. xxiv. and xxvii. (comp. xxvi. 19).   But I regard the term "Cush"—the Cushite, Ethiopian—as an equivalent for "Edomite," and explain the expression "the Benjamite," as referring to Doeg's identification (as a proselyte) with the Benjamites, and his probable settlement among them, as evidenced by 1 Sam. xxii. 7, 9.   The Rabbis have a curious conceit on this point, which, as it has not been told by any previous critic, and is incorrectly alluded to by Delitzsch and Moll, may here find a place.   It occurs in *Sifré* 27 *a*, where the expression, Numb. xii. 1, is applied to Zipporah, it being explained that she is called "a Cushite" (Ethiopian), because, as the Ethiopian differed by his skin from all other men, so Zipporah by her beauty from all women.   Similarly the inscription, Ps. vii. 1, is applied to Saul, the term Cush, or Ethiopian, being explained by a reference to 1 Sam. ix. 2.   On the same principle, Amos ix. 7 is accounted for, because Israel differed from all others, the Law being given to them only, while, lastly, the Ebed-melech, or servant of the king, in Jer. xxxviii. 7, is supposed to have been Baruch, because he differed by his deeds from all the other servants.

dicating what not only his real feelings but his true policy towards Philistia must be, however differently it might suit his present purpose to bear himself (comp. 1 Sam. xxix. 3–5). The danger which now threatened David must have been very great. In fact, to judge from Ps. lvi. 1, the Philistine lords must have actually "taken" him, to bring him before Achish, with a view to his imprisonment, if not his destruction. We are probably warranted in inferring that it was when thus led before the king, and waiting in the court before being admitted to the audience, that he feigned madness by scribbling[1] on the doors of the gate, and letting his spittle fall upon his beard. The device proved successful. The Philistine lords with true Oriental reverence for madness as a kind of spiritual possession, dared not harm him any more ; while Achish himself, however otherwise previously disposed (comp. xxvii. 2, 3), would not have him in his house, under the apprehension that he might "rave against"[2] him, and in a fit of madness endanger his life. And as Ps. lvi. described the feelings of David in the hour of his great danger, so Ps. xxxiv. expresses those on his deliverance therefrom. Accordingly the two should be read in connection. Indeed the eight Psalms which date from the time of the persecutions by Saul (lix., vii., lvi., xxxiv., lvii., lii., cxlii., liv.[3]) are closely connected, the servant of the Lord gradually rising to full and triumphant anticipation of deliverance. They all express the same trustfulness in God, the same absolute committal to Him, and the same sense of undeserved persecution. But what seems of such special interest, regarding, as we do, the history of David in its typical aspect, is that in these Psalms David's view is always enlarging, so that in

---

[1] The LXX., by a slight alteration in the Hebrew lettering, have rendered it "beating" or "drumming."

[2] Instead of, "that ye have brought this fellow to play the madman in my presence" (xxi. 15), as in our Authorised Version, translate, "that ye have brought this one to rave against me."

[3] We have arranged these Psalms in the chronological order of the events to which they refer, although we would not, of course, be understood as implying that they were exactly composed at those very periods.

the judgment of his enemies he beholds a type of that of the heathen who oppose the kingdom of God and its King (comp. for example, Ps. lvi. 7 ; vii. 9 ; lix. 5) ; thus showing that David himself must have had some spiritual understanding of the prophetic bearing of his history.

And now David was once more a fugitive—the twofold lesson which he might have learned being, that it needed no subterfuges to ensure his safety, and that his calling for the present was within, not outside the land of Israel. A comparatively short distance—about ten miles—from Gath runs " the valley of the terebinth," the scene of David's great combat with Goliath. The low hills south of this valley are literally burrowed by caves, some of them of very large dimensions. Here lay the ancient city of Adullam (Gen. xxxviii. 1 ; Josh. xii. 15 ; xv. 35, and many other passages), which has, with much probability, been identified with the modern Aid el Mia (Adlem). In the largest of the caves close by, David sought a hiding-place. What his feelings were either at that time, or later, in similar circumstances (1 Sam. xxiv.), we learn from Ps. lvii.

It has been well observed, [1] that hitherto David had always remained within easy distance of Bethlehem. This would secure him not only the means of information as to Saul's movements, but also of easy communication with his own family, and with those who would naturally sympathise with him. Adullam was only a few hours distant from Bethlehem, and David's family, who no longer felt themselves safe in their home, soon joined him in his new refuge. But not only they. Many there must have been in the troublous times of Saul's reign who were " in distress," oppressed and persecuted ; many who under such misgovernment would fall "into debt" to unmerciful and violent exactors ; many also, who, utterly

---

[1] See Lieutenant Conder's very interesting paper on *The Scenery of David's Outlaw Life*, in the Quarterly Report of the Palestine Exploration Fund, for Jan. 1875, p. 42. I regret, however, that in reference to this, as to other papers of the same kind, I have to dissent from not a few of the exegetical reasonings and inferences.

dissatisfied with the present state of things, would, in the expressive language of the sacred text, " be bitter of soul." Of these the more active and ardent now gathered around David, first to the number of about four hundred, which soon increased to six hundred (xxiii. 13). They were not a band in rebellion against Saul. This would not only have been utterly contrary to David's constantly avowed allegiance and oft proved loyalty to Saul, but to the higher purpose of God. The latter, if we may venture to judge, seems to have been spiritually to fit David for his calling, by teaching him constant dependence on God, and by also outwardly training him and his followers for the battles of the Lord—not against Saul, but against Israel's great enemy, the Philistines ; in short, to take up the work which the all-absorbing murderous passion of Saul, as well as his desertion by God, prevented him from doing. Thus we see once more how, in the Providence of God, the inward and the outward training of David were the result of circumstances over which he had no control, and which seemed to threaten consequences of an entirely different character. How in those times of persecution outlaws became heroes, and of what deeds of personal bravery they were capable in the wars of the Lord, we learn from the record of their names (1 Chron. xii.), and of some of their achievements (2 Sam. xxiii. 13, etc. comp. 1 Chron. xi. 15, etc.).

But there were among them those nearest and dearest to David, his own aged father and mother, whose presence could only impede the movements of his followers, and whose safety he must secure. Besides, as such a band could not long escape Saul's notice, it seemed desirable to find a better retreat than the caves about Adullam. For this twofold object David and his followers now passed to the other side of Jordan. From the account of the war between Saul and Moab in 1 Sam. xiv. 47, we infer that the latter had advanced beyond their own territory across the border, and were now occupying the southern part of the trans-Jordanic country which belonged to Israel. This was within easy reach of Bethlehem. Accordingly David now went to Mizpeh Moab, the "outlook," mountain-height or "Tor" (as we might call it) of Moab, probably over against Jericho in the "Arboth of Moab" (Numb. xxii. 1; Deut. xxxiv. 1, 8; Josh. xiii. 32), perhaps, as the name seems to indicate, on the fields of the Zophim (or outlookers), on the top of Pisgah (Numb. xxiii. 14 [1]). To the king of Moab, whose protection he could invoke in virtue of their descent from Ruth the Moabitess, he commended his father and mother, with the expressive remark, till he should know "what Elohim [2] would do" unto him. He himself and his followers meantime entrenched on that "mountain-height," [3] associated with the prophecy there delivered by Balaam concerning Israel's future.

It was impossible that such a movement on the part of David could long remain unknown. In two quarters it excited deep feelings, though of a very different character. It seems highly probable that the tidings reached the Naioth, and that it was from thence that Gad (afterwards David's "seer" and spiritual adviser, 2 Sam. xxiv. 11–19; 1 Chron. xxi. 9, and the chronicler of his reign, 1 Chron. xxix. 29) went to David by Divine commission.[4] But the stay in the land of Moab was not in accordance with the purpose of God. David must not flee from the discipline of suffering, and God had some special work for him in the land of Israel which Saul could no longer do. In accordance with this direction, David left his entrenched position, recrossed the Jordan, and sought shelter in "the forest of Hareth," [5] within the boundaries of

---

[1] See Vol. II. of this History, p. 199.

[2] It is significant that David speaks to the king of Moab of *Elohim*, not of Jehovah.

[3] This is the meaning of what is rendered in our Authorised Version "in the hold" (xxii. 4). We infer that this entrenched mountain-height was Mizpeh of Moab.

[4] Of course, this is only our *inference*, but it seems in accordance with the whole narrative. It is impossible to say whether Gad was sent by Samuel, or had received the message from God directly.

[5] Lieutenant Conder proposes to follow the LXX., and by a slight change of the letters, to read "the city of Hareth." But such a city is not otherwise known, nor would David's unmolested stay there agree with the after history.

Judah. But meantime Saul also had heard that "David had become known, and the men that were with him" (xxii. 6). Being aware of his position, he would secure his prey.

A royal court is held at Gibeah. The king sits, as so often before, "under the tamarisk-tree on the height," his spear as sceptre in his hand, and surrounded by all his officers of state, among them Doeg, the "chief of the herdsmen." Characteristically Saul seems now to have surrounded himself exclusively by "Benjamites," either because no others would serve him, or more probably because he no longer trusted any but his own clansmen. Still more characteristic is the mode in which he appeals to their loyalty and seeks to enlist their aid. He seems to recognise no motive on the part of others but that of the most sordid selfishness. Probably some of the words that had passed between Jonathan and David, when they made their covenant of friendship (xx. 42), had been overheard, and re-peated to Saul in a garbled form by one of his many spies. That was enough. As he put it, his son had made a league with David, of which the only object could be to deprive him of his throne. This could only be accomplished by violence. Everyone was aware that David and his men then held a strong position. A conspiracy so fully organised must have been known to his courtiers. If they had no sympathy with a father betrayed by his own son, at least what profit could they as Benjamites hope to derive from such a plot? It was to defend the courtiers from guilty knowledge of such a plot that Doeg now reported what he had seen and heard at Nob. David's was a conspiracy indeed, but one hatched not by the laity but by the priesthood; and of which, as he had had personal evidence, the high-priest himself was the chief abettor.

The suggestion was one which would only too readily approve itself to a mind and conscience like Saul's. There could be nothing in common between Saul and the ministers of that God Who by His prophet had announced his rejection and appointed his successor. A priestly plot against himself, and in favour of David, had every appearance of likelihood. It is only when we thus understand the real import of Doeg's account to the king, that we perceive the extent of his crime, and the meaning of the language in which David characterised it in Ps. lii.   A man of that kind was not likely to shrink from any deed.   Saul summoned Ahimelech and all his father's house to his presence. In answer to the charge of conspiracy, the priest protested his innocence in language the truth of which could not have been mistaken by any impartial judge.[1]   But the case had been decided against the priesthood before it was heard.   Yet, callous as Saul's men-at-arms were, not one of them would execute the sentence of death against the priests of Jehovah.   It was left to the Edomite to carry out what his reckless malice had instigated. That day no fewer than eighty-five of the priests in actual ministry were murdered in cold blood.   Not content with this, the king had "the ban" executed upon Nob.   As if the priest-city had been guilty of idolatry and rebellion against Jehovah (Deut. xiii. 15), every living being, both man and beast, was cut down by the sword.   Only one escaped the horrible slaughter of that day.   Abiathar, the son of Ahimelech,[2] had probably received timely warning.   He now fled to David, to whom he reported what had taken place.   From him he received such assurance of protection as only one could give who in his strong faith felt absolute safety in the shelter of Jehovah's wings.   But here also the attentive reader will trace a typical parallel between the murder at Nob and that of the children at Bethlehem—all the more striking, that in the latter case also an Edomite was the guilty party, Herod the king having been by descent an Idumæan.

When Abiathar reached David, he was already on his way from the forest of Hareth to Keilah.[3]   Tidings had come to

[1] Ver. 14 reads thus : "And who among all thy servants is approved like David, and son-in-law to the king, and having access to thy private audience, and honoured in all thy house?"

[2] He may have remained behind in Nob to attend to the Sanctuary during the absence of the other priests.

[3] As from the expression, "enquired of Jehovah" (xxiii. 2, 4), it is evident that the enquiry was made by the Urim and Thummim, we must conclude

David of a Philistine raid against Keilah, close on the border —the modern Kilah, about six miles to the south-east of Adullam. Keilah was a walled city, and therefore not itself in immediate danger. But there was plenty of plunder to be obtained outside its walls; and henceforth no threshing-floor on the heights above the city was safe from the Philistines. Here was a call for the proper employment of a band like David's. But his followers had not yet learned the lessons of trust which he had been taught. Although the expedition for the relief of Keilah had been undertaken after "enquiry," and by direction of the Lord, his men shrank from provoking an attack by the Philistines at the same time that they were in constant apprehension of what might happen if Saul overtook them. So little did they as yet understand either the source of their safety or the object of their gathering! What happened—as we note once more in the course of ordinary events—was best calculated to teach them all this. A second formal enquiry of the Lord by the Urim and Thummim, and a second direction to go forward, brought them to the relief of the city. The Philistines were driven back with great slaughter, and rich booty was made of their cattle.

But soon the danger which David's men had apprehended seemed really at hand. When Saul heard that David had "shut himself in by coming into a town with gates and bars," it seemed to him almost as if judicial blindness had fallen upon him, or, as the king put it: "Elohim has rejected him into my hand." So thinking, Saul rapidly gathered a force to march against Keilah. But, as we learn from the course of this narrative, each side was kept well informed of the movements and plans of the other. Accordingly David knew his danger, and

---

that Abiathar had reached David either after he had been preparing his expedition to Keilah, or more probably on his way thither. But, in general, it seems to me that the language in xxiii. 6 must not be too closely pressed. The enquiry mentioned in ver. 4 must have taken place on the road to Keilah, probably near to it, and ver. 6 is manifestly intended only to explain the mode of David's enquiry.

in his extremity once more appealed to the Lord.   It was not a needless question which he put through the Urim and Thummim,[1] but one which was connected with God's faithfulness and the truth of His promises.   With reverence be it said, God could not have given up David into the hands of Saul. Nor did his enquiries of God resemble those by heathen oracles. *Their main element seems to have been prayer.*   In most earnest language David spread his case before the Lord, and entreated His direction.   The answer was not withheld, although, significantly, each question had specially and by itself to be brought before the Lord (xxiii. 11, 12).

Thus informed of their danger, David and his men escaped from Keilah, henceforth to wander from one hiding-place to another.   No other district could offer such facilities for eluding pursuit as that large tract, stretching along the territory of Judah, between the Dead Sea and the mountains of Judah. It bore the general designation of "the wilderness of Judah," but its various parts were distinguished as "the wilderness of Ziph," "of Maon," etc., from the names of neighbouring towns. In general it may be said of this period of his wanderings (ver. 14), that during its course David's head-quarters were on "mountain heights," [2] whence he could easily observe the approach of an enemy, while "Saul sought him every day," but in vain, since "God gave him not into his hand."

The first station in these wanderings was the "wilderness of Ziph," on the outskirts of the town of that name, about an hour and three-quarters to the south-east of Hebron.   South of it a solitary mountain-top rises about one hundred feet, commanding a full prospect of the surrounding country.   On the other hand, anything that passed there could also easily be observed from below.   It seems that this was "the mountain" (ver. 14), or, as it is afterwards (ver. 19) more particularly

[1] This is implied in David's direction to Abiathar : "Bring hither the ephod" (xxiii. 9).
[2] This is the correct rendering, and not "in strongholds," as in the Authorised Version.

described, "the hill of Hachilah, on the south of the wilderness,"[1] where David had his principal station, or rather, to be more accurate, in "the thicket," or "brushwood,"[2] which covered its sides (vers. 15, 16). It was thither that in the very height of these first persecutions, Jonathan came once more to see his friend, and, as the sacred text emphatically puts it, "strengthened his hand in God." It is difficult to form an adequate conception of the courage, the spiritual faith, and the moral grandeur of this act. Never did man more completely clear himself from all complicity in guilt, than Jonathan from that of his father. And yet not an undutiful word escaped the lips of this brave man. And how truly human is his fond hope that in days to come, when David would be king, he should stand next to his throne, his trusted adviser, as in the days of sorrow he had been the true and steadfast friend of the outlaw! As we think of what it must have cost Jonathan to speak thus, or again of the sad fate which was so soon to overtake him, there is a deep pathos about this brief interview, almost unequalled in Holy Scripture, to which the ambitious hopes of the sons of Zebedee form not a parallel but a contrast.

But yet another bitter experience had David to make. As so often in the history of the Church, and never more markedly than in the case of Him Who was the great Antitype of David, it appeared that those who should most have rallied around him were his enemies and betrayers. The "citizens"[3] of

---

[1] Not, as in the Authorised Version, "on the south of Jeshimon" (ver. 19), where the word is left untranslated.

[2] Lieutenant Conder labours to show that there never could have been "a wood" in Ziph. But the text does not call it a *yaar*, "wood" or "forest," but a *choresh*, which conveys the idea of a thicket of brushwood. Our view is fully borne out by the portraiture of a scene exactly similar to that on Hachilah in Isa. xvii. 9: "In that day shall his strong cities be like the forsakenness of the thicket (*choresh*) and of the mountain-top." In the Jer. Targum to Gen. xxii. 13 the term is applied to the thicket in which the ram was caught.

[3] There is a difference between the "inhabitants" of Keilah (xxiii. 5), and the "citizens," burghers, "lords of Keilah" (the *Baalé Keilah*), ver. 12, who were ready to sell David for their own advantage.

Keilah would have given him up from fear of Saul. But the men of Ziph went further. Like those who hypocritically pretended that they would have no other king but Cæsar, they feigned a loyalty for which it is impossible to give them credit. Of their own accord, and evidently from hatred of David, they who were his own tribesmen betrayed his hiding-place to Saul, and offered to assist in his capture. It is pitiable to hear Saul in the madness of his passion invoking on such men "the blessing of Jehovah," and characterising their deed as one of "compassion" on himself (xxiii. 21). But the danger which now threatened David was greater than any previously or afterwards. On learning it he marched still further south-east, where "the Jeshimon," or desert, shelves down into the Arabah, or low table-land.[1] Maon itself is about two hours south-east from Ziph ; and amidst the mountains between Maon and the Dead Sea on the west, we must follow the track of David's further flight and adventures.

But meantime the plan which Saul had suggested was being only too faithfully carried out. Slowly and surely the men of Saul, guided by the Ziphites, were reaching David, and drawing the net around him closer and closer. Informed of his danger, David hastily "came down the rock,"[2]—perhaps the round mountain-top near Maon. It was high time, for already Saul and his men had reached and occupied one side of it, while David and his men retreated to the other. The object of the king now was to surround David, when he must have succumbed to superior numbers. We are told that "David was anxiously endeavouring to go away from before Saul ; and Saul and his men were surrounding David and his men to seize them."[3] *Almost* had they succeeded—but that "almost," which as so often in the history of God's people, calls out earnest faith

---

[1] In our Authorised Version (xxiii. 24) : "the plain on the south of Jeshimon."

[2] Our Authorised Version has erroneously (ver. 25), "he came down into a rock."

[3] Such is the correct rendering of the second half of ver. 26.

and prayer, only proves the real impotence of this world's might as against the Lord. How David in this danger cried unto the Lord, we learn from Ps. liv.[1] How God "delivered him out of all trouble," appears from the sacred narrative. Once more all is in the natural succession of events ; but surely it was in the wonder-working Providence of God that, just when David seemed in the power of his enemies, tidings of an incursion by the Philistines reached Saul, which obliged him hastily to turn against them. And ever afterwards, as David or others passed through that " wilderness," and looked up the face of that cliff, they would remember that God is " the Helper " of His people— for to all time it bore the name " Cliff of Escape." And so we also may in our wanderings have our " cliff of escape," to which ever afterwards we attach this precious remembrance, " Behold, God is thine Helper."

CHAPTER XIII.

Saul in David's power at En-gedi—The Story of Nabal—Saul a second time in David's power.

(1 SAM. XXIV.—XXVI.)

WHEN Saul once more turned upon his victim, David was no longer in the wilderness of Maon. Passing to the north-west, a march of six or seven hours would bring him to En-gedi, "the fountain of the goat," which, leaping down a considerable height in a thin cascade, converts that desert into the most lovely oasis. In this plain, or rather slope, about one mile and a half from north to south, at the foot of abrupt limestone mountains, sheltered from every

[1] We suppose that Psa. liv. refers to this rather than to the second betrayal by the Ziphites, recorded in 1 Sam. xxvi.

storm, in climate the most glorious conceivable, the city of En-gedi had stood, or, as it used to be called, Hazazon Tamar (the Cutting of the Palm-trees), perhaps the oldest place in the world (2 Chron. xx. 2). Through this town (Gen. xiv. 7) the hordes of Chedorlaomer had passed; unchanged it had witnessed the destruction of Sodom and Gomorrah, which must have been clearly visible from the heights above, where the eye can sweep the whole district far up the Jordan valley, and across the Dead Sea to the mountains of Moab. Quite close to the waters of that sea, on which the doom of judgment has ever since rested, a scene of tropical beauty and wealth stretched, such as it is scarcely possible to describe. Bounded by two perennial streams, between which the En-gedi itself makes its way, it must of old have been a little paradise; the plain covered with palm-trees, the slopes up the mountains with the choicest vineyards of Judæa, scented with camphire (Sol. Song i. 14). But all above was "wilderness," bare round limestone hills rising from two hundred to four hundred feet, burrowed by numberless caves, to which the entrance is sometimes almost inaccessible. These were "the rocks of the wild goats," and here was the cave—perhaps that of Wady Charitun, which is said to have once given shelter to no less than thirty thousand men—where David sought safety from the pursuit of the king of Israel.

Wild, weird scenery this, and it reads like a weird story, when the king of Israel enters alone one of those caverns, the very cave in the farthest recesses of which David and his men are hiding. Shall it be life or death? The goal is within easy reach! They have all seen Saul coming, and now whisper it to David with bated breath, to rid himself for ever of his persecutor. The mixture of religion and personal revenge —the presenting it as "the day of which Jehovah had spoken unto him," is entirely true to Oriental nature and to the circumstances. Who would let such an opportunity pass? But it is not by our own hands that we are to be freed from our wrongs, nor is every opportunity to attain our aims, whatever they be, God-sent. There is ever the prior question of plain duty, with which nothing else, however tempting or promising of success, can come into conflict; and such seasons may be only those when our faith and patience are put on trial, so as to bring it clearly before us, whether or not, quite irrespective of all else, we are content to leave everything in the hands of God. And David conquered, as long afterwards his great Antitype overcame the tempter, by steadfast adherence to God's known will and ordinance. Stealthily crawling along, he cut off a corner from the robe which the king had laid aside. That was all the vengeance he took.

It was with some difficulty that David had restrained his men. And now the king had left the cave to rejoin his followers. But still David's conscience smote him, as if he had taken undue liberty with the Lord's anointed. Climbing one of those rocks outside the cave, whence flight would have been easy, his voice startled the king. Looking back into the wild solitude, Saul saw behind him the man who, as his disordered passion had suggested, was seeking his life. With humblest obeisance and in most dutiful language, David told what had just happened. In sharp contrast with the calumnies of his enemies, he described the king's danger, and how he had cast from him the suggestion of his murder. Then bursting into the impassioned language of loyal affection, which had been so cruelly wronged, he held up the piece of the king's mantle which he had cut off, as evidence of the fact that he was innocent of that of which he was accused. But if so—if he had refused to avenge himself even in the hour of his own great danger, leaving judgment to God, and unwilling to put forth his own hand to wickedness, since, as the common proverb had it, "wickedness proceedeth from the wicked"—then, what was the meaning of the king's humiliating pursuit after him? Rather would he, in the conscious innocence of his heart, now appeal to Jehovah, alike for judgment between them two, and for personal deliverance, should these persecutions continue.

Words like these, of which the truth was so evident, could not but make their way even to the heart of Saul. For a moment it seemed as if the dark clouds, which had gathered around his soul and prevented the light penetrating it, were to be scattered. Saul owned his wrong; he owned the justice of David's cause; he even owned the lesson which the events of the past must have so clearly taught, which, indeed, his own persecution of David had, all unconsciously to himself, prophetically indicated, just as did the words of Caiaphas the real meaning of what was done to Jesus (John xi. 49–52). He owned the future of David, and that in his hand the kingdom of Israel would be established; and all this not in words only, but practically, by insisting on a sworn promise that in that future which he foresaw, Oriental vengeance would not be taken of his house.

And yet David himself was not secure against the temptation to personal vengeance and to self-help, although he had resisted it on this occasion. The lesson of his own weakness in that respect was all the more needed, that this was one of the most obvious moral dangers to an ordinary Oriental ruler. But David was not to be such; and when God in His good Providence restrained him as he had almost fallen, He showed him the need of inward as well as of outward deliverance, and the sufficiency of His grace to preserve him from spiritual as from temporal dangers. This may have been one reason why the history of Nabál and Abigail is preserved in Holy Scripture. Another we may find in the circumstance that this incident illustrates not only God's dealings with David, but also the fact that even in the time of his sorest persecutions David was able to take upon himself the care and protection of his countrymen, and so, in a certain sense, proved their leader and king.

The whole story is so true to all the surroundings of place, time, and people, that we can almost portray it to ourselves. Samuel had died, mourned by all Israel. Although his work had long been finished, his name must always have been a tower of strength. He was the link which connected two very different periods, being the last representative of a past which could never come back, and seemed almost centuries behind, and also marking the commencement of a new period, intended to develop into Israel's ideal future. Samuel was, so to speak, the John the Baptist who embodied the old, and initiated the new by preaching repentance as its preparation and foundation. It was probably the death of Samuel which determined David to withdraw still farther south, to the wilderness of Paran,[1] which stretched from the mountains of Judah far to the desert of Sinai. Similarly our blessed Lord withdrew Himself after the death of John the Baptist. In the wilderness of Paran David was not only safe from pursuit, but able to be of real service to his countrymen by protecting the large flocks which pastured far and wide from the predatory raids of the wild tribes of the desert. It was thus (xxv. 7, 15, 16) that David had come into contact with one whom we only know by what was apparently his by-name, Nabal, "fool"—an ominous designation in Old Testament parlance, where "the fool" represented the headstrong, self-willed person, who followed his own course, as if there were "no God" alike in heaven and on earth. And so he is described as "hard"—stubborn, stiff,—and "evil of doings" (ver. 3). His wife Abigail was the very opposite: "good of understanding, and fair of form." Nabal, as Scripture significantly always calls him was a descendant of Caleb. His residence was in Maon, while his "business" was in Carmel, a place about half an hour to the north-west of Maon. Here, no doubt, were his large cotes and folds, whence his immense flocks of sheep and goats pastured the land far and wide. It was the most joyous time for such a proprietor—that of sheep-shearing, when every heart would be open. A time of festivity this (ver. 36), which each would keep according to what was in him. And Nabal had cause for gladness. Thanks to the

---

[1] The LXX., as it seems to us needlessly, alter the text by making it the wilderness of Maon.

ever watchful care of David and his men, he had not suffered the slightest loss (vers. 15, 16); and the rich increase of his flocks crowned another year's prosperity. It was quite in the spirit of an Eastern chieftain in such circumstances, that David sent what would be a specially respectful embassy of ten of his men, with a cordial message of congratulation,[1] in the expectation that at such a time some acknowledgment would be made to those who not only deserved, but must have sorely needed the assistance of a rich Judæan proprietor. But Nabal received David's message with language the most insulting to an Oriental.

The provocation was great, and David was not proof against it. Arming about four hundred of his men, he set out for Carmel, with the determination to right himself and take signal vengeance. Assuredly this was not the lesson which God had hitherto made David learn, nor that which He wished His anointed to teach to others. It was the zeal of the sons of Boanerges, not the meekness of Him Who was David's great Antitype. And so God kept His servant from presumptuous sin.[2] Once more God's interposition came in the natural course of events. A servant who had overheard what had passed, and naturally dreaded the consequences, informed Abigail. Her own resolve was quickly taken. Sending forward a present princely in amount,[3] even in comparison with that which at a later period Barzillai brought to King David when on his flight from Absalom (2 Sam. xvii. 27–29), she hastily followed. Coming down the hollow of a hill ("the covert of a hill"), she found herself of a sudden in the presence of David and his armed men. But her courage was not shaken.

[1] Ver. 6, which is somewhat difficult, should, I think, be thus rendered : "And ye shall say thus : To life! Both to thee peace, to thy house peace, and to all that is thine peace !"

[2] Although guilty of a rash imprecation (ver. 22), it was at least not upon himself.

[3] The "bottles" were, of course, "skins of wine;" "the clusters" and "cakes" of fruit were large compressed cakes, such as are common in the East.

With humblest Oriental obeisance, she addressed David, first taking all the guilt on herself, as one on whom David would not stoop to wreak vengeance. Surely one like Nabal was not a fit object for controversy; and, as for herself, she had known nothing of what had passed.

But there were far weightier arguments for David's forbearance. Was it not evidently God's Providence which had sent her for a high and holy purpose? "And now, my lord, as Jehovah liveth, and as thy soul liveth, that (it is) Jehovah who has withheld thee from coming into blood-guiltiness, and from thy hand delivering thyself." This twofold sin had been averted. Such was her first argument. But further, was it not well to leave it to God—would not Jehovah Himself avenge His servant, and make all his enemies as Nabal—showing them to be but "Nabal," "fools" in the Scriptural sense, with all the impotence and ruin which this implied? It was only after having urged all this, that Abigail ventured to ask acceptance of her gift, offering it, as if unworthy of him, to David's men rather than to himself (ver. 27). Then returning to the prayer for forgiveness, she pointed David to the bright future which, she felt assured, was reserved for him, since he was not pursuing *private* aims, nor would he afterwards charge himself with any wrong in this matter. How closely all this tallied with her former pleas will be evident. In pursuance of her reasoning she continued : " And (though) a man is risen to pursue thee, and to seek thy soul, and (yet) the soul of my lord is bound up in the bundle of life with Jehovah thy God; and the soul of thine enemies shall He sling out from the hollow of the sling." Finally, she reminded him that when God had fulfilled all His gracious promises, this would not become a "stumbling-block" to him, nor yet be a burden on his conscience, that he had needlessly shed blood and righted himself.

Wiser speech, in the highest as well as in a worldly sense, than that of Abigail can scarcely be imagined. Surely if any one, she was fitted to become the companion and adviser of

David.   Three things in her speech chiefly impress themselves on our minds as most important for the understanding
of this history.   The fact that David was God's anointed,
on whom the kingdom would devolve, seems now to have
been the conviction of all who were godly in Israel.   They
knew it, and they expected it.   Equally strong was their
belief that David's present, as his future mission, was simply to
contend for God and for His people.   But most important of
all was the deep feeling prevalent, that David must not try
to right himself, nor work his own deliverance.   This was a
thoroughly spiritual principle, which had its foundation in absolute, almost childlike trust in Jehovah the living God, whatever
might were arrayed against David, and however the probabilities
might seem other to the outward observer.   Viewed in this
light, the whole contest between David and Saul would assume
spiritual proportions.   There was nothing personal now in the
conflict; least of all, was it to be regarded as an attempt at
rebellion against, or dethronement of Saul.   The cause was
altogether God's; only David must not right himself, but in
faith and patience await the fulfilment of God's sure and steadfast promises.   To have the matter thus set before him, was
to secure the immediate assent of David's conscience.   Recognising the great spiritual danger from which he had just been
delivered, he gave thanks to God, and then to the wise and
pious woman who had been the instrument in His hand.

Meantime Nabal had been in ignorance alike of what had
threatened him, and of what his wife had done to avert it.
On her return, she found him rioting and in drunkenness.
Not till next morning, when he was once more capable of
understanding what had passed, did she inform him of all.   A
fit of impotent fury on the part of one who was scarcely sobered,
resulted in what seems to have been a stroke of apoplexy.
If this had been brought on by himself, the second and
fatal stroke, which followed ten days later, is set before us as
sent directly by God.   It is not often that Divine vengeance
so manifestly and so quickly overtakes evil-doing.   David

fully recognised this. Nor can we wonder, that on reviewing his own deliverance from spiritual danger, and the advice which had led to it, he should have wished to have her who had given it always by his side. In connection with this the sacred text also notes the union of David with Ahinoam of Jezreel,[1] consequent probably on Saul's cruel and heartless separation between David and Michal, whom he gave to one Phalti, or Phaltiel (2 Sam. iii. 15) of Gallim in Benjamin (Isa. x. 30). Thus Saul himself had wilfully and recklessly severed the last ties which had bound David to him.

Yet another bitter experience of betrayal and persecution was in store for David. Probably trusting to his new connection with two, no doubt, powerful families in the district—those of Ahinoam and of Abigail — David seems again to have advanced northwards from the wilderness of Paran. Once more we find David in the wilderness of Ziph—the most northern and the nearest to the cities of Judah. And once more the Ziphites were negociating with Saul for his betrayal, and the king of Israel was marching against him with the three thousand men, who apparently formed the nucleus of his standing army.[2] Some years before, when betrayed by the Ziphites, David had on the approach of Saul retired to the wilderness of Maon, and been only preserved by tidings to Saul of a Philistine incursion. On yet another somewhat similar occasion, in the wilderness of En-gedi, David had had his enemy in his power, when Saul had entered alone a cave in which David and his men lay concealed. In this instance, however, the circumstances were different, alike as concerned the situation of Saul's camp, the location of David, the manner in which he came into contact with Saul, and even the communication

[1] This Jezreel is, of course, not the place of that name in the north (Josh. xix. 18), but a town in Judah near Carmel (Josh. xv. 56).

[2] Such a nucleus seems implied in 1 Sam. xiii. 2, where we have the same number, constituting apparently Saul's standing army. From our remarks it will be seen that we entirely repudiate the rash assertion that this is only another account of what had been related in 1 Sam. xxiii. 19–xxiv. 22.

which subsequently passed between them.   The points of
resemblance are just those which might have been expected :
the treachery of the Ziphites, tne means taken by Saul against
David, the suggestion made to David to rid himself of his
enemy, his firm resolve not to touch the Lord's anointed,
as well as an interview between David and his persecutor,
followed by temporary repentance.   But the two narratives
are essentially different.   On learning that Saul and his army
were encamped on the slope of the hill Hachilah, David and
two of his bravest companions—Ahimelech, the Hittite, and
Abishai, the son of Zeruiah, David's sister—resolved to ascertain the exact situation of the enemy.   Creeping under cover
of night through the brushwood, which as we know covered the
sides of the hill (xxiii. 19), they found themselves soon where
the camp of Israel lay open to them.   As we imagine the
scene, the three had gained the height just above the camp.
Faithful as was the Hittite, and none more true or brave than
he (comp. 2 Sam. xi. 3, 6 ; xxiii. 39), it was David's nephew
Abishai, probably of the same age, who now volunteered to
share with him the extremely perilous attempt of "going down"
into the camp itself.   But there was no murderous intent in
the heart of David ; rather the opposite, of proving his innocence of it.   And so God blessed it.   A deep sleep—evidently
from the Lord—weighed them all down.   In the middle, by the
" waggons " of the camp, lay Saul, at his head the royal spear
stuck in the ground, and a cruse of water beside him.   Close
by lay Abner, as chief of the host, to whom, so to speak, the
custody of the king was entrusted—and all round in wide
circle, the people.   Once more comes the tempting suggestion
to David.   This time it is not his own hand, but Abishai's,
that is to deal the blow.   But what matters it : " For who
has stretched out his hand against the anointed of Jehovah,
and been unpunished ?   If Jehovah do not (literally, ' unless
Jehovah ') smite him [like Nabal], or his day be come and
he die, or he go down into the war and be swept away—far
be it from me, through Jehovah !—to stretch forth mine hand

against Jehovah's anointed."[1]   And so David stayed the hand of his companion.

Noiselessly the two have removed the royal spear and the cruse from the side of Saul.   They have crept back through the camp of sleepers, and through the brushwood, crossed the intervening valley, and gained a far-off height on the other side.   Who dares break the king's slumber in the middle of his camp?   But another ear than Abner's has heard, and has recognised the voice of David.   It has gone right to the heart of Saul, as he learns how once more his life had been wholly in the power of him whom he has so unrelentingly and so wickedly persecuted.   Again he seems repentant, though he heeds not David's advice that, if these constant persecutions were the effect produced on his mind by the spirit of evil from the Lord, he should seek pardon and help by means of sacrifice; but if the outcome of calumnious reports, those who brought them should be regarded as sure of the Divine judgment, since, as he put it, "They drive me out this day, that I cannot join myself to the heritage of Jehovah, saying (thereby in effect): Go, serve other gods" (xxvi. 19).   It is useless to follow the matter farther.   Saul's proposal for David's return, and his promise of safety, were, no doubt, honestly meant at the time, just as are the sorrow and resolutions of many into whose consciences the light has for a time fallen.   But David knew otherwise of Saul; and it marks an advance in his spiritual experience that he preferred committing himself to God rather than trusting in man.

[1] We have translated as literally as possible.   David considers that the guilt would have been equally his, although the deed had been done by Abishai.

CHAPTER XIV.

David's Second Flight to Gath—Residence at Ziklag—Expedition of the Philistines against Israel—Saul at Jezreel—He resorts to the Witch at Endor—Apparition and Message of Samuel—David has to leave the Army of the Philistines—Capture of Ziklag by the Amalekites—Pursuit and Victory of David.

(I SAM. XXVII.—XXX.)

THE parting appeal of David sounds specially solemn when we remember that this was the last meeting of these two. Feeling that some day he might "fall into the hand of Saul,"[1] and that henceforth there was "no good for him,"[1] he resolved once more to seek shelter with King Achish at Gath. His reception this time was very different from that on the former occasion. For years David had been treated by Saul as his avowed enemy. He came now not as a solitary fugitive, but at the head of a well-trained band of brave men, to place himself and them, as it would seem, at the disposal of Achish. He met a most friendly welcome, and for a time was located with his men in the royal city itself. This, of course, entailed restraints such as would have proved most irksome, if not impossible, to David. The pretext that the presence of such a large band under their own chieftain was scarcely becoming in the capital of his new royal master, furnished the plea for asking and obtaining another place of residence. For this purpose Ziklag was assigned to him— a city first belonging to Judah (Josh. xv. 31), and afterwards to Simeon (Josh. xix. 5), which lay close to the southern border of the land of Israel. Of course, the inference is fair that, at the time of which we write, it had been in the possession of the

---

[1] So literally (xxvii. 1).

Philistines, and was probably deserted by its former inhabitants. No other place could have suited David so well. Whether we regard his raids against the heathen tribes, which was "his manner" during the whole year and four months that he was with the Philistines, as intended to repel their inroads into the territory of Israel, or else as incursions into heathen lands, the situation of Ziklag would afford him equal facilities. On every such occasion, as he returned laden with spoil, he took care to report himself at Gath, partly to disarm suspicion,[1] and partly, no doubt, to secure the good will of Achish by giving him a large share of the booty. His reports may have been true to the letter—giving it a forced meaning,—but they were certainly untrue in spirit. But David never brought captives with him to Gath,[2] who might have betrayed him, but always destroyed all who had witnessed his attacks.

If by means of these reported frequent successes in the land of Israel David secured the confidence of Achish, as one who had irretrievably broken with his own people, and if by the rich booty which he brought he besides obtained the favour of the Philistine, he was once more to experience that real safety was not to be gained by untruthfulness. Again there was to be war between the Philistines and Israel, this time on a larger scale than any since the first contest with Saul. It was but natural that Achish should have wished to swell his contingent to the army of the united Philistine princes by so large, well-trained, and, as he believed, trusty band as that of David. Of course, there was no alternative but to obey such a summons, although it must be admitted that the words of David, both on this occasion (xxviii. 2), and afterwards, when dismissed the camp of the Philistines (xxix. 8), are capable of

[1] The words of the question in xxvii. 10 are so dark in the original as to need slight alteration. The rendering of the LXX., "Against whom made ye invasion?" is evidently the correct reading of the text.

[2] The Authorised Version supplies erroneously in ver. 11 "to bring *tidings*"—the reference is clearly to captives. The last clause of ver. 11 is a substantive sentence, being part of the narrative, and not of what the captives had said.

two interpretations. Achish, however, took them in what seemed their obvious meaning, and promised in return ("there- fore"—for that) to make David the chief of his body-guard. It need scarcely be told, what terrible anxieties this unexpected turn of events must have brought to David, or how earnestly he must have prayed and trusted that, at the right moment, some "way of escape" would be made for him.

The sacred narrative now carries us successively to the camp of Israel and to that of the Philistines. The battle- field was to be once more the Plain of Jezreel, where of old Gideon with his three hundred had defeated the hosts of Midian (Judg. vii.). A spot this full of happy, glorious memo- ries; but, ah, how sadly altered were the circumstances! Gideon had been the God-called hero, who was to conquer in His might; Saul was the God-forsaken king, who was hastening to judgment and ruin. And each knew and felt it— Gideon when he was content to reduce his forces to three hundred men, and then crept down with his armour-bearer to hear the enemy foretell his own destruction; and Saul when viewing the host of the Philistines across the plain, "he was afraid, and his heart greatly trembled" (xxviii. 5), and when all his enquiries of the Lord remained without answer. It seems strange, and yet, as we think, it is most truthfully cha- racteristic of Saul, that, probably after the death of Samuel, he displayed special theocratic zeal by a systematic raid upon all necromancy in the land, in accordance with Lev. xix. 31; xx. 27; Deut. xviii. 10, etc. Such outward conformity to the law of God, not only from political motives, but from those of such religiousness as he was capable of, seems to us one of the most striking psychological confirmations of the history of Saul.

The reason why the scene of battle was laid so far north, distant alike from the cities of the Philistine princes and from the residence of Saul, was, in all probability, that the Philistines now wished to obtain such undoubted supremacy in the north of Palestine as they seem to have virtually possessed in the south.

A great victory in Jezreel would not only cut the land, so to speak, in two, but give them the key both to the south and to the north. With this view, then, the Philistines chose their ground. Where the great plain of Esdraelon shelves down to the Jordan it is broken in the east by two mountain-ranges. On the southern side of the valley, which is here about three miles wide, are the mountains of Gilboa, and at their foot, or rather spur, lies Jezreel, where the spring which gushes down is gathered into a pool of considerable size. On the northern side of the valley is Little Hermon, and at its foot the rich village of Shunem (the "twain rest"). Behind and to the north of Little Hermon runs another narrow branch of the plain. On its other side is the mountain where Endor lay amidst most desolate scenery; and in one of its many lime-stone caves was the scene of Saul's last interview with Samuel. Nor is it void of significance to us that Endor was but a few miles from Nazareth; for it is the close contiguity of these contrasting scenes which often sheds such lurid light upon events.

From his camp on the slopes of Gilboa and by the spring of Jezreel, Saul had anxiously watched the gathering hosts of Philistia on the opposite side at Shunem, and his heart had utterly failed him. Where was now the Lord God of Israel? Certainly not with Saul. And where was there now a David to meet another Goliath? Saul had successively "enquired of Jehovah" by all the well-known means, from the less to the more spiritual,[1] but without answer. That alone

---

[1] We venture to regard the "dreams," the "Urim," and the "prophets," as marking progress from the lower to the higher modes of enquiry. In accordance with the principles implied when treating of the gatherings of the "prophets," it seems to us that the more passive the instrumentality employed, the lower the stage in the mode of Divine communication. What we have ventured to call the lower or more mechanical stages of communication were adapted to the varying stages of spiritual development. But the absolutely highest stage of intercourse with God is the indwelling of the Holy Ghost in the New Testament Church, when man's individuality is not superseded nor suppressed, but transformed, and thus conformed to Him in spiritual fellowship.

should have been sufficient, had Saul possessed spiritual under-standing to perceive its meaning. Had his been real enquiry of *the Lord*,[1] he would have felt his desertion, and even now returned to Him in humble penitence; just as Judas, if his repentance had been genuine and true, would have gone out to seek pardon like Peter, instead of rushing in despair to self-destruction. As the event proved, Saul did *not* really enquire of the Lord, in the sense of seeking direction from Him, and of being willing to be guided by it. Rather did he, if we may so express it, wish to use the Lord as the means by which to obtain his object. But that was essen-tially the heathen view, and differed only in detail, not in principle, from the enquiry of a familiar spirit, to which he afterwards resorted. Accordingly the latter must be regarded as explaining his former " enquiry," and determining its cha-racter. In this sense the notice in 1 Chron. x. 14 affords a true and spiritual insight into the transaction.

Already the utter darkness of despair had gathered around Saul. He was condemned : he knew it, felt it, and his con-science assented to it. What was to happen on the morrow? To that question he must have an answer, be it what it may. If he could not have it from God, he must get it somewhere else. To whom should he turn in his extremity? Only one person, sufficiently powerful with God and man, occurred to his mind. It was Samuel,—the very incarnation to him of Divine power, the undoubted messenger of God, the one man who had ever confronted and overawed him. It seems like fate which drives him to the very man who had so sternly, unrelentingly, and in the hour of his triumph, told him his downfall. But how was he to meet Samuel? By necromancy —that is, by devilry ! The Divine through the anti-Divine,

---

[1] If it be asked how Saul could enquire by Urim, since Abiathar, and with him "the Ephod," were with David, we reply that Saul had evidently appointed Zadok successor to Abiathar (1 Chron. xvi. 39, comp. vi. 8, 53), and located the tabernacle at Gibeon. This explains the mention of two high-priests in the early years of David's reign (comp. 2 Sam. viii. 17; xv. 24, 29, 35; 1 Chron. xv. 11; xviii. 16).

communication from on high by means of witchcraft: terrible
contrasts these—combined, alas! in the life of Saul, and strangely
connecting its beginning with its ending.   But no matter; if it
be at all possible, he must see Samuel, however he had parted
from him in life.   Samuel had announced his elevation, let him
now come to tell him his fate; he had pushed him to the brow
of the hill, let him show what was beneath.   And yet who could
say what might happen, or to what that interview might lead?
For deep down in the breast of each living there is still, even
in his despairing, the possibility of hope.

It is the most vivid description in Holy Scripture, next to
that of the night of Judas' betrayal.   Putting on the disguise
of a common man, and only attended by two companions,
Saul starts at dark.   It was eight miles round the eastern
shoulder of Hermon to Endor.   None in the camp of Israel
must know whither and on what errand the king has gone;
and he has to creep round the back of the position of the
Philistines, who lie on the front slope of Hermon.   Nor must
"the woman, possessor of an *Ob*"—or spirit by which the
dead can be conjured up (Lev. xx. 27)—know it, that he who
enquires of her is the one who "hath cut off those that have
familiar spirits and the wizards out of the land."

It was night when Saul and his companions wearily reached
their destination.   They have roused the wretched impostor,
"the woman, possessor of an *Ob*," and quieted her fears by
promise that her nefarious business should not be betrayed.
To her utter horror it is for once truth.   God has allowed
Samuel to obey Saul's summons; and, to be unmistakeable,
he appears, as he was wont in life, wrapped in his prophet's
meïl, or mantle.   The woman sees the apparition,[1] and from
her description Saul has no difficulty in recognising Samuel,

[1] 1 Sam. xxviii. 13: "I saw gods" (or rather, *Elohim*) "ascending out
of the earth."   The expression Elohim here refers not to a Divine, but simply
to a supernatural appearance, indicating its *character* as not earthly.   But
in that supernatural light she has also recognised her visitor as the king of
Israel.   Verses 13 and 14 show that Saul had *not* himself seen the apparition.   The question whether the vision of the woman was objective or

and he falls in lowly reverence on his face. During the whole interview between them the king remains on his knees. What a difference between the last meeting of the two and this! But the old prophet has nothing to abate, nothing to alter. There is inexpressible pathos in the king's cry of despair: " Make known to me what I shall do!" What he shall do! But Samuel had all his life-time made it known to him, and Saul had resisted. The time for doing was now past. In quick succession it comes, like thunderbolt on thunderbolt: " Jehovah thine enemy " ; "Jehovah hath rent the kingdom out of thine hand, and given it to David " ; " thy sins have overtaken thee ! All this Saul knew long ago, although he had never realised it as now. And then as to his fate : *to-morrow—* defeat, death, slaughter, to Saul, to his sons, to Israel!

One by one, each stroke heavier than the other, they had pitilessly fallen on the kneeling king, weary, faint from want of food, and smitten to the heart with awe and terror ; and now he falls heavily, his gigantic length, to the ground. The woman and Saul's companions had stood aside, nor had any heard what had passed between the two. But the noise of his fall brought them to his side. With difficulty they persuade him to eat ere he starts on his weary return to Jezreel. At last he yields ; and, rising from his prostrate position, sits down on the divan, while they wait on him. But he has no longer speech, or purpose, or thought. As one driven to the slaughter, he goes back to meet his doom. It must have been early morning when once more he reached Gilboa—the morning of the dread and decisive battle.[1]

---

subjective, is really of no importance whatever. Suffice that it was *real*, and came to her *ab extra*.

[1] As will be seen, we regard the apparition of Samuel not as trickery by the woman, but as real—nor yet as caused by the devil, but as allowed and willed of God. A full discussion of our reasons for this view would be evidently out of place. Of two things only will we remind the reader : the story must not be explained on our modern Western ideas of the ecstatic, somnambulistic, magnetic state (Erdmann), nor be judged according to the standpoint which the Church has *now* reached. It was *quite* in accordance with the stage in which the kingdom of God was in the days of Saul.

The sacred narrative now turns once more to the Philistine host. The trysting-place for the contingents of the five allied "lords" or kings of the Philistines was at Aphek, probably the same as on a previous occasion (1 Sam. iv. 1).[1] As they marched past, the division of Achish formed "the rearward." When the Philistine leaders saw David and his men amongst them, they not unnaturally objected to their presence. In vain Achish urged their faithfulness since they had "fallen away" to him. As it appeared to them, one who had in the past taken such a stand as David could never be trusted; and how better could he make his peace with his master than by turning traitor to the Philistines in the hour of their supreme need? And so, however reluctantly, Achish had to yield. David's remonstrance, couched in ambiguous language, was perhaps scarcely such (1 Sam. xxix. 8), but rather intended to make sure of the real views of Achish in regard to him. But it must have been with the intense relief of a realised God-given deliverance, that early next morning, ere the camp was astir, David and his men quitted its outskirts, where the rear-guard lay, to return to Ziklag.

It was the third day when the Hebrews reached their Philistine home. But what a sight greeted them here! Broken walls, blackened ruins, and the desolateness of utter silence all around! The Amalekites had indeed taken vengeance for David's repeated raids upon them (xxvii. 8). They had made an incursion into the *Negeb*, or south country, and specially upon Ziklag. In the absence of its defenders, the place fell an easy prey. After laying it waste, the Amalekites took with them all the women and children, as well as the cattle, and any other booty on which they could lay hands. It was a

---

[1] Most writers suppose that this Aphek was close to Shunem, though the supposition by no means tallies with the narrative. There is, however, this insuperable objection to it, that as Shunem is between eighty and ninety miles from where Ziklag must be sought, David and his men could not possibly have reached the latter "on the third day."

terrible surprise, and the first effect upon David and his men was truly Oriental (xxx. 4). But it is both characteristic of David's followers, and indicates with what reluctance they must have followed him to Aphek, that they actually thought of killing David, as if he had been the author of that ill-fated expedition after Achish which had brought them such hopeless misery. It was bitter enough to have lost his own family, and now David was in danger of his life from the mutiny of his men. Had God spared him for this? On the very morning when they had broken up from Aphek, making almost forced marches to traverse the fifty miles to Ziklag, their homes had been utterly laid waste. Why all this? Did the Lord make him tarry, as Jesus did "beyond Jordan," till Lazarus had been three days dead? Never more than on occasion of extreme and seemingly hopeless straits did David prove the reality of his religion by rising to the loftiest heights of faith and prayer. The text gives a marked emphasis to the contrast : " But David strengthened himself in Jehovah his God." His resolve was quickly taken. The first thing was to enquire of the Lord whether he should pursue the Amalekites. The answer was even fuller than he had asked, for it promised him also complete success. The next thing was hasty pursuit of the enemy. So rapid was it, that when they reached the brook Besor, which flows into the sea to the south of Gaza, two hundred of his men, who, considering the state in which they had found Ziklag, must have been but ill-provisioned, had to be left behind.[1]

They soon came on the track of the Amalekites. They had found an Egyptian slave, whom his inhuman master had, on the hasty retreat from Ziklag, left by the wayside to starve rather than hamper himself with the care of a sick man. Food soon

[1] It is a curious instance of the resemblance of the popular parlance of all nations and ages, that the word in vers. 10, 21, rendered by "faint," literally means " were corpsed "—the same as in some districts of our own country. The Hebrew word is evidently a vulgarism, for it occurs only in these two verses.

revived him ; and, on promise of safety and freedom, he offered
to be the guide of the party to the place which, as he knew,
the Amalekites had fixed upon as sufficiently far from Ziklag to
permit them to feast in safety on their booty. A short-lived
security theirs. It was the twilight—the beginning, no doubt,
of a night of orgies—when David surprised them, "lying
about on the ground," "eating and drinking, and dancing."
No watch had been set; no weapon was in any man's hands;
no danger was apprehended. We can picture to ourselves the
scene : how David probably surrounded the camping-place ;
and with what shouts of vengeance the infuriated Hebrews fell
on those who could neither resist nor flee. All night long, all
the next day the carnage lasted. Only four hundred servant-
lads, who had charge of the camels, escaped. Everything that
had been taken by the Amalekites was recovered, besides the
flocks and herds of the enemy, which were given to David as
his share of the spoil. Best of all, the women and children
were safe and unhurt.

It was characteristic of the wicked and worthless among
the followers of David, that when on their return march they
came again to those two hundred men who had been left
behind "faint," they proposed not to restore to them what of
theirs had been recovered from the Amalekites, except their
wives and children. Rough, wild men were many among
them, equally depressed in the day of adversity, and recklessly elated and insolent in prosperity. Nor is it merely the
discipline which David knew to maintain in such a band that
shows us "the skilfulness of his hands" in guiding them, but
the gentleness with which he dealt with them, and, above
all, the earnest piety with which he knew to tame their wild
passions prove the spiritual "integrity," or "perfectness, of
his heart" (Ps. lxxviii. 72). Many a wholesome custom, which
ever afterwards prevailed in Israel, as well as that of equally
dividing the spoil among combatants and non-combatants in
an army (1 Sam. xxx. 24, 25), must have dated not only from
the time of David, but even from the period of his wanderings

and persecutions. Thus did he prove his fitness for the government long ere he attained to it.

Yet another kindred trait was David's attachment to friends who had stood by him in seasons of distress. As among his later servants and officials we find names connected with the history of his wanderings (1 Chron. xxvii. 27–31), so even now he sent presents from his spoil to "the elders" of the various cities of the South,[1] where his wanderings had been, and who had proved "his friends" by giving him help in the time of need. It may indeed have been that the south generally had suffered from the incursion of the Amalekites against Ziklag (xxx. 1). But such loss could scarcely have been made up by "presents" from David. His main object, next to grateful acknowledgment of past aid, must have been to prepare them for publicly owning him, at the proper time, as the chosen leader of God's people, who would make "spoil of the enemies of Jehovah." At the proper time! But while these gifts were passing, all unknown to David, that time had already come.

[1] The places enumerated in 1 Sam. xxx. 27–31 were all in the south country. The Bethel mentioned in ver. 27, was, of course, not the city of that name in the tribe of Benjamin, but Bethuel, or Bethul (1 Chron. iv. 30), in the tribe of Simeon (Josh. xix. 4).

CHAPTER XV.

(1 Sam. xxxi.—2 Sam. iv.)

BRIEF as are the accounts of the battle of Gilboa (1 Sam.
xxxi. ; 1 Chron. x.), we can almost picture the scene. The
attack seems to have been made by the Philistines. Slowly
and stubbornly the Israelites yielded, and fell back from Jezreel
upon Mount Gilboa. All day long the fight lasted ; and the
darkness seems to have come on before the Philistines knew
the full extent of their success, or could get to the sad work of
pillaging the dead. Ill had it fared with Israel that day.
Their slain covered the sides of Mount Gilboa. The three
sons of Saul—foremost among them the noble Jonathan—
had fallen in the combat. Saul himself had retreated on
Gilboa. But the battle had gone sore against him. And now
the enemy's sharpshooters had "found him "[1]—come up with
him. Thus the fatal moment had arrived : " Saul was sore
afraid." But if he fell, let it at least not be by the hand of
the Philistines, lest Israel's hereditary enemy "make sport "[2]
of the disabled, dying king. Saul will die a king. The
last service he asks of his armour-bearer is to save him from
falling into Philistine hands by thrusting him through. But
the armour-bearer dares not lift his sword against the Lord's
anointed, and Saul plants his now otherwise useless sword

[1] So correctly, and not, as in our Authorised Version (ver. 3), "the archers
hit him, and he was sore wounded."
[2] So literally in ver. 4, rendered in the Authorised Version, "abuse me."

on the ground, and tnrows himself upon it.   The faithful
armour-bearer follows his master's example.   Soon all Saul's
personal attendants have likewise been cut down (1 Sam.
xxxi. 6 ; comp. 1 Chron. x. 6).

And now darkness stayed further deeds of blood.   Before
the morning light the tidings of Israel's defeat had spread
far and wide.   North of the valley of Jezreel, and even across
the Jordan,[1] which rolled close by, the people deserted the
cities and fled into the open country, leaving their strongholds to the conquerors.   Meantime the plunderers were busy
searching and stripping the dead in Jezreel and on Mount
Gilboa.   They found what they could scarcely have expected :
the dead bodies of Saul and of his three sons.   To strip
them would have been comparatively little ; but to add every
insult, they cut off the heads of the king and of his sons,
leaving the naked carcases unburied.   The gory heads and the
bloody armour were sent round through Philistia, "to publish it
in the houses of their idols, and among the people."   Finally,
the armour was distributed among the temples of the Ashtaroth
(the Phœnician Venus), while the skull of Saul was fastened up
in the great temple of Dagon.

But the Philistine host had not halted.   They advanced to
occupy the towns deserted by the Hebrews.   The main body
occupied Bethshan, the great mountain-fortress of Central
Palestine, which from the top of a steep brow, inaccessible to
horsemen, seemed to command not only the Jordan valley,
but also all the country round.   As if in utter scorn and
defiance, they hung out on the walls of Bethshan the headless trunks of Saul and of his sons.   And now night with
her dark mantle once more covered these horrible trophies.
Shall the eagles and vultures complete the work which, no
doubt, they had already begun ?   The tidings had been carried

[1] Commentators have raised, as it seems to me, needless difficulties about
an expression which always means "east of the Jordan."   There cannot
be anything incredible in the border-towns on the other side of Jordan
being deserted by their inhabitants.   If such a strong fortress as Bethshan
was given up, why not smaller places across the Jordan ?

across the Jordan, and wakened echoes in one of Israel's cities. It was to Jabesh-gilead that Saul, when only named but not yet acknowledged king, had by a forced night-march brought help, delivering it from utter destruction (1 Sam. xi.). That had been the morning of Saul's life, bright and promising as none other; his first glorious victory, which had made him king by acclamation, and drawn Israel's thousands to that gathering in Gilgal, when, amidst the jubilee of an exultant people, the new kingdom was inaugurated. And now it was night; and the headless bodies of Saul and his sons, deserted by all, swung in the wind on the walls of Bethshan, amid the hoarse music of vultures and jackals.

But it must not be so; it cannot be so. There was still truth, gratitude, and courage in Israel. And the brave men of Jabesh-gilead marched all the weary night; they crossed Jordan ; they climbed that steep brow, and silently detached the dead bodies from the walls. Reverently they bore them across the river, and ere the morning light were far out of reach of the Philistines. Though it had always been the custom in Israel to bury the dead, they would not do so to these mangled remains, that they they might not, as it were, perpetuate their disgrace. They burned them just sufficiently to destroy all traces of insult, and the bones they reverently laid under their great tamarisk tree, themselves fasting for seven days in token of public mourning. All honour to the brave men of Jabesh-gilead, whose deed Holy Scripture has preserved to all generations !

It was the third day after the return of David and his men to Ziklag. Every heart must have been heavy with anxiety for tidings of that great decisive struggle between the Philistines and Saul which they knew to be going on, when all at once a messenger came, whose very appearance betokened disaster and mourning (comp. 1 Sam. iv. 12). It was a stranger, the son of an Amalekite settler in Israel, who brought sad and strange tidings. By his own account, he had fled to Ziklag straight out of the camp of Israel, to tell of the defeat and slaughter of Israel, and of the death of Saul and of Jonathan.

As he related the story, he had, when the tide of battle turned against Israel, come by accident upon Saul, who stood alone on the slope of Gilboa leaning upon his spear, while the Philistine chariots and horsemen were closing in around him. On perceiving him, and learning that he was an Amalekite, the king had said, "Stand now to me and slay me, for cramp has seized upon me—for my life is yet wholly in me."[1] On this the Amalekite had "stood to" him, and killed him, "for"—as he added in explanation, probably referring to the illness which from fear and grief had seized Saul, forcing him to lean for support on his spear—"I knew that he would not live after he had fallen;[2] and I took the crown that was on his head, and the arm-band which was upon his arm, and I brought them to my lord—here!"

Improbable as the story would have appeared on calm examination, and utterly untrue as we know it to have been, David's indignant and horrified expostulation, how he had dared to destroy Jehovah's anointed (2 Sam. i. 14), proves that in the excitement of the moment he had regarded the account as substantially correct. The man had testified against himself: he held in his hand as evidence the king's crown and arm-band. If he had not murdered Saul, he had certainly stripped him when dead. And now he had come to David, evidently thinking he had done a deed grateful to him, for which he would receive reward, thus making David a partaker in his horrible crime. David's inmost soul recoiled from such a deed as murder of his sovereign and daring presumption against Jehovah, Whose anointed he was. Again and again, when defending precious life, Saul had been in his power, and he had rejected with the strongest energy of which he was capable the suggestion to ensure his own safety by the death of his persecutor. And that from which in the hour of his supreme

---

[1] This is the correct rendering of 2 Sam. i. 9.

[2] Most critics understand the expression "after he had fallen," to refer to his defeat. But there really seems no occasion for this. It is quite rational to suppose that the Amalekite meant that, in his state of body, Saul would be unable to defend himself against an attack.

danger he had recoiled, this Amalekite had now done in cold blood for hope of a reward ! Every feeling would rise within him to punish the deed ; and if he failed or hesitated, well might he be charged before all Israel with being an accomplice of the Amalekite. " Thy blood on thy head ! for thy mouth hath testified upon thyself, saying, I have slain the anointed of Jehovah." And the sentence thus spoken was immediately executed.

It was real and sincere grief which led David and his men to mourn, and weep, and fast until even for Saul and for Jonathan, and for their fallen countrymen in their twofold capacity as belonging to the Church and the nation (" the people of Jehovah and the house of Israel," ver. 12). One of the finest odes in the Old Testament perpetuated their memory. This elegy, composed by David " to teach the children of Israel," bears the general title of *Kasheth*, as so many of the Psalms have kindred inscriptions. In our text it appears as extracted from that collection of sacred heroic poetry, called *Sepher hajjashar*, "book of the just." It consists, after a general superscription, of two unequal stanzas, each beginning with the line : " Alas, the heroes have fallen !" The second stanza refers specially to Jonathan, and at the close of the ode the head-line is repeated, with an addition, indicating Israel's great loss. The two stanzas mark, so to speak, a descent from deepest grief for those so brave, so closely connected, and so honoured, to expression of personal feelings for Jonathan, the closing lines sounding like the last sigh over a loss too great for utterance. Peculiarly touching is the absence in this elegy of even the faintest allusion to David's painful relations to Saul in the past. All that is merely personal seems blotted out, or rather, as if it had never existed in the heart of David. In this respect we ought to regard this ode as casting most valuable light on the real meaning and character of what are sometimes called the vindictive and imprecatory Psalms. Nor should we omit to notice, what a German divine has so aptly pointed out : that, with the exception of the lament of Jabesh-gilead, the only real mourning for Saul was on the part of David, whom the king had so bitterly persecuted to the death—reminding us in this also of David's great Antitype, Who alone of all wept over that Jerusalem which was preparing to betray and crucify Him ! The elegy itself reads as follows :

"The adornment of Israel on thy heights thrust through !
       Alas,[1] the heroes have fallen !
Announce it not in Gath, publish it not as glad tidings in the streets
    of Askelon,
       Lest the daughters of the Philistines rejoice,
       Lest the daughters of the uncircumcised jubilee !
O mountains in Gilboa—no dew, nor rain upon you, nor fields of first-
    fruit offerings—
    For there defiled is the shield of the heroes,
    The shield of Saul, no more anointed with oil !
    From blood of slain, from fat of heroes
    The bow of Jonathan turned not backward,
    And the sword of Saul returned not void (lacking) !
    Saul and Jonathan, the loved and the pleasant,
    In their life and in their death were not parted—
    Than eagles were they lighter, than lions stronger !
    Daughters of Israel, over Saul weep ye,
    Who clad you in purple with loveliness,
    Who put jewels of gold upon your clothing !
    Alas, the heroes have fallen in the midst of the contest—
       Jonathan, on thy heights thrust through !
    Woe is me for thee, my brother Jonathan,—
    Pleasant wast thou to me exceedingly,
    More marvellous thy love to me than the love of women !
    Alas, the heroes have fallen—
    And perished are the weapons of war ! "[2]

But the present was not a time for mourning only. So far as men could judge, there was no further necessity for David's exile. But even so he would not act without express Divine

---

[1] Our translation is an attempt at a literal rendering, which in poetry is specially desirable. The word rendered in our Authorised Version "How," has been translated "Alas," not only because this gives more fully the real meaning, but also because our word "how" might be taken interrogatively instead of exclamatively.

[2] The attentive reader will notice that throughout the body of the ode, the thoughts move forward in sentences of three lines each, indicated in our translation by a sign of exclamation.

guidance. In answer to his enquiry by the Urim and Thummim he was directed to take up his residence in Hebron, where he was soon anointed king by his own tribe of Judah. As yet, however, and for the next seven and a half years, his rule only extended over that tribe. It is further evidence of the entire submission of David to the leading of Jehovah, and of his having fully learned the lesson of not seeking to compass his own "deliverance," that he took no steps to oppose the enthronement of Saul's son, however contrary this was to the Divine appointment; and that the contest which ultimately ensued originated not with David, but with his rival. On the contrary, David's first act as king of Judah was to send an embassy to Jabesh-gilead to express his admiration of their noble loyalty to Saul.[1] Nor does it detract from this mark of his generosity that, now their master was dead, he intimated his own elevation, to bespcak, if possible, their allegiance. The support of such men was well worth seeking. Besides, Jabesh-gilead was the capital of the whole of that district; and already the standard had there been set up of a rival, whose claims were neither founded on the appointment of God, nor on the choice of the people.

As we infer from the sacred narrative, there had been among the fugitives from the battle of Gilboa a son of Saul—whether the youngest or not must remain undetermined.[2] From the lan-

[1] Keil has well noticed the frequent conjunction of the expressions "mercy and truth" (2 Sam. ii. 6; comp. Ex. xxxiv. 6; Psa. xxv. 10). It is ever so with God: first, "mercy"—free, gracious, and forgiving; then "truth"—faithfulness to His promises, and experience of their reality. The expression rendered in our Authorised Version, "And I also will requite you this kindness," should be translated: "And I also am showing you this goodness," referring to the kind message which David sent them.

[2] Although Ish-bosheth is always mentioned fourth among the sons of Saul, it does not necessarily follow that he was the youngest. He may have been the son of another mother, and stand last in respect of dignity rather than of age. The different cast of his name from that of the others, seems rather to point in that direction. This would also account for his age —thirty-five at least—at the time of his father's death. At the same time we would not put too much stress on *numerals* in the Hebrew text, in which, from the nature of the case, clerical errors would most easily arise.

guage of the text (2 Sam. ii. 8), as well as from his subsequent
history, he seems to have been a weak character—a puppet in
the hands of Abner, Saul's uncle, whom that ambitious and
unscrupulous soldier used for his own purposes.   His original
name, Esh-Baal, "fire of Baal" (1 Chron. viii. 33; ix. 39),
became in popular designation Ish-Bosheth, "man of shame,"
—Baal and Bosheth being frequently interchanged according
to the state of popular religion (Judg. vi. 32; Jer. xi. 13;
Hos. ix. 10).   Even this may be regarded as indicating the
popular estimate of the man.   Immediately after the battle of
Gilboa, Abner had taken him across the Jordan to Mahanaim,
"the twain camp," where probably the broken remnants of
Saul's army also gathered.   The place was well chosen, not
only from the historical remembrances attaching to the spot
where angels' hosts had met Jacob on his return to the land of
promise (Gen. xxxii. 2), but also as sufficiently far from the
scene of the recent war to afford safe shelter.   Here Abner
raised the standard of the Pretender to the throne of Israel;
and, probably in the course of five and a half years,[1] succeeded
in gradually clearing the country from the Philistines, and sub-
jecting it, with the exception of the territory of Judah, to the
nominal rule of the "man of shame."

The first conflict between the armies of the rival kings was
undoubtedly provoked by Abner.   With all the forces at his
disposal he marched upon Gibeon, primarily with the view of
again establishing the royal residence at "Gibeah of Saul," but
with the ulterior object of placing Ish-bosheth in the room of
his father, and gradually pushing back David.   Upon this, Joab
advanced with the seasoned troops of David, to oppose his
progress.   The town of Gibeon was built on the slope of a hill,

---

[1] This probably explains the seeming discrepancy between the two years
of his reign and the seven and a half of David's over Judah.   Erdmann has
well remarked that the preposition "over," which occurs six times in ver. 9,
is represented in the Hebrew three times by *el*, and three times by *al*—the
latter indicating the gradual subjection of territory.   The word "*Ashurites*"
should probably read *Geshurites*, their land lying on the borders of Gilead
and Bashan (Deut. iii. 14; Josh. xii. 5).

overlooking a wide and fertile valley. On the eastern side of the hill deep down in a rock is a beautiful spring, the waters of which are drained into a large rectangular pool, about seventy-two feet long and forty-two feet wide (comp. also Jer. xli. 12). South of this pool lay the army of Joab, north of it that of Abner. The two generals seem to have been previously acquainted (ver. 22); and perhaps Abner may from the first have had in his mind the contingency of having to make his peace with David. Be this as it may, the provocation to actual hostilities came once more from Abner. On his proposal,— perhaps with a view to decide the conflict by a kind of duel, instead of entering upon an internecine civil war—twelve young men from either side were to engage in a personal combat.[1] But such was the embitterment and determination of parties, that each one rushed on his antagonist, and, taking hold of him, buried his sword in his side; whence the spot obtained the name : " Plot of the sharp blades." This bloody and, in the event, useless " game " having proved indecisive, a fierce battle ensued ; or rather, a rout of the Israelites, in which three hundred and sixty of them fell, as against nineteen of David's seasoned and trained warriors. The pursuit was only stopped when night had fallen, and Abner had rallied his scattered forces in a strong position on the top of a hill and then only at Abner's special request.[2]

An incident in that day's pursuit is specially recorded for its bearing on the after-history. Of the three sons of Zeruiah, David's sister (1 Chron. ii. 16),—Abishai (1 Sam. xxvi. 6), Joab, David's general-in-chief, and Asahel—the youngest was " light of foot as one of the roes in the field." Flushed with the fight, the youth singled out Abner, and followed

[1] The expression, ver. 14, " Let the young men play before us," refers here to the terrible "game" of single combat.

[2] The Hebrew construction of ver. 27 is difficult. The probable meaning is as follows : " As the Elohim liveth ! For unless thou hadst spoken— then if before the morning the people had returned, each from after his brother !" In other words, the pursuit would have been continued till the morning.

him in his flight.   After a little Abner, recognising his pursuer, stood still.   Probably the youth thought this meant surrender.   But Abner, having ascertained that his pursuer was
really Asahel, and deeming that his ambition would be satisfied if he carried away the armour of some enemy, bade him
gratify his wish on one of the men-at-arms around.   When
the youth, bent on the glory of slaying Abner himself, nevertheless continued the pursuit, the captain once more stopped
to expostulate.   But neither the well-meant and kindly-spoken
warning of Abner, nor the manifest discrepancy of fighting
power between the two, could stay a lad intoxicated by perhaps a first success.   To get rid of him, and almost in necessary self-defence, Abner now struck behind him with the
butt-end of his lance, which was probably sharpened with a
point, to be capable of being stuck in the ground (1 Sam.
xxvi. 7).   Mortally wounded in "the abdomen,"[1] the lad fell,
and soon "died in the same place."   The sight of one so
young and brave weltering in his blood and writhing in
agony no doubt greatly increased the bitterness of that day's
pursuit (ver. 23).

The battle of Gibeon seems to have been followed rather
by a protracted state of war[2] than by any other actual
engagement between the forces of the two kings.   The general
result is described as the house of Saul waxing weaker and
weaker, and that of David stronger and stronger.   Of both
evidence appeared.   The increasing political strength of David
was shown, as usual among Eastern monarchs, by the fresh
alliances through marriage into which he now entered.   These
would not only connect him with powerful families throughout
the country, but prove to his subjects that he felt himself safe
in his position, and could now in the Oriental fashion found
a royal house.   On the other hand, the dependence of Ish-

[1] This is the correct rendering, and not "under the fifth rib," as in the
Authorised Version (2 Sam. ii. 23).

[2] The expression in 2 Sam. iii. 1 : "Now there was long war," refers
not to actual war, of which there is no evidence in the record, but to a state
of chronic warfare.

bosheth upon Abner became constantly more evident and humiliating. At last the all-powerful general took a public step which in those days was regarded as implying an open claim to the succession to Saul's throne (comp. 2 Sam. xvi. 21 ; 1 Kings ii. 21). Whether or not Abner had intended this when he took Rizpah, Saul's concubine, or merely wished to gratify his passion, with utter and marked disregard of the puppet whom it had suited his purpose to keep on the throne, Ish-bosheth at any rate resented this last and crowning insult. But Abner, who had no doubt for some time seen the impossibility of maintaining the present state of affairs (comp. ver. 17), was in no mood to brook even reproof. He broke into coarse invective,[1] and vowed to Ish-bosheth's face that he would henceforth espouse the cause of David, and soon bring it to a successful issue. Nor did the wretched king even dare to reply.

If Ish-bosheth had regarded it as only the threat of an angry man, Abner at least was in full earnest. Negotiations with David were forthwith set on foot. But they met with a preliminary condition—right and proper not only in itself, but also from political considerations. It was a standing memento of David's weakness in the past, and a lasting disgrace, that his wife Michal should be parted from him, and continue the wife of another—a mere subject of the kingdom. Besides, as the husband of Saul's daughter, and as recalling how he had obtained her hand, her restoration would place him on a manifest political vantage ground. Accordingly David sent Abner this message in reply : "Well, I will make a covenant with thee ; only one thing I demand of thee, viz. : Thou shalt not see my face, unless thou before bringest Michal, the daughter of Saul, when thou comest to see my face." But it would have ill become David to address such a demand to Abner, except as all-powerful with Ish-bosheth, and therefore really responsible for his acts. The formal demand

[1] The words of Abner (ver. 8) should be thus rendered : "Am I a dog's head which belongeth to Judah ? This day" (at present) "I show kindness to the house of Saul thy father," etc.

was made to Ish-bosheth himself, and grounded on David's rights. The son of Saul immediately complied—of course, under the direction of Abner, who himself executed the commission to fetch her from her present husband, and restore her to David. The publicity with which this was done—the husband being allowed to accompany her with his lamentations as far as the boundary of Judah—and the influential character of the embassy, as well as the act of restoration itself, must have given to the whole nation an idea of David's acknowledged position, and contributed to their speedy submission to his rule.

When Abner brought Michal to Hebron, at the head of an embassy of twenty men—whether sent by Ish-bosheth, or coming as a sort of representative deputation from Israel—he had, with characteristic energy, already taken all his measures. First he had assured himself of the co-operation of the tribal "elders," who had long been weary of a nominal rule which left them defenceless against the Philistines and others. After that he had entered into special negotiations with the tribe of Benjamin, which might naturally be jealous of a transference of royalty from themselves to Judah. Having secured the consent of all, he was able to offer to David the undivided allegiance of Israel. The king had favourably received Abner and his suite, and entertained them at a great banquet. Already the embassy was on its way back to accomplish its mission, when Joab and his men returned to Hebron from some raid, such as in the then circumstances of David might still be necessary for the support of the troops. On learning what had passed in his absence, he made his way to the king, and violently expostulated with him for not having acted treacherously towards his guest. Abner had come bent on treachery, and he ought not to have been allowed to escape. We can scarcely suppose that this pretence of zeal imposed upon any one, any more than afterwards, when he had murdered Abner, that of having acted as avenger of blood. In both instances his motives, no doubt, were envy, personal jealousy, and fear lest his position might be endangered. As David gave him no encouragement, he acted on his own responsibility, whether or not he used the name of David in so doing. A swift messenger soon brought back Abner to Hebron. Joab, who had concerted his measures with Abishai, his brother (ver. 30), met the unsuspecting victim " in the gate ;" and taking him aside from the pathway into the interior and darker roofed part, as if for some private communication, "slew" him by a wound in "the abdomen," similar to that by which Asahel had died.[1]

As we understand it, the murderers would then turn round, and addressing the bystanders, declare that they were justified, since they had acted as "avengers of blood." But that such plea could not be urged in this instance must have been evident to all, since Abner's had been an act of self-defence, and certainly not intentional murder (comp. Deut. iv. 42, etc.; Josh. xx.). Abner, however, represented a low type of Israelitish valour. If we were to credit his protestations (vers. 9, 10, 18) of desiring to carry out the Divine will in the elevation of David, we should, of course, have to regard him as having previously acted in conscious opposition to God, and that from the most selfish motives. But probably—put in an Oriental and Jewish fashion—it meant no more than the thousand protestations of "God wills it" and the "Te Deums" which in all ages of the world have covered human ambition with a garb of religiousness.

But none the less foul and treacherous was Joab's deed, and it behoved David not only to express his personal abhorrence of it, but to clear himself of all suspicion of complicity. In this instance it was impossible for human justice to overtake the criminals. Probably public feeling would not have supported the king; nor could he at this crisis in his affairs afford the loss of such generals, or brave the people and the army. But David did all that was possible. Those whom human justice could not overtake he left in the hands of Divine

---

[1] The difference is marked in the original of ver. 30: Joab and Abishai *slew* or murdered Abner because *he made* Asahel *die.*

vengeance to mete out the punishment appropriate to the inordinate desire after leadership which had prompted such a
crime (ver. 29).[1] A public mourning was ordered, in which
the murderers themselves had to take part. The king in his
official character followed the murdered man to his burying,
pronounced over him an appropriate elegy, and publicly
announced his intention to fast, in token of personal mourning. From the remark added in the sacred text (ver. 37), it
seems that such proofs of sincerity were requisite to counter-
balance the suspicions otherwise excited by such an instance
of treachery and deception in high places. To his own immediate surroundings—his "servants" (vers. 38, 39)—David
spoke more unreservedly, lamenting the circumstances which
still made him comparatively powerless in face of such reckless chiefs as the sons of Zeruiah.

But, on the other hand, increasing public confidence rewarded David's integrity of purpose. It was needed, if high-
handed crime was to be suppressed in the land. Another
glaring instance of the public demoralisation consequent on
Saul's long misrule soon occurred. The death of Abner had
naturally the most discouraging effect, not only upon Ish-
bosheth, but upon all his adherents. No one was now left of
sufficient prominence and influence to carry out the peaceable
revolution which Abner had planned. The present weak
government could not long be maintained ; and if Ish-bosheth
died, the only representative of Saul's line left was a crippled
child, Mephi-bosheth ("the exterminator of shame," or "of
Baal"[2]), the son of Jonathan, whose deformity had been caused
by the nurse letting him fall when snatching him up for hasty
flight on receiving tidings of the disastrous day at Jezreel.
Not even the most ardent partisan could have wished to see on
the throne of Israel a child thus permanently incapacitated.

---

[1] Of course, we must in all such instances not lose out of view the
religious standpoint of the times, even in the case of a David.

[2] I explain the word : "He who blows down Baal," which seems best
to correspond with the parallel name Merib-Baal, in 1 Chron. viii. 34.

But few could have been prepared for the tragedy which was so soon to put an end to all difficulties.

It seems that two of Ish-bosheth's "captains of bands," prompted, no doubt, by the hope of rich reward, had in the most deliberate and treacherous manner planned the murder of Ish-bosheth. They were brothers, from Beeroth, on the western boundary of Benjamin, but included in its territory (Josh. xviii. 25). Hence they were of the same tribe with Saul, which, of course, aggravated their crime. For some unexplained reason the Beerothites had fled *en masse* to Gittaim—perhaps, as has been suggested, on the occasion of Saul's slaughter of the Gibeonites (2 Sam. xxi. 1, 2). This, however, can scarcely be regarded as the motive of their crime.[1] Probably on pretence of superintending the receipt of what was necessary for the provisioning of their men, they entered the royal residence at the time when Ish-bosheth was taking the customary Eastern midday rest, made their way into his bed-chamber, stabbed him in his sleep in the abdomen, and cut off his head, to carry it to David as gory evidence of their deed.[2] The reception which they met was such as might have been expected. To the daring appeal of those interested murderers that they had been the instruments of Jehovah's vengeance upon Saul's wrongs to David, the king gave no further reply than to point to what had hitherto been the faith and experience of his heart and the motto of his life : " Jehovah liveth, Who hath redeemed my soul out of all adversity ! " It needed not man's help, least of all the aid of crime. Never—not even in his darkest hour—had he either desponded, doubted, or sought to right himself. His strength, as his confidence, had lain in realising Jehovah as the living God and his all-sufficient

[1] So in *The Speaker's Commentary*, Vol. II. p. 380.

[2] There is no real difficulty about the repetition in the narrative, 2 Sam. iv. 5, 6—the latter verse taking up and continuing the interrupted narrative in ver. 5. Accordingly, there is no need for the addition made in the LXX., which must be regarded not as an emendation of, but as a gloss upon, the text.

Saviour.   No other deliverance did he either need or seek.
But as for this crime—had not his conduct to the lying
messenger at Ziklag sufficiently shown his abhorrence of such
deeds?   How much more in regard to a murder so foul as
this!   Swift, sure, and signally public punishment was the
the only possible reply in such a case.

And thus at last, not by his own act, but through circumstances over which he had had no control,—allowed by Him
Who gives full liberty to each man, though He overrules even
the darkest deeds of the wicked for the evolving of good—
David was left undisputed claimant to the throne of Israel.
Faith, patience, and integrity were vindicated; the Divine
promises to David had come true in the course of natural
events—and all this was better far than even if Saul had
voluntarily resigned his place, or Abner succeeded in his plans.

CHAPTER XVI.

*David anointed King over all Israel—Taking of Fort Zion—Philistine
Defeat—The Ark brought to Jerusalem—Liturgical arrangements and
Institutions.*

(2 SAM. V., VI.; I CHRON. XI.—XVI.)

THE cessation of the long-pending rivalry and the prospect of
a strong monarchy under David must have afforded sincere
relief and satisfaction to all the well-disposed in Israel.   Even
during the time when his fortunes were at the lowest, David had
had constant accessions of valiant and true men from all tribes,
not excluding Saul's tribe of Benjamin and the country east of
the Jordan.   Yet it implied no ordinary courage to face the
dangers and difficulties of the life of an outlaw; no common
determination to leave home and country in such a cause.   The
Book of Chronicles furnishes in this as in other instances

most welcome notices supplemental to the other historical writings of the Old Testament.[1] Thus it gives us (1 Chron. xii. 1–22) the names of the leading men who joined David at different periods, with their tribal connection, and even helps us to guess what motives may have actuated at least some of their number. From these notices we learn that considerable accessions had taken place on four different occasions. When David was at Ziklag (vers. 1–7), he was joined by certain tribesmen ("brothers") of Saul (vers. 1–8), and by some men from Judah (vers. 4, 6, 7). While in the mountain-fastnesses, in the wilderness of Judah (1 Sam. xxii.–xxiv), certain of the Gadites separated themselves unto him, "men of the army for war"—soldiers trained for war (ver. 8), "chief of the host" (*not* "captains of the host," ver. 14), "one to a hundred the least, and the greatest one to a thousand," who when breaking away from the army of Saul had not only crossed Jordan in the dangerous floodtime of early spring, but cut their way through those who would have barred it (ver. 15). A third contingent from Benjamin and Judah came during the same period (vers. 16–18). Their names are not mentioned; but they were headed by Amasai, probably another nephew of

---

[1] Without here entering on a detailed analysis of the Books of Chronicles (for which see the Table at the beginning of this Volume), we may remark that their position in the canon appropriately indicates their character relatively to the Books of Samuel and of the Kings. These latter are *prophetic*, while the Books of Chronicles are *hagiographic*. In the one series all is viewed from the *prophetic* standpoint; in the other, from that of the "sacred writer." In the one case, it is the theocracy, with its grand world-wide principles, which dominates the view; in the other, it is rather the sanctuary which is in Judah—God-appointed in its location, ordinances, priesthood, and law, allegiance to which brings blessing, while unfaithfulness entails judgments. Accordingly, after general genealogical tables (in which the work abounds), the kingdom of David is traced to the Babylonish captivity, while the history of the kingdom of Israel is wholly omitted. Even in the history of the kingdom of David and of his successors—especially in that of David and Solomon—all the merely *personal* parts are passed over, and the narrative is, if one may use the expression, rather objective than subjective. The reader will easily find for himself what parts of history are omitted, although the plan is not always consistently carried out, especially in regard to the later reigns.

David—the son of Abigail, David's younger sister (1 Chron. ii. 16, 17). When challenged by David as to their intentions, Amasai had, under the influence of the Spirit, broken forth in language which showed the character of their motives (ver. 18). The last and perhaps most important contingent joined David on his road back to Ziklag, when dismissed from the armies of the Philistines. It consisted of seven chieftains of thousands of Manasseh, who gave David most valuable aid against the Amalekites.

If such had been David's position and influence in Israel even during Saul's lifetime, we can readily understand the rush of enthusiasm at his accession to the throne of a people once more united, now that there was no longer any rival claimant left. As they afterwards told David at Hebron, they all felt that he was their own,—just as Israel will feel when at last in repentant faith they will turn to their Messiah King; that in the past, even in Saul's life-time, he alone had been the victorious leader and chief of all; and that to him had pointed the express Divine promise as spoken through Samuel (1 Chron xi. 3). And while the "elders of Israel" made a regular "covenant" with David, and anointed him king over Israel, hundreds and thousands of the men of war marched down to Hebron from the most remote parts of the country (1 Chron. xii. 23–40). Such enthusiasm had never before been witnessed. Not bidden to the war, but voluntarily they came, some bringing with them even from the northernmost parts of the land—from Issachar, Zebulun, and Naphtali—contributions in kind for the three days' popular feast which David's former subjects of Judah, and especially those around Hebron, were preparing in honour of this great and most joyous event. From both banks of the Jordan they came. Of course, we do not look for a large representation from Judah and Simeon (the latter being enclosed in the terri- tory of Judah), since they were already David's, nor from the Levites, many of whom may previously have been in David's territory (1 Chron. xii. 24–26). Issachar was represented by two hunared of its most prominent public leaders, " knowing (possessing) understanding of the times, to know what Israel should do." [1] Only the contingents from Ephraim and Benjamin were comparatively small : the former, owing either to the old tribal jealousy between Ephraim and Judah, or else from a real diminution in their number, such as had appeared even in the second census taken by Moses,[2] while in the case of Benjamin it is sufficiently accounted for by the circumstance that " even till then the greatest part of them were keeping their allegiance to the house of Saul " (ver. 29). Taking all these circumstances into account, the grand total of warriors that appeared in Hebron—339,600 men, with 1222 chiefs,[3] and so many of them from the other side Jordan,—afforded a truly marvellous exhibition of national unanimity and enthusiasm. And the king who was surrounded by such a splendid array was in the prime of his vigour, having just reached the age of thirty-seven and a half years (2 Sam. v. 5). What a prospect before the

---

[1] The expression refers, of course, to these two hundred representative men, and not to the tribe as a whole.

[2] Comp. Vol. II. of this *Bible History*, p. 146.

[3] Bearing in mind our above remarks, and that, of course, units are not given, the following are the numbers of warriors and of their leaders, given in 1 Chron. xii. 24–37 :

Of Judah	6,800 men	
„ Simeon	7,100 „	
„ Levi	4,600 „	
With Jehoiada, the "prince" (not high-priest of Aaron)	3,700 „	
Zadok and his father's house	—	22 chiefs.
Of Benjamin	3,000 „	
„ Ephraim	20,800 „	
„ half Manasseh	18,000 „	
„ Issachar	—	200 leaders.
„ Zebulon	50,000 „	
„ Naphtali	37,000 „	... 1,000 chiefs.
„ Dan	28,600 „	
„ Asher	40,000 „	
„ the 2½ tribes east of Jordan	120,000 „	
Total	339,600 men ... 1222 chiefs, etc.	

nation! Well might they joy at the national feast which
David gave in Hebron! Viewing this history in its higher
bearing, and remembering the grounds on which the elders of
Israel in Hebron based the royal claims of David, we venture
to regard it as typical of Israel at last returning to their
Saviour-King. And surely it is not to strain the application,
if thoughts of this feast at Hebron carry us forward to that
other and better feast in the "latter days," which is destined
to be so full of richest joy alike to Israel and to the world
(Isa. xxv. 6–10).

Surrounded by a force of such magnitude and enthusiasm,
David must have felt that this was the proper moment for
the greatest undertaking in Jewish history since the conquest
of the land under Joshua. The first act of David's government must appropriately be the conquest of Israel's capital.[1]
The city of the Jebusites must become truly Jerusalem—
"the inheritance," "the abode" "of peace:" the peace of
the house of David. The town itself had indeed already
been taken immediately upon Joshua's death (Judg. i. 8).
But "the stronghold" on Mount Zion, which dominated the
city, still continued to be held by "the Jebusites." Yet
Jerusalem was almost marked out by nature to be Israel's
capital, from its strength, its central position, and its situation between Benjamin and Judah. Far more than this, it
was the place of which the Lord had made choice: to be,
as it were, a guarded sanctuary within the holy land. So long
as Zion was in possession of the Jebusites, as the original
Canaanite "inhabitants of the land," the land itself could not
be said to have been wholly won. Thither accordingly David
now directed the united forces of his people. Yet such was
the natural and artificial strength of Zion that "to say (express), David shall not come hither" (ver. 5), the Jebusites

---

[1] This might have been inferred from the circumstance that both in
2 Sam. v. and in 1 Chron. xi. the capture of Jerusalem is recorded immediately after David's coronation. But the wording of 2 Sam. v. 5
places it beyond doubt.

taunted him with what afterwards became a proverb, per-
petuating among the people the fact that no conquest is too
difficult for God and with God : " He will not come in
hither, for even the blind and the lame shall drive thee
away !"[1]   It was wise and right in David to take up this
defiant taunt of the heathen, when he gave his men charge
—perhaps directing them to scale the bare rock by the
water-course,[2] which may at that time have come down the
brow of Zion : " Whoever smiteth Jebusites—let him throw
(them) down the water-course : both ' the blind and the lame '
who are hated of David's soul !"[3]   At the same time no
means were neglected of encouraging the leaders in the attack.   As we learn from the Book of Chronicles (1 Chron.
xi. 6), the leader who first scaled the walls was to be made
general-in-chief.   This honour was won by Joab, who had
commanded David's separate army, before his elevation to the
throne had united the whole host of Israel.   And so, in face
of the Jebusite boast, the impregnable fort was taken, and
called " the City of David,"—a lesson this full of encouragement to the people of God at all times.   Henceforth David
made it his residence.   To render it more secure, " he built,"
or rather fortified, " round about from (fort) Millo and inwards,"[4] or, as in 1 Chron. xi. 8 : " From the surrounding
(wall) and to the surrounding,"—that is, as we understand
it : Zion, which had hitherto been surrounded by three walls,
had now a fourth added on the north, reaching from Castle

---

[1] So the words in the original, and not as in our Authorised Version.

[2] The expression rendered in the Authorised Version "gutter," occurs only
again in the *plural* in Ps. xlii. 7, where it undoubtedly means "cataracts"
or "waterfalls."   Accordingly we translate the singular of the noun by
"watercourse down a steep brow."   Keil, Ewald, and Erdmann render
it "abyss."   The interpretation of this difficult verse (ver. 8) in *The
Speaker's Bible* seems to us not warranted by the language of the text.

[3] This is the best rendering of this somewhat difficult verse.

[4] Mr. Lewin's theory (*Siege of Jerusalem*, pp. 256, etc.) that Millo was
the Temple-area is wholly untenable.   There was, for example, another
Millo in Shechem (Judg. ix. 6), which is also designated as the migdal,
or tower of Shechem (vers. 46, 49).

Millo (either at the north-eastern or at the north-western angle)
to where the other wall ended. Similarly, Joab repaired the
rest of the city walls (1 Chron. xi. 8).

What we have just related must, of course, not be taken as
indicating a strict chronological succession of events. The
building of these walls no doubt occupied some time, and many
things occurred in the interval, which are related afterwards.
Apparently the intention of the sacred historian was to complete
his sketch of all connected with David's conquest of Zion and
his making it the royal residence, not to write in chronological
order. Hence we have also here notices of the palace which
David built on Mount Zion, and of the help which Hiram,
king of Tyre, gave him both in men and materials, and even of
David's fresh alliances and of their issues, although the children
were born at a much later period than this.[1] As we understand
it, soon after his accession, probably after the capture of Jerusalem and the final defeat of the Philistines, Hiram sent an
embassy of congratulation to David, which led to an interchange
of courtesies and to the aid which the king of Tyre gave in
David's architectural undertakings.[2]

Different feelings from those in Israel were awakened in Philistia by the tidings of David's elevation to the throne of united
Israel, and of his conquest of the Jebusite fort. The danger to
their supremacy was too real to be overlooked. On their approach,
David retired to the stronghold of Zion. While the Philistines
advanced unopposed as far as the valley of Rephaim, which is
only separated by a mountain-ridge from that of Ben-Hinnom,
David "enquired of Jehovah." So near had danger come,
and so strongly did the king feel that he must take no step

[1] So, notably, the four sons of Bathsheba or Bathshua (comp. 1 Chron.
iii. 5), and, of course, the others also. In 1 Chron. iii. 6, 7, two names
(Eliphelet and Nogah) are mentioned, which do not occur in 2 Sam. These
two must have died.

[2] The building of David's palace must have taken place in the first years
of his reign in Jerusalem. This is evident from many allusions to this
palace. We must, therefore, in this, as in so many other instances, consider
the *dates* given by Josephus as incorrect (*Ant.* viii. 3, 1 ; *Ag. Ap.* i. 18).

without Divine direction to avert it. For, placing ourselves on the standpoint of those times, this was the best, if not the only way of manifesting entire dependence on God's guidance —even to the incurring of what seemed near danger in so doing, and also the best if not the only way of teaching his followers much-needed lessons of allegiance to Jehovah, with all that religiously and morally followed from it.

The answer of the Lord conveyed promised assurance of help, and hence of victory. And in this light David afterwards described his triumph, exclaiming, "Broken in hath Jehovah upon mine enemies before me." To perpetuate this higher bearing of the victory, the spot was ever afterwards called "Baal-perazim" ("possessor of breaches"),—and from Isa. xxviii. 21, we know that the solemn import of the name never passed from memory. The victory and its meaning were the more notable that the Philistines had brought their gods with them to the battle, as Israel the Ark on a former occasion. Their idols were now burned by command of David, in accordance with Deut. vii. 5, 25. Yet a second time did the Philistines come up to Rephaim to retrieve their disaster. On this occasion also David was divinely directed—no doubt the more clearly to mark the Divine interposition : "Thou shalt not go up (viz., against them *in front*) ; turn thyself upon their rear, and come upon them from opposite the Bacha-trees.[1] And when thou hearest the sound of marching in the tops of the Bacha-trees, then be quick, for then shall Jehovah go forth before thee to smite in the host of the Philistines." It was as David had been told ; and the rout of the Philistines extended from Gibeon [2] to the Gazer road, which runs from Nether Bethhoron to the sea.

[1] I have left the word untranslated. The guess of the Rabbis, who render it by *mulberry-trees*, is as unsupported as that of the LXX. who translate : *pear-trees*. The word is derived from *bacha*, to flow, then to weep. Ewald and Keil suggest with much probability that it was a balsam-tree (as in the Arabic), of which the sap dropped like tears.

[2] So in 1 Chron. xiv. 16. The word *Geba*, in 2 Sam. v. 25, is evidently a clerical error, since Geba lay in quite another direction.

Thus far for the political results of David's elevation, which are placed first in the "Book of Samuel," as dealing primarily with the political aspect of his kingdom, while in the Book of Chronicles, which views events primarily in their theocratic bearing, they are recorded after another of greatest importance for the religious welfare of the new kingdom.[1]   For the same reason also, the Book of Chronicles adds details not recorded in that of Samuel, about David's consultation with his chiefs, and the participation of the priests and Levites in what related to the removal of the ark of the Lord.

About seventy years had passed since the ark of Jehovah had stood in the Tabernacle,[2] according to the express ordinance of God.   And now that Israel was once more united, not only in a political, but in the best and highest sense, and its God-appointed capital had at last been won, it was surely time to restore the ancient worship which had been so sadly disturbed.   Nor could there be any question as to the location of the Ark.   No other place fit for it but the capital of the land.   For was it not the "ark of God" over which the Lord specially manifested His Presence and His glory to His people? —or, in the language of Holy Scripture[3] (2 Sam. vi. 2): "over which is called the Name, the NAME of Jehovah Zevaoth, Who throneth upon the cherubim."   Much, indeed, had still to be left in a merely provisional state.   We cannot doubt that David from the first contemplated a time when the Lord would no longer dwell, so to speak, in tents, but when a stable form would be given to the national worship by the erection of a

---

[1] If the reader will keep in view this fundamental difference in the object of the two histories, he will readily understand not only why events are differently arranged in them, but also the reason why some events are left unrecorded, or more briefly narrated in one or the other of these works.

[2] Keil reckons about twenty years to the victory of Ebenezer, forty years in the time of Samuel and Saul, and about ten in that of David.

[3] We have translated the verse correctly, as our Authorised Version is manifestly in error.

central sanctuary. But for the present it must remain—if in Jerusalem—yet in a "tabernacle." Nay, more than that, the tent which David would prepare would not be the tabernacle which Moses had made. This was in Gibeah, and there, since the murder of the priests at Nob, Zadok officiated, while Abiathar acted as high-priest with David. Neither of these two could be deposed ; and so there must be two tabernacles, till God Himself should set right what the sin of men had made wrong. And for this, as we believe, David looked forward to the building of a house for the God of Israel.

An undertaking of such solemn national importance as the transference of the Ark to Jerusalem must be that of the whole people, and not of David alone. Accordingly representatives from the whole land assembled to the number of thirty thousand, with whom he went to bring in solemn procession the Ark from [1] Baalah of Judah, as Kirjath-Jearim ("the city of the woods") also used to be called [2] (Josh. xv. 9 ; 1 Chron. xiii. 6 ; comp. also Ps. cxxxii. 6). One thing only David had omitted, but its consequences proved fatal. The act of David and of Israel was evidently intended as a return to the Lord, and as submission to His revealed ordinances. But if so, the obedience must be complete in every particular. Viewed symbolically and typically, all these ordinances formed one complete whole, of which not the smallest detail could be altered without disturbing the symmetry of all, and destroying their meaning. Viewed legally, and, so far as Israel was concerned, even morally, the neglect of any single ordinance involved a breach of all, and indeed, in principle, that of obedience and absolute submission to Jehovah, in consequence of which the people had already so terribly suffered. Once more we must here place ourselves on the stand-point of the stage

---

[1] In our text (2 Sam. vi. 2) we have it : "David arose and went . . . . from Baale"—probably a clerical error instead of "to Baale" (comp. 1 Chron. xiii. 6).

[2] Baalah "of Jehudah," to distinguish it from others of that name (Josh. xix. 8, 44), or also Kirjath-Baal (Josh. xv. 60 ; xviii. 14) was the same as Kirjath-Jearim. Comp. also Delitzsch *Com.* ii. d., Ps. vol. II. p. 264.

of religious development then attained.   For only thus can we understand either the grave fault committed by David, or the severity of the punishment by which it was followed.

The arrangements which David had made for the transport of the Ark differed in one most important particular from those which God had originally prescribed.   According to God's ordinance (Numb. iv.) the Ark was only to be handled by the Levites—for symbolical reasons on which we need not now enter—nor was any other even to touch it (Numb. iv. 15). Moreover the Levites were to carry it on their shoulders, and not to place it in a waggon.   But the arrangements which David had made for the transport of the Ark were those of the heathen Philistines when they had restored it to Israel (1 Sam. vi. 7, etc.), not those of the Divine ordinance.   If such was the case on the part of the king, we can scarcely wonder at the want of reverence on the part of the people.   It was a question of the safe transport of a sacred vessel, not of the reverent handling of the very symbol of the Divine Presence.   It had been placed in a new cart, driven by the sons of Abinadab,[1] in whose house the Ark had been these many years, while David and all Israel followed with every demonstration of joy,[2] and with praise. At a certain part of the road, by the threshing-floor of "the stroke" (*Nachon*, 2 Sam. vi. 6 ; or, as in 1 Chron. xiii. 9, *Chidon*, "accident"), the oxen slipped, when Uzzah, one of Abinadab's sons, took hold of the Ark.   It scarcely needs the comment on this act, so frequently made, that Uzzah was a type of those who honestly but with unhallowed hands try to steady the ark of God when, as they think, it is in danger, to show us that some lesson was needed alike by the king and his people to remind them

---

[1] By a copyist's mistake the first two clauses of 2 Sam. vi. 3, are repeated in ver. 4.   The text of ver. 3 should continue in ver. 4 with these words : "with the ark of God : and Ahio went before the ark."

[2] A clerical error, similar to that just mentioned, occasion the wording of ver. 5, "on all manner of *instruments made of* cypress wood."   The expression should read as in 1 Chron. xiii. 8 : "with all their might and with singing."   The instruments translated in the Authorised Version (2 Sam. vi. 5) "cornets," are the *sistra*, consisting of two iron rods furnished with little bells.

that this was not merely a piece of sacred furniture, but the very emblem of God's Presence among His people. It was a sudden and terrible judgment which struck down Uzzah in his very act before all the people ; and though David was "displeased" at the unexpected check to his cherished undertaking, the more so that he must have felt that the blame lay with himself, he seems also to have learnt its lesson at least thus far, to realise, more than ever before, that holiness befitted every contact with God (2 Sam. vi. 9).

The meaning of this judgment was understood by David. When three months later the Ark was fetched from where it had been temporarily deposited in the house of Obed-Edom, a Levite of Gath-Rimmon (Josh. xxi. 24; xix. 45), and of that family of that Korahites (1 Chron. xxvi. 4; comp. Ex. vi. 21), to whom the custody of the Ark was specially entrusted (1 Chron. xv. 18, 24), David closely observed the Divine ordinance. Of this, as indeed of all the preparations made by David on this occasion, we have, as might be expected, a very full account in 1 Chron. xv. 1–25. As the procession set forward a sacrifice of an ox and a fatling[1] was offered (2 Sam. vi. 13); and again when the Levites had accomplished their task in safety, a thank-offering of seven bullocks and seven rams was brought (1 Chron. xv. 26). David himself, dressed as the representative of the priestly nation, in an ephod, took part in the festivities, like one of the people. It is a sad sign of the decay into which the public services of the sanctuary had fallen in the time of Saul, that Michal saw in this nothing but needless humiliation of the royal dignity. She had loved the warrior, and she could honour the king, but "the daughter of Saul"[2] could neither understand nor sympathise with such a demonstration as that in which David now took part. As she looked from her window upon the scene below, and mentally contrasted the proud grandeur of her father's court with what she regarded

[1] The text uses the singular, and not, as in our Authorised Version, the *plural*.

[2] Thus Michal is here significantly designated, and not as the wife of David.

as the triumph of the despicable priesthood at the cost of
royalty, other thoughts than before came into her mind alike
as to the past and the present, and "she despised David in
her heart."

The lengthened services of that happy day were past. David
had prepared for the reception of the Ark a "tabernacle," no
doubt on the model of that which Moses had made. The
introduction of the Ark into its "most holy place"[1] was made
the feast of the dedication of the new sanctuary which had
been reared for its reception, when burnt-offerings and peace-
offerings were brought. But there was more than this to mark
the commencement of a new religious era. For the first time
the service of praise was now introduced in the public worship
of Israel.[2] Shortly after it was fully organised, as also the
other ritual of the sanctuary (1 Chron. xvi.). The introduction
of fixed hymns of praise, with definite responses by the people
(as in 1 Chron. xvi. 34–36), marks the commencement of that
liturgy which, as we know, was continued in the Temple, and
afterwards in the Synagogues throughout the land. The grand
hymn composed for this occasion was no doubt Ps. xxiv., as its
contents sufficiently indicate. But besides we have in the
Book of Chronicles (xvi. 8–36), what must be considered either
as a liturgical arrangement and combination of parts from other
Psalms introduced at that time into the public worship, or else
as a separate Psalm, parts of which were afterwards inserted
into others. This question is, however, of little practical importance. In favour of the first view is the undoubted fact that
the successive parts of the hymn in the Book of Chronicles
occur in Ps. cv. (1–15), xcvi., cvii. (1), and cvi. (47, 48), and
the circumstance that the expressions (1 Chron. xvi. 4) "to
record, and to thank, and to praise," mark a liturgical division
and arrangement of the Psalms. The first of the three classes
indicated, the Ascharah or "memorial" Psalms, were sung

---

[1] The Hebrew expression implies the innermost part.
[2] This is expressly stated in 1 Chron. xvi. 7, omitting, of course, the
words in *italics.*

when meat-offerings were brought [1] (Lev. ii. 2). Ps. xxxviii. and lxx. in our Psalter may be mentioned as examples of this class. As to the second and third classes, we need only remark that Ps. cv. is the first of the Hodim, or Thank-Psalms, and Ps. cvi. of the "Hallelujah," or "Praise" Psalms. Nor is it said that the hymn in Chronicles was actually sung in the form there indicated, the inference to that effect being derived from the words in italics in our Authorised Version (1 Chron. xvi. 7). These are, of course, not in the Hebrew text, which has it : "On that day then gave" (appointed) "David first" (for the first time) "to thank Jehovah" (*i.e.* the service of song) "by the hand of Asaph and his brethren." On the other hand, however, the hymn in the Book of Chronicles is so closely and beautifully connected in its various parts, as to give the impression of one whole, parts of which may afterwards have been inserted in different Psalms, just as similar adaptations are found in other parts of the Psalter (comp., for example, Ps. xl. 17, etc., with Ps. lxx.).

But, whatever may be thought of its original form, this "Psalm" of eight stanzas,[2] as given in the Book of Chronicles, is one of the grandest hymns in Holy Scripture. If the expression might be allowed, it is New Testament praise in Old Testament language. Only we must beware of separating the two dispensations, as if the faith and joy of the one had differed from that of the other except in development and form. From first to last the hymn breathes a missionary spirit, far beyond any narrow and merely national aspirations. Thus, in the fifth

[1] At the time of our Lord the Psalms for the day were chanted when the drink-offering was poured out. Comp. my *Temple: its Ministry and Services at the time of Jesus Christ*, pp. 143, 144. But the arrangement then prevailing may not date further back than the time of the Maccabees—at any rate, it forms no criterion for the order of the services in the time of David.

[2] Stanza i. (vers. 8–11) : Eulogy of God and of His wonders ; stanza ii. (vers. 12–14) : Memorial of God's great doings ; stanza iii. (vers. 15–18) : Memorial of the covenant and its promises ; stanza iv. (ver. 19–22) : Record of gracious fulfilment ; stanza v. (vers. 23–27) : Missionary ; stanza vi. (vers. 28–30) : The Universal Kingdom of God ; stanza vii. (vers. 31–33) : The reign of God upon earth ; stanza viii. (vers. 34–36) : Eucharistic, with doxology and liturgical close.

stanza (vs. 23–27), we have anticipation of the time when God's promise to Abraham would be made good, and all nations share in his spiritual blessing,—a hope which, in the sixth (28–30) and seventh stanzas (31–33), rises to the joyous assurance of Jehovah's reign over all men and over ransomed earth itself.

That this hymn is deeply Messianic, not only in its character but in its basis, needs no proof. In truth, we regard it and the earlier hymns of the same spirit, as that by the Red Sea (Ex. xv.) and that of Hannah (1 Sam. ii. 1–10), as forming links connecting the earlier with the later (prophetic) portions of the Old Testament, showing that, however gradually the knowledge may have come of the precise manner in which the promise would ultimately be fulfilled, the faith and hope of believers were, in substance, always the same. Nor, to pass from this to what to some may seem a comparatively secondary point, ought we to neglect noticing as an important advance, marked even by this Psalm, the establishment of a liturgical worship, apparent even in the introduction of a fixed hymnody, instead of occasional outbursts of sacred poetry, and by very distinct though brief liturgical formulas—the whole last stanza being, in fact, of that character.[1]

The solemn services of the consecration ended, David dismissed the people, giving to each individual, probably for the journey homewards, needful provisions.[2]   But in that most

---

[1] If the reader will compare the last stanza of this hymn with corresponding parts in Ps. cvi., cvii., cxviii., and cxxxvi.—not to speak of the liturgical close of each of the five books of which the Psalter consists,—and consider such passages as 2 Chron. v. 13; vii. 3; xx. 21, or Jer. xxxiii. 11, he will understand what is meant in the text.

[2] Of the three expressions in 2 Sam. vi. 19, there can be no doubt as to the meaning of the first and the last : "a cake of bread . . . and a cake of raisins" (not "flagon of wine," as in our Authorised Version). Much doubt prevails about what the Rabbis and our Authorised Version render by "a good piece of flesh"—probably on the assumption that it had formed part of the "peace-offerings." But such a distribution of "peace-offerings" would have been quite contrary to custom—nor does the gift of "cakes of raisins" accord with it. The most probable rendering of the word in question is : "measure," viz., of wine. We venture to think that our explanation of these gifts as provisions for the journey will commend itself to the reader.

joyous hour David had once more to experience, how little sympathy he could expect, even in his own household. Although we can understand the motives which influenced Michal's "contempt" of David's bearing, we would scarcely have been prepared for the language in which she addressed him when, in the fulness of his heart, he came to bless his assembled household, nor yet for the odious representation she gave of the scene. Such public conduct on her part deserved and, in the circumstances, required the almost harsh rebuke of the king. The humiliation of the proud woman before man was ratified by her humiliation on the part of God: "Therefore Michal, the daughter of Saul, had no child unto the day of her death."

The placing of the Ark in the capital of Israel, thus making it "the city of God," was an event not only of deep national but of such typical importance, that it is frequently referred to in the sacred songs of the sanctuary. No one will have any difficulty in recognising Ps. xxiv. as the hymn composed for this occasion. But other Psalms also refer to it, amongst which, without entering on details that may be profitably studied by each reader, we may mention Ps. xv., lxviii., lxxviii., and especially Ps. ci., as indicating, so to speak, the moral bearing of the nearness of God's ark upon the king and his kingdom.

CHAPTER XVII.

*David's purpose of building the Temple, and its Postponement — The
"Sure Mercies" of David in the Divine Promise—David's Thanksgiving.*

(2 SAM. VII.; 1 CHRON. XVII.)

THOSE who, with devout attention, have followed the course
of this history, and marked in it that of the kingdom
of God in its gradual unfolding, will feel that a point had
now been reached when some manifestation of the Divine
purpose, fuller and clearer than ever before, might be expected. As we look back upon it, not only the whole history,
but every event in it, has been deeply significant, and fraught
with symbolical and typical meaning. Thus we have marked
how as each event, so to speak, kindled a light, which was
reflected from the polished mirror of the Psalter, it seemed
to throw its brightness far beyond its own time into that
future on which the day had not yet risen. But even to the
men of that generation what had taken place must have carried a meaning far beyond the present. The foundation of
a firm kingdom in Israel, its concentration in the house of
David, and the establishment of a central worship in the capital
of the land as the place which God had chosen, must have
taken them back to those ancient promises which were now
narrowing into special fulfilment, and have brought into greater
prominence the points in these predictions which, though still
towering aloft, sprung out of what was already reached, and
formed part of it. A never-ending kingdom, a never-passing
king ; a sanctuary never to be abolished : such were the hopes
still before them in the world-wide application of the promises of which they already witnessed the national and typical
fulfilment. These hopes differed, not in character, but only

in extent and application, from what they already enjoyed. To use our former illustration, they were not other heights than those on which they stood, but only peaks yet unclimbed. These considerations will help us properly to understand the narrative of David's purpose to build a temple, and the Divine communication consequent upon it. For clearness' sake we first sketch the facts as stated in sacred history, and then indicate their deeper meaning.

To complete the history of the religious movement of that period, the sacred writers insert in this place the account of David's purpose to build a temple. The introduction to the narrative (2 Sam. vii. 1), and the circumstance that at the time most if not all the wars mentioned in 2 Sam. viii. and x. were past, sufficiently indicate that in this, as in other instances, the history is *not* arranged according to strict chronological succession. Still it must have taken place when David's power was at its zenith, and before his sin with Bath-sheba. The king had been successful in all his undertakings. Victorious and world-famed, he inhabited his splendid palace on Mount Zion. The contrast between his own dwelling and that in which His ark abode [1] to Whom he owed all, and Who was Israel's real King, was painfully great. However frequent and unheeded a similar contrast may be in our days between the things of God and of man, David too vividly apprehended spiritual realities to remain contented under it. Without venturing to express a wish which might have seemed presumptuous, he told his feelings on this subject to his trusted friend and adviser, the prophet Nathan.[2] As might have been expected,

---

[1] The expression (2 Sam. vii. 2) is : "Abideth in the midst (within) the *Yeriah,*" or "curtain," that is the *Yeriah* (in the singular), composed of the ten *Yerioth* (in the plural), mentioned in Ex. xxvi. 1. These formed the *Mishcan,* or dwelling—thus proving that "the curtains" hung *within* the wooden framework, and constituted the "dwelling" itself.

[2] *Nathan,* "given"—a *prophet* (whereas Gad is designated as a "seer," 1 Sam. ix. 9), whose name here appears for the first time. For further notices of him see 2 Sam. xii. ; 1 Kings i. 10, 22, 34 ; 1 Chron. xxix. 29 ; 2 Chron. ix. 29. From the latter two passages it appears that Nathan wrote a history of David and (at least in part also) of Solomon.

Nathan responded by a full approval of the king's unspoken purpose, which seemed so accordant with the glory of God. But Nathan had spoken—as ancient writers note—from his own, though pious, impulse, and not by direction of the Lord. Ofttimes our thoughts, although springing from motives of real religion, are not God's thoughts; and the lesson here conveyed is most important of not taking our own impressions, however earnestly and piously derived, as necessarily in accordance with the will of God, but testing them by His revealed word,—in short, of making our test in each case not subjective feeling, but objective revelation.

That night, as Nathan was busy with thoughts of the great future which the king's purpose seemed to open, God spake to him in vision, forbidding the undertaking; or rather, while approving the motive, delaying its execution. All this time, since He had brought them up out of Egypt, God's Presence had been really among Israel; He had walked about with them in all their wanderings and state of unsettledness. Thus far, then, the building of an house could not be essential to God's Presence, while the "walking about in tent and dwelling" had corresponded to Israel's condition. Another period had now arrived. Jehovah Zevaoth[1] had chosen David, and established his kingdom. And in connection with it as concerned Israel (ver. 10) and David (ver. 11): "And I have appointed a place for My people Israel, and have planted it that it may abide in its place, and no more tremble; and that the children of wickedness" (malice) "may no more oppress it as at the first, and from the day when I appointed judges over My people Israel.[2] And I give thee rest from all thine enemies, and Jehovah intimates to thee that a house will Jehovah make to thee."

[1] The use here of the name "Jehovah of Hosts" is very significant. It marks, on the one hand, the infinite exaltation of the Lord above all earthly dwellings, and, on the other, the real source of David's success in war.

[2] It is quite evident that the sentences must be arranged and punctuated as we have done, and not as in our Authorised Version. The same remark applies to the tenses of the verbs.

Thus much for the present. As for the future, it was to be as always in the Divine arrangement. For God must build us a house before we can build one to Him. It was not that David was first to rear a house for God, but that God would rear one for David. Only afterwards, when all Israel's wanderings and unrest were past, and He had established the house of His servant, would the son of that servant, no longer a man of war (1 Chron. xx. 8; xxviii. 3), but a man of peace, "Solomon," build the house of peace. There was inward and even outward congruity in this: a kingdom which was peace; a king the type of the Prince of peace; and a temple the abode of peace. This, then, was the main point: a promise alike to David, to Israel, and in regard to the Temple, that God would build David a house, and make his kingdom not only lasting, but everlasting, in all the fulness of meaning set out in Ps. lxxii. What followed will be best giver in the words of Holy Scripture itself: "I shall be to him a Father, and he shall be to Me a son, whom, if he transgress, I will correct with the rod of men, and with stripes of the children of men; but My mercy shall not depart from him as I made it depart from Saul, whom I put away from before thee. And unfailing" (sure) "thy house and thy kingdom for ever before thee; and thy throne shall be established for ever!"

That this promise included Solomon is as plain as that it was not confined to him. No unprejudiced reader could so limit it; certainly no sound Jewish interpreter would have done so. For on this promise the hope of a Messianic kingdom in the line of David and the title of the Messiah as the Son of David were based. It was not only the Angel, who pointed to the fulfilment of this promise in the Annunciation to the Virgin (Luke i. 32, 33), but no one, who believed in a Messiah, would have thought of questioning his application. All the predictions of the prophets may be said to rest upon it. While, therefore, it did not exclude Solomon and his successors, and while some of its terms are only applicable to them, the *fulfilment* of this promise was in Christ. In this view we are not hampered but helped by the clause which speaks of human chastisements as eventual on sins in the successors of David. For we regard the whole history from David to Christ as one, and as closely connected. And this prophecy refers neither only to Solomon nor only to Christ; nor has it a twofold application, but it is a covenant-promise which, extending along the whole line, culminates in the Son of David, and in all its fulness applies only to Him. These three things did God join in it, of which one necessarily implies the other, alike in the promise and in the fulfilment : a unique relationship, a unique kingdom, and a unique fellowship and service resulting from both. The unique relationship was that of Father and Son, which in all its fulness only came true in Christ (Heb. i. 5). The unique kingdom was that of the Christ, which would have no end (Luke i. 32, 33; John iii. 35). And the unique sequence of it was that brought about through the temple of His body (John ii. 19), which will appear in its full proportions when the New Jerusalem comes down out of heaven (Rev. xxi. 1–3).

Such was the glorious hope opening up wider and wider, till at its termination David could see " afar off " the dawn of the bright morning of eternal glory ; such was the destiny and the mission which, in His infinite goodness, God assigned to His chosen servant. Much there was still in him that was weak, faltering, and even sinful ; nor was he, whose was the inheritance of such promises, even to build an earthly temple. Many were his failings and sins, and those of his successors ; and heavy rods and sore stripes were to fall upon them. But that promise never failed. Apprehended from the first by the faith of God's people, it formed the grand subject of their praise, not only in Ps. lxxxix., but in many others, such as Ps. ii., xlv., lxxii., cx., cxxxii., and continued the hope of the Church, as expressed in the burning language and ardent aspirations of all the prophets. Brighter and brighter this light grew, even unto the perfect day; and when all else seemed to fail, these were still "the sure mercies of David " (Isa. lv. 3), steadfast and stable, and at last fully realised in the resurrection of our Blessed Lord and Saviour Jesus Christ (Acts xiii. 32–34).

It was significant that when David received, through Nathan, this Divine communication, " he went in," no doubt, into that " tabernacle," which was to be to him what the Pisgah-view of the land had been to Moses, and " remained "[1] before Jehovah, uttering prayer, in which confession of unworthiness formed the first element, soon followed by thanksgiving and praise, and concluding with earnest entreaty. And such must all true prayer be—mingling humble confession with thanksgiving and with petition for the promised blessing.

CHAPTER XVIII.

Wars of David—Great Ammonite and Syrian Campaign against Israel— The Auxiliaries are Defeated in turn—The capital of Moab is taken —Edom subdued—Record of David's officers—His kindness to Mephibosheth.

(2 SAM. VIII., IX.; I CHRON. XVIII.—XX.)

B Y a fitting arrangement, the record of God's promise to establish the kingdom of David is followed by an account of all his wars, though here also the order is not strictly chronological. In fact, we have merely a summary of results, which is all that was necessary in a history of the kingdom of God— the only exception being in the case of the war with Ammon and their allies the Syrians, which is described in detail in 2 Sam. x. and xi. because it is connected with David's great sin.

As might be expected, the first war was with the Philistines, whom David subdued, taking " out of the hand of the Philis-

---

[1] Not "sat," as in our Authorised Version (2 Sam. vii. 18). *Sitting* was not the attitude of prayer, either under the old dispensation or in Apostolic times.

tines the bridle of the mother"[1]—that is, as we learn from
I Chron. xviii. I, the command of Gath, "the mother," or
principal city of the Philistine confederacy—which henceforth
became tributary to Israel.   The next victory was over the
Moabites, who must have, in some way, severely offended
against Israel, since the old friendship between them was not
only broken (I Sam. xxii. 3, 4), but terrible punishment meted
out to them—the whole army being made to lie down, when
two-thirds, measured by line, were cut down, and only one
third left alive. It was, no doubt, in this war that Benaiah,
one of David's heroes, "slew two lion-like men of Moab"
(I Chron. xi. 22).

The next contest, mentioned in 2 Sam. viii. 3–6, evidently
formed only an incident in the course of the great war against
Ammon and its confederates, which is detailed at length in
the tenth and eleventh chapters of 2 Samuel. From the number
of auxiliaries whom the Ammonites engaged against Israel,
this was by far the greatest danger which threatened the
kingdom of David.   As such it is brought before the Lord
in Ps. xliv. and lx., while the deliverance Divinely granted,
with all that it typically implied concerning the future victory
of God's kingdom, is gratefully celebrated in Ps. lxviii.   In
fact, Ammon had succeeded in girdling the whole Eastern
frontier of the land with steel. Up in the far north-east
rose Hadad-Ezer (*Hadad*, the sun-god, is *help*), and arrayed
against Israel his kingdom of Zobah, which probably lay to the
north-east of Damascus.   Nor was he alone. With him were
the forces of the Syrian (probably) vassal-territory, south of
Hamath, between the Orontes and the Euphrates, of which
Rehob (Numb. xiii. 21 ; Judg. xviii. 28), or Beth-Rehob, was
the capital. Descending still further south, along the north-
eastern frontier of Palestine, was the kingdom of Maacah
(Deut. iii. 14), which joined in the war against Israel, as well as

---

[1] The expression "taking the bridle," means taking the command or
supremacy (comp. Job xxx. 11).   The term "mother" is applied to the
principal city in a district, the other towns being designated "daughters."

the men of Tob, who inhabited the territory between Syria and Ammon, where Jephthah had erewhile found refuge (Judg. xi. 5). Next we reach the territory of Ammon, from which the war originally proceeded. In the far south Moab had been only just subdued, while the Edomites made a diversion by overrunning the valley south of the Dead Sea—and a stubborn enemy they proved. Thus, as already stated, the whole eastern, north-eastern, and south-eastern frontier was threatened by the enemy.

The occasion of this war was truly Oriental. Nahash, the king of the Ammonites, seems on some occasion, not otherwise known, to have shown kindness to David (2 Sam. x. 2). On his death, David, who never lost grateful remembrance, sent an embassy of sympathy to Hanun, the son and successor of Nahash. This the Ammonite princes chose to represent as only a device, preparatory to an attack on their capital, similar in character to that which so lately had laid Moab waste (viii. 2). There was something cowardly and deliberately provocative in the insult which Hanun put upon David's ambassadors, such as Orientals would specially feel, by shaving off the beard on one side of their face, and cutting off their long flowing dress from below up to the middle. It was an insult which, as they well knew, David could not brook; and Ammon accordingly prepared for war by raising, as we have described, all the border tribes as auxiliaries against Israel. A sum of not less than a thousand talents, or about £375,000, was spent on these auxiliaries (1 Chron. xix. 6), who amounted altogether to thirty-two thousand men—consisting of chariots, horsemen, and footmen [1]—besides the one thousand men whom the king of Maacah furnished (2 Sam. x. 6; 1 Chron. xix. 6, 7).

Against this formidable confederacy David sent Joab, at the head of "all the host—the mighty men," that is, the choicest

---

[1] By combining the accounts in 2 Sam. and 1 Chron., it will be seen that the army consisted, as might be expected, of these three kinds of forces, although only chariots and horsemen are mentioned in Chronicles, and footmen in Samuel. In general these two narratives supplement each other, and also not unfrequently enable us to detect and correct from the one text clerical errors that have crept into the other.

of his troops (2 Sam. x. 7). Joab found the enemy in double battle-array. The Ammonite army stood a short distance outside their capital, Rabbah, while the Syrian auxiliaries were posted on the wide unwooded plateau of Medeba (1 Chron. xix. 7), about fifteen miles south-west of Rabbah. Thus Joab found himself shut in between two armies. But his was not the heart to sink in face of such danger. Dividing his men into two corps, he placed the best soldiers under his brother Abishai, to meet a possible attack of the Ammonites, encouraging him with brave and pious words, while he himself, with the rest of the army, fell upon the Syrians. From the first the victory was his. When the Ammonites saw the flight of their auxiliaries, they retired within the walls of Rabbah without striking a blow. But the war did not close with this almost bloodless victory, although Joab returned to Jerusalem. It rather commenced with it. Possibly this may explain why only the second act in this bloody drama is recorded in the summary account given in 2 Sam. viii. 3, etc., and in 1 Chron. xviii. 4, etc. Combining these narratives with the fuller details in 2 Sam. x. and 1 Chron. xix., we gather that, on his defeat, or rather after his precipitate flight, Hadad - Ezer "went to turn again his hand at the river [Euphrates]," that is, to recruit his forces there (2 Sam. viii. 3 ; in 1 Chron. xviii. 3 : "to establish his hand"[1])—a statement which is further explained in 2 Sam. x. 16 and 1 Chron. xix. 16 by the notice, that the Syrian auxiliaries thence derived were placed under the command of Shobach, the captain of the host of Hadad-Ezer. The decisive battle was fought at Helam (2 Sam. x. 17), near Hamath (1 Chron. xviii. 3), and resulted in the total destruction of the Syrian host. No less than 1000 chariots, 7000[2] horsemen, and 20,000 footmen, were

---

[1] This is the correct rendering, and not as in our Authorised Version.

[2] In 2 Sam. viii. 4 by a clerical error the number is given as 700. In general, as already stated, the details of the two accounts must be compared, so as to correct copyists' omissions and mistakes in either of them. It need scarcely be pointed out how readily such might occur in numerals, and where the details were so numerous and intricate.

taken; while those who fell in the battle amounted to 700, or rather (according to 1 Chron. xix. 18) 7000 charioteers and horsemen, and 40,000 footmen (in 2 Sam., "horsemen"). Shobach himself was wounded, and died on the field of battle.[1] David next turned against the Syrians of Damascus, who had come to the succour of Hadad-Ezer, slew 22,000 of them, put garrisons throughout the country, and made it tributary. But all the spoil taken in that war—notably the "golden shields," and the brass from which afterwards "the brazen sea, and the pillars and the vessels of brass," were made for the Temple (1 Chron. xviii. 8)—was carried to Jerusalem. The immediate results of these victories was not only peace along the borders of Palestine, but that all those turbulent tribes became tributary to David. One of the kings or chieftains, Toi, the king of Hamath, had always been at war with Hadad-Ezer. On his complete defeat, Toi sent his son Hadoram[2] to David to seek his alliance. The gifts which he brought, as indeed all the spoil of the war, were dedicated to the Lord, and deposited in the treasury of the sanctuary for future use.

But still the formidable combination against Israel was not wholly broken up. On the return of David's army from their victory over the Syrians, they had to encounter the Edomites[3] (2 Sam. viii. 13, 14), who had advanced as far as the "valley of salt," south of the Dead Sea. The expedition was entrusted to Abishai, Joab's brother (1 Chron. xviii. 12, 13), and resulted in the total rout of the enemy, and the garrisoning of the prin-

[1] If the reader will attentively compare the brief notices in 2 Sam. viii. 3, 4 and 1 Chron. xviii. 3, 4 with those in 2 Sam. x. 15–18 and 1 Chron. xix. 16–18, no doubt will be left on his mind that they refer to one and the same event, viz., *not* to the beginning of the war with Hadad-Ezer, but to its second stage after his precipitate flight from the battle of Medeba. For detailed proof we must refer to the Commentaries.

[2] So in 1 Chron. xviii. 10. The writing *Joram*, in 2 Sam. viii. 10, is either a clerical error or the translation of the heathen into the Jewish form of the name—by changing "Hadad," or sun-god, into "Jehovah."

[3] In 2 Sam. viii. 13 the words "he smote Edom," have evidently fallen out after "when he returned from smiting of the Syrians."

cipal places in Edom by David's men; though, to judge by
1 Kings xi. 15, 16, the operations took some time, and were
attended with much bloodshed.   The account just given of
the wars of David appropriately closes with a notice of his
principal officers of state, among whom we mark Joab as
general-in-chief, Jehoshaphat as chancellor (*magister memoriæ*),
or recorder and adviser, Zadok as high-priest at Gibeon (1 Chron.
xvi. 39), and Jonathan as assistant of his father Abiathar
(1 Kings i. 7, 42 ; ii. 22–27) at Jerusalem, Seraiah as secretary
of state, and Benaiah as captain of the body-guard — the
Cherethi and *Pelethi*, or "executioners and runners"[1]—while
the king's sons acted as intimate advisers.[2]

The record of this period of David's reign — indeed, of
his life — would have been incomplete if the memory of his
friendship with Jonathan had passed without leaving a trace
behind.   But it was not so.   When he had reached the climax
of his power,[3] he made enquiry for any descendant of Saul to
whom he might show "the kindness of God" for Jonathan's
sake.   There is something deeply touching alike in this loving
remembrance of the past, and in the manner of it, while David
was at the zenith of his power, which shows his true character,
and proves that success had not yet injured his better nature.
There was but one legitimate scion of the royal house left—
Mephibosheth, who bore in his lamed body the memorial of
that sad day on Mount Gilboa.   It is another bright glimpse
into the moral state of the people that all this time the poor
neglected descendant of fallen royalty should have found a
home and support in the house of the wealthy chieftain Machir,

[1] This seems to us the most rational interpretation of the terms, though
not a few have regarded them as names of nationalities, in which case they
would represent a guard of foreign mercenaries.

[2] The term here used in the Hebrew is *cohen*, which is always translated
"priest," but is here employed in its root-meaning : one who represents and
pleads the case of a person.

[3] This is evident from the circumstance that, on the death of Saul, Mephibosheth was only five years old (2 Sam. iv. 4), while in the account before
us he is represented as having a young son (2 Sam. ix. 12), so that a
considerable period must have intervened.

the son of Ammiel, at Lodebar,[1] near Mahanaim, the scene of Ishbosheth's murder (2 Sam. iv.). Yet another evidence was afterwards given of the worth and character of Machir. He had evidently known to appreciate David's conduct toward Mephibosheth, and in consequence become one of his warmest adherents, not only in the time of prosperity, but in that of direst adversity, when he dared openly to espouse David's cause, and to supply him in his flight with much needed help (2 Sam. xvii. 27–29).

But to return. The first care of the king was to send for Ziba, well known as a servant of Saul's—perhaps formerly the steward of his household. It is curious to note how, even after David assured him of his friendly intentions, Ziba on mentioning Mephibosheth, immediately told that he was "lame on his feet," as if to avert possible evil consequences. So strongly did the Oriental idea seem rooted in his mind, that a new king would certainly compass the death of all the descendants of his predecessor. Something of the same feeling appeared also in the bearing of Mephibosheth when introduced to David. But far other thoughts were in the king's heart. Mephibosheth was henceforth to be treated as one of the royal princes. His residence was to be at Jerusalem, and his place at the king's table while, at the same time, all the land formerly belonging to Saul was restored to him for his support. Ziba, whom David regarded as a faithful adherent of his old master's family, was directed, with his sons and servants, to attend to the ancestral property of Mephibosheth.

[1] Much ingenious use has been made of the name "Lo Debar," as meaning "no pasture." It may help to control such fancies if we point out that the Masoretic writing "Lo-debar" in two words is manifestly incorrect, the place being probably the *Lidbir* of Josh. xiii. 26 (in our Authorised Version *Debir*). But even were it otherwise, Lo-Debar could only mean "no pasture," if the "Lo" were spelt with an *aleph*, which it is in 2 Sam. xvii. 27, but not in ix. 4, 5, where it is spelt with a *vav*, and hence would mean the *opposite* of "no pasture." We have called attention to this as one of many instances of certain interpretations of Holy Scripture, wholly unwarranted by a proper study of the text, from which, however, too often, dogmatic inferences are drawn.

We love to dwell upon this incident in the history of David, which forms, so to speak, an appendix to the narrative of the first period of his reign, not merely for what it tells us of the king, but as the last bright spot on which the eye rests. Other thoughts, also, seem to crowd around us, as we repeat to ourselves such words as "the kindness of God" and "for Jonathan's sake." Thus much would a man do, and so earnestly would he enquire for the sake of an earthly friend whom he had loved. Is there not a higher sense in which the "for Jonathan's sake" can bring us comfort and give us direction in the service of love?

CHAPTER XIX.

Siege of Rabbah—David's great Sin—Death of Uriah—Taking of Rabbah —David's seeming Prosperity — God's Message through Nathan— David's Repentance—The Child of Bathsheba dies—Birth of Solomon.

(2 SAM. XI., XII.)

THERE is one marked peculiarity about the history of the most prominent Biblical personages, of which the humbling lesson should sink deep into our hearts. As we follow their onward and upward progress, they seem at times almost to pass beyond our reach, as if they had not been compassed with the same infirmities as we, and their life of faith were so far removed as scarcely to serve as an example to us. Such thoughts are terribly rebuked by the history of their sudden falls, which shed a lurid light on the night side of their character— showing us also, on the one hand, through what inward struggles they must have passed, and, on the other, how Divine grace alone had supported and given them the victory in their many untold contests. But more than that, we find this specially exhibited just as these heroes of faith attain, so to speak, the spiritual climax of their life, as if the more clearly to set it forth from the eminence which they had reached. Accordingly, the climax of their history often also marks the commencement of their decline. It was so in the case of Moses and of Aaron, in that of David,[1] and of Elijah. But there is one exception to this—or rather we should say, one history to which the opposite of this remark applies : that of our Blessed Lord and Saviour. The climax in the history of His life among men was on the Mount of Transfiguration ; and though what followed marks His descent into the valley of humiliation, even to the bitter end, yet the glory around Him only grew brighter and brighter to the Resurrection morning.

Once more spring-time had come, when the war against the Ammonites could be resumed. For hitherto only their auxiliaries had been crushed. The importance attached to the expedition may be judged from the circumstance that the ark of God now accompanied the army of Israel (2 Sam. xi. 11). Again success attended David. His army, having in its advance laid waste every town, appeared before Rabbah, the strong capital of Ammon. Here was the last stand which the enemy could make—or, indeed, so far as man could judge, it was the last stand of David's last enemy. Henceforth all would be prosperity and triumph ! It was in the intoxication of hitherto unbroken success, on the dangerous height of absolute and unquestioned power, that the giddiness seized David which brought him to his fall. It is needless to go over the sad, sickening details of his sin—how he was literally "drawn away of his lust, and enticed ;" and how when lust had conceived it brought forth sin—and then sin, when it was finished, brought forth death (James i. 14, 15). The heart sinks as we watch his rapid

[1] It need scarcely be pointed out, how this truthful account of the sins of Biblical heroes evinces the authenticity and credibility of the Scriptural narratives. Far different are the legendary accounts which seek to palliate the sins of Biblical personages, or even to deny their guilt. Thus the *Talmud* (Shab., 55. 6) denies the adultery of David on the ground that every warrior had, before going to the field, to give his wife a divorce, so that Bathsheba was free. We should, however, add, that this view was controverted. In the Talmudic tractate *Avodah Sarah* (4. *b*, 5. *a*) a very proper application is made of the sin of David, while that of Israel in making the golden calf is not only excused but actually given thanks for !

downward course—the sin, the attempt to conceal it by en-
ticing Uriah, whose suspicions appear to have been aroused,
and then, when all else had failed, the despatch of the murderous missive by Uriah's own hands, followed by the contest,
with its foreseen if not intended consequences, in which Uriah,
one of David's heroes and captains, who never turned his back
to the foe (2 Sam. xxiii. 39), fell a victim to treachery and lust.

It was all past. "The wife of Uriah"—as the text significantly calls Bathsheba, as if the murdered man were still alive,
since his blood cried for vengeance to the Lord—had completed her seven days' hypocritical "mourning," and David
had taken her to his house. And no worse had come of it.
Her husband had simply fallen in battle; while the wife's
shame and the king's sin were concealed in the harem. Everything else was prosperous. As the siege of Rabbah can scarcely
have lasted a whole year, we assume that also also to have been
past. The undertaking had not been without serious difficulty. It had been comparatively easy to penetrate through
the narrow gorge, and, following the "fish - stocked stream,
with shells studding every stone and pebble," which made
"Rabbah most truly 'a city of waters,'" to reach "the turfed
plain," "completely shut in by low hills on every side," in
which "the royal city" stood. This Joab took. But there
still remained "the city itself," or rather the citadel, perched
in front of Rabbah on "a round, steep, flat-topped mamelon,"
past which the stream flowed rapidly "through a valley contracted at once to a width of five hundred paces." As if to
complete its natural defences, on its other side were valleys,
gullies, and ravines, which almost isolated the citadel.[1] But
these forts could not hold out after the lower city was taken.
Only it was a feat of arms in those days — and Joab, unwilling to take from the king the credit of its capture,
sent for David, who in due time reduced it. The spoil was
immense — among it the royal crown of Ammon, weighing

[1] Our description is taken from Canon Tristram's *Land of Israel*,
pp. 549, 55c

no less than a talent of gold,[1] and encrusted with precious stones, which David took to himself. The punishment meted out to those who had resisted was of the most cruel, we had almost said, un-Israelitish character, not justified even by the terrible war which the Ammonites had raised, nor by the cruelties which they seem to have practised against helpless Israelitish mothers (Amos i. 13), and savouring more of the ferocity of Joab than of the bearing of David—at least before his conscience had been hardened by his terrible sin. And so David returned triumphant to his royal city!

A year had passed since David's terrible fall. The child of his sin had been born. And all this time God was silent! Yet like a dark cloud on a summer's day hung this Divine sentence over him : " But the thing that David had done was evil in the eyes of Jehovah" (2 Sam. xi. 27). Soon it would burst in a storm of judgment. A most solemn lesson this to us concerning God's record of our deeds, and His silence all the while. Yet, blessed be God, if judgment come on earth—if we be judged here, that we may "not be condemned with the world!" (1 Cor. xi. 32). And all this time was David's conscience quiet? To take the lowest view of it, he could not be ignorant that the law of God pronounced sentence of death on the adulterer and adulteress (Lev. xx. 10). Nor could he deceive himself in regard to the treacherous, foul murder of Uriah. But there was far more than this. The man whom God had so exalted, who had had such fellowship with Him, had sunk so low ; he who was to restore piety in Israel had given such occasion to the enemy to blaspheme ; the man who, when his own life was in danger, would not put

[1] Keil and other commentators are disposed to regard this weight as approximative, as the crown would, in their opinion, have been too heavy to wear. But the text does not imply that it was habitually worn, nor was its weight really so excessive. Comp. Erdmann, *die Bücher Samuelis*, p. 442, col. *b*. The question is very fully discussed in the Talmud (*Av. S.* 44. *a*). Among the strange explanations offered—such as that there was a magnet to draw up the crown ; that it was worn over the phylactery, etc. —the only one worth mention is, that its gems made up its value to a talent of gold.

forth his hand to rid himself of his enemy, had sent into pitiless death his own faithful soldier, to cover his guilt and to gratify his lust! Was it possible to sink from loftier height or into lower depth? His conscience could not be, and it was not silent. What untold agonies he suffered while he covered up his sin, he himself has told us in the thirty-second Psalm. In general, we have in this respect also in the Psalter a faithful record for the guidance of penitents in all ages—to preserve them from despair, to lead them to true repentance, and to bring them at last into the sunlight of forgiveness and peace. Throughout one element appears very prominently, and is itself an indication of "godly sorrow." Besides his own guilt the penitent also feels most keenly the dishonour which he has brought on God's name, and the consequent triumph of God's enemies. Placing these Psalms, so to speak, in the chronological order of David's experience, we would arrange them as follows : Psa. xxxviii., vi., li., and xxxii.[1]—when at last it is felt that all "transgression is forgiven," all "sin covered."

It was in these circumstances that Nathan the prophet by Divine commission presented himself to David. A parabolic story, simple, taken from every-day life, and which could awaken no suspicion of his ulterior meaning, served as introduction. Appealed to on the score of right and generosity, the king gave swift sentence. Alas, he had only judged himself, and that in a cause which contrasted most favourably with his own guilt. How the prophet's brief, sharp rejoinder : "Thou art the man" must have struck to his heart! There was no disguise now; no attempt at excuse or palliation. Stroke by stroke came down the hammer—each blow harder and more crushing than the other. What God had done for David; how David had acted towards Uriah and towards his wife—and how God would avenge what really was a despising of Himself: such was the burden of Nathan's brief-worded

[1] Comp. Delitzsch *Commentar ü. d. Psalter*, Vol. I. pp. 44, 45, 297. For reasons which, I hope, will approve themselves on careful comparison of these Psalms, I have somewhat altered the arrangement proposed by Delitzsch.

message. Had David slain Uriah with the sword of the Ammonites? Never, so long as he lived, would the sword depart from the house of David. Had he in secret possessed himself adulterously of Uriah's wife? Similar and far sorer evil would be brought upon him, and that not secretly but publicly. And we know how the one sentence came true from the murder of Amnon (2 Sam. xiii. 29) to the slaughter of Absalom (xviii. 14), and even the execution of Adonijah after David's death (1 Kings ii. 24, 25); and also how terribly the other prediction was fulfilled through the guilt of his own son (2 Sam. xvi. 21, 22).

The king had listened in silence, like one staggering and stunned under the blows that fell. But it was not sorrow unto death. Long before his own heart had told him all his sin. And now that the Divine messenger had broken through what had hitherto covered his feelings, the words of repentance sprang to his long-parched lips, as under the rod of Moses the water from the riven rock in the thirsty wilderness. They were not many words which he spoke — and in this also lies evidence of their depth and genuineness (comp. Luke xviii. 13)—but in them he owned two realities : sin and God. But to own them in their true meaning : sin as against God, and God as the Holy One, and yet God as merciful and gracious—was to have returned to the way of peace. Lower than this penitence could not descend; higher than this faith could not rise. And God *was* Jehovah—and David's sin *was* put away.

Brief as this account reads, we are not to imagine that all this passed, and passed away, in the short space of time it takes to tell it. Again we say : in this respect also let the record be searched of the penitential Psalms, that Old Testament comment, as it were, on the three days' and three nights' conflict, outlined in Rom. vii. 5–25, the history of which is marked out by the words " blasphemer," " persecutor," " injurious," and " exceeding abundant grace " (1 Tim. i. 13–16). For, faith is indeed an *act*, and *immediate ;* and pardon also is an *act, immediate* and *complete ;* but only the soul that has passed through it knows the terrible reality of a personal sense of sin, or the wondrous surprise of the sunrise of grace.

Assuredly it was so in the case of David. But the sting of that wound could not be immediately removed. The child who was the offspring of his sin must die : for David's own sake, that he might not enjoy the fruit of sin ; because he had given occasion for men to blaspheme, and that they might no longer have such occasion ; and because Jehovah was God. And straightway the child sickened unto death. It was right that David should keenly feel the sufferings of the helpless innocent child; right that he should fast and pray for it without ceasing ; right 'even that to the last he should hope against hope. that this, the seemingly heaviest punishment of his guilt, might be remitted. We can understand how all the more dearly he loved his child ; how he lay on the ground night and day, and refused to rise or be comforted of man's comforts. We can also understand—however little his servants might—how, when it was all over, he rose of his own accord, changed his apparel, went to worship in the house of Jehovah, and then returned to his own household : for, if the heavy stroke had not been averted, but had fallen—his child was not gone, only gone before.

And once more there came peace to David's soul. Bathsheba was now truly and before God his wife. Another child gladdened their hearts. David named him, symbolically and prophetically, Solomon, "the peaceful :" the seal, the pledge, and the promise of peace. But God called him, and he was "Jedidiah," the Jehovah-loved. Once more, then, the sunshine of God's favour had fallen upon David's household—yet was it, now and ever afterwards, the sunlight of autumn rather than that of summer ; a sunlight, not of undimmed brightness, but amidst clouds and storm.

THE BIBLE HISTORY

VOLUME V

HISTORY

OF

JUDAH AND ISRAEL

FROM THE

BIRTH OF SOLOMON TO THE REIGN OF AHAB

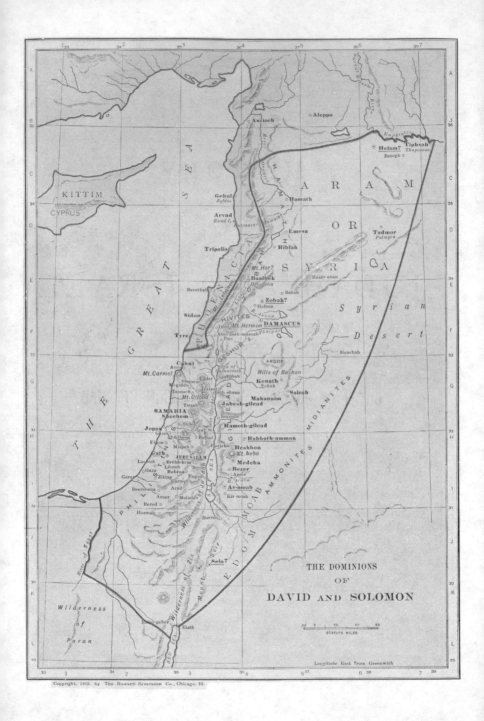

THE DOMINIONS

OF

DAVID AND SOLOMON

PREFACE

THE period of Israel's history treated in this Volume has a two-fold special interest : political and religious. Beginning with the later years of David's reign, when the consciousness and the consequences of the great sin of his life had, so to speak, paralysed the strong hand which held the reins of government, we are, first, led to see how, in the Providence of God, the possibility of a great military world-monarchy in Israel (comp. Ps. xviii. 43-45)—such as those of heathen antiquity—was for ever frustrated. Another era began with Solomon : that of peaceful development of the internal resources of the country ; of rapid increase of prosperity ; of spread of culture ; and, through friendly intercourse with other nations, of introduction of foreign ideas and foreign civilisation. When it is remembered that the building of the Temple preceded the legislation of Lycurgus in Sparta by about one hundred and twenty years ; that of Solon in Athens by more than four hundred years ; and the building of Rome by about two hundred and fifty years, it will be perceived that the kingdom of Solomon presented the dim possibility of the intellectual, if not the political Empire of the world. What Jerusalem was in the high-day of Solomon's glory is described in a chapter of this history. But, in the Providence of God, any such prospect passed away, when, after only eighty years' duration, the Davidic kingdom was rent into two rival and hostile states. Yet, although this catastrophe was intimated by prophecy, as Divine judgment upon Solomon's unfaithfulness, there was nothing either abrupt or out of the order of rational causation in its accomplishment. On the contrary, the causes of this separation lay far back in the tribal relations of Israel ; they manifested themselves once and again in the history of the Judges and of Saul; made themselves felt in the time of David; appeared in that of Solomon; and only reached their final issue, when the difficult task of meeting them devolved upon the youthful inexperience and misguided folly of a Rehoboam. All this is fully explained in the course of this history. After their separation, the two kingdoms passed, in their relations, through three stages: the first one of hostility; the second one of alliance, which commenced with the reign of Jehoshaphat and of Ahab, and ended with the slaughter of the kings of Judah and Israel by Jehu; and the third again one of estrangement and of hostility. Of these three periods the first is fully traced, and the beginning of the second marked in the present Volume.

From the political we turn to the religious aspect of this history. It was indeed true, that the empire of the world was to be connected with the Davidic kingdom (Ps. ii.)—but not in the sense of founding a great military monarchy, nor in that of attaining universal intellectual supremacy, least of all, by conformity to the ways and practices of heathen worship, magic, and theurgy. The exaltation of Zion above the hills, and the flowing of all nations unto it, was to be brought about by the going forth of the Law out of Zion, and of the Word of Jehovah from Jerusalem (Is. ii. 2, 3). This—to confine ourselves to the present period of our history—had been distinctly implied in the great promise to David (2 Sam. vii.); it was first typically realised in the choice of Jerusalem as the City of God (Ps. xlvi.; xlviii.; lxxxvii.); and further presented in its aspect of peace, prosperity, and happiness in the reign of Solomon (Ps. lxxii.) to which the prophets ever afterwards pointed as the emblem of the higher blessings in the Kingdom of God (Mic. iv. 4; Zech. iii. 10, comp. with 1 Kings iv. 25). But the great work of that reign, alike in its national and typical importance, was the building of the Temple at Jerusalem. This also has been fully described in the following pages.

But already other elements were at work. The introduction of heathen worship commenced with the decline of Solomon's spiritual life. After his death, the apostasy from God attained fearful proportions, partially and temporarily in Judah, but permanently in Israel. In the latter, from the commencement of its separate national existence under Jeroboam, the God-chosen Sanctuary at Jerusalem, and the God-appointed priesthood were discarded ; the worship of Jehovah transformed ; and by its side spurious rites and heathen idolatry introduced, till, under the reign of Ahab, the religion of Baal became that of the State. This marks the highpoint of apostasy in Israel. The evolving of principles of contrariety to the Divine Covenant slowly but surely led up to the final destruction of the Jewish Commonwealth. But, side by side with it, God in great mercy placed an agency, the origin, character, and object of which have already been indicated in a previous Volume. The Prophetic Order may be regarded as an extraordinary agency, by the side of the ordinary economy of the Old Testament ; and as intended, on the one hand, to complement its provisions, and, on the other, to supplement them, either in times of religious declension, or when, as in Israel, the people were withdrawn from their influences. Hence the great extension of the Prophetic Order in such periods, and especially in the kingdom of the ten tribes. But when, during the reign of Ahab, the religion of Jehovah was, so to speak, repudiated, and the worship of Baal and Astarte substituted in its place, something more than even the ordinary exercise of the Prophetic Office was required. For the prophet was no longer acknowledged, and the authority of the God, Whose Messenger he was, disowned. Both these had therefore to be vindicated, before the prophetic agency could serve its purpose. This was achieved through what must be regarded, not so much as a new phase, but as a further development of the agency already at work. We mark this chiefly in the ministry of Elijah and Elisha, which was contemporary with the first open manifestation of Israel's national apostasy.

Even a superficial reader will observe in the ministry of these two prophets, as features distinguishing it from that of all other prophets—indeed, we might almost say, from the whole history of the Old Testament—the *frequency* and the *peculiar character* of their miracles. Three points here stand out prominently : their *unwonted accumulation;* their seeming characteristic of *mere assertion of power;* and their apparent purpose of *vindicating the authority of the prophet.* The reason and object of these peculiarities have already been indicated in our foregoing remarks. But in reference to the characteristic of *power* as connected with these miracles, it may be remarked that its exhibition was not only necessary for the vindication of the authority of the prophet, or rather of Him in Whose Name he spake, but that they also do not present a mere display of power. For, it was always associated with an ultimate moral purpose : in regard to the Gentiles or to Israel—the believing or the unbelieving among them ; and in all the leading instances (which must rule the rest) it was brought about not only in the Name of Jehovah, but by calling upon Him as the direct Agent in it (comp. for the present Volume 1 Kings xvii. 4, 9, 14, 20–22). Thus viewed, this extraordinary display of the miraculous appears, like that in the first proclamation of Christianity among the heathen, "for a sign, not to them that believe, but to them that believe not" (1 Cor. xiv. 22)—as Bengel explains, in order that, drawn and held thereby, they might be made to listen.

But even so, some further remarks may here be allowed ; not, indeed, in the way of attempted disquisition on what must always be a prime postulate in our faith, but as helps in our thinking. It seems to me, that miracles require for their (objective) possibility— that is, subjectively viewed for their credibility[1]—only one postulate : that of the True and the Living God. It is often asserted, that miracles are not the traversing of the established, but the outcome of a higher order of things. This, no doubt, must be metaphysically true ; but practically it is only a hypothetical statement, since, admittedly, and, as the very idea of miracles implies, we know nothing of this higher nature or order of things. But may we not

---

[1] I do not mean for the credibility of one or another special miracle, but for that of miracles in general.

assert that a miracle does not seem so much an interference with the laws of Nature—of which at most we have only partial and empirical knowledge—as with the laws and habits of our own thinking concerning Nature? And if so, does not this place the question on quite another footing?

Given, that there is a God (be the seeming hypothetication forgiven!), and in living connection with His rational creatures—and it seems to follow that He must teach and train them. It equally follows, that such teaching must be adapted to their stage and capacity (power of receptiveness). Now in this respect all times may be arranged into two periods : that of outward, and that of inward spiritual communication (of Law and Persuasion). During the former the miraculous could scarcely be called an extraordinary mode of Divine communication, since men generally, Jews and Gentiles alike, expected miracles. Outside this general circle (among deeper thinkers) there was only a "feeling after God," which in no case led up to firm conviction. But in the second stage personal determination is the great characteristic. Reason has taken the place of sense ; the child has grown to the man. The ancient world as much expected an argument from the miraculous as we do from the purely rational or the logically evidential. That was their mode of apprehension, this is ours. To them, in one sense, the miraculous was really not the miraculous, but the expected ; to us it is and would be interference with our laws and habits of thinking. It *was* adapted to the first period ; it is *not* to the second.

It would lead beyond our present limits to inquire into the connection of this change with the appearance of the God-Man and the indwelling of the Holy Ghost in the Church. As we have shown in a previous Volume, under the Old Testament the Holy Spirit was chiefly known and felt as a *power*. The "still small voice" marks the period of transition. "Prophetism" was, so to speak, the introduction of the "still small voice" into the world—first in a preparatory manner ; in the fulness of time, as in all fulness, in the Christ ; and finally as indwelling in the Church of God.

These remarks will show what kind of questions are incidentally raised in the course of this history. Even in this respect the reader will have noticed progression in the successive Volumes of this Bible History. Otherwise also, it is hoped, he will mark it in these pages and in the Notes, in the fuller and more critical treatment of all questions. A new feature here is the introduction of a few Jewish and Rabbinical notices, which may prove interesting and useful. In general, while I have endeavoured to make my investigations thoroughly independent, and, so far as I could, original, it will, I trust, be also found that I have not neglected any sources of information within my reach. But above all, I would ever seek to keep steadily in view, as my main object, the practical and spiritual interest of this history. It all leads up to the Person of Christ, the Miracle of Miracles—the Miracle which gives meaning and unity to all others, and which is the truest evidence of them all. Thank God, we have sufficient and most firm historical ground for our faith in Him, as well as the inward teaching and the assurance of the Holy Ghost; sufficient, not indeed to supersede the necessity of faith, but to make that "blessed faith," so well grounded, so glorious, so joyous, and so transforming in its power, not only reasonable to us, but of obligatory duty to all men.

ALFRED EDERSHEIM.

LODERS VICARAGE, BRIDPORT:
Easter, 1880.

CONTENTS

CHAPTER I.

Close of David's Reign.

CHAPTER II.

CHAPTER III.

Appendix to the History of David.

CHAPTER IV.

Reign of Solomon.

CHAPTER XI.

Jeroboam, first King of Israel.

CHAPTER XII.

Abijah and Asa, Kings of Judah.

CHAPTER XIII.

Asa, King of Judah.—Nadab, Baasha, Elah, Zimri, Tibni, and Omri, Kings of Israel.

CHAPTER XIV.

Asa and Jehoshaphat, Kings of Judah.—Ahab, King of Israel.

CHAPTER XV.

Ahab, King of Israel.

THE

HISTORY OF JUDAH AND ISRAEL

FROM THE BIRTH OF SOLOMON.

CHAPTER I.

*Jewish View of the History of David—Amnon's Crime—Absalom's Ven-
geance—Flight of Absalom—The Wise Woman of Tekoah—Absalom
returns to Jerusalem—His Conspiracy—David's Flight.*

(2 SAM. XIII.—XVI.)

IN studying the history of the Old Testament, every thoughtful Christian must feel that a special interest attaches to
the views and interpretations of the ancient Synagogue. Too
often they are exaggerated, carnal, and even contrary to the
real meaning of Holy Scripture. But, on the other hand,
there are subjects on which we may profitably learn from
Jewish teaching. Among them are some of the opinions
expressed by the Rabbis on the history and character of
David. A brief review of these may be helpful, and serve
both as retrospect of the past, and as preparation for the study
of the closing years of his reign.

Considering the important part which David sustains in
the history of Israel, the views expressed by the ancient
Synagogue are, on the whole, remarkably free from undue
partiality. But beyond this there is a shrewd discernment of
real under apparent motives, and a keen appreciation of the
moral bearing of actions. The bright side of David's character
is dwelt upon: his true humility,[1] the affectionateness of his

---

[1] Tradition instances this curious (if not historically accurate) evidence
of it, that the coins which he had struck bore on one side the emblem of
a shepherd's staff and scrip, and on the reverse a tower (*Ber. R.* 39).

disposition, the faithfulness of his friendship, and, above all, his earnest heart-piety, which distinguished him not only from the monarchs of heathen nations, but from all his contem- poraries, and made him for all time one of the heroes of faith. On the other hand, his failings and sins are noted, and traced to self-indulgence, to rashness in arriving at conclusions, to suspiciousness in listening to every breath of slander, and even to a tendency to revengefulness,—all, we may observe, truly Oriental failings, the undisguised account of which is, of course, evidential of the truthfulness of the narrative. But what the Rabbis lay special stress upon is, that, while David kept indwelling sin in check, he failed in the full subdual, or rather in the moral renovation, of the heart. This led to his final and terrible sin. Of course, the Rabbis take a defective view of the case, since it would be more correct to reverse their statement. Nor should we omit to notice their conception of the higher aspects of his history. The typical bearing of his life is not lost sight of, and in every phase of it they point forward to " David's better Son." They also delight in marking throughout the overruling guidance of God : how the early training and history of David were intended to fit him for his calling; how, in Divine Providence, his failings and sins were, so to speak, ever reflected in their punishment,—as, for example, his rashness in dividing the inheritance of Mephi- bosheth with his unworthy servant in the similar loss sustained by Rehoboam, David's grandson; how his life is full of deeper lessons; and how in the fifteenth Psalm he embodies in brief summary the whole spiritual outcome of the Law (this is noticed in *Macc.* 24 *a*).

But of special interest in this history are the views taken of David's repentance, and of the consequences which followed from his great sin. David is here set before us as the model and ideal of, and the encouragement to, true repentance. In fact, tradition goes even further. It declares that the sin of Israel in making the golden calf and the fall of David were only recorded—it might almost seem, that they were only allowed—for the sake of their lessons about repentance. The former showed that, even if the whole congregation had erred and strayed, the door of mercy was still open to them; the latter, that not only for Israel as a whole, but for each individual sinner, however low his fall, there was assurance of forgiveness, if with true penitence he turned to God. The one case proved that nothing was too great for God to pardon; the other that there was not any one beneath His gracious notice. Be they many, or only one solitary individual, the ear of God was equally open to the cry of the repentant (comp. *Av. Sar.* 4. *b*, 5. *a*). The other point to which the Rabbis call attention is, that all the trials of David's later life, and all the judgments which overtook him and his house, might be traced up to his great sin, which, though personally pardoned, made itself felt in its consequences throughout the whole of his after-history (comp. especially *Sanh.* 107. *a* and *b*, where there are some interesting notices about David).

It cannot be doubted that there is deep truth in this view. For, although David was graciously forgiven, and again received into God's favour, neither he nor his government ever wholly recovered from the moral shock of his fall. It is not merely that his further history was attended by an almost continuous succession of troubles, but that these troubles, while allowed of God in judgment, were all connected with a felt and perceptible weakness on his part, which was the consequence of his sin. If the figure may be allowed : henceforth David's hand shook, and his voice trembled ; and both what he did and what he said, alike in his own household and in the land, bore evidence of it.

As we reckon, it must have been about the twentieth year of his reign,[1] when the sin of his son Amnon proved the beginning of a long series of domestic and public troubles. In

---

[1] Both Absalom and Tamar were the children of Maacah, daughter of the king of Geshur, whom David married after his enthronement in Hebron (2 Sam. iii. 3). Amnon was the son of Ahinoam, the Jezreelitess (2 Sam. iii. 2).

this instance also it was carnal lust which kindled the devouring flame. The gloss of the LXX. is likely to be correct, that David left unpunished the incest of Amnon with Tamar, although committed under peculiarly aggravating circumstances, on account of his partiality for him as being his first-born son. This indulgence on the part of his father may also account for the daring recklessness which marked Amnon's crime. The sentence of the Divine law upon such sin was, indeed, unmistakeable (Lev. xx. 17). But a doting father, smitten with moral weakness, might find in the remembrance of his own past sin an excuse for delay, if not a barrier to action; for it is difficult to wield a heavy sword with a maimed arm.

Two years had passed since this infamous deed. But there was one who had never forgiven it. Absalom had not forgotten the day when his brave and noble sister, after having vainly offered such resistance as she could, driven with her shame from the door of her heartless brother, had brought back the tale of her disgrace,—her maiden-princess's "sleeved upper garment"[1] rent, in token of mourning, her face defiled with ashes, her hand upon her head, as if staggering under its burden,[2] and bitterly lamenting her fate. So fair had she gone forth on what seemed her errand of mercy; so foully had she been driven back! These two years had the presence in his home of a loved sister, now "desolate" for ever, kept alive the remembrance of an irreparable wrong. The king had been "very wroth"—no more than that; but Absalom would be avenged, and his revenge should not only be signal, but overtake Amnon when least suspecting it, and in the midst of his pleasures. Thus Amnon's sin and punishment would, so to speak, be in equipoise. Such a scheme could not, however, be immediately carried out. It required time, that so all suspicion might be allayed. But then, as Absalom's plan of revenge was

---

[1] This is the correct rendering, and not "garment of divers colours," as in our Authorised Version (2 Sam. xiii. 18, 19). The maiden princesses seem to have worn as mark of distinction a sleeved cloak-like upper garment. Comp. the Hebrew of ver. 18.

[2] In the East burdens are carried on the head.

peculiarly Oriental, these long delays to make sure of a victim are also characteristic of the lands of still, deep passion. At the same time, the readiness with which Jonadab, Amnon's cousin (xiii. 3) and clever adviser in wickedness, could suggest, before it was correctly known, what had taken place (vers. 32, 33), shows that, despite his silence, Absalom had not been able effectually to conceal his feelings. Perhaps the king himself was not quite without suspicion, however well Absalom had played his part. And now follows the terrible history. It is the time of sheep-shearing on Absalom's property, not very far from Jerusalem—a merry, festive season in the East. Absalom pressingly invites to it the king and his court, well knowing that such an invitation would be declined. But if the king himself will not come, at least let the heir-presumptive be there; and, if the king somewhat sharply takes up this suspicious singling out of Amnon, Absalom does not ask him only, but all the king's sons.

The consent has been given, and the rest of the story is easily guessed. Absalom's well-concerted plan; the feast; the merriment; the sudden murder; the hasty flight of the affrighted princes; the exaggerated evil tidings which precede them to Jerusalem; the shock to the king and his courtiers; then the partial relief on the safe arrival of the fugitives, followed by the horror produced as they tell the details of the crime—all this is sketched briefly, but so vividly that we can almost imagine ourselves witnesses of the scene. It was well for Absalom that he had fled to his maternal grandfather at Geshur. For all his life long the king could not forget the death of his firstborn, although here also time brought its healing to the wound. Absalom had been three years in Geshur—and "King David was restrained from going out after Absalom,[1] because he was comforted concerning Amnon."

Great as Absalom's crime had been, we can readily understand

[1] That is, in a hostile sense, as the same expression is used in Deut. xxviii. 7. The Hebrew text seems to admit no other translation than that which we have given. The Authorised Version, through following the Rabbis, is evidently incorrect.

that popular sympathy would in large measure be on the side of the princely offender. He had been provoked beyond endurance by a dastardly outrage, which the king would not punish because the criminal was his favourite. To the popular, especially the Eastern mind, the avenger of Tamar might appear in the light of a hero rather than of an offender. Besides, Absalom had everything about him to win the multitude. Without any bodily blemish from head to foot, he was by far the finest-looking man in Israel. Common report had it that, when obliged once a year, on account of its thickness, to have his long flowing hair cut, it was put, as a matter of curiosity, in the scales, and found amounting to the almost incredible weight of twenty shekels.[1] How well able he was to ingratiate himself by his manners, the after history sufficiently shows. Such was the man who had been left in banishment these three years, while Amnon had been allowed—so far as the king was concerned—to go unpunished !

Whether knowledge of this popular sympathy or other motives had induced Joab's interference, there seems no doubt that he had repeatedly interceded for Absalom ;[2] till at last he felt fully assured that "the heart of the king was against[3] Absalom" (xiv. 1). In these circumstances Joab resorted to a not uncommon Eastern device. At Tekoah, about two hours south of Bethlehem, lived "a wise woman," specially capable of aiding Joab in a work which, as we judge, also commanded her sympathy. Arrayed in mourning, she appeared before the king to claim his interference and protection. Her two sons—so she said—had quarrelled ; and as

[1] The Hebrew "200 shekels" must depend on a copyist's mistake, the lower stroke of ב, 20, having been obliterated, thereby making the numeral ר, 200.

[2] We infer this not only from 2 Sam. xiv. 22, but also from the ready guess of the king (ver. 19).

[3] This is certainly the correct translation. Comp. the similar use of the expression in Dan. xi. 28. If, as the Authorised Version puts it, the king's heart had been *toward* Absalom, there would have been no need to employ the woman of Tekoah, nor would the king have afterwards left Absalom for two full years without admitting him to his presence (xiv. 28).

no one was present to interpose, the one had killed the other. And now the whole family sought to slay the murderer !

True, he was guilty—but what mattered the "avenging of blood" to her, when thereby she would lose her only remaining son, and so her family become extinct ? Would the death of the one bring back the life of the other—"gather up the water that was spilt"? Was it needful that she should be deprived of both her sons ? Thus urged, the king promised his interference on her behalf. But this was only the introduction to what the woman really wished to say. First, she pleaded, that if it were wrong thus to arrest the avenging of blood, she would readily take the guilt upon herself (ver. 9). Following up this plea, she next sought and obtained the king's assurance upon oath, that there should be no further "destroying" merely for the sake of avenging blood (ver. 11). Evidently the king had now yielded in principle what Joab had so long sought. It only remained to make clever application of the king's concession. This the woman did; and, while still holding by the figment of her story (vers. 16, 17), she plied the king with such considerations, as that he was always acting in a public capacity; that lost life could not be restored ; that pardon was God-like, since He "does not take away a soul, but deviseth thoughts not to drive away one driven away ;"[1] and, lastly, that, to her and to all, the king was like the Angel of the Covenant, whose "word" was ever "for rest."

David could have no further difficulty in understanding the real meaning of the woman's mission. Accordingly, Joab obtained permission to bring back Absalom, but with this condition, that he was not to appear in the royal presence. We regard it as evidence of the prince's continued disfavour, that Joab afterwards twice refused to come to him, or to take a message to the king. It was a grave mistake to leave such a proud, violent spirit to brood for two years over supposed wrongs. Absalom now acted towards Joab like one wholly

---

1 This is the correct rendering of the latter clauses of 2 Sam. xiv. 14.

reckless—and the message which Joab finally undertook to deliver was in the same spirit. At last a reconciliation took place between the king and his son—but only outwardly, not really, for already Absalom had other schemes in view.

Once more we notice here the consequences of David's fatal weakness, as manifest in his irresolution and half-measures. Morally paralysed, so to speak, in consequence of his own guilt, his position sensibly and increasingly weakened in popular estimation, that series of disasters, which had formed the burden of God's predicted judgments, now followed in the natural sequence of events. If even before his return from Geshur Absalom had been a kind of popular hero, his presence for two years in Jerusalem in semi-banishment must have increased the general sympathy. Whatever his enemies might say against him, he was a splendid man—every inch a prince : brave, warm-hearted, and true to those whom he loved —witness even the circumstance, told about Jerusalem, that he had called that beautiful child, his only daughter, after his poor dishonoured sister (2 Sam. xiv. 27), while, unlike an Oriental, he cared not to bring his sons prominently forward.[1] Daring he was—witness his setting Joab's barley on fire ; but an Eastern populace would readily forgive, rather like in a prince, what might almost be called errors on the side of virtue. And now Absalom was coming forward like a real prince ! His state-carriage and fifty outrunners would always attract the admiration of the populace. Yet he was not proud—quite the contrary. In fact, never had a prince taken such cordial interest in the people, nor more ardently wished to see their wrongs redressed ; nor yet was there one more condescending. Day by day he might be seen at the entering of the royal palace, where the crowd of suppliants for redress were gathered. Would that he had the power, as he had the will, to see them righted ! It might not be the king's blame ; but there was a lack of proper officials to take cognisance of

[1] It is remarkable and exceptional that the name of his daughter is mentioned, and not those of his sons.

such appeal-cases—in short, the government was wrong, and the people must suffer in consequence. As we realize the circumstances, we can scarcely wonder that thus "Absalom stole the hearts of the men of Israel."[1]

How long this intrigue was carried on we cannot accurately determine,[2] and only once more wonder at the weakness of the king who left it so entirely unnoticed. That the conspiracy which Absalom had so carefully prepared, though kept very secret, was widely ramified, appears from the circumstance, that, immediately on its outbreak, he could send "spies throughout all the tribes," to ascertain and influence the feelings of the people generally, and to bid his adherents, on a preconcerted signal, gather around him. More than that, it seems likely that Ahithophel, one of David's privy councillors, and deemed the ablest of his advisers, had, from the first, been in the secret, and, if so, probably directed the conspiracy. This would explain the strange coincidence of Ahithophel's absence from Jerusalem at the time of the outbreak, and his presence at his native Giloh, not far from Hebron (Josh. xv. 51). Nor is it likely that a man like Ahithophel would so readily have obeyed the summons of Absalom if he had been till then a stranger to his plans, and had not had good reason to expect success. And, indeed, if his advice had been followed, the result would have answered his anticipations.

The place chosen for the rising was Hebron, both on account of the facilities it offered for retreat in case of failure, and as the city where formerly (in the case of David) a new royalty had been instituted; perhaps also as the birthplace of Absalom, and, as has been suggested, because the transference of the royal residence to Jerusalem may have left dissatisfaction

[1] Keil notices that by similar means Agamemnon obtained the supreme command of the Greek army (*Euripides*, Iphigenia, v. 337, seq.).

[2] The notice in the text: "after forty years" (2 Sam. xv. 7) is manifestly a clerical error. Most interpreters (with the Syrian, Arabic, and Josephus) read "four years;" but it is impossible to offer more than a hypothesis.

in Hebron. Absalom obtained the king's permission to go
thither, on pretence of paying a vow made at Geshur. It
was a clever device for entrapping two hundred influential
persons from Jerusalem to invite them to accompany him, on
pretext of taking part in the sacrificial feast. Arrived at
Hebron, the mask was thrown off, and the conspiracy rapidly
assumed most formidable proportions. Tidings of what had
passed speedily reached Jerusalem. It was a wise measure
on the part of the king to resolve on immediate flight from
Jerusalem, not only to avoid being shut up in the city, and to
prevent a massacre in its streets, but to give his adherents
the opportunity of gathering around him. Indeed, in the hour
of danger, the king seemed, for a brief space, his old self
again. We can quite understand how, in David's peculiar state
of mind, trials in which he recognised the dealings of God
would rouse him to energy, while the even tenor of affairs left
him listless. No weakness now—outward or inward! Prudence,
determination, and courage in action; but, above all, a constant acknowledgment of God, self-humiliation, and a continuous
reference of all to Him, marked his every step. In regard
to this, we may here notice the progress of David's spiritual
experience, marking how every act in this drama finds expression
in the Book of Psalms. As Abraham perpetuated his progress
through the land by rearing an altar unto Jehovah in every place
where he sojourned, so David has chronicled every phase in his
inner and outer life by a Psalm—a waymark and an altar for
lone pilgrims in all ages. First, we turn to Psalms xli. and
lv.—the former in which the designation Jehovah, the latter
in which that of Elohim, prevails,[1]—which become more full of
meaning if (with Professor Delitzsch) we infer from them, that
during the four years Absalom's plot was ripening, the king
was partially incapacitated by some illness. These two Psalms,
then, mark the period *before* the conspiracy actually broke
out, and find their typical counterpart in the treachery of Judas

[1] The circumstance that some are "Jehovah" and some "Elohim"
Psalms often determines their position in the Psalter.

Iscariot.[1] Read in this light, these Psalms afford an insight into the whole history of this rising—political as well as religious. Other two Psalms, iii. and lxiii., refer to David's flight ; while the later events in, and the overthrow of the conspiracy, form the historical background of Psalms lxi.. xxxix., and lxii.

When leaving Jerusalem in their flight, the king and his followers made a halt at "the far house."[2] Besides his family, servants and officials, his body-guard (the *Cherethi* and *Pelethi*), and the six hundred tried warriors, who had been with him in all his early wanderings, accompanied him.[3] In that hour of bitterness the king's heart was also cheered by the presence and stedfast adherence of a brave Philistine chieftain, *Ittai*, who had cast in his lot with David and with David's God. He had brought with him to Jerusalem his family (2 Sam. xv. 22) and a band of adherents (ver. 20); and his fidelity and courage soon raised him to the command of a division in David's army (xviii. 2).

It was winter, or early spring,[4] when the mournful procession passed through a crowd of weeping spectators over the Kidron, to take the way of the wilderness that led towards Jericho and the Jordan. At the foot of the Mount of Olives they again paused. Here the Levites, headed by Zadok the priest, put down the Ark, which had accompanied David, until the high-priest Abiathar, and the rest of the people who were to join the king, came up out of the city. They were wise as well as good words with which David directed the Ark of God to be

[1] Psa. lv. 22, in the version of the LXX., is quoted by St. Peter (1 Pet. v. 7).

[2] Probably the last house in the suburbs of Jerusalem. The rendering in our Authorised Version (2 Sam. xv. 17): "in a place that was far off," is not only incorrect, but absolutely meaningless.

[3] It is impossible to suppose that these six hundred were natives of Gath. Everything points to his old companions-in-arms, probably popularly called "Gathites," as we might speak of our Crimean or Abyssinian warriors.

[4] Kidron—"the dark flowing"—was only a brook during the winter and early spring rains.

taken back. At the same time he established communication with the city through the priests.[1] He would wait by "the fords" of the wilderness [2] till the sons of the two priests should bring him trustworthy tidings by which to guide his further movements.

It reads almost like prophecy, this description of the procession of weeping mourners, whom Jerusalem had cast out, going up "the ascent of the olive-trees," and once more halting at the top, "where it was wont to worship God !"[3] A little before, the alarming news had come that Ahithophel had joined the conspiracy. But now a welcome sight greeted them. Hushai, the Archite (comp. Josh. xvi. 2), David's friend and adviser, came to meet the king, and offered to accompany him. But the presence of unnecessary non-combatants would manifestly have entailed additional difficulties, especially if of the age of Hushai. Besides, a man like the Archite might render David most material service in Jerusalem, if, by feigning to join the conspirators, he could gain the confidence of Absalom, and so, perhaps, counteract the dreaded counsels of Ahithophel. Accordingly, Hushai was sent back to the city, there to act in concert with the priests.

Twice more David's progress was interrupted before he and his men reached *Ayephim*.[4] First it was Ziba, who, deeming this a good opportunity for securing to himself the coveted property of his master, came on pretext of bringing provisions for the fugitives, but really to falsely represent Mephibosheth

[1] The expression (2 Sam. xv. 27), rendered in the Authorised Version : "Art thou not a seer?" is very difficult. Keil and others, by slightly altering the punctuation, translate : "Thou seer !"

[2] So the *Chethib*, or written text, has it ; the *Keri*, or emendated text, has "plains." The former seems the more correct. The "fords" were, of course, those where the Jordan was crossed.

[3] This is the correct rendering, and not as in the Authorised Version (2 Sam. xv. 32) : "where he worshipped God."

[4] The Authorised Version translates 2 Sam. xvi. 14 : "they came *weary* ;" but the word *Ayephim* is evidently intended as the name of a place, though it may mean "weary," somewhat in the sense of our "Traveller's Rest."

as engaged in schemes for recovering the throne of Israel amidst the general confusion. The story was so manifestly improbable, that we can only wonder at David's haste in giving it credence, and according to Ziba what he desired. Another and sadder interruption was the appearance of Shimei, a distant kinsman of Saul. As David, surrounded by his soldiers and the people, passed Bahurim, on the farther side of the Mount of Olives, Shimei followed on the opposite slope of the hill, casting earth and stones at the king, and cursing him with such words as these : "Get away! get away! thou man of blood! thou wicked man!" thus charging him, by implication, with the death, if not of Saul and Jonathan, yet of Abner and Ishbosheth. Never more truly than on this occasion did David act and speak like his old self, and, therefore, also as a type of the Lord Jesus Christ in similar circumstances (comp. Luke ix. 52–56). At that moment, when he realised that all which had come upon him was from God, and when the only hope he wished to cherish was not in human deliverance, but in God's mercy, he would feel more than ever how little he had in common with the sons of Zeruiah, and how different were the motives and views which animated them (2 Sam. xvi. 10). Would that he had ever retained the same spirit as in this the hour of his deepest humiliation, and had not, after his success, relapsed into his former weakness! But should not all this teach us, that, however necessary a deep and true sense of guilt and sin may be, yet if sin pardoned continueth sin brooded over, it becomes a source, not of sanctification, but of moral weakness and hindrance? Let the dead bury their dead, but let *us* arise and follow Christ—and, "forgetting those things which are behind, and reaching forth unto those things which are before," let us "press toward the mark for the prize of the high calling of God in Christ Jesus" (Phil. iii. 13, 14).

CHAPTER II.

Ahithophel's twofold Advice—Hushai prevents imminent Danger—David is informed, and crosses the Jordan—The Battle in the Forest—Death of Absalom—Mourning of David—David's Measures—Return to Gilgal— Barzillai and Joab as Representative Men of their Period — Federal Republican Rising under Sheba—Murder of Amasa—Death of Sheba.

(2 SAM. XVI.—XX.)

DAVID had not left the capital a moment too soon. He had scarcely quitted the city when Absalom and his forces appeared, and took possession of it. Hushai the Archite was one of the first to welcome him with feigned allegiance. There was a touch of boastful self-confidence about the manner in which the new king received his father's old counsellor, which the experienced man of the world well knew how to utilise. By skilful flattery of his vanity, Absalom was soon gained, and Hushai obtained access to his counsels. Thus far everything had prospered with Absalom. Jerusalem had been occupied without a struggle; and the new king now found himself at the head of a very large force, though of wholly undisciplined troops. But Ahithophel at least must have known that, though David had fled, his cause was far from lost. On the contrary, he was at the head of veteran warriors, filled with enthusiasm for their leader, and commanded by the ablest generals in the land. Besides, account must also be taken of the reaction which would undoubtedly set in. The flush of confidence on the part of Absalom's raw levies, caused by success where no resistance had been offered, would pass away in measure as the real difficulties of their undertaking daily more and more appeared; while, on the other hand, sympathy with David, and adherents to his cause, would increase in the same proportion. In these circumstances even a much less sagacious adviser than Ahithophel, whose counsel was regarded in those days as if a man had inquired of the oracle of God, would have felt that Absalom's chief, if not his sole chance of success, lay in a quick and decisive stroke, such as should obviate the necessity of a protracted campaign. But first Ahithophel must secure himself, and, indeed, all the adherents of Absalom.

Considering the vanity and folly of Absalom, of which his easy reception of Hushai must have afforded fresh evidence to Ahithophel, and David's well-known weakness towards his children, it was quite possible that a reconciliation might yet take place between the usurper and his father. In that case Ahithophel would be the first, the other leaders in the rebellion the next, to suffer. The great aim of an unscrupulous politician would therefore be to make the breach between father and son publicly and absolutely permanent. This was the object of the infamous advice which Ahithophel gave Absalom (2 Sam. xvi. 21, 22), though, no doubt, he represented it as affording, in accordance with Oriental custom, public evidence that he had succeeded to the throne. While recoiling with horror from this unnatural crime, we cannot but call to mind the judgment predicted upon David (2 Sam. xii. 11, 12), and note how, as so often was the case, the event, supernaturally foretold, happened, not by some sudden interference, but through a succession of natural causes.

Having thus secured himself and his fellow-conspirators, Ahithophel proposed to select 12,000 men, make a rapid march, and that very night surprise David's followers—weary, dispirited, greatly outnumbered, and not yet properly organised. Had this advice been followed, the result would probably have been such as Ahithophel anticipated. A panic would have ensued, David fallen a victim, and with his death his cause been for ever at an end. But a higher power than the wisdom of the renowned Gilonite guided events. In the language of

Holy Scripture, "Jehovah had appointed to defeat the good counsel of Ahithophel" (2 Sam. xvii. 14). But, as first explained to Absalom and the council of Israelitish elders, Ahithophel's advice at once commended itself to their acceptance. Hushai seems not to have been present at that meeting. He was too prudent to intrude unbidden into the king's council-chamber. Besides, he had made arrangements for communicating with David before any measure of his enemies could have been executed. Just outside the city-wall, by the "*En-Rogel*," "the Fuller's Fountain"—for they dared not show themselves in the city—the two young priests, Jonathan and Ahimaaz the swift-footed (2 Sam. xviii. 23), waited in readiness to carry tidings to David.

Although Absalom had followed Ahithophel's vile advice, by which no immediate danger was incurred, it was another thing to take so decisive a step as to risk the flower of his army in a night attack upon David. If Ahithophel had retired from the royal presence in the expectation of seeing his counsel immediately carried out, he was soon to find himself disappointed. Hushai was next sent for, and consulted as to the measure proposed by Ahithophel. It was easy for the old statesman to conjure up difficulties and dangers to one so inexperienced and so irresolute as Absalom, and still more, by means of unlimited flattery, to turn one so vain into another course. Absalom had only to speak, and all Israel would gather to him from Dan even to Beer-sheba,—they would light upon David like the dew upon the grass; or if he fled into a city, why, cart-ropes would suffice to drag it, to the smallest stone, into the nearest river! On the other hand, this was the worst time for attacking David and his men when they were desperate. The idea of a night surprise was altogether inadmissible, bearing in mind David's great experience in such warfare; while any mishap, however small, would be fatal to Absalom's cause. We scarcely wonder, even taking the merely rational view of it, that in such a council-chamber the advice of Hushai should have prevailed, although we recognise none the less devoutly, the

Hand of God in ordering all. There was one, however, who did not deceive himself as to the consequences of this fatal mistake. Ahithophel knew, as if he had already witnessed it, that from this hour Absalom's cause was lost. His own course was soon and decisively chosen. He returned to his city, set his affairs in order, and, with the deliberate cynicism of a man who has lost all faith, committed that rare crime in Israel, suicide. Typical as the history of David is throughout, we cannot fail to see here also a terrible prefigurement of the end of him, who, having been the friend and companion of the Lord Jesus—perhaps regarded as the "wise adviser" among the simple disciples—betrayed his Master, and, like Ahithophel, ended by hanging himself (Matt. xxvii. 5).

Meanwhile, Hushai had communicated with the priests in Jerusalem. His counsel had, indeed, been adopted; but it was impossible to know what one so irresolute as Absalom might ultimately do. At any rate, it was necessary David should be informed, so as to secure himself against a surprise. A trusty maidservant of the priest carried the message to the young men by the "Fuller's Fountain." At the last moment their enterprise was almost defeated. A lad—probably one of those stationed to watch any suspicious movement—noticed their hurried departure in the direction of David's camp. Happily, the young men had observed the spy, and got the start of those sent after them. It was not the first nor yet the last time that an Israelitish woman wrought deliverance for her people, when at Bahurim the two young priests were successfully hidden in an empty well, and their pursuers led astray (2 Sam. xvii. 18-20). And here we gladly mark how different from the present inmates of Eastern harems were the mothers, wives, and daughters of Israel, — how free in their social intercourse, and how powerful in their influence : the religious and social institutions of the Old Testament forming in this respect also a preparation for the position which the New Testament would assign to woman. But to return. Coming out of their concealment, the two priests reached the encampment safely, and informed David of his danger. Ere the morning light he and all his followers had put the Jordan between them and their enemies; and anything like a surprise was henceforth impossible.

It all happened as Ahithophel had anticipated. The revolution now changed into a civil war, of which the issue could not be doubtful. David and his forces fell back upon Mahanaim, " a strong city in a well-provisioned country, with a mountainous district for retreat in case of need, and a warlike and friendly population."[1] Here adherents soon gathered around him, while wealthy and influential heads of clans not only openly declared in his favour, but supplied him with all necessaries. We are inclined to regard the three mentioned in the sacred narrative (2 Sam. xvii. 27) as representative men : *Shobi*, of the extreme border-inhabitants, or rather foreign tributaries (comp. 2 Sam. x. 2); *Machir*, of the former adherents of Saul; and *Barzillai*, of the wealthy land-owners generally.

With Absalom matters did not fare so well. Intrusting the command of his army to a relative, Amasa, the natural son of one Ithra, an Ishmaelite,[2] and of Abigail, David's step-sister,[3] he crossed the Jordan to offer battle to his father's forces. These must have considerably increased since his flight from Jerusalem (comp. 2 Sam. xviii. 1, 2), though, no doubt, they were still greatly inferior in number to the undisciplined multitude which followed Absalom. David divided his army into three corps, led by Joab, Abishai, and Ittai—the chief command being entrusted to Joab, since the people would not allow the king himself to go into battle. The field was most skilfully chosen for an engagement with undisciplined

---

[1] *Speaker's Commentary*, Vol. II. p. 429.

[2] This is the correct reading, as in 1 Chron. ii. 17. The word "Israelite " in 2 Sam. xvii. 25 is evidently a clerical error.

[3] From 2 Sam. xvii. 25, it appears that both Abigail and Zeruiah, though David's sisters, were not the daughters of Jesse, David's father, but of Nahash. It follows, that David's mother had been twice married : first to Nahash and then to Jesse, and that Abigail and Zeruiah were David's step-sisters.

superior numbers, being a thick forest near the Jordan,[1] which, with its pitfalls, morasses, and entanglements, destroyed more of Absalom's followers than fell in actual contest. From the first the battle was not doubtful; it soon became a carnage rather than a conflict.

One scene on that eventful day had deeply and, perhaps, painfully impressed itself on the minds of all David's soldiers. As they marched out of Mahanaim on the morning of the battle, the king had stood by the side of the gate, and they had defiled past him by hundreds and by thousands. One thing only had he been heard by all to say, and this he had repeated to each of the generals. It was simply : " Gently,[2] for my sake, with the lad, with Absalom !" If the admonition implied the existence of considerable animosity on the part of David's leaders against the author of this wicked rebellion, it showed, on the other hand, not only weakness, but selfishness, almost amounting to heartlessness, on the part of the king. It was, as Joab afterwards reproached him, as if he had declared that he regarded neither princes nor servants, and that it would have mattered little to him how many had died, so long as his own son was safe (2 Sam. xix. 6). If such was the impression produced, we need not wonder that it only increased the general feeling against Absalom. This was soon to be brought to the test. In his pursuit of the rebels, one of Joab's men came upon a strange sight. It seems that, while Absalom was riding rapidly through the dense wood in his flight, his head had somehow been jerked in between the branches of one of the large spreading terebinths—perhaps, as Josephus has it (*Ant.* vii. 10, 2), having been entangled by the flowing hair. In this position the mule which he rode—perhaps David's royal mule —had run away from under him ; while Absalom, half suf- focated and disabled, hung helpless, a prey to his pursuers.

[1] It is impossible to decide whether this " Wood of Ephraim " was west or east of the Jordan. From the context, the latter seems the more probable.
[2] So literally in the Hebrew text.

But the soldier who first saw him knew too well the probable consequences of killing him, to be tempted to such an act by any reward, however great. He only reported it to Joab, but would not become his tool in the matter. Indeed, Joab himself seems to have hesitated, though he was determined to put an end to Absalom's schemes, which he must have resented the more, since but for his intervention the prince would not have been allowed to return to Jerusalem. And so, instead of killing, he only wounded Absalom with pointed staves,[1] leaving it to his armour-bearers finally to despatch the unhappy youth. His hacked and mangled remains were cast into a great pit in the wood, and covered by a large heap of stones. A terrible contrast, this unknown and unhonoured criminal's grave, to the splendid monument which Absalom had reared for himself after the death of his sons! Their leader being dead, Joab, with characteristic love for his countrymen, sounded the *rappel*, and allowed the fugitive Israelites to escape.

But who was to carry to the king tidings of what had happened? Joab knew David too well to entrust them to any one whose life he specially valued. Accordingly, he sent a stranger, a Cushite; and only after repeated entreaty and warning of the danger, allowed Ahimaaz also to run with the news to Mahanaim. Between the outer and the inner gates of that city sat the king, anxiously awaiting the result of that decisive day. And now the watchman on the pinnacle above descried one running towards the city. Since he was alone, he could not be a fugitive, but must be a messenger. Soon the watchman saw and announced behind the first a second solitary runner. Presently the first one was so near that, by the swiftness of his running the watchman recognised Ahimaaz. If so, the tidings which he brought must be good, for on no other errand would Ahimaaz have come. And so it was! Without giving the king time for question, he rapidly announced

---

[1] The Hebrew word here used (*Shevet*) generally means sceptre, or else staff or rod, but not dart, as in the Authorised Version (2 Sam. xviii. 14).

the God-given victory. Whatever relief or comfort the news must have carried to the heart of David, he did not express it by a word. Only one question rose to his lips, only one idea of peace[1] did his mind seem capable of contemplating: "Peace to the lad, to Absalom?" Ahimaaz could not, or rather would not, answer. Not so the Cushite messenger, who by this time had also arrived. From his language—though even he feared to say it in so many words—David speedily gathered the fate of his son. In speechless grief he turned from the two messengers, and from the crowd which, no doubt, was rapidly gathering in the gateway, and crept up the stairs leading to the chamber over the gate, while those below heard his piteous groans, and these words, oft repeated : "My son Absalom—my son! My son Absalom! Oh, would that I had died for thee! Absalom, my son—my son!"

That was not a joyous evening at Mahanaim, despite the great victory. The townsmen went about as if there were public mourning, not gladness. The victorious soldiers stole back into the city as if ashamed to show themselves—as if after a defeat, not after a brilliant and decisive triumph. It was more than Joab could endure. Roughly forcing himself into the king's presence, he reproached him for his heartless selfishness, warning him that there were dangers, greater than any he had yet known, which his recklessness of all but his own feelings would certainly bring upon him. What he said was, indeed, true, but it was uttered most unfeelingly— especially remembering the part which he himself had taken in the death of Absalom—and in terms such as no subject, however influential, should have used to his sovereign. No doubt David felt and resented all this. But, for the present, it was evidently necessary to yield; and the king received the people in the gate in the usual fashion.

---

[1] The first word of Ahimaaz as he came close to the king was : "Shalom," "Peace" (in our Authorised Version "All is well"). David's first word to Ahimaaz also was "Shalom." Only Ahimaaz referred to the public weal, David to his personal feelings.

The brief period of insurrectionary intoxication over, the reaction soon set in. David wisely awaited it in Mahanaim. The country recalled the national glory connected with his reign, and realised that, now Absalom had fallen, there was virtually an interregnum equally unsatisfactory to all parties. It certainly was neither politic nor right on the part of David under such circumstances to employ the priests in secret negotiations with the tribe of Judah for his restoration to the throne. Indeed, all David's acts now seem like the outcome of that fatal moral paralysis into which he had apparently once more lapsed. Such, notably, was the secret appointment of Amasa as commander-in-chief in the room of Joab, a measure warranted neither by moral nor by military considerations, and certainly, to say the least, a great political mistake, whatever provocation Joab might have given. We regard in the same light David's conduct in returning to Jerusalem on the invitation of the tribe of Judah only (2 Sam. xix. 14). Preparations for this were made in true Oriental fashion. The men of Judah went as far as Gilgal, where they had in readiness a ferry-boat, in which the king and his household might cross the river. Meantime, those who had cause to dread David's return had also taken their measures. Both Shimei, who had cursed David on his flight, and Ziba, who had so shamefully deceived him about Mephibosheth, went over Jordan "to meet the king."[1] As David was "crossing,"[2] or, rather, about to embark, Shimei, who had wisely brought with him a thousand men of his own tribe, Benjamin—the most hostile to David— entreated forgiveness, appealing, as evidence of his repentance, to his own appearance with a thousand of his clansmen, as the first in Israel to welcome their king. In these circumstances it would have been almost impossible not to pardon Shimei, though David's rebuff to Abishai, read in the light

---

[1] This is the correct rendering, and not, as in the Authorised Version, 2 Sam. xix. 17, last clause : "They went over Jordan before the king."

[2] This is the proper translation of the Hebrew word, and not, as in our Authorised Version (xix. 18) : "As he was come over Jordan."

of the king's dying injunctions to Solomon (1 Kings ii. 8, 9),
sounds somewhat like a magniloquent public rebuke of the
sons of Zeruiah, or an attempt to turn popular feeling against
them. At the same time, it is evident that Shimei's plea would
have lost its force, if David had not entered into separate secret
negotiations with the tribe of Judah.

Ziba's motives in going to meet David need no comment.
There can be little doubt that, well-informed as David must have
been of all that had passed in Jerusalem, he could not but
have known that the bearing and feelings of Mephibosheth had
been the reverse of what his hypocritical servant had represented them (comp. 2 Sam. xix. 24). All the more unjustifiable
was his conduct towards the son of Jonathan.[1] Both the language of irritation which he used towards him, and the compromise which he attempted (xix. 29), show that David felt.
though he would not own, himself in the wrong. Indeed,
throughout, David's main object now seemed to be to conciliate
favour and to gain adherents—in short, to compass his own
ends by his own means, which were those of the natural, not
of the spiritual man ; of the Oriental, though under the influence
of religion, rather than of the man after God's own heart. For,
at the risk of uttering a truism, we must insist that there are
only two courses possible—either to yield ourselves wholly to
the guidance of the Holy Spirit, or else to follow our natural
impulses. These impulses are not such as we may, perhaps,
imagine, or suppose them to have become under the influence
of religion. For the natural man always remains what he had
been—what birth, nationality, education, and circumstances
had made him. This consideration should keep us from harsh
and, probably, erroneous judgments of others, and may likewise serve for our own warning and instruction.

Happily, this history also presents a brighter picture. It is

[1] The Talmud makes the following significant application : "In the
hour when David said to Mephibosheth, Thou and Ziba shall divide the
land, a *Bath Kol* (voice of God) came forth and said to him : Rehoboam
and Jeroboam shall divide the kingdom" (*Shabb.* 56 b.).

that of the grand patriarchal chieftain, Barzillai, who had supported David in his adversity, and now came, despite the weight of his years, to escort the king over the Jordan. No reward or acknowledgment did he seek—in fact, the suggestion seemed almost painful. A good and true man this, happy in his independence, though not too proud to allow his son Chimham to go to court—all the more that he had nothing to gain by it. May we not legitimately infer, that his conduct was influenced not merely by loyalty to his earthly sovereign, but by the recognition of the higher spiritual truths, and the hope for Israel and the world, symbolised by the reign of David? For nearly eighty years Barzillai had watched in distant Rogelim the varying fortunes of his loved people. He remembered the time when Samuel was "judge;" he recalled the hopes enkindled in the hearts of Israel when, after the brilliant exploit in his own Jabesh-gilead, Saul was proclaimed king. He had followed the waning glory of that same Saul— for far and wide are tidings carried in the East, told by watch-fires, and borne from home to home—until hope had almost died out in his soul. Then came the story of David, and increasingly, as he followed his career, or when some one would repeat one of those new Psalms—so different from the old war-songs in which Jewish deeds of valour had been recorded—ascribing all to Jehovah, and making man of no account, it all seemed to mark a new period in the history of Israel, and Barzillai felt that David was indeed God's Anointed, the symbol of Israel's real mission, and the type of its accomplishment. And at last, after the shameful defeat of Israel and the sad death of Saul, he had hailed what had taken place in Hebron. The capture of Jerusalem, the erection of a central sanctuary there, and the subjection of Israel's enemies round about, would seem to him bright links in the same chain. And though David's sad fall must have grieved him to the heart, it could never have influenced his views of Absalom's conduct, nor yet shaken his own allegiance. And now that David's reign, so far as its spiritual bearing was concerned, was evidently coming to a close — its great results achieved, its spiritual meaning realised—he would feel that nothing could undo the past, which henceforth formed part of the spiritual inheritance of Israel, or rather of that of the world at large. And so, in the spirit of Simeon, when he had witnessed the incipient fulfilment of Israel's hopes, Barzillai was content to "turn back again" to his own city, to die there, and be laid in the grave of his father and mother, who had lived in times far more troubled than his own, and had seen but "far off" that of which he had witnessed the happy accomplishment.

On the other hand, we may, at this stage of our inquiries, be allowed to place by the side of Barzillai another representative man of that period. If Barzillai was a type of the spiritual, Joab was of the national aspect of Judaism. He was intensely Jewish, in the tribal meaning of the word, not in its higher, world-wide bearing : only Judæan in everything that outwardly marked Judaism, though not as regarded its inward and spiritual reality. Fearless, daring, ambitious, reckless, jealous, passionate, unscrupulous, but withal most loving of his country and people, faithful to, and, no doubt, zealous for his religion, so far as it was ancestral and national—Joab represented the one phase of Judaism, as Barzillai the other. Joab stands before us as a typical Eastern, or rather as the typical Eastern Judæan. Nor is it without deep symbolical meaning, as we trace the higher teaching of history, that Joab, the typical Eastern Judæan,—may we not say, the type of Israel after the flesh?—should, in carrying out his own purposes and views, have at last compassed his own destruction.

David's difficulties did not end with the crossing of Jordan. On the contrary, they seemed rather to commence anew. He had been received by the tribe of Judah ; a thousand Benjamites had come for purposes of their own ; and probably a number of other tribesmen may have joined the king during his progress.[1] But the tribes, in their corporate capacity, had

---

[1] It is thus that we interpret the expression—" half the people of Israel "—in 2 Sam. xix. 40. Of course, it must not be taken literally, as appears from the whole context.

not been asked to take part in the matter, and both David and Judah had acted as if they were of no importance. Accordingly, when the representatives of Israel arrived in Gilgal, there was fierce contention between them and the men of Judah about this unjustifiable slight—the men of Judah being the more violent, as usual with those who do a wrong.

It needed only a spark to set the combustible material on fire. A worthless man, one Sheba, a Benjamite, who happened to be there, blew a trumpet, and gave it forth to the assembled representatives of the tribes that, since they had no part in David, they should leave him to reign over those who had selected him as their king. It was just such a cry as in the general state of excitement would appeal to popular feeling. David soon found himself deserted by his Israelitish subjects, obliged to return to Jerusalem with only his own tribesmen, and threatened by a formidable revolution in front. To suppress the movement before it had time to spread and disintegrate the country by everywhere exciting tribal jealousies —such was David's first care on his return to Jerusalem, after setting his household in order (2 Sam. xx. 3). But the fatal consequences of David's late conduct now appeared. True to his promise, he proposed to entrust to Amasa the command of the expedition against Sheba and what, to borrow a modern term, we may call the "Federal Republic." But, whether from personal incapacity, or, more probably, from the general want of confidence in, and dissatisfaction with, the new commander, Amasa did not even succeed in bringing together a force. As time was of the greatest importance,[1] David felt himself obliged again to have recourse to Abishai, or rather, through him, to Joab.[2] There was now no lack

---

[1] To use the pictorial Hebrew expression (2 Sam. xx. 6) : "lest he find him fenced cities, and tear out our eye." This seems to us a more suitable rendering than that either of our Authorised Version or of Ewald.

[2] The text mentions only dealings between David and Abishai, but the subsequent narrative shows that Joab was in command. From the relations between Joab and the king, it seems likely that David may have preferred to communicate with Joab through his brother.

of trusty warriors, and the expedition at once moved north-wards.

The forces, under the leadership of Abishai and Joab, had reached the great stone at Gibeon, when Amasa "came to meet them"[1] from the opposite direction, no doubt, on his way to Jerusalem. Joab was, as usual, "girt with his armour-coat as a garment, and upon it the girdle of the sword, bound upon his loins, in its scabbard; and it [the scabbard] came out, and it [the sword] fell out."[2] Amasa seems to have been so startled by this unexpected appearance of a host with another leader as to have lost all presence of mind. He saw not the sword which Joab picked up from the ground, and now held low down in his left hand, but allowed his treacherous relative to take him by the beard, as if to kiss him, so that the sword ran into the lower part of his body. Probably Joab, while determined to rid himself of his rival, had adopted this plan, in the hope of leaving it open to doubt whether Amasa's death had been the result of accident or of criminal intention. Then, as if there were not time for delay, Joab and Abishai left the body weltering where it had fallen, and hastened on their errand.

It was a dreadful sight; and not all the urgency of the soldier whom Joab had posted by the dead or dying man could prevent the people from lingering, horror-stricken, around him. At last the body had to be removed. It had been left on the ground, probably alike as a mark of contempt and a warning to others not to provoke the jealousy of Joab. And now David's army was in full chase after Sheba and his adherents. They followed him through the whole land up to the far north among the fortresses[3] by the Lake Merom,

[1] So 2 Sam. xx. 8, and not, as in the Authorised Version, "went before them."

[2] This is the correct rendering of the rest of ver. 8.

[3] These fortresses are grouped together in 1 Kings xv. 20; 2 Kings xv. 29; 2 Chron. xvi. 4. It has been ingeniously suggested that the expression: "all the Berites" (2 Sam. xx. 14), which gives no meaning, should be regarded as a masculine form of the word, and rendered: "all the fortresses."

where he was at last tracked to Abel, or rather, Abel-Beth-maachah. To this fortress Joab now laid siege. Its destruction, however, was averted by the wisdom of one of its women. Demanding speech of Joab from the city-wall, she reminded the general that the people of Abel had been famed, not for being rash in action, but rather wise and deliberate in counsel. Had Joab ever asked whether the town of Abel, which he was about to destroy, shared the views of Sheba, or took part in the rebellion? She, and, by implication, her fellow-citizens, were quite the contrary of turbulent conspirators. How, then, could Joab act so unpatriotically, so un-Jewishly, as to wish to destroy a city and a mother in Israel, and to swallow up the inheritance of Jehovah? And when Joab explained that it was not the destruction of a peaceable city, but the suppression of a rebellion which he sought, she proposed, as a speedy end to all trouble, that Sheba should be killed, and, in evidence of it, his head thrown over the wall. It was an easy mode of ridding themselves both of a troublesome visitor and of a terrible danger,—and the gory head cast at his feet convinced Joab that the rebellion was at an end, that he might retire from the city, dismiss his army, and return to Jerusalem. So ended the last rising against David—and, we may add, the political history of his reign.

CHAPTER III.

Appendix to the History of David.

The Famine—The Pestilence—The Temple Arrangements—David's Last Hymn and Prophetic Utterance.

(2 SAM. XXI.—XXIV.; 1 CHRON. XXI.—XXVII.)

WITH the suppression of the federal revolution under Sheba, the political history of David, as related in the Second Book of Samuel, closes. Accordingly, the account of this, the second part of his reign, concludes, like that of the first (2 Sam. viii. 16), with an enumeration of his principal officers (2 Sam. xx. 23 to the end). What follows in the Second Book of Samuel (xxi.–xxiv.), must be regarded as an Appendix, giving, first, an account of the famine which desolated the land (xxi. 1–14), probably in the *earlier* part, and of the pestilence which laid it waste, probably towards the *close* of David's reign (xxiv.); secondly, some brief notices of the Philistine wars (xxi. 15–22), and a detailed register of David's heroes (xxiii. 8–39), neither of which will require comment on our part; and, lastly, David's final Psalm of thanksgiving (xxii.), and his last prophetic utterances (xxiii. 1–7). All these are grouped together at the end of the Second Book of Samuel, probably because it was difficult to insert them in any other place consistently with the plan of the work, which, as we have repeatedly noted, was not intended to be a biography or a history of David, chronologically arranged. Perhaps we should add, that the account of the pestilence was placed last in the book (xxiv.), because it forms an introduction to the preparations made for the building of the Temple by Solomon. For, as we understand it, no sooner had the place been divinely pointed out where the Sanctuary should be reared, than David commenced such preparations for it as he could make. And here the First Book of Chronicles supplements most valuable notices, not recorded in any other part of Scripture. From these we learn what David did and ordered in his kingdom with a view to the building of the Temple and the arrangement of its future services (1 Chron. xxii.–xxix.). We have thus four particulars under which to group our summary of what we have designated as the Appendix to the History of David : the *famine ;* the *pestilence ;* the *Temple arrangements ;* and the *last Psalm and prophecy of the king.*

1. *The Famine* (2 Sam. xxi. 1–14).—There is not a more harrowing narrative in Holy Scripture than that connected with the famine which for three years desolated Palestine. Properly to understand it, we require to keep two facts in view. First, the Gibeonites, who, at the time of Joshua, had secured themselves from destruction by fraud and falsehood (Josh. ix. 3, etc.), were really heathens—Hivites, or, as they are called in the sacred text, Amorites, which was a general designation for all the Canaanites (Gen. x. 16; xv. 16; Josh. ix. 1; xi. 3; xii. 8, etc.). We know, only too well, the character of the Canaanite inhabitants of the land ; and although, after their incorporation with Israel, the Gibeonites must have been largely influenced for good, their habits of thinking and feeling would change comparatively little,[1]—the more so because, as there would be few, if any, intermarriages between them and native Israelites, they would be left, at least socially, isolated. This will account for their ferocious persistence in demanding the uttermost punishment prescribed by the law. The provisions of this law must be our second point of consideration. Here we have again to bear in mind the circumstances of the times, the existing moral, social, and national conditions, and the spiritual stage which Israel had then reached. The fundamental principle, laid down in Numb.

---

[1] In a previous volume of this *History* we have shown how much even a woman like Jael was influenced by tribal traditions—so to speak, the inherited taint of blood.

xxxv., was that of the holiness of the land in which Jehovah dwelt among His people. This holiness must be guarded (ver. 34). But one of the worst defilements of a land was that by innocent blood shed in it. According to the majestic view of the Old Testament, blood shed by a murderer's hand could not be covered up—it was, so to speak, a living thing which cried for vengeance, until the blood of him that had shed it silenced its voice (ver. 33), or, in other words, till the moral equipoise had been restored. While, therefore, the same section of the law provided safety in case of unintentional homicide (vers. 10–29), and regulated the old practice of "avenging blood," it also protected the land against crime, which it would not allow to be compensated for by money (ver. 31). Hence the Gibeonites were strictly within the letter of the law in demanding retaliation on the house of Saul, in accordance with the universally acknowledged Old Testament principle of the solidarity of a family; and David had no alternative but to concede their claim. This is one aspect of the question. The other must be even more reverently approached. We can only point out how they who lived in those times (especially such as the Gibeonites) would feel that they might cry to God for vengeance, and expect it from the Just and True One; and how the sternest lessons concerning public breach of faith and public crimes would be of the deepest national importance after such a reign as that of Saul.

The story itself may be told in few sentences. For some reason unrecorded—perhaps in the excess of his carnal zeal, but certainly without sufficient grounds—Saul had made havoc among the Gibeonites, in direct contravention of those solemn engagements into which Israel had entered, and which up to that time had been scrupulously observed. When, afterwards, a famine desolated the land for three years, and David sought the face of Jehovah, he was informed that it was due to the blood-guilt[1] which still rested on the house of Saul.

[1] It is thus we understand the expression (2 Sam. xxi. 1): "It is for Saul, and for his bloody house."

Upon this the king summoned the Gibeonites, and asked them what atonement they desired for the wrong done them, so that the curse which they had invoked might no longer rest on the inheritance of Jehovah. Their answer was characteristic. " It is not *a matter* to us of silver or of gold, in regard to Saul and his house, nor is it ours to put to death any one in Israel." "And he said : What say ye then? and I will do it for you."[1] Then came the demand, made with all the ferocity and irony of which they were capable, that the blood-vengeance which they, as Gibeonites, did not venture to take, should be executed for them, and that seven of Saul's descendants should be handed over to them that they might be nailed to the cross —of course *after* they were dead, for so the law directed[2]— as they termed it : " To Jehovah in Gibeah of Saul, the chosen of Jehovah."

Terrible as their demand was, it could not be refused, and the two sons of Rizpah, a foreign concubine of Saul, and five sons of Merab,[3] Saul's eldest daughter, were selected as the victims. Then this most harrowing spectacle was presented. From the commencement of the barley harvest in April till the early rains of autumn evidenced the removal of the curse from the land, hung those lifeless, putrescent bodies, which a fierce Syrian sun shrivelled and dried; and beneath them, ceaseless, restless, was the weird form of Saul's concubine. When she lay down at night it was on the coarse hair-cloth of mourners,

[1] We have translated literally 2 Sam. xxi. 4.

[2] The punishment of crucifixion, or impaling, is mentioned in Numb. xxv. 4. But that criminals were not crucified or impaled *alive*, but only *after* they were slain, appears from ver. 5. Similarly, in hanging, death always preceded the hanging (Deut xxi. 22, where our Authorised Version is not sufficiently distinct). The same remark applies to the punishment of *burning*, which was only executed on the dead body of the criminal (Lev. xx. 14), as appears from Josh. vii. 15 comp. with ver. 11. In these respects the Rabbinical Law was much more cruel, ordering literal strangulation, and burning by pouring down molten lead (comp. specially *Mishnah Sanh.* vii. 1–3).

[3] In 2 Sam. xxi. 8, by a clerical error, we have *Michal* instead of *Merab*. But it was the latter, not the former, who was married to Adriel the Meholathite (comp. 1 Sam. xviii. 19).

which she spread upon the rock ; but day and night was she on her wild, terrible watch to chase from the mangled bodies the birds of prey that, with hoarse croaking, swooped around them, and the jackals whose hungry howls woke the echoes of the night. Often has *Judæa capta* been portrayed as weeping over her slain children. But as we realise the innocent Jewish victims of Gentile persecution in the Middle Ages, and then remember the terrible cry under the Cross, this picture of Rizpah under the seven crosses, chasing from the slaughtered the vultures and the jackals, seems ever to come back to us as its terrible emblem and type.

" And it was told David what Rizpah, the daughter of Aiah, the concubine of Saul, had done. And David went [himself] and took the bones of Saul, and the bones of Jonathan his son, from the men of Jabesh-gilead, who had stolen them from the street of Bethshan, where the Philistines had hanged them, when the Philistines had slain Saul in Gilboa : and he brought up from thence the bones of Saul and the bones of Jonathan his son; and they gathered the bones of them that were crucified. And the bones of Saul and Jonathan his son buried they in the country of Benjamin in Zelah, in the sepulchre of Kish his father."

2. *The Pestilence.*—In regard to this event, it is of the greatest importance to bear in mind that it was sent in consequence of some sin of which Israel, as a people, were guilty. True, the direct cause and immediate occasion of it were the pride and carnal confidence of David, perhaps his purpose of converting Israel into a military monarchy. But this state of mind of their king was, as we are expressly told (2 Sam. xxiv. 1), itself a judgment upon Israel from the Lord, when Satan stood up to accuse Israel, and was allowed thus to influence David (1 Chron. xxi. 1). If, as we suppose, the popular rising under Absalom and Sheba was that for which Israel was thus punished, there is something specially corresponding to the sin alike in the desire of David to have the people numbered, and in the punishment which followed. Nor ought we to overlook

another Old Testament principle evidenced in this history: that of the solidarity of a people and their rulers.

It seems a confirmation of the view, that the sin of David, in wishing to ascertain the exact number of those capable of bearing arms, was due to carnal elation and pride, and that the measure was somehow connected with military ambition on his part, that both in 2 Sam. and in 1 Chron. this story follows an enumeration of the three classes of David's heroes, and of some of their most notable feats of arms.[1] The unwillingness of Joab and of the other captains, to whom the king entrusted the census, arose partly from the knowledge that such an attempt at converting all Israel into a large camp would be generally disliked and disapproved—a feeling with which he and his fellow-captains would, as Israelitish patriots, fully sympathise. But religious considerations also came in, since all would feel that a measure prompted by pride and ambition would certainly bring judgment upon the people (1 Chron. xxi. 3). Remonstrance having been vain, the military census was slowly and reluctantly taken, the Levites being, however, excluded from it (Numb. i. 47–54), and the royal order itself recalled before the territory of Benjamin was reached.[2] For already David's conscience was alive to the guilt which he had incurred. It was after a night of confession and prayer on the part of David, that Gad was sent to announce to him the punishment of his sin. For, the temporal punishment appropriately followed—not preceded—the confession of public sin. Left to choose between famine,[3] defeat, and pestilence, David

[1] The same inference may be drawn from 1 Chron. xxvii. 23, 24, where the enumeration is evidently connected with the military organisation of the nation.

[2] Comp. 1 Chron. xxi. 6; xxvii. 24. From this latter notice we also gather that the result of the census was *not* entered in the Chronicles of King David. We can therefore the less hesitate in supposing some want of accuracy in the numbers given. Of the two enumerations we prefer that in 2 Sam. xxiv. 9. However, 1,300,000, or even, according to 1 Chron. xxi. 5, 1,570,000 men capable of bearing arms, would only imply a total population of about five or six millions, which is not excessive.

[3] According to 1 Chron. xxi. 12, the famine was to be of *three* years' duration. The number "*seven*" in 2 Sam. xxiv. 13 must be a clerical error.

wisely and well cast himself upon the Lord, finding comfort only in the thought, which has so often brought relief to those who realise it, that, even when suffering for sin, it is well to fall into the hands of Jehovah. Nor was his unuttered hope disappointed. The pestilence, terrible as it was in its desolations, was shortened from three days to less than one day : "from the morning to the time of the assembly," viz., for the evening sacrifice.[1]

Meanwhile "David and the elders, clothed in sackcloth" (1 Chron. xxi. 16), were lying on their faces in humiliation before the Lord. Significantly, it was as the Divine command of mercy sped to arrest the arm of the Angel messenger of the judgment, that he became visible to David and his companions in prayer. Already he had neared Jerusalem, and his sword was stretched towards it—just above Mount Moriah, at that time still outside the city, where Aravnah[2] the Jebusite had his threshing-floor. It was a fitting spot for mercy upon Israel, this place where of old faithful Abraham had been ready to offer his only son unto God ; fitting also as still outside the city ; but chiefly in order that the pardoning and sparing mercy now shown might indicate the site where, on the great altar of burnt-offering, abundant mercy in pardon and acceptance would in the future be dispensed to Israel. At sight of the Angel with his sword pointed towards Jerusalem, David lifted his voice in humblest confession, entreating that, as the sin had been his, so the punishment might descend on him and his household, rather than on his people. This prayer marked the beginning of mercy. By Divine direction, through Gad, David and they who were with him, went to Aravnah to purchase the place thus rendered for ever memorable, in order to consecrate it to the Lord by an altar, on which burnt and peace-offerings were brought. And this was to be the site for the future "house of Jehovah God," and

[1] This is the proper rendering of 2 Sam. xxiv. 15.
[2] This seems to have been the original, while that of Ornan (1 Chron. xxi. 15) and others are the Hebraised forms of the name.

for "the altar of the burnt-offering for Israel" (1 Chron. xxii. 1).

And God had both prepared and inclined the heart of the Jebusite for the willing surrender of the site for its sacred purposes. No doubt he was a proselyte, and probably (analogously to Rahab) had been an ally in the taking of Jerusalem under Joab. It seems that Aravnah and his four sons, while busy in that threshing-floor, had also seen the figure of the Angel high above them, and that it had struck terror into their hearts (1 Chron. xxi. 20). When, therefore, David and his followers came, they were prepared freely to give. not only the threshing-floor, but also all within it,[1] if only Jehovah were pleased to accept the prayer of the king (2 Sam. xxiv. 23). Thus most significantly, in its typical aspect, were Jew and Gentile here brought together to co-operate in the dedication of the Temple-site. It, no doubt, showed insight into Oriental character, though we feel sure it was neither from pride nor narrow national prejudice, that David refused to accept as a gift what had been humbly and, as we believe, heartily offered. But there was evident fitness in the acquisition of the place by money[2] on the part of David, as the representative of all Israel. And as if publicly and from heaven to ratify what had been done, fire, unkindled by man, fell upon the altar and consumed the sacrifices (1 Chron. xxi. 26). But from that moment the destroying sword of the Angel was sheathed at the command of God.

3. *David's Temple arrangements.*—Since the Lord had, in

---

[1] 2 Sam. xxiv. 23, reads in the Hebrew : "The whole, O king, does Aravnah give unto the king," and not as in the Authorised Version.

[2] Of the two statements of the price, we unhesitatingly take that in 1 Chron. xxi. 25 (the other in 2 Sam. depending on a clerical error, very common and easily accounted for in numerals). Bearing in mind that the common shekel was of half the value of the sacred, and that the proportion of gold to silver was about ten to one, the six hundred shekels of gold would amount to about £380. In *Siphré* 146 a., various attempts are made to conciliate the two diverging accounts—it need scarcely be said ineffectually. The learned reader will find a full discussion of the question in Ugolini's tractate *Altare Exterius* (Ugolini Thesaurus, Fol. Vol. x. pp. 504–506).

His Providence, pointed out the place where the Sanctuary was to be reared, David, with characteristic energy, began immediate preparations for a work, the greatness of which the king measured by his estimate of Him for Whose service it was designed (1 Chron. xxii. 5). It almost seems as if in these arrangements all David's former vigour had come back, showing where, despite his weaknesses and failings, the king's heart really was. Besides, the youth of his son and successor Solomon,[1] and the consideration that probably no other monarch would wield such influence in the land as he had possessed, determined David not to neglect nor defer anything that he might be able to do. First, he took a census of the "strangers,"[2] and set them to prepare the stone, iron, and timber work. His next care was to give solemn charge to Solomon concerning what was so much on his own heart. Recapitulating all that had passed, when he first proposed to "build an house unto the Name of Jehovah," he laid this work upon his son and God-appointed successor, as the main business of his reign. Yet not as a merely outward work to be done, but as the manifestation of spiritual religion, and as the outcome of allegiance to God and His law (1 Chron. xxii. 6–12). Only such principles would secure true prosperity to his reign (ver. 13). For himself, he had "by painful labour"[3] gathered great treasures,[4] which

---

[1] Solomon was probably at this time about twenty years of age.

[2] These were not only foreign settlers, but the descendants of the original inhabitants of the land whose lives had been spared. Such was their number that Solomon could employ no fewer than one hundred and fifty thousand of them to bear burdens, and to hew stones (1 Kings v. 15; 2 Chron. ii. 17).

[3] This, and not "in my trouble," is the correct rendering of 1 Chron. xxii. 14.

[4] Although, as we have often explained, clerical errors occur in the numerals in the historical books, it may be well to give the real equivalent of the silver and gold, mentioned in 1 Chron. xxii. 14. Bearing in mind the distinction between the sacred and the common shekel (2 Sam. xiv. 26; 1 Kings x. 17, compared with 2 Chron. ix. 16), it would amount to under £4,000,000. Immense as this sum is, Keil has shown that it is by no means out of proportion with the treasures taken as booty in antiquity (comp. *Bibl. Comment.* Vol. v. pp. 181–184).

were to be devoted to the building of the new Temple ; and he had made all possible preparations for it. Finally, summoning "the princes of Israel, with the priests and the Levites" (1 Chron. xxiii. 1, 2), and presenting to them his son Solomon as successor in the kingdom, he entreated their co-operation with him in what was to be the great work of the future—making it not a personal, but a national undertaking, expressive of this, that they had "set heart and soul to seek Jehovah" their God (1 Chron. xxii. 19).

It was in this solemn assembly of laity and priesthood that Solomon's succession was announced and accepted, and that the future organisation of the Temple Services was determined and fixed.[1] A census of the Levites gave their number, from thirty years and upwards, at 38,000 men. Of these 24,000 were appointed to attend to the general ministry of the sanctuary (xxiii. 28–32), 6,000 to act as "officers and judges," 4,000 for instrumental music, and 4,000 as choristers—the latter (and probably also the former class) being subdivided into adepts, of which there were 288 (xxv. 7), and learners (xxv. 8). As all the Levites, so these 288 adepts or trained choristers were arranged by lot into twenty-four courses, a certain number of "learners" being attached to each of them. Each course of Levites had to undertake in turn such services as fell to them. Those who had charge of the gates were arranged into classes, there being altogether twenty-four posts in the Sanctuary in which watch was to be kept (1 Chron. xxvi. 1–19). Similarly, the priests, the descendants of Aaron, were arranged by lot into twenty-four courses for their special ministry (1 Chron. xxiv. 1–19). Lastly, the sacred text gives a brief account of the work of those 6000 Levites whom David appointed as "scribes and judges" (1 Chron. xxvi. 29–32), and of the final arrangement of the army, and of all the other public offices (1 Chron. xxvii.).

---

[1] It is, of course, impossible here to enter into any critical examination of the chapters in 1 Chron., summarised in our text.

4. *David's last hymn and prophetic utterance* (2 Sam. xxii.–xxiii. 2–7).—The history of David appropriately closes with a grand hymn, which may be described as alike the programme and the summary of his life and reign in their spiritual aspect. Somewhat altered in language, so as to adapt it to liturgical purposes, it is inserted in our present Psalter as Ps. xviii., to which we accordingly refer. This grand hymn of thanksgiving is followed—to use the language of an eminent German critic[1]—by the prophetic testament of the king, in which he indicates the spiritual import and bearing of his kingdom. If Ps. xviii. was a grand Hallelujah, with which David quitted the scene of life, these his "last words" are the Divine attestation of all that he had sung and prophesied in the Psalms concerning the spiritual import of the kingdom which he was to found, in accordance with the Divine message that Nathan had been commissioned to bring to him. Hence these "last words" must be regarded as an inspired prophetic utterance by David, before his death, about *the King* and *the Kingdom* of God in their full and real meaning. The following is the literal rendering of this grand prophecy:

The Spirit of Jehovah speaks by me,[2]
And His Word *is* on my tongue![3]

Saith the God of Israel,
Speaks to me the Rock of Israel:
A Ruler over man,[4] righteous,
A Ruler in the fear of God—
And as the light of morning,[5] *when* riseth the sun[6]—

---

[1] Keil. We quote, of course, only the substance of his remarks.

[2] According to some "in me" or "into me," as Hos. i. 2. In that case, the first clause would indicate inspiration, and the second its human utterance.

[3] The Rabbis and others regard this as referring to all David's Psalms and prophecies.

[4] Not merely over Israel, but over mankind, indicating the future Kingdom of God, and the full application of the prophecy in its Messianic sense.

[5] Here the effects of that great salvation are described. The Rabbis, however, connect it with the previous verse, and regard it as a farther description of this ruler.

[6] The light of the morning of salvation—in opposition to the previous darkness of the night, the sun being the Sun of Righteousness.

Morning without clouds—
From the shining forth out of (after) rain (sprouts) the green out of the
　　earth ! [1]
For is not thus my house with God? [2]
Since an everlasting covenant He hath made with me,
Provided (prepared) in all things, and preserved (kept, watched over)—
Then, all my salvation and all good pleasure,
Shall He not cause it to spring forth?

And (the sons of) Belial, as thorns cast away are they all [3]—
For they are not taken up in the hand [3]
And the man who toucheth them,
Provides himself (*lit.*, fills) with iron and shaft of spear, [4]
And in fire [5] are they utterly burned in their dwelling [6] (where
　　they are).

---

[1] After a night of rain the sun shines forth and the earth sprouts. Comp.
Ps. lxxii. 6 ; Is. xlv. 8.

[2] Pointing to the promise in 2 Sam. vii.—as it were : Does not my house
stand in this relationship towards God, that alike the Just Ruler and the
blessings connected with His reign shall spring from it ?

[3] Here is an indication of the judgment to come upon the enemies of the
Messianic Kingdom.　Mark here the contrast between the consequences of
Belial and those of the morning light when green sprouts from the earth.
Mark also how, while the sprouting of the grass is a gradual and continuous
process, the burning of the castaway thorns is the final but immediate
judgment.　Comp. Matt. xiii. 30.

[4] That is, they are not gathered together with the naked hand in order
to burn them, but people provide themselves with iron instruments held
by wooden handles.

[5] The fire a symbol of the Divine wrath.

[6] Other renderings have been proposed, but the one in the text conveys
the idea that the thorns are burned where they lie.

CHAPTER IV.

Adonijah's Attempt to Seize the Throne—Anointing of Solomon—Great Assembly of the Chiefs of the People—Dying Charge of David—Adonijah's Second Attempt and Punishment—Execution of Joab and of Shimei.

(I KINGS I., II. ; I CHRON. XXIII. I, XXVIII., XXIX.)

THE history of David, as told in the Book of Chronicles, closes with an account of what, in its bearing on the *theocracy*, was of greatest importance—the public charge to Solomon in regard to the building of the Temple and the preparations for the work. On the other hand, the Book of Kings[1] takes up the thread of *prophetic history* where the

[1] It should always be kept in view that (as stated in Vol. iv. p. 163) the history of Israel is presented in the Book of Kings from the *prophetic* point of view. In other words, it is a history written from the standpoint of 2 Sam. vii. 12-16. In the language of Winer (*Real-Wörterb.* vol. i. p. 412, note), "The history of the Old Testament was not regarded as an aggregate of facts, to be ascertained by diligent research and treated with literary ability, but as the manifestation of Jehovah in the events which occurred, for the understanding of which the influence of the Spirit of God was an essential condition." The Old Testament contains not merely secular history. Accordingly, its writers are designated in the Canon as "prophets." The "Book of Kings" was originally one work. Its division into two books was made by the LXX translators. Thence it passed into the *Vulgate,* and was introduced into our printed editions of the Hebrew Bible by Dan. Bomberg, at the beginning of the 16th century. In the LXX and *Vulgate* the books of Samuel and of Kings form one work, divided into four books. The Talmud (*Baba B.* 15 *a*) ascribes the authorship of the Book of Kings to Jeremiah, but the evidence seems insufficient. The author of the "Book of Kings" mentions three sources from which, at least partially, his information was derived : the Acts of Solomon (*once,* 1 Kings xi. 41), the Book of the Chronicles of the Kings of Judah (*sixteen* times), and the Book of the Chronicles of the Kings of Israel (*seventeen* times)—making in all thirty-four references. At the time of the composition of the Book of Chronicles the two last-mentioned works seem to have been either combined, or re-cast into one : the Book of the Kings of Judah and Israel (2 Chron.

previous writers had dropped it. The birth of Solomon had been the beginning of the fulfilment of that glorious promise (2 Sam. vii. 12–16), which gave its spiritual meaning and import to the institution of royalty in Israel. And the promises and the warnings embodied in that prediction form, so to speak, the background of the whole later history of the people of God.

Naturally, the first event recorded in this history is the formal installation of Solomon as the God-appointed successor of David (2 Sam. vii. 12 ; xii. 25 ; 1 Kings viii. 20 ; 1 Chron. xxviii. 5–7). It was somewhat hastened by an incident which, like so many others that caused trouble in Israel, must ultimately be traced to the weakness of David himself. It has already been noticed, in the history of Amnon and in that of Absalom, to what length David carried his indulgence towards his children, and what terrible consequences resulted from it. Both Amnon and Absalom had died violent deaths. A third son of David, Chileab, whose mother was Abigail,

---

xvi. 11 ; xxiv. 27, and other passages). Another important inference is to be derived from a comparison of the Books of Kings with those of Chronicles. Not unfrequently the two relate the same event in almost the same words. But while in the history of Solomon, as told in the Book of Kings, the reference is to the Acts of Solomon, in Chronicles (2 Chron. ix. 29) it is to the "Book of Nathan the prophet, the Prophecy of Ahijah the Shilonite, and the Visions of Iddo the Seer," showing that the work called the Acts of Solomon was based on these three prophetic compositions. Again, in the history of Rehoboam, we have in 2 Chron. xii. 15, a reference to the "Book of Shemaiah the Prophet," and to that of " Iddo the Seer, concerning genealogies ;" in the history of Abijah to the "Midrash of the prophet Iddo " (2 Chron. xiii. 22) ; in that of Uzziah to "the writing of Isaiah the prophet " (2 Chron. xxvi. 22); and in that of Manasseh to "the Book of Chosai" (2 Chron. xxxiii. 19). Without entering into further details, we only remark that passages from the prophecies of Isaiah (xxxvi.–xxxix.), and of Jeremiah (lii.) are inserted in 2 Kings, where, however, they are ascribed not to these prophetic books, but to the "Book of the Kings of Judah" (2 Kings xx. 20). These facts seem to show that the works from which the author of the Book of Kings quoted, were themselves based on earlier prophetic writings. It is only necessary to add in this note that the period embraced in the Books of Kings extends over 455 years.

seems also to have died. At least, so we infer from the silence of Scripture concerning him. These were the three eldest sons of David. The next in point of age was Adonijah the son of Haggith (2 Sam. iii. 2–4). Like his elder brother, Amnon, he had been born in Hebron;[1] like Absalom, he was distinguished by personal attractions. But he also, as Amnon and Absalom, had all his life been fatally indulged by David. In the expressive language of Holy Scripture: "his father had not made him sorry all his days, saying, Why hast thou done so?" (1 Kings i. 6.) The consequence may be easily guessed. By right of primogeniture the succession to the throne seemed his. Why, then, should he not attempt to seize upon a prize so coveted? His father had, indeed, sworn to Bathsheba that Solomon should be his successor (1 Kings i. 13, 30), and that on the ground of express Divine appointment; and the prophet Nathan (ver. 11), as well as the leading men in Church and State, not only knew (as did most people in the land), but heartily concurred in it. But what mattered this to one who had never learned to subject his personal desires to a higher will? This supposed Divine appointment of his younger brother might, after all, have been only a matter of inference to David, and Nathan and Bath-sheba have turned it to account, the one because of the influence which he possessed over Solomon, the other from maternal fondness and ambition. At any rate, the prospect of gaining a crown was worth making an effort; and the more quickly and boldly, the more likely of success.

It must be admitted that circumstances seemed specially to favour Adonijah's scheme. David was indeed only seventy years old; but premature decay, the consequence of a life of exposure and fatigue, had confined him not only to his room (ver. 15), but to his bed (ver. 47). Such was his weakness, that the body had lost its natural heat, which could not be restored even by artificial means; so that the physicians,

---

[1] Accordingly, Adonijah must have been between thirty-three and forty years of age at the time of his attempt to seize the throne.

according to the medical views of those times, had advised bodily contact with a young, healthy subject.[1] For this purpose Abishag,[2] a fair maiden from Shunem, had been brought into the king's harem. In David's utter physical prostration, Adonijah might reckon on being able to carry on his scheme without interference from the king. Indeed, unless David had been specially informed, tidings of the attempt would not even have reached his sick-chamber till it was too late. The rebellion of Absalom had failed because David was in full vigour at the time, and so ably supported by Abiathar the priest and Joab the captain of the host. But Adonijah had attached these two to his interests. It is not difficult to understand the motives of Joab in trying to secure the succession for one who would owe to him his elevation, not to speak of the fact that the rival candidate for the throne was Solomon, the "man of peace," the pupil of Nathan, and the representative of the "religious party" in the land. But it is not so easy to account for the conduct of Abiathar, unless it was prompted by jealousy of Zadok, who officiated at Gibeon (1 Chron. xvi. 39). As the latter was considered the principal Sanctuary (1 Kings iii. 4), the high-priest who officiated there might have been regarded as entitled to the Pontificate, when the temporary dual service of Gibeon and Jerusalem should give place to the permanent arrangements of the Temple. If such was his motive, Abiathar may have also wished to lay the new king under personal obligations.

From such a movement—which took advantage first of the

---

[1] Josephus (*Ant.* vii. 2) expressly states this to have been the advice given by his *physicians*. The practice was in accordance with the medical views entertained not only in ancient, but even in comparatively modern times. Dr. Trusen devotes to the medical consideration of this subject a special paragraph (§ 21, pp. 257–260) in his curious work, *Sitten, Gebr. u. Krankh. d. alten Hebr.*

[2] The story of Abishag is only introduced in order to explain the occasion of Adonijah's later execution. Of course it must be viewed in the light of the toleration of polygamy—nor could the object which the physicians had in view have been otherwise secured.

indulgence, and then of the illness of David ; which compassed aims that every one would know to be equally contrary to the Divine appointment and the express declarations of the aged king ; and in which the chief agents were an ambitious priest and an unscrupulous military chieftain—those who were faithful to their God or to their monarch would, of course, keep aloof. Adonijah knew this, and accordingly excluded such from the invitation to the feast, at which it had been arranged his accession to the throne should be proclaimed. In other respects his measures closely resembled those taken by Absalom. For some time previous to his attempt he had sought to accustom the people to regard him as their future king by assuming royal state (1 Kings i. 5).[1] At length all seemed ready. It is characteristic that, in order to give the undertaking the appearance of religious sanction, the conspirators prepared a great sacrificial feast. We know the scene, and we can picture to ourselves that gathering in the shady retreat of the king's gardens, under an over-arching rock, close by the only perennial spring in Jerusalem—that of the Valley of Kidron—which now bears the name of the "fountain of the Virgin,"[2] at that time the *En-Rogel* (" Spring of the Spy," or else " of the Fuller "). But a higher power than man's overruled events. To outward appearance the danger was indeed most urgent, the more so that it was not known in the palace. But already help was at hand. Nathan hastened to Bathsheba, and urged on her the necessity of immediate and decisive action. If Adonijah were proclaimed king, Solomon, Bathsheba, and all their adherents would immediately be put out of the way. In such circumstances court-ceremonial must be set aside ; and Bathsheba made her way into the king's sick-chamber. She spoke respectfully but earnestly ; she told him fully what at that very moment was taking place in the king's gardens ; she reminded him of his solemn oath about the succession, which had hitherto determined

[1] Comp. Josephus, *Ant.* vii. 14. 4.
[2] Comp. Bonar, *Land of Promise*, pp. 492-496.

her own conduct and that of Solomon's adherents ; and, finally, she appealed to him as alone competent at this crisis to determine who was to be king. The interview had not terminated when, according to previous arrangement, Nathan was announced. He had come on the same errand as Bathsheba : to inform the king of what Adonijah and his adherents were doing, and that Solomon and the king's most trusted servants had been excluded from a feast, the object of which was not concealed. Had all this been done by direction of the king? If so, why had not he, so old and faithful a counsellor, been informed that Adonijah was to be proclaimed successor to the throne?

With whatever weakness David may have been chargeable, he always rose to the requirements of the situation in hours of decisive importance, when either the known will of God or else the interests of his kingdom were in question. In this instance his measures were immediate and decisive. Recalling Bathsheba, who had withdrawn during the king's interview with Nathan, he dismissed her with words of reassurance. Then he sent for Zadok, Nathan, and Benaiah, and gave them his royal command for the immediate anointing of Solomon as king over Judah and Israel. The scene is vividly portrayed in Scripture. The king's body-guard—the *Cherethi* and *Pelethi*—under the command of Benaiah, was drawn up in front of the royal palace. Soon a vast concourse of people gathered. And now the king's state-mule, richly caparisoned, was brought out. It was an unwonted sight, which betokened some great state event. Presently, the great news became known, and rapidly spread through the streets and up the bazaars : Solomon was about to be anointed king! The people crowded together, in hundreds and thousands, from all parts of the city. And now Solomon appeared, attended by Zadok the high priest, Nathan the prophet, and Benaiah the chief of the royal guard. The procession formed, and moved forward. To avoid collision with the party of Adonijah, it took an opposite or western direction to the valley of Gihon.[1] Here, by authority and express command of David, Solomon was anointed king with the sacred oil by the joint ministry of the high priest and the prophet. The ceremony ended, the blast of the trumpets proclaimed the accession of the new monarch, and the people burst into a ringing shout: " God save King Solomon !" The enthusiastic demonstrations of joy were truly Eastern. There were music of pipes and acclamations of the people, till the ground beneath seemed to rend with the noise. As the procession returned, the city rang with the jubilee, till it reached the royal palace, where King Solomon seated himself in solemn state on his father's throne, and received the homage of the court, while David gave public thanks that he had lived to see that day.

Meanwhile, out in the king's gardens, the strange shouts from the city had reached Adonijah and his guests. Joab had grown uneasy as he heard the well-known sound of the trumpet. The tidings travelled quickly, and already one was in waiting to explain its meaning. But it was not as Adonijah had hoped against hope. The son of Abiathar had come to inform the conspirators of what had just taken place in Gihon and in the royal palace. And now sudden terror seized those who had but lately been so confident in their feasting. Every one of the conspirators fled, foremost among them Adonijah; nor did he deem himself safe till he had reached the sacred precincts, and laid hold on the horns of the altar. This asylum he refused to quit, until Solomon had assured him by oath that his life would be spared—though on condition that his future conduct should give the king no cause for complaint.

The events just recorded, which are only briefly indicated in 1 Chron. xxiii. 1, were followed by a great assembly of the chief dignitaries in Church and State (1 Chron. xxviii., xxix.), when the accession of Solomon to the throne was formally confirmed, and he was anointed a second time (1 Chron. xxix. 22). We remember, that similarly both Saul and David were

---

[1] Such seems to me the right location of Gihon, and not that suggested in the *Speaker's Commentary*, vol. ii. p. 485.

anointed a second time, on publicly receiving the homage of their subjects (1 Sam. xi. 15 ; 2 Sam. ii. 4 ; v. 3). It was in this great assembly that the aged king, speaking, as it were, from his death-bed, laid before his people the deepest wishes of his heart, and told his inmost thoughts concerning the character, the stability, and the object of royalty in Israel. Beginning with an evident reference to the great promise given to him and his house, David first solemnly owned, that the appointment to the royal office—more particularly his own election and that of Solomon as his successor—was of God as Israel's supreme King, and that the stability and welfare of the kingdom depended upon faithful allegiance to Jehovah, to which he accordingly admonished Solomon and the people (1 Chron. xxviii. 2–10). Then, following further the line indicated in the covenant-promise, David pointed out that the grand object of his son's reign must be to build an house unto the LORD. This would be the initial typical fulfilment of that to which the prophetic promise pointed. So deeply had the king this work at heart, that he had already prepared all the plans for the Temple ; and that he dedicated to this work the vast treasures which during his long reign he had accumulated, always with this great purpose in view (1 Chron. xxviii. 11–xxix. 5). But this was not a work which Solomon either could or should undertake by himself. He must be supported in it by a willing people. And when the representatives of Israel in that great assembly readily and liberally promised of their substance, David seemed to feel that the work of his life was indeed done, and that God would now let "His servant depart in peace." The solemn and joyous eulogy, and the earnest prayer for his people, and for his son and successor on the throne, with which David dismissed this assembly, form a most appropriate close to his public career.

Gladly would we here end our record of David's life. But Scripture, in its truthful narration, calls us to witness yet another scene. We stand by the death-bed of David, and hear his last injunctions to his son and successor. At this time Solomon could not have been more than twenty years of age. Probably he was even younger. However wise and well-disposed, the temptations and difficulties of his position could not but awaken fears in the heart of his father, and that in proportion as he kept in view the terms of the Divine prediction concerning his house, with its warnings as well as its promises. In regard to matters Divine and spiritual, only one plain advice need he give to Solomon. Spiritual decidedness, faithfulness, and obedience to God : such simply were the means by which the promises given to David and his house would be inherited. But all the greater were the political dangers which beset the path of the youthful king: an unscrupulous military party, headed by Joab ; a dissatisfied priestly faction, ready to plot and join any rebellious movement ; and ill-suppressed tribal jealousies, of whose existence Shimei had, at a critical period, given such painful evidence. The leaders of two of these parties had long forfeited their lives ; indeed, only the necessities of the time could have excused either the impunity with which Joab's treachery and his murder of Abner and Amasa had been passed over, or the indulgence extended to such conduct as that of Shimei. On the other hand, gratitude to such tried adherents in adversity as the family of Barzillai had proved, was alike dictated by duty and by policy. It was not, as some would have us believe, that on his death-bed David gave utterance to those feelings of revenge which he was unable to gratify in his lifetime, but that, in his most intimate converse with his son and successor, he looked at the dangers to a young and inexperienced monarch from such powerful and unscrupulous partisans. In these circumstances it was only natural that, before dying, he should have given to his son and successor such advice for his future guidance as his long experience would suggest; and similarly that, in so doing, he should have reviewed the chief dangers and difficulties which had beset his own patn, and have referred to the great public crimes which, during his reign, had necessarily been left unpunished. The fact that, even before his death, an attempt had been made to elevate Adonijah to the throne, contrary alike to the known will of God and the appointment of David, and that the chief actors in this had been Joab and Abiathar, must have recalled the past to his mind, and shown him that the fire had been smouldering these many years, and might at any time burst into flame.   But, however natural, and even lawful, such feelings on the part of David, it is impossible to read his parting directions and suggestions to Solomon without disappointment and pain.   Truly, even the most advanced of the "children were in bondage under the elements of the world" (Gal. iv. 3). How far did the type fall short of the reality, and how dim and ill-defined were the foreshadowings of Him, "Who when He was reviled, reviled not again; when He suffered, He threatened not; but committed Himself to Him that judgeth righteously!"

And yet events soon proved that David's apprehensions had been only too well grounded.   The aged king died, and was buried in his own "City of David," amidst the laments of a grateful nation, which ever afterwards cherished his memory (Acts ii. 29).   It seems that Adonijah, although obliged to submit to Solomon's rule, had not given up all hope of his own ultimate accession.   The scheme which he conceived for this purpose lacked, indeed, the courage of open rebellion, but was characterised by the cunning and trickery of a genuine Oriental intrigue.   To marry any of the late king's wives or concubines was considered in the East as publicly claiming his rights (2 Sam. xii. 8; xvi. 21, 22).   If such were done by a rival, it would be regarded as implying an insult to which not even the weakest monarch could submit without hopelessly degrading his authority in public opinion (2 Sam. iii. 7).   If Adonijah's primary object was to lower Solomon in public estimate, and that in a manner which he could neither resist nor resent, no better scheme could have been devised than that of his application for the hand of Abishag.   By combined flattery and parade of his supposed wrongs and injuries, he gained the queen-mother as unconscious accomplice and even instrument of his intrigue. Any scruples might be set aside by the plea, that there could be no wrong in his request, since, in the strict sense, Abishag had neither been the wife nor the concubine of David. To punish with death so cunning and mean an intrigue can scarcely be called excessive severity on the part of Solomon. It was rather a measure necessary, if tranquillity was to be preserved in the land, all the more that, by his own admission, Adonijah still entertained the opinion that rightfully the kingdom was his, and that " all Israel set their faces on him that *he* should reign" (1 Kings ii. 15).

Whether or not Abiathar and Joab were involved in this intrigue, is matter of uncertainty. At any rate an attempt so daring, and coming so soon after that in which these two had taken a leading part, called for measures which might prevent rebellion in the future, and serve as warning to the turbulent in Israel. That Joab felt conscious his conduct deserved the severest punishment, appears from the circumstance that he anticipated his sentence. On hearing of Adonijah's execution, he sought refuge within the sacred precincts of the Tabernacle. It would have been not only a dangerous precedent, but contrary to the express direction of the law (Ex. xxi. 12; Deut. xix. 11–13), to have allowed a criminal by such means to escape justice. However, it was not for his part in Adonijah's recent schemes that Joab now suffered the extreme penalty of the law, but for his former and still unpunished crimes, which his recent treasonable conduct seemed to bring afresh to view, just as some accidental ailment does a long latent fatal disease. As for Abiathar, in consideration of his office and former services to David, he was only removed from the Pontificate, and banished to his ancestral property at Anathoth, the city of the priests. But Holy Scripture calls us to mark, how by the deposition of Abiathar the Divine prediction against the house of Eli (1 Sam. ii. 31–36) was fulfilled, though in this instance also through a concurrence of intelligible causes.

There was now only one other left, who in heart and

mind, as well as in popular opinion, belonged to the party
opposed to the reigning house.   That old offender, Shimei,
was still at large, and enjoying ill-deserved safety.   Had he
during those years learned to respect the dynasty which he
had once so wantonly insulted, or did he still consider it
too weak to resent insubordination on his part?   The question
was soon to be decided; for Solomon now ordered Shimei to
remain permanently within the bounds of Jerusalem, at the
same time warning him that any infringement of this command,
from whatever cause, would be punished by death.   Shimei,
who had probably expected a far more severe sentence, received
with gratitude this comparatively slight restriction upon his
liberty.   He must have known that most Eastern monarchs
would have acted towards him in a very different spirit.   Besides,
the restriction was not more irksome than that which limited
the safety of an ordinary manslayer by the condition of his
remaining within the bounds of the city of refuge.   Nor was the
command in itself unreasonable, considering the necessity of
watching Shimei's movements, and the importance of convincing
the people that a strong hand now held the reins of government.   But whatever outward acquiescence Shimei had shown,
he had no idea of yielding such absolute obedience as in his
circumstances seemed called for.   On the first apparently
trivial occasion,[1] Shimei left Jerusalem for the capital of
Philistia without having sought the king's permission, and, upon
his return, suffered the penalty which, as he well knew, had
been threatened.   By such measures of vigour and firmness
"the kingdom was established in the hand of Solomon."

---

[1] It can scarcely be pretended that Shimei's personal presence at Gath
was absolutely necessary for the recovery of his fugitive slaves.   But even
had it been so, if Shimei had been allowed to transgress the king's injunction, his obedience in this or any other matter could never afterwards have
been enforced.

CHAPTER V.

Solomon marries the Daughter of Pharaoh—His Sacrifice at Gibeon—His Dream and Prayer—Solomon's Wisdom—Solomon's Officers and Court —Prosperity of the Country—Understanding and Knowledge of the King.

(1 KINGS III., IV., 2 CHRON. I.)

IT is remarkable, how often seemingly unimportant details in the sacred narrative gain a fresh meaning and new interest if viewed in their higher bearing and spiritual import. Nor is such application of them arbitrary. On the contrary, we conclude that Scripture was intended to be so read. This is evident from the circumstance that it is, avowedly, not a secular but a prophetic history,[1] and that, being such, it is not arranged according to the chronological succession of events, but grouped so as to bring into prominence that which concerns the kingdom of God. This plan of Scripture history is not only worthy of its object, but gives it its permanent interest and application.

What has just been stated is aptly illustrated by the opening account of King Solomon's reign. Of course, no chronological arrangement could have been here intended, since the list of Solomon's officers, given in 1 Kings iv., contains the names of at least two of the king's sons-in-law (vers. 11, 15), whose appointment must, therefore, date from a period considerably later than the commencement of his reign. What, then, we may ask, is the object of not only recording in a "prophetic history" such apparently unimportant details, but grouping them together irrespective of their dates? Without undervaluing them, considered as purely historical notices, we may venture to suggest a higher object in their record and arrange-

---

[1] As noticed in the previous part, and even indicated by the position in the Hebrew Canon of the historical books among "the Prophets."

ment. This detailed account of all the court and government appointments serves as evidence, how thoroughly and even elaborately the kingdom of Solomon was organised—and by obvious inference, how fully God had made good in this respect His gracious promises to King David. But may we not go even beyond this, and see in the literal fulfilment of these outward promises a pledge and assurance that the spiritual realities connected with them, and of which they were the symbol and type, would likewise become true in the Kingdom of Him Who was "David's better Son?" Thus viewed, the Divine promise made to David (2 Sam. vii.) was once more like a light casting the lengthening shadows of present events towards the far-off future.

The first event of national interest that occurred was the marriage of Solomon with the daughter of Pharaoh. It was of almost equal political importance to Egypt and to Palestine. An alliance with the great neighbouring kingdom of Egypt might have seemed an eventuality almost unthought of among the possibilities of the new and somewhat doubtful monarchy in Israel. But, on the other hand, it may have been also of importance to the then reigning Egyptian dynasty (the 21st Tanite), which, as we know, was rapidly declining in authority.[1] To Israel and to the countries around, such a union would now afford evidence of the position and influence which the Jewish monarchy had attained in the opinion of foreign politicians. All the more are we involuntarily carried back in spirit to the period when Israel was oppressed and in servitude to Egypt. As we contrast the relations in the past and in the time of Solomon, we realise how marvellously God had fulfilled His promises of deliverance to His people. And here we again turn to the great promise in 2 Sam. vii., as alike instructive to Israel as regarded their present, and as full of blessed hope for their future. The time of the Judges had been one of struggle and disorganisation ; that of David one of war and conflicts. But with Solomon the period of peace had begun, emblematic

---

[1] Comp. Stuart Poole, in Smith's *Bible Dict.*, vol. i. p. 511.

of the higher peace of the ", Prince of Peace." Thus viewed, the account of the prosperity of the land and people, as further evidenced by the wealth displayed in the ordinary appointments of the Court; by the arrangement of the country into provinces under officers for fiscal administration and civil government; and, above all, by the wisdom of Solomon, — who, while encouraging by example literature and study of every kind, chiefly aimed after that higher knowledge and understanding which is God-given, and leads to the fear and service of the Lord,—acquires a new and a spiritual meaning.

But to return to the sacred narrative. This marriage of Solomon with the daughter of Pharaoh—to which, from its frequent mention, so much political importance seems to have been attached—took place in the first years of his reign, although some time after the building of the Temple and of his own palace had commenced.[1] Such a union was not forbidden by the law,[2] nor was the daughter of Pharaoh apparently implicated in the charge brought against Solomon's other foreign wives of having led him into idolatry (1 Kings xi. 1–7). In fact, according to Jewish tradition, the daughter of Pharaoh actually became a Jewish proselyte. Still, Solomon seems to have felt the incongruity of bringing her into the palace of David, within the bounds of which " the Ark of the Lord " appears to have been located (2 Chron. viii. 11), and she occupied a temporary abode "in the City of David," till the new palace of Solomon was ready for her reception.

But the great prosperity which, as we shall presently see, the country enjoyed during the reign of Solomon, was due to higher than merely outward causes. It was the blessing of the Lord which in this instance also made rich—that blessing which

---

[1] From 1 Kings xi. 42, comp. with xiv. 21, we might infer that Solomon had married the Ammonitess Naamah before the death of his father. But as this seems incompatible with 2 Chron. xiii. 7, and for other reasons which will readily occur to the reader, the numeral indicating the age of Rehoboam (1 Kings xiv. 21) seems to be a copyist's mistake for 21.

[2] The law only forbade alliance with the Canaanites (Ex. xxxiv. 16 Deut. vii. 3).

it was Solomon's chief concern to obtain. From the necessity of the case, Israel, and even Solomon, still worshipped on the ancient "high places"[1] Of these the principal was naturally *Gibeon*—the twin height. For, right over against the city itself, on one of the two eminences ("mamelons") which gave it its name, the ancient Tabernacle which Moses had reared had been placed. Here Solomon, at the commencement of his reign, celebrated a great festival, probably to inaugurate and consecrate his accession by a public acknowledgment of Jehovah as the God of Israel. All the people took part in what was a service of hitherto unparalleled magnificence.[2] But something far better than the smoke of a thousand burnt-sacrifices offered in Israel's ancient Sanctuary, attested that the God, Who had brought Israel out of Egypt and led them through the Wilderness, st.ll watched over His people. The services of those festive days were over, and king and people were about to return to their homes. As Solomon had surveyed the vast multitude which, from all parts of the country, had gathered to Gibeon, the difficulty must have painfully forced itself on him of wisely ruling an empire so vast as that belonging to him, stretching from Tiphsach (the Greek *Thapsacus*), "the fords," on the western bank of the Euphrates, in the north-east, to Gaza on the border of Egypt, in the south-west (1 Kings iv. 24). The conquests so lately made had not yet been consolidated : the means at the king's disposal were still comparatively scanty ; tribal jealousies were scarcely appeased ; and Solomon himself was young and wholly inexperienced. Any false step might prove fatal ; even want of some brilliant success might disintegrate what was but imperfectly welded together. On the other hand, had Israel's history not been a series of constant miracles, through the gracious Personal interposition of the Lord? What, then, might Solomon not expect from His help?

Busy with such thoughts, the king had laid him down to rest

---

[1] Comp. the views expressed in the *Mishnah* on the lawfulness of such worship in vol. iii. of this "Bible History," p. 78.

[2] Similarly Xerxes offered a thousand oxen at Troy (Herod. vii. 43)

on the last night of his stay in Gibeon. Ordinarily dreams are without deeper significance. So Solomon himself afterwards taught (Eccles. v. 7); and so the spiritually enlightened among other nations, and the prophets in Israel equally declared (Job xx. 8; Is. xxix. 7). And yet, while most fully admitting this (as in Ecclus. xxxiv. 1–6), it must have been also felt, as indeed Holy Scripture teaches by many instances, that dreams might be employed by the Most High in the time of our visitation (Ecclus. xxxiv. 6). So was it with Solomon on that night. It has been well remarked, that Adonijah would not have thus dreamed after his feast at En-Rogel (1 Kings i. 9, 25), even had his attempt been crowned with the success for which he had hoped. The question which on that night the Lord put before Solomon, "Ask what I shall give thee?" was not only an answer to the unspoken entreaty for help expressed in the sacrifices that had been offered, but was also intended to search the deepest feelings of his heart. Like that of our Lord addressed to St. Peter, "Simon, son of Jonas, lovest thou Me?" it sounded the inmost depths of the soul. Such questions come, more or less distinctly, to us all, and that in every crisis of our lives. They may become fresh spiritual starting-points to us, seasons of greater nearness to God, and of spiritual advancement; or they may prove times of "temptation," if we allow ourselves to be "drawn away" and "enticed" of our own "lust."

The prayer of Solomon on this occasion once more combined the three elements of thanksgiving, confession, and petition. In his thanksgiving, acknowledgment of God mingled with humiliation; in his confession, a sense of inability with the expression of felt want; while his petition, evidently based on the Divine promise (Gen. xiii. 16; xxxii. 12), was characterised by singleness of spiritual desire. For, in order to know what he sought, when so earnestly craving for "understanding," we have only to turn to his own "Book of Proverbs." And, as in the case of all whose spiritual aim is single, God not only granted his request, but also added to what He gave "all things" other-

wise needful, thus proving that the "promise of the life that
now is" is ever connected with that of the life "which is to
come" (1 Tim. iv. 8), just as in our present condition the soul is
with the body. Perhaps we may put it otherwise in this manner :
As so often, God extended the higher wisdom granted Solomon
even to the lower concerns of this life, while He added to it the
promise of longevity and prosperity—but only on condition
of continued observance of God's statutes and commandments
(1 Kings iii. 14). [1] Such gracious condescension on the part
of the LORD called for the expression of fresh public thanksgiving, which Solomon rendered on his return to Jerusalem
(1 Kings iii. 15).

Evidence of the reality of God's promise soon appeared, and
that in a manner peculiarly calculated to impress the Eastern
mind. According to the simple manners of the times, a cause
too difficult for ordinary judges was carried direct to the
king, who, as God's representative, was regarded as able to
give help to his people in all time of need. In such paternal
dispensation of justice, there was no appeal to witnesses nor to
statute-books, which indeed would have been equally accessible
to inferior judges ; but the king was expected to strike out some
new light, in which the real bearings of a case would so appear
as to appeal to all men's convictions, and to command their
approval of his sentence. There was here no need for anything
recondite—rather the opposite. To point out to practical
common sense what *was* there, though unperceived till suddenly
brought to prominence, would more than anything else appeal
to the people, as a thing within the range of all, and yet showing
the wise guidance of the king. Thus sympathy and universal
trust, as well as admiration, would be called forth, especially
among Orientals, whose wisdom is that of common life, and
whose philosophy that of proverbs.

The story of the contention of the two women for the one
living child, when from the absence of witnesses it seemed

[1] Accordingly, Solomon forfeited this promise on account of his later
idolatry. He died at the age of about fifty-nine or sixty.

impossible to determine whose it really was, is sufficiently known. The ready wisdom with which Solomon devised means for ascertaining the truth would commend itself to the popular mind. It was just what they would appreciate in their king. Such a monarch would indeed be a terror to evil-doers, and a protection and praise to them that did well. It is probably in order to explain the rapid spread of Solomon's fame that this instance of his wisdom is related in Holy Scripture (1 Kings iii. 28).

The prosperity of such a reign was commensurate with the fact that it was based upon the Divine promises, and typical of far greater blessings to come. The notices in 1 Kings iv. and v. are strung together to indicate that prosperity by presenting to our view the condition of the Israelitish monarchy in the high-day of its glory. Wise and respected councillors surrounded the king.[1] The administration of the country was orderly, and the taxation not arbitrary but regulated. The land was divided, not according to the geographical boundaries of the "tribes," but according to population and resources, into twelve provinces, over each of which a governor was appointed. Among their number we find two sons-in-law of the king (iv. 11, 15), and other names well-known in the land (such as those of Baana, ver. 12, probably the brother of "the recorder," ver. 3, and Baanah, the son of Hushai, probably David's councillor, ver. 16). Had this policy of re-arranging the country into provinces been sufficiently consolidated, many of the tribal jealousies would have ceased. On the other hand, the financial administration, entrusted to these governors, was of the simplest kind. Apparently, no direct taxes were levied, but all that was requisite for the royal court and government had to be provided, each province supplying in turn what

[1] The word *Cohen* in 1 Kings iv. 2 ("Azariah, the son of Zadok the *priest*") should *not* be rendered "priest," but refers to a civil office—that of the king's representative to the people and his most intimate adviser. The same term is used of Zabud in ver. 5, where the Authorised Version translates "principal officer," and also of David's sons, 2 Sam. viii. 18. A grandson of Zadok could not have been old enough to be high-priest (comp. 1 Chron. vi. 10.)

was required for one month. Such a system could not indeed press heavily, so long as the country continued prosperous; but with a luxurious court, in hard times, or under harsh governors, it might easily become an instrument of oppression and a source of discontent. From 1 Kings xii. 4 we gather that such was ultimately the case. It need scarcely be added, that in each province the supreme civil government was in the hands of these royal officials; and such was the general quiet prevailing, that even in the extensive district east of the Jordan, which bordered on so many turbulent tributary nations, "one sole officer" (1 Kings iv. 19) was sufficient to preserve the peace of the country.

Quite in accordance with these notices are the references both to the prosperity of Israel, and to the extent of Solomon's dominions (1 Kings iv. 20, 21). They almost read like an initial fulfilment of that promise to Abraham: "Multiplying I will multiply thy seed as the stars of the heaven, and as the sand which is upon the sea shore; and thy seed shall possess the gate of his enemies" (Gen. xxii. 17). And if, compared with the simplicity of Saul's and even of David's court, that of Solomon seems luxurious in its appointments,[1] we must remember that it was intended to show the altered state of the Israelitish monarchy, and that even so the daily consumption was far smaller than at the court of the Persian monarchs in the high-day of their power and glory.[2]

---

[1] The provision made was not only for the court and its dependants, but also for the royal stables (1 Kings iv. 26–28). In verse 26 the number of his horses is by a clerical error given as 40,000 instead of 4000 (comp. 2 Chron. ix. 25). If, according to 1 Kings x. 26, 2 Chron. i. 14, Solomon had 1,400 chariots, each with two horses, and with, in most of them, a third horse as reserve, we have the number 4000.

[2] It is difficult to give the exact equivalent of the "thirty measures of fine flour and threescore of meal" (in all, ninety measures), 1 Kings iv. 22. According to the calculation of the Rabbis (*Bibl. Dict.* vol. iii. p. 1742) they would yield ninety-nine sacks of flour. Thenius (*Studien u. Krit.* for 1846, p. 73, etc.) calculates that they would yield two pounds of bread for 14,000 persons. But this computation is exaggerated. On competent authority I am informed that one bushel of flour makes up fourteen (four

But the fame which accrued to the kingdom of Solomon from its prosperity and wealth would have been little worthy of the Jewish monarchy, had it been uncombined with that which alone truly exalteth a nation or an individual. The views of Solomon himself on this subject are pithily summed up in one of his own " Proverbs" (iii. 13, 14): " Happy is the man that findeth wisdom, and the man that causeth understanding to go forth ; for merchandise (trading) with it, is better than merchandise with silver, and the gain from it than the most fine gold." [1] All this the " wise king" exemplified in his own person. God gave him "wisdom" not only far wider in its range, but far other in its character (Prov. i. 7 ; ix. 10) than that of the East, or of far-famed Egypt, or even of those deemed wisest in Israel,[2] "and understanding exceeding much, and largeness of heart, even as the sand that is on the sea-shore" [3] (1 Kings iv. 29). Not satisfied with the idle life of an Eastern monarch, he set

---

pound) loaves of bread ; consequently, one sack (= four bushels) fifty-six loaves, or 224 pounds of bread. This for ninety-nine sacks would give 22,176 pounds of bread, which at two pounds per person would supply 11,088—or, with waste, about 11,000 persons. Of this total amount of bread, the thirty-three sacks of "fine flour"—probably for court use—would yield 1,848 loaves, or 7,392 pounds of bread. The number of persons fed daily at the court of the kings of Persia is said to have been 15,000 (see *Speaker's Comm.*, p. 502). Thenius further calculates that, taken on an average, the thirty oxen and one hundred sheep would yield one and a half pounds of meat for each of the 14,000 persons. At the court of Cyrus, the daily provision seems to have been, 400 sheep, 300 lambs, 100 oxen, 30 horses, 30 deer, 400 fatted geese, 100 young geese, 300 pigeons, 600 small fowls, 3,750 gallons of wine, 75 gallons of new milk, and 75 of sour milk (comp. Bähr in Lange's *Bibel W.*, vol. vii. p. 29). But here also the computation of Thenius seems too large, bearing in mind that cattle and sheep in the East are much smaller than in the West.

[1] We translate literally.

[2] Comp. 1 Chron. ii. 6. Ethan, 1 Chron. vi. 44 ; xv. 17, 19 ; Ps. lxxxix. (inscr.) Heman, 1 Chron. vi. 33 ; xxv. 5 ; Ps. lxxxviii. (inscr.) Chalcol and Darda, sons of Mahol, perhaps—" *sacras choreas ducendi periti.*"

[3] A hyperbole not uncommon in antiquity. I feel tempted here to quote the similar expression of Horace (*Odes*, i. 28) :

"Te maris et terræ numeroque carentis arenæ
Mensorem cohibent, Archyta."

the example of, and gave encouragement to study and literature—the range of his inquiries extending not only to philosophy and poetry,[1] but also to natural science in all its branches.[2] It must have been a mighty intellectual impulse which proceeded from such a king; it must have been a reign unparalleled in that age, as well as among that people, which Solomon inaugurated.

CHAPTER VI.

The Building of Solomon's Temple—Preparations for it—Plan and Structure of the Temple—Internal Fittings—History of the Temple—Jewish Traditions.

(1 KINGS V., VI., VII. 13–51, VIII. 6–9; 2 CHRON. II. III., IV., V. 7–10).

WHILE Solomon thus wisely and in the fear of God ordered his government, and the country enjoyed a measure of prosperity, wealth, and power never before or afterwards attained, the grand work of his reign yet remained to be done. This was the building of an " house unto the Name of Jehovah God." We have already seen how earnestly David had this at heart; how fully it corresponded with the Divine promise; and how fitly its execution was assigned to Solomon as the great task of his reign, viewing it as typical of that of " David's greater Son." As might be expected, all outward circumstances contributed to further the work. Israel, as a nation, was not intended to attain pre-eminence either in art or science. If

---

[1] Of these " Proverbs " only 915 verses have been preserved in the Book of that name; of " the Songs," besides the Song of Songs, only Ps. lxxii. and cxxvii.

[2] The word rendered " hyssop" in the Authorised Version is either the mint, the marjoram, the *Orthotricum saxatile*, or, according to Tristram (*Nat. Hist. of the Bible*," p. 457), the caper (*Capparis spinosa*).

we may venture to pronounce on such a matter, this was the part assigned, in the Providence of God, to the Gentile world. To Israel was specially entrusted the guardianship of that spiritual truth, which in the course of ages would develop in all its proportions, till finally it became the common property of the whole world. On the other hand, it was the task assigned to that world, to develop knowledge and thought so as to prepare a fitting reception for the truth, that thus it might be presented in all its aspects, and carried from land to land in a form adapted to every nation, meeting every want and aspiration. This was symbolically indicated even in the building of Solomon's Temple. For, if that Temple had been exclusively the workmanship of Jewish hands, both the materials for it and their artistic preparation would have been sadly defective, as compared with what it actually became. But it was not so; and, while in the co-operation of Gentiles with Israel in the rearing of the Temple we see a symbol of their higher union in the glorious architecture of that "spiritual house built up" of "lively stones," we also recognise the gracious Providence of God, which rendered it possible to employ in that work the best materials and the best artificers of the ancient world.

For it was in the good Providence of God that the throne of Tyre was at the time occupied by Hiram,[1] who had not only been a friend and ally of David, but to whom the latter had communicated his plans of the projected Temple-buildings. Indeed, Hiram had already furnished David with a certain proportion of the necessary materials for the work (1 Chron. xxii. 4). The extraordinary mechanical skill of the Phœnicians —especially of the Sidonians—was universally famed in the ancient world.[2] Similarly, the best materials were at their command. On the slopes of Lebanon, which belonged to their territory, grew those world-famed cedars with which the palaces

---

[1] Also written *Hirom* (1 Kings v. 10, 18—in the Hebrew, iv. 24, 32), and in 2 Chron. ii. *Huram.*

[2] Comp. the quotations in the *Speaker's Comment.* (II, p. 507*a*,) and Movers, *Phöniz.* II, i. pp. 86, etc.

of Assyria were adorned, and, close by, at Gebal (the ancient Byblos, the modern *Jebeil*) were the most skilled workmen [1] (Ezek. xxvii. 9). On the same slopes grew also the cypress,[2] so suitable for flooring, its wood being almost indestructible, and impervious to rot and worms; while the Phœnician merchantmen brought to Tyre that "almug," "algum," or red sandal-wood which was so valued in antiquity (comp. 1 Kings x. 11)[3] The same skill as in the preparation of woodwork distinguished the Phœnician carvers, stone-cutters, dyers, modellers, and other craftsmen. To have at his disposal the best artificers of Phœnicia, and these under a trained and cele-brated "master" (2 Chron. ii. 13, 14), must have been of immense advantage to Solomon. At the same time the extensive preparations which David had made rendered the work comparatively so easy, that the Temple-buildings, with their elaborate internal fittings, were completed in the short space of seven years (1 Kings vi. 37, 38), while the later rearing of the king's palace occupied not less than thirteen years (1 Kings vii. 1). But, although Solomon thus availed himself of Phœnician skill in the execution of the work, the plan and design were strictly Jewish, having, in fact, been drawn long before, in the time of King David.

[1] Our Authorised Version translates wrongly, "stone-squarers" (1 Kings v. 18), where the original has "Gebalites," *i.e.*, inhabitants of Gebal.

[2] There has been much controversy as to the meaning of the word *berosh*, rendered in the Authorised Version (1 Kings v. 8, and many other passages) by "fir." Differing from Canon Rawlinson, it seems to me, for many reasons, most improbable that it was "the juniper," and on the grounds explained in Gesenius' *Thesaurus* I. 246 *b*, 247 *a*, I regard it, with almost all authorities, as the cypress. The Targumim and the Talmud have the words *berotha* and *beratha*, with apparently the same signification. Comp. Levy, *Chald. Wörterb. ü. d. Targ.* p. 118 *b*. Canon Tristram, who is always trustworthy (*Nat. Hist. of the Bible*), speaks of it with caution.

[3] Most commentators are agreed that it was the "red sandal" wood. It is curious to notice that this was apparently an article of ordinary commerce. The "Ophir" (or Red Sea) fleet of King Solomon, on the other hand, is only said to have brought "gold" (1 Kings ix. 28 ; 2 Chron. viii. 17, 18). Remembering that this wood had to come from *Tyre*, there is not the slightest inaccuracy in 2 Chron. ii. 8, as Zöckler and even Keil seem to imagine.

The building of the Temple commenced in the second month ("*Siv*," "splendour"—the month of opening beauty of nature) of the fourth year of Solomon's reign, being the 480th from the Exodus [1] (1 Kings vi. 1). But there was this peculiarity about the work, that no sound of axe, hammer, or chisel was heard on Mount Moriah while the Holy House was rising, day by day, in beauty and glory. As Jewish tradition has it : "The iron is created to shorten the days of man, and the altar to lengthen them ; therefore it is not right that that which shortens should be lifted upon that which lengthens" (*Midd.* iii. 4). The massive timber used was not merely prepared but dressed before it was brought to the sea, to be conveyed in floats to Joppa, whence the distance to Jerusalem was only about forty miles (1 Kings v. 9). Similarly, those great, splendid (*not* "costly," as in the Authorised Version) hewed stones (1 Kings v. 17), bevelled at the edges, of which to this day some are seen in what remains of the ancient Temple-wall—the largest of them being more than thirty feet long by seven and a half high, and weighing above one hundred tons—were all chiselled and carefully marked before being sent to Jerusalem (1 Kings vi. 7). An undertaking of such magnitude would require, especially in the absence of modern mechanical appliances, a very large number of workmen. They amounted in all to 160,000 Palestinians, who were divided into two classes. The first comprised native Israelites, of whom 30,000 were raised by a "levy," which, taking the census of David as our basis, would be at the rate of considerably less than one in forty-four of the able-bodied male population. These 30,000 men worked by relays, 10,000 being employed during one month, after which they returned for two months to their homes. The second class of workmen, which consisted of strangers resident in Palestine (1 Kings v. 15 ; 2 Chron. ii. 17, 18), amounted to 150,000, of

[1] Doubt has been thrown on the accuracy of this date, which indeed is altered by the LXX; but this, as it seems to us, on wholly insufficient grounds. Compare the Chronological Table at the beginning of Vol. III. of this "Bible History," and the detailed remarks of Bähr in Lange's *Bibel-Werk*, vol. vii. pp. 40*b*, 41*a*.

whom 70,000 were burden-bearers, and 80,000 "hewers in the mountains," or rather, as the expression always means, "stone-cutters." The two classes are carefully distinguished—the Israelites being free labourers, who worked under the direction of Hiram's skilled men ; while the others, who were the representatives of the ancient heathen inhabitants of Palestine, were really held to "bond-service" (1 Kings ix. 20, 21 ; 2 Chron. ii. 17, 18 ; viii. 7–9). The total number of men employed (160,000), though large, cannot be considered excessive, when compared, for example, with the 360,000 persons engaged for twenty years on the building of one pyramid (Pliny, *Hist. Nat.* xxxvi. 12. *apud* Bähr *u. s.*) Over these men 3,300 officers were appointed (1 Kings v. 16), with 550 "chiefs" (1 Kings ix. 23), of whom 250 were apparently native Israelites (2 Chron. viii. 10.)[1]

The number of skilled artificers furnished by Hiram is not mentioned, though probably the proportion was comparatively small. A very vivid impression is left on our minds of the transaction between the two kings. When Hiram sent a friendly embassy to congratulate Solomon on his accession, the latter replied by another, which was charged formally to ask help in the building about to be undertaken. The request was entertained by Hiram in the most cordial manner. At the same time, bearing in mind Eastern phraseology, and that a Phœnician ally of David would readily recognise the God of Israel as a "national Deity," there is no reason for inferring, from the terms of his reply, that Hiram was personally a worshipper of Jehovah (1 Kings v. 7; 2 Chron. ii. 12). The agreement seems to have been, that Solomon would undertake to provide for the support of Hiram's men, wheat, barley, and oil, to the amount specified in 2 Chron. ii. 10 ; while, so long as building materials were required, Hiram charged for them at an annual rate of 20,000 measures of wheat, and twenty

---

[1] There is no real discrepancy between the number of the "officers," as given respectively in Chronicles and in Kings. The sum total (3850) is in both cases the same—the arrangement in Chronicles being apparently according to nationality, and in the Book of Kings according to office (1 Kings, 3300 + 550 ; 2 Chron., 3600 + 250)

measures (about ten hogsheads) of "beaten oil,"—that is, the best in the market, which derived its name from its manufacture, the oil being extracted by beating the olives before they were quite ripe (1 Kings v. 11). In regard to these terms, it should be remembered that Phœnicia was chiefly dependent on Palestine for its supply of grain and oil (Ezek. xxvii. 17 ; Acts xii. 20). Lastly, the name of the "master-workman," whom Hiram sent, has also been preserved to us as Huram, or rather Churam,[1] a man of Jewish descent by the mother's side (2 Chron. ii. 13, 14; comp. 1 Kings vii. 14 ; 2 Chron. iv. 16).[2] Even the completeness and entirely satisfactory character of these arrangements proved, that in this respect also "Jehovah gave Solomon wisdom, as He had promised him" (1 Kings v. 12).

Without entering into details,[3] the general appearance and proportions of the Temple which Solomon built can be described without much difficulty. The Temple itself faced east—that is to say, the worshippers entered by the east, and, turning to the Most Holy Place, would look west ; while, if the veil had been drawn aside, the Ark in the innermost Sanctuary would have been seen to face eastwards. Entering then by the east, the worshipper would find himself in front of "a porch," which extended along the whole width of the Temple,—that is, twenty cubits, or about thirty feet—and went back a depth of ten cubits, or fifteen feet. The Sanctuary itself was sixty cubits (ninety feet) long, twenty cubits (thirty feet) wide, and thirty cubits (forty-five feet) high. The height of the porch is not mentioned in the Book of Kings, and the numeral given for it in 2 Chron. iii. 4, is evidently a copyist's error.[4] Probably it rose to a height

[1] The name is the same as that of the king himself.
[2] Our Authorised Version of 2 Chron. ii. 13 is entirely misleading. The sacred text mentions "Huram" as "Abi," "my father,"—not the father of King Hiram, but a title of distinction given to this able man (comp. the use of the word "*Ab*" in regard to Joseph, Gen. xlv. 8), and equivalent to "master."
[3] The literature of this subject is very large, and details are often most difficult.
[4] A height of 120 cubits would be out of all proportion, and, indeed, considering the width and length, almost impossible.

of about thirty cubits.[1] Of the total length of the Sanctuary, forty cubits were apportioned to the Holy Place, (which was thus sixty feet long, thirty wide, and forty-five high), and twenty cubits (thirty feet) to the Most Holy Place, which (1 Kings vi. 20) is described as measuring twenty cubits[2] (thirty feet) in length, width, and height. The ten cubits (fifteen feet) left above the Most Holy Place were apparently occupied by an empty room. Perhaps, as in the Temple of Herod, this space was used for letting down the workmen through an aperture, when repairs were required in the innermost Sanctuary. In that case the access to it would have been from the roof. The latter was, no doubt, flat.[3]

The measurements just given apply, of course, only to the *interior* of these buildings. As regards their *exterior* we have to add not only the thickness of the walls on either side, and the height of the roof, but also a row of side-buildings, which have, not inaptly, been designated as a "lean-to." These side-

[1] Of the textual alterations proposed, the first (מאה, 100, into אמות "cubits") seems the easiest, although it involves the elimination of the ו with which the next word in the Hebrew begins. On the other hand, "thirty cubits" seems a more suitable height, especially as the absence of its measurement in 1 Kings seems to convey that the "porch" had the same height as the main building. But this implies *two* alterations in the text, it being difficult to understand how, if the *numeral* 30 was originally written by a letter (ל, of which, it is supposed, the blotting out of the upper half made it appear like כ = 20), the copyist finding אמות written in full could have mistaken it for מאה, 100, which also ought to have been written with a letter (ק). It is, however, possible that instead of the full word, אמות, the MS. may have borne אמי, and the copyist have been thus misled.

[2] Thus the Most Holy Place would have had exactly double the proportions of that in the Tabernacle, while the height of the Holy Place was ten cubits (fifteen feet) higher.

[3] It is with great reluctance and becoming modesty—though without misgiving—that I differ from so justly famous an authority as Mr. Ferguson (Smith's *Bibl. Dict.* vol. III., Art. "Temple"). Mr. Ferguson, and after him most English writers, have maintained that the roof, both of the Tabernacle and of the Temple, was *sloping*, and not flat. This view is, to say the least, wholly unsupported by the text of Holy Scripture. Canon Rawlinson, indeed, speaks of Mr. Ferguson's view as "*demonstrated*," but, surely, without weighing the meaning of the word which he has italicised.

buildings consisted of three tiers of chambers, which surrounded the Temple, south, west, and north—the east front being covered by the "porch." On the side where these chambers abutted on the Temple they seem to have had no separate wall. The beams, which formed at the same time the ceiling of the first and the floor of the second tier of chambers, and similarly those which formed the ceiling of the second and the floor of the third tier, as also those on which the roof over the third tier rested, were *not* inserted within the Temple wall, but were laid on graduated buttresses which formed part of the main wall of the Temple. These buttresses receded successively one cubit in each of the two higher tiers of chambers, and for the roofing of the third, thus forming, as it were, narrowing steps, or receding rests on which the beams of the chambers were laid. The effect was that, while the walls of the Temple decreased one cubit in thickness with each tier, the chambers increased one cubit in width, as they ascended. Thus, if at the lowest tier the wall including the buttress was, say, six cubits thick, at the next tier of chambers it was, owing to the decrease in the buttress, only five cubits thick, and at the third only four cubits, while above the roof, where the buttress ceased, the walls would be only three cubits thick. For the same reason each tier of chambers, built on gradually narrowing or receding rebatements, would be one cubit wider than that below, the chambers on the lowest tier being five cubits wide, on the second six cubits, and on the third seven cubits. If we suppose these tiers with their roof to have been altogether sixteen to eighteen cubits high (1 Kings vi. 10), and allow a height of two cubits for the roof of the Temple, whose walls were thirty cubits high (the total height, including roof, thirty-two cubits), this would leave an elevation of twelve to fourteen cubits (eighteen to twenty-one feet) for the wall of the Temple above the roof of "the chambers." Within this space of twelve to fourteen cubits we suppose the "windows" to have been inserted—south and north, the back of the Most Holy Place (west) having no windows, and the front (east) being covered by the "porch." The use of the "chambers" is not mentioned in the sacred text, but it seems more probable that they served for the deposit of relics of the ancient Tabernacle, and for the storage of sacred vessels, than that they were the sleeping apartments of the ministering priesthood. Access to these "chambers" was gained by a door in the middle of the southern façade, whence also a winding stair led to the upper tiers (1 Kings vi. 8). The windows of the Temple itself, which we have supposed to have been above the roof of the "chambers," were with "fixed lattices"[1] (1 Kings vi. 4), which could not be opened, as in private dwellings, and were probably constructed, like the windows of old castles and churches, broad within, but mere slits externally. While these protracted works were progressing, the LORD in His mercy gave special encouragement alike to Solomon and to the people. The word of the LORD, which on this occasion came to the king (1 Kings vi. 11–13)—no doubt through a prophet—not only fully confirmed the promise made to David (2 Sam. vii. 12, etc.), but also connected the "house" that was being built to the LORD with the ancient promise (Ex. xxv. 8; xxix. 45) that God would dwell in Israel as among His people. Thus it pointed king and people beyond that outward building which, rising in such magnificence, might have excited only national pride, to its spiritual meaning, and to the conditions under which alone it would fulfil its great purpose.[2]

Thus far we have given a description of the exterior of the Temple.[3] It still remains to convey some idea of its internal arrangements. If we may judge by the description of Ezekiel's Temple (Ezek. xl. 49), and by what we know of the Temple of Herod, some steps would lead up to the porch,

[1] Not as in our Authorised Version : "windows of narrow lights."

[2] A fuller description of the Temple, and a detailed discussion of the various points in controversy among writers on the subject, would lead beyond the limit which we must here assign ourselves.

[3] Some have imagined that the Most Holy Place was, like the chancel in most churches, lower than the Holy Place (ten feet). Lundius has drawn the porch to the height of a gigantic steeple. Many (mostly fanciful) sketch-plans of the Temple have been drawn ; but it would be out of place here to enter into further details.

which, as we imagine, presented the appearance of an open colonnade of cedar, set in a pavement of hewn stones, and supporting a cedar-roof covered with marble. The most prominent objects here were the two great pillars, Jachin and Boaz, which Hiram cast by order of Solomon (1 Kings vii. 15–22). These pillars stood, as we are expressly told, *within* "the porch" (1 Kings vii. 21), and must have served alike architectural, artistic, and symbolical purposes. Added after the completion of the "House," perhaps for the better support of the roof of the "porch," their singular beauty must have attracted the eye, while their symbolical meaning appeared in their names. Jachin ("He supports"), Boaz ("in Him is strength"), pointed beyond the outward support and strength which these pillars gave, to Him on Whom not only the Sanctuary but every one who would truly enter it must rest for support and strength. Some difficulty has been experienced in computing the height of these pillars, including their "chapiters," or "capitals" (1 Kings vii. 15–22). It seems most likely that they consisted of single shafts, each eighteen cubits high and twelve in circumference,[1] surmounted by a twofold "chapiter"—the lower of five cubits, with fretted network depending, and ornamented with two rows of one hundred pomegranates; the higher chapiter four cubits high (1 Kings vii. 19), and in the form of an opening lily. The symbolical significance of the pomegranate and of the lily—the one *the* flower, the other *the* fruit of the Land of Promise, and both emblematic of the pure beauty and rich sweetness of holiness —need scarcely be pointed out. If we compute the height of these pillars with their chapiters at twenty-seven cubits,[2] we have three cubits left for the entablature and the roofing of the porch (18+5+4+3 = 30).

"The porch," which (in its tablature) was overlaid with gold (2 Chron. iii. 4), opened into the Holy Place by folding doors,

---

[1] Canon Rawlinson has shown that the columns of the Egyptian temples were thicker than those of Solomon's.

[2] Other calculations have also been proposed, as by Bähr and Merz.

each of two leaves, folding back upon each other. These doors, which were the width of a fourth of the wall (1 Kings vi. 33), or five cubits, were made of cypress-wood, and hung by golden hinges on door-posts of olive-wood. They were decorated with carved figures of cherubim between palm-trees,[1] and above them opening flower-buds and garlands, the whole being covered with thin plates of gold, which showed the design beneath. Within the Sanctuary all the sacred furniture was of gold, while that outside of it was of brass. In truth, the Sanctuary was a golden house. The floor, which was of cypress-wood, was overlaid with gold; the walls, which were panelled with cedar, on which the same designs were carved as on the doors, were covered with gold, and so was the ceiling. It need scarcely be said, how it must have glittered and shone in the light of the sacred candlesticks, especially as the walls were encrusted with gems (2 Chron. iii. 6). There were ten candlesticks in the Holy Place, each seven-branched, and of pure gold. They were ranged right and left before the Most Holy Place[2] (1 Kings vii. 49). The entrance to the Most Holy Place was covered by a veil "of blue and purple, and crimson, and byssus," with "wrought cherubs thereon" (2 Chron. iii. 14). Between the candlesticks stood the "altar of incense," made of cedar-wood and overlaid with gold (1 Kings vi. 20, 22; vii. 48); while ten golden tables of shewbread (2 Chron. iv. 8) were ranged right and left. The implements necessary for the use of this sacred furniture were also of pure gold (1 Kings vii. 49, 50).

Two folding-doors, similar in all respects to those already described, except that they were of oleaster wood, and not a fourth, but a fifth of the wall (=4 cubits), opened from the

---

[1] Probably they were in panels, each having two cherubs and a palm tree.

[2] Keil supposes that only two of these candlesticks stood before the Most Holy Place, while the other eight were ranged, four and four, along the side walls, five tables of shewbread being placed in the interstices *behind* them, along each of the side walls. In that case, however, it would not have been easy to go round the tables.

Holy Place into the Most Holy.   These doors we suppose
to have always stood open, the entrance being concealed by
the great veil, which the High-priest lifted, when on the Day of
Atonement he went into the innermost Sanctuary.[1]   Considerable difficulty attaches to a notice in 1 Kings vi. 21, which
has been variously translated and understood.   Two interpretations here specially deserve attention.   The first regards
the "chains of gold before the Oracle," as chain-work that
fastened together the cedar-planks forming the partition between the Holy and the Most Holy Place—somewhat like the
bars that held together the boards in the Tabernacle.   The
other, which to us seems the more likely,[2] represents the
partition boards between the Holy and the Most Holy Place, as
not reaching quite to the ceiling, and this "chain-work" as
running along the top of the boarding.   For some opening of
this kind seems almost necessary for ventilation, for letting out
the smoke of the incense on the Day of Atonement, and to
admit at least a gleam of light, without which the ministrations
of the High-priest on that day, limited though they were, would
have been almost impossible.   The only object within the Most
Holy Place was the Ark overshadowed by the Cherubim.   It
was the same which had stood in the Tabernacle.   But
Solomon placed on either side of it (south and north) a gigantic
figure of a Cherub, carved out of oleaster wood, and overlaid
with gold.   Each was ten cubits high ; and the two, with their
outspread wings, which touched over the Mercy - Seat, ten
cubits wide.   Thus, the two cherubim with their outspread
wings reached (south and north) from one wall of the Sanctuary
to the other (1 Kings vi. 23–28).   But, whereas the Mosaic
Cherubim looked inwards and downwards towards the Mercy-

---

[1] This we conclude from the circumstance, that otherwise there would
have been no use of a veil, and that we do not read of the High-priest
opening the doors on the Day of Atonement.

[2] Most writers suppose that these chains were drawn inside to furthe.
bar access to the Most Holy Place.   But no mention is made of their
existence or removal on the Day of Atonement.   The view we have expressed
is that of the Rabbis.

Seat, those made by Solomon looked outwards towards the Holy Place, with probably a slight inclination downwards (2 Chron. iii. 13). Another notice has raised differences of opinion. From 1 Kings viii. 8, we learn that the "staves" by which the Ark was carried were "drawn forward" ("lengthened," not "drawn out," as in the Authorised Version), so that their heads were visible from the Holy Place. As these "staves" were never to be drawn out (Ex. xxv. 15), and as all view of the interior of the Most Holy Place was precluded, this could only have been effected (as the Rabbis suggest) by drawing the staves forward, so that their heads would slightly bulge out on the veil. Of course this would imply that the staves faced east and west—not, as is generally supposed, south and north. Nor is there any valid objection to this supposition.

Descending from "the Porch," we stand in the "inner" (1 Kings vi. 36) or "Court of the Priests" (2 Chron. iv. 9). This was paved with great stones, as was also the outer or "Great Court" (2 Chron. iv. 9) of the people. Within the "inner" or Priests' Court, facing the entrance to the Sanctuary, was "the altar of burnt-offering" (1 Kings viii. 64), made of brass, and probably filled within with earth and unhewn stones. It was ten cubits high, and twenty cubits in length and breadth at the base—probably narrowing as it ascended, like receding buttresses [1] (2 Chron. iv. 1). Between the altar and the porch stood the colossal "sea of brass," five cubits high, and thirty cubits in circumference (1 Kings vii. 23–26; 2 Chron. iv. 2–5). Its upper rim was bent outwards, "like the work of the brim of a cup, in the shape of a lily-flower." Under the brim it was ornamented by two rows of opening flower-buds, ten to a cubit. This immense basin rested on a pedestal of twelve oxen, three looking to each point of the compass. Its object was to hold

---

[1] This was certainly the structure of the altar in the Temple of Herod (comp. *Midd.* iii. 1). In general, I must here refer the reader to the description of that Temple in *The Temple, its Ministry and Services at the Time of Jesus Christ,* and to my translation of the Mishnic Tractate *Middoth,* in the Appendix to *Sketches of Jewish Social Life in the Days of Christ.* Our present limits prevent more than the briefest outline.

the water in which the priests and Levites performed their ablutions. For the washing of the inwards and of the pieces of the sacrifices, ten smaller "lavers" of brass were provided, which stood on the right and left "side of the House" (1 Kings vii. 38 ; 2 Chron. iv. 6). They were placed on square "bases," or, rather, waggons of brass, four cubits long and broad, and three cubits high, which rested on "four feet" (not "corners," as in the Authorised Version, 1 Kings vii. 30) upon wheels, so as to bring them readily to the altar. Bearing in mind the height of the altar, this accounts for their being four cubits high ($+4$ cubits for the laver itself). The sides of these waggons were richly ornamented with figures of lions, oxen, and cherubs, and beneath them were "garlands, pensile work."[1] Although it is not easy to make out all the other details, it seems that the tops of these "bases" or waggons had covers, which bulged inwards to receive the lavers, the latter being further steadied by supports ("undersetters" in the Authorised Version, or rather "shoulder-pieces"). The covers of the waggons were also richly ornamented. Lastly, in the Priests' Court, and probably within full view of the principal gate, stood the brazen scaffold or stand (2 Chron. vi. 13) from which King Solomon offered his dedicatory prayer, and which seems to have always been the place occupied in the Temple by the kings (2 Kings xi. 14 ; xxiii. 3). To this a special "ascent" led from the palace (1 Kings x. 5), which was, perhaps afterwards, roofed over for protection from the weather.[2] The Priests' Court was enclosed by a wall consisting of three tiers of hewn stones and a row of cedar beams (1 Kings vi. 36).

From the court of the priests steps led down to the "outer court" of the people (comp. Jer. xxxvi. 10), which[3] was surrounded by a solid wall, from which four massive gates, covered

---

[1] See *Speaker's Comment.* ii., p. 521—not, as in our Authorised Version, "certain additions made of thin work" (1 Kings vii. 29).

[2] This was "the covert for the Sabbath" (2 Kings xvi. 18). The Rabbis hold it to have been the exclusive privilege of the kings to sit down within the Priests' Court.   [3] This appears from 1 Chron. xxvi. 13–16.

with brass, opened upon the Temple-mount (2 Chron. iv. 9). In this court were large colonnades and chambers, and rooms for the use of the priests and Levites, for the storage of what was required in the services, and for other purposes. The principal gate was, no doubt, the eastern (Ezek. xi. 1), corresponding to the "Beautiful Gate" of New Testament times. To judge by the analogy of the other measurements, as compared with those of the Tabernacle, the Court of the Priests would be 100 cubits broad, and 200 cubits long, and the Outer Court double these proportions (comp. also Ezek. xl. 27).[1]

Such, in its structure and fittings, was the Temple which Solomon built to the Name of Jehovah God. Its further history to its destruction, 416 years after its building, is traced in the following passages of Holy Scripture : 1 Kings xiv. 26 ; xv. 18, etc. ; 2 Chron. xx. 5 ; 2 Kings xii. 5, etc. ; xiv. 14 ; xv. 35 ; 2 Chron. xxvii. 3 ; 2 Kings xvi. 8 ; xviii. 15, etc. ; xxi. 4, 5, 7 ; xxiii. 4, 7, 11 ; xxiv. 13 ; xxv. 9, 13–17).[2]

[1] It is with exceeding reluctance that I forbear entering on the symbolical import of the Temple, of its materials, structure, and arrangements. But such discussions would evidently be outside the plan and limits of this Bible History.

[2] Comparing the Temple of Solomon with that of Herod, the latter was, of course, much superior, not only as regards size, but architectural beauty. To understand the difference, plans of the two should be placed side by side. We add a few remarks which may interest the reader. From being so largely constructed of cedar-wood, the Temple is also figuratively called "Lebanon" (Zech. xi. 1). Among the Jewish legends connected with the Temple, one of the strangest is that about a certain worm Shamir, which, according to *Aboth* v. 6, was among the ten things created on the eve of the world's first Sabbath, just before sunset (see also *Sifré on Deut.* p. 147, *a*). In *Gitt.* 86, *a* and *b*, we are informed by what artifices Solomon obtained possession of this worm from Ashmedai, the prince of the demons. This worm possessed the power, by his touch, to cut the thickest stones, and was therefore used by Solomon for this purpose (comp. also generally *Gitt.* 68 *a*, and *Sotah* 48 *b*). According to *Joma* 53*b*, 54*b*, the Ark was placed upon what is called the "foundation stone of the world." So early as in the *Targum Pseudo-Jonathan* on Exod. xxviii. 30, we read that the ineffable Name of God was engraved upon this stone, and that God at the first sealed up with it the mouth of the great deep. This may serve as a specimen of these legends. Perhaps we should add that, according to later Rabbis, the roof of the Temple was not quite flat, but slightly sloping, yet probably not higher in any part than the parapet around

CHAPTER VII.

(1 KINGS VIII. ; 2 CHRON. V.—VII. 11.)

A T length the great and beautiful house, which Solomon had raised to the Name of Jehovah, and to which so many ardent thoughts and hopes attached, was finished. Its solemn dedication took place in the year following its completion, and, very significantly, immediately before, and in connection with, the Feast of Tabernacles. Two questions, of some difficulty and importance, here arise. The first concerns the circumstance that the sacred text (1 Kings vii. 1-12) records the building of Solomon's palace immediately after that of the Temple, and, indeed, almost intermingles the two accounts. This may partly have been due to a very natural desire on the part of the writer not to break the continuity of the account of Solomon's great buildings, the more so as they were all completed by the aid of Tyrian workmen, and under the supervision of Hiram. But another and more important consideration may also have influenced the arrangement of the narrative. For, as has been suggested, these two great undertakings of Solomon bore a close relation to each other. It was not an ordinary Sanctuary, nor was it an ordinary royal residence which Solomon reared. The building of the Temple marked that the preparatory period of Israel's unsettledness had passed, when God had walked with them " in tent and tabernacle "— or, in other words, that the Theocracy had attained not only fixedness, but its highest point, when God would set "His Name for ever" in its chosen centre. But this new stage of the Theocracy was connected with the establishment of a firm and settled kingdom in Israel, when He would "establish the throne of that kingdom for ever" (compare 2 Sam. vii. 5–16). Thus the dwelling of God in His Temple and that of Solomon in his house were events between which there was deep internal connection, even as between the final establishment of the Theocracy and that of David's royal line in Israel. Moreover, the king was not to be a monarch in the usual Oriental, or even in the ancient Western sense. He was to be regarded, not as the *Vicegerent* or *Representative* of God, but as *His Servant,* to do His behest and to guard His covenant. And this might well be marked, even by the conjunction of these two buildings in the Scripture narrative.

These considerations will also help us to understand why the Feast of the Dedication of the Temple was connected with that of Tabernacles (of course, in the year following). It was not only that, after "the eighth month," when the Temple was completed, it would have been almost impossible, considering the season of the year, to have gathered the people from all parts of the country, or to have celebrated for eight days a great popular festival; nor yet that of all feasts, that of Tabernacles, when agricultural labour was at an end, probably witnessed the largest concourse in Jerusalem.[1] But the Feast of Tabernacles had a threefold meaning. It pointed back to the time when, "strangers and pilgrims" on their way to the Land of Promise, Israel, under its Divine leadership, had dwelt in tents. The full import of this memorial would be best realised at the dedication of the Temple, when, instead of tent and tabernacle, the glorious house of God was standing in all its beauty, while the stately palace of Israel's king was rising. Again, the Feast of Tabernacles was essentially one of thanksgiving, when at the

---

[1] The Temple was completed in the eighth month; its dedication took place in the seventh of the next year. Ewald suggests that it was dedicated before it was quite finished. But this idea can scarcely be maintained.

completion, not only of the harvest, but of the ingathering of the fruits, a grateful people presented its homage to the God to Whom they owed all, and to Whom all really belonged. But what could raise this hymn of praise to its loudest strains, if not that they uplifted it within those sacred walls, symbolical of God's gracious Presence as King in His palace in the midst of His people, whose kingdom He had established? Lastly, the Feast of Tabernacles—the only still unfulfilled Old Testament type—pointed forward to the time of which the present state of Israel was an initial realisation, when the Name of the LORD should be known far and wide to earth's utmost bounds, and all nations seek after Him and offer worship in His Temple. Thus, however viewed, there was the deepest significance in the conjunction of the dedication of the Temple with the Feast of Tabernacles.

But, as previously stated, there is yet another question of somewhat greater difficulty which claims our attention. To judge by the arrangement of the narrative, the dedication of the Temple (1 Kings viii.) might seem to have taken place *after* the completion of Solomon's palace, the building of which, as we know, occupied further thirteen years (1 Kings vii. 1). Moreover, from the circumstance that the second vision of God was vouchsafed "when Solomon had finished the building of the house of the LORD, and the king's house, and all Solomon's desire which he was pleased to do" (1 Kings ix. 1), it has been argued, that the dedication of the Temple must have taken place immediately before this vision, especially as what was said to him seems to contain pointed reference to the consecration prayer of Solomon (1 Kings ix. 3, 7, 8). But, even if that vision took place at the time just indicated,[1] the supposed inference from it cannot be maintained.

---

[1] At the same time, I confess that I am by no means convinced that such was the case. The language of 1 Kings ix. 1 should not be too closely pressed, and may be intended as a sort of general transition from the subject previously treated to that in hand. The brief notices in 2 Chron. vii. seem rather to favour this idea.

For, although part of the sacred vessels may have been made during the time that Hiram was engaged upon Solomon's palace, it is not credible that the Temple should, after its completion, have stood deserted and unused for thirteen years. Nor are the arguments in favour of this most improbable assumption valid. The appeal to 1 Kings ix. 1 would oblige us to date the dedication of the Temple even later than the completion of Solomon's palace, viz., after he had finished all his other building operations. As for the words which the LORD spake to Solomon in vision (2 Kings ix. 3-9), although bearing reference to the Temple and the king's dedication prayer, they are evidently intended rather as a general warning, than as an answer to his petition, and are such as would befit the period of temptation, *before* Solomon, carried away by the splendour of his success, yielded himself to the luxury, weakness, and sin of his older age. From all these considerations we conclude that the Feast of the Dedication, which lasted seven days, took place in the seventh month, that of Ethanim, or of "flowing brooks "[1] (the later Tishri), of the year after the completion of the Temple (eleven months after it), and immediately before the Feast of Tabernacles, which, with the concluding solemnity, lasted eight days.

The account of the dedication of the Temple may be conveniently ranged under these three particulars : the *Consecration-Services*, the *Consecration-Prayer*, and the *Consecration-Thanksgiving* and *Festive Offerings*. But before describing them, it is necessary to call attention to the remarkable circumstance that the chief, if not almost the sole prominent agent in these services, was the *king*, the high-priest not being even mentioned. Not that Solomon in any way interfered with, or arrogated to himself the functions of the priesthood, but that, in the part which he took, he fully acted up to the spirit of the monarchical institution as founded in Israel. Solomon was not "king" according to the Saxon idea of *cyning*—cunning,

---

[1] This rendering of the term "Ethanim," seems preferable to that of "gifts," viz., fruits (Thenius), or of "stand still," viz., equinox (Böttche).

mighty, illustrious, the embodiment of strength. According to the terms of the Covenant, all Israel were God's *servants* (Lev. xxv. 42, 55 ; comp. Isa. xli. 8, 9 ; xliv. 1, 2, 21 ; xlv. 4 ; xlix. 3, 6 ; Jer. xxx. 10, and others). As such they were to be "a kingdom of priests" (Exod. xix. 6)—"the priest," in the stricter sense of the term, being only the representative of the people, with certain distinctive functions *ad hoc.* But what the nation was, as a whole, that Israel's theocratic king was *pre-eminently :* the servant of the LORD (1 Kings viii. 25, 28, 29, 52, 59). It was in this capacity that Solomon acted at the dedication of the Temple, as his own words frequently indicate (see the passages just quoted). In this manner the innermost and deepest idea of the character of Israel and of Israel's king as "the servant" of the LORD, became, so to speak, more and more individualized during the progress of the Old Testament dispensation, till it stood out in all its fulness in the Messiah—the climax of Israel and of Israelitish institutions—Who is *the* Servant of Jehovah. Thus we perceive that the common underlying idea of the three great institutions in Israel, which connected them all, was that of the *Servant* of Jehovah. The prophet who uttered the voice of heaven upon earth was the servant of Jehovah (comp., for example, Numb. xii. 7, 8 ; Josh. i. 2 ; Isa. xx. 3, etc.).[1] So was the priest, who spake the voice of earth to heaven ; and the king, who made heaven's voice to be heard on earth. That which gave its real meaning equally to this threefold function—downwards, upwards, outwards—was the grand fact that in each of them it was the Servant of Jehovah who was acting, or, in other words, that *God was all in all.* With these general principles in view we shall be better able to understand what follows.

1. *The Consecration-Services* (1 Kings viii. 1–21).—These commenced with the transference of the Ark and of the other

---

[1] It is impossible here to do more than indicate this train of thought. The reader will be able to make out a perfect *catena* of confirmatory passages, extending over almost all the books of Holy Scripture, or from age to age.

holy vessels from Mount Zion, and of the ancient Mosaic Tabernacle from Gibeon. The latter and the various other relics of those earlier services were, as we have suggested, placed in the chambers built around the new Sanctuary. In accordance with the Divine direction, the whole of this part of the service was performed by the Priests and Levites, attended by the king, " the elders of Israel, the heads of the tribes, and the princes (of the houses) of the fathers of Israel," who, as representatives of the people, had been specially summoned for the purpose. As this solemn procession entered the sacred courts, amidst a vast concourse of people, numberless offerings were brought. Then the Ark was carried to its place in the innermost Sanctuary.[1] As the priests reverently retired from it, and were about to minister in the Holy Place [2]—perhaps to burn incense on the Golden Altar—"the cloud," as the visible symbol of God's Presence, came down, as formerly at the consecration of the Tabernacle (Ex. xl. 34, 35), and so filled the whole of the Temple itself, that the priests, unable to bear "the glory," had to retire from their ministry. But even here also we mark the characteristic difference between the Old and the New Dispensations, to which St. Paul calls attention in another connection (2 Cor. iii. 13–18). For whereas, under the preparatory dispensation God dwelt in a "cloud" and in "thick darkness," we all now behold "the glory of God" in the Face of His Anointed.[3]

[1] The expression, 1 Kings viii. 9, seems to be incompatible with the notice in Hebrews ix. 4. But not only according to the Talmud (*Joma* 52. *b*), but according to uniform Jewish tradition (see *apud* Delitzsch *Comm. z. Br. an die Hebr.* p. 361), what is mentioned in Heb. ix. 4 had been really placed in the Ark, although the emphatic notice in 1 Kings viii. 9 indicates that it was no longer there in the time of Solomon. It may have been removed previous to, or after the capture of the Ark by the Philistines.

[2] The Book of Chronicles (2 Chron. v. 12–14) characteristically notes that the Priests and Levites were raising holy chant and music.

[3] Bähr here quotes this ancient comment : *Nebulâ Deus se et repre-sentabat et velabat,* and Buxtorf (*Hist. Arcæ Foed.* ed. Bas. 1659, p. 115) adduces a very apt passage from Abarbanel.

This was the real consecration of the Temple. And now the king, turning towards the Most Holy Place, filled with the Sacred Presence, spake these words of dedication, brief as became the solemnity : " Jehovah hath said : to dwell in darkness—Building, I have built an house of habitation to Thee, and a settling-place for Thy dwelling ever !" In this reference to what Jehovah had said, it would not be any single utterance which presented itself to Solomon's mind. Rather would he think of them in their connection and totality—as it were, a golden chain of precious promises welded one to the other, of which the last link seemed riveted to the solemnity then enacting. Such sayings as Ex. xix. 9 ; xx. 21 ; Lev. xvi. 2 ; Deut. iv. 11 ; v. 22 would crowd upon his memory, and seem fully realised as he beheld the Cloudy Presence in the Holy House. Thus it is often not one particular promise or prophecy which is referred to when we read in Holy Scripture these words : " That it might be fulfilled," but rather a whole series which culminate in some one great fact (as, for example, in Matt. ii. 15, 23). Nor should we forget that, when the king spoke of the Temple as God's dwelling for *ever*, the symbolical character alike of the manifestation of His Presence and of its place could not have been absent from his mind. But the *symbolical* necessarily implies the *temporary*, being of the nature of an accommodation to circumstances, persons, and times. What was *for ever* was not the form, but the substance—not the manner nor the place, but the fact of God's Presence in the midst of His people. And what is real and eternal is the Kingdom of God in its widest sense, and God's Presence in grace among His worshipping people, as fully realised in Jesus Christ.

When the king had spoken these words, he turned from the Sanctuary to the people who reverently stood to hear his benedictory "address." [1] Briefly recounting the gracious promises and experiences of the past, he pointed to the present as their

---

[1] It is thus, and not as implying any actual benediction, either uttered or silent, that I understand the words 1 Kings viii. 14.

fulfilment, specially applying to it, in the manner already described, what God had said to David (2 Sam. vii. 7, 8).[1]

2. *The Prayer of Consecration.*—This brief address concluded, the king ascended the brazen pulpit-like platform "before the altar" (of burnt offering), and with his face, probably sideways, towards the people, knelt down with hands outspread in prayer (comp. 2 Chron. vi. 12, 13).

It seems like presumption and impertinence to refer in laudatory terms to what for comprehensiveness, sublimeness, humility, faith, and earnestness has no parallel in the Old Testament, and can only be compared with the prayer which our Lord taught His disciples.[2] Like the latter, it consists of an introduction (1 Kings viii. 23–30), of seven petitions (the covenant-number, vers. 31–53), and of a eulogetic close (2 Chron. vi. 40–42). The Introduction sounds like an Old Testament version of the words "Our Father" (vers. 23–26), "which art in heaven" (vers. 27–30). It would be out of place here to enter into any detailed analysis. Suffice it to indicate the leading Scriptural references in it—as it were, the spiritual stepping-stones of the prayer—and one or another of its outstanding points. Marking how a review of the gracious dealings in the past should lead to *confidence* in present petitions (comp. Matt. xxi. 22; Mark xi. 24; James i. 6), reference should

---

[1] Compare the fuller account in 2 Chron. vi. 5, 6.

[2] It is one of its many extraordinary instances of "begging the question," that modern criticism boldly declares this whole prayer spurious, or rather relegates its composition to a much later date, even so far as the Babylonish exile! The only *objective* ground by which this *dictum* is supported, is the circumstance that the prayer is full of references to the Book of Deuteronomy—which modern criticism has *ruled* to be non-Mosaic, and of much later date—*ergo*, this prayer must share its fate! This kind of reasoning is, in fact, to derive from one unproved hypothesis another even more unlikely! For we have here, first, the accordant accounts (with but slight variations) in 1 Kings and 2 Chron.; while, secondly (as Bleek has remarked), the wording of the prayer implies a time and conditions when the Temple, Jerusalem, and the Davidic throne were still extant. To this we may add, that the whole tone and conception is not at all in accordance with, or what we would have expected at, the time of the exile.

be made in connection with verses 23–26 to the following passages : Ex. xv. 11 ; Deut. iv. 39 ; vii. 9 ; Josh. ii. 11 ; 2 Sam. vii. 12–22 ; xxii. 32 ; Ps. lxxxvi. 8. In regard to the second part of the Introduction (vers. 27–30), we specially note the emphatic assertion, that He, Whose Presence they saw in the cloud, was really *in* " *heaven,*" and yet "*our* Father," who art upon earth. These two ideas seem carried out in it : (1) Not as heathenism does, do we locate God here ; nor yet will we, as carnal Israel did (Jer. vii. 4 ; Mic. iii. 11), imagine that *ex opere operato* (by any mere deed of ours) God will necessarily attend even to His own appointed services in His house. Our faith rises higher—from the Seen to the Unseen—from the God of Israel to our Father ; it realises the spiritual relationship of *children,* which alone contains the pledge of His blessing ; and through which, though He be in heaven, yet faith knows and addresses Him as an ever-present help. Thus Solomon's prayer avoided alike the two extremes of unspiritual realism and of unreal spiritualism.

The *first petition* (vers. 31, 32) in the stricter sense opens the prayer, which in ver. 28 had been outlined, according to its prevailing characteristics, as " petition," " prayer for mercy" (forgiveness and grace), and " thanksgiving " (praise).[1] It is essentially an Old Testament " Hallowed be Thy Name," in its application to the sanctity of an oath as its highest expression, inasmuch as thereby the reality of God's holiness is challenged. The analogy between the *second petition* (vers. 33, 34) and that in the Lord's Prayer is not so evident at first sight. But it is none the less real, since its ideal fulfilment would mark the coming of the kingdom of God, which neither sin from within nor enemy from without could endanger. The references in this petition seem to be to Lev. xxvi. 3, 7, 14, 17 ; Deut. xxviii. 1–7, 15–25 ; and again to Lev. xxvi. 33, and 40–42, and Deut. iv. 26–28 ; xxviii. 64–68, and iv. 29–31 ; xxx. 1–5. The organic

---

[1] In the Authorised Version, inaccurately, " prayer," " supplication," " cry ;" in the Hebrew, *Tephillah* (from the *Hithpael* of *Palal*), *Techinnah* (from the *Hithp.* of *Chanan*), and *Rinnah* (from *Ranan*).

connection, so to speak, between heaven and earth, which lies
at the basis of the *third petition* in the Lord's Prayer, is also
expressed in that of Solomon (vers. 35, 36). Only in the one
case we have the New Testament realisation of that grand idea,
or rather ideal, while in the other we have its Old Testament
aspect. The references here are to Lev. xxvi. 19; Deut. xi. 17 ;
xxviii. 23, 24. At the same time the rendering of our Authorised Version (1 Kings viii. 35): "When Thou afflictest them,"
should be altered to, " Because Thou humblest them," which
indicates the moral effect of God's discipline, and the last link
in the chain of true repentance.

The correspondence between the *fourth petition* in the
Solomonic (vers. 37–40) and in our Lord's Prayer will be evident
— always keeping in view the difference between the Old
and the New Testament standpoint. But perhaps verses
38–40 may mark the transition from, and connection between
the first and second parts of the prayer. The *fifth petition*
(vers. 41–43), which concerns the acceptance of the prayers of
strangers (not proselytes), is based on the idea of the great
mutual forgiveness by those who are forgiven of God, fully
realised in the abolition of the great *enmity* and separation, which
was to give place to a common brotherhood of love and service
—"that all the people of the earth may know Thy Name, to
fear Thee, as Thy people Israel." Here also we note the difference between the Old and the New Testament form of the
petition—a remark which must equally be kept in view in
regard to the other two petitions. These, indeed, seem to bear
only a very distant analogy to the concluding portion of the
Lord's Prayer. Yet that there was real " temptation" to Israel,
and real " deliverance from evil" sought in these petitions,
appears from the language of confession put into the mouth of
the captives (ver. 47), which, as we know, was literally adopted
by those in Babylon[1] (Dan. ix. 5; Ps. cvi. 6). Here sin is

---

[1] It would seem almost too great a demand upon our credence, even by
" advanced criticism," that, because these expressions were taken up by
the exiles in Babylon, they originated at that time.

presented in its threefold aspect as *failure,* so far as regards the goal, or *stumbling* and *falling* (in the Authorised Version "we have sinned"); then as *perversion* (literally, making crooked); and, lastly, as *tumultuous rebellion* (in the Authorised Version "committed wickedness"). Lastly, the three concluding verses (vers. 51–53) may be regarded either as the argument for the last petitions, or else as an Old Testament version of "Thine is the kingdom, and the power, and the glory." But the whole prayer is the opening of the door into heaven—a door moving, if the expression be lawful, on the two hinges of *sin* and of *grace,* of *need* and of *provision.*

3. *The Consecration-Thanksgiving and Offerings.*—To the prayer of Solomon, the descent of fire upon the great altar—probably from out the Cloudy Presence [1]—which is recorded in 2 Chron. vii. 1, seems a most appropriate answer [2] (comp. Lev. ix. 24). Little requires to be added to the simple account of what followed. Rising from his knees, the king turned once more to the people, and expressed the feelings of all in terms of mingled praise and prayer, basing them on such Scriptural passages as Deut. xii. 9, 10; Josh. xxi. 44, etc.; xxiii. 14, and, in the second part of his address, on Lev. xxvi. 3–13; Deut. xxviii. 1–14. But it deserves special notice, that throughout (as Thenius has well remarked) the tone is of the loftiest spirituality. For, if the king asks for continued help and blessing from the Lord, it is for the express purpose "that He may incline our hearts to Him" (comp. Ps. cxix. 36; cxli. 4), "to keep His commandments" (1 Kings viii. 58); and, if he looks for answers to prayer (ver. 59), it is "that all the people of the earth may know that Jehovah is God, and that there is none else" (ver. 60).

[1] 2 Chron. vii. 1 does *not* necessarily imply that there was a second manifestation of "the glory of Jehovah."

[2] It is certainly a fact, that this circumstance is not mentioned in the narrative in the Book of Kings. But from this it is a very long and venturesome step to the conclusion, that this is an addition or interpolation on the part of the writer or editor of the Books of Chronicles, the more so as "Kings" and "Chronicles" alternately record or omit other important events.

Lastly, we have an account of the vast number [1] of festive offerings which Solomon and all Israel [2] brought, and of the Feast of Tabernacles [3] with which the solemn dedication-services concluded.

CHAPTER VIII.

The Surroundings of the Temple—Description of Jerusalem at the time of Solomon—The Palace of Solomon—Solomon's fortified Cities— External relations of the Kingdom—Internal State—Trade—Wealth —Luxury—The visit of the Queen of Sheba.

(1 KINGS IX., X.; 2 CHRON. VII. 11–IX. 28.)

WE have now reached the period of Solomon's greatest worldly splendour, which, as alas! so often, marks also that of spiritual decay. The building of the Temple was not the first, nor yet the last, of his architectural undertakings. Mount Moriah was too small to hold on its summit the Temple itself, even without its courts and other buildings. Accordingly,

---

[1] Canon Rawlinson (*Speaker's Commentary*, II. p. 533) has shown, by numerous quotations, that these sacrifices were not out of proportion to others recorded in antiquity. As to the time necessarily occupied in these sacrifices, we have the historical notice of Josephus (*Jewish War*, vi. 9, 3), that on one occasion not fewer than 256,000 Passover-lambs were offered, the time occupied being just *three hours* of an afternoon. It is also to be borne in mind that the killing and preparing of the sacrifices was *not* necessarily the duty of priests or even Levites, the strictly priestly function being *only that of sprinkling the blood*. Lastly, we are distinctly informed (1 Kings viii. 64) that supplementary altars—besides the great altar of burnt offering—were used on this occasion.

[2] We are expressly told in ver. 62, that these offerings were brought not only by the king but by all Israel.

[3] The Feast of Tabernacles lasted seven days and closed on the afternoon of the eighth with the *clausura* or solemn dismissal (comp. Lev. xxiii. 33–39).

as we learn from Josephus (*Ant.* xv. 11, 3), extensive substructures had to be reared.   Thus, the level of the Temple-mount
was enlarged both east and west, in order to obtain a sufficient
area for the extensive buildings upon it.   These rose terrace
upon terrace—each court higher than the other, and the Sanctuary itself higher than its courts.   We are probably correct in
the supposition that the modern Mosque of Omar occupies the
very site of the ancient Temple of Solomon, and that over
the celebrated rock in it—according to Jewish tradition, the
very spot where Abraham offered up Isaac—the great altar of
burnt-offering had risen.   Before the building of the Sanctuary
itself could have been commenced, the massive substructures
of the Temple must have been at least partially completed,
although these and the outbuildings were probably continued
during many years, perhaps many reigns, after the completion
of the Temple.

The same remarks apply to another structure connected
with the Temple, called "Parbar" (1 Chron. xxvi. 18).   As
already explained, the outer court of the Temple had *four*
massive gates (1 Chron. xxvi. 13–16), of which the western-
most opened upon "Parbar" or "Parvarim" (perhaps "colonnade").   This seems to have been an annex to the western
side of the Temple, fitted up as chambers, stables for sacrificial animals, etc. (2 Kings xxiii. 11, where our Authorised
Version wrongly renders "Parvarim" by "suburbs").   From
Parbar steps led down to the Tyropœon, or deep valley which
intersected the city east and west.

Although anything like an attempt at detailed description
would here be out of place, it seems desirable, in order to realise
the whole circumstances, to give at least a brief sketch of
Jerusalem, as Solomon found, and as he left it.   Speaking
generally, Jerusalem was built on the two opposite hills (east
and west), between which the Tyropœon runs south-east and
then south.   The eastern hill is about 100 feet lower than
the western.   Its northern summit is Mount Moriah, which
slopes down into Ophel (about 50 feet lower), afterwards the

suburb of the priests. Some modern writers have regarded this as the ancient fort of the Jebusites, and as the site of the "City of David," the original Mount Zion. Although this is opposed to the common traditional view, which regards the *western* hill as Mount Zion, the arguments in favour of identifying it with the eastern hill seem very strong. These it would, of course, be impossible here to detail. But we may say that the history of David's purchase of the threshing-floor of Ornan the Jebusite (2 Sam. xxiv. 16–24; 1 Chron. xxi. 15–25) conveys these two facts : that the Jebusites *had* settlements on the western hill, and that David's palace (which, as we know, was in the City of David) was close by, only a little lower than Mount Moriah, since David so clearly saw from his palace the destroying Angel over the threshing-floor of Ornan. All this agrees with the idea, that the original stronghold of the Jebusites was on the slopes of Moriah and Ophel, and that David built his palace in that neighbourhood, below the summit of Moriah.[1] Lastly, if the term "Mount Zion" included Moriah, we can understand the peculiar sacredness which throughout Holy Scripture attaches to that name. Be this as it may, the regular quarter of the Jebusites was on the western hill, towards the slope of the Tyropœon, while the Jewish Benjamite quarter (the Upper City) was on the higher terrace above it (eastwards). Fort Millo was on the north-eastern angle of the Western City. Here King David had continued the wall, which had formerly enclosed the western hill northward and westward, drawing it eastward, so as to make (the western) Jeru-

---

[1] The above would give a new view of the taking of the fortress of Jebus by Joab. There undoubtedly existed a subterranean watercourse dug through the solid rock on which Jebus stood on Ophel, leading down to the "En-Rogel," or "Fountain of the Virgin." It is suggested, that with the connivance of Aravnah, Joab undertook the daring feat of climbing up into Jebus by this "gutter," and opening the gates to his comrades. This would also account for the presence of the Jebusite Aravnah on the neighbouring Moriah during the later years of David's reign, and explain the somewhat difficult passage, 2 Sam. v. 8. Comp. Warren's *Recovery of Jerusalem*, pp. 244–255.

salem a complete fortress (2 Sam. v. 9; 1 Chron. xi. 8). On the opposite (eastern) side of the Tyropœon was the equally fortified (later) Ophel. Solomon now connected these two fortresses by enlarging Millo and continuing the wall across the Tyropœon (1 Kings iii. 1; ix. 15; xi. 27).

Without referring to the various buildings which Solomon reared, it may be safely asserted that the city must have rapidly increased in population. Indeed, during the prosperous reign of Solomon it probably attained as large, if not larger, proportions than at any time before the Exile. The wealthier part of the population occupied the western terraces of the west hill—the Upper City—the streets running north and south. The eastern slopes of the west hill were covered by "the middle city" (2 Kings xx. 4, marginal rendering). It will have been noticed, that as yet only the *southern* parts of both the eastern and western hills of Jerusalem had been built over King Solomon now reared the Temple on Mount Moriah, which formed the northern slope of the eastern hill, while the increase of the population soon led to building operations on the side of the western hill opposite to it. Here the city extended beyond the old wall, north of "the middle city," occupying the northern part of the Tyropœon. This was "the other" or "second part of the city" (2 Kings xxii. 14; 2 Chron. xxxiv. 22; Neh. xi. 9, the "maktesh" or "mortar" of Zeph. i. 11). Here was the real business quarter, with its markets, "fishgate," "sheepgate," and bazaars, such as the "Baker Street" (Jer. xxxvii. 21), the quarters of the goldsmiths and other merchants (Neh. iii. 8, 32), the "valley of the cheesemongers," etc. This suburb must have been soon inclosed by a wall. We do not know when or by whom the latter was commenced, but we have notices of its partial destruction (2 Kings xiv. 13; 2 Chron. xxv. 23), and of its repair (2 Chron. xxxii. 5).

We have purposely not taken account of the towers and gates of the city, since what has been described will sufficiently explain the location of the great palace which Solomon built during the thirteen years after the completion of the Temple

(1 Kings vii. 1–12; 2 Chron. viii. 1). Its site was the eastern terrace of the western hill, probably the same as that afterwards occupied by the palace of the Asmonæans (Maccabees) and of Agrippa II. The area covered by this magnificent building was four times that of the Holy House (not including its courts). It stood right over against the Temple. A descent led from the Palace into the Tyropœon, and thence a special magnificent "ascent" (2 Chron. ix. 4) to the royal entrance (2 Kings xvi. 18), probably at the south-western angle of the Temple. The site was happily chosen—protected by Fort Millo, and looking out upon the Temple-Mount, while south of it stretched the wealthy quarter of the city. Ascending from the Tyropœon, one would pass through a kind of ante-building into a porch, and thence into a splendid colonnade. This colonnade connected "the house of the forest of Lebanon," so called from the costly cedars used in its construction, with "the porch for the throne," where Solomon pronounced judgment (1 Kings vii. 6, 7). Finally, there was in the inner court, still further west, "the house where Solomon dwelt," and "the house for Pharaoh's daughter," with, of course, the necessary side and outbuildings (1 Kings vii. 8). Thus, the royal palace really consisted of three separate buildings. Externally it was simply of "costly stones" (ver. 9), the beauty of its design only appearing in its interior. Here the building extended along three sides. The ground-floor consisted of colonnades of costly cedar, the beams being fastened into the outer walls. These colonnades would be hung with tapestry, so as to be capable of being formed into apartments. Above these rose, on each side of the court, three tiers of chambers, fifteen on each tier, with large windows looking out upon each other. Here were the State apartments for court feasts, and in them were kept, among other precious things, the golden targets and shields (1 Kings x. 16, 17). Passing through another colonnade, one would next reach the grand Judgment- and Audience-halls, with the magnificent throne of ivory, described in 1 Kings x. 18–20; 2 Chron. ix. 17–19. And,

lastly, the innermost court contained the royal dwellings themselves.[1]

But this great Palace, the Temple, and the enlargement of Millo and of the city wall, were not the only architectural undertakings of King Solomon. Remembering that there were watchful foes on all sides, he either built or repaired a number of strong places. In the north, as defence against Syria, rose the ancient stronghold of Hazor (Josh. xi. 13 ; Judges iv. 2). The plain of Jezreel, the traditional battlefield of, as well as the highway into Palestine from the west and the north, was protected by Megiddo; while the southern approach from Egypt and the Philistine plain was guarded by Gezer, which Pharaoh had before this taken from the Canaanites and burnt, but afterwards given to his daughter as dowry on her marriage with Solomon. Not far from Gezer, and serving a similar defensive purpose, rose the fortress of Baalath, in the possession of Dan (comp. Josephus, *Ant.* viii., 6, 1). The eastern and northeastern parts of Solomon's dominions were protected by Tamar or Tadmor, probably the Palmyra of the ancients,[2] and by Hamath-Zobah (2 Chron. viii. 4), while access to Jerusalem and irruptions from the north-western plain were barred by the fortification of Upper and Nether Bethhoron (1 Kings ix. 15–19; 2 Chron. viii. 3–6). Besides these fortresses, the king provided magazine-cities, and others where his chariots and cavalry were stationed—most of them, probably, towards the north. In all such undertakings Solomon employed the forced labour of the descendants of the ancient Canaanite inhabitants of Palestine, his Jewish subjects being chiefly engaged as overseers and officers in various departments (1 Kings ix. 20–23). But even thus, the diversion of so much labour and the taxation which his undertakings must have involved were felt as a

[1] In the description of Jerusalem and of Solomon's palace, I have largely availed myself of the Article in Riehm's *Hand-Wörterb. d. Bibl. Alterth.* Part viii. pp. 679–683, with which compare Unruh, *Das alte Jerusalem.*
[2] Comp. the admirable article of Mr. Twistleton, in Smith's *Bibl. Dict.* iii., pp. 1428–1430.

"grievous service" and "heavy yoke" (1 Kings xii. 4), all the more that Solomon's love of building and of Oriental splendour seems to have rapidly grown upon him. Thus, once more by a natural process of causation, the inner decay marked by luxury led to the weakening of the kingdom of Solomon, and scattered the seeds of that disaffection which, in the days of his degenerate son, ripened into open rebellion. So true is it, that in the history of Israel the inner and the outer always keep pace. But as yet Solomon's devotion to the services of Jehovah had not lessened. For we read that on the great festivals of the year (2 Chron. viii. 12, 13) he was wont to bring numerous special offerings.[1]

As regards the *foreign* relations of Solomon, reference has already been made (in ch. v.) to his marriage with the daughter of Pharaoh (1 Kings iii. 1), which took place in the first years of his reign. In all likelihood this Pharaoh was one of the last rulers of the (21st) Tanite dynasty. We know that their power had of late greatly declined, and Pharaoh may have been glad to ally himself with the now powerful ruler of the neighbouring country. On the new kingdom, however, such an alliance would shed great lustre, especially in the eyes of the Jews themselves. The frequent references to Pharaoh's daughter show what importance the nation attached to this union. It may be well here again to note, that the Egyptian princess, who brought to her husband the dowry of an important border-fortress (Gezer), was not in any way responsible for Solomon's later idolatry, no Egyptian deities being named among those towards whom he turned (1 Kings xi. 5-7).

Solomon's relations to Hiram, king of Tyre, at one time

---

[1] The expression "he burnt incense" (1 Kings ix. 25) has been regarded by Keil as a mistranslation—the text only implying the burning of the sacrifices. Bähr, more satisfactorily, refers it to the burning of incense on the great altar which accompanied all meat-offerings (Lev. ii. 1, 2). But on no consideration can it be supposed to imply, that Solomon arrogated to himself the priestly function of burning incense on the golden altar in the Holy Place (Thenius). How such an idea can be harmonised with the theory of the later origin of these books may be left to its advocates to explain.

threatened to become less friendly than they had been at first, and afterwards again became. It appears that, besides furnishing him with wood, Hiram had also advanced gold to Solomon (1 Kings ix. 11), amounting, if we may connect with this the notice in ver. 14, to 120 talents of gold, variously computed at £1,250,000 (Poole), £720,000 (S. Clarke), and £471,240 (Keil, whose estimate seems the most probable). We suppose it was in repayment of this sum that Solomon ceded to Hiram twenty cities in Northern Galilee, adjoining the possessions of Tyre. With these he might the more readily part, since the district was partially "Gentile" (Is. ix. 1). But Hiram, who probably coveted a strip of land along the coast, was dissatisfied with his new acquisition, and gave it the contemptuous designation of "the land of Cabul."[1] The district seems, however, to have been afterwards restored to Solomon[2] (2 Chron. viii. 2), no doubt on repayment of the loan and other compensation.

The later relations between Hiram and Solomon consisted chiefly in mercantile alliances. Although most writers regard the fleet which sailed to Ophir (1 Kings ix. 27, 28) as identical with "the navy of Tarshish" (1 Kings x. 22), yet the names, the imports, as well as the regularity in the passages of the latter ("every three years"), and the express statement that its destiny was Tarshish (2 Chron. ix. 21) seem opposed to this view. Opinions are also divergent as to the exact location of Ophir, and the share which Hiram had in the outfit of this expedition, whether he only furnished sailors (1 Kings ix. 27), or also the ships (2 Chron. viii. 18). In all probability the wood for these ships was cut in Lebanon by order of Hiram, and floated to Joppa, whence it would be transported by land (comp. 2 Chron. ii. 16) to Ezion-Geber and Elath, at the head of the Gulf of Akabah (the Red Sea), where the vessels would

[1] The derivation and meaning of the name are in dispute. Probably it is equivalent to "as nothing."

[2] This view is, however, opposed by some critics, though, as I think, on insufficient grounds.

be built under the direction of Phœnician shipwrights. Upon the whole, it seems most likely that the Ophir whence they fetched gold was Arabia. The sacred text does not inform us whether these expeditions were periodical, the absence of such notice rather leading to the supposition that this was not the case, or at least that they were not continued. The total result of these expeditions was an importation of gold to the amount of 420 talents[1] (according to Keil about 1½ million sterling). It was not only the prospect of such addition to the wealth of the country, but that this was the first Jewish maritime expedition—in fact, the first great national trading undertaking, which gave it such importance in public estimation that Solomon went in person to visit the two harbours where the fleet was fitting out (2 Chron. viii. 17). According to 1 Kings x. 11, the Phœnician fleet also brought from "Ophir" "precious stones" and "almug-trees," or sandal-wood, which King Solomon used for "balustrades" in the Temple, for his own palace, and for making musical instruments.

The success of this trading adventure may have led to another similar undertaking, in company with the Phœnicians, to Tartessus (Tarshish),[2] the well-known great mercantile emporium on the south coast of Spain. The duration of such an expedition is stated in round numbers as *three years;* and the trade became so regular that afterwards all the large merchantmen were popularly known as "Tarshish-ships" (comp. 1 Kings xxii. 48 ; Ps. xlviii. 7 ; Is. ii. 16).[3] The imports from Tarshish consisted of gold, silver, ivory,[4] apes, and peacocks (1 Kings x. 22).

---

[1] According to 2 Chron. viii. 18, by a clerical error (ב for כ), 450 talents.

[2] Critics are generally agreed that Tarshish is the Tartessus of Spain. This was the great place for the export of silver, and a central depot whence the imports from Africa, such as sandal-wood, ivory, ebony, apes, and peacocks, would be shipped to all parts of the world. Compare here the very conclusive reasoning of Canon Rawlinson, *u. s.* pp. 545, 546.

[3] From this passage Bähr and others have concluded that the Tarshish fleet of King Solomon went to Ophir ; but the inference is incorrect.

[4] The Hebrew terms are not easy to render. Most critics have, by a slight alteration, translated them "ivory, ebony." But Keil and Bähr have shown that this rendering is not sufficiently supported.

The two last-mentioned articles of import indicate the commencement of a very dangerous decline towards Oriental luxury. It has been well observed (by Ewald), that there was a moment in Israel's history when it seemed possible that David might have laid the foundation of an empire like that of Rome, and another when Solomon might have led the way to a philosophy as sovereign as that of Greece.[1] But it was an equally, if not more dangerous path on which to enter, and one even more opposed to the Divine purpose concerning Israel, when foreign trade, and with it foreign luxury, became the object of king and people. The danger was only too real, and the public display appeared in what the Queen of Sheba saw of Solomon's court (1 Kings x. 5), in the magnificence of his throne (vers. 19, 20), and in the sumptuousness of all his appointments (ver. 21). Two hundred large targets and three hundred smaller shields, all covered with beaten gold,[2] hung around the house of the forest of Lebanon; all the king's drinking vessels, and all the other appurtenances for State receptions were of pure gold; the merchants brought the spices of the East into the country (ver. 15); while traders, importers, and vassal chiefs swelled the immense revenue, which in one year[3] rose to the almost incredible sum of 666 talents of gold, which at the lowest computation amounts to upwards of $2\frac{1}{2}$ millions of our money, or only one million less than that of the Persian kings (Herod. iii. 95). Add to this the number of Solomon's chariots and horsemen, the general wealth of the country, and the importation of horses[4] from Egypt, which

[1] See Sir Edward Strachey's very thoughtful book on *Hebrew Politics in the Times of Sargon and Sennacherib*, p. 200.

[2] These shields were made of wood or of twisted material, and covered with gold, the amount of the latter being calculated for the targets at 9lbs., and for the smaller shields at $4\frac{1}{2}$lbs (Keil).

[3] 1 Kings x. 14 does not necessarily imply that this was the *annual* revenue, only that it came to him in one year. The 666 talents may perhaps be a round sum.

[4] Our Authorised Version renders 1 Kings x. 28 "linen yarn," but this is a mistranslation for: "And the bringing out of horses which was for Solomon from Egypt— and the troop of the merchants of the king brought a

made Palestine almost an emporium for chariots and horses;[1] and it will not be difficult to perceive on what a giddy height king and people stood during the later years of Solomon's reign.

It was this scene of wealth and magnificence, unexampled even in the East, as well as the undisputed political influence and supremacy of the king, combined with the highest intellectual activity and civilization in the country, which so much astounded the Queen of Sheba on her visit to Solomon's dominions. Many, indeed, were the strangers who had been attracted to Jerusalem by the fame of its king (1 Kings x. 24). But none of them had been so distinguished as she, whose appearance was deeply symbolical of the glorious spiritual destiny of Israel (Ps. lxxii. 10, 11; Is. lx. 6), and indicative of the future judgment on the unbelief of those who were even more highly favoured (Matt. xii. 42; Luke xi. 31). Sheba, which is to be distinguished from Seba, or Meroë in Ethiopia, was a kingdom in Southern Arabia,[2] on the shores of the Red Sea, and seems to have been chiefly governed by Queens. Owing to its trade, the population was regarded as the wealthiest in Arabia. It may have been that Solomon's fame had first reached the ears of the Queen through the fleet of Ophir. In consequence, she resolved to visit Jerusalem, to see, to test, and to learn for herself whether the extraordinary reports

---

troop (of horses) for a (definite) price." This would imply that there was a regular trading company which purchased the horses by contract. But the text seems to be here corrupt, and the LXX render, "From Egypt and from Koa" (doubtfully Thekoa), and that "the royal merchants fetched them from Koa for a definite price." In this case there would seem to have been annual horse fairs at Koa, at which the royal merchants bought at a contract price.

[1] The price mentioned in 1 Kings x. 29 amounts (according to Keil) for a chariot—of course, complete, with two or rather three horses, to £78, and for a (cavalry) horse, to £19 10s.

[2] Accordingly the story of the descent of the Ethiopian royal line from Solomon and the Queen of Sheba must be dismissed as unhistorical, although Judaism may have spread into Ethiopia from the opposite shores of Arabia.

which had reached her were true. But, whatever may have *specially* influenced her to undertake so novel a pilgrimage, three things in regard to it are beyond question. She was attracted by the fame of Solomon's *wisdom* ; she viewed that wisdom in connection with "the Name of Jehovah" (1 Kings x. 1[1]); and she came to *learn.* What the higher import of this "wisdom" was, is explained by Solomon himself in Prov. iii. 14–18, while its source is indicated in Prov. ii. 4–6. Thus viewing it, no event could have been more important, alike typically and in its present bearing on the ancient world. The Queen had come, scarcely daring to hope that Eastern exaggeration had not led her to expect more than she would find. It proved the contrary. Whatever difficulty, doubt, or question she propounded, in the favourite Oriental form of "riddles,"[2] "whatever was with her heart,"[3] "Solomon showed (disclosed to) her all her words"[4] (the spoken and unspoken). And here she would learn chiefly this : that all the prosperity she witnessed, all the intellectual culture and civilisation with which she was brought into contact, had their spring above, with "the Father of lights." She had come at the head of a large retinue, bearing richest presents, which she left in remembrance and also in perpetuation of her visit—at least, if we may trust the account of Josephus, that the cultivation of balsam in the gardens of Jericho owed its origin to plants which the Queen had brought (Jos., *Ant.* viii. 6, 6). The notice is at least deeply symbolical. The spices of Sheba, so sweet and strong

---

[1] Without here entering on a detailed criticism of the precise meaning of the Hebrew expression *leShem Jehovah* ("to the name of Jehovah"), our inference from it can scarcely be called in question.

[2] Our Authorised Version renders "hard questions"— accurately as regards the import, but not the literal meaning of the word. Josephus relates, on the authority of Dius and Menander, some curious legends about "problems" propounded by Solomon to Hiram, which the latter could not solve, and had to pay heavy fines in consequence,—a like fate, however, overtaking Solomon in regard to the problems propounded to him by Abdemon (*Ag. Ap.* i. 17, 18). The love of the Easterns—especially the Arabs—for "riddles" is well known.

[3] So literally. [4] So literally.

that, according to ancient accounts, their perfume was carried out far to sea, were to be brought to Jerusalem, and their plants to strike root in sacred soil (Ps. lxxii. 10, 11; Is. lx. 6). But now the balsam-gardens of Jericho, into which they were transplanted, are lying bare and desolate—for "the Queen of the South" hath risen up in judgment with that "generation;" and what further "sign" can or need be given to the generation that turned from Him Who was "greater than Solomon?"

CHAPTER IX.

Solomon's Court—His Polygamy—Spread of Foreign Ideas in the Country —Imitation of Foreign Manners—Growing Luxury—Solomon's spiritual Decline—Judgment predicted—Solomon's Enemies: Hadad, Rezon, Jeroboam—Causes of popular discontent—Ahijah's prediction of the separation of the two Kingdoms—Jeroboam's Rebellion and Flight into Egypt—Death of Solomon.

(1 KINGS XI.)

A GREATER contrast could scarcely be imagined than that between the state of Solomon's court and of the country generally, and the directions and restrictions laid down in Deut. xvii. 16, 17 for the regulation of the Jewish monarchy. The first and most prominent circumstance which here presents itself to the mind, is the direct contravention of the Divine command as regarded the number of "princesses" and concubines which formed the harem of Solomon.[1] Granting that the notice in Cant. vi. 8 affords reason for believing that the numerals in 1 Kings xi. 3 may have been due to a mistake on the part of a copyist, still the sacred narrative expressly

[1] Bähr gives a number of instances, both from ancient and modern history, of far larger harems than that ascribed to Solomon.

states, that the polygamy of Solomon, and especially his alliances with nations excluded from intermarriage with Israel,[1] was the occasion, if not the cause, of his later sin and punishment. While on this subject we may go back a step further, and mark (with Ewald) what sad consequences the infringement of the primitive Divine order in regard to marriage wrought throughout the history of Israel. It is undoubtedly to polygamy that we have to trace the troubles in the family of David; and to the same cause were due many of those which came on David's successors. If Moses was obliged to tolerate the infringement of the original institution of God, "the hardness of heart" which had necessitated it brought its own punishment, especially when the offender was an Eastern king. Thus the sin of the people, embodied, as it were, in the person of their representative, carried national judgment as its consequence.

But the elements which caused the fall of Solomon lay deeper than polygamy. Indeed, the latter was among the effects, as well as one of the further causes of his spiritual decline. First among these elements of evil at work, we reckon the growing luxury of the court. The whole atmosphere around, so to speak, was different from what it had been in the primitive times which preceded the reign of Solomon, and still more from the ideal of monarchy as sketched in the Book of Deuteronomy. Everything had become un-Jewish, foreign, purely Asiatic. Closely connected with this was the evident desire to emulate, and even outdo neighbouring nations. Such wisdom, such splendour, such riches, and finally, such luxury, and such a court were not to be found elsewhere, as in the kingdom of which Jerusalem was the capital. An ominous beginning this of that long course of Jewish pride and self-exaltation which led to

---

[1] Properly speaking, only Canaanite women were excluded by the Law (Ex. xxxiv. 11–16; Deut. vii. 1–3). But alliance with those of other nations was contrary to the spirit of the law, at any rate so long as they continued idolaters. Comp. Ezra ix. 1; Neh. xiii. 23. There is a legend that Solomon married a daughter of Hiram, king of Tyre.

such fearful consequences. It is to this desire of surpassing other Eastern courts that the size of Solomon's harem must be attributed. Had it been coarse sensuality which influenced him, the earlier, not the later years of his reign, would have witnessed the introduction of so many strange wives. Moreover, it deserves special notice that the 700 wives of Solomon are designated as "princesses" (1 Kings xi. 3). Without pressing this word in its most literal meaning, we may at least infer that Solomon courted influential connections with the reigning and other leading families of the clans around, and that the chief object of his great harem was, in a worldly sense, to strengthen his position, to give evidence of his wealth and power as an Eastern monarch, and to form promising alliances, no matter what spiritual elements were thus introduced into the country. Closely connected with all this was the rapidly growing intercourse between Israel and foreign nations. For one reason or another, strangers, whom Israel hitherto had only considered as heathens, crowded to Jerusalem. By their presence king and people would not only become familiar with foreign ideas, but so-called toleration would extend to these strangers the right of public worship, or rather, of public idolatry. And so strong was this feeling, that, although Asa, Jehoshaphat, Joash, and Hezekiah put an end to all idolatry, yet the high places which Solomon had built on the southern acclivity of the Mount of Olives remained in use till the time of Josiah (2 Kings xxiii. 13), avowedly for the worship of those foreigners who came to, or were resident in, Jerusalem. Viewed in connection with what has just been stated, even the intellectual culture in the time of Solomon may have proved a source of serious danger.

All this may help us to form a more correct conception of the causes which led to the terrible decline in the spiritual history of Solomon, and this without either extenuating his guilt or, as is more commonly the case, exaggerating his sin. As Holy Scripture puts it, when Solomon was old, and less able to resist influences around, he so far yielded to his foreign wives as to build altars for their worship. This in the Scriptural and real sense was already to "go after Ashtoreth and Milcom" (1 Kings xi. 5). But the sacred text does not state that Solomon personally "served them;"[1] nor is there any reason for supposing that he either relinquished the service of Jehovah, or personally took part in heathen rites. To have built altars to "the abominations of the Gentiles,"[2] and to have tolerated, if not encouraged, the idolatrous rites openly enacted there by his wives, implied great public guilt. In the language of Scripture: "Solomon's heart was not perfect with Jehovah his God;" he "did evil in the sight of Jehovah, and went not fully after Jehovah." His sin was the more inexcusable, that he had in this respect the irreproachable example of David. Besides, even closer allegiance to the LORD might have been expected from Solomon than from David, since he had been privileged to build the Temple, and had on two occasions received personal communication from the Lord, whereas God had never *appeared* to David, but only employed prophets as intermediaries to make known His good pleasure.

It need scarcely be said, that public sin such as that of Solomon would soon bring down judgment. As preparatory to it we regard that solemn warning, when the LORD a second time appeared in vision to Solomon (1 Kings ix. 4–9). This being misunderstood or neglected, the actual announcement of judgment followed, probably through Ahijah. The terms of the sentence were terribly explicit. Solomon's kingdom would be rent from him, and given to his servant.

[1] Whenever the Jewish kings were personally guilty of idolatry, the Hebrew word *avad*, "served," is used. Comp. 1 Kings xvi. 31; xxii. 53; 2 Kings xvi. 3; xxi. 2–6, 20–22. Jewish tradition also emphatically asserts (*Shab.* 56 b.) that Solomon was not *personally* guilty of idolatry. The account of Josephus (*Ant.* viii. 7, 5) is worthless.

[2] Ashtoreth, the goddess of the Phœnicians, was worshipped with impure rites. Milcom, Malcom, or Molech, was the principal deity of the Ammonites, but must be distinguished from Moloch, whose terrible rites were only introduced at a later period (2 Kings xvi. 3). Chemosh was the sun-god and war-god of the Moabites; his name frequently occurs on the celebrated Moabite Stone.

Yet even so Divine mercy would accord a twofold limitation: the event foretold should not happen in the days of Solomon himself, and when it took place the kingdom should not be wholly taken away, but partially remain in his line. And this for the sake of David—that is, not from partiality for him, nor on account of any supposed superabundant merit, but because of God's promise to David (2 Sam. vii. 14–16), and for God's own glory, since He had made choice of Jerusalem as the place where He would for ever reveal His Name (1 Kings ix. 3).

But although execution of the judgment was stayed, indications of its reality and nearness soon appeared. Once more we mark a succession of natural and intelligible causes, of which the final outcome was the fulfilment of the Divine prediction. It will be remembered that, of the two great wars in which David was involved after his accession, the most formidable was that against the hostile combination of tribes along the eastern boundary of his kingdom.[1] The distance, the character of the country, the habits of the enemy—the alliance of so many nationalities, their determination, and the stubborn resistance which they offered, made this a really great war. We know that the armies of David, under the leadership of Joab and Abishai, were victorious at all points (2 Sam. viii.; x.; 1 Chron. xix.). But, although the enemy may have been subdued and even crushed for a time, it was, in the nature of things, impossible wholly to remove the elements of resistance. In the far south-east, terrible, almost savage, vengeance had been taken on Edom (1 Chron. xviii. 12). From the slaughter of the people a trusty band of Edomites had rescued one of the youthful royal princes, Hadad[2] (or Adad), and brought him

---

[1] Comp. the account of this war in vol. iv. of this Bible History, chapter xviii.

[2] Hadad, "the Sun," or "Sun-god"—an ancient name, perhaps a royal title among the Edomite princes (comp. Gen. xxxvi. 35). But it seems an ungrounded inference (by Ewald, Thenius, and even Canon Rawlinson) to connect him (as grandson) with the last king of the Edomites, who in 1 Chron. i. 50 is by a clerical error called Hadad instead of Hadar (comp. Gen. xxxvi. 39.)

ultimately to Egypt, where he met a hospitable reception from the then reigning Pharaoh—probably the predecessor of Solomon's father-in-law. If Pharaoh had at first been influenced by political motives in keeping near him one who might become a source of trouble to the growing Israelitish power, the young prince of Edom soon enlisted the sympathy and affection of his host (1 Kings xi. 14–19). He married the sister of Tahpenes,[1] the Gevirah, or queen dominant (principal) of Pharaoh's harem ; and their child was acknowledged and brought up among the royal princes of Egypt. When tidings of the death of David and afterwards of Joab reached Hadad, he insisted on returning to Edom, even against the friendly remonstrances of Pharaoh, who by this time would rather have seen him enjoying his peaceful retreat in Egypt than entering upon difficult and dangerous enterprises. But, although Hadad returned to his own country in the beginning of Solomon's reign, it was only towards its close—when growing luxury had enervated king and people—that his presence there became a source of trouble and anxiety.[2] This we infer, not only from 1 Kings iv. 24, but from such a notice as that in 1 Kings ix. 26.

But in the extreme north-east, as well as in the far south-east, a dark cloud gathered on the horizon. At the defeat of Hadadezer by the troops of David (2 Sam. viii. 3 ; x. 18) one of the Syrian captains, Rezon by name, had "fled from his lord." In the then disorganized state of the country he gradually gathered around him a band of followers, and ultimately fell back upon Damascus, of which he became king. The sacred text leads us to infer that, although he probably did not venture on open warfare with Solomon, he cast off the

---

[1] The name occurs also on Egyptian monuments. Tahpenes, or rather Thacpenes, was also the name of an Egyptian goddess (Gesenius, *Thesaurus*, vol. iii., p. 1500 a.).

[2] The LXX have here an addition, upon which Josephus bases a notice (*Ant.* viii. 7, 6), to the effect that Hadad (Ader) raised the standard of revolt in Edom, but, being unsuccessful, combined with Rezon, and became king of part of Syria. The notice cannot be regarded as of historical authority.

Jewish suzerainty, and generally "was an adversary"—or, to use the pictorial language of the Bible, "abhorred Israel." [1]

Ill-suppressed enmity in Edom (far south-east), and more active opposition and intrigue at Damascus (in the north-east)—in short, the danger of a combination like that which had so severely taxed the resources of David: such, then, so far as concerned external politics, were the darkening prospects of Solomon's later years. But the terms in which Holy Scripture speaks of these events deserve special notice. We are told, that "Jehovah stirred up" or, rather, "raised up" these adversaries unto Solomon (1 Kings xi. 14, 23). The expression clearly points to Divine Causality in the matter (comp. Deut. xviii. 15, 18; Judges ii. 18; 1 Sam. ii. 35; Jer. xxix. 15; Ez. xxxiv. 23). Not, indeed, that the ambitious or evil passions of men's hearts are incited of God, but that while each, in the exercise of his free will, chooses his own course, the LORD overrules all, so as to serve for the chastisement of sin and the carrying out of His own purposes (comp. Psa. ii. 1, 2; Is. x. 1-3).

But yet another and far more serious danger threatened Solomon's throne. Besides "adversaries" without, elements of dissatisfaction were at work within Palestine, which only needed favouring circumstances to lead to open revolt. First, there was the old tribal jealousy between Ephraim and Judah. The high destiny foretold to Ephraim (Gen. xlviii. 17-22; xlix. 22-26) must have excited hopes which the leadership of Joshua, himself an Ephraimite (Numb. xiii. 8), seemed for a time to warrant. Commanding, perhaps, the most important territorial position in the land, Ephraim claimed a dominating power over the tribes in the days of Gideon and of Jephthah (Judg. viii. 1; xii. 1). In fact, one of the successors of these Judges, Abdon, was an Ephraimite (Judg. xii. 13). But, besides, Ephraim

---

[1] Canon Rawlinson (in the *Speaker's Commentary*, vol. ii., p. 550) arranges the succession of the Damascus kings as follows: Hadad-Ezer (Hadad I.), contemporary of David; Rezon (usurper), contemporary of Solomon; Hezion (Hadad II.), contemporary of Rehoboam; Tabrimon (Hadad III.), contemporary of Abijam; Ben-hadad (Hadad IV.), contemporary of Asa.

could boast not only of secular, but of ecclesiastical supremacy, since Shiloh and Kirjath-jearim were within its tribal possession. And had not Samuel, the greatest of the Judges, the one outstanding personality in the history of a decrepit priesthood, been, though a Levite, yet "from Mount Ephraim" (1 Sam. i. 1)? Even the authority of Samuel could not secure the undisputed acknowledgment of Saul, who was only too painfully conscious of the objections which tribal jealousy would raise to his elevation (1 Sam. ix. 21). It needed that glorious God-given victory at Jabesh-Gilead to hush, under strong religious convictions, those discordant voices, and to unite all Israel in acclamation of their new king. And yet the tribe of Benjamin, to which Saul belonged, was closely allied to that of Ephraim (Judg. xxi. 19–23). Again, it was the tribe of Ephraim which mainly upheld the cause of Ishbosheth (2 Sam. ii. 9); and though the strong hand of David afterwards kept down all active opposition, no sooner did his power seem on the wane than "a man of Mount Ephraim" (2 Sam. xx. 21) roused the tribal jealousies, and raised the standard of rebellion against him. And now, with the reign of King Solomon, all hope of tribal pre-eminence seemed to have passed from Ephraim. There was a new capital for the whole country, and that in the possession of Judah. The glory of the ancient Sanctuary had also been taken away. Jerusalem was the ecclesiastical as well as the political capital, and Ephraim had to contribute its wealth and even its forced labour to promote the schemes, to support the luxury, and to advance the glory of a new monarchy, taken from, and resident in, Judah!

But, secondly, the burden which the new monarchy imposed on the people must, in the course of time, have weighed very heavily on them (1 Kings xii. 4). The building of a great national Sanctuary was, indeed, an exceptional work which might enlist the highest and best sympathies, and make the people willing to submit to any sacrifices. But this was followed by the construction of a magnificent palace, and then by a succession of architectural undertakings (1 Kings ix. 15, 17–

19) on an unprecedented scale. However useful some of these
might be, they not only marked an innovation, but involved a
continuance of forced labour (1 Kings iv. 6; v. 13, 14; xi.
28), wholly foreign to the spirit of a free people, and which
diverted from their proper channels the industrial forces of the
country. Nor was this all. The support of such a king and
court must have proved a heavy demand on the resources of
the nation (1 Kings iv. 21–27). To have to pay enormous
taxes, and for many long years to be deprived during so many
months of the heads and the bread-winners of the family,
that they might do what seemed slaves' labour for the glori-
fication of a king, whose rule was every year becoming weaker,
would have excited dissatisfaction even among a more enduring
people than those tribes who had so long enjoyed the freedom
and the privileges of a federated Republic.

It only needed a leader—and once more Ephraim furnished
him. Jeroboam, the son of Nebat and of a widow named
Zeruah, was a native of Zereda or Zererath [1] (Judg. vii. 22),
within the territory of Ephraim. The sacred text describes
him as a "mighty man of valour." His energy, talent, and
aptitude pointed him out as a fit permanent overseer of the
forced labour of his tribe. It was a dangerous post to assign
to a man of such power and ambition. His tribesmen, as a
matter of course, came to know him as their chief and leader,
while in daily close intercourse he would learn their grievances
and sentiments. In such circumstances the result which
followed was natural. The bold, strong, and ambitious
Ephraimite, "ruler over all the burden of the house of
Joseph," became the leader of the popular movement against
Solomon.

It was, no doubt, in order to foment the elements of discontent already existing, as well as because his position in the

---

[1] Most critics erroneously identify it with Zarthan (1 Kings vii. 46), or
Zeredathah (2 Chron. iv. 17), which, however, lay outside the possession
of Ephraim.

city must have become untenable, that "Jeroboam went out of Jerusalem" (1 Kings xi. 29). When "the prophet Ahijah the Shilonite found him in the way," Jeroboam had already planned, or rather commenced, his revolt against Solomon. Himself an Ephraimite (from Shiloh), the prophet would not only be acquainted with Jeroboam, but also know the sentiments of his tribesmen and the views of their new leader. It was not, therefore, Ahijah who incited Jeroboam to rebellion [1] by the symbolical act of rending his new garment in twelve pieces, giving him ten of the pieces, [2] while those retained were emblematic of what would be left to the house of David. Rather did he act simply as the Divine messenger to Jeroboam, *after* the latter had resolved on his own course. The event was, indeed, ordered of God in punishment of the sin of Solomon (vers. 11–13); and the intimation of this fact, with its lessons of warning, was the principal object of Ahijah's mission and message. But the chief actor had long before chosen his own part, being prompted, as Holy Scripture puts it, by a settled ambition to usurp the throne (1 Kings xi. 37); while the movement of which he took advantage was not only the result of causes long at work, but might almost have been forecast by any observer acquainted with the state of matters. Thus we learn once more how, in the Providence of God, a result which, when predicted, seems miraculous, and is really such, so far as the Divine operation is concerned, is brought about, not only through the free agency of man, but by a series of natural causes, while at the same time all is guided and overruled of God for His own wise and holy purposes.

Indeed, closely considered, the words of the prophet, so far from inciting Jeroboam to rebellion against Solomon, should

---

[1] This is the view of some German critics.

[2] Much needless ingenuity has been employed to show in what sense Jeroboam had ten "pieces" or tribes, and Rehoboam "one"—or rather two—assigned to him. The language must not be too closely pressed. The "one" tribe left to the house of David was no doubt Judah, including "little Benjamin" as the second of the twelve "pieces" or tribes.

rather have deterred him from it. The scene is sketched in vivid outline: Jeroboam, in whose soul tribal pride, disgust at his work, contempt for the king, irrepressible energy, and high-reaching ambition, combined with a knowledge of the feelings of his tribesmen, have ripened into stern resolve, has left Jerusalem. The time for secret intrigue and dissimulation is past; that for action has arrived. As he leaves the hated city-walls—memorials of Ephraim's servitude—and ascends to-wards the heights of Benjamin and Ephraim, a strange figure meets him. It is his countryman from Shiloh, the prophet Ahijah. No salutation passes between them, but Ahijah takes hold of the new square cloth or upper mantle in which he has been wrapped, and rends it in twelve pieces. It is not, as usually, in token of mourning (Gen. xxxvii. 29; xliv. 13; 2 Sam. xiii. 19), though sadness must have been in the prophet's heart, but as symbol of what is to happen—as it were, God's answer to Jeroboam's thoughts. Yet the judgment predicted is *not* to take effect in Solomon's lifetime (1 Kings xi. 34, 35);[1] and any attempt at revolt, such as Jeroboam seems to have made (vers. 26, 40),[2] was in direct contravention of God's declared will.

There were other parts of the prophet's message which Jeroboam would have done well to have borne in mind. David was always to "have a light before God" in Jerusalem, the city "which He had chosen to put His Name there" (1 Kings xi. 36). In other words, David was always to have a descendant on the throne,[3] and Jerusalem with its Temple was always to be God's chosen place; that is, Israel's worship was to continue in the great central Sanctuary, and the descendants of David were to be the rightful occupants of the throne till He came Who was

---

[1] I cannot adopt Canon Rawlinson's proposed rendering of ver. 34: "I will not take aught of the kingdom out of his hand."

[2] The expression "to lift up the hand," means actual revolt. Comp. 2 Sam. xviii. 28; xx. 21.

[3] That this is the meaning of the figurative expression "light," may be gathered from 1 Kings xv. 4; 2 Kings viii. 19; 2 Chron. xxi. 7; Psa. xviii. 28; lxxii. 17.

David's greater Son. God had linked the Son of David with His City and the Temple, so that the final destruction of the latter marked the fulfilment of the prophecies concerning the house of David. Thus gloriously did the promise stretch beyond the immediate future, with its troubles and afflictions. Lastly, so far as regarded Jeroboam, the promise of succession to the kingdom of Israel in his family was made conditional on his observance of the statutes and commandments of God, as David had kept them (ver. 38). But Jeroboam was of far other spirit than David. His main motive had been personal ambition. Unlike David, who, though anointed king, would make no attempt upon the crown during Saul's lifetime, Jeroboam, despite the express warning of God, "lifted up his hand against the king." The result was failure[1] and flight into Egypt. Nor did Jeroboam keep the statutes and commandments of the LORD ; and after a brief reign his son fell by the hand of the assassin (1 Kings xv. 28). Lastly, and most important of all—the Messianic bearing of the promise to David, and the Divine choice of Jerusalem and its Temple, were fatally put aside or forgotten by Jeroboam and his successors on the throne of Israel. The schism in the kingdom became one from the Theocracy; and the rejection of the central Sanctuary resulted, as might have been expected, in the establishment of idolatry in Israel.

Nor did King Solomon either live or die as his father David. A feeble attempt—perhaps justifiable—to rid himself of Jeroboam, and no more is told of him than that, at the close of a reign of forty years,[2] he "slept with his fathers, and was buried in the city of David his father." So far as we know, in that death-chamber no words of earnest, loving entreaty to serve Jehovah were spoken to his successor, such as David

---

[1] Of course this is only an inference from the narrative.

[2] Josephus (*Ant.* viii. 7, 8) assigns him a reign of eighty years. But this must either be a clerical error, or depend on one in Josephus' copy of the LXX. Solomon probably died at the age of about sixty. The question of his final repentance, so largely discussed at one time by theologians, may be safely left—where the Bible has left it.

had uttered; no joyous testimony here as regarded the past, nor yet strong faith and hope as concerned the future, such as had brightened the last hours of David. It is to us a silent death-chamber in which King Solomon lay. No bright sunset here, to be followed by a yet more glorious morning. He had done more than any king to denationalise Israel. And on the morrow of his death: rebellion within the land; outside its borders—Edom and Syria ready to spring to arms, Egypt under Shishak gathering up its might; and only a Rehoboam to hold the rudder of the State in the rising storm.

CHAPTER X.

REHOBOAM, FIRST KING OF JUDAH.

Family of Solomon—Age of Rehoboam—His Character—Religious History of Israel and Judah—The Assembly at Shechem—Jeroboam's return from Egypt—Rehoboam's Answer to the Deputies in Shechem—Revolt of the Ten Tribes—The Reigns of Rehoboam and of Jeroboam—Invasion of Judah by Shishak—Church and State in Israel—Rehoboam's attempt to recover rule over the Ten Tribes—His Family History—Religious Decline in Israel, and its consequences.

(1 KINGS XII.; XIV. 21-31; 2 CHRON. X.-XII.)

STRANGE as it may seem, despite the multifarious marriages of the king, his alliances with neighbouring nations, and his immense wealth, "the house of Solomon" was far from strong at the time of his decease. It may have been that Solomon left other sons besides Rehoboam, though it is strange that we find no notice of them, nor, indeed, of any child, except a casual remark about two of Solomon's daughters (1 Kings iv. 11, 15). If other children survived him, their position must have been far less influential than that of the sons of David, nor does Rehoboam's succession appear to have been ever contested by any member of the family.

Rehoboam, or rather *Rechavam* ("he who enlargéth the people"), must have been very young at his accession. This we gather from the expression by which they "who had grown up with him" are described, and from the manner in which his son and successor, Abijah, characterised the commencement of his reign (2 Chron. xiii. 7). There seems, therefore, considerable probability attaching to the suggestion, that the notice of his age at his accession—forty-one (1 Kings xiv. 21; 2 Chron. xii. 13)—is the mistake of a copyist, who in transcribing the figures misread the two letters כא—twenty-one—for מא—forty-one. This supposition is strengthened by the fact that Rehoboam was not the son of the Egyptian princess, who seems to have been Solomon's first wife, but of Naamah, an Ammonitess ;[1] and we know that it was only after his religious decline (1 Kings xi. 1) that Solomon entered upon alliances with "strange women," among whom Ammonitesses are specially mentioned.[2]

Of the character of Rehoboam we know sufficient to form an accurate estimate. David had taken care to commit the upbringing of his son and successor to the prophet Nathan ; and, so far as we can judge, the early surroundings of Solomon were such as not only to keep him from intimacy with light or evil associates, but to train him in earnest piety. But when Rehoboam was born, King Solomon had already entered upon the fatal path which led to the ruin of his race ; and the prince

---

[1] The LXX notice that she was the granddaughter of Nahash, king of Ammon.

[2] It is hardly credible that Solomon should have contracted such an alliance before his accession to the throne, which, of course, would be implied if Rehoboam was forty-one years old at the time of his father's death. The Rabbis find a parallel to the marriage of Solomon with Naamah in that of Ruth with Boaz (Jalkut, vol. ii., p. 32 *a*).

was brought up, like any other Eastern in similar circumstances, with the young nobles of a court which had learned foreign modes of thinking and foreign manners. The relation between the aristocracy and the people, between the king and his subjects, had changed from the primitive and God-sanctioned to that of ordinary Eastern despotism; and the notions which Rehoboam and his young friends entertained, appeared only too clearly in the first act of the king's reign. In general, we gather that Rehoboam was vain, weak, and impulsive; ready to give up under the influence of fear what he had desired and attempted when he deemed himself secure. Firm religious principles he had not, and his inclinations led him not only towards idolatry, but to a form of it peculiarly dissolute in its character (1 Kings xiv. 23, 24; 2 Chron. xi. 13–17; xii. 1). During the first three years of his reign he remained, indeed, faithful to the religion of his fathers, either through the influence of the Levites who had gathered around him from all Israel—though even in this case his motives might be rather political than conscientious—or else under the impression of the outward consequences of his first great mistake. But this mood soon passed away, and when the state-reasons for his early adherence to the worship of Jehovah had ceased to be cogent, or he felt himself secure on his throne, he yielded, as we have seen, to his real inclinations in the matter.

Here, at the outset of the separate history of the kingdoms of Judah and Israel, it may be well to take a general view of the relation of these two divisions of the Jewish people to Jehovah, their King. That the sin of Israel was much deeper, and their apostasy from God much sooner and more fully developed than in the case of Judah, appears from the circumstance, that the Divine judgment in the banishment of the people from their land overtook Israel 123 years earlier than Judah.[1] Yet at first sight it seems almost strange that such should have been the case. Altogether, the period of the

---

[1] See the Chronological Table at the end of this volume, and the remarks on the chronology of that period there appended.

separate existence of the two kingdoms (to the deportation of the ten tribes under Shalmaneser, about 722 B.C.) extended over 253 years. During that time, thirteen monarchs reigned over Judah, and twenty over Israel—besides two periods of probable interregnum, or rather of anarchy in Israel. The religious history of the ten tribes during these two and a half centuries may be written in very brief compass. Of all the kings of Israel it is uniformly said, that they "walked in the ways of Jeroboam, the son of Nebat," except of Ahab and his two sons (Ahaziah and Joram), under whose reigns the worship of Baal became the established religion of the country. It follows, that there was not a single king in Israel who really served the LORD or worshipped in His Temple. On the other hand, there were at least *five* kings in Judah distinguished for their piety (Asa, Jehoshaphat, Uzziah, Jotham, and Hezekiah), while of the other eight, *two* (Joash and Amaziah) continued for a considerable, and a *third* (Rehoboam) for a short period their profession of the religion of their fathers. Four of the other *five* kings acquired, indeed, a terrible notoriety for daring blasphemy. Abijam, the son and successor of Rehoboam, adopted all the practices of his father during the last fourteen years of that monarch's reign. During the reign of Joram the worship of Baal was introduced into Judah; and we know with what terrible consistency it was continued under Ahaziah and Athaliah, the measure of iniquity being filled by Ahaz, who ascended the throne twenty years before the deportation of the ten tribes, when the doors of the Sanctuary were actually closed, and an idol-altar set up in the Temple court. But, despite all this, idolatry never struck its roots deeply among the people, and this for three reasons. There was, *first*, the continued influence for good of the Temple at Jerusalem; and in this we see at least one providential reason for the existence of a central Sanctuary, and for the stringency of the Law which confined all worship to its courts. *Secondly*, the idolatrous kings of Judah were always succeeded by monarchs distinguished for piety, who swept away the rites of their pre-

decessors; while, *lastly* and most remarkably, the reign of
the idolatrous kings was uniformly brief as compared with
that of the God-fearing rulers. Thus, on a review of the
whole period, we find that, of the 253 years between the accession of Rehoboam and the deportation of the ten tribes,
200 passed under the rule of monarchs who maintained the
religion of Jehovah, while only during 53 years His worship
was more or less discarded by the kings of Judah.[1]

We repeat, it were a mistake to ascribe the separation of the
ten tribes entirely to the harsh and foolish refusal of Rehoboam
to redress the grievances of the people. This only set the
spark to the inflammable material which had long been ac-
cumulating. We have seen how dissatisfaction had spread,
especially in the northern parts of the kingdom, during the
later part of Solomon's reign; how, indeed, a rising seems to
have been actually attempted by Jeroboam, though for the
time it failed. We have also called attention to the deep-seated
tribal jealousy between Ephraim and Judah, which ever and
again broke into open hostility (Judg. viii. 1–3; xii. 1–6;
2 Sam. ii. 9; xix. 42, 43). This, indeed, may be described
as the ultimate (secondary) cause of the separation of the two
kingdoms. And, if proof were required that the rebellion
against Rehoboam was only the outcome of previously existing
tendencies, we would find it even in the circumstance that
the language used by the representatives of Israel, when renouncing the rule of Rehoboam, was exactly the same as that
of Sheba when he raised against David the standard of
what would be represented as the ancient federal Republic
of Israel (2 Sam. xx. 1 comp. with 1 Kings xii. 16). Still
more wrongful would it be to account for the conduct either
of Israel or of Jeroboam, or even to attempt vindicating it,

[1] We arrive at this result by the following computation:—Years of
public idolatry: under Rehoboam, 14; under Abijah, 3; under Joram, 6;
under Ahaziah, 1; under Athaliah, 6; under Ahaz, 16; or in all 46 years,
to which we add 7, for the later idolatrous reigns of Joash and Amaziah.
See Keil, *Bibl. Commentar*, vol. iii., pp. 137, 138.

on the ground of the prophecy of Ahijah (1 Kings xi. 29--39). The latter foretold an event in history, and explained the reason of what, in view of the promises to David, would otherwise have been unaccountable. But such prediction and announcement of judgment—even if known to the tribes—warranted neither their rebellion nor the usurpation of Jeroboam. It is, indeed, true that, as the Old Testament considers all events as directly connected with God, its fundamental principle being: Jehovah reigneth—and that not merely in a pseudo-spiritual, but in the fullest sense—this, as all other things that come to man, is ultimately traced up to the living God. So was the resistance of Pharaoh, and so are the sword, the pestilence, and the famine. For, all things are of Him, Who sendeth blessings upon His people, and taketh vengeance of their inventions; Who equally ruleth in the armies of heaven, and among the inhabitants of the earth; Who maketh the wrath of man as well as the worship of His people to praise Him; Who always doeth marvellously, whether He accomplish His purposes by direct interposition from heaven, or, as much more frequently, through a chain of natural causation, of which He holds the first, and man the last, link. This grand truth, as fully expressed and applied in the sublime language of Ps. cxlvii., is the sheet-anchor of faith by which it rides out the storms of this world. Ever to look up straight to God, to turn from events and secondary causations to Jehovah as the living God and the reigning King, is that denial of things seen and affirmation of things unseen, which constitute the victory of faith over the world.

On the death of his father, Rehoboam seems to have at once, and without opposition, assumed the reins of government. His enthronement at Jerusalem implied the homage of Judah and its neighbour-tribe Benjamin. According to ancient custom, the representatives of the more distant tribes should have assembled at the residence of the king, when in a great popular assembly the royal dignity would be solemnly conferred, and public homage rendered to the new monarch

(comp. 1 Sam. xi. 15 ; 2 Sam. ii. 4 ; v. 3 ; 1 Chron. xxix. 22).
But, instead of repairing to Jerusalem, the representatives
of the ten tribes gathered at Shechem, the ancient capital
of Ephraim, where important popular assemblies had previously been held (Josh. viii. 30–35 ; xxiv. 1–28), and the
first claimant of royalty in Israel, Abimelech, had set up his
throne (Judg. ix. 1–23). Only one meaning could attach
to their choice of this place.[1]   They had indeed come to
make Rehoboam king, but only with full concessions to their
tribal claims.   All that they now required was an energetic
leader.   Such an one was to hand in the person of Jeroboam,
who in the reign of King Solomon had headed the popular
movement.   After the failure of his attempt, he had fled into
Egypt, and been welcomed by Shishak.   The weak (21st
Tanite) dynasty, with which King Solomon had formed a
matrimonial alliance, had been replaced by the vigorous and
martial rule of Shishak (probably about fifteen years before
the death of Solomon).   The rising kingdom of Palestine
—allied as it was with the preceding dynasty—was too
close, and probably too threatening a neighbour not to be
attentively watched by Shishak.   It was obviously his policy
to encourage Jeroboam, and to support any movement which
might divide the southern from the northern tribes, and
thus give Egypt the supremacy over both.   In point of fact,
five years later Shishak led an expedition against Rehoboam,
probably not so much for the purpose of humbling Judah as
of strengthening the new kingdom of Israel.

The sacred text leaves it doubtful whether, after hearing of
the accession of Rehoboam, Jeroboam continued in Egypt till
sent for by the representatives of the ten tribes, or returned
to Ephraim of his own accord.[2]   In any case, he was not in

---

[1] Jewish commentators expressly account for the gathering of the ten
tribes at Shechem on the ground of their intention to make Jeroboam their
king.

[2] The LXX version has here several additions about the mother of Jeroboam, his stay in Egypt, his conduct after his return, etc.   This is not the
place to discuss them in detail, but they may safely be rejected as *legendary*,
and, indeed, quite in the spirit of later Jewish tradition.

Shechem when the assembly of the Israelitish deputies met there, but was expressly sent for to conduct negotiations on their behalf.[1] It was a mark of weakness on the part of Rehoboam to have gone to Shechem at all ; and it must have encouraged the deputies in their demands. Moderate as these sound, they seem to imply not only a lightening of the "heavy" burden of forced labour and taxation, but of the "grievous yoke" of what they regarded as a despotism, which prevented their free movements. It is on this supposition alone that we can fully account for the reply which Rehoboam ultimately gave them. The king took three days to consider the demand. First, he consulted Solomon's old advisers, who strongly urged a policy of at least temporary compliance. The advice was evidently ungrateful, and the king—as Absalom of old, and most weak men in analogous circumstances—next turned to another set of counsellors. They were his young companions—as the text throughout contemptuously designates them : "the children (the boys) who had grown up with him." With their notions of the royal supremacy, they seem to have imagined that such daring attempts at independence arose from doubt of the king's power and courage, and would be best repressed if sternly met by an overawing assertion of authority. Rehoboam was not to discuss their demands, but to tell them that they would find they had to deal with a monarch far more powerful and far more strict than his father had been. To put it in the vain-glorious language of the Eastern "boy-counsellors," he was to say to them : " My little finger is bigger than my father's hips. And now my father did lade upon you a heavy yoke, and I will add to your yoke ; my father chastised you with whips [those of ordinary slaves], but I will chastise you with [so-called] 'scorpions'"[2]—or wnips

---

[1] Probably Jeroboam returned of his own account, but did not go to Shechem till he was sent for by the deputies of Israel. This accords with the two versions. There is no need further to discuss here the reading, or rather the proper punctuation of 1 Kings xii. 2, 3.

[2] So literally

armed with hooks, such as were probably used upon criminals or recalcitrants.

Grossly foolish as this advice was, Rehoboam followed it —the sacred writer remarking, in order to account for such an occurrence: "for the turn (of events) was from Jehovah, that He might perform His word which Jehovah spake by the hand of Ahijah the Shilonite to Jeroboam the son of Nebat."[1] The effect was, indeed, immediate. To the shout of Sheba's ancient war-cry of rebellion the assembly renounced their allegiance to the house of David, and the deputies returned to their homes. Rehoboam perceived his fatal error, when it was too late to retrieve its consequences. Even his attempt in that direction was a mistake. The king sent Adoram,[2] the superintendent of the tribute and of forced labour[3]—the two forming apparently one department of the king's dues—to arrange, if possible, matters with the rebellious tribes. But this seemed only like trifling with their grievances, and a fresh insult. The presence of the hated official called forth such feelings, that he was stoned, and Rehoboam himself narrowly escaped[4] the same fate by flight to Jerusalem.

The rebellion of the ten tribes was soon followed by their formation into an independent kingdom. When, on their return from Shechem, the deputies made known the presence of Jeroboam, the tribes sent for him, and in a popular assembly appointed him king over all Israel. Still, it must not be thought that the whole land was absolutely subject to him. When thinking of monarchy in Palestine, it is always necessary to bear in mind the long-established and great municipal rights and liberties which made every city

---

[1] So literally.

[2] As three persons of that name are mentioned (2 Sam. xx. 24; 1 Kings v. 6; xii. 18) who must have lived at different times, may not "Adoram" be the appellation of the office?

[3] The one Hebrew word means both—and probably the two belonged to the same department of royal dues.

[4] This is implied in ver. 18; see the marginal rendering.

with its district, under its Elders, almost an independent state within the state. Accordingly, we find it chronicled as a note worthy fact (1 Kings xii. 17), that King Rehoboam reigned over those Israelites who were settled in Judæan towns— either wholly inhabiting, or forming the majority in them; while it is marked as a wise measure on the part of Reho- boam, that he distributed "his children throughout all the countries (districts) of Judah and Benjamin unto every fenced city"—no doubt, with the view of making sure of their allegiance. It seems to have been otherwise within the domains of Jeroboam. From 2 Chron. xi. 13–16 we learn that, on the substitution by Jeroboam and his successors of the worship of the golden calves for the service of Jehovah, the old religion was disestablished, and the Levites deprived of their ecclesiastical revenues, the new priesthood which took their place being probably supported by the dues of their office, and, if we may judge from the history of Ahab (1 Kings xviii. 19), by direct assistance from the royal treasury. In consequence of these changes, many of the Levites seem to have settled in Judæa, followed perhaps by more or less extensive migrations of the pious laity, varying according to the difficulties put in the way of resorting to the great festivals in Jerusalem. It would, however, be a mistake to infer the entire exodus of the pious laity or of the Levites.[1] But even if such had been the case, the feeling in the ancient Levitical cities would for some time have con- tinued sufficiently strong to refuse allegiance to Jeroboam.

And here a remarkable document throws unexpected light upon our history. On the wall of the great Egyptian Temple of Karnak, Shishak has left a record of his victorious expe- dition against Judah. Among the conquests there named 133 have been deciphered—although only partially identi- fied—while 14 are now illegible. The names ascertained have

---

[1] In point of fact, 2 Chron. xi. 16 does *not* necessarily imply any settle- ment of the pious laity in Judah; and even the evidence for that of the priests and Levites is not *quite* convincing (see the next chapter).

been arranged into three groups [1]—those of Judæan cities
(the smallness of their number being accounted for by the
erasures just mentioned); those of Arab tribes, south of
Palestine; and those of Levitical and Canaanite cities within
the territory of the new kingdom of Israel. It is the latter which
here alone claim our attention. Any conquest of cities within
the territory of Jeroboam might surprise us, since the expedition of Shishak was against Judah, and *not* against Israel—
indeed, rather in alliance with Jeroboam and in support of
his new kingdom. Another remarkable circumstance is, that
these Israelitish conquests of Shishak are *all* of Levitical or
else of ancient Canaanite cities, and that they are of towns in
all parts of the territory of the ten tribes, and at considerable
distances from one another, there being, however, no mention
of the taking of the intervening cities. All these facts point
to the conclusion, to which we have already been directed on
quite independent grounds, that the Levitical and ancient
Canaanite cities within the territory of Jeroboam did not
acknowledge his rule. This is why they were attacked and
conquered by Shishak on his expedition against Judah, as
virtually subject to the house of David, and hence constituting
an element not only of rebellion but of danger within the new
kingdom of Israel. Before quitting this subject, these two
remarks may be allowed: how wonderfully, and we may add,
unexpectedly, documents of secular history—apparently accidentally discovered—confirm and illustrate the narratives of
the Bible; and how wise, politically and religiously, how suited
to the national life, were the institutions of the Old Testament,
even when to our notions they seem most strange, as in the
case of Levitical cities throughout the land. For, these cities,
besides serving other most important purposes, formed also
the strongest bond of political union, and at the same time
the most powerful means of preserving throughout the country
the unity of the faith in the unity of the central worship of

---

[1] Compare Mr. Poole's admirable article on "Shishak," in Smith's
Dictionary of the Bible, vol. iii., pp. 1287–1295.

Jehovah at Jerusalem. Thus national union and religious purity were bound up together, and helped to preserve each other.

But to return. On the elevation of Jeroboam to the new throne of Israel, Rehoboam made one more attempt to recover the lost parts of David's kingdom. He assembled an army of 180,000 men [1] from Judah and Benjamin—the latter tribe having apparently become almost unified with Judah since the establishment of the political and religious capital in Jerusalem, through which ran the boundary-line between Judah and Benjamin. But the expedition was at its outset arrested by Divine direction through the prophet Shemaiah. [2] This abandonment of an expedition and dispersion of a host simply upon the word of a prophet, are quite as remarkable as the courage of that prophet in facing an army in such circumstances, and his boldness in so fully declaring as a message from Jehovah what must have been a most unwelcome announcement alike to king and people. Both these considerations are very important in forming an estimate, not only of the religious and political state of the time, and their mutual inter-relations, but of the character of " Prophetism " in Israel.

The expedition once abandoned was not again renewed, although throughout the reign of Rehoboam there were constant incursions and border-raids—probably chiefly of a predatory character—on the part of Judah and of Israel (1 Kings xiv. 30). The remaining notices of Rehoboam's reign concern the *internal* and *external* relations of Judah, as well as the *sad religious change* which passed over the country after the first three years of his rule. They are recorded, either solely or with much fuller details, in the Book of Chronicles (2 Chron. xi. 4 to xii. 16). The first measure referred to is the building of fifteen fortresses, of which thirteen were in the land of

---

[1] The LXX has 120,000, but the number in the Hebrew text is moderate (comp. 2 Sam. xxiv. 9).

[2] From 2 Chron. xii. 15 we learn that Shemaiah wrote a history of the reign of Rehoboam.

Judah—Hebron forming, as it were, the centre of them—and only two (Zorah and Aijalon) within the later possession of Benjamin.[1] They served as a continuous chain of forts south of Jerusalem, and to defend the western approaches into the country. The northern boundary was left wholly unprotected. From this it would appear that Rehoboam chiefly dreaded an incursion from Egypt, though it does not by any means follow that these fortresses were only built after the campaign of Shishak, which took place five years after the accession of Solomon's son.

The next notice concerns the family relations of Rehoboam. It appears that he had eighteen wives and sixty concubines (thirty, according to Josephus, *Ant.* viii. 10, 1), following in this respect the evil example of Solomon. Of his wives only *two*[2] are named : his cousin Mahalath, the daughter of Jerimoth, a son of David (either the same as Ithream, 1 Chron. iii. 3, or the son of one of David's concubines, 1 Chron. iii. 9), and of Abihail, the daughter of Eliab, David's eldest brother; and Maachah, the daughter, or rather, evidently, the granddaughter of Absalom,[3] through his only child, Tamar (2 Sam. xiv. 27; xviii. 18; comp. Jos. *Ant.* viii. 10, 1), who had married Uriel of Gibeah (2 Chron. xiii. 2). Maachah, named after her paternal great-grandmother (the mother of Absalom, 1 Chron. iii. 2), was the favourite of the king, and her eldest son, Abijah, made "chief among his brethren," with succession to the throne. As already noticed, Rehoboam took care to locate his other sons in the different districts of

[1] Originally they belonged to Dan (Josh. xix. 41, 42), but see 1 Chron. vi. 66–69.

[2] Some commentators have regarded Abihail (2 Chron. xi. 18) as the name of a *third* wife, and accordingly represented her, not as a daughter but as a granddaughter of Eliab. But even if this were not contrary to the plain meaning of vers. 18, 19, a granddaughter of Eliab would have been too old for the wife of Rehoboam.

[3] This appears clearly from 2 Chron. xiii. 2. At the death of Solomon the daughter of Absalom would be about fifty years of age. In 2 Chron. xiii. 2 the name is misspelt *Michaiah.*

his territory, giving them ample means for sustaining their rank, and forming numerous and influential alliances for them.[1] Altogether Rehoboam had twenty-eight sons and sixty daughters.

From these general notices, which must be regarded as referring not to any single period, but to the whole reign of Rehoboam, we pass to what, as regards the Scripture narrative, is the most important event in this history. The fact itself is told in fullest detail in the Book of Kings (1 Kings xiv, 22–24); its punishment at the hand of God in the Book of Chronicles (2 Chron. xii. 2, 12).

After the first three years of Rehoboam's reign a great change seems to have come over the religious aspect of the country. Rehoboam and Judah did not, indeed, openly renounce the worship of Jehovah. On the contrary, we find that the king continued to attend the house of the LORD in royal state, and that after the incursion of Shishak there was even a partial religious revival[2] (2 Chron. xii. 11, 12). Still the general character of this period was, that " Rehoboam forsook the law of Jehovah, and all Israel with him," that " he did evil in that he did not set his heart on seeking Jehovah " (2 Chron. xii. 1, 14, *lit.*), and, lastly, that " Judah did the evil in the sight of Jehovah, and provoked Him to jealousy (viewing the relation between the LORD and Israel as one of marriage, Numb. v. 14)—more than anything which their fathers had done by their sins which they sinned " (1 Kings xiv. 22). These sins consisted in building *Bamoth*, or " high places," *i.e.*, altars on every high hill, and setting up

---

[1] Our Authorised Version renders 2 Chron. xi. 23 : " he desired many wives," which seems to imply that Rehoboam sought them for himself. But this is not the case. The original has it, that he " demanded (or sought) " these alliances for his sons, evidently to strengthen his connection with the noble families of the land.

[2] It must not be thought that there was a formal renunciation in Judah of the worship of Jehovah ; but, side by side with it, other services were carried on, which Holy Scripture rightly describes as so inconsistent with it as to amount to idolatry.

in every grove *Mazzeboth*, or memorial-stones and pillars dedicated to Baal, and *Asherim*, or trunks of trees dedicated to
Astarte (with all the vileness which their service implied).[1]
This idolatry was, indeed, not new in Israel—though it had
probably not been practised to the same extent. But in
addition to this we now read of persons "consecrated" to
the Syrian goddess, with the nameless abominations connected
therewith. This form of heathen pollution was of purely
Canaanite origin. As indicating the influence of the Canaanites
upon Judah, it may perhaps be regarded as another evidence
of the connection subsisting between Rehoboam and the
ancient Canaanite cities within the territory of Israel.

The Divine punishment was not long withheld. Once
more it came in the course of natural causation, through
the political motives which influenced Shishak, and led him
to support Jeroboam. In the fifth year of Rehoboam's reign
Shishak marched a large army of Egyptians, Lybians, Sukkiim,
("tent-dwellers"?   Arabs?), and Ethiopians, with 1200
chariots [2] and 60,000 horsemen, into Judæa, and, after taking
the fenced cities along his route, advanced upon Jerusalem,
where Rehoboam and his army were gathered. Once more
the prophet Shemaiah averted a contest, which could only
have ended in disaster. On showing them that the national
danger, though apparently arising from political causes, was
really due to their sin against Jehovah (2 Chron. xii. 2); and
that it was needless to fight, since, as they had been God-for-
saking, they were now God-forsaken (ver. 5)—the king and his
princes humbled themselves. Thereupon the LORD intimated
through His prophet, that He would "grant them deliverance
for a little while," on condition of their submitting to Shishak.
The reason for this: "that they may know My service, and the
service of the kingdoms of the countries," as well as the

---

[1] The *Bamoth* would be on the heights, the Baal- and Astarte-worship
in the groves.

[2] This number is thoroughly consistent with such notices as Exod. xiv.
7; 1 Kings x. 26, and other well-ascertained historical instances.

terms by which the promised deliverance was qualified, contained the most solemn warning of the ultimate consequences of apostasy. Yet the Divine forbearance continued other 370 years before the threatened judgment burst upon the nation. But at this time Jerusalem was spared. Voluntary submission having been made, Shishak entered the city, and contented himself with carrying away the treasures of the Temple and of the Palace, including among the latter the famous golden shields used by Solomon's body-guard on state occasions,[1] for which Rehoboam now substituted shields of brass.[2]

---

[1] These were kept in the guard-house, or "house of the runners," who kept watch at the entrance of the king's house—and not, as before, in the house of the forest of Lebanon (1 Kings x. 17).

[2] And yet the Rabbis speak of the reign of Rehoboam as one of the five brilliant periods (those of David, Solomon, Rehoboam, Asa, and Abijah, *Shem. R.* 15). The Rabbinical notices are collated in the *Nachalath Shim.*, p. 61, cols. *c* and *d*. There is a curious legend (*Pes.* 119, *a*), that Joseph gathered in Egypt all the gold and silver of the world, and that the children of Israel brought it up with them from Egypt. On the capture of Jerusalem, Shishak is said to have taken it, and the possession of this treasure is then traced through various wars to Rome, where it is said now to be.

CHAPTER XI.

JEROBOAM, FIRST KING OF ISRAEL.

Political Measures of Jeroboam—The Golden Calves—The New Priesthood and the New Festival—The Man of Elohim from Judah—His Message and Sign—Jeroboam Struck by Jehovah and miraculously Restored —Invitation to the Man of Elohim—Heathen view of Miracles—The Old Prophet—Return of the Man of Elohim to Bethel—Judgment on his Disobedience—Character of the Old Prophet and of the Man of Elohim—Sickness of the Pious Child of Jeroboam—Mission of his Mother to Ahijah—Predicted Judgment—Death of the Child—Remaining Notices of Jeroboam.

(1 KINGS XII. 25–XIV. 20.)

FROM the history of Judah under Rehoboam, we turn to that of the newly-established kingdom of Israel, the record of which is only found in the Book of Kings (1 Kings xii. 25—xiv. 20). The first object of Jeroboam ("He shall increase the people") was to strengthen the defences of his throne. For this purpose he fortified Shechem, the modern Nablûs—which he made his residence till he exchanged it for Tirzah (1 Kings xiv. 17)—and also the ancient Penuel (Gen. xxxii. 30, 31; Judges viii. 8), on the other side Jordan. As the latter place commanded the great caravan-route to Damascus and Palmyra, its fortification would serve the double purpose of establishing the rule of Jeroboam in the territory east of the Jordan, and of protecting the country against incursions from the east and north-east. His next measure, though, as he deemed it, also of a protective character, not only involved the most daring religious innovation ever attempted in Israel, but was fraught with the most fatal consequences to

Jeroboam and to Israel. How deeply Israel had sunk appears alike from the fact that the king acted with the approbation of his advisers [1]—no doubt the representatives of the ten tribes—and that the people, with the exception of the Levites and a minority among the laity, readily acquiesced in the measure. It implied no less than a complete transformation of the religion of Jehovah, and that for a purely political object.

The danger that, if the people regularly resorted to the great festivals at Jerusalem, their allegiance might be won back to their rightful king, who held rule in the God-chosen capital, was too obvious not to have occurred to a mind even less suspicious than that of an Oriental despot, who had gained his throne by rebellion. To cut off this source of dynastic and even personal peril, Jeroboam, with the advice of his council, introduced a complete change in the worship of Israel. In so doing, his contention would probably be, that he had not abolished the ancient religion of the people, only given it a form better suited to present circumstances—one, moreover, derived from primitive national use, and sanctioned by no less an authority than that of Aaron, the first High-priest.[2] It was burdensome and almost impossible to go up to the central Sanctuary at Jerusalem. But there was the ancient symbol of the "golden calf," [3] made by Aaron himself, under which the people had worshipped Jehovah in the wilderness. Appealing, perhaps at the formal consecration of these symbols, to the very words which Aaron had used (Ex. xxxii. 4), Jero-

---

[1] It has been suggested that the expression (1 Kings xii. 28): "the king took counsel," only refers to deliberation in his own mind. But the view given in the text seems the more rational, consistent, and accordant with the language of the original.

[2] The idea, that these golden calves of Jeroboam were intended as imitations of the cherubim over the ark (*Speaker's Comment.*), is manifestly untenable.

[3] It has been objected, that Jeroboam could not have wished to have recalled to Israel the service of the golden calf in the wilderness, in view of the punishment which followed that sin. But the words and the fact clearly point to it; and many ways might be found of either ignoring or explaining away the consequences of Israel's conduct at that time.

boam made two golden calves, and located them at the southern
and the northern extremities of the territory of the ten tribes.
This was the more easy, since there were both in the south
and north "sacred" localities, associated in popular opinion
with previous worship. Such in the extreme south was Beth-el
—"the house of God and the gate of heaven"—consecrated
by the twofold appearance of God to Jacob; set apart by
the patriarch himself (Gen. xxviii. 11–19; xxxv. 1, 7, 9–15);
and where of old Samuel had held solemn assemblies (1 Sam.
vii. 16). Similarly, in the extreme north Dan was a "consecrated" place, where "strange worship" may have lingered
from the days of Micah (Judges xviii. 30, 31).

The setting up of the golden calves as the symbol of
Jehovah brought with it other changes. An "house of Bamoth,"
or Temple for the high-place altars, probably with priests'
dwellings attached, was reared. The Levitical priesthood was
extruded, either as inseparably connected with the old worship,
or because it would not conform to the new order of things,
and a new priesthood appointed, not confined to any tribe
or family, but indiscriminately taken from all classes of the
people,[1] the king himself apparently acting, in true heathen
fashion, as Chief Pontiff (1 Kings xii. 32, 33).[2] Lastly, the
great Feast of Tabernacles was transferred from the 7th to the
8th month, probably as a more suitable and convenient time for
a harvest-festival in the northern parts of Palestine, the date
(the 15th) being, however, retained, as that of the full moon.
That this was virtually, and would in practice almost immediately become idolatry, is evident. Indeed, it is expressly
attested in 2 Chron. xi. 15, where the service of the "Calves"
is not only associated with that of the *Bamoth,* or high-place
altars, but even with that of "goats"[3]—the ancient Egyptian

---

[1] Our Authorised Version renders "the lowest of the people." But this
is not implied in the original, which uses an expression conveying the idea
of all ranks and classes, in opposition to the Levites.

[2] This is implied in his offering the incense, which was the highest act
in worship.

[3] So literally, and not "devils," as in our Authorised Version and
according to the Rabbis.

worship of Pan under the form of a goat (Lev. xvii. 7). It is true, the text does not imply, as our Authorised Version suggests, that the new priests were taken " from the lowest of the people." But the emphatic and more detailed repetition of the mode of their appointment (1 Kings xii. 31, comp. xiii. 33), of which apparently the only condition was to bring an offering of one young bullock and seven rams (2 Chron. xiii. 9), enables us to judge on what class of people the conduct of the religious services must soon have devolved.

A more daring attempt against that God-ordained symbolical religion, the maintenance of which was the ultimate reason for Israel's call and existence—so to speak, Israel's very *raison d'être*—could not be conceived. It was not only an act of gross disobedience, but, as the sacred text repeatedly notes, a system devised out of Jeroboam's own heart, when every religious institution in Israel had been God-appointed, symbolical, and forming a unity of which no part could be touched without impairing the whole. It was a movement which, if we may venture so to say, called for immediate and unmistakable interposition from on high. Here, then, if anywhere, we may look for the miraculous, and that in its most startling manifestation. Nor was it long deferred.

It was, as we take it, the first occasion on which this new Feast of Tabernacles was celebrated—perhaps at the same time also the dedication of the new Temple and the inauguration of its services. Bethel was in festive array, and thronged by pilgrims—for no less a personage than the king himself was to officiate as Chief Pontiff on that occasion. Connecting, as we undoubtedly should do, the last verse of 1 Kings xii. with the first of chapter xiii., and rendering it literally, we read that on this feast which he " made " (*i.e.* of his own devising) " to the children of Israel," the king " went up on the altar," that is, up the sloping ascent which led to the circuit around the altar on which the officiating priest stood. The sacrifices had already been offered, and their smouldering embers and fat

had mingled with the ashes (1 Kings xiii. 3).[1] And now the
most solemn and central part of the service was reached. The
king went up the inclined plane to the middle of the altar [2]
to burn the incense, when he was suddenly arrested, and the
worshippers startled by a voice from among the crowd (comp.
here the similar event in John vii. 37). It was a stranger
who spoke, and, as we know him, a Judæan, "a man of
Elohim." He had come "in [3] the word of Jehovah" (1 Kings
xiii. 1)—not merely in charge of it, nor only in its constraining
power, but as if the Word of Jehovah itself had come, and this
"man of God" been carried in it to deliver the message which
he "cried to the altar in the word of Jehovah" (ver. 2). It was
to the spurious and rival altar that he spake, and not to the
king—for it was a controversy with spurious worship, and King
Jeroboam was as nothing before Jehovah. That altar, and the
policy which had reared it, would be shivered — the altar
desecrated,[4] and that by a son of David [5]—whereof he gave

---

[1] 1 Kings xiii. 3, not "ashes," as in the Authorised Version, but "fat"
—or rather ashes laden with fat.

[2] Ver. 1 in the original: "Jeroboam stood upon the altar"—this because
"going up" the inclined plane to the middle of the altar, he would stand
on the circuit of the altar, when laying on it either sacrifices or incense.

[3] So literally.

[4] The most effectual mode of desecration would be by the bones of
dead men (comp. Numb. xix. 16). For the fulfilment of this prediction,
see 2 Kings xxiii. 16.

[5] We would put the words in 1 Kings xiii. 2, "Josiah by name," within
hyphens, thus: "—Josiah by name—," as not those of the original prophecy, but of the writer of the Book of Kings, being added for the purpose
of pointing to the fulfilment of that prediction. Our reasons for this view
are: 1. That there is a similar, and in that case, unquestionable, explanatory addition by the writer in ver. 32, where the "cities of Samaria"
are mentioned (see our note below); 2. That prophecy never deals in
details ; 3. That the present would be the only exception to this rule.
For, the mention of Cyrus by name in Isa. xliv. 28 ; xlv. 1, affords no
parallel instance, since Cyrus, or Coresh, means "Sun," and may be regarded
as the designation (appellation) of the Persian kings, which Cyrus afterwards made his own name (like Augustus Cæsar). Keil, indeed, argues
that Josiah was also an appellative title, meaning "Jehovah supports
him"—but this explanation seems, to say the least, strained. There is no

them immediate symbolic evidence that Jehovah had spoken by his mouth that day,[1] by this "wondrous sight,"[2] that the altar would be rent, and the ashes laden with the fat of the sacrifices poured out. Arrested by this uncompromising announcement from one whom he regarded as a daring fanatical intruder, the king turned quickly round, and stretching out his hand towards him, commanded : "Seize him !" But already a mightier Hand than King Jeroboam's was stretched out. Now, if ever, would Jehovah vindicate His authority, prove His Word, and show before all the people that He, Whose authority they had cast off, was the Living God. Then and there must it be shown, in the idol-temple, at the first consecration of that spurious altar, at the first false feast, and upon King Jeroboam, in the pomp of his splendour and the boastfulness of his supposed power (comp. here Acts xii. 22, 23). The king had put forth his hand, but he could not draw it back : the Hand of the LORD held it. Some mysterious stroke had fallen upon him ; and while he thus stood, himself a sign, the top of the altar suddenly parted, and the ashes, clogged and heavy with the fat of idol-sacrifices, poured out around him. No hand was stretched out to seize the "man of God." Nor was there need of it—the "man of God" had neither design nor desire to escape. Rather was it now the king's turn, not to command but to entreat. In the expressive language of the original : "And the king answered" (to the unspoken word of Jehovah in the stroke that had arrested his hand), "and said,

---

need to suppose that, contrary to the universal canon of prophecy, a prediction would give a name 300 years before the time. Of course, fully believing, as we do, in the reality of prophecy, we admit that this would be quite possible ; but on the grounds mentioned, and on others which will readily suggest themselves, it seems so unlikely, that we have adopted a view, supported, if not suggested, by the reference to Samaria in ver. 32. True and reverent faith in Divine revelation will make us only the more careful in our study of its exact meaning.

[1] 1 Kings xiii. 3 reads : "This is the portent (marvellous sign) that Jehovah hath spoken " (not "which Jehovah hath spoken," as in our Authorised Version).

[2] The Hebrew word means a *marvellous sign.*

Soften now the Face of Jehovah thy God, and make entreaty
on my behalf, and " (or, that) " my hand shall return to me."

It was as he craved—for the prophecy and controversy were
not with the king, but with the Altar.   And all this had been
only a sign, which had fulfilled its purpose, and would fulfil
it still more, if the same Power that had appeared in the
sudden stroke would again become manifest in its equally
sudden removal.   As for Jeroboam, Jehovah had no controversy with him then and there, nor indeed anywhere.   The
judgment of his sins would soon enough overtake him and his
house.   It might, indeed, seem passing strange that the king
could now invite this "man of God" to his palace and table,
and even promise him "a reward," if we did not bear in mind
the circumstances of the times, and the heathen idea of
miracles.   To the heathen the miraculous, as direct Divine
manifestation, was not something extraordinary and unexpected.
Heathenism—may we not say, the ancient world ?—*expected* the
miraculous ; and hence in those times God's manifestation by
miracles might almost be designated not as an extraordinary,
but, according to the then notions, as the ordinary mode of
teaching.   Moreover, heathenism regarded miracles as simply
manifestations of *power*, and the worker of miracles as a
magician, possessed of power—the question being, whether the
power of the deity whom he represented was greater than that
of other gods, or not.   It was, no doubt, in this light that
Jeroboam regarded this "man of *Elohim*"—the name Elohim
itself expressing especially "*power.*" [1]   This, as well as knowledge of the character of his own "prophets," and perhaps a
secret hope that he might attach him to himself by a "reward,"
prompted the words of the king.   He would do honour to the
man of power, and, through him, to the deity whom he represented—perhaps even gain the man of God.[2]

---

[1] In contradistinction to *Jehovah*, which added the idea of the *covenant*
to that of power.

[2] I prefer this to the view that Jeroboam's conduct was merely prompted
by the wish to nullify the effect upon the people.   Such a motive seems,
psychologically, unlikely in the circumstances.

It need scarcely be said, that the mere fact of the "man of God" entering the king's palace and sharing his feast—probably a sacrificial idol-feast—would not only have been contrary to the whole scope and spirit of his embassy, but have destroyed the moral effect of the scene enacted before the people. So, to mention a much lower parallelism, is the moral effect of all Christian testimony, whether by word or life, annulled by every act of conformity to, and fellowship with the world (comp. Rom. xii. 1, 2). But in the present instance any danger of this kind had by anticipation been averted. God had given His messenger express command, neither to eat bread nor to drink water in that place, nor even to return by the way that he had come. These directions had, of course, a much deeper and symbolical meaning. They indicated that Bethel lay under the ban; that no fellowship of any kind was to be held with it; and that even the way by which the messenger of God had come, was to be regarded as consecrated, and not to be retraced.[1] In the discharge of the commission entrusted to him, the "man of God," who had "come in the word of Jehovah," was to consider himself as an impersonal being—till he was beyond the place to which, and the road by which he had been sent. Whatever view, therefore, we may take of his after-conduct, it cannot at least surprise us, that at that moment no earthly temptation could have induced him to accept the king's offer (1 Kings xiii. 8, 9).

Yet, as we think of it, the answer of the "man of God" seems to us disappointing. It is like that of Balaam to the messengers of Balak (Numb. xxii. 13, 18), and yet we know that all along his heart was with them, and that he afterwards yielded to their solicitations, to his own destruction. We would have expected more from the "man of God" than a mere recital of his orders—some expression of feeling like that of Daniel under analogous circumstances (Dan. v. 17). But, in repeating

---

[1] The general explanation, that this was added, in order that it should not be known what route he took, so that he might be fetched back, needs no refutation.

before all the people the express command which God had given him, the "man of God," like Balaam of old, also pronounced his own necessary doom, if he swerved from the injunction laid upon him. He had borne testimony—and by the testimony of his own mouth he must be content to be judged; he was quite certain of the command which God had laid upon him, and by that certainty he must abide.

And at first it seemed as if he would have done so. His message delivered, he left Bethel by another way than that which he had come. Among his astonished audience that day had been the sons of an old resident in Bethel, whose real character it is not easy to read.[1] In the sacred narrative he is throughout designated as *Navi*, or Prophet (literally : one who "wells forth"), while the Divine messenger from Judah is always described as "man of Elohim"—a distinction which must have its meaning. On their return from the idol-temple, the eldest of his sons [2] described to the old prophet the scene which they had witnessed. Inquiring from them what road the "man of God" had taken—which they, and probably many others had watched [3]—he hastily rode after him, and overtook him. The "man of Elohim" was resting under "the terebinth"—apparently a well-known spot where travellers were wont to unlade their beasts of burden, and to halt for shelter and repose (a kind of "Travellers' Rest"). Repeating the invitation of Jeroboam, he received the same answer as the king. There could be even less hesitation now, since the "man of God" had actually left Bethel, nor could he possibly have

[1] See the remarks further on.

[2] In the second clause of ver. 11 the singular is used, "his son," not, as in our Authorised Version, "sons." The plural which follows shows, however, that several sons were present, though one was the spokesman. From the presence of the "old prophet" in Bethel, and that of Ahijah in Shiloh, we infer that, if there was a migration of pious laity into the territory of Rehoboam—which, however, is *not* expressly stated in 2 Chron. xi. 16— it must have been that of a minority.

[3] This disposes of the argument quoted in the previous page as to the reason why the "man of God" was to return by another road.

deemed it right to return thither. Upon this the old prophet
addressed him as a colleague, and falsely pretended, not indeed
that Jehovah, but that "*an angel* in the word of Jehovah," had
directed him to fetch him back, when the other immediately
complied. As the two sat at table in Bethel, suddenly "the
word of Jehovah was upon the prophet [1] who had brought him
back." Because he had "resisted (rebelled against) the mouth
of Jehovah, and not kept the commandment which Jehovah
had commanded him," [2] his dead body should not come into
the sepulchre [3] of his fathers. Startling as such an announcement must have been, it would set two points vividly before
him : his disobedience and his impending punishment—the
latter very real, according to the views prevailing at the time
(Gen. xlvii. 30; xlix. 29; l. 25; 2 Sam. xix. 37, etc.), although
not implying either immediate or even violent death. It is
very surprising to us—and indicative of the absence of the
higher moral and spiritual elements — that this announcement was not followed by any expression of sorrow or repentance, but that the meal seems to have continued uninter-
rupted to the end. Did the old prophet seem to the other
only under an access of ecstatic frenzy? Did the fact that
he announced not immediate death blunt the edge of his
message? Had disobedience to the Divine command carried
as its consequence immediate spiritual callousness? Or had
the return of the "man of God" to Bethel after all been the
result of a deeper estrangement from God, of which the first
manifestation had already appeared in what we have described
as his strangely insufficient answer to Jeroboam's invitation and
offer? These are necessarily only suggestions—and yet it
seems to us as if all these elements had been present and at
work to bring about the final result.

[1] So literally.　　　[2] So literally.

[3] The sepulchres in Palestine were not like ours, but generally rock-
hewn, and consisted of an ante-chamber and an inner cave in which the
bodies were deposited in niches—the entrance to the sepulchre being
guarded by a stone. For details, comp. *Sketches of Jewish Social Life in
the Days of Christ*, p. 171.

The meal was past, and the "old prophet" saddled his ass to convey his guest to his destination. But the end of the journey was never reached. As some travellers were passing that way, they saw an unwonted spectacle which must have induced them to hasten on their journey. Close by the roadside lay a dead body, and beside it stood the ass[1] which the unhappy man had ridden—both guarded, as it were, by the lion, who had killed the man, evidently by the weight of his paw as he knocked him down,[2] without, however, rending him, or attempting to feed on his carcase. Who the dead man was, the travellers seem not to have known, nor would they, of course, pause by the road. On passing through Bethel—which from the narrative does not seem to have been their ultimate destination, but the first station which they reached—they naturally "talked in the town" about what they had just seen in its neighbourhood. When the rumour reached the "old prophet," he immediately understood the meaning of all. Riding to the spot, he reverently carried home with him the dead body of the "man of God," mourned over, and buried him in his own sepulchre, marking the place by a monumental pillar to distinguish this from other tombs, and to keep the event in perpetual remembrance. But to his sons he gave solemn direction to lay him in the same tomb—in the rock-niche by the side of that in which the "man of God" rested. This was to be a dying testimony to "the man of God:" that his embassy of God had been real, and that surely the "thing would be" (that it would happen) "which he had cried in the word of Jehovah against the altar which (was) at Bethel, and against all the *Bamoth*-houses which (are)[3] in the cities of Samaria." With this

---

[1] From 2 Kings ii. 24 we gather, that the forest around Bethel was the haunt of wild beasts. It will be easily understood, that it was almost necessary the lion should remain by the dead body, alike to show the Divine character of the judgment, and to induce the passers-by to make haste on their journey.

[2] This is clearly implied by the word "broken" in 1 Kings xiii. 26, marginal rendering.

[3] So literally. The reference to the other *Bamoth*-houses, besides those of Bethel and Dan, is, of course, prophetic.

profession of faith in the truth of Jehovah's message, and in the power of the LORD certainly to bring it to pass at some future time, would the old prophet henceforth live. With it would he die and be buried—laying his bones close to those of the "man of God," sharing his grave, and nestling, as it were, for shelter in the shadow of that great Reality which "the man of God" had cast over Bethel. So would he, in life and death, speak of, and cling to Jehovah—as the True and the Living God.

More than three hundred years later, and nearly a century had passed since the children of Israel had been carried away from their homes. *Then* it was that what, centuries before, the "man of God" had foretold, became literally true (2 Kings xxiii. 15-18). The idol-temple, in which Jeroboam had stood in his power and glory on that opening day, was burned by Josiah; the *Bamoth* were cast down; and on that altar, to defile it, they gathered from the neighbouring sepulchres the bones of its former worshippers, and burned them there. Yet in their terrible search of vengeance one monument arrested their attention. They asked of them at Bethel. It marked the spot where the bones of "the man of God" and of his host the "old prophet" of Samaria [1] lay. And they reverently left the bones in their resting-places, side by side—as in life, death, and burial, so still and for aye witnesses to Jehovah; and safe in their witness-bearing. But three centuries and more between the prediction and the final fulfilment: and in that time symbolic rending of the altar, changes, wars, final ruin, and desolation! And still the word seemed to slumber all those centuries of silence, before it was literally fulfilled. There is something absolutely overawing in this absence of all haste on the part of God, in this certainty of the final event, with apparent utter unconcern of what may

---

[1] The mention of Samaria here and in 1 Kings xiii. 32 must have been explanatory additions by the writer, since Samaria was only built by Omri (1 Kings xvi. 24). This, of course, confirms the view we have expressed about the mention of the name of Josiah. It need scarcely be stated, that this in no way invalidates the truthfulness of the narrative, but rather confirms it.

happen during the long centuries that intervene, which makes us tremble as we realise how much of buried seed of warning or of promise may sleep in the ground, and how unexpectedly, but how certainly, it will ripen as in one day into a harvest of judgment or of mercy.

But too many questions and lessons are involved in this history to pass it without further study. Who was this "old prophet?" was he a true prophet of Jehovah? and why did he thus "lie" to the destruction of the "man of God?" Again, why was such severe punishment meted out to the "man of God?" did he deserve any for what might have been only an error of judgment? and why did his tempter and seducer apparently escape all punishment? To begin with the old "prophet" of Bethel—we do not regard him as simply a false prophet, whose object it was to seduce "the man of God," either from jealousy or to destroy the effect of his mission.[1] On the other hand, it seems equally incorrect to speak of him as a true prophet of God, roused from sinful conformity with those around by the sudden appearance of the Judæan messenger of Jehovah, and anxious to recover himself by fellowship with "the man of God," even if that intercourse could only be secured by means of a falsehood.[2] Nor would we describe his conduct as intended to try the steadfast obedience of the "man of God." The truth seems to lie between these extreme opinions. Putting aside the general question of heathen divination, which we have not sufficient materials satisfactorily to answer, it is at least certain that not every *Navi* was a prophet of Jehovah. That God should have sent a message through one who was not His prophet, need not surprise us when we recall the history of Balaam. Moreover, it was peculiarly appropriate, that the announcement of guilt and punishment should come to the "man of God" through the person who had misled him by false pretence

---

[1] This, in one form or another, is the view of Josephus, the Targum, and of most of the Rabbinical and Christian commentators.

[2] So Ephr. Syr., Theodor., Witsius, Hengstenberg, Keil, and Bähr.

of an angelic command, and at the very meal to which the
"man of God" should never have sat down. Again, it is
evident that, from the moment he heard of the scene in
the idol-temple, the " old prophet" believed in the genuineness and authority of the message brought to Bethel. Every
stage in the history deepened this conviction, till at last it
became, so to speak, the fundamental fact of his religious
life, which must have determined his whole after-conduct.
May it not have been that this " old *Navi*" was one of
the fruits of the " Schools of the Prophets "—the prophetic
order having apparently been widely revived during the later
part of Solomon's reign? Settling in Bethel (as Lot in
Sodom), he may have gradually lapsed into toleration of
evil—as the attendance of his children in the idol-temple
seems to imply —without, however, surrendering his character,
perhaps his office of " Prophet," the more so as the service
of Jehovah might be supposed to be only altered in form, not
abolished, by the adoption of the symbol of the Golden Calves.
In that case his immediate recognition of the " man of God,"
and his deepening conviction may be easily understood ; his
earnest desire to claim and have fellowship with a direct
messenger of God seems natural ; and even his unscrupulous
use of falsehood is accounted for.

These considerations will help to show that there was an
essential difference between him and " the man of God,"
and that the punishment which overtook the latter bears
no possible relation to the apparent impunity of the " old
prophet." That terrible judgment ought to be viewed from
two different points : as it were, absolutely—from heaven
downwards ; and relatively to the person whom it overtook
—from earth heavenwards. The most superficial consideration will convince, that, from the nature of the case, the
authority of God must have been vindicated, and that by a
patent and terrible judgment, if the object and meaning of
the message which He had sent were not to be nullified.
When " the man of God " publicly proclaimed in the temple

the terms which God had prescribed, he pronounced his own sentence in case of disobedience. Besides, the main idea underlying the Divine employment of such messengers was that of their absolute and unquestioning execution of the exact terms of their commission. This essential condition of the prophetic office it was the more necessary to vindicate in Bethel, as also at the commencement of a period marked by a succession of prophets in Israel, who, in the absence of the God-ordained services, were to keep alive the knowledge of Jehovah, and, by their warnings and teaching, to avert, if possible, the catastrophe of national judgment which would overtake apostate Israel.

As regards "the man of God" himself, we have already noticed the increasing spiritual callousness, consequent upon his first unfaithfulness. But putting this aside, surely there never could have been any serious question in his mind as to his duty. By his own testimony, he had received express and unmistakable command of God, which Scripture again and again repeats, for the sake of emphasis; and his conduct should have been guided on the plain principle, that an obvious and known duty can never be set aside by another seeming duty. Besides, what evidence had he that an angel had really spoken to the "old prophet;" or even that his tempter was a "prophet" at all, or, if a prophet, acted in the prophetic spirit? All these points are so obvious, that the conduct of the "man of God" would seem almost incredible, if we did not recall how often in every-day life we are tempted to turn aside from the plain demands of right and duty by a false call in contravention to it. In all moral and spiritual questions it is ever most dangerous to reason: simple obedience and not argument is the only safe path (comp. here Gal. i. 8). One duty can never contravene another—and the plainly known and clear command of God must silence all side-questions.

Viewing the conduct of the man of God" as a fall and a sin, all becomes plain. He had publicly announced his duty, and he had publicly contravened it; and his punishment was, through the remarkable, though not miraculous, circumstances [1] under which it overtook him, equally publicly known. Throughout the whole history there is, so to speak, a remarkable equipoise in the circumstances of his sin and of his punishment, as also in the vindication of God's authority. And yet even so, the moral effect of God's message was apparently weakened through the sin of His messenger. So terribly fatal in their consequences are our sins, even when publicly punished. For it is scarcely possible to believe that, had it not been so, Jeroboam would "after this thing" have uninterruptedly continued his former course of defiance of the authority of God. But here the history also turns from Israel to its wretched king, and in a narrative of deepest pathos shows us at the same time the punishment of his sin, and the wonderful tenderness of God's dealings towards those who, in the midst of greatest temptations, have kept their hearts true to Him, and are preserved by His mercy from the evil to come. And most comforting is it to know that God has and keeps His own—even though it be in the family of a Jeroboam, and that true piety finds its respectful acknowledgment, even among a people so sunken as was Israel at that time.

If it were necessary to show how unhappiness and sin go hand in hand, the history about to be told would furnish ample evidence of it. The main reason of its insertion in the Biblical record is, of course, that it gave occasion to announce the Divine punishment upon the race of Jeroboam, as having traversed the fundamental condition on which the possibility of the new dynasty rested (1 Kings xi. 38). At the same time, it seems also to cast an important side-light on the transaction between Ahijah the prophet and Jeroboam, when the former first announced to him his future elevation to the kingdom (1 Kings xi. 29–39). Keil renders 1 Kings xiv. 7 : "Thus saith Jehovah, the God of Israel: Therefore, because thou hast

---

[1] It is well known that lions do not prey upon dead bodies, except through stress of hunger.

elevated thyself from amongst the people, and I have given thee ruler over My people Israel " If this rendering is correct, it would imply that his elevation, or leadership of Israel, was in the first place entirely Jeroboam's own act, and that, having so elevated himself and assumed the leadership, God afterwards bestowed on him the rule to which he aspired, leaving for future trial the fitness of his race for the kingdom.

But, besides the higher Divine meaning of this history, it possesses also a deep human interest. It gives us a glimpse into the inner family-life of the wretched king, as, divested of crown and purple, and having cast aside state-craft and religious falsehood, he staggers under a sore blow. For once we see the man, not the king, and, as each man appears truest, when stricken to the heart by a sorrow which no earthly power can turn aside. From Shechem the royal residence had been transferred to the ancient Canaanite city (Josh. xii. 24) Tirzah, the beautiful (Cant. vi. 4), two hours to the north of Samaria, amidst cultivated fruit-and-olive-clad hills, up on a swelling height, with glorious outlook over the hills and valleys of rich Samaria.[1] The royal palace seems to have stood at the entering in of the city (comp. 1 Kings xiv. 17 with ver. 12). But within its stately apartments reigned silence and sorrow. Abijah, Jeroboam's son, and apparently the intended successor to his throne, lay sick. He seems like the last link that bound Jeroboam to his former better self. The very name of the child—*Abijah,* " Jehovah is my Father," or else " my Desire "—indicates this, even if it were not for the touching notice, that in him was " found a good thing towards Jehovah, the God of Israel, in the house of Jeroboam " (ver. 13) We can conceive how this " good thing " may have sprung up; but to keep and to cause it to grow in such surroundings, surely needed the gracious tending of the Good Husbandman. It was the one green spot in Jeroboam's life and home; the

---

[1] The fullest description is that in Guérin's *Samarie,* tome i., pp. 365–368. It is the modern *Thailusah* : comp. Böttger, *Topogr. Histor. Lex. zu Flavius Josephus,* p. 243.

one germ of hope. And as his father loved him truly, so all Israel had set their hopes on him. Upon the inner life of this child—its struggles and its victories—lies the veil of Scripture-silence ; and best that it should be so. But now his pulses were beating quick and weak, and that life of love and hope seemed fast ebbing. None with the father in those hours of darkness—neither counsellor, courtier, prophet, nor priest—save the child's mother. As they two kept sad watch, helpless and hopeless, the past, to which this child bound him, must have come back to Jeroboam. One event in it chiefly stood out : it was his first meeting with Ahijah the Shilonite. That was a true prophet—bold, uncompromising withal. With that impulse of despair which comes upon men in their agony, when all the delusions of a misspent life are swept away, he turned to the opening of his life, so full of hope and happy possibility, ere ambition had urged him upon the path of reckless sacrifice of all that had been dearest and holiest; ere unlimited possession had dazzled his sight and the sound of flattery deafened his ears. As to Saul of old on the eve of that fatal battle, when God and man had become equally silent to him, the figure of Samuel had stood out—that which to us might seem the most unlikely he could have wished to encounter—so now to Jeroboam that of Ahijah. Could he have wished to blot out, as it were, all that had intervened, and to stand before the prophet as on the day when first he met him, when great but not yet unholy thoughts rose within him ? Had he some unspoken hope of him who had first announced to him his reign ? Or did he only in sheer despair long to know what would come to the child, even though he were to learn the worst ? Be this as it may, he must have word from Ahijah, whatever it might be.

In that hour he has no friend nor helper save the mother of his child. She must go, in her love, to the old prophet in Shiloh. But how dare she, Jeroboam's wife, present herself there ? Nay, the people also must not know what or whither her errand was. And so she must disguise herself as a poor woman, carrying with her, indeed, as customary, a gift to the prophet, but one such as only the poorest in the land would offer.   While alone and in humble disguise the wife of Jeroboam goes on her heavy embassy, across the hills of Samaria, past royal Shechem, Another has already brought her message to Shiloh.   No need for the queen to disguise herself, so far as Ahijah was concerned, since age had blinded his eyes. But Jehovah had spoken to His aged servant, and charged him concerning this matter.   And as he heard the sound of her feet within the door, he knew who his unseen visitor was, and addressed her not as queen but as the wife of Jeroboam. Stern, terrible things they were which he was commissioned to tell her ; and with unswerving faithfulness and unbending truth he spake them, though his heart must have bled within him as he repeated what himself called "hard *tidings.*"[1]   All the more deeply must the aged prophet have felt them, that it was he who had announced to Jeroboam his future elevation. They concerned Jeroboam ; but they also touched every heart-string in the wife and the mother, and must well nigh have torn each one of them as they swept across her.   First :[2] an uncompromising recital of the past, and a sternly true representation of the present—all glare, dazzle, and self-delusion dispelled, till it stood in naked reality before her.   Only two persons are in this picture, Jehovah and Jeroboam—all else is in the far background.   That is enough ; and now once in full sight of those two persons, the wife, the mother, must hear it all, though her ears tingle and her knees tremble.   Not this child only, but every child, nay, every descendant, down to the meanest, whether it be child or adult[3]—swept away : "And I will sweep

---

[1] In the original it is simply "*hard.*"

[2] Commentators have noted in the ten verses of Ahijah's message (vers. 7–16) a rhythmic arrangement, viz., twice 5 verses—the first stanza (vers. 7–11) consisting of 3 + 2, the last stanza (vers. 12–16) of 2 + 3 verses.

[3] This seems to be the correct meaning of a proverbial expression which scarcely occurs except during the period from the time of David to that of Jehu.

out after the house of Jeroboam, as one sweepeth out dirt till it is quite gone" (1 Kings xiv. 10).[1] And not only this, but also horrible judgment; the carcases of her children lying like carrion in street and on field, their flesh torn and eaten by the wild, unclean dogs that prowl about, or picked from their limbs by birds of prey who swoop round them with hoarse croaking.[2] Thus far for Jeroboam. And now as for the child that lay sick in the palace of Tirzah—it shall be in God's keeping, removed from the evil to come. As her feet touched the threshold of her doomed home, it would die. As it were, such heavy tidings shall not be brought within where he sleeps; its terrors shall not darken his bed. Before they can reach him, he shall be beyond their shadow and in the light. But around that sole-honoured grave all Israel shall be the mourners, and God Himself wills to put this mark of honour upon His one child in that now cursed family. Lastly, as for apostate Israel, another king raised up to execute the judgment of God—nay, all this not merely in the dim future, but the scene seems to shift, and the prophet sees it already in the present.[3] Israel shaken as a reed in the water by wind and waves; Israel uprooted from their land,—cast away and scattered among the heathen beyond the river, and given up to be trampled under foot. Such is the end of the sins of Jeroboam and of his people; such, in the bold figure of Scripture, is the sequel of casting Jehovah "behind their back."[4]

Of the further course of this history we know no more.

---

[1] This is the literal, and, as will be perceived, much more forcible rendering.

[2] Comp. here Exod. xx. 4, 5; Deut. xxviii. 26. Even the alteration of this latter passage in 1 Kings xiv. 11 is in favour of the earlier age of the Book of Deuter.—since the addition about the "dogs" points to Eastern *town*-life, where the wild dogs act as scavengers of cities.

[3] The words of the original are somewhat difficult to render on account of the abruptness of the speech; but the above, which corresponds with our Authorised Version, gives the correct meaning.

[4] It is remarkable, that the same strong expression occurs only in Ezek. xxiii. 35, in reference to the same sin of apostate Judah as followed by the same punishment as that of Israel.

The queen and mother went back, stricken, to her home; and it was as the prophet had told her from Jehovah. And this literal fulfilment would be to her for ever afterwards the terrible pledge of what was yet to come.

Nor do we read any more of Jeroboam. It almost seems as if Holy Scripture had nothing further to say of him—not even concerning his later and disastrous war with the son of Rehoboam (2 Chron. xiii. 2–20). That is told in connection with the reign of the second king of Judah. Of Jeroboam we only read that he "reigned two and twenty years," that "he slept with his fathers," and that "Nadab his son reigned in his stead."[1]

---

[1] We subjoin the following as the most interesting of the Rabbinical notices about Jeroboam (comp. the *Nachalath Shimoni*, vol. i., p. 37, *b* and *c*) : The name of Jeroboam is explained as "making contest among the people," either in reference to their relationship to God, or as between Israel and Judah (*Sanh.* 101, *b*). His father Nebat is identified with Micah, and even with Sheba, the son of Bichri (*Sanh.* ib.). The Talmud records various legendary accounts of Jeroboam's quarrel with Solomon, in which the former appears more in the right (*Sanh.* ib.), although he is blamed alike for the public expression of his feelings and for his rebellion. That rebellion is regarded as the outward manifestation of long-existing disunion. The government of Jeroboam is looked upon as distinguished by firmness, and he is praised for his wisdom, which had given rise to great hope. Pride is stated to have been the reason of his apostasy from God (*Sanh.* 102 *a*). The promise to Jacob in Gen. xxxv. 11, "Kings shall come out of thee," is applied in *Bereshith R.* 82 (ed. Warsh. p. 146, *b*), to Jeroboam ; but he is regarded as not having share in the world to come. Seven such are mentioned : three kings—Jeroboam, Ahab, and Manasseh, and four private persons—Balaam, Doeg, Ahithophel, and Gehazi (*Sanh.* 90, *a*). He is also mentioned among those who are condemned eternally to Gehenna in *Rosh ha-Shanah,* 17, *a*.

CHAPTER XII.

ABIJAH AND ASA (*2nd & 3rd*) KINGS OF JUDAH.

Accession of Abijah—His Idolatry—War between Judah and Israel—Abijah's Address to Israel and Victory—Deaths of Jeroboam and of Abijah— Accession of Asa—Religious Reformation in Judah—Invasion by Zerah the Ethiopian—Victory of Zephathah—Azariah's Message to the Army of Asa—Great Sacrificial Feast at Jerusalem—Renewal of the Covenant with Jehovah.

(1 KINGS XV. 1-15; 2 CHRON. XIII.-XV.)

JEROBOAM did not only survive Rehoboam, but he witnessed the accession of two other kings of Judah, Abijah and Asa. The reign of Abijah[1] was very brief. Both in 1 Kings xv. 2 and in 2 Chron. xiii. 2 it is said to have lasted *three* years—an expression which must be understood according to this canon laid down by the Rabbis, that the commencement of a year in the reign of a king is to be reckoned as a full year. Thus, as Abijah ascended the throne in the eighteenth (1 Kings xv. 1), and Asa in the twentieth (ver. 9) year of Jeroboam's reign, it follows that the former actually reigned only somewhat over two years. Two things are specially noticed concerning Abijah: his relation towards Jehovah (in 1 Kings xv. 3-5), and his relation to the kingdom of Jeroboam (2 Chron. xiii. 2-20).

To begin with the former. It is stated that "he walked in

---

[1] *Abijah*—"my father Jehovah!" Two other forms of the name occur. In the Book of Kings he is always called *Abijam*, while in 2 Chron. xiii. 21 he is also designated (in the Hebrew) *Abijahu*. Probably *Abijam* (in 1 Kings) was the older form—and it is not impossible that it may have been altered into *Abijah*, when that monarch made his loud profession of Jehovahism (2 Chron. xiii. 4, etc.).

all the sins of his father," and that "his heart was not perfect
with Jehovah his God." These two statements are not explanatory of, but supplementary to, each other. We know that
Rehoboam had not abolished the service of Jehovah (see, for
example, 1 Kings xiv. 28), but that, by its side, a spurious
worship had been tolerated, if not encouraged, which, in the
view of Holy Scripture, was equal to idolatry. In this matter
Rehoboam had not only followed the example of his father
Solomon, during his later years, but greatly increased the evil
which had then begun. A similar remark applies to the
reign of Abijah, as compared with that of Rehoboam. That
the idolatry of the reign of Rehoboam had grown both worse
in character and more general in practice under that of Abijah,
appears from the notices of the reformation instituted by his
successor, Asa. The former circumstance is implied in the
terms by which the idolatry of that period is described (2 Chron.
xiv. 3, 5), and by the circumstance that "the queen-mother"
(Maachah, Abijah's mother and Asa's grandmother),[1] who
under Abijah held the official rank of *Gevirah*, "Queen" (the
modern *Sultana Valide*), had made and set up "a horror for
Asherah"[2]—some horrible wooden representation, equally vile
and idolatrous in its character. Again, that idolatry had
become more widely spread, and that its hold was stronger, we
infer from the fact that, despite Asa's example, admonitions,
and exertions (2 Chron. xiv. 4, 5), "the high places did not
cease" (1 Kings xv. 14). This progressive spiritual decline
under the reigns of Solomon, Rehoboam, and Abijah was so
marked as to have deserved the removal of the family of
David from the throne, had it not been for God's faithfulness to
His covenant-promises (1 Kings xv. 4, 5). But, although such

[1] As Maachah, the daughter (granddaughter) of Abishalom (Absalom)
was the mother of Abijah, she must have been the grandmother of Asa.
She is designated as "Queen," or rather (in the original) as *Gevirah*, which
is an *official* title.

[2] It is needless to inquire into the nameless abominations connected with
what the original designates as a "horror," rendered in the Authorised
Version "idol."

was the state of religion, Abijah not only made loud profession of the worship of Jehovah, but even brought votive offerings to the Temple, probably of part of the spoil taken in war (1 Kings xv. 15; comp. 2 Chron. xiii. 16–19).

Concerning the relations of Judah to the neighbouring kingdom of Israel, it may be said that the chronic state of warfare which had existed during the time of Rehoboam now changed into one of open hostilities. Two reasons for this may be given. Abijah was a much more vigorous ruler than his father, and the power of Egypt, on which Jeroboam relied for support, seems at that time to have decreased. This we gather, not only from the non-interference of Egypt in the war between Abijah and Jeroboam, but from the fact that, when Egypt at length sought to recover its lost ascendancy, it was under the rule of Zerah the Ethiopian (probably Osorkon II.), who was not the son, but the son-in-law, of the preceding monarch (2 Chron. xiv. 9); and we know the fate that overtook the huge, undisciplined army which Zerah led.

The language of the sacred narrative (2 Chron. xiii. 2, 3) implies, that the war between Judah and Israel was begun by Abijah. On both sides a levy of all capable of bearing arms was raised, though, so far as the numerical strength of the two armies was concerned, the response seems not to have been so universal in Judah as in Israel.[1] But perhaps the

---

[1] The numbers : 400,000 for Judah, 800,000 for Israel, and 500,000 killed, have always seemed a difficulty. Bishop Kennicott and others have regarded these numerals as a copyist's mistake. But it seems difficult to imagine three consecutive errors in copying. Professor Rawlinson (in the *Speaker's Commentary*, vol. iii., p. 306) thinks, that both the combatants and the slain represent those engaged throughout the whole war. But this scarcely removes the difficulty. Two points may help our better understanding of the matter, though we would only suggest them hypothetically. First, comparing these numbers with more exact numerical details, as in 2 Chron. v.–vii., and xii., they read rather like what might be called "round numbers" than as precise numeration. Secondly, comparing these numbers with the census under King David (2 Sam. xxiv. 9), we find that the number of the Israelites is exactly the same in both cases, while that of Judah is larger by 100,000 in the census of David

seeming discrepancy may be explained by the necessity of
leaving strong garrisons in the south to watch the Egyptian
frontier (comp. 2 Chron. xiv. 9).   The two armies met at the
boundary of the two kingdoms, though, as we judge, within the
territory of Israel.   They camped in close proximity, only
separated by Mount Zemaraim,[1] a height to the east of Bethel
and some distance north of Jericho, forming part of the ridge
known as "Mount Ephraim," which stretched from the plain
of Esdraelon southwards.   From this height Abijah addressed
the army of Israel just before the battle began, in the hope
of securing their voluntary submission, or at least weakening
their resistance.   Ignoring all that told against himself,[2] Abijah
tried to impress on his opponents that right was wholly on
his side.[3]   In language full of irony he set before them their
weakness, as the necessary result of their apostasy from Jehovah,
the God of their fathers, and of their adoption of a worship
neither conformable to their ancient faith nor even respectable
in the sight of men.   Lastly, he loudly protested that, since
Judah had gone to war under the leadership of Jehovah and
in the manner appointed by Him, Israel was really fighting
against Jehovah, the God of their fathers, and could not expect
success.   Whatever hollowness there may have been in this
profession on the part of Abijah, it was at least the true war-
cry of Israel which he raised.   It found an echo in the hearts

---

than in the army of Abijah, though it included Benjamin. If we assume that
Abijah invaded Israel with a regular army — "began the war with an
army of war-heroes," and that in defence Jeroboam raised a levy of all
capable of bearing arms, we can understand the use of these "round
numbers," derived from a previous census.   In that case the number of the
slain would represent rather the proportion of those who fell during the
war than a numerically exact statement.

[1] The *Semaron* of Josephus (*Ant.* viii. 11, 2), probably the modern
Kharbet-es-Somera (Guerin, *La Samarie*, vol. i. pp. 226, 227 ; vol. ii.
p. 175).   But this localisation is by no means certain.

[2] Such as the conditions of David's royalty (Ps. cxxxii. 12), the sin of
Solomon, the folly and sin of Rehoboam, and his own unfaithfulness to
the LORD.

[3] "A covenant of salt"—comp. Lev. ii. 13 ; Numb. xviii. 19.

of his followers. In vain Jeroboam, by a cleverly executed movement, attacked Judah both in front and rear. The terror excited by finding themselves surrounded only led the people to cry unto Jehovah (2 Chron. xiii. 14), and He was faithful to His promise (Numb. x. 9). The shout of the combatants mingled with the blast of the priests' trumpets, as Judah rushed to the attack. Israel fled in wild disorder, and a terrible carnage ensued. The fugitives were followed by the army of Judah, and Abijah recovered from Israel the border-cities,[1] with the districts around them. In consequence of this victory the power of Jeroboam was henceforth on the wane, and that of Abijah in the ascendancy Not long afterwards Jehovah struck Jeroboam, either suddenly or with lingering disease, of which he died. He had, however, survived his rival, Abijah,[2] for more than two years.

Abijah was succeeded on the throne of Judah by his son, Asa, probably at the time a boy of only ten or eleven years.[3] This may in part account for his pious up-bringing, as, during his minority he would be chiefly under the official guardianship of the High-priest (comp. 2 Chron. xxii. 12). It also explains how a bold, resolute woman, such as Maachah, could still retain her official position as *Gevirah*, or "queen-mother," till, on attaining majority, the young king commenced his religious reformation. During the first ten years of Asa's reign the land had rest (2 Chron. xiv. 1). While devoutly acknowledging the goodness of God in this, it is easy to understand the outward circumstances by which it was brought about. The

---

[1] The localisation of "Jeshanah" and "Ephrain" has not been satisfactorily made out. But in all probability these towns were not at a great distance from Bethel.

[2] The expression (2 Chron. xiii. 21): "Abijah waxed mighty," or rather "strengthened himself," may also refer to his league with Syria (2 Chron. xvi. 3). The notice of his wives and children includes, of course, an earlier period of his life.

[3] If Rehoboam was twenty-one years old at his accession, and reigned eighteen years, and then after two or three years was followed by his grandson, the latter could scarcely have been more than ten or eleven years old.

temporary weakness of Egypt, the defeat of Jeroboam, and an alliance which Abijah seems to have contracted with Syria (2 Chron. xvi. 3), as well as afterwards the rapid succession of rival dynasties in Israel, sufficiently explain it. For, during his long reign of forty-one years, Asa saw no fewer than seven kings ascend the throne of Israel.[1] The first work which Asa took in hand was a thorough religious reformation ; his next, the strengthening of the defences of the country. For this the temporary state of security prevailing offered a happy opportunity—" the land " being " still before them "—open and free from every enemy, though it was not difficult to foresee that such would not long be the case. And, as king and people owned that this time of rest had been granted them by Jehovah, so their preparations [2] against future attacks were carried on in dependence upon Him. The period of trial came only too soon.

An almost countless [3] Egyptian host, under the leadership of Zerah,[4] the Ethiopian, swarmed into Judah. Advancing by the south-west, through the border of the Philistines, who, no doubt, made common cause with the Egyptians (2 Chron. xiv. 14), they appeared before Mareshah (comp. Josh. xv. 44). This was one of the border fortresses which Jeroboam had built (2 Chron. xi. 8). The natural capabilities of the place and its situation, so near the south-western angle of the country, and almost midway between Hebron and Ashdod, must have marked it as one of the most important strategical points in the Jewish line of defensive works against Philistia, or rather,

---

[1] At his accession Jeroboam reigned in Israel. The other seven were : Nadab, Baasha, Elah, Zimri, Tibni, Omri, and Ahab. These seven kings represented four rival dynasties.

[2] Evidently all the males capable of bearing weapons were trained to arms. The proportion of Benjamin relatively to Judah, though great, is not excessive (comp. Gen. xlix. 27).

[3] We regard these numerals also as round numbers.

[4] Brügsch regards Zerah not as Osorkon, but as an independent Ethiopian monarch. But there is no evidence in support of this hypothesis.

against Egypt.[1] About two miles north of Mareshah a
beautiful valley debouches from between the hills.[2] This
is the valley of Zephathah, where the relieving army of Asa,
coming from the north-east, now took up its position. Here a
decisive battle took place, which ended in the complete rout of
the Egyptians. It has been well noted,[3] that this is the only
occasion on which the armies of Judah ventured to meet, and
with success, either Egypt or Babylon *in the open field* (not
behind fortifications). On the only other occasion when a battle
in the open was fought (2 Chron. xxv. 20–24), it ended in the
signal defeat of Judah. But this is only one of the circumstances which made the victory of Asa so remarkable. Although
the battle-field (a valley) must have been unfavourable for
handling so unwieldy a mass of soldiers and for deploying their
war-chariots, yet the host of Egypt was nearly double that of
Asa, and must have included well-disciplined and long-trained
battalions. But, on the other hand, never before had a battle
been fought in the same manner ; never had there been more
distinct negation of things seen and affirmation of things unseen—which constitutes the essence of faith—nor yet more
trustful application of it than in Asa's prayer before the battle :
" Is it not with Thee to help between the much (the mighty)
relatively to no strength (in regard to the weak) ?[4] Help us,
Jehovah our God, for upon Thee do we put our trust ; and in
Thy name have we come (do we come) upon this multitude.
O Jehovah, Thou art our God (the God of power, *Elohim*) : let
not man retain *strength* by the side of Thee (have power before

---

[1] The *Marissa* of Josephus, the modern *Marâsh*. Comp. Robinson's
Bibl. Researches, vol. ii. pp. 67, 68. Its importance as a fortress is shewn
by the part it sustained in later Jewish history, having been taken and
retaken several times at different periods.

[2] Not where Robinson finds it (*u.s.* p. 31).

[3] Professor Rawlinson in the *Speaker's Commentary.*

[4] The words are not easy of exact rendering, though their meaning is
plain. Different translations have been proposed. We have ventured to
put it interrogatively. If this view be not adopted, that which would most
commend itself to us would be : "It is nothing with Thee, Jehovah, to
help between the mighty in regard to the weak."

Thee)!" Such an appeal could not be in vain. In the significant language of Holy Scripture, it was "Jehovah" Who "smote" the Ethiopians, and "Asa and the people that were with him" only "pursued them."[1] Far away to Gerar, three hours south-east from the border-city, Gaza, continued the chase amidst unnumbered slain, and still the destroying sword of Jehovah was before His host (2 Chron. xiv. 13), and His fear fell upon all the cities round about. To wrest the hostile cities of the Philistines and to carry away much spoil was only one sequence. Henceforth Egypt ceased to be a source of terror or of danger, and full 330 years passed before its army was again arrayed against Judah.[2]

The occasion was too favourable not to have been improved. Asa had entered on a course of right-doing, and the LORD, upon Whom he and his people had called, had proved a faithful and prayer-hearing God. If the religious reformation so happily begun, and the religious revival which had appeared, only issued in a thorough return to the LORD, the evil which had been in the far and near past and which threatened in the future, might yet be averted. The morrow of the great God-given victory seemed the most suitable time for urging this upon Judah. Accordingly, Azariah, the son of Oded,[3] was Divinely commissioned to meet the returning victorious army of Asa, and to urge such considerations upon the people. "The Spirit of Elohim" was upon him, and what he spake bore reference not only to the past and the present, but also to the future. Hence his message is rightly described as both "words" and "a prophecy" (2 Chron. xv. 8). Carefully examined, it contains alike an address and a prophecy. For it were a mistake to suppose,

---

[1] In 2 Chron. xiv. 13 the Hebrew expression is : "they were broken before Jehovah"—as it were by the weight of His Hand.

[2] In the reign of Josiah (2 Chron. xxxv. 20–24).

[3] There is no reason for supposing that Oded was Iddo the prophet. In 2 Chron. xv. 8 the words : "Of Oded the prophet," are either defective, or more probably a gloss. This is evident, not only from the ascription of the prophecy to Oded, but from the fact that the grammatical structure requires either the omission of these words or the addition to them of others.

that the picture which Azariah drew of Israel's sin and its consequence in vers. 3, 5, 6 was only that of the far past in the time of the Judges, of the religious decline under Jeroboam and Abijah, or even of their future apostasy and its punishment. *All these* were included in what the prophet set before the people.[1] And not only so, but his words extended beyond Judah, and applied to all Israel, as if the whole people were viewed as still united, and ideally one in their relation to the Lord.[2] Accordingly, it deserves special notice, that neither in ver. 3 nor in ver. 5 any verb is used, as if to indicate the general application of the "prophecy." But its present bearing, alike as regarded Judah's sin and repentance, and God's judgment and mercy, was an earnest call to carry on and complete the good work which had already been begun (ver. 7).

And king and people hearkened to the voice of God through His prophet. Again and more energetically than before, the religious reformation was taken in hand. The idol-"abominations" were removed, not only from Judah and Benjamin, but from the conquered cities of the north, and the great altar of burnt-offering in the Temple was repaired. The earnestness of this movement attracted the pious laity from the neighbouring tribes, and even led those of Simeon (in the far south) who, apparently, had hitherto sympathised with the northern kingdom, as they shared their idolatry (comp. Amos iv. 4; v. 5; viii. 14), to join the ranks of Judah. At a great sacrificial feast, which the king held in Jerusalem, the solemn covenant into which Israel had originally entered with Jehovah (Ex. xxiv. 3–8) was renewed, in repentant acknowledgment that it had been broken, and in believing choice of Jehovah as henceforth their God— just as it was afterwards renewed on two analogous occasions:

---

[1] As regards the past compare Judges ii. 10; iii. 14; v. 6; vi. 2; xii. 4; xx. As regards the future compare here, Deut. iv. 27–30; xxviii. 20; Is. ix. 17–20; lv. 6; Jer. xxxi. 1; Ezek. xxxvi. 24; Amos iii. 9; Zechar. xiv. 13.

[2] In regard to Israel comp. here Hos. iii. 5; v. 13–15.

in the time of Josiah (2 Kings xxiii. 3; 2 Chron. xxxiv. 31), and in that of Nehemiah (Nehem. x. 28–39). The movement was the outcome of heart-conviction and earnest purpose, and consisted, on the one hand, in an undertaking that any introduction of idolatry should be punished by death[1] (according to Deut. xiii. 9), and, on the other, in an act of solemn national consecration to Jehovah.

To Asa at least all this was a reality, although, as regarded his subjects, the religious revival does not seem to have been equally deep or permanent (2 Chron. xv. 17). But the king kept his part of the solemn engagement. However difficult it might be, he removed "the Queen-mother" from her exalted position, and thus showed an example of sincerity and earnestness in his own household. And, in token of his consecration to Jehovah, he brought into His House alike those war-spoils which his father had, after the victory over Jeroboam, set apart as the portion for God, and what he himself now consecrated from the spoil taken in the war with Egypt. These measures were followed by a period of happy rest for the land —even to the twenty-fifth[2] year of King Asa's reign.

---

[1] The Authorised Version conveys the impression, that in every case want of personal piety would be punished by death. Such, however, is not the meaning of the original. It only implies, that the introduction of idolatry by any person should be punishable by death (comp. Deut. xvii. 2–7).

[2] As the dates in 2 Chron. xv. 19; xvi. 1 are incompatible with that of Baasha's death (1 Kings xvi. 8), and consequently, of course, with that of Baasha's war against Asa, commentators have tried to obviate the difficulty, either by supposing that the numeral 35 refers, not to the date of Asa's accession, but to that of the separation of the kingdoms of Judah and Israel, or else by emendating the numeral in the Book of Chronicles. The latter is, evidently, the only satisfactory solution. There is manifestly here a copyist's mistake, and the numeral which we would substitute for 35 is not 15 (as by most German commentators) but 25—and this for reasons too long to explain (כה instead of לה).

CHAPTER XIII.

ASA (3rd) KING OF JUDAH — NADAB, BAASHA, ELAH, ZIMRI, TIBNI, AND OMRI (2nd, 3rd, 4th, 5th, 6th, 7th) KINGS OF ISRAEL.

Reign of Nadab—His Murder by Baasha—War between Judah and Israel—
Baasha's Alliance with Syria—Asa gains over Ben-hadad—Prophetic
Message to Asa—Resentment of the King—Asa's Religious Decline—
Death of Asa—Death of Baasha—Reign of Elah—His Murder by Zimri
—Omri dethrones Zimri—War between Omri and Tibni—Rebuilding
of Samaria.

(1 KINGS XV. 16–XVI. 28; 2 CHRON. XVI.)

WHILE these things were going on in Judah, the judgment, which the LORD had, through Ahijah, pronounced upon Jeroboam and his house, was rapidly preparing. After an apparently uneventful reign of only two years, Nadab, the son and successor of Jeroboam, was murdered while engaged in the siege of Gibbethon (the *Gabatha* and *Gabothane* of Josephus). This border-city, on the edge of the plain of Esdraelon (not many miles south-west of Nazareth, and originally in the possession of Dan, Josh. xix. 44), must have been of great importance as a defence against incursions from the west—to judge from the circumstance that not only Nadab but his successors sought, although in vain, to wrest it from the Philistines (comp. 1 Kings xvi. 15). No other event in the reign of Nadab is recorded. " He walked in the way of his father, and in his sin," and sudden destruction overtook him. Baasha—probably the leader of a military revolution—murdered him, and usurped his throne. The first measure of the new king was, in true Oriental fashion, to kill the whole family of his predecessor. Although the judgment of God upon Jeroboam and his house, as announced by the prophet, was thus fulfilled, it must not for a moment be thought that the foul deed of Baasha was thereby lessened in guilt. *On the contrary, Holy Scripture expressly marks this crime as one of the grounds of Baasha's later judgment* (1 Kings xvi. 7). It is perhaps not easy, and yet it is of supreme importance for the understanding of the Old Testament, to distinguish in these events the action of man from the overruling direction of God. Thus when, after his accession, the prophet Jehu, the son of Hanani,[1] was commissioned to denounce the sin, and to announce the judgment of Baasha, these two points were clearly put forward in his message : The sin of Baasha in the murder of Jeroboam's house, and the fact that his exaltation was due to the LORD (1 Kings xvi. 7 ; comp. ver. 2).[2]

Baasha had sprung from a tribe wholly undistinguished by warlike achievements,[3] and from a family apparently ignoble and unknown (1 Kings xvi. 2). His only claim to the crown lay in his military prowess, which the neighbouring kingdom of Judah was soon to experience. Under his reign the state of chronic warfare between the two countries once more changed into one of active hostility. From the concordant accounts in the Books of Kings and Chronicles (1 Kings xv. 16–22 ; 2 Chr. xvi. 1–6), we gather what was Baasha's object in this war, and what his preparations for it had been. It seems, that Asa's father, Abijah, had formed an alliance with the rising power of Syria under Tabrimon ("good is Rimmon "),[4] with the view

[1] As to Jehu comp. 2 Chron. xix. 2, 3 ; his death xx. 34. As to Hanani, comp. 2 Chron. xvi. 7–10.

[2] In fact the last clause in 1 Kings xvi. 7 seems added to explain the statement in ver. 2.

[3] The tribe of Issachar ; comp. Gen. xlix. 14, 15. That tribe furnished the Judge Jola (Judg. x. 1).

[4] The god Rimmon—or more probably Hadad-Rimmon, the Sun-god of the Syrians, 2 Kings v. 18. Hadad, "the sun," seems from ancient history to have been a royal title both in Syria and Edom. As stated

of holding Israel in check by placing it between two enemies—
Syria in the north and Judah in the south. This "league"
was, as we infer, discontinued by Asa during the earlier part
of his reign, when his confidence was more entirely placed
in Jehovah his God. In these circumstances Baasha eagerly
sought and entered upon an alliance with Syria. His primary
object was to arrest the migration of Israelites into the kingdom
of Judah, and the growing influence of Asa upon his own
subjects, consequent, as we know, upon his great religious
reformation (1 Kings xv. 17). His secondary object was so
to overawe Jerusalem, as virtually to paralyse the power of
Judah. The invasion was at first successful, and Baasha
penetrated as far as Ramah, about midway between Bethel
and Jerusalem, thus obtaining command of the two roads
which led from the north and the east to the Jewish capital.
This, of course, implied not only the re-conquest of the towns
which Abijah had taken from Israel (2 Chron. xiii. 19 ; comp.
also xv. 8), but the complete isolation and domination of
Jerusalem. Ramah was to be immediately converted into a
strong fortress.

In these straits Asa seems to have forgotten the manner in
which his former brilliant victory over Zerah had been obtained.
Instead of relying wholly on Jehovah his God, he appears to
have imagined that his former policy in regard to Syria had
been a mistake. Like many who, on losing the first freshness
of their faith, seek to combine trust in the LORD with what they
regard as most likely means of worldly success, Asa entered
into a new alliance [1] with Ben-Hadad, purchasing it with the
silver and gold treasured up in the Temple and in the royal

---

in a previous note, there seem to have been four kings of Syria who
bore that name : Hadad-ezer, in time of David ; Hezion (Hadad II.) in
that of Rehoboam ; Tab-Rimmon (Hadad III.) in the time of Abijah ; and
Ben-Hadad (Hadad IV.) in the time of Asa. It is doubtful, whether the
Rezon in the time of Solomon (1 Kings xi. 23–25) was identical with Hezion,
or whether the former was a usurper.

[1] The meaning of 1 Kings xv. 19 is : Let there be a league.

palace. He may have argued, that this did not imply a renunciation of his former allegiance to Jehovah ; that he had no
personal intercourse with Syria, which, indeed, was far separated from his dominions ; that his was only a countermove
to Baasha's schemes; and that a similar league had, during
the reign of his father, proved eminently successful. But the
result of an alliance so incongruous, and purchased in so
dubious a manner, proved the beginning of spiritual declension
and of little honour or real benefit to his country.

Ben-Hadad was only too ready to entertain Asa's proposals.
It could never have been his real policy to strengthen the
neighbour-state of Israel, and to weaken that of Judah. On
receiving the rich bribe, which made Judah virtually tributary
to him, he broke his league with Baasha, and immediately
invaded Israel, overrunning the northern territory, penetrating
as far as the district of Chinneroth (Josh. xi. 2 ; xii. 3 ; xix.
35),—which gave its name to the Lake of Gennesaret,—
and occupying the land of Naphtali. This threatening danger
in the north of his dominions obliged Baasha hastily to quit
Ramah. Asa now summoned all Judah. The materials accumulated for the fortress of Ramah were removed, and used
for building two new forts : Geba ("the height") and Mizpah
("the outlook") (comp. Josh. xviii. 24, 26 ; also Jer. xli. 5–9).
Both these cities lay within the territory of Benjamin, about
three miles to the north of Ramah, in very strong positions,
and commanded the two roads to Jerusalem.

But with the retreat of Baasha from Ramah, the troubles of
Asa did not end ; rather did they only then begin. When, alone
and unaided, he had, in the might of Jehovah, encountered the
hosts of Egypt, signal success had been his ; peace and prosperity had followed ; and God's prophet had been specially sent
to meet the returning army with good and encouraging tidings.
It was all otherwise now. Hanani the prophet was directed to
meet Asa with a message of reproof and judgment ; instead of,
as formerly, peace, there would henceforth be continual warfare
(2 Chron. xvi. 9) ; and the alliance with Syria would prove

neither to honour nor profit. On the other hand, even had his fears been realised, and the combined armies of Israel and Syria invaded Judah, yet if, instead of buying the alliance of Ben-Hadad, he had gone forward in the name of the LORD, victory such as that over the Ethiopians would again have been his (2 Chron. xvi. 7). As it was, Asa had chosen a worldly policy, and by its issue he must abide. Henceforth it was no more Jehovah Who was arrayed against the might of man, but the contest would be simply one of cunning and strength, as between man and man (2 Chron. xvi. 9).

Hanani had spoken, as all the prophets of Jehovah, fearlessly, faithfully, and only too truly. It was probably conviction of this which, in the unhumbled state of the king, kindled his anger against "the seer." Once more it might seem to Asa as not implying rebellion against God, only a necessary precaution against disunion and dissatisfaction among his own subjects, threatening to upset his political calculations and combinations, to use measures of severity against the prophet from which he would have shrunk at a former period of his reign. All the more requisite might these appear, since his unwelcome monitor evidently commanded the sympathies of an influential part of the community. But it was an unheard-of proceeding, which happily found imitation only in the worst times of Israel (1 Kings xxii. 26–29; Jer. xx. 2; xxix. 26; Acts xvi. 24), to put the prophet of the LORD "in the house of stocks"[1] on account of his faithfulness, and by a series of persecutions to oppress, and, if possible, crush[2] those who sympathised with him.

Nor was this all. The fatal tendency which had showed itself in the Syrian alliance, and still more in the measures

---

[1] Two terms are used in Hebrew for "the stocks." That here employed combined the pillory for the body with the stocks for the legs. It was, in fact, an instrument of torture, the neck and arms being confined, and the body in a bent position.

[2] The verb really means "to crush." It is generally used in connection with cruel oppression, as in Deut. xxviii. 33; 1 Sam. xii. 3, etc.

against Hanani and his sympathisers, continued and increased
with the lapse of years. Two years before his death, Asa was
attacked by some disease[1] in his feet. In this "also"[2] "he
sought not Jehovah but in (by) the physicians."[3] It is not
necessary to explain the blame which Holy Scripture evidently
attaches to this, on the ground that these physicians were
so called "medicine-men" (as among the heathen), nor to
suppose that they used idolatrous or even superstitious means.
The example of Hezekiah (2 Kings xx. ; 2 Chron. xxxii. 24)
sufficiently shows, how one who fully trusted in the LORD
would have felt and acted in these circumstances. On the
other hand, Asa displayed in this instance the same want of
practical religion as in his alliance with Syria—a state of mind
which Bengel rightly characterises as theoretical orthodoxy
combined with practical atheism. And—as formerly the prophet had summed up what Asa had no doubt regarded as the
height of political wisdom in the curt, if somewhat harsh,
criticism : "Thou hast acted stupidly over this " (2 Chron. xvi.
9)—so might it have been said of him in this matter also.
He had not sought Jehovah, but had sought in the physicians
—and by the help which he had sought he must abide. He
had not trusted in the supernatural, but applied to the natural :
and in the natural course of events his disease ended in death.
It was not wrong to employ means, indeed such were used in
the miraculous cure of Hezekiah (2 Kings xx. 7), just as in
the miraculous rescue of St. Paul's companions from shipwreck
(Acts xxvii. 23, 24, 43, 44). And, if one lesson more than
another has been impressed on our minds in the course of this
history, it is that of the use of natural means, in the ordinary

---

[1] According to the Talmud (*Sotah* 10 *a*) it was the gout.

[2] So 2 Chron. xvi. 12 literally.

[3] It deserves to be noticed that, when the true seeking of Jehovah is referred
to, the original uses simply the accusative, as if to indicate the directness of
the address ; while in all spurious enquiries or requests the preposition *in*
or *by* is employed, as if, while marking the means by which the object is
sought, at the same time to indicate that any result still comes only from God.
For, the Hebrew may be designated as the only theologically true language.

and rational succession of events, for the accomplishment of supernatural and Divinely-announced purposes. But the error and sin of Asa consisted in seeking an object, however lawful and even desirable, in, by, and through secondary means, without first seeking Jehovah. Such conduct carried with it its natural result. For, what a man soweth, that—the very kind of grain—shall he also reap ; just as, none the less, that we work for it (or perhaps have it supplied to our hands), but on the contrary, all the more because of it, we first pray : "Give us this day our daily bread," and then receive as directly from His hand the consecrated fruit of our labour.

There was the same sad consistency about Asa's death as in his life. He seems to have built him a special mausoleum in the city of David ; and there they laid him in almost Egyptian pomp on a bed of spices, and burnt at his burying, whether for the first time in royal funerals, or according to a more ancient practice,[1] a large quantity of costly spices and perfumes.

But in following the narrative of Holy Scripture, we have been really anticipating the course of this history. For, as previously stated, Asa not only outlived Baasha, but altogether saw eight kings on the throne of Israel. Baasha seems to have survived his defeat little more than a year. He was succeeded by his son Elah, in the twenty-sixth year of King Asa's reign. The rule of Elah lasted only two years, or, more exactly, part of two years. Baasha had set the example of military revolutions, in which the favourite of the soldiery ascended the throne by the murder of his predecessor, and the extirpation of all who might have rival claims to the crown. The precedent was a dangerous one ; and henceforth the throne of Israel was occupied by a series of military adventurers, whose

---

[1] The former seems to me the most probable. It need scarcely be said that the heathen practice of *cremation* was unknown. On this subject, and on the burning of spices at such funerals, comp. Geier, *De Ebræorum Luctu*, pp. 104–119. According to Rabbinical writings, Asa was one of the model-kings.

line did not extend beyond their immediate successors. The son of Baasha was a cowardly debauchee, who, forgetful even of the decorum of Eastern princes, indulged in orgies in the houses of his favourites, while his army was fighting before Gibbethon. He fell a victim to a court conspiracy. We know only two of the actors in it : Arza, the steward of the king's palace (or rather, his *major-domo*), in whose house Elah was drinking himself drunk, and the king's murderer and successor Zimri, who filled the post of chief over half his "chariots," or perhaps his cavalry. The reign of Zimri lasted only seven days, but they were stained by even more than the bloodshed usual on such occasions. For Zimri destroyed not only the family of his predecessor, but killed all the "blood-avengers" (relatives, kinsfolk), and even "the friends" of the late king.

Whether, as Josephus explains (*Ant.* viii. 12, 4), Zimri had chosen for his rebellion the moment when all the leading officers were in camp, or Omri himself was originally in the conspiracy, certain it is that the army was not disposed to acknowledge the new usurper. It immediately proclaimed their general Omri, and under his leadership marched back upon Tirzah. Zimri held out till the city was taken, when he retired into "the citadel of the king's palace,"[1] which he set on fire, perishing in its flames. But Omri had not at first undisputed possession of the throne. For four years the people were divided between him and another pretender to the crown, Tibni, the son of Genath. At length Omri prevailed, and "Tibni died"—either in battle or, as Josephus seems to imply (*Ant.* viii. 12, 5), by command of his rival.

Omri occupied the throne altogether twelve (or part of twelve) years. The first four of these passed in contests with Tibni. During the next two years he resided in Tirzah. After that he bought from Shemer for two talents of silver (about £780) the hill of Samaria. On this commanding position he built the new capital of Israel, which, according to the sacred text, he named

---

[1] This is the correct rendering of the original.

Shomeron,[1] after the former owner of the site. But on other grounds it deserved to be called "watch-mountain," as the name may be rendered. Situated about the centre of the land, six miles north-west of Shechem, it occupied a commanding hill, rising from a broad valley, and surrounded on all sides by mountains, through which there was only a narrow entrance from the west. The approach to the plateau on which Samaria stood is steep on all sides. Thus the site of the new capital, which was also distinguished by great beauty, was singularly adapted both for observation and defence. The country around was very rich, and the place well supplied with water. A more suitable spot could not have been chosen by monarch or general. This accounts for the continued importance of Samaria through all the varying fortunes of the country and its people. The modern miserable village of *Sebustiyeh* (the ancient *Sebaste*), inhabited by less than one thousand people, which occupies the site of the once splendid city, where Omri, Ahab, and their successors held high court, contains but few remains of its ancient grandeur. But these are sufficiently remarkable.[2] The ancient Acropolis, or temple, palace, and citadel, seems to have stood on the western brow of the hill, and its site is still marked by the ruins of a most magnificent colonnade composed of graceful monoliths. The approach to the castle must have been by ascending terraces, which, no doubt, were covered with houses and palaces. Of these not a trace is left. Only on the topmost height—from which, west-wards, the Mediterranean, and eastwards, across swelling mountains, a landscape of unrivalled beauty and fertility were full in view—a few broken and upturned pillars mark the site of the royal castle. The dynasties that reigned

[1] It is remarkable that in the older Assyrian monuments the city is still denominated as that of Omri, its later name appearing only in the time of Tiglath-pileser, nearly two hundred years after its building by Omri. This is a noteworthy confirmation of the Scriptural narrative. According to tradition, John the Baptist was buried in Samaria.

[2] See the very full description by M. Guérin (*La Samarie*, vol. ii. pages 188–210).

there have long been swept away; the people over whom they ruled carried into a captivity over which the veil of impenetrable mystery lies.   Only the word of the LORD has stood firm and immovable.   Of Nadab, of Baasha, of Elah, of Zimri, and of Omri, Scripture has only one and the same thing to say: that they walked in the way and in the sin of Jeroboam, the son of Nebat, "wherewith he made Israel to sin, to provoke Jehovah, the God of Israel, to anger."   And over each and all did the same judgment sweep.   And yet there were more grievous sins to follow, and more terrible judgments to come.[1]

<center>~~~~~~</center>

CHAPTER XIV.

ASA AND JEHOSHAPHAT (*3rd and 4th*) KINGS OF JUDAH—AHAB (*8th*) KING OF ISRAEL.

Accession of Ahab—Further Religious Decline in Israel—Political Relations between Israel and Judah—Accession of Jehoshaphat—Ahab's marriage with Jezebel—The Worship of Baal and Astarte established in Israel— Character of Ahab—Religious Reforms in Judah—Jehoshaphat joins affinity with Ahab—Marriage of Jehoram with Athaliah, and its consequences.

(1 KINGS XVI. 29-33; XXII. 41-44; 2 CHRON. XVII.; XVIII. 1, 2.)

OMRI was succeeded on the throne of Israel by his son Ahab, in the thirty-eighth year of the reign of Asa, king of Judah With the accession of Ahab a new period may be said to commence in the history of Israel, and this alike religiously and politically.   In regard to the former, Omri had already prepared the way for further terrible progression in Israel's

---

[1] The Talmud (*Sanh.* 102 *b*) asks whether Omri was worthy of the kingdom—the answer being, that he added a city to the land of Israel.

apostasy. In the language of Holy Scripture (1 Kings xvi. 25), he "did worse than all that were before him." Whatever the special "statutes" or ordinances in this respect which he introduced, they marked an era in the history of Israel's religious decline (Micah vi. 16). But Ahab far out-distanced even his father's wickedness, first by entering into a matrimonial alliance with the vile dynasty of Ethbaal, and then by formally making the worship of Baal the established religion of Israel, with all of vileness and of persecution which this implied. In these circumstances, surely, we may look for extraordinary interposition on the part of Jehovah. For, with such a king and queen, and with a people, not only deprived of the Temple-services and the Levitical priesthood, but among whom the infamous rites of Baal and Astarte had become the established worship, ordinary means would manifestly have been in vain. Again and again had messengers sent from God spoken His Word and announced His judgments, without producing even a passing effect. It needed more than this, if the worship of Baal was to be effectually checked. Accordingly, this period of Israel's history is also marked by a great extension of the Prophetic order and mission. It was theirs to keep alive the knowledge of Jehovah in the land; theirs also to meet the gross and daring idolatry of king and people by a display of *power* which could neither be resisted nor gainsaid. Hence the unparalleled frequency of miracles, mostly intended to prove the vainness of idols as against the power of the Living God, the reality of the prophets' mission, and of the authority which the LORD had delegated to His messengers. Only thus could any effect be produced. It was an extraordinary period—and God raised up in it an extraordinary agency. We have already indicated that, in general, considering the notions and expectations of the times, miracles might almost be said to have been God's ordinary mode of teaching the men of that age. This holds specially true of the period now under consideration. Hence the unusual accumulation of the miraculous—and that chiefly in its aspect of power—as displayed by an Elijah and an Elisha, so far from seeming strange or unaccountable, appears eminently called for.

Politically speaking also, this was a period of great change. For, whereas hitherto the two kingdoms of Israel and Judah had been in a state of constant warfare, an alliance between them was now formed. At first, indeed, it seemed otherwise. As Ahab ascended the throne of Israel during the lifetime of Asa, the relations between the two kingdoms continued as before. And when, in the fourth year of King Ahab's reign, Jehoshaphat succeeded his father Asa (1 Kings xxii. 41), it appeared as if the prospect of an alliance between the sister-countries were more remote than ever. Jehoshaphat began his reign by strengthening the defences of his country against Israel (2 Chron. xvii. 1, 2). His religious measures were in the opposite direction from those of Ahab. Himself earnestly and decidedly pious, it is expressly stated that he walked "not after the doings of Israel." On the other hand, Ahab entered, probably at the beginning of his reign, into an alliance with the most wicked dynasty then in power, by marrying Jezebel,[1] the daughter of Ethbaal (or Ithobalus, "Baal is with him"). Josephus has preserved to us the history of this royal family (*Against Ap.* i. 18). It appears that Ethbaal was originally the High-priest of the great temple of Astarte in Tyre; that he murdered his king, and usurped the throne, which he occupied for thirty-two years; and that his dynasty continued for at least sixty-two years after his death. These notices will sufficiently explain the upbringing of Jezebel. A clever, strong, bold, and unscrupulous woman, she was by conviction a devotee to the most base and revolting idolatry which the world has ever known, combining with this the reckless contempt of the rights and consciences of others, and the utter indifference as to the means employed, which characterise the worst aspect of Eastern despotism. That she would hate the religion of Jehovah, and

---

[1] The classical student will be interested to know that Jezebel was the grand-aunt of Dido, the founder of Carthage. The notices in Josephus are taken from Menander.

seek utterly to destroy it—and, indeed, whatever would not bend to her imperious will; that she would prove the implacable foe of all that was pious or even free in Israel; and that she would not shrink from the wholesale murder of those who resisted or opposed her, follows almost as a matter of course. Yet, strange as it may sound, there is something grand about this strong, determined, bold woman, which appears all the more strikingly from its contrast with her husband. Jezebel was every inch a Queen—though of the type of the Phœnician Priest-King who had usurped the throne by murder.

The immediate consequence of this ill-fated union was, that the religion of Jezebel became the worship of the land of Israel. Ahab built in Samaria a temple to "the Baal"[1]—the Sun-god (the producing principle in Nature)—in which he erected not only an altar, but, as we gather from 2 Kings iii. 2; x. 27, also one of those pillars which were distinctive of its vile services. As usual, where these rites were fully carried out, he also "made the Asherah"[2]—Astarte, the Moon-goddess (the receptive principle in Nature)—so that the Phœnician worship was now established in its entirety. As we infer from later notices, there was a "vestry" attached to these temples, where special festive garments, worn on great occasions, were kept (2 Kings x. 22). Ahab—or perhaps rather Jezebel—appointed not less than 450 priests of Baal and 400 of Asherah, who were supported by the bounty of the queen (1 Kings xviii. 19; xxii. 6). The forced introduction of this new worship led to a systematic persecution of the prophets, and even of the openly professed worshippers of Jehovah, which had their complete extermination for its object (1 Kings xviii. 13; xix. 10; 2 Kings ix. 7).

[1] With the article—the supreme Phœnician and Assyrian deity, worshipped under different designations throughout that part of Asia. The critical study of the mythology of these countries has yielded many interesting results, and shown, with striking similarities in designation of the deity, the most absolute contrast to the religion of Jehovah as regards doctrine and life, so as to bring the heavenly origin of the latter into marked prominence.

[2] *Not* as in the Authorised Version (1 Kings xvi. 33): "And Ahab made a grove."

These measures were wholly due to the absolute power which Jezebel exercised over her husband. Left to himself, Ahab might have yielded to better influences (comp. 1 Kings xviii. 39–46; xx. 13, etc.; xxi. 27–29). Altogether Ahab presents a strange, though by no means uncommon mixture of the good and the evil, the noble and the mean, issuing finally not in decision for God and what was right and true, but in the triumph of evil, to his own destruction and that of his race. For he possessed qualities which, if directed by the fear of God, might have made him even a great king. He was at times brave, even chivalrous (comp. for example 1 Kings xx. 11, and even verse 32); royal in his tastes and undertakings (1 Kings xxii. 39; 2 Chron. xviii. 2); and ready, under temporary emotion, to yield to the voice of conscience. But all this was marred by fatal weakness, selfishness, uncontrolled self-indulgence, an utter want of religion, and especially the influence of his wife, so that in the language of Holy Scripture he "sold himself to work wickedness in the sight of Jehovah," incited thereto by his wife Jezebel (1 Kings xxi. 25).

While these influences were at work in Israel, Jehoshaphat, encouraged by the blessing which rested on his kingdom, once more vigorously resumed the work of religious reformation in Judah (2 Chron. xvii. 6–9). Not only did he take away the "high places and groves," but, in the third year of his reign,[1] he sent five of his princes, accompanied by nine of the principal Levites and two priests, throughout the towns of Judah to teach the people the Law—no doubt the Pentateuch,[2] of which they took with them an authorised copy. The actual instruction would unquestionably be committed to the priestly members of this commission (comp. Lev. x. 11; Deut. xvii. 8, 9), whilst the presence of the princes would not only secure the authority of the teachers and the efficiency of their work, but also be

---

[1] It has been ingeniously suggested (by Hitzig), that this was a Year of Jubilee, viz. 912 B.C.

[2] Thus the Pentateuch in its present form circulated ten centuries before the time of our LORD.

requisite for civil purposes, since the Law of Moses affected many of the social relations of life, and accordingly required for its enforcement the authority of the magistrates. Once more signal marks of the Divine approbation followed. Some of the Philistine chiefs rendered voluntary homage to Jehoshaphat; the Arab tribes, whom Asa had subdued during his pursuit of Zerah, the Ethiopian, again paid their tribute; new castles for the defence of the country were built, "store-cities" provided, and the various towns provisioned;[1] while a large army was ready prepared,[2] of which the five chiefs resided in Jerusalem, to be under the personal orders of the king.[3]

It was in circumstances of such marked prosperity that Jehoshaphat "joined affinity with Ahab." The sacred text specially notes this (2 Chron. xviii. 1), partly to show that Jehoshaphat had not even an excuse for such a step, and partly, as we think, to indicate that this alliance must, in the first place, have been sought by Ahab. The motives which would influence the King of Israel are not difficult to understand. The power of the country had been greatly weakened by Syria during the reign of Omri. Not only had Ben-Hadad possessed himself of a number of cities, both east (Ramoth-Gilead, for example) and west of the Jordan, but the country had become virtually subject to him, since he claimed even in the capital, Samaria, the right of having "streets," or rather "squares," that is, Syrian quarters of the town, which owned his dominion (comp. 1 Kings xx. 34). And now Ben-Hadad had been succeeded by a son of the same name, equally warlike

[1] This seems the real meaning of the Hebrew, and not "much business," as in the Authorised Version of 2 Chron. xvii. 13.

[2] A very ingenious defence of the accuracy of the numbers of this army has been lately attempted. But to us these numerals seem corrupt, though it is impossible in this place to furnish proof for the assertion. Probably they were illegible or blotted out, and the copyist seems to have supplied the two first from chap. xiv. 8, while the other three were formed by deducting 100,000 from each of them. The sum total is *double* that of chapter xiv. 8.

[3] This seems to be the true meaning of the Hebrew text.

and ambitious. In these circumstances it was of the utmost importance to Ahab to secure permanent peace on his southern or Judæan frontier, and, if possible, to engage as an active ally so powerful and wealthy a monarch as Jehoshaphat. On the other hand, it is not so easy to perceive the reasons which influenced the King of Judah. Of course he could not have wished to see the power of Syria paramount so close to his borders. Did he, besides, desire to have the long-standing (seventy years') breach between Judah and Israel healed? Had he a dim hope that, by the marriage of his son with the daughter of Ahab, the two realms might again be joined, and an undivided kingdom once more established in the house of David? Or did he only allow himself to be carried along by events, too weak to resist, and too confident to dread evil? We can only make these suggestions, since the sacred text affords no clue to this political riddle.

It was, as we reckon, about the eighth year of Jehoshaphat's reign, and consequently about the twelfth of that of Ahab, that Jehoram, the son of Jehoshaphat—then a lad of about fifteen or sixteen years—was married to Athaliah, the daughter of Ahab and Jezebel (2 Chron. xxi. 6).[1] Jehoshaphat lived to see some

---

[1] We arrive at this conclusion as follows : When eight or nine years later — that is, in the seventeenth year of Jehoshaphat, the latter paid his memorable visit to Ahab (1 Kings xxii. 2), Ahaziah, the son of Jehoram, must have been already about eight or nine years old, since he ascended the throne about thirteen years later, after the death of his grandfather and his father, at the age of twenty-two (2 Kings viii. 26). But it must be admitted that the chronology of these reigns is involved and somewhat difficult. Indeed, a perfect agreement is impossible. For the dates are given not according to any *fixed* standard (such as the Creation, or the Birth of Christ), but according to the reigns of the various kings. But, according to Jewish practice, a year of a king's reign is counted from *Nisan* (April) to *Nisan*, so that any time before or after Nisan would be counted as an integral year. Thus a prince who ascended the throne in *Adar* (March) of one year and died in *Ijar* (May) of the next, although only reigning fourteen months, would be said to have reigned *three years*. This difference, when applied to the reigns of the various kings, or to a comparison between the dates of the kings of Israel and Judah, constitutes one of the main practical difficulties in establishing a perfect agreement.

of the bitter fruits of the rash and unholy alliance which he had sanctioned. Eight or nine years later, he went on that visit to Ahab which led to the disastrous war with Syria, in which Ahab himself perished (2 Chron. xviii.). Then followed the joint maritime expedition of Jehoshaphat and the son of Ahab, which ended in loss. But the worst was to come after the death of Jehoshaphat. His son and successor, the husband of Athaliah, introduced in Judah the idolatry of his wife, and brought shame and loss upon his people. The next occupant of the throne—the son of Athaliah—followed the example of his father, and perished by command of Jehu. Lastly came the terrible tragedy of the wholesale murder of the royal princes by Athaliah, then her reign, and finally her tragic death.

It was not by means such as those which Jehoshaphat employed that good could come to Judah, the breach be healed between the severed tribes, the kingdom of David restored, or even peace and righteousness return to Israel. But already God had been preparing a new instrumentality to accomplish His own purposes. A Voice would be raised loud enough to make itself heard to the ends of the land; a Hand, strong enough not only to resist the power of Ahab and Jezebel, but to break that of Baal in the land. And all this not by worldly might or craftiness, but by the manifestation of the power of Jehovah as the Living God.[1]

---

[1] A few Talmudic notices about Ahab may here find a place. They are chiefly derived from the Tractate *Sanhedrin* (102 *b*—103 *b*). His outward prosperity, and enjoyment of the pleasures of this world in contrast with those of the next, are emphatically dwelt upon. He is characterised as naturally cold and weak—his sinfulness being chiefly ascribed to his wife ; hence this proverb : He who walks in the counsel of his wife will fall into Gehenna (*Baba Mez.* 59). The heaviest sins of Jeroboam had only been like the lightest of Ahab ; in fact, he was guilty of all kinds of idolatry, and even inscribed on the gates of Samaria : Ahab denies the God of Israel ! Nevertheless he was allowed to reign twenty-two years because he had shown respect to the Law (as in the embassy of Ben-Hadad to him, in his temporary repentance, etc.), the Law being written with twenty-two letters (which constitute the Hebrew alphabet). Ahab was one of those who were supposed to have no part in the world to come. To dream of King Ahab was an evil omen (*Ber.* 57 *b*).

CHAPTER XV.

AHAB, (*8th*) KING OF ISRAEL.

Rebuilding of Jericho—The Mission of Elijah—His Character and Life—
Elijah's First Appearance—Parallelism with Noah, Moses, and John
the Baptist—Elijah's Message to King Ahab—Sojourn by the Brook
Cherith—Elijah with the Widow of Sarepta—The Barrel of Meal wastes
not, nor does the Cruse of Oil fail—Lessons of his Sojourn—Sickness
and Death of the Widow's Son—He is miraculously restored to life.

(1 KINGS XVI. 34–XVII.)

WITH the enthronement of Ahab and Jezebel, the establishment of the worship of Baal as the state-religion, and
the attempted extermination of the prophets and followers of
the LORD, the apostasy of Israel had reached its high point.
As if to mark alike the general disregard in Israel of the
threatened judgments of God, and the coming vindication
of Jehovah's Kingship, Holy Scripture here inserts a notice
of the daring rebuilding of the walls of Jericho, and of the
literal fulfilment of Joshua's curse upon its builder [1] (1 Kings
xvi. 34; comp. Josh. vi. 26). Indeed, the land was now ripe
for the sickle of judgment. Yet as the long-suffering of God
had waited in the days of Noah, so in those of Ahab; and as
then the preacher of righteousness had raised the voice of
warning, while giving evidence of the coming destruction, so
was Elijah now commissioned to present to the men of his
age in symbolic deed the alternative of serving Jehovah or Baal,
with all that the choice implied. The difference between Noah

---

[1] Jericho seems to have belonged to Ahab. On its rebuilding see Vol.
III. of this History, p. 66. The remarks of the Talmud on the subject
(*Sanh.* 113 *a*) are, to say the least, very far-fetched.

and Elijah was only that of times and circumstances : the one was before, the other after the giving of the Law; the one was sent into an apostate world, the other to an apostatising covenant-people. But there is also another aspect of the matter. On the one side were arrayed Ahab, Jezebel, Baal, and Israel—on the other stood Jehovah. It was a question of reality and of power : and Elijah was to be, so to speak, the embodiment of the Divine Power, the Minister of the Living and True God. The contest between them could not be decided by words, but by deeds. The Divine would become manifest in its reality and irresistible greatness, and whoever or whatever came in contact with it would, for good or for evil, experience its Presence. We might almost say, that in his prophetic capacity Elijah was an impersonal being—the mere medium of the Divine. Throughout his history other prophets also were employed on various occasions : he only to do what none other had ever done or could do. His path was alone, such as none other had trodden nor could tread. He was the impersonation of the Old Testament in one of its aspects : that of grandeur and judgment—the living realisation of the topmost height of the mount, which burned with fire, around which lightnings played and thunder rolled, and from out of whose terrible glory spake the Voice of Jehovah, the God of Israel. We have the highest authority for saying that he was the type of John the Baptist. But chiefly in this respect, that he lifted the axe to the root of the tree, yet, ere it fell, called for fruits meet for repentance. He was not the forerunner of the Lord, save in judgment; he was the forerunner of the King, not of the Kingdom; and the destruction of the state and people of Israel, not the salvation of the world, followed upon his announcement.

A grander figure never stood out even against the Old Testament sky than that of Elijah. As Israel's apostasy had reached its highest point in the time of Ahab, so the Old Testament antagonism to it in the person and mission of Elijah. The analogy and parallelism between his history and that of Moses, even to minute details, is obvious on comparison of the two ;[1] and accordingly we find him, significantly, along with Moses on the Mount of Transfiguration. Yet much as Scripture tells of him, we feel that we have only dim outlines of his prophetic greatness before us. By his side other men, even an Elisha, seem small. As we view him as Jehovah's representative, almost plenipotentiary, we recall his unswerving faithfulness to, and absolutely fearless discharge of his trust. And yet this strong man had his hours of felt weakness and loneliness, as when he fled before Ahab and Jezebel, and would fain have laid him down to die in the wilderness. As we recall his almost unlimited power, we remember that its spring was in constant prayer. As we think of his unbending sternness, of his sharp irony on Mount Carmel, of his impassioned zeal, and of his unfaltering severity, we also remember that deep in his heart soft and warm feelings glowed, as when he made himself the guest of the poor widow, and by agonising prayer brought back her son to life. Such as this must have been intended by God, in His mercy, as an outlet and precious relief to his feelings, showing him that all his work and mission were not of sorrow and judgment, but that the joy of Divine comfort was his also. And truly human, full of intense pathos, are those days of wilderness-journey, and those hours on Mount Horeb, when in deepest sadness of soul the strong man, who but yesterday had defiantly met Ahab and achieved on Mount Carmel such triumph as none other, bent and was shaken, like the reed in the storm. A life this full of contrasts—of fierce light and deep shadows—not a happy, joyous, prosperous life ; not one even streaked with peace or gladness, but wholly devoted to God : a bush on the wilderness-mount, burning yet not consumed. A life full of the miraculous it is

---

[1] Jewish tradition extols him almost to blasphemy, to show how absolutely God had delegated to Elijah His power—or, as the Rabbis express it : His three keys—those of rain, of children, and of raising to life. With special application of Hos. xii. 13 to Moses and Elijah, Jewish tradition traces a very minute and instructive parallelism between the various incidents in the lives of Moses and Elijah (*Yalkut* vol. ii. p. 32. *d*).

and must be, from the character of his mission—and yet himself one of the greatest wonders in it, and the success of his mission the best attestation of, because the greatest of the miracles of his history. For, alone and unaided, save of God, he *did* conquer in the contest, and he *did* break the power of Baal in Israel.

His first appearance—alike in the manner and suddenness of it—was emblematic of all that was to follow. Of his birth and early circumstances, we know next to nothing. Josephus assumes (*Ant.* viii. 13, 2) that the Tishbah which gave him his name (1 Kings xvii. 1) lay on the eastern side of Jordan, in the land of Gilead; and some modern writers have found the name in the village of *Tisieh*, to the south of Busrah. But this view has been shown (by Keil) to be untenable. Even more fanciful is the suggestion, that the Hebrew expression means that he was "a stranger among the strangers of Gilead" —possibly a Gentile by birth. Most likelihood attaches to the generally received view, that his birthplace was the Tishbi in Upper Galilee (within the territory of Naphtali), known to us from apocryphal story (Tobit i, 2, LXX) — and that, for some unascertained reason, he had migrated into Gilead, without, however, becoming one of its citizens. This the sacred text conveys by the expression, " Elijah the Tishbite from among the dwellers (strangers dwelling) in Gilead." Another inference as to his character may be drawn from his name *Elijah:* My God . Jehovah! though it is scarcely necessary to say that he did not assume it himself.[1]

With the same, or perhaps with even more startling unexpectedness and strangeness than that which characterised the appearance of John the Baptist—and with precisely the same object in it—Elijah suddenly presented himself in Samaria and

[1] Later Jewish tradition has represented him as of priestly descent, presumably on account of his sacrifice on Mount Carmel. But even so the illegality of a sacrifice outside Jerusalem would require special vindication. Even Jewish legalism, however, admits the plea of exceptional necessity in this instance. Tradition represents Elijah as a disciple of Ahijah, the Shilonite.

before Ahab.   It was, and intended to be—to adapt the figure of the Son of Sirach (Ecclus. xlviii. 1)—like a fire that kindled suddenly, like a torch that blazed up in the still darkness of the night.   There was, indeed, sufficient here to rouse the dullest mind.   We can imagine the stern figure of the Tishbite, arrayed in an upper garment of black camel's hair [1]—which henceforth seems to have become the distinctive garb of the prophets (Zechar. xiii. 4)—girt about his loins with a leathern girdle.   The dress betokened poverty, renunciation of the world, mourning, almost stern judgment, while the girdle, which, as the badge of office, was always the richest part of the dress, was such as only the poorest of the land wore.   It was an unwonted sight, and, as he made his way up through the terraced streets of rich luxurious Samaria, its inhabitants would whisper with awe that this was a new prophet come from the wilds of Gilead, and follow him.   What a contrast between those Baal-debauched Samaritans and this man ; what a greater contrast still between the effeminate decrepit priests of Baal, in their white linen garments and high-pointed bonnets,[2] and this stern prophet of Jehovah !   And now he had reached the height where palace and castle stand, and met Ahab himself, perhaps at the magnificent entrance to that splendid colonnade which overlooked such a scene of beauty and fertility.   His message to the king was abrupt and curt, as became the cir-cumstances [3]—after all, only a repetition of Jehovah's denun-ciation of judgment upon an apostate people (Lev. xxvi. 19,

---

[1] The rendering, 2 Kings i. 8, "a hairy man" is incorrect.   The ex-pression means a man arrayed in a hairy garment—as we gather, of black camel's hair.

[2] This was the official dress of the priests of Baal.

[3] The Talmud (*Sanh.* 113. *a*) mars the whole subject by a discussion, at the close of which Elijah's words are introduced.   Both he and King Ahab are supposed to have come on a visit of condolence to Hiel, after the death of his children (1 Kings xvi. 34).   Elijah explains that this terrible calamity was the consequence of the neglect of Joshua's warning, to which Ahab objects that it was incredible the disciple's word should become true, if the master's were not.   But since the threatening of Moses in regard to idolatry had not been fulfilled, he could not believe in the warning of Joshua.   Upon this Elijah bursts into the words mentioned in the text.

etc. ; Deut. xi. 16, etc. ; xxviii. 23, etc. ; comp. 1 Kings viii. 35 ; Amos iv. 7) ; but with this addition, that the cessation of dew and rain should last these years—whether many or few —" except" by his word. This latter perhaps was intended to emphasize the impotence of Ahab's prophets and priests as against Jehovah.

It was all most startling : the sudden, strange, wild apparition ; the bold confronting of king and people there in Samaria ; the announcement apparently so incredible in itself, and in such contrast to the scene of wealth and fruitfulness all around ; the unexpected pronunciation of the name Jehovah in such a place ; the authority which he pleaded and the power which he claimed—in general, even the terms of his message : " Lives Jehovah, the God of Israel, which I stand before His Face ! If there be these years dew or rain, except by the mouth (the spoken means) of my word !" [1] What answer Ahab made, what impression it produced on him or his people, Holy Scripture, in its Divine self-consciousness and sublime indifference to what may be called " effect," does not condescend even to notice. Nay, here also silence is best— and the prophet himself must withdraw as suddenly as he had come, hide himself from human ken, not be within reach of question or answer, and let God work, alone and unseen. An absolute pause with that thunder-cloud overhead—unremoved and apparently unremovable—in presence of which man and Baal shall be absolutely powerless : such was the fitting sequence to Elijah's announcement.

Elijah's first direction was to the Wady Cherith—probably east of the Jordan [2]—one of those many wide water-courses which drain into the river of Palestine. In this wild solitude, like Moses, nay, like our LORD Himself, he was to be alone with God—to plead for Israel, and to prepare for his further

[1] So in strict literality.

[2] This appears probable from the Hebrew expression rendered in the Authorised Version " before Jordan," but meaning literally, "in face of Jordan."

work. So long as water was left in the brook—for there is nothing needlessly miraculous, even in the story of Elijah— and so long as Jehovah had such strange provisioners as "the ravens"[1] to act as His messengers — for there is nothing that is merely natural in this history, and the miraculous always appears by the side of the natural,—the prophet would not want needed support. In this also there were lessons of deepest significance to Elijah (compare as to God's strange messengers, Job xxxvii. 10; Psa. lxxviii. 23; Isa. v. 6; Amos ix. 3). When in the course of time the waters of Cherith failed, owing to the long drought, Elijah was directed to go to Zarephath (*Sarepta*, Luke iv. 26 [2]), where God had "commanded" for him even a more strange provisioner than the ravens : a poor, almost famishing widow, and she a Gentile![3]

Here again everything is significant. Sarepta was not only a heathen city, outside the bounds of Israel, midway between Sidon and Tyre, but actually within the domains of Jezebel's father. The prophet, who was not safe from Jezebel in Israel, would be safe within Jezebel's own country; he for whom Ahab had so earnestly but vainly searched, not only throughout his own land, but in all neighbouring countries (1 Kings xviii.

---

[1] Surely, it is one of the strangest freaks of criticism (Jewish and Christian) to make of these "ravens" either "Arabs," or "merchants," or "Orebites," from a supposed town of Oreb. We can understand the difficulty of the Rabbis, arising from the circumstance that Elijah should be fed by ravens, which were unclean animals. Those of them who take the literal translation comfort themselves with the fact, that the ravens at least brought him levitically clean food, either from one of the 7000 in Israel who had not bent the knee to Baal, or from the table of Ahab, or from that of Jehoshaphat. But these Rabbinical comments are so far evidential of the truth of this narrative, that we see how differently a later writer would have constructed this history, had he invented a Jewish legend. Hess adduces parallel instances of the support of people by wild beasts ; but they are of little interest, since the provision for Elijah was manifestly miraculous.

[2] Corresponding to the modern village of *Surafend*, though the latter seems farther from the sea than the ancient Sarepta.

[3] The Rabbis represent her as a Jewess, and make her the mother of Jonah.

10), would be securely concealed in the land most hostile to Elijah's mission, and most friendly to Ahab's purposes. But there are even deeper lessons. It is only one of these, that, cast out of his own country and by his own people, God can find a safe refuge for His servant in most unlikely circumstances; and that, when faith seems to fail, where most we might have expected it, God will show that He has His own where least we would look for them. Again, the reference of our LORD to this history (Luke iv. 25), shows these three things: that the entertainment of Elijah was a distinguishing honour conferred on the widow of Sarepta; that it proved of real spiritual benefit to her (as will be shown in the course of this history); and that it implied, that God had purposes of grace beyond the narrow bounds of Israel, unbelieving as it was—in the language of St. Paul, that He was not the God of the Jews only, but also of the Gentiles (Rom. iii. 29). May we not go a step farther, and see in this mission of Elijah to, and entertainment by a heathen widow, an anticipation at least of the announcement of that "Kingdom of God" in its world-wide bearing, which formed part of the message of his antitype, John the Baptist?

Once more the support of Elijah, though miraculous, was to be secured in the course of natural and easily intelligible events. Yet withal, as it had been Jehovah Who "commanded"[1] the ravens, so it was He also Who "commanded" the widow of Sarepta, all unconscious as she was of it, to sustain Elijah. But how should the prophet recognise her? He must go, trusting to God's direction, and, watching such natural indications as would appear, be guided to whither he was supernaturally sent. Arrived at the gate of Sarepta, he saw a widow, whose poverty was evidenced by her searching for a little brushwood. Was she the woman who would sustain him? There was a preliminary test ready to hand. She must have recognised the stranger by his dress as a

---

[1] The Rabbis note, that, when God is said to have "commanded" the ravens. He put it in their heart—a gloss this of manifold application.

prophet of Jehovah. Would she, the heathen, be willing to hold friendly communication with him? So he handed her the drinking-vessel which he had brought, with the request to interrupt her weary work in order to fetch him some water. Even this first test proved that God had, as of old (Gen. xxiv. 12–21), and as afterwards (Luke xix. 30–34; xxii. 9–12), by anticipation provided for His servant. And, assuredly, as ever, "the cup of cold water" given in the name of the LORD was soon to receive rich reward.

But there was yet another and a sharper test by which to ascertain whether she were the widow to whom Elijah was Divinely sent. If she would hold communion with a servant of Jehovah—did she truly believe in Jehovah Himself; and if so, was her faith such that she would venture her last means of support upon her trust in Him and in His word? To put it in another manner: heathen as she was, though thus far prepared, was there, if not activeness, yet receptiveness of faith in her, of sufficient capacity for such spiritual provision as that which was afterwards miraculously supplied for her temporal wants? This would be the last and decisive test. As she was going to fetch the water, without hesitating or murmuring at the interruption of the old, or at the imposition of the new task, Elijah arrested her with a request yet stranger and far harder than the first. She was evidently a poor widow, and we know from profane history [1] that the famine, consequent on the want of rain in Israel, had also extended to Tyre. But when Elijah addressed to her what, even in these circumstances, would have seemed the modest request for "a morsel of the bread" in her hand—that is, in her possession [2]—he could

---

[1] Menander in Josephus' *Ant.* viii. 13, 2. According to Menander the actual famine in Tyre lasted one whole year. We may here remark, that if any one wishes to be impressed with the sublimeness of the Scriptural account of this event he can do no better than compare it with the wretched rationalistic prose of Josephus' version of it.

[2] The words "in thine hand" do not refer to the verb "bring," but to "bread," and mean that Elijah spoke as if she had some bread at home. So the LXX render it.

not have been aware of the terrible straits to which his future hostess was reduced. It was not unwillingness to give even to a complete stranger part of her scanty provision, but that she had absolutely none left. Despair breaks down the barriers of reserve—at least to fellow-sufferers, and, as in this case, to fellow-believers. With the adjuration: " Lives Jehovah, thy God," which attested alike her knowledge of Elijah's profession and her own faith, she told how nothing but a handful of meal was left in the small *Cad* [1] that held her provisions, and a little oil in her cruse. She had now come to gather by the highway a few sticks, with which to cook a last meal for herself and her child. After that they must lie down and die.

It is difficult to know which most to wonder at : Elijah's calmness, consistency, and readiness of faith, or the widow's almost incredible simplicity of trustfulness. Elijah was not taken aback; he did not hesitate to go on with the trial of his hostess to the end ; least of all, was he afraid of the possible consequences. As in every real trial of our trust, there was first a general promise, and, on the ground of it, a specific demand, followed by an assurance to conquering faith (" the cad of meal shall not come to an end, nor the cruse of oil fail "). But, if it was as he told her, why this demand in its sharply trying severity : *first*, to use for Elijah part of the very little she had, and to bring it to him, and only after that to go back [2] and prepare for herself and her son? Needless, indeed, the trial would seem, except as a test of her faith ; yet not a mere test, since if she stood it and inherited the promise, it would be such confirmation of it, such help and blessing to her—alike spiritually and temporally—as to constitute the beginning of a new life. And so it ever is ; and therefore

[1] The *Cad* was a small—probably the smallest—barrel. The word has passed into the Latin, the Greek, and the Sanscrit. Curiously enough, our English representative of it is the word "Caddy."

[2] This is clearly implied in the original, and must have been a much greater trial of her faith than if Elijah had at once returned with her, and the miracle begun then and there.

does every specific demand upon our faith stand between a general promise and a special assurance, that, resting upon the one, we may climb the other; and thus every specific trial—and every trial is also one of our faith—may become a fresh starting-point in the spiritual life.

And the widow of Sarepta obeyed. It requires no exercise of imagination to realise what her difficulties in so doing must have been. Did Elijah go back with her after she had brought him the cake, almost the last provision for herself and her child,—to watch as, with wonderment and awe, she prepared the first meal from her new store; or did he allow her to return home alone, perhaps wondering as she went whether it would be as the prophet had said, or whether perhaps she would never again see the Israelite stranger? One thing at least is clear: that this heathen woman, whose knowledge of Jehovah could only have been rudimentary and incipient, and who yet, at the word of a stranger, could give up her own and her son's last meal, because a prophet had bidden it, and promised her miraculous supply for the future, must have had the most simple childlike trustfulness in the God of Israel. What a lesson this, and how full of comfort, to Elijah! There *was* faith not only in Israel, but wherever He had planted its seed. Elijah had spread the wings of the God of Israel's promise (1 Kings xvii. 14), and this poor heathen had sought shelter under them. There, almost hourly these many "days," [1] the promise proved true, and, day by day, as when Israel gathered the manna in the wilderness, did an unseen Hand provide—and that not only for herself and her son, but for all " her household." It was a constant miracle; but then we need, and we have a God Who doeth wonders — not one of the idols of the heathen, nor yet a mere abstraction, but the Living and the True God. And we need in our Bible such a history as this,

---

[1] The word "many " in 1 Kings xvii. 15 is not in the original (as indicated by the italics). The expression marks an indefinite period of time—yet, as it seems to me, with the peculiar Old Testament idea of time, as "day by day."

to give us the pledge of personal assurance, when our hearts well-nigh sink within us in the bitter trials of life—something which to all time may serve as evidence that Jehovah reigneth, and that we can venture our all upon it. And yet as great as this miracle of daily providing seems that other of the faith of the widow of Sarepta!

It was soon to be put to even greater trial—and, as before, not only she, but Elijah also, would learn precious lessons by it. "Days" (time) had passed in happy quiet since God had daily spread the table in the widow's home, when her son became ill. The sickness increased, till, in the language of the sacred text, "there was not left in him breath."[1] There is something in the immediate contact with the Divine, which, from its contrast, brings sin to our remembrance, and in consequence makes us feel as if it were impossible to stand unpunished before Him—until our thoughts of the Divine Holiness, which in this view seems as consuming fire, pass into the higher realisation of the infinite love of God, which seeks and saves that which is lost (comp. Luke v. 8; also Isa. vi. 5). It was certainly not the wish that the prophet should be gone from her home, nor yet regret that he had ever come to it, which wrung from the agonised woman, as she carried to him her dead child in her bosom, these wild words, in which despair mingled with the consciousness of sin and the searching after the higher and better: "What have I to do with thee (what to [between] me and thee[2]), man of the Elohim? Come art thou to me to bring to remembrance my sin, and (thus) to cause the death of my son!" The Divine, as represented by Elijah, having no commonality with her; its fierce light

---

[1] Since the same or at least a very similar expression in Dan. x. 17 does not imply actual death, it would be rash to assert that the child was really dead. This is well pointed out by Kimchi. Similarly, Josephus has it that the child only seemed dead (was "as one dead," in New Testament language). The circumstance that his mother still carried him in her bosom seems to imply the same.

[2] Comp. Judg. xi. 12; 2 Sam. xvi. 10; 2 Kings iii. 13; Matt. viii. 29; John ii. 4.

bringing out her sin, and her sin bringing down condign punishment—such were the only clearly conscious thoughts of this incipient believer—though with much of the higher and better, as yet unconsciously, in the background.

Elijah made no other answer than to ask for her son. He took him from her bosom, carried him to the *Alijah* (upper chamber) where he dwelt, and there laid him on his own bed. In truth, it was not a time for teaching by words, but by deeds. And Elijah himself was deeply moved. These "many days" had been a happy, quiet, resting time to him—perhaps the only quiet happy season in all his life. And as day by day he had been the dispenser of God's goodness to the widow and her household, and had watched the unfolding of her faith, it must have been a time of strengthening and of joy to his heart. As St. Chrysostom has it : Elijah had to learn compassion in the house of the widow of Sarepta, before he was sent to preach to his own people. He learned more than this in that heathen home. Already he had learned that experience of faith, which, as St. Paul tells us, worketh a hope that maketh not ashamed (Rom. v. 4, 5). But now it seemed as if it were all otherwise ; as if he were only a messenger of judgment; as if his appearance had not only boded misery to his own people Israel, but brought it even upon the poor widow who had given him shelter. But it could not be so—and in the agony of prayer he cast this burden upon his God. Three times—as when the Name of Jehovah is laid in blessing on His people (Numb. vi. 24, etc.), and as when the Seraphim raise their voice of praise (Isa. vi. 3)— he stretched himself in symbolic action upon the child, calling upon Jehovah as his God : laying the living upon the dead, pouring his life, as it were, into the child, with the agony of believing prayer. But it was *Jehovah* Who restored the child to life, hearkening to the voice of His servant.

They are truly human traits, full of intense pathos, which follow—though also fraught with deep spiritual lessons. We can almost see Elijah as he takes down the child to his mother in that darkened room, and says to her only these words of deep emotion, not unmingled with loving reproof: " See, thy son liveth !" Words these, which our blessed LORD has said to many a weeping mother when holding her child, whether in life or in death. And thus we can understand the words of the mother of Sarepta, and those of many a mother in like circumstances : " Now—thus—I know that a Man of Elohim thou, and that the Word of Jehovah in thy mouth *is* truth !" She had learned it when first she received him ; she had seen it day by day at her table ; she had known it when God had answered her unspoken thought, her unuttered prayer, by showing that mercy and not judgment, love and forgiveness, not punishment and vengeance, were the highest meaning of His dealings.

The Rabbis see in this story an anticipation of the resurrection of the dead. We perceive this and more in it—an emblem also of the resurrection from spiritual death : a manifestation to Elijah and to us all, that " He quickeneth the dead, and calleth those things which be not as though they were" (Rom. iv. 17).

CHRONOLOGICAL TABLE

OF THE KINGS OF JUDAH AND ISRAEL, AND OF CONTEMPORARY EVENTS,

According to Keil, Winer, Ewald, Clinton, and the Margin of our Authorised Version (Ussher[1]).

Year from the Separation of the Two Kingdoms.	Kings of Judah. Reigned:	Year from the Accession of the Kings of Judah.	Kings of Israel. Reigned:	Year from the Accession of the Kings of Israel.	Contemporary Events.	Keil.	Winer.	Ewald.	Clinton.	Authorised Version.
1	Rehoboam, 17 years	1st	Jeroboam, 22 years	1st	Shishak King of Egypt	975	975	985	976	975
					Shishak enters Jerusalem	971	970			
18	Abijam, 3 years	2nd				957	957	968	959	958
20	Asa, 41 years	3rd				955	955	965	956	955
22			Nadab, 2 years	18th		953	954	963	955	954
23			Baasha, 24 years	20th		952	953	961	954	953
					Zerah the Ethiopian	940				
					Ben-Hadad I. of Syria	939				
45			Elah, 2 years	26th		930	930	937	930	930
46			Zimri, 7 days	27th		929	928	935	930	929
46			Omri and Tibni, 4 years	27th		929	928	935	930	929
50			Omri, sole king 8 years	31st		925	924			
					Building of Samaria	924	923			
					Ethbaal, King of Tyre and Sidon					
57	Jehoshaphat, 25 years	38th	Ahab, 22 years	4th		918	918	919	919	918
61					Ben-Hadad II. of Syria / Battle of Ramoth-gilead	914	914	917	915	914
78	Jehoram, co-regent for 2 years?	17th	Ahaziah, 2 years			897	897	897	896	898
79	Jehoram, sole ruler 6 yrs	18th	Jehoram, 12 years	5th	War of Israel and Judah against Moab (Moabite Stone)	897	897	895	895	896
						896	896			
86	Ahaziah, 1 year					891	889	893	891	892
					Hazael, King of Syria	889	885	885	884	885
91				12th	Second Battle of Ramoth-gilead	884				

№	Kings of Judah	Kings of Israel	Events					
92	ATHALIAH, 6 years	JEHU, 28 years	Murder of Ahaziah and Jehoram by Jehu, 884	884	883	883	884	883
			Lycurgus in Sparta, 884					
98	JOASH, 40 years		(7th) Athaliah slain	878	877	877	878	877
			Pygmalion, King of Tyre. His sister					
			Dido founds Carthage, 143 years after the building of the Temple					
119		(22nd?) JEHOAHAZ, 17 years	(2nd) Judah invaded and Jerusalem threatened by the Syrians	856	855	855	856	856
135		(37th) JOASH, 16 years	Ben-Hadad III., King of Syria	841	839	839	840	840
			Joash, King of Judah, murdered					
137	AMAZIAH, 29 years		War of Amaziah against Edom	839	837	837	838	838
			Attack of Moab upon Israel					
			War between Judah and Israel					
			Jerusalem occupied by the Israelites					
151		(15th) JEROBOAM II, 41 years	Successful War of Israel against Syria	825	823	823	825	824
165	UZZIAH, 52 years		(15th?) Ammon becomes tributary to Judah	810	808	808	809	810
			The Philistines humbled					
192		Death of JEROBOAM II, Interregnum for 11 yrs.					784	783
			First year of the Olympiads, 776					
203		(38th) ZACHARIAH, 6 months		773	771	770	772	772
204		(39th) SHALLUM, 1 month		772	770	770	771	771
204		(39th) MENAHEM, 10 years		772	770	769	771	771
			Pul, King of Assyria					
			Israel becomes tributary to Assyria					
215		(50th) PEKAHIAH, 2 years	Murder of Pekahiah	761	759	759	760	760
216		(52nd) PEKAH, 20 years	(2nd)	759	757	757	758	759
217	JOTHAM, 16 years		Building of Rome, 753	758	756	756	753	758
			Nabonassar, King of Babylon, 747					
			Rezin, King of Syria					
233	AHAZ, 16 years		(17th) Ahaz invokes the help of Assyria against Syria and Israel	742	741	740	741	742
			Tiglath-pileser, King of Assyria					
			The Assyrians occupy the land east of the Jordan, and the north of Palestine, and lead the people captive					

¹ For Events from the Exodus to the building of the Temple by Solomon, see the Chronological Table at the beginning of Vol. III. of this History.

Year from the Separation of the Two Kingdoms.	Kings of Judah. Reigned:	Year from the Accession of the Kings of Judah.	Kings of Israel. Reigned;	Year from the Accession of the Kings of Israel.	Contemporary Events.	Keil.	Winer.	Ewald.	Clinton.	Authorised Version.
236		4th	PEKAH murdered. Interregnum 8½ years?		The Philistines conquer the western part of Judah	739	738			
245		12th	HOSHEA, 9 years, tributary to Assyria		So, King of Egypt	730	729	728	730	730
248	HEZEKIAH, 29 years			3rd	Shalmaneser, King of Assyria (Media and Babylonia). Growth of the Assyrian Empire in Asia	727	725 722	724	726	726
					Attempt of Hoshea to rebel against Assyria. Invasion of the Assyrians. Siege of Samaria					
253		6th	DESTRUCTION OF THE COMMONWEALTH OF ISRAEL		Deportation of the Ten Tribes	722	721	719	721	721
261					Sargon, King of Assyria. Siege of Ashdod (Isa. xx. 1)	714	712			
					Alliance between Judah and Egypt					
					Siege of Jerusalem by Sennacherib					
					War between Sennacherib and Tirhakah					
					Destruction of the Assyrians by "the Angel of the Lord"					
					Embassy from Merodach-baladan					
277	MANASSEH, 55 years				Esarhaddon, King of Assyria, sends fresh Colonists to Samaria	698	696	695	697	698
332	AMON, 2 years				Scythian hordes pass through Palestine (Herod. I, 104, etc.)	643	641	640	642	643
					Murder of Amon	641	639	638	640	641
334	JOSIAH, 31 years				Nabopolassar, founder of the Babylonian Temple, father of Nebuchadnezzar	626	625			
					Draco in Athens					

365	JEHOAHAZ, 3 months	Invasion of Assyria by Egypt. Alliance of Assyria and Judah. Victory of Megiddo by Pharaoh-necoh, Josiah slain	610				609
365	JEHOIAKIM, 11 years	Jehoiakim put on the throne by the King of Egypt. Judah subject to Egypt	610	609	608		609
		The Egyptians beaten by the Chaldees in the Battle of Carchemish. Taking of Jerusalem by Nebuchadnezzar	610	609	607		609
369	Commencement of the Exile		606	605			607
376	JEHOIACHIN, 3 months	Second Conquest of Jerusalem and Deportation	599	598	597	598	599
376	ZEDEKIAH, 11 years	Jerusalem and the Temple plundered by the Chaldees					
		Zedekiah made king by the Chaldees					
		Zedekiah rebels against Nebuchadnezzar, and turns towards Pharaoh-hophra, King of Egypt (Jer. xliv. 30; Ezek. xvii. 15). Jerusalem besieged. Attempted relief of Jerusalem by the Egyptians (Jer. xxxvii. 5, etc.; Ezek. xvii. 17, etc.)	599	598	596	598	599 / 590
387	DESTRUCTION OF JERUSALEM	Death of Zedekiah. Majority of the Jews carried to Babylon (3rd deportation)	588	587	588		588
387	Gedaliah Babylonian Governor in Judah, 2 mths.	Gedaliah murdered. Many of the Jews retire into Egypt	588	588			
391	Last Deportation of the Jews to Babylon (Jos. Ant. x. 97; comp. Jer. lii. 30?)		584		534		

Judah lies desolate (2 Chron. xxxvi. 21; Zech. vii. 14). Occupation of part of the country by the Philistines and Edomites. The latter take the southern territory (Ezek. xxxv. 10). Hebron part of Idumea (Jos. Jew. Wars, iv. 9, 7).

The Chronology of the two Kingdoms after their separation is in many respects involved, and, from the want of sufficient data to guide us, sometimes so difficult as to baffle all efforts at certain solution. But the final result shows that these divergences are rather nice than important, the total difference being at most only that of a few years. Special difficulties are considered in the text as they arise. Two points ought to be here kept in view, as on the one hand accounting for, and on the other helping us to solve most of the minor difficulties. They are : *first*, the dates are not computed according to a fixed standard, such as the Creation of the World, or the Exodus, but according to the accession of the various kings of Judah and Israel; while *secondly*, the duration of the reign of these kings is computed from the month Nisan to the month Nisan of each year, so that even a single day before or after the 1st of Nisan is reckoned equivalent to a whole year. This mode of computation, which is distinctly asserted in the Talmud (*Rosh-ha-Sh. 2a–3a passim*), was that according to which Josephus reckoned. Compare the detailed proof in Wieseler's *Synopse*, pp. 53, etc.

THE BIBLE HISTORY

VOLUME VI

THE HISTORY

OF

ISRAEL AND JUDAH

FROM

THE REIGN OF AHAB TO THE DECLINE
OF THE TWO KINGDOMS.

THE KINGDOMS OF
JUDAH AND ISRAEL

PREFACE

———◆———

THE present Volume of this Bible History traces the period of the commencing decline alike in the kingdom of Israel and in that of Judah, although in the latter its progress was retarded by the gracious faithfulness of God in regard to the house of David, and by seasons of temporary repentance on the part of the people. The special interest of the period lies in this, that it was critical of the future of the nation. And of this its history also bears evidence in the more marked and direct—we had almost said, realistic—interpositions, or, perhaps more correctly, self-manifestations on the part of the God of Israel: whether by more emphatic evidence of His constant Presence and claims, or in the more continuous mission and direct qualifications of the Prophets whom He commissioned. This, as indicated in a previous Volume, accounts for the intensified miraculous character of that Biblical period—notably in connection with the history of Elijah and Elisha. For such prophetic mission was necessary, if in a crisis—when destruction, or at least severest judgment, was impending, or else national recovery, and with it great expansion of national influence—Israel was to be roused to a realization of the truth at issue, such as was, for example, presented by Elijah at the sacrifice on Mount Carmel. And not only as regarded that fundamental truth, but also its application to all the details of public and private life in Israel. In this, therefore, we find the rational vindication—we avoid the obnoxious designation, apologetic—of the otherwise strange, and certainly exceptional, manifestation of miraculous prophetic power in so many private as well as public affairs. In the state of Israel, and at that period, an Elijah and an Elisha were required, and, if required, their mission and their message must be thus evidenced : alike before all friends and against all gainsayers.

If, from this point of view, the application of the miraculous during this period, in private as well as in public concerns, is not, as some would have it, a retrogression, it marks in other and more important aspects a great progression—and that towards the perfectness of the New Testament. We must explain what we mean by a seeming retrogression. Very markedly the Old Testament history differs from all others, which in their earliest stages are legendary, in this, that whereas in them the miraculous is introduced in what may be called the prehistoric period, then speedily, almost abruptly, to cease ; it is otherwise in that of the Old Testament. The patriarchal history (notably that of Isaac and Jacob) has comparatively less of the miraculous. It appears in the desert-history of new-born Israel, and on their entrance in the land. It disappears again in great measure, to reappear once more in manner altogether unprecedented at the period of which this Volume treats—that is, at a comparatively advanced time, when the history of Israel runs parallel to the trustworthy records of that of other nations as perpetuated on their monuments. Assuredly, this has its various lessons in regard to the credibility of the miraculous in the Old Testament. Most notably this, which, as before stated, marks that, which to some seems a retrogression, as a real progression : that the miraculous now stands with increasing clearness in direct connection with moral relationship towards God. So to speak : the miraculous interpositions are now not so much *for* Israel as *to* Israel; not so much on behalf of Israel as such, but whether in judgment or in mercy, with direct reference and application to Israel's moral and spiritual condition. And this, as we have said, points to the perfectness of the New Testament, in which the relation of God to each soul, as well as to the Church, and the spiritual condition of the soul, or of the Church : the outward and the inward, are correlative. Thus, in the wider application, these miraculous elements in the history of Israel are themselves prophecies, of which the fulfilment is in Christ.

Thus much must for the present suffice—the more so, as in the next Volume (which will conclude the Old Testament History) the opportunity will necessarily present itself for larger retrospect and wider survey. It only remains to add that the treatment of the subject in this Volume will be found in accordance with the progressive plan of this work, repeatedly indicated in previous Volumes. Alike the critical and exegetical notes will be found more frequent and more full, and the general treatment more detailed, and designed for more advanced readers. A new element in the present Volume is the light brought to bear on this period from the ancient monuments. We live in days when more attention than ever before is given to the critical study of the Old Testament; in days also when attacks are chiefly directed against the trustworthiness, the credibility, and, as it seems to us, the Divine Authority, in its true sense, of the Old Testament. There are those, we will gladly believe, who can disjoint, and in logical connection with it, re-interpret the Old Testament, and yet retain their full faith in its direct Divine character, and in its preparation for the Christ. We must frankly confess that we are not of their number. There is, indeed, a general Divine character in the Old Testament, and a general preparation in it for the New,

whatever historical views we may take of it, or whatever interpretations we may give of it. We would even advance beyond
this, and say that Christ and Christianity have their absolute
truth, quite irrespective of the Old Testament. But to us at
least Jesus of Nazareth as the Christ is the direct outcome of
the Old Testament, as well as its higher fulfilment : not only
"a light to lighten the Gentiles," but, and even in this very
respect also : "the glory of Thy people Israel."

ALFRED EDERSHEIM

8, BRADMORE ROAD, OXFORD :
 1st November, 1885.

CONTENTS

CHAPTER I.
Ahab, King of Israel.

CHAPTER II.

CHAPTER III.

CHAPTER IV.

CHAPTER V.
Ahab and Ahaziah, (Eighth and Ninth) Kings of Israel. Jehoshaphat, (Fourth) King of Judah.

CHAPTER VI.

Jehoshaphat, (Fourth) King of Judah.

CHAPTER VII.

Jehoshaphat, (Fourth) King of Judah, Ahaziah and (Jehoram) Joram, (Ninth and Tenth) Kings of Israel.

CHAPTER VIII.

Elisha the Prophet.

CHAPTER IX.

Jehoshaphat, (Fourth) King of Judah—Joram, (Tenth) King of Israel.

CHAPTER XIV.

𝔄𝔩𝔬𝔰𝔢 𝔬𝔣 𝔈𝔩𝔦𝔰𝔥𝔞'𝔰 𝔓𝔲𝔟𝔩𝔦𝔠 𝔐𝔦𝔫𝔦𝔰𝔱𝔯𝔶: 𝔱𝔥𝔢 𝔅𝔢𝔤𝔦𝔫𝔫𝔦𝔫𝔤 𝔬𝔣 𝔍𝔲𝔡𝔤𝔪𝔢𝔫𝔱.

CHAPTER XV.

𝔍𝔢𝔥𝔬𝔯𝔞𝔪 𝔞𝔫𝔡 𝔄𝔥𝔞𝔷𝔦𝔞𝔥, (𝔉𝔦𝔣𝔱𝔥 𝔞𝔫𝔡 𝔖𝔦𝔵𝔱𝔥) 𝔎𝔦𝔫𝔤𝔰 𝔬𝔣 𝔍𝔲𝔡𝔞𝔥. 𝔍𝔬𝔯𝔞𝔪, (𝔗𝔢𝔫𝔱𝔥) 𝔎𝔦𝔫𝔤 𝔬𝔣 𝔈𝔰𝔯𝔞𝔢𝔩.

CHAPTER XVI.

𝔍𝔬𝔯𝔞𝔪 𝔞𝔫𝔡 𝔍𝔢𝔥𝔲, (𝔗𝔢𝔫𝔱𝔥 𝔞𝔫𝔡 𝔈𝔩𝔢𝔳𝔢𝔫𝔱𝔥) 𝔎𝔦𝔫𝔤𝔰 𝔬𝔣 𝔈𝔰𝔯𝔞𝔢𝔩. 𝔄𝔥𝔞𝔷𝔦𝔞𝔥, (𝔖𝔦𝔵𝔱𝔥) 𝔎𝔦𝔫𝔤 𝔬𝔣 𝔍𝔲𝔡𝔞𝔥.

CHAPTER XVII.

𝔍𝔢𝔥𝔲, (𝔈𝔩𝔢𝔳𝔢𝔫𝔱𝔥) 𝔎𝔦𝔫𝔤 𝔬𝔣 𝔈𝔰𝔯𝔞𝔢𝔩. 𝔄𝔱𝔥𝔞𝔩𝔦𝔞𝔥, (𝔖𝔢𝔳𝔢𝔫𝔱𝔥) 𝔔𝔲𝔢𝔢𝔫 𝔬𝔣 𝔍𝔲𝔡𝔞𝔥.

THE

HISTORY OF JUDAH AND ISRAEL

FROM THE SACRIFICE ON CARMEL.

———◆———

CHAPTER I.

Ahab, King of Israel.

*Three years' Famine in Israel—Elijah meets Obadiah and Ahab—The
Gathering on Mount Carmel—The Priests of Baal—Description of their
Rites—The time of the Evening Sacrifice—Elijah prepares the Sacrifice
—Elijah's Prayer—The Answer by Fire—Israel's Decision—Slaughter
of the Priests of Baal—The Cloud not bigger than a Man's Hand—
Elijah runs before Ahab to Jezreel.*

(1 KINGS XVIII.)

THREE and a half years had passed since the ban of Elijah
had driven clouds and rain from the sky of Israel, and
the dry air distilled no dew on the parched and barren ground
(comp. Luke iv. 25 ; James v. 17[1]). Probably one of these
years had been spent by the prophet in the retirement of Wadi
Cherith ; another may have passed before the widow's son
was restored from death to life ; while other eighteen months
of quiet may have followed that event. Surely, if ever, the
terrible desolation which the prophet's word had brought
upon the land must by this time have had its effect upon
Israel. Yet we meet no trace of repentance in king or people :

---

[1] Not only the New Testament writers (as above quoted), but the Rabbis
fix the period of rainlessness at three years and a half, and every explanation which attempts to date this period as beginning before the appearance
of Elijah is forced and unnatural. Accordingly the expression "the third
year" in 1 Kings xviii. 1 must refer to Elijah's stay at Sarepta—about two
years and a half after his arrival there.

only the sullen silence of hopeless misery. What man could do, had been attempted, but had signally failed. As the want and misery among the people became more pressing, King Ahab had searched both the land and all neighbouring countries for Elijah, but in vain (1 Kings xviii. 10), while Jezebel had wreaked her impotent vengeance on all the prophets of Jehovah on whom she could lay hands, as if they had been Elijah's accomplices, to be punished for what she regarded as his crime. If all the representatives of Jehovah were exterminated, His power could no longer be exercised in the land, and she would at the same time crush resistance to her imperious will, and finally uproot that hated religion which was alike the charter of Israel's spiritual allegiance and of civil liberty. Yet neither Ahab nor Jezebel succeeded. Though Elijah was near at hand, either in Ahab's dominions or in those of Jezebel's father, neither messenger nor king could discover his place of retreat. Nor could Jezebel carry out her bloody design. It affords most significant illustration of God's purpose in raising up "prophets," and also of the more wide sense in which we are here to understand that term, that such was their number, that, however many the queen may have succeeded in slaying, at least a hundred of them could still be hid, by fifties, in the limestone caverns with which the land is burrowed. And this, we infer, must have been in the immediate neighbourhood of the capital, as otherwise Obadiah (the "servant of Jehovah"), the pious governor of Ahab's palace (comp. 1 Kings iv. 6 ; 2 Kings xviii. 18 ; Isa. xxii. 15), could scarcely have supplied their wants without being detected (1 Kings xviii. 4). Nor was Obadiah the only one in Israel who "feared Jehovah," though his position may have been more trying than that of others. As we know, there were still thousands left in Israel who had not bowed to Baal (1 Kings xix. 18).

But there was at least one general effect throughout the land of this terrible period of drought. Every one must have learned that it had followed upon the announcement of Elijah ;

every one must have known what that announcement had been, with all concerning Jehovah and His prophet that it implied ; and, lastly, if no general repentance had taken place, every one must at least have been prepared for the grand decisive trial between God and Baal, which was so soon to take place. And still the weary days crept on as before ; the sun rose and sank on a cloudless sky over an arid land ; and there was no sign of change, nor hope of relief. It was summer. Jezebel had left the palace of Samaria, and was in her delicious cool summer-residence at Jezreel, to which more full reference will be made in the sequel (comp. 1 Kings xviii. 45, 46 ; and the inference from 1 Kings xxi. 2). But Ahab was still in Samaria, busy with cares, caused by the state of the land. This temporary absence of Jezebel explains not only Ahab's conduct, but how he went to meet Elijah, attempted no violence, and even appeared in person on Mount Carmel. So great was the strait even in Samaria itself, that the king was in danger of losing every horse and mule, whether for the public or his own service. To discover if any fodder were left in the country, the king and Obadiah were each to make careful survey of part of the land. Obadiah had not proceeded far on his mission, when the sight least ex-pected—perhaps least desired—presented itself to his view. It was none other than Elijah, who had been Divinely directed to leave Sarepta and meet Ahab. As there is not anything in Holy Scripture without meaning and teaching, we may here mark, that, when this is assigned by the Lord as the reason for Elijah's mission : " I will send rain upon the ground " (1 Kings xviii. 1), it is intended to teach that, although it was Jehovah Himself (and not Elijah, as the Rabbis imagine) who held "the keys of the rain," yet He would not do anything except through His chosen messenger.

Obadiah could have no difficulty in immediately recognising Elijah, even if he had not, as seems most likely, met him before. With lowliest reverence he saluted the prophet, and then received command to announce his presence to Ahab. But timid and only partially enlightened, although God-fearing, as Obadiah was, this was no welcome message to him. Ahab had so long and so systematically sought for Elijah, that Obadiah could only imagine the prophet had been miraculously removed from shelter to shelter, just in time to save him from being detected by the messengers of Ahab. In point of fact, we know that such was not the case ; but those who have lost the habit of seeing God in the ordinary Providence of every-day life—as is the case with all who are conformed to the world—are too often in the habit of looking for things strange, or for miracles, and thus become at the same time superstitious and unbelieving. What—so argued Obadiah— if, after he had intimated Elijah's presence to the king, the prophet were once more miraculously removed? Would he not have to pay with his life for Elijah's escape ; would not suspicious Ahab or bloodthirsty Jezebel wreak their vengeance on him as an abettor of the prophet? Most ground-less fears these, as all which are prompted by the faint-heart-edness of partially enlightened piety ; and so Elijah hastened to assure him, not, as it seems to us, without a touch of pitying reproof.

The meeting which followed between the king of Israel and the representative of Jehovah was characteristic of each. It is a mistake to suppose, as interpreters generally do, that the words with which Ahab accosted Elijah, " Art thou the one [1] who troubleth Israel? " were intended to frighten the prophet by a display of authority. Even Ahab could not have imagined that such would be their effect. It seems rather like an appeal. See what thou hast done ; and what now? In truth, a man such as Ahab must have felt it difficult to know how to address the prophet. But Elijah was not, even momentarily, to be drawn into a personal controversy. With a sharp reproof, which pointed out that it was not he but the sin of Ahab and of his house which had brought trouble upon Israel, he directed

---

[1] I have given this the primary meaning of the Hebrew word ("this," "that one "), and not, as interpreters generally, the rare derivation "here."

the king to gather unto Mount Carmel the representatives of all Israel, as well as the 450 prophets of Baal and the 400 prophets of Astarte who enjoyed the special favour of the queen.

Putting aside for the moment the thought of the overruling guidance of God in the matter, it is not difficult to understand why Ahab complied with Elijah's direction. Naturally he could not have anticipated what turn matters would take. Certain it was that the land was in a terrible strait from which, if any one, Elijah alone could deliver it. Should he provoke him to fresh judgments by a refusal? What was there to fear from one unarmed man in presence of a hostile assembly? If Elijah could remove the curse, it was worth any temporary concession; if he refused or failed, the controversy with him would be easily settled, and that with popular approbation. Besides these, there may have been other secondary reasons for Ahab's compliance. As we have noticed, Jezebel was not then in Samaria; and Ahab may have felt that secret misgiving which is often the outcome of superstition rather than of partial belief. Lastly, he may at the moment have been under the influence of the overawing power of Elijah. It could scarcely have been otherwise in the circumstances.

That day Carmel witnessed one of the grandest scenes in the history of Israel. Three such scenes on mountain-tops stand out before the mind : the first on Mount Sinai, when the Covenant was made by the ministry of Moses; the second on Mount Carmel, when the Covenant was restored by the ministry of Elijah; the third on "the Mount of Transfiguration," when Moses and Elijah bare worshipful witness to the Christ in Whom and by Whom the Covenant was completed, transfigured, and transformed. In each case the scene on the Mount formed the high point in the life and mission of the agent employed, from which henceforth there was a descent, save in the history of Christ, where the descent to Gethsemane was in reality the commencement of the ascent to the Right Hand of God. Moses died and was buried at the Hand of God,

Elijah went up with chariot of fire ; Jesus died on the cross. Yet whereas from the mountain-top Moses and Elijah really descended, so far as their work and mission were concerned, the seeming descent of Jesus was the real ascent to the topmost height of His work and glory.

No spot in Palestine is more beautiful, more bracing, or healthful than *Carmel*, " the Park-like." Up in the north-west, it juts as a promontory into the Mediterranean, rising to a height of five hundred feet. Thence it stretches about twelve miles to the s.s.e., rising into two other peaks. The first of these, about four miles from the promontory, is not less than 1740 feet high. Still further to the south-east is a third peak, 1687 feet high,[1] which to this day bears the name of *El-Mahrakah*, or " place of burning " (sacrifice). This, there can scarcely be a doubt, was the place of Elijah's sacrifice. Let us try to realise the scene. On whichever side the mountain be ascended, the scene is one of unsurpassed beauty. The rich red soil, where not cultivated, is covered by a thick brushwood of luxurious evergreens. Not only flowering trees and delicious fragrant herbs, but all the flora of the North of Palestine seems gathered in this favoured spot. So early as November, the crocus, narcissus, pink cistus, and large daisy are in bloom, and the hawthorn in bud. In spring, wild tulips, dark red anemones, pink phlox, cyclamen, purple stocks, marigolds, geranium, and pink, yellow, and white rock-roses make it bright with gay colouring. For numerous springs trickle along the foot of the mountain and fertilise the soil. Ascending to El-Mahrakah we catch glimpses of cliffs, which in some places descend sheer down to the plain. At last we reach a plateau where at the edge of a steep slope there is a perennial well, filled with water even in the driest season. Yet a little higher rises another

---

[1] For these measurements and other interesting notices I am indebted to Conder's *Tent-work in Palestine*, vol. i., pp. 168, etc. See also Dean Stanley's description in his *Sinai and Palestine*, Mr. Grove's article in Smith's *Bible Dict.*, and other accounts.

plateau of rich soil, shaded by olives ; and finally we reach the topmost peak, a semi-isolated knoll. This was the place of the two altars : that of Baal, and that ruined one of Jehovah restored by Elijah, and dating from before the building of the Temple, when such worship was lawful. On the plateau beneath, under the shade of the olives, full in view of the highest altar-peak, were on the one side Elijah, and on the other King Ahab, the priests of Baal, and the people. Yet a little lower was the well whence the water for Elijah's sacrifice was drawn. Some 1400 feet beneath, where the rapid descent is close to steep precipices and by sharp crags, rolls that "ancient river" Kishon, where the wild slaughter of the priests of Baal formed the closing scene in the drama of that day. But up on the topmost altar-height what an outlook ! Westwards over Carmel and far to the sandhills around Cæsarea ; northwards, the Galilean hills, Lebanon and Hermon ; eastwards, across the plain of Esdraelon, some six miles off, to Jezreel,—further away, to Shunem, Endor, Nain, Tabor, Nazareth, and even distant Gilead. A theatre this truly befitting what was to be enacted on it.

Among those who on that day had gathered under the olives on that shady plateau just beneath the topmost peak, the four hundred priests of Astarte were not found. Whether they had shrunk from the encounter, or had deemed it inconsistent with the wishes of their spiritual patroness, the queen, to appear on such an occasion, certain it is that they were not with their four hundred and fifty colleagues of the priesthood of Baal. These must have been conspicuous amid king, courtiers, and the motley gathering from all parts of the land, by their white dresses and high pointed caps. Over against them, his upper garment of black camel-hair girt with a leathern girdle, stood the stern figure of the prophet ; in the foreground was King Ahab. It was, indeed, a unique gathering, a wondrous array of forces, a day of tremendous import. To this Elijah had bidden king, priests, and people, and he left them not long in doubt of his object. First, he turned to the people with these words, which must have alike shown them their real condition and appealed to their judgment : " How long halt ye " (pass ye from one to the other [1]) "as to the two opinions " (divisions, parties [2]) ?   If Jehovah be the Elohim—go after Him ; but if the Baal, go after him ! To an appeal so trenchantly true there could in the then condition of the public mind be no answer.   Their very appearance on Mount Carmel was an attestation of this mental passing to and fro on the part of Israel—irrational, unsatisfactory, and self-condemnatory (Deut. vi. 4, etc.).   But the question of Elijah also formed a most apt preparation for what was to follow.   The two divided opinions were now to be brought to the test of truth ; the two parties to measure their strength.   Let Israel see and decide !

In the breathless silence that ensued upon this challenge Elijah now stood forward, and pointing to the white-robed crowd of priests over against him, he recalled to king and people that he and he only remained—that is, in active office and open profession [3]—a prophet of Jehovah.   Single-handed, therefore, he would go to the contest, if contest of power it were against that multitude.   Power !   They worshipped as God the powers of nature : [4] let them then make trial on whose side the powers which are in nature were arrayed.   Let this be the test : the priests of Baal on their side, and he on his, would each choose a bullock and prepare it for sacrifice, but

[1] The word is used in verse 26 of the wild dance or leaping of the priests of Baal.

[2] It is not easy to render the Hebrew word exactly.   It occurs in Psa. cxix. 113 (" I hate divided *thoughts* ") ; Isa. ii. 21 ; lvii. 5 (" clefts ") ; Ezek. xxxi. 6 (" boughs," divided branches).   The expression was probably proverbial.

[3] The others being hid in caves, were for all practical purposes for the present as non-existing.

[4] It deserves more than passing notice, that the modern denial of God may be reduced to the same ultimate principle as the worship of Baal.   For, if the great First Cause—God as the Creator—be denied, then the only mode of accounting for the origin of all things is to trace it to the operation of forces in matter.   And what really is this but a deification of Nature ?

not kindle the fire beneath, "and it shall be the Elohim who shall answer by fire, He *is* the Elohim." A shout of universal assent greeted the proposal. In the circumstances it would be of the greatest practical importance that the futility of Baal-worship should be exhibited in the fullest manner. This explains the details of all that follows. Besides, after a whole day's vain appliance of every resource of their superstition, the grandeur of Jehovah's majestic interposition would also make the deeper impression. But although from Elijah's point of view it was important that the priests of Baal should first offer their sacrifice, the proposition was one to which no objection could be taken, since Elijah not only gave them the choice of the sacrificial animal, but they were many as against one. Nor could they complain so far as regarded the test proposed by Elijah, since their Baal was also the god of fire, the very Sun-god.[1]

Now commenced a scene which baffles description. Ancient writers have left us accounts of the great Baal-festivals, and they closely agree with the narrative of the Bible, only furnishing further details. First rose a comparatively moderate, though already wild, cry to Baal; followed by a dance around the altar, beginning with a swinging motion to and fro.[2] The howl then became louder and louder, and the dance more frantic. They whirled round and round, ran wildly through each other's ranks, always keeping up a circular motion, the head low bent, so that their long dishevelled hair swept the ground. Ordinarily the madness now became infectious, and the onlookers joined in the frenzied dance. But Elijah knew how to prevent this. It was noon—and for hours they had kept up their wild rites. With cutting taunts and bitter irony

---

[1] As already stated, Baal was the real deity of Asia, worshipped under different forms (hence the plural : *Baalim*). Moloch was only Baal under another aspect, that of destruction, comp. Jer. xix. 5; xxxii. 35.

[2] In the original the word, as before noted, is the same as that rendered "halt" (in verse 21). The expression, no doubt, refers to the pantomimic dances around the altar.

Elijah now reminded them that, since Baal was Elohim, the fault must lie with them. He might be otherwise engaged, and they must cry louder. Stung to madness, they became more frantic than before, and what we know as the second and third acts in these feasts ensued. The wild howl passed into piercing demoniacal yells. In their madness the priests bit their arms and cut themselves with the two-edged swords which they carried and with lances.[1] As blood began to flow the frenzy reached its highest pitch, when first one, then others, commenced to "prophesy," moaned and groaned, then burst into rhapsodic cries, accusing themselves, or speaking to Baal, or uttering incoherent broken sentences. All the while they beat themselves with heavy scourges, loaded or armed with sharp points, and cut themselves with swords and lances— sometimes even mutilated themselves—since the blood of the priests was supposed to be specially propitiatory with Baal.

Two more hours had this terrible scene lasted—and their powers of endurance must have been all but exhausted. The sun had long passed its meridian, and the time of the regular evening-sacrifice in the Temple of Jehovah at Jerusalem had come. From the accounts of Temple-times left us we know that the evening sacrifice was offered "between the evenings," as it was termed—that is, between the downgoing of the sun and the evening.[2] In point of fact the service commenced between two and three p.m. It must have been about the same time when Elijah began the simple yet solemn preparations for his sacrifice. Turning from the frantic priests to the astonished people, he bade them draw nigh. They must gather around him, not only in order to be convinced that no deception was practised, but to take part with him, as it were, in the service. And once more Israel was to appear as the Israel of old in

---

[1] This is the correct rendering of verse 28, and not "knives and lancets," as in the Authorised Version.

[2] For a full description and explanation of the time of the Evening Sacrifice, see *The Temple, its Ministry and Services at the time of Jesus Christ*, p. 116.

happier times, undivided in nationality as in allegiance to Jehovah. This was the meaning of his restoring the broken place of former pious worship by rolling to it twelve of the large pieces of rock that strewed the ground, according to the number of the tribes. And as he built the altar, he consecrated it by prayer: "in the name of Jehovah." Next, the soft crumbling calcareous soil around the altar was dug into a deep and wide trench. Then the wood, and upon it the pieces of the sacrifice were laid in due order. And now, at the prophet's bidding, willing hands filled the pitchers from the well close by.[1] Once, twice, thrice he poured the water over the sacrifices, till it ran down into the trench, which he also filled. This, as we suppose, not merely to show the more clearly that the fire, which consumed the sacrifice in such circumstances, was sent from heaven, but also for symbolic reasons, as if to indicate that Israel's penitent confession was poured upon the offering.

And now a solemn silence fell on the assembly. The sun was going down, a globe of fire, behind Carmel, and covered it with purple glow. It was the time of the evening sacrifice. But Jehovah, not Elijah, would do the miracle; the Hand of the living God Himself must be stretched out. Once more it was prayer which moved that Hand. Such prayer was not heard before—so calm, so earnest, so majestic, so assured, so strong. Elijah appeared in it as only the servant of Jehovah, and all that he had previously done as only at His Word: but Jehovah was the covenant-God, the God of Abraham, of Isaac, and of Israel, manifesting Himself as of old as the Living and True, as Elohim in Israel: the conversion of Israel to Him as their God being the great object sought for.[2]

He had said it, and, as when first the Tabernacle was consecrated (Lev. ix. 24), or as when King Solomon (1 Chron.

---

[1] The Rabbis note that, each time, four pitchers of water were poured, or twelve in all, corresponding to the twelve stones of which the altar was built, and for the same symbolic reason.

[2] 1 Kings xviii. 37 indicates the final (moral) purpose not only of this but of every miracle. The last clause of the verse should be rendered in the *present* tense: "and that Thou turnest their heart back again."

xxi. 26 ; 2 Chron. vii. 1) brought the first offering in the
Temple which he had reared to Jehovah, so now the fire of
Jehovah leaped from heaven, consumed the sacrifice and the
wood, enwrapped and burnt up the limestone rocks of which
the altar was constructed, and with burning tongue licked up
even the water that was in the trench.   One moment of solemn
silence, when all who had seen it fell in awe-stricken worship
on their faces; then a shout which seemed to rend the very air,
and found its echo far and wide in the glens and clefts of
Carmel : " Jehovah, He the Elohim ! Jehovah, He the
Elohim !"

And so Israel was once more converted unto God. And
now, in accordance with the Divine command in the Law (Deut.
xiii. 13 ; xvii. 2, etc.), stern judgment must be executed on the
idolaters and seducers, the idol-priests. The victory that day
must be complete ; the renunciation of Baal-worship beyond
recall. Not one of the priests of Baal must escape. Down
the steep mountain sides they hurried them, cast them over
precipices, those fourteen hundred feet to the river Kishon,
which was reddened with their blood.[1] But up on the mountain-top lingered King Ahab, astonished, speechless, himself
for the time a convert to Jehovah. He also was to share in
the sacrifice ; he was to eat the sacrificial meal. But it must be
in haste, for already Elijah heard the sighing and low moaning
of the wind in the forest of Carmel. Himself took no part in
the feast. He had other bread to eat whereof they wot not.
He had climbed the topmost height of Carmel out of sight
of the king. None had accompanied him save his servant,
whom tradition declares to have been that son of the widow of
Sarepta who had been miraculously restored to life. Most
fitting minister, indeed, he would have been in that hour.
Once more it was agonising prayer—not once, but seven times
repeated.[2] At each break in it the faithful attendant climbed

[1] It is scarcely credible, in view of the words of our Lord, Luke ix. 55,
56 ; and yet this scene has been adduced as a precedent for the persecution
of so-called "heretics."   [2] *Seven*—the number of the Covenant.

the highest knoll, and looked earnestly and anxiously over the broad expanse of the sea, there full in view. At last it had come—a cloud, as yet not bigger than a man's hand. But when God begins to hear prayer, He will hear it abundantly; when He gives the blessing, it will be without stint. Ahab must be up, and quick in his chariot, or the rain, which will descend in floods, will clog the hard ground, so that his chariot would find it difficult to traverse the six miles across the plain to the palace of Jezreel. And now as the foot of the mountain was reached, the heaven was black with clouds, the wind moaned fitfully, and the rain came in torrents. But the power of Jehovah[1] was upon the Tishbite. He girded up his loins and ran before the chariot of Ahab. On such a day he hesitated not to act as outrunner to the convert-king; nay, he would himself be the harbinger of the news to Jezreel. Up to the entrance of Jezreel he heralded them; to the very gate of Jezebel's palace he went before them, like the warning voice of God, ere Ahab again encountered his tempter. But there the two must part company, and the king of Israel must henceforth decide for himself to whom he will cleave, whether to Jehovah or to the god of Jezebel.

[1] The *Targum* renders: "And the spirit of strength from before Jehovah."

CHAPTER II.

Different Standpoint of the Old and the New Testament—Analogy between Elijah and John the Baptist—Jezebel threatens Elijah's life—The Prophet's Flight—His Miraculous Provision—Analogy between Moses and Elijah—Elijah at Mount Horeb—What doest thou here, Elijah? —The Wind, the Earthquake, the Fire, and the Still Small Voice—The Divine Message and Assurance to Elijah—Call of Elisha.

(I Kings xix.)

UNSPEAKABLY grand as had been the scene on Mount Carmel, we instinctively feel that it was the outcome of the Old Testament. We cannot conceive it possible under the New dispensation. In so saying we do not so much refer to the ironical taunts which Elijah had addressed to the priests of Baal, when compassion, gentleness, and meekness might have seemed befitting, since it was necessary effectually to expose the folly as well as the sin of idolatry, and this was best done in such manner (comp. Isa. xl. 18, etc.; xli. 7; xliv. 8-22; xlvi. 5-11; Jer. x. 7, etc.). Nor do we allude only or mainly to the destruction of the priests of Baal. This was simply in obedience to the Old Testament Law, and was grounded alike on its economy [1] and on the circumstances of the time. Taking the lowest view, it was an act of necessary self-preservation, since the two religions could not co-exist, as the conduct of Jezebel had recently proved. But there is a higher view than this of the event. For the fundamental object of Israel's calling and existence—the whole typical import and preparatory purpose of the nation—was incompatible with even the existence of idolatry among them. Finally, there is this essential difference between the Old and the New Testament

---

[1] I use the term "economy" here in its original meaning, as denoting the household arrangement, the household legislation and order.

dispensation—that under the latter, religion is of personal choice, heart-willingness being secured by the persuasion of the Holy Ghost; while under the Old Testament (from its nature) religion was of Law. Religious liberty is a principle which necessarily follows from a religion of free choice, where God no longer addresses Himself to man merely, or mainly, with the authority of a general Law, but appeals to the individual conscience with the persuasion of a special invitation. Under the Old Testament, of which the fundamental principle was the sole Divine authority of Jehovah (Ex. xx. 2, 3), idolatry was not only a crime, but a revolt against the Majesty of heaven, Israel's King, which involved the most fatal consequences to the nation. Yet even so, we repeat it, the scene on Mount Carmel could not have been enacted in New Testament times.

But while fully admitting this distinctive standpoint of the preparatory dispensation, it were a most serious mistake to forget that the Old Testament itself points to a higher and fuller manifestation of God, and never more distinctly than in this history of Elijah. Attention has already been called to the analogy between Elijah and John the Baptist. At this stage we specially recall three points in the history of the latter. It seems as if the Baptist had expected that his warning denunciations would be immediately followed either by visible reform, or else by visible judgment. But instead of this he was cast, at the instigation of Herod's wife, into a dungeon which he was never to leave; and yet judgment seemed to slumber, and the Christ made no movement either for the deliverance of His forerunner, or the vindication of his message. And, lastly, in consequence of this disappointment, spiritual darkness appears to have gathered around the soul of the Baptist. One almost feels as if it had been needful for such a messenger of judgment to become consciously weak, that so in the depression of the human the Divine element might appear the more clearly. And it was also good that it should be so, since it led to the inquiring embassy to Christ, and

thus to a fuller revelation of the Divine character of the kingdom. The same expectation and the same disappointment
are apparent in the history of Elijah on the morrow of the
victory at Carmel. But they also led up to a fuller manifestation of the meaning and purpose of God. Thus we see how
the Old Testament itself, even where its distinctive character
most clearly appeared, pointed to that fuller and more glorious
manifestation of God, symbolised, not by storm, earthquake,
or fire, but by "the still small voice."

If Elijah had lingered in Jezreel in the hope that the reformation proclaimed on Mount Carmel would be followed up
by the king, he was soon to experience bitter disappointment.
There is, however, good reason for inferring that the impression
then made upon the mind of Ahab was never wholly effaced.
This appears not only from the subsequent relations between
the king and prophets of the LORD (1 Kings xx.), but even
from his tardy repentance after the commission of his great
crime (1 Kings xxi. 27–29). Indeed, it might almost seem
as if, but for the influence of Jezebel upon the weak king,
matters might at least temporarily have taken a different turn
in Israel. But if such was the effect produced upon Ahab
by the scene on Mount Carmel, we can understand that
Jezebel's first wish must have been as soon as possible to
remove Elijah from all contact with the king. For this purpose
she sent a message, threatening the prophet with death within
twenty-four hours. It need scarcely be said, that, if she had
been so bold as really to purpose his murder, she would not
have given him warning of it, and that the reference to twenty-
four hours as the limit of his life must rather have been intended to induce Elijah to immediate flight. And she succeeded in her purpose—not, indeed, from fear on the part of
the prophet,[1] but from deep disappointment and depression,
for which we may in some measure find even a physical cause

---

[1] The LXX. (and some *Codd.*) by a slight change alter the word "saw"
(1 Kings xix. 3) into one which means "feared:" it need scarcely be said,
erroneously.

in the reaction that must have followed on the day after Carmel.

Strange as it may seem, these felt weaknesses of men like Elijah come upon us with almost a sense of relief. It is not only that we realise that these giants of faith are men of like passions with ourselves, but that the Divine in their work is thereby the more prominently brought out. It deserves special notice that Elijah proceeded on his hasty journey without any Divine direction to that effect. Attended only by his faithful servant, he passed without pausing to the farthest boundary of the neighbouring kingdom of Judah. But even that was not his final destination, nor could he in his then mood brook any companionship. Leaving his servant behind, he went into the wilderness of Paran. In its awful solitude he felt himself for the first time free to rest. Utterly broken down in body and in spirit, he cast himself under one of those wide-spreading brooms,[1] which seemed as if they indicated that even in the vast, howling wilderness, the hand of the Great Creator had provided shelter for His poor, hardly bestead wanderers. There is something almost awful in the life-and-death conflicts of great souls. We witness them with a feeling akin to reverence. The deep despondency of Elijah's soul found utterance in the entreaty to be released from work and suffering. He was not better than his fathers; like them he had vainly toiled; like them he had failed; why should his painful mission be prolonged? But not so must he pass away. Like Moses of old, he must at least gain distant view of the sweet land of beauty and rest. As so often, God in His tender mercy gave His beloved the precious relief of sleep. And more than that— he was to have evidence that even there he was not forsaken. An angel awakened him to minister to his wants. God careth for the body ; and precious in His sight is not only the death, but also the felt need of His people. The same great Jehovah,

---

[1] The *Rothem* is not a juniper-tree (as in the Authorised Version), but a species of large, wide-spreading broom, which generally grows near watercourses, and serves as protection alike from the sun and the wind.

Whose manifestation on Carmel had been so awful in its grandeur, condescended to His servant in the hour of his utmost need, and with unspeakable tenderness, like a mother, tended His weary child. Once more a season of sleep, and again the former heaven-given provision for the journey which he was to make—now in the guidance of God.[1]

The analogy between Moses, as he through whom the Covenant was given, and Elijah, as he through whom the Covenant was restored, has already been indicated. There is, however, one great difference between the two. When Israel broke the Covenant which Moses was about to make, he pleaded for them with the most intense agony of soul (Ex. xxxiii.–xxxiv. 9). When once more Israel broke the Covenant on the morrow of Carmel, Elijah fled in utter despondency of spirit. In both cases God granted light to His servants by such manifestation of Himself as gave deepest insight into His purposes of grace and anticipation of the manner in which they would be ultimately realised in all their fulness through Jesus Christ. And hence it was in this respect also fitting that Moses and Elijah should be with Jesus on the Mount of Transfiguration. But Elijah had not been like Moses ; rather had he been like the children of Israel. And therefore, like them, must he wander for symbolic forty days in the wilderness, before liberty and light were granted,[2] to learn the same lesson which God would have had Israel learn during their forty years of wandering. And so he came ultimately unto "the mount of God," to "the cave"[3]—perhaps the very "clift of the rock" where Moses had first been permitted to hear the glorious revelation of what Jehovah was and of what He purposed.

---

[1] Kimchi marks that the second meal was not newly brought, but must have been the remainder of the old. He also points out how Elijah was led in the wilderness by a higher direction than his own.

[2] The journey straight to Mount Horeb would have taken scarcely more than a fourth of that time.

[3] The Hebrew has the definite article, to mark a special, well-known cave.

It was a wondrous place in which to spend the night,[1] and to hear amidst its silence the voice of Jehovah.[2] The one question—afterwards repeated in different circumstances— "What doest thou here, Elijah?"[3] was intended to bring his state of mind clearly to the consciousness of the prophet. In tender mercy, no reproach was uttered, not even reproof of the rash request for release from seemingly hopeless, burdensome toil. But was it really hopeless? Did Elijah rightly apprehend God's final purpose in it; did he even know what in God's Providence would follow that seeming defeat of the prophet on the day after his great victory: how God would vindicate His cause, punish the rebellious, and take care of His own? What then had brought Elijah thither; what was his purpose in coming? Although the same question was twice asked and the same answer twice returned, it seems in each case to bear a somewhat different meaning. For the words of Elijah (vv. 10, 14) imply two things: an accusation against the children of Israel and a vindication of his own conduct in fleeing into the wilderness. The *first* of these seems to have been the meaning of his reply *before* the special manifestation of God (Rom. xi. 2, 3); the *second*, that *after* that revelation of God which the vision conveyed. This manifestation, so deeply symbolical, appears to us to have also wrought an entire change in the prophet.

The first question came to Elijah while still in the cave. As already stated, it elicited from him an accusation of His people, as if to appeal for vengeance to the LORD (Rom. xi. 2, 3)—"It is time for Thee to work, O LORD, for men have made void Thy Law" (Psa. cxix. 126)! Upon this Elijah was bidden to go forth out of the dark, narrow cave, and behold, as

---

[1] This is the meaning of the word "*lodge*" in verse 9.

[2] Some commentators regard the first part of what is related as having been a *vision*. But there seems no indication of this in the text.

[3] The question bears manifold application. By recalling it, the children of God have not unfrequently been preserved from sin, from improper association, and from worldly conformity.

Jehovah passed by.[1] Not a word was spoken. But first burst "wind great and strong, rending mountains, shivering rocks before the face of Jehovah—not in storm Jehovah! And after the wind earthquake—not in earthquake Jehovah! And after the earthquake fire—not in fire Jehovah! And after the fire sound of soft silencing (audible gentle stilling)!"[2] Elijah could not but have understood the meaning of this. He knew it when, at the "sound of soft stilling," he wrapped his face in the mantle and came forth in most reverent attitude to stand before Jehovah (comp. Ex. iii. 6; xxxiii. 20, 22; Isa vi. 2). The storm which rends, the earthquake which shakes all to its foundations, the fire which consumes—these are but His messengers which at most precede His coming. But Jehovah Himself is not in them. When He cometh it is not in these, but in the gentle stilling of them. To learn this was a real, though not an expressed, answer to Elijah's despondency and to his accusing appeal against Israel, the more touchingly conveyed that, being indirect, like the answer of Jesus to the inquiry of the Baptist, it carried instruction but not rebuke. The mood of both was the same, their doubts, and the reply given to them. It was in effect, See what the LORD really is, purposes, and doeth; and learn reverently to bow and to adore. God is greater, higher, better than appears only in judgment: do thy work, and leave the result to Him—He will make it plain. And so, we suppose that, when *after* this manifestation the same question again came to Elijah, his answer was no longer in the spirit of accusation, but rather a

---

[1] The LXX. seem to have read more correctly the first clauses of verse 11. We translate: "And he said, Go forth and stand on the mount before Jehovah—and behold, Jehovah passing by (passeth by)." The *narrative* portion only begins after this: "And wind, great and strong," etc. It deserves notice that the expression "pass by" is only used here and in Ex. xxxiii. and xxxiv. 6 of Jehovah. Generally the opposite—that of *dwelling* (whence *Shechinah*)—is connected with Him. Of these glorious manifestations only *passing* glimpses could be caught under the Old Testament.

[2] So literally.

statement of fact in vindication or explanation of his own presence on Mount Horeb.

With reverence be it said that, in the mood in which Elijah had come, no more fitting answer could have been made to him than this awful and glorious self-manifestation of Jehovah. If the LORD Himself had not been in the desolating messengers of terror, why should Elijah have expected it in the judgments which he was commissioned to execute? Nay, if Elijah himself had come forth to worship not in the storm, the earthquake, nor the fire, but had waited for the Presence of the LORD in the soft, gentle, stilling sound, why should he wonder if the revival of Israel's worship awaited a similar manifestation? But God would in the meantime take care of His own cause. The storm must burst from without on an unrepentant people : Hazael was to be anointed king of Syria, and foreign wars, more desolating than any that had preceded, would sweep over Israel. The earthquake would shake the house of Ahab to its foundations : and Jehu was to be appointed the minister of vengeance. That fire which Elijah had kindled would burn more brightly and fiercely : the mission of Elijah was to be continued in Elisha. To prepare all[1] this was now the only work left for the aged and weary prophet. And in each case he did prepare it.[2] Elisha was called by the prophet himself. The destruction of the house of Ahab, which involved the elevation of Jehu, through whom it was accomplished, was distinctly announced to Ahab by Elijah in the field of Naboth (1 Kings xxi. 19, 21, 22); while the future power of Syria over Israel, which involved the elevation of

[1] The expressions in 1 Kings xix. 15–17 must, of course, not be pressed in a literal sense. As a matter of fact, only Jehu was anointed, and that neither by Elijah nor by Elisha. Similarly the expression about Elisha slaying those who had escaped the sword of Jehu must be taken in its obvious figurative meaning. But in the sight of God these three were from that moment "anointed to their work" (comp. 2 Kings viii. 13, leaving out the words in *italics*, and 2 Kings ix. 3).

[2] It is strange that commentators should so generally have failed to see this.

Hazael, was similarly prophetically intimated (1 Kings xx. 42)
—as we conjecture from the expression "a certain man of the
sons of the prophets" (1 Kings xx. 35)—by direction of
Elijah.

Yet one precious assurance, or rather visible token that
Jehovah was still in Israel, in the voice of soft stilling, was
granted to the prophet. All unknown to him God had even in
corrupt Israel His own, a "remnant according to the election
of grace" (Rom. xi. 2–5), a sacred covenant-number which
could be counted by thousands [1]—"still ones" in the land, who
had never bent the knee to Baal nor kissed in worship the
abominable image.[2] And yet further consolation was to be
granted to the weary servant of the LORD. In each case the
actual judgment was to be only intimated, not executed, through
Elijah himself, or in his lifetime. But this comfort would he
have, that, even in his lifetime, and while engaged in his mission, a yoke-fellow true in sympathy, ministry, and likeness of
spirit, should attend him to make the burden seem easier to
bear.

It was as had been told him. With a sense that his mission
was well-nigh completed, and that what remained was chiefly
to prepare Elisha for his work, the prophet turned again towards
the land of Israel. As he proceeded on his way, nature itself
must have seemed to reflect the gladsome revelation of stillness
and peace which had been vouchsafed on Horeb. The abundant rain which had descended must have softened the long-
parched fields. The country was putting on the garb of a new
spring. Everywhere the work of the husbandman was resumed ;
herds and flocks were browsing in the meadows ; busy hands
were rapidly putting in the seed. Upwards he travelled along
the rich Jordan valley, till, past the borders of Judah, he

[1] The term 7000 must not be pressed literally, as if it were the exact
number of the faithful. *Seven* is the well-known sacred and covenant-
number.
[2] To kiss the idol—its feet, beard, etc.—was the common practice in
heathen worship.

reached the ancient possession of Issachar. No more happy scene than on the fields of *Abel Meholah*, the "meadow of the dance," of which the very name seems to suggest the joyous time of rich harvest and the merry dances of the reapers. These fields, far as the eye could reach, were the possession of one Shaphat, and he was of those seven thousand who had not bent to Baal, as we infer even from the name which he had given to his son : Elisha, "the God of salvation," or better, "my God salvation." And now twelve yoke of oxen were ploughing up the land—eleven guided by the hands of servants, the twelfth, in good old Hebrew simple fashion, by the son of the owner of those lands.

With characteristic sparingness of detail the sacred text does not inform us whether Elijah had before known his successor, nor how he came now to recognize him. Suffice it, that he knew and called him, not in words, indeed, but by the unmistakable symbolic action of casting over him his prophet's mantle, as he passed. This was Elisha's first test. There was no absolute need for responding, nor yet for showing that he had understood an unspoken call, which could have offered so little to attract even one whose lot had been cast in circumstances much less happy than those of Elisha. But Elisha showed his inward and spiritual preparedness by at once responding to Elijah's call, with only this one request : to be allowed to take leave of his father and mother.[1] It was not stern rebuke nor reproof which prompted the reply of Elijah : " Go back, for what have I done to thee ? " Precisely because he understood the greatness of the sacrifice which immediate obedience implied, would he leave Elisha entirely unswayed and free, and his service the outcome of his own heart's conviction and choice.[2]

---

[1] Matthew Henry quaintly remarks, " to *take* leave, not to *ask* leave of them."

[2] However reasonable and evident these details, we could scarcely conceive them possible in a narrative that was not based upon historical facts. Their invention would be almost inconceivable. Hence all these details furnish evidence of the reality of these events and of the truth of the Scriptural narrative.

Thus only could he be fitted for a calling which required such entire self-denial and self-sacrifice.

This further test also, which reminds us how our LORD set before intending followers the difficulties of their choice (Matt. viii. 20) and before His disciples the absolute necessity of willing self-denial (Luke xiv. 26), did Elisha endure, as must every one who is to do service for God. It seems almost symbolic that the oxen with which he had been working, the yoke which bound them, and the wooden ploughshare which they had drawn, were now used to prepare the farewell-feast of Elisha. To forsake and give up all for the service of the LORD is only one lesson, which must be complemented, not so much by abandoning all of the past, as by consecrating to our new life-work all that we formerly had or did. Nor let us forget two other considerations, suggested by the history of Elisha's call. All personal decision for God, and all work undertaken for Him, implies a leave-taking and a forsaking of the old, which must "pass away " when "all things become new" (2 Cor. v. 17). But this forsaking, though necessarily involving pain and loss, should not be sad—rather joyous, as leading through pain to real joy, and through seeming loss to real gain : [1] a "feast," such as was the parting of Elisha from his home, and that of St. Matthew from his calling and friends. Thus the end of the old will at the same time be the beginning of the new ; the giving up of the former calling the first act of the new ministry. And however humble that ministry, or however indirectly it may seem to bear upon the LORD, it is really ministry of Him. Then, and for many years afterwards, Elisha did but "pour water on the hands of Elijah " (2 Kings iii. 11) —yet from the moment that "he arose and went after Elijah " he was really, and in the judgment of God, "anointed to be prophet; " nor had he, nor needed he, other earthly consecration.

---

[1] It is probably in this that the difference lies between the case of Elisha and that in which our LORD returned so different an answer to a request, which to a superficial reader might seem substantially the same as that of the son of Shaphat (comp. Luke ix. 59--62).

CHAPTER III.

General effect of Elijah's Mission—The Two Expeditions of Syria and the Twofold Victory of Israel—Ahab releases Ben-hadad—The Prophet's Denunciation and Message.

(1 KINGS xx.)

BUT the mission of Elijah must also have had other and, in some respects, even more deep-reaching results than those with which God had comforted His servant in his deep dejection of spirit. Thus the "seven thousand" who had never bent the knee to Baal, must have been greatly quickened and encouraged by what had taken place on Carmel. Nay, it could not but have made lasting impression on King Ahab himself. Too self-indulgent to decide for Jehovah, too weak to resist Jezebel, even when his conscience misgave him, or directed him to the better way, the impression of what he had witnessed could never have wholly passed from his mind. Even if, as in the case of Israel after the exile, it ultimately issued only in pride of nationality, yet this feeling must ever afterwards have been in his heart, that Jehovah He was God—"the God of Gods"[1]—and that Jehovah was in Israel, and the God of Israel.

It is this which explains the bearing of Ahab in the first wars with Ben-hadad of Syria.[2] It need scarcely be said that this monarch was not the same, but the son of him who during the reigns of Baasha (1 Kings xv. 20) and Omri had possessed himself of so many cities, both east and west

[1] Although this special Psalm (cxxxvi.) may not be David's, we must remember that a considerable portion of the Psalter must have been in existence, and, at least in part, known to Ahab.

[2] Ben-hadad, "the Son of the Sun." *Hadad* was the official title of the kings of Syria. On the monarchs of that name, see Vol. V. pp. 114, 168, 181.

of the Jordan, and whose sovereignty had, in a sense, been owned within the semi-independent Syrian bazaars and streets of Samaria itself (1 Kings xx. 34). To judge from various notices, both Biblical and on Assyrian monuments, this Ben-hadad had inherited the restless ambition, although not the sterner qualities of his father. The motives of his warfare against Ahab are not difficult to understand. It was the settled policy of Syria to isolate and weaken the neighbouring kingdom of Israel. With this object in view, Ben-hadad IV. (the father of this king of Syria) had readily broken his league with Baasha, and combined with Asa against Israel.[1] But since the days of Omri the policy of both Israel and Judah had changed. Their former internecine wars had given place, first to peace, and then to actual alliance between the two kingdoms, cemented at last by the marriage of the son of Jehoshaphat with the daughter of Ahab (2 Chron. xviii. 1; 2 Kings viii. 18). To this cause for uneasiness to Syria must be added the close alliance between Israel and Tyre, indicated, if not brought about, by the marriage of Ahab with Jezebel. Thus the kingdom of Israel was secure both on its southern and western boundaries, and only threatened on that towards Syria. And the increasing prosperity and wealth of the land appear not only from the internal tranquillity that obtained during the thirty-six years of the reign of Ahab and his two descendants, but also from the circumstance that Ahab built so many cities, and adorned his capital by a magnificent palace made of ivory (1 Kings xxii. 39). Lastly, the jealousy and enmity of Ben-hadad must have been increased by his own relations to the great neighbouring power of Assyria, which (as we shall see) were such as to make a dangerous alliance between the latter and Israel an event of political probability.

In these circumstances, Ben-hadad resolved to strike such a blow at Samaria as would reduce it to permanent impotence. At the head of all his army, and followed by thirty-two vassal

---

[1] Compare Vol. V. p. 170.

kings, or probably rather chieftains, who ruled over towns with adjoining districts within the territory between the Euphrates and the northern boundary of Israel,[1] he invaded Samaria. He met with no opposition, for, as Josephus notes (*Ant.* viii. 14, 1), Ahab was not prepared for the attack. But even if it had been otherwise, sound policy would have dictated a retreat, and the concentration of the Israelitish forces behind the strong walls of the capital. This proved a serious check to the plans of Ben-hadad. The Syrian army laid, indeed, siege to Samaria, but the heat of the summer season,[2] the character and habits of his allies, and even the circumstance that his own country seems to have been divided among a number of semi-savage chiefs, must have proved unfavourable to a prolonged warfare. Ben-hadad might have succeeded if at the first onset he could have crushed the small, hastily-raised forces of Ahab by sheer weight of numbers. But the slow systematic siege of a well-defended city, into which Ahab had evidently gathered all the leading personages in his realm and all their wealth,[3] must have appeared even to a boastful Oriental a doubtful undertaking, which might at any time be converted into a disaster by the sudden appearance of allies to Israel from Judah, Tyre, or perhaps even from Assyria.

It was probably shortly after the commencement of the siege of Samaria, that Ben-hadad sent envoys to demand in

[1] Josephus erroneously represents them as from "beyond the Euphrates." But from Assyrian inscriptions we know that at that period the country between the Euphrates and the northern border of Jordan, was parcelled out among a number of states, such as those of the Hittites, the Hamathites, and others (comp. *Schrader, d. Keilinschriften u. d. A. Test.*, 2nd ed., pp. 200–204). This affords undesigned, but most important, confirmation of the Biblical narrative. So does the mention of "the chariots." (ver. 1) which, according to the Assyrian inscriptions, formed a very important part of the Syrian forces (Comp. *Schrader, u. s.*).

[2] This seems implied in the term "booths" (*sukkoth*), ver. 12—not "pavilions," as in the Authorised Version.

[3] The former seems implied by the presence in Samaria of "all the elders of the land," (ver. 7) ; the latter by the demand of Ben-hadad in ver. 6.

imperious terms the absolute submission of Ahab (1 Kings
xx. 2). At least so the latter seems to have understood it,
when he declared his readiness to agree to his enemy's terms.
But whether Ben-hadad had from the first meant more, or his
insolence had grown with what he regarded as the necessities
and fears of Ahab, the next day other heralds came from
Ben-hadad, requiring in terms of extreme and wanton
insult, not only the surrender of Ahab, but that of Samaria ;
and especially of the palaces of its nobility, for the avowed
purpose of plunder. It was evident that Ben-hadad intended,
not the surrender of Ahab, but the destruction (" evil ") of the
capital, and the ruin of the whole land (ver. 7). Possibly the
apparently strange demand of Ben-hadad (ver. 6) may indicate
a deeper scheme. To oblige Ahab formally to submit, would
be of comparatively small, at most, of only temporary use. On
the withdrawal of Ben-hadad the hostility of Israel would, as
experience had shown, once more break forth under Ahab, or
some new military leader, and threaten Syria with the same or
even graver danger than before. But if the spirit of the
leaders could be crushed by having their substance taken from
them, then the chiefs of the people would not only be detached
from their native monarchy, which had proved powerless to
protect them, but in future rendered dependent on Syria, and
hence led to seek the favour of Ben-hadad, instead of giving
their allegiance to their own Israelitish rulers.

But the scheme was foiled by the clumsy frankness of its
avowal. Ahab summoned to his council the elders of Israel.
He told them how on the previous day he had expressed to
Ben-hadad his willingness to make absolute personal submission and surrender of all that he possessed—as Josephus,
no doubt, correctly puts into his mouth—for the sake of their
preservation and peace. But the new terms which Ben-hadad
proposed involved the leaders of the people as well as himself,
and meant ruin equally to them all. In these circumstances,
"the elders" counselled the absolute rejection of the terms demanded. Their advice was ratified by a popular assembly

(ver. 8). These measures of Ahab were wise. Besides, the bearing of Ben-hadad must have indicated even to a ruler less astute than Ahab, the weakness and folly of his opponent. And, instead of attacking the city, on the refusal of his terms, as he would have done had he been sure of his army, Ben-hadad now only sent a message of ridiculously boastful threatening,[1] to which Ahab replied with calm dignity (vv. 10, 11).

Thus, for a time at least, Ahab seems in the school of adversity to have learned some of the lessons which his contact with Elijah might have taught him. Besides, it is only reasonable to suppose that both the composition of the force outside the city, and the utter demoralization of its leaders, were known in Samaria. A summer campaign in Palestine would have tried even the best disciplined troops. But the Syrian host contained a motley following of thirty-two Eastern chiefs, who probably had little other interest in the campaign than the hope of plunder. It was an army incoherent in its composition, and unwieldy from its very numbers. Hitherto their advance had been unchecked, and its progress, no doubt, marked by the desolation of the country along their straggling line of march. Their easy success would make them not only more reckless, but also unwilling to engage in serious fighting, especially in those hot and enervating days, when their leaders lay in the cool shadow of their booths, indulging in drunken orgies. It was a dissipated rabble, rather than an army.

Ben-hadad and his allies were engaged in a midday bout when the reply of Ahab to the Syrian challenge arrived. Received under such circumstances, we scarcely wonder that it provoked the order of Ben-hadad to make immediate prepara-

---

[1] The words of Ben-hadad (ver. 10) are generally regarded as meaning that "the dust of Samaria," about to be reduced to ashes and ruins, would not "suffice for the hollow hands" of all the people that were in his following. But it may have been only a general boast as against the popular assembly in Samaria that had ratified the resistance to him, that if all Samaria were reduced to dust there were more people in his following than could fill their hands with it.

tion for an assault on the city. But in whatever these preparations consisted,—whether in the advance of siege engines, or a massing of the troops,[1] they could scarcely have been very effective, since all the Syrian chiefs continued at their orgies, so that the hour of battle surprised them while incapacitated by intoxication (ver. 16).

Matters were very different within Samaria. There a prophet appeared,[2] to announce not only deliverance from the LORD, but to point its lesson in the contrast between the great multitude of the enemy, and the small number of Israel's host, by which they were to be defeated. This, with the view of showing to Ahab and to Israel that He was Jehovah, the living Covenant God, Who gave the victory. Thus the teaching of Elijah on Mount Carmel was now to find its confirmation and application in national blessing. And that the influence of that scene had not been, as Elijah had feared, only temporary and transient, appears even from the presence of a prophet in Samaria,[3] and from the whole bearing of Ahab. He is neither doubtful nor boastful, but, as having learned the prophetic lesson, anxious to receive plain Divine direction, and to follow it implicitly. Apparently the land was parcelled out among "princes of the shires," either hereditary chieftains of districts, or governors appointed by the king: an arrangement which throws further light on Ben-hadad's previously expressed purpose permanently to break the power of these leaders of Israel. These "princes of the shires" seem to have been each surrounded by a small armed retinue: "the young men" (comp. 2 Sam. xviii. 15). By these, numbering in all only 232 men, the victory over the great Syrian host was to be achieved. It only remained for Ahab to inquire, "Who shall commence

---

[1] The former seems the more likely meaning of verse 12.

[2] According to the Rabbis, Micaiah, the son of Imlah (xxii. 8; see *Rashi* and *Kimchi* ad loc.) But this seems a mere guess.

[3] This is the real meaning of the presence of the prophet in Samaria, and there is not, rightly understood, any inconsistency between this and 1 Kings xviii. 4, 22; xix. 10, as negative critics assert.

the warfare?"[1] For in such a victory the main condition
would be exact conformity to all Divine directions, in order
to show that all was of God, and to give evidence of the
principle of faith on the part of the combatants.

Having received the direction that he was to begin the
battle, Ahab lost no time. At midday—probably of the
following day—when, as no doubt was well-known in Samaria,
Ben-hadad and his thirty-two confederates were "drinking"
themselves "drunk" in the booths, the 232 of the body-guard
of the princes marched forth, followed by the 7000 men which
formed the army of Israel. Although this number naturally
reminds us of the 7000 who had not bent the knee to Baal,
there is no need to regard it as referring to them, or (with the
Rabbis) to "the true children of Israel." The precise number
(232) of the body-guard points to an exact numeration, nor
need we perhaps wonder if in the wonder-working Providence
of God there was a striking coincidence between the number
of the faithful and that of Israel's victorious host.[2]

The same wonder-working Providence appears in the manner
in which victory was granted. As so often, we mark the
accomplishment of a result, miraculous when viewed by itself,
yet, as regards the means, brought about in the order of natural
causation. And thus we ever learn anew that, although too
frequently we do not perceive it, we are constantly surrounded
by miracles, since Jehovah is the living God ; and that hence
ours should be the faith of a constant expectancy. It reads
as we might have expected in the circumstances, that, when
Ben-hadad was informed that men had come out from
Samaria, he commanded in his drunken conceit and boastfulness, they should not be attacked, but made captives
and brought to him. It may have been that those who were

---

[1] Or "battle." This, and not "*order* the battle," as in the A.V. The
same expression occurs in 2 Chron. xiii. 3, and corresponds to the French
entammer.

[2] On the other hand, the 7000 may represent only what is called a
"round number."

sent to execute this command went not fully armed. At any rate they seem to have been quite unprepared for resistance; and when these 232 Israelitish soldiers cut down each a man, no doubt following it up by further onslaught, the Syrians might naturally imagine that this was only an advanced guard, which was intended to precede a sortie of the whole garrison of Samaria. A panic, not uncommon among Orientals, seized the unprepared and unmarshalled masses, whose officers the while lay drunken in the booths. The very number of the Syrians would make a formation or rally more difficult, while it would afterwards increase the confusion of what soon became an indiscriminate flight. At this moment King Ahab issued from Samaria with his whole army. Whether, as our present Hebrew text bears, the king struck at the war-horses and war-chariots of the enemy, with the view of capturing them, or, as the ancient Greek translators (the LXX.) seem to have read, he "took" them,—implying that there had not been time to harness the war-chariots when the Israelitish host was among them—the result would be the same. Ben-hadad, followed by a few horsemen, escaped by hasty flight, as the word used in the original conveys, on a "chariot-horse," showing how sore was the stress when the king was obliged hastily to escape on the first horse to hand.

If it were necessary to demonstrate the compatibility of direct Divine help, and of reliance upon it, with the most diligent use of the best means, the narrative which follows would show it. After this great victory the king and people might have indulged in outward, or still worse, in professedly religious security, to the neglect of what was plain duty. But the same prophet who before had announced Divine deliverance, now warned Ahab to gather all his forces, and prepare, for that— "at the turn of the year," that is, in the spring (comp. 2 Sam. xi. 1), he might expect another attack from Syria. And to make best preparation for the coming danger, in obedience to the Divine word, would not supersede but presuppose faith, even as we shall work best when we feel that we have